Contents

II Travel information

- II Driving regulations
- V Ski resorts
- VII Sights of Europe
- XVIII History and culture of Europe
- XXI European politics and economics

1 Route planning maps

- 1 Key map • Distance table

17 Road maps

- 17 Key map

111 City plans and approach maps

- 111 Legend to city plans and approach maps

111 Alicante, Antwerpen
112 Amsterdam, Athínai approaches, Athínai
113 Barcelona approaches, Barcelona, Bruxelles
114 Berlin approaches, Berlin
115 Bordeaux approaches, Bordeaux, Budapest, Dublin
116 Düsseldorf – Ruhrgebiet approaches
117 Düsseldorf, Edinburgh, Firenze, Frankfurt
118 Genève, Göteborg, Hamburg approaches, Hamburg
119 Helsinki approaches, Helsinki
120 København approaches, København
121 Köln, Luxembourg, Lisboa approaches, Lisboa
122 London approaches
123 London, Lyon approaches, Lyon
124 Madrid approaches, Madrid, Marseille
125 Milano approaches, Milano
126 München approaches, München, Nápoli approaches, Nápoli
127 Oslo approaches, Oslo
128 Paris approaches
129 Paris, Praha approaches, Praha
130 Roma approaches, Roma
131 Stockholm approaches, Stockholm
132 Strasbourg approaches, Strasbourg, Sevilla, Stuttgart
133 Torino approaches, Torino, Warszawa
134 Wien approaches, Wien, Zürich

135 Index to road maps

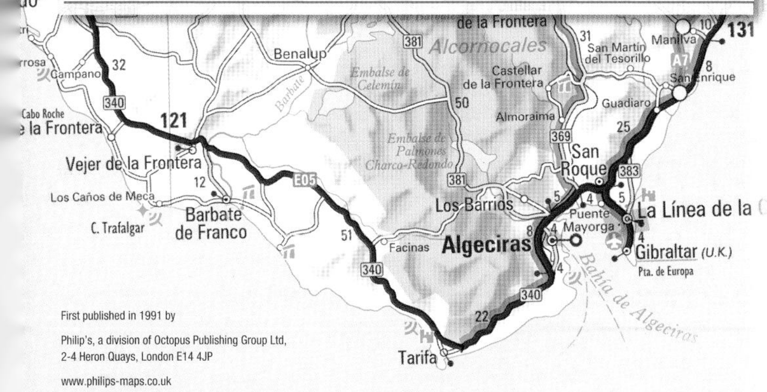

First published in 1991 by

Philip's, a division of Octopus Publishing Group Ltd,
2-4 Heron Quays, London E14 4JP

www.philips-maps.co.uk

Twelfth edition 2004 First impression 2004

Cartography by Philip's. Copyright © Philip's 2004
Printed and bound in Spain by Cayfosa-Quebecor

Legend to rout…

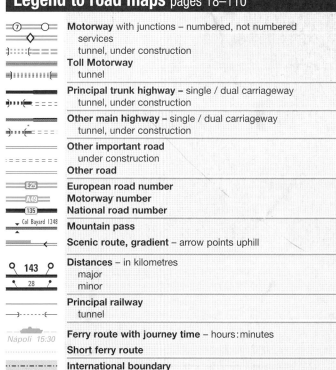

- **Motorway** - …
  - tunnel, ur…
- **Toll motorw…**
- **Main throug…**
  - under con…
- **Other major…**
- **Other road**
- 25 **European road number**
- 56 **Motorway number**
- 55 **National road number**
- 56 **Distances** – in kilometres
- **International boundary**
- **National boundary**
- LE HAVRE **Car ferry and destination**
- **Mountain pass**
- **International airport**
- 1089 **Height** – in metres
- **National park**

Town – population

MOSKVA	5 million +	Ikast	10000–20000
BERLIN	2–5 million	Skjern	5000–10000
MINSK	1–2 million	Lillesand	0–5000
Oslo	500000–1million		
Århus	200000-500000		
Turku	100000-200000		
Gävle	50000–100000		
Nybro	20000–50000		

Scale 1: 4 250 000
approximately 67 miles to 1 inch

0 20 40 60 80 miles
0 40 80 120 km

Legend to road maps pages 18–110

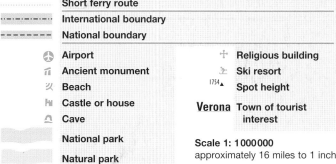

- **Motorway** with junctions – numbered, not numbered
  - services
  - tunnel, under construction
- **Toll Motorway**
  - tunnel
- **Principal trunk highway –** single / dual carriageway
  - tunnel, under construction
- **Other main highway –** single / dual carriageway
  - tunnel, under construction
- **Other important road**
  - under construction
- **Other road**
- E25 **European road number**
- A49 **Motorway number**
- 135 **National road number**
- Col Bayard 1248 **Mountain pass**
- **Scenic route, gradient** – arrow points uphill
- **Distances** – in kilometres
  - 143 major
  - 28 minor
- **Principal railway**
  - tunnel
- Nápoli 15:30 **Ferry route with journey time** – hours:minutes
- **Short ferry route**
- **International boundary**
- **National boundary**

- **Airport**
- **Ancient monument**
- **Beach**
- **Castle or house**
- **Cave**
- **National park**
- **Natural park**
- **Other place of interest**
- **Park or garden**
- **Religious building**
- **Ski resort**
- 1754 **Spot height**
- Verona **Town of tourist interest**

Scale 1: 1 000 000
approximately 16 miles to 1 inch

0 5 10 15 20 miles
0 10 20 30 km

Driving regulations

A national vehicle identification plate is always required when taking a vehicle abroad.

It is important for your own safety and that of other drivers to fit headlamp converters or beam deflectors when taking a right-hand drive car to a country where driving is on the right (every country in Europe except the UK and Ireland). When the headlamps are dipped on a right-hand drive car, the lenses of the headlamps cause the beam to shine upwards to the left – and so, when driving on the right, into the eyes of oncoming motorists.

The symbols used are:

- Motorway
- Dual carriageway
- Single carriageway
- Urban area
- Speed limit in kilometres per hour (kph)
- Seat belts
- Children
- Blood alcohol level
- Warning triangle
- First aid kit
- Spare bulb kit
- Fire extinguisher
- Motorcycle helmet
- Minimum driving age
- Additional documents required
- Mobile phones
- Other information

All countries require that you carry a driving licence, green card/insurance documentation, registration document or hire certificate, and passport.

The penalties for infringements of regulations vary considerably from one country to another. In many countries the police have the right to impose on-the-spot fines (you should always request a receipt for any fine paid). Penalties can be severe for serious infringements, particularly for drinking when driving which in some countries can lead to immediate imprisonment. Insurance is important, and you may be forced to take out cover at the frontier if you cannot produce acceptable proof that you are insured.

Please note that driving regulations often change, particularly in the new democracies of eastern Europe. Reliable information for Belarus and Ukraine was not available at the time of going to press.

The publishers have made every effort to ensure that the information given here was correct at the time of going to press. No responsibility can be accepted for any errors or their consequences.

Andorra (AND)

	Motorway	Dual carriageway	Single carriageway	Urban area
Speed	n/a	70	70	40

- Compulsory in front seats and if fitted in rear seats
- Over 10 only allowed in front seats if over 150cm
- 0.08%
- Recommended
- Recommended
- Recommended
- Recommended
- Compulsory for all riders
- 18
- Use not permitted whilst driving

Austria (A)

	Motorway	Dual carriageway	Single carriageway	Urban area
Speed	130	100	100	50
If towing trailer under 750kg	100	100	100	50
If towing trailer over 750kg	100	100	80	50

- Compulsory in front seats and rear seats
- Under 14 and under 150cm in front seats only in child safety seat; under 14 and over 150cm, must wear adult seat belt
- 0.05%
- Compulsory
- Compulsory
- Recommended
- Recommended
- Compulsory for all riders
- 18 (16 for mopeds)
- Third party insurance
- Use permitted only with hands-free speaker system
- ★ If you intend to drive on motorways or expressways, a motorway tax disk must be purchased at the border. There are additional tolls on the A9, A10, A13, S16
- ★ Dipped headlights must be used at all times on motorbikes

Belgium (B)

	Motorway	Dual carriageway	Single carriageway	Urban area
Speed	120*	120	90	50
If towing trailer	90	90	90	50

*Minimum speed of 70kph on motorways

- Compulsory in front and rear seats
- Under 12 in front seats only in child safety seat
- 0.05%
- Compulsory
- Compulsory
- Recommended
- Compulsory
- Compulsory for all riders
- 18 (16 for mopeds)
- Third party insurance
- Use only permitted with hands-free kit

Bulgaria (BG)

	Motorway	Dual carriageway	Single carriageway	Urban area
Speed	120	80	80	50-60
If towing trailer	100	70	70	50

- Compulsory in front seats; advised in rear
- Under 12 not allowed in front seats
- 0.00%
- Compulsory
- Compulsory
- Compulsory
- Compulsory for all riders
- 18
- Driving licence with translation or international driving permit; third party insurance
- Use only permitted with hands-free kit
- ★ $10 fee at border plus $2 disinfection fee

Croatia (HR)

	Motorway	Dual carriageway	Single carriageway	Urban area
Speed	130	80	80	50
If towing	110	80	80	50

- Compulsory if fitted
- Under 12 not allowed in front seats
- 0.05%
- Compulsory
- Compulsory
- Compulsory
- Compulsory for all riders
- 18
- No legislation

Czech Republic (CZ)

	Motorway	Dual carriageway	Single carriageway	Urban area
Speed	130	130	90	50
If towing	80	80	80	50

- Compulsory in front seats and, if fitted, in rear
- Under 12 or under 150cm not allowed in front seats
- 0.00%
- Compulsory
- Compulsory
- Compulsory
- Compulsory for all riders (unless maximum speed is 40kph or less)
- 18 (17 for motorcycles over 50cc, 16 for motorcycles under 125 cc)
- International driving permit; visa
- Use only permitted with hands-free kit
- ★ Permit needed for motorway driving

Denmark (DK)

	Motorway	Dual carriageway	Single carriageway	Urban area
Speed	110	80	80	50
If towing	80	70	70	50

- Compulsory in front seats and, if fitted, in rear
- Under 3 not allowed in front seat except in a child safety seat; in rear, 3 to 6 years in a child safety seat or on a booster cushion
- 0.05%
- Compulsory
- Recommended
- Recommended
- Compulsory for all riders
- 18

- Third party insurance
- Use only permitted with hands-free kit
- ★ Dipped headlights must be used at all times

Estonia (EST)

	Motorway	Dual carriageway	Single carriageway	Urban area
Speed	n/a	90	70	50

- Compulsory in front seats and if fitted in rear seats
- Under 12 not allowed in front seats; under 7 must have child safety seat in rear
- 0.00%
- Compulsory
- Compulsory
- Recommended
- Compulsory
- Compulsory for all riders
- 18 (16 for motorcycles, 14 for mopeds)
- International driving permit recommended
- Use only permitted with hands-free kit

Finland (FIN)

	Motorway	Dual carriageway	Single carriageway	Urban area
Speed	120	100	80	30-60
If towing	80	80	80	30-60

Maximum of 80 kph for vans and lorries

Speed limits are often lowered in winter

- Compulsory in front and rear
- Children must travel with a safety belt or in special child's seat
- 0.05%
- Compulsory
- Recommended
- Recommended
- Recommended
- Compulsory for all riders
- 18
- Third party insurance compulsory
- Use only permitted with hands-free kit
- ★ Dipped headlights must be used at all times

France (F)

	130	110	90	50
On wet roads				
	110	90	80	50

50kph on all roads if fog reduces visibility to less than 50m. Licence will be lost and driver fined for exceeding speed limit by over 40kph

Compulsory in front seats and,if fitted, in rear

Under 10 not allowed in front seats unless in approved safety seat facing backwards; in rear, if 4 or under, must have a child safety seat (rear facing if up to 9 months); if 5 to 10 may use a booster seat with suitable seat belt

0.05%

Compulsory unless hazard warning lights are fitted; compulsory for vehicles over 3,500kgs or towing a trailer

Recommended

Recommended

Compulsory for all riders

18 (16 for light motorcycles, 14 for mopeds)

No specific legislation but fine applies if deemed that concentration is impaired

★ Tolls on motorways

Germany (D)

	no limit*	no limit*	100	50
If towing				
	no limit*	no limit*	80	50

*130 kph recommended

Compulsory

Children under 12 and under 150cm must have a child safety seat, in front and rear

0.05%

Compulsory

Compulsory

Recommended (compulsory bus & coach)

Recommended

Compulsory for all riders

18 (motorbikes: 16 if not more than 125cc and limited to 11 kW)

Third party insurance

Use only permitted with hands-free - also applies to drivers of motorbikes and bicycles

★ Dipped headlights must be used on motorbikes at all times

Greece (GR)

	120	110	110	50
If towing				
	90	70	70	40

Compulsory in front seats and if fitted in rear seats

Under 12 not allowed in front seats except with suitable safety seat; under 10 not allowed in front seats

0.025%

Compulsory

Compulsory

Recommended

Compulsory

Compulsory for all riders

18 (16 for low cc motorcycles)

Third party insurance

Use only permitted with hands-free kit

Hungary (H)

	120	100	80	50
If towing				
	80	70	70	50

Compulsory in front seats and if fitted in rear seats

Under 12 or under 140cm not allowed in front seats

0.00%

Compulsory

Compulsory

Compulsory

Compulsory for all riders

18

Third party insurance

Use only permitted with hands-free kit

★ Dipped headlights must be used at all times

Ireland (IRL)

	112	96	96	48
If towing				
	80	80	80	48

Compulsory in front seats and if fitted in rear seats. Driver responsible for ensuring passengers under 17 comply

Under 4 not allowed in front seats unless in a child safety seat or other suitable restraint

0.08%

Recommended

Recommended

Recommended

Compulsory for all riders

17 (16 for motorbikes up to 125cc; 18 for over 125cc; 18 for lorries; 21 bus/minibus)

Third party insurance; international driving permit for non-EU drivers

Use only permitted with hands-free kit

★ Driving is on the left

Italy (I)

	130	110	90	50
If towing				
	80	70	70	50

Compulsory in front seats and, if fitted, in rear

Under 12 not allowed in front seats except in child safety seat; children under 3 must have special seat in the back

0.08%

Compulsory

Recommended

Compulsory

Recommended

Compulsory for all motorcyclists

18 (14 for mopeds, 16 for up to 125cc, 20 for up to 350cc)

International Driving Licence unless you have photocard licence

Use only permitted with hands-free kit

Latvia (LV)

	n/a	90	90	50
If towing				
	n/a	80	80	50

In residential areas limit is 20kph

Compulsory in front seats and if fitted in rear

If under 150cm must use child restraint in front and rear seats

0.05%

Compulsory

Compulsory

Recommended

Compulsory

Compulsory for all riders

18 (14 for mopeds, 16 for up to 125cc, 21 for up to 350cc)

International driving permit if licence is not in accordance with Vienna Convention

No legislation

★ Cars must use dipped headlights day and night 1Oct-1Apr, all year for motorbikes

★ Cars and minibuses under 3.5 tonnes must have winter tyres from 1Dec-1Mar

Lithuania (LT)

	130	110	90	60
If towing				
	70	70	70	60

Compulsory in front seats and if fitted in rear seats

Under 12 not allowed in front seats unless In a chlld safety seat

0.04%

Compulsory

Compulsory

Recommended

Compulsory

Compulsory for all riders

18 (14 for mopeds)

Visa

No legislation

★ Dipped headlights must be used day and night from Nov to Mar (all year for motorcyclists) and from 1–7 Sept

Luxembourg (L)

	130/110	90	90	50
If towing				
	90	75	75	50

Compulsory

Under 12 or 150cm not allowed in front seats unless in a child safety seat; under 12 must have child safety seat or belt in rear seats

0.08%

Compulsory

Recommended

Recommended

Recommended

Compulsory for all riders

18 (16 for mopeds)

Third party insurance

Use only permitted with hands-free speaker system

★ Motorcyclists must use dipped headlights at all times

Macedonia (MK)

	120	100	60	60
If towing				
	80	70	50	50

Compulsory in front seats; compulsory if fitted in rear seats

Under 12 not allowed in front seats

0.05%

Compulsory

Compulsory

Compulsory

Recommended

Compulsory for all riders

18 (mopeds 16)

International driving permit; visa

No legislation

Moldova (MD)

	90	90	60	60

Compulsory in front seats

Under 12 not allowed in front seats

0.00%

Compulsory

Compulsory

Compulsory

Recommended

Compulsory for all riders

18 (mopeds 16)

Visa

No legislation

Netherlands (NL)

	120	80	80	50

Compulsory in front seats and, if fitted, rear

Under 12 not allowed in front seats except in child restraint; in rear, 0-3 child safety restraint, 4-12 child restraint or seat belt

0.5%

Recommended

Recommended

Recommended

Recommended

Compulsory for all riders

18 (16 for mopeds)

Third party insurance

Use only permitted with hands-free kit

Norway (N)

	90	80	80	50
If towing trailer with brakes				
	80	80	80	50
If towing trailer without brakes				
	60	60	60	50

Compulsory in front seats and, if fitted, in rear

Under 4 must have child restraint; over 4 child restraint or seat belt

0.02%

Compulsory

Recommended

Recommended

Compulsory for all riders

18 (16 mopeds, heavy vehicles 18/21)

Use only permitted with hands-free kit

★ Dipped headlights must be used at all times

★ Tolls apply on some bridges, tunnels and access roads into major cities

Poland (PL)

	110*	100	90	60
If towing				
	80*	80	70	60

*40kph minimum • 20kph in residential areas

Compulsory in front seats and, if fitted, in rear

Under 10 not allowed in front seats unless in a child safety seat

0.02%

Compulsory

Recommended

Recommended

Compulsory

Compulsory for all riders

17 (mopeds: 15, motorbikes: 16)

International permit (recommended)

Use only permitted with hands-free kit

★ Between 1 Nov and 1 Mar dipped headlights must be used day and night

Portugal (P)

	120*	100	90	50
If towing				
	100*	80	70	50

*40kph minumum; 90kph maximum if licence held under 1 year

Compulsory in front seats; compulsory if fitted in rear seats

Under 3 not allowed in front seats unless in a child seat; 3–12 not allowed in front seats except in approved restraint system

0.05%. Imprisonment for 0.12% or more

Compulsory

Recommended

Compulsory for all riders

18 (motorcycles under 50cc 16)

Use not permitted

★ Tolls on motorways

Romania (RO)

Cars				
	120	90	90	50
Vehicles seating eight persons or more				
	90	80	80	50
Motorcycles				
	100	80	80	50

Jeep-like vehicles: 70kph outside built-up areas but 60kph in all areas if diesel

Compulsory in front seats and, if fitted, in rear

Under 12 not allowed in front seats

0.0%

Recommended

Compulsory

Recommended

Recommended

Compulsory for all riders

18 (16 for mopeds)

Visa (only if stay over 30 days for EU citizens): third party insurance

Use only permitted with hands-free kit

★ Tolls on Bucharest to Constanta motorway and bridges over Danube

Russia (RUS)

	130	120	110	60

Compulsory in front seats

Under 12 not allowed in front seats

0.00%

Compulsory

Compulsory

Recommended

Compulsory

Compulsory

18

International driving licence with translation;visa

No legislation

Serbia & Montenegro (YU)

	120	100	80	60

Compulsory in front and rear seats

Under 12 not allowed in front seats

0.05%

Compulsory

Compulsory

Recommended

Compulsory

Compulsory

18 (16 for motorbikes less than 125cc; 14 for mopeds)

International driving permit; visa

No legislation

★ Tolls on motorways and some primary roads

★ All types of fuel available at petrol stations

★ 80km/h speed limit if towing a caravan

Slovak Republic (SK)

	130	90	90	60

Compulsory in front seats and, if fitted, in rear

Under 12 not allowed in front seats unless in a child safety seat

0.0

Compulsory

Compulsory

Compulsory

Recommended

Compulsory for motorcyclists

18 (15 for mopeds)

International driving permit

Use only permitted with hands-free kit

★ Tow rope recommended

★ Passport must be valid for at least eight months after entry

Slovenia (SLO)

	130	100*	90*	50
If towing				
	80	80*	80*	50

*70kph in urban areas

Compulsory in front seats and, if fitted, in rear

Under 12 only allowed in the front seats with special seat; babies must use child safety seat

0.05%

Compulsory

Compulsory

Compulsory

Recommended

Compulsory for all riders

18 (motorbikes up to 125cc - 16, up to 350cc - 18)

Use only permitted with hands-free kit

★ Dipped headlights must be used at all times

Spain (E)

	120	100	90	50
If towing				
	80	80	70	50

Compulsory in front seats and if fitted in rear seats

Under 12 not allowed in front seats except in a child safety seat

0.05% (0.03% if vehicle over 3,500 kgs or carries more than 9 passengers, and in first two years of driving licence)

Two compulsory (one for in front, one for behind)

Compulsory in adverse weather conditions

Compulsory for all riders

18 (18/21 heavy vehicles; 18 for motorbikes over 125cc; 16 for motorbikes up to 125cc; 14 for mopeds up to 75cc)

Third party insurance

Use only permitted with hands-free kit

★ Tolls on motorways

Sweden (S)

	110	90	70	50
If towing trailer with brakes				
	80	80	70	50

- Compulsory in front and rear seats
- Under 7 must have safety seat or other suitable restraint
- 0.02%
- Compulsory
- Recommended
- Recommended
- Compulsory for all riders
- 18
- Third party insurance
- No legislation
- ★ Dipped headlights must be used at all times

Switzerland (CH)

	120	100	80	50/30
If towing up to 1 ton				
	80	80	80	50/30
If towing over 1 ton				
	80	80	60	50/30

- Compulsory in front and, if fitted, rear
- Under 12 not allowed in front seats unless in child restraint
- 0.05%
- Compulsory
- Compulsory
- Recommended
- Recommended
- Compulsory for all riders
- 18 (mopeds up to 50cc - 14)
- Third party insurance
- Use only permitted with hands-free kit
- ★ If you intend to drive on motorways, however short the journey, a motorway tax disk (vignette) must be purchased at the border

Turkey (TR)

	120	90	90	50
If towing				
	70	70	70	40

- Compulsory in front seats
- Under 12 not allowed in front seats
- 0.05%
- Two compulsory (one in front, one behind)
- Compulsory
- Compulsory
- Compulsory for all riders (except on freight motorcycles)
- 18
- International driving permit advised; note that Turkey is in both Europe and Asia
- Use only permitted with hands-free kit
- ★ Tow rope and tool kit must be carried

United Kingdom (GB)

	112	112	96	48
If towing				
	96	96	80	48

- Compulsory in front seats and if fitted in rear seats
- Under 3 not allowed in front seats except with appropriate restraint, and in rear must use child restraint if available; 3-12 and under 150cm must use appropriate restraint or seat belt in front seats, and in rear if available
- 0.08%
- Recommended
- Recommended
- Compulsory for all riders
- 17 (16 for mopeds)
- Use only permitted with hands-free kit
- ★ Driving is on the left

Ski resorts

The resorts listed are popular ski centres, therefore road access to most is normally good and supported by road clearing during snow falls. However, mountain driving is never predictable and drivers should make sure they take suitable snow chains as well as emergency provisions and clothing.

Listed for each resort are: the atlas page and grid square; the altitude; the number of lifts; the season start and end dates; the nearest town (with its distance in km) and the telephone number of the local tourist information centre ('00' prefix required for calls from the UK).

Andorra

Pyrenees

Pas de la Casa / Grau Roig 77 A4
2050m, 31 lifts, Dec-May • Andorra La Vella (30km) +376 801060
www.pasgrau.com • *Access via Envalira Pass (2407m), highest in Pyrenees, snow chains essential.*

Austria

Alps

A 24-hour driving conditions information line is provided by the Tourist Office of Austria www.austria-tourism.at +43 1 588 660.

Bad Gastein 58 A3
1002m, 51 lifts, Dec-Apr • Bad Hofgastein (6km) +43 6434 25310
www.skigastein.at
Snow report: +43 6432 64555.

Bad Hofgastein 58 A3
860m, 51 lifts, Dec-Apr • Salzburg (90km) +43 6432 7110
www.badhofgastein.com
Snow report: +43 64323393260.

Bad Kleinkirchheim 58 B3
1100m, 32 lifts, Dec-Apr • Villach (35km) +43 4240 8212
www.badkleinkirchheim.com
Snowfone:+43 4240 8222. Near Ebene Reichenau.

Ehrwald 57 A5
1000m, 22 lifts, Dec-Apr • Imst (30km) +43 5673 2395
www.tiscover.at/ehrwald
Weather report: +43 5673 3329.

Innsbruck 57 A6
574m, 59 lifts, Dec-Apr • Innsbruck +43 5125 9850
www.innsbruck-tourismus.com
Motorway normally clear. The motorway through to Italy and through the Arlberg Tunnel West to Austria are both toll roads.

Ischgl 57 A5
1400m, 42 lifts, Dec-May • Landeck (25km) +43 5444 52660 www.ischgl.com
Car entry to resort prohibited between 2200hrs and 0600hrs.

Kaprun 58 A2
800m, 56 lifts, Jan-Dec • Zell am See (10km) +43 6547 86430
www.zellkaprun.at
Snowfone:+43 6547 8444

Kirchberg in Tyrol 58 A2
860m, 59 lifts, Dec-Apr • Kitzbühel (6km) +43 5357 2309 www.kirchberg.at
Easily reached from Munich International Airport (120 km).

Kitzbühel 58 A2
800m, 59 lifts, Dec-Apr • Wörgl (40km) +43 5356 621550
www.kitzbuehel.com

Lech/Oberlech 57 A5
1450m, 84 lifts, Dec-Apr • Bludenz (50km) +43 5583 21610 www.Lech.at
Roads normally cleared but keep chains accessible because of altitude. Road conditions report tel +43 5583 1515.

Mayrhofen 58 A1
630m, 29 lifts, Dec-Apr • Jenbach (35km) +43 5285 6760 www.mayrhofen.com
Chains rarely required.

Obertauern 58 A3
1740m, 27 lifts, Nov-May • Radstadt (20km) +43 6456 7252
www.top-obertauern.com
Roads normally cleared but chains accessibility recommended. Camper vans and caravans not allowed; park these in Radstadt.

Saalbach Hinterglemm 58 A2
1003m, 52 lifts, Dec-Apr • Zell am See (19km) +43 6541 6800 68
w www.saalbach.com • Both village centres are pedestrianised and there is a good ski bus service during the daytime.

St Anton am Arlberg 57 A5
1304m, 84 lifts, Nov-May • Innsbruck (104km) +43 5446 22690
www.stantonamarlberg.com
Snow report tel +43 5446 2565.

Schladming 58 A3
745m, 86 lifts, Nov-Apr • Schladming +43 3687 222680
www.schladming.com

Serfaus 57 A5
1427m, 53 lifts, Dec-Apr • Landeck (30km) +43 5476 6239 www.serfaus.com
Cars banned from village, use world's only 'hover' powered underground railway.

Sölden 57 B6
1377m, 32 lifts, all year • Imst (50km) +43 5254 22120 www.soelden.com
Roads normally cleared but snow chains recommended because of altitude. The route from Italy and the south over the Timmelsjoch via Obergurgl is closed in the winter and anyone arriving from the south should use the Brenner Pass motorway. Snow information tel +43 5254 2666.

Zell am See 58 A2
758m, 56 lifts, Dec-Mar • Zell am See +43 6542 770 www.zellkaprun.at
Snowfone +43 6542 73694 Low altitude, therefore good access and no mountain passes to cross.

Zell im Zillertal (Zell am Ziller) 58 A1
580m, 47 lifts, Dec-Apr • Jenbach (25km) +43 5282 2281 www.tiscover.at/zell
Snowfone +43 5202 716526.

Zürs 57 A5
1720m, 84 lifts, Dec-May • Bludenz (30km) +43 5583 2245 www.zuers.com
Roads normally cleared but keep chains accessible because of altitude. Village has garage with 24-hour self-service gas/petrol, breakdown service and wheel chains supply.

France

Alps

Alpe d'Huez 65 A5
1860m, 85 lifts, Dec-Apr • Grenoble (63km) +33 4 76 11 44 44
www.alpedhuez.com • *Snow chains may be required on access road to resort. Road report tel +33 4 76 11 44 50.*

Avoriaz 56 B1
2277m, 38 lifts, Dec-May • Morzine (14km) +33 4 50 74 02 11
www.avoriaz.com
Chains may be required for access road from Morzine. Car free resort, park on edge of village. Horse-drawn sleigh service available.

Chamonix-Mont-Blanc 56 C1
1035m, 49 lifts, Nov-May +33 4 50 53 00 24 www.chamonix.com

Chamrousse 65 A4
1700m, 26 lifts, Dec-Apr • Grenoble (30km) +33 4 76 89 92 65
www.chamrousse.com • *Roads normally cleared, keep chains accessible because of altitude.*

Châtel 56 B1
2200m, 40 lifts, Dec-Apr • Thonon Les Bains (35km) +33 450 732244
www.chatel.com

Courchevel 56 C1
1850m, 197 lifts, Dec-Apr • Moûtiers (23km) +33 47 9 0800 29
www.courchevel.com • *Roads normally cleared but keep chains accessible. Traffic 'discouraged' within the four resort bases. Traffic info: +33 4 79 37 73 37.*

Flaine 56 B1
1800m, 74 lifts, Dec-Apr • Cluses (25km) +33 450 908001 www.flaine.com
Keep chains accessible for D6 from Cluses to Flaine. Car access for depositing luggage and passengers only. 1500-space car park outside resort. Near Sixt-Fer-á-Cheval.

La Clusaz 55 C6
1100m, 55 lifts, Dec-Apr • Annecy (32km) +33 4 50 32 65 00 www.laclusaz.com
Roads normally clear but keep chains accessible for final road from Annecy.

La Plagne 56 C1
2100m, 110 lifts, Dec-Apr Moûtiers (32km) +33 4 79 09 02 01
www.la-plagne.com • *Ten different centres up to 2100m altitude. Road access via Bozel, Landry or Aime normally cleared.*

Les Arcs 56 C1
2600m, 77 lifts, Dec-Apr • Bourg-St-Maurice (15km) +33 4 79 07 12 57
www.lesarcs.com • *Three base areas up to 2000 metres; keep chains accessible. Pay parking at edge of each base resort.*

Les Carroz d'Araches 56 B1
1140m, 74 lifts, Dec-Apr • Cluses (13km) +33 4 50 90 00 04
www.lescarroz.com

Les Deux-Alpes 65 B5
1650m, 63 lifts, Dec-May • Grenoble (75km) +33 4 76 79 22 00
www.les2alpes.com • *Roads normally cleared, however snow chains recommended for D213 up from valley road (N91).*

Les Gets 56 B1
1172m, 53 lifts, Dec-May • Cluses (18km) +33 4 50 75 80 80 www.lesgets.com

Les Ménuires 55 C6
1815m, 197 lifts, Dec-Apr • Moûtiers (27km) +33 4 79 00 73 00
www.lesmenuires.com • *Keep chains accessible for N515A from Moûtiers.*

Les Sept Laux 55 C6
1350m, 29 lifts, Dec-Apr • Grenoble (38km) +33 4 76 08 17 86 www.les7laux.com
Roads normally cleared, however keep chains accessible for mountain road up from the A41 motorway. Near St Sorlin d'Arves.

Megève 55 C6
2350m, 117 lifts, Dec-Apr • Sallanches (12km) +33 4 50 21 27 28
www.megeve.com
Horse-drawn sleigh rides available.

Méribel 55 C6
1400m, 197 lifts, Dec-May • Moûtiers (18km) +33 4 79 08 60 01
www.meribel.com
Keep chains accessible for 18km to resort on D90 from Moûtiers.

Morzine 56 B2
1000m, 217 lifts, Dec-May • Thonon-Les-Bains (30km) +33 4 50 74 72 72
www.morzine.com

Pra Loup 65 B5
1500m, 53 lifts, Dec-Apr • Barcelonnette (10km) +33 4 92 84 10 04
www.praloup.com
Roads normally cleared but chains accessibility recommended.

Risoul 65 B5
1850m, 58 lifts, Dec-Apr • Briançon (40km) +33 4 92 46 02 60 www.risoul.com • *Keep chains accessibie . Near Guillestre.*

St Gervais 56 C1
850m, 121 lifts, Dec-Apr • Sallanches (10km) +33 4 50 47 76 08
www.st-gervais.com

Serre-Chevalier 65 B5
1350m, 79 lifts, Dec-May • Briançon (10km) +33 4 92 24 98 98
www.serre-chevalier.com
Made up of 13 small villages along the valley road, which is normally cleared.

Tignes 56 C1
2100m, 97 lifts, Jan-Dec • Bourg St Maurice (26km) +33 4 79 40 04 40
www.tignes.net
Keep chains accessible because of altitude. Parking information tel +33 4 79 06 39 45.

Val d'Isère 56 C1
1850m, 97 lifts, Nov-May • Bourg-St-Maurice (30km) +33 4 79 06 06 60
www.valdisere.com • *Roads normally cleared but keep chains accessible .*

Val Thorens 55 C6
2300m, 197 lifts, Nov-May • Moûtiers (37km) +33 4 79 00 08 08
www.valthorens.com
Chains essential – highest ski resort in Europe. Obligatory paid parking on edge of resort.

Valloire 55 C6
1430m, 36 lifts, Dec-May • Modane (20km) +33 4 79 59 03 96 www.valloire.net
Road normally clear up to the Col du Galbier, to the south of the resort, which is closed from 1st November to 1st June.

Valmeinier 55 C6
2600m, 32 lifts, Dec-Apr • St Michel de Maurienne (47km) +33 4 79 59 53 69
www.valmeinier.com
Access from north on N9 / N902. Col du Galbier, to the south of the resort closed from 1st November to 1st June. Near Valloire.

Valmorel 55 C6
1400m, 55 lifts, Dec-Apr • Moûtiers (15km) +33 4 79 09 85 55
www.valmorel.com
Near St Jean-de-Belleville.

Vars Les Claux 65 B5
1850m, 58 lifts, Dec-Apr • Briançon (40km) +33 4 92 46 51 31
www.vars-ski.com • *Four base resorts up to 1850 metres. Keep chains accessible. Road and weather information tel +33 4 36 68 02 05 and +33 4 91 78 78 78. Snowfone +33 492 46 51 04*

Villard-de-Lans 65 A4
1050m, 29 lifts, Dec-Apr • Grenoble (32km) +33 476 951038
www.ot-villard-de-lans.fr

Pyrenees

Font-Romeu 77 A5
1800m, 33 lifts, Dec-Apr • Perpignan (87km) +33 4 68 30 68 30
www.fontromeu.com • *Roads normally cleared but keep chains accessibie.*

St Lary-Soulan 63 D3
830m, 32 lifts, Dec-Apr • Tarbes (75km) +33 5 62 39 50 81 www.saintlary.com
Access roads constantly cleared of snow.

Vosges

La Bresse-Hohneck 46 B2
900m, 20 lifts, Dec-Mar • Cornimont (6km) +33 3 29 25 41 29
www.labresse-remy.com

Germany

Alps

Garmisch-Partenkirchen 57 A6
702m, 38 lifts, Dec-Apr • Munich (95km) +49 8821 180 700
www.garmisch-partenkirchen.de • *Roads usually clear, chains rarely needed.*

Oberaudorf 48 C3
483m, 21 lifts, Dec-Apr • Kufstein (15km) +49 8033 301 20 www.oberaudorf.de
Motorway normally kept clear. Near Bayrischzell.

Oberstdorf 57 A5
815m, 31 lifts, Dec-Apr • Sonthofen (15km) +49 8322 7000 www.oberstdorf.de
Snow information on tel +49 8322 3035 or 1095 or 5757.

Rothaargebirge

Winterberg 37 C1
700m, 55 lifts Dec-Mar • Brilon (30km) +49 2981 92500 www.winterberg.de
Roads usually cleared, chains rarely required.

Italy

Alps

Bardonecchia 65 A5
1312m, 24 lifts, Dec-Apr • Bardonecchia +39 122 907778
Snowfone +39 122 99137
www.goski.com/rit/bardon.htm
Resort reached through the 11km Frejus tunnel from France, roads normally cleared.

Bormio 57 B5
1225m, 16 lifts, Dec-Apr • Tirano (40km) +39 342 903300 www.bormio.com
Tolls payable in Ponte del Gallo Tunnel, open 0800hrs-2000hrs.

Breuil-Cervinia 56 C2
2050m, 73 lifts, Jan-Dec • Aosta (54km) +39 166 940986
www.breuil-cervinia.it
Snow chains strongly recommended. Bus from Milan airport

Courmayeur 56 C1
1224m, 27 lifts, Dec-Apr • Aosta (40km) +39 165 842370
www.courmayeur.net • *Access through the Mont Blanc tunnel from France. Roads constantly cleared.*

Limone Piemonte 66 B1
1050m, 29 lifts, Dec-Apr • Cuneo (27km) +39 171 92101
www.limonepiemonte.it
Roads normally cleared, chains rarely required. Snow report tel +39 171 926254

Livigno 57 B5
1816m, 33 lifts, Dec-May • Zernez (CH) (27km) +39 342 996379
www.aptlivigno.it • *Keep chains accessible. La Drosa Tunnel from Zernez, Switzerland, is open only from 0800hrs to 2000hrs.*

Sestrière 65 B5
2035m, 91 lifts, Dec-Apr • Oulx (22km) +39 122 755444
www.sestriere.it • *One of Europe's highest resorts; although roads are normally cleared, chains should be accessible.*

Appennines

Roccaraso – Aremogna 90 A1
1285m, 31 lifts, Dec-Apr • Castel di Sangro (7km) +39 864 62210
www.roccaraso.net

Dolomites

Andalo – Pai della Paganella 57 B5
1042m, 22 lifts, Dec-Apr • Trento (40km) +39 461 585836 www.paganella.net

Arabba 58 B1
2500m, 30 lifts, Dec-Apr • Brunico (45km) +39 436 79130
www.dolomitisuperski.com/arabba1
Roads normally cleared but keep chains accessible.

Cortina d'Ampezzo 58 B2
1224m, 48 lifts, Dec-Apr • Belluno (72km) +39 436 3231
www.cortinadampezzo.it
Access from north on route 51 over the Cimabanche Pass may require chains.

Corvara (Alta Badia) 58 B1
1568m, 57 lifts, Dec-Apr • Brunico (38km) +39 471 836176
www.altabadia.it/inverno
Roads normally clear but keep chains accessible.

Madonna di Campiglio 57 B5
1550m, 60 lifts, Dec-Apr • Trento (60km) +39 465 442000
www.campiglio.net• *Roads normally cleared but keep chains accessible.*

Moena di Fassa (Sorte/Ronchi) 58 B1
1184m, 29 lifts, Dec-Apr • Bolzano (40km) +39 462 573122
www.dolomitisuperski.com/valfassa

Passo del Tonale 57 B5
1883m, 30 lifts, Dec-Aug • Breno (50km) +39 364 903838
www.adamelloski.com
Located on high mountain pass; keep chains accessible.

Selva di Val Gardena/Wolkenstein Groden 58 B1 1563m, 82 lifts, Dec-Apr • Bolzano (40km) +39 471 795122
www.valgardena.it • *Roads normally cleared but keep chains accessible.*

Norway

Hemsedal 2 F11
650m, 16 lifts, Nov-May Honefoss (150km) +47 32 060156 www.hemsedal.com
Be prepared for extreme weather conditions.

Trysil (Trysilfjellet) 2 F13
465m, 24 lifts, Nov-May • Elverum (100km) +47 62 450911 www.trysil.com
Be prepared for extreme weather conditions.

Spain

Pyrenees

Baqueira/Beret 76 A3
1500m, 24 lifts, Dec-Apr • Viella (15km) +34 973 644455 www.baqueira.es
Roads normally clear but keep chains accessible. Snowfone tel +34 973 645025. Near Salardú

Sistema Penibetico

Sierra Nevada 86 B2
2102m, 21 lifts, Dec-May • Granada (32km) +34 958 249100
www.sierranevadaski.com• *Access road designed to be avalanche safe and is snow cleared. Snowfone +34 958 249119 .*

Sweden

Idre Fjäll 2 F13
710m, 30 lifts, Oct-May • Mora (140km) +46 253 40000 www.idrefjall.se
Be prepared for extreme weather conditions.

Sälen 2 F13
360m, 101 lifts, Nov-Apr
Malung (70km) +46 280 20250
www.salen.se, www.salenfjallen.se
Be prepared for extreme weather conditions.

Switzerland

Alps

Adelboden 56 B2
1353m, 50 lifts, Dec-Apr • Frutigen (15km) +41 33 6738080 www.adelboden.ch

Arosa 57 B4
1800m, 16 lifts, Dec-Apr • Chur (30km) +41 81 3877020 www.arosa.ch
Roads cleared but keep chains accessible because of high altitude (1800m).

Crans Montana 56 B2
1500m, 35 lifts, Dec-Apr, Jul-Oct • Sierre (15km) +41 27 4850404
www.crans-montana.ch
Roads normally cleared, however keep chains accessible for ascent from Sierre.

Davos 57 B4
1560m, 54 lifts, Nov-Apr • Davos +41 81 4152121 www.davos.ch

Engelberg 56 B3
1000m, 26 lifts, Nov-Jun • Luzern (39km) +41 41 6397777 www.engelberg.ch
Straight access road normally cleared.

Iums (Flumserberg) 57 A4
1400m, 17 lifts, Dec-Apr • Buchs (25km) +41 81 7201818
www.flumserberg.com
Roads normally cleared, but 1000 metre vertical ascent; keep chains accessible.

Grindelwald 56 B3
1034m, 30 lifts, Dec-Apr • Interlaken (20km) +41 36 8541212 www.grindelwald.ch

Gstaad – Saanenland 56 B2
1050m, 66 lifts, Dec-Apr • Gstaad +41 33 7488181 www.gstaad.ch

Klosters 57 B4
1191m, 61 lifts, Dec-Apr • Davos (10km) +41 81 4102020 www.klosters.ch

Leysin 56 B2
1263m, 19 lifts, Dec-Apr • Aigle (6km) +41 24 4942244 www.leysin.ch

Mürren 56 B2
1650m, 37 lifts, Dec-Apr • Interlaken (18km) +41 33 8568686
www.wengen-muerren.ch
No road access. Park in Strechelberg (1500 free places) and take the two-stage cable car.

Nendaz 56 B2
1365m, 91 lifts, Nov-Apr • Sion (16km) +41 27 2895589 www.nendaz.ch • *Roads normally cleared, however keep chains accessible for ascent from Sion. Near Vex.*

Saas-Fee 56 B2
1800m, 25 lifts, Jan-Dec • Brig (35km) +41 27 9581858 www.saas-fee.ch • *Roads normally cleared but keep chains accessible because of altitude.*

St Moritz 57 B4
1856m, 58 lifts, Nov-May • Chur (89km) +41 81 8373333 www.stmoritz.ch • *Roads normally cleared but keep chains accessible because of altitude.*

Samnaun 57 B5
1846m, 42 lifts, Dec-May • Scuol (30km) +41 81 8685858 www.samnaun.ch • *Roads normally cleared but keep chains accessible.*

Verbier 56 B2
1500m, 95 lifts, Nov-May, Jun-Jul • Martigny (27km) +41 27 7753888
www.verbier.ch • *Roads normally cleared.*

Villars 56 B2
1253m, 37 lifts, Nov-Apr, Jun-Jul • Montreux (35km) +41 24 4953232
www.villars.ch • *Roads normally cleared but ckeep chains accessible for ascent from N9. Near Bex.*

Wengen 56 B2
1270m, 37 lifts, Dec-Apr • Interlaken (12km) +41 33 8551414 www.wengen-muerren.ch •*No road access. Park at Lauterbrunnen and take mountain railway.*

Zermatt 56 B2
1620m, 73 lifts, all year • Brig (42km) +41 27 9668100 www.zermatt.ch • *Cars not permitted in resort, park in Täsch (3km) and take shuttle train.*

Ski resort information based on data compiled by Snow24 plc. www.snow24.com email: info@snow24.com. To the best of the Publisher's knowledge the information in this table was correct at the time of going to press. No responsibility can be accepted for any errors or their consequences.

300 greatest sights of Europe

Majolicahaus, Wien, Austria

Albania *Shquipëria*

Berat Fascinating old town with picturesque Ottoman Empire buildings and traditional Balkan domestic architecture.

Tiranë Capital of Albania. Skanderbeg Square has main historic buildings. Also: 18c Haxhi Ethem Bey Mosque; Art Gallery (Albanian); National Museum of History. Nearby: medieval Krujë; Roman monuments.

Austria *Österreich*

Graz University town, seat of imperial court to 1619. Historic centre around Hauptplatz. Imperial monuments: Burg; mausoleum of Ferdinand II; towers of 16c schloss; 17c Schloss Eggenburg. Also: 16c Town Hall; Zeughaus; 15c cathedral. Museums: Old Gallery (Gothic, Flemish); New Gallery (good 19–20c).

Innsbruck Old town is reached by Maria-Theresien-Strasse with famous views. Buildings: Goldenes Dachl (1490s); 18c cathedral; remains of Hofburg imperial residence; 16c Hofkirche (tomb of Maximilian I).

Krems On a hill above the Danube, medieval quarter has Renaissance mansions. Also: Gothic Piaristenkirche; Wienstadt Museum.

Linz Port on the Danube. Historic buildings are concentrated on Hauptplatz below the imperial 15c schloss. Notable: Baroque Old Cathedral; 16c Town Hall; New Gallery.

Melk Set on a rocky hill above the Danube, the fortified abbey is the greatest Baroque achievement in Austria – particularly the Grand Library and abbey church.

Salzburg Set in subalpine scenery, the town was associated with powerful 16-17c prince-archbishops. The 17c cathedral has a complex of archiepiscopal buildings: the Residence and its gallery (excellent 16–19c); the 13c Franciscan Church (notable altar). Other sights: Mozart's birthplace; the Hohensalzburg fortress; the Collegiate Church of St Peter (cemetery, catacombs); scenic views from Mönchsberg and Hettwer Bastei. The Grosse Festspielhaus runs the Salzburg festival.

Salzkammergut Natural beauty with 76 lakes (Wolfgangersee, Altersee, Gosausee, Traunsee, Grundlsee) in mountain scenery. Attractive villages (St Wolfgang) and towns (Bad Ischl, Gmunden) include Hallstatt, famous for Celtic remains.

Wien Capital of Austria. The historic centre lies within the Ring. Churches: Gothic St Stephen's Cathedral; 17c Imperial Vault; 14c Augustine Church; 14c Church of the Teutonic Order (treasure); 18c Baroque churches (Jesuit Church, Franciscan Church, St Peter, St Charles). Imperial residences: Hofburg; Schönbrunn. Architecture of Historicism on Ringstrasse (from 1857). Art Nouveau: Station Pavilions, Postsparkasse, Looshaus, Majolicahaus. Exceptional museums: Art History Museum (antiquities, old masters); Cathedral and Diocesan Museum (15c); Academy of Fine Arts (Flemish); Belvedere (Gothic, Baroque, 19–20c).

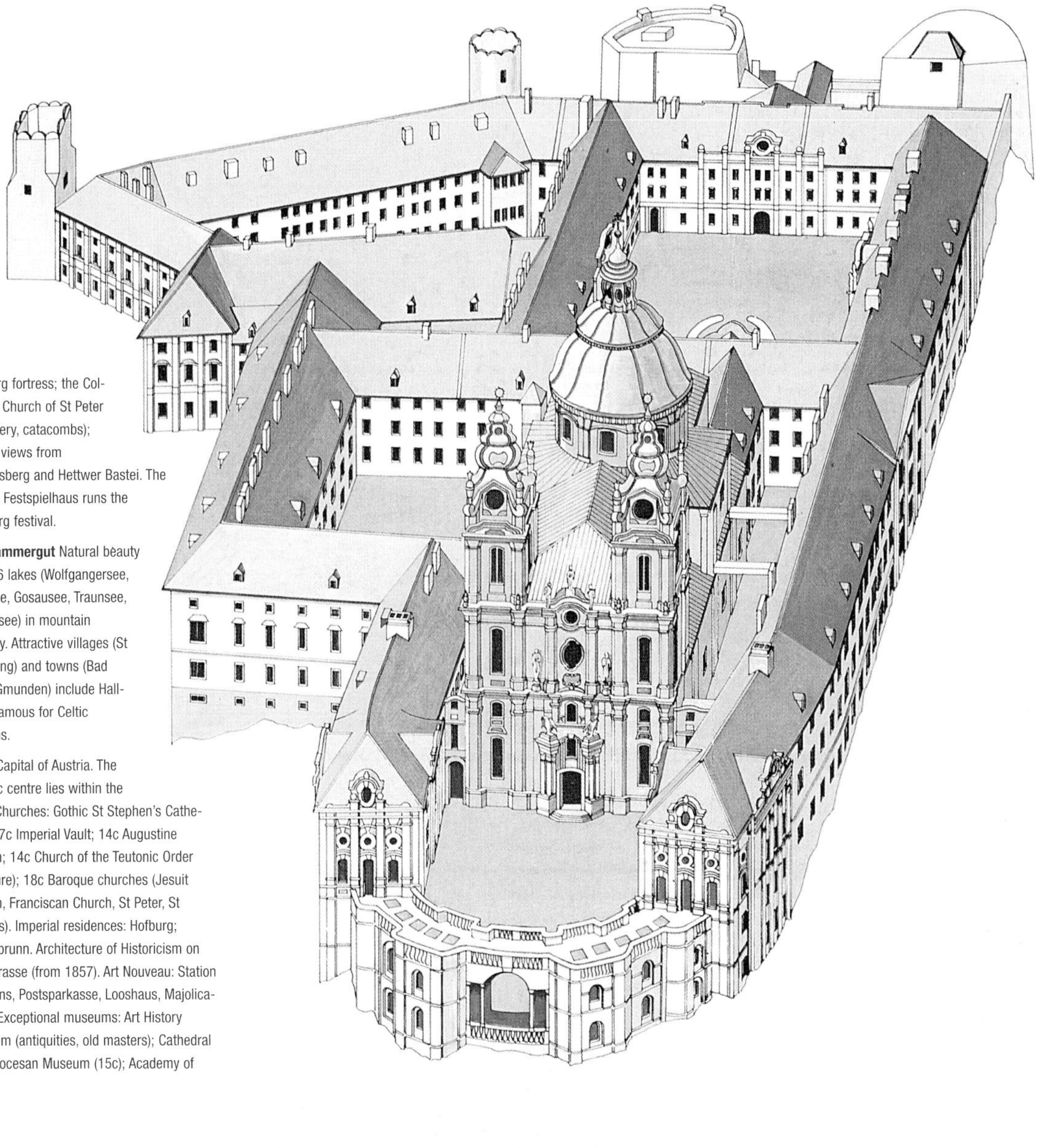

Belgium *Belgique*

Antwerpen City with many tall gabled Flemish houses on the river. Heart of the city is Great Market with 16–17c guildhouses and Town Hall. 14–16c Gothic cathedral has Rubens paintings. Rubens also at the Rubens House and his burial place in St Jacob's Church. Excellent museums: Mayer van den Berg Museum (applied arts); Koninklijk Museum of Fine Arts (Flemish, Belgian).

Brugge Well-preserved medieval town with narrow streets and canals. Main squares: the Market with 13c Belfort and covered market; the Burg with Basilica of the Holy Blood and Town Hall. The Groeninge Museum and Memling museum in St Jans Hospital show 15c Flemish masters. The Onze Lieve Vrouwekerk has a famous *Madonna and Child* by Michelangelo

Bruxelles Capital of Belgium. The Lower Town is centred on the enormous Grand Place with Hôtel de Ville and rebuilt guildhouses. Symbols of the city include the Manneken Pis and Atomium (giant model of a molecule). The 13c Notre Dame de la Chapelle is the oldest church. The Upper Town contains: Gothic cathedral; Neoclassical Place Royale; 18c King's Palace; Royal Museums of Fine Arts (old and modern masters). Also: much Art Nouveau (Victor Horta Museum, Hôtel Tassel, Hôtel Solvay); Place du Petit Sablon and Place du Grand Sablon; 19c Palais de Justice.

Gent Medieval town built on islands surrounded by canals and rivers. Views from Pont St-Michel. The Graslei and Koornlei quays have Flemish guild houses. The Gothic cathedral has famous Van Eyck altarpiece. Also: Belfort; Cloth Market; Gothic Town Hall; Gravensteen. Museums: Bijloke Museum in beautiful abbey (provincial and applied art); Museum of Fine Arts (old masters).

Namur Reconstructed medieval citadel is the major sight of Namur, which also has a cathedral and provincial museums.

Tournai The Romanesque-Gothic cathedral is Belgium's finest (much excellent art). Fine Arts Museum has a good collection (15–20c).

Town Hall, Antwerpen, Belgium

Bulgaria *Bulgariya*

Black Sea Coast Beautiful unspoiled beaches (Zlatni Pyasŭtsi). The delightful resort Varna is popular. Nesebŭr is famous for Byzantine churches. Also: Danube Delta in Hungary.

Plovdiv City set spectacularly on three hills. The old town has buildings from many periods: 2c Roman stadium and amphitheatre; 14c Dzumaiya Mosque; 19c Koyumdjioglu House and Museum (traditional objects). Nearby: Bačkovo Monastery (frescoes).

Rila Bulgaria's finest monastery, set in the most beautiful scenery of the Rila mountains. The church is richly decorated with frescoes.

Sofiya Capital of Bulgaria. Sights: exceptional neo-Byzantine cathedral; Church of St Sofia; 4c rotunda of St George (frescoes); Byzantine Boyana Church (frescoes) on panoramic Mount Vitoša. Museums: National Historical Museum (particularly for Thracian artefacts); National Art Gallery (icons, Bulgarian art).

Veliko Tŭrnovo Medieval capital with narrow streets. Notable buildings: House of the Little Monkey; Hadji Nicoli Inn; ruins of medieval citadel; Baudouin Tower; churches of the Forty Martyrs and of SS Peter and Paul (frescoes); 14c Monastery of the Transfiguration.

Croatia *Hrvatska*

Dalmacija Exceptionally beautiful coast along the Adriatic. Among its 1185 islands, those of the Kornati Archipelago and Brijuni Islands are perhaps the most spectacular. Along the coast are several attractive medieval and Renaissance towns, most notably Dubrovnik, Split, Šibenik, Trogir, Zadar.

Dubrovnik Surrounded by medieval and Renaissance walls, the city's architecture dates principally from 15–16c. Sights: many churches and monasteries including Church of St Vlah and Dominican monastery (art collection); promenade street of Stradun, Dubrovnik Museums; Renaissance Rector's Palace; Onofrio's fountain; Sponza Palace. The surrounding area has some 80 16c noblemen's summer villas.

Istra (Croatian) Peninsula with a number of ancient coastal towns (Rovinj, Poreč, Pula, Piran in Slovene Istria) and medieval hill-top towns (Motovun). Pula has Roman monuments (exceptional 1c amphitheatre). Poreč has narrow old streets; the mosaics in 6c Byzantine basilica of St Euphrasius are exceptional. See also Slovenia.

Plitvička Jezera Outstandingly beautiful world of water and woodlands with 16 lakes and 92 waterfalls interwoven by canyons.

Split Most notable for the exceptional 4c palace of Roman Emperor Diocletian, elements of which are incorporated into the streets and buildings of the town itself. The town also has a cathedral (11c baptistry) and a Franciscan monastery.

Trogir The 13–15c town centre is surrounded by medieval city walls. Romanesque-Gothic cathedral includes the chapel of Ivan the Blessed. Dominican and Benedictine monasteries house art collections.

Czech Republic *Česka Republica*

Brno Capital of Moravia. Sights: Vegetable Market and Old Town Hall; Capuchin crypt decorated with bones of dead monks; hill of St Peter with Gothic cathedral; Mies van der Rohe's buildings (Bata, Avion Hotel, Togendhat House). Museums: UPM (modern applied arts); Pražáků Palace (19c Czech art).

České Budějovice Famous for Budvar beer, the medieval town is centred on náměsti Přemysla Otokara II. The Black Tower gives fine views. Nearby: medieval Český Krumlov.

Olomouc Well-preserved medieval university town of squares and fountains. The Upper Square has the Town Hall. Also: 18c Holy Trinity; Baroque Church of St Michael.

Praha Capital of Czech Republic and Bohemia. The Castle Quarter has a complex of buildings behind the walls (Royal Castle; Royal Palace; cathedral). The Basilica of St George has a fine Romanesque interior. The Belvedere is the best example of Renaissance architecture. Hradčani Square has aristocratic palaces and the National Gallery. The Little Quarter has many Renaissance (Wallenstein Palace) and Baroque mansions and the Baroque Church of St Nicholas. The Old Town has its centre at the Old Town Square with the Old Town Hall (astronomical clock), Art Nouveau Jan Hus monument and Gothic Týn church. The Jewish quarter has 14c Staranova Synagogue and Old Jewish Cemetery. The Charles Bridge is famous. The medieval New Town has many Art Nouveau buildings and is centred on Wenceslas Square.

Spas of Bohemia Before World War I, the spa towns of Karlovy Vary (Carlsbad), Máriánske Lázně (Marienbad) and Frantiskovy Lázně (Franzenbad) were the favourite resorts of the Habsburg aristocracy.

Denmark *Danmark*

Hillerød Frederiksborg is a fine red-brick Renaissance castle set among three lakes.

København Capital of Denmark. Old centre has fine early 20c Town Hall. Latin Quarter has 19c cathedral. 18c Kastellet has statue of the Little Mermaid nearby. The 17c Rosenborg Castle was a royal residence, as was the Christianborg (now government offices). Other popular sights: Nyhavn canal; Tivoli Gardens. Excellent art collections: Ny Carlsberg Glypotek; State Art Museum; National Museum.

Roskilde Ancient capital of Denmark. The marvellous cathedral is a burial place of the Danish monarchy.

Estonia *Eesti*

Kuressaare Main town on the island of Saaremaa with the 14c Kuressaare Kindlus.

Pärnu Sea resort with an old town centre. Sights: 15c Red Tower; neoclassical Town Hall; St Catherine's Church.

Tallinn Capital of Estonia. The old town is centred on the Town Hall Square. Sights: 15c Town Hall; Toompea Castle; Three Sisters houses. Churches: Gothic St Nicholas; 14c Church of the Holy Spirit; St Olaf's Church.

Tartu Historic town with 19c university. The Town Hall Square is surrounded by neoclassical buildings. Also: remains of 13c cathedral; Estonian National Museum.

Finland *Suomi*

Finnish Lakes Area of outstanding natural beauty covering about one third of the country with thousands of lakes, of which Päijänne and Saimaa are the most important. Tampere, industrial centre of the region, has numerous museums, including the Sara Hildén Art Museum (modern). Savonlinna has the medieval Olavinlinna Castle. Kuopio has the Orthodox and Regional Museums.

Helsinki Capital of Finland. The 19c neoclassical town planning between the Esplanade and Senate Square includes the Lutheran cathedral. There is also a Russian Orthodox cathedral. The Constructivist Stockmann Department Store is the largest in Europe. The Main Train Station is Art Nouveau. Gracious 20c buildings in Mannerheimintie avenue include Finlandiatalo by Alvar Aalto. Many good museums: Art Museum of the Ateneum (19–20c); National Museum; Museum of Applied Arts; Helsinki City Art

Château de Chenonceaux, Châteaux of the Loire, France

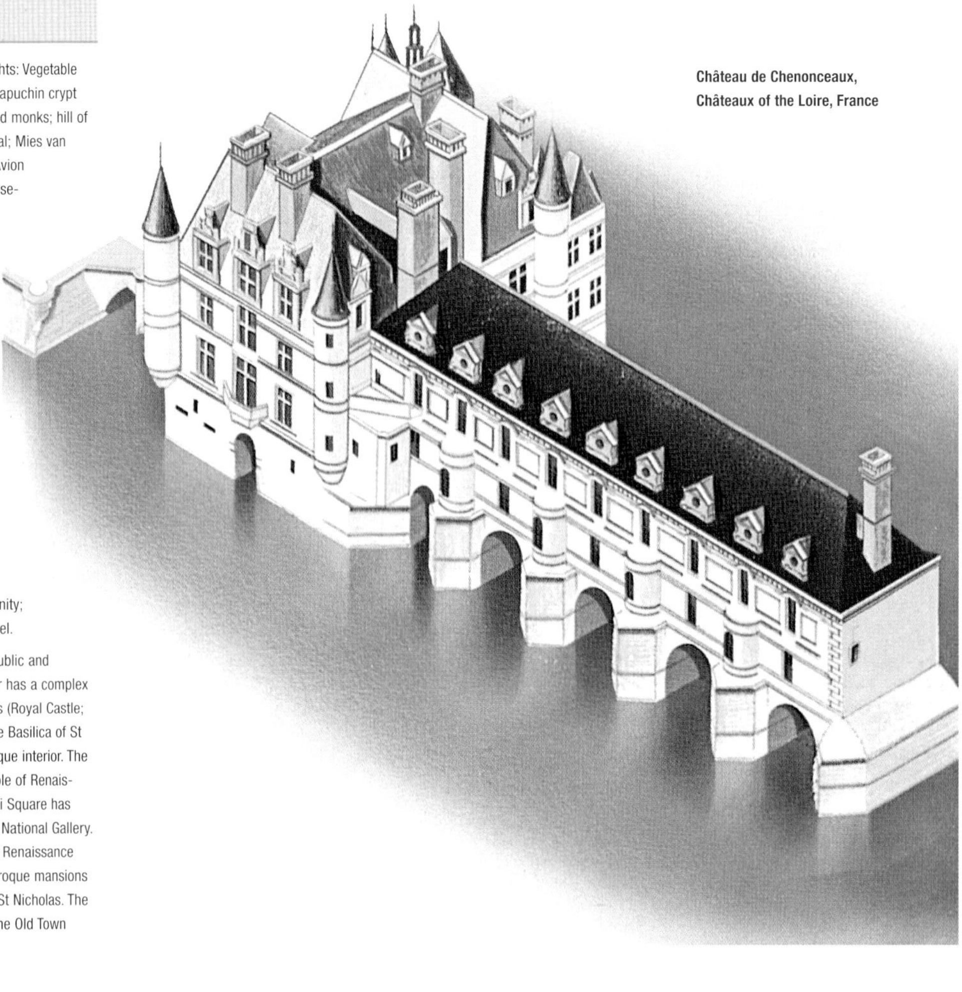

Abbaye aux Hommes, Caen, France

Museum (modern Finnish); Open Air Museum (vernacular architecture); 18c fortress of Suomenlinna has several museums.

Lappland (Finnish) Vast unspoiled rural area. Lappland is home to thousands of nomadic Sámi living in a traditional way. The capital, Rovaniemi, was rebuilt after WWII in the form of reindeer antlers; museums show Sámi history and culture. Nearby is the Artic Circle with the famous Santa Claus Village. Inarim is a centre of Sámi culture. See also Norway and Sweden.

France

Albi Old town with rosy brick architecture. The vast Cathédrale Ste-Cécile (begun 13c) holds some good art. The Berbie Palace houses the Toulouse-Lautrec museum.

Alpes (French) Grenoble, capital of the French Alps, has a good 20c collection in the Museum of Painting and Sculpture. The Vanoise Massif has the greatest number of resorts (Val d'Isère, Courchevel). Chamonix has spectacular views on Mont Blanc, France's and Europe's highest peak.

Amiens France's largest Gothic cathedral has beautiful decoration. The Museum of Picardy has unique 16c panel paintings.

Arles Ancient, picturesque town with Roman relics (1c amphitheatre), 11c cathedral, Archaeological Museum (Roman art).

Avignon Medieval papal capital (1309–77) with 14c walls and many ecclesiastical buildings. Vast Palace of the Popes has stunning frescoes. The Little Palace has fine Italian Renaissance painting. The 12–13c Bridge of St Bénézet is famous.

Bourges The Gothic Cathedral of St Etienne, one of the finest in France, has a superb sculptured choir. Also notable is the House of Jacques Coeur.

Bourgogne Rural wine region with a rich Romanesque, Gothic and Renaissance heritage. The 12c cathedral in Autun and 12c basilica in Vézelay have fine Romanesque sculpture. Monasteries include 11c L'Abbaye de Cluny (ruins) and L'Abbaye de Fontenay. Beaune has beautiful Gothic Hôtel-Dieu and 15c Nicolas Rolin hospices.

Bretagne Brittany is famous for cliffs, sandy beaches and wild landscape. It is also renowned for megalithic monuments (Carnac) and Celtic culture. Its capital, Rennes, has the Palais de Justice and good collections in the Museum of Brittany (history) and Museum of Fine Arts. Also: Nantes; St-Malo.

Caen City with two beautiful Romanesque buildings: Abbaye aux Hommes; Abbaye aux Dames. The château has two museums (15–20c painting; history). The *Bayeux Tapestry* is displayed in nearby Bayeux.

Carcassonne Unusual double-walled fortified town of narrow streets with an inner fortress. The fine Romanesque Church of St Nazaire has superb stained glass.

Chartres The 12–13c cathedral is an exceptionally fine example of Gothic architecture (Royal Doorway, stained glass, choir screen). The Fine Arts Museum has a good collection.

Châteaux of the Loire The Loire Valley has many 15–16c châteaux built amid beautiful scenery by French monarchs and members of their courts. Among the most splendid are Azay-le-Rideau, Chenonceaux and Loches. Also: Abbaye de Fontévraud.

Clermont-Ferrand The old centre contains the cathedral built out of lava and Romanesque basilica. The Puy de Dôme and Puy de Sancy give spectacular views over some 60 extinct volcanic peaks (*puys*).

Colmar Town characterised by Alsatian half-timbered houses. The Unterlinden Museum has excellent German religious art including the famous Isenheim altarpiece. The Dominican church also has a fine altarpiece.

Corse Corsica has a beautiful rocky coast and mountainous interior. Napoleon's birthplace of Ajaccio has: Fesch Museum with Imperial Chapel and a large collection of Italian art; Maison Bonaparte; cathedral. Bonifacio, a medieval town, is spectacularly set on a rock over the sea.

Côte d'Azur The French Riviera is best known for its coastline and glamorous resorts. There are many relics of artists who worked here: St-Tropez has Musée de l'Annonciade; Antibes has 12c Château Grimaldi with the Picasso Museum; Cagnes has the Renoir House and Mediterranean Museum of Modern Art; St-Paul-de-Vence has the excellent Maeght Foundation and Matisse's Chapelle du Rosaire. Cannes is famous for its film festival. Also: Marseille, Monaco, Nice.

Dijon Great 15c cultural centre. The Palais des Ducs et des Etats is the most notable monument and contains the Museum of Fine Arts. Also: the Charterhouse of Champmol.

Disneyland Paris Europe's largest theme park follows in the footsteps of its famous predecessors in the United States.

Le Puy-en-Velay Medieval town bizarrely set on the peaks of dead volcanoes. It is dominated by the Romanesque cathedral (cloisters). The Romanesque chapel of St-Michel is dramatically situated on the highest rock.

Lyon France's third largest city has an old centre and many museums including the Museum of the History of Textiles and the Museum of Fine Arts (old masters).

Marseille Second lagest city in France. Spectacular views from the 19c Notre-Dame-de-la-Garde. The Old Port has 11-12c Basilique St Victor (crypt, catacombs). Cantini Museum has major collection of 20c French art. Château d'If was the setting of Dumas' *The Count of Monte Cristo*.

Mont-St-Michel Gothic pilgrim abbey (11–12c) set dramatically on a steep rock island rising from mud flats and connected to the land by a road covered by the tide. The abbey is made up of a complex of buildings.

Nancy A centre of Art Nouveau. The 18c Place Stanislas was constructed by dethroned Polish king Stanislas. Museums: School of Nancy Museum (Art Nouveau furniture); Fine Arts Museum.

Nantes Former capital of Brittany, with the 15c Château des ducs de Bretagne. The cathedral has a striking interior.

Nice Capital of the Côte d'Azur, the old town is centred on the old castle on the hill. The seafront includes the famous 19c Promenade des Anglais. The aristocratic quarter of the Cimiez Hill has the Marc Chagall Museum and the Matisse Museum. Also: Museum of Modern and Contemporary Art (especially neo-Realism and Pop Art).

Paris Capital of France, one of Europe's most interesting cities. The Île de la Cité area, an island in the River Seine has the 12–13c Gothic Notre Dame (wonderful stained glass) and La Sainte-Chapelle (1240–48), one of the jewels of Gothic art. The Left Bank area: Latin Quarter with the famous Sorbonne university; Museum of Cluny housing medieval art; the Panthéon; Luxembourg Palace and Gardens; Montparnasse, interwar artistic and literary centre; Eiffel Tower; Hôtel des Invalides with Napoleon's tomb. Right Bank: the great boulevards (Avenue des Champs-Élysées joining the Arc de Triomphe and Place de la Concorde); 19c Opéra Quarter; Marais, former aristocratic quarter of elegant mansions (Place des Vosges); Bois de Boulogne, the largest park in Paris; Montmartre, centre of 19c bohemianism, with the Basilique Sacré-Coeur. The Church of St Denis is the first gothic church and the mausoleum of the French monarchy. Paris has three of the world's greatest art collections: The Louvre (to 19c, *Mona Lisa*), Musée d'Orsay (19–20c) and National Modern Art Museum in the Pompidou Centre. Other major museums include: Orangery Museum; Paris Museum of Modern Art; Rodin Museum; Picasso Museum. Notable cemeteries with graves of the famous: Père-Lachaise, Montmartre, Montparnasse. Near Paris are the royal residences of Fontainebleau and Versailles.

Pyrenees (French) Beautiful unspoiled mountain range. Towns include: delightful sea resorts of St-Jean-de-Luz and Biarritz; Pau, with access to the Pyrenees National Park; pilgrimage centre Lourdes.

Reims Together with nearby Epernay, the centre of champagne production. The 13c Gothic cathedral is one of the greatest architectural achievements in France (stained glass by Chagall). Other sights: Palais du Tau (with cathedral sculpture, 11c Basilica of St Rémi; cellars on Place St-Niçaise and Place des Droits-des-Hommes.

Rouen Old centre with many half-timbered houses and 12–13c Gothic cathedral and the Gothic Church of St Maclou with its fascinating remains of a dance macabre on the former cemetery of Aître St-Maclou. The Fine Arts Museum has a good collection.

St-Malo Fortified town (much rebuilt) in a fine coastal setting. There is a magnificent boat trip along the river Rance to Dinan, a splendid well-preserved medieval town.

Strasbourg Town whose historic centre includes a well-preserved quarter of medieval half-timbered Alsatian houses, many of them set on the canal. The cathedral is one of the best in France. The Palais Rohan contains several museums.

Toulouse Medieval university town characterised by flat pink brick (Hôtel Assézat). The Basilique St Sernin, the largest Romanesque church in France, has many art treasures. Marvellous Church of the Jacobins holds the body of St Thomas Aquinas.

Tours Historic town centred on Place Plumereau. Good collections in the Guilds Museum and Fine Arts Museum.

Versailles Vast royal palace built for Louis XIV, primarily by Mansart, set in large formal gardens with magnificent fountains. The extensive and much-imitated state apartments include the famous Hall of Mirrors and the exceptional Baroque chapel.

Vézère Valley Caves A number of prehistoric sites, most notably the cave paintings of Lascaux (some 17,000 years old), now only seen in a duplicate cave, and the cave of Font de Gaume. The National Museum of Prehistory is in Les Eyzies.

Germany *Deutschland*

Aachen Once capital of the Holy Roman Empire. Old town around the Münsterplatz with magnificent cathedral. An exceptionally rich treasure is in the Schatzkammer. The Town Hall is on the medieval Market.

Augsburg Attractive old city. The Town Hall is one of Germany's finest Renaissance buildings. Maximilianstrasse has several Renaissance houses and Rococo Schaezler Palace (good art collection). Churches: Romanesque-Gothic cathedral; Renaissance St Anne's Church. The Fuggerei, founded 1519 as an estate for the poor, is still in use.

Bamberg Well-preserved medieval town. The island, connected by two bridges, has the Town Hall and views of Klein Venedig. Romanesque-Gothic cathedral (good art) is on an exceptional square of Gothic, Renaissance and Baroque buildings – Alte Hofhaltung; Neue Residenz with State Gallery (German masters); Ratstube.

Berlin Capital of Germany. Sights include: the Kurfürstendamm avenue; Brandenburg Gate, former symbol of the division between East and West Germany; Tiergarten; Unter den Linden; 19c Reichstag. Berlin has many excellent art and history collections. Museum Island includes: Pergamon Museum (classical antiquity, Near and Far East, Islam); Bode Museum (Egyptian, Early Christian, Byzantine and European); Old National Gallery (19–20c German). Dahlem Museums: Picture Gallery (13–18c); Sculpture Collection (13–19c); Prints and Drawings Collection; Die Brücke Museum (German Expressionism). Tiergarten Museums: New National Gallery (19–20c); Decorative Arts Museum; Bauhaus Archive. In the Kreuzberg area: Berlin Museum; Grupius Building with Jewish Museum and Berlin Gallery; remains of Berlin Wall and Checkpoint Charlie House. Schloss Charlottenburg houses a number of collections including the National Gallery's Romantic Gallery; the Egyptian Museum is nearby.

Bodensee Lake Constance, with many pleasant lake resorts. Lindau, on an island, has numerous gabled houses. Birnau has an 18c Rococo church. Konstanz (Swiss side) has the Minster set above the Old Town.

Deutsche Alpenstrasse German Alpine Road in the Bavarian Alps, from Lindau on Bodensee to Berchtesgaden. The setting for 19c fairy-tale follies of Ludwig II of Bavaria (Linderhof, Hohenschwangau, Neuschwanstein), charming old villages (Oberammergau) and Baroque churches (Weiss, Ottobeuren). Garmisch-Partenkirchen has views on Germany's highest peak, the Zugspitze.

Dresden Historic centre with a rich display of Baroque architecture. Major buildings: Castle of the Electors of Saxony; 18c Hofkirche; Zwinger Palace with fountains and pavilions (excellent old masters); Albertinum with excellent Gallery of New Masters; treasury of Grünes Gewölbe. The Baroque-planned New Town contains the Japanese Palace and Schloss Pillnitz.

Frankfurt Financial capital of Germany. The historic centre around the Römerberg Square has 13–15c cathedral, 15c Town Hall, Gothic St Nicholas Church, Saalhof (12c chapel). Museums: Museum of Modern Art (post-war); State Art Institute.

Freiburg Old university town with system of streams running through the streets. The Gothic Minster is surrounded by the town's finest buildings. Two towers remain of the medieval walls. The Augustine Museum has a good collection.

Hamburg Port city with many parks, lakes and canals. The Kunsthalle has Old Masters and 19-20c German art. Buildings: 19c Town Hall; Baroque St Michael's Church.

Heidelberg Germany's oldest university town, majestically set on the banks of the river and romantically dominated by the ruined schloss. The Gothic Church of the Holy Spirit is on the Market Place with the Baroque Town Hall. Other sights include the 16c Knight's House and the Baroque Morass Palace with a museum of Gothic art.

Hildesheim City of Romanesque architecture (much destroyed). Principal sights: St Michael's Church; cathedral (11c interior, sculptured doors, St Anne's Chapel); superb 15c Tempelhaus on the Market Place.

Köln Ancient city with 13–19c cathedral (rich display of art). In the old town are the Town Hall and many Romanesque churches (Gross St Martin, St Maria im Kapitol, St Maria im

Lyskirchen, St Ursula, St Georg, St Severin, St Pantaleon, St Apostolen). Museums: Diocesan Museum (religious art); Roman-German Museum (ancient history); Wallraf-Richartz/Ludwig Museum (14–20c art).

Lübeck Beautiful old town built on an island and characterised by Gothic brick architecture. Sights: 15c Holsten Gate; Market with the Town Hall and Gothic brick St Mary's Church; 12–13c cathedral; St Ann Museum.

Mainz The Electoral Palatinate schloss and Market fountain are Renaissance. Churches: 12c Romanesque cathedral; Gothic St Steven's (with stained glass by Marc Chagall).

Marburg Medieval university town with the Market Place and Town Hall, St Elizabeth's Church (frescoes, statues, 13c shrine), 15–16c schloss.

München Old town centred on the Marienplatz with 15c Old Town Hall and 19c New Town Hall. Many richly decorated churches: St Peter's (14c tower); Gothic red-brick cathedral; Renaissance St Michael's (royal portraits on the façade); Rococo St Asam's. The Residenz palace consists of seven splendid buildings holding many art objects. Schloss Nymphenburg has a palace, park, botanical gardens and four beautiful pavilions. Superb museums: Old Gallery (old masters), New Gallery (18–19c), Lenbachhaus (modern German). Many famous beer gardens.

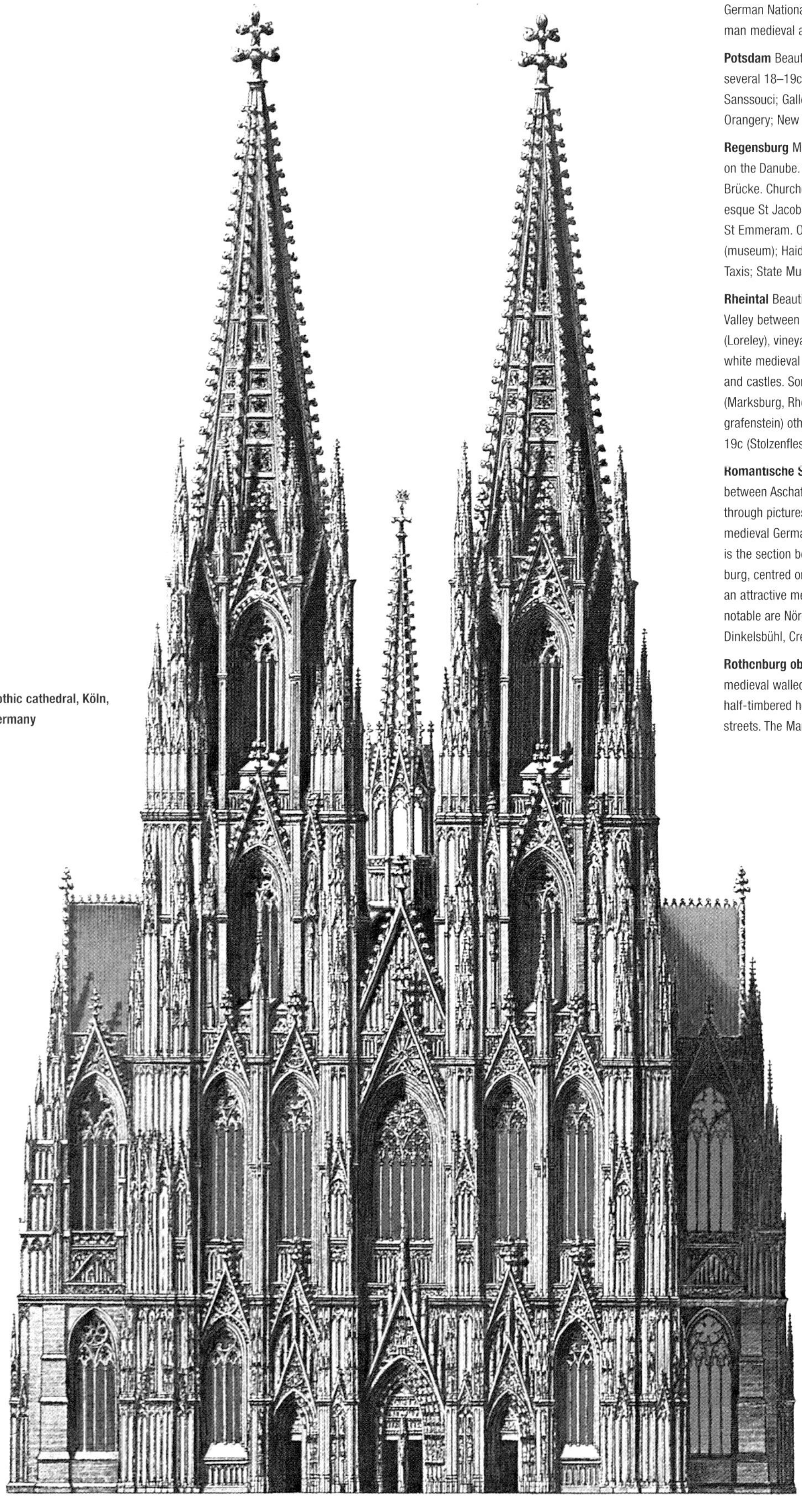

Gothic cathedral, Köln, Germany

Münster Historic city with well-preserved Gothic and Renaissance buildings: 14c Town Hall; Romanesque-Gothic cathedral. The Westphalian Museum holds regional art.

Nürnberg Beautiful medieval walled city dominated by the 12c Kaiserburg. Romanesque-Gothic St Sebaldus Church and Gothic St Laurence Church are rich in art. On Hauptmarkt is the famous 14c Schöner Brunnen. Also notable is 15c Dürer House. The German National Museum has excellent German medieval and Renaissance art.

Potsdam Beautiful Sanssouci Park contains several 18–19c buildings including: Schloss Sanssouci; Gallery (European masters); Orangery; New Palace; Chinese Teahouse.

Regensburg Medieval city set majestically on the Danube. Views from 12c Steinerne Brücke. Churches: Gothic cathedral; Romanesque St Jacob's; Gothic St Blaisius; Baroque St Emmeram. Other sights: Old Town Hall (museum); Haidplatz; Schloss Thurn und Taxis; State Museum.

Rheintal Beautiful 80km gorge of the Rhein Valley between Mainz and Koblenz with rocks (Loreley), vineyards (Bacharach, Rüdesheim), white medieval towns (Rhens, Oberwesel) and castles. Some castles are medieval (Marksburg, Rheinfles, island fortress Pfalzgrafenstein) others were built or rebuilt in the 19c (Stolzenfles, Rheinstein).

Romantische Strasse Romantic route between Aschaffenburg and Füssen, leading through picturesque towns and villages of medieval Germany. The most popular section is the section between Würzburg and Augsburg, centred on Rothenburg ob der Tauber, an attractive medieval walled town. Also notable are Nördlingen, Harburg Castle, Dinkelsbühl, Creglingen.

Rothenburg ob der Tauber Attractive medieval walled town with tall gabled and half-timbered houses on narrow cobbled streets. The Market Place has Gothic-Renaissance Town Hall, Rattrinke-stubbe and Gothic St Jacob's Church (altarpiece).

Schwarzwald Hilly region between Basel and Karlsruhe, the largest and most picturesque woodland in Germany, with the highest summit, Feldberg, lake resorts (Titisee), health resorts (Baden-Baden) and clock craft (Triberg). Freiburg is regional capital.

Speyer 11c cathedral is one of the largest and best Romanesque buildings in Germany. 12c Jewish Baths are well-preserved.

Stuttgart Largely modern city with old centre around the Old Schloss, Renaissance Alte Kanzlei, 15c Collegiate Church and Baroque New Schloss. Museums: Regional Museum; post-modern State Gallery (old masters, 20c German). The 1930s Weissenhofsiedlung is by several famous architects.

Trier Superb Roman monuments: Porta Nigra; Aula Palatina (now a church); Imperial Baths; amphitheatre. The Regional Museum has Roman artefacts. Also, Gothic Church of Our Lady; Romanesque cathedral.

Ulm Old town with half-timbered gabled houses set on a canal. Gothic 14–19c minster has tallest spire in the world (161m).

Weimar The Neoclassical schloss, once an important seat of government, now houses a good art collection. Church of SS Peter and Paul has a Cranach masterpiece. Houses of famous people: Goethe, Schiller, Liszt. The famous Bauhaus was founded at the School of Architecture and Engineering.

Würzburg Set among vineyard hills, the medieval town is centred on the Market Place with the Rococo House of the Falcon. The 18c episcopal princes' residence (frescoes) is magnificent. The cathedral is rich in art. Work of the great local Gothic sculptor, Riemenschneider, is in Gothic St Mary's Chapel, Baroque New Minster, and the Mainfränkisches Museum.

Greece *Ellas*

Athínai Capital of Greece. The Acropolis, with 5c BC sanctuary complex (Parthenon, Propylaia, Erechtheion, Temple of Athena Nike), is the greatest architectural achievement of antiquity in Europe. The Agora was a public meeting place in ancient Athens. Pláka has narrow streets and small Byzantine churches (Kapnikaréa). The Olympeum was the largest temple in Greece. Also: Olympic Stadium; excellent collections of ancient artefacts (Museum of Cycladic and Ancient Greek Art; Acropolis Museum; National Archeological Museum; Benáki Museum).

Delphí At the foot of the Mount Parnassós, Delphi was the seat of the Delphic Oracle of Apollo, the most important oracle in Ancient Greece. Delphi was also a political meeting place and the site of the Pythian Games. The Sanctuary of Apollo consists of: Temple of Apollo, led to by the Sacred Way; Theatre; Stadium. The museum has a display of objects from the site (5c BC *Charioteer*).

Epídavros Formerly a spa and religious centre focused on the Sanctuary of Asclepius (ruins). The enormous 4c BC theatre is probably the finest of all ancient theatres.

Greek Islands Popular islands with some of the most beautiful and spectacular beaches in Europe. The many islands are divided into various groups and individual islands: The major groups are the Kikládhes and Dhodhekanisos in the Aegean Sea, the largest islands are Kérkira (Corfu) in the Ionian Sea and Kríti.

Kórinthos Ancient Corinth (ruins), with 5c BC Temple of Apollo, was in 44BC made capital of Roman Greece by Julius Caesar. Set above the city, the Greek-built acropolis hill of Acrocorinth became the Roman and Byzantine citadel (ruins).

Kriti Largest Greek island, Crete was home to the great Minoan civilization (2800–1100 BC). The main relics are the ruined Palace of Knossós and Mália. Gortys was capital of the Roman province. Picturesque Réthimno has narrow medieval streets, a Venetian fortress and a former Turkish mosque. Mátala has beautiful beaches and famous caves cut into cliffs. Iráklio (Heraklion), the capital, has a good Archeological Museum.

Metéora The tops of bizarre vertical cylinders of rock and towering cliffs are the setting for 14c Cenobitic monasteries, until recently only accessible by baskets or removable ladders. Méga Metéoron is the grandest and set on the highest point. Roussánou has the most extraordinary site. Varlaám is one of the oldest and most beautiful, with the Ascent Tower and 16c church with frescoes. Áyiou Nikólaou also has good frescoes.

Mistrás Set in a beautiful landscape, Mystra is the site of a Byzantine city, now in ruins, with palaces, frescoed churches, monasteries and houses.

Mykenai The citadel of Mycenae prospered between 1950BC and 1100BC and consists of the royal complex of Agamemnon: Lion Gate, royal burial site, Royal Palace, South House, Great Court.

Óros Ólimpos Mount Olympus, mythical seat of the Greek gods, is the highest, most dramatic peak in Greece.

Olympia In a stunning setting, the Panhellenic Games were held here for a millennium. Ruins of the sanctuary of Olympia consist of the Doric temples of Zeus and Hera and the vast Stadium. There is also a museum (4c BC figure of Hermes).

Ródhos One of the most attractive islands with wonderful sandy beaches. The city of Rhodes has a well-preserved medieval centre with the Palace of the Grand Masters and the Turkish Süleymaniye Mosque

Thessaloníki Largely modern city with Byzantine walls and many fine churches: 8c Ayía Sofia; 11c Panayía Halkéon; 14c Dhódheka Apóstoli; 14c Áyios Nikólaos Orfanós; 5c Áyios Dhimítrios (largest in Greece, 7c Mosaics).

Hungary *Magyarorszàg*

Balaton The 'Hungarian sea', famous for its holiday resorts: Balatonfüred, Tihany, Badasconytomaj, Keszthely.

Budapest Capital of Hungary on River Danube, with historic area centring on the Castle Hill of Buda district. Sights include: Matthias church; Pest district with late 19c architecture, centred on Ferenciek tere; neo-Gothic Parliament Building on river; Millennium Monument. The Royal Castle houses a number of museums: Hungarian National Gallery, Budapest History Museum; Ludwig Collection. Other museums: National Museum of Fine Arts (excellent Old and Modern masters); Hungarian National Museum (Hungarian history). Famous for public thermal baths: Király and Rudas baths, both made under Turkish rule; Cellért baths, the most visited.

Esztergom Medieval capital of Hungary set in scenic landscape. Sights: Hungary's largest basilica (completed 1856); royal palace ruins.

Pécs Attractive old town with Europe's fifth oldest university (founded 1367). Famous for Turkish architecture (Mosque of Gazi Kasim Pasha, Jakovali Hassan Mosque).

Sopron Beautiful walled town with many Gothic and Renaissance houses. Nearby: Fertöd with the marvellous Eszergázy Palace.

Ireland

Aran Islands Islands with spectacular cliffs and notable pre-Christian and Christian sights, especially on Inishmore.

Cashel Town dominated by the Rock of Cashel (61m) topped by ecclesiastical ruins including 13c cathedral; 15c Halls of the Vicars; beautiful Romanesque 12c Cormac's Chapel (fine carvings).

Connemara Beautiful wild landscape of mountains, lakes, peninsulas and beaches. Clifden is the capital.

Cork Pleasant city with its centre along St Patrick's Street and Grand Parade lined with fine 18c buildings. Churches: Georgian St Anne's Shandon (bell tower); 19c cathedral.

County Donegal Rich scenic landscape of mystical lakes and glens and seascape of cliffs (Slieve League cliffs are the highest in Europe). The town of Donegal has a finely preserved Jacobean castle.

Dublin Capital of Ireland. City of elegant 18c neoclassical and Georgian architecture with gardens and parks (St Stephen's Green, Merrion Square with Leinster House – now seat of Irish parliament). City's main landmark, Trinity College (founded 1591), houses in its Old Library fine Irish manuscripts (7c Book of Durrow, 8c Book of Kells). Two Norman cathedrals: Christ Church; St Patrick's. Other buildings: originally medieval Dublin Castle with State Apartments; James Gandon's masterpieces: Custom House; Four Courts. Museums: National Museum (Irish history); National Gallery (old masters, Impressionists, Irish painting); Guinness Brewery Museum; Dublin Writers' Museum (Joyce, Wilde, Yeats and others).

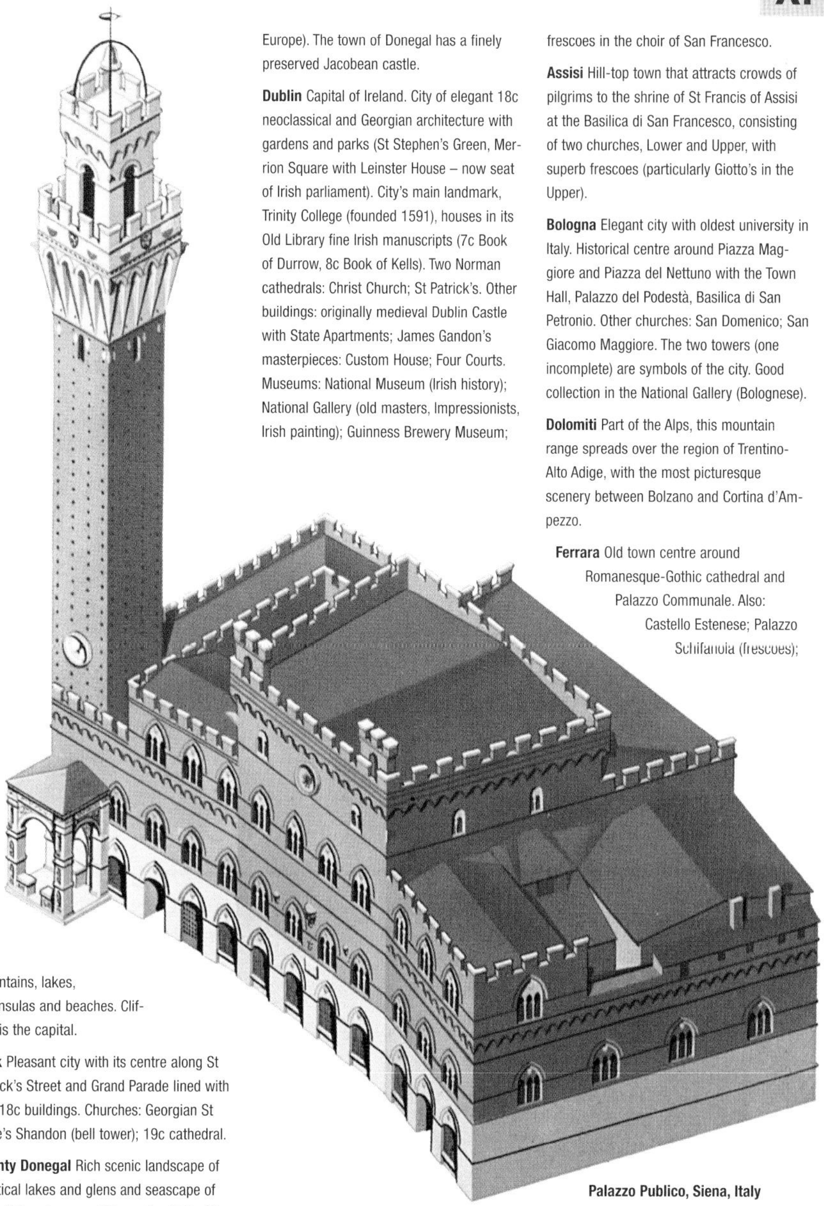

Palazzo Publico, Siena, Italy

Glendalough Impressive ruins of an important early Celtic (6c) monastery with 9c cathedral, 12c St Kevin's Cross, oratory of St Kevin's Church.

Kilkenny Charming medieval town, with narrow streets dominated by 12c castle (restored 19c). The 13c Gothic cathedral has notable tomb monuments.

Newgrange One of the best passage graves in Europe, the massive 4500-year-old tomb has stones richly decorated with patterns.

Ring of Kerry Route around the Iveragh peninsula with beautiful lakes (Lough Leane), peaks overlooking the coastline and islands (Valencia Island, Skelling). Also: Killarney; ruins of 15c Muckross Abbey.

Italy *Italia*

Alpi (Italian) Wonderful stretch of the Alps running from the Swiss and French borders to Austria. The region of Valle d'Aosta is one of the most popular ski regions, bordered by the highest peaks of the Alps.

Agrigento Set on a hill above the sea and famed for the Valley of the Temples. The nine originally 5c Doric temples are Sicily's best-preserved Greek remains.

Arezzo Beautiful old town set on a hill dominated by 13c cathedral. Piazza Grande is surrounded by medieval and Renaissance palaces. Main sight: Piero della Francesca's frescoes in the choir of San Francesco.

Assisi Hill-top town that attracts crowds of pilgrims to the shrine of St Francis of Assisi at the Basilica di San Francesco, consisting of two churches, Lower and Upper, with superb frescoes (particularly Giotto's in the Upper).

Bologna Elegant city with oldest university in Italy. Historical centre around Piazza Maggiore and Piazza del Nettuno with the Town Hall, Palazzo del Podestà, Basilica di San Petronio. Other churches: San Domenico; San Giacomo Maggiore. The two towers (one incomplete) are symbols of the city. Good collection in the National Gallery (Bolognese).

Dolomiti Part of the Alps, this mountain range spreads over the region of Trentino-Alto Adige, with the most picturesque scenery between Bolzano and Cortina d'Ampezzo.

Ferrara Old town centre around Romanesque-Gothic cathedral and Palazzo Communale. Also: Castello Estenese; Palazzo Schifanoia (frescoes); Palazzo dei Diamanti housing Pinacoteca Nazionale.

Firenze City with exceptionally rich medieval and Renaissance heritage. Piazza del Duomo has:13–15c cathedral (first dome since antiquity); 14c campanile; 11c baptistry (bronze doors). Piazza della Signoria has: 14c Palazzo Vecchio (frescoes); Loggia della Signoria (sculpture); 16c Uffizi Gallery with one of the world's greatest collections (13–18c). Other great paintings: Museo di San Marco; Palatine Gallery in 15–16c Pitti Palace surrounded by Boboli Gardens. Sculpture: Cathedral Works Museum; Bargello Museum; Academy Gallery (Michelangelo's *David*). Among many other Renaissance palaces: Medici-Riccardi; Rucellai; Strozzi. The 15c church of San Lorenzo has Michelangelo's tombs of the Medici. Many churches have richly frescoed chapels: Santa Maria Novella, Santa Croce, Santa Maria del Carmine. The 13c Ponte Vecchio is one of the most famous sights.

Italian Lakes Beautiful district at the foot of the Alps, most of the lakes with holiday resorts. Many lakes are surrounded by aristocratic villas (Maggiore, Como, Garda).

Mántova Attractive city surrounded by three lakes. Two exceptional palaces: Palazzo Ducale (Sala del Pisanello; Camera degli Sposi, Castello San Giorgio); luxurious Palazzo Tè (brilliant frescoes). Also: 15c Church of Sant'Andrea; 13c law courts.

Romanesque cathedral, Pisa, Italy

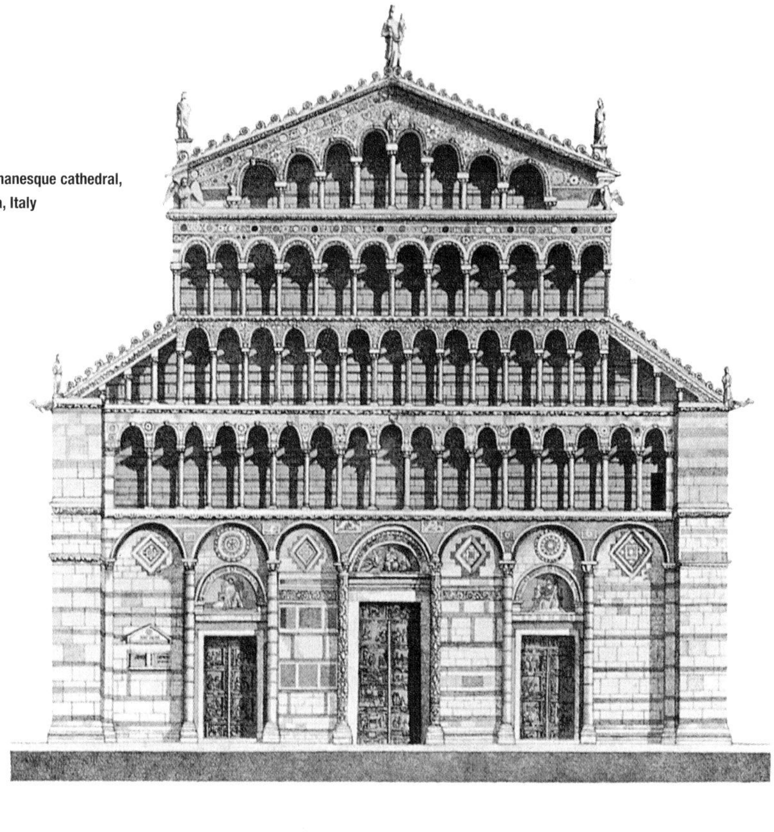

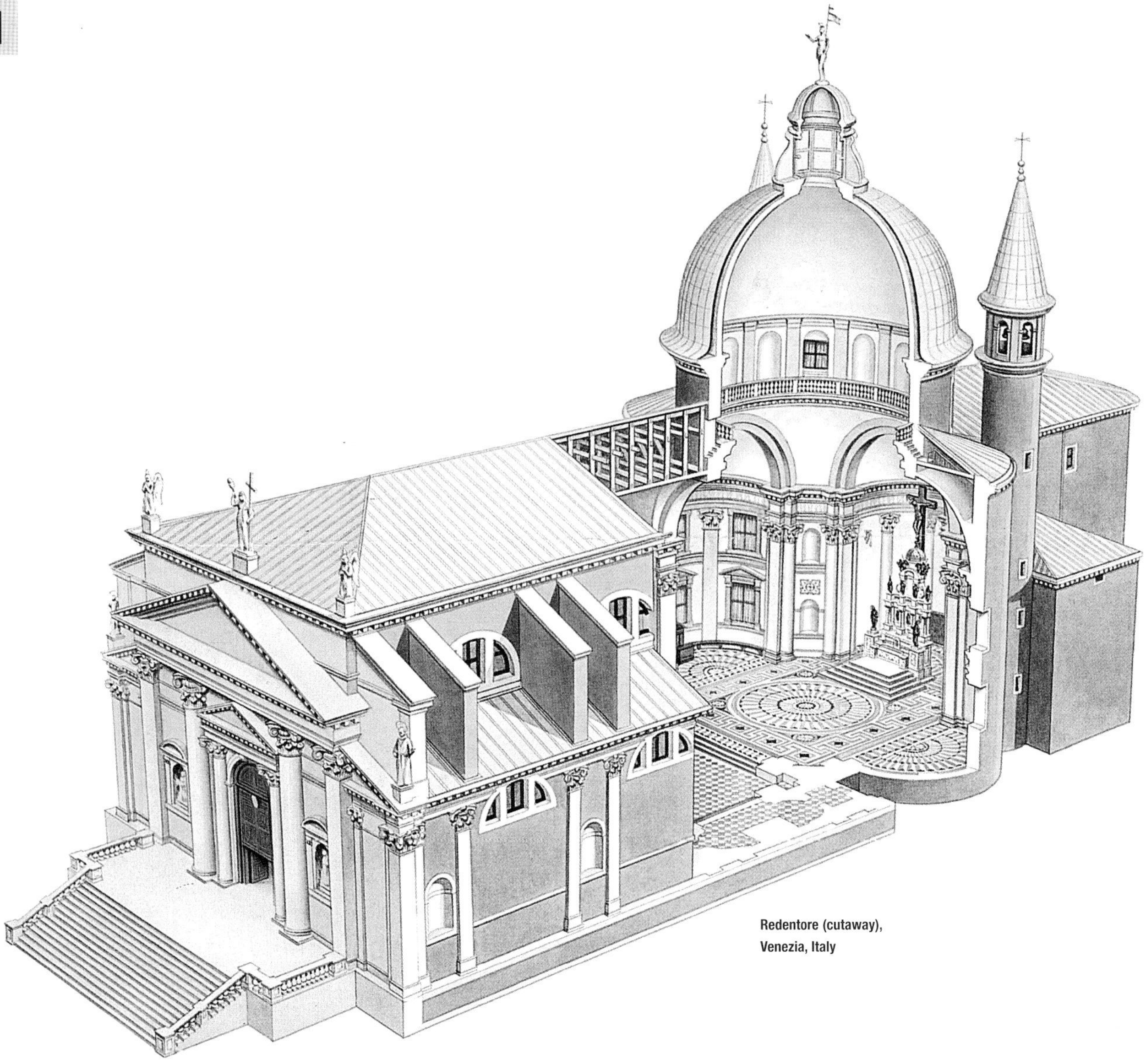

Redentore (cutaway), Venezia, Italy

Milano Modern city, Italy's fashion and design capital (Corso and Galleria Vittoro Emmanuelle II). Churches include: Gothic cathedral (1386–1813), the world's largest (4c baptistry); Romanesque St Ambrose; 15c San Satiro; Santa Maria delle Grazie with Leonardo da Vinci's *Last Supper* in the convent refectory. Great art collections, Brera Gallery, Ambrosian Library, Museum of Contemporary Art. Castello Sforzesco (15c, 19c) also has a gallery. The famous La Scala theatre opened in 1778. Nearby: monastery at Pavia.

Napoli Historical centre around Gothic cathedral (crypt). Spaccanapoli area has numerous churches (bizarre Cappella Sansevero, Gesù Nuovo, Gothic Santa Chiara with fabulous tombs). Buildings: 13c Castello Nuovo; 13c Castel dell'Ovo; 15c Palazzo Cuomo. Museums: National Archeological Museum (artefacts from Pompeii and Herculaneum); National Museum of Capodimonte (Renaissance painting). Nearby: spectacular coast around Amalfi; Pompeii; Herculaneum.

Orvieto Medieval hill-top town with a number of monuments including the Romanesque-Gothic cathedral (façade, frescoes).

Pádova Pleasant old town with arcaded streets. Basilica del Santo is a place of pilgrimage to the tomb of St Anthony. Giotto's frescoes in the Scrovegni chapel are exceptional. Also: Piazza dei Signori with Palazzo del Capitano; vast Palazzo della Ragione; church of the Eremitani (frescoes).

Palermo City with Moorish, Norman and Baroque architecture, especially around the main squares (Quattro Canti, Piazza Pretoria, Piazza Bellini). Sights: remains of Norman palace (12c Palatine Chapel); Norman cathedral; Regional Gallery (medieval); some 8000 preserved bodies in the catacombs of the Cappuchin Convent. Nearby: 12c Norman Duomo di Monreale.

Parma Attractive city centre, famous for Corregio's frescoes in the Romanesque cathedral and church of St John the Evangelist, and Parmigianino's frescoes in the church of Madonna della Steccata. Their works are also in the National Gallery.

Perúgia Hill-top town centred around Piazza Quattro Novembre with the cathedral, Fontana Maggiore and Palazzo dei Priori. Also: Collegio di Cambio (frescoes); National Gallery of Umbria; many churches.

Pisa Medieval town centred on the Piazza dei Miracoli. Sights: famous Romanesque Leaning Tower, Romanesque cathedral (excellent façade, Gothic pulpit); 12–13c Baptistry; 13c Camposanto cloistered cemetery (fascinating 14c frescoes).

Ravenna Ancient town with exceptionally well-preserved Byzantine mosaics. The finest are in 5c Mausoleo di Galla Placidia and 6c Basilica di San Vitale. Good mosaics also in the basilicas of Sant'Apollinare in Classe and Sant'Apollinare Nuovo.

Roma Capital of Italy, exceptionally rich in sights from many eras. Ancient sights: Colosseum; Arch of Constantine; Trajan's Column; Roman and Imperial fora; hills of Palatino and Campidoglio (Capitoline Museum shows antiquities); Pantheon; Castel Sant' Angelo; Baths of Caracalla). Early Christian sights: catacombs (San Calisto, San Sebastiano, Domitilla); basilicas (San Giovanni in Laterano, Santa Maria Maggiore, San Paolo Fuori le Mura). Rome is known for richly decorated Baroque churches: il Gesù, Sant'Ignazio, Santa Maria della Vittoria, Chiesa Nuova. Other churches, often with art treasures: Romanesque Santa Maria in Cosmadin, Gothic Santa Maria Sopra Minevra, Renaissance Santa Maria del Popolo, San Pietro in Vincoli. Several Renaissance and Baroque palaces and villas house superb art collections (Palazzo Barberini, Palazzo Doria Pamphilj, Palazzo Spada, Palazzo Corsini, Villa Giulia, Galleria Borghese) and are beautifully frescoed (Villa Farnesina). Fine Baroque public spaces with fountains: Piazza Navona; Piazza di Spagna with the Spanish Steps, Trevi Fountain). Nearby: Tivoli; Villa Adriana. Rome also contains the Vatican City (Città del Vaticano).

Sardegna Sardinia has some of the most beautiful beaches in Italy (Alghero). Unique are the nuraghi, some 7000 stone constructions (Su Nuraxi, Serra Orios), the remains of an old civilization (1500–400 BC). Old towns include Cagliari and Sássari.

Sicilia Surrounded by beautiful beaches and full of monuments of many periods, Sicily is the largest island in the Mediterranean. Taormina with its Greek theatre has one of the most spectacular beaches, lying under the mildly active volcano Mount Etna. Also: Agrigento; Palermo, Siracusa.

Siena Outstanding 13–14c medieval town centred on beautiful Piazza del Campo with Gothic Palazzo Publico (frescoes of secular life). Delightful Romanesque-Gothic Duomo (Libreria Piccolomini, baptistry, art works). Many other richly decorated churches. Fine Sienese painting in Pinacoteca Nazionale and Museo dell'Opera del Duomo.

Siracusa Built on an island connected to the mainland by a bridge, the old town has a 7c cathedral, ruins of the Temple of Apollo; Fountain of Arethusa; archaeological museum. On the mainland: 5c BC Greek theatre with seats cut out of rock; Greek fortress of Euralus; 2c Roman amphitheatre; 5–6c Catacombs of St John.

Torino City centre has 17-18c Baroque layout dominated by twin Baroque churches. Also: 15c cathedral (holds Turin Shroud);Palazzo Reale; 18c Superga Basilica; Academy of Science with two museums (Egyptian antiquities; European painting.

Urbino Set in beautiful hilly landscape, Urbino's heritage is mainly due to the 15c court of Federico da Montefeltro at the magnificent Ducal Palace (notable Studiolo), now also a gallery.

Venezia Stunning old city built on islands in a lagoon, with some 150 canals. The Grand Canal is crossed by the famous 16c Rialto Bridge and is lined with elegant palaces (Gothic Ca'd'Oro and Ca'Foscari, Renaissance Palazzo Grimani, Baroque Rezzonico). The district of San Marco has the core of the best known sights and is centred on Piazza San Marco with 11c Basilica di San Marco (bronze horses, 13c mosaics); Campanille (exceptional views) and Ducal Palace (connected with the prison by the famous Bridge of Sighs). Many churches (Santa Maria Gloriosa dei Frari, Santa Maria della Salute, Redentore, San Giorgio Maggiore, San Giovanni e Paolo) and scuole (Scuola di San Rocco, Scuola di San Giorgio degli Schiavoni) have excellent works of art. The Gallery of the Academy houses superb 14–18c Venetian art. The Guggenheim Museum holds 20c art.

Verona Old town with remains of 1c Roman Arena and medieval sights including the Palazzo degli Scaligeri; Arche Scaligere; Romanesque Santa Maria Antica; Castelvecchio; Ponte Scaliger. The famous 14c House of Juliet has associations with *Romeo and Juliet*. Many churches with fine art works (cathedral; Sant'Anastasia; basilica di San Zeno Maggiore).

Vicenza Beautiful town, famous for the architecture of Palladio, including the Olympic Theatre (extraordinary stage), Corso Palladio with many of his palaces, and Palazzo Chiericati. Nearby: Villa Rotonda, the most influential of all Palladian buildings.

Volcanic Region Region from Naples to Sicily. Mount Etna is one of the most famous European volcanoes. Vesuvius dominates the Bay of Naples and has at its foot two of Italy's finest Roman sites, Pompeii and Herculaneum, both destroyed by its eruption in 79AD. Stromboli is one of the beautiful Aeolian Islands.

Legend

This guide to sights of Europe has been compiled particularly with the motorist in mind. While many of the places are excellent holiday destinations in themselves, they are all worth a stop or detour on your journey should you be driving that way. With the higher-rated places particularly, it is well worth adapting your travel arrangements to make time for a visit.

- Mont-St-Michel ■ **Do not miss**
- El Escorial ◆ **Exceptional**
- Urbino • **First rate**
- *Wroclaw* • **Worth visiting**

There are descriptions of the places on this map in the accompanying three pages of text. These point you to the most famous, fascinating or beautiful sights you will find if you visit.

Latvia *Latvija*

Riga Well-preserved medieval town centre around the cathedral. Sights: Riga Castle; medieval Hanseatic houses; Great Guild Hall; Gothic Church of St Peter; Art Nouveau buildings in the New Town. Nearby: Baroque Rundale Castle.

Lithuania *Lietuva*

Vilnius Baroque old town with fine architecture including: cathedral; Gediminas Tower; university complex; Archbishop's Palace; Church of St Anne. Also: remains of Jewish life; Vilnius Picture Gallery (16–19c regional); Lithuanian National Museum.

Luxembourg

Luxembourg Capital of Luxembourg, built on a rock with fine views. Old town is around the Place d'Armes. Buildings: Grand Ducal Palace; fortifications of Rocher du Bock; cathedral. Museum of History and Art holds an excellent regional collection.

Macedonia *Makedonija*

Skopje Historic town with Turkish citadel, fine 15c mosques, oriental bazaar, ancient bridge. Superb Byzantine churches nearby.
Ohrid Old town, beautifully set by a lake, with houses of wood and brick, remains of a Turkish citadel, many churches (two cathedrals; St Naum south of the lake).

Malta

Valletta Capital of Malta. Historic walled city, founded in 16c by the Maltese Knights, with 16c Grand Master's Palace and a richly decorated cathedral.

Monaco

Monaco Major resort area in a beautiful location. Sights include: Monte Carlo casino, Prince's Palace at Monaco-Ville; 19c cathedral; oceanographic museum.

The Netherlands *Nederland*

Amsterdam Capital of the Netherlands. Old centre has picturesque canals lined with distinctive elegant 17–18c merchants' houses. Dam Square has 15c New Church and Royal Palace. Other churches include Westerkerk. The Museumplein has three world-famous museums: Rijksmuseum (several art collections including 15–17c painting); Van Gogh Museum; Municipal Museum (art from 1850 on). Other museums: Anne Frank House; Jewish Historical Museum; Rembrandt House.

Delft Well-preserved old Dutch town with gabled red-roofed houses along canals. Gothic churches: New Church; Old Church. Famous for Delftware (two museums).

Den Haag Seat of Government and of the royal house of the Netherlands. The 17c Mauritshuis houses the Royal Picture Gallery (excellent 15–18c Flemish and Dutch). Other good collections: Prince William V Gallery; Hesdag Museum; Municipal Museum

Haarlem Many medieval gabled houses centred on the Great Market with 14c Town Hall and 15c Church of St Bavon. Museums: Frans Hals Museum; Teylers Museum.

Het Loo Former royal palace and gardens set in a vast landscape (commissioned by future Queen of England, Mary Stuart).

Keukenhof Landscaped gardens, planted with bulbs of many varieties, are the largest flower gardens in the world.

Leiden University town of beautiful gabled houses set along canals. The Rijksmuseum Van Oudheden is Holland's most important home to archaeological artefacts from the Antiquity. The 16c Hortus Botanicus is one of the oldest botanical gardens in Europe. The Cloth Hall with van Leyden's *Last Judgement.*

Rotterdam The largest port in the world. The Boymans-van Beuningen Museum has a huge and excellent decorative and fine art collection (old and modern). Nearby: 18c Kinderdijk with 19 windmills.

Utrecht Delightful old town centre along canals with the Netherlands' oldest university and Gothic cathedral. Good art collections. Central Museum; National Museum.

Norway *Norge*

Bergen Norway's second city in a scenic setting. The Quay has many painted wooden medieval buildings. Sights: 12c Romanesque St Mary's Church; Bergenhus fortress with 13c Haakon's Hall; Rosenkrantztårnet; Grieghallen; Rasmus Meyer Collection (Norwegian art); Bryggens Museum.

Lappland (Norwegian) Vast land of Finnmark is home to the Sámi. Nordkapp is the northern point of Europe. Also Finland, Sweden.

Norwegian Fjords Beautiful and majestic landscape of deep glacial valleys filled by the sea. The most thrilling fjords are between Bergen and Ålesund.

Oslo Capital of Norway with a modern centre. Buildings: 17c cathedral; 19c city hall, 19c royal palace; 19c Stortinget (housing parliament); 19c University; 13c Akershus (castle); 12c Akerskirke (church). Museums: National Gallery; Munch Museum; Viking Ship Museum; Folk Museum (reconstructed buildings).

Stavkirker Wooden medieval stave churches of bizarre pyramidal structure, carved with images from Nordic mythology. Best preserved in southern Norway.

Tromsø Main arctic city of Norway with a university and two cathedrals.

Trondheim Set on the edge of a fjord, a modern city with the superb Nidaros cathedral (rebuilt 19c). Also: Stiftsgaard (royal residence); Applied Arts Museum.

Poland *Polska*

Częstochowa Centre of Polish Catholicism, with the 14c monastery of Jasna Góra a pilgrimage site to the icon of the Black Madonna for six centuries.

Gdańsk Medieval centre with: 14c Town Hall (state rooms); Gothic brick St Mary's Church, Poland's largest; Long Market has fine buildings (Artus Court); National Art Museum.

Kraków Old university city, rich in architecture, centred on superb 16c Marketplace with Gothic-Renaissance Cloth Hall containing the Art Gallery (19c Polish), Clock Tower, Gothic red-brick St Mary's Church (altarpiece). Czartoryski Palace has city's finest art collection. Wawel Hill has the Gothic cathedral and splendid Renaissance Royal Palace. The former Jewish ghetto in Kazimierz district has 16c Old Synagogue, now a museum.

Poznań Town centred on the Old Square with Renaissance Town Hall and Baroque mansions. Also: medieval castle; Gothic cathedral; National Museum (European masters).

Tatry One of Europe's most delightful mountain ranges with many beautiful ski resorts (Zakopane). Also in Slovakia.

Warszawa Capital of Poland, with many historic monuments in the Old Town with the Royal Castle (museum) and Old Town Square surrounded by reconstructed 17–18c merchants' houses. Several churches including: Gothic cathedral; Baroque Church of the Nuns of Visitation. Richly decorated royal palaces and gardens: Neoclassical Łazienki Palace; Baroque palace in Wilanów. The National Museum has Polish and European art.

Wrocław Historic town centred on the Market Square with 15c Town Hall and mansions. Churches: Baroque cathedral; St Elizabeth; St Adalbert. National Museum displays fine art. Vast painting of Battle of Racławice is specially housed.

Portugal

Alcobaça Monastery of Santa Maria, one of the best examples of a Cistercian abbey, founded in 1147 (exterior 17–18c). The church is Portugal's largest (14c tombs).

Algarve Modern seaside resorts among picturesque sandy beaches and rocky coves (Praia da Rocha). Old towns: Lagos; Faro.

Batalha Abbey is one of the masterpieces of French Gothic and Manueline architecture (tombs, English Perpendicular chapel, unfinished pantheon).

Braga Historic town with cathedral and large Archbishop's Palace.

Coimbra Old town with narrow streets set on a hill. The Romanesque cathedral is particularly fine (portal). The university (founded 1290) has a fascinating Baroque library. Also: Museum of Machado de Castro; many monasteries and convents.

Évora Centre of the town, surrounded by walls, has narrow streets of Moorish character and medieval and Renaissance architecture. Churches: 12–13c Gothic cathedral; São Francisco with a chapel decorated with bones of some 5000 monks; 15c Convent of Dos Lóis. The Jesuit university was founded in 1559. Museum of Évora holds fine art (particularly Flemish and Portugese).

Guimarães Old town with a castle with seven towers on a vast keep. Churches: Romanesque chapel of São Miguel; São Francisco. Alberto Sampaio Museum and Martins Sarmento Museum are excellent.

Lisboa Capital of Portugal. Baixa is the Neoclassical heart of Lisbon with the Praça do Comércio and Rossío squares. São Jorge castle (Visigothic, Moorish, Romanesque) is surrounded by the medieval quarters. Bairro Alto is famous for *fado* (songs). Monastery of Jerónimos is exceptional. Churches: 12c cathedral; São Vicente de Fora; São Roque (tiled chapels); Torre de Belém; Convento da Madre de Deus. Museums: Gulbenkian Museum (ancient, oriental, European), National Museum of Antique Art (old masters), Modern Art Centre; Azulejo Museum (decorative tiles). Nearby: palatial monastic complex Mafra; royal resort Sintra.

Porto Historic centre with narrow streets. Views from Clérigos Tower. Churches: São Francisco; cathedral. Soares dos Reis Museum holds fine and decorative arts (18–19c). The suburb of Vila Nova de Gaia is the centre for port wine.

Tomar Attractive town with the Convento de Cristo, founded in 1162 as the headquarters of the Knights Templar (Charola temple, chapter house, Renaissance cloisters).

Romania

Bucovina Beautiful region in northern Romanian Moldova renowned for a number of 15–16c monasteries and their fresco cycles. Of particularly note are Moldovita, Voroneţ and Suceviţa.

Bucureşti Capital of Romania with the majority of sites along the Calea Victoriei and centring on Piaţa Revoluţei with 19c Romanian Athenaeum and 1930s Royal Palace housing the National Art Gallery. The infamous 1980s Civic Centre with People's Palace is a symbol of dictatorial aggrandisement.

Carpaţii The beautiful Carpathian Mountains have several ski resorts (Sinaia) and peaks noted for first-rate mountaineering (Făgă raşuiui, Rodnei).

Danube Delta Europe's largest marshland, a spectacular nature reserve. Travel in the area is by boat, with Tulcea the starting point for visitors. The Romanian Black Sea Coast has a stretch of resorts (Mamaia, Eforie) between Constantaţ and the border, and well-preserved Roman remains in Histria.

Transilvania Beautiful and fascinating scenic region of medieval citadels (Timişoara, Sibiu) provides a setting for the haunting image of the legendary Dracula (Sighişoara, Braşov, Bran Castle). Cluj-Napoca is the main town.

Russia *Rossiya*

Moskva Capital of Russia, with many monuments. Within the Kremlin's red walls are: 15c Cathedral of the Dormition; 16c Cathedral of the Archangel; Cathedral of the Annunciation (icons), Armour Palace. Outside

Westerkerk, Amsterdam, The Netherlands

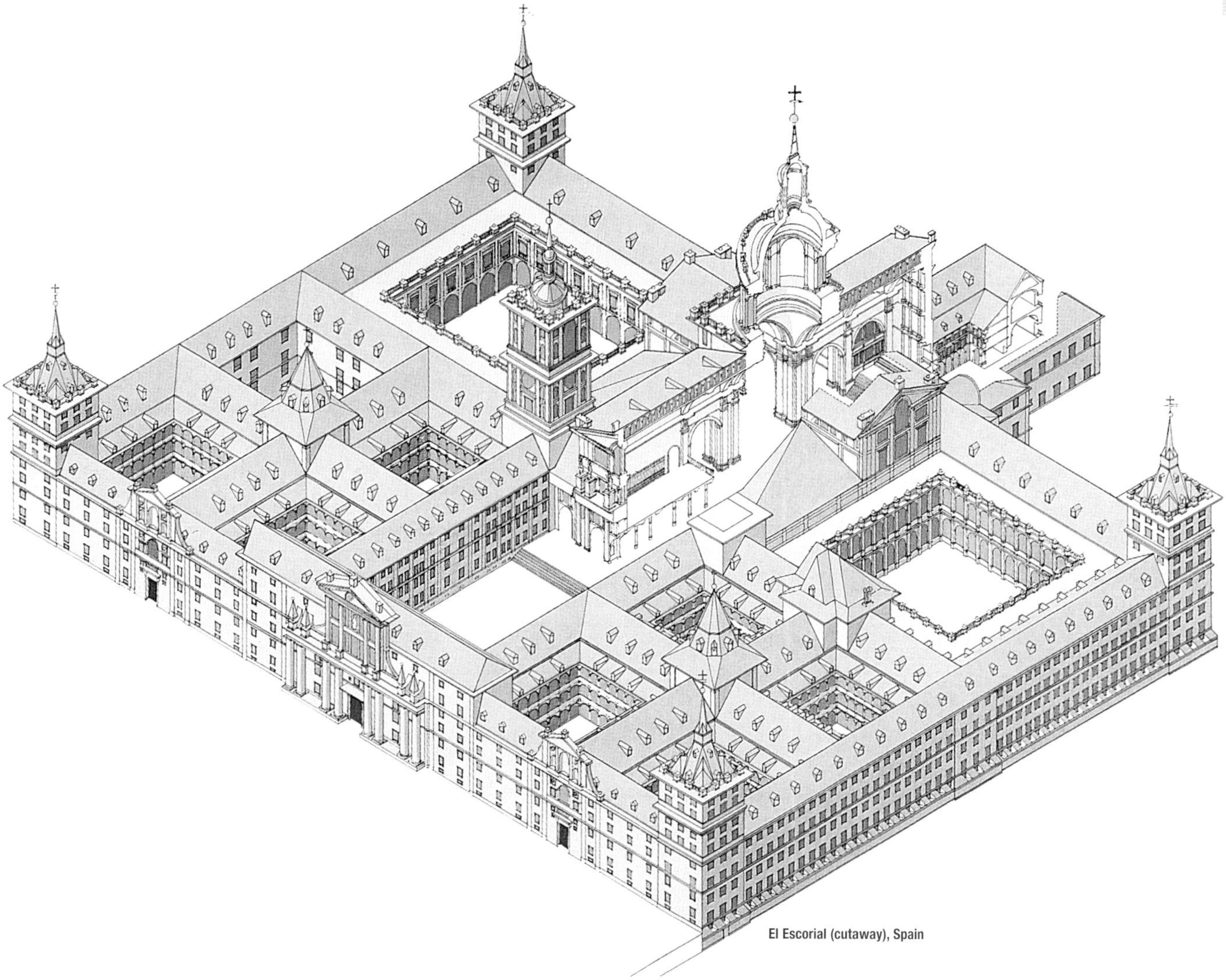

El Escorial (cutaway), Spain

the walls, Red Square has the Lenin Mausoleum and 16c St Basil's Cathedral. There are a number of monasteries (16c Novodevichi). Two superb museums: Tretiakov Art Gallery (Russian); Pushkin Museum of Fine Art (European). Kolomenskoe, once a royal summer retreat, has the Church of the Ascension. The VDNKh is a symbol of the Stalinist era.

Novgorod One of Russia's oldest towns, centred on 15c Kremlin with St Sophia Cathedral (iconostasis, west door). Two other cathedrals: St Nicholas; St George. Museum of History, Architecture and Art has notable icons and other artefacts.

Petrodvorets Grand palace with numerous pavilions (Monplaisir) set in beautiful parkland interwoven by a system of fountains, cascades and waterways connected to the sea.

Pushkin (Tsarskoye Selo) Birthplace of Alexander Pushkin, with the vast Baroque Catherine Palace – splendid state apartments, beautiful gardens and lakes.

Sankt Peterburg Founded in 1703 with the SS Peter and Paul Fortress and its cathedral by Peter the Great, and functioning as seat of court and government until 1918. Many of the most famous sights are around elegant Nevski Prospekt. The Hermitage, one of the world's largest and finest art collections is housed in five buildings including the Baroque Winter and Summer palaces. The Mikhailovsky Palace houses the Russian Museum (Russian art). Other sights: neoclassical Admiralty; 19c St Isaac's Cathedral and St Kazan Cathedral; Vasilievsky Island with 18c Menshikov Palace; Alexander Nevsky Monastery; 18c Smolny Convent.

Sergiev Posad (Zagorsk) Trinity St Sergius monastery with 15c cathedral.

Serbia & Montenegro *Srbija i Crna Gora*

Beograd Capital of Serbia & Montenegro. The largely modern city is set between the Danube and Sava rivers. The National Museum holds European art. To the south there are numerous fascinating medieval monasteries, richly embellished with frescoes.

Spain *España*

Ávila Medieval town with 2km-long 11c walls. Pilgrimage site to shrines to St Teresa of Ávila (Convent of Santa Teresa, Convent of the Incarnation).

Barcelona Showcase of Gothic ('Barri Gòtic': cathedral; Santa María del Mar; mansions on Carrer de Montcada) and *modernista* architecture ('Eixample' area with Manzana de la Discòrdia; Sagrada Familia, Güell Park, La Pedrera). Many elegant boulevards (La Rambla, Passeig de Gràcia). Museums: Modern Catalan Art; Picasso Museum, Miró Museum; Tàpies Museum. Nearby: monastery of Montserrat (Madonna); Figueres (Dali Museum).

Burgos Medieval town with Gothic cathedral, Moorish-Gothic Royal Monastery and Charterhouse of Miraflores.

Cáceres Medieval town surrounded by originally Moorish walls and with several aristocratic palaces with solars.

Córdoba Capital of Moorish Spain with a labyrinth of streets and houses with tile-decorated patios. The 8–10c Mezquita is the finest mosque in Spain. A 16c cathedral was added at the centre of the building and a 17c tower replaced the minaret. The old Jewish quarter has 14c synagogue

El Escorial Immense Renaissance complex of palatial and monastic buildings and mausoleum of the Spanish monarchs..

Granada The Alhambra was hill-top palace-fortress of the rulers of the last Moorish kingdom and is the most splendid example of Moorish art and architecture in Spain. The complex has three principal parts: Alcazaba fortress (11c); Casa Real palace (14c, with later Palace of Carlos V); Generalife gardens. Also: Moorish quarter; gypsy quarter; Royal Chapel with good art in the sacristy.

León Gothic cathedral has notable stained glass. Royal Pantheon commemorates early kings of Castile and León.

Madrid Capital of Spain, a mainly modern city with 17–19c architecture at its centre around Plaza Mayor. Sights: Royal Palace with lavish apartments; Descalzas Reales Convent (tapestries and other works); Royal Armoury museum. Spain's three leading galleries: Prado (15–18c); Queen Sofia Centre (20c Spanish, Picasso's *Guernica*); Thyssen-Bornemisza Museum (medieval to modern).

Oviedo Gothic cathedral with 12c sanctuary. Three Visigoth (9c) churches: Santullano, Santa María del Naranco, San Miguel de Lillo.

Palma Situated on Mallorca, the largest and most beautiful of the Balearic islands, with an impressive Gothic cathedral.

Picos de Europa Mountain range with river gorges and peaks topped by Visigothic and Romanesque churches.

Pyrenees (Spanish) Unspoiled mountain range with beautiful landscape and villages full of Romanesque architecture (cathedral of Jaca). The Ordesa National Park has many waterfalls and canyons.

Salamanca Delightful old city with some uniquely Spanish architecture: Renaissance Plateresque is famously seen on 16c portal of the university (founded 1215); Baroque Churrigueresque on 18c Plaza Mayo; both styles at the Convent of San Estaban. Also: Romanesque Old Cathedral; Gothic-Plateresque New Cathedral; House of Shells.

Santiago di Compostella Medieval city with many churches and religious institutions. The famous pilgrimage to the shrine of St James the Apostle ends here in the magnificent cathedral, originally Romanesque with many later elements (18c Baroque façade).

Segovia Old town set on a rock with a 1c Roman aqueduct. Also: 16c Gothic cathedral; Alcázar (14–15c, rebuilt 19c); 12-sided 13c Templar church of Vera Cruz.

Sevilla City noted for festivals and flamenco. The world's largest Gothic cathedral (15c) retains the Orange Court and minaret of a mosque. The Alcazar is a fine example of Moorish architecture. The massive 18c tobacco factory, now part of the university, was the setting for Bizet's *Carmen*. Barrio de Santa Cruz is the old Jewish quarter with narrow streets and white houses. Casa de Pilatos (15–16c) has a fine domestic patio. Hospital de la Caridad has good Spanish painting. Nearby: Roman Italica with amphitheatre.

Tarragona The city and its surroundings have some of the best-preserved Roman heritage in Spain. Also: Gothic cathedral (cloister); Archaeological Museum.

Toledo Historic city with Moorish, Jewish and Christian sights. The small 11c mosque of El Cristo de la Luz is one of the earliest in Spain. Two synagogues have been preserved: Santa María la Blanca; El Tránsito. Churches: San Juan de los Reyes; Gothic cathedral (good artworks). El Greco's *Burial of the Count of Orgaz* is in the Church of Santo Tomé. More of his works are in the El Greco house and, with other art, in Hospital de Santa Cruz.

Valencia The old town has houses and palaces with elaborate façades. Also: Cothic cathedral and Lonja de la Seda church.

Zaragoza Town notable for Moorish architecture (11c Aljafería Palace). The Basilica de Nuestra Señora del Pilar, one of two cathedrals, is highly venerated.

Slovenia *Slovenija*

Istra (Slovene) Two town centres, Koper and Piran, with medieval and Renaissance squares and Baroque palaces. See also Croatia.

Julijske Alpe Wonderfully scenic section of the Alps with lakes (Bled, Bohinj), deep valleys (Planica, Vrata) and ski resorts (Kranjska Gora, Bohinjska Bistrica).

Karst Caves Numerous caves with huge galleries, extraordinary stalactites and stalagmites, and underground rivers. The most spectacular are Postojna (the most famous, with Predjamski Castle nearby) and Škocjan.

Château de Chillon, Switzerland

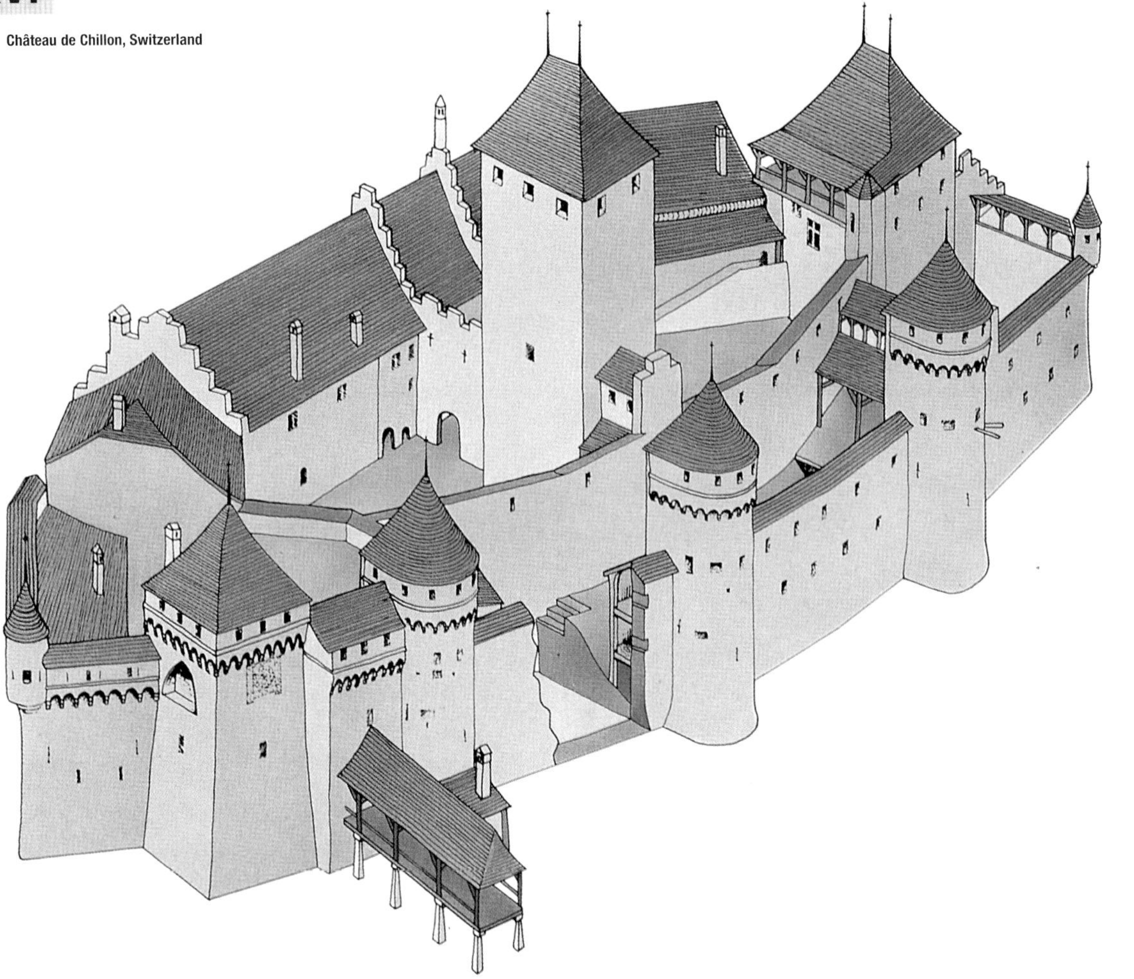

Ljubljana Capital of Slovenia. The old town, dominated by the castle (good views), is principally between Prešeren Square and Town Hall (15c, 18c), with the Three Bridges and colonnaded market. Many Baroque churches (cathedral, St Jacob, St Francis, Ursuline) and palaces (Bishop's Palace, Seminary, Gruber Palace). Also: 17c Križanke church and monastery complex; National Gallery and Modern Gallery show Slovene art.

Slovakia *Slovenska Republika*

Bratislava Capital of Slovakia, dominated by the castle (Slovak National Museum, good views). Old Town centred on the Main Square with Old Town Hall and Jesuit Church. Many 18–19c palaces (Mirbach Palace, Pálffy Palace, Primate's Palace), churches (Gothic cathedral, Corpus Christi Chapel) and museums (Slovak National Gallery).

Košice Charming old town with many Baroque and neoclassical buildings and Gothic cathedral.

Spišské Podhradie Region, east of the Tatry, full of picturesque medieval towns (Levoča, Kežmarok, Prešov) and architectural monuments (Spišský Castle).

Tatry Beautiful mountain region. Poprad is an old town with 19c villas. Starý Smokovec is a popular ski resort. See also Poland.

Sweden *Sverige*

Abisko Popular resort in the Swedish part of Lapland set in an inspiring landscape of lakes and mountains.

Göteborg Largest port in Sweden, the historic centre has 17–18c Dutch architectural character (Kronhuset). The Art Museum has interesting Swedish works.

Gotland Island with Sweden's most popular beach resorts (Ljugarn) and unspoiled countryside with churches in Baltic Gothic style (Dahlem, Bunge). Visby is an pleasant walled medieval town.

Lappland (Swedish) Swedish part of Lappland with 18c Arvidsjaur the oldest preserved Sámi village. Jokkmokk is a Sámi cultural centre, Abisko a popular resort in fine scenery. Also Finland, Norway.

Lund Charming university city with medieval centre and a fine 12c Romanesque cathedral (14c astronomical clock, carved tombs).

Malmö Old town centre set among canals and parks dominated by a red-brick castle (museums) and a vast market square with Town Hall and Gothic Church of St Peter.

Mora Delightful village on the shores of Siljan Lake in the heart of the Dalarna region, home to folklore and traditional crafts.

Stockholm Capital of Sweden built on a number of islands. The Old Town is largely on three islands with 17–18c houses, Baroque Royal Castle (apartments and museums), Gothic cathedral, parliament. Riddarholms church has tombs of the monarchy. Museums include: Modern Gallery (one of world's best modern collections); Nordiska Museet (cultural history); open-air Skansen (Swedish houses). Baroque Drottningholm Castle is the residence of the monarchy.

Swedish Lakes Beautiful region around the Vättern and Vänern Lakes. Siljan Lake is in the Dalarna region where folklore and crafts are preserved (Leksand, Mora, Rättvik).

Uppsala Appealing university town with a medieval centre around the massive Gothic cathedral.

Switzerland *Schweiz*

Alpen (Swiss) The most popular Alpine region is the Berner Oberland with the town of Inter-laken a starting point for exploring the large number of picturesque peaks (Jungfrau). The valleys of the Graubünden have famous ski resorts (Davos, St Moritz). Zermatt lies below the highest and most recognizable Swiss peak, the Matterhorn.

Basel Medieval university town with Romanesque-Gothic cathedral (tomb of Erasmus). Superb collections: Art Museum; Museum of Contemporary Art.

Bern Capital of Switzerland. Medieval centre has fountains, characteristic streets (Spital-gasse) and tower-gates. The Bärengraben is famed for its bears. Also: Gothic cathedral; good Fine Arts Museum.

Genève Wonderfully situated on the lake with the world's highest fountain. The historic area is centred on the Romanesque cathedral and Place du Bourg du Four. Excellent collections: Art and History Museum; Museum of Modern Art in 19c Petit Palais. On the lake shore: splendid medieval Château de Chillon.

Interlaken Starting point for excursions to the most delightful part of the Swiss Alps, the Bernese Oberland, with Grindelwald and Lauterbrunnen – one of the most thrilling valleys leading up to the ski resort of Wengen with views on the Jungfrau.

Luzern On the beautiful shores of Vierwald-stättersee, a charming medieval town of white houses on narrow streets and of wooden bridges (Kapellbrücke, Spreuer-brücke). It is centred on the Kornmarkt with the Renaissance Old Town Hall and Am Rhyn-Haus (Picasso collection).

Zürich Set on Zürichsee, the old quarter is around Niederdorf with 15c cathedral. Gothic Fraumünster has stained glass by Chagall. Museums: Swiss National Museum (history); Art Museum (old and modern masters); Bührle Foundation (Impressionists, Post-impressionists).

Turkey *Türkiye*

Istanbul Divided by the spectcular Bosphorus, the stretch of water that separates Europe from Asia, the historic district is surrounded by the Golden Horn, Sea of Marmara and the 5c wall of Theodosius. Major sights: 6c Byzantine church of St Sophia (converted first to a mosque in 1453 and then a museum in 1934); 15c Topkapi Palace; treasury and Archaeological Museum; 17c Blue Mosque; 19c Bazaar; 16c Süleymaniye Mosque; 12c Kariye Camii; European district with Galata Tower and 19c Dolmabahçe Palace.

Ukraine *Ukraina*

Kyïv Capital of Ukraine, known for its cathedral (11c, 17c) with Byzantine frescoes and mosaics. The Monastery of the Caves has churches, monastic buildings and catacombs.

United Kingdom

Antrim Coast Spectacular coast with diverse scenery of glens (Glenarm, Glenariff), cliffs (Murlough Bay) and the famous Giant's Causeway, consisting of some 40,000 basalt columns. Carrickefergus Castle is the largest and best-preserved Norman castle in Ireland.

Bath Elegant spa town with notable 18c architecture: Circus, Royal Crescent, Pulteney Bridge, Assembly Rooms; Pump Room. Also: well-preserved Roman baths; superb Perpendicular Gothic Bath Abbey. Nearby: Elizabethan Longleat House; exceptional 18c landscaped gardens at Stourhead.

Belfast Capital of Northern Ireland. Sights: Donegall Square with 18c Town Hall; neo-Romanesque Protestant cathedral; University Square; Ulster Museum (European painting).

Brighton Resort with a sea-front of Georgian, Regency and Victorian buildings with the Palace Pier, and an old town of narrow lanes. The main sight is the 19c Royal Pavilion in Oriental styles.

Bristol Old port city with the fascinating Floating Harbour. Major sights include Gothic 13–14c Church of St Mary Redcliffe and 19c Clifton Suspension Bridge.

Caernarfon Town dominated by a magnificent 13c castle, one of a series built by Edward I in Wales (others include Harlech, Conwy, Beaumaris, Caerphilly).

Cambridge City with university founded in the early 13c. Peterhouse (1284) is the oldest college. Most famous colleges were founded in 14–16c: Queen's, King's (with the superb Perpendicular Gothic 15–16c King's College Chapel), St John's (with famous 19c Bridge of Sighs), Trinity, Clare, Gonville and Caius, Magdalene. Museums: excellent Fitzwilliam Museum (classical, medieval, old masters). Kettle's Yard (20c British).

Canterbury Medieval city and old centre of Christianity. The Norman-Gothic cathedral has many sights and was a major medieval pilgrimage site (as related in Chaucer's *Canterbury Tales*). St Augustine, sent to convert the English in 597, founded St Augustine's Abbey, now in ruins.

Cardiff Capital of Wales, most famous for its medieval castle, restored 19c in Greek, Gothic and Oriental styles. Also: National Museum and Gallery.

Chatsworth One of the richest aristocratic country houses in England (largely 17c) set in a large landscaped park. The palatial interior has some 175 richly furnished rooms and a major art collection.

Chester Charming medieval city with complete walls. The Norman-Gothic cathedral has several abbey buildings.

Cornish Coast Scenic landscape of cliffs and sandy beaches with picturesque villages (Fowey, Mevagissey). St Ives has the Tate Gallery with work of the St Ives Group. The island of St Michael's Mount holds a priory.

Durham Historic city with England's finest Norman cathedral and a castle, both placed majestically on a rock above the river.

Edinburgh Capital of Scotland, built on volcanic hills. The medieval Old Town is dominated by the castle set high on a volcanic rock (Norman St Margaret's Chapel, state apartments, Crown Room). Holyrood House (15c and 17c) has lavishly decorated state apartments and the ruins of Holyrood Abbey (remains of Scottish monarchs). The 15c cathedral has the Crown Spire and Thistle Chapel. The New Town has good Georgian architecture (Charlotte Square, Georgian House). Excellent museums: Scottish National Portrait Gallery, National Gallery of Scotland; Scottish National Gallery of Modern Art.

Glamis Castle In beautiful, almost flat landscaped grounds, 14c fortress, rebuilt 17c, gives a fairy-tale impression.

Glasgow Scotland's largest city, with centre around George Square and 13–15c Gothic cathedral. The Glasgow School of Art is the masterpiece of Charles Rennie Mackintosh. Fine art collections: Glasgow Museum and Art Gallery; Hunterian Gallery; Burrell Collection.

Hadrian's Wall Built to protect the northernmost border of the Roman Empire in the 2c AD, the walls originally extended some 120km with castles every mile and 16 forts. Best-preserved walls around Hexam; forts at Housesteads and Chesters.

Lake District Beautiful landscape of lakes (Windermere, Coniston) and England's high

Radcliffe Camera (cutaway), Oxford, United Kingdom

The facade of Basilica san Pietro, Vatican City

peaks (Scafell Pike, Skiddaw, Old Man), famous for its poets, particularly Wordsworth.

Leeds Castle One of the oldest and most romantic English castles, standing in the middle of a lake. Most of the present appearance dates from 19c.

Lincoln Old city perched on a hill with narrow streets, majestically dominated by the Norman-Gothic cathedral and castle.

Loch Ness In the heart of the Highlands, the lake forms part of the scenic Great Glen running from Inverness to Fort William. Famous as home of the fabled Loch Ness Monster (exhibition at Drumnadrochit). Nearby: ruins of 14–16c Urquhart Castle.

London Capital of UK and Europe's largest city. To the east of the medieval heart of the city – now the largely modern financial district and known as the City of London – is the Tower of London (11c White Tower, Crown Jewels) and 1880s Tower Bridge. The popular heart of the city and its entertainment is the West End, around Piccadilly Circus, Leicester Square and Trafalgar Square (Nelson's Column). Many sights of political and royal power: Whitehall (Banqueting House, 10 Downing Street, Horse Guards); Neo-Gothic Palace of Westminster (Houses of Parliament) with Big Ben; The Mall leading to Buckingham Palace (royal residence, famous ceremony of the Changing of the Guard). Numerous churches include: 13–16c Gothic Westminster Abbey (many tombs, Henry VII's Chapel); Wren's Baroque St Paul's Cathedral, St Mary-le-Bow, spire of St Bride's, St Stephen Walbrook. Museums of world fame: British Museum (prehistory, oriental and classical antiquity, medieval); Victoria and Albert Museum (decorative arts); National Gallery (old masters to 19c); National Portrait Gallery (historic and current British portraiture); Tate – Britain and Modern; Science Museum; Natural History Museum. Madame Tussaud's waxworks museum is hugely popular. Other sights include: Kensington Palace; Greenwich with Old Royal Observatory (Greenwich meridian), Baroque Royal Naval College, Palladian Queen's House; Tudor Hampton Court Palace; Syon House. Nearby: Windsor Castle (art collection, St George's Chapel).

Longleat One of the earliest and finest Elizabethan palaces in England. The palace is richly decorated. Some of the grounds have been turned into a pleasure park, with the Safari Park, the first of its kind outside Africa.

Norwich Medieval quarter has half-timbered houses. 15c castle keep houses a museum and gallery. Many medieval churches include the Norman-Gothic cathedral..

Oxford Old university city. Earliest colleges date from 13c: University College; Balliol; Merton. 14–16c colleges include: New College; Magdalen; Christ Church (perhaps the finest). Other buildings: Bodleian Library; Radcliffe Camera; Sheldonian Theatre; cathedral. Good museums: Ashmolean Museum (antiquity to 20c); Museum of Modern Art; Christ Church Picture Gallery (14–17c). Nearby: outstanding 18c Blenheim Palace.

Petworth House (17c) with one of the finest country-house art collections (old masters), set in a huge landscaped park.

Salisbury Pleasant old city with a magnificent 13c cathedral built in an unusually unified Gothic style. Nearby: Wilton House.

Stonehenge Some 4000 years old, one of the most famous and haunting Neolithic monuments in Europe. Many other Neolithic sites are nearby.

Stourhead Early 18c palace famous for its grounds, one of the finest examples of neoclassical landscaped gardening, consisting of a lake surrounded by numerous temples.

Stratford-upon-Avon Old town of Tudor and Jacobean half-timbered houses, famed as the birth and burial place of William Shakespeare. Nearby: Warwick Castle.

Wells Charming city with beautiful 12–16c cathedral (west facade, scissor arches, chapter house, medieval clock). Also Bishop's Palace; Vicar's Close.

Winchester Historic city with 11–16c cathedral (tombs of early English kings). Also: 13c Great Hall; Winchester College; St Cross almshouses.

York Attractive medieval city surrounded by well-preserved walls with magnificent Gothic 13–15c Minster. Museums: York City Art Gallery (14–19c); Jorvik Viking Centre. Nearby: Castle Howard.

Vatican City

Città del Vaticano

Città del Vaticano Independent state within Rome. On Piazza San Pietro is the 15–16c Renaissance-Baroque Basilica San Pietro (Michelangelo's dome and *Pietà*), the world's most important Roman Catholic church. The Vatican Palace contains the Vatican Museums with many fine art treasures including Michelangelo's frescoes in the Sistine Chapel.

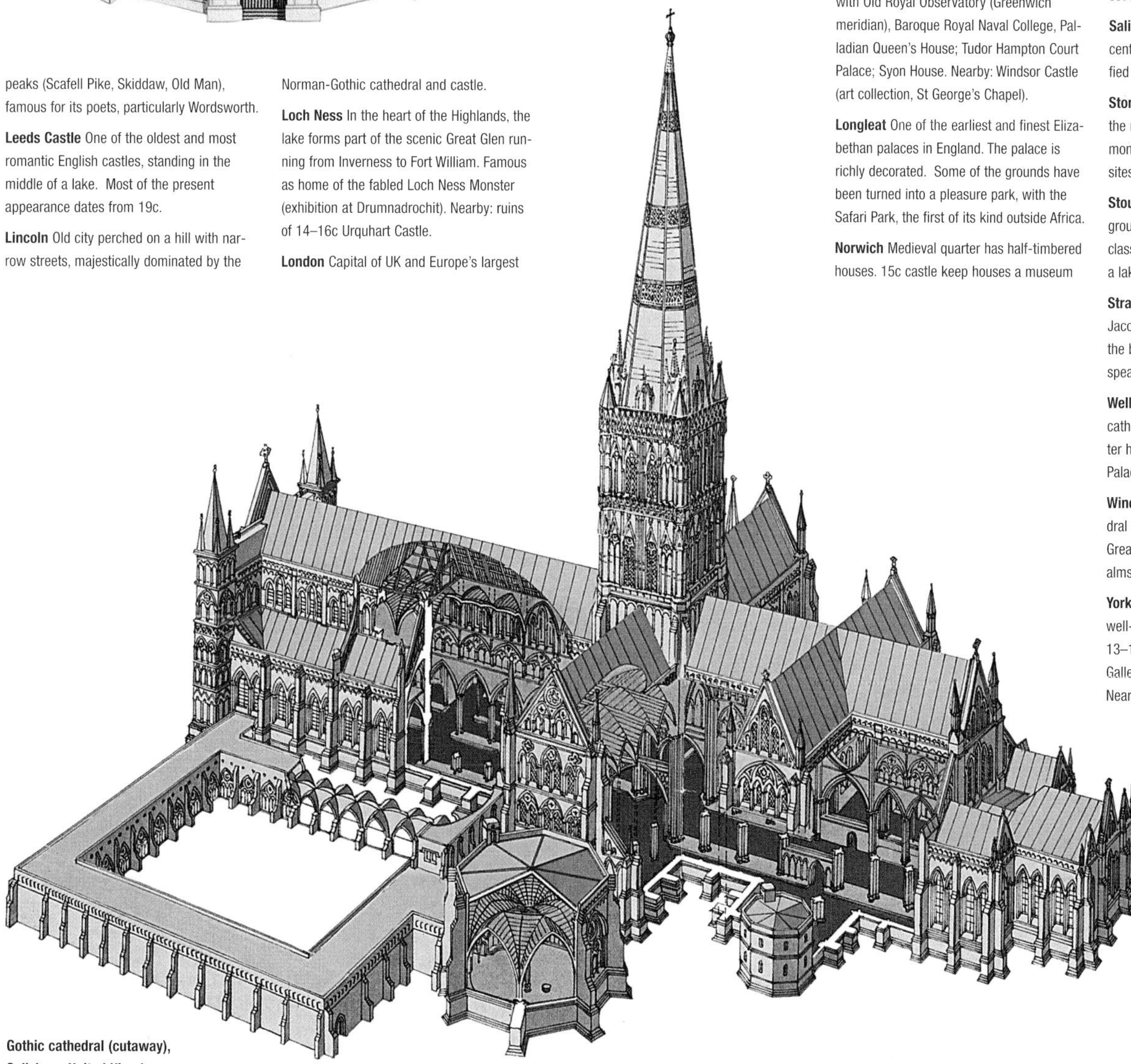

Gothic cathedral (cutaway), Salisbury, United Kingdom

History and culture of Europe

The following definitions describe some of the key terms in the timeline below.

Aegean civilization Bronze Age cultures, chiefly Minoan (on Crete, at its height c.1700BC-c.1100BC) and Mycenaean (at its height c.1580BC-c.1120BC).

baroque Style of art and architecture which at its best was a blend of light, colour, and movement calculated to overwhelm through emotional appeal. Buildings were heavily decorated with ornament and free-standing sculpture. Baroque became increasingly complex and florid. The term is often used to describe the period in history as well as the style.

Byzantine Empire Christian, Greek-speaking, Eastern Roman Empire that outlasted the Western Empire by nearly 1000 years. The area of the Byzantine Empire varied greatly, and its history from c.600 was marked by continual military crisis and recovery.

Carolingian period Cultural revival in France and Italy beginning under the encouragement of Charlemagne, who gathered notable educators and artists to his court at Aachen.

Counter-Reformation Revival of the Roman Catholic Church in Europe, beginning as a reaction to the Reformation. The reforms were largely conservative, trying to remove many of the abuses of the late medieval church and win new prestige for the papacy. The Council of Trent (1545-63) generated many of the key decisions and doctrines.

Dark Ages Term that at one time historians used to imply cultural and economic backwardness, but now is used mainly to indicate our ignorance of the period due to lack of historical evidence.

Enlightenment (Age of Reason) Philosophical movement that influenced many aspects of 18th-century society. It was inspired by the scientific and philosophical revolutions of the late 17th century and stressed the use of reason and the rational side of human nature.

Gothic Architecture and painting characterized by the pointed arch and ribbed vault. Religious in inspiration, its greatest expression was the cathedral. Gothic sculpture was elegant and more realistic than Romanesque. The Gothic style was also well expressed in manuscript illumination.

High Renaissance Brief period regarded as the height of Italian (particularly Roman) Renaissance art, brought to an end by the sack of Rome by the troops of Charles V.

Historicism, 19th-century Revival of past architectural styles. Ancient Greek and Gothic forms predominated, though buildings were constructed in a wide range of styles, including Renaissance, Romanesque and baroque.

Holy Roman Empire Empire centred on Germany, which aimed to echo ancient Rome. It was founded when Otto I was crowned in Rome (some date it from the coronation of Charlemagne). The Emperor claimed to be the worldly sovereign of Christendom ruling in co-operation with the Pope. After 1648 the

1500

c.1250-1200 Trojan War

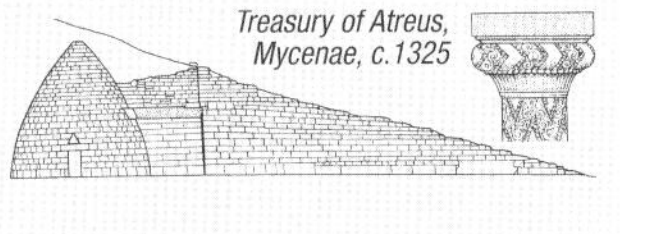

Treasury of Atreus, Mycenae, c.1325

1000

776 First Olympic Games held in Greece

753 Traditional date for the foundation of Rome by Romulus and Remus

c.750 *Odyssey* and *Iliad* complete in known forms

582?-500? Pythagoras

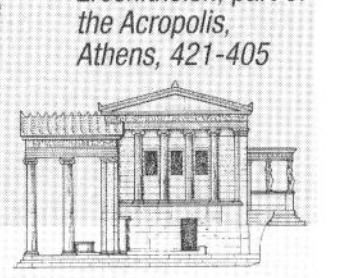

Erechtheion, part of the Acropolis, Athens, 421-405

500

336-323 Alexander the Great's campaigns

218 Hannibal crosses Alps with elephants

58-51 Romans conquer Gaul

43 Romans invade Britain

428?-347? Plato

384-322 Aristotle

356-323 Alexander the Great

c.140 *Venus de Milo* sculpted

100-44 Julius Caesar

69-30 Cleopatra

BC

AD

63BC-14AD Augustus

37-68 Nero

c.58 St Paul's Letter to the Corinthians

79 Vesuvius erupts burying Pompeii and Herculaneum

75-80 Coliseum built in Rome

53-117 Trajan

Arch of Titus, Rome, 81

Pantheon, Rome, 120-124

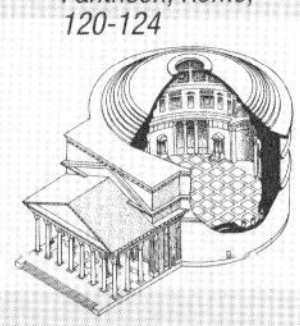

100

101–2, 105–6 Trajan's Dacian campaigns (recounted on Trajan's Column)

121-126 Hadrian's wall built across northern England

121-180 Marcus Aurelius

200

245-313 Diocletian

c.274-337 Constantine the Great

Temple of Vesta, Rome, 205

285 Roman Empire first split – Rome in the West and Byzantium (Constantinople) in the East

300

313 Edict of Milan: tolerance of Christianity in Empire

330 Constantinople founded

391 Christianity official religion of Roman Empire

395 Final division of Roman Empire into E and W

313-315 Arch of Constantine

c.329-379 St Basil

354-430 St Augustine

Palace of Diocletian, Split, Croatia, c.300

400

410 Visigoths sack Rome

455 Vandals sack Rome

476 Last Western Roman emperor overthrown

465-511 Clovis I, Frankish (Merovingian) king

483-565 Justinian I, ruler in first Byzantine Golden Age

San Apollinare Nuovo, Ravenna, Italy, detail of apse mosaic, 6th century

500

527–530 Slavs cross Danube

c.550 Major outbreak of bubonic plague in Europe

c.550 Height of Byzantine power and art

532-37 Church of Santa Sophia (Hagia Sophia) built in Constantinople

532-37 Church of San Vitale, Ravenna, built

San Apollinare in Classe, Ravenna, Italy, begun 532

600

603 Slavs invade Balkans

c.679–1018 First Bulgarian Empire

700

711-718 Muslims invade Spain

732 Franks defeat Muslims in Spain, preventing further conquests

742-814 Charlemagne

790-800 Palatine Chapel at Aachen

Great Mosque, Cordoba, Spain, detail of arches, begun 785

800

800 Charlemagne crowned Emperor by Pope

835-71 Danes establish settlements in England

c.860 Vikings raiders reach Mediterranean

Timeline bars (BC–AD 800):

- Bronze age to **c.1000**
- Aegean civilization to **c.1200**
- **c1000** Ancient Greek civilisation **c.27**
- ▼**c.753** Early Romans **c.500**
- ▼**c.500** Rise of Roman power **c.27**
- ▼**c.900** Etruscans **c.500**
- ▼**c.800** Carthaginian power **146**
- ▼**27BC** Imperial Rome **AD476**
- ▼**27BC** Pax Romana **AD180**
- ▼**c.150** Major Slavic invasions of eastern Europe **c.900**
- ▼**180** Germanic (barbarian) tribes invade Roman empire **476**
- ▼**285** Byzantine empire **1453**
- **476** Middle Ages **c.1400**
- **476** Dark Ages **c.1000**
- ▼**c.481** Frankish power in western Europe **962**
- ▼**c.800** Vikings raid...

900

911 Vikings take control of Normandy

962 Holy Roman Empire founded

972 Hungarian state established

912-973 Otto I, first Holy Roman Emperor

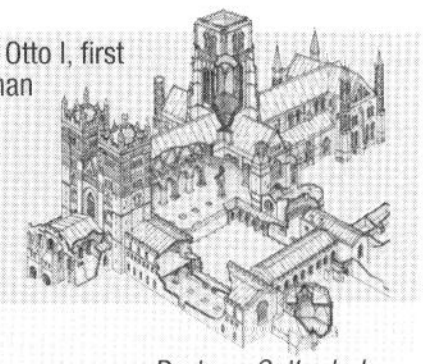

Durham Cathedral, England, 1093-c.1130

1000

1054 Church splits into Roman Catholic and Eastern Orthodox

1066 Norman conquest of England begins

1094 El Cid takes Valencia from the Moors

1050 Work begins on St Marks, Venice

1063 Pisa Romanesque cathedral started

c.1077-97 White Tower of the Tower of London begun

Worms Cathedral, Germany, c.1110-81

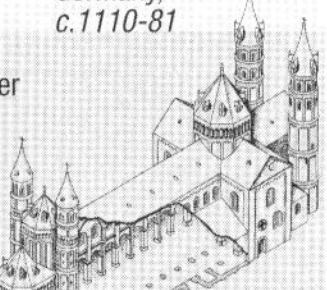

1100

1130 Normans take control of Sicily, having conquered much of southern Italy

1186–1393 Second Bulgarian Empire

1140 First gothic cathedral, St Denis near Paris, begun

1200

1204 Fourth Crusade and sack of Constantinople

1209-1229 Wars against Albigensians in France

1209 St Francis of Assisi establishes rules for Franciscans

1194-1250 Frederick II Barbarossa Holy Roman Emperor and King of Sicily

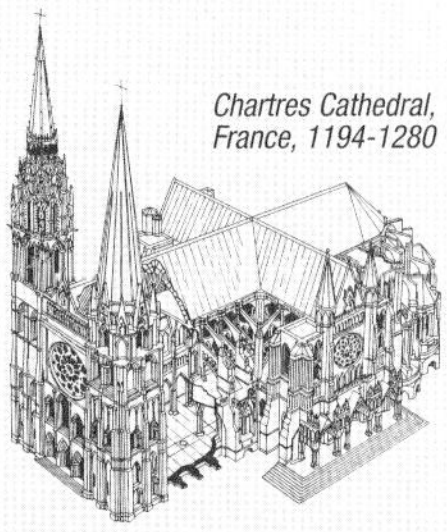

Chartres Cathedral, France, 1194-1280

1236 Christian forces take Córdoba from Moors

1237-1241 Tartar Golden Horde ravage Russia and much of north-east Europe

1250

Angel Choir, Lincoln Cathedral, England, 1256-1280

1265-1321 Dante Alighieri

c.1266-1337 Giotto

1261-1431 Paleologue age in Byzantium

1265 First English parliament in Westminster Hall, London

1271 Marco Polo's first visit to China

1282 Sicilian Vespers massacre of French in Sicily

c.1290 Invention of spectacles

1291 Swiss Confederation formed

Salisbury Cathedral, England, 1220-1380

1300

c.1300 Gunpowder appears in Europe

1309-77 Papacy moves from Rome to Avignon

1304-74 Francesco Petrarch

1309 Doge's Palace, Venice, started

1313-1321 Dante works on the *Divine Comedy*

Church of the Holy Apostles, Salonica, Greece, an Orthodox continuation of the Byzantine style, 1312-15

1347-50 Worst outbreaks of plague (the Black Death), which kill about a quarter of Europe's population

Gothic window tracery

Timeline bars (900–1350):

- **476** Middle Ages **c.1400**
- **476** Dark Ages **c.1000**
- **285** Byzantine empire **1453**
- ▼**c.800** Vikings raid many parts of Europe **c.1050**
- ▼**c.1000** Romanesque **c.1180**
- ▼**c.1135** Gothic period **c.1450**
- ▼**1096** Crusades **1291**
- ▼**1337** Hundred Years War...

Empire became a loose confederation, containing hundreds of virtually independent states. It was abolished by Napoleon I.

Imperial Rome Period of Roman history starting when Augustus declared himself emperor, ending the Roman republic. Most of the empire had already been conquered.

international gothic Style of painting characterized by naturalistic detail, elegant elongated figures and jewel-like colour.

mannerism Loose term applied to the art and architecture of Italy between the High Renaissance and the Baroque. A self-conscious style, it aimed to exceed earlier work in emotional impact. Painting is characterized by elongated figures in distorted poses, often using lurid colours.

Middle Ages Period between the disintegration of the Roman Empire and the Renaissance. The Middle Ages were, above all, the age of the Christian church and of the social structure known as the feudal system.

modern art Loose term that describes painting and sculpture that breaks from traditions going back to the Renaissance. There have been many movements, including fauvism, cubism, surrealism and expressionism.

neoclassicism Movement in art and architecture that grew out of the Enlightenment. Exponents admired and imitated the order and clarity of ancient Greek and Roman art.

Pax Romana Period when ancient Rome was so powerful that its authority could not be challenged by outside forces and peace was maintained in the empire.

Reformation Sixteenth-century movement that sought reform of the Catholic Church and resulted in the development of Protestantism. The starting date is often given as 1517, when Martin Luther nailed his 95 theses to the door of the Schlosskirche in Wittenberg, Germany, protesting against abuses of the clergy. In Zurich, the Reformation was led by Ulrich Zwingli and then by John Calvin.

Renaissance Period of rapid cultural and economic development. An important element in this was humanism, which involved a revival of interest in classical learning and emphasis on the philosophical and moral importance of the human individual. There was a great flowering of all the arts. Architectural and artistic style emerged in Italy and was heavily influenced by Greek and Roman models and by humanism. There was development of perspective, increasing use of secular and pagan subjects, a rise of portraiture, constant experimentation, and growing concern for the expression of the individual artist. The ideas spread and were emulated with national variations.

rococo Playful, light style of art, architecture and decoration that developed from baroque. Rococo brought to interior decoration swirls, scrolls, shells and arabesques. It was also applied to furniture, porcelain and silverware.

Romanesque Medieval architectural style preceding gothic. It was characterized by heavy round arches and massive walls, often decorated with carving or, originally, painted scenes.

romanticism Movement that valued individual experience and intuition, rather than the orderly, structured universe of neoclassicism. An emphasis on nature was also a characteristic. In music, the term refers to the rather later period from c.1800 to 1910.

1350

1353 First Ottoman (Turkish) invasion of Europe

1378-81 War of Chioggia – Venice takes control of Mediterranean

1378-1417 Great Schism in the Papacy between Rome and Avignon

1389 Battle of Kosovo - Turks gain firm foothold in the Balkans

Periods:
- **476** Middle Ages **c.1400**
- **c.1135** Gothic period **c.1450**
- **285** Byzantine empire **1453**
- **c.1370** International Gothic style **c.1450**
- **1337** Hundred Years War between England and Franc **1453**

1353 Giovanni Boccaccio writes the *Decameron*

1377-1446 Filippo Brunelleschi

1378-1455 Lorenzo Ghiberti

1386-1466 Donatello

1387/1400-55 Fra Angelico

c.1390-1441 Jan van Eyck

1386-1400 Geoffrey Chaucer's *Canterbury Tales*

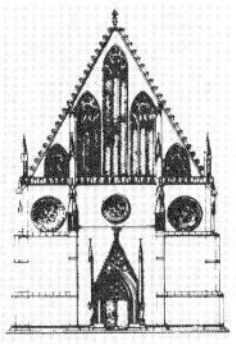

Church of the Holy Cross, Schwabish-Gemund, Germany, begun c.1350

1400

c.1400 onward Full plate armour begins to be used instead of chain main

1414 Discovery of Vitruvius' ancient treatise on architecture

1415 Introduction of oil paints by Jan and Hubert van Eyck in the Netherlands

1434-94 Medici family gain power in Florence

1431 Joan of Arc executed at Rouen

c.1440 Gutenberg invents moveable type allowing large-scale printing

Periods:
- **c.1400** Renaissance **c.1600**

c.1400-1464 Roger van der Weyden

1401-c1428 Masaccio

1404-72 Leon Battista Alberti

1415-92 Piero della Francesca

c.1420 Work begins on dome of Florence Cathedral

1434 Van Eyck paints the *Arnolfini Marriage*

c.1445-1510 Sandro Botticelli

Foundling Hospital, Florence, Italy, from 1429

Town Hall, Louvain, Belgium, 1448-63

1450

1453 Turks capture Constantinople

1479 Aragon and Castile unite to become Spain

1479 Start of Spanish Inquisition

1492 Christopher Columbus reaches the Americas; Spanish and Portuguese colonization begins

1494 Spanish take Granada, the last Moorish stronghold

1499 Portuguese discover sea route to India

Periods:
- **c.1450** Late Gothic period **c.1550**
- **c.1480** Great age of European discovery **c.1580**
- **1495** High Renaissance **1527**

c.1450-1516 Hieronymus Bosch

1452-1519 Leonardo da Vinci

1466?-1536 Erasmus of Rotterdam

1471-1528 Albrecht Dürer

1475-1564 Michelangelo Buonarotti

1473-1543 Nicolaus Copernicus

1483-1512 Raphael Sanzio

c.1487-1576 Titian

1492/9-1546 Giuliano Romano

1497/8-1543 Hans Holbein the Younger

c.1480 Botticelli paints *The Birth of Venus*

St Georges Chapel, Windsor Castle, England, 1481-1528

St Maria Novella, Florence, Italy, from 1458

1500

1506 Antique statue of the Laocöon discovered near Rome, sparking increased interest in the forms of Hellenistic sculpture

1517 Martin Luther publishes his 95 Theses in Wittenberg

1522 Magellan's expedition completes circumnavigation of the globe

1527 Sack of Rome by Imperial troops

1541 John Calvin founds church in Geneva

1543 Copernicus publishes idea that Earth revolves around the Sun

Periods:
- **1517** Reformation **c.1600**
- **c.1520** Mannerism **c.1610**

1500 Bosch paints *The Garden of Earthly Delights*

1503 Leonardo da Vinci paints *Mona Lisa*

1504 Michelangelo sculpts *David*

1506 St Peter's, Rome, begun on Boromini's plan

1508-1512 Michelangelo paints Sistine Chapel

1508-80 Andrea Palladio

1513 Machiavelli's *The Prince*

1541-1614 El Greco

1547 Ivan IV (the Terrible) Tsar of Russia

Palazzo Strozzi, Florence, Italy, from 1490

Bibliotecha Laurenziana, door to library, Florence, Italy, from 1524

1550

1545-63 Council of Trent

1562 Netherlands revolt against Spanish rule

1562-98 Wars of Religion in France; end with religious tolerance under Edict of Nantes

1557-82 Livonia War between Sweden and its Baltic neighbours

1571 Ottoman Turk navy defeated by Holy League at Battle of Lepanto

1572 St Bartholomew's Day Massacre in Paris

1572-1648 Dutch revolt against Spanish rule

1581 Independence of United Provinces (Netherlands)

1588 English fleet defeats Spanish Armada

Periods:
- **c.1400** Renaissance **c.1600**
- **1545** Counter Reformation **1648**
- **c.1520** Mannerism **c.1610**
- **c.1480** Great age of European discovery **c.1580**

1558-1603 Elizabeth I Queen of England

1564-1616 William Shakespeare

1571-1610 Michelangelo Merisi da Caravaggio

1573-1652 Inigo Jones

1577-1640 Peter Paul Rubens

1581/5-1666 Frans Hals

1594-1665 Nicolas Poussin

1598-1680 Gianlorenzo Bernini

1599-1660 Diego Velazquez

1599-1641 Sir Anthony Van Dyck

1598-1666 Françcois Mansart

Palace of Charles V, Granada, Spain, detail, begun 1526

S. Georgio Maggiore, Venice,

1600

1607 First English colony in North America at Jamestown

1618 Defenestration of Prague starts Thirty Years' War

1630 Sweden enters Thirty Year's War

1635 Peace of Prague ends German involvement in Thirty Years' War

1635 France enters Thirty Years' War

1642-5 English Civil War

1648 Treaty of Westphalia ends Thirty Years' War

1649 Execution of Charles I of England

Periods:
- **c.1600** Baroque **c.1750**
- **1618** Thirty Years' War **1648**

1600-92 Claude Lorraine

1603 *Hamlet* written by Shakespeare

1606-69 Rembrandt van Rijn

1624 Frans Hals paints *The Laughing Cavalier*

1624 Palace of Versailles started

1627-1725 Peter I, the Great, of Russia

1632-75 Jan Vermeer

1632-1723 Sir Christopher Wren

1633 Galileo tried for heresy

1642 Rembrandt paints *The Night Watch*

Mauritzhuis, The Hague, Netherlands, c.1633

1650

1652-3, 1665-7, 1672-4 1st, 2nd and 3rd Anglo-Dutch wars

1660 Restoration of English monarchy

1666 Great Fire of London

1671 Spain and United Provinces ally against France

1671 Hungarian Revolt and Reign of Terror

1682 Spain and Holy Roman Empire ally against France

1683 Turks besiege Vienna

1685 Edict of Nantes revoked and Huguenots leave France

1689 English Parliament passes Bill of Rights

1699 Habsburgs recover Hungary from Turks

1661 Louis XIV takes power in France

1667 John Milton, *Paradise Lost*

1667-70 Main façade of Louvre

1687 Isaac Newton publishes *Principia Mathematica*

1696 Peter I, the Great, becomes Tsar of Russia

1696-1770 Giovanni Battista Tiepolo

S. Carlo alle Quatro Fontane, Rome, Italy, detail, begun 1633

Troja Palace, Prague, Czech Republic, 1679-96

1700

1700-21 Great Northern War between Sweden and Russia and its allies

1702-1713 War of Spanish Succession (ends with Peace of Utrecht)

1703 St Petersburg founded

1704 "Grand Alliance" of Holland, England and Austria defeat France at Blenheim

1707 Act of Union between England and Scotland

1730 Methodism founded by John and Charles Wesley

1740-86 Prussia under Frederick the Great

1740-8 War of Austrian Succession

Periods:
- **c.1700** Rococo **c.1750**
- **c.1700** Age of Enlightenment **1789**
- **c.1730** Gothic Revival **c.1780**

1719 Daniel Defoe, *Robinson Crusoe*

1720 J.S.Bach *Brandenburg Concertos*

1726 Jonathan Swift, *Gulliver's Travels*

1728-92 Robert Adam

1742 Handel's *Messiah*

1746-1828 Goya

1748-1825 Jacques-Louis David

1749-1832 Johann Wolfgang von Goethe

Baroque interior, St John Nepomuk, Munich, Germany 1732-46

Amalienburg Palace, near Munich, Rococo detail and decoration, 1734

1750

1755 Earthquake destroys Lisbon

1756-63 Britain defeats France in Seven Years' War (ends with Treaty of Paris)

1772 Partition of Poland between Austria and Russia

1776 Britain's North American colonies declare indepence (gained 1783)

1783 Montgolfier brothers ascend in hot-air balloon

1789-99 French Revolution

1797 Fall of Venetian Republic to forces of Napoleon

1799 Napoleon Bonaparte seizes power in France

1762-96 Catherine the Great Empress of Russia

1769-1821 Napoleon Bonaparte

1775-1851 JMW Turner

1780-1867 Jean Auguste Dominique Ingres

1781 Kant *Critique of Pure Reason*

1798 Wordsworth and Coleridge *Lyrical Ballads*

1799 Beethoven's First Symphony

Kedleston Hall, England, 1757-70

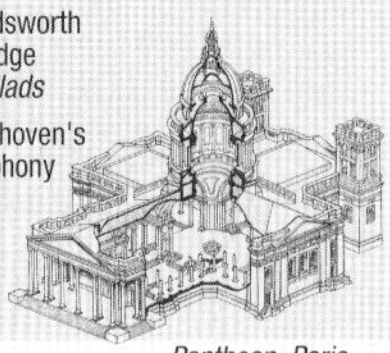

Pantheon, Paris, France, 1757-80

1800

1803-1815 Napoleonic Wars

1805 Battle of Trafalgar

1806 End of Holy Roman Empire

1812 Napoleon invades Russia

1815 Battle of Waterloo

1820-28 War of Greek Independence

c.1825 Joseph Niépce produces first known photograph

1830 July Revolution in France

1830 Independence of Belgium from Netherlands

1845 Irish potato famine

1848 Revolutions all round Europe, particularly France, Germany, Hungary, Italy

1821 Constable *The Hay Wain*

1830-40 Helsinki Cathedral

1832-83 Edouard Manet

1834-96 William Morris

1834-1917 Edgar Degas

1839 Dickens *Oliver Twist*

1839-1906 Paul Cezanne

1840-1917 Auguste Rodin

1840-1926 Claude Monet

1841-1919 Pierre Auguste Renoir

1848 Marx and Engels *Communist Manifesto*

1848-55 Pre-Raphaelites (style continues later)

1848-1903 Paul Gauguin

Crystal Palace, London England, 1851

1850

1853-6 Crimean War

1860 Garibaldi's Expedition of the Thousand leads to founding of Kingdom of Italy (1861)

1870-1 Franco-Prussian War

1871-1940 Third Republic in France

1885 Karl Benz in Germany builds first car with internal combustion engine

1893 Lumiére brothers invent cinematograph

1897-9 Marconi demonstrates radio communication

1853 Verdi *La Traviata*

1853-90 Vincent van Gogh

1859 Charles Darwin *The Origin of Species*

1859-91 Georges Seurat

1863 Manet paints *Dejeuner sur l'Herbe*, often regarded as the first modern painting

1863-1944 Edvard Munch

1865-69 Tolstoy *War and Peace*

1867 Marx *Das Kapital*

1869-1954 Henri Matisse

1874 First Impressionist exhibition in Paris

1878-1953 Stalin

1875 Bizet *Carmen*

1898-1976 Alvar Aalto

Votivkirche, Vienna 1856-79

1900

1903 Wright brothers make first powered flight

1914-1918 World War I

1917 Russian Revolution

1919 Treaty of Versailles

1922 USSR established

1922 Mussolini in power in Italy

1923 Hitler leads Munich Putsch

1929 Wall Street Crash heralds Great Depression of the 1930s

1933 Hitler becomes Chancellor of Germany

1936-39 Spanish Civil War

1939 Germany invades Poland, provoking World War II

1900 Sigmund Freud *The Interpretation of Dreams*

1902 Edvard Munch *The Scream* exhibited

1904-89 Salvador Dali

1905 Einstein publishes special theory of relativity

1907 First cubist exhibition

1913 Stravinsky *The Rite of Spring*

1916 Einstein publishes general theory of relativity

1919 Bauhaus movement founded

1932 Aldous Huxley *Brave New World*

1937 Pablo Picasso *Guernica*

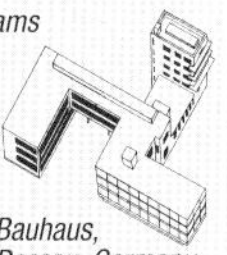

Bauhaus, Dessau, Germany, 1925

Gruntvig Church, Copenhagen, Denmark, 1920-40

1950

1957 Treaty of Rome establishes European Economic Community (EEC)

1961 Soviet authorities build Berlin Wall

1967 EEC become European Community (EC)

1968 Soviet invasion ends 'Prague Spring'

1989 Berlin Wall dismantled

1992 Maastrict Treaty establishes European Union (EU)

1999 Serb actions in Kosovo prompt NATO intervention

1953 Tito president of Yugoslavia

1953 Crick and Watson discover structure of DNA

1905–1989 Samuel Beckett

1927– Günter Grass

1936– Vaclav Havel

1961–70 The Beatles

1979 Margaret Thatcher becomes UK Prime Minister

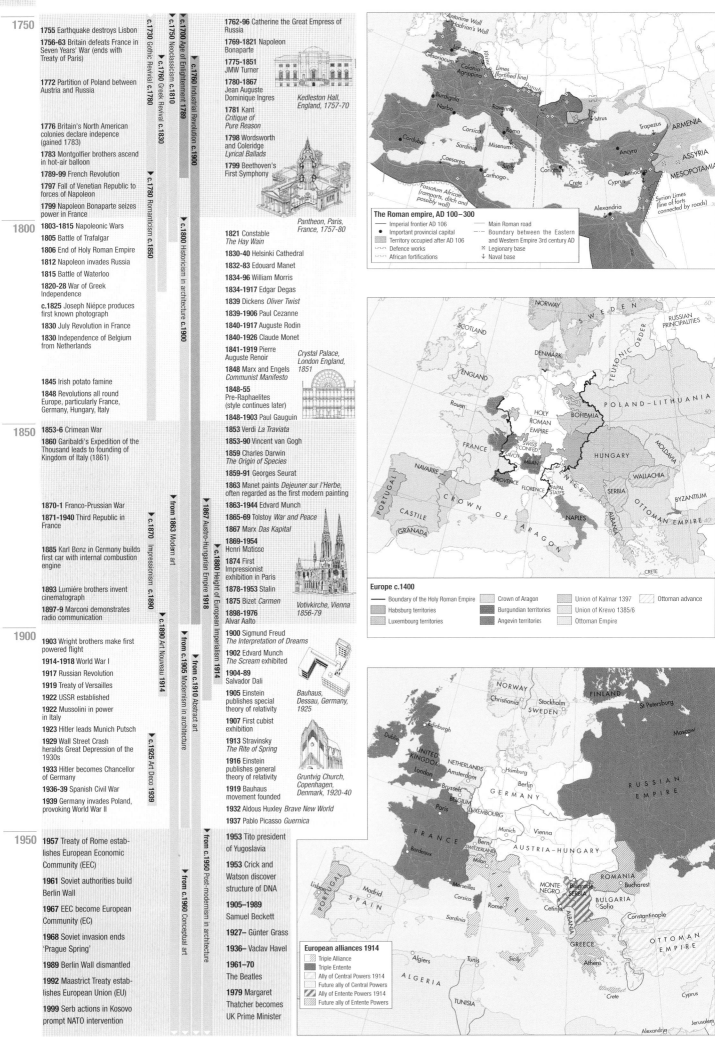

Styles and periods

- c.1730 Gothic Revival c.1780
- c.1750 Neoclassicism c.1810
- c.1760 Greek Revival c.1830
- c.1700 Age of Enlightenment 1789
- c.1760 Industrial Revolution c.1900
- c.1780 Romanticism c.1850
- c.1800 Historicism in architecture c.1900
- c.1870 Impressionism c.1890
- from 1863 Modern art
- 1867 Austro-Hungarian Empire 1918
- c.1880 Height of European Imperialism 1914
- c.1890 Art Nouveau 1914
- from c.1905 Modernism in architecture
- from c.1910 Abstract art
- c.1925 Art Deco 1939
- from c.1960 Conceptual art
- from c.1950 Post-modernism in architecture

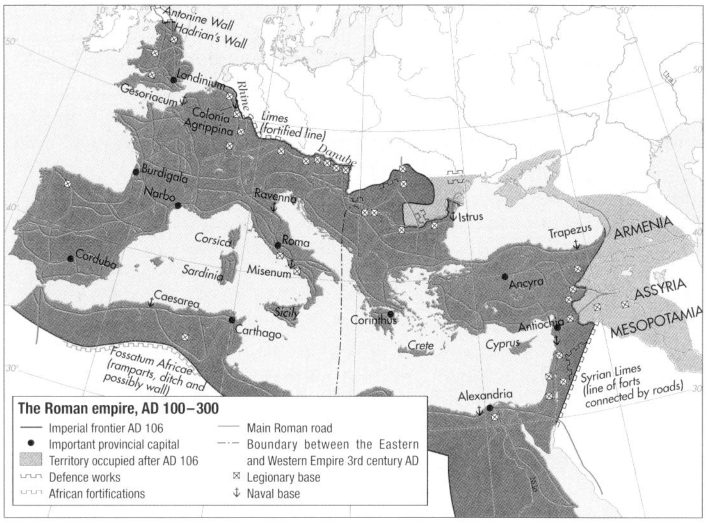

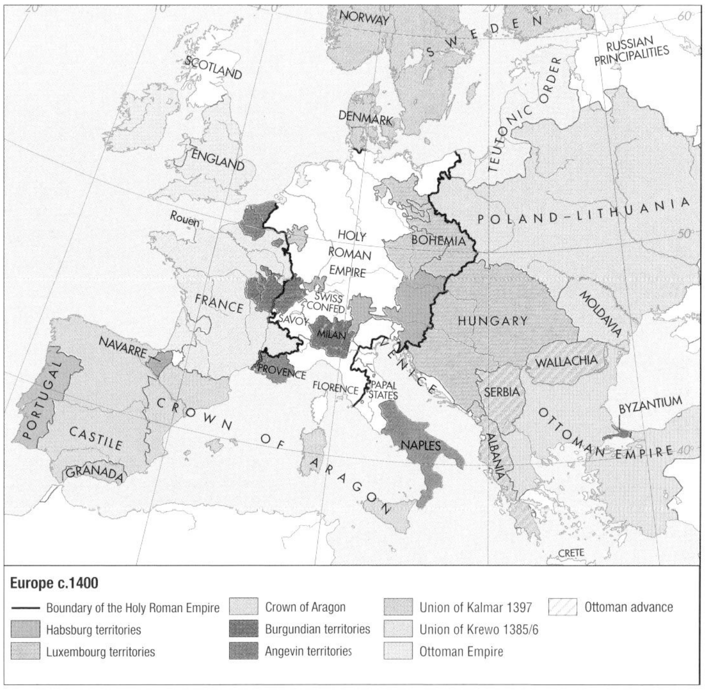

European politics and economics

Albania *Shqipëria*

Area 28,750 sq km (11,100 sq miles)
Population 3,331,000
Capital Tirana/Tiranë (pop 251,000)
Languages Albanian (official), Greek
GDP per capita 1997 US$723
Currency Lek = 100 Quindars
Government multiparty republic
Head of state President Alfred Moisiu, 2002
Head of Government Fatos Nano (Socialist Party), 2002
Recent events
In 1997 the collapse of nationwide pyramid finance schemes sparked a large-scale rebellion in southern Albania. A government was formed in 2001 by the Socialist Party.
Economy
Albania is Europe's poorest country, and 56% of the workforce are engaged in agriculture. Private ownership of land has been encouraged since 1991. Crops include fruits, maize, olives, potatoes, sugar beet, vegetables, and wheat. Livestock farming is also important. Chromite, copper, and nickel are exported. Other resources include oil, brown coal, and hydroelectricity.
Website www.parlament.al

Andorra *Principat d'Andorra*

Area 453 sq km (175 sq miles)
Population 69150
Capital Andorra la Vella
Languages Catalan (official), French, Spanish
GDP per capita 2000 US$ 18,000
Currency Euro = 100 cents
Government independent state and co-principality
Head of state co-princes: Joan Enric Vives Sicilia, Bishop of Urgell, 2003 and Jacques Chirac (see France), 1995
Head of government Chief Executive Marc Forné Molné, 1994
Recent events
In 1993 a new democratic constitution was adopted that reduced the roles of the President of France and the Bishop of Urgell to purely constitutional figureheads.
Economy
The main sources of income include agriculture; the sale of water and hydroelectricity to Catalonia; tourism, particularly skiing.
Website www.andorra.ad

Austria *Österreich*

Area 83,850 sq km (32,374 sq miles)
Population 8,134,000
Capital Vienna/Wien (1,560,000)
Languages German (official)
GDP per capita 1999 US$25,948
Currency Euro = 100 cents
Government federal republic
Head of state President Thomas Klestil, Party (OVP), 1992
Federal Chancellor Wolfgang Schüssel (OVP), 2000
Recent events
Austria became a member of the European Union in 1995. In general elections in 1999, the extreme right Freedom Party, under Jörg Haider, made gains at the expense of the Social Democrats. He subsequently resigned as leader. Peoples' Party electoral win in 2002 wasn't sufficient to form a government so a coalition was formed with the Freedom Party despite first having talks with the Social Democrats and the Greens.
Economy
Austria is a wealthy nation which, despite plenty of hydroelectric power, is dependent on the import of fossil fuels. Austria's leading economic activity is the manufacture of metals. Dairy and livestock farming are the principal agricultural activities. Tourism is an important industry.
Website www.austria.gv.at/e/

Belarus

Area 207,600 sq km (80,154 sq miles)
Population 10,322,151
Capital Minsk (1,680,000)
Languages Belarussian, Russian (both official)
GDP per capita 2000 US$8,200
Currency Belarussian rouble = 100 kopek
Head of state Alexander Lukashenko, 1994
Head of government Sergei Sidorsky, 2003
Recent events
Belarus was a founder member of the CIS. The administrative centre of the CIS is in Minsk. In 1997, despite opposition from nationalists, Belarus signed a Union Treaty with Russia, committing it to integration with Russia. Currency union is scheduled for 2008. Lukashenko was elected for a second term in 2001 though the elections were deemed undemocratic by western observers.
Economy
Belarus has faced problems in the transition to a free-market economy. In 1995 an agreement with Russia enabled Belarus to receive subsidised fuel. Agriculture, especially meat and dairy farming, is important.
Website www.government.by/eng

Belgium *Belgique*

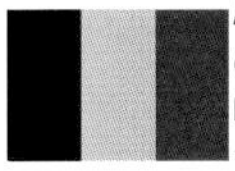

Area 30,510 sq km (11,780 sq miles)
Population 10,175,000
Capital Brussels/Bruxelles (952,000)
Languages Dutch, French, German (all official)
GDP per capita 1999 US$24,344
Currency Euro = 100 cents
Government federal constitutional monarchy
Head of state King Albert II, 1993
Head of government Guy Verhofstadt, Flemish Liberal Democrats (VLD), 1999
Recent events.
A central domestic issue has been the tension between Dutch-speaking Flemings and French-speaking Walloons. In 1993 Belgium adopted a federal system of government, and each of the regions has its own parliament.
Economy
Belgium is a major trading nation. The leading activity is manufacturing and products include steel and chemicals. Agriculture employs only 3% of the workforce, but the country is mostly self-sufficient. Barley and wheat are the chief crops, but the most valuable activities are dairy farming and livestock rearing.
Website www.belgium.be

Bosnia-Herzegovina *Bosna i Hercegovina*

Area 51,129 sq km (19,745 sq miles)
Population 3,366,000
Capital Sarajevo (526,000)
Language Serbian/Croatian
GDP per capita 2000 US$1,770
Currency Convertible Mark = 100 paras
Government federal republic
Head of state Chairman of the Presidency Dragan Covic, 2003
Heads of government Chairman of the Council of Ministers Adrian Terzic
Recent events
In 1992 a referendum approved independence from the Yugoslav federation. The Bosnian Serb population was against independence and in the resulting war occupied over two-thirds of the land. Croat forces seized other parts of the country. After many attempts at a settlement, the Dayton Peace Accord affirmed that Bosnia-Herzegovina was a single state but partitioned it into a Muslim-Croat federation and a Serbian republic. A tripartite presidency was set up, the other members of which are Sulejman Tihic (Bosniak) and Borislav Paravac (Serb).NATO troops remain as a peace-keeping force.
Economy
Excluding Macedonia, Bosnia was the least developed of the former republics of Yugoslavia. Currently receiving substantial aid, though this will be reduced.
Website www.fbihvlada.gov.ba

Bulgaria *Bulgariya*

Area 110,910 sq km (42,822 sq miles)
Population 8,240,000
Capital Sofia (1,117,000)
Languages Bulgarian (official), Turkish
GDP per capita 1995 US$4,480
Currency Lev = 100 stotinki
Government multiparty republic
Head of state President Georgi Purvanov, 2002
Head of government Simeon Saxe-Coburg-Gotha, 2001
Recent events
In 1990 the first non-communist president for 40 years, Zhelyu Zhelev, was elected. A new constitution (1991) saw the adoption of free-market reforms. Elections in 1997, prompted by the resignation of the previous government, were won by a centre-right coalition.
Economy
Bulgaria is a lower-middle-income developing country, faced with a difficult transition to a market economy. Manufacturing is the leading economic activity but has outdated technology. The main products are chemicals, metals, machinery and textiles. Mineral reserves include molybdenum. Wheat and maize are the main crops. The valleys of the Maritsa are ideal for winemaking, plums and tobacco. Tourism is increasing rapidly.
Website www.president.bg/en

Croatia *Hrvatska*

Area 56,538 sq km (21,824 sq miles)
Population 4,672,000
Capital Zagreb (931,000)
Language Croatian
GDP per capita 1991 US$ 5,600
Currency Kuna = 100 lipas
Government multiparty republic
Head of state President Stjepan Mesic, 2000
Head of government Ivica Racan, Social Democratic Party of Croatia (SDP). Coalition with Croatian Social Liberal Party (HSLS), 2000.
Recent events
A 1991 referendum voted overwhelmingly in favour of independence. Serb-dominated areas took up arms to remain in the federation. Serbia armed Croatian Serbs, war broke out between Serbia and Croatia, and Croatia lost much territory. In 1992 United Nations peacekeeping troops were deployed. In 1995 Croatian government forces occupied Krajina and 150,000 Serbs fled. Following the Dayton Peace Accord (1995), Croatia and Yugoslavia established diplomatic relations (1996). An agreement between the Croatian government and Croatian Serbs provided for the eventual reintegration of Krajina into Croatia (1998). Elections called after the death of President Tudjman in December 1999. Stjepan Mesic elected president in 2000.
Economy
The wars have badly disrupted Croatia's relatively prosperous economy. Croatia has a wide range of manufacturing industries, such as steel, chemicals, oil refining, and wood products. Agriculture is the principal employer. Crops include maize, soya beans, sugar beet and wheat.
Website www.hr

Czech Republic *Česka Republica*

Area 78,864 sq km (30,449 sq miles)
Population 10,286,000
Capital Prague/Praha (1,213,000)
Languages Czech (official), Moravian
GDP per capita 2000 US$15,300
Currency Czech Koruna = 100 haler
Government multiparty republic
Head of state President Václav Klaus, 2003
Head of government Prime minister Vladimir Spidla, Czech Social Democrat Party, 2002
Recent events
Free elections were held in 1990, resulting in the re-election of Vaclav Havel. In 1992 the government agreed to the secession of the Slovak Republic, and on 1 January 1993 the Czech Republic was created. The Czech Republic will join the EU in May 2004.
Economy
The country has deposits of coal, uranium, iron ore, magnesite, tin and zinc. Industries include chemicals, beer, iron and steel, and machinery. Private ownership of land is gradually being restored. Agriculture employs 12% of the workforce. Livestock raising is important. Crops include grains, fruit, and hops for brewing. Prague is now a major tourist destination.
Website www.czech.cz

Denmark *Danmark*

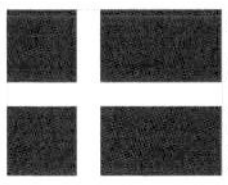

Area 43,070 sq km (16,629 sq miles)
Population 5,334,000
Capital Copenhagen/København (1,353,000)
Language Danish (official)
GDP per capita 1999 US$33,124
Currency Krone = 100 øre
Government parliamentary monarchy
Head of state Queen Margrethe II, 1972
Head of government Poul Nyrop Rasmussen, Social Democrats (SD), 1993
Recent events
In 1992 Denmark rejected the Maastricht Treaty, but reversed the decision in a second referendum (1993). In 1998 the Amsterdam Treaty was ratified by a further referendum. Currency pegged to euro but still independent.
Economy
Danes enjoy a high standard of living. Denmark is self-sufficient in oil and natural gas. Products include furniture, electrical goods and textiles. Services, including tourism, form the largest sector (63% of GDP). Farming employs only 4% of the workforce but is highly productive. Fishing is also important.
Website www.denmark.dk

Estonia *Eesti*

Area 44,700 sq km (17,300 sq miles)
Population 1,421,000
Capital Tallinn (435,000)
Languages Estonian (official), Russian
GDP per capita 2000 US$5,600
Currency Kroon = 100 sents
Government multiparty republic
Head of state President Arnold Rüütel, Estonian Peoples' Union, 2001
Head of government Juhan Parts, Res Publica, 2003
Recent events
In 1992 Estonia adopted a new constitution and multiparty elections were held. Since independence Estonia has been ruled by a succession of coalition or minority governments. Estonia will join the EU in May 2004.
Economy
Privatisation and free-trade reforms have increased foreign investment and trade with the European Union. Chief natural resources are oil shale and forests. Manufactures include petrochemicals, fertilisers and textiles. Agriculture and fishing are important. Barley, potatoes and oats are major crops.
Website www.riik.ee/en

Finland *Suomi*

Area 338,130 sq km (130,552 sq miles)
Population 5,149,000
Capital Helsinki (525,000)
Languages Finnish, Swedish (both official)
GDP per capita 1999 US$25,046
Currency Euro = 100 cents
Government multiparty republic
Head of state President Tarja Kaarina Halo-

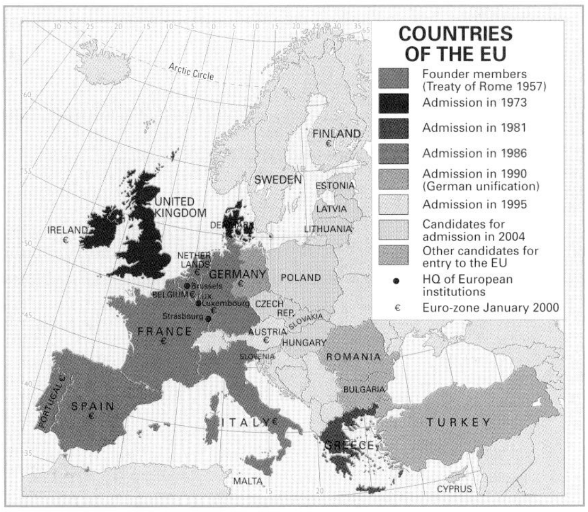

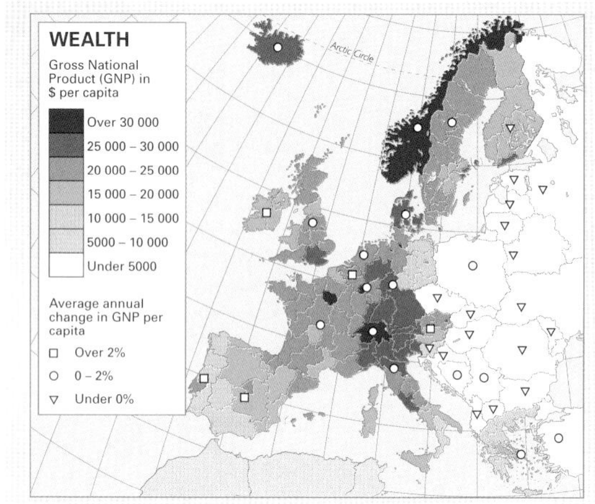

nen, 2000
Head of government Matti Vanhanen, Centre Party, 2003
Recent events
In 1986 Finland became a member of EFTA, and in 1995 it joined the European Union. A new constitution was established in March 2000. A coalition was set up between the Social Democrats and the Swedish Peoples' Party after a close election result in 2003
Economy
Forests are Finland's most valuable resource, with wood and paper products accounting for 35% of exports. Engineering, shipbuilding and textile industries have grown. Farming employs 9% of the workforce. Livestock and dairy farming are the chief activities.
Website www.government.fi

France

Area 551,500 sq km (212,934 sq miles)
Population 58,805,000
Capital Paris (9,469,000)
Languages French (official), Breton, Occitan
GDP per capita 1999 US$23,912
Currency Euro = 100 cents
Government multiparty republic
Head of state President Jacques Chirac, Assembly for the Republic (RPR), 1995
Head of government Jean-Pierre Raffarin (DL), 2002
Recent events
Jacques Chirac's welfare economic reforms in order to meet the criteria for European Monetary Union (EMU) brought strikes and unemployment and led to the election in 1997 of a socialist prime minister, Lionel Jospin. In 2002 voter apathy led to FN leader Jean-Marie Le Pen reaching second round of voting in presidential elections above Lionel Jospin, who resigned as PM after the presidential elections which Jacques Chirac won with 82% of the vote.As a result of their oppostion to the 2003 war in Iraq France and Germany have forged closer ties.
Economy
France is a leading industrial nation. It is the world's fourth-largest manufacturer of cars. Industries include chemicals and steel. It is the leading producer of farm products in western Europe. Livestock and dairy farming are vital sectors. It is the world's second-largest producer of cheese and wine. Tourism is a major industry.
Website www.gouv.fr

Germany *Deutschland*

Area 356,910 sq km (137,803 sq miles)
Population 82,079,000
Capital Berlin (3,472,000)
Language German (official)
GDP per capita 1999 US$25,729
Currency Euro = 100 cents
Government federal multiparty republic
Head of state Johannes Rau, Social Democratic Party (SPD), 1999
Head of government Chancellor Gerhard Schröder, Social Democratic Party in coalition with the Green Party (SPD/Grüne), 1998
Recent events
Germany is a major supporter of the European Union, and former chancellor Helmut Köhl was the driving force behind the creation of the euro. During 1999 state elections in the former German Democratic Republic saw massive losses for the Social Democrats. As a result of their oppostion to the 2003 war in Iraq Germany and France have forged closer ties
Economy
Germany is one of the world's greatest economic powers. Services form the largest economic sector. Machinery and transport equipment account for 50% of exports. It is the world's third-largest car producer. Other major products: ships, iron, steel, petroleum, tyres. It has the world's second-largest lignite mining industry. Other minerals: copper, potash, lead, salt, zinc, aluminium. Germany is the world's second-largest producer of hops and beer, and fifth-largest of wine. Other products: cheese and milk, barley, rye, pork.
Website www.deutschland.de

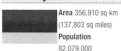

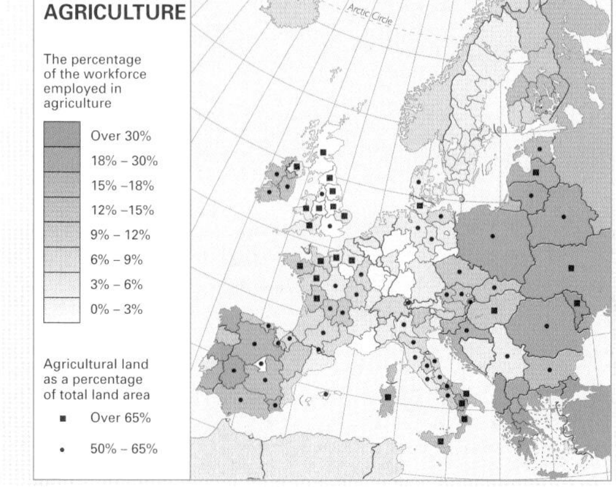

Greece *Ellas*

Area 131,990 sq km (50,691 sq miles)
Population 10,662,000
Capital Athens/Athinai (3,097,000)
Language Greek (official)
GDP per capita 2000 US$13,900
Currency Euro = 100 cents
Government multiparty republic
Head of state President Konstantinos Stephanopoulos, Political Spring Party (PA), 1995
Head of government Kostas Simitis, Panhellenic Socialist Movement (PASOK), 1996
Recent events In 1981 Greece joined the European Community and Andreas Papandreou became Greece's first socialist prime minister (1981-89, 1993-96). Konstantinos Stephanopoulos became president in 1995. The Olympic Games will take place in Greece in 2004.
Economy
Greece is one of the poorest members of the European Union. Manufacturing is important. Products: textiles, cement, chemicals, metallurgy. Minerals: lignite, bauxite, chromite. Farmland covers 33% of Greece, grazing land 40%. Major crops: tobacco, olives, grapes, cotton, wheat. Livestock are raised. Shipping and tourism are also major sectors.
Website www.greece.gr

Hungary *Magyarorszàg*

Area 93,030 sq km (35,919 sq miles)
Population 10,208,000
Capital Budapest (1,909,000)
Language Hungarian (official)
GDP per capita 1999 US$4,772
Currency Forint = 100 filler
Government multiparty republic
Head of state President Ferenc Madl, 2000
Head of government Peter Medgyessy, 2002
Recent events
Peter Medgyessy is not a member of any political party but was selected by the Socialists in 2001. Narrowly avoided having to resign in 2002 when he admitted to having worked for the secret services in the late 70s/early 80s, but denied working for the KGB. Hungary will join the EU in May 2004.
Economy
Since the early 1990s, Hungary has adopted market reforms and privatisation programmes. The economy has suffered from the collapse in exports to the former Soviet Union and Yugoslavia. The manufacture of machinery and transport is the most valuable sector. Hungary's resources include bauxite, coal and natural gas. Major crops include grapes for wine-making, maize, potatoes, sugar beet and wheat. Tourism is a growing sector.
Website www.magyarorszag.hu/angol

Ireland, Republic of *Eire*

Area 70,280 sq km (27,135 sq miles)
Population 3, 619,000
Capital Dublin (1,024,000)
Languages Irish, English (both official)
GDP per capita 1999 US$24,943
Currency Euro = 100 cents
Government multiparty republic
Head of state President Mary McAleese, 1997
Head of government Taoiseach Bertie Ahern, 1997 (Fianna Fáil)
Recent events
The Anglo-Irish Agreement (1985) gave Ireland a consultative role in the affairs of Northern Ireland. Following a 1995 referendum, divorce was legalised. Abortion remains a contentious political issue. In 1997 elections Bertie Ahern became taoiseach and Mary McAleese became president. In the Good Friday Agreement (1998) the Irish Republic gave up its constitutional claim to Northern Ireland and a North-South Ministerial Council was established.
Economy
Ireland has benefited greatly from its membership of the European Union. Grants have enabled the modernisation of farming, which employs 14% of the workforce. Major products include cereals, cattle and dairy products, sheep, sugar beet and potatoes. Fishing is important. Traditional sectors, such as brewing, distilling and textiles, have been supplemented by high-tech industries, such as electronics. Tourism is the most important component of the service industry.
Website www.irlgov.ie

Italy *Italia*

Area 301,270 sq km (116,320 sq miles)
Population 56,783,000
Capital Rome/Roma (92,688,000)
Language Italian (official)
GDP per caplta 2000 US$21,400
Currency Euro = 100 cents
Government multiparty republic
Head of state President Carlo Ciampi, 1997
Head of government Silvio Berlosconi, Casa della Libertà coalition, 2001
Recent events
In 2001 Silvio Berlosconi won the general election as leader of the Casa della Libertà coalition. In 2003 he was tried for matters relating to his business affairs in the 1980s, however the trial was halted when parliament approved a law giving serving prime ministers immunity from prosecution. There was a controversial start to the EU presidency when Berlusconi rebuffed criticism from a German MEP by comparing him to a Nazi guard. A fierce diplomatic row ensued.
Economy
Italy's main industrial region is the northwestern triangle of Milan, Turin and Genoa. It is the world's eighth-largest car and steel producer. Machinery and transport equipment account for 37% of exports. Agricultural production is important. Italy is the world's largest producer of wine. Tourism is a vital economic sector.
Website www.enit.it

Latvia *Latvija*

Area 64,589 sq km (24,938 sq miles)
Population 2,385,000
Capital Riga (840,000)
Languages Latvian (official), Russian
GDP per capita 2000 US$4,200
Currency Lats = 100 santimi
Government multiparty republic
Head of state President Vaira Vike-Freiberga
Head of government Einars Repse, 2002
Recent events
In 1993 Latvia held its first multiparty elections. In 1994 it adopted a law restricting the naturalisation of non-Latvians, including many Russian settlers. In 1995 Latvia joined the Council of Europe and formally applied to join the EU. In 1998 elections the People's Party emerged as the largest single party, but a coalition government was formed by Vilis Kristopans of Latvia's Way who then resigned on the election of Vaira Vike-Freiberga as president. She was then re-elected for a second four-year term in June 2003. Latvia will join the EU in May 2004.
Economy
Latvia is a lower-middle-income country. The country has to import many of the materials needed for manufacturing. Latvia produces only 10% of the electricity it needs, and the rest has to be imported from Belarus, Russia and Ukraine. Manufactures include electronic goods, farm machinery and fertiliser. Farm exports include beef, dairy and pork.
Website www.lv

Liechtenstein

Area 157 sq km (61 sq miles)
Population 32,000
Capital Vaduz
Language German (official)
GDP per capita 1991 US$34,000
Currency Swiss franc = 100 centimes
Government independent principality
Head of state Prince Hans Adam II, 1989
Head of government Otmar Hasler, Progressive Citizens Party, 2001
Recent events
Independent principality in western central Europe in a currency and customs union with Switzerland. Women finally got the vote in 1984. The principality joined the UN in 1990. In 2003 the people voted in a referendum to give Prince Hans Adam II new political powers thus rendering the country Europe's only absolute monarchy with the prince having power of veto over the government.
Economy
Liechtenstein is the fourth-smallest country in the world and one of the richest per capita. Since 1945 it has rapidly developed a specialised manufacturing base. The major part of state revenue is derived from international companies attracted by low taxation rates. Tourism is increasingly important.
Website www.liechtenstein.li

Lithuania *Lietuva*

Area 65,200 sq km (25,200 sq miles)
Population 3, 600,000
Capital Vilnius (576,000)
Languages Lithuanian (official), Russian, Polish
GDP per capita 1995 US$4,120
Currency Litas = 100 centai
Government multiparty republic
Head of state President Rolandas Paksas, 2003
Head of government Algirdas Mykolas Brazauskas, 2001
Recent events
The Soviet Union recognised Lithuania as independent in September 1991. In 1993 Soviet troops completed their withdrawal. In 1996 Lithuania signed a treaty of association with the EU. When Rolandas Paksas was elected president in Januwary 2003, he was chairman of the Liberal Democratic Party but had to relinquish this position as president. Lithuania will join the EU in May 2004.
Economy
Lithuania is a developing country. It is dependent on Russian raw materials. Manufacturing is the most valuable export sector: major products include chemicals, electronic goods and machine tools. Dairy and meat farming and fishing are also important activities.
Website www.lithuania.lt

Luxembourg

Area 2,590 sq km (1,000 sq miles)
Population 425,000
Capital Luxembourg

(pop. 76,000)
Languages Luxembourgian/Letzeburgish (official), French, German
GDP per capita 1999 US$44,688
Currency Euro = 100 cents
Government constitutional monarchy (or grand duchy)
Head of state Grand Duke Henri,2000
Head of government Jean-Claude Juncker, coalition between Christian Social People's Party (PCS) and the Conservative Democratic Party (PDL), 1999
Recent events
Following 1994 elections, the Christian Social People's Party (CD) and the Luxembourg Socialist Workers' Party (SOC) formed a coalition government. Jean-Claude Juncker (CD) became prime minister. Grand Duke Jean abdicated in favour of his son Prince Henri in October 2000
Economy
There are rich deposits of iron ore, and Luxembourg is a major producer of iron and steel. Other industries include chemicals, textiles, tourism, banking and electronics. Farmers raise cattle and pigs. Major crops include cereals, fruits and grapes for winemaking. The city of Luxembourg is a major centre of European administration and finance.
Website www.luxembourg.lu

Macedonia *Makedonija*

Area 25,710 sq km (9,927 sq miles)
Population 2,009,000
Capital Skopje (541,000)
Languages Macedonian (official), Albanian
GDP per capita 2000 US$3,800
Currency Denar = 100 deni
Government multiparty republic
Head of state Boris Trajkovski, Internal Macedonian Revolutionary Organisation-Democratic Party for Macedonian National Unity (VMRO/DPMNE), 1999
Head of government Prime Minister Branko Crvenkovski (SDSM), 2002
Recent events
In 1993 the UN accepted the new republic as a member. In 1994 Greece banned Macedonian trade through Greece. The ban was lifted in 1995, when Macedonia agreed to redesign its flag and remove any claims to Greek Macedonia from its constitution. Internal tensions exist between Macedonians and the Albanian minority. In 2002 Social Democrat Alliance won the election and formed a coalition cabinet including a deputy prime minister from the Democratic Union for Integration - a party with Albanian sympathies.
Economy
Macedonia is a developing country. The poorest of the six former republics of Yugoslavia, its economy was devastated by UN trade damaged by sanctions against Yugoslavia and by the Greek embargo.The GDP is increasing each year and successful privatisation in 2000 boosted the country's reserves to over $700 Million Manufactures, especially metals, dominate exports. Agriculture employs 17% of the workforce. Major crops include cotton, fruits, maize, tobacco and wheat.
Website www.gov.mk/english

Malta

Area 316 sq km (122 sq miles)
Population 379,000
Capital Valetta (pop. 102,000)
Languages Maltese, English (both official)
GDP per capita 1992 US$8,281
Currency Maltese lira = 100 cents
Government multiparty republic
Head of state President Guido de Marco, Christian Democratic Nationalist Party, 1999
Head of government Edward Fenech Adami, Christian Democratic Nationalist Party, 1998
Recent events
In 1990 Malta applied to join the European Community. In 1997 the newly elected Malta Labour Party pledged to rescind the application. The Nationalist Party, led by the pro-European Edward Fenech Adami, regained power in 1998 elections. Malta will join the EU in May 2004.
Economy
Malta is an upper-middle-income developing country. Machinery and transport equipment account for more than 50% of exports. Malta's historic naval dockyards are now used for commercial shipbuilding and repair. The state-owned Malta Drydocks is Malta's leading industry. Manufactures include chemicals, electronic equipment and textiles. The largest sector is services, especially tourism. The main crops are barley, fruits, vegetables and wheat. Privatisation of state-controlled companies and liberalisation of markets in preparation for membership of EU is still a contentious issue.
Website www.gov.mt

Moldova

Area 33,700 sq km (13,010 sq miles)
Population 4,458,000
Capital Chisinau (700,000)
Language Moldovan/Romanian (official)
GDP per capita 1992 US$3,670
Currency Leu = 100 bani
Government multiparty republic
Head of state President Vladimir Voronin, 2001
Head of government Vasile Tarlev, 2001
Recent events
In 1994 multiparty elections were won by the former communists of the Agrarian Democratic Party. A referendum rejected reunification with Romania. Parliament voted to join the CIS. A new constitution (1994) established a presidential parliamentary republic. In 1996 Petru Lucinschi was elected president but lost to Vladimir Voronin in 2001.
Economy
Moldova is a lower-middle-income developing economy. Agriculture is important and major products include fruits and grapes for wine-making. Farmers also raise livestock, including dairy cattle and pigs. Moldova has to import materials and fuels for its industries. Major manufactures include agricultural machinery and consumer goods. Exports include food, wine, tobacco, textiles and footwear.
Website www.parliament.md/eng

Monaco

Area 1.5 sq km (0.6 sq miles)
Population 32,000
Capital Monaco-Ville
Languages French (official), Italian, Monegasque
GDP per capita 2000 US$27,000
Currency Euro = 100 cents
Government principality
Head of state Prince Rainier III, 1949
Minister of State Patrick Leclerque, 2000.
Recent events
Monaco has been ruled by the Grimaldi family since the end of the 13th century. and under the protection of France since 1860.
Economy
The chief source of income is tourism, attracted by the casinos of Monte Carlo. There is some light industry, including printing, textiles and postage stamps.
Website www.monaco.gouv.mc

The Netherlands
Nederland

Area 41,526 sq km (16,033 sq miles)
Population 15,731,000
Capital Amsterdam (1,100,000); administrative capital 's-Gravenhage (The Hague)
Languages Dutch (official), Frisian
GDP per capita 1999 US$ 24,906
Currency Euro = 100 cents
Government constitutional monarchy
Head of state Queen Beatrix, 1980
Head of government Jan Peter Bakenende (CDA), 2002
Recent events
In 2002 Pim Fortuyn, leader of right wing anti-immigrant party Lijst Pim Fortuyn was assassinated. Subsequently Wim Kok lost power to Jan Peter Bakenende who formed a coalition Cabinet with the Democrats-66 and VVD (Peoples' Party for Freedom and Democracy).
Economy
The Netherlands has prospered through its close European ties. Private enterprise has successfully combined with progressive social policies. It is highly industrialised. Products include aircraft, chemicals, electronics and machinery. Natural resources include natural gas. Agriculture is intensive and mechanised, employing only 5% of the workforce. Dairy farming is the leading agricultural activity. Major products are cheese, barley, flowers and bulbs.
Website www.holland.com

Norway *Norge*

Area 323,900 sq km (125,000 sq miles)
Population 4,420,000
Capital Oslo (714,000)
Languages Norwegian (official), Lappish, Finnish
GDP per capita 1999 US$34,410
Currency Krone = 100 øre
Government constitutional monarchy
Head of state King Harald V, 1991
Head of government Kjell Magne Bondevik (Christian People's Party), 2001
Recent events
In 1991 Olav V was succeeded by his son, Harald V. In referenda in 1972 and 1994 Norway rejected joining the EU. A centre-right coalition of Christian Peoples' Party, Conservative Party and Liberal Party rules with a minority
Economy
Norway has one of the world's highest standards of living. Its chief exports are oil and natural gas. Norway is the world's eighth-largest producer of crude oil. Per capita, Norway is the world's largest producer of hydroelectricity. Major manufactures include petroleum products, chemicals, aluminium, wood pulp and paper. The chief farming activities are dairy and meat production, but Norway has to import food. Norway has the largest fish catch in Europe after Russia.
Website www.norge.no

Poland *Polska*

Area 312,680 sq km (120,726 sq miles)
Population 38,607,000
Capital Warsaw/Warszawa (1,638,000)
Language Polish (official)
GDP per capita 1999 US$4,811
Currency Zloty = 100 groszy
Government multiparty republic
Head of state Aleksander Kwasniewski, Alliance of the Democratic Left (SdRP/SLD), 1995

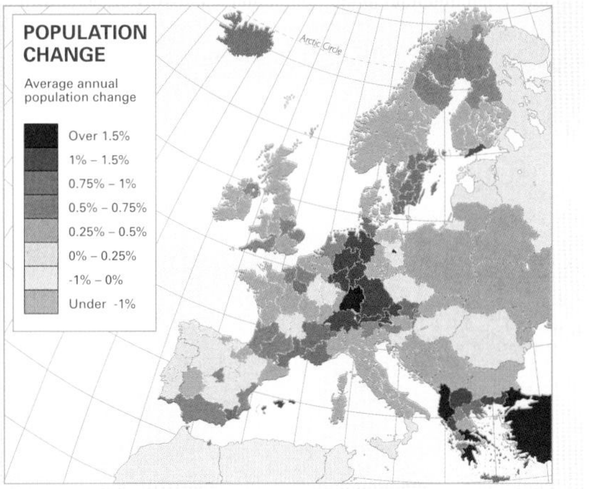

Head of government Leszek Miller, Democratic Left Alliance, 2001
Recent events
In 1996 Poland joined the OECD. In 1997 it was invited to join NATO. In 2001 the Democratic Left Alliance formed a coaltion with the Polish Peasants Party (PSL) and the Labour Union, however the PSL were ordered out after voting against government tax proposals. Poland will join the EU in May 2004.
Economy
Of the workforce, 27% is employed in agriculture and 37% in industry. Poland is the world's fifth-largest producer of lignite and seventh-largest producer of bituminous coal. Copper ore is also a vital resource. Manufacturing accounts for 24% of exports. Poland is the world's fifth-largest producer of ships. Agriculture remains important. Major crops include barley, potatoes and wheat. The transition to a free-market economy has caused many problems, but economic growth is slowly returning.
Website www.poland.pl

Portugal

Area 92,390 sq km (35,670 sq miles)
Population 9,928,000
Capital Lisbon/Lisboa (2,561,000)
Language Portuguese (official)
GDP per capita 2000 US$15,300
Currency Euro = 100 cents
Government multiparty republic
Head of state Jorge Sampaio, 1996, PS
Head of government Jose Manuel Durao Barroso (PSD), 2002
Recent events
In 1986 Portugal joined the European Community. In 1996 Jorge Sampaio became president. In 2002 the Social Democrat Party won the election and formed a coalition government with the Popular Party.
Economy
In 1999 Portugal adopted the euro. Its commitment to the European Union (EU) has seen the economy emerge from recession. Manufacturing accounts for 33% of exports. Textiles, footwear and clothing are major exports. Portugal is the world's fifth-largest producer of tungsten and the world's eighth-largest producer of wine. Olives, potatoes and wheat are also grown. Tourism is a rapidly growing sector.
Website www.portugal.gov.pt

Romania

Area 237,500 sq km (91,699 sq miles)
Population 22,396,000
Capital Bucharest/Bucuresti (2,061,000)
Languages Romanian (official), Hungarian
GDP per capita 1995 U$4,360
Currency Romanian leu = 100 bani
Government multiparty republic
Head of state President Ion Iliescu
Head of government Adrian Nastase, 2000
Recent events
A new constitution was introduced in 1991. 1995 saw Romania applying to join the European Union. Ion Iliescu, a former communist official, was re-elected in 2000. Romania could join the EU in 2007 if it continues with current reforms.
Economy
Industry accounts for 40% of GDP. Oil, natural gas and antimony are the main mineral resources. Agriculture employs 29% of the workforce. Romania is the world's second-largest producer of plums (after China). It is the world's ninth-largest producer of wine. Other major crops include maize and cabbages. Economic reform is slow.
Website www.gov.ro

Russia *Rossiya*

Area 17,075,000 sq km (6,592,800 sq miles)
Population 146,861,000
Capital Moscow/Moskva (9,233,000)
Languages Russian (official), and many others
GDP per capita 1995 US$4,480
Currency Russian rouble = 100 kopeks
Government federal multiparty republic
Head of state Vladimir Putin. 2000
Head of government Mikail Kassianov
Recent events
In 1992 the Russian Federation became a co-founder of the CIS, composed of former Soviet Republics. A new Federal Treaty was signed between the central government and the autonomous republics within the Russian Federation. Chechnya refused to sign, and declared independence. In December 1993 a new democratic constitution was adopted. From 1994 to 1996, Russia fought a costly civil war in Chechnya. In 1998 the stock market collapsed and the rouble was devalued by 50%. In 1999 war flared up again in Chechnya. Vladimir Putin was officially elected president in spring 2000. Russia continues to suffer considerable political and economic instability. Having supported the US led campaign against terrorism in 2002 a Nato-Russian Council was formed with an eye on terrorism policy. Russia did not support the war in Iraq of 2003.
Economy
In 1993 mass privatisation began. By 1996, 80% of the Russian economy was in private hands. A major problem remains the size of Russia's foreign debt. Industry employs 46% of the workforce and contributes 48% of GDP. Mining is the most valuable activity. Russia is the world's leading producer of natural gas and nickel, the second largest pro-

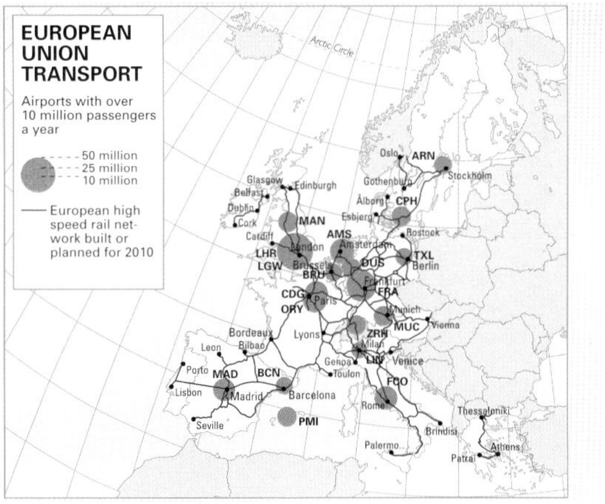

ducer of aluminium and phosphates. and the third-largest of crude oil, lignite and brown coal. Light industries are growing in importance. Most farmland is still government-owned or run as collectives, with important products barley, oats, rye, potatoes, beef and veal.

Website www.gov.ru

San Marino

Area 61 sq km (24 sq miles)
Population 25,000
Capital San Marino (4,335)
GDP per capita 2000 US$20,000
Currency Euro = 100 cents
Language Italian (official)
Government multiparty republic
Heads of state co-Captains Regent: Giovanni Lonternini, Valeria Ciavatta

Recent events
World's smallest republic and perhaps Europe's oldest state, San Marino's links with Italy led to the adoption of the euro.

Economy
The economy is largely agricultural. Tourism is vital to the state's income.

Website www.sanmarinosite.com

Serbia & Montenegro *Srbija i Crna Gora*

Area 102,170 sq km (39,449 sq miles)
Population 10,393.177
Capital Belgrade/Beograd (1,137,000)
Languages Serbian (official), Albanian
GDP per capita 1992 US$4,000
Currency Dinar = 100 paras (Serbia)
Euro = 100 cents (Montenegro)
Government federal republic
Head of state Svetozvar Marovic, 2003; Nastasa Misic (Serbia), 2003; Filip Vujanovic (Montenegro), 2003
Head of government Zoran Zivkovic (Serbia), 2002; Milo Djukanovic (Montenegro), 2002

Recent events
In 1989 Slobodan Milosevic´ became president of Serbia and called for the creation of a "Greater Serbia". Serbian attempts to dominate the Yugoslav federation led to the secession of Slovenia and Croatia (with which Serbia fought a brief war) in 1991 and to Bosnia-Herzegovina's declaration of independence in March 1992. In April 1992 Serbia and Montenegro announced the formation of a new Yugoslav federation and invited Serbs in Croatia and Bosnia-Herzegovina to join. Serbian aid to the Bosnian Serb campaign of "ethnic cleansing" in the civil war in Bosnia led the United Nations to impose sanctions on Serbia, Milosevic´ severed support for the Bosnian Serbs. In 1995 Milosevic´ signed the Dayton Peace Accord, which ended the Bosnian war. In 1997 Milosevic´ became president of Yugoslavia. In 1998 fighting erupted in Kosovo between Albanian nationalists and Serbian security forces. In 1999, following the forced expulsion of Albanians from Kosovo, NATO bombed Yugoslavia, forcing withdrawal of Serbian forces from Kosovo. Kostunica won the elections of September 2000, but Milosevic´ refused to hand over power. After a week of civil unrest and increased support for Kostunica, Milosevic´ was finally ousted. A constitutional charter for the union of Serbia & Montenegro was agreed in December 2002. There is a federal presidency with federal foreign & defence ministries, but the two republics are semi-independent states in charge of their own economies. This arrangement will remain for a minimum of three years. Kosovo is legally part of Serbia, but is an international protectorate.

Economy
Yugoslavia's lower-middle income economy has been devastated by war and economic sanctions. Hyperinflation is one of the greatest problems. Industrial production has collapsed. Natural resources include bauxite, coal and copper. There is some oil and natural gas. Manufacturing includes aluminium, cars, machinery, plastics, steel and textiles. Agriculture is important.

Website www.serbia-tourism.org; montenegro.yu

Slovakia *Slovenska Republika*

Area 49,035 sq km (18,932 sq miles)
Population 5,393,000
Capital Bratislava (451,000)
Languages Slovak (official), Hungarian
GDP per capita 1999 US$3,653
Currency Koruna = 100 halierov
Government multiparty republic
Head of state President Rudolf Schuster, Party of Civic Understanding (SOP), 1999
Head of government Mikulás Dzurinda, coalition government led by Slovak Democratic Coalition (SDK), 1998

Recent events
In 1993 the Slovak Republic became a sovereign state, breaking peaceably from the Czech Republic, with which it maintains close relations. In 1996 the Slovak Republic and Hungary ratified a treaty confirming their borders and stipulating basic rights for the 560,000 Hungarians in Slovakia. Following elections in 1998, a coalition government was formed, led by Mikulás Dzurinda of the Slovak Democratic Coalition. Slovakia will join the EU in May 2004.

Economy
The transition from communism to private ownership has been painful with industrial output falling, unemployment and inflation rising. In 1995 the privatisation programme was suspended. Manufacturing employs 33% of the workforce. Bratislava and Kosiče are the chief industrial cities. Major products include ceramics, machinery and steel. Farming employs 12% of the workforce. Crops include barley and grapes. Tourism is growing.

Website www.slovakia.org

Slovenia *Slovenija*

Area 20,251 sq km (7,817 sq miles)
Population 1,972,000
Capital Ljubljana (280,000)
Languages Slovene
GDP per capita 1992 US$6,330
Currency Tolar = 100 stotin
Government multiparty republic
Head of state Janez Drnovsek, Liberal Democrats of Slovenia (LDS), 2002
Head of government Anton Rop, LDS, 2002

Recent events
In 1990 Slovenia declared itself independent, which led to brief fighting between Slovenes and the federal army. In 1992 the European Community recognised Slovenia's independence. Janez Drnovsek was elected president in December '02 and immediately stepped down as prime minister. Slovenia will join the EU in May 2004.

Economy
The transformation of a centrally planned economy and the fighting in other parts of former Yugoslavia have caused problems for Slovenia. Manufacturing is the leading activity. Major manufactures include chemicals, machinery, transport equipment, metal goods and textiles. Major crops include maize, fruit, potatoes and wheat.

Website www.gov.si

Spain *España*

Area 504,780 sq km (194,896 sq miles)
Population 39,134,000
Capital Madrid (3,041,000)
Languages Castilian Spanish (official), Catalan, Galician, Basque
GDP per capita 1999 US$17,300
Currency Euro = 100 cents
Government constitutional monarchy
Head of state King Juan Carlos, 1975
Head of government José María Aznar, People's Party (PP), 1996

Recent events
From 1959 the militant Basque organization ETA waged a campaign of terror but announced a ceasefire in 1998. José María Aznar formed a minority administration. In 2002 Basque separatist party Batasuna was suspended for three years pending investigation into its links with ETA.

Economy
Spain has rapidly transformed from a largely poor, agrarian society into a prosperous industrial nation. Agriculture now employs only 10% of the workforce. Spain is the world's third-largest wine producer. Other crops include citrus fruits, tomatoes and olives. Industries: cars, ships, chemicals, electronics, metal goods, steel, textiles.

Website www.tourspain.es

Switzerland *Schweiz*

Area 41,290 sq km (15,942 sq miles)
Population 7,260,000
Capital Bern (324,000)
Languages French, German, Italian, Romansch (all official)
GDP per capita 1999 US$36,247
Currency Swiss Franc = 100 centimes
Government federal republic
Head of state and **Head of government** Pascal Couchepin, 2003

Recent events
A referendum (1986) rejected Swiss membership of the UN to avoid compromising its neutrality. EU membership was similarly rejected (1992).The President of the Confederation is elected annually. 2003 elections led to 28% share for right-wing Swiss Peoples' Party, but their fixed share of Federal Council is only 14% so they demanded an extra post.

Economy
Switzerland is wealthy and industrialised. Manufactures include chemicals, electrical equipment, machinery, precision instruments, watches and textiles. Livestock raising, notably dairy farming, is the chief agricultural activity. Tourism is important, and Swiss banks attract worldwide investment

Website www.gov.ch

Sweden *Sverige*

Area 449,960 sq km (173,730 sq miles)
Population 8,887,000
Capital Stockholm (1,553,000)
Languages Swedish (official), Finnish
GDP per capita 1999 US$27,256
Currency Swedish krona = 100 ore
Government constitutional monarchy
Head of state King Carl XVI Gustaf, 1973
Head of government Göran Persson, Social Democratic Workers' Party (SSA), 1996

Recent events
In 1995 Sweden joined the European Union. Göran Persson was re-elected in 2002. The cost of maintaining Sweden's extensive welfare services has become a major political issue. In September 2003 Sweden was shocked by the murder of popular minister Anna Lindh, thus reigniting discussion over the relaxed attitude to security. Days later Sweden said no to the euro.

Economy
Sweden Is a hlghly developed Industrlal country. It has rich iron ore deposits, but other industrial materials are imported. Steel is a major product, used to manufacture aircraft, cars, machinery and ships. Forestry and fishing are important. Livestock and dairy farming are valuable activities; crops include barley and oats.

Website www.sweden.gov.se

Turkey *Türkiye*

Area 779,450 sq km (300,946 sq miles)
Population 69,568,000
Capital Ankara (3,028,000)
Languages Turkish (official), Kurdish
GDP per capita 1999 US$2,809
Currency Turkish lira = 100 kurus
Government multiparty republic
Head of state President Ahmet Necdet Sezer, 2000
Head of government Recep Tayyip Erdogan, Justice and Development Party (AK), 2002

Recent events
Since 1984 Turkey has been fighting the Kurdish Workers Party (PKK) in south-eastern Turkey, Syria and northern Iraq. Turkey has often been accused of violating the human rights of Kurds. In 1999 Turkey captured the PKK leader, Abdullah Ocalan. In 1999 earthquakes caused severe damage and loss of 20,000 lives in north western Turkey.

Economy
Turkey is a lower-middle income developing country. Agriculture employs 47% of the workforce. Turkey is a leading producer of citrus fruits, barley, cotton, wheat, tobacco and tea. It is a major producer of chromium and phosphate fertilisers. Tourism is a vital source of foreign exchange.

Website www.tourismturkey.org

Ukraine *Ukraina*

Area 603,700 sq km (233,100 sq miles)
Population 50,125,000
Capital Kiev/Kyviv (2,630,000)
Languages Ukrainian (official), Russian
GDP per capita 1995 US$2,400
Currency Hryvna = 100 kopiykas
Government multiparty republic
Head of state President Leonid Kuchma, 1994
Head of government Prime Minister Anatoliy Kimakh

Recent events
The Chernobyl disaster of 1986 contaminated large areas of Ukraine. Tensions with Russia over the Crimea, the Black Sea fleet, the control of nuclear weapons and oil and gas reserves were eased by a 1992 treaty. Leonid Kuchma was elected president in 1994. He continued the policy of establishing closer ties with the West and sped up the pace of privatisation. Kuchma was re-elected in 1999. There are continuing disputes over the the powers of the Crimean legislature.

Economy
Ukraine is a lower-middle-income economy. Agriculture is important. It is the world's leading producer of sugar beet, the second-largest producer of barley, and a major producer of wheat. Ukraine has extensive raw materials, including coal (though many mines are exhausted), iron ore and manganese ore. Ukraine is reliant on oil and natural gas imports. Ukraine's debt to Russia has been partly offset by allowing Russian firms majority shares in many Ukrainian industries.

Website www.kmu.gov.ua/control.en

United Kingdom

Area 243,368 sq km (94,202 sq miles)
Population 58,970,000
Capital London (8,089,000)
Languages English (official), Welsh (also official in Wales), Gaelic
GDP per capita 1999 US$24,228
Currency Sterling (pound) = 100 pence
Government constitutional monarchy
Head of state Queen Elizabeth II, 1952
Head of government Tony Blair, Labour Party, 1997

Recent events
The United Kingdom of Great Britain and Northern Ireland is a union of four countries - England, Northern Ireland, Scotland and Wales. In 1997 referenda on devolution saw Scotland and Wales gain their own legislative assemblies. The Scottish assembly was given tax-varying power. The Good Friday Agreement (1998) offered the best chance of peace in Northern Ireland for a generation. Tony Blair was re-elected prime minister in 2001 and controversially gave full support to Bush over the war in Iraq in 2003.

Economy
The UK is a major industrial and trading nation. Cars remain a significant product, but the economy has become more service-centred and high-technology industries have grown in importance. The UK is a producer of oil, petroleum products, natural gas, potash, salt and lead. Agriculture employs only 2% of the workforce. Major crops include hops for beer, potatoes, carrots, sugar beet and strawberries. Sheep are the leading livestock, with poultry, beef and dairy cattle important. Fishing is a major activity. Financial services and tourism are the leading service industries.

Website www.parliament.uk

1: 4 250 000

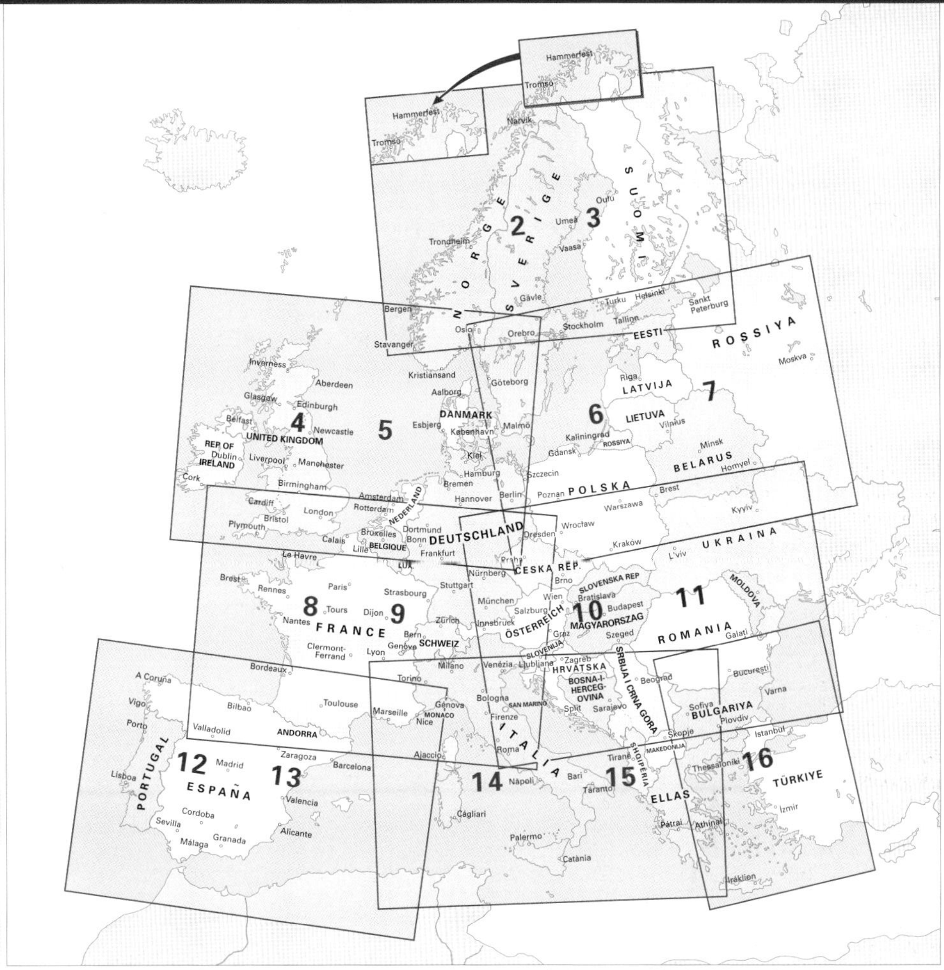

Calais					
548	Dublin				
726	346	Edinburgh			
575	1123	1301	Frankfurt		
1342	477	176	1067	Göteborg	
760	477	1486	485	582	Hamburg

Dublin ▶ Göteborg = 477 km

000 =

	Amsterdam	Athínai	Barcelona	Bergen	Berlin	Bruxelles	Bucuresti	Budapest	Calais	Dublin	Edinburgh	Frankfurt	Göteborg	Hamburg	Helsinki	Istanbul	København	Köln	Lisboa	London	Luxembourg	Madrid	Marseille	Milano	Moskva	München	Oslo	Paris	Praha	Roma	Sevilla	Sofiya	Stockholm	Warszawa	Wien
Athínai	2945
Barcelona	1505	3192
Bergen	1484	3742	2803
Berlin	650	2412	1863	1309
Bruxelles	197	2895	1308	1586	764
Bucuresti	2245	1219	2644	3037	1707	2181
Budapest	1420	1530	1999	2212	882	1358	852
Calais	367	3100	1269	1783	956	215	2398	1573
Dublin	533	3630	1817	270	1504	763	3021	2196	548
Edinburgh	1093	3826	1995	176	1696	941	3124	2299	726	346
Frankfurt	441	2499	1313	1508	550	383	1804	979	575	1123	1301
Göteborg	1029	3080	2362	819	668	1145	1734	1550	1342	477	176	1067
Hamburg	447	2719	1780	1023	286	563	2014	1189	760	477	1486	485	582
Helsinki	1560	2539	2338	1063	475	1239	1834	1009	1431	1318	1236	1598	505	1113
Istanbul	2756	1145	2990	3653	2223	2706	690	1341	2911	3537	3657	2314	2891	2530	2350
København	965	2782	2090	1103	370	1081	2077	1252	1278	752	479	795	284	518	803	2593
Köln	256	2684	1376	1427	566	198	1983	1158	390	938	1116	180	986	404	1517	2499	714
Lisboa	2331	4460	1268	3723	2869	3141	3917	3222	2069	2617	2795	2400	3282	2700	3817	4342	3014	2339
London	480	3200	1387	458	1074	333	2591	1766	118	430	608	693	122	878	1991	3107	1188	508	2187
Luxembourg	406	2661	1190	1613	749	209	2052	1227	424	972	1150	240	1172	590	1703	2472	900	186	2160	542
Madrid	1790	3809	617	3183	2364	1600	3262	2622	1528	1634	2254	1930	2742	2160	3276	3589	2473	1798	651	1646	1628
Marseille	1210	2683	509	2435	1541	1030	2154	1505	1063	1588	1789	1023	1994	1412	2525	2479	1722	1006	1777	1182	822	1126
Milano	1085	2182	1038	2141	1060	890	1668	992	1072	1620	1798	683	1700	1118	1535	1993	1428	868	2315	1190	679	1655	538
Moskva	2457	2930	3655	2223	1821	2585	1761	2099	2800	3348	3526	2312	1665	2115	1160	2605	2325	2387	4875	2918	2852	4224	3270	3027
München	839	2106	1340	1788	594	789	1497	672	994	1524	1720	398	1347	765	1069	1907	969	580	2545	1094	555	2010	1011	473	2305
Oslo	1347	3372	2680	503	960	1463	2667	1842	1660	773	729	1385	316	900	697	3089	590	1304	3604	1778	1490	3063	2312	2018	1823	1559
Paris	510	2917	988	1922	1051	320	2307	1482	281	829	1007	591	1481	899	2012	2727	1209	495	1821	399	351	1280	782	857	2903	810	1799
Praha	950	2067	1750	1675	345	888	1362	537	1097	1635	1816	512	1013	652	770	1878	715	690	2870	1205	753	2329	1399	853	1853	388	1305	1061
Roma	1691	1140	1385	2706	1502	1520	1904	1263	1678	2226	2404	1289	2265	1683	1977	2237	1993	1474	2653	1796	1285	2002	876	606	3362	918	2583	1389	1309
Sevilla	2347	4223	1031	3736	2894	2150	3709	3010	2078	2626	2804	2344	3295	2713	3826	4034	3023	2318	401	2196	2178	550	1540	2078	4774	2371	3613	1830	2781	2446
Sofiya	2206	828	2453	3103	1673	2156	391	790	2361	2891	3087	1764	2341	1980	1800	550	2043	1949	3706	2461	1922	3037	1929	1443	2252	1367	2632	2177	1328	1687	3484
Stockholm	1393	3418	2726	1063	1006	1509	2713	1888	1673	2254	1069	1431	505	946	167	3185	590	1350	3650	1824	1536	3109	2358	2064	1228	1600	530	1845	1351	2629	3659	2679
Warszawa	1256	2128	2366	1909	606	1350	1473	648	1542	2110	2268	1136	1274	886	361	1989	956	1152	3480	1680	1345	2960	2015	1469	1245	996	1506	1677	616	1853	3397	1439	1612
Wien	1168	1772	1856	1970	640	1114	1067	242	1308	1954	2034	731	1308	947	1088	1583	1010	916	3100	1524	993	2473	1353	818	2137	430	1600	1240	295	1126	2876	1033	1646	727
Zürich	816	2426	1030	1938	863	619	1810	985	804	1352	1530	464	1497	915	2164	2323	1433	589	2296	922	410	1647	699	292	2552	303	1815	592	691	898	2061	1173	1861	1307	743

km

Nordkapp
Magerøya
Havøysund
Kjøllefjord
Honningsvåg
Nordkinn-
halvøya
Berlevåg
Båtsfjord
Sørøya
Akkarfjord
Porsanger-
halvøya
Hammerfest
Kvaløya
Breivikbotn
Loppahavet
Seiland
Stjernøya
Arnøy
Vanna
Gamvik
Talvik
Alta
Ringvassøy
Tromsø
Kvaløy
Lakselv
Tana
Vardø
Varanger-
halvøya
Vadsø
Varangerfjorden
Finnmark
Utsjoki
Kirkenes
Bjørnevatn
Pechenga
Nikel
Zapolyarnyi
Karasjok
Storfjord
Halti
Andselv
Kaamanen
Partakko
Kautokeino
Inari
Inarijärvi
Vesterålen
Andenes
Senja
Andøya
Risøyhamn
Harstad
Sortland
Hinnøya
Langøya
Austvågøy
Stokmarknes
Lødingen
Narvik
Vestvågøy
Svolvær
Stamsund
Bognes
Skarberget
Frostisen
Bodø
Fauske
Sulitjelma
Saltfjorden
Vastenjaure
Virihaure
Pieskehaure
Svartisen
Helgeland
Tomma
Mo i Rana
Dønna
Hemnesberget
Sandnessjøen
Alsten
Korgen
Strimasund
Norra Storfjället
Mosjøen
Vega
Brønnøysund
Trofors
Tärnaby
Sorsele
Strömsund
Vennesund
Austra
Leka
Storuman
Vikna
Rørvik
Folda
Namsos
Grong
Vilhelmina
Gäddede
Trøndelag
Frøya
Hitra
Smøla
Frohavet
Åfjord
Follafoss
Steinkjer
Brekstad
Fosna
Verdalsøra
Levanger
Stranda
Sandvika
Trondheimsfjorden
Trondheim
Stjørdalshalsen
Heimdal
Hommelvik
Melhus
Kristiansund
Vinje
Orkanger
Åre
Mörsil
Storlien
Duved
Järpen
Krokom
Lit
Östersund
Hustadvika
Molde
Tingvoll
Løkken
Støren
Jämtland
Brunflo
Sollefteå
Ålesund
Spjelkavik
Sunndalsøra
Haltdalen
Ulsberg
Sylarna
Fosnavåg
Hareid
Ørsta
Volda
Stranda
Åndalsnes
Oppdal
Kvikne
Os
Røros
Brekken
Funäsdalen
Tännäs
Bräcke
Hede
Åsarna
Ånge
Rätansbyn
Måløy
Nordfjordeid
Hellesylt
Grotli
Stryn
Videseter
Lesjaskog
Lesjaverk
Snøhetta
Hjerkinn
Dombås
Folldal
Alvdal
Tynset
Tufsingdalen
Sundsvall
Florø
Eikefjord
Naustdal
Førde
Sandane
Olden
Lom
Dovre
Idre
Sveg
Ljusdal
Galdhøpiggen
Skagastølstindane
Skjolden
Engerdal
Särna
Hudiksvall
Vadheim
Høyanger
Balestrand
Sogndalsfjøra
Kaupanger
Øvre Årdal
Vangsnes
Vik
Lærdalsøyri
Sognefjorden
Gudvangen
Koppang
Trysil
Iggesund
Tretten
Fagernes
Lillehammer
Brumunddal
Sälen
Älvdalen
Bollnäs
Söderhamn
Ljusne
Lerwick
Tórshavn
Seyðisfjörður
Flåm
Hemsedal
Voss
Askøy
Ytre Arna
Bergen
Nesttun
Osøyro
Norheimsund
Gol
Geilo
Nesbyen
Gjøvik
Raufoss
Hamar
Stange
Elverum
Mora
Orsa
Rättvik
Siljan
Gävle
Älvkarleby
Stord
Bømlo
Odda
Skare
Folgefonna
Brandbu
Sand
Eidsvoll
Malungsfors
Malung
Sysslebäck
Stöllet
Vansbro
Björbo
Falun
Hofors
Borlänge
Sandviken
Hedemora
Avesta
Leirvik
Etne
Sauda
Røldal
Hønefoss
Jevnaker
Skarnes
Kongsvinger
Rjukan
Gausta
Vikersund
Oslo
Lillestrøm
Åmot
Torsby
Hagfors
Ludvika
Sala
Haugesund
Kopervik
Åkrahamn
Tinnoset
Kongsberg
Drammen
Ski
Charlottenberg
Sunne
Fagersta
Uppsala
Bykle
Dalen
Seljord
Notodden
Holmestrand
Drøbak
Svelvik
Moss
Askim
Mysen
Töcksfors
Arvika
Filipstad
Hällefors
Västerås
Sigtuna
Enköping
Boknafjorden
Telemark
Hylestad
Ulefoss
Horten
Tønsberg
Rakkestad
Årjäng
Karlstad
Karlskoga
Köping
Stavanger
Jørpeland
Sandnes
Skien
Sandefjord
Sarpsborg
Fredrikstad
Halden
Grums
Skoghall
Kristinehamn
Degerfors
Örebro
Kumla
Eskilstuna
Södertälje
Bryne
Ålgård
Nærbø
Treungen
Porsgrunn
Stathelle
Larvik
Stavern
Bengtsfors
Åmål
Säffle
Oslofjorden
NORGE
SVERIGE

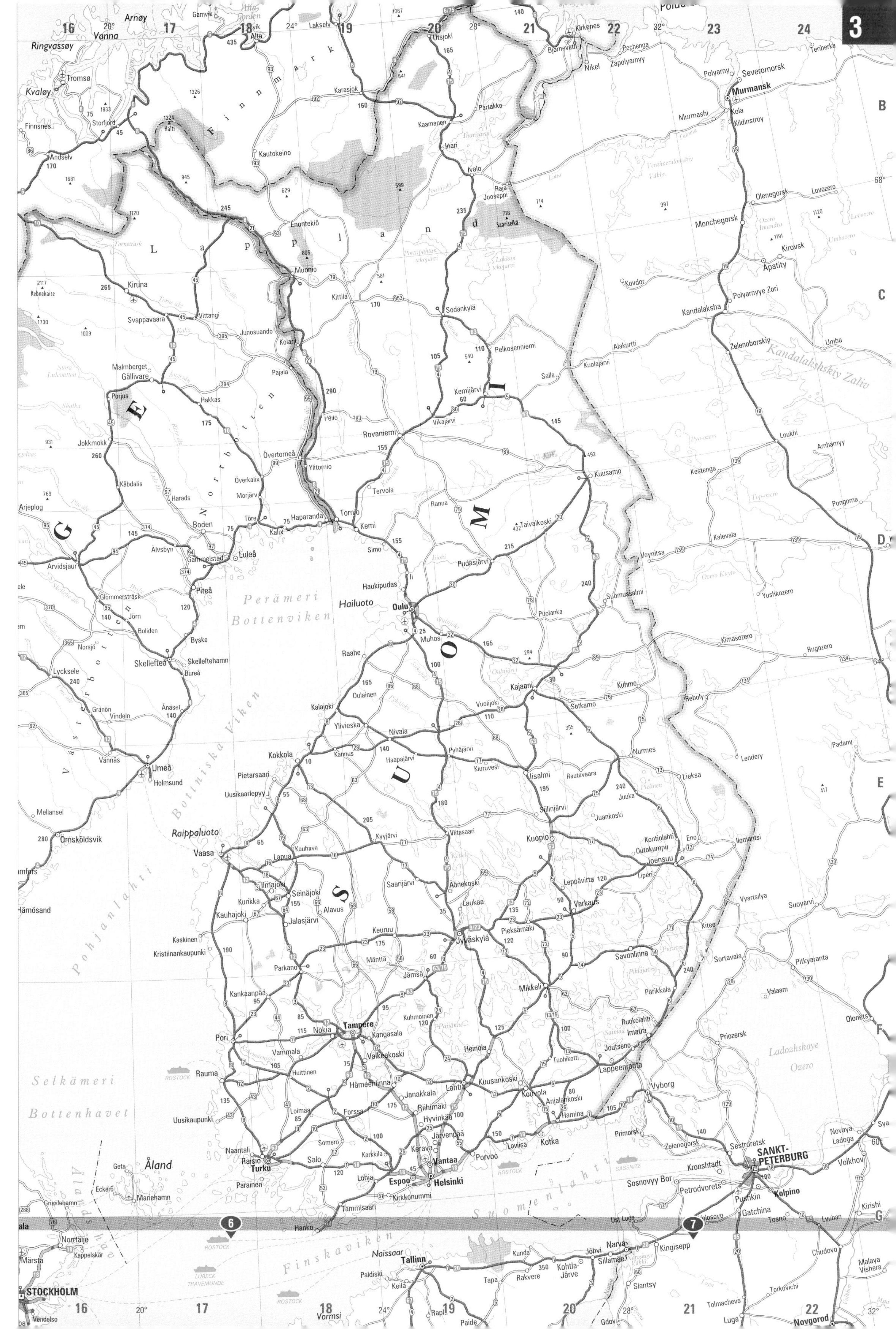

Finnmark
Lappland
Norrbotten
Västerbotten
SUOMI
Perämeri
Bottenviken
Bottniska Viken
Pohjanlahti
Selkämeri
Bottenhavet
Åland
Ålands hav
Suomenlahti
Finskaviken
Kandalakshskiy Zaliv
Ladozhskoye Ozero
Hailuoto
Raippaluoto
Ringvassøy
Kvaløy
Vanna
Arnøy
Tromsø
Alta
Lakselv
Karasjok
Kautokeino
Utsjoki
Kirkenes
Bjørnevatn
Nikel
Pechenga
Zapolyarnyy
Polyarny
Severomorsk
Murmansk
Kola
Kildinstroy
Murmashi
Teriberka
Olenegorsk
Lovozero
Monchegorsk
Kirovsk
Apatity
Kovdor
Polyarnyye Zori
Kandalaksha
Zelenoborskiy
Umba
Alakurtti
Kuolajärvi
Salla
Loukhi
Ambarnyy
Kestenga
Pongoma
Kalevala
Voynitsa
Yushkozero
Kimasozero
Rugozero
Reboly
Padany
Lendery
Inari
Ivalo
Kaamanen
Partakko
Raja Jooseppi
Saariselkä
Enontekiö
Muonio
Kittilä
Sodankylä
Pelkosenniemi
Kemijärvi
Vikajärvi
Rovaniemi
Pello
Kolari
Pajala
Övertorneå
Ylitornio
Tervola
Ranua
Kuusamo
Taivalkoski
Pudasjärvi
Tornio
Haparanda
Kemi
Simo
Ii
Haukipudas
Oulu
Muhos
Raahe
Puolanka
Suomussalmi
Kajaani
Kuhmo
Sotkamo
Vuolijoki
Oulainen
Kalajoki
Ylivieska
Nivala
Haapajärvi
Pyhäjärvi
Kiuruvesi
Iisalmi
Rautavaara
Nurmes
Lieksa
Juuka
Siilinjärvi
Juankoski
Kuopio
Kontiolahti
Outokumpu
Eno
Joensuu
Ilomantsi
Liperi
Kokkola
Kannus
Pietarsaari
Uusikaarlepyy
Vaasa
Kauhava
Lapua
Seinäjoki
Ilmajoki
Kurikka
Alavus
Kauhajoki
Jalasjärvi
Kaskinen
Kristiinankaupunki
Kyyjärvi
Viitasaari
Saarijärvi
Äänekoski
Laukaa
Keuruu
Jyväskylä
Pieksämäki
Varkaus
Leppävirta
Savonlinna
Kitee
Parkano
Mänttä
Jämsä
Mikkeli
Parikkala
Kankaanpää
Pori
Nokia
Tampere
Kangasala
Kuhmoinen
Vammala
Valkeakoski
Heinola
Rauma
Huittinen
Hämeenlinna
Lahti
Kuusankoski
Kouvola
Anjalankoski
Hamina
Imatra
Ruokolahti
Joutseno
Lappeenranta
Tuohikotti
Uusikaupunki
Loimaa
Forssa
Riihimäki
Hyvinkää
Järvenpää
Kerava
Janakkala
Naantali
Raisio
Turku
Somero
Salo
Karkkila
Lohja
Vantaa
Espoo
Helsinki
Porvoo
Loviisa
Kotka
Parainen
Kirkkonummi
Tammisaari
Hanko
Geta
Eckerö
Mariehamn
Kiruna
Kebnekaise
Svappavaara
Vittangi
Junosuando
Malmberget
Gällivare
Porjus
Hakkas
Jokkmokk
Kåbdalis
Harads
Överkalix
Morjärv
Töre
Kalix
Boden
Luleå
Gammelstad
Älvsbyn
Arvidsjaur
Arjeplog
Piteå
Glommersträsk
Jörn
Boliden
Byske
Norsjö
Skellefteå
Skelleftehamn
Bureå
Lycksele
Granön
Vindeln
Ånäset
Vännäs
Umeå
Holmsund
Mellansel
Örnsköldsvik
Härnösand
Finnsnes
Storfjord
Andselv
Halti
Vyborg
Primorsk
Zelenogorsk
Sestroretsk
Kronshtadt
SANKT-PETERBURG
Sosnovyy Bor
Petrodvorets
Pushkin
Kolpino
Gatchina
Tosno
Lyuban
Kirishi
Volkhov
Novaya Ladoga
Priozersk
Sortavala
Pitkyaranta
Valaam
Olonets
Vyartsilya
Suoyarvi
Kingisepp
Narva
Sillamäe
Jõhvi
Kohtla-Järve
Kunda
Rakvere
Tapa
Tallinn
Naissaar
Paldiski
Keila
Vormsi
Slantsy
Chudovo
Malaya Vishera
Novgorod
Tolmachevo
Luga
Ust Luga
Volosovo
Norrtälje
Kappelskär
Märsta
STOCKHOLM
Grisslehamn
ROSTOCK
LÜBECK TRAVEMÜNDE
SASSNITZ

1
2
3
4
5
6
7
G
H
J
K
L
58°
54°
50°
8°
4°
0°
Shetland Is.
Yell
Unst
Fetlar
Mainland
Foula
Lerwick
Sumburgh Hd.
Fair Isle
Orkney Is.
Westray
Sanday
Stronsay
Mainland
Stromness
Hoy
Kirkwall
South Ronaldsay
Pentland Firth
Thurso
John o' Groats
Wick
Helmsdale
Outer Hebrides
Eilean Leodais
Stornoway
St. Kilda
Na Hearadh
Tairbeart
Uibhist a Tuath
Loch nam Madadh
Beinn na Faoghla
Loch Baghasdail
Uibhist a Deas
Bagh a Chaisteil
Eilean Bharraigh
Inner Hebrides
Skye
Rum
Eigg
Coll
Tobermory
Tiree
Mull
Oban
Colonsay
Jura
Islay
Port Askaig
Port Ellen
Arran
Brodick
Campbeltown
Rubha Robhanais
C. Wrath
Lochinver
Ullapool
Tongue
Lairg
Golspie
Tain
Invergordon
Dingwall
Inverness
Nairn
Elgin
Buckie
Banff
Fraserburgh
Rattray Hd.
Peterhead
Huntly
Inverurie
Aberdeen
Stonehaven
Ballater
Braemar
Ben Macdhui
Aviemore
Newtonmore
Fort Augustus
Portree
Kyle of Lochalsh
Armadale
Mallaig
Fort William
Ben Nevis
Ballachulish
Pitlochry
Aberfeldy
Blairgowrie
Forfar
Brechin
Montrose
Arbroath
Dundee
Perth
St. Andrews
Glenrothes
Kirkcaldy
Dunfermline
Stirling
Edinburgh
North Berwick
Dunbar
Firth of Forth
Moray Firth
North West Highlands
North Minch
Grampian Mts.
SCOTLAND
Lochgilphead
Tarbert
Greenock
Dumbarton
Dunoon
Rothesay
Paisley
Glasgow
East Kilbride
Hamilton
Ardrossan
Irvine
Kilmarnock
Ayr
Cumnock
Girvan
Peebles
Galashiels
Berwick-upon-Tweed
Coldstream
Hawick
Jedburgh
Moffat
Southern Uplands
Dumfries
Lockerbie
Newton Stewart
Cairnryan
Stranraer
Kirkcudbright
Gretna Green
Annan
Carlisle
Mull of Kintyre
Mull of Galloway
North Channel
Firth of Clyde
Solway Firth
Malin Hd.
Aran I.
Buncrana
Letterkenny
Londonderry
Strabane
Lifford
Coleraine
Ballycastle
Ballymena
Larne
Antrim
Omagh
Donegal
NORTHERN IRELAND
Bangor
Newtownards
Belfast
Lisburn
Dungannon
Portadown
Lurgan
Armagh
Downpatrick
Newry
Newcastle
Enniskillen
Bundoran
Sligo
Ballina
Achill I.
Castlebar
Westport
Claremorris
Leitrim
Clones
Castleblaney
Cavan
Longford
Roscommon
Tuam
Athlone
Ballinasloe
Mullingar
Ceanannus Mor
An Uaimh
Ardee
Dunleer
Drogheda
Dublin
Dun Laoghaire
Bray
Naas
Wicklow
Arklow
Gorey
Enniscorthy
Wexford
Rosslare
Waterford
Kilkenny
Carlow
Athy
Kildare
Port Laoise
Tullamore
Birr
Portumna
Loughrea
Galway
Galway Bay
Aran Is.
Ennis
Kilkee
Kilrush
Shannon
Limerick
Nenagh
Thurles
Tipperary
Cahir
Carrick-on-Suir
Clonmel
Bunclody
Listowel
Tralee
Dingle
Killarney
Mallow
Mitchelstown
Fermoy
Newcastle West
Cahersiveen
Macroom
Cork
Cobh
Dungarvan
Youghal
Bandon
Kinsale
Bantry
C. Clear
REP OF IRELAND
UNITED KINGDOM
I. of Man
Ramsey
Douglas
Castletown
Irish Sea
Workington
Whitehaven
Scafell Pike
Kendal
Penrith
Barrow-in-Furness
Morecambe
Lancaster
Blackpool
Preston
Southport
Blackburn
Burnley
Bolton
Bury
Liverpool
Birkenhead
Manchester
Oldham
Stockport
Warrington
Wigan
Chester
Crewe
Macclesfield
Buxton
Stoke on Trent
Newcastle-under-Lyme
Stafford
Shrewsbury
Telford
Lichfield
Walsall
Wolverhampton
BIRMINGHAM
Coventry
Nuneaton
Leicester
Rugby
Warwick
Redditch
Stratford-upon-Avon
Worcester
Hereford
Leominster
Ludlow
Welshpool
Oswestry
Llangollen
Wrexham
Denbigh
Rhyl
Llandudno
Conwy
Bangor
Anglesey
Holyhead
Caernarfon
Porthmadog
Pwllheli
Harlech
Dolgellau
Snowdon
Cambrian Mts.
WALES
Machynlleth
Aberdyfi
Aberystwyth
Aberaeron
Cardigan Bay
Cardigan
Fishguard
Haverfordwest
Milford Haven
Pembroke
Tenby
Carmarthen
Llandovery
Llandrindod Wells
Builth Wells
Rhayader
Brecon
Abergavenny
Llanelli
Swansea
Neath
Merthyr Tydfil
Port Talbot
Bridgend
Cardiff
Barry
Newport
Cwmbran
Monmouth
Gloucester
Cheltenham
Cirencester
Bristol
Bath
Frome
Weston-super-Mare
Bristol Channel
St. George's Channel
Ilfracombe
Barnstaple
Minehead
Bideford
Bridgwater
Taunton
Glastonbury
Shepton Mallet
Bude
Okehampton
Exeter
Launceston
Newton Abbot
Torquay
Torbay
Plymouth
Dartmouth
Start Pt.
Bodmin
Newquay
St. Austell
Truro
Redruth
Penzance
Falmouth
Land's End
Lizard Pt.
Isles of Scilly
Sidmouth
Exmouth
Bridport
Dorchester
Weymouth
Portland Bill
Poole
Bournemouth
Swanage
Salisbury
Yeovil
Shaftesbury
Southampton
Winchester
Newport
Isle of Wight
Portsmouth
Gosport
Havant
Worthing
Brighton
Newhaven
Eastbourne
Hastings
Bexhill
Horsham
Crawley
Reigate
Guildford
Dorking
Woking
Basingstoke
Andover
Newbury
Reading
Slough
Swindon
Abingdon
Oxford
Witney
High Wycombe
Aylesbury
Watford
St. Albans
Luton
Stevenage
Harlow
Chelmsford
Basildon
Southend-on-Sea
LONDON
Chatham
Gillingham
Maidstone
Tonbridge
Royal Tunbridge Wells
Ashford
Canterbury
Margate
Ramsgate
North Foreland
Dover
Folkestone
English Channel
La Manche
Milton Keynes
Bedford
Northampton
Kettering
Corby
Peterborough
Cambridge
Sudbury
Colchester
Clacton-on-Sea
Harwich
Felixstowe
Ipswich
Bury St. Edmunds
Thetford
Ely
Wisbech
King's Lynn
Hunstanton
Wells-next-the-Sea
Cromer
Norwich
Great Yarmouth
Lowestoft
Saxmundham
The Wash
Boston
Skegness
Grantham
Loughborough
Nottingham
Derby
Ashbourne
Newark-on-Trent
Lincoln
Mansfield
Chesterfield
Sheffield
Rotherham
Gainsborough
Doncaster
Barnsley
Huddersfield
Halifax
Bradford
Leeds
Keighley
Skipton
Ilkley
Harrogate
Ripon
York
Selby
Goole
Scunthorpe
Grimsby
Louth
Mablethorpe
Kingston upon Hull
Beverley
Driffield
Spurn Hd.
Flamborough Hd.
Scarborough
Thirsk
Middlesbrough
Stockton-on-Tees
Darlington
Bishop Auckland
Durham
Hartlepool
Redcar
Sunderland
Gateshead
South Shields
Newcastle-upon-Tyne
Hexham
Ashington
Alnwick
Pennines
ENGLAND
North Sea
CELTIC SEA
Boulogne-sur-Mer
Calais
Dunkerque
Le Touquet-Paris-Plage
Berck
Abbeville
Le Tréport
Dieppe
St.-Valery-en-Caux
Fécamp
Neufchâtel-en-Bray
Blangy-sur-Bresle
Montreuil
Hesdin
Auderville
C. de la Hague
Alderney
Pte. de Barfleur
Tunnel
TORSHAVN SEYDISFJÖRDUR
BERGEN
ZEEBRUGGE
STAVANGER HAUGESUND BERGEN
KRISTIANSAND GÖTEBORG
AMSTERDAM
CHERBOURG
CHERBOURG ROSCOFF
ROSCOFF
SANTANDER ST. MALO ROSCOFF
ST. MALO GUERNSEY
CHANNEL ISLANDS ST. MALO CHERBOURG
BILBAO ST. MALO CHERBOURG LE HAVRE CAEN CHANNEL ISLANDS
8

NORGE
SVERIGE
DANMARK
DEUTSCHLAND
NEDERLAND
BELGIQUE
Nordsjøen
Vesterhavet
Nordsee
Noordzee
Skagerrak
Kattegat
Østersøen
Oslofjorden
Telemark
Nordfriesische Inseln
Ost-friesische Inseln
Westfriesche Eilanden
Bornholm (Danmark)
Oslo
Bergen
Stavanger
Kristiansand
Drammen
Göteborg
Malmö
Helsingborg
Jönköping
Borås
Karlstad
Örebro
Linköping
KØBENHAVN
Århus
Ålborg
Odense
Esbjerg
Kiel
HAMBURG
Bremen
Lübeck
Rostock
Schwerin
Hannover
Braunschweig
Magdeburg
BERLIN
Potsdam
Halle
Leipzig
Dresden
Chemnitz
Kassel
Göttingen
Erfurt
Osnabrück
Münster
Bielefeld
Dortmund
Essen
Duisburg
Düsseldorf
Köln
Bonn
Koblenz
Frankfurt
Wiesbaden
Mainz
Darmstadt
Würzburg
Nürnberg
Erlangen
Plzeň
AMSTERDAM
ROTTERDAM
's-Gravenhage
Utrecht
Eindhoven
Antwerpen
BRUXELLES
Gent
Brugge
Liège
Lille
LUX.

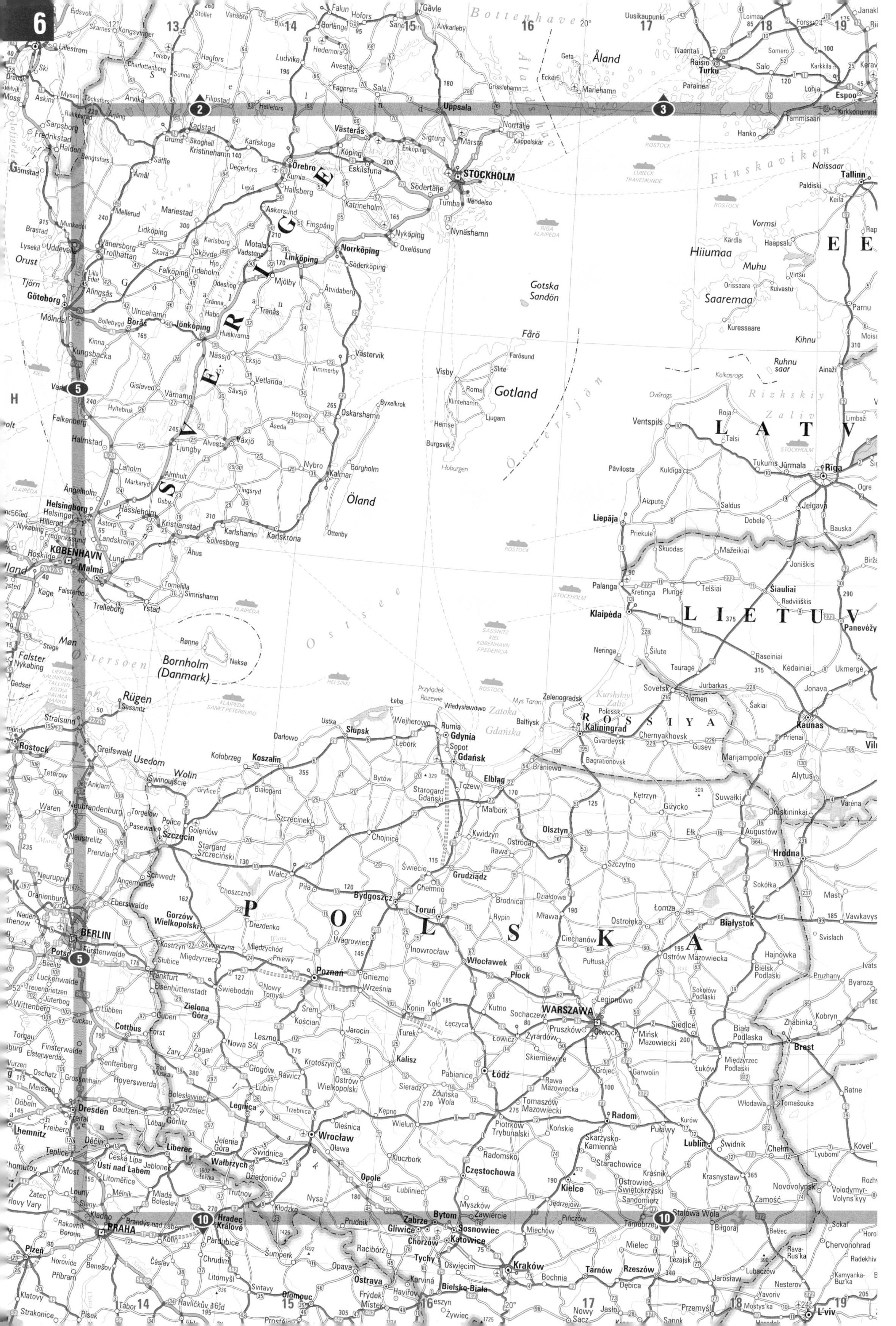
SVERIGE
POLSKA
LATV
LIETUV
ROSSIYA
EE
Bottenhave
Ålands hav
Finskaviken
Östersjön
Østersøen
Ostsee
Rizhskiy Zaliv
Zatoka Gdańska
Åland
Mariehamn
Turku
Espoo
Tallinn
Hiiumaa
Saaremaa
Gotland
Visby
Gotska Sandön
Fårö
Öland
Bornholm (Danmark)
Rønne
Rügen
STOCKHOLM
Uppsala
Västerås
Örebro
Norrköping
Linköping
Jönköping
Göteborg
Borås
Helsingborg
Malmö
KØBENHAVN
Karlskrona
Kalmar
Växjö
Halmstad
Kristianstad
Ventspils
Liepāja
Riga
Jelgava
Šiauliai
Klaipėda
Panevėžys
Kaunas
Sovetsk
Kaliningrad
Gdańsk
Gdynia
Elbląg
Słupsk
Koszalin
Szczecin
Stralsund
Rostock
Olsztyn
Białystok
Hrodna
Bydgoszcz
Toruń
Poznań
WARSZAWA
Łódź
Radom
Lublin
Brest
Wrocław
Opole
Katowice
Kraków
Częstochowa
Kielce
Rzeszów
Tarnów
BERLIN
Frankfurt
Cottbus
Dresden
Chemnitz
PRAHA
Plzeň
Hradec Králové
Ostrava
Olomouc
L'viv
Kovel'
2
3
5
10
13
14
15
16
17
18
19

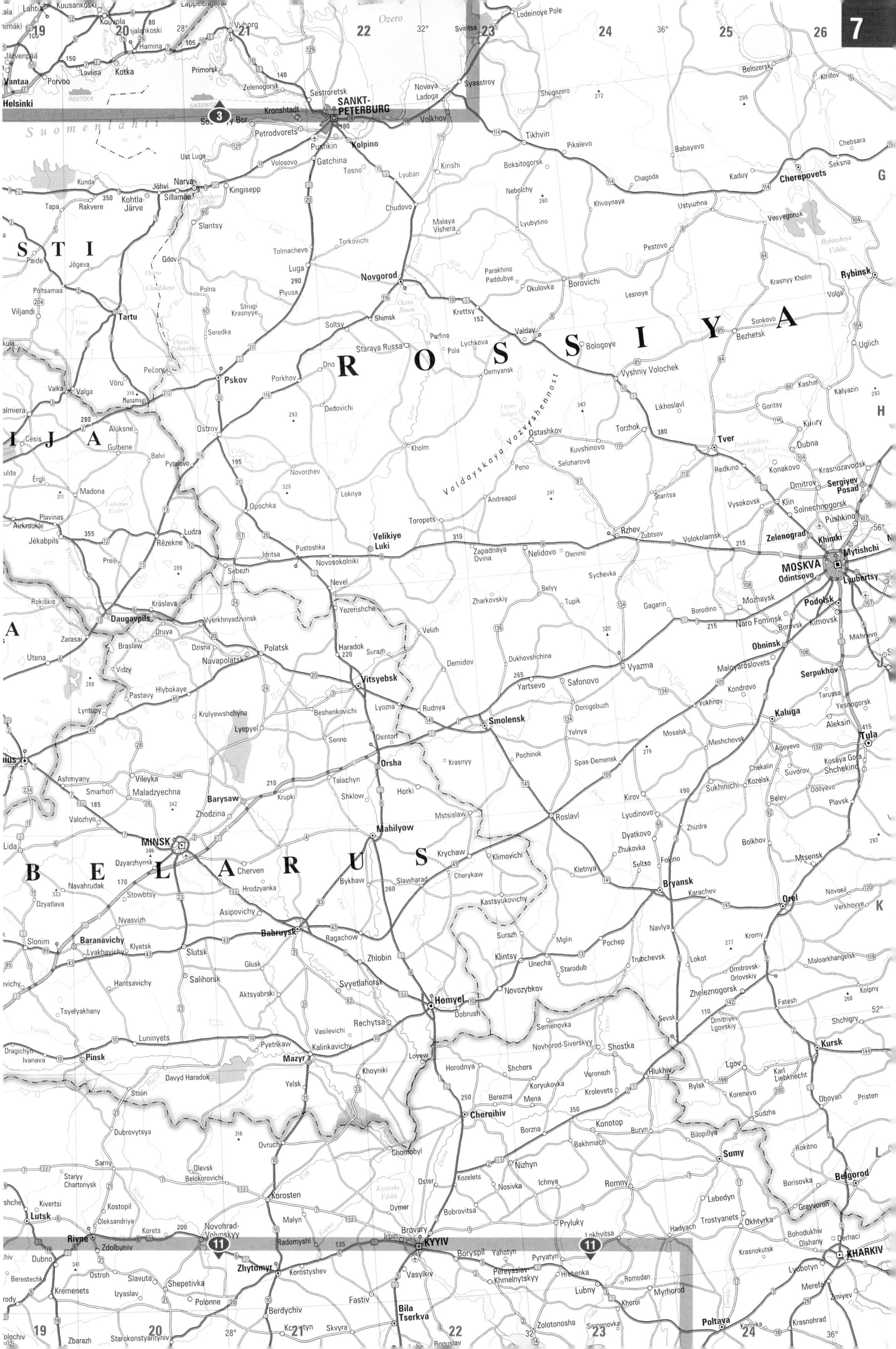
ROSSIYA
BELARUS
Helsinki
Vantaa
Porvoo
Loviisa
Kotka
Hamina
Vyborg
Primorsk
Zelenogorsk
Sestroretsk
SANKT-PETERBURG
Kronshtadt
Petrodvorets
Pushkin
Kolpino
Gatchina
Tosno
Lyuban
Kirishi
Volkhov
Novaya Ladoga
Syasstroy
Lodeinoye Pole
Sviritsa
Tikhvin
Pikalevo
Boksitogorsk
Shugozero
Belozersk
Kirillov
Babayevo
Chebsara
Cherepovets
Kaduy
Chagoda
Sheksna
Suomenlahti
Ust Luga
Kunda
Narva
Jõhvi
Sillamäe
Kingisepp
Volosovo
Kohtla-Järve
Rakvere
Tapa
Paide
Jõgeva
Põltsamaa
Viljandi
Tartu
Slantsy
Gdov
Polna
Strugi Krasnyye
Seredka
Luga
Plyusa
Tolmachevo
Torkovichi
Chudovo
Malaya Vishera
Novgorod
Shimsk
Soltsy
Staraya Russa
Parfino
Pola
Lychkova
Demyansk
Krettsy
Valday
Okulovka
Borovichi
Parakhino Paddubye
Lyubytino
Nebolchy
Khvoynaya
Ustyuzhna
Pestovo
Lesnoye
Vesyegonsk
Krasnyy Kholm
Rybinsk
Volga
Sonkovo
Bezhetsk
Uglich
Bologoye
Vyshniy Volochek
Likhoslavl
Torzhok
Tver
Kashin
Kalyazin
Goritsy
Kimry
Dubna
Konakovo
Redkino
Ostashkov
Kuvshinovo
Selizharovo
Peno
Andreapol
Valdayskaya Vozvyshennost
Staritsa
Rzhev
Zubtsov
Volokolamsk
Klin
Solnechnogorsk
Dmitrov
Sergiyev Posad
Krasnozavodsk
Pushkino
Zelenograd
Khimki
Mytishchi
MOSKVA
Odintsovo
Lyubertsy
Podolsk
Vysokovsk
Pskov
Pechory
Võru
Valga
Valka
Porkhov
Dno
Dedovichi
Kholm
Ostrov
Pytalovo
Novorzhev
Opochka
Loknya
Toropets
Velikiye Luki
Nelidovo
Olenino
Zapadnaya Dvina
Sychevka
Belyy
Tupik
Zharkovskiy
Gagarin
Borodino
Mozhaysk
Naro Fominsk
Borovsk
Klimovsk
Obninsk
Maloyaroslavets
Serpukhov
Tarussa
Yasnogorsk
Kaluga
Aleksin
Tula
Alūksne
Gulbene
Balvi
Cēsis
Ērgli
Madona
Pļaviņas
Aizkraukle
Jēkabpils
Rēzekne
Ludza
Preiļi
Sebezh
Idritsa
Pustoshka
Novosokolniki
Nevel
Yezerishche
Velizh
Krāslava
Daugavpils
Rokiškis
Zarasai
Utena
Druya
Braslaw
Dzisna
Verkhnyadzvinsk
Polatsk
Navapolatsk
Vidzy
Pastavy
Hlybokaye
Haradok
Surazh
Vitsyebsk
Demidov
Dukhovshchina
Vyazma
Yartsevo
Safonovo
Dorogobuzh
Yukhnov
Kondrovo
Rudnya
Lyozna
Beshenkovichi
Senno
Osintorf
Orsha
Smolensk
Yelnya
Pochinok
Spas-Demensk
Krasnyy
Mosalsk
Meshchovsk
Sukhinichi
Kozelsk
Chekalin
Suvorov
Ageyevo
Kosaya Gora
Shchekino
Odoyevo
Belev
Plavsk
Kirov
Lyudinovo
Zhizdra
Dyatkovo
Zhukovka
Seltso
Fokino
Bolkhov
Mtsensk
Roslavl
Krulyewshchyna
Lyepyel
Lyntupy
Vilnius
Ashmyany
Smarhon
Vileyka
Maladzyechna
Barysaw
Zhodzina
Krupki
Talachyn
Shklow
Horki
Mstsislaw
Krychaw
Klimovichi
Cherykaw
Kastsyukovichy
Mahilyow
Valozhyn
MINSK
Lida
Dzyarzhynsk
Cherven
Navahrudak
Stowbtsy
Hrodzyanka
Dzyatlava
Asipovichy
Bykhaw
Slawharad
Nyasvizh
Slonim
Baranavichy
Lyakhavichy
Klyetsk
Slutsk
Babruysk
Ragachow
Zhlobin
Glusk
Salihorsk
Hantsavichy
Aktsyabrski
Svyetlahorsk
Homyel
Dobrush
Surazh
Klintsy
Unecha
Starodub
Mglin
Pochep
Novozybkov
Bryansk
Karachev
Navlya
Trubchevsk
Lokot
Dmitrovsk-Orlovskiy
Kromy
Orel
Novosil
Verkhovye
Maloarkhangelsk
Zheleznogorsk
Fatesh
Kolpny
Dmitriyev Lgovskiy
Shchigry
Kursk
Sevsk
Tsyelyakhany
Luninyets
Pinsk
Dragichyn
Ivanava
Pyetrikaw
Kalinkavichy
Mazyr
Vasilevichi
Rechytsa
Khoyniki
Loyew
Yelsk
Davyd Haradok
Stolin
Dubrovytsya
Ovruch
Chornobyl
Horodnya
Shchors
Semenovka
Novhorod-Siverskyy
Shostka
Voronezh
Koryukovka
Krolevets
Hlukhiv
Rylsk
Lgov
Karl Liebknecht
Korenevo
Oboyan
Pristen
Sudzha
Chernihiv
Berezna
Mena
Konotop
Buryn
Borzna
Bakhmach
Bilopillya
Sumy
Rokitno
Belgorod
Borisovka
Grayvoron
Nizhyn
Kozelets
Oster
Nosivka
Ichnya
Romny
Lebedyn
Trostyanets
Okhtyrka
Bohodukhiv
Olshany
Derhachi
KHARKIV
Lyubotyn
Merefa
Zmiyev
Krasnohrad
Krasnokutsk
Sarny
Olevsk
Belokorovichi
Staryy Chartoriysk
Kivertsi
Lutsk
Kostopil
Oleksandriya
Rivne
Zdolbuniv
Korets
Novohrad-Volynskyy
Korosten
Malyn
Radomyshl
Dymer
Bobrovitsa
Pryluky
Lokhvitsa
Hadyach
Brovary
Irpin
KYYIV
Boryspil
Yahotyn
Pyryatyn
Pereyaslav-Khmelnytskyy
Hrebenka
Romodan
Lubny
Myrhorod
Khorol
Dubno
Ostroh
Berestechko
Kremenets
Slavuta
Shepetivka
Izyaslav
Polonne
Zhytomyr
Korostyshev
Vasylkiv
Fastiv
Bila Tserkva
Berdychiv
Koростyn
Skvyra
Zolotonosha
Poltava
Zbarazh
Starokonstyantyniv
Boguslav
Zhytomyr

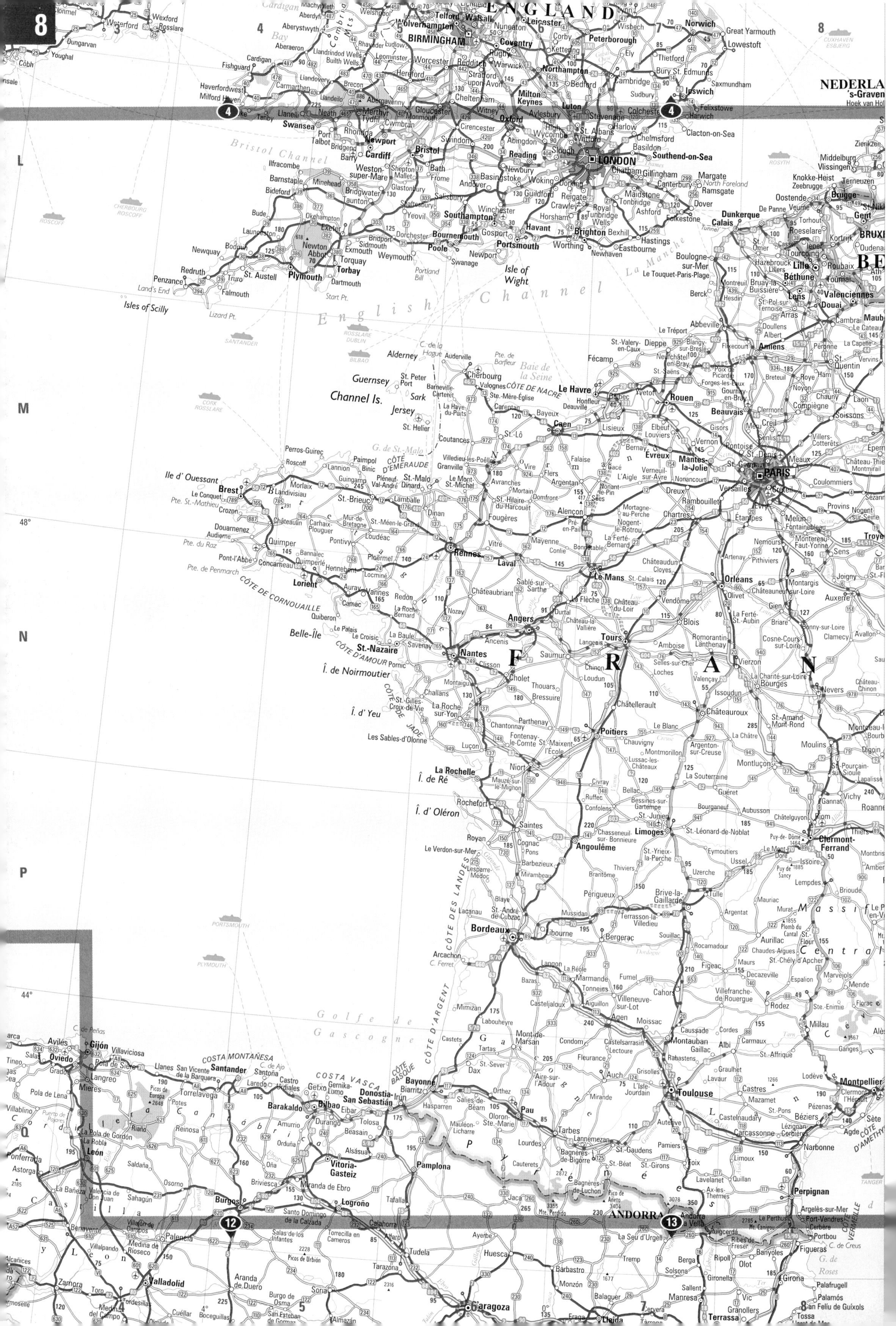
ENGLAND
BIRMINGHAM
LONDON
Bristol Channel
English Channel
La Manche
Channel Is.
Alderney
Guernsey
Jersey
Sark
Isle of Wight
Isles of Scilly
FRANCE
PARIS
Le Havre
Rouen
Caen
Cherbourg
Brest
Rennes
Nantes
Le Mans
Tours
Orléans
Angers
Poitiers
Limoges
Bordeaux
Toulouse
Montpellier
Perpignan
Clermont-Ferrand
Lille
Calais
Dunkerque
Amiens
Golfe de Gascogne
Massif Central
Pyrénées
ANDORRA
Bilbao
Santander
San Sebastián
Pamplona
Burgos
Valladolid
Zaragoza
Lleida
Oviedo
Gijón
León
NEDERLAND
BELGIQUE
Ipswich
Norwich
Plymouth
Cardiff
Southampton
Oxford
Côte de Cornouaille
Côte d'Émeraude
Côte d'Amour
Côte de Jade
Côte d'Argent
Côte Basque
Costa Vasca
Costa Montañesa
Côte Vermeille
Côte d'Améthyste
Belle-Île
Î. de Noirmoutier
Î. d'Yeu
Î. de Ré
Î. d'Oléron
Ile d'Ouessant

DEUTSCHLAND
ÖSTERREICH
SCHWEIZ
ITALIA
ČESKÁ REP.
SLOVENIJA
BELGIQUE
LUX.
LIECHTENSTEIN
MONACO
SAN MARINO
CITTÀ DEL VATICANO
MARE LIGURE
Golfo di Génova
Golfo di Venézia
Corse
AMSTERDAM
BERLIN
PRAHA
MÜNCHEN
Innsbruck
Zürich
Bern
Genève
MILANO
TORINO
Génova
LYON
MARSEILLE
ROMA
Firenze
Venézia
Ljubljana
Frankfurt
Köln
Stuttgart
Nürnberg
Dresden
Leipzig
Hannover
Salzburg
Bologna
Trieste
Nice
Basel
Strasbourg
9
10
11
12
13
14

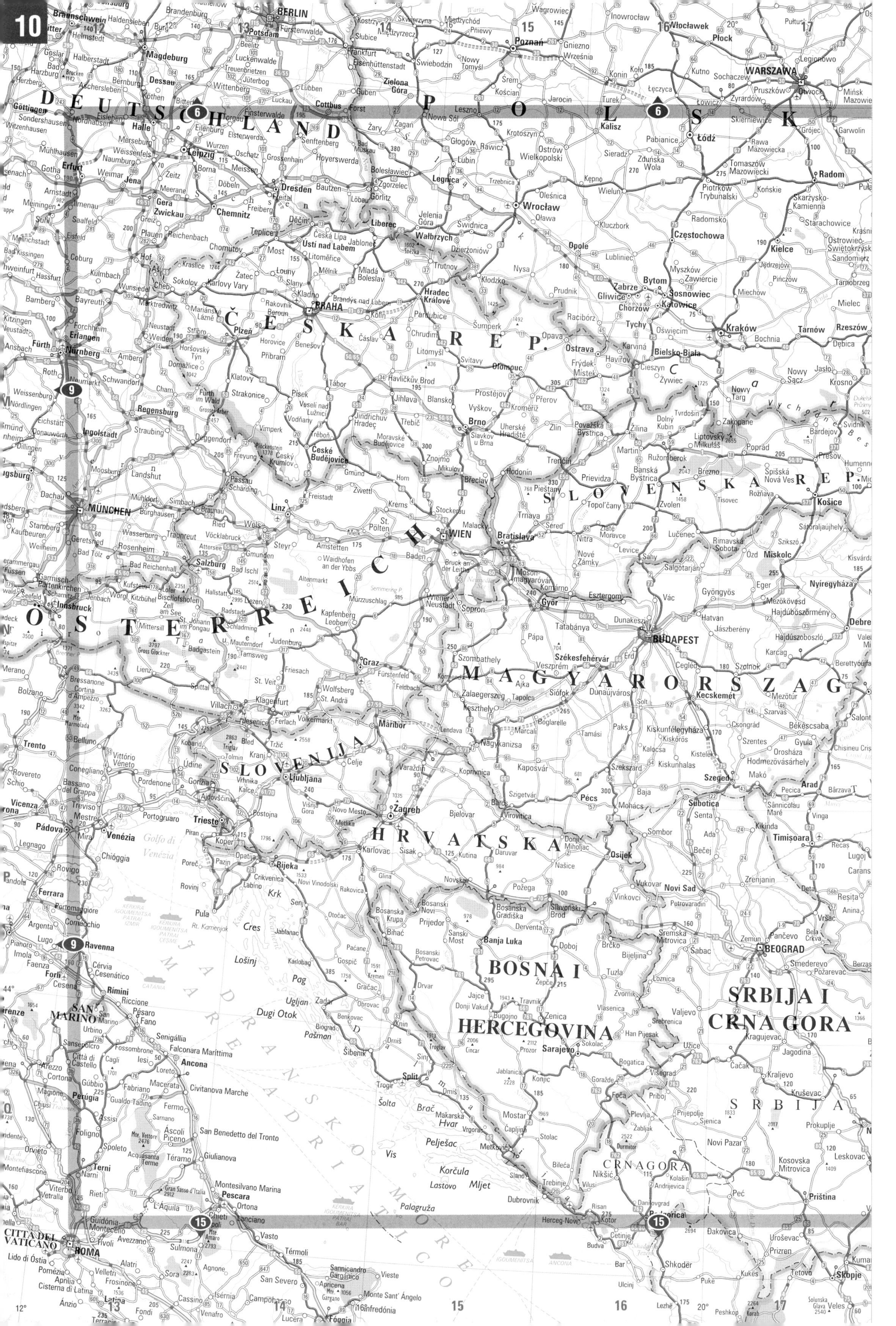
DEUTSCHLAND
POLSKA
ČESKÁ REP.
SLOVENSKÁ REP.
ÖSTERREICH
MAGYARORSZÁG
SLOVENIJA
HRVATSKA
BOSNA I HERCEGOVINA
SRBIJA I CRNA GORA
SRBIJA
CRNA GORA
SAN MARINO
CITTÀ DEL VATICANO
JADRANSKO MORE
12
13
14
15
16
17
20°
12°
6
9
15
BERLIN
Potsdam
Braunschweig
Magdeburg
Halle
Leipzig
Dresden
Chemnitz
Zwickau
Erfurt
Jena
Gera
Göttingen
Cottbus
Frankfurt
Bamberg
Bayreuth
Nürnberg
Fürth
Erlangen
Regensburg
Ingolstadt
MÜNCHEN
Augsburg
Passau
Landshut
Rosenheim
Garmisch-Partenkirchen
Poznań
Wrocław
Legnica
Wałbrzych
Opole
Kalisz
Łódź
WARSZAWA
Radom
Kielce
Częstochowa
Katowice
Gliwice
Zabrze
Bytom
Sosnowiec
Kraków
Tarnów
Rzeszów
Bielsko-Biała
Płock
Włocławek
Konin
Zielona Góra
Liberec
Ústí nad Labem
PRAHA
Plzeň
Hradec Králové
Pardubice
Jihlava
Brno
Olomouc
Ostrava
České Budějovice
Zlín
Bratislava
Žilina
Banská Bystrica
Košice
Prešov
Poprad
Nitra
Trenčín
Trnava
WIEN
Linz
Salzburg
Innsbruck
Graz
Klagenfurt
Villach
St. Pölten
BUDAPEST
Győr
Miskolc
Debrecen
Nyíregyháza
Szeged
Pécs
Kecskemét
Székesfehérvár
Szombathely
Veszprém
Eger
Ljubljana
Maribor
Celje
Koper
Zagreb
Rijeka
Osijek
Split
Dubrovnik
Zadar
Šibenik
Karlovac
Sarajevo
Banja Luka
Mostar
Tuzla
Zenica
BEOGRAD
Novi Sad
Subotica
Niš
Kragujevac
Podgorica
Priština
Skopje
Timişoara
Arad
Venézia
Trieste
Pádova
Vicenza
Treviso
Trento
Bolzano
Ferrara
Ravenna
Rímini
Ancona
Perúgia
Pescara
ROMA
Foggia
Latina
Kerkira Igoumenitsa Patrai

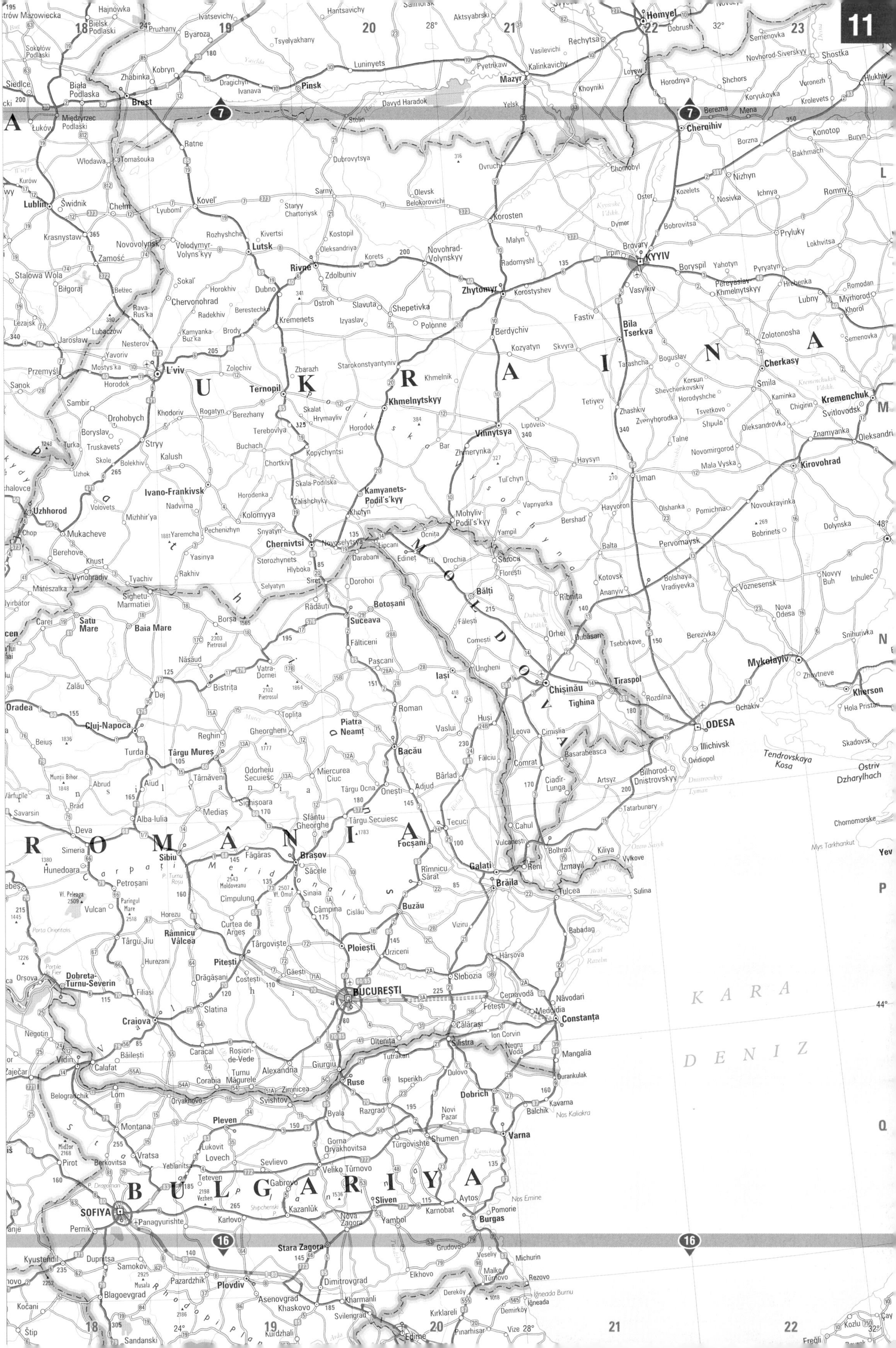
UKRAINA
MOLDOVA
ROMÂNIA
BULGARIYA
KARA DENIZ
Homyel
Mazyr
Pinsk
Brest
Biała Podlaska
Lublin
Chełm
Kovel'
Lutsk
Rivne
Korosten
Zhytomyr
KYYIV
Chernihiv
Brovary
Boryspil
Bila Tserkva
Cherkasy
Kremenchuk
Kirovohrad
Uman
Vinnytsya
Khmelnytskyy
Ternopil
L'viv
Ivano-Frankivsk
Uzhhorod
Mukacheve
Chernivtsi
Kamyanets-Podil's'kyy
Mohyliv-Podil's'kyy
Bălţi
Chişinău
Tighina
Tiraspol
ODESA
Mykolayiv
Kherson
Illichivsk
Bilhorod-Dnistrovskyy
Izmayil
Reni
Galaţi
Brăila
Tulcea
Sulina
Suceava
Botoşani
Iaşi
Bacău
Piatra Neamţ
Vaslui
Focşani
Buzău
Braşov
Sibiu
Cluj-Napoca
Oradea
Satu Mare
Baia Mare
Târgu Mureş
Deva
Hunedoara
Râmnicu Vâlcea
Piteşti
Ploieşti
BUCUREŞTI
Constanţa
Craiova
Dobreta-Turnu-Severin
Vidin
Ruse
Pleven
Dobrich
Varna
Shumen
Veliko Tŭrnovo
Burgas
Sliven
Stara Zagora
Plovdiv
SOFIYA
Pernik
Blagoevgrad
Kŭrdzhali
Edirne
Kırklareli

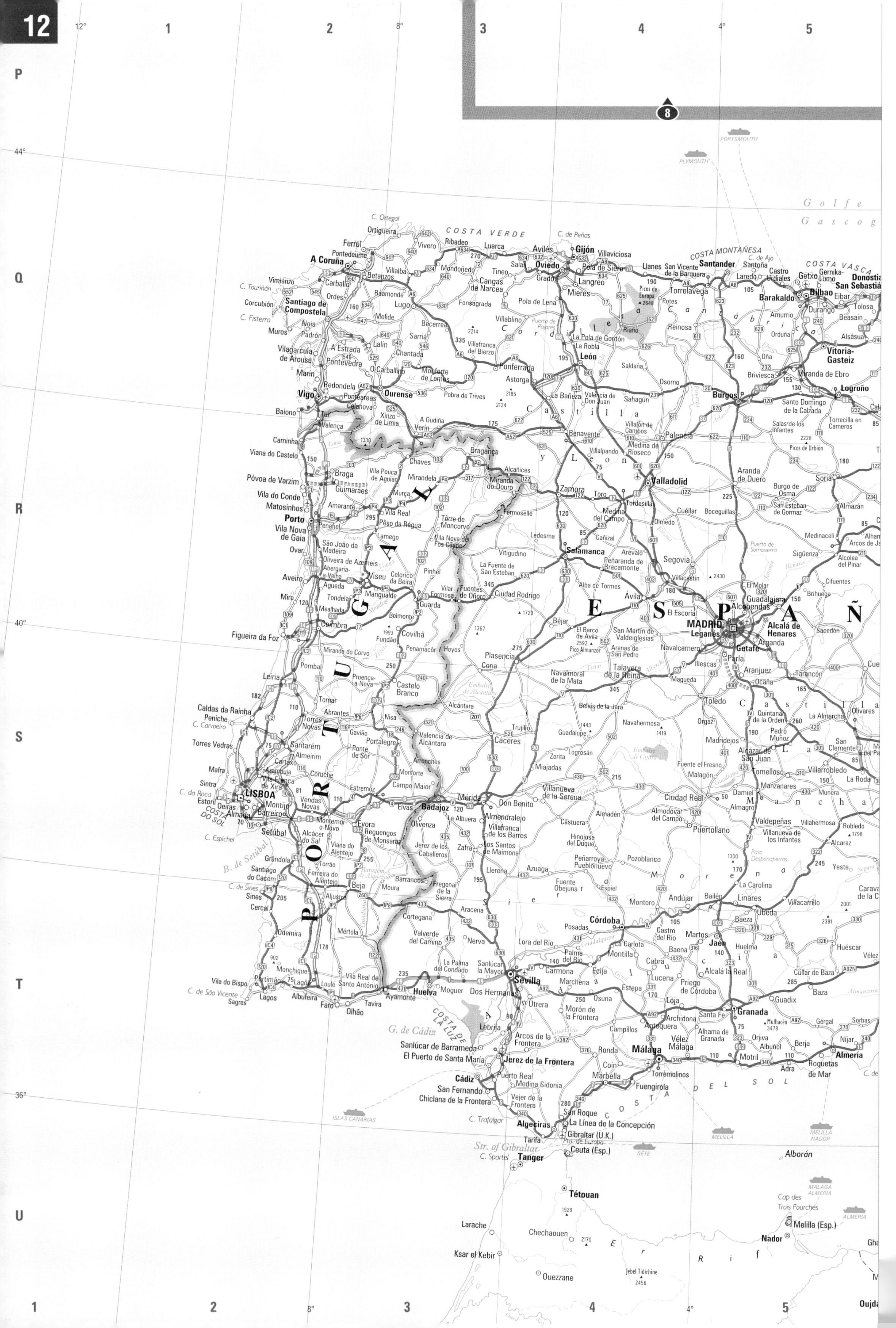

1
2
3
4
5
P
Q
R
S
T
U
44°
40°
36°
12°
8°
4°
8
PORTSMOUTH
PLYMOUTH
Golfe
Gascog
COSTA VERDE
COSTA MONTAÑESA
COSTA VASCA
C. Ortegal
Ortigueira
Ferrol
Pontedeume
A Coruña
Vivero
Ribadeo
Luarca
Avilés
Gijón
Villaviciosa
C. de Peñas
Oviedo
Pola de Siero
Llanes
San Vicente de la Barquera
Santander
C. de Ajo
Santoña
Castro Urdiales
Laredo
Getxo
Gernika-Lumo
Donostia
San Sebastián
Bilbao
Barakaldo
Eibar
Durango
Tolosa
Beasain
Alsasua
Vitoria-Gasteiz
Vimianzo
C. Touriñán
Carballo
Betanzos
Villalba
Mondoñedo
Tineo
Salas
Grado
Cangas de Narcea
Langreo
Mieres
Picos de Europa
2648
Torrelavega
Potes
Corcubión
Santiago de Compostela
Ordes
Baamonde
Lugo
Fonsagrada
Pola de Lena
C. Fisterra
Muros
Noia
Padrón
Melide
Becerrea
Villablino
Puerto de Pajares
Riaño
Reinosa
Amurrio
Orduña
Sarria
2214
Villafranca del Bierzo
La Pola de Gordón
La Robla
Vilagarcía de Arousa
A Estrada
Lalín
Chantada
Ponferrada
León
Oña
Marín
Pontevedra
O Carballiño
Monforte de Lemos
Astorga
Saldaña
Briviesca
Miranda de Ebro
Logroño
Redondela
Vigo
Ponteareas
Ourense
Pobra de Trives
2185
2124
La Bañeza
Valencia de Don Juan
Sahagún
Osorno
Burgos
Santo Domingo de la Calzada
Baiona
Tui
Celanova
Xinzo de Limia
A Gudiña
Verín
Valença
Benavente
Villalón de Campos
Palencia
Salas de los Infantes
Torrecilla en Cameros
Caminha
Viana do Castelo
Chaves
Bragança
Picos de Urbión
Villalpando
Medina de Rioseco
Póvoa de Varzim
Braga
Vila Pouca de Aguiar
Mirandela
Alcañices
Miranda do Douro
Valladolid
Aranda de Duero
Soria
Vila do Conde
Guimarães
Murça
Zamora
Toro
Tordesillas
Burgo de Osma
Matosinhos
Amarante
Vila Real
San Esteban de Gormaz
Almazán
Porto
Penafiel
Pêso da Régua
Torre de Moncorvo
Fermoselle
Medina del Campo
Cuéllar
Boceguillas
Vila Nova de Gaia
Lamego
Olmedo
Ovar
São João da Madeira
Vila Nova de Fos Côa
Ledesma
Cañizal
Medinaceli
Salamanca
Arévalo
Puerto de Somosierra
Sigüenza
Oliveira de Azeméis
Vitigudino
Peñaranda de Bracamonte
Segovia
Alcolea del Pinar
Aveiro
Águeda
Viseu
Celorico da Beira
Pinhel
La Fuente de San Esteban
Villacastín
2430
Cifuentes
Mira
Tondela
Mangualde
Vilar Formoso
Fuentes de Oñoro
Ciudad Rodrigo
Alba de Tormes
Ávila
El Molar
Guadalajara
Brihuega
Mealhada
Guarda
1723
El Escorial
Alcobendas
Coimbra
Belmonte
Béjar
MADRID
Leganés
Alcalá de Henares
Figueira da Foz
1993
Fundão
Covilhã
1367
El Barco de Ávila
2592
Pico Almanzor
San Martín de Valdeiglesias
Arenas de San Pedro
Navalcarnero
Getafe
Arganda
Sacedón
Miranda do Corvo
Penamacor
Hoyos
Plasencia
Parla
Illescas
Pombal
Coria
Talavera de la Reina
Aranjuez
Tarancón
Leiria
Proença-a-Nova
Castelo Branco
Navalmoral de la Mata
Maqueda
Ocaña
Embalse de Alcántara
Toledo
Caldas da Rainha
Peniche
C. Carvoeiro
Tomar
Abrantes
Alcántara
Belvís de la Jara
Quintanar de la Orden
Olivares
La Almarcha
Torres Novas
Nisa
Gavião
Trujillo
Navahermosa
1443
1419
Orgaz
Pedro Muñoz
Torres Vedras
Santarém
Almeirim
Portalegre
Ponte de Sor
Valencia de Alcántara
Cáceres
Guadalupe
Madridejos
San Clemente
Cartaxo
Arronches
Logrosán
Zorita
Alcázar de San Juan
Mafra
Azambuja
Vila Franca de Xira
Coruche
Monforte
Miajadas
Fuente el Fresno
Malagón
Tomelloso
Villarrobledo
Sintra
LISBOA
Estremoz
Campo Maior
Villanueva de la Serena
La Roda
C. da Roca
Estoril
Oeiras
Almada
Montijo
Barreiro
Vendas Novas
Elvas
Badajoz
Mérida
Don Benito
Ciudad Real
Daimiel
Manzanares
Munera
COSTA DO SOL
Montemor-o-Novo
Évora
Almendralejo
Almagro
Setúbal
C. Espichel
Alcácer do Sal
Reguengos de Monsaraz
Olivenza
La Albuera
Villafranca de los Barros
Castuera
Almadén
Almodóvar del Campo
Puertollano
Valdepeñas
Villahermosa
Robledo
Villanueva de los Infantes
Viana do Alentejo
Jerez de los Caballeros
Zafra
Los Santos de Maimona
Hinojosa del Duque
Alcaraz
B. de Setúbal
Grândola
Torrão
Barrancos
Llerena
Azuaga
Peñarroya-Pueblonuevo
Pozoblanco
Paso Despeñaperros
Yeste
Santiago do Cacém
Ferreira do Alentejo
Moura
Fregenal de la Sierra
Fuente Obejuna
Espiel
C. de Sines
Sines
Beja
La Carolina
Cercal
Aljustrel
Aracena
Montoro
Andújar
Bailén
Linares
Villacarrillo
Cortegana
Córdoba
Úbeda
Baeza
Odemira
Mértola
Valverde del Camino
Nerva
Lora del Río
Posadas
Palma del Río
La Carlota
Castro del Río
Martos
Jaén
Huéscar
Monchique
La Palma del Condado
Sanlúcar la Mayor
Carmona
Écija
Montilla
Cabra
Baena
Huelma
Alcalá la Real
Cúllar de Baza
Vila do Bispo
Portimão
Lagoa
Loulé
Vila Real de Santo António
Huelva
Moguer
Sevilla
Marchena
Lucena
Priego de Córdoba
Baza
C. de São Vicente
Sagres
Lagos
Albufeira
Faro
Olhão
Tavira
Ayamonte
Dos Hermanas
Utrera
Osuna
Estepa
Loja
Granada
Guadix
Morón de la Frontera
Archidona
Antequera
Santa Fe
Alhama de Granada
Mulhacén
3478
Gérgal
Sorbas
G. de Cádiz
COSTA DE LA LUZ
Lebrija
Arcos de la Frontera
Campillos
Vélez Málaga
Órgiva
Albuñol
Berja
Níjar
Sanlúcar de Barrameda
El Puerto de Santa María
Jerez de la Frontera
Ronda
Málaga
Motril
Almería
Adra
Roquetas de Mar
Cádiz
Puerto Real
Medina Sidonia
Coín
Marbella
Fuengirola
Torremolinos
COSTA DEL SOL
San Fernando
Chiclana de la Frontera
Vejer de la Frontera
San Roque
La Línea de la Concepción
ISLAS CANARIAS
C. Trafalgar
Algeciras
Gibraltar (U.K.)
Tarifa
Pta. de Europa
MELILLA
MELILLA NADOR
Str. of Gibraltar
C. Spartel
Tanger
Ceuta (Esp.)
SÈTE
Alborán
Tétouan
MALAGA ALMERIA
Cap des Trois Fourches
1928
ALMERIA
Larache
Chechaouen
2170
Melilla (Esp.)
Nador
Ksar el Kebir
Rif
Jebel Tidirhine
2456
Ouezzane
Oujda
PORTUGAL
ESPAÑA
Castilla y León
Cordillera Cantábrica
Castilla La Mancha
Sierra Morena

Royan
Cognac
Angoulême
Eymoutiers
Ussel
Issoire
Ambert
St.-Chamond
Vienne
Voiron
St.-Jean-de-Maurienne
St.-Michel-de-Maurienne
Chivasso
Le Verdon-sur-Mer
Pons
Barbezieux
Thiviers
St.-Yrieix-la-Perche
Uzerche
Lempdes
Firminy
St.-Étienne
Grenoble
Modane
Rivoli
TORINO
Lesparre-Médoc
Mirambeau
Brantôme
Périgueux
Brive-la-Gaillarde
Tulle
Mauriac
Murat
Brioude
Le Puy-en-Velay
Annonay
Yssingeaux
Romans-sur-Isère
Vizille
La Mure
Corps
Briançon
Pinerolo
Asti
Savigliano
Bra
Alba
Blaye
St.-André-de-Cubzac
Lacanau
Mussidan
Terrasson-la-Villedieu
Argentat
Plomb du Cantal
St.-Flour
Mt. Mézenc
St.-Agrève
Tournon-sur-Rhône
Valence
Monestier-de-Clermont
St.-Bonnet
Saluzzo
Mte. Viso
Fossano
Ceva
Voltri
Varazze
Savona
Bordeaux
Libourne
Bergerac
Souillac
Rocamadour
Aurillac
Chaudes-Aigues
St.-Chély-d'Apcher
Vals-les-Bains
Privas
Livron-sur-Drôme
Crest
Die
Gap
Embrun
Cuneo
Mondovì
Limone Piemonte
Arcachon
C. Ferret
Langon
La Réole
Marmande
Bazas
Figeac
Decazeville
Espalion
Marvejols
Mende
Aubenas
Montélimar
Serres
Veynes
Barcelonette
Col di Tenda
Fumel
Cahors
Tonneins
Villeneuve-sur-Lot
Villefranche-de-Rouergue
Rodez
Ste.-Enimie
Florac
Pierrelatte
Bollène
Orange
Pont-St.-Esprit
Mt. Ventoux
Sisteron
Château-Arnoux
Digne-les-Bains
Isola
Casteljaloux
Aiguillon
Agen
Moissac
Millau
Alès
Carpentras
Sospel
Impéria
San Remo
Mimizan
Labouheyre
Caussade
Cordes
Carmaux
Villeneuve-lès-Avignon
Avignon
Remoulins
Cavaillon
Manosque
Castellane
MONACO
Menton
Monte-Carlo
Cagnes-sur-Mer
Nice
Antibes
Cannes
Mont-de-Marsan
Condom
Castelsarrasin
Montauban
Gaillac
Albi
St.-Affrique
Ganges
Nîmes
Tarascon
Pertuis
Grasse
Castets
Tartas
Lectoure
Rabastens
Graulhet
Lodève
Montpellier
Lunel
Arles
Salon-de-Provence
Aix-en-Provence
Draguignan
Vidauban
St.-Raphaël
Ste.-Maxime
Côte d'Azur
St.-Sever
Dax
Fleurance
Grisolles
Lavaur
Castres
Clermont-l'Hérault
Aigues-Mortes
Martigues
Brignoles
Le Luc
Bayonne
Biarritz
Irún
Aire-sur-l'Adour
Auch
L'Isle-Jourdain
Toulouse
Mazamet
Pézenas
Béziers
Sète
Stes.-Maries-de-la-Mer
MARSEILLE
Aubagne
St.-Tropez
Hasparren
Orthez
Salies-de-Béarn
Pau
Mirande
Castelnaudary
St.-Pons
Lézignan-Corbières
Agde
La Ciotat
Toulon
Hyères
Cavalaire-sur-Mer
Côte de l'Esterel
Mauléon-Licharre
Oloron-Ste.-Marie
Tarbes
Lannemezan
Autérive
Carcassonne
Narbonne
La Seyne-sur-Mer
Côte des Calanques
Îles d'Hyères
Lourdes
Bagnères-de-Bigorre
St.-Gaudens
Pamiers
Limoux
Golfe du Lion
Pamplona
Cauterets
St.-Béat
St.-Girons
Foix
Lavelanet
Quillan
Perpignan
Bagnères-de-Luchon
Pico de Aneto
Ax-les-Thermes
Argelès-sur-Mer
Port-Vendres
Cerbère
Portbou
Côte Vermeille
Tafalla
Jaca
Mte. Perdido
ANDORRA
Andorra La Vella
Puigcerdà
Mt. Canigou
Le Perthus
Ribes de Freser
Figueras
C. de Creus
La Seu d'Urgell
Ayerbe
Tremp
Berga
Ripoll
Olot
Banyoles
G. de Roses
Tudela
Huesca
Barbastro
Solsona
Gironella
Girona
Palafrugell
Palamós
Sant Feliu de Guíxols
Costa Brava
Monzón
Sallent
Manresa
Vic
Granollers
Tossa
Lloret de Mar
Blanes
Zaragoza
Balaguer
Cervera
Terrassa
Sabadell
Mataró
Badalona
BARCELONA
Fraga
Lleida
Tàrrega
Igualada
Vilafranca del Penedès
La Almunia de Doña Godina
Cariñena
Montblanc
Valls
Sitges
El Prat de Llobregat
Calatayud
Belchite
Hijar
Caspe
Reus
Falset
Vilanova i la Geltrú
Tarragona
Costa Dorada
Daroca
Calamocha
Alcañiz
Gandesa
G. de Sant Jordi
Montalbán
Tortosa
C. Tortosa
Monreal del Campo
Morella
Vinaròs
Benicarló
Sant Mateu
Albocàcer
Teruel
Alcalá de Xivert
Costa del Azahar
Cañete
Onda
Castelló de la Plana
Vila-real de los Infantes
Is. Columbretes
Chelva
La Vall de Uixó
Liria
Sagunt
Golfo de Valencia
Utiel
Requena
Chiva
Valencia
Torrent
Casas Ibáñez
Algemesí
Sueca
Cullera
Alberic
Alcira
Gandía
Albacete
Chinchilla de Monte Aragón
Xàtiva
Denia
C. de la Nao
Almansa
Alcoy
Villena
Yecla
Tobarra
Hellín
Jumilla
Elda
Altea
Benidorm
Villajoyosa
Elche de la Sierra
Novelda
Alicante
Elche
Cieza
Mula
Orihuela
Torrevieja
Costa Blanca
Alcantarilla
Murcia
San Pedro del Pinatar
San Javier
Mar Menor
Totana
Cartagena
C. de Palos
Rubio
Lorca
La Unión
Águilas
Huércal Overa
Cuevas del Almanzora
Vera
Gata
Islas Baleares
Menorca
Fornells
C. de Formentor
Ciudadela de Menorca
Maó
Sóller
Palma de Mallorca
Calvià
Inca
Manacor
Llucmajor
Mallorca
B. de Palma
Cabrera
Ibiza/Eivissa
Sant Antoni Abat
Eivissa
Formentera
MER MÉDITERRANÉE
MAR MEDITERRANEO
TANGER
PORTO-VECCHIO TUNIS
ALICANTE ORAN
ALGER BEJAIA SKIKDA ANNABA
GENOVA
MARSEILLE
BARCELO
C. Bougaroun
Collo
Jijel
El Milia
Skikda
Azzaba
Bejaia
Bordj el Kiffan
C. Matifou
Bordj Menaiel
Aïn Benian
Koléa
ALGER
Tizi-Ouzou
Dj. Babor
Mila
Constantine
Bou Ismaël
Blida
Boufarik
El Arba
Akbou
El Khroub
C. Ténès
C. Kramis
Bouïra
Sétif
El Eulma
Aïn M'lila
Ech Cheliff
Miliana
Khemis Miliana
Medéa
Berrouaghia
Sour el Ghozlane
Bordj bou Arreridj
Oum-el-Bouaghi
O. Chéliff
Ras el Oued
Mostaganem
Arzew
Oued Rhiou
Ksar el Boukhari
Sidi-Aïssa
M'sila
Batna
C. Falcon
Oran
Relizane
ALGERIE
Tissemsilt
Barika
Aïn Touta
Chott el Hodna
Mohammadia
Sig
Aïn Oussera
Zahrez Chergui
Bou Saâda
Mascara
Tiaret
Beni Saf
Aïn Témouchent
Sidi-bel-Abbès
Sougueur
Ksar Chellala
Hassi Bahbah
Biskra
Frenda
Remchi
Tlemcen
Saïda
Zahrez Rharbi
Djelfa
Tolga
Ouled Djellal
Sidi Khaled
Q
R
S
T
U
44°
40°
36°
0°
4°
6
7
8
9
10

Lyon
St.-Étienne
Grenoble
Chambéry
Valence
Montélimar
Avignon
Marseille
Aix-en-Provence
Toulon
Hyères
Cannes
Nice
Monaco
Menton
San Remo
Torino
Milano
Génova
La Spézia
Livorno
Pisa
Firenze
Bologna
Módena
Parma
Piacenza
Alessándria
Novara
Bérgamo
Bréscia
Verona
Vicenza
Pádova
Venézia
Trento
Trieste
Ljubljana
Rijeka
Ravenna
Rímini
San Marino
Ancona
Perúgia
Siena
Grosseto
Terni
Pescara
Roma
Città del Vaticano
Latina
Napoli
Salerno
Capri
Sorrento
Ventotene
Ísole Ponziane
Bastia
Ajaccio
Corse
Bonifacio
Porto-Vecchio
Maddalena
Ólbia
Sássari
Alghero
Nuoro
Oristano
Cágliari
Sardegna
Elba
Capraia
Pianosa
Montecristo
Giglio
Mare Ligure
Mare Tirreno
Golfo di Génova
Ústica
Ísole Eólie
Palermo
Trápani
Marsala
Agrigento
Caltanissetta
Enna
Gela
Ísole Égadi
Pantelleria
Ísole Pelagie
Lampedusa
Linosa
Lampione
Malta
Valletta
Gozo
Tunis
Bizerte
Sousse
Kairouan
Hammamet
Golfe de Tunis
Golfe de Hammamet
Annaba
Skikda
Constantine
Jijel
Guelma
Souk-Ahras
Tébessa
Batna
Is. de la Galite
9
13
P
Q
R
S
T
U
40°
36°
8°
12°
10
11
12
13
14

HRVATSKA
BOSNA I HERCEGOVINA
SRBIJA I CRNA GORA
SRBIJA
CRNA GORA
ROMANIA
BULGARIYA
MAKEDONIJA
SHQIPËRIA
ELLAS
Zagreb
Osijek
Novi Sad
Timişoara
BEOGRAD
Banja Luka
Sarajevo
Split
Dubrovnik
Podgorica
Niš
Priština
Skopje
SOFIYA
Plovdiv
Craiova
Piteşti
Pleven
Tiranë
Durrës
Bitola
Thessaloniki
Lárisa
Vólos
Pátrai
ATHÍNAI
Pireévs
Kérkira
Bari
Táranto
Brindisi
Lecce
Fóggia
Messina
Réggio di Calábria
Catánia
Siracusa
Peloponnisos
MARE ADRIATICO
MARE IONIO
IÓNIO PÉLAGOS
Iónioi Nísoi
Golfo di Táranto
Kefallinía
Zákinthos
Kíthira
Vorίai Sporádhes
Évvoia
10
11
16
14
15
16
17
18
16°
20°
24°
36°
40°
44°

ROMANIA
BULGARIYA
TÜRKIYE
KARA DENIZ
AIYAÍON PELAGOS
Marmara Denizi
Kikládhes
Dhodhekánisos
BUCUREŞTI
SOFIYA
İSTANBUL
ATHÍNAI
İZMIR
Constanţa
Varna
Burgas
Plovdiv
Thessaloníki
Bursa
Eskişehir
Antalya
Brașov
Ploiești
Pitești
Craiova
Galați
Brăila
Tulcea
Ruse
Pleven
Shumen
Dobrich
Stara Zagora
Edirne
Tekirdağ
Kocaeli (İzmit)
Adapazarı
Balıkesir
Manisa
Kütahya
Denizli
Isparta
Burdur
Aydın
Muğla
Piraiévs
Lárisa
Vólos
Kavála
Alexandroúpolis
Thásos
Samothráki
Gökçeada
Límnos
Lésvos
Khíos
Sámos
Ikaría
Évvoia
Ándros
Tínos
Míkonos
Náxos
Páros
Mílos
Thíra
Kos
Ródhos
Kárpathos
Kíthira
Iráklion
Kriti
Gávdhos
Zonguldak
Afyonkarahisar
Çanakkale
Vidin
Veliko Tŭrnovo
Sliven
11
15
44°
40°
36°
24°
28°
18
19
20
21
22
P
Q
R
S
T
U

1:1000000

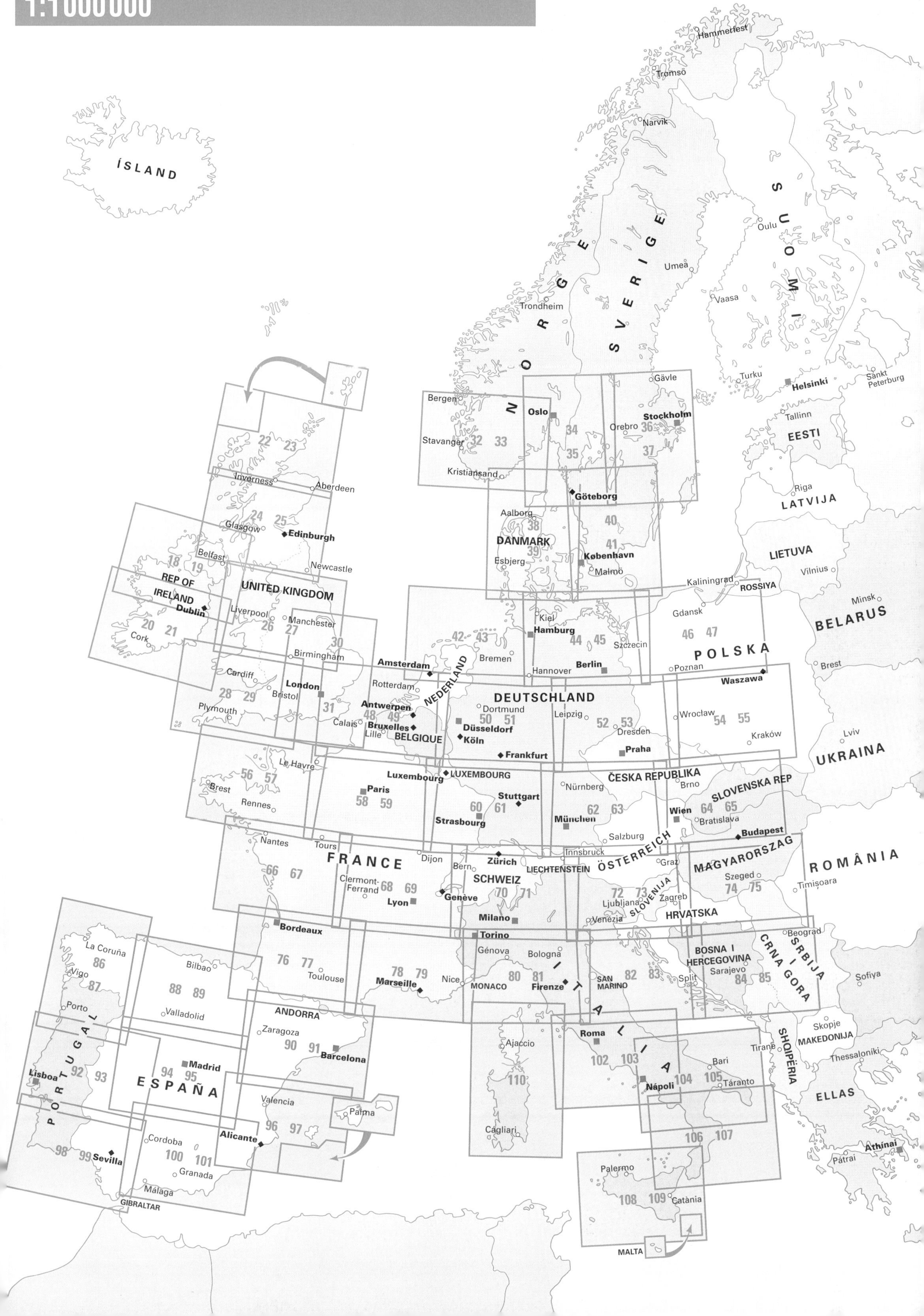

ÍSLAND
Hammerfest
Tromsö
Narvik
NORGE
SVERIGE
SUOMI
Oulu
Umeå
Vaasa
Trondheim
Gävle
Turku
Helsinki
Sankt Peterburg
Bergen
Oslo
Stockholm
Tallinn
EESTI
Stavanger
32 33
34 35
Örebro 36 37
Kristiansand
Göteborg
Riga
LATVIJA
Aalborg 38
DANMARK
39
Esbjerg
40 41
København
Malmö
LIETUVA
Vilnius
22 23
Inverness
Aberdeen
24 25
Glasgow
Edinburgh
Belfast
18 19
Newcastle
REP OF IRELAND
Dublin
UNITED KINGDOM
20 21
Cork
Liverpool
26 27
Manchester
30
Birmingham
Cardiff
28 29
Bristol
Plymouth
London
31
Calais
Kaliningrad
ROSSIYA
Minsk
BELARUS
Gdansk
46 47
POLSKA
Kiel
Hamburg
44 45
Szczecin
42 43
Bremen
Amsterdam
NEDERLAND
Hannover
Berlin
Poznan
Waszawa
Brest
Rotterdam
Antwerpen
48 49
Bruxelles
Lille
BELGIQUE
DEUTSCHLAND
Dortmund
50 51
Düsseldorf
Köln
Frankfurt
Leipzig
52 53
Dresden
Praha
Wrocław
54 55
Kraków
Lviv
UKRAINA
Le Havre
56 57
Brest
Rennes
Luxembourg
LUXEMBOURG
Paris
58 59
60 61
Strasbourg
Stuttgart
Nürnberg
62 63
München
ČESKA REPUBLIKA
Brno
SLOVENSKA REP
Wien
64 65
Bratislava
Budapest
Salzburg
ÖSTERREICH
Innsbruck
Nantes
Tours
FRANCE
Dijon
66 67
Clermont-Ferrand
68 69
Lyon
Bern
Zürich
SCHWEIZ
Genève
70 71
LIECHTENSTEIN
Graz
72 73
Ljubljana
SLOVENIJA
Zagreb
MAGYARORSZAG
Szeged
74 75
ROMÂNIA
Timişoara
HRVATSKA
Milano
Venézia
Torino
Bordeaux
Génova
Bologna
76 77
Toulouse
78 79
Marseille
Nice
MONACO
80 81
Firenze
ITALIA
SAN MARINO
82 83
Split
BOSNA I HERCEGOVINA
Sarajevo
84 85
CRNA GORA
SRBIJA
Beograd
Sofiya
La Coruña
86
Vigo
87
Bilbao
88 89
Valladolid
Porto
PORTUGAL
ANDORRA
Zaragoza
90 91
Barcelona
Ajaccio
Roma
102 103
Nápoli
104 105
Bari
Táranto
Tiranë
SHQIPËRIA
Skopje
MAKEDONIJA
Thessaloníki
Lisboa
92 93
Madrid
94 95
ESPAÑA
Valencia
Palma
96 97
110
ELLAS
Cagliari
106 107
Athínai
Pátrai
Cordoba
100 101
Granada
98 99
Sevilla
Alicante
Málaga
GIBRALTAR
Palermo
108 109
Catània
MALTA

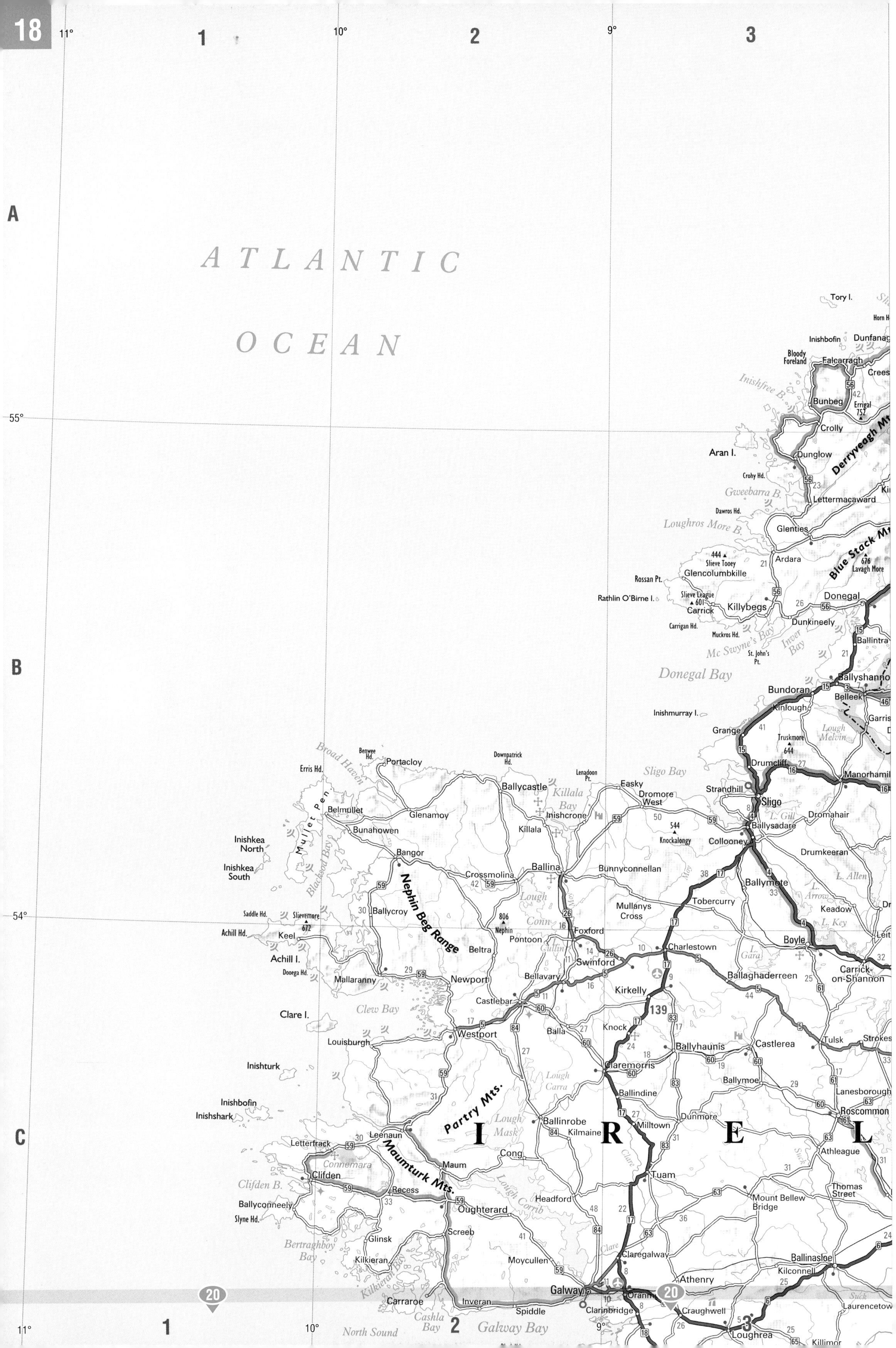

ATLANTIC OCEAN
Tory I.
Horn Hd.
Inishbofin
Dunfanaghy
Bloody Foreland
Falcarragh
Creeslough
Inishfree B.
Bunbeg
Errigal 752
Crolly
Derryveagh Mts.
Aran I.
Dunglow
Crohy Hd.
Gweebarra B.
Lettermacaward
Dawros Hd.
Loughros More B.
Glenties
Ardara
Blue Stack Mts.
444 Slieve Tooey
676 Lavagh More
Glencolumbkille
Rossan Pt.
Rathlin O'Birne I.
Slieve League 601
Carrick
Killybegs
Donegal
Carrigan Hd.
Muckros Hd.
Dunkineely
Mc Swyne's Bay
St. John's Pt.
Inver Bay
Ballintra
Donegal Bay
Ballyshannon
Bundoran
Belleek
Kinlough
Garrison
Inishmurray I.
Grange
Lough Melvin
Truskmore 644
Drumcliff
Manorhamilton
Benwee Hd.
Broad Haven
Portacloy
Erris Hd.
Downpatrick Hd.
Lenadoon Pt.
Sligo Bay
Easky
Dromore West
Strandhill
Sligo
Ballycastle
Killala Bay
Inishcrone
Belmullet
Mullet Pen.
Glenamoy
Killala
Bunahowen
544 Knockalongy
Ballysadare
Collooney
L. Gill
Dromahair
Inishkea North
Inishkea South
Blacksod Bay
Bangor
Nephin Beg Range
Crossmolina
Ballina
Bunnyconnellan
Drumkeeran
Ballymote
L. Allen
L. Arrow
Lough Conn
Mullanys Cross
Tobercurry
Keadow
Saddle Hd.
Slievemore 672
Achill Hd.
Keel
Achill I.
Dooega Hd.
Ballycroy
806 Nephin
Pontoon
Foxford
Charlestown
Boyle
L. Key
Beltra
Lough Cullin
Swinford
L. Gara
Ballaghaderreen
Carrick-on-Shannon
Mallaranny
Newport
Bellavary
Kirkelly
Clare I.
Clew Bay
Castlebar
139
Westport
Balla
Knock
Louisburgh
Ballyhaunis
Castlerea
Tulsk
Strokestown
Inishturk
Claremorris
Ballymoe
Lanesborough
Inishbofin
Inishshark
Partry Mts.
Lough Carra
Ballindine
Roscommon
Lough Mask
Ballinrobe
Kilmaine
Milltown
Dunmore
Leenaun
Maumturk Mts.
IRELAND
Letterfrack
Connemara
Maum
Cong
Athleague
Clifden B.
Clifden
Tuam
Lough Corrib
Recess
Headford
Ballyconneely
Oughterard
Mount Bellew Bridge
Thomas Street
Slyne Hd.
Screeb
Glinsk
Bertraghboy Bay
Kilkieran
Kilkieran Bay
Moycullen
Claregalway
Ballinasloe
Kilconnell
Athenry
Galway
Oranmore
Carraroe
Inveran
Spiddle
Clarinbridge
Craughwell
Laurencetown
Cashla Bay
North Sound
Galway Bay
Loughrea
Killimor
20
1
2
3
A
B
C
11°
10°
9°
55°
54°

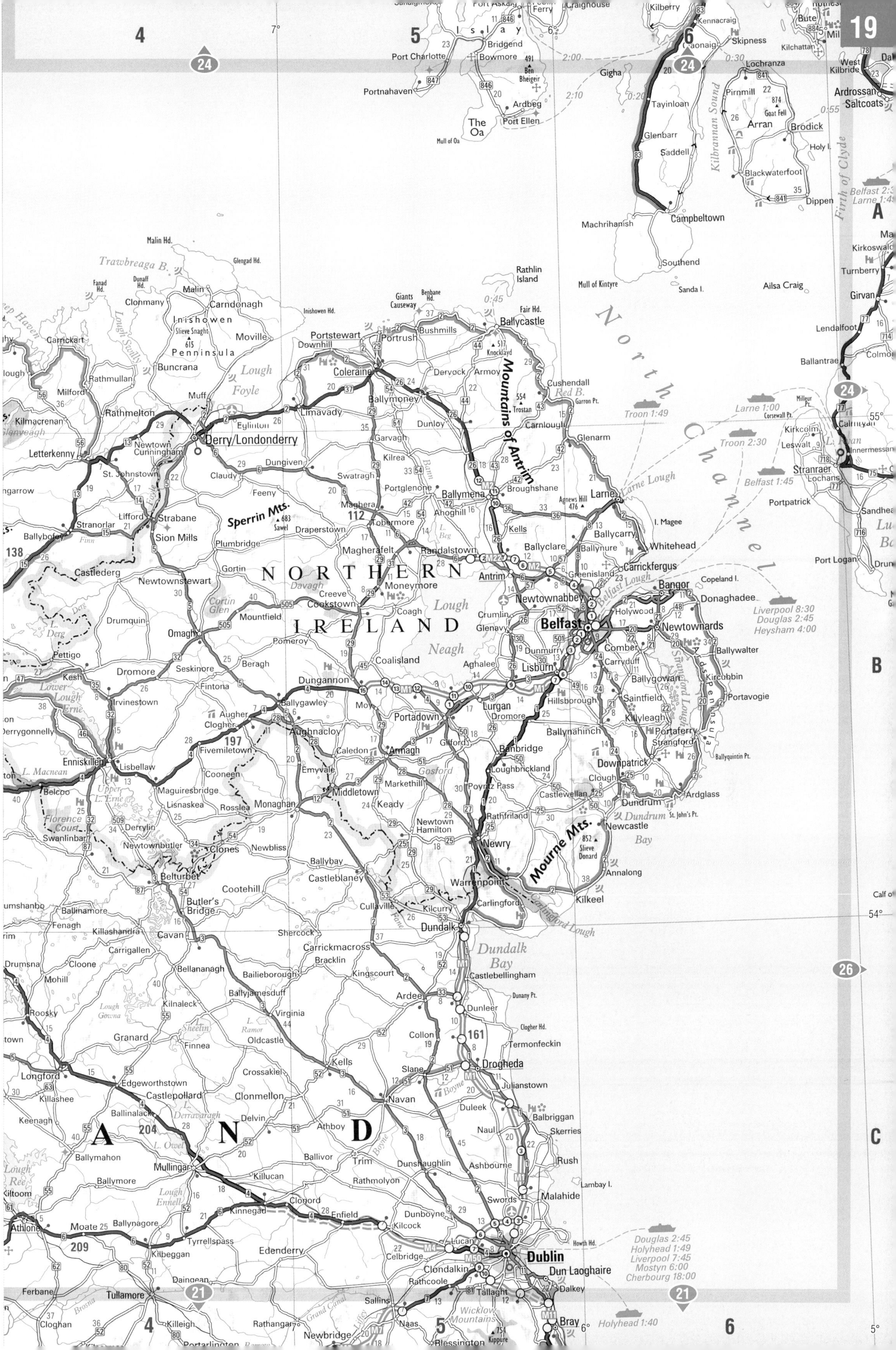

Islay
Port Askaig
Bridgend
Port Charlotte
Bowmore
Portnahaven
Ardbeg
Port Ellen
The Oa
Mull of Oa
Kilberry
Kennacraig
Skipness
Claonaig
Gigha
Tayinloan
Lochranza
Pirnmill
Goat Fell
Arran
Brodick
Kilbrannan Sound
Glenbarr
Saddell
Holy I.
Blackwaterfoot
Dippen
Firth of Clyde
Machrihanish
Campbeltown
Southend
Sanda I.
Mull of Kintyre
Ailsa Craig
Ardrossan
Saltcoats
West Kilbride
Kilchattan
Bute
Kirkoswald
Turnberry
Girvan
Lendalfoot
Ballantrae
Colmonell
Cairnryan
Kirkcolm
Leswalt
L. Ryan
Stranraer
Lochans
Portpatrick
Port Logan
Sandhead
Belfast 2:3
Larne 1:4
Troon 1:49
Larne 1:00
Troon 2:30
Belfast 1:45
Liverpool 8:30
Douglas 2:45
Heysham 4:00
North Channel
Malin Hd.
Glengad Hd.
Trawbreaga B.
Fanad Hd.
Dunaff Hd.
Malin
Carndonagh
Clonmany
Inishowen Peninsula
Slieve Snaght
Moville
Inishowen Hd.
Lough Swilly
Buncrana
Rathmullan
Carrickart
Milford
Lough Foyle
Muff
Rathmelton
Kilmacrenan
Glenveagh
Letterkenny
Newtown Cunningham
Derry/Londonderry
Eglinton
Limavady
St. Johnston
Lifford
Strabane
Sion Mills
Stranorlar
Ballybofey
Finn
Castlederg
Claudy
Dungiven
Feeny
Sperrin Mts.
Sawel
Plumbridge
Gortin
Newtownstewart
Cortin Glen
Drumquin
Omagh
Mountfield
Seskinore
Beragh
Fintona
Dromore
Pettigo
Kesh
Lower Lough Erne
Irvinestown
Lough Derg
Derrygonnelly
Enniskillen
Lisbellaw
L. Macnean
Belcoo
Upper L. Erne
Florence Court
Swanlinbar
Derrylin
Newtownbutler
Lisnaskea
Maguiresbridge
Rosslea
Clones
Belturbet
Cooneen
Fivemiletown
Augher
Clogher
Ballygawley
Aughnacloy
Caledon
Emyvale
Middletown
Monaghan
Keady
Armagh
Markethill
Gosford
Newtown Hamilton
Newbliss
Ballybay
Castleblaney
Cootehill
Butler's Bridge
Cavan
Killashandra
Ballinamore
Fenagh
Carrigallen
Cloone
Drumsna
Mohill
Bellananagh
Bailieborough
Kingscourt
Shercock
Carrickmacross
Bracklin
Cullaville
Kilcurry
Dundalk
Dundalk Bay
Castlebellingham
Dunany Pt.
Ardee
Dunleer
Collon
Clogher Hd.
Termonfeckin
Drogheda
Slane
Julianstown
Boyne
Navan
Duleek
Balbriggan
Skerries
Naul
Rush
Lambay I.
Malahide
Swords
Ashbourne
Dunshaughlin
Dunboyne
Kilcock
Enfield
Clonard
Kinnegad
Trim
Rathmolyon
Ballivor
Athboy
Delvin
Kells
Virginia
Ballyjamesduff
Kilnaleck
Oldcastle
Crossakiel
Clonmellon
Finnea
Granard
Lough Sheelin
Lough Gowna
L. Ramor
Roosky
Longford
Killashee
Edgeworthstown
Castlepollard
L. Derravaragh
Ballinalack
Keenagh
Ballymahon
L. Owel
Mullingar
Killucan
Lough Ennell
Ballymore
Lough Ree
Athlone
Moate
Ballynagore
Kilbeggan
Tyrrellspass
Edenderry
Daingean
Tullamore
Ferbane
Clogham
Killeigh
Rathangan
Portarlington
Newbridge
Naas
Sallins
Grand Canal
Celbridge
Lucan
Clondalkin
Rathcoole
Tallaght
Dublin
Dun Laoghaire
Dalkey
Howth Hd.
Bray
Blessington
Wicklow Mountains
Kippure
Douglas 2:45
Holyhead 1:49
Liverpool 7:45
Mostyn 6:00
Cherbourg 18:00
Holyhead 1:40
Portstewart
Downhill
Portrush
Giants Causeway
Benbane Hd.
Bushmills
Ballycastle
Fair Hd.
Rathlin Island
Knocklayd
Coleraine
Dervock
Armoy
Mountains of Antrim
Ballymoney
Cushendall
Red B.
Garron Pt.
Trostan
Carnlough
Glenarm
Dunloy
Garvagh
Kilrea
Swatragh
Portglenone
Bann
Ballymena
Broughshane
Ahoghill
Larne
Larne Lough
Agnews Hill
I. Magee
Maghera
Tobermore
Draperstown
Kells
Ballycarry
Whitehead
Magherafelt
Randalstown
Ballyclare
Ballynure
Carrickfergus
Antrim
Greenisland
Belfast Lough
Newtownabbey
Bangor
Copeland I.
Donaghadee
Moneymore
Creeve
Cookstown
Coagh
NORTHERN IRELAND
Lough Neagh
Crumlin
Glenavy
Belfast
Holywood
Newtownards
Dunmurry
Comber
Ballywalter
Pomeroy
Coalisland
Aghalee
Lisburn
Carryduff
Strangford Lough
Ards Peninsula
Kircubbin
Dungannon
Moy
Lurgan
Hillsborough
Ballygowan
Saintfield
Portavogie
Portadown
Dromore
Killyleagh
Portaferry
Strangford
Ballyquintin Pt.
Gilford
Ballynahinch
Banbridge
Loughbrickland
Downpatrick
Clough
Poyntz Pass
Castlewellan
Ardglass
Dundrum
Dundrum Bay
St. John's Pt.
Rathfriland
Newcastle
Mourne Mts.
Slieve Donard
Newry
Annalong
Warrenpoint
Kilkeel
Carlingford
Carlingford Lough
Calf of Man

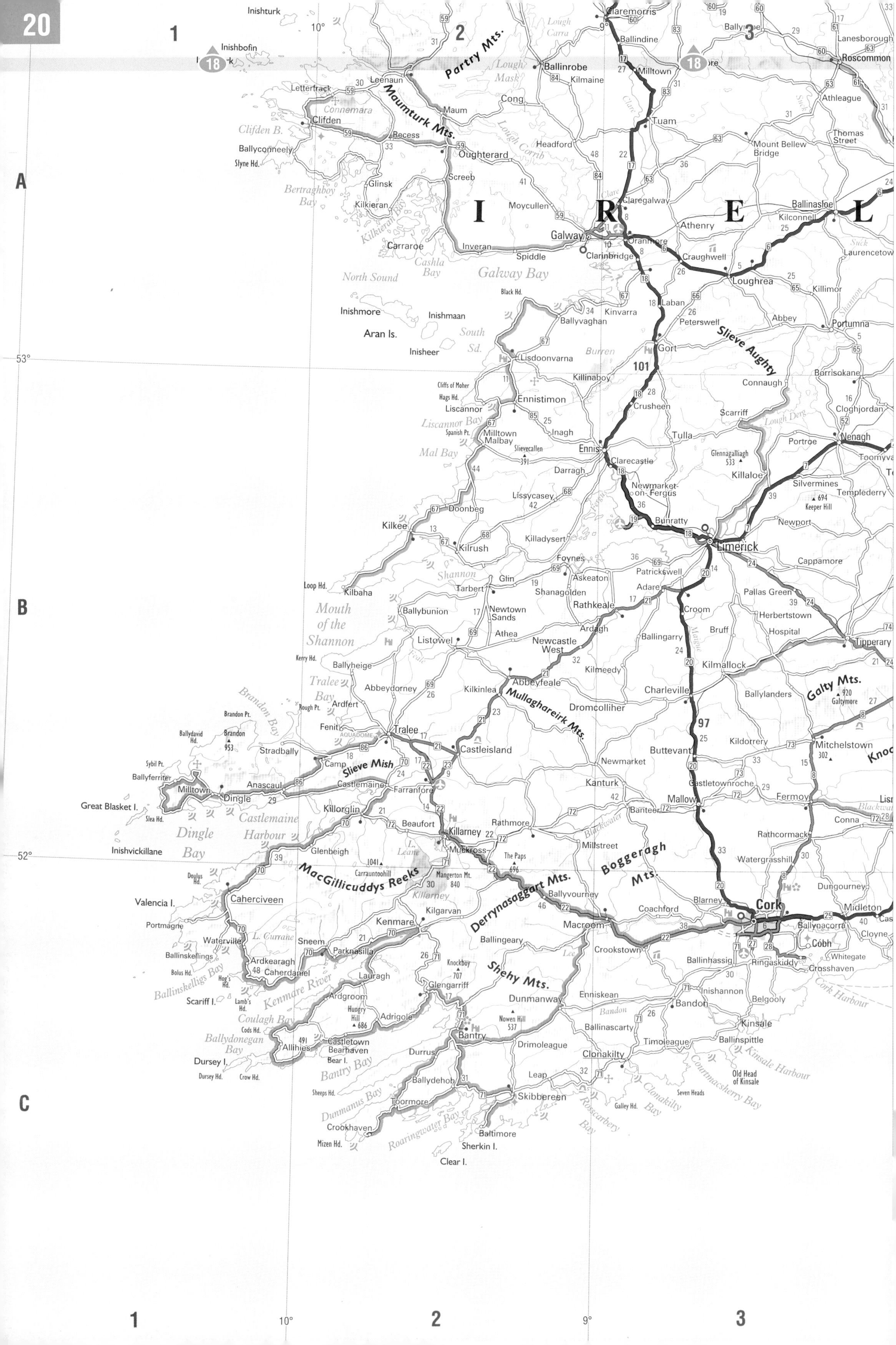
I R E L
Inishturk
Inishbofin
Partry Mts.
Lough Carra
Claremorris
Ballindine
Ballinrobe
Lough Mask
Kilmaine
Milltown
Lanesborough
Roscommon
Leenaun
Letterfrack
Connemara
Maumturk Mts.
Maum
Cong
Tuam
Athleague
Clifden
Clifden B.
Recess
Ballyconneely
Slyne Hd.
Oughterard
Lough Corrib
Headford
Mount Bellew Bridge
Thomas Street
Bertraghboy Bay
Screeb
Glinsk
Kilkieran
Kilkieran Bay
Moycullen
Claregalway
Ballinasloe
Kilconnell
Athenry
Galway
Oranmore
Clarinbridge
Carraroe
Inveran
Spiddle
Cashla Bay
Craughwell
Loughrea
Laurencetown
Galway Bay
North Sound
Black Hd.
Kinvarra
Killimor
Inishmore
Inishmaan
Aran Is.
Inisheer
South Sd.
Ballyvaghan
Laban
Peterswell
Abbey
Portumna
Slieve Aughty
Burren
Lisdoonvarna
Gort
Killinaboy
Connaugh
Borrisokane
Cliffs of Moher
Hags Hd.
Liscannor
Liscannor Bay
Ennistimon
Crusheen
Cloghjordan
Scarriff
Lough Derg
Spanish Pt.
Milltown Malbay
Inagh
Tulla
Nenagh
Mal Bay
Slievecallen
391
Ennis
Clarecastle
Glennagalliagh 533
Portroe
Toomyva
Darragh
Killaloe
Silvermines
Newmarket-on-Fergus
Lissycasey
694 Keeper Hill
Templederry
Doonbeg
Bunratty
Newport
Kilkee
Kilrush
Killadysert
Limerick
Cappamore
Foynes
Shannon
Askeaton
Patrickswell
Loop Hd.
Kilbaha
Glin
Tarbert
Shanagolden
Adare
Pallas Green
Mouth of the Shannon
Ballybunion
Newtown Sands
Rathkeale
Croom
Herbertstown
Athea
Ardagh
Bruff
Hospital
Listowel
Newcastle West
Ballingarry
Tipperary
Kerry Hd.
Ballyheige
Kilmeedy
Kilmallock
Tralee Bay
Abbeydorney
Abbeyfeale
Kilkinlea
Charleville
Ballylanders
Galty Mts.
920 Galtymore
Brandon Bay
Rough Pt.
Ardfert
Mullaghareirk Mts.
Dromcolliher
Brandon Pt.
Fenit
Tralee
Ballydavid Hd.
Brandon 953
Stradbally
Castleisland
Buttevant
Kildorrery
Mitchelstown
302
Sybil Pt.
Camp
Slieve Mish
Newmarket
Ballyferriter
Castlemaine
Farranfore
Kanturk
Castletownroche
Fermoy
Milltown
Anascaul
Dingle
Mallow
Great Blasket I.
Slea Hd.
Killorglin
Banteer
Castlemaine Harbour
Dingle Bay
Beaufort
Rathmore
Blackwater
Conna
Killarney
Millstreet
Rathcormack
Inishvickillane
Glenbeigh
L. Leane
Muckross
The Paps 696
Boggeragh Mts.
Watergrasshill
1041 Carrauntoohill
Mangerton Mt. 840
MacGillicuddys Reeks
Doulus Hd.
Derrynasaggart Mts.
Dungourney
Valencia I.
Cahirciveen
Ballyvourney
Blarney
Cork
Midleton
Kilgarvan
Coachford
Portmagne
Kenmare
Macroom
Ballynacorra
Cloyne
Waterville
L. Currane
Sneem
Ballingeary
Crookstown
Cobh
Whitegate
Ballinskelligs
Parknasilla
Ballinhassig
Ringaskiddy
Crosshaven
Ardkearagh
Caherdaniel
Knockboy 707
Shehy Mts.
Bolus Hd.
Ballinskelligs Bay
Hog's Hd.
Lauragh
Glengarriff
Cork Harbour
Kenmare River
Ardgroom
Dunmanway
Enniskean
Inishannon
Belgooly
Scariff I.
Lamb's Hd.
Hungry Hill 686
Adrigole
Bandon
Coulagh Bay
Nowen Hill 537
Cods Hd.
Ballydonegan Bay
Allihies
Castletown Bearhaven
Bantry
Ballinascarty
Kinsale
Bear I.
Durrus
Drimoleague
Clonakilty
Timoleague
Ballinspittle
Dursey I.
Dursey Hd.
Crow Hd.
Bantry Bay
Kinsale Harbour
Courtmacsherry Bay
Old Head of Kinsale
Ballydehob
Leap
Clonakilty Bay
Sheeps Hd.
Dunmanus Bay
Toormore
Skibbereen
Seven Heads
Rosscarbery Bay
Galley Hd.
Roaringwater Bay
Crookhaven
Baltimore
Mizen Hd.
Sherkin I.
Clear I.
53°
52°
10°
9°
A
B
C
1
2
3

Longford
Edgeworthstown
Crossakiel
Kells
Slane
Drogheda
Julianstown
Killashee
Castlepollard
Clonmellon
Navan
Keenagh
Ballinalack
Delvin
Athboy
Duleek
Balbriggan
Skerries
Nauls
Ballymahon
L. Owel
Mullingar
Killucan
Ballivor
Trim
Dunshaughlin
Ashbourne
Rush
Lough Ree
Ballymore
Rathmolyon
Lambay I.
Kiltoom
Lough Ennell
Clonard
Dunboyne
Swords
Malahide
Kinnegad
Enfield
Kilcock
Athlone
Moate
Ballynagore
Tyrrellspass
Edenderry
Lucan
Howth Hd.
Kilbeggan
Celbridge
Dublin
Douglas 2:45
Holyhead 1:49
Liverpool 7:45
Mostyn 6:00
Cherbourg 18:00
Clondalkin
Dun Laoghaire
A N D
Ferbane
Daingean
Rathcoole
Tallaght
Dalkey
Tullamore
Sallins
Bray
Holyhead 1:40
Grand Canal
Cloghan
Killeigh
Rathangan
Naas
Newbridge
Blessington
Kippure
Portarlington
Kilcormac
Kildare
Kilcullen
Wicklow Mountains
Greystones
Slieve Bloom
Monasterevin
Poulaphouca Res.
Newtownmount-kennedy
Mountmellick
Birr
Kinnitty
Dunlavin
Roundwood
Fontstown
Portlaoise
Arderin
Laragh
Rathnew
Mountrath
Timolin
Lugnaquilla
Wicklow
Athy
Glenealy
Wicklow Hd.
Roscrea
Baltinglass
Borris-in-Ossory
Ballylynan
Rathdrum
Abbeyleix
Castledermot
Hacketstown
Aughrim
Moneygall
Rathvilly
Clogh
Mizen Hd.
Durrow
Carlow
Arklow
Templemore
Croghan Mt.
Ballyragget
Castlecomer
Tullow
Coolgreany
Borrisoleigh
Johnstown
Shillelagh
Kilmichael Pt.
Freshford
Leighlinbridge
Ballon
Urlingford
Thurles
Paulstown
Muine Bheag
Carnew
Gorey
Kilkenny
Bunclody
Holycross
Blackstairs Mts.
Littleton
Gowran
Borris
Mt. Leinster
Ballycanew
Ballingarry
Ferns
Killenaule
Cahore Pt.
Cashel
Callan
Graiguenamanagh
Thomastown
Enniscorthy
Knocktopher
Fethard
Ninemilehouse
Clonroche
Blackwater
Newinn
Slievenamon
Oilgate
New Ross
Carrick-on-Suir
Castlebridge
Caher
Clonmel
Mullinavat
Wexford
Wexford Harbour
Comeragh Mts.
Monavullagh Mts.
Waterford
Rosslare
Fishguard 3:30
Pembroke 3:45
Clogheen
Arthurstown
Wellingtonbridge
Rosslare Harbour
Knockmealdown Mts.
Kilmeadan
Killinick
Greenore Pt.
Knockmealdown
Passage East
Kilmacthomas
Cappoquin
Millstreet
Tramore
Fethard
Dunmore East
Crossfarnoge Pt.
Kilmore Quay
Carnsore Pt.
Cherbourg 18:00
Roscoff 15:00
Bunmahon
Annestown
Hook Hd.
Tallow
Dungarvan
Dungarvan Harbour
Helvick Hd.
Tramore Bay
Waterford Harbour
Rosslare 3:30
Strumble Hd.
Goodwick
Fishguard
Clashmore
Youghal
Youghal Bay
St. David's Hd.
St. David's
Ramsey I.
Solva
St. Brides Bay
Haverfordwest
Ballycotton
Broad Haven
Skomer I.
Milford Haven
Skokholm I.
Dale
Angle
Swansea 10:00
Roscoff 14:00
St. George's Channel
Rosslare 3:45
A
B
C
4
5
6
7°
6°
53°
52°
19
26
28

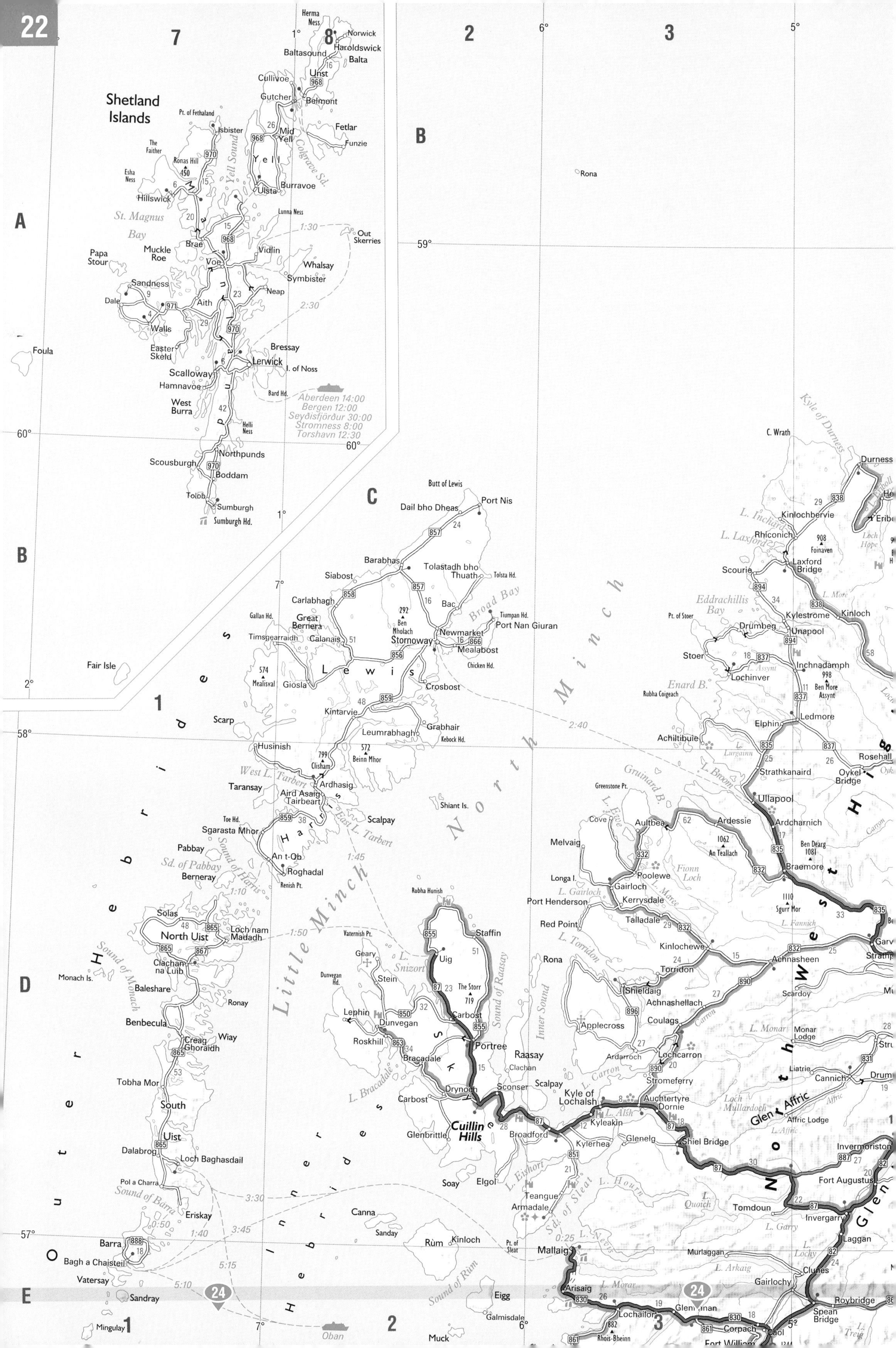
7
8
2
3
1°
6°
5°
Herma Ness
Norwick
Haroldswick
Baltasound
Balta
Unst
Cullivoe
Gutcher
Belmont
Shetland Islands
Pt. of Fethaland
Isbister
Fetlar
Funzie
Mid Yell
Yell
Yell Sound
Colgrave Sd.
The Faither
Ronas Hill 450
Esha Ness
Hillswick
Ulsta
Burravoe
Lunna Ness
St. Magnus Bay
Out Skerries
Papa Stour
Muckle Roe
Brae
Vidlin
Whalsay
Voe
Symbister
Sandness
Neap
Dale
Aith
Walls
Foula
Easter Skeld
Bressay
Lerwick
I. of Noss
Scalloway
Hamnavoe
Bard Hd.
Aberdeen 14:00
Bergen 12:00
Seyðisfjörður 30:00
Stromness 8:00
Torshavn 12:30
West Burra
Helli Ness
60°
Northpunds
Scousburgh
Boddam
Toab
Sumburgh
Sumburgh Hd.
Fair Isle
2°
B
Rona
A
59°
C
Butt of Lewis
Port Nis
Dail bho Dheas
Barabhas
Tolastadh bho Thuath
Tolsta Hd.
Siabost
Carlabhagh
Bac
Broad Bay
Gallan Hd.
Great Bernera
Ben Mholach 292
Tiumpan Hd.
Port Nan Giuran
Timsgearraidh
Calanais
Newmarket
Stornoway
Mealabost
Chicken Hd.
Mealisval 574
Giosla
Lewis
Crosbost
Scarp
Kintarvie
Grabhair
Leumrabhagh
Kebock Hd.
58°
Husinish
Clisham 799
Beinn Mhor 572
West L. Tarbert
Taransay
Ardhasig
Aird Asaig
Tairbeart
Harris
East L. Tarbert
Shiant Is.
Scalpay
Toe Hd.
Sgarasta Mhor
Pabbay
Sound of Harris
Sd. of Pabbay
An t-Ob
Roghadal
Berneray
Renish Pt.
North Minch
Little Minch
Rubha Hunish
Solas
North Uist
Loch nam Madadh
Clachan na Luib
Monach Is.
Sound of Monach
Baleshare
Ronay
Benbecula
Creag Ghoraidh
Wiay
Tobha Mor
South Uist
Dalabrog
Loch Baghasdail
Pol a Charra
Sound of Barra
Eriskay
Barra
Bagh a Chaisteil
Vatersay
Sandray
Mingulay
Outer Hebrides
57°
E
1
2
3
7°
Oban
Vaternish Pt.
Geary
L. Snizort
Dunvegan Hd.
Stein
Uig
Staffin
The Storr 719
Sound of Raasay
Lephin
Dunvegan
Roskhill
Bracadale
L. Bracadale
Carbost
Portree
Raasay
Clachan
Skye
Drynoch
Sconser
Scalpay
Glenbrittle
Cuillin Hills
Broadford
Soay
Elgol
L. Eishort
Inner Sound
Inner Hebrides
Canna
Sanday
Rùm
Kinloch
Sound of Rùm
Eigg
Galmisdale
Muck
Pt. of Sleat
Mallaig
Sd. of Sleat
Teangue
Armadale
Kyle of Lochalsh
Kyleakin
L. Alsh
Kylerhea
Glenelg
Dornie
Auchtertyre
Shiel Bridge
L. Hourn
L. Nevis
Arisaig
L. Morar
Lochailort
Glenfinnan
Corpach
Caol
Fort William
Rhois-Bheinn 882
Spean Bridge
Roybridge
Gairlochy
Clunes
L. Lochy
L. Arkaig
Murlaggan
Laggan
Invergarry
L. Garry
Tomdoun
L. Quoich
Fort Augustus
Invermoriston
Glen Affric
Affric Lodge
L. Affric
Loch Mullardoch
Cannich
Drum
Liatrie
Monar Lodge
L. Monar
Scardoy
Achnasheen
Garve
Strathpeffer
Lochcarron
Stromeferry
Ardarroch
Applecross
Coulags
Achnashellach
Shieldaig
Torridon
L. Torridon
Kinlochewe
Talladale
Kerrysdale
L. Maree
Gairloch
L. Gairloch
Port Henderson
Red Point
Rona
Longa I.
Poolewe
Fionn Loch
Melvaig
Cove
L. Ewe
Aultbea
Greenstone Pt.
Gruinard B.
Ardessie
An Teallach 1062
Braemore
Sgurr Mor 1110
L. Fannich
Ben Dearg 1081
Ardcharnich
Ullapool
L. Broom
Strathkanaird
Achiltibuie
Rubha Coigeach
L. Lurgainn
Elphin
Ledmore
Oykel Bridge
Rosehall
Ben More Assynt 998
Inchnadamph
Enard B.
L. Assynt
Lochinver
Stoer
Pt. of Stoer
Drumbeg
Unapool
Kylestrome
Kinloch
L. More
Eddrachillis Bay
Scourie
Laxford Bridge
Foinaven 908
Rhiconich
L. Laxford
L. Inchard
Kinlochbervie
Loch Hope
Durness
Kyle of Durness
C. Wrath
North West Highlands
Carron
Oykel
Glen
24

Orkney Islands
Mull Head
Papa Westray
Hollandstoun
Dennis Hd.
N. Ronaldsay
Westray
Pierowall
The North Sound
Midbea
Burness
Start Pt.
Sanday
Rapness
Calfsound
Overbister
Eday
Store
Sanday Sound
Sacquoy Hd.
Wasbister
Eynhallow Sd.
Rousay
Veness
Brinyan
Odie
Brough Hd.
The Barony
Twatt
Redland
Aith
Stronsay
Dounby
Stronsay Firth
Lamb Hd.
Balfour
Shapinsay
Voy
Finstown
Kirkwall
Mull Head
Stromness
Mainland
Lerwick 8:00
Invergordon 8:30
Orphir
Gritley
Linksness
Copinsay
St. Mary's
Scrabster 2:00
Aberdeen 10:00
Old Man of Hoy
Scapa Flow
Rose Ness
Hoy
Flotta
Burray
Lyness
St. Margaret's Hope
Longhope
South Ronaldsay
Tor Ness
South Walls
Burwick
Pentland Firth
Stromness 2:00
Dunnet Hd.
Stroma
John o' Groats
Mey
Duncansby Head
Holborn Hd.
Scrabster
Dunnet
Strathy Pt.
Kyle of Tongue
Whiten Hd.
Dounreay
Thurso
Castletown
Melvich
Nybster
Keiss
Bettyhill
Strathy
Sordale
Halkirk
Hastigrow
Tongue
Olgrinmore
Reiss
Noss Hd.
Dalhalvaig
Watten
Mybster
Wick
Forsinain
Loch Loyal
Thrumster
Achavanich
Ulbster
Lybster
Altnaharra
L. Naver
L. nan Clar
Latheron
Kinbrace
Dunbeath
Morven
Strath of Kildonan
Meall Nan Con
Kildonan
Berriedale
Ousdale
Helmsdale
Sallachy
Lairg
Pittentrail
Brora
Golspie
Inveran
Kirkwall 8:30
Bonarbridge
Clashmore
Dornoch
Dornoch Firth
Ardgay
Tarbat Ness
Edderton
Tain
Portmahomack
Moray Firth
Fearn
Balintore
Kilmuir
Lossiemouth
Burghead
Findochty
Portknockie
Troup Hd.
Rosehearty
Kinnairds Hd.
Fraserburgh
Inverallochy
Alness
Invergordon
Balnapaling
Burghead B.
Spey B.
Kingston
Buckie
Portsoy
Macduff
Banff
New Aberdour
Cromarty Firth
Findhorn
Kinloss
Elgin
Cromarty
Craibstone
Rattray Hd.
Strichen
Crimond
Dingwall
Fortrose
Nairn
Forres
Fochabers
New Pitsligo
Conon Bridge
Ardersier
Auldearn
Kellas
Mulben
Aberchirder
Mintlaw
Peterhead
North Kessock
Cawdor
Rothes
Keith
Turriff
Maud
Old Deer
Buchan Ness
Boddam
Beauly
Inverness
Ferness
Archiestown
Charlestown of Aberlour
Fortrie
Huntly
Methlick
Cruden Bay
Dores
Moy
Lettoch
Marypark
Dufftown
Colpy
Insch
Tarves
Ellon
Grantown-on-Spey
Tomnavoulin
Oldmeldrum
Newburgh
Tomatin
Cabrach
Rhynie
Lerwick 14:00
Stromness 8:00
Torness
Carrbridge
Tomintoul
Lumsden
Inverurie
Newmachar
Foyers
Boat of Garten
Strath Spey
Ladder Hills
Carn Mor
Kemnay
Kintore
Dyce
Balmedie
White Bridge
Aviemore
Cairngorms
Strathdon
Alford
Ordhead
Bridge of Don
Aberdeen
Girdle Ness
Westhill
Monadhliath Mts.
Cairn Gorm
Kincraig
Morven
Cults
Carn Ban
Kingussie
Cairngorm Mts.
Tarland
Torphins
Peterculter
Newtonmore
Ruthven
Ben Macdhui
Crathie
Aboyne
Banchory
Portlethen
Ballater
Strachan
Newtonhill
Drumgask
Braemar
Mt. Keen
Stonehaven
Lochnagar
L. Laggan
Dalwhinnie
Forest of Atholl
N. Esk
Ben Dearg
Beinn a' Ghlo
Glas Maol
Spittle of Glenshee
Clova
Fettercairn
Laurencekirk
Inverbervie

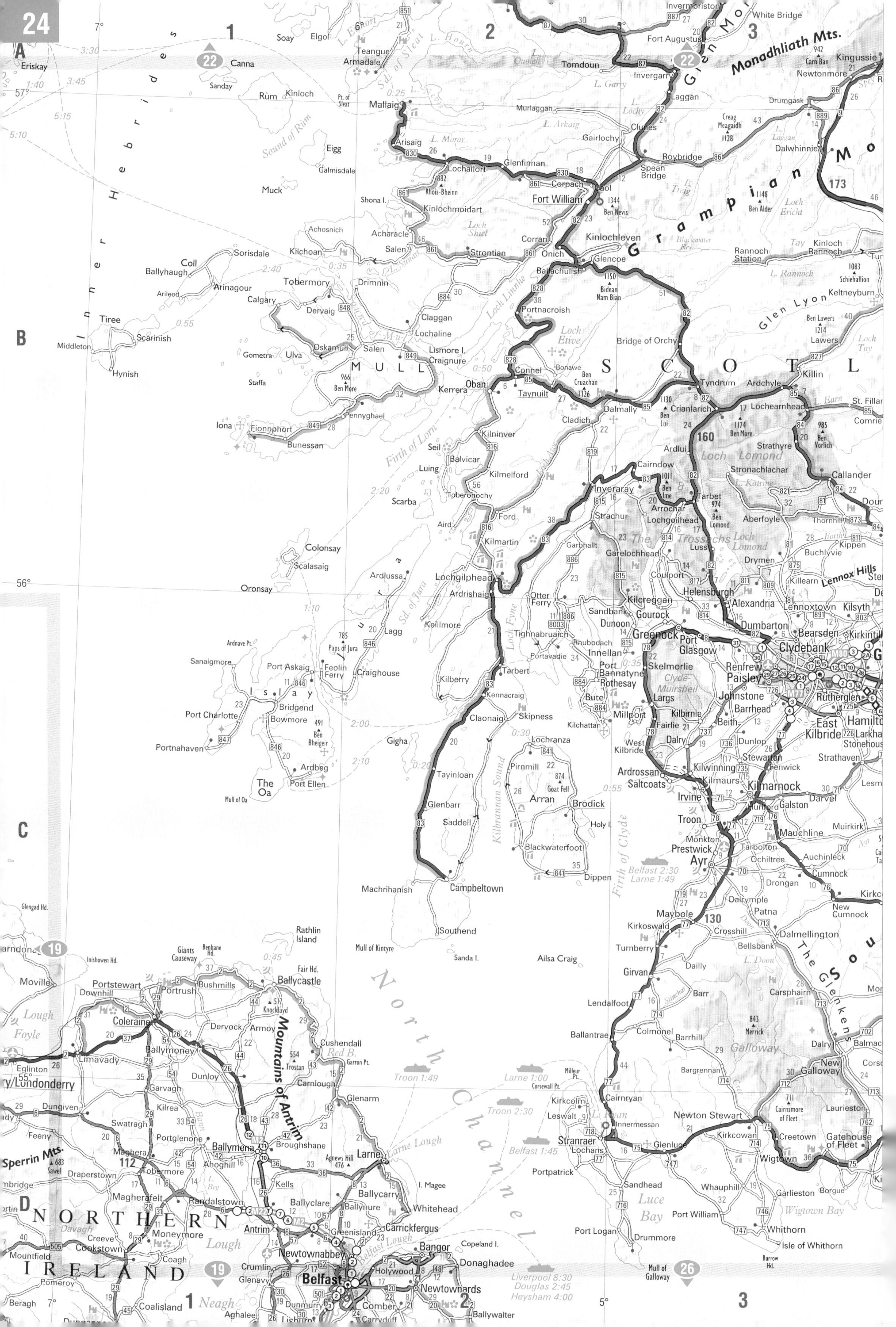

Inner Hebrides
Eriskay
Canna
Sanday
Soay
Elgol
Rùm
Kinloch
Eigg
Galmisdale
Muck
Sound of Rum
Armadale
Teangue
Sd. of Sleat
Pt. of Sleat
Mallaig
Arisaig
L. Morar
Lochailort
Glenfinnan
Rhois-Bheinn
Kinlochmoidart
Shona I.
Acharacle
Achosnich
Kilchoan
Salen
Strontian
Loch Shiel
Coll
Sorisdale
Ballyhaugh
Arinagour
Arileod
Tiree
Scarinish
Middleton
Hynish
Tobermory
Calgary
Dervaig
Drimnin
Claggan
Lochaline
Sound of Mull
Gometra
Ulva
Oskamull
Salen
MULL
Ben More
Staffa
Iona
Fionnphort
Bunessan
Pennyghael
Lismore I.
Craignure
Kerrera
Oban
Connel
Taynuilt
Bonawe
Loch Etive
Ben Cruachan
Dalmally
Cladich
Kilninver
Seil
Balvicar
Luing
Kilmelford
Firth of Lorn
Toberonochy
Scarba
Aird
Ford
Kilmartin
Colonsay
Scalasaig
Oronsay
Ardlussa
Jura
Sd. of Jura
Paps of Jura
Lochgilphead
Ardrishaig
Lagg
Craighouse
Port Askaig
Feolin Ferry
Ardnave Pt.
Sanaigmore
Islay
Bridgend
Bowmore
Port Charlotte
Portnahaven
Ardbeg
Port Ellen
The Oa
Mull of Oa
Gigha
Kilberry
Tarbert
Kennacraig
Claonaig
Skipness
Tayinloan
Glenbarr
Saddell
Kilbrannan Sound
Machrihanish
Campbeltown
Southend
Mull of Kintyre
Sanda I.
Rathlin Island
Invermoriston
White Bridge
Fort Augustus
Glen Mor
Monadhliath Mts.
Carn Ban
Kingussie
Newtonmore
Tomdoun
L. Quoich
L. Garry
Invergarry
Laggan
Drumgask
Murlaggan
L. Arkaig
Gairlochy
L. Lochy
Clunes
Creag Meagaidh
Dalwhinnie
Roybridge
Spean Bridge
Corpach
Caol
Fort William
Ben Nevis
L. Treig
Grampian Mountains
Ben Alder
Loch Ericht
Kinlochleven
Corran
Onich
Glencoe
Ballachulish
Blackwater Res.
Rannoch Station
Kinloch Rannoch
L. Rannoch
Schiehallion
Keltneyburn
Bidean Nam Bian
Loch Linnhe
Portnacroish
Bridge of Orchy
Glen Lyon
Ben Lawers
Lawers
Loch Tay
Killin
Tyndrum
Ardchyle
Crianlarich
Ben Lui
Lochearnhead
L. Earn
St. Fillans
Comrie
Ben More
Ben Vorlich
Strathyre
Ardlui
Loch Lomond
Stronachlachar
L. Katrine
Callander
Cairndow
Ben Ime
Inveraray
Loch Fyne
Tarbet
Ben Lomond
Arrochar
Strachur
Lochgoilhead
Aberfoyle
Thornhill
The Trossachs
Luss
Loch Lomond
Kippen
Buchlyvie
Garbhallt
Garelochhead
Drymen
Coulport
Helensburgh
Killearn
Lennox Hills
Alexandria
Otter Ferry
Kilcreggan
Lennoxtown
Kilsyth
Sandbank
Gourock
Dunoon
Dumbarton
Bearsden
Kirkintilloch
Greenock
Port Glasgow
Clydebank
Tighnabruaich
Rhubodach
Portavadie
Innellan
Renfrew
Paisley
Port Bannatyne
Rothesay
Skelmorlie
Clyde-Muirsheil
Largs
Johnstone
Rutherglen
Bute
Millport
Kilbirnie
Barrhead
East Kilbride
Hamilton
Kilchattan
Fairlie
Beith
Dalry
Dunlop
Lochranza
West Kilbride
Stewarton
Stonehouse
Strathaven
Pirnmill
Goat Fell
Arran
Ardrossan
Saltcoats
Kilwinning
Kilmaurs
Fenwick
Kilmarnock
Brodick
Irvine
Galston
Darvel
Holy I.
Troon
Hurlford
Mauchline
Muirkirk
Monkton
Prestwick
Tarbolton
Ayr
Ochiltree
Auchinleck
Blackwaterfoot
Dippen
Firth of Clyde
Cumnock
Drongan
New Cumnock
Dalrymple
Patna
Maybole
Kirkoswald
Crosshill
Dalmellington
Turnberry
Dailly
Bellsbank
L. Doon
Ailsa Craig
Girvan
Barr
Carsphairn
The Glenkens
Lendalfoot
Merrick
Colmonell
Barrhill
Ballantrae
Galloway
Dalry
Balmaclellan
Bargrennan
New Galloway
Cairnryan
Cairnsmore of Fleet
Laurieston
Milleur Pt.
Corsewall Pt.
Kirkcolm
Leswalt
L. Ryan
Innermessan
Newton Stewart
Kirkcowan
Creetown
Gatehouse of Fleet
Stranraer
Lochans
Glenluce
Wigtown
Portpatrick
Sandhead
Whauphill
Garlieston
Luce Bay
Port William
Wigtown Bay
Sorbie
Port Logan
Drummore
Whithorn
Isle of Whithorn
Mull of Galloway
Burrow Hd.
SCOTLAND
North Channel
Belfast 2:30
Larne 1:49
Troon 1:49
Larne 1:00
Troon 2:30
Belfast 1:45
Liverpool 8:30
Douglas 2:45
Heysham 4:00
Glengad Hd.
Inishowen Hd.
Giants Causeway
Benbane Hd.
Fair Hd.
Ballycastle
Bushmills
Portstewart
Portrush
Downhill
Moville
Lough Foyle
Coleraine
Knocklayd
Mountains of Antrim
Armoy
Dervock
Cushendall
Red B.
Garron Pt.
Trostan
Limavady
Ballymoney
Dunloy
Eglinton
Londonderry
Carnlough
Garvagh
Glenarm
Dungiven
Kilrea
Swatragh
Portglenone
Feeny
Sperrin Mts.
Sawel
Maghera
Ballymena
Broughshane
Larne
Larne Lough
Agnews Hill
I. Magee
Draperstown
Tobermore
Ahoghill
Kells
Ballycarry
Magherafelt
Randalstown
Ballyclare
Ballynure
Whitehead
NORTHERN IRELAND
Davagh
Antrim
Carrickfergus
Greenisland
Belfast Lough
Creeve
Moneymore
Lough Neagh
Cookstown
Newtownabbey
Bangor
Copeland I.
Donaghadee
Mountfield
Coagh
Crumlin
Holywood
Glenavy
Belfast
Newtownards
Pomeroy
Dunmurry
Comber
Beragh
Coalisland
Aghalee
Lisburn
Carryduff
Ballywalter

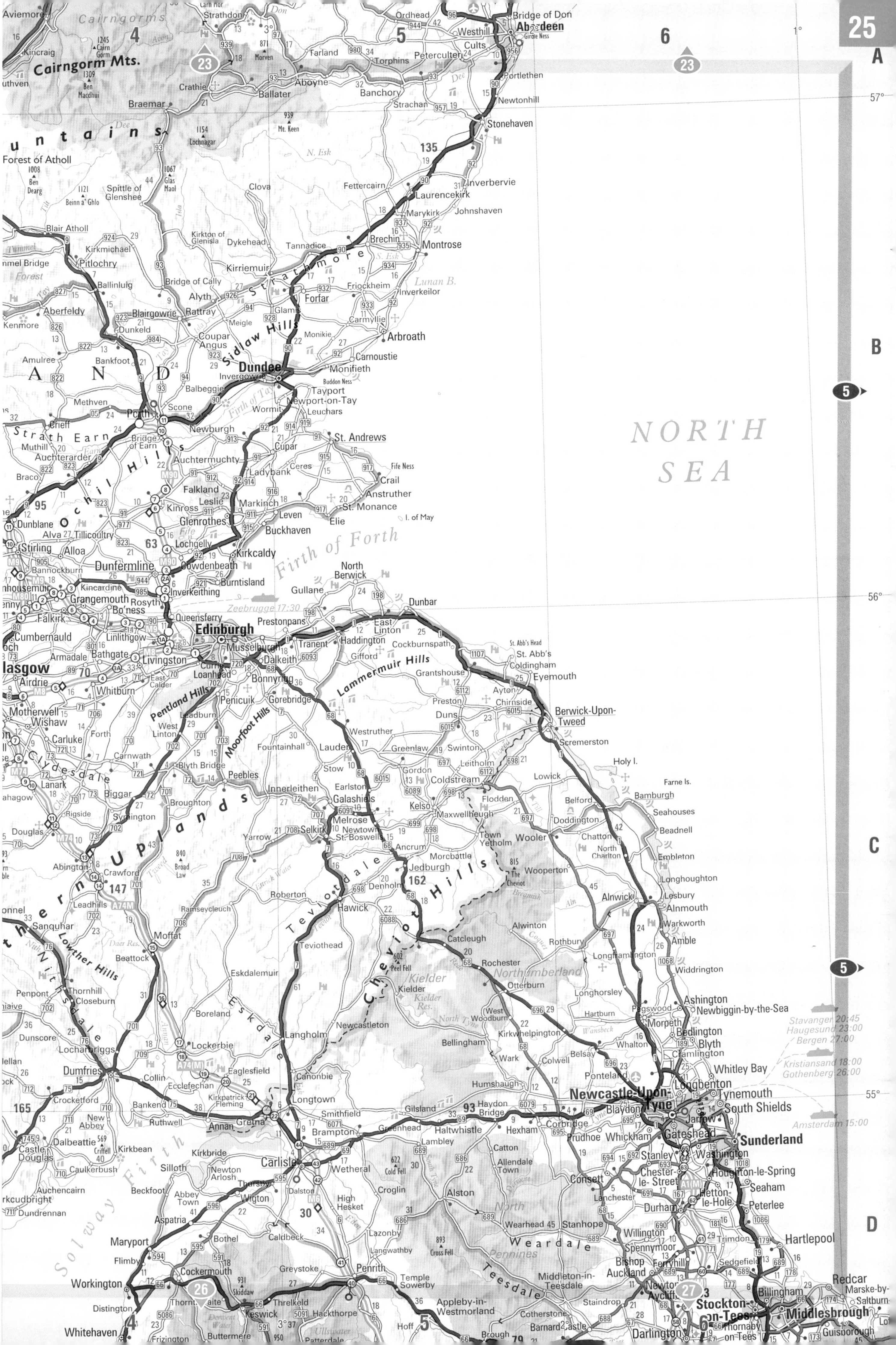

Aviemore
Cairngorms
Cairngorm Mts.
Ben Macdhui
Strathdon
Ordhead
Westhill
Bridge of Don
Aberdeen
Girdle Ness
Cults
Peterculter
Tarland
Torphins
Aboyne
Ballater
Crathie
Banchory
Portlethen
Newtonhill
Braemar
Strachan
Mt. Keen
Lochnagar
Stonehaven
Forest of Atholl
Ben Dearg
Beinn a' Ghlo
Spittle of Glenshee
Glas Maol
Clova
Fettercairn
Inverbervie
Laurencekirk
Marykirk
Johnshaven
Blair Atholl
Kirkmichael
Kirkton of Glenisla
Dykehead
Tannadice
Brechin
Montrose
Pitlochry
Kirriemuir
Strathmore
Ballinluig
Bridge of Cally
Friockheim
Lunan B.
Inverkeilor
Aberfeldy
Alyth
Forfar
Blairgowrie
Rattray
Meigle
Glamis
Carmyllie
Kenmore
Dunkeld
Coupar Angus
Monikie
Arbroath
Sidlaw Hills
Amulree
Bankfoot
Carnoustie
Dundee
Monifieth
Invergowrie
Buddon Ness
Balbeggie
Tayport
Newport-on-Tay
Methven
Wormit
Leuchars
Scone
Perth
Crieff
Newburgh
Strath Earn
Firth of Tay
St. Andrews
Bridge of Earn
Cupar
Muthill
Auchterarder
Auchtermuchty
Ceres
Fife Ness
Braco
Ochil Hills
Ladybank
Crail
Falkland
Leslie
Anstruther
Kinross
Markinch
St. Monance
Dunblane
Leven
Glenrothes
Elie
I. of May
Alva
Tillicoultry
Buckhaven
Stirling
Alloa
Lochgelly
Kirkcaldy
Firth of Forth
Dunfermline
Cowdenbeath
North Berwick
Bannockburn
Kincardine
Burntisland
Grangemouth
Inverkeithing
Gullane
Rosyth
Bo'ness
Zeebrugge 17:30
Dunbar
Falkirk
Queensferry
Prestonpans
East Linton
Edinburgh
Cumbernauld
Linlithgow
Musselburgh
Tranent
Haddington
Cockburnspath
St. Abb's Head
St. Abb's
Coldingham
Armadale
Bathgate
Livingston
Dalkeith
Gifford
Lammermuir Hills
Eyemouth
Glasgow
Airdrie
Currie
Loanhead
East Calder
Bonnyrigg
Grantshouse
Ayton
Whitburn
Pentland Hills
Penicuik
Gorebridge
Chirnside
Berwick-Upon-Tweed
Preston
Motherwell
Wishaw
Leadburn
Duns
Moorfoot Hills
West Linton
Westruther
Scremerston
Carluke
Forth
Fountainhall
Lauder
Greenlaw
Swinton
Holy I.
Carnwath
Blyth Bridge
Leitholm
Clydesdale
Stow
Gordon
Lowick
Farne Is.
Lanark
Peebles
Innerleithen
Earlston
Coldstream
Bamburgh
Biggar
Galashiels
Flodden
Belford
Seahouses
Broughton
Kelso
Doddington
Rigside
Symington
Melrose
Maxwellheugh
Chatton
Beadnell
Douglas
Selkirk
Newtown St. Boswells
Town Yetholm
Wooler
Yarrow
Ancrum
North Charlton
Embleton
Southern Uplands
Morebattle
Abington
Broad Law
Jedburgh
The Cheviot
Wooperton
Crawford
Denholm
Longhoughton
Leadhills
Robertson
Hawick
Cheviot Hills
Alnwick
Lesbury
Alnmouth
Ramseycleuch
Sanquhar
Teviotdale
Alwinton
Warkworth
Amble
Moffat
Lowther Hills
Teviothead
Catcleugh
Rothbury
Longframlington
Beattock
Rochester
Northumberland
Widdrington
Eskdalemuir
Peel Fell
Kielder
Kielder Res.
Otterburn
Thornhill
Closeburn
Longhorsley
Ashington
Newbiggin-by-the-Sea
Penpont
Eskdale
Boreland
Pegswood
Morpeth
Newcastleton
Woodburn
Hartburn
Bedlington
Stavanger 20:45
Haugesund 23:00
Bergen 27:00
Dunscore
Langholm
Kirkwhelpington
Whalton
Blyth
Nithsdale
Locharbriggs
Lockerbie
Bellingham
Cramlington
Dumfries
Eaglesfield
Belsay
Whitley Bay
Kristiansand 18:00
Gothenberg 26:00
Collin
Canonbie
Wark
Colwell
Ponteland
Longbenton
Ecclefechan
Humshaugh
Tynemouth
Crocketford
Kirkpatrick Fleming
Longtown
Haydon Bridge
Newcastle-Upon-Tyne
South Shields
Bankend
Annan
Gretna
Smithfield
Gilsland
Blaydon
Jarrow
New Abbey
Ruthwell
Haltwhistle
Hexham
Corbridge
Amsterdam 15:00
Brampton
Greenhead
Prudhoe
Whickham
Gateshead
Sunderland
Dalbeattie
Criffell
Kirkbean
Solway Firth
Lambley
Catton
Washington
Castle Douglas
Kirkbride
Carlisle
Allendale Town
Stanley
Caulkerbush
Silloth
Newton Arlosh
Wetheral
Cold Fell
Chester-le-Street
Houghton-le-Spring
Auchencairn
Thursby
Consett
Seaham
Kirkcudbright
Beckfoot
Abbey Town
Dalston
Croglin
Alston
Lanchester
Hetton-le-Hole
Dundrennan
Wigton
High Hesket
North Pennines
Durham
Peterlee
Aspatria
Wearhead
Stanhope
Willington
Maryport
Bothel
Caldbeck
Lazonby
Weardale
Trimdon
Hartlepool
Spennymoor
Langwathby
Cross Fell
Flimby
Greystoke
Penrith
Pennines
Ferryhill
Sedgefield
Cockermouth
Bishop Auckland
Redcar
Workington
Skiddaw
Temple Sowerby
Teesdale
Middleton-in-Teesdale
Newton Aycliffe
Billingham
Marske-by-the-Sea
Saltburn
Threlkeld
Distington
Thornthwaite
Keswick
Hackthorpe
Appleby-in-Westmorland
Cotherstone
Staindrop
Stockton-on-Tees
Middlesbrough
Whitehaven
Derwent Water
Ullswater
Hoff
Barnard Castle
Thornaby-on-Tees
Guisborough
Frizington
Buttermere
Patterdale
Brough
Darlington
NORTH SEA

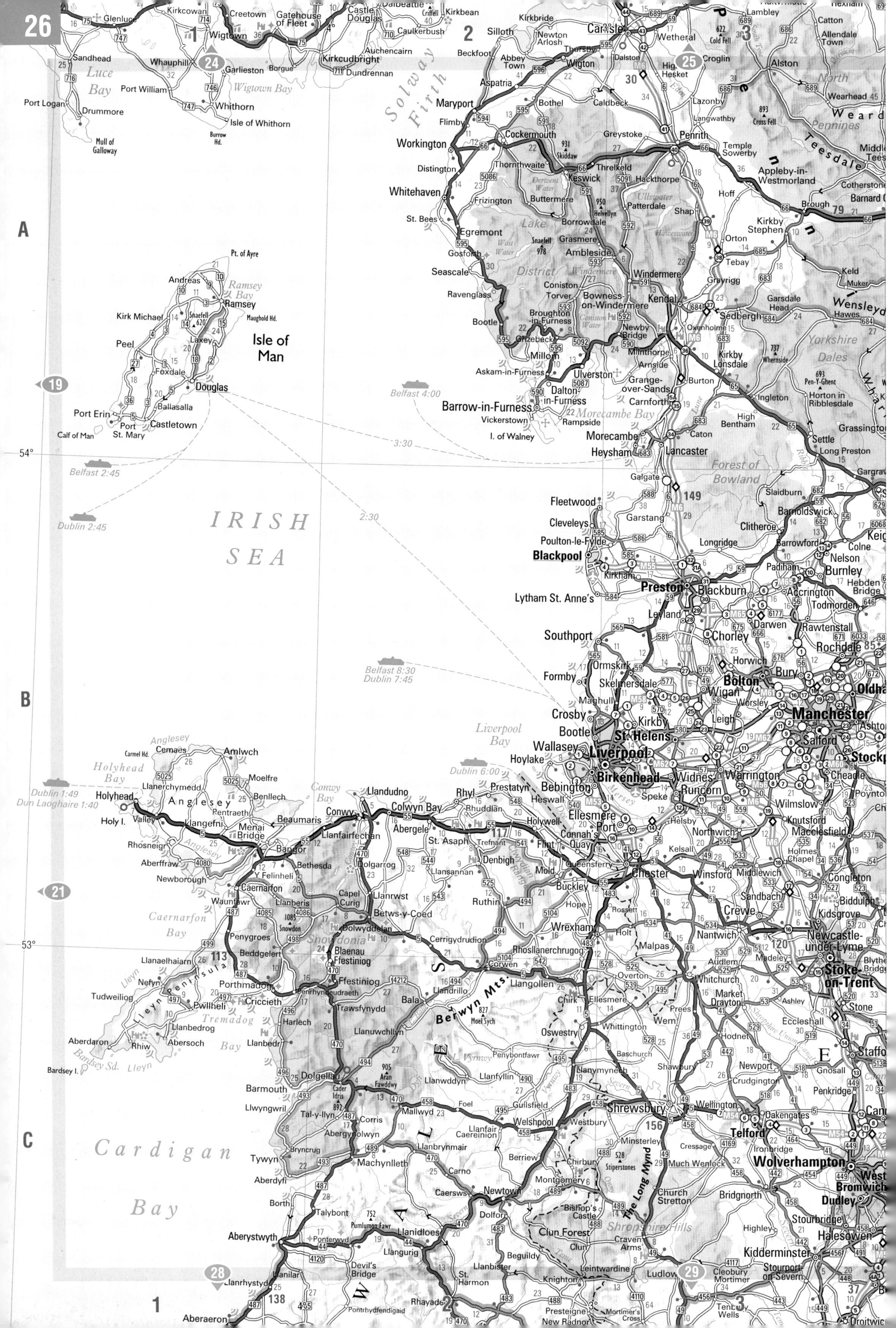

Glenluce
Kirkcowan
Creetown
Gatehouse of Fleet
Castle Douglas
Dalbeattie
Kirkbean
Caulkerbush
Wigtown
Auchencairn
Kirkcudbright
Dundrennan
Sandhead
Luce Bay
Whauphill
Garlieston
Borgue
Wigtown Bay
Port William
Port Logan
Drummore
Whithorn
Isle of Whithorn
Burrow Hd.
Mull of Galloway
Kirkbride
Silloth
Newton Arlosh
Carlisle
Wetheral
Lambley
Catton
Allendale Town
Beckfoot
Abbey Town
Thursby
Dalston
Wigton
Highr Hesket
Croglin
Alston
Aspatria
Solway Firth
Maryport
Bothel
Caldbeck
Lazonby
Cold Fell
North Pennines
Wearhead
Weardale
Flimby
Cockermouth
Greystoke
Langwathby
Cross Fell
Workington
Skiddaw
Penrith
Temple Sowerby
Teesdale
Distington
Thornthwaite
Keswick
Threlkeld
Hackthorpe
Appleby-in-Westmorland
Cotherstone
Whitehaven
Derwent Water
Frizington
Buttermere
Helvellyn
Ullswater
Patterdale
Hoff
Brough
Barnard Castle
St. Bees
Lake District
Borrowdale
Shap
Kirkby Stephen
Egremont
Scafell
Grasmere
Haweswater
Orton
Gosforth
Wast Water
Ambleside
Tebay
Seascale
Windermere
Grayrigg
Keld
Muker
Ravenglass
Coniston
Torver
Bowness-on-Windermere
Kendal
Garsdale Head
Hawes
Wensleydale
Broughton-in-Furness
Sedbergh
Bootle
Coniston Water
Newby Bridge
Oxenholme
Yorkshire Dales
Whernside
Grizebeck
Millom
Milnthorpe
Kirkby Lonsdale
Arnside
Pen-Y-Ghent
Askam-in-Furness
Ulverston
Grange-over-Sands
Burton
Horton in Ribblesdale
Ingleton
Dalton-in-Furness
Carnforth
Barrow-in-Furness
Vickerstown
Rampside
Morecambe Bay
High Bentham
Grassington
I. of Walney
Morecambe
Caton
Settle
Heysham
Lancaster
Long Preston
Forest of Bowland
Galgate
Slaidburn
Fleetwood
Garstang
Barnoldswick
Cleveleys
Clitheroe
Poulton-le-Fylde
Longridge
Barrowford
Colne
Blackpool
Nelson
Kirkham
Padiham
Burnley
Preston
Blackburn
Accrington
Hebden Bridge
Lytham St. Anne's
Todmorden
Leyland
Darwen
Southport
Chorley
Rawtenstall
Rochdale
Ormskirk
Horwich
Bury
Formby
Skelmersdale
Bolton
Oldham
Wigan
Maghull
Worsley
Manchester
Crosby
Kirkby
Leigh
Bootle
St. Helens
Salford
Stockport
Wallasey
Liverpool
Hoylake
Birkenhead
Widnes
Warrington
Cheadle
Liverpool Bay
Bebington
Heswall
Runcorn
Speke
Wilmslow
Ellesmere Port
Helsby
Knutsford
Macclesfield
Holywell
Connah's Quay
Northwich
Flint
Kelsall
Holmes Chapel
Queensferry
Chester
Winsford
Middlewich
Congleton
Mold
Sandbach
Buckley
Crewe
Biddulph
Hope
Kidsgrove
Wrexham
Nantwich
Newcastle-under-Lyme
Holt
Malpas
Audlem
Madeley
Stoke-on-Trent
Rhosllanerchrugog
Overton
Whitchurch
Llangollen
Chirk
Ellesmere
Market Drayton
Ashley
Stone
Prees
Wem
Oswestry
Whittington
Eccleshall
Hodnet
Baschurch
Llanymynech
Shawbury
Newport
Gnosall
Crudgington
Penkridge
Wellington
Oakengates
Shrewsbury
Welshpool
Westbury
Telford
Minsterley
Cressage
Ironbridge
Wolverhampton
Chirbury
Stiperstones
Much Wenlock
West Bromwich
Berriew
Montgomery
The Long Mynd
Church Stretton
Bridgnorth
Dudley
Newtown
Bishop's Castle
Stourbridge
Dolfor
Clun Forest
Shropshire Hills
Highley
Halesowen
Clun
Craven Arms
Kidderminster
Beguildy
Llanbister
Leintwardine
Ludlow
Cleobury Mortimer
Stourport-on-Severn
Knighton
Presteigne
New Radnor
Tenbury Wells
Droitwich
Isle of Man
Pt. of Ayre
Andreas
Ramsey Bay
Ramsey
Maughold Hd.
Kirk Michael
Snaefell
Laxey
Peel
Foxdale
Douglas
Ballasalla
Port Erin
Castletown
Port St. Mary
Calf of Man
Belfast 4:00
3:30
Belfast 2:45
Dublin 2:45
IRISH SEA
2:30
Belfast 8:30
Dublin 7:45
Dublin 6:00
Dublin 1:49
Dun Laoghaire 1:40
Anglesey
Carmel Hd.
Cemaes
Amlwch
Holyhead Bay
Llanerchymedd
Moelfre
Benllech
Holyhead
Holy I.
Valley
Llangefni
Pentraeth
Menai Bridge
Beaumaris
Rhosneigr
Aberffraw
Newborough
Conwy Bay
Llandudno
Conwy
Colwyn Bay
Rhyl
Prestatyn
Rhuddlan
Abergele
Llanfairfechan
St. Asaph
Trefnant
Bangor
Bethesda
Dolgarrog
Llansannan
Denbigh
Y Felinheli
Caernarfon
Llanrwst
Capel Curig
Llanberis
Betws-y-Coed
Ruthin
Waunfawr
Caernarfon Bay
Snowdon
Dolwyddelan
Cerrigydrudion
Penygroes
Snowdonia
Blaenau Ffestiniog
Beddgelert
Llanaelhaearn
Corwen
Nefyn
Porthmadog
Ffestiniog
Penrhyndeudraeth
Llandrillo
Berwyn Mts.
Moel Sych
Tudweiliog
Lleyn Peninsula
Pwllheli
Criccieth
Tremadog Bay
Bala
Trawsfynydd
Llanbedrog
Harlech
Llanuwchllyn
Aberdaron
Rhiw
Abersoch
Llanbedr
Penybontfawr
Bardsey Sd.
Bardsey I.
Dolgellau
Aran Fawddwy
Llanwddyn
Llanfyllin
Barmouth
Cader Idris
Guilsfield
Llwyngwril
Tal-y-llyn
Corris
Mallwyd
Foel
Llanfair Caereinion
Aberdyfi
Abergynolwyn
Bryncrug
Tywyn
Machynlleth
Llanbrynmair
Carno
Caersws
Cardigan Bay
Borth
Talybont
Pumlumon Fawr
Llanidloes
Aberystwyth
Ponterwyd
Llangurig
Devil's Bridge
Llanilar
Llanrhystyd
St. Harmon
Rhayader
Pontrhydfendigaid
Aberaeron
WALES
ENGLAND
1
2
3
A
B
C
54°
53°
19
21
24
25
28
29

Sunderland
Gateshead
Prudhoe
Whickham
Stanley
Washington
Consett
Chester-le-Street
Houghton
Spring
Lanchester
Hetton-le-Hole
Durham
Peterlee
Stanhope
Willington
Hartlepool
Spennymoor
Trimdon
Bishop Auckland
Ferryhill
Sedgefield
Newton Aycliffe
Redcar
Marske-by-the-Sea
Saltburn-by-the-sea
Staindrop
Billingham
Stockton-on-Tees
Middlesbrough
Staithes
Loftus
Darlington
Thornaby on Tees
Yarm
Guisborough
Whitby
Bowes
Stokesley
Scotch Corner
Sleights
Robin Hood's Bay
Richmond
Cleveland Hills
North York Moors
Reeth
Catterick
Northallerton
Burniston
Leyburn
Bedale
Kirkbymoorside
Scalby
Scarborough
Aysgarth
Thirsk
Thornton Dale
Pickering
Sowerby
Helmsley
Snainton
Filey
Masham
Kirkby Malzeard
Hovingham
Nidderdale
Howardian Hills
Norton
Flamborough
Pateley Bridge
Ripon
Stillington
Yorkshire Wolds
Rudston
Sledmere
Bridlington
Boroughbridge
Burton Agnes
Bridlington Bay
Fridaythorpe
Driffield
Knaresborough
Harrogate
York
Stamford Bridge
Skipsea
Bainton
North Frodingham
Skipton
Spofforth
Wetherby
Hutton Cranswick
Hornsea
Pocklington
Ilkley
Otley
Elvington
Leven
Collingham
Tadcaster
Escrick
Market Weighton
Baildon
Bingley
Holme-on-Spalding-moor
Beverley
Aldbrough
Leeds
Bradford
Garforth
Selby
South Cave
Cottingham
Sproatley
Kingston upon Hull
Hedon
Withernsea
Castleford
Howden
Halifax
Brighouse
Batley
Goole
Keyingham
Snaith
Barrow upon Humber
Dewsbury
Wakefield
Pontefract
Burton upon Stather
Barton-upon-Humber
Patrington
Easington
Huddersfield
Meltham
Hemsworth
Thorne
Ulceby
Immingham
Darton
Adwick le Street
Scunthorpe
Grimsby
Spurn Hd.
Barnsley
Barnetby le Wold
Holmfirth
Wombwell
Hatfield
Cleethorpes
Penistone
Epworth
Brigg
Laceby
Humberston
Rotterdam 12:30
Zeebrugge 12:45
Mexborough
Doncaster
Scotter
Haxey
Lincolnshire Wolds
Caistor
Ashton-under-Lyne
Kirton in Lindsey
North Thoresby
North Somercotes
Glossop
Stocksbridge
Rotherham
Saltfleet
Bawtry
Walkeringham
Binbrook
Market Rasen
Sheffield
Maltby
Gainsborough
Beckingham
Louth
Mablethorpe
New Mills
Castleton
Blyth
Lea
Peak District
Hathersage
Eckington
Worksop
Retford
Faldingworth
Withern
Sutton-on-Sea
Chapel en le Frith
Dronfield
Sturton
Wragby
Huttoft
Buxton
Baslow
Staveley
Clowne
Saxilby
Scamblesby
Alford
Bolsover
East Markham
Lincoln
Chesterfield
Bardney
Horncastle
Partney
Bakewell
Market Warsop
Ollerton
Sutton-on-Trent
Burgh le Marsh
Clay Cross
Woodhall Spa
Skegness
Waddington
Mareham le Fen
Spilsby
Matlock
Mansfield
Collingham
Navenby
Coningsby
Wainfleet All Saints
Alfreton
Sutton-in-Ashfield
Wirksworth
Southwell
Billinghay
The Wash
Ripley
Hucknall
Newark-on-Trent
Ruskington
Sibsey
Wrangle
Norfolk Coast
Belper
Heanor
Ashbourne
Arnold
Sleaford
Brancaster
Wells-next-the-Sea
Carlton
Long Bennington
Benington
Burnham Market
Cheadle
Duffield
Nottingham
Bottesford
Ancaster
Heckington
Boston
Hunstanton
Alton
Rocester
Derby
Ilkeston
Bingham
Kirton
Docking
Little Walsingham
Mickleover
West Bridgford
Grantham
Swineshead
Heacham
Uttoxeter
Long Eaton
Donington
Fakenham
Billingborough
Gosberton
Dersingham
Abbots Bromley
Burton upon Trent
Kegworth
Waltham on the Wolds
Pinchbeck
Weston
Swadlincote
Loughborough
Colsterworth
Spalding
Holbeach
Long Sutton
King's Lynn
Gayton
ENGLAND
Rugeley
Ashby de la Zouch
Shepshed
Melton Mowbray
Bourne
Deeping St. Nicholas
Litcham
Mountsorrel
Coalville
Dereham
Lichfield
Ibstock
Thurmaston
Baston
Market Deeping
Crowland
Wisbech
Downham Market
Fincham
Swaffham
Tamworth
Leicester
Oakham
Stamford
Rutland Water
Brownhills
Sutton Coldfield
Atherstone
Earl Shilton
Oadby
Duddington
Eye
Outwell
Stoke Ferry
Watton
Walsall
Hinckley
Wigston
Uppingham
Peterborough
March
Hilgay
Attleborough
Nuneaton
Wansford
Whittlesey
Methwold
Breckland
BIRMINGHAM
Bedworth
Market Harborough
Corby
Oundle
Yaxley
The Fens
Chatteris
Littleport
Brandon
Lutterworth
Husbands Bosworth
Brigstock
Ramsey
Lakenheath
Thetford
Solihull
Coventry
Rothwell
Thrapston
Sawtry
Somersham
Ely
Mildenhall
Knowle
Kettering
Raunds
St. Ives
Needingworth
Isleham
Kenilworth
West Haddon
Burton Latimer
Irthlingborough
Huntingdon
Godmanchester
Fordham
Ixworth
Bromsgrove
Royal Leamington Spa
Southam
Wellingborough
Rushden
Cottenham
Burwell
Redditch
Warwick
Earls Barton
Newmarket
Bury St.
Studley
Great Whernside

St. George's Channel
Bristol Channel
Wexford
Wexford Harbour
Blackwater
Castlebridge
Rosslare
Rosslare Harbour
Killinick
Greenore Pt.
Kilmore Quay
Carnsore Pt.
Fishguard 3:30
Pembroke 3:45
Cherbourg 18:00
Roscoff 15:00
Rosslare 3:30
Rosslare 3:45
Cork 10:00
Roscoff 6:00
Santander 24:00
Aberystwyth
Borth
Talybont
Ponterwyd
Devil's Bridge
Llanrhystyd
Llanilar
Aberaeron
New Quay
Tregaron
Cambrian Mts.
Llangranog
Aberporth
Cardigan
St. Dogmaels
Lampeter
Llanwrtyd Wells
W
A
L
Newcastle Emlyn
Llandysul
Llanybydder
Llansawel
Pumsaint
Llandovery
Strumble Hd.
Goodwick
Newport
Fishguard
Mynydd Prescelly
Greenway
Pembrokeshire
St. David's Hd.
St. David's
Ramsey I.
Solva
Wolf's Castle
St. Brides Bay
Haverfordwest
Camrose
Broad Haven
Skomer I.
Milford Haven
Skokholm I.
Dale
Angle
Pembroke Dock
Pembroke
Neyland
Coast
Narberth
St. Clears
Carmarthen
Trelech
Alltwalis
Llandeilo
Llangadog
Mynydd Du
Brynamman
Pontardulais
Ammanford
Cross-Hands
Llanelli
Kidwelly
Burry Port
Pendine
Laugharne
Saundersfoot
Tenby
Manorbier
Caldey I.
St. Govan's Hd.
Carmarthen Bay
Gorseinon
Gowerton
Clydach
Neath
Swansea
Port Talbot
Margam
Swansea Bay
Porthcawl
Gower
Rhossili
Worms Hd.
The Mumbles
Port Eynon
Oxwich Pt.
Lundy
Lynmouth
Lynton
Exmoor
Ilfracombe
Morte Pt.
Morte Bay
Woolacombe
Croyde
Barnstaple or Bideford Bay
North Devon
Barnstaple
Simonsbath
Challacombe
Instow
Appledore
Westward Ho!
Bideford
Hartland Pt.
Hartland
Clovelly
South Molton
North Molton
Great Torrington
Stibb Cross
Chulmleigh
Morwenstow
Venn Green
Winkleigh
Lapford
Bude Bay
Bude
Stratton
Widemouth
Holsworthy
Hatherleigh
North Tawton
Colebrooke
Poundstock
Okehampton
South Tawton
High Willhays
Chagford
Dunsford
Moretonhampstead
Dartmoor
Boscastle
Tintagel Hd.
Tintagel
Hallworthy
Launceston
Lydford
Delabole
Port Isaac Bay
Port Isaac
Pentire Pt.
Camelford
Brown Willy
St. Teath
Marytavy
Widecombe in the Moor
Padstow
Trevose Hd.
Wadebridge
St. Issey
Bodmin Moor
Tavistock
Princetown
Kingsteignton
Gunnislake
Callington
Ashburton
Buckfastleigh
Bodmin
Tamar Valley
Bere Alston
Yelverton
Newquay
St. Columb Major
Dobwalls
Liskeard
South Brent
St. Enoder
Lostwithiel
Saltash
Torpoint
Plymouth
Ivybridge
Devonport
Plymstock
Modbury
Yealmpton
Perranporth
St. Blazey
Bodinnick
Looe
Fowey
Polruan
Polperro
Whitesand Bay
St. Agnes
Perranzabuloe
St. Austell
Wembury
Newton Ferrers
Bigbury
Bigbury Bay
Kingsbridge
Portreath
Probus
Tregony
Mevagissey Bay
Mevagissey
Gorran Haven
Redruth
Truro
St. Ives
Carbis Bay
Zennor
Hayle
Camborne
Gwennap
Veryan
Marlborough
Salcombe
Bolt Head
Pendeen
Penryn
St. Mawes
St. Just
Marazion
Helston
Falmouth
Falmouth Bay
Newlyn
Penzance
Mousehole
Sennen
Land's End
Porthleven
Mount's Bay
St. Keverne
The Manacles
Mullion
Coverack
Lizard
Lizard Pt.
Cornwall
ISLES OF SCILLY
Tresco
St. Martin's
Hugh Town
Crow Sound
St. Mary's
Wolf Rock

BIRMINGHAM
Dudley
Stourbridge
Halesowen
Solihull
Coventry
Bedworth
Kidderminster
Stourport-on-Severn
Bromsgrove
Redditch
Kenilworth
Royal Leamington Spa
Warwick
Droitwich Spa
Worcester
Stratford-upon-Avon
Daventry
Northampton
Kettering
Wellingborough
Shropshire Hills
Clun Forest
Ludlow
Leominster
Hereford
Ledbury
Great Malvern
Evesham
Banbury
Tewkesbury
Gloucester
Cheltenham
Cotswolds
Stow-on-the-Wold
Chipping Norton
Bicester
Buckingham
Aylesbury
Oxford
Witney
Cirencester
Stroud
Monmouth
Abergavenny
Black Mountains
Brecon Beacons
Brecon
Merthyr Tydfil
Pontypool
Cwmbran
Newport
Cardiff
Caerphilly
Rhondda
Pontypridd
Bridgend
Barry
Penarth
Chepstow
Bristol
Bath
Weston-super-Mare
Clevedon
Swindon
Chippenham
Marlborough
Hungerford
Newbury
Reading
Wokingham
Basingstoke
High Wycombe
Henley-on-Thames
Maidenhead
Chiltern Hills
Vale of White Horse
Berkshire Downs
North Wessex Downs
Marlborough Downs
Vale of Pewsey
Devizes
Trowbridge
Frome
Salisbury Plain
Salisbury
Andover
Winchester
Hampshire Downs
Farnham
Aldershot
Fleet
Eastleigh
Southampton
Portsmouth
Havant
Gosport
Fareham
Isle of Wight
Newport
Ryde
Cowes
Sandown
Shanklin
Ventnor
The Solent
New Forest
Lymington
Christchurch
Bournemouth
Poole
Poole Harbour
Swanage
Purbeck
Weymouth
I. of Portland
Portland Bill
Chesil Beach
Dorchester
South Dorset Downs
North Dorset Downs
Blackmoor Vale
Bridport
Lyme Regis
Lyme Bay
Sherborne
Yeovil
Shaftesbury
Cranborne Chase & West Wiltshire Downs
Blandford Forum
Wimborne Minster
Taunton
Bridgwater
Bridgwater Bay
Burnham-on-Sea
Quantock Hills
Polden Hills
Mendip Hills
Glastonbury
Wells
Minehead
Brendon Hills
Blackdown Hills
Tiverton
Honiton
Exeter
Exmouth
Sidmouth
Teignmouth
Torquay
Paignton
Tor Bay
Brixham
Start Bay
Start Pt.
ENGLAND
WALES
Guernsey 2:30
Jersey 3:45
Cherbourg 2:15
Cherbourg 4:15
St. Malo 5:25
Guernsey 6:30
Jersey 10:00
Bilbao 35:00
Caen 6:00
Cherbourg 2:45
Cherbourg 5:00
Le Havre 5:30
St. Malo 8:45
50°
3°
2°
1°
4
5
6
7
A
B
C
D

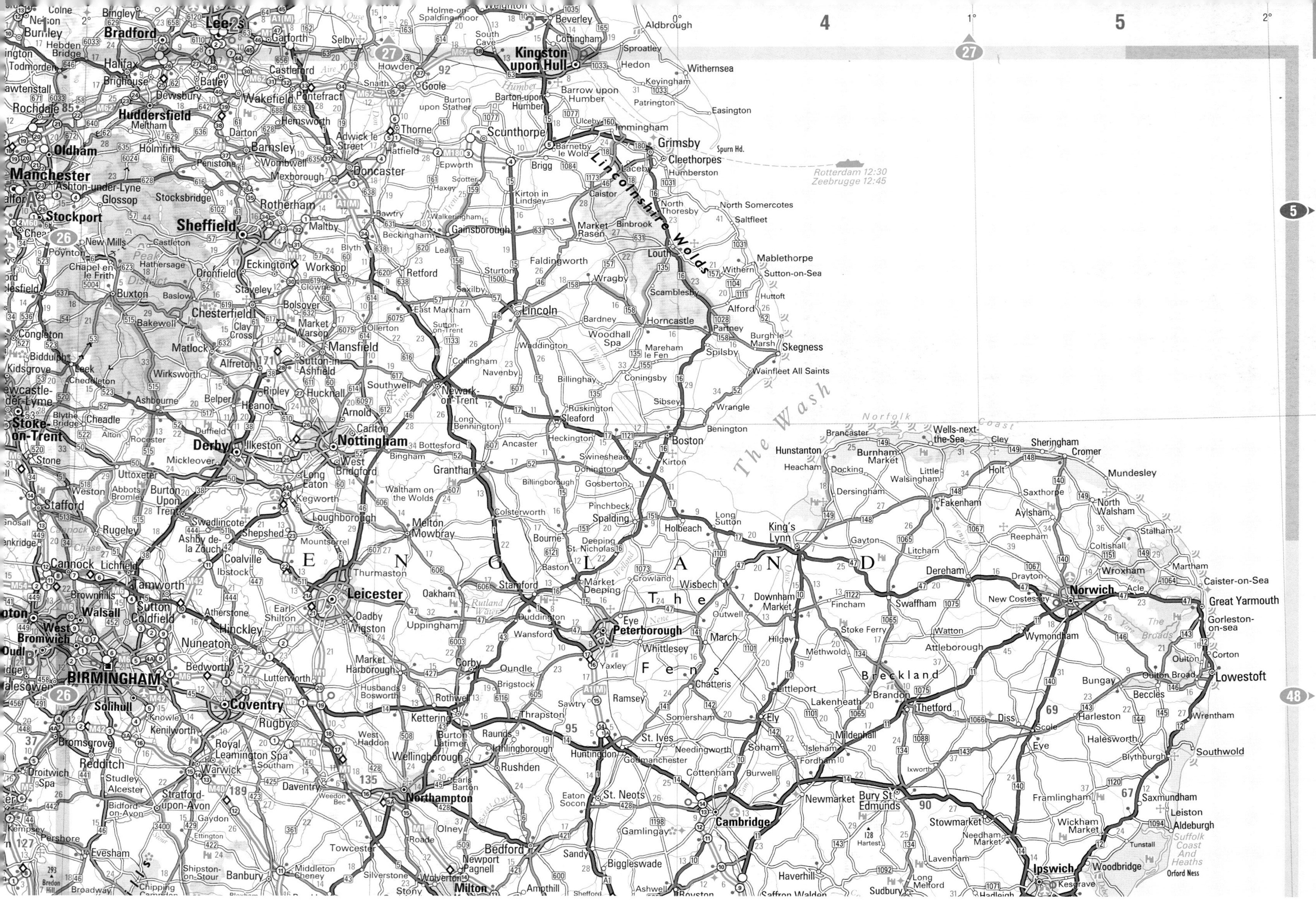
Leeds
Bradford
Halifax
Huddersfield
Wakefield
Castleford
Pontefract
Selby
Howden
Goole
Kingston upon Hull
Beverley
Cottingham
Aldbrough
Withernsea
Hedon
Easington
Spurn Hd.
Scunthorpe
Grimsby
Cleethorpes
Immingham
Brigg
Barton-upon-Humber
Thorne
Doncaster
Barnsley
Rotherham
Sheffield
Oldham
Manchester
Stockport
Rochdale
Glossop
Buxton
Chesterfield
Worksop
Retford
Gainsborough
Lincolnshire Wolds
Louth
Mablethorpe
Sutton-on-Sea
Skegness
Wainfleet All Saints
Spilsby
Horncastle
Lincoln
Market Rasen
Newark-on-Trent
Mansfield
Nottingham
Derby
Stoke-on-Trent
Stafford
Leicester
Loughborough
Melton Mowbray
Grantham
Sleaford
Boston
The Wash
Rotterdam 12:30
Zeebrugge 12:45
Norfolk Coast
Hunstanton
King's Lynn
Wells-next-the-Sea
Sheringham
Cromer
Fakenham
Dereham
Swaffham
Norwich
Great Yarmouth
Lowestoft
Southwold
Beccles
Thetford
Breckland
Bury St Edmunds
Newmarket
Ely
Cambridge
Peterborough
Spalding
Stamford
Wisbech
The Fens
Huntingdon
St. Neots
Bedford
Northampton
Kettering
Corby
Wellingborough
Rugby
Coventry
Birmingham
Solihull
Walsall
Tamworth
Nuneaton
Warwick
Stratford-upon-Avon
Banbury
Ipswich
Stowmarket
Woodbridge
Aldeburgh
Orford Ness
Suffolk Coast And Heaths
Haverhill
Sudbury
E N G L A N D
A
B
1
3
4
5
0°
1°
2°
53°

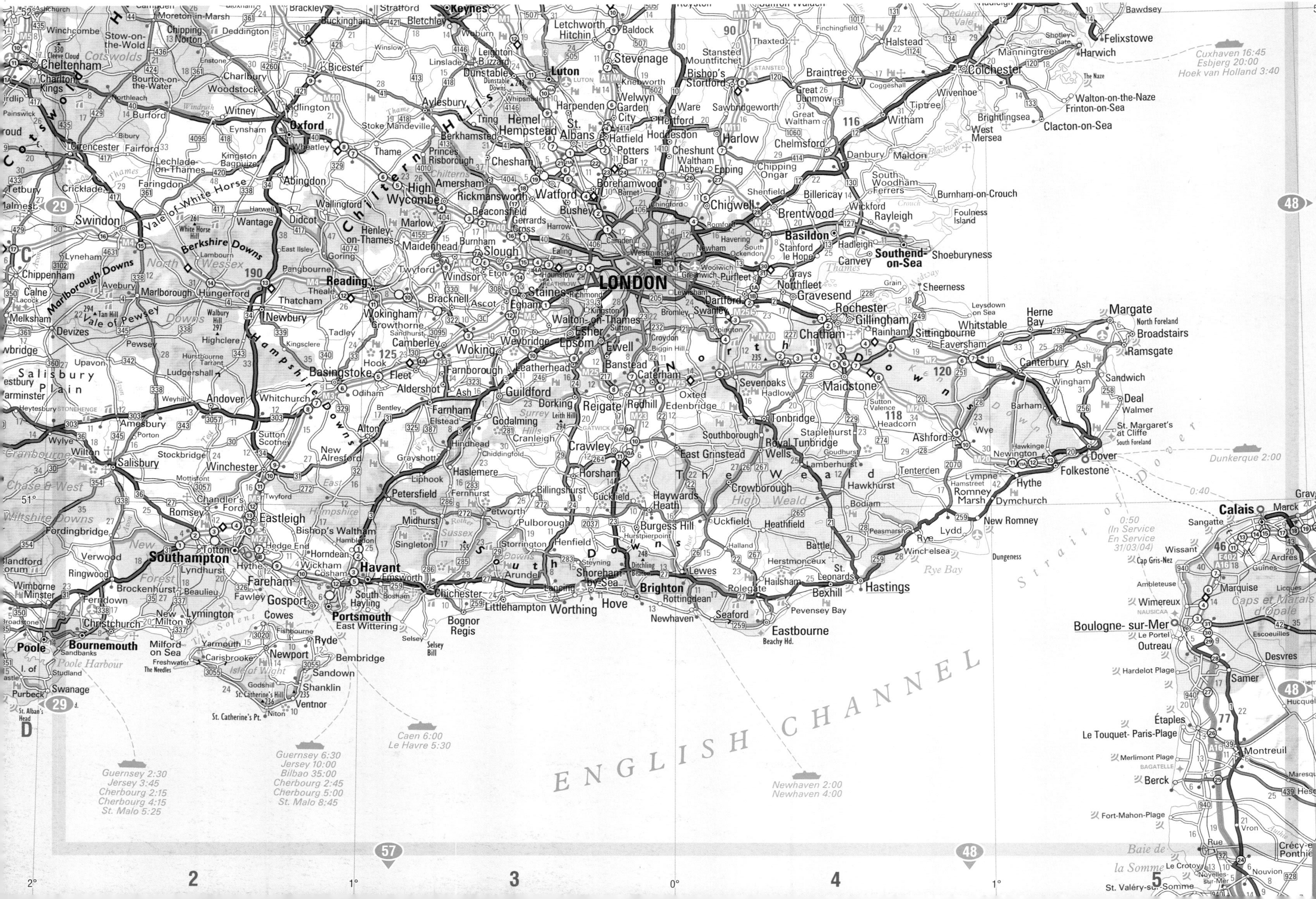
ENGLISH CHANNEL
Strait of Dover
LONDON
Oxford
Reading
Swindon
Cheltenham
Southampton
Portsmouth
Brighton
Hastings
Eastbourne
Dover
Folkestone
Canterbury
Margate
Ramsgate
Maidstone
Chatham
Rochester
Gillingham
Southend-on-Sea
Basildon
Chelmsford
Colchester
Harwich
Felixstowe
Clacton-on-Sea
Luton
Stevenage
St. Albans
Watford
Slough
Guildford
Crawley
Reigate
Salisbury
Winchester
Basingstoke
Newbury
Bournemouth
Poole
Isle of Wight
Newport
Calais
Boulogne-sur-Mer
Le Touquet-Paris-Plage
Montreuil
Berck
Cotswolds
Chiltern Hills
North Downs
South Downs
The Weald
Salisbury Plain
Berkshire Downs
Hampshire Downs
Marlborough Downs
Vale of White Horse
Vale of Pewsey
Caps et Marais d'Opale
Cuxhaven 16:45
Esbjerg 20:00
Hoek van Holland 3:40
Dunkerque 2:00
Newhaven 2:00
Newhaven 4:00
Caen 6:00
Le Havre 5:30
Guernsey 6:30
Jersey 10:00
Bilbao 35:00
Cherbourg 2:45
Cherbourg 5:00
St. Malo 8:45
Guernsey 2:30
Jersey 3:45
Cherbourg 2:15
Cherbourg 4:15
St. Malo 5:25
0:50
(In Service
En Service
31/03/04)
0:40
Rye Bay
Pevensey Bay
Baie de la Somme

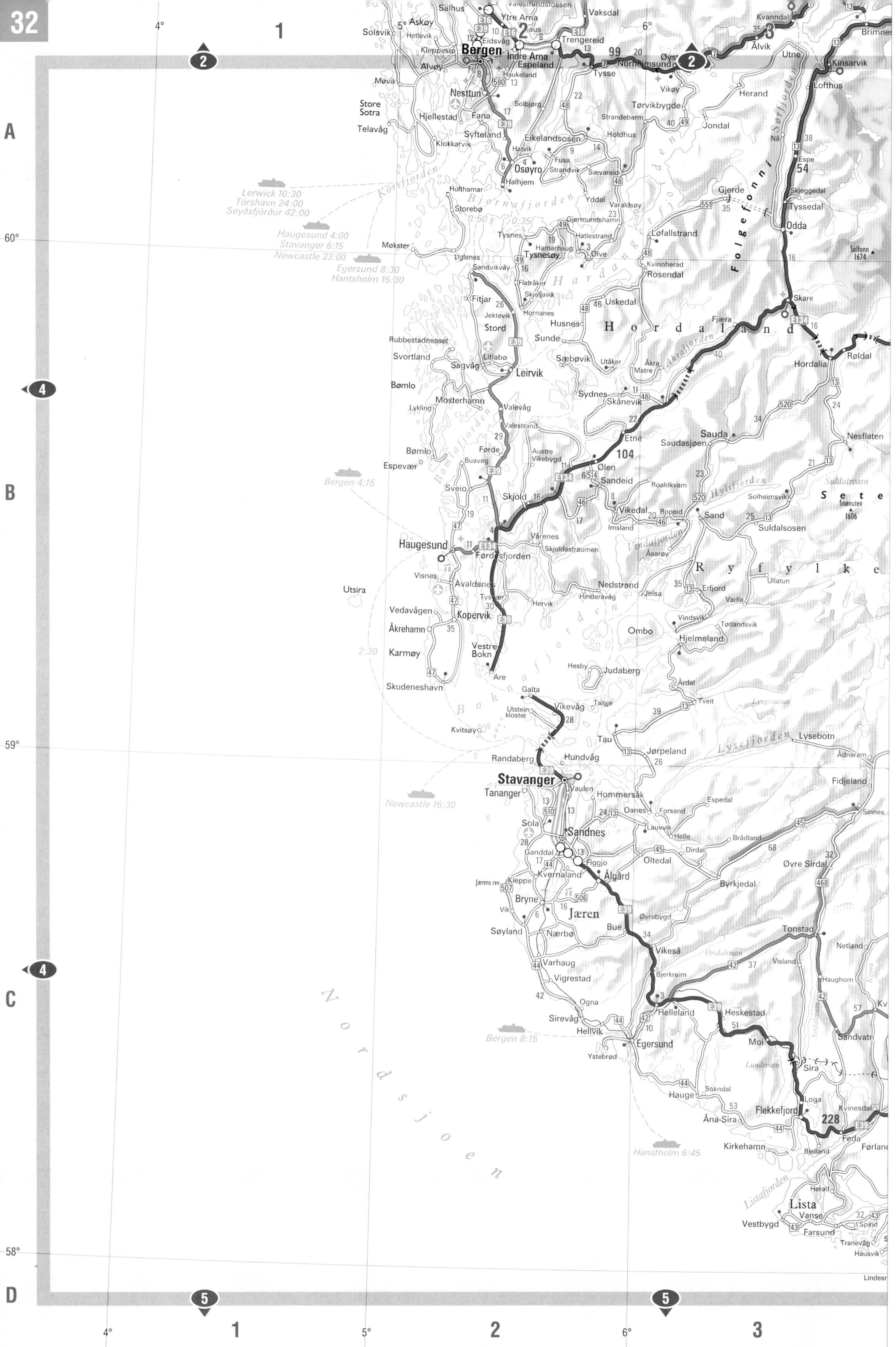
Bergen
Salhus
Askøy
Solsvik
Ytre Arna
Vaksdal
Kvanndal
Brimnes
Eidsvåg
Indre Arna
Espeland
Trengereid
Norheimsund
Øystese
Ålvik
Utne
Kinsarvik
Lofthus
Hetlevik
Kleppestø
Alvøy
Møvik
Haukeland
Nesttun
Store Sotra
Hjellestad
Fana
Solbjørg
Tysse
Vikøy
Tørvikbygde
Herand
Strandebarm
Jondal
Telavåg
Syfteland
Klokkarvik
Eikelandsosen
Holdhus
Hatvik
Fusa
Strandvik
Osøyro
Sævareid
Halhjem
Nå
Espe
Sørfjorden
Korsfjorden
Hufthamar
Storebø
Bjørnafjorden
Yddal
Varaldsøy
Gjerde
Skjeggedal
Tyssedal
Odda
Lerwick 10:30
Tórshavn 24:00
Seyðisfjörður 42:00
Haugesund 4:00
Stavanger 6:15
Newcastle 23:00
Egersund 8:30
Hantsholm 15:30
Gjermundshamn
Tysnes
Hatlestrand
Løfallstrand
Møkster
Hamarhaug
Tysnesøy
Ølve
Uglenes
Kvinnherad
Rosendal
Folgefonni
Solfonn 1674
Sandvikvåg
Flatråker
Hardangerfjorden
Skjelfavik
Fitjar
Jektevik
Hornanes
Uskedal
Skare
Stord
Husnes
Fjæra
Hordaland
Rubbestadneset
Sunde
Åkrafjorden
Svortland
Litlabø
Sæbøvik
Utåker
Åkra
Matre
Hordalia
Røldal
Sagvåg
Leirvik
Bømlo
Sydnes
Skånevik
Mosterhamn
Lykling
Valevåg
Etne
Sauda
Saudasjøen
Nesflaten
Valestrand
Bømlafjorden
Austre Vikebygd
Førde
Bømlo
Ølen
Buaveg
Espevær
Sandeid
Roaldkvam
Hylsfjorden
Suldalsvatn
Bergen 4:15
Sveio
Skjold
Solheimsvik
Setesdal
Snønuten 1606
Vikedal
Ropeid
Sand
Imsland
Suldalsosen
Haugesund
Vårenes
Skjoldastraumen
Vindafjorden
Åsarøy
Førdesfjorden
Ryfylke
Visnes
Avaldsnes
Nedstrand
Utsira
Erfjord
Ullatun
Hinderavåg
Jelsa
Tysvær
Hervik
Vadla
Vedavågen
Kopervik
Vindsvik
Tøtlandsvik
Åkrehamn
Boknafjorden
Ombo
Hjelmeland
Karmøy
Vestre Bokn
Hesby
Judaberg
Årdal
Are
Skudeneshavn
Galta
Tveit
Talgje
Utstein kloster
Vikevåg
Lyngsvatnet
Kvitsøy
Tau
Lysefjorden
Lysebotn
Jørpeland
Ådneram
Randaberg
Hundvåg
Stavanger
Fidjeland
Tananger
Vaulen
Hommersåk
Espedal
Newcastle 16:30
Oanes
Forsand
Sinnes
Sola
Lauvvik
Sandnes
Helle
Brådland
Ganddal
Dirdal
Figgjo
Oltedal
Øvre Sirdal
Kvernaland
Ålgård
Jærens rev
Kleppe
Byrkjedal
Bryne
Vik
Jæren
Øvrebygd
Søyland
Bue
Nærbø
Tonstad
Vikeså
Netland
Orsdalsvatn
Varhaug
Vigrestad
Visland
Bjerkreim
Haughom
Nordsjøen
Heskestad
Ogna
Helleland
Sirevåg
Sandvatn
Hellvik
Egersund
Bergen 8:15
Moi
Ystebrød
Lundevatn
Sira
Hauge
Sokndal
Loga
Flekkefjord
Kvinesdal
Åna-Sira
Feda
Kirkehamn
Bjelland
Førland
Hanstholm 6:45
Listafjorden
Herad
Lista
Vanse
Spind
Vestbygd
Farsund
Tranevåg
Hausvik
Lindesnes

Hardangervidda
Hårteigen 1690
Sandflot 1719
Haukeliseter
Haukeligrend
Edland
Grungedal
Rauland
Berge
TELEMARK
Vinje
Åmot
Bjåen
Hovden
Setesdal
Bykle
Berehommen
Dalen
Lårdal
Kviteseid
Vrådal
Seljord
Lifjell
Flatdal
Hjartdal
Sauland
Ofte
Rjukan
Gausta 1883
Møsstrand
Møsvatn
Tuddal
Kalhovd
Atrå
Miland
Dal
Ingolfsland
Bondal
Kråmvik
Uvdal
Rødberg
Imingen
Brostrud
Dagali
Tunnhovd
Ustaoset
Fagerheim
Tråastølen
Eidfjord
Tveit
Numedal
Hvåle
Karlsrud
Veggli
Rollag
Austbygda
Flesberg
Svene
Bakka
Blefjell
Høymyr
Tinnoset
Gransherad
Kongsberg
Notodden
Heddal
Skrimfjella
Hjukse
Sauherad
Bø
Gvarv
Nordagutu
Lunde
Ulefoss
Helgen
Skotfoss
Skien
Porsgrunn
Herøya
Brevik
Stathelle
Langesund
Larvik
Stavern
Sandefjord
Tønsberg
Horten
Holmestrand
Drammen
Mjøndalen
Hokksund
Vestfossen
Krokstad-elva
Lierbyen
Asker
Sandvika
Hønefoss
Norderhov
Noresund
Norefjell
Gulsvik
Sigdal
Vikersund
Geithus
Åmot
Sylling
Tyrifjorden
Sokna
Drangedal
Nissedal
Treungen
Fyresdal
Fyresvatn
Nisser
Tovdal
Åmli
Vegårshei
Kragerø
Risør
Tvedestrand
Arendal
Tromøy
Grimstad
Lillesand
Birkeland
Vennesla
Kristiansand
Søgne
Mandal
Vigeland
Lyngdal
Evje
Hornnes
Bygland
Byglandsfjord
Valle
Hylestad
Austad
Sandes
NORGE
Skagerrak
Frederikshavn 6:15
Göteborg 8:30
Newcastle 15:45
Hirtshals 2:30
59°
58°
60°
8°
9°
10°
A
B
C
D
4
5
6
7

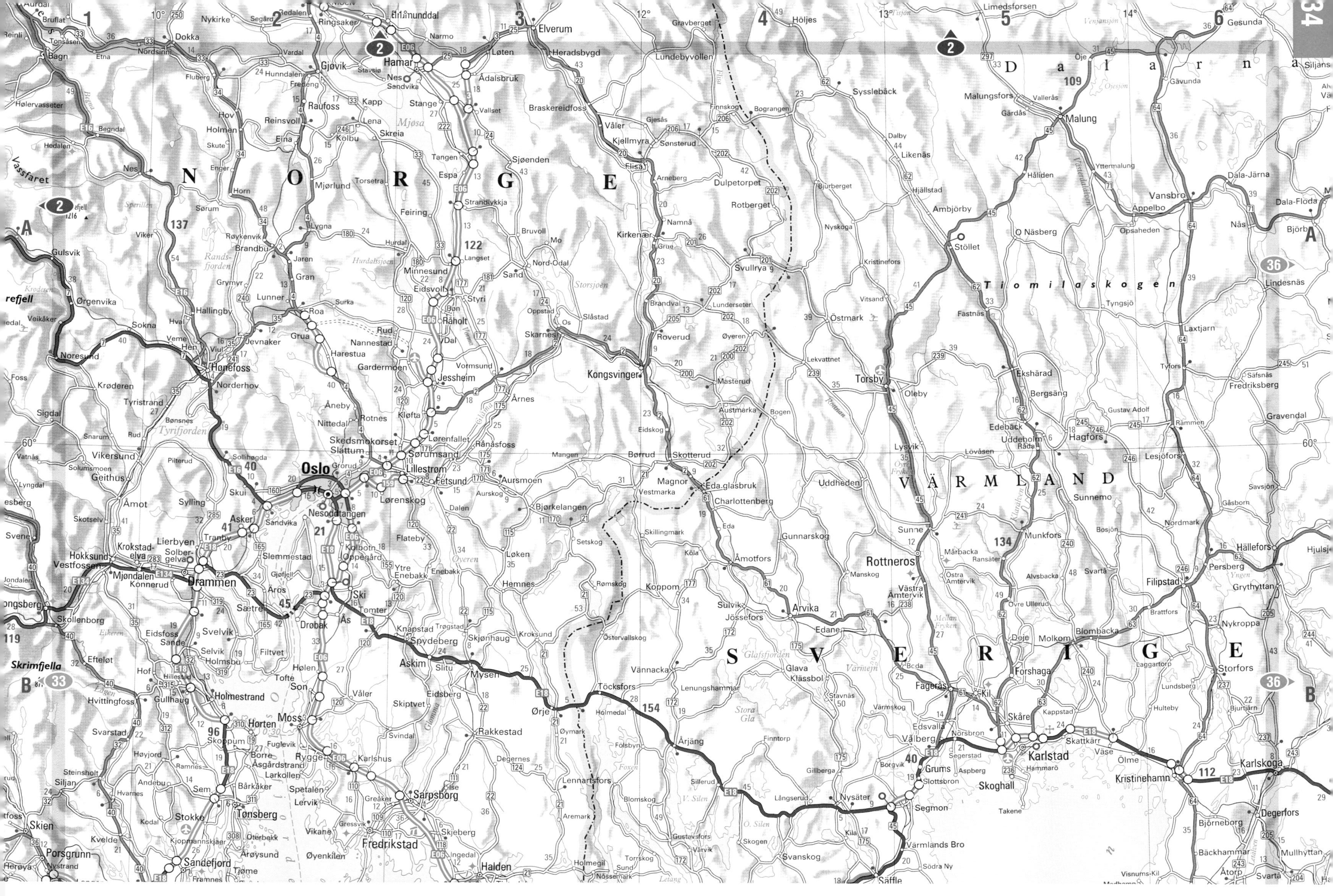
NORGE
SVERIGE
VÄRMLAND
Dalarna
Tiomilaskogen
Oslo
Drammen
Hamar
Gjøvik
Elverum
Kongsvinger
Lillestrøm
Moss
Horten
Tønsberg
Sandefjord
Fredrikstad
Sarpsborg
Halden
Porsgrunn
Skien
Hønefoss
Karlstad
Kristinehamn
Karlskoga
Degerfors
Filipstad
Hagfors
Torsby
Arvika
Säffle
Grums
Kil
Forshaga
Sunne
Malung
Vansbro
Hällefors
Charlottenberg
Eda glasbruk
Töcksfors
Årjäng
Ørje
Mysen
Askim
Ski
Asker
Sandvika
Jessheim
Gardermoen
Eidsvoll
Rottneros
Skoghall
Storfors
Ekshärad
Munkfors
Uddeholm
Stöllet
Lesjöfors
Sysslebäck
Höljes
Kirkenær
Flisa
Skarnes
Bjørkelangen
Magnor
Åmotfors
Glava
Nysäter
Svanskog
Mjøsa
Storsjøen
Randsfjorden
Tyrifjorden
Glafsfjorden
Skrimfjella
Vassfaret
Kongsberg
Hokksund
Vestfossen
Mjøndalen
Lierbyen
Holmestrand
Svelvik
Drøbak
Ås
Hvittingfoss
Noresund
Sokna
Dokka
Brandbu
Jevnaker
Gran
Roa
Harestua
Stange
Løten
Vikersund
Geithus
Sylling
Nesoddtangen
Spydeberg
Rakkestad
Larkollen
Rygge
Stokke
Skoppum
Åsgårdstrand
Sande
Eidsfoss
Gullhaug
Svarstad
Siljan
Värmlands Bro
Gesunda
Limedsforsen
E6
E16
E18
E134
112
122
134
137
154
96
109
40
41
45
21
36
2
33
A
B
1
2
3
4
5
6
10°
12°
13°
14°
60°

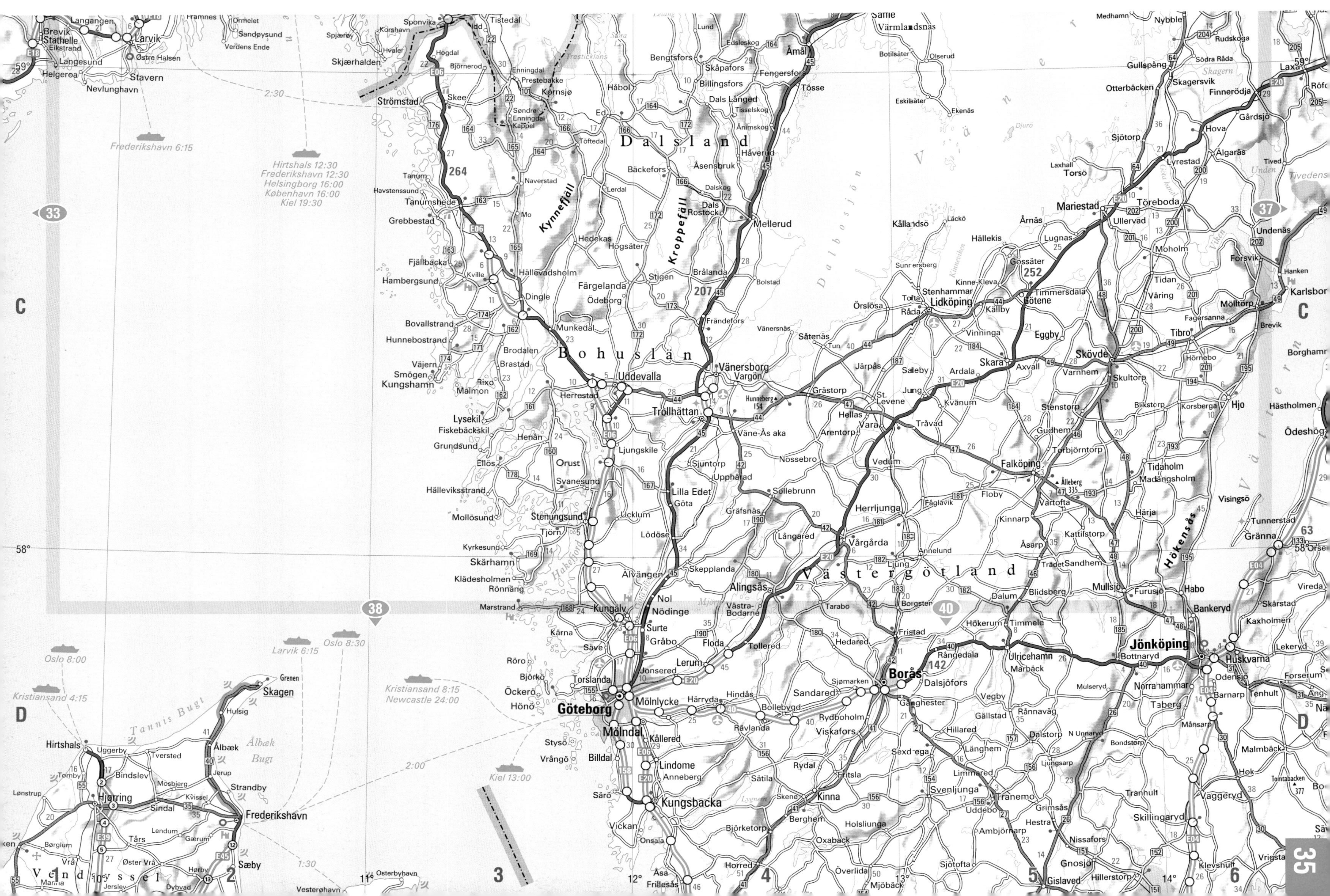
Dalsland
Bohuslän
Västergötland
Vendsyssel
Kynnefjäll
Kroppefjäll
Hökensås
Vänern
Dalbosjön
Vättern
Tannis Bugt
Ålbæk Bugt
Göteborg
Borås
Jönköping
Trollhättan
Vänersborg
Uddevalla
Lidköping
Skövde
Mariestad
Skara
Falköping
Alingsås
Kungsbacka
Mölndal
Kungälv
Strömstad
Lysekil
Stenungsund
Ulricehamn
Huskvarna
Åmål
Mellerud
Frederikshavn
Hjørring
Skagen
Hirtshals
Larvik
Gislaved
Kinna
Tidaholm
Hjo
Götene
Herrljunga
Vårgårda
Lilla Edet
Orust
Tjörn
Marstrand
Hirtshals 12:30
Frederikshavn 12:30
Helsingborg 16:00
København 16:00
Kiel 19:30
Frederikshavn 6:15
Oslo 8:00
Kristiansand 4:15
Larvik 6:15
Oslo 8:30
Kristiansand 8:15
Newcastle 24:00
Kiel 13:00
2:30
2:00
1:30
58°
59°
12°
13°
14°
11°
10°
C
D
1
2
3
4
5
6
33
37
38
40
63

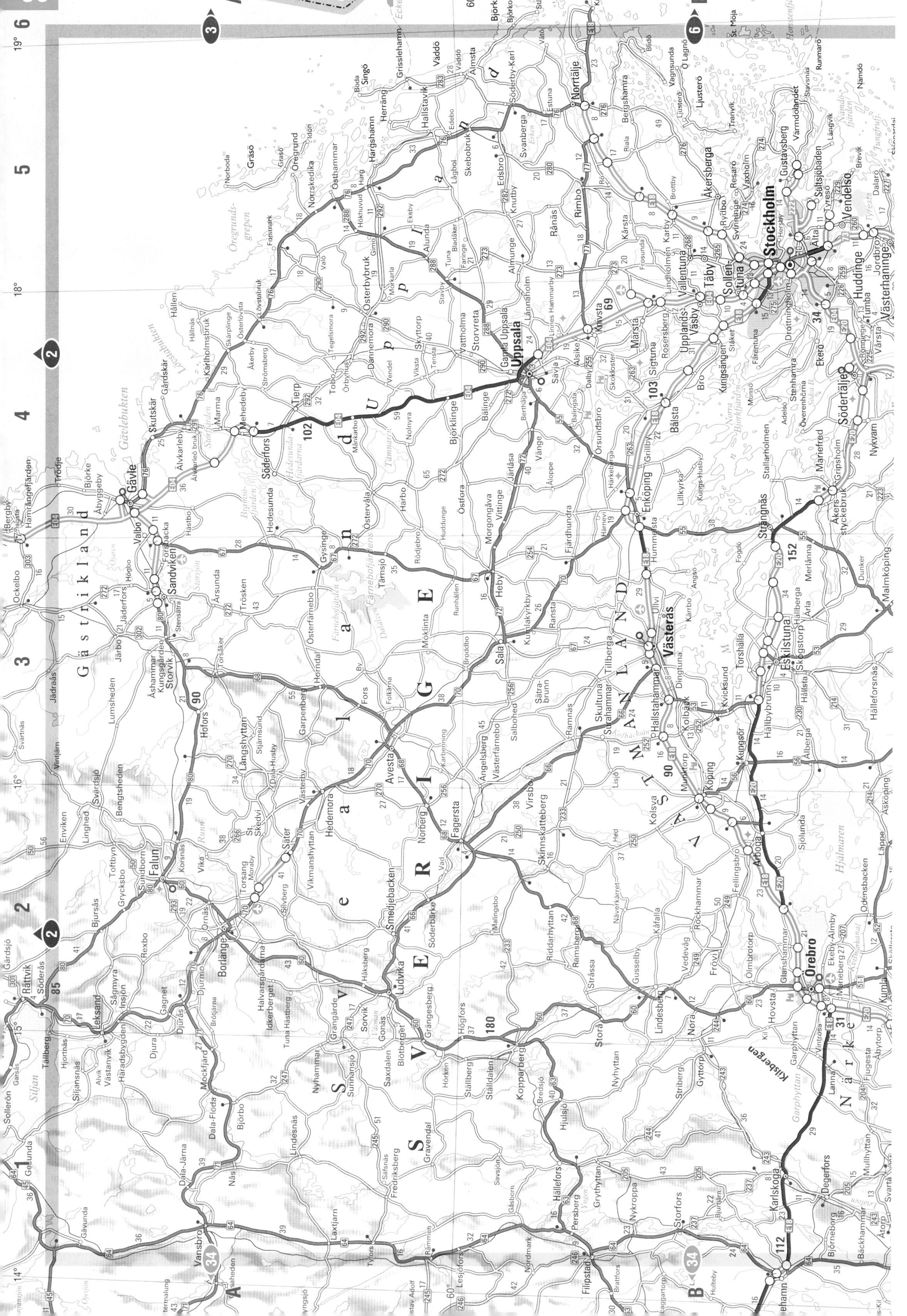
Gästrikland
Uppland
Västmanland
Dalarna
Närke
SVERIGE
Stockholm
Uppsala
Västerås
Örebro
Gävle
Falun
Borlänge
Sandviken
Norrtälje
Enköping
Sala
Avesta
Hedemora
Ludvika
Fagersta
Köping
Arboga
Eskilstuna
Strängnäs
Södertälje
Sigtuna
Märsta
Knivsta
Bålsta
Tierp
Östhammar
Öregrund
Hallstavik
Rimbo
Åkersberga
Täby
Vallentuna
Sollentuna
Upplands-Väsby
Kungsängen
Huddinge
Vendelso
Saltsjöbaden
Gustavsberg
Nynäshamn
Hallstahammar
Kungsör
Lindesberg
Nora
Kopparberg
Smedjebacken
Säter
Hofors
Storvik
Karlskoga
Kumla
Filipstad
Hällefors
Leksand
Rättvik
Vansbro
Gävlebukten
Hjälmaren
Siljan
Kilsbergen

Östergötland
Norrköping
Linköping
Nyköping
Oxelösund
Nynäshamn
Katrineholm
Motala
Vadstena
Mjölby
Tranås
Eksjö
Nässjö
Vetlanda
Hultsfred
Vimmerby
Västervik
Gamleby
Valdemarsvik
Söderköping
Åtvidaberg
Finspång
Askersund
Hallsberg
Karlsborg
Hjo
Gränna
Huskvarna
Ödeshög
Visingsö
Gotland
Visby
Klintehamn
Norrköpings Bukten
Bråviken
Vättern
Tivedens
Holaveden
Gdansk 18:30
Ölands norra udde
Flen
Järna
Trosa
Gnesta
Vingåker
Kisa
Boxholm
Skänninge
Borensberg
Ljungsbro
Aneby
Sävsjö
Vaggeryd
59°
58°
16°
18°
C
D
1
2
3
4
5

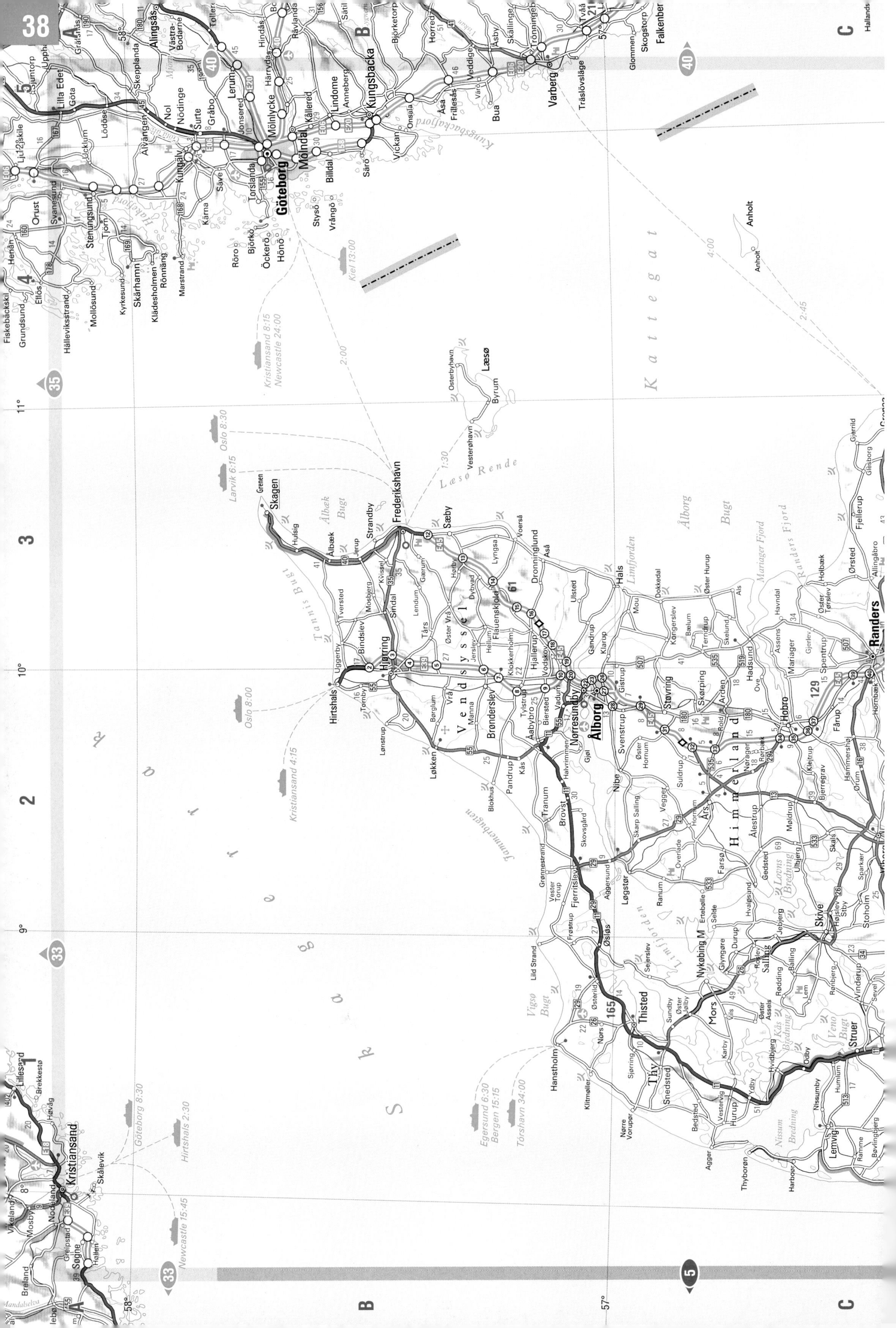
Göteborg
Kungsbacka
Mölndal
Mölnlycke
Alingsås
Kungälv
Stenungsund
Orust
Lilla Edet
Varberg
Falkenberg
Anholt
Læsø
Kattegat
Skagen
Frederikshavn
Sæby
Hirtshals
Hjørring
Brønderslev
Nørresundby
Ålborg
Løkken
Vendsyssel
Himmerland
Hobro
Randers
Løgstør
Fjerritslev
Thisted
Nykøbing M
Mors
Skive
Struer
Lemvig
Hanstholm
Thy
Limfjorden
Ålborg Bugt
Jammerbugten
Tannis Bugt
Læsø Rende
Kristiansand
Søgne
Lillesand
Skagerrak
Oslo 8:30
Larvik 6:15
Oslo 8:00
Kristiansand 4:15
Kristiansand 8:15
Newcastle 24:00
Kiel 13:00
Göteborg 8:30
Hirtshals 2:30
Newcastle 15:45
Egersund 6:30
Bergen 15:15
Tórshavn 34:00
Hallands

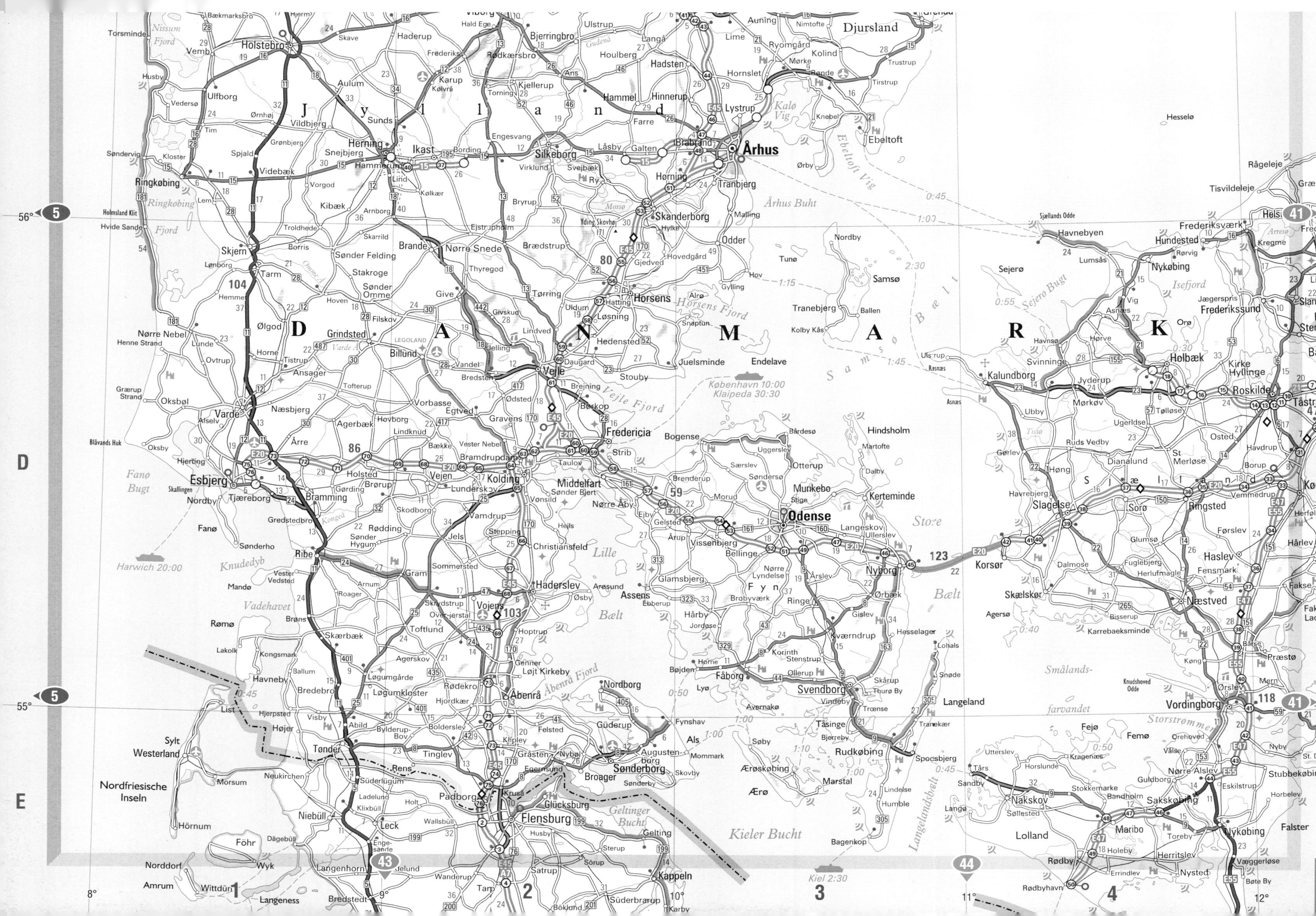
DANMARK
Jylland
Fyn
Sjælland
Djursland
Holstebro
Herning
Ikast
Silkeborg
Århus
Skanderborg
Horsens
Vejle
Fredericia
Kolding
Middelfart
Odense
Nyborg
Svendborg
Fåborg
Esbjerg
Varde
Ribe
Haderslev
Åbenrå
Sønderborg
Tønder
Flensburg
Niebüll
Ringkøbing
Skjern
Grindsted
Billund
Brande
Give
Kalundborg
Holbæk
Roskilde
Slagelse
Sorø
Ringsted
Næstved
Køge
Korsør
Vordingborg
Nakskov
Maribo
Nykøbing
Rødby
Rødbyhavn
Lolland
Falster
Langeland
Rudkøbing
Ærø
Als
Samsø
Fanø
Rømø
Sylt
Föhr
Amrum
Nordfriesische Inseln
Kieler Bucht
Store Bælt
Lille Bælt
Århus Buht
Ebeltoft Vig
Horsens Fjord
Vejle Fjord
Ringkøbing Fjord
Nissum Fjord
Sejerø Bugt
Isefjord
Smålands-farvandet
Storstrømmen
Langelandsbælt
Geltinger Bucht
Vadehavet
Knudedyb
Fanø Bugt
Harwich 20:00
København 10:00
Klaipeda 30:30
Kiel 2:30
Sejerø
Hesselø
Hundested
Frederikssund
Helsinge
Hillerød
Farum
Ballerup
Tåstrup
Greve
Fakse
Præstø
Stege
Sakskøbing
Marstal
Ærøskøbing
Assens
Bogense
Kerteminde
Juelsminde
Odder
Ebeltoft
Grenå
Hammel
Hadsten
Bjerringbro
Viborg
Padborg
Gråsten
Vojens
Gram
Rødding
Brørup
Vejen
Holsted
Bramming
Ølgod
Tarm
Videbæk
Lemvig
Leck
Kappeln
Westerland
Wyk
Wittdün
56°
55°
8°
9°
10°
11°
12°
1
2
3
4
D
E
5
41
43
44
E20
E45
E47
E55

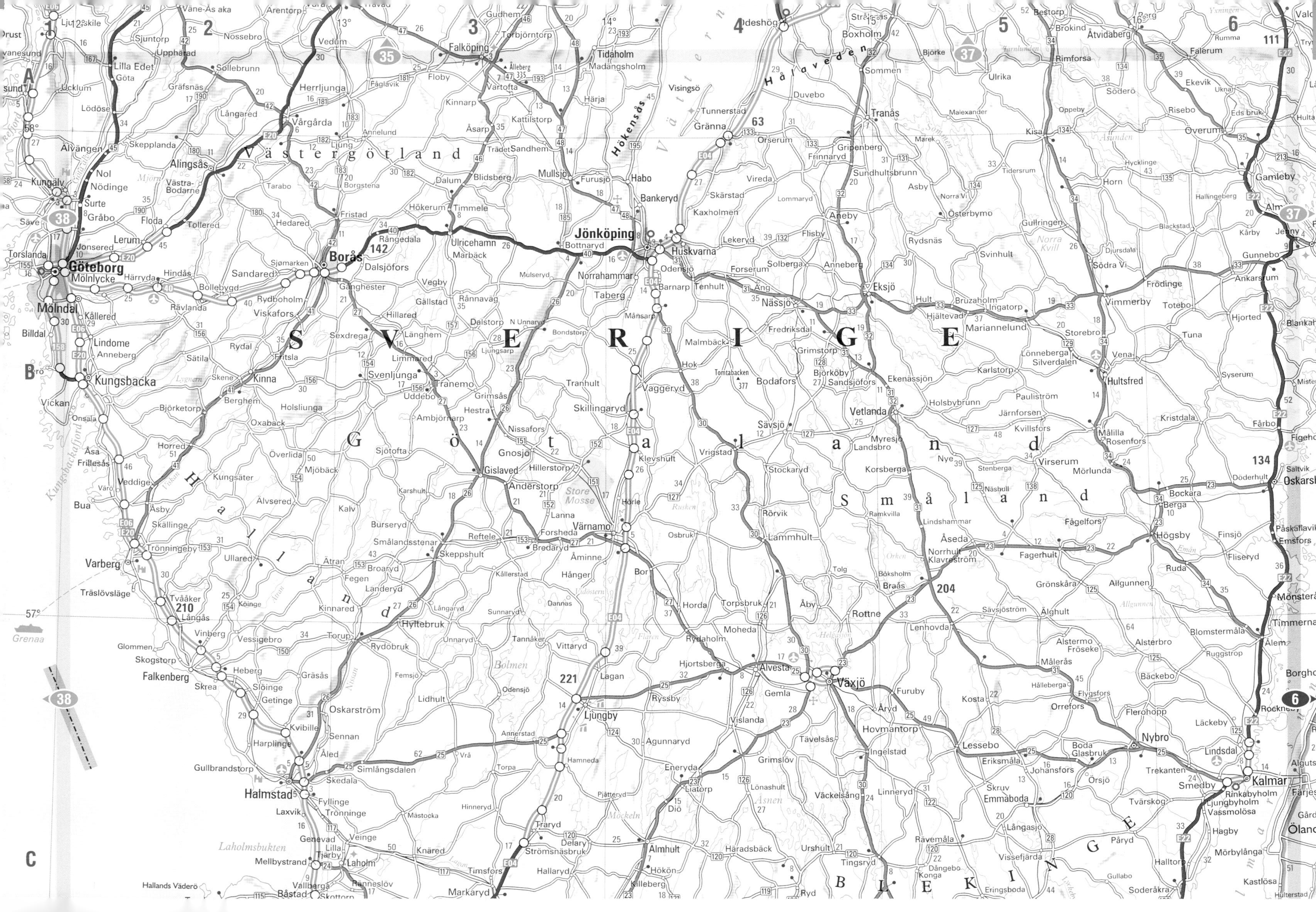
S V E R I G E
Västergötland
Småland
Halland
Blekinge
Öland
Vättern
Göteborg
Borås
Jönköping
Huskvarna
Växjö
Kalmar
Halmstad
Varberg
Falkenberg
Kungsbacka
Alingsås
Kungälv
Mölndal
Falköping
Tidaholm
Gränna
Tranås
Eksjö
Nässjö
Vetlanda
Värnamo
Ljungby
Alvesta
Hultsfred
Vimmerby
Oskarshamn
Västervik
Nybro
Åtvidaberg
Ulricehamn
Gislaved
Laholm
Båstad
Markaryd
Älmhult
Tingsryd
Lessebo
Emmaboda
Västervik
Mönsterås
Högsby
Gamleby
Vaggeryd
Sävsjö
Grenaa
Laholmsbukten
Kungsbackafjord
Bolmen
Åsnen
Store Mosse
Hökensås
Hålaveden
57°
58°

KØBENHAVN
Malmö
Helsingborg
Helsingør
Lund
Landskrona
Trelleborg
Ystad
Simrishamn
Kristianstad
Hässleholm
Karlshamn
Ronneby
Karlskrona
Sölvesborg
Olofström
Ängelholm
Höganäs
Hillerød
Køge
Roskilde
Bornholm
Rønne
Hanöbukten
Bornholmsgattet
Öresund
Køge Bugt
Fakse Bugt
Skälderviken
Pukaviksbukten
Skåne
Falster
Møn
Oslo 16:00
Fredericia 10:00
Rønne 6:00
Klaipeda 21:30
Swinoujście 9:00
Rostock 2:45
Tavemünde 7:00
Swinoujście 6:30
København 6:00
Swinoujście 5:15
Gdynia 10:30
56°
55°
12°
13°
14°
15°
16°
D
E
2
3
4
5
6

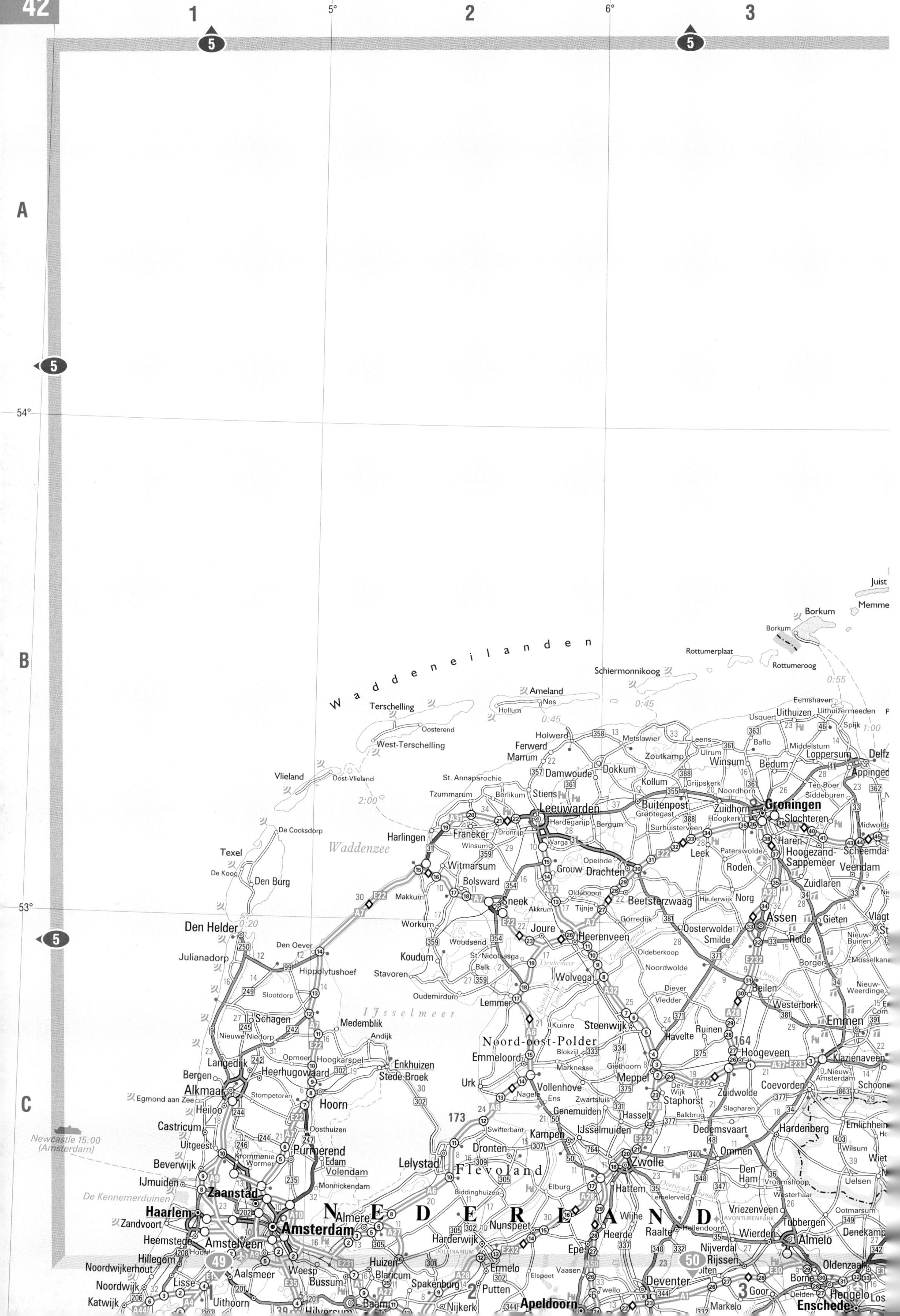
1
2
3
5°
6°
A
B
C
54°
53°
Waddeneilanden
Waddenzee
IJsselmeer
Noord-oost-Polder
Flevoland
NEDERLAND
Terschelling
West-Terschelling
Oosterend
Vlieland
Oost-Vlieland
Ameland
Nes
Hollum
Schiermonnikoog
Rottumerplaat
Rottumeroog
Borkum
Juist
Memmert
Texel
De Cocksdorp
De Koog
Den Burg
Den Helder
Julianadorp
Den Oever
Hippolytushoef
Slootdorp
Schagen
Medemblik
Andijk
Enkhuizen
Stede Broek
Hoorn
Heerhugowaard
Langedijk
Bergen
Alkmaar
Egmond aan Zee
Heiloo
Castricum
Uitgeest
Beverwijk
IJmuiden
Zaanstad
Purmerend
Edam
Volendam
Monnickendam
Haarlem
Zandvoort
Heemstede
Amstelveen
Amsterdam
Almere
Hillegom
Noordwijkerhout
Noordwijk
Katwijk
Lisse
Aalsmeer
Uithoorn
Weesp
Bussum
Huizen
Blaricum
Hilversum
Baarn
Nijkerk
Spakenburg
Putten
Ermelo
Harderwijk
Nunspeet
Elburg
Lelystad
Dronten
Biddinghuizen
Swifterbant
Kampen
Urk
Emmeloord
Lemmer
Harlingen
Franeker
Witmarsum
Bolsward
Makkum
Workum
Koudum
Stavoren
Sneek
Joure
Heerenveen
Wolvega
Leeuwarden
Dokkum
Damwoude
Holwerd
Ferwerd
Marrum
St. Annaparochie
Tzummarum
Stiens
Drachten
Grouw
Beetsterzwaag
Oosterwolde
Steenwijk
Meppel
Zwolle
Hattem
Heerde
Epe
Apeldoorn
Deventer
Raalte
Wijhe
Ommen
Hardenberg
Dedemsvaart
Hoogeveen
Coevorden
Emmen
Klazienaveen
Beilen
Westerbork
Assen
Groningen
Leek
Roden
Haren
Hoogezand-Sappemeer
Veendam
Zuidlaren
Winsum
Bedum
Appingedam
Delfzijl
Uithuizen
Uithuizermeeden
Eemshaven
Nijverdal
Rijssen
Almelo
Wierden
Vriezenveen
Tubbergen
Oldenzaal
Denekamp
Hengelo
Enschede
Borne
Goor
Markelo
Uelsen
Emlichheim
Newcastle 15:00 (Amsterdam)
De Kennemerduinen

4
5
6
8° Nordfriesische Inseln
Morsum
Neukirchen
Süderlügum
Ladelund
Klixbüll
Niebüll
Leck
39
Padborg
Kruså
Glücksburg
Flensburg
Geltinger Bucht
Gelting
Holt
Wallsbüll
Husby
Sterup
Sörup
Kappeln
Hörnum
Föhr
Dägebüll
Wyk
Enge-sande
Norddorf
Amrum
Wittdün
Langeness
Hooge
Langenhorn
Goldelund
Wanderup
Tarp
Satrup
Süderbrarup
Karby
Bredstedt
Böklund
Schlei
Waabs
Schleswig-Holsteinisches Wattenmeer
Pellworm
Ostersiel
Süderoogsand
Suden
Nordstrand
Hattstedt
Viöl
Jübek
Schleswig
Husum
Silberstedt
Ostenfeld
Jagel
Fleckeby
Eckernförde
Osdorf
Hüttener Berge
Schleswig-Holstein
Kropp
Osterhever
Friedrichstadt
Norderstapel
Garding
Tönning
Lunden
Erfde
Hohn
Bovenau
Kronshagen
Büdelsdorf
Rendsburg
St. Peter-Ording
Hennstedt
Jevenstedt
Westensee
Molfs
Wesselburen
Heide
Tellingstedt
Hamdorf
Nortorf
Bordesh
Aukrug
Nord-Ostsee-Kanal
Hemmingstedt
Albersdorf
Hanerau-Hademarschen
Hohenwestedt
Helgoland
Düne
Deutsche Bucht
Büsum
Meldorf
Schafstedt
Nindorf
Trischen
Schenefeld
Hennstedt
Friedrichskoog
Hochdonn
Burg
St. Michaelisdonn
Hohenlockstedt
Kellinghusen
Bad Bramstedt
Marne
Wilster
Itzehoe
Scharhörn
Neuwerk
Harwich 16:45
Lägerdorf
Lentföhrden
Brunsbüttel
Cuxhaven
Wewelsfleth
Brande-Hornerkirchen
Kaltenkirch
Altenwalde
Altenbruch
Freiburg
Krempe
Glückstadt
Barmstedt
Henstedt-Ulzburg
Ostfriesische Inseln
Niedersächsisches Wattenmeer
Wangerooge
Spiekeroog
Langeoog
Baltrum
Mellum
Nordholz
Otterndorf
Neuhaus
Geversdorf
Wischhafen
Cadenberge
Elmshorn
Quickborn
Bülkau
Midlum
Wanna
Ihlienworth
Norderney
Juist
Neuharlingersiel
Carolinensiel
Minsen
Dorum
Neuenwalde
Hemmoor
Drochtersen
Tornesch
Uetersen
Pinneberg
Nessmersiel
Hohenkirchen
Hooksiel
Dornum
Esens
Steinau
Hechthausen
Assel
Bützfleth
Wremen
Debstedt
Lamstedt
Schenefeld
Norddeich
Sengwarden
Langwarden
Burhave
Bad Bederkesa
Stade
Norden
Hage
Westerholt
Wittmund
Sillenstede
Langen
Himmelpforten
Wedel
Jever
Schortens
Nordenham
Bremerhaven
Elm
Jork
HAMBURG
Leerhafe
Wilhelmshaven
Kutenholz
Horneburg
Harburg
Moordorf
Sandhorst
Aurich
Sande
Stollhamm
Abbehausen
Seefeld
Jade-busen
Wehdel
Ebersdorf
Bremervörde
Buxtehude
Ostfriesland
Friedeburg
Horsten
Zetel
Loxstedt
Beverstedt
Harsefeld
Apensen
Harburger Berge
Emden
Wiesmoor
Varel
Schweiburg
Stotel
Rodenkirchen
Kuhstedt
Gnarrenburg
Selsingen
Karlshöfen
Wangersen
Neuenburg
Bockhorn
Jade
Brake
Hagen
Buchholz
Oldersum
Strackholt
Warsingsfehn
Hesel
Remels
Spohle
Ovelgönne
Oldenbrok
Hambergen
Rhade
Zeven
Tostedt
Jesteburg
Ditzum
Dollard
Neermoor
Jemgum
Wiefelstede
Rastede
Schwanewede
Osterholz-Scharmbeck
Tarmstedt
Sittensen
Hanstedt
Lüneburger Heide
Westerstede
Elsfleth
Worpswede
Weener
Augustfehn
Apen
Bad Zwischenahn
Leer
Bunde
Finsterwolde
Nieuweschans
Ritterhude
Grasberg
Scheessel
Barssel
Collinghorst
Oldenburg
Berne
Lemwerder
Lilienthal
Ottersberg
Sottrum
Rotenburg
Schneverdingen
Winschoten
Harkebrügge
Strücklingen
Edewecht
Hude
Bremen
Oyten
Hemslingen
Oude-Pekela
Ostrhauderfehn
Scharrel
Küstenkanal
Delmenhorst
Brockel
Neuenkirchen
Rhede
Papenburg
Wardenburg
Stuhr
Achim
Aschendorf
Burlage
Friesoythe
Hatten
Ganderkesee
Wittorf
Visselhövede
Soltau
Munster
Heede
Bösel
Weyhe
Langwedel
Esterwegen
Surwold
Garrel
Grossenkneten
Syke
Verden
Kirchlinteln
Theding-hausen
Dörpen
Markhausen
Lorup
Dötlingen
Harpstedt
Bomlitz
Dorfmark
Börger
Ahlhorn
Wildeshausen
Walsrode
Fallingbostel
Ter Apel
Lathen
Hümmling
Werlte
Lindern
Molbergen
Wildeshauser Geest
Bassum
Bruchhausen-Vilsen
Martfeld
Sögel
Cloppenburg
Emstek
Visbek
Twistringen
Dörverden
Bergen
Haren
Lastrup
Cappeln
Langförden
Neubruchhausen
Hoya
Rethem
Hodenhagen
Lahden
Löningen
Bakum
Goldenstedt
Asendorf
Eystrup
Vechta
Barnstorf
Sulingen
Marklohe
Schwarmstedt
Winsen
Niedersachsen
Meppen
Herzlake
Essen
Quakenbrück
Steimbke
Haselünne
Menslage
Dinklage
Lohne
Jacobidrebber
Barver
Nienburg
Wietze
Diepholz
Rehden
Liebenau
Mandelsloh
Hambühren
Twist
Berge
Bawinkel
Bersenbrück
Ankum
Holdorf
Steinfeld
Kirchdorf
Wagenfeld
Steyerberg
Landesbergen
Mellendorf
Fuhrberg
Lengerich
Dalum
Lingen
Fürstenau
Schwagstorf
Neuenkirchen
Damme
Ströhen
Stolzenau
Steinhuder Meer
Neustadt
Wedemark
Grossburgw
Alfhausen
Vorden
Dümmer
Leese
Rehburg
Loccum
Uchte
Garbsen
Freren
Messingen
Merzen
Rahden
Lemförde
Haldem
Lavelsloh
Sachsenhagen
Wunstorf
Seelze
Hannover
Nordhorn
Emsbüren
Lünne
Hopsten
Recke
Wiehengebirge
Bramsche
Meyerhöfen
Engter
Espelkamp
Petershagen
Levern
Bohmte
Bad Essen
Hille
Nenndorf
Gehrden
Laatzen
Bad Bentheim
Schüttorf
Rheine
Horstel
Westerkappeln
Wallenhorst
Ostercappeln
Mittelland kanal
Lübbecke
Minden
Stadthagen
Obernkirchen
Barsinghausen
Pattensen
Hohenh
Ibbenbüren
Osnabrück
Bückeburg
Wennigsen
Sarstedt
Gestorf
Ochtrup
Neuenkirchen
Bissendorf
Bad Oeynhausen
Neesen
Holzh
Weserbergland
Springe
Georgsmarien
Melle
Bünde
Dörenthe
Tecklenburg
Verdinkel
Gronau
50
51
44
88
96
97
52
56
104
112
129
135
152
171
1:00

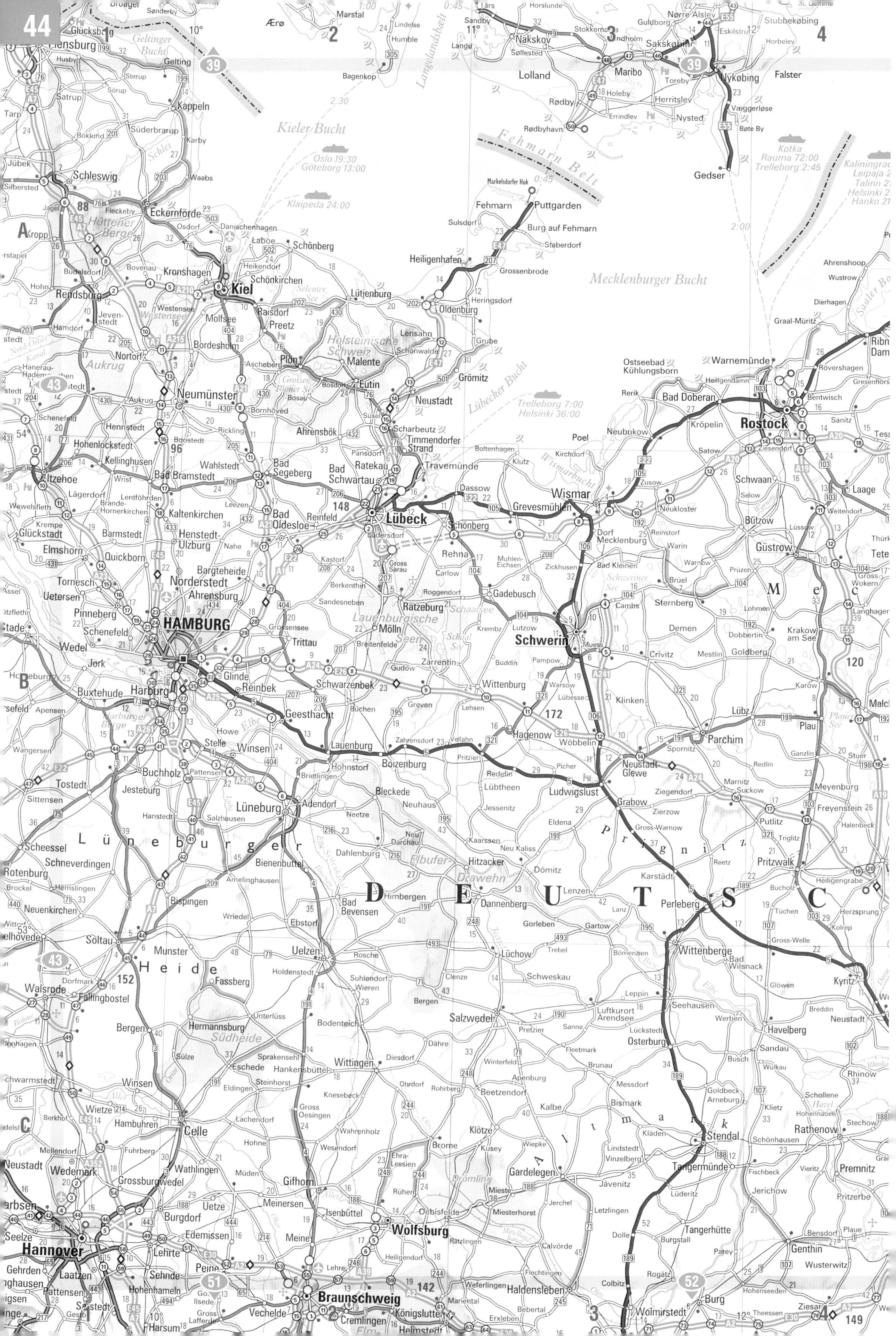
Flensburg
Glücksburg
Geltinger Bucht
Gelting
Kappeln
Marstal
Ærø
Lindelse
Humble
Bagenkop
Langelandsbælt
Tårs
Sandby
Nakskov
Søllested
Langø
Lolland
Maribo
Sakskøbing
Nørre Alslev
Nykøbing
Falster
Stubbekøbing
Holeby
Rødby
Rødbyhavn
Toreby
Herritslev
Nysted
Væggerløse
Bøte By
Gedser
Kieler Bucht
Oslo 19:30
Göteborg 13:00
Klaipeda 24:00
Fehmarn Belt
Markelsdorfer Huk
Puttgarden
Fehmarn
Burg auf Fehmarn
Heiligenhafen
Grossenbrode
Kotka
Rauma 72:00
Trelleborg 2:45
Mecklenburger Bucht
Schleswig
Süderbrarup
Eckernförde
Hüttener Berge
Kropp
Rendsburg
Kronshagen
Kiel
Schönberg
Laboe
Schönkirchen
Lütjenburg
Oldenburg
Heringsdorf
Raisdorf
Preetz
Molfsee
Westensee
Bordesholm
Holsteinische Schweiz
Plön
Malente
Eutin
Lensahn
Grube
Grömitz
Neustadt
Lübecker Bucht
Trelleborg 7:00
Helsinki 36:00
Aukrug
Neumünster
Nortorf
Itzehoe
Hohenlockstedt
Kellinghusen
Bad Bramstedt
Bad Segeberg
Ahrensbök
Scharbeutz
Timmendorfer Strand
Travemünde
Bad Schwartau
Lübeck
Bad Oldesloe
Reinfeld
Kaltenkirchen
Henstedt-Ulzburg
Glückstadt
Elmshorn
Barmstedt
Quickborn
Norderstedt
Bargteheide
Ahrensburg
Tornesch
Uetersen
Pinneberg
Schenefeld
Wedel
HAMBURG
Stade
Jork
Buxtehude
Harburg
Glinde
Reinbek
Geesthacht
Trittau
Grosshansdorf
Ratzeburg
Mölln
Schwarzenbek
Büchen
Lauenburg
Boizenburg
Gadebusch
Rehna
Dassow
Grevesmühlen
Wismar
Poel
Neubukow
Dorf Mecklenburg
Schwerin
Crivitz
Hagenow
Wittenburg
Zarrentin
Ludwigslust
Neustadt-Glewe
Grabow
Parchim
Lübz
Plau
Goldberg
Sternberg
Bützow
Güstrow
Laage
Schwaan
Bad Doberan
Kröpelin
Kühlungsborn
Warnemünde
Rostock
Graal-Müritz
Teterow
Krakow am See
Buchholz
Tostedt
Winsen
Lüneburg
Adendorf
Bleckede
Neuhaus
Dahlenburg
Hitzacker
Dömitz
Lenzen
Lüneburger Heide
Soltau
Munster
Bispingen
Schneverdingen
Rotenburg
Scheessel
Walsrode
Fallingbostel
Bad Bevensen
Uelzen
Bienenbüttel
Dannenberg
Lüchow
Gartow
Gorleben
Wittenberge
Perleberg
Karstädt
Pritzwalk
Meyenburg
Kyritz
Bad Wilsnack
Havelberg
Seehausen
Osterburg
Salzwedel
Prignitz
Elbe
Fassberg
Bergen
Hermannsburg
Südheide
Unterlüss
Celle
Winsen
Wietze
Hambühren
Wedemark
Burgwedel
Burgdorf
Uetze
Lehrte
Sehnde
Hannover
Laatzen
Gehrden
Seelze
Peine
Braunschweig
Wolfsburg
Gifhorn
Wittingen
Hankensbüttel
Klötze
Gardelegen
Kalbe
Bismark
Stendal
Tangermünde
Tangerhütte
Rathenow
Altmark
Haldensleben
Königslutter
Helmstedt
Wolmirstedt
Burg
Genthin
Ziesar
Premnitz

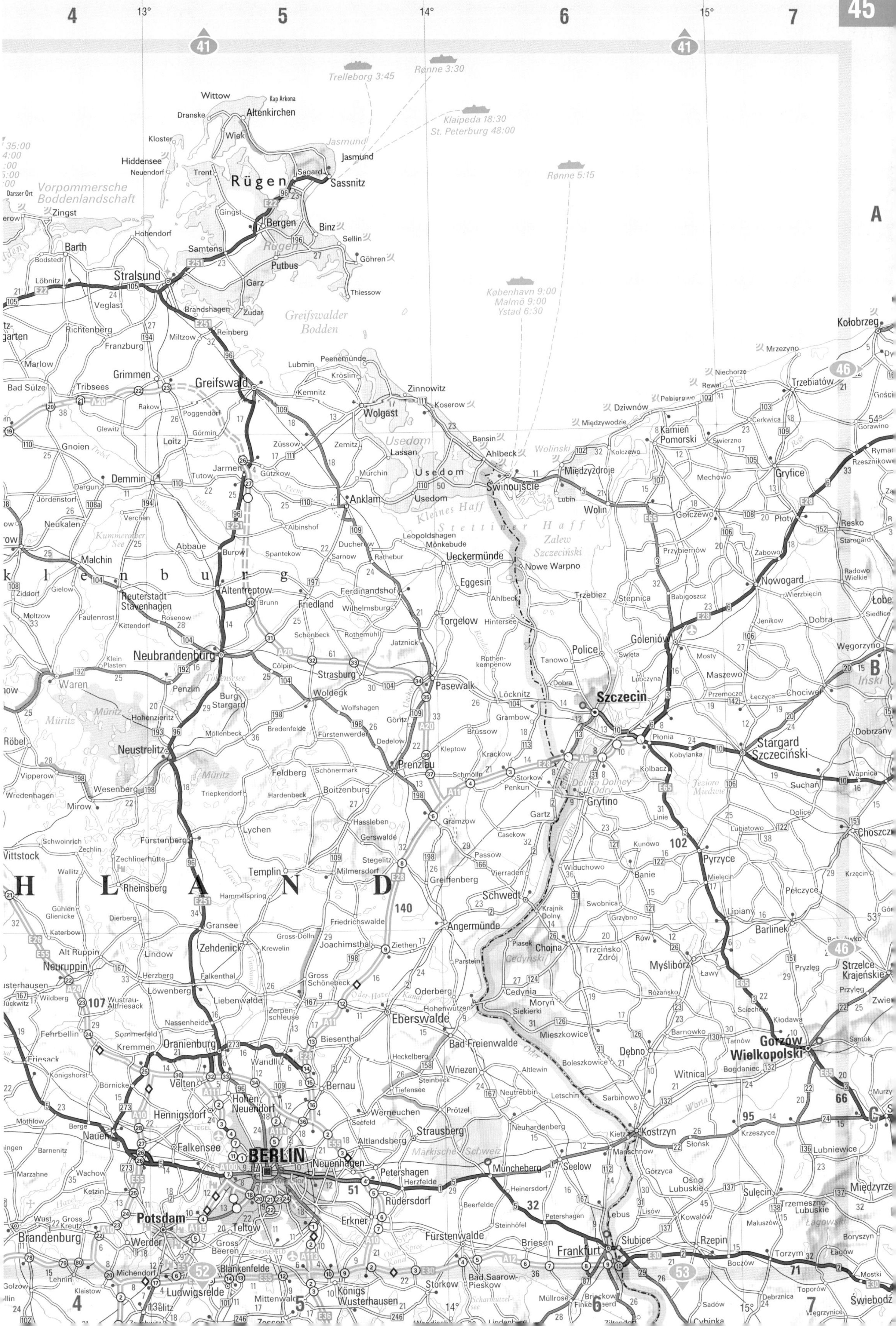
Trelleborg 3:45
Rønne 3:30
Klaipeda 18:30
St. Peterburg 48:00
Rønne 5:15
København 9:00
Malmö 9:00
Ystad 6:30
Rügen
Sassnitz
Bergen
Binz
Stralsund
Vorpommersche Boddenlandschaft
Greifswalder Bodden
Greifswald
Wolgast
Usedom
Anklam
Kleines Haff
Stettiner Haff
Zalew Szczeciński
Ueckermünde
Świnoujście
Międzyzdroje
Wolin
Kamień Pomorski
Kołobrzeg
Trzebiatów
Gryfice
Nowogard
Goleniów
Police
Szczecin
Stargard Szczeciński
Gryfino
Pyrzyce
Neubrandenburg
Demmin
Malchin
Pasewalk
Prenzlau
Neustrelitz
Templin
Schwedt
Angermünde
Chojna
Myślibórz
Gorzów Wielkopolski
Eberswalde
Oranienburg
Bad Freienwalde
Kostrzyn
BERLIN
Potsdam
Brandenburg
Strausberg
Müncheberg
Frankfurt
Słubice
Fürstenwalde
Sulęcin
Międzyrzecz
Świebodzin

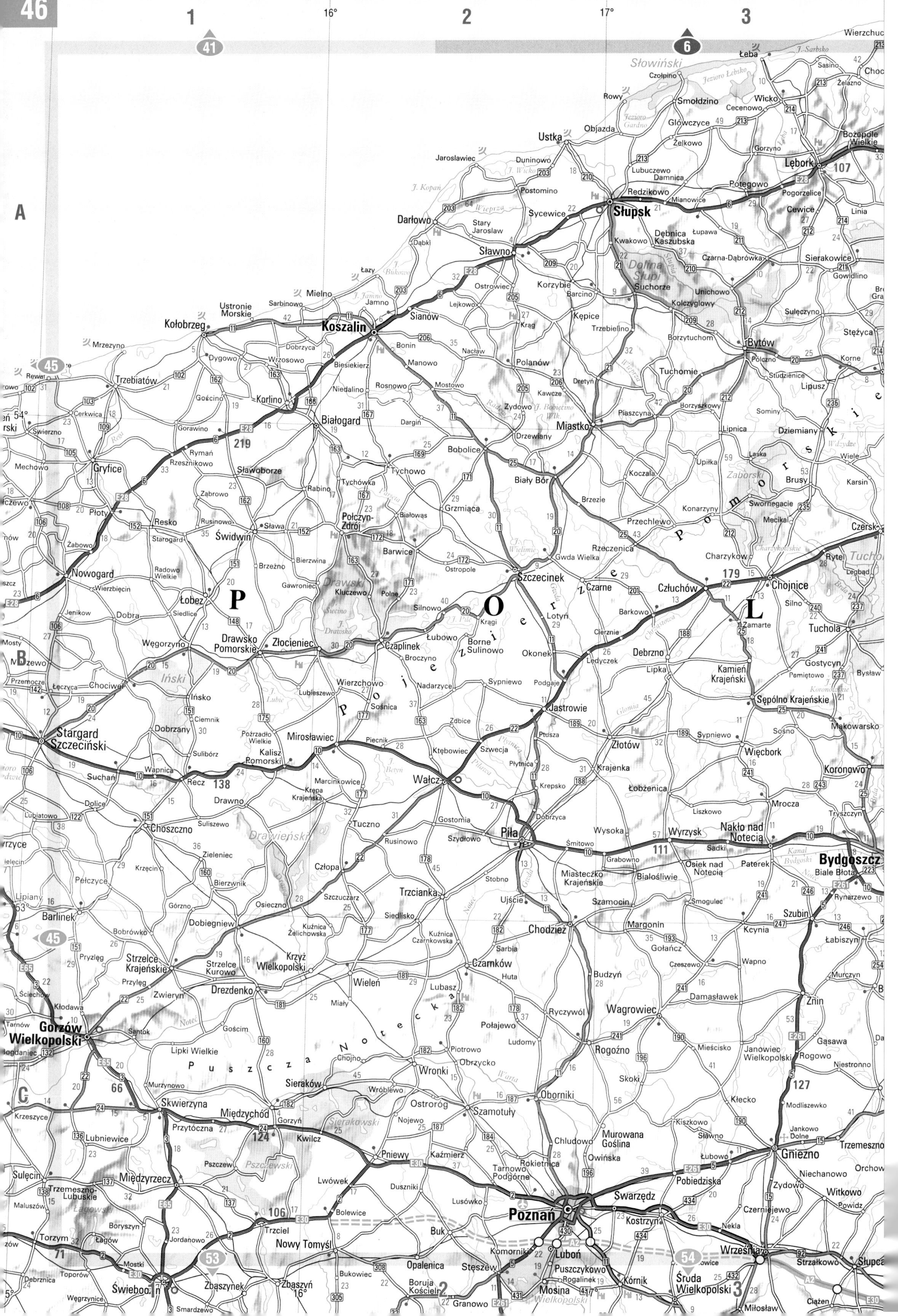

1
2
3
16°
17°
A
B
C
Słupsk
Koszalin
Kołobrzeg
Darłowo
Sławno
Ustka
Łeba
Lębork
Bytów
Miastko
Białogard
Szczecinek
Człuchów
Chojnice
Tuchola
Czersk
Bobolice
Biały Bór
Połczyn-Zdrój
Świdwin
Łobez
Drawsko Pomorskie
Złocieniec
Czaplinek
Nowogard
Gryfice
Trzebiatów
Stargard Szczeciński
Choszczno
Barlinek
Myślibórz
Recz
Kalisz Pomorski
Mirosławiec
Wałcz
Jastrowie
Złotów
Okonek
Krajenka
Piła
Wyrzysk
Nakło nad Notecią
Bydgoszcz
Szubin
Więcbork
Sępólno Krajeńskie
Kamień Krajeński
Chodzież
Trzcianka
Czarnków
Wągrowiec
Rogoźno
Oborniki
Wronki
Sieraków
Szamotuły
Międzychód
Drezdenko
Strzelce Krajeńskie
Gorzów Wielkopolski
Skwierzyna
Międzyrzecz
Pniewy
Poznań
Swarzędz
Gniezno
Kostrzyn
Września
Środa Wielkopolska
Kórnik
Mosina
Luboń
Buk
Opalenica
Nowy Tomyśl
Trzciel
Zbąszyń
Zbąszynek
Świebodzin
Żnin
Janowiec Wielkopolski
Kcynia
Margonin
Budzyń
Murowana Goślina
Pobiedziska
Wielkie
P O L
Pojezierze
Pomorskie
Puszcza Notecka

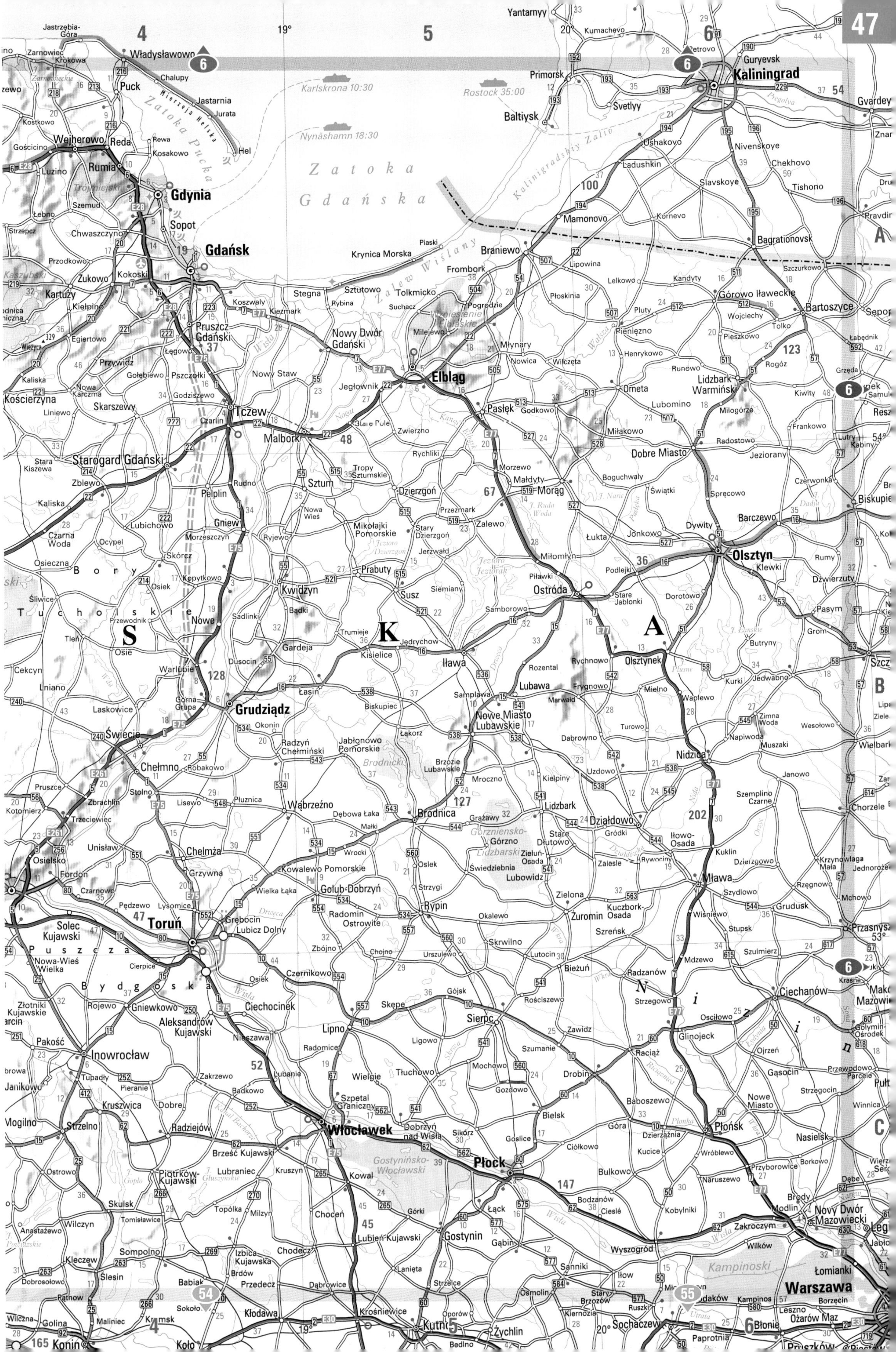

Jastrzębia-Góra
4
19°
5
Yantarnyy
20°
Kumachevo
6
Władysławowo
Karlskrona 10:30
Rostock 35:00
Primorsk
Petrovo
Guryevsk
Kaliningrad
Gvardey
Zarnowiec
Krokowa
Chalupy
Puck
Mierzeja Helska
Jastarnia
Jurata
Zatoka Pucka
Baltiysk
Svetlyy
Pregolya
Kostkowo
Nynäshamn 18:30
Ushakovo
Nivenskoye
Wejherowo
Reda
Rewa
Kosakowo
Hel
Gościcino
Luzino
Rumia
Zatoka Gdańska
Kaliningradskiy Zaliv
Ladushkin
Chekhovo
Slavskoye
Tishono
Trójmiejski
Gdynia
Szemud
Łebno
Sopot
Mamonovo
Kornevo
Bagrationovsk
Chwaszczyno
Strzepcz
Przodkowo
Gdańsk
Krynica Morska
Piaski
Braniewo
Lipowina
Kaszubski
Żukowo
Kokoski
Zalew Wiślany
Frombork
Lelkowo
Kandyty
Szczurkowo
Kartuzy
Sztutowo
Stegna
Tolkmicko
Płoskinia
Górowo Iławeckie
Bartoszyce
Kiełpino
Koszwaly
Kiezmark
Rybina
Suchacz
Pogrodzie
Wzniesienie Elbląskie
Pluty
Wojciechy
Tolko
Pruszcz Gdański
Egiertowo
Nowy Dwór Gdański
Milejewo
Pieniężno
Pieszkowo
Łabędnik
Wieżyca
Przywidz
Łęgowo
Młynary
Henrykowo
Rogóz
Grzęda
Kaliska
Gołębiewo
Pszczółki
Nowy Staw
Elbląg
Nowica
Wilczęta
Runowo
Lidzbark Warmiński
Kościerzyna
Nowa Karczma
Godziszewo
Jegłownik
Orneta
Kiwity
Samulewo
Skarszewy
Tczew
Pasłęk
Godkowo
Lubomino
Liniewo
Czarlin
Stare Pole
Milogórze
Frankowo
Malbork
Zwierzno
Miłakowo
Radostowo
Lutry
Kabiny
Starogard Gdański
Stara Kiszewa
Rychliki
Dobre Miasto
Jeziorany
Zblewo
Tropy Sztumskie
Morzewo
Boguchwały
Czerwonka
Sztum
Rudno
Małdyty
Morąg
Świątki
Spręcowo
Biskupiec
Pelplin
Dzierzgoń
Kaliska
Nowa Wieś
Przezmark
Barczewo
Lubichowo
Gniew
Mikołajki Pomorskie
Stary Dzierzgoń
Zalewo
Dywity
Czarna Woda
Ocypel
Morzeszczyn
Ryjewo
Jerzwałd
Jonkowo
Łukta
Olsztyn
Klewki
Osieczna
Skórcz
Prabuty
Miłomłyn
Rumy
Bory
Kopytkowo
Osiek
Kwidzyn
Susz
Siemiany
Piławki
Ostróda
Podlejki
Dorotowo
Dźwierzuty
Śliwice
Tucholskie
Przewodnik
Nowe
Sadlinki
Bądki
Samborowo
Stare Jabłonki
Pasym
Tleń
Trumieje
Jedrychow
Grom
Osie
Gardeja
Kisielice
Iława
Rozental
Rychnowo
Olsztynek
Butryny
Cekcyn
Warlubie
Dusocin
Lubawa
Frygnowo
Mielno
Kurki
Jedwabno
Lniano
Łasin
Marwald
Waplewo
Laskowice
Górna Grupa
Grudziądz
Biskupiec
Samplawa
Nowe Miasto Lubawskie
Turowo
Zimna Woda
Wesołowo
Świecie
Okonin
Radzyń Chełmiński
Jabłonowo Pomorskie
Łąkorz
Dąbrowno
Napiwoda
Muszaki
Wielbark
Chełmno
Robakowo
Brodnicki
Brzozie Lubawskie
Uzdowo
Nidzica
Janowo
Pruszcz
Mroczno
Kiełpiny
Szemplino Czarne
Kotomierz
Zbrachlin
Stolno
Lisewo
Płużnica
Wąbrzeźno
Brodnica
Grążawy
Lidzbark
Działdowo
Chorzele
Trzeciewiec
Dębowa Łąka
Małki
Górzno
Stare Dłutowo
Gródki
Iłowo-Osada
Unisław
Chełmża
Wrocki
Lidzbarski
Zieluń-Osada
Kuklin
Dzierzgowo
Krzynowłoga Mała
Osielsko
Grzywna
Kowalewo Pomorskie
Oślek
Świedziebnia
Lubowidz
Zalesie
Rywociny
Mława
Jednorożec
Fordon
Czarnowo
Wielka Łąka
Golub-Dobrzyń
Strzygi
Zielona
Szydłowo
Rzęgnowo
Pędzewo
Lysomice
Drwęca
Rypin
Żuromin
Kuczbork-Osada
Mchowo
Solec Kujawski
Toruń
Grębocin
Lubicz Dolny
Radomin
Ostrowite
Okalewo
Szreńsk
Wiśniewo
Grudusk
Stupsk
Przasnysz
53°
Puszcza
Zbójno
Skrwilno
Nowa-Wieś Wielka
Cierpice
Chojno
Urszulewo
Lutocin
Mdzewo
Szulmierz
Bieżuń
Radzanów
Krasne
Bydgoska
Osiek
Czernikowo
Gójsk
Strzegowo
Ciechanów
Maków Mazowiecki
Złotniki Kujawskie
Rojewo
Gniewkowo
Ciechocinek
Skępe
Rościszewo
Aleksandrów Kujawski
Nieszawa
Lipno
Sierpc
Zawidz
Osciłowo
Gołymin-Ośrodek
Pakość
Ligowo
Glinojeck
Inowrocław
Radomice
Szumanie
Raciąż
Ojrzeń
Przewodowo Parcele
Mochowo
Drobin
Gąsocin
Janikowo
Tupadły
Pieranie
Zakrzewo
Lubanie
Wielgie
Tłuchowo
Gozdowo
Pułtusk
Kruszwica
Dobre
Bądkowo
Szpetal Graniczny
Bielsk
Baboszewo
Nowe Miasto
Strzegocin
Mogilno
Strzelno
Radziejów
Kanał Bachorze
Włocławek
Dobrzyń nad Wisłą
Sikórz
Goślice
Góra
Dzierzążnia
Płońsk
Winnica
Nasielsk
Brześć Kujawski
Gostynińsko-Włocławski
Płock
Ciółkowo
Kucice
Wróblewo
Ostrowo
Piotrków-Kujawski
Lubraniec
Kruszyn
Kowal
Bulkowo
Naruszewo
Przyborowice
Borkowo
Dębe
Skulsk
Gopło
Topólka
Milżyn
Choceń
Łąck
Bodzanów
Ciesle
Kobylniki
Brody
Modlin
Nowy Dwór Mazowiecki
Tomisławice
Wilczyn
Górki
Gąbin
Zakroczym
Anastażewo
Lubień Kujawski
Gostynin
Wilków
Sompolno
Izbica Kujawska
Chodecz
Łanięta
Sanniki
Wyszogród
Kampinoski
Łomianki
Kleczew
Ślesin
Brdów
Przedecz
Dąbrowice
Strzelce
Iłow
Warszawa
Dobrosołowo
Babiak
Osmolin
Stary Brzozów
Ruszki
Młodzieszyn
Kampinos
Borzęcin
Patnów
Sokołów
Kłodawa
Krośniewice
Oporów
Kiernozia
Sochaczew
Leszno
Ożarów Maz.
Wilczna
Golina
Maliniec
Kramsk
Kutno
Żychlin
20°
Papro tnia
Błonie
Konin
Koło
Bedlno
Pruszków

Littleport
Ely
Lakenheath
Brandon
Thetford
Diss
Bungay
Oulton Broad
Lowestoft
Beccles
Harleston
Wrentham
Soham
Mildenhall
Scole
Eye
Halesworth
Southwold
Blythburgh
Cottenham
Burwell
Fordham
Ixworth
Newmarket
Bury St. Edmunds
Framlingham
Saxmundham
Leiston
Aldeburgh
Cambridge
Stowmarket
Wickham Market
Needham Market
Hartest
Tunstall
Suffolk Coast And Heaths
Lavenham
Haverhill
Long Melford
Ipswich
Woodbridge
Orford Ness
Saffron Walden
Sudbury
Hadleigh
Kesgrave
Bawdsey
Finchingfield
Dedham Vale
Thaxted
Halstead
Felixstowe
Shotley Gate
Manningtree
Harwich
Stansted Mountfitchet
Bishop's Stortford
Braintree
Coggeshall
Colchester
The Naze
Cuxhaven 16:45
Esbjerg 20:00
Hoek van Holland 3:40
Great Dunmow
Wivenhoe
Sawbridgeworth
Great Waltham
Tiptree
Walton-on-the-Naze
Frinton-on-Sea
Witham
Harlow
Chelmsford
Brightlingsea
West Mersea
Clacton-on-Sea
Chipping Ongar
Danbury
Maldon
South Woodham Ferrers
Shenfield
Billericay
Burnham-on-Crouch
Chigwell
Brentwood
Wickford
Rayleigh
Foulness Island
Romford
Basildon
LONDON
Stanford le Hope
Hadleigh
Southend-on-Sea
Shoeburyness
Canvey
Purfleet
Grays
Northfleet
Thames
Dartford
Gravesend
Grain
Sheerness
Hull 12:45
Rosyth 17:30
Swanley
Rochester
Leysdown on Sea
Gillingham
Orpington
Chatham
Rainham
Sittingbourne
Whitstable
Herne Bay
Margate
North Foreland
Broadstairs
Ramsgate
Faversham
North Downs
Sevenoaks
Hadlow
Maidstone
Canterbury
Ash
Sandwich
Wingham
Sutton Valence
Barham
Deal
Walmer
Tonbridge
Headcorn
Staplehurst
Wye
Ashford
St. Margaret's at Cliffe
South Foreland
Southborough
Royal Tunbridge Wells
Goudhurst
Hawkinge
Newington
Dover
Folkestone
Crowborough
Lamberhurst
The Weald
High Weald
Tenterden
Hawkhurst
Lympne
Hythe
Romney Marsh
Dymchurch
Bodiam
Uckfield
Heathfield
Peasmarsh
Lydd
New Romney
Rye
Battle
Winchelsea
Herstmonceux
Rye Bay
Dungeness
Hailsham
St. Leonards
Hastings
Polegate
Bexhill
Pevensey Bay
Seaford
Eastbourne
Beachy Hd.
Strait of Dover
0:40
0:50
(In Service En Service 31/03/04)
2:00
Blankenberge
De Haan
Oostende
Middelkerke
Oudenburg
Nieuwpoort
Koksijde
De Panne
Ichtegem
Bray Dunes
Veurne
Diksmuide
Koekelare
St. Pol-sur-Mer
Dunkerque
Adinkerke
Gravelines
Loone-Plage
Woumen
Zarren
Calais
Marck
Sangatte
Bergues
Hondschoote
Bourbourg
Vleteren
Roesbrugge
Roeselare
Langemark-Poelkapelle
Wissant
Cap Gris-Nez
Ardres
Audruicq
Wormhout
Poperinge
Guines
Nordausques
Watten
Licques
Steenvoorde
Ieper
Ambleteuse
Marquise
Caps et Marais d'Opale
Cassel
Wimereux
Nausicaa
St. Omer
Arques
Bailleul
Comines
Boulogne-sur-Mer
Le Portel
Escoeuilles
Lumbres
Hazebrouck
Armentières
Outreau
Desvres
Aire-sur-la-Lys
Merville
Hardelot Plage
Samer
Thérouanne
Estaires
Fauquembergues
Estrée-Blanche
Norrent-Fontes
St. Venant
Lille
Hucqueliers
Lillers
Béthune
Étaples
Auchy-au-Bois
Seclin
Le Touquet-Paris-Plage
Fruges
Bruay-la-Buissière
La Bassée
Carvin
Merlimont Plage
Montreuil
Heuchin
Divion
Noeux-les-Mines
Bagatelle
Anvin
Houdain
Berck
Maresquel
St. Pol-sur-Ternoise
Liévin
Lens
Hesdin
Vimy
Hénin-Beaumont
Le Parcq
Cambligeu
Fort-Mahon-Plage
Tincques
Aubigny-en-Artois
Vron
Baie de la Somme
Rue
Frévent
Arras
Crécy-en-Ponthieu
Auxi-le-Château
Avesnes-le-Comte
Le Crotoy
Beaumetz-lès-Loges
Noyelles-sur-Mer
Nouvion
Bouquemaison
La Herlière
St. Valéry-sur-Somme
Cayeux-sur-Mer
Ayette
St. Riquier
Bernaville
Doullens
Vaulx-Vraucourt
Ault
Abbeville
Marieux
Puisieux
Mers-les-Bains
Fressenville
Beauval
Acheux-en-Amienois
Bapaume
Bertincourt
Newhaven 2:00
Newhaven 4:00
Le Tréport
Pont-Remy
Picardie
Puchevillers
Criel-sur-Mer
Eu
Flixecourt
Contay
Albert
Bray-sur-Somme
Biville-sur-Mer
Gamaches
Le Translay
Airaines
Villers-Bocage
Dieppe
Bouttencourt
Oisemont
Picquigny
Corbie
Varengeville-sur-Mer
Ouiberville
Blangy-sur-Bresle
St. Valery-en-Caux
Senarpont
Ailly-sur-Somme
Amiens
Péronne
Veulettes-sur-Mer
Veules-les-Roses
Offranville
Envermeu
Arques-la-Bataille
Fresnoy-Folny
Longueau
Villers-Bretonneux
Villers-Carbonnel
St. Pierre-en-Port
Bacqueville-en-Caux
Londinières
Hornoy-le-Bourg
Chaulnes
Athies
Fontaine-le-Dun
Torcy-le-Petit
Les Grandes-Ventes
Quevauvillers
Rosières
Fécamp

4
5
6
4°
42
Haarlem
Amsterdam
Zaanstad
Almere
Harderwijk
Apeldoorn
Hilversum
Amersfoort
Leiden
Utrecht
's-Gravenhage
Zoetermeer
Gouda
Arnhem
Rotterdam
Dordrecht
Nijmegen
's-Hertogenbosch
Breda
Tilburg
Eindhoven
Helmond
Roosendaal
Bergen op Zoom
Goes
Middelburg
Vlissingen
Hull 12:30
Harwich 3:40
Zeeuws Vlaanderen
Brugge
Antwerpen
Gent
Kortrijk
Mouscron
Roubaix
Tournai
Mechelen
Leuven
Bruxelles
Hasselt
Genk
Maastricht
Liège
Namur
Charleroi
Mons
La Louvière
Valenciennes
Douai
Cambrai
Maubeuge
B E L G I Q U E
Dinant
Rochefort
St. Quentin
Thiérache
Hirson
Bastogne
59
50

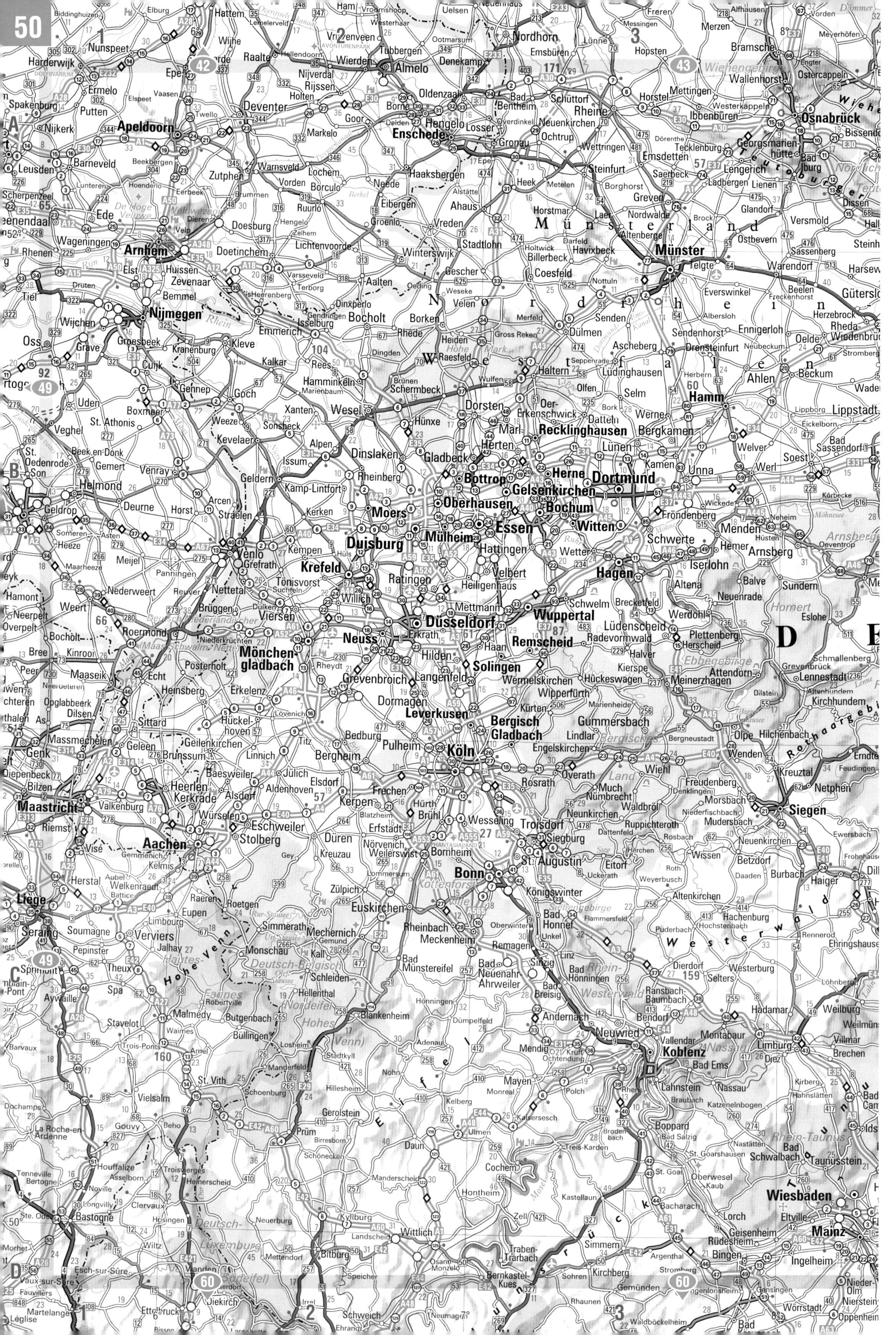
Apeldoorn
Arnhem
Nijmegen
Deventer
Almelo
Enschede
Hengelo
Nordhorn
Osnabrück
Münster
Münsterland
Nordrhein-Westfalen
Dorsten
Recklinghausen
Bottrop
Herne
Dortmund
Gelsenkirchen
Oberhausen
Bochum
Witten
Essen
Moers
Duisburg
Mülheim
Krefeld
Venlo
Hagen
Iserlohn
Hamm
Unna
Düsseldorf
Wuppertal
Neuss
Mönchen-
gladbach
Remscheid
Solingen
Leverkusen
Bergisch
Gladbach
Köln
Roermond
Maastricht
Aachen
Liège
Bonn
Siegen
Koblenz
Wiesbaden
Mainz
Verviers
Hohe Venn
Eifel
Westerwald
Hunsrück
Taunus
Teutoburger Wald
D

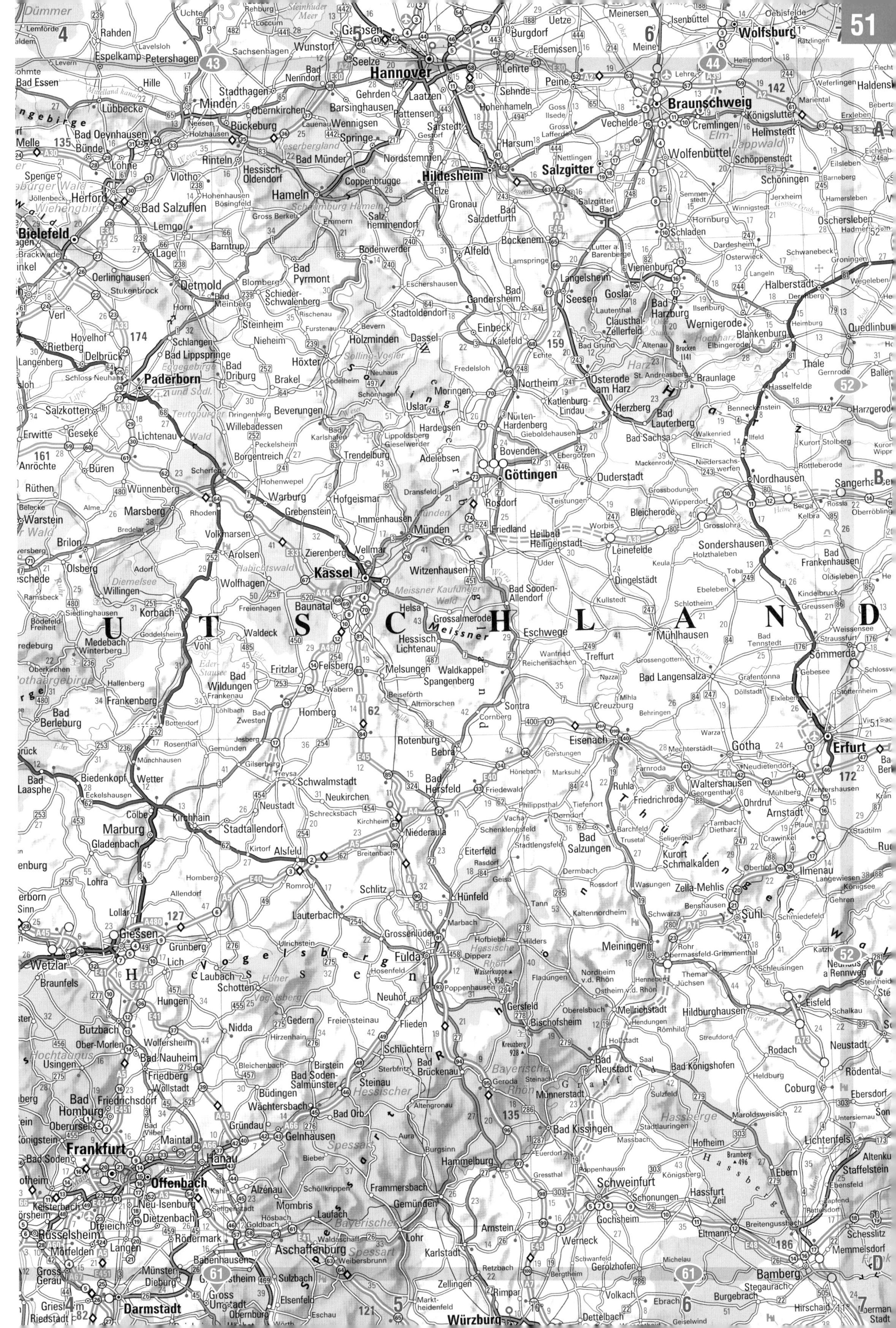

Dümmer
Lemförde
Rahden
Uchte
Rehburg
Steinhuder Meer
Loccum
Garbsen
Burgdorf
Uetze
Meinersen
Isenbüttel
Wolfsburg
Espelkamp
Petershagen
Wunstorf
Seelze
Hannover
Lehrte
Edemissen
Meine
Bad Essen
Hille
Stadthagen
Nenndorf
Gehrden
Laatzen
Sehnde
Peine
Lehre
Flechtingen
Lübbecke
Minden
Obernkirchen
Barsinghausen
Pattensen
Hohenhameln
Braunschweig
Königslutter
Bückeburg
Wennigsen
Sarstedt
Vechelde
Cremlingen
Helmstedt
Melle
Bad Oeynhausen
Bünde
Springe
Harsum
Salzgitter
Wolfenbüttel
Schöppenstedt
Löhne
Rinteln
Bad Münder
Nordstemmen
Hildesheim
Spenge
Vlotho
Hessisch Oldendorf
Coppenbrügge
Elze
Gronau
Schöningen
Herford
Bad Salzuflen
Hameln
Salzhemmendorf
Bad Salzdetfurth
Salzgitter Bad
Oschersleben
Bielefeld
Lemgo
Bockenem
Schladen
Lage
Barntrup
Bodenwerder
Alfeld
Lamspringe
Vienenburg
Halberstadt
Oerlinghausen
Detmold
Bad Pyrmont
Langelsheim
Goslar
Bad Harzburg
Wernigerode
Blankenburg
Quedlinburg
Verl
Horn
Bad Meinberg
Schieder-Schwalenberg
Stadtoldendorf
Bad Gandersheim
Seesen
Clausthal-Zellerfeld
Hovelhof
Rietberg
Delbrück
Schlangen
Bad Lippspringe
Steinheim
Holzminden
Dassel
Einbeck
Kalefeld
Brocken
Thale
Paderborn
Bad Driburg
Brakel
Höxter
Northeim
Osterode am Harz
Braunlage
Hasselfelde
Salzkotten
Beverungen
Uslar
Moringen
Katlenburg-Lindau
Herzberg
Bad Lauterberg
Lichtenau
Willebadessen
Bad Karlshafen
Hardegsen
Nörten-Hardenberg
Bad Sachsa
Erwitte
Geseke
Büren
Borgentreich
Trendelburg
Adelebsen
Bovenden
Göttingen
Duderstadt
Nordhausen
Rüthen
Wünnenberg
Warburg
Hofgeismar
Dransfeld
Rosdorf
Bleicherode
Sangerhausen
Warstein
Marsberg
Grebenstein
Immenhausen
Münden
Friedland
Heilbad Heiligenstadt
Leinefelde
Sondershausen
Brilon
Volkmarsen
Arolsen
Zierenberg
Vellmar
Kassel
Witzenhausen
Bad Frankenhausen
Olsberg
Wolfhagen
Baunatal
Helsa
Bad Sooden-Allendorf
Dingelstädt
Willingen
Korbach
Großalmerode
Mühlhausen
Medebach
Winterberg
Waldeck
Hessisch Lichtenau
Eschwege
Sömmerda
D E U T S C H L A N D
Vöhl
Fritzlar
Felsberg
Melsungen
Waldkappel
Spangenberg
Treffurt
Bad Langensalza
Bad Wildungen
Frankenberg
Bad Berleburg
Homberg
Sontra
Creuzburg
Gotha
Erfurt
Rotenburg
Bebra
Eisenach
Biedenkopf
Wetter
Schwalmstadt
Neukirchen
Bad Hersfeld
Ruhla
Friedrichroda
Waltershausen
Ohrdruf
Arnstadt
Bad Laasphe
Marburg
Kirchhain
Stadtallendorf
Neustadt
Niederaula
Gladenbach
Alsfeld
Eiterfeld
Bad Salzungen
Schmalkalden
Ilmenau
Lohra
Schlitz
Hünfeld
Zella-Mehlis
Suhl
Lauterbach
Giessen
Grünberg
Grossenlüder
Fulda
Meiningen
Wetzlar
Lich
Laubach
Schotten
Braunfels
Hungen
Neuhof
Gersfeld
Bischofsheim
Mellrichstadt
Hildburghausen
Eisfeld
Neustadt
Butzbach
Nidda
Gedern
Flieden
Schlüchtern
Bad Neustadt
Bad Königshofen
Rodach
Coburg
Usingen
Bad Nauheim
Friedberg
Wölfersheim
Bad Soden-Salmünster
Bad Brückenau
Münnerstadt
Bad Homburg
Friedrichsdorf
Büdingen
Wächtersbach
Bad Orb
Steinau
Bad Kissingen
Gründau
Gelnhausen
Maintal
Hanau
Hammelburg
Hofheim
Lichtenfels
Frankfurt
Offenbach
Neu-Isenburg
Dietzenbach
Alzenau
Mombris
Frammersbach
Gemünden
Schweinfurt
Hassfurt
Zeil
Staffelstein
Rüsselsheim
Dreieich
Langen
Rödermark
Aschaffenburg
Lohr
Arnstein
Werneck
Gochsheim
Eltmann
Mörfelden
Babenhausen
Karlstadt
Gerolzhofen
Bamberg
Groß-Gerau
Münster
Dieburg
Sulzbach
Zellingen
Rimpar
Volkach
Burgebrach
Darmstadt
Gross Umstadt
Elsenfeld
Würzburg
Dettelbach
Ebrach
Riedstadt

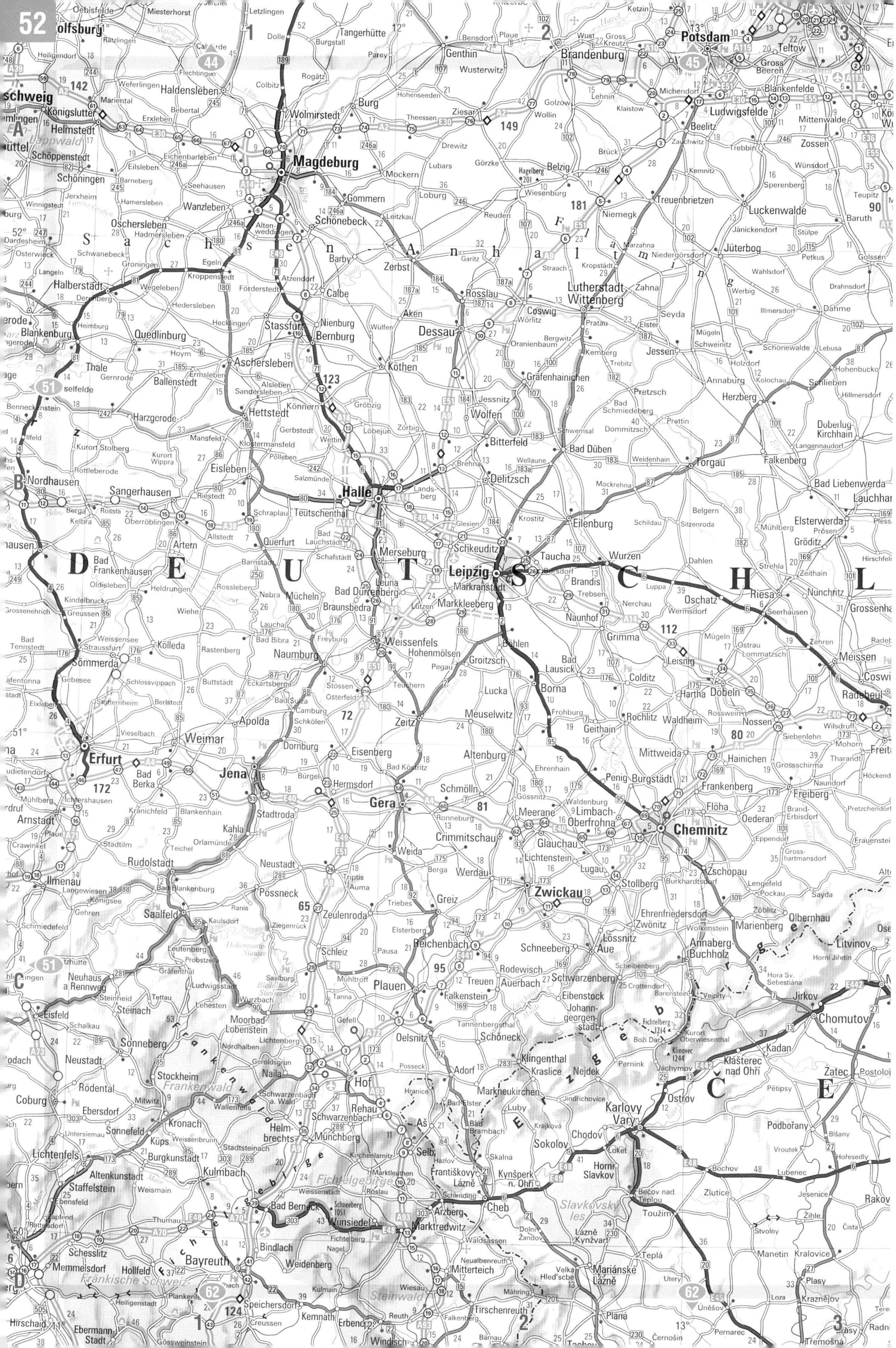
Wolfsburg
Tangerhütte
Genthin
Brandenburg
Potsdam
Teltow
Braunschweig
Königslutter
Helmstedt
Haldensleben
Wolmirstedt
Burg
Ludwigsfelde
Magdeburg
Schöningen
Belzig
Zossen
Oschersleben
Wanzleben
Gommern
Schönebeck
Treuenbrietzen
Luckenwalde
Sachsen-Anhalt
Fläming
Jüterbog
Halberstadt
Zerbst
Calbe
Roßlau
Coswig
Lutherstadt Wittenberg
Blankenburg
Quedlinburg
Staßfurt
Nienburg
Bernburg
Aken
Dessau
Jessen
Aschersleben
Köthen
Gräfenhainichen
Herzberg
Hettstedt
Könnern
Wolfen
Bitterfeld
Bad Düben
Torgau
Eisleben
Delitzsch
Nordhausen
Sangerhausen
Halle
Eilenburg
Bad Liebenwerda
Elsterwerda
Querfurt
Merseburg
Schkeuditz
Leipzig
Taucha
Wurzen
DEUTSCHLAND
Bad Frankenhausen
Mücheln
Markkleeberg
Oschatz
Riesa
Großenhain
Sömmerda
Weißenfels
Naumburg
Grimma
Meißen
Borna
Colditz
Döbeln
Apolda
Zeitz
Nossen
Erfurt
Weimar
Jena
Eisenberg
Altenburg
Mittweida
Freital
Arnstadt
Gera
Schmölln
Burgstädt
Frankenberg
Freiberg
Stadtroda
Meerane
Glauchau
Chemnitz
Rudolstadt
Kahla
Crimmitschau
Ilmenau
Neustadt
Pößneck
Werdau
Zwickau
Stollberg
Saalfeld
Greiz
Zschopau
Zeulenroda
Reichenbach
Marienberg
Olbernhau
Litvínov
Schleiz
Aue
Annaberg-Buchholz
Plauen
Auerbach
Schwarzenberg
Eisfeld
Chomutov
Jirkov
Sonneberg
Oelsnitz
Erzgebirge
Kadaň
Coburg
Naila
Hof
Klingenthal
Kraslice
Nejdek
Klášterec nad Ohří
Žatec
Kronach
Rehau
Schwarzenbach
Karlovy Vary
Ostrov
Lichtenfels
Selb
Sokolov
Chodov
Kulmbach
Fichtelgebirge
Cheb
Wunsiedel
Marktredwitz
Bayreuth
Mariánské Lázně
Bamberg
Tirschenreuth
Plasy

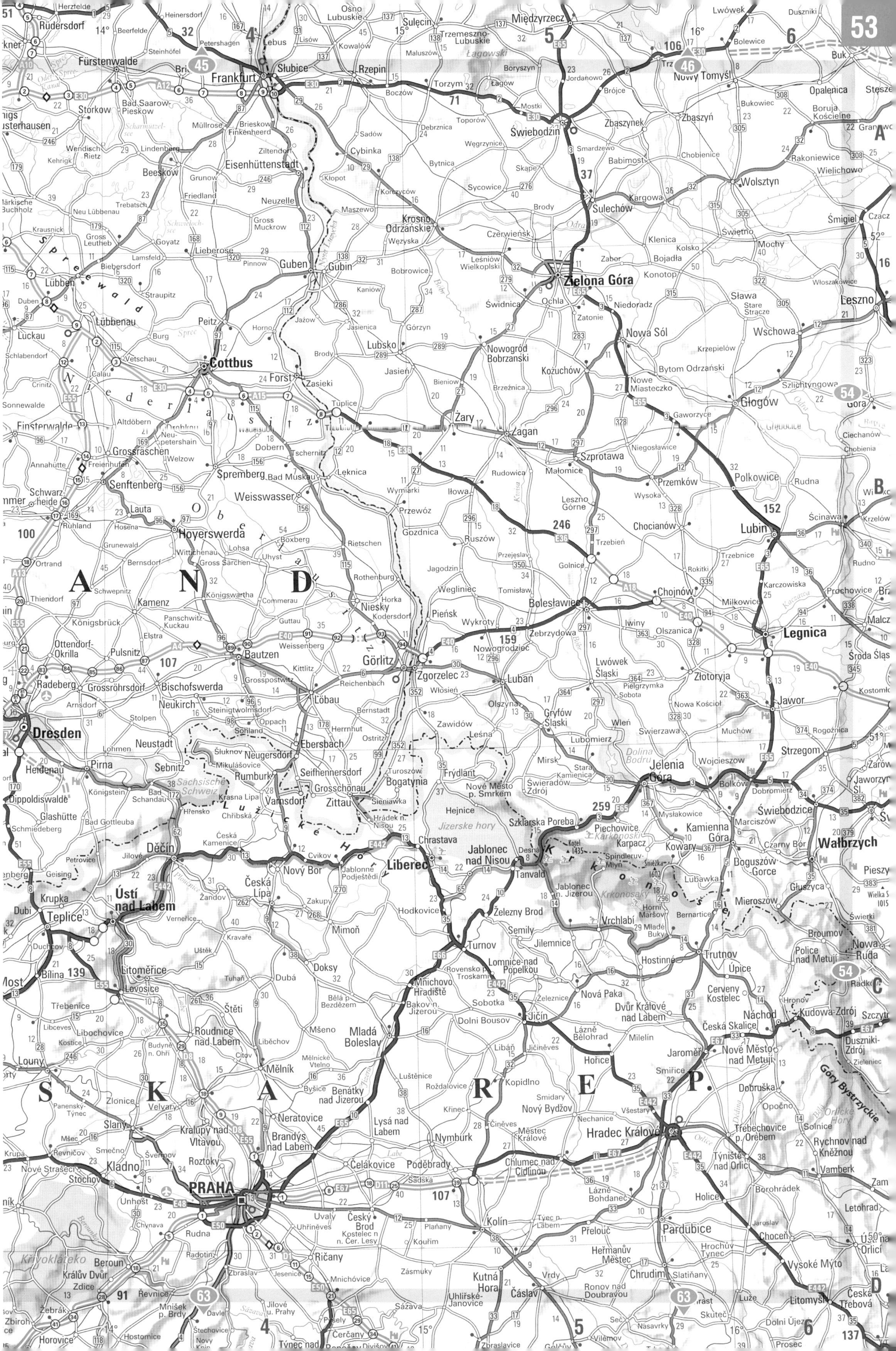

Frankfurt
Słubice
Fürstenwalde
Rüdersdorf
Storkow
Eisenhüttenstadt
Beeskow
Guben
Gubin
Lübben
Lübbenau
Cottbus
Forst
Spremberg
Senftenberg
Hoyerswerda
Weisswasser
Bad Muskau
Niesky
Görlitz
Zgorzelec
Bautzen
Löbau
Kamenz
Bischofswerda
Dresden
Pirna
Sebnitz
Neugersdorf
Rumburk
Varnsdorf
Zittau
Ebersbach
Děčín
Ústí nad Labem
Teplice
Litoměřice
Lovosice
Česká Lípa
Nový Bor
Liberec
Jablonec nad Nisou
Turnov
Mladá Boleslav
Mělník
Kralupy nad Vltavou
Kladno
PRAHA
Beroun
Brandýs nad Labem
Nymburk
Poděbrady
Kolín
Kutná Hora
Čáslav
Pardubice
Hradec Králové
Jičín
Trutnov
Náchod
Jaroměř
Litomyšl
Vysoké Mýto
Wałbrzych
Jelenia Góra
Legnica
Lubin
Głogów
Polkowice
Bolesławiec
Lubań
Żary
Żagań
Nowa Sól
Zielona Góra
Sulechów
Świebodzin
Międzyrzecz
Nowy Tomyśl
Wolsztyn
Leszno
Krosno Odrzańskie
Lubsko
Szprotawa
Chojnów
Złotoryja
Jawor
Kudowa-Zdrój
Karkonosze
Jizerske hory
Krkonoše
Lužické Hory
SAND
SKA
REP

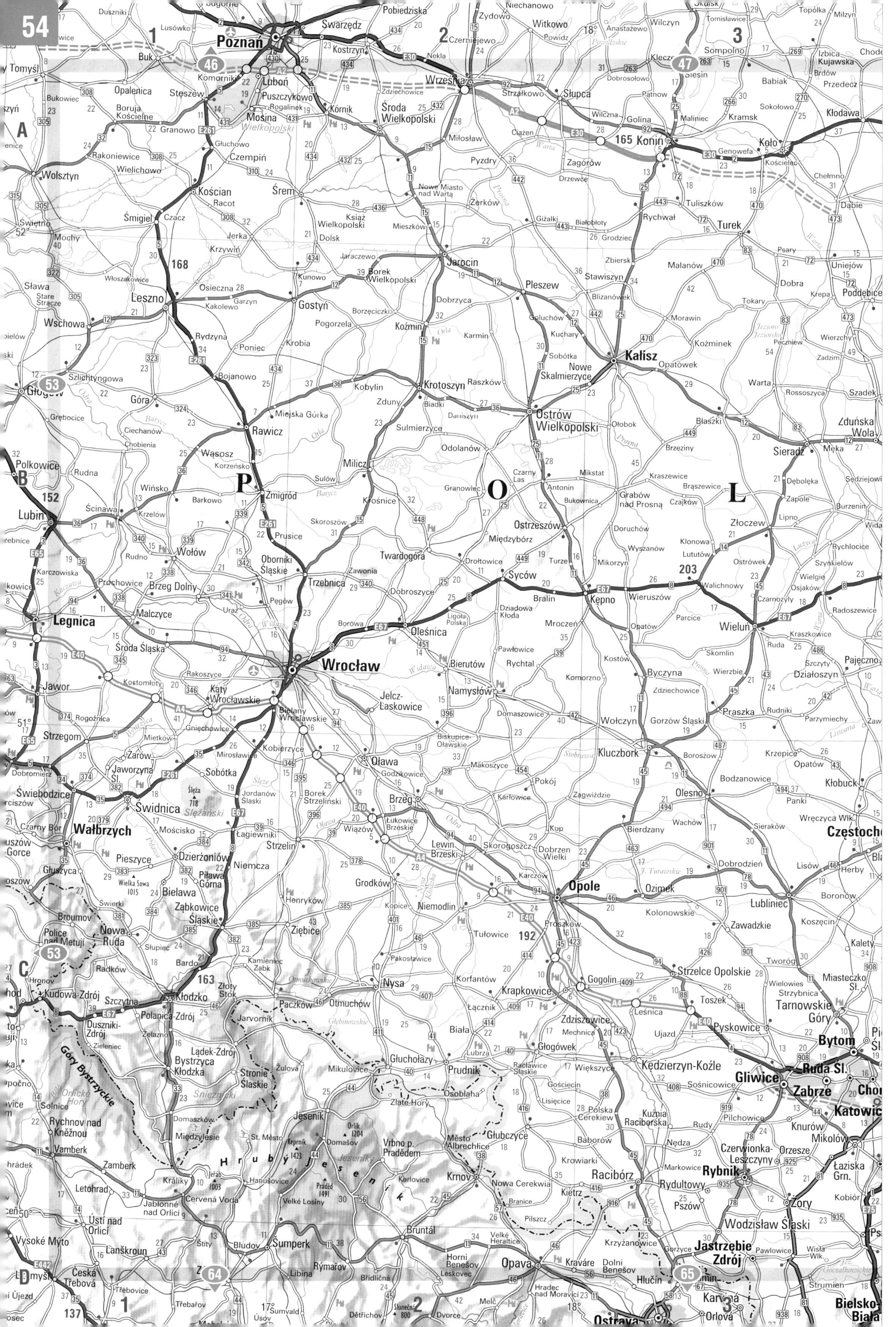
Poznań
Swarzędz
Kostrzyn
Września
Komorniki
Luboń
Puszczykowo
Mosina
Kórnik
Środa Wielkopolski
Konin
Koło
Kłodawa
Słupca
Wolsztyn
Kościan
Śmigiel
Śrem
Leszno
Gostyń
Jarocin
Pleszew
Kalisz
Turek
Wschowa
Głogów
Rawicz
Krotoszyn
Ostrów Wielkopolski
Sieradz
Zduńska Wola
Polkowice
Lubin
Legnica
Wołów
Trzebnica
Oleśnica
Syców
Kępno
Wieluń
Wrocław
Oława
Brzeg
Namysłów
Kluczbork
Opole
Strzelce Opolskie
Świdnica
Wałbrzych
Dzierżoniów
Kłodzko
Nysa
Prudnik
Kędzierzyn-Koźle
Racibórz
Gliwice
Zabrze
Rybnik
Wodzisław Śląski
Jastrzębie Zdrój
Tarnowskie Góry
Bytom
Częstochowa
Lubliniec
Ostrava
Opava
Krnov
Šumperk
Jeseník
Bruntál
P
O
L
A
B
C
D
1
2
3
46
47
53
64
65

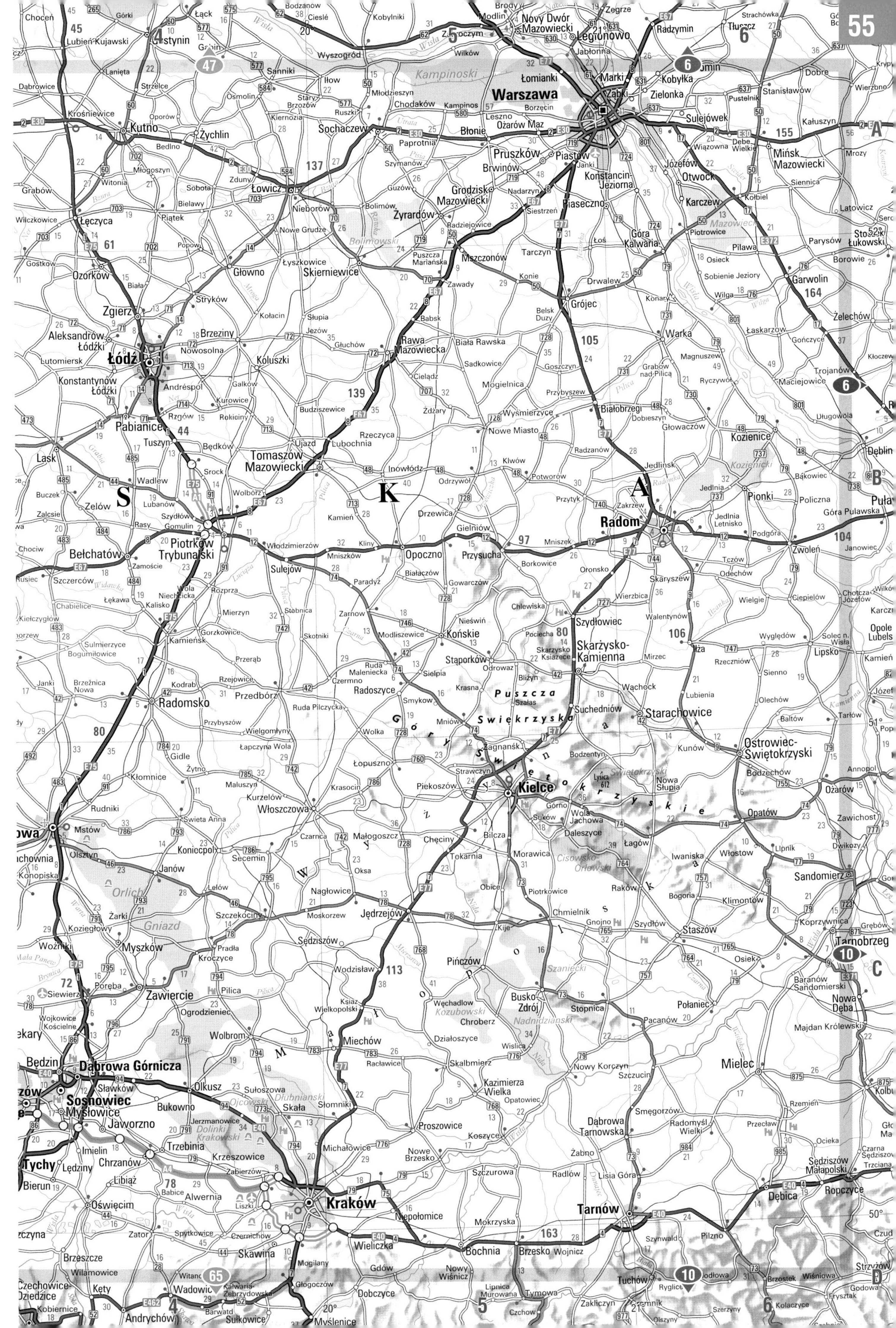
Chocen
Lubień Kujawski
Gostynin
Gąbin
Łąck
Bodzanów
Ciesłe
Kobylniki
Modlin
Nowy Dwór Mazowiecki
Zegrze
Legionowo
Radzymin
Tłuszcz
Strachówka
Wyszogród
Zakroczym
Wilków
Jabłonna
Łaniętą
Sanniki
Iłow
Kampinoski
Łomianki
Marki
Kobyłka
Dobre
Dąbrowice
Strzelce
Osmolin
Młodzieszyn
Warszawa
Ząbki
Zielonka
Stanisławów
Krośniewice
Kutno
Oporów
Brzozów
Chodaków
Kampinos
Borzęcin
Pustelnik
Sulejówek
Kałuszyn
Żychlin
Kiernozia
Sochaczew
Leszno
Ożarów Maz
Błonie
Paprotnia
Wiązowna
Dębe Wielkie
Mińsk Mazowiecki
Mrozy
Bedlno
Szymanów
Pruszków
Piastów
Grabów
Witonia
Łowicz
Brwinów
Janki
Józefów
Otwock
Konstancin-Jeziorna
Grodzisk Mazowiecki
Nadarzyn
Siennica
Sobota
Zduny
Guzów
Nieborów
Bolimów
Żyrardów
Radziejowice
Piaseczno
Karczew
Kołbiel
Latowicz
Wilczkowice
Łęczyca
Piątek
Bielawy
Siestrzeń
Mazowiecki
Nowe Grudze
Puszcza Mariańska
Mszczonów
Tarczyn
Góra Kalwaria
Piotrowice
Parysów
Stoczek Łukowski
Pilawa
Osieck
Borowie
Ozorków
Gostków
Łyszkowice
Skierniewice
Głowno
Konie
Drwalew
Sobienie Jeziory
Garwolin
Biała
Zawady
Grójec
Konary
Wilga
Zgierz
Stryków
Kołacin
Słupia
Babsk
Belsk Duży
Żelechów
Aleksandrów Łódzki
Brzeziny
Jeżów
Rawa Mazowiecka
Biała Rawska
Warka
Łaskarzew
Gończyce
Łódź
Nowosolna
Głuchów
Koluszki
Sadkowice
Goszczyn
Magnuszew
Grabów nad Pilicą
Ryczywół
Trojanów
Maciejowice
Kłoczew
Lutomiersk
Konstantynów Łódzki
Andrespol
Galków
Cielądz
Mogielnica
Przybyszew
Kurowice
Rzgów
Rokiciny
Budziszewice
Żdżary
Wyśmierzyce
Białobrzegi
Dobieszyn
Głowaczów
Długowola
Pabianice
Tuszyn
Nowe Miasto
Rzeczyca
Lubochnia
Kozienice
Radzanów
Dęblin
Lask
Będków
Ujazd
Tomaszów Mazowiecki
Inowłódz
Odrzywół
Klwów
Potworów
Jedlińsk
Bąkowiec
Srock
Wadlew
Buczek
Zelów
Lubanów
Wolbórz
Drzewica
Przytyk
Zakrzew
Jedlnia
Pionki
Policzna
Puławy
Zalesie
Szydłów
Gomulin
Rasy
Kamień
Gielniów
Radom
Jedlnia Letnisko
Góra Puławska
Podgóra
Zwoleń
Janowiec
Chociw
Bełchatów
Piotrków Trybunalski
Włodzimierzów
Kliny
Opoczno
Przysucha
Mniszek
Mniszków
Borkowice
Orońsko
Tczów
Odechów
Chotcza Józefów
Rusiec
Szczerców
Zamoście
Sulejów
Białaczów
Paradyż
Gowarczów
Skaryszew
Chabielice
Łękawa
Wola Niechcicka
Kalisko
Rozprza
Stobnica
Chlewiska
Wierzbica
Wielgie
Ciepielów
Kiełczygłów
Mierzyn
Żarnów
Nieświń
Szydłowiec
Walentynów
Karczmiska
Gorzkowice
Skotniki
Modliszewice
Końskie
Pociecha
Skarżysko Książęce
Skarżysko-Kamienna
Wyględów
Opole Lubelskie
Solec n. Wisłą
Sulmierzyce
Bogumiłowice
Kamieńsk
Przerąb
Ruda Maleniecka
Stąporków
Odrowąż
Mirzec
Iłża
Lipsko
Rzeczniów
Kamień
Janki
Brzeźnica Nowa
Rzejowice
Kodrab
Radomsko
Przedbórz
Czermno
Radoszyce
Siełpia
Krasna
Bliżyn
Wąchock
Sienno
Lubienia
Olechów
Józefów
Ruda Pilczycka
Smyków
Puszcza Świętokrzyska
Szałas
Suchedniów
Starachowice
Bałtów
Tarłów
Przybyszów
Wielgomłyny
Mniów
Wolka
Góry Świętokrzyskie
Łapczyna Wola
Gidle
Żytno
Łopuszno
Zagnańsk
Bodzentyn
Kunów
Ostrowiec-Świętokrzyski
Kłomnice
Maluszyn
Kurzelów
Krasocin
Piekoszów
Strawczyn
Kielce
Łysica 612
Nowa Słupia
Bodzechów
Ożarów
Annopol
Rudniki
Włoszczowa
Górno
Wola Jachowa
Suków
Opatów
Zawichost
Święta Anna
Mstów
Czarnca
Małogoszcz
Chęciny
Bilcza
Daleszyce
Łagów
Iwaniska
Włostów
Lipnik
Dwikozy
Olsztyn
Koniecpol
Secemin
Tokarnia
Morawica
Cisowsko-Orłowski
Sandomierz
Konopiska
Janów
Oksa
Orlich
Obice
Piotrkowice
Raków
Bogoria
Klimontów
Lelów
Nagłowice
Chmielnik
Żarki
Gniazd
Szczekociny
Moskorzew
Jędrzejów
Kije
Gnojno
Szydłów
Staszów
Koprzywnica
Grębów
Tarnobrzeg
Koziegłowy
Woźniki
Myszków
Pradła
Kroczyce
Sędziszów
Osiek
Pińczów
Szaniecki
Siewierz
Poręba
Zawiercie
Pilica
Wodzisław
Książ Wielkopolski
Węchadłów
Kozubowski
Chroberz
Busko Zdrój
Stopnica
Nadnidziański
Połaniec
Baranów Sandomierski
Nowa Dęba
Wojkowice Kościelne
Ogrodzieniec
Wolbrom
Miechów
Działoszyce
Wiślica
Pacanów
Majdan Królewski
Będzin
Dąbrowa Górnicza
Racławice
Skalbmierz
Nowy Korczyn
Szczucin
Mielec
Sosnowiec
Sławków
Olkusz
Sułoszowa
Kazimierza Wielka
Opatowiec
Mysłowice
Bukowno
Jerzmanowice
Ojcowski
Dłubniański
Skała
Słomniki
Smęgorzów
Radomyśl Wielki
Rzemień
Kolbuszowa
Jaworzno
Dolinki Krakowskie
Proszowice
Koszyce
Dąbrowa Tarnowska
Przecław
Imielin
Trzebinia
Krzeszowice
Michałowice
Nowe Brzesko
Żabno
Ocieka
Tychy
Lędziny
Chrzanów
Zabierzów
Szczurowa
Radłów
Lisia Góra
Sędziszów Małopolski
Trzciana
Bieruń
Libiąż
Babice
Alwernia
Liszki
Kraków
Niepołomice
Tarnów
Dębica
Ropczyce
Oświęcim
Zator
Spytkowice
Czernichów
Mokrzyska
Brzesko
Wojnicz
Szynwałd
Pilzno
Brzeszcze
Skawina
Wieliczka
Bochnia
Wilamowice
Mogilany
Gdów
Nowy Wiśnicz
Lipnica Murowana
Tymowa
Tuchów
Ryglice
Jodłowa
Brzostek
Wiśniowa
Strzyżów
Czechowice-Dziedzice
Kęty
Wadowice
Kalwaria Zebrzydowska
Głogoczów
Dobczyce
Czchów
Zakliczyn
Gromnik
Szerzyny
Frysztak
Godowa
Kobiernice
Andrychów
Barwałd
Sułkowice
Myślenice
Olszyny
Kolaczyce
S
K
A

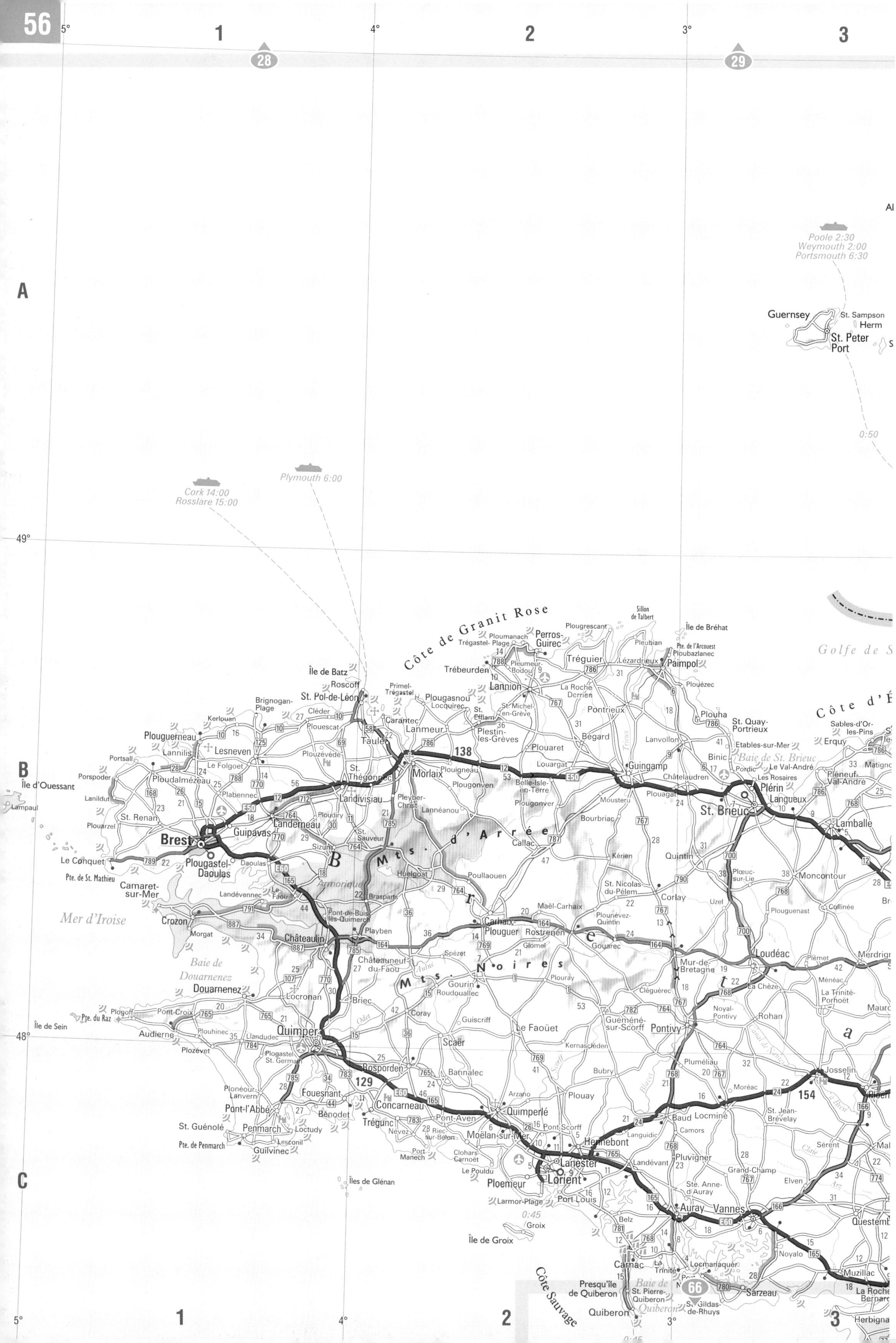

28
29
Poole 2:30
Weymouth 2:00
Portsmouth 6:30
Guernsey
St. Sampson
Herm
St. Peter Port
0:50
Plymouth 6:00
Cork 14:00
Rosslare 15:00
Côte de Granit Rose
Golfe de S
Côte d'É
Sillon de Talbert
Île de Bréhat
Plougrescant
Perros-Guirec
Ploumanach
Trégastel-Plage
Pleubian
Pte. de l'Arcouest
Ploubazlanec
Paimpol
Tréguier
Lézardrieux
Trébeurden
Lannion
Pleumeur-Bodou
La Roche Derrien
Plouézec
Pontrieux
Plouha
St. Quay-Portrieux
Île de Batz
Roscoff
St. Pol-de-Léon
Primel-Trégastel
Plougasnou
Locquirec
St. Efflam
St. Michel-en-Grève
Plestin-les-Grèves
Brignogan-Plage
Kerlouan
Cléder
Plouescat
Carantec
Lanmeur
Taulé
Plouguerneau
Lannilis
Lesneven
Le Folgoet
Portsall
Porspoder
Plouzévédé
St. Thégonnec
Morlaix
Plouigneau
138
Plougonven
Plouaret
Bégard
Lanvollon
Etables-sur-Mer
Erquy
Sables-d'Or-les-Pins
Binic
Baie de St. Brieuc
Pordic
Le Val-André
Les Rosaires
Pléneuf-Val-André
Matignon
Louargat
Guingamp
Belle-Isle-en-Terre
Plougonver
Mousteru
Châtelaudren
Plouagat
Plérin
Langueux
St. Brieuc
Lamballe
Île d'Ouessant
Lampaul
Ploudalmézeau
Plabennec
Landivisiau
Pleyber-Christ
Lannéanou
Lanildut
St. Renan
Plouarzel
Brest
Guipavas
Landerneau
Ploudiry
Sizun
St. Sauveur
Mts. d'Arrée
Callac
Bourbriac
Kérien
Quintin
Moncontour
Le Conquet
Pte. de St. Mathieu
Plougastel-Daoulas
Daoulas
Huelgoat
Poullaouen
St. Nicolas-du-Pélem
Corlay
Plœuc-sur-Lie
Camaret-sur-Mer
Landévennec
Le Faou
Armorique
Brasparts
Uzel
Plouguenast
Collinée
Mer d'Iroise
Crozon
Morgat
Pont-de-Buis-lès-Quimerch
Carhaix-Plouguer
Maël-Carhaix
Plounévez-Quintin
Rostrenen
Gouarec
Playben
Châteaulin
Loudéac
Plémet
Merdrignac
Baie de Douarnenez
Douarnenez
Locronan
Châteauneuf-du-Faou
Spézet
Glomel
Mts. Noires
Plouray
Mur-de-Bretagne
Ménéac
La Trinité-Porhoët
La Chèze
Île de Sein
Pte. du Raz
Plogoff
Pont-Croix
Audierne
Plouhinec
Plozévet
Landudec
Quimper
Briec
Coray
Gourin
Roudouallec
Guiscriff
Le Faouët
Cléguérec
Guémené-sur-Scorff
Pontivy
Noyal-Pontivy
Rohan
Mauron
Kernascléden
Plogastel-St. Germain
Scaër
Bannalec
Rosporden
129
Bubry
Pluméliau
Josselin
Ploërmel
154
Moréac
Ploneour-Lanvern
Fouesnant
Concarneau
Bénodet
Pont-l'Abbé
Arzano
Quimperlé
Plouay
Baud
Locminé
St. Jean-Brévelay
St. Guénolé
Pte. de Penmarch
Penmarch
Loctudy
Lesconil
Guilvinec
Trégunc
Nevez
Pont-Aven
Riec-sur-Bélon
Port Manech
Clohars-Carnoët
Le Pouldu
Moëlan-sur-Mer
Pont-Scorff
Hennebont
Languidic
Camors
Sérent
Malestroit
Lanester
Lorient
Ploemeur
Landévant
Pluvigner
Grand-Champ
Elven
Îles de Glénan
Larmor-Plage
Port Louis
Ste. Anne-d'Auray
Auray
Vannes
Questembert
0:45
Groix
Île de Groix
Belz
Côte Sauvage
Carnac
La Trinité
Locmariaquer
Noyalo
Muzillac
Presqu'île de Quiberon
Baie de Quiberon
St. Pierre-Quiberon
Quiberon
Sarzeau
St. Gildas-de-Rhuys
La Roche-Bernard
Herbignac
66
E50
E60
5°
4°
3°
49°
48°
A
B
C
1
2
3

2° 4 1° 5 0° 6

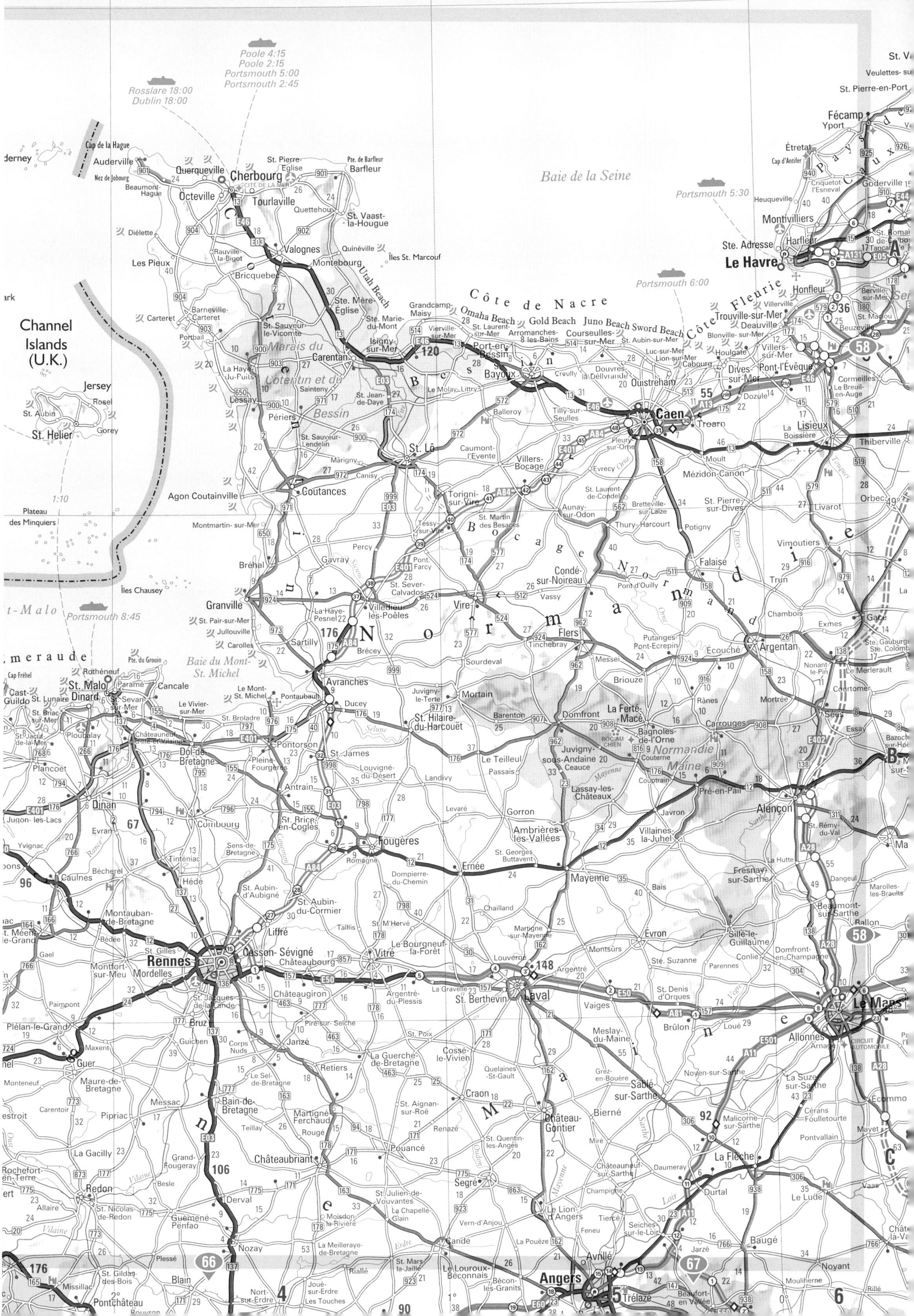
Channel Islands (U.K.)
Jersey
St. Helier
St. Aubin
Gorey
Rosel
Plateau des Minquiers
Îles Chausey
Poole 4:15
Poole 2:15
Portsmouth 5:00
Portsmouth 2:45
Rosslare 18:00
Dublin 18:00
Portsmouth 5:30
Portsmouth 6:00
Portsmouth 8:45
Baie de la Seine
Baie du Mont-St. Michel
Côte de Nacre
Côte Fleurie
Omaha Beach
Gold Beach
Juno Beach
Sword Beach
Utah Beach
Cap de la Hague
Auderville
Nez de Jobourg
Beaumont-Hague
Querqueville
Cherbourg
Octeville
Tourlaville
St. Pierre-Église
Pte. de Barfleur
Barfleur
Quettehou
St. Vaast-la-Hougue
Diélette
Les Pieux
Valognes
Montebourg
Quinéville
Îles St. Marcouf
Rauville-la-Bigot
Bricquebec
Carteret
Barneville-Carteret
Portbail
St. Sauveur-le-Vicomte
Ste. Mère-Église
Marais du Cotentin et du Bessin
Carentan
La Haye-du-Puits
Lessay
Périers
Sainteny
St. Jean-de-Daye
Isigny-sur-Mer
Grandcamp-Maisy
Port-en-Bessin
Bayeux
Arromanches-les-Bains
Courseulles-sur-Mer
Creully
Douvres-la-Délivrande
Ouistreham
Luc-sur-Mer
Lion-sur-Mer
Cabourg
Houlgate
Dives-sur-Mer
Caen
Troarn
Tilly-sur-Seulles
Balleroy
Le Molay-Littry
St. Lô
Coutances
Agon Coutainville
Marigny
Canisy
Caumont-l'Evente
Villers-Bocage
Evrecy
Fleury-sur-Orne
Torigni-sur-Vire
Tessy-sur-Vire
Montmartin-sur-Mer
Bréhal
Percy
Gavray
Granville
Villedieu-les-Poêles
La Haye-Pesnel
St. Pair-sur-Mer
Jullouville
Carolles
Sartilly
Brécey
Vire
Aunay-sur-Odon
Thury-Harcourt
Condé-sur-Noireau
Vassy
Flers
Tinchebray
St. Martin des Besaces
Bretteville-sur-Laize
Falaise
Pont d'Ouilly
Potigny
Mézidon-Canon
Moult
Le Havre
Ste. Adresse
Harfleur
Montivilliers
Honfleur
Trouville-sur-Mer
Deauville
Villers-sur-Mer
Pont-l'Évêque
Lisieux
Cormeilles
Thiberville
Livarot
Orbec
Vimoutiers
St. Pierre-sur-Dives
Trun
Chambois
Argentan
Écouché
Putanges-Pont-Ecrepin
Gacé
Exmes
Sées
Mortrée
Carrouges
Rânes
Briouze
La Ferté-Macé
Bagnoles-de-l'Orne
Domfront
Mortain
Barenton
Juvigny-le-Tertre
St. Hilaire-du-Harcouët
Avranches
Ducey
Pontaubault
Le Mont-St. Michel
St. Malo
Dinard
Cancale
Dol-de-Bretagne
Pontorson
St. James
Antrain
Louvigné-du-Désert
Fougères
Dinan
Combourg
Tinténiac
Hédé
Caulnes
Montauban-de-Bretagne
Rennes
Cesson-Sévigné
Liffré
Vitré
Châteaubourg
Bruz
Janzé
La Guerche-de-Bretagne
Ernée
Mayenne
Laval
St. Berthevin
Vaiges
Château-Gontier
Craon
Sablé-sur-Sarthe
La Flèche
Alençon
Le Mans
Allonnes
Fresnay-sur-Sarthe
Beaumont-sur-Sarthe
Sillé-le-Guillaume
Évron
Pré-en-Pail
Villaines-la-Juhel
Lassay-les-Châteaux
Ambrières-les-Vallées
Gorron
Juvigny-sous-Andaine
Couterne
Normandie Maine
Châteaubriant
Pouancé
Segré
Redon
Guémené-Penfao
Nozay
Derval
Blain
Candé
Angers
Avrillé
Trélazé
Beaufort-en-Vallée
Baugé
Durtal
Le Lude
Fécamp
Yport
Étretat
Pays de Caux
Normandie
Bocage
Cotentin
Bretagne
Maine
Anjou
Fécamp
Lisieux
Le Mans

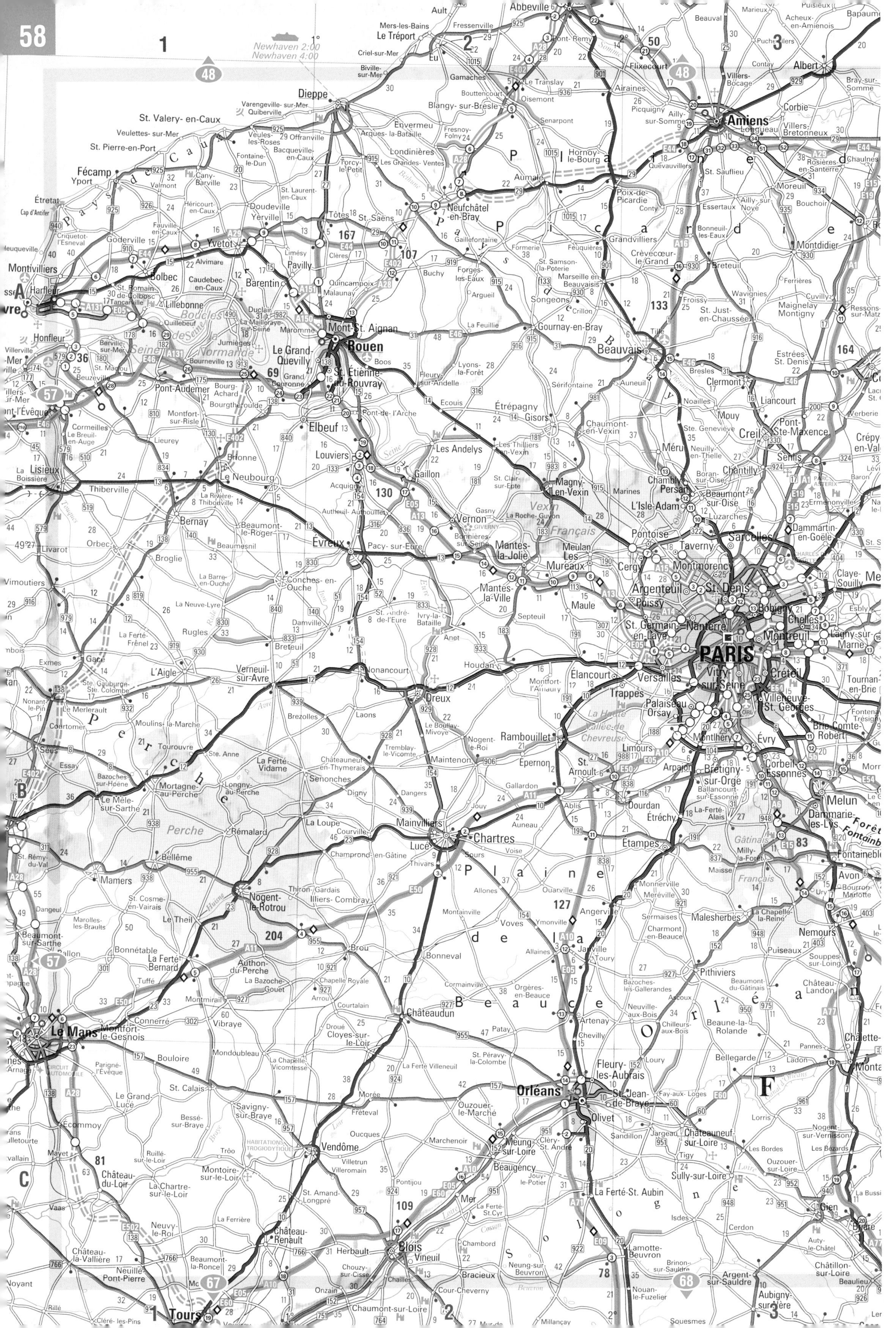
Newhaven 2:00
Newhaven 4:00
Abbeville
Le Tréport
Mers-les-Bains
Ault
Fressenville
Criel-sur-Mer
Eu
Gamaches
Dieppe
Varengeville-sur-Mer
Quiberville
St. Valery-en-Caux
Veulettes-sur-Mer
St. Pierre-en-Port
Fécamp
Yport
Étretat
Cap d'Antifer
Pays de Caux
Montivilliers
Harfleur
Honfleur
Goderville
Bolbec
Yvetot
Lillebonne
Caudebec-en-Caux
Barentin
Pavilly
Tôtes
St. Saëns
Envermeu
Arques-la-Bataille
Londinières
Neufchâtel-en-Bray
Blangy-sur-Bresle
Aumale
Oisemont
Hornoy-le-Bourg
Poix-de-Picardie
Airaines
Flixecourt
Amiens
Albert
Corbie
Villers-Bretonneux
Moreuil
Montdidier
Breteuil
Crèvecœur-le-Grand
Grandvilliers
Forges-les-Eaux
Songeons
Gournay-en-Bray
Beauvais
Clermont
St. Just-en-Chaussée
Estrées-St. Denis
Liancourt
Pont-Ste-Maxence
Creil
Senlis
Chantilly
Méru
Noailles
Mont-St. Aignan
Rouen
Maromme
Le Grand-Quevilly
Grand Couronne
St. Étienne-du-Rouvray
Boucles de la Seine Normande
Jumièges
Elbeuf
Louviers
Gaillon
Les Andelys
Étrépagny
Gisors
Lyons-la-Forêt
Pont-Audemer
Bourg-Achard
Bourgtheroulde
Montfort-sur-Risle
Brionne
Le Neubourg
Bernay
Lisieux
Cormeilles
Thiberville
Orbec
Livarot
Vimoutiers
Évreux
Pacy-sur-Eure
Vernon
Giverny
Bonnières-sur-Seine
Mantes-la-Jolie
Mantes-la-Ville
Magny-en-Vexin
Vexin Français
Chaumont-en-Vexin
Meulan
Les Mureaux
Pontoise
Cergy
L'Isle-Adam
Beaumont-sur-Oise
Persan
Luzarches
Taverny
Montmorency
Sarcelles
Argenteuil
St. Denis
Poissy
St. Germain-en-Laye
Nanterre
PARIS
Bobigny
Montreuil
Chelles
Créteil
Vitry-sur-Seine
Versailles
Trappes
Palaiseau
Orsay
Villeneuve-St. Georges
Évry
Montlhéry
Corbeil-Essonnes
Brétigny-sur-Orge
Arpajon
Dammartin-en-Goële
Conches-en-Ouche
Breteuil
Rugles
L'Aigle
Verneuil-sur-Avre
Nonancourt
Anet
Ivry-la-Bataille
Houdan
Dreux
Montfort-l'Amaury
Élancourt
Rambouillet
Maintenon
Épernon
Nogent-le-Roi
Limours
Dourdan
Étréchy
Étampes
Milly-la-Forêt
Melun
Dammarie-les-Lys
Fontainebleau
Forêt de Fontainebleau
Nemours
Gâtinais Français
Malesherbes
Pithiviers
Gace
Sées
Mortagne-au-Perche
Longny-au-Perche
La Ferté-Vidame
Senonches
Perche
Rémalard
Bellême
Mamers
Nogent-le-Rotrou
La Loupe
Courville
Lucé
Mainvilliers
Chartres
Illiers-Combray
Plaine de la Beauce
Voves
Janville
Angerville
Toury
Artenay
Patay
Brou
Bonneval
Châteaudun
Cloyes-sur-le-Loir
La Ferté-Bernard
Le Mans
Montfort-le-Gesnois
Connerré
Vibraye
Montmirail
Bouloire
St. Calais
Mondoubleau
Vendôme
Montoire-sur-le-Loir
Château-du-Loir
La Chartre-sur-le-Loir
Château-Renault
Amboise
Blois
Vineuil
Chambord
Mer
Beaugency
Meung-sur-Loire
Orléans
Fleury-les-Aubrais
St. Jean-de-Braye
Olivet
Châteauneuf-sur-Loire
Sully-sur-Loire
La Ferté-St. Aubin
Lamotte-Beuvron
Sologne
Orléanais
Beaune-la-Rolande
Bellegarde
Montargis
Gien
Briare
Châtillon-sur-Loire
Argent-sur-Sauldre
Aubigny-sur-Nère
Tours
Chaumont-sur-Loire
Cour-Cheverny
Bracieux
Neung-sur-Beuvron
Château-la-Vallière
Neuillé-Pont-Pierre
Écommoy
Mayet
Beaumont-sur-Sarthe
Mayenne
Chelles
Melun
Avon
Fontainebleau
Montereau
Brie-Comte-Robert
Tournan-en-Brie
Lagny-sur-Marne
Claye-Souilly

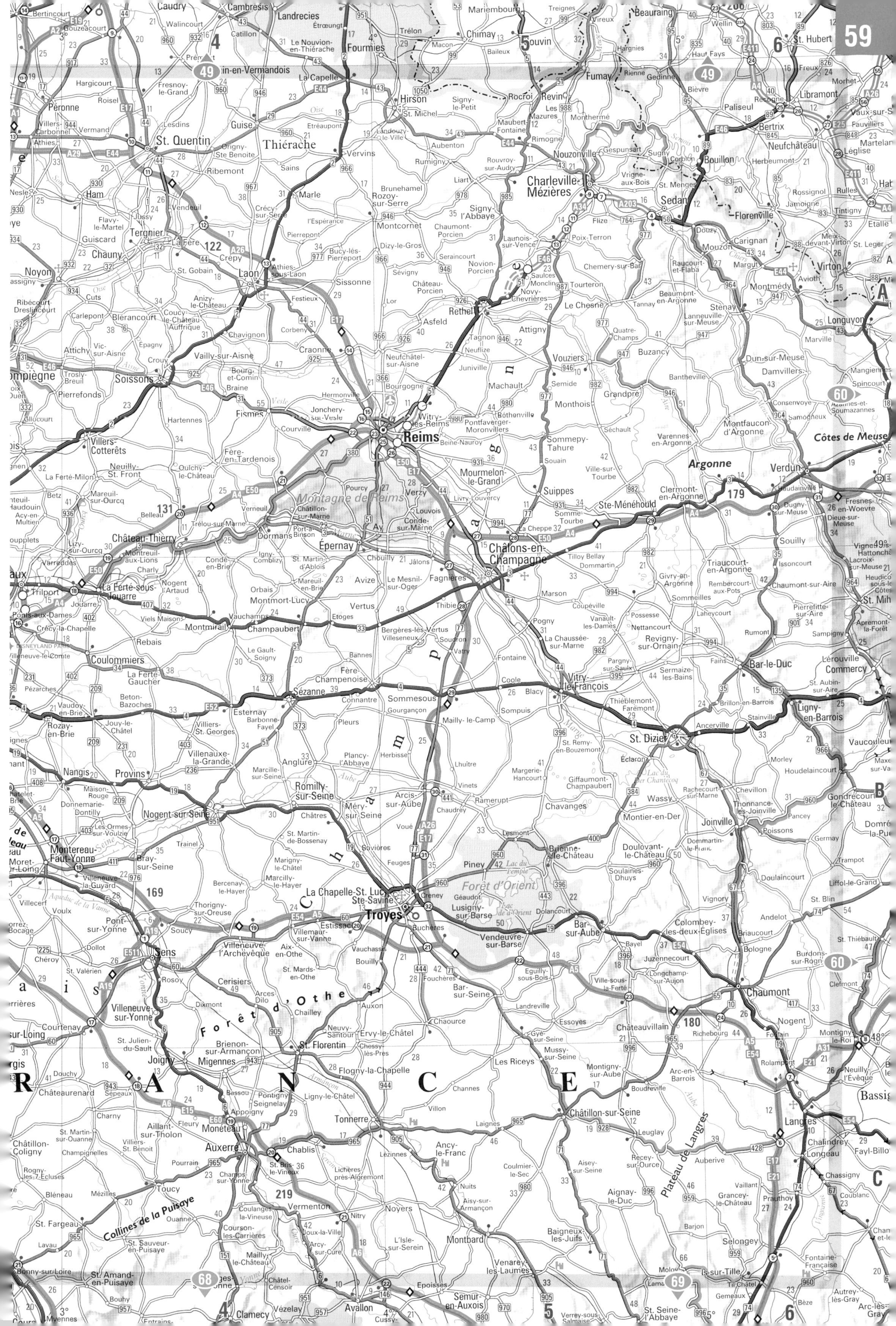

Cambrésis
Landrecies
Fourmies
Chimay
Couvin
Beauraing
St. Hubert
Guise
St. Quentin
Thiérache
Hirson
Rocroi
Revin
Fumay
Bièvre
Libramont
Péronne
Vervins
Nouzonville
Charleville-Mézières
Sedan
Bouillon
Bertrix
Neufchâteau
Ham
Tergnier
La Fère
Marle
Florenville
Chauny
Noyon
Laon
Sissonne
Rethel
Carignan
Virton
Montmédy
Stenay
Longuyon
Soissons
Vouziers
Asfeld
Craonne
Pierrefonds
Fismes
Reims
Dun-sur-Meuse
Damvillers
Villers-Cotterêts
Montagne de Reims
Argonne
Verdun
Côtes de Meuse
Château-Thierry
Épernay
Dormans
Châlons-en-Champagne
Ste-Ménehould
Suippes
La Ferté-sous-Jouarre
Montmirail
Vertus
Avize
Coulommiers
Sézanne
Vitry-le-François
Bar-le-Duc
Commercy
St. Dizier
Ligny-en-Barrois
Provins
Nangis
Nogent-sur-Seine
Romilly-sur-Seine
Arcis-sur-Aube
Montereau-Faut-Yonne
Brienne-le-Château
Joinville
Wassy
Troyes
Forêt d'Orient
Bar-sur-Aube
Sens
Chaumont
Bar-sur-Seine
Forêt d'Othe
St. Florentin
Joigny
Châteauvillain
Les Riceys
Tonnerre
Châtillon-sur-Seine
Auxerre
Chablis
Langres
Plateau de Langres
Collines de la Puisaye
Montbard
Noyers
Avallon
Semur-en-Auxois
Clamecy
Vézelay
F R A N C E
C h a m p a g n e

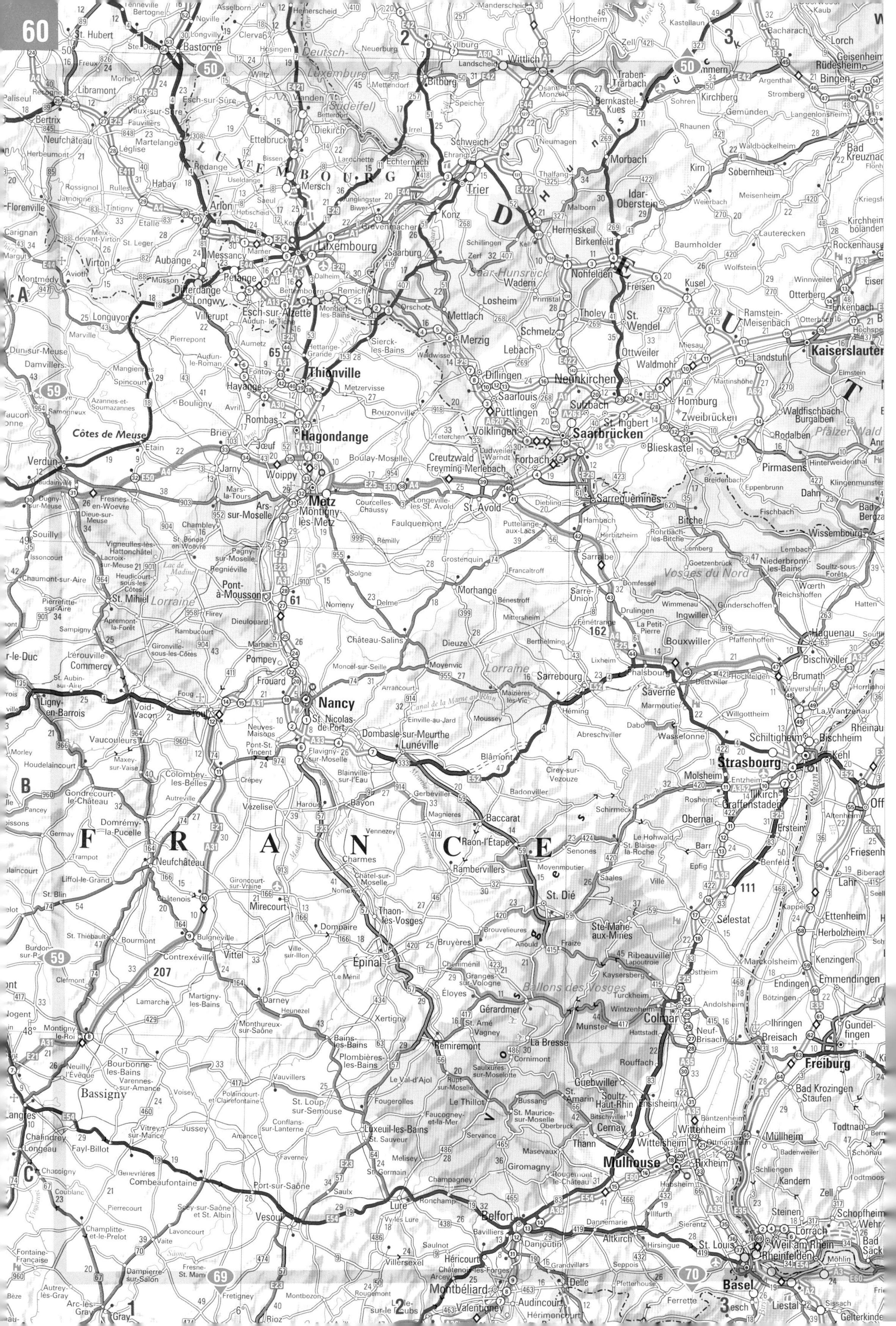
LUXEMBOURG
D
E
U
T
FRANCE
Vosges
Hunsrück
Côtes de Meuse
Lorraine
Vosges du Nord
Ballons des Vosges
Pfälzer Wald
Saar-Hunsrück
Deutsch-Luxemburg (Südeifel)
St. Hubert
Bastogne
Libramont
Bertrix
Neufchâteau
Florenville
Arlon
Virton
Aubange
Differdange
Longwy
Longuyon
Esch-sur-Alzette
Mersch
Luxembourg
Ettelbruck
Diekirch
Vianden
Echternach
Bitburg
Wittlich
Trier
Konz
Saarburg
Schweich
Bernkastel-Kues
Traben-Trarbach
Morbach
Idar-Oberstein
Hermeskeil
Birkenfeld
Nohfelden
Kusel
Kirn
Bingen
Rüdesheim
Bacharach
Bad Kreuznach
Kaiserslautern
Landstuhl
Homburg
Zweibrücken
Pirmasens
St. Ingbert
Neunkirchen
St. Wendel
Saarbrücken
Saarlouis
Völklingen
Dillingen
Merzig
Mettlach
Losheim
Lebach
Forbach
Sarreguemines
Bitche
Wissembourg
Haguenau
Saverne
Thionville
Hagondange
Metz
Verdun
Étain
Briey
St. Avold
Creutzwald
Faulquemont
Morhange
Dieuze
Château-Salins
Pont-à-Mousson
St. Mihiel
Commercy
Toul
Nancy
Lunéville
Sarrebourg
Phalsbourg
Strasbourg
Kehl
Molsheim
Obernai
Sélestat
Colmar
Freiburg
Breisach
St. Dié
Baccarat
Raon-l'Étape
Rambervillers
Épinal
Mirecourt
Charmes
Neufchâteau
Vittel
Contrexéville
Remiremont
Gérardmer
Munster
Guebwiller
Thann
Cernay
Mulhouse
Belfort
Montbéliard
Héricourt
Lure
Vesoul
Luxeuil-les-Bains
Plombières-les-Bains
Langres
Bourbonne-les-Bains
Chaumont-sur-Aire
Bar-le-Duc
Ligny-en-Barrois
Vaucouleurs
Gondrecourt-le-Château
Domrémy-la-Pucelle
Altkirch
St. Louis
Basel
Lörrach
Weil am Rhein
Rheinfelden
Liestal
Müllheim
Gray
50
59
69
70
1
2
3
A
B
C

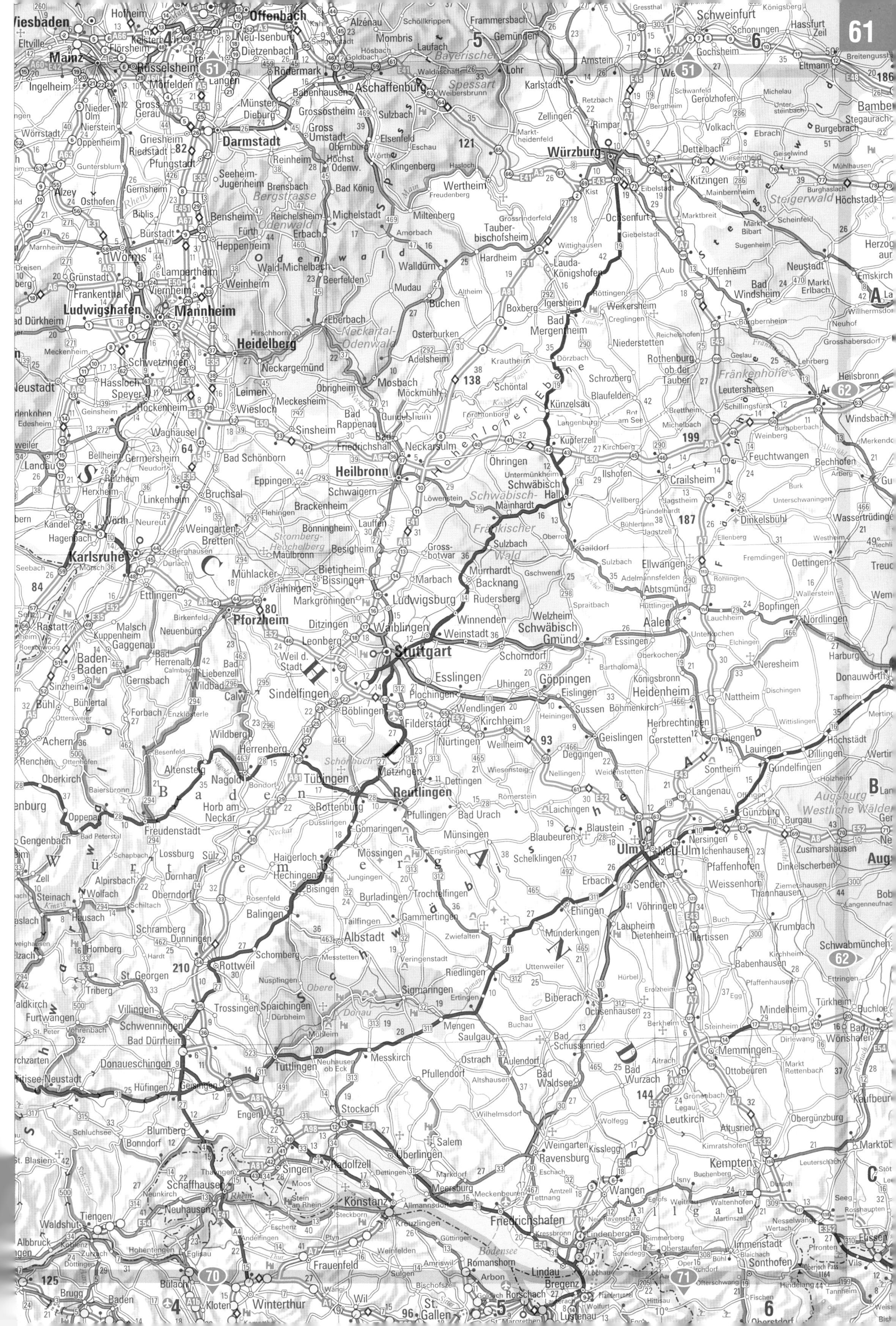
Wiesbaden
Mainz
Offenbach
Rüsselsheim
Aschaffenburg
Schweinfurt
Würzburg
Darmstadt
Worms
Ludwigshafen
Mannheim
Heidelberg
Speyer
Heilbronn
Karlsruhe
Pforzheim
Stuttgart
Ludwigsburg
Esslingen
Reutlingen
Tübingen
Ulm
Neu-Ulm
Aalen
Schwäbisch Hall
Schwäbisch Gmünd
Göppingen
Heidenheim
Crailsheim
Dinkelsbühl
Nördlingen
Rothenburg ob der Tauber
Ansbach
Baden-Baden
Rastatt
Offenburg
Freudenstadt
Rottweil
Villingen
Schwenningen
Donaueschingen
Tuttlingen
Sigmaringen
Biberach
Memmingen
Kempten
Ravensburg
Friedrichshafen
Konstanz
Singen
Schaffhausen
Lindau
Bregenz
Winterthur
St. Gallen
Füssen
Augsburg
Spessart
Odenwald
Bergstrasse
Steigerwald
Frankenhöhe
Schwäbische Alb
Schwarzwald
Baden-Württemberg
Allgäu
Bodensee
Donau
Neckar
Main
Rhein

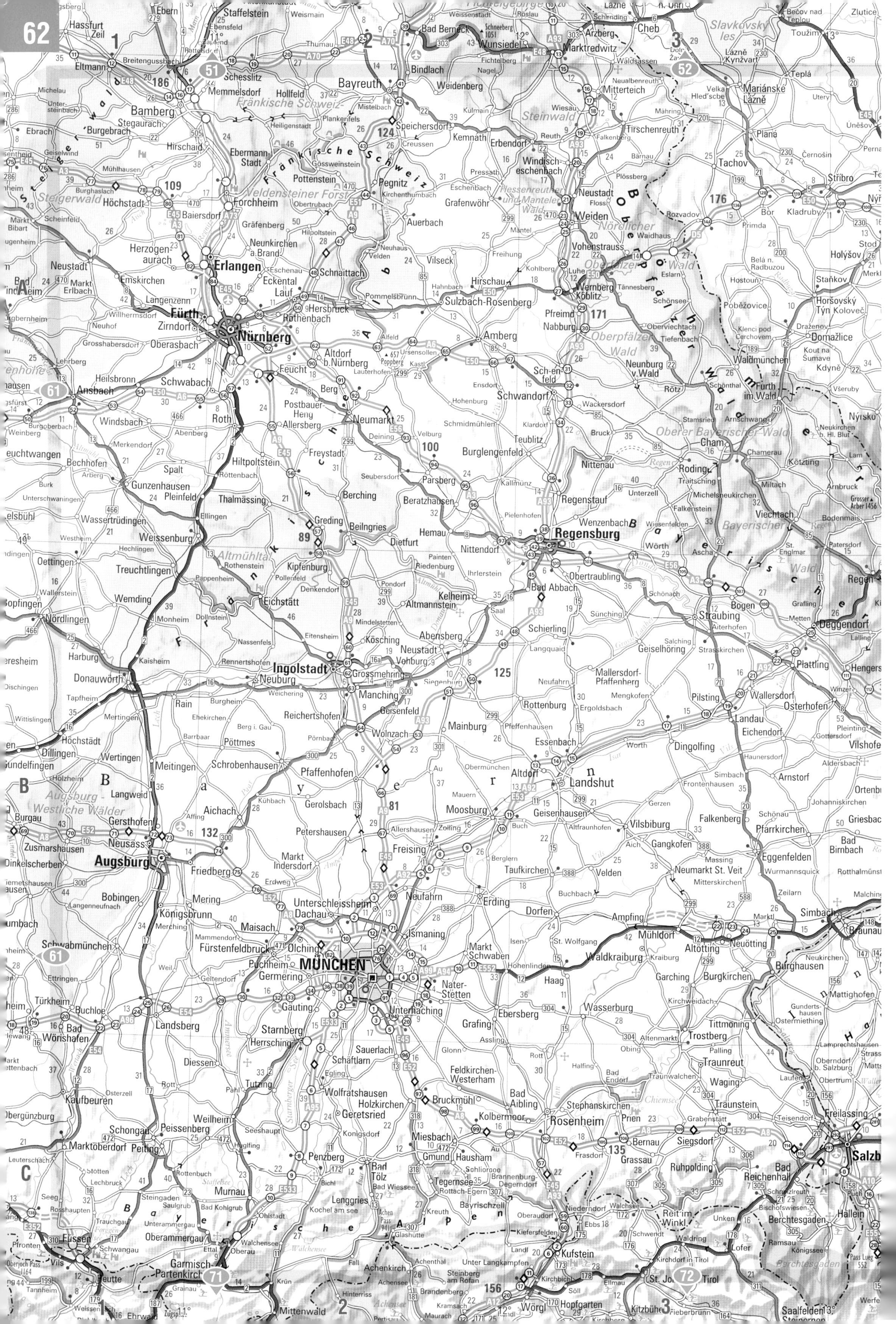
Bamberg
Bayreuth
Fränkische Schweiz
Steinwald
Cheb
Marktredwitz
Wunsiedel
Bad Berneck
Mariánské Lázně
Steigerwald
Forchheim
Erlangen
Fürth
Nürnberg
Schwabach
Ansbach
Roth
Neumarkt
Amberg
Weiden
Sulzbach-Rosenberg
Schwandorf
Oberpfälzer Wald
Regensburg
Straubing
Deggendorf
Cham
Domažlice
Bayerischer Wald
Oberer Bayerischer Wald
Weissenburg
Eichstätt
Ingolstadt
Kelheim
Landshut
Freising
Dingolfing
Landau
Donauwörth
Nördlingen
Augsburg
MÜNCHEN
Dachau
Erding
Mühldorf
Altötting
Burghausen
Rosenheim
Starnberg
Landsberg
Kaufbeuren
Füssen
Garmisch-Partenkirchen
Kufstein
Traunstein
Bad Reichenhall
Salzb
Kitzbühel
Wörgl
Bayerische Alpen

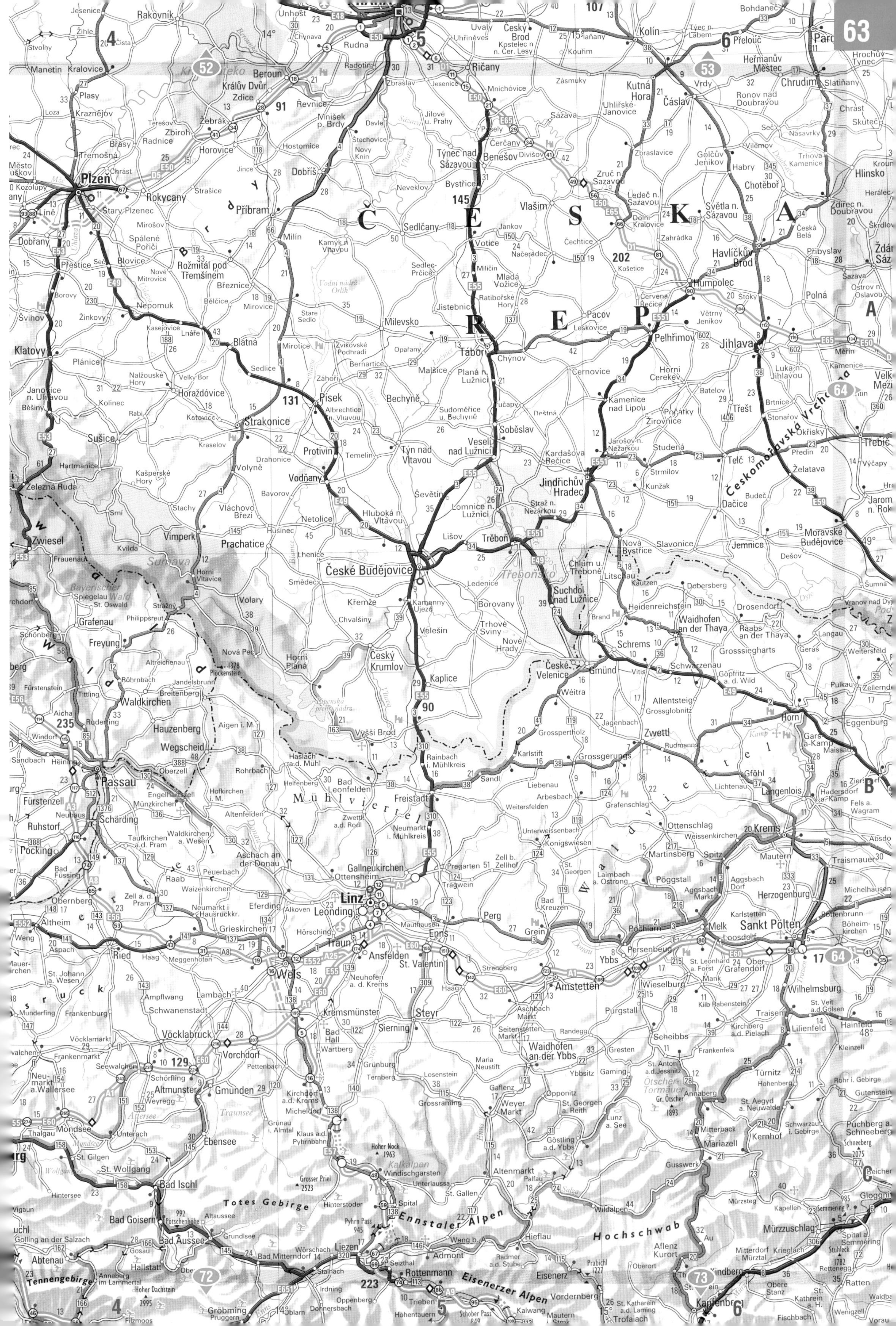
Č E S K Á
R E P
Rakovník
Kolín
Beroun
Říčany
Kutná Hora
Čáslav
Přelouč
Chrudim
Plzeň
Rokycany
Příbram
Dobříš
Benešov
Sedlčany
Vlašim
Havlíčkův Brod
Humpolec
Hlinsko
Klatovy
Blatná
Milevsko
Tábor
Pelhřimov
Jihlava
Písek
Strakonice
Horažďovice
Sušice
Vodňany
Protivín
Týn nad Vltavou
Soběslav
Veselí nad Lužnicí
Jindřichův Hradec
Telč
Dačice
Třebíč
Moravské Budějovice
Železná Ruda
Zwiesel
Vimperk
Prachatice
České Budějovice
Třeboň
Třeboňsko
Šumava
Český Krumlov
Kaplice
Horní Planá
Vyšší Brod
České Velenice
Gmünd
Waidhofen an der Thaya
Zwettl
Horn
Krems
Grafenau
Freyung
Waldkirchen
Passau
Schärding
Freistadt
Mühlviertel
Waldviertel
Linz
Leonding
Traun
Wels
Enns
Steyr
Amstetten
Melk
Sankt Pölten
Ybbs
Ried
Vöcklabruck
Gmunden
Bad Ischl
Bad Aussee
Liezen
Rottenmann
Eisenerz
Totes Gebirge
Ennstaler Alpen
Eisenerzer Alpen
Hochschwab
Mürzzuschlag
Kapfenberg
Kindberg
Lilienfeld
Wilhelmsburg
Scheibbs
Waidhofen an der Ybbs
Mariazell
Českomoravská Vrchovina

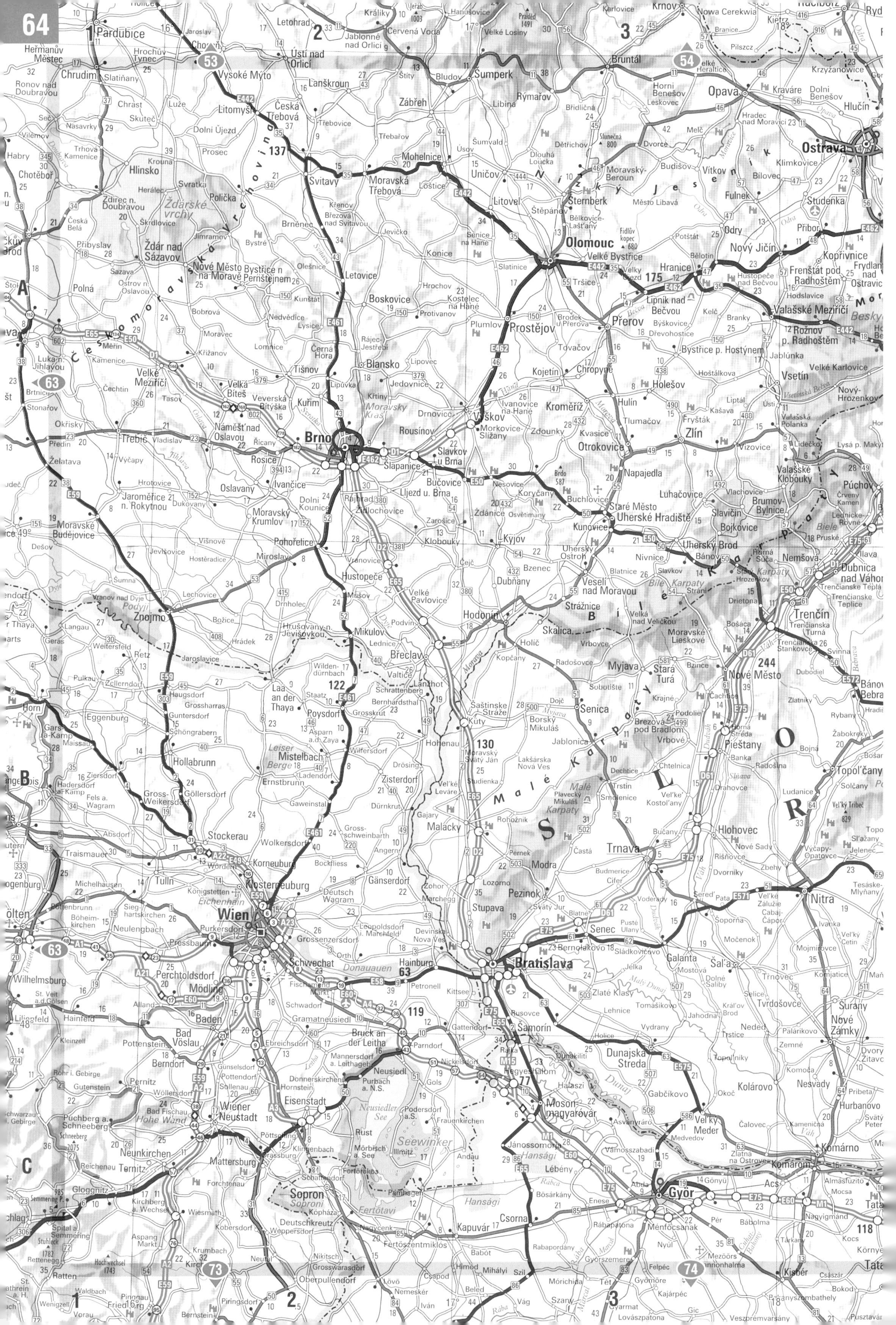
Pardubice
Chrudim
Vysoké Mýto
Ústí nad Orlicí
Šumperk
Bruntál
Opava
Ostrava
Hlinsko
Polička
Svitavy
Mohelnice
Olomouc
Přerov
Prostějov
Hranice
Nový Jičín
Valašské Meziříčí
Žďár nad Sázavou
Jihlava
Velké Meziříčí
Třebíč
Brno
Blansko
Boskovice
Vyškov
Kroměříž
Zlín
Uherské Hradiště
Moravské Budějovice
Znojmo
Mikulov
Břeclav
Hodonín
Trenčín
Senica
Trnava
Piešťany
Nitra
Malacky
Mistelbach
Hollabrunn
Stockerau
Korneuburg
Wien
Bratislava
Schwechat
Baden
Mödling
Wiener Neustadt
Eisenstadt
Sopron
Győr
Mosonmagyaróvár
Dunajská Streda
Komárno
Neunkirchen
Bruck an der Leitha
Tulln
Krems
Nové Zámky
Hlohovec
Pezinok
Senec
Galanta

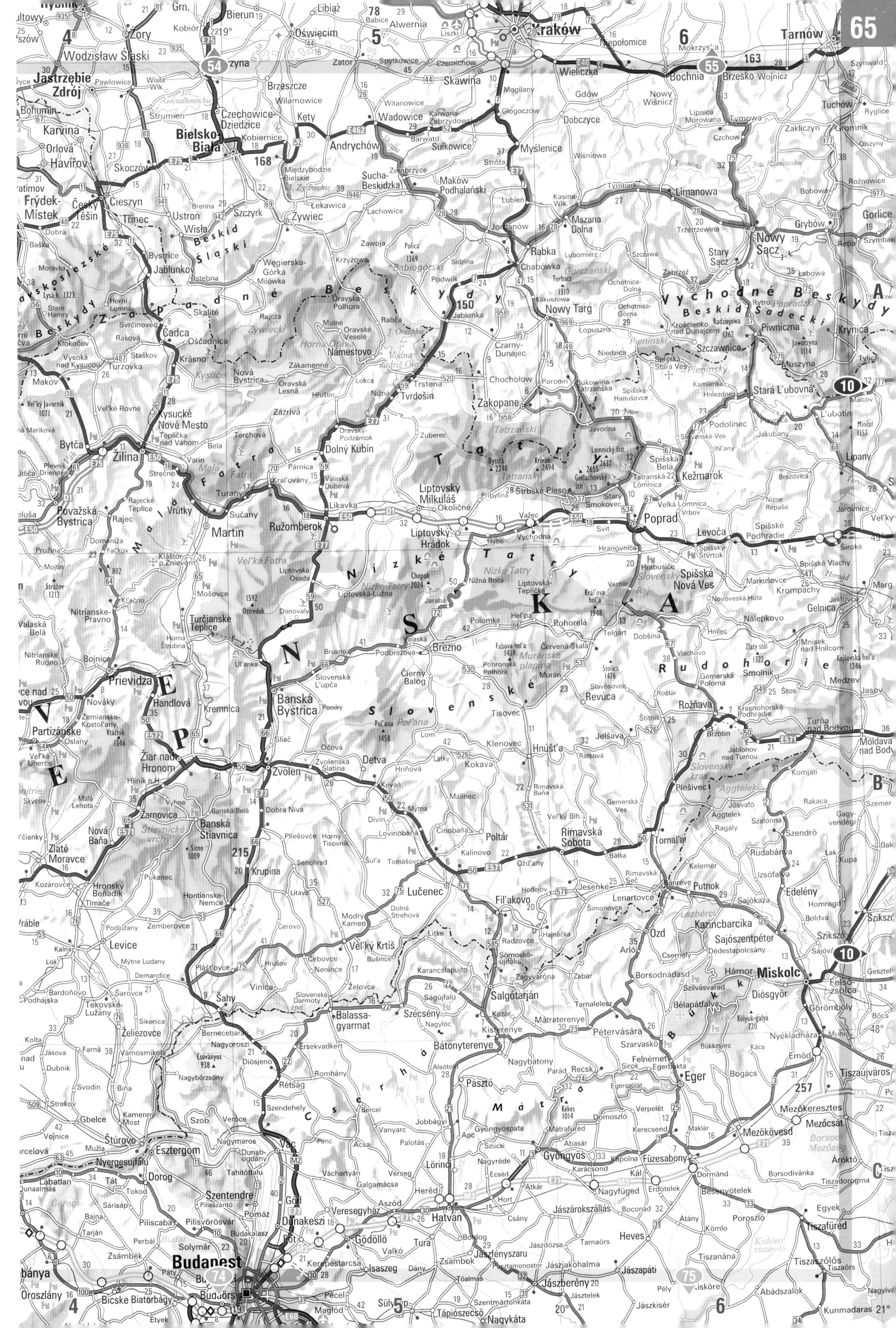

Kraków
Tarnów
Oświęcim
Wieliczka
Bochnia
Brzesko
Niepołomice
Jastrzębie Zdrój
Wodzisław Śląski
Żory
Bielsko-Biała
Czechowice-Dziedzice
Skawina
Wadowice
Andrychów
Kęty
Myślenice
Dobczyce
Limanowa
Nowy Sącz
Stary Sącz
Grybów
Gorlice
Karviná
Havířov
Frýdek-Místek
Český Těšín
Cieszyn
Třinec
Ustroń
Wisła
Żywiec
Sucha-Beskidzka
Maków Podhalański
Jordanów
Rabka
Nowy Targ
Zakopane
Krynica
Piwniczna
Szczawnica
Čadca
Námestovo
Tvrdošín
Dolný Kubín
Kysucké Nové Mesto
Bytča
Žilina
Považská Bystrica
Martin
Ružomberok
Liptovský Mikuláš
Liptovský Hrádok
Poprad
Kežmarok
Spišská Belá
Stará Ľubovňa
Levoča
Spišská Nová Ves
Gelnica
Prievidza
Handlová
Partizánske
Žiar nad Hronom
Banská Bystrica
Brezno
Zvolen
Detva
Banská Štiavnica
Žarnovica
Nová Baňa
Krupina
Lučenec
Fiľakovo
Rimavská Sobota
Revúca
Rožňava
Hnúšťa
Tornaľa
Veľký Krtíš
Levice
Šahy
Štúrovo
Esztergom
Salgótarján
Balassagyarmat
Szécsény
Bátonyterenye
Pásztó
Gyöngyös
Hatvan
Eger
Miskolc
Kazincbarcika
Ózd
Putnok
Edelény
Mezőkövesd
Tiszaújváros
Füzesabony
Heves
Jászberény
Gödöllő
Vác
Szentendre
Budapest
Budaörs
Tiszafüred
Beskid Śląski
Západné Beskydy
Východné Beskydy
Beskid Sądecki
Malá Fatra
Veľká Fatra
Tatry
Nízke Tatry
Slovenské Rudohorie
Slovenský Raj
Cserhát
Mátra
Bükk
SLOVENSKÁ
NEPEP

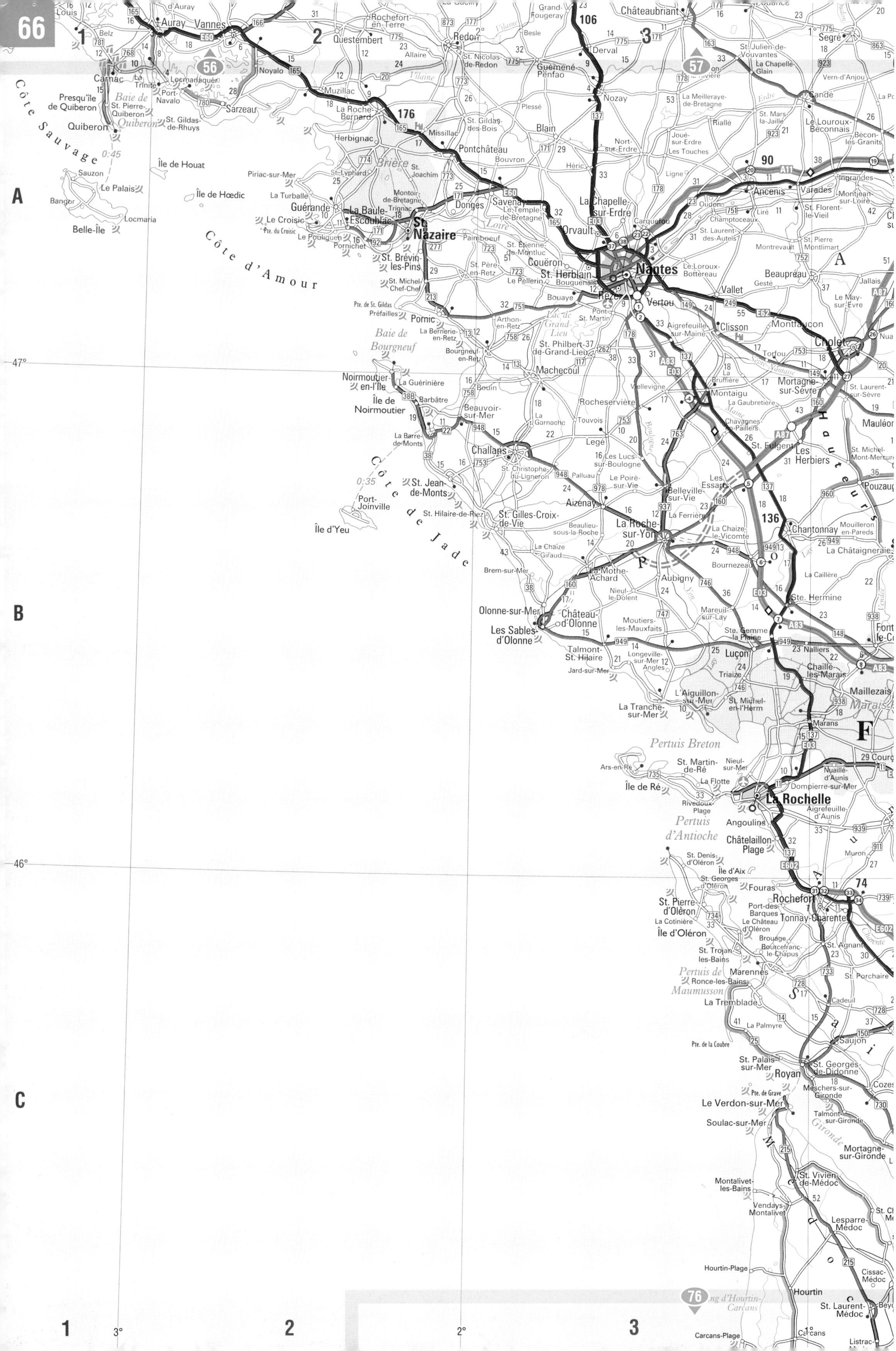
Auray
Vannes
Questembert
Rochefort-en-Terre
Redon
St. Nicolas-de-Redon
Grand-Fougeray
Châteaubriant
Derval
Guémené-Penfao
Segré
St. Julien-de-Vouvantes
La Chapelle-Glain
Vern-d'Anjou
Candé
Carnac
La Trinité
Locmariaquer
Port-Navalo
Sarzeau
St. Gildas-de-Rhuys
Presqu'île de Quiberon
Baie de Quiberon
St. Pierre-Quiberon
Quiberon
Côte Sauvage
Muzillac
Noyalo
Allaire
La Roche-Bernard
Herbignac
Missillac
St. Gildas-des-Bois
Pontchâteau
Plessé
Blain
Nozay
La Meilleraye-de-Bretagne
Riallé
Joué-sur-Erdre
Les Touches
Nort-sur-Erdre
St. Mars-la-Jaille
Le Louroux-Béconnais
Bécon-les-Granits
Île de Houat
Sauzon
Le Palais
Bangor
Locmaria
Belle-Île
Île de Hœdic
Piriac-sur-Mer
La Turballe
Guérande
Brière
St. Lyphard
St. Joachim
Montoir-de-Bretagne
Trignac
Bouvron
Héric
Ligne
Ancenis
Varades
Ingrandes
Montjean-sur-Loire
St. Florent-le-Vieil
Le Croisic
Pte. du Croisic
Le Pouliguen
La Baule-Escoublac
Pornichet
St. Nazaire
Donges
Savenay
Le Temple-de-Bretagne
La Chapelle-sur-Erdre
Carquefou
Oudon
Liré
Champtoceaux
St. Laurent-des-Autels
Montrevault
St. Pierre-Montlimart
Côte d'Amour
Paimbœuf
St. Étienne-de-Montluc
Orvault
Couëron
St. Herblain
Nantes
Le Pellerin
Bouguenais
Rezé
Le Loroux-Bottereau
Beaupréau
Gesté
Jallais
St. Brevin-les-Pins
St. Michel-Chef-Chef
St. Père-en-Retz
Bouaye
Vertou
Vallet
Le May-sur-Èvre
Pte. de St. Gildas
Préfailles
Pornic
Arthon-en-Retz
Lac de Grand-Lieu
Pont-St. Martin
Aigrefeuille-sur-Maine
Clisson
Montfaucon
Cholet
La Bernerie-en-Retz
Baie de Bourgneuf
Bourgneuf-en-Retz
St. Philbert-de-Grand-Lieu
Machecoul
Torfou
Noirmoutier-en-l'Île
La Guérinière
Île de Noirmoutier
Barbâtre
Bouin
Vieillevigne
La Bruffière
Montaigu
Mortagne-sur-Sèvre
St. Laurent-sur-Sèvre
Beauvoir-sur-Mer
Rocheservière
La Garnache
Touvois
Legé
La Gaubretière
Chavagnes-en-Paillers
St. Fulgent
Les Herbiers
Mauléon
La Barre-de-Monts
Challans
St. Christophe-du-Ligneron
Palluau
Les Lucs-sur-Boulogne
Le Poiré-sur-Vie
Belleville-sur-Vie
Les Essarts
St. Michel-Mont-Mercure
Pouzauges
Côte de Jade
St. Jean-de-Monts
Port-Joinville
Île d'Yeu
St. Hilaire-de-Riez
St. Gilles-Croix-de-Vie
Aizenay
Beaulieu-sous-la-Roche
La Roche-sur-Yon
La Ferrière
La Chaize-le-Vicomte
Chantonnay
Mouilleron-en-Pareds
La Châtaigneraie
La Chaize-Giraud
Brem-sur-Mer
La Mothe-Achard
Aubigny
Bournezeau
La Caillère
Ste. Hermine
Olonne-sur-Mer
Château-d'Olonne
Les Sables-d'Olonne
Nieul-le-Dolent
Moutiers-les-Mauxfaits
Mareuil-sur-Lay
Ste. Gemme-la-Plaine
Talmont-St. Hilaire
Longeville-sur-Mer
Angles
Jard-sur-Mer
Luçon
Nalliers
Chaillé-les-Marais
Triaize
L'Aiguillon-sur-Mer
St. Michel-en-l'Herm
Maillezais
La Tranche-sur-Mer
Marans
Pertuis Breton
Ars-en-Ré
St. Martin-de-Ré
Nieul-sur-Mer
La Flotte
Île de Ré
Rivedoux-Plage
La Rochelle
Nuaillé-d'Aunis
Dompierre-sur-Mer
Aigrefeuille-d'Aunis
Pertuis d'Antioche
Angoulins
Châtelaillon-Plage
Muron
St. Denis-d'Oléron
Île d'Aix
St. Georges-d'Oléron
Fouras
St. Pierre-d'Oléron
Port-des-Barques
Rochefort
Tonnay-Charente
La Cotinière
Le Château-d'Oléron
Île d'Oléron
Brouage
Bourcefranc-le-Chapus
St. Agnant
St. Trojan-les-Bains
Pertuis de Maumusson
Marennes
Ronce-les-Bains
St. Porchaire
La Tremblade
Cadeuil
La Palmyre
Saujon
Pte. de la Coubre
St. Palais-sur-Mer
Royan
St. Georges-de-Didonne
Meschers-sur-Gironde
Pte. de Grave
Le Verdon-sur-Mer
Talmont-sur-Gironde
Soulac-sur-Mer
Gironde
Mortagne-sur-Gironde
Montalivet-les-Bains
St. Vivien-de-Médoc
Vendays-Montalivet
Lesparre-Médoc
Hourtin-Plage
Cissac-Médoc
Hourtin
Étang d'Hourtin-Carcans
St. Laurent-Médoc
Carcans-Plage
Carcans
Listrac
A
B
C
F
1
2
3
47°
46°
3°
2°
56
57
76
E60
E62
E03
E602
A11
A83
A87

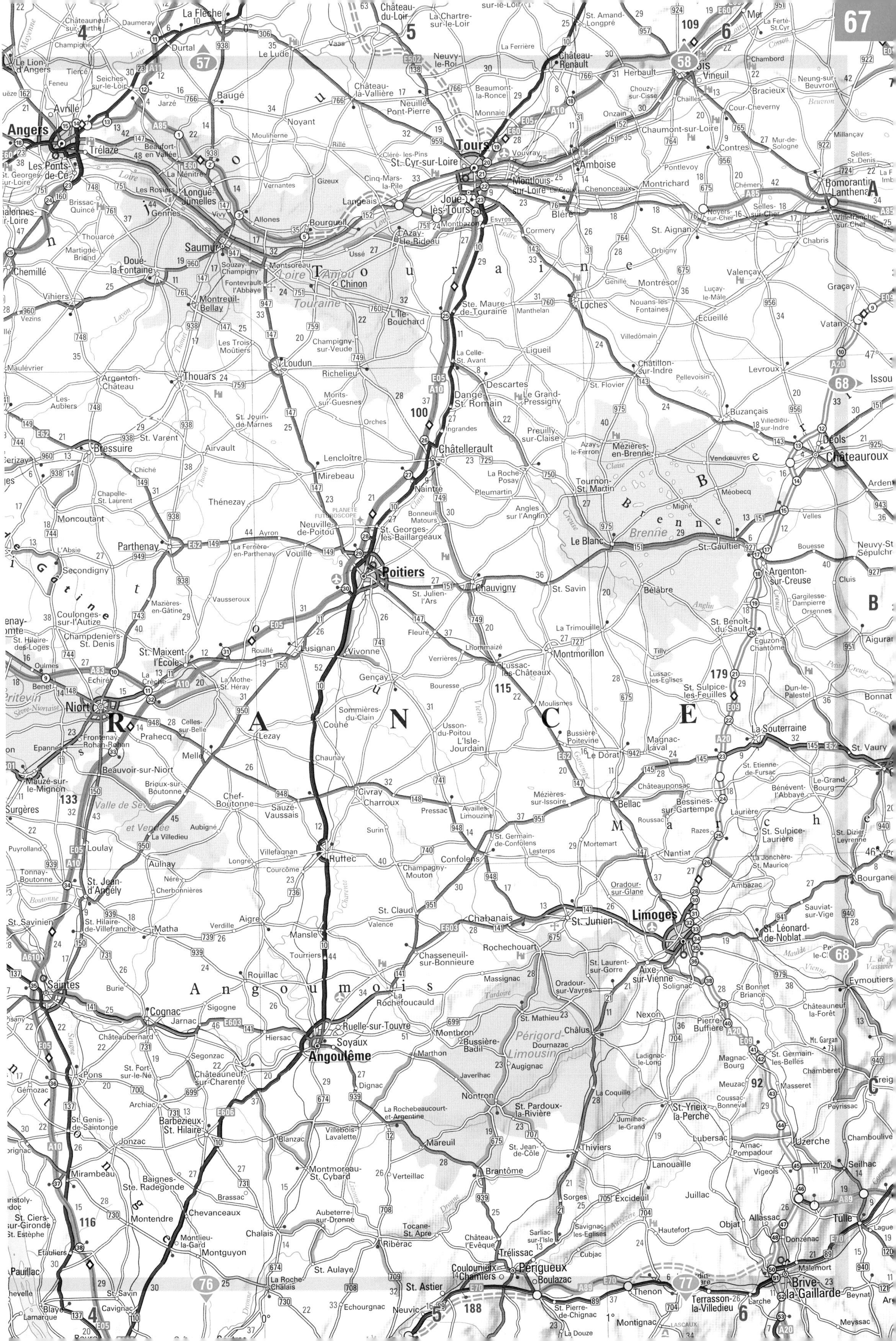
La Flèche
Château-du-Loir
La Chartre-sur-le-Loir
St. Amand-Longpré
Mer
Angers
Trélazé
Les Ponts-de-Cé
Durtal
Le Lude
Baugé
Château-la-Vallière
Neuvy-le-Roi
Château-Renault
Herbault
Blois
Vineuil
Chambord
Bracieux
Neung-sur-Beuvron
Avrillé
Seiches-sur-le-Loir
Beaufort-en-Vallée
Longué-Jumelles
Saumur
Tours
St.-Cyr-sur-Loire
Vouvray
Amboise
Montlouis-sur-Loire
Joué-lès-Tours
Langeais
Cinq-Mars-la-Pile
Bourgueil
Azay-le-Rideau
Chaumont-sur-Loire
Cour-Cheverny
Contres
Montrichard
Chenonceaux
Bléré
Romorantin-Lanthenay
Selles-sur-Cher
Noyers-sur-Cher
St. Aignan
Chinon
Doué-la-Fontaine
Montreuil-Bellay
Fontevrault-l'Abbaye
Montsoreau
L'Ile-Bouchard
Ste. Maure-de-Touraine
Loches
Montrésor
Valençay
Ecueillé
Vatan
Graçay
Chemillé
Vihiers
Thouars
Loudun
Richelieu
Descartes
Ligueil
Le Grand-Pressigny
Châtillon-sur-Indre
Levroux
Buzançais
Châteauroux
Déols
Bressuire
Airvault
Châtellerault
Lencloître
Mirebeau
Preuilly-sur-Claise
Mézières-en-Brenne
La Roche-Posay
Tournon-St. Martin
Parthenay
Neuville-de-Poitou
St. Georges-lès-Baillargeaux
Le Blanc
St.-Gaultier
Argenton-sur-Creuse
Poitiers
Chauvigny
St. Savin
Bélâbre
Vouillé
St. Maixent-l'École
Lusignan
Vivonne
Montmorillon
Lussac-les-Châteaux
La Trimouille
Niort
Melle
Couhé
L'Isle-Jourdain
Le Dorat
Magnac-Laval
La Souterraine
Eguzon-Chantôme
Dun-le-Palestel
Civray
Charroux
Bellac
Confolens
Chef-Boutonne
Sauzé-Vaussais
Ruffec
Aulnay
St. Jean-d'Angély
Surgères
Limoges
St. Junien
Chabanais
Rochechouart
St. Léonard-de-Noblat
Aixe-sur-Vienne
Saintes
Cognac
Jarnac
Angoulême
Soyaux
Ruelle-sur-Touvre
La Rochefoucauld
Mansle
Châlus
Nontron
St. Yrieix-la-Perche
Eymoutiers
Pons
Barbezieux-St. Hilaire
Jonzac
Montmoreau-St. Cybard
Brantôme
Thiviers
Uzerche
Mirambeau
Montendre
Chevanceaux
Chalais
Aubeterre-sur-Dronne
Ribérac
Périgueux
Trélissac
Boulazac
Excideuil
Hautefort
Tulle
Brive-la-Gaillarde
Donzenac
Terrasson-la-Villedieu
Montguyon
St. Astier
Neuvic
Blaye
Pauillac
A n g o u m o i s
F R A N C E
T o u r a i n e
B e r r y
B r e n n e
M a r c h e
Périgord-Limousin

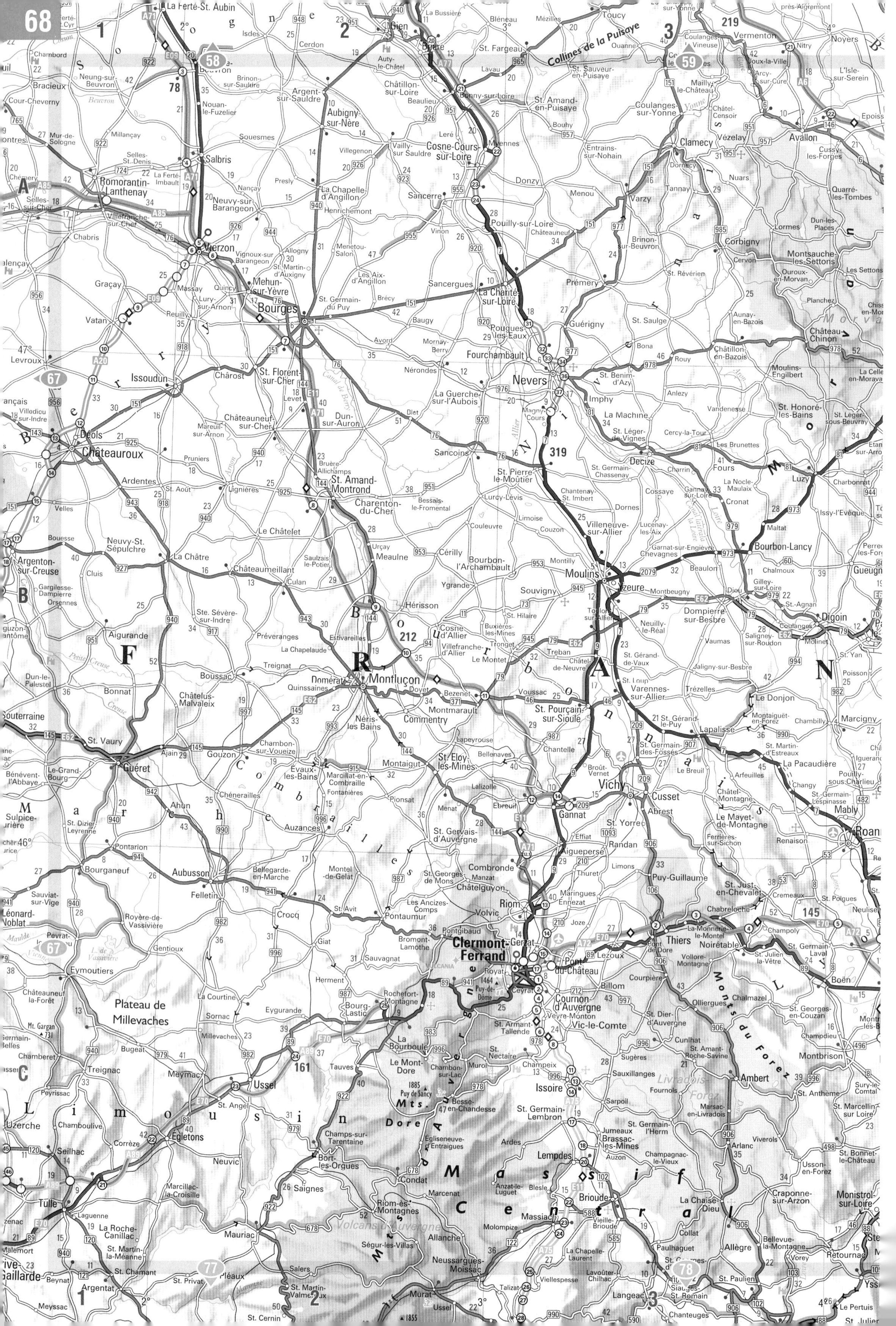
La Ferté-St. Aubin
Gien
Briare
Toucy
Collines de la Puisaye
St. Fargeau
Vermenton
Noyers
Chambord
Bracieux
Cour-Cheverny
Neung-sur-Beuvron
Nouan-le-Fuzelier
Argent-sur-Sauldre
Aubigny-sur-Nère
Châtillon-sur-Loire
Bonny-sur-Loire
St. Amand-en-Puisaye
Coulanges-sur-Yonne
Clamecy
Vézelay
Avallon
Salbris
Romorantin-Lanthenay
Selles-sur-Cher
Cosne-Cours-sur-Loire
Sancerre
Donzy
Varzy
Quarré-les-Tombes
Neuvy-sur-Barangeon
La Chapelle-d'Angillon
Henrichemont
Pouilly-sur-Loire
Corbigny
Vierzon
Mehun-sur-Yèvre
Bourges
Sancergues
La Charité-sur-Loire
Prémery
Montsauche-les-Settons
Vatan
Issoudun
Levroux
Château-Chinon
Châtillon-en-Bazois
Nevers
Fourchambault
St. Florent-sur-Cher
Dun-sur-Auron
La Guerche-sur-l'Aubois
Imphy
Moulins-Engilbert
Déols
Châteauroux
Sancoins
St. Pierre-le-Moûtier
Decize
St. Honoré-les-Bains
Luzy
St. Amand-Montrond
Charenton-du-Cher
Ardentes
Lignières
Le Châtelet
Bourbon-Lancy
Argenton-sur-Creuse
La Châtre
Châteaumeillant
Bourbon-l'Archambault
Moulins
Yzeure
Dompierre-sur-Besbre
Digoin
Hérisson
Cosne-d'Allier
Aigurande
Boussac
Montluçon
Commentry
St. Pourçain-sur-Sioule
Varennes-sur-Allier
Le Donjon
Lapalisse
Guéret
Gouzon
Évaux-les-Bains
Montaigut
St. Eloy-les-Mines
Vichy
Cusset
Gannat
La Pacaudière
Roanne
Bourganeuf
Aubusson
Felletin
Aigueperse
Randan
Riom
Volvic
Thiers
Clermont-Ferrand
Pont-du-Château
Lezoux
Noirétable
Boën
Eymoutiers
Plateau de Millevaches
Rochefort-Montagne
Puy-de-Dôme
Cournon-d'Auvergne
Vic-le-Comte
Ambert
Montbrison
La Bourboule
Le Mont-Dore
Mts. Dore
Issoire
Monts du Forez
Ussel
Meymac
Egletons
Tulle
Uzerche
Bort-les-Orgues
Condat
Massif Central
Brioude
La Chaise-Dieu
Craponne-sur-Arzon
Riom-ès-Montagnes
Volcans d'Auvergne
Mauriac
Allanche
Massiac
Monistrol-sur-Loire
Neussargues-Moissac
Salers
Argentat
Murat
Langeac
St. Paulien
Limousin
Bourbonnais
Combrailles
Berry
Morvan
Nivernais
Sologne
Livradois-Forez
Millevaches
Vienne
Creuse
Allier
Loire
Cher
Yonne
1885 Puy de Sancy
1464
58
59
67
77
78

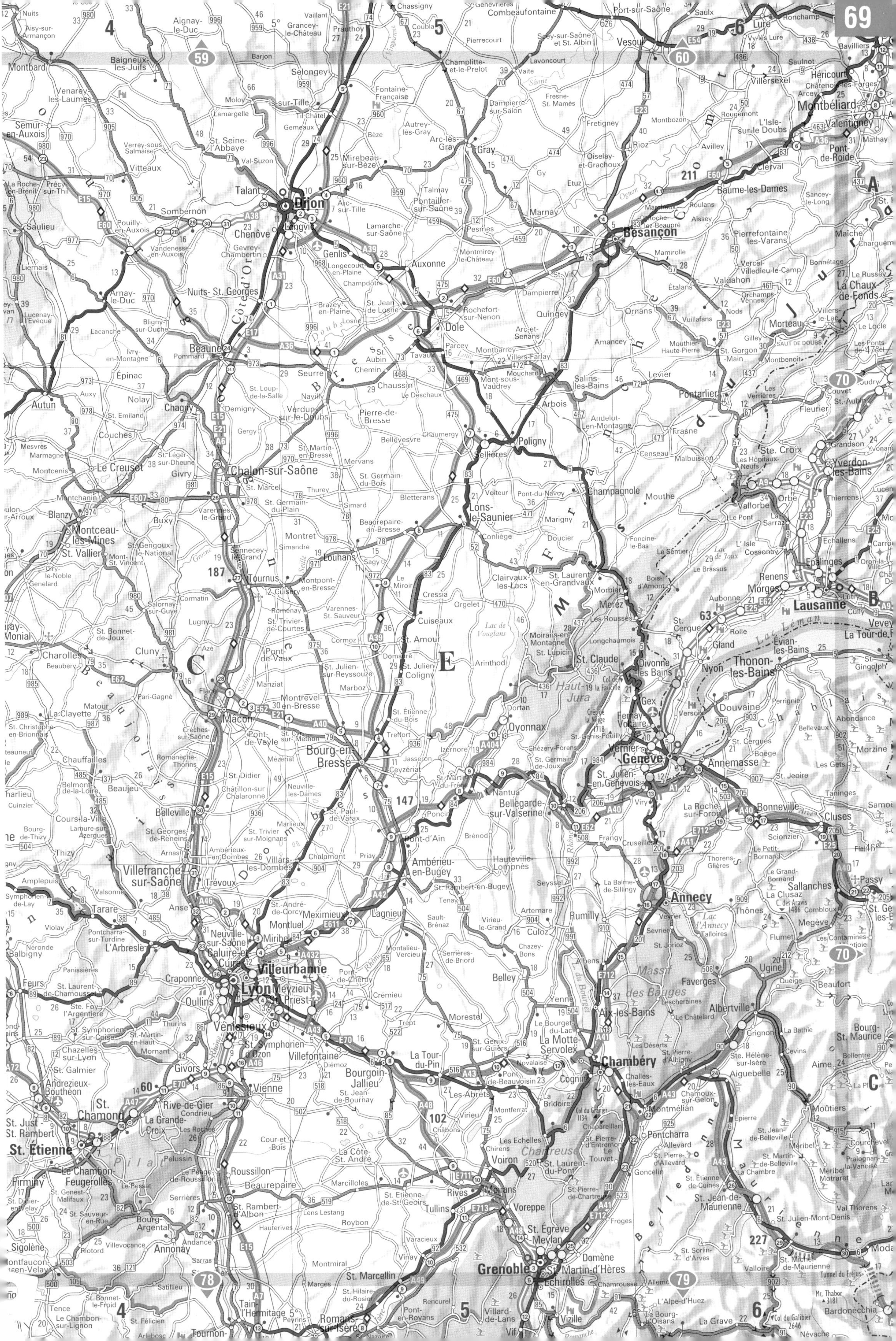
59
60
70
78
79
4
5
6
A
B
C
E
Dijon
Besançon
Montbéliard
Lausanne
Genève
Annecy
Chambéry
Grenoble
Lyon
Villeurbanne
St. Étienne
Mâcon
Chalon-sur-Saône
Beaune
Dole
Lons-le-Saunier
Bourg-en-Bresse
Oyonnax
Vesoul
Gray
Auxonne
Autun
Le Creusot
Montceau-les-Mines
Villefranche-sur-Saône
Vienne
Bourgoin-Jallieu
Voiron
Aix-les-Bains
Albertville
Thonon-les-Bains
Annemasse
Pontarlier
Morteau
La Chaux-de-Fonds
Yverdon-les-Bains
Montbard
Semur-en-Auxois
Tournus
Louhans
Poligny
Arbois
St. Claude
Nantua
Bellegarde-sur-Valserine
Ambérieu-en-Bugey
Vénissieux
Givors
St. Chamond
Annonay
Romans-sur-Isère
St. Marcellin
Tullins
Meylan
Échirolles
St. Jean-de-Maurienne
Moûtiers
Bonneville
Cluses
Sallanches
Lac Léman
Lac d'Annecy
Côte-d'Or
Bresse
Jura
Beaujolais
Dombes
Chartreuse
Massif des Bauges
Pilat
Chablais
Belledonne
Maurienne

Belfort
Montbéliard
Basel
Lörrach
Weil am Rhein
Rheinfelden
Bad Säckingen
Waldshut
Tiengen
Schaffhausen
Neuhausen
Frauenfeld
Winterthur
Bülach
Kloten
Zürich
Dübendorf
Uster
Baden
Brugg
Aarau
Olten
Zofingen
Liestal
Delémont
Porrentruy
Solothurn
Grenchen
Biel
La Chaux-de-Fonds
Le Locle
Neuchâtel
Bern
Burgdorf
Langenthal
Sursee
Luzern
Emmen
Zug
Schwyz
Altdorf
Thun
Spiez
Interlaken
Meiringen
Brienz
Sarnen
Stans
Andermatt
Airolo
Fribourg
Bulle
Yverdon-les-Bains
Lausanne
Vevey
Montreux
Aigle
Monthey
Martigny
Sion
Sierre
Visp
Brig
Naters
Zermatt
Domodóssola
Locarno
Lugano
Bellinzona
Biasca
Verbania
Varese
Gallarate
Busto Arsízio
Legnano
Rho
Novara
Vercelli
Biella
Ivrea
Aosta
Chamonix-Mont Blanc
Courmayeur
Torino
Chivasso
Casale Monferrato
Vigévano
Mortara
Evian-les-Bains
Thonon
Cluses
Sallanches
Megève
Bourg-St. Maurice
Moûtiers
Modane
Bardonécchia
S C H W E I Z
Alpi Lepontine
Alpes Pennine
Alpi Pennine
Alpi Graie
Monte Rosa
Matterhorn 4482
Dufourspitze 4634
Mont Blanc 4807
Gran Paradiso 4061
Eiger 3970
Jungfrau 4158
Finsteraarhorn 4274
Aletschhorn 4195
Tödi 3614
Simplon P. 2005
Furkapass 2431
Grimselpass 2165
Sustenpass 2224
P. del San Gottardo 2108
Col du Grd. St. Bernard
Tunnel du Mt. Blanc
Lötschberg Tunnel
Simplon Tunnel
St. Gotthard Tunnel
60
61
69
79
80

Allgäu
Bodensee
Friedrichshafen
Lindau
Bregenz
Kempten
Wangen i. A.
Immenstadt
Sonthofen
Oberstdorf
Füssen
Reutte
Garmisch-Partenkirchen
Mittenwald
Murnau
Oberammergau
Innsbruck
Hall in Tirol
Jenbach
Telfs
Imst
Landeck
St. Anton am Arlberg
Bludenz
Feldkirch
Dornbirn
Vaduz
LIECHTENSTEIN
St. Gallen
Rorschach
Chur
Davos
Klosters
St. Moritz
Samedan
Pontresina
Scuol
Allgäuer Alpen
Lechtaler Alpen
Karwendelgebirge
Stubaier Alpen
Ötztaler Alpen
Rätikon
Tuxer Alpen
Alpi Atesine
Vipiteno
Merano
Bolzano
Silandro
Bórmio
Livigno
Sóndrio
Tirano
Valtellina
Alpi Oróbie
Chiavenna
Colico
Lecco
Como
Bergamo
Monza
MILANO
Lodi
Crema
Cremona
Brescia
Lombardia
Salò
Desenzano del Garda
Lago di Garda
Riva del Garda
Rovereto
Trento
Verona
Vicenza
Mántova
Legnago
Dolomiti
Adamello
Stelvio
Edolo
Schio
Thiene
Cavalese
Predazzo
Ortisei
Bressanone
Asiago
Maróstica
Lonigo
Piacenza

Innsbruck
Kufstein
Wörgl
Jenbach
Schwaz
Hall in Tirol
Wattens
Kitzbühel
St. Johann in Tirol
Lofer
Reichenhall
Berchtesgaden
Hallein
Bad Ischl
Bad Goisern
Bad Aussee
Hallstatt
Abtenau
Saalfelden a. Steinernen Meer
Bischofshofen
St. Johann im Pongau
Radstadt
Schladming
Zell am See
Mittersill
Mayrhofen
Zell am Ziller
Bad Hofgastein
Badgastein
Tamsweg
ÖSTERREICH
Hohe Tauern
Zillertaler Alpen
Kitzbüheler Alpen
Tuxer Alpen
Karwendelgebirge
Tennengebirge
Niedere Tauern
Grossvenediger 3674
Grossglockner 3797
Matrei in Osttirol
Heiligenblut
Mallnitz
Obervellach
Spittal an der Drau
Lienz
Villach
Hermagor
Arnoldstein
Gailtaler Alpen
Karnische Hochalpen
Alpi Atesine
Mittenwald
Vipiteno
Bressanone
Brunico
Dobbiaco
Cortina d'Ampezzo
Ortisei
Canazei
Moena
Cavalese
Predazzo
Agordo
Belluno
Feltre
Pieve di Cadore
Tolmezzo
Gemona del Friuli
Údine
Cividale del Friuli
Gorizia
Nova Gorica
Monfalcone
Trieste
Koper
Izola
Piran
Umag
Poreč
Rovinj
Pordenone
Sacile
Conegliano
Vittório Véneto
Treviso
Castelfranco Véneto
Bassano del Grappa
Vicenza
Pádova
Mestre
Venézia
Chióggia
Rovigo
Portogruaro
Latisana
Lignano Sabbiadoro
Grado
Cáorle
Lido di Jésolo
San Donà di Piave
Palmanova
Cervignano del Friuli
Codroipo
Spilimbergo
Maniago
Aviano
Tarvisio
Julijske Alpe
Bovec
Kobarid
Tolmin
ITALIA
Dolomiti
G. di Trieste
Golfo di Venézia
Kérkira 22:00
Igoumenitsa 22:30
Pátrai 29:00
Çeşme 65:00
Kérkira Igoumenitsa Pátrai Izmir 64:00
Pula 6:00
62
63
71
82
1
2
3
A
B
C
12°
13°
47°

Windischgarsten
Grosser Priel 2523
Liezen
Rottenmann
Admont
Hieflau
Ennstaler Alpen
Hochschwab
Eisenerz
Eisenerzer Alpen
Vordernberg
Trofaiach
Seckauer Alpen
Wölzer Tauern
Leoben
Bruck an der Mur
Kapfenberg
Kindberg
Mürzzuschlag
Gloggnitz
Ternitz
Semmering
Aspang Markt
Kirchschlag
Deutschkreutz
Oberpullendorf
Friedberg
Pinkafeld
Oberwart
Hartberg
Pöllau
Birkfeld
Fohnsdorf
Knittelfeld
Judenburg
Zeltweg
Murau
Gleinalpe
Frohnleiten
Peggau
Weiz
Gleisdorf
Graz
Köflach
Voitsberg
Bärnbach
Fürstenfeld
Riegersburg
Feldbach
Fehring
Jennersdorf
Güssing
Körmend
Szombathely
Kőszeg
Szentgotthárd
Őrségi
Friesach
Wolfsberg
St. Andrä
Deutschlandsberg
Leibnitz
Wildon
Bad Radkersburg
Mureck
Murska Sobota
Lendava
Lenti
St. Veit an der Glan
Klagenfurt
Völkermarkt
Villach
Velden am Worther See
Ferlach
Bleiburg
Dravograd
Maribor
Ptuj
Ormož
Čakovec
Varaždin
Slovenj Gradec
Ravne na Koroškem
Pohorje
Karawanken
Jesenice
Bled
Radovljica
Kranj
Tržič
Kamniške in Savinjske Alpe
Velenje
Celje
Slovenska Bistrica
Rogaška Slatina
Krapina
Ivanšćica
Kalnik
Kamnik
Škofja Loka
Domžale
Ljubljana
Trbovlje
Zagorje
Hrastnik
Laško
Sevnica
Krško
Brežice
Litija
Vrhnika
Logatec
Idrija
SLOVENIJA
Grosuplje
Novo Mesto
Trebnje
Gorjanci
Zaprešić
Zagreb
Sesvete
Medvednica
Samobor
Velika Gorica
Dugo Selo
Vrbovec
Križevci
Ivanić Grad
Sisak
Petrinja
Postojna
Cerknica
Kočevje
Ribnica
Črnomelj
Metlika
Jastrebarsko
Karlovac
Duga Resa
HRVATSKA
Rijeka
Opatija
Delnice
Vrbovsko
Ogulin
Velika Kapela
Crikvenica
Novi Vinodolski
Labin
Slunj
Petrova Gora
Velika Kladuša
Zrinska Gora
Glina
Topusko
Bosanski Novi
Dvor

Sopron
Fertő tavi
Nagycenk
Kapuvár
Csorna
Győr
Ménfőcsanak
Komárom
Tata
Tatabánya
Oroszlány
Dorog
Budapest
Bicske
Biatorbágy
Érd
Kisbér
Pannonhalma
Pápa
Zirc
Mór
Várpalota
Székesfehérvár
Gárdony
Martonvásár
Kőszeg
Bük
Sárvár
Szombathely
Celldömölk
Vasvár
Körmend
Ajka
Veszprém
Balatonfüred
Balatonalmádi
Siófok
Tihany
Sümeg
Tapolca
Badacsonytomaj
Keszthely
Hévíz
Fonyód
Balatonboglár
Zalaegerszeg
Lenti
Nagykanizsa
Marcali
Kaposvár
Dombóvár
Tamási
Paks
Szekszárd
Bonyhád
Komló
Pécs
Szigetvár
Barcs
Mohács
Siklós
Harkány
Osijek
Đakovo
Slavonski Brod
Požega
Nova Gradiška
Okučani
Daruvar
Virovitica
Bjelovar
Koprivnica
Đurđevac
Križevci
Kutina
Sisak
Novska
Pakrac
Lipik
Slatina
Našice
Valpovo
Varaždin
Čakovec
Vukovar
Županja
Bosanska Gradiška
Bosanska Dubica
Bosanski Novi
Bosanski Brod
M A G Y A R
H R V A T S K A
Bakony
Mecsek
Papuk
Bilo Gora
Moslavačka Gora
Kalnik
Balaton
Drava
Sava
Duna
Rába
268

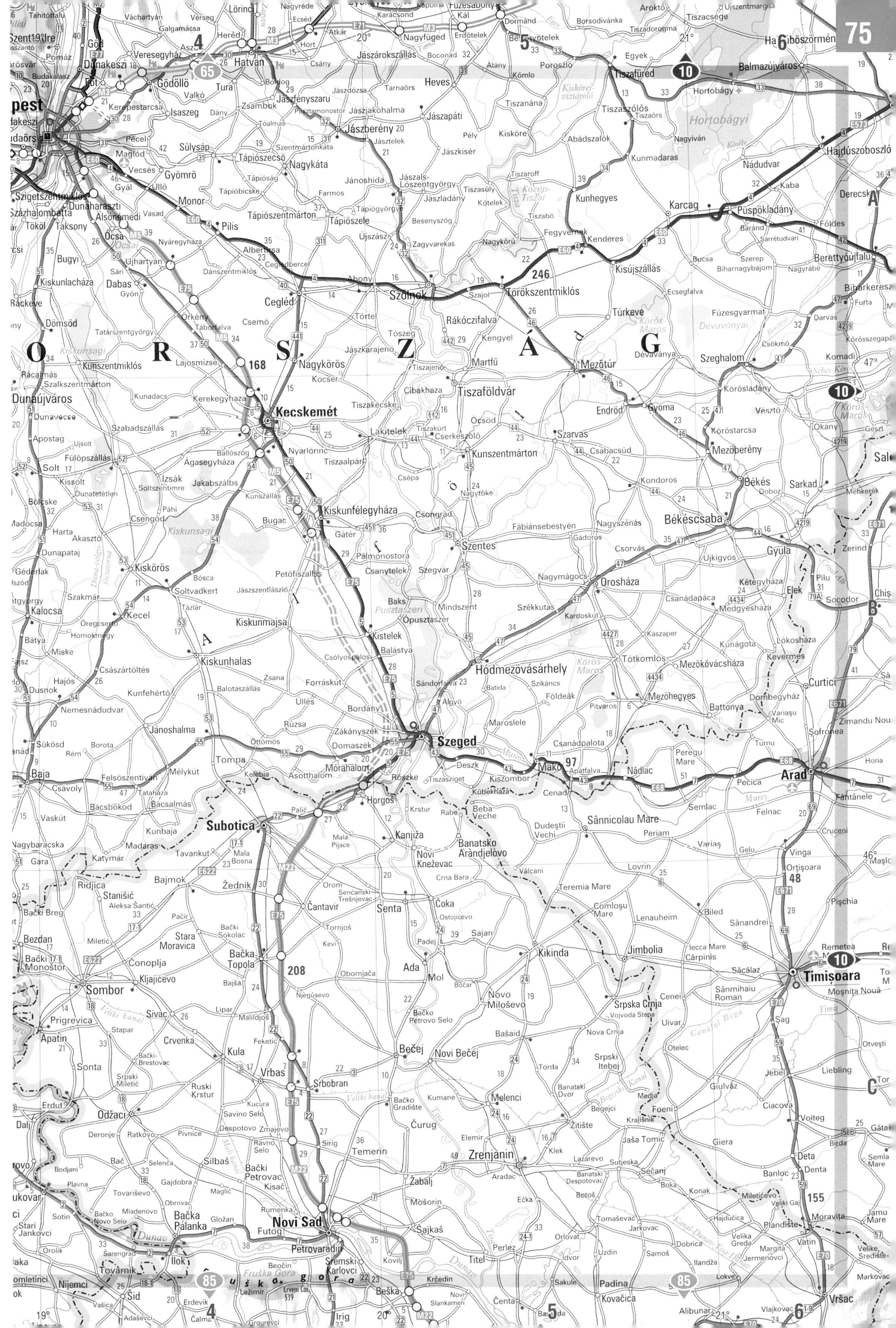
O R S Z Á G
Kecskemét
Szeged
Szolnok
Cegléd
Nagykőrös
Kiskunfélegyháza
Kiskunhalas
Hódmezővásárhely
Makó
Szentes
Csongrád
Békéscsaba
Gyula
Orosháza
Békés
Mezőtúr
Szarvas
Törökszentmiklós
Karcag
Kisújszállás
Püspökladány
Hajdúszoboszló
Berettyóújfalu
Tiszafüred
Heves
Jászberény
Gödöllő
Hatvan
Dunakeszi
Kalocsa
Kiskőrös
Baja
Dunaújváros
Subotica
Senta
Kikinda
Zrenjanin
Novi Sad
Sombor
Bačka Topola
Bečej
Vrbas
Kula
Arad
Timişoara
Vršac
Jimbolia
Sânnicolau Mare
Nădlac
Hortobágy
Kiskunsági
Pusztaszeri
Fruška Gora
Dunav
Tisza
Maros
Körös
E60
E75
E68
E70
E671
M5
M3
M22
10
65
85
168
208
246
97
155
48

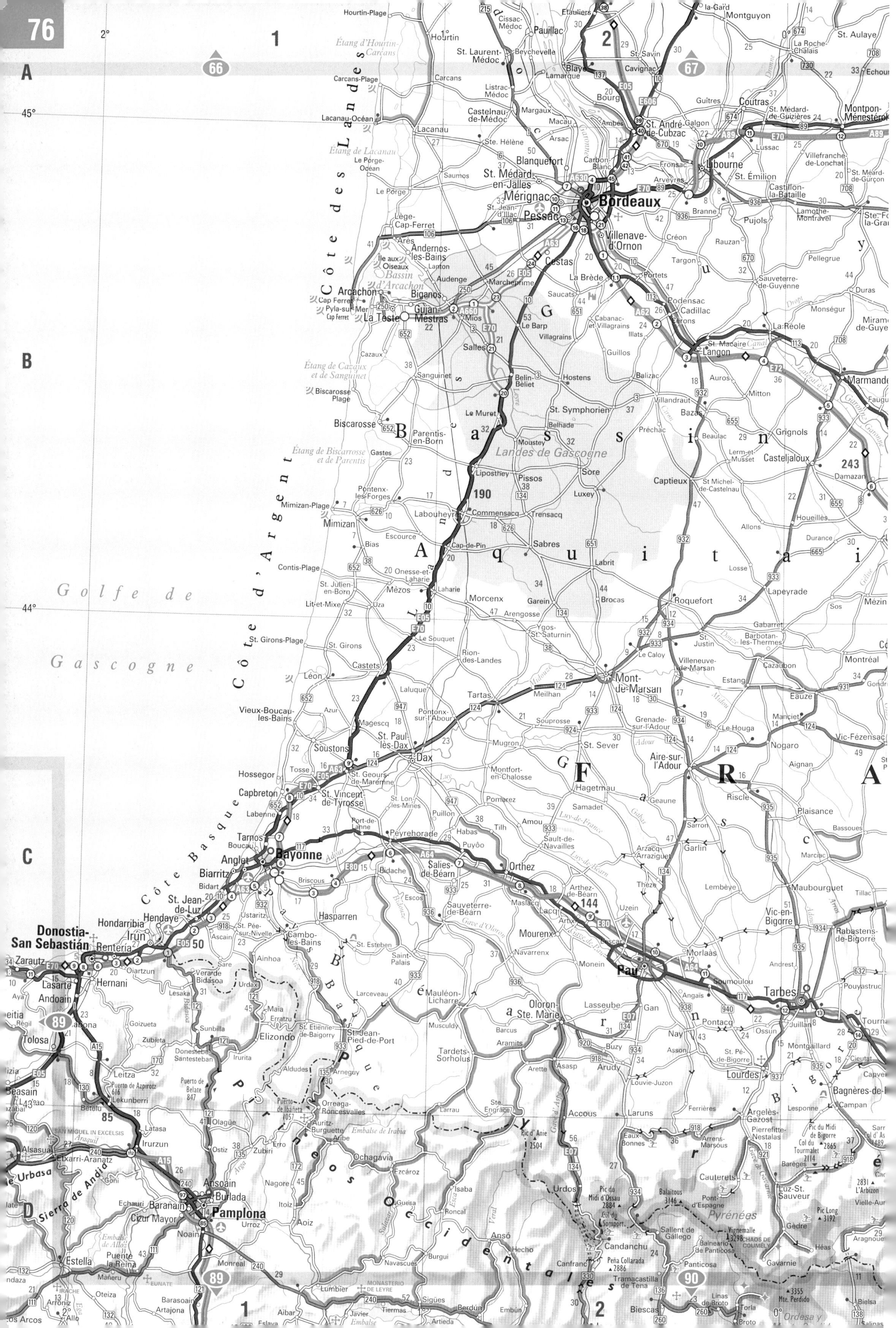
Bordeaux
Mérignac
Pessac
St. Médard-en-Jalles
Blanquefort
Villenave-d'Ornon
Cestas
Libourne
St. Émilion
Coutras
St. André-de-Cubzac
Blaye
Pauillac
Lacanau
Lacanau-Océan
Carcans
Hourtin
Arcachon
La Teste
Gujan-Mestras
Biganos
Andernos-les-Bains
Lège-Cap-Ferret
Bassin d'Arcachon
Langon
La Réole
Marmande
Bazas
Casteljaloux
Captieux
Biscarosse
Parentis-en-Born
Mimizan
Labouheyre
Sabres
Pissos
Morcenx
Mont-de-Marsan
Roquefort
Tartas
Dax
St. Paul-lès-Dax
Soustons
Hossegor
Capbreton
Bayonne
Anglet
Biarritz
St. Jean-de-Luz
Hendaye
Irun
Donostia-San Sebastián
Hernani
Tolosa
Pamplona
Burlada
Estella
Orthez
Pau
Tarbes
Lourdes
Oloron-Ste. Marie
Mauléon-Licharre
St. Jean-Pied-de-Port
Aire-sur-l'Adour
Nogaro
Eauze
Vic-en-Bigorre
Bagnères-de-Bigorre
Landes de Gascogne
Côte d'Argent
Côte des Landes
Côte Basque
Golfe de Gascogne
Aquitaine
Pays Basque
Bigorre
Pyrénées
Pyrénées Occidentales
Pic du Midi d'Ossau 2884
Balaitous 3146
Vignemalle 3298
Pic Long 3192
Mte. Perdido 3355
Col du Tourmalet 2114
Pic du Midi de Bigorre 2865
66
67
89
90
A
B
C
D
1
2

Périgueux
Trélissac
Coulounieix-Chamiers
Boulazac
St. Astier
Neuvic
Mussidan
Villamblard
Vergt
La Douze
Thenon
Montignac
Terrasson-la-Villedieu
Le Lardin-St. Lazare
Larche
Brive-la-Gaillarde
Malemort
Beynat
Argentat
St. Chamant
St. Privat
Pléaux
St. Martin-Valmeroux
Salers
St. Cernin
Jussac
Thiézac
Vic-sur-Cère
Murat
Plomb du Cantal
Aurillac
Arpajon-sur-Cère
Polminhac
St. Mamet-la-Salvetat
Le Rouget
Sousceyrac
Laroquebrou
Beaulieu-sur-Dordogne
Meyssac
Vayrac
Martel
Bretenoux
St. Céré
Cressensac
Salignac-Eyvigues
Sarlat-la-Canéda
Souillac
Le Bugue
Les Eyzies-de-Tayac
St. Cyprien
Pezuls
Campsegret
Pont-St. Mamet
Périgord
Dordogne
Bergerac
Lalinde
Le Buisson-Cadouin
Siorac-en-Périgord
Belvès
La Roque-Gageac
Domme
Monbazillac
Beaumont
Issigeac
Payrac
Rocamadour
Alvignac
Gramat
Gourdon
Latronquière
Maurs
Calvinet
Lacapelle-Marival
Le Bourg
Causses de Quercy
Montsalvy
Mur-de-Barrez
Lacroix-Barrez
Cassuéjouls
St. Hippolyte
Laguiole
Entraygues-sur-Truyère
Le Cayrol
Conques
Decazeville
Firmi
Aubin
Capdenac-Gare
Figeac
Livernon
Grèzec
Labastide-Murat
Lamothe-Cassel
Lauzès
Frayssinet
Salviac
Cazals
Villefranche-du-Périgord
Monpazier
Castillonès
Eymet
Villeréal
Lauzun
Monbahus
Seyches
Cancon
Tombeboeuf
Monflanquin
Fumel
Puy-l'Évêque
Prayssac
Luzech
Frayssinet-le-Gélat
Cahors
Cajarc
Villeneuve
Limogne-en-Quercy
Concots
Villecomtal
Espalion
Bozouls
Gabriac
Marcillac-Vallon
Montbazens
Roussennac
Rignac
Sebazac-Concourès
Rodez
Laissac
Villefranche-de-Rouergue
Villeneuve-sur-Lot
Castelmoron-sur-Lot
Tonneins
Ste. Livrade-sur-Lot
Tournon-d'Agenais
Penne-d'Agenais
Montaigu-de-Quercy
St. Antoine-de-Ficalba
Bourran
Aiguillon
Port-Ste. Marie
Laroque-Timbaut
Montcuq
Sauzet
Lalbenque
Castelnau-Montratier
Bourg-de-Visa
Lauzerte
Beauville
Puylaroque
Caylus
Parisot
Memer
Najac
La Fouillade
Rieupeyroux
La Salvetat-Peyralès
Baraqueville
Pont-de-Salars
La Primaube
Lac de Pont-de-Salars
Salmiech
Cassagnes-Bégonhès
Naucelle
Agen
Bon-Encontre
Puymirol
Nérac
Lamagistère
Valence-d'Agen
Moissac
Auvillar
Laplume
Astaffort
Francescas
Ligardes
Montpezat-de-Quercy
Molières
Caussade
Lafrançaise
Nègrepelisse
Montricoux
Vaour
St. Antonin-Noble-Val
Laguépie
Cordes-sur-Ciel
Monestiés
Carmaux
Blaye-les-Mines
Tanus
Villefranche-de-Panat
Réquista
Broquiès
Valence-d'Albigeois
St. Izaire
La Ville Dieu-du-Temple
Montauban
Castelsarrasin
Miradoux
Lavit
Lectoure
Montech
Bourret
Larrazet
Labastide-St. Pierre
Monclar-de-Quercy
Castelnau-de-Montmirail
Gaillac
Marsac
Albi
St. Juéry
Plaisance
St. Sernin-sur-Rance
Grands Causses
Valence-sur-Baïse
Fleurance
St. Clar
Beaumont-de-Lomagne
Verdun-sur-Garonne
Grisolles
Fronton
Villemur-sur-Tarn
Salvagnac
Rabastens
Lisle-sur-Tarn
Montans
Cadalen
Florentin
Villefranche-d'Albigeois
Alban
Teillet
Belmont-sur-Rance
Montestruc-sur-Gers
Solomiac
Mauvezin
Cox
Grenade
Cépet
St. Sulpice
Montastruc-la-Conseillère
Briatexte
Graulhet
Réalmont
Montredon-Labessonnié
Lacaune
Vabre
Col de la Bassine
Mts. de Lacaune
Jegun
Preignan
Nougaroulet
Cologne
Cadours
Montaigut-sur-Save
Lavaur
Lautrec
Roquecourbe
Brassac
Auch
Aubiet
Gimont
L'Isle-Jourdain
Léguevin
Colomiers
Blagnac
Toulouse
Verfeil
St. Paul-Cap-de-Joux
Vielmur-sur-Agout
Puylaurens
Castres
Anglès
La Salvetat-sur-Agout
Haut Languedoc
L'Isle-de-Noé
Montesquiou
Mirande
Seissan
Saramon
Samatan
Lombez
Plaisance
Cugnaux
St. Lys
Ramonville-St. Agne
Lanta
Caraman
Fourquevaux
Soual
Labruguière
Dourgne
Mazamet
Labastide-Rouairoux
Montagne Noire
Sorèze
Revel
St. Amans-Soult
Courniou
Col des Usclats
Miélan
St. Michel
Masseube
St. Foy-de-Peyrolières
Muret
Lherm
Baziège
Villefranche-de-Lauragais
St. Félix-Lauragais
Mas-Cabardès
Col de Serieres
Molas
L'Isle-en-Dodon
Rieumes
Montgiscard
Vernet
Gardouch
Saissac
Trie-sur-Baïse
Bérat
Noé
Auterive
Nailloux
Castelnaudary
Cintegabelle
Caunes-Minervois
Peyriac Minervois
Olonzac
Boulogne-sur-Gesse
Pouy-de-Touges
Carbonne
Lézat-sur-Lèze
Salles-sur-l'Hers
Montolieu
Conques-sur-Orbiel
Castelnau-Magnoac
Le Fousseret
Rieux
St. Ybars
Saverdun
Mazères
Bram
Alzonne
Carcassonne
Capendu
Galan
Blajan
Aurignac
Cazères
Montesquieu-Volvestre
Belpech
Fanjeaux
Montréal
Lannemezan
St. Plancard
St. Marcet
Boussens
Martres Tolosane
Tapio
Gaja-la-Selve
Villeneuve-de-Rivière
St. Martory
Mazères-sur-Salat
Ste. Croix-Volvestre
Le Fossat
Mirepoix
Pinas
Montréjeau
St. Gaudens
Valentine
Salies-du-Salat
Le Mas-d'Azil
Pailhès
Pamiers
Lagrasse
St. Laurent-de-la-Cabrerisse
Limoux
St. Hilaire
La Barthe-de-Neste
Barbazan
Aspet
Prat
Varilhes
La Bastide-de-Sérou
Malléon
Lagarde
Ajac
Loures-Barousse
Mauléon-Barousse
Sengouagnet
Arbas
Cazavet
St. Girons
Foix
Lieurac
Laroque-d'Olmes
Chalabre
Alet-les-Bains
Vignevieille
Mouthoumet
Corbières
Arreau
Cierp
St. Béat
Burret
Lavelanet
Espéraza
Puivert
Couiza
Rennes-les-Bains
Granges-de-Crouhens
Orgibet
Castillon-en-Couserans
Nalzen
Bélesta
Quillan
Soulatgé
Tuchan
Paziols
Col de Peyresourde
Picde Bacanère
Oust
Massat
Pic des 3 Seigneurs
Saurat
Tarascon-sur-Ariège
Pic de St. Barthelemy
St. Paul-de-Fenouillet
Caudiès-de-Fenouillèdes
Maury
St. Lary-Soulan
Bagnères-de-Luchon
Eylie
Mt. Valier
Aulus-les-Bains
Couflens
Belcaire
Axat
Estagel
Bossost
Vall d'Aran
Vicdessos
Les Cabannes
Usson-les-Bains
Sournia
Millas
Perpignan
Vielha
Salau
Ax-les-Thermes
Quérigut
Ille-sur-Têt
Maladeta
Tunel de Vielha
Pico de Aneto
Puerto de la Bonaigua
Alos d'Ensil
Pic de Montcalm
Pic d'Estats
Tavescan
El Serrat
Andorra
Formiguères
Prades
Vinca
Boule-d'Amont
Fourques
Vernet-les-Bains
Caldas de Boi
Esterri d'Aneu
Areo
Espot
Ordino
L'Hospitalet
Col de Puymorens
Pic du
Benasque
Nestier
Lot
Tarn
Aveyron
Garonne
Canal du Midi
Gers
Save
Ariège
Viaur
Cère
Dadou
Agout
Thoré
Lac de Pont-de-Salars

Massif Central
Volcans d'Auvergne
Allanche
Ségur-les-Villas
Neussargues-Moissac
Murat
Plomb du Cantal
Thiezac
Vic-sur-Cère
Aurillac
Arpajon-sur-Cère
St. Flour
Pierrefort
Chaudes-Aigues
Mur-de-Barrez
Lacroix-Barrez
Mts. d'Aubrac
Cassuéjouls
St. Hippolyte
Laguiole
Entraygues-sur-Truyère
Espalion
St. Come-d'Olt
St. Geniez-d'Olt
Bozouls
Rodez
Laissac
Sévérac-le-Château
Pont-de-Salars
Salles-Curan
Millau
St. Beauzély
St. Rome-de-Tarn
St. Affrique
Grands Causses
Camarès
Belmont-sur-Rance
Lacaune
Mts. de Lacaune
Murat-sur-Vèbre
Haut-Languedoc
Olargues
St. Pons-de-Thomières
Lodève
Le Caylar
Causse du Larzac
La Cavalerie
Nant
Meyrueis
Causse-Méjean
Mts. de la Margeride
St. Chély-d'Apcher
Aumont-Aubrac
Marvejols
Mende
La Canourgue
Ste. Enimie
Florac
Cévennes
Mt. Aigoual 1567
Le Vigan
Ganges
St. Hippolyte-du-Fort
Anduze
Alès
La Grand-Combe
Villefort
Langogne
Pradelles
Mts. du Velay
Le Puy-en-Velay
Yssingeaux
Annonay
Tournon-sur-Rhône
Valence
Lamastre
Le Cheylard
Mt. Mézenc 1754
Privas
La Voulte-sur-Rhône
Aubenas
Vals-les-Bains
Largentière
Joyeuse
Les Vans
Montélimar
Le Teil
Viviers
Pierrelatte
Bourg-St. Andéol
Pont-St. Esprit
Bollène
Orange
Bagnols-sur-Cèze
Uzès
Avignon
Villeneuve-lès-Avignon
Remoulins
Beaucaire
Tarascon
Nîmes
St. Rémy-de-Provence
Arles
St. Gilles
Vauvert
Lunel
Sommières
Montpellier
Aigues-Mortes
La Grande-Motte
Le Grau-du-Roi
Camargue
Stes-Maries-de-la-Mer
Port-St.-Louis-du-Rhône
Fos-sur-Mer
Istres
Miramas
Sète
Frontignan
Mèze
Agde
Le Cap d'Agde
Pézenas
Clermont-l'Hérault
Bédarieux
Béziers
Sérignan
Valras-Plage
Narbonne
Narbonne-Plage
Gruissan
Port-la-Nouvelle
Sigean
Lézignan-Corbières
Corbières
Leucate
Port-Barcarès
Rivesaltes
Perpignan
Canet-Plage
St. Cyprien
Elne
Thuir
Côte d'Améthyste
Golfe du Lion
Côte Vermeille
Tanger 36:00
Alicante
Oran 23:00
Alger 18:00
Annaba 23:00
Bejaia 21:00
Skikda 23:00
F R A
A
B
C
D
1
2
3
4°
43°
44°
45°
68
69
77
91

Grenoble
Meylan
Domène
St. Martin-d'Hères
Échirolles
Chamrousse
Vizille
Villard-de-Lans
Vif
Romans-sur-Isère
St. Marcellin
Pont-en-Royans
St. Jean-en-Royans
Vercors
Valence
Chabeuil
Crest
Die
Saillans
Châtillon-en-Diois
Luc-en-Diois
Dieulefit
Nyons
Vaison-la-Romaine
Buis-les-Baronnies
Carpentras
Pernes-les-Fontaines
L'Isle-sur-la-Sorgue
Cavaillon
Apt
Sault
Mt. Ventoux
Banon
Forcalquier
Manosque
Pertuis
Lourmarin
Cadenet
Aix-en-Provence
Gardanne
Marseille
Aubagne
Cassis
La Ciotat
Bandol
Sanary-sur-Mer
La Seyne-sur-Mer
Toulon
Hyères
Giens
Porquerolles
Î. de Porquerolles
Îs. d'Hyères
Î. de Port-Cros
Î. du Levant
Parc National de Port-Cros
Le Lavandou
Bormes-les-Mimosas
Cavalaire-sur-Mer
St. Tropez
Ste. Maxime
Cogolin
Grimaud
Fréjus
St. Raphaël
Côte de l'Esterel
Mandelieu-la-Napoule
Cannes
Antibes
Juan-les-Pins
Grasse
Cagnes-sur-Mer
Vence
Nice
Villefranche-sur-Mer
Côte d'Azur
Draguignan
Le Muy
Brignoles
St. Maximin-la-Ste. Baume
Trets
Le Luc
Vidauban
Lorgues
Salernes
Barjols
Riez
Moustiers-Ste. Marie
Castellane
Digne-les-Bains
Château-Arnoux
Sisteron
Laragne-Montéglin
Serres
Veynes
Gap
Tallard
Embrun
Barcelonnette
Jausiers
Allos
Colmars
Annot
Entrevaux
Puget-Théniers
Guillaumes
Valberg
St. Martin-Vésubie
Massif du Pelvoux
Ecrins
La Mure
Corps
St. Bonnet
Orcières
Vallouise
L'Argentière-la-Bessée
Guillestre
Briançon
Montgenèvre
Le Monêtier-les-Bains
La Grave
Les Deux-Alpes
L'Alpe-d'Huez
Le Bourg-d'Oisans
Valloire
Modane
Tunnel du Fréjus
Bardonécchia
Oulx
Sestriere
Susa
Bussoleno
Avigliana
Rívoli
Giaveno
Pinerolo
Saluzzo
Cúneo
Dronero
Borgo San Dalmazzo
Alpes Maritimes
Mercantour
Provence
FRANCE
Tunis 20:00
Porto Tórres 14:15
Ajaccio 8:30
Bastia 10:00
Calvi 12:00
L'Ile Rousse 11:30
Porto-Vecchio 13:30
Propriano 8:30
Ajaccio 8:00
Bastia 8:30
Propriano 8:30
Porto Tórres 9:30
Bastia 3:30
L'Ile Rousse 3:00
Calvi 2:45
Ajaccio 4:05
Propriano 4:10
69
70
80
4
5
6
B
C
D
6°
7°
43°

A
B
C
D
1
2
3
Torino
Chivasso
Crescentino
Trino
Casale Monferrato
Mortara
Garlasco
Pavia
Lodigiano
Casalpusterlengo
Belgioioso
Venaria
Caselle Torinese
Settimo Torinese
Rivoli
Avigliana
Giaveno
Orbassano
Moncalieri
Chieri
Castelnuovo Don Bosco
Montiglio
Moncalvo
Ozzano Monferrato
Occimiano
Valenza
Mede
Lomello
Sannazzaro de' Burgondi
Voghera
Broni
Stradella
Castel San Giovanni
Casteggio
Pinerolo
Torre Pellice
None
Carignano
Poirino
Villanova d'Asti
Carmagnola
Asti
San Damiano d'Asti
Alessándria
Tortona
Felizzano
Quargnento
Oviglio
Nizza Monferrato
Costigliole d'Asti
Canelli
Acqui Terme
Novi Lígure
Serravalle Scrívia
Gavi
Ovada
Varzi
Bóbbio
Ottone
Cavour
Racconigi
Barge
Cavallermaggiore
Bra
Alba
Saluzzo
Savigliano
Verzuolo
Cherasco
Fossano
Dogliani
Busca
Cúneo
Caráglio
Borgo San Dalmazzo
Mondovì
Carrù
Ceva
Millesimo
Cairo Montenotte
Busalla
Ronco Scrivia
Torriglia
Génova
Nervi
Recco
Camogli
Rapallo
Santa Margherita Ligure
Portofino
Chiávari
Lavagna
Sestri Levante
Moneglia
Déiva Marina
Lévanto
Vernazza
Voltri
Pegli
Arenzano
Varazze
Celle Ligure
Albisola Marina
Savona
Vado Lígure
Spotorno
Noli
Finale Lígure
Pietra Ligure
Loano
Borghetto Santo Spirito
Albenga
Alássio
Laiguéglia
Diano Marina
Impéria
Tággia
Riva Ligure
San Remo
Ospedaletti
Bordighera
Ventimiglia
Menton
MONACO
Monte-Carlo
Beaulieu-sur-Mer
Villefranche-sur-Mer
Nice
Cap Ferrat
Antibes
Limone Piemonte
Tende
Sospel
Breil-sur-Roya
Saorge
Ormea
Garéssio
Calizzano
Pieve di Teco
Triora
Mercantour
P i e m o n t e
L i g u r i a
A p p e n n i n o L i g u r e
A l p e s M a r i t i m e s
Golfo di Génova
Riviera di Ponente
Riviera di Levante
Côte d'Azur
MARE LIGURE
Bastia 3:05
L'Île Rousse 5:45
Palermo 20:00
Tunis 24:00
Palau
Olbia 10:00
Porto Tórres 10:00
Árbatax
Cágliari 20:00
Bastia 6:30
Barcelona 17:00
Bastia 3:30
L'Ile Rousse 3:00
Calvi 2:45
Ajaccio 4:05
Propriano 4:10
Savona 5:45
Nice 2:45
Marseille 12:00
Nice 3:00
Marseille 11:30
C. Corse
Ersa
Macinaggio
Rogliano
Pino
Luri
Santa Severa
Marine de Sisco
Nonza
Brando
Erbalunga
G. de St. Florent
San-Martino-di-Lota
Ville-di-Pietrabugno
Patrimonio
St. Florent
Bastia
Biguglia
Oletta
Santo-Pietro-di-Tenda
l'Île-Rousse
Belgodere
44°
43°
8°
9°
70
71
79
110

Cremona
Mántova
Legnago
Rovigo
Fidenza
Parma
Réggio nell'Emília
Modena
Carpi
Mirándola
Ferrara
Cento
Bologna
Ímola
Faenza
Forlì
Lugo
Comácchio
Argenta
Pontrémoli
Aulla
La Spézia
Sarzana
Carrara
Massa
Viaréggio
Lucca
Pisa
Livorno
Pistóia
Prato
Firenze
Empoli
Pontedera
San Miniato
Volterra
Poggibonsi
Siena
Arezzo
Cortona
Montepulciano
Chiusi
Orvieto
Grosseto
Follónica
Piombino
Portoferraio
Elba
Capraia
Gorgona
Cécina
Massa Maríttima
Montalcino
Appennino
Alpi Apuane
Toscana
Maremma
Colline Metallifere
Arcipelago Toscano
Mar Ligure
Levante
Canale di Piombino
Bastia 2:00
Porto Vecchio 7:30
Golfo Aranci 9:00
Ólbia 10:00
Palermo 17:00
Marseille 10:00
Toulon 8:30
Nice 3:30
Génova 6:30
La Spezia 5:00
Savona 3:05
Livorno 2:00
Tunis 21:00
Bastia 3:00
Piombino 3:00
Parco Nazionale dell'Arcipélago Toscano

1
2
13°
14°
12°
45°
A
B
C
D
72
81
102
103
105
115
152
178
199
87
Sottomarina
Cona
Cavárzere
Rosalina
Adria
Loreo
Rovigo
Táglio di Po
Contarina
Ariano nel Polésine
Ca'Pisani
Porto Tolle
Scardovari
Crespino
Iolanda di Savoia
Mésola
Delta del Po
Codigoro
Pomposa
Foci del Po
Tresigallo
Massa Fiscáglia
Migliarino
Lagosanto
Lido di Volano
Lido della Nazioni
Lido di Pomposa
Lido degli Scacchi
Porto Garibaldi
Lido degli Estensi
Portomaggiore
Comácchio
Valli di Comacchio
Longastrino
Consélice
Alfonsine
San Alberto
Lamone
Marina Romea
Marina di Ravenna
Punta Marina
Massa Lombarda
Mezzano
Lugo
Ravenna
Russi
Catánia 35:00
Lido di Classe
Lido di Savio
Savio
Faenza
Milano Marittima
Cérvia
Pinerella
Forlì
Forlimpopoli
Cesenático
Gatteo a Mare
Bellária
Igea Marina
Bertinoro
Méldola
Cesena
Predáppio
Rocca San Casciano
Viserba
Savignano sul Rubicone
Rímini
Santarcángelo di Romagna
Borello
Civitella di Romagna
Galeata
Mercato Saraceno
Ránchio
Miramare
Riccione
Sogliano al Rubicone
Cattólica
SAN MARINO
San Marino
Santa Sofia
Sársina
Talamello
San Leo
Novaféltria
Pésaro
San Piero in Bagno
Sant'Agata Feltria
Morciano di Romagna
Saludécio
Mercatino Conca
Bagno di Romagna
Pennabilli
Macerata Féltria
Montécchio
Fano
Badia Pratáglia
Carpegna
Sassocorvaro
Mombaróccio
Marotta
Saltara
Calcinelli
Sestino
Lunano
Urbino
Fossombrone
Costanzo
San Mondolfo
Senigállia
Badia Tedalda
Pieve S. Stefano
Borgo Pace
Sant'Angelo in Vado
Urbánia
Monte Porzio
Marzocca
Mondavio
Rocca Priora
Falconara Maríttima
Ancona
Corinaldo
Chiaravalle
Sansepolcro
Piobbico
Ostra
Cónero
Subbiano
San Giustino
Apécchio
Cagli
Pérgola
San Lorenzo in Campo
San Marcello
Anghiari
Montecarotto
Moie
Iesi
Agugliano
Camerano
Sirolo
Numana
Arezzo
Città di Castello
Arcévia
Cantiano
Serra S. Quírico
Ósimo
Castelfidardo
Loreto
Porto Recanati
Pietralunga
Mte. Cátria 1701
Cupramontana
Filottrano
Recanati
Palazzo del Pero
Scheggia
Sassoferrato
Apiro
Cíngoli
Montefano
Rigutino
Trestina
Monte Cucco
Montecassiano
Potenza Picena
Porto Potenza Picena
Castiglion Fiorentino
Gúbbio
Camporeggiano
Fabriano
Cerreto d'Esi
Tréia
Passo di Tréia
Civitanova Alta
Cortona
Niccone
Umbértide
Sigillo
Fossato di Vico
Macerata
Civitanova Marche
Chiana
Mercatale
Branca
San Severino Marche
Sforzacosta
Porto Sant'Elpídio
Tuoro sul Trasimeno
Passignano sul Trasimeno
Scritto
Matélica
Tolentino
Corridónia
Sant'Elpídio a Mare
Lido di Fermo
L. Trasimeno
Gualdo Tadino
Casa Castalda
Castelraimondo
Montegranaro
Magione
Piccione
Serrapetrona
Abbadia di Fiastra
Mogliano
Porto San Giórgio
Castiglione del Lago
Pozzuolo
Ponte Felcino
Valfabbrica
Pióraco
Camerino
Caldarola
Fermo
Perúgia
Ponte San Giovanni
Nocera Umbra
Monte Subasio
Montegiórgio
San Ginésio
Mte. Pennino 1571
Serravalle di Chienti
Múccia
Pedaso
Mugnano
Bastia
Assisi
Servigliano
Monterubbiano
Chiusi
Tavernelle
Bettona
Spello
Valtopina
Colfiorito
Pieve Torina
Sarnano
Santa Vittória in Matenano
Cupra Maríttima
Città della Pieve
Piegaro
Deruta
Cannara
Casenove
Appennino
Bolognola
Amándola
Montalto delle Marche
Ripatransone
Grottammare
Cerqueto
Monteleone d'Orvieto
Casalina
Bevagna
Foligno
Visso
Montefortino
Comunanza
Rotella
San Benedetto del Tronto
Marsciano
Collepepe
Monte Sibillini
Offida
Acquaviva Picena
Porto d'Áscoli
Piazze
Casciano
San Venanzo
Bastardo
Montefalco
Trevi
Sellano
Castelsantángelo
Montemónaco
Áscoli Piceno
Martinsicuro
Fratta Todina
Ficulle
Tevere
Mte. Vettore 2476
Balzo
Nereto
Alba Adriática
Massa Martana
San Giácomo
Tripónzo
Nórcia
Arquata del Tronto
Sant'Egídio alla Vibrata
Tortoreto Lido
Acquapendente
Prodo
Todi
Piedipaterno
Serravalle
Civitella di Tronto
Orvieto
Capretta
Spoleto
Acquasanta Terme
Mosciano Sant'Angelo
Giulianova
San Lorenzo Nuovo
Bolsena
Baschi
Acquasparta
Cáscia
Accúmoli
Valle Castellana
Campli
Gran Sasso e Monti della Laga
Montecastri
Monteleone di Spoleto
Téramo
Roseto degli Abruzzi
Bagnorégio
Guardea
San Gémini Fonte
Civita
Notaresco
Pineto
Montório al Vomano
Ferentillo
Amatrice
Amélia
Montefranco
Roccapassa
Poreč
Baderna
Šušnjevica
Mošćenice
Kanfanar
Žminj
Kršan
Brestova
Porozina
Vrsar
Plomin
Labin
Dragozet
Rovinj
Svetvinčenat
Raša
Rabac
Bale
Barban
Barbariga
Vodnjan
Koromačno
ISTARSKA
Marčana
Venézia 6:00
Brijuni
Brionski
Pula
Medulin
Martinšćica
Premantura
Rt. Kamenjak
Unije
Nerezine
3:10
Susak
MARE ADRIATICO
JADRANSKO MORE
Zadar 6:00
Bríndisi 11:30
Kérkira 19:00
Igoumenítsa 16:00
Pátrai 19:00
Šibenik 8:30
Split 4:30
Starigrad 9:30
Vis 8:00
Hvar 5:00
Vela Luka 6:20
Ubli 7:30
Bar 32:00
Durrës 18:00
Romagna
Appennino Umbro-Marchigiano

BOSNA I
HERCEGOVINA
HRVATSKA
Velebit
Mala Kapela
Plješevica
Grmeč Planina
Krajina
Dinara Planina
Svilaja
Kozara
Kvarnerić
Velebitski Kanal
Virsko more
Splitski Kanal
Brački Kanal
Hvarski Kanal
Viški Kanal
Korčulanski Kanal
Lastovski Kanal
Kornati
Telašćica
Paklenica
Plitvička Jezera
Vransko Jezero
Prokljansko Jezero
Peručko Jezero
Krka
MORE
ADRIATICO
Omišalj
Crikvenica
Njivice
Selce
Malinska
Novi Vinodolski
Vrbnik
Krk
Punat
Baška
Senj
Cres
Rab
Lopar
Kampor
Supetarska Draga
Osor
Lun
Novalja
Pag
Mali Lošinj
Veli Lošinj
Silba
Olib
Premuda
Ist
Molat
Vir
Privlaka
Nin
Sestrunj
Petrčane
Zadar
Ugljan
Preko
Kali
Božava
Brbinj
Dugi Otok
Kukljica
Pašman
Sali
Žut
Kornat
Murter
Tisno
Vodice
Šibenik
Zablaće
Krapanj
Žirje
Primošten
Rogoznica
Trogir
Marina
Kaštel Stari
Split
Solin
Stobreč
Čiovo
Omiš
Dugi Rat
Klis
Sinj
Trilj
Žrnovica
Šolta
Maslinica
Grohote
Rogač
Supetar
Sutivan
Postira
Pučišća
Milna
Nerežišća
Bol
Brač
Hvar
Starigrad
Vrboska
Jelsa
Šćedro
Vis
Komiža
Biševo
Svetac
Jabucka
Vela Luka
Blato
Korčula
Pigradic
Sušac
Lastovo
Kopište
Ubli
Gospič
Otočac
Lički Osik
Perušić
Udbina
Gračac
Obrovac
Benkovac
Biograd na Moru
Pakoštane
Knin
Drniš
Skradin
Kistanje
Vrlika
Bihać
Cazin
Velika Kladuša
Bosanska Krupa
Bosanski Petrovac
Drvar
Bosansko Grahovo
Glamoč
Livno
Ključ
Sanski Most
Prijedor
Bosanski Novi
Bosanska Kostajnica
Dvor
Slunj
Plaški
Brinje
Rakovica
Titova Korenica
Karlobag
Jablanac
Starigrad-Paklenica
Novigrad
Posedarje
Bibinje
Sukošan
Ancona 6:00
Ancona 8:30
Ancona 9:00
Ancona 5:00
Split 5:15
Zadar 5:15
Rijeka 12:00
Rijeka
E65
E71
E761
E66
73
84
103
199
149
3
4
5
A
B
C
D
15°
16°
45°
44°
43°

BOSNA I
HERCEGOVINA
Bosanska Dubica
Bosanska Gradiška
Slavonski Brod
Bosanski Brod
Županja
Prijedor
Derventa
Modriča
Bosanski Šamac
Orašje
Brčko
Laktaši
Prnjavor
Banja Luka
Sanski Most
Doboj
Gradačac
Gračanica
Kotor Varoš
Teslić
Tešanj
Maglaj
Tuzla
Lukavac
Ključ
Mrkonjić Grad
Žepče
Zavidovići
Živinice
Jajce
Šipovo
Travnik
Novi Travnik
Zenica
Vitez
Donji Vakuf
Kakanj
Bugojno
Kupres
Visoko
Vareš
Olovo
Vlasenica
Livno
Gornji Vakuf
Prozor
Kiseljak
Ilidža
Sarajevo
Vogošća
Pale
Sokolac
Tomislavgrad
Jablanica
Konjic
Goražde
Foča
Kalinovik
Mostar
Široki Brijeg
Ljubuški
Čapljina
Stolac
Nevesinje
Gacko
Metković
Ploče
Opuzen
Neum
Makarska
Omiš
Sinj
Trebinje
Bileća
Ljubinje
Dubrovnik
Cavtat
Nikšić
Plužine
Korčula
Lastovo
Mljet
Brač
Pelješac
Kozara
Manjača
Vlašić
Vranica
Bitovnja
Bjelašnica
Jahorina
Treskavica
Prenj
Čvrsnica
Zelengora
Maglić
Romanija
Konjuh
Ozren
Cincar
Majevica
Javornik
Durmitor
Golija
Njegoš
E70
E73
E661
E761
E762
E65
74
83
15
A
B
C
D
1
2
3
17°
18°
19°
45°
43°

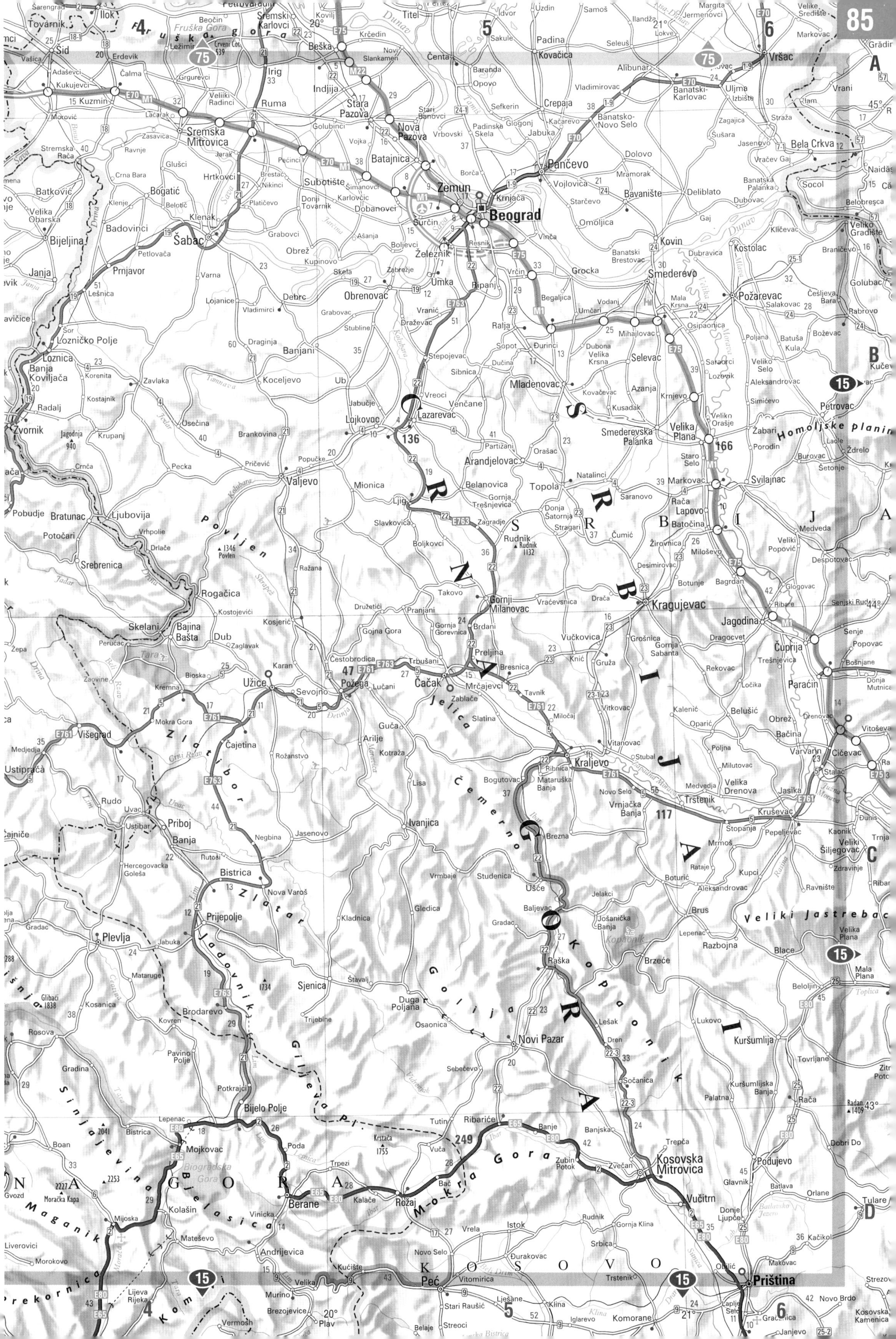
Beograd
Zemun
Krnjača
Pančevo
Smederevo
Požarevac
Novi Sad
Sremska Mitrovica
Šabac
Bijeljina
Zvornik
Loznica
Valjevo
Obrenovac
Lazarevac
Arandjelovac
Mladenovac
Smederevska Palanka
Velika Plana
Kragujevac
Jagodina
Ćuprija
Paraćin
Kruševac
Kraljevo
Čačak
Gornji Milanovac
Užice
Požega
Višegrad
Priboj
Prijepolje
Plevlja
Bijelo Polje
Mojkovac
Kolašin
Berane
Rožaj
Andrijevica
Novi Pazar
Raška
Kosovska Mitrovica
Vučitrn
Priština
Peć
Sjenica
Ivanjica
Trstenik
Vrnjačka Banja
Kuršumlija
Podujevo
Vršac
Bela Crkva
Kovin
Inđija
Ruma
Stara Pazova
Nova Pazova
Batajnica
Surčin
Železnik
Umka
Vrčin
Grocka
Vinča
Ripanj
Ralja
Sopot
Topola
Lapovo
Batočina
Svilajnac
Petrovac
Kučevo
Golubac
Veliko Gradište
Dubovac
Deliblato
Kovačica
Alibunar
Crepaja
Opovo
Čenta
Padina
Beška
Irig
Titel
Sremski Karlovci
Ilok
Šid
Tovarnik
Bajina Bašta
Ljubovija
Kosjerić
Arilje
Nova Varoš
Tutin
Zvečan
Istok
S R B I J A
C R N A G O R A
K O S O V O
Fruška gora
Homoljske planine
Povljen
Zlatibor
Zlatar
Jadovnik
Golija
Kopaonik
Čemerno
Jelica
Mokra Gora
Bjelasica
Sinjajevina
Maganik
Veliki Jastrebac
Dunav
Sava
Drina
Morava
Ibar
Lim
E70
E75
E763
E761
E65
E80
M1
15
75
4
5
6
A
B
C
D

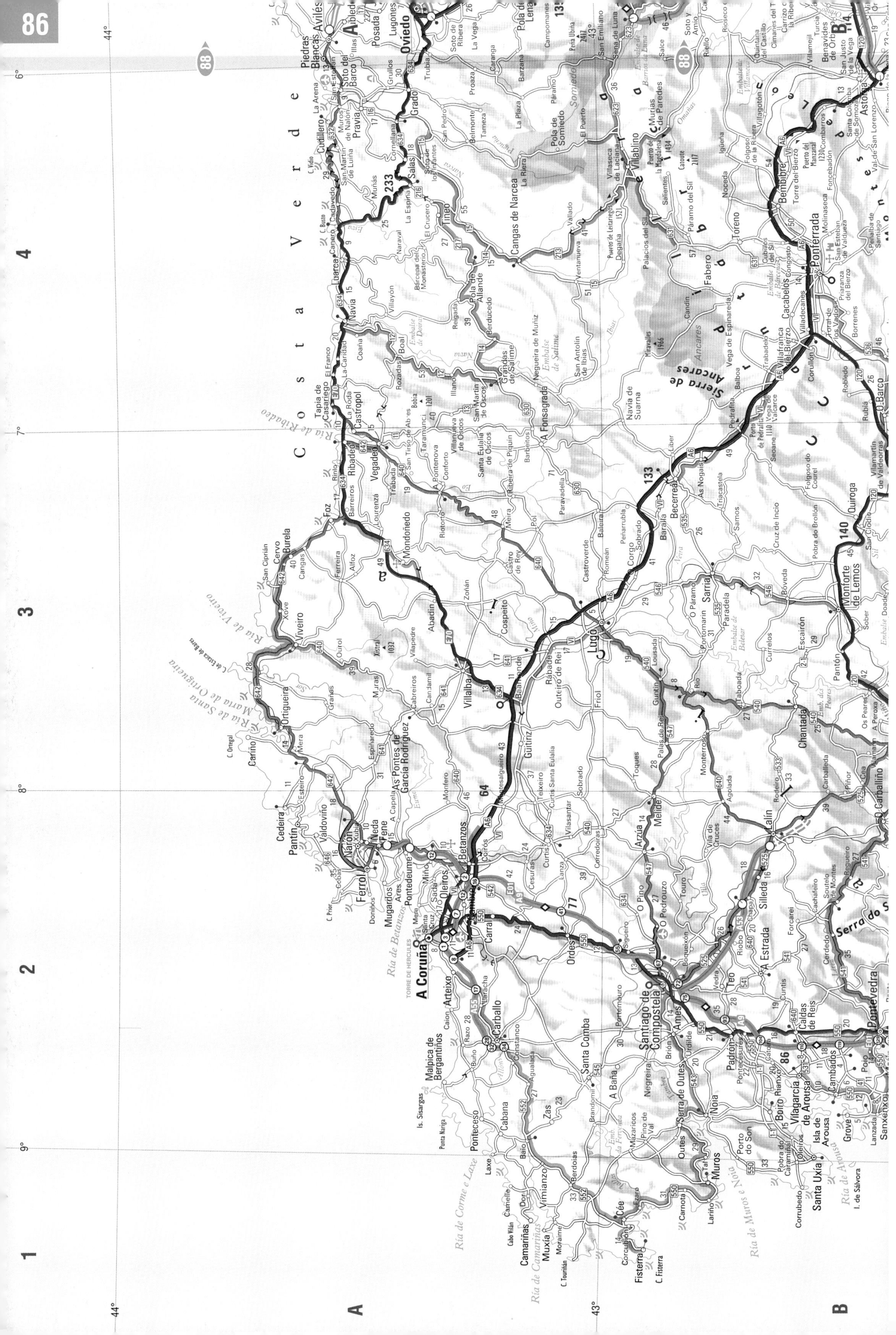
Costa Verde
A Coruña
Ferrol
Betanzos
Santiago de Compostela
Lugo
Oviedo
Avilés
Pontevedra
Ponferrada
Monforte de Lemos
Vilagarcía de Arousa
Carballo
Viveiro
Ribadeo
Luarca
Cangas de Narcea
Villablino
Sierra de Ancares
Ría de Ribadeo
Ría de Viveiro
Ría de Betanzos
Ría de Corme e Laxe
Ría de Camariñas
Ría de Muros e Noia
Ría de Arousa
Fisterra
C. Fisterra
Muros
Noia
Padrón
Lalín
Chantada
Sarria
Mondoñedo
Vilalba
Astorga
Bembibre
88
44°
43°
6°
7°
8°
9°
1
2
3
4
A
B

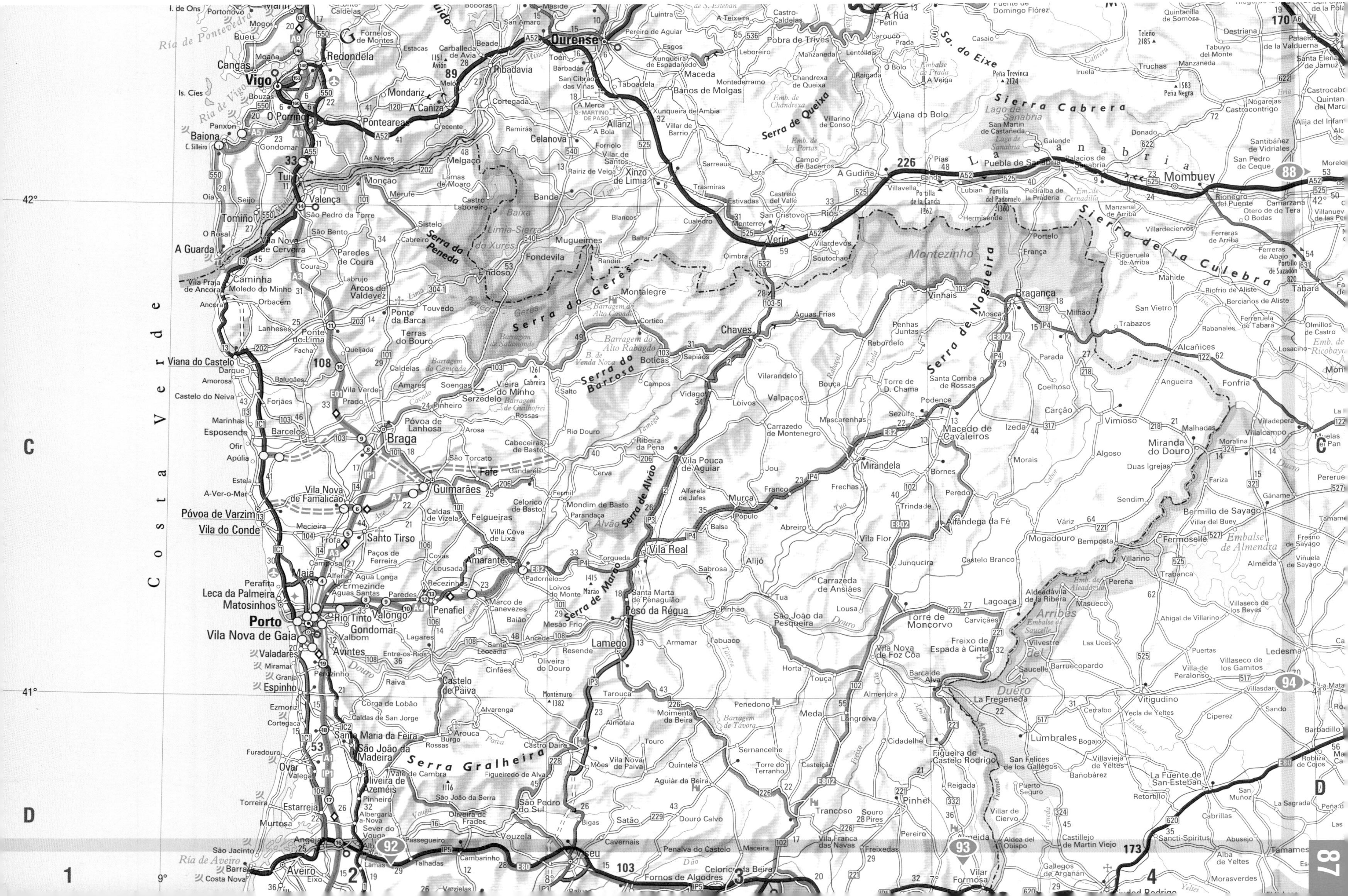
Costa Verde
Porto
Vila Nova de Gaia
Matosinhos
Leça da Palmeira
Braga
Guimarães
Viana do Castelo
Póvoa de Varzim
Vila do Conde
Barcelos
Esposende
Vila Nova de Famalicão
Santo Tirso
Valongo
Gondomar
Penafiel
Amarante
Vila Real
Peso da Régua
Lamego
Chaves
Bragança
Mirandela
Macedo de Cavaleiros
Miranda do Douro
Torre de Moncorvo
Vila Nova de Foz Côa
Viseu
Aveiro
Ovar
Espinho
Valença
Tui
Vigo
Ourense
Verín
Puebla de Sanabria
Mombuey
Vitigudino
Figueira de Castelo Rodrigo
Trancoso
Serra do Gerês
Serra da Peneda
Serra do Alvão
Serra do Marão
Serra de Nogueira
Sierra de la Culebra
Sierra Cabrera
Serra de Queixa
Serra Gralheira
Montezinho
Douro
Lago de Sanabria
Arribes del Duero
Ría de Vigo
Ría de Aveiro

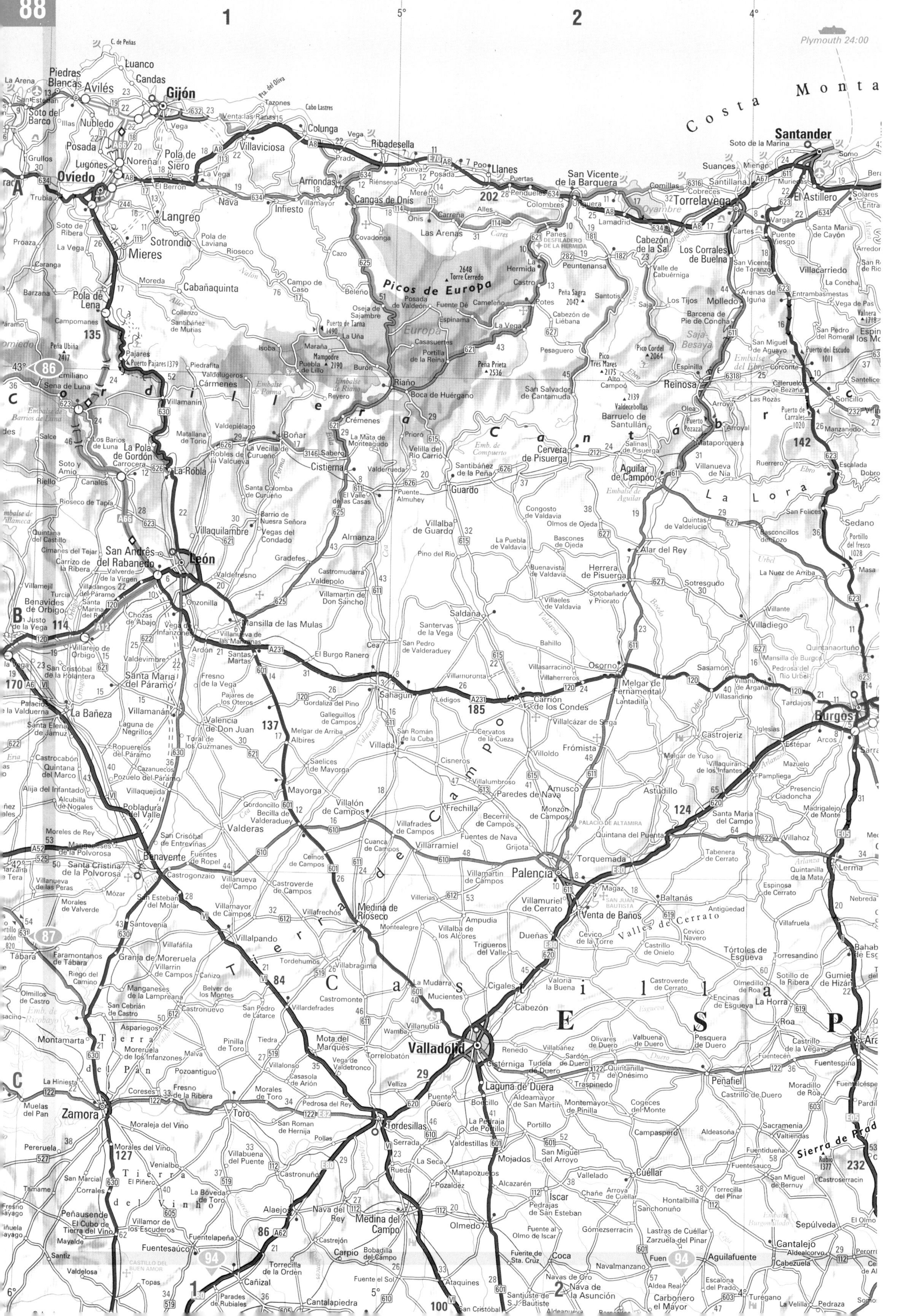
1
2
5°
4°
Plymouth 24:00
Costa Monta
C. de Peñas
Luanco
Candas
Gijón
Piedras Blancas
Avilés
La Arena
Soto del Barco
Nubledo
Posada
Lugones
Noreña
Pola de Siero
Oviedo
Villaviciosa
Colunga
Ribadesella
Llanes
Arriondas
Cangas de Onís
Infiesto
Nava
Langreo
Sotrondio
Mieres
Pola de Laviana
Cabañaquinta
Pola de Lena
Campomanes
Covadonga
Picos de Europa
2648 Torre Cerredo
Posada de Valdeón
Fuente Dé
Potes
San Vicente de la Barquera
Comillas
Santillana
Torrelavega
Santander
Soto de la Marina
Suances
El Astillero
Cabezón de la Sal
Los Corrales de Buelna
Puente Viesgo
Villacarriedo
Reinosa
Pico Cordel 2064
Peña Sagra 2042
Peña Prieta 2536
Riaño
Boca de Huérgano
Cistierna
Boñar
La Robla
La Pola de Gordón
Villamanín
Puerto Pajares 1379
Peña Ubiña 2417
Sena de Luna
León
San Andrés del Rabanedo
Villaquilambre
Mansilla de las Mulas
Valencia de Don Juan
Sahagún
Guardo
Cervera de Pisuerga
Aguilar de Campóo
La Lora
Alar del Rey
Herrera de Pisuerga
Saldaña
Osorno
Carrión de los Condes
Frómista
Villadiego
Sasamón
Burgos
Castrojeriz
Melgar de Fernamental
Astudillo
Palencia
Torquemada
Dueñas
Venta de Baños
Baltanás
Valles de Cerrato
Lerma
La Bañeza
Astorga
Benavente
Santa Cristina de la Polvorosa
Valderas
Mayorga
Villalón de Campos
Medina de Rioseco
Tierra de Campos
Villalpando
Villafrechós
Zamora
Toro
Tordesillas
Valladolid
Cigales
Simancas
Laguna de Duera
Tudela de Duero
Peñafiel
Roa
Aranda
Cuéllar
Iscar
Portillo
Olmedo
Medina del Campo
Alaejos
Nava del Rey
Fuentesaúco
Cantalejo
Sepúlveda
Coca
Aguilafuente
Navas de Oro
Nava de la Asunción
Carbonero el Mayor
Santiuste de S.J. Bautiste
Tierra del Pan
Tierra del Vino
Montamarta
Castilla
E S P
Sierra de Prad
Cañizal
Cantalapiedra
Ataquines
Fuente el Sol
43°
42°
6°
86
87
94
135
114
137
185
142
124
84
127
29
100
170
232
202

3
4
5
Portsmouth 29:00
Côte Basque
Bilbao
Barakaldo
Portugalete
Getxo
Sestao
Basauri
Galdakao
Amorebieta
Gernika-Lumo
Bermeo
Mungia
Lekeitio
Ondarroa
Zumaia
Zarautz
Donostia-San Sebastián
Hernani
Rentería
Irún
Hondarribia
Hendaye
St. Jean-de-Luz
Biarritz
Anglet
Bayonne
Capbreton
Hossegor
St. Vincent-de-Tyrosse
Hasparren
Cambo-les-Bains
Elizondo
Laredo
Colindres
Santoña
Noja
Castro-Urdiales
Ampuero
Ramales de la Victoria
Balmaseda
Zalla
Güeñes
Llodio
Amurrio
Orduña
Medina de Pomar
Trespaderne
Durango
Eibar
Elgoibar
Bergara
Arrasate
Oñati
Zumárraga
Azpeitia
Azcoitia
Tolosa
Andoain
Beasain
Ordizia
Alsasua
Irurzun
Vitoria-Gasteiz
Sierra de Urbasa
Sierra de Andía
Pamplona
Burlada
Barañáin
Noain
Estella
Puente la Reina
Tafalla
Olite
Sangüesa
Miranda de Ebro
Pancorvo
Briviesca
Haro
Sierra de Cantabria
Laguardia
Logroño
Viana
Los Arcos
Lodosa
Calahorra
Arnedo
Alfaro
Corella
Tudela
Tarazona
Borja
Mallén
Santo Domingo de la Calzada
Nájera
Navarrete
Ezcaray
Sierra de la Demanda
Picos de Urbión
Sierra Cebollera
Tierra de Cameros
Sierra del Madero
Sierra del Moncayo
Ágreda
Olvega
Soria
Almazán
El Burgo de Osma
San Esteban de Gormaz
Aranda de Duero
Peñaranda de Duero
Ayllón
Riaza
Atienza
Medinaceli
Arcos de Jalón
Ariza
Alhama de Aragón
Calatayud
La Almunia de Doña Godina
Ricla
Épila
Daroca
Illueca
San Leonardo de Yagüe
Salas de los Infantes
Santo Domingo de Silos
Quintanar de la Sierra
Covaleda
Vinuesa
Castilla y León
Cordillera Ibérica

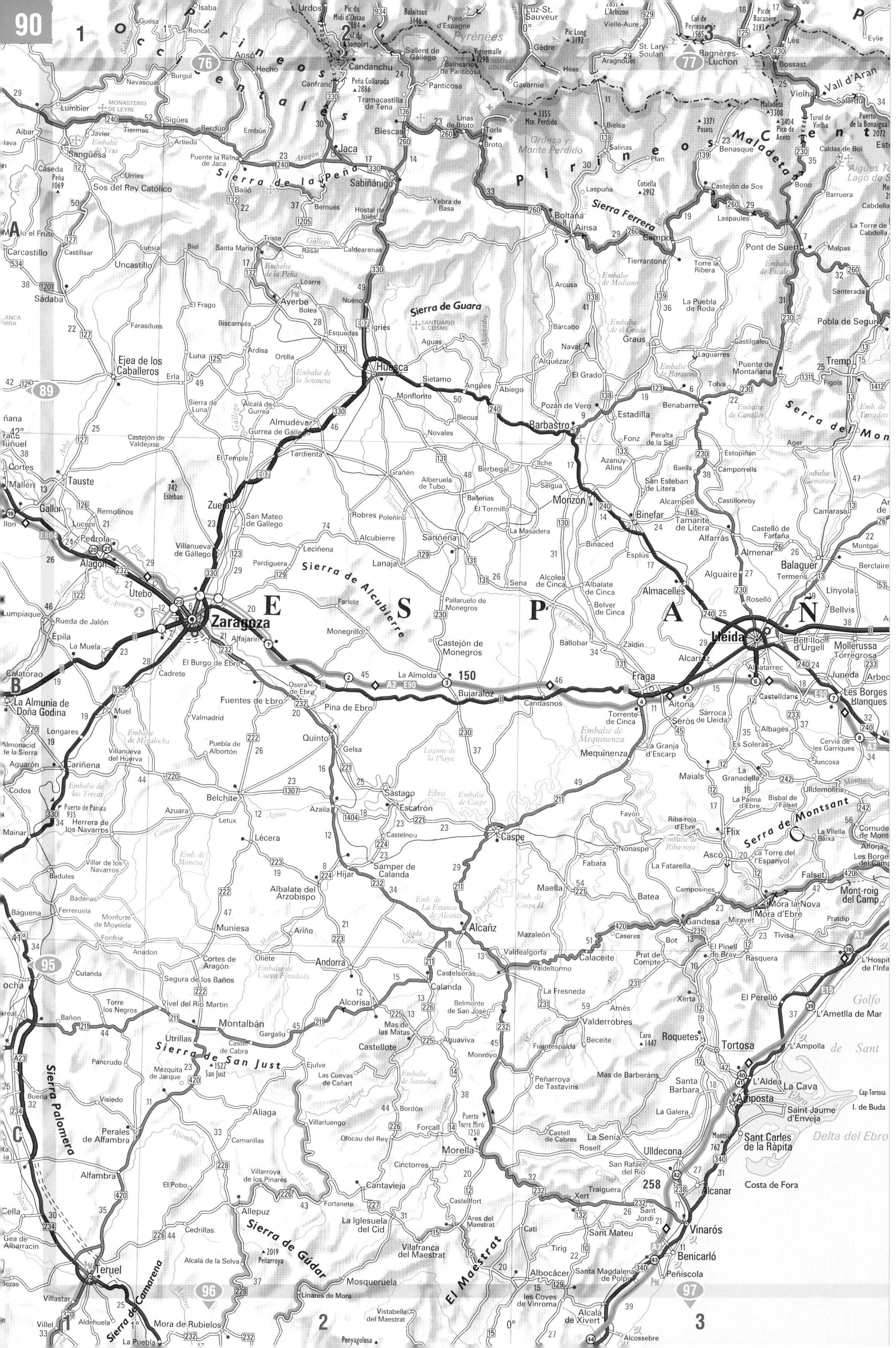
1
2
3
Pirineos Occidentales
Pyrénées
Pirineos Centrales
Isaba
Guesa
Roncal
Urdos
Pic du Midi d'Ossau 2884
Col du Somport
Balaïtous 3146
Pont-d'Espagne
Luz-St.-Sauveur
L'Arbizon
Vielle-Aure
Col de Peyresourde 1569
Pic de Bacanère 2193
Eylie
Ansó
Hecho
Candanchu
Sallent de Gállego
Vignemalle 3298
Chaos de Coumély
Gèdre
Pic Long 3192
St. Lary-Soulan
Aragnouet
Bagnères-de-Luchon
Les
Bossast
Navascués
Burgui
Canfranc
Peña Collarada 2886
Balneario de Panticosa
Panticosa
Gavarnie
Héas
Vielha
Vall d'Aran
Salardú
Lumbier
Monasterio de Leyre
Sigües
Tramacastilla de Tena
Mte. Perdido 3355
Maladeta 3308
Pico de Aneto 3404
Posets 3371
Túnel de Vielha
Puerto de la Bonaigua 2072
Aibar
Javier
Embalse de Yesa
Tiermas
Berdún
Embún
Biescas
Linas de Broto
Torla
Broto
Ordesa y Monte Perdido
Bielsa
Salinas
Plan
Benasque
Maladeta
Caldas de Boi
Aigües Tortes Lago de S.
Sangüesa
Artieda
Puente la Reina de Jaca
Jaca
Aragón
Sabiñánigo
Sierra de la Peña
Cáseda
Peña 1069
Urries
Sos del Rey Católico
Bailó
Bernués
Yebra de Basa
Hostal de Ipiés
Laspuña
Cotiella 2912
Castejón de Sos
Bono
Barruera
Cabdella
Boltaña
Aínsa
Sierra Ferrera
Campo
Laspaules
La Torre de Cabdella
Mélida
El Frugo
Carcastillo
Castilisar
Luesia
Biel
Santa María
Triste
Rasal
Gállego
Caldearenas
Embalse de la Peña
Tierrantona
Pont de Suert
Malpas
Uncastillo
Loarre
Embalse de Mediano
Torre la Ribera
Embalse de Escales
Sádaba
Ayerbe
Bolea
Nuéno
Arcusa
La Puebla de Roda
Senterada
El Frago
Biscarrués
Esquedas
Igriés
Sierra de Guara
Santuario S. Cosme
Embalse de el Grado
Graus
Pobla de Segur
Farasdues
Aguas
Bárcabo
Castigaleu
Ardisa
Naval
Laguarres
Ejea de los Caballeros
Luna
Ortilla
Embalse de la Sotonera
Huesca
Alquézar
Embalse de Barasona
Puente de Montañana
Tremp
Erla
Sietamo
Angües
El Grado
Tolva
Figols
Monflorite
Abiego
Pozán de Vero
Estadilla
Benabarre
Embalse de Canelles
Emb. de Terradets
Sierra de Luna
Alcalá de Gurrea
Almudévar
Blecua
Barbastro
Novales
Fonz
Peralta de la Sal
Serra del Montsec
Castejón de Valdejasa
Gurrea de Gállego
Estopiñán
Ager
Tardienta
Azanúy-Alins
Baells
Camporrells
El Temple
Grañén
Berbegal
Ilche
Alberuela de Tubo
Selgua
San Esteban de Litera
Embalse de Camarasa
Tauste
742 Esteban
Monzón
Ballerías
El Tormillo
Alcampell
Castillonroy
Mallén
Zuera
Binéfar
Tamarite de Litera
Camarasa
Gallur
Remolinos
Robres
Poleñino
Castelló de Farfaña
Luceni
San Mateo de Gallego
Alcubierre
Sariñena
La Masadera
Alfarràs
Pedrola
Leciñena
Binaced
Almenar
Montgai
Alagón
Villanueva de Gállego
Perdiguera
Lanaja
Esplús
Balaguer
Termens
Berclaire
Sierra de Alcubierre
Sena
Alcolea de Cinca
Albalate de Cinca
Almacelles
Alguaire
Linyola
Utebo
Farlete
Pallaruelo de Monegros
Belver de Cinca
Rosselló
Bellvís
Lumpiaque
Rueda de Jalón
Zaragoza
E S P A Ñ A
Lleida
Bell-lloc d'Urgell
Mollerussa
Torregrossa
Épila
La Muela
Alfajarín
Monegrillo
Castejón de Monegros
Ballobar
Zaidín
Alcarràs
Albatàrrec
Juneda
Arbeca
Calatorao
El Burgo de Ebro
Cadrete
La Almolda
150
Fraga
Les Borges Blanques
La Almunia de Doña Godina
Osera de Ebro
Bujaraloz
Candasnos
Aitona
Castelldans
Fuentes de Ebro
Pina de Ebro
Torrente de Cinca
Sarroca de Lleida
Muel
Valmadrid
Seròs
L'Albagès
Longares
Embalse de Mezalocha
Quinto
Embalse de Mequinenza
Es Soleràs
Cervià de les Garrigues
Almonacid de la Sierra
Villanueva del Huerva
Puebla de Albortón
Gelsa
Laguna de la Playa
Mequinenza
La Granja d'Escarp
Juncosa
Aguarón
Cariñena
Maials
La Granadella
Montsant
Codos
Embalse de las Torcas
Belchite
Sástago
Embalse de Caspe
Ulldemolins
Puerto de Paniza 935
Azuara
Azaila
Escatrón
Fayón
La Palma d'Ebre
Bisbal de Falset
Serra de Montsant
Mainar
Herrera de los Navarros
Letux
Lécera
Castelnou
Caspe
Riba-roja d'Ebre
Embalse de Riba-roja
Flix
La Vilella Baixa
Cornudella de Montsant
Alforja
Villar de los Navarros
Emb. de Moneva
Hijar
Samper de Calanda
Nonaspe
Fabara
Ascó
La Torre de l'Espanyol
Les Borges del Camp
Badules
Albalate del Arzobispo
La Fatarella
Falset
Bádenas
Maella
Emb. de Caspe II
Batea
Camposines
Mont-roig del Camp
Báguena
Ferreruela
Emb. de La Estanca de Alcañiz
Guadalope
Móra la Nova
Móra d'Ebre
Monforte de Moyuela
Muniesa
Salada Grande
Alcañiz
Gandesa
Miravet
Pratdip
Fonfría
Ariño
Mazaleón
Caseres
Bot
Tivisa
Anadón
Oliete
Andorra
Valdealgorfa
Calaceite
El Pinell de Bray
Rasquera
L'Hospitalet de l'Infant
Cutanda
Cortes de Aragón
Embalse de Cueva Foradada
Castelserás
Valdeltormo
Prat de Comte
Segura de los Baños
Calanda
La Fresneda
Torre los Negros
Vivel del Río Martín
Alcorisa
Belmonte de San José
Arnes
Xerta
El Perelló
Golfo
L'Ametlla de Mar
Baños
Montalbán
Gargallo
Mas de las Matas
Valderrobres
Utrillas
Castel de Cabra
Aguaviva
Roquetes
Caro 1447
Beceite
Sierra de San Just
Castellote
Monroyo
Fuentespalda
Tortosa
L'Ampolla
Golfo de Sant Jordi
Pancrudo
Mezquita de Jarque
1522 San Just
Ejulve
Las Cuevas de Cañart
Embalse de Santolea
Peñarroya de Tastavins
Mas de Barberáns
Santa Bàrbara
L'Aldea
La Cava
Sierra Palomera
Buena
Visiedo
Aliaga
Bordón
Puerto Torre Miró 1250
Amposta
Cap Tortosa
I. de Buda
Sant Jaume d'Enveja
Villarluengo
Forcall
La Galera
Perales de Alfambra
Camarillas
Olocau del Rey
Morella
Castell de Cabres
La Sénia
Rosell
Ulldecona
Montsià 762
Sant Carles de la Ràpita
Delta del Ebro
Alfambra
Alfambra
Cinctorres
San Rafael del Río
Mal Burgo
El Pobo
Villarroya de los Pinares
Cantavieja
Traiguera
258
Alcanar
Costa de Fora
Fortanete
Castellfort
Xert
Sant Jordi
Cella
Allepuz
La Iglesuela del Cid
Ares del Maestrat
Cedrillas
Sierra de Gúdar
Cati
Sant Mateu
Vinaròs
Gea de Albarracín
Tirig
Benicarló
Alcalá de la Selva
2019 Peñarroya
Vilafranca del Maestrat
El Maestrat
Peníscola
Teruel
Mosqueruela
Albocàsser
Santa Magdalena de Polpís
Linares de Mora
Les Coves de Vinromà
Villastar
Sierra de Camarena
Vistabella del Maestrat
Alcalà de Xivert
Villel
Aldehuela
Mora de Rubielos
La Puebla
Penyagolosa
Alcossebre
0°
42°
76
77
89
95
96
97
A
B
C
E07
E804
E90
A2
A7
E15

Pyrénées
Pirineos Orientales
Serra del Cadí
Cadí Moixeró
Cerdaña
Roussillon
Mts. Albères
Côte Vermeille
Costa Brava
Costa Dorada
Cataluña
Golfo de Roses
ANDORRA
Andorra la Vella
Encamp
Les Escaldes
Ordino
El Serrat
St. Julià de Loria
Port d'Envalira
Pas de la Casa
L'Hospitalet
Col de Puymorens
Pic Carlit
Ax-les-Thermes
Tarascon-sur-Ariège
Vicdessos
Cabannes
Massat
Oust
Aulus-les-Bains
Couflens
Salau
Mt. Valier
Pic des 3 Seigneurs
Pic de St. Barthelemy
Pic de Montcalm
Pic d'Estats
Quillan
Axat
Belcaire
Usson-les-Bains
Quérigut
Formiguères
Madrès
St. Paul-de-Fenouillet
Caudiès-de-Fenouillèdes
Paziols
Maury
Vingrau
Rivesaltes
Estagel
Salses-le-Château
Étang de Leucate
Port-Barcarès
St. Laurent-de-la-Salanque
Perpignan
Millas
Ille-sur-Têt
Thuir
Canet-Plage
Sournia
Prades
Vinca
Boule-d'Amont
Fourques
Elne
St. Cyprien
Argelès-sur-Mer
Port-Vendres
Banyuls-sur-Mer
Cerbère
Portbou
Colera
El Port de Llança
Llançà
El Port de la Selva
C. de Creus
Cadaqués
Roses
Vernet-les-Bains
Pic du Canigou
Olette
Font-Romeu
Mont-Louis
Fontpédrouse
Col de la Perche
Saillagouse
Puigcerdà
Bourg-Madame
Llívia
Ur
Puigmal
Queixans
La Molina
Queralbs
Amélie-les-Bains-Palalda
Céret
Arles-sur-Tech
Prats-de-Mollo-la-Preste
La Preste
Le Boulou
Le Perthus
La Jonquera
Espolla
Maçanet de Cabrenys
Garriguella
Mollet de Peralada
Peralada
Vilajuïga
Figueres
Castelló d'Empúries
Sant Pere Pescador
L'Escala
Empúries
Colomers
Verges
Torroella de Montgrí
Estartit
Flaça
Parlavà
La Bisbal d'Empordà
Pals
Begur
Cap de Begur
Aiguablava
Tamariu
Palafrugell
Calella
Llafranc
Palamós
Calonge
Sant Antoni de Calonge
Platja d'Aro
S'Agaró
Sant Feliu de Guíxols
Tossa de Mar
Lloret de Mar
Blanes
Malgrat de Mar
Pineda de Mar
Calella
Canet de Mar
Arenys de Mar
Arenys de Munt
Vilassar de Mar
Premià de Mar
El Masnou
Badalona
Mataró
Argentona
Santa Coloma de Gramenet
BARCELONA
L'Hospitalet de Llobregat
El Prat de Llobregat
Sant Boi de Llobregat
Gavà
Castelldefels
Club de Garraf
Sitges
Vilanova i la Geltrú
Cubelles
Calafell
Coma-ruga
El Vendrell
Torredembarra
Tamarit de Mar
Tarragona
Salou
C. de Salou
Cambrils
Vila-seca
Reus
Constantí
Universal Mediterranea
Gènova 17:00
Maó 9:00
Palma de Mallorca 3:00
Eivissa 9:30
Girona
Salt
Sarrià de Ter
Cassà de la Selva
Caldas de Malavella
Llagostera
Anglès
Amer
Santa Coloma de Farners
Sant Hilari Sacalm
Arbúcies
Hostalric
Breda
Sils
Tordera
Banyoles
Besalú
Olot
Santa Pau
Mieres
Castellfollit de la Roca
Sadernes
Cabanelles
Albanyà
Pont de Molins
Camprodon
Sant Pau de Segúries
Sant Joan de les Abadesses
Ribes de Freser
Setcases
Molló
Ripoll
Sant Quirze de Besora
Torelló
Manlleu
Roda de Ter
Vic
Tona
Taradell
Vilanova de Sau
Santa Maria de Corco
Les Planes d'Hostoles
Viladrau
Espinelves
El Montseny
Montseny
Sant Celoni
La Garriga
Cardedeu
Granollers
Canovelles
Centelles
Sant Feliu de Codines
Caldes de Montbui
Castellar del Vallès
Sant Llorenç del Munt i l'Obac
Sant Llorenç Savall
Terrassa
Sabadell
Rubí
Molins de Rei
Sant Feliu
Martorell
Esparreguera
Olesa de Montserrat
Monistrol de Montserrat
Montserrat
Castellbell i el Vilar
St. Vicenç de Castellet
Manresa
Navarcles
Castellterçol
Moià
Calders
Artés
Sallent
Súria
Santpedor
Callús
Avinyó
L'Estany
Balsareny
Navás
Puig Reig
Gironella
Olost
Sant Feliu Sasserra
Sant Hipòlit de Voltregà
Sant Agustí de Lluçanès
Borredà
Palmerola
La Pobla de Lillet
Guardiola de Bergueda
Baga
Cercs
Berga
Avià
Llinars
L'Espunyola
Sant Llorenç de Morunys
Solsona
Navès
Cardona
Emb. de Sant Ponç
Lladurs
Castellar de la Ribera
Bassella
Oliana
Emb. d'Oliana
Graho de la Grande
Alinyà
Organyà
Garganta de Organyà
Coll de Nargó
Boixols
Noves de Segre
Els Castells
La Seu d'Urgell
Montella
Bellver de Cerdanya
Adrall
Pallerols
La Farga de Moles
Lles
Sort
Llavorsí
Llessui
Ribera de Cardós
Areo
Tavescan
Alòs d'Ensil
Esterri d'Aneu
Espot
Isona
Tremp
La Serra
Ponts
Agramunt
Torà
Castellfollit de Riubregos
Guisona
Calaf
St. Pere Sallavinera
La Manresana dels Prats
Sant Ramon
Cervera
Tàrrega
Verdú
Bellpuig d'Urgell
Ciutadilla
Vallfogona de Riucorb
Sant Martí de Maldà
Belltall
Igualada
Jorba
Castelloli
Sta. Margarida de Montbui
Capellades
Santa Coloma de Queralt
Piera
La Llacuna
Rocafort de Queralt
Sarral
Solivella
Montblanc
Espluga de Francolí
Poblet
Prades
El Pla de Santa Maria
Vila-Rodona
Valls
Alcover
La Selva del Camp
El Morell
Roda de Barà
La Riera de Gaià
Rodonyà
Aquapark
Sant Jaume dels Domenys
L'Arboç
Castellet
Vilafranca del Penedès
St. Pere de Riudebitlles
Sant Martí Sarroca
El Pont d'Armentera
St. Sadurní d'Anoia
Gelida
Begues
Stas Creus
Fluvià
Museo Dalí
Water World
Sant Marti de Llémana
Viladamat
Sant Juan
Jordi
A
B
C
4
5
6
2°
3°
41°
42°
77
78
97

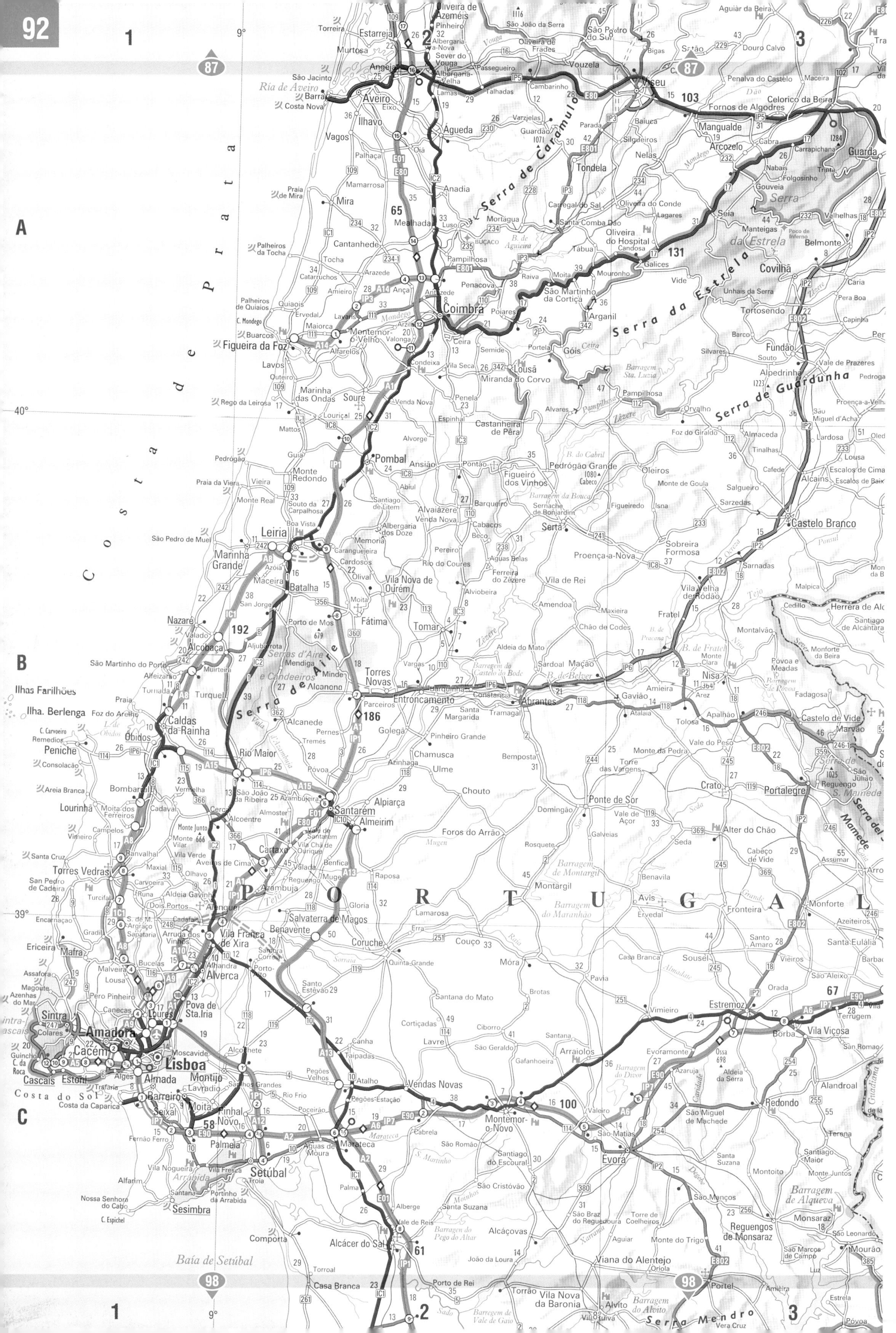

1
2
3
87
98
A
B
C
9°
40°
39°
Costa de Prata
Costa do Sol
Ría de Aveiro
Baía de Setúbal
PORTUGAL
Serra do Caramulo
Serra da Estrela
Serra de Guardunha
Serras d'Aire e Candeeiros
Serra de Aire
Serra de Mamede
Serra Mendro
Ilhas Farilhões
Ilha. Berlenga
Oliveira de Azeméis
Estarreja
Aveiro
Ílhavo
Vagos
Águeda
Viseu
Mangualde
Guarda
Tondela
Mira
Cantanhede
Mealhada
Coimbra
Figueira da Foz
Montemor-o-Velho
Lousã
Seia
Covilhã
Gouveia
Belmonte
Fundão
Arganil
Góis
Pombal
Leiria
Marinha Grande
Batalha
Fátima
Nazaré
Alcobaça
Tomar
Torres Novas
Entroncamento
Abrantes
Caldas da Rainha
Óbidos
Peniche
Rio Maior
Santarém
Almeirim
Cartaxo
Azambuja
Torres Vedras
Alenquer
Vila Franca de Xira
Mafra
Ericeira
Sintra
Amadora
Cacém
Cascais
Estoril
Lisboa
Loures
Almada
Barreiro
Montijo
Seixal
Moita
Palmela
Setúbal
Sesimbra
Alcácer do Sal
Montemor-o-Novo
Évora
Estremoz
Vila Viçosa
Borba
Redondo
Reguengos de Monsaraz
Portel
Viana do Alentejo
Castelo Branco
Sertã
Proença-a-Nova
Vila Velha de Ródão
Nisa
Castelo de Vide
Marvão
Portalegre
Crato
Ponte de Sor
Alter do Chão
Avis
Fronteira
Monforte
Coruche
Benavente
Mora
Arraiolos
Vendas Novas
Salvaterra de Magos
Chamusca
Golegã
Alpiarça
Barragem de Alqueva
Barragem de Montargil
Barragem do Maranhão

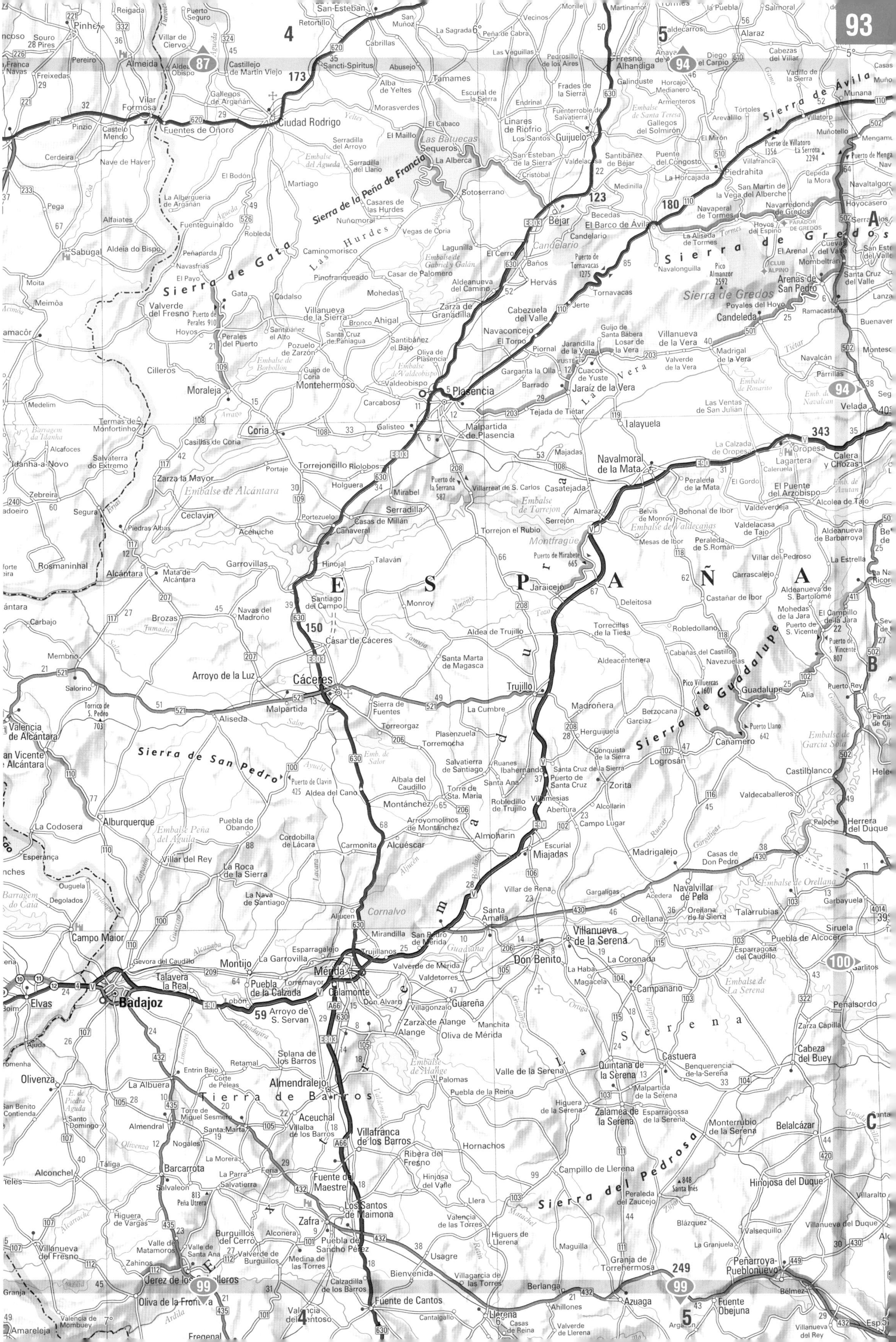
4
5
87
94
99
100
E S P A Ñ A
A
B
C
Sierra de la Peña de Francia
Sierra de Gata
Las Hurdes
Las Batuecas
Sierra de Ávila
Sierra de Gredos
Sierra de San Pedro
Sierra de Guadalupe
Sierra del Pedrosa
Tierra de Barros
La Serena
La Vera
Montfragüe
Cornalvo
San Esteban
Reigada
Pinhel
Puerto Seguro
Villar de Ciervo
Almeida
Castillejo de Martín Viejo
Sancti-Spiritus
Retortillo
San Muñoz
Cabrillas
La Sagrada
Peña de Cabra
Vecinos
Morille
Martinamor
Tormes
La Puebla
Salmoral
Aldeacarros
Alaraz
Cabezas del Villar
Souro Pires
Pereiro
Freixedas
Vilar Formoso
Fuentes de Oñoro
Ciudad Rodrigo
Gallegos de Argañán
Pinzio
Castelo Mendo
Cerdeira
Nave de Haver
Alba de Yeltes
Tamames
Abusejo
Escurial de la Sierra
Frades de la Sierra
Las Veguillas
Pedrosillo de los Aires
Fresno Alhándiga
Galinduste
Horcajo-Medianero
Diego del Carpio
Vadillo de la Sierra
Armenteros
Tórtoles
Arevalillo
Villatoro
Muñotello
Munana
Morasverdes
El Cabaco
El Maíllo
Serradilla del Arroyo
Serradilla del Llano
Embalse del Águeda
Sequeros
La Alberca
Endrinal
Linares de Riofrío
Los Santos
Guijuelo
Fuenterroble de Salvatierra
Embalse de Santa Teresa
Gallegos del Solmirón
El Mirón
Puerto de Villatoro 1356
La Serrota 2294
Villafranca
Piedrahíta
Cepeda la Mora
Mengamuñoz
Puerto de Menga
Navaltalgordo
San Esteban de la Sierra
Valdelacasa
Santibáñez de Béjar
Puente del Congosto
La Horcajada
Cristóbal
El Bodón
Martiago
La Alberguería de Argañán
Pega
Alfaiates
Fuenteguinaldo
Robleda
Sabugal
Aldeia do Bispo
Peñaparda
Navasfrías
El Payo
Casares de las Hurdes
Nuñomoral
Sotoserrano
Medinilla
San Martín de la Vega del Alberche
Navarredonda de Gredos
Hoyocasero
Béjar
Becedas
El Barco de Ávila
Navapeal de Tormes
Hoyos del Espino
Parador de Gredos
Candelario
La Aliseda de Tormes
El Arenal
Cuevas del Valle
San Esteban del Valle
Mombeltrán
Santa Cruz del Valle
Vegas de Coria
Caminomorisco
Lagunilla
Embalse de Gabriel y Galán
El Cerro
Baños
Puerto de Tornavacas 1275
Navalonguilla
Pico Almanzor 2592
Club Alpino
Arenas de San Pedro
Lanzahíta
Moita
Meimoa
Valverde del Fresno
Puerto de Perales 910
Gata
Pinofranqueado
Casar de Palomero
Aldeanueva del Camino
Hervás
Tornavacas
Cadalso
Mohedas
Zarza de Granadilla
Cabezuela del Valle
Jerte
Poyales del Hoyo
Candeleda
Ramacastañas
Buenaventura
Hoyos
Villanueva de la Sierra
Bronco
Ahigal
Santibáñez el Alto
Perales del Puerto
Santa Cruz de Paniagua
Pozuelo de Zarzón
Santibáñez el Bajo
Navaconcejo
El Torno
Guijo de Santa Bárbara
Jarandilla de la Vera
Losar de la Vera
Villanueva de la Vera
Madrigal de la Vera
Valverde de la Vera
Montesclaros
Cilleros
Embalse de Borbollón
Guijo de Coria
Montehermoso
Oliva de Plasencia
Embalse de Valdeobispo
Valdeobispo
Piornal
Garganta la Olla
Barrado
Yuste
Cuacos de Yuste
Jaraíz de la Vera
Navalcán
Parrillas
Embalse de Rosarito
Emb. de Navalcán
Velada
Moraleja
Carcaboso
Plasencia
Tejada de Tiétar
Las Ventas de San Julián
Medelim
Termas de Monfortinho
Coria
Galisteo
Malpartida de Plasencia
Talayuela
Barragem da Idanha
Alcafoces
Salvaterra do Extremo
Idanha-a-Nova
Casillas de Coria
Majadas
Navalmoral de la Mata
La Calzada de Oropesa
Oropesa
Lagartera
Calera y Chozas
Zarza la Mayor
Torrejoncillo
Riolobos
Portaje
Holguera
Puerto de la Serrana 587
Villarreal de S. Carlos
Casatejada
Peraleda de la Mata
El Gordo
Calzeruela
El Puente del Arzobispo
Emb. de Azután
Alcolea de Tajo
Zebreira
Segura
Embalse de Alcántara
Mirabel
Serradilla
Embalse de Torrejón
Almaraz
Belvis de Monroy
Bohonal de Ibor
Valdeverdeja
Ceclavín
Portezuelo
Casas de Millán
Cañaveral
Serrejón
Embalse de Valdecañas
Valdelacasa de Tajo
Aldeanueva de Barbarroya
Piedras Albas
Acehuche
Torrejón el Rubio
Mesas de Ibor
Peraleda de S. Román
Rosmaninhal
Alcántara
Mata de Alcántara
Garrovillas
Hinojal
Talaván
Puerto de Miravete 665
Villar del Pedroso
La Estrella
Carrascalejo
Jaraicejo
Castañar de Ibor
Aldeanueva de S. Bartolomé
Brozas
Navas del Madroño
Santiago del Campo
Monroy
Deleitosa
Mohedas de la Jara
El Campillo de la Jara
Puerto de S. Vicente
Carbajo
Almonte
Aldea de Trujillo
Torrecillas de la Tiesa
Robledollano
Puerto de S. Vicente 807
Membrío
Casar de Cáceres
Santa Marta de Magasca
Aldeacentenera
Cabañas del Castillo
Navezuelas
Arroyo de la Luz
Cáceres
Salorino
Pico Villuercas 1601
Guadalupe
Puerto Rey
Alía
Torrico de S. Pedro 703
Malpartida
Sierra de Fuentes
La Cumbre
Trujillo
Madroñera
Berzocana
Garciaz
Valencia de Alcántara
Aliseda
Torreorgaz
Plasenzuela
Torremocha
Herguijuela
Conquista de la Sierra
Puerto Llano 642
Cañamero
Embalse de García Sola
San Vicente de Alcántara
Salvatierra de Santiago
Ruanes
Ibahernando
Santa Cruz de la Sierra
Puerto de Santa Cruz
Logrosán
Castilblanco
Puerto de Clavín 425
Aldea del Cano
Albalá del Caudillo
Torre de Sta. María
Santa Ana
Zorita
Valdecaballeros
Alburquerque
Montánchez
Robledillo de Trujillo
Villamesías
Abertura
Alcollarín
Campo Lugar
Herrera del Duque
Peloche
La Codosera
Embalse Peña del Águila
Puebla de Obando
Arroyomolinos de Montánchez
Almoharín
Cordobilla de Lácara
Carmonita
Alcuéscar
Escurial
Miajadas
Madrigalejo
Casas de Don Pedro
Esperança
Villar del Rey
La Roca de la Sierra
Villar de Rena
Gargáligas
Acedera
Navalvillar de Pela
Embalse de Orellana
Garbayuela
Ouguela
Degolados
Barragem do Caia
La Nava de Santiago
Aljucén
Santa Amalia
Orellana la Vieja
Orellana de la Sierra
Talarrubias
Siruela
Campo Maior
Mirandilla
San Pedro de Mérida
Trujillanos
Villanueva de la Serena
Puebla de Alcocer
Esparragalejo
La Garrovilla
Montijo
Gévora del Caudillo
Mérida
Valverde de Mérida
Don Benito
La Coronada
Esparragosa del Caudillo
Garlitos
Elvas
Talavera la Real
Badajoz
Puebla de la Calzada
Torremayor
Calamonte
Valdetorres
La Haba
Magacela
Campanario
Embalse de La Serena
Lobón
Arroyo de S. Serván
Don Álvaro
Villagonzalo
Guareña
Zarza de Alange
Alange
Oliva de Mérida
Manchita
Peñalsordo
Zarza Capilla
Ajuda
Solana de los Barros
Embalse de Alange
Castuera
Cabeza del Buey
Olivenza
La Albuera
Retamal
Entrín Bajo
Corte de Peleas
Almendralejo
Palomas
Valle de la Serena
Quintana de la Serena
Benquerencia de la Serena
Puebla de la Reina
Malpartida de la Serena
San Benito de la Contienda
Torre de Miguel Sesmero
Aceuchal
Villalba de los Barros
Higuera de la Serena
Zalamea de la Serena
Esparragosa de la Serena
Monterrubio de la Serena
Belalcázar
Almendral
Santa Marta
Nogales
Villafranca de los Barros
Santo Domingo
Táliga
Hornachos
La Morera
Barcarrota
La Parra
Feria
Ribera del Fresno
Campillo de Llerena
Alconchel
Salvaleón
Salvatierra
Fuente del Maestre
Hinojosa del Valle
Peraleda del Zaucejo
Santa Inés 848
Hinojosa del Duque
Villaralto
Peña Utrera 813
Higuera de Vargas
Los Santos de Maimona
Llera
Valencia de las Torres
Higuera de Llerena
Blázquez
Valsequillo
Villanueva del Duque
Villanueva del Fresno
Valle de Matamoros
Valle de Santa Ana
Burguillos del Cerro
Valverde de Burguillos
Alconera
Zafra
Puebla de Sancho Pérez
Medina de las Torres
Usagre
Maguilla
Granja de Torrehermosa
La Granjuela
Peñarroya-Pueblonuevo
Zahinos
Jerez de los Caballeros
Bienvenida
Villagarcía de las Torres
Berlanga
Azuaga
Bélmez
Oliva de la Frontera
Calzadilla de los Barros
Fuente de Cantos
Llerena
Ahillones
Fuente Obejuna
Valencia de Mombuey
Valencia del Ventoso
Cantalgallo
Casas de Reina
Valverde de Llerena
Argallón
Villanueva del Rey
Amareleja
Fregenal

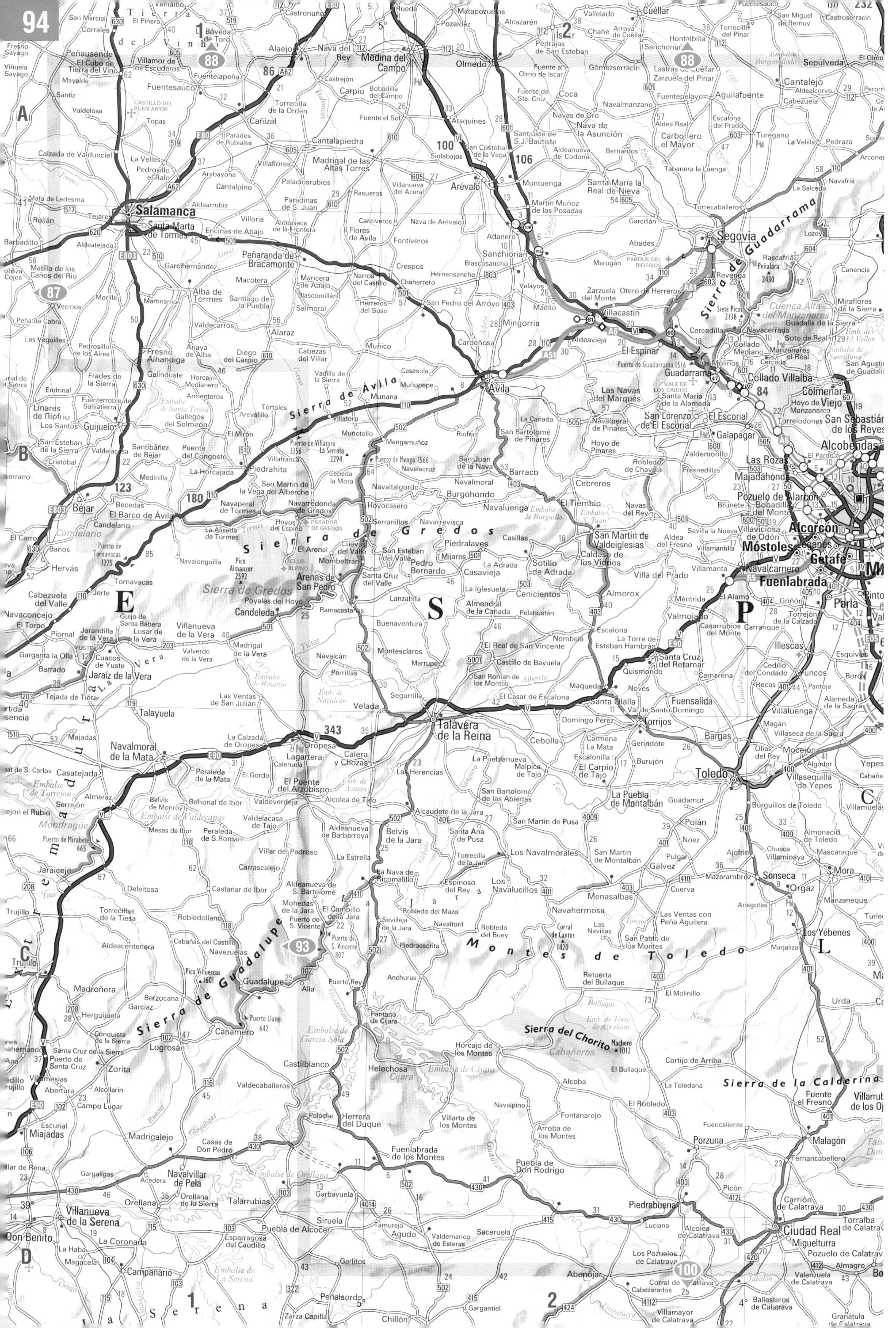
Salamanca
Santa Marta de Tormes
Alba de Tormes
Peñaranda de Bracamonte
Medina del Campo
Olmedo
Cuéllar
Sepúlveda
Arévalo
Madrigal de las Altas Torres
Segovia
Sierra de Guadarrama
Ávila
Sierra de Ávila
Sierra de Gredos
Guadarrama
San Lorenzo de El Escorial
Collado Villalba
Colmenar Viejo
Alcobendas
Las Rozas
Majadahonda
Pozuelo de Alarcón
Alcorcón
Móstoles
Leganés
Getafe
Fuenlabrada
Parla
Béjar
Piedrahita
El Barco de Ávila
Arenas de San Pedro
Candeleda
Guijuelo
Jaraíz de la Vera
Navalmoral de la Mata
Oropesa
Talavera de la Reina
Maqueda
Torrijos
Toledo
Illescas
Sonseca
Mora
Orgaz
Los Yébenes
Guadalupe
Sierra de Guadalupe
Montes de Toledo
Sierra del Chorito
Sierra de la Calderina
Herrera del Duque
Miajadas
Villanueva de la Serena
Don Benito
Malagón
Ciudad Real
Miguelturra
Piedrabuena
Porzuna
Almadén
A
B
C
D
E
S
P
L

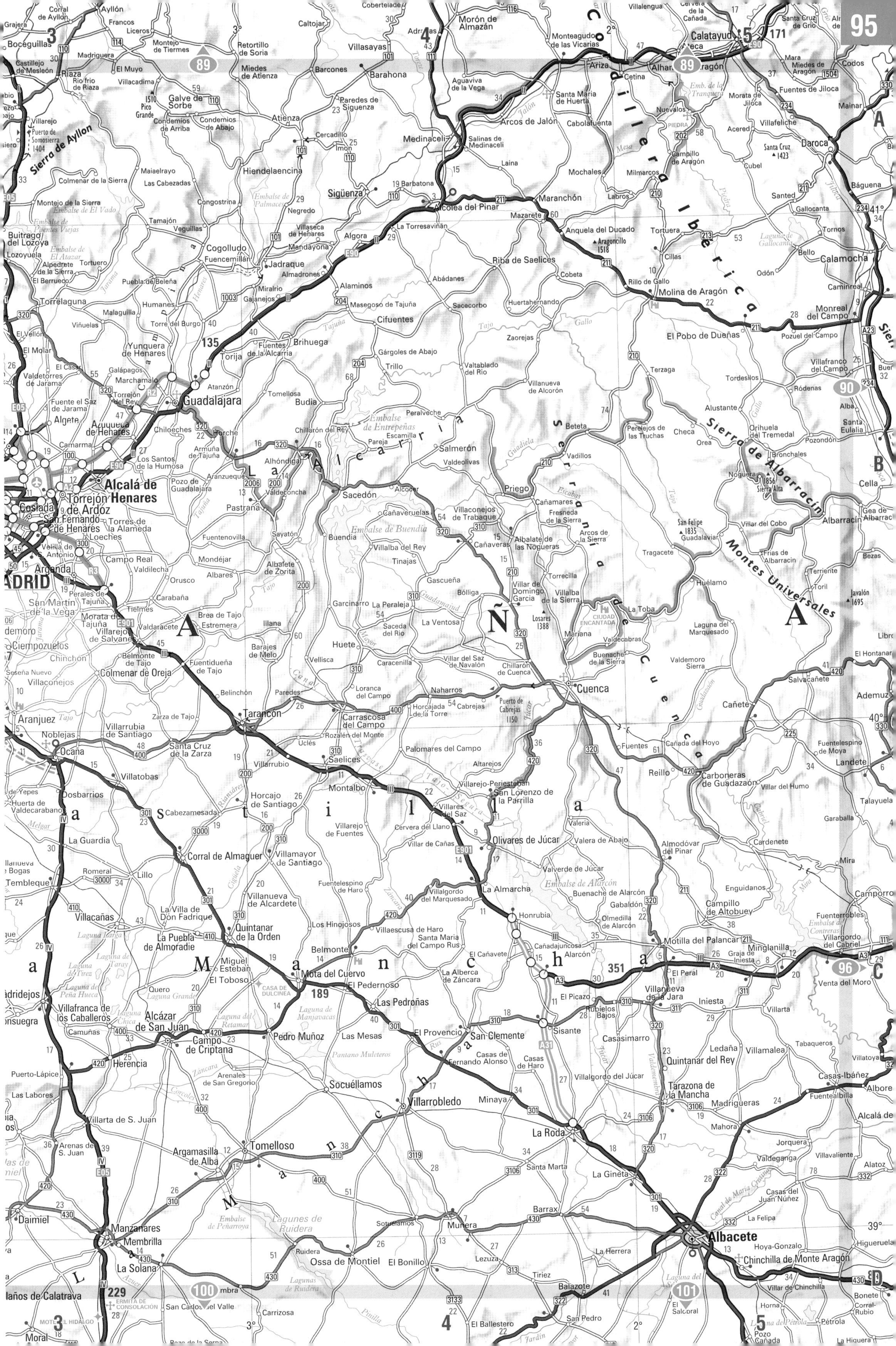
Corral de Ayllón
Ayllón
Grajera
Boceguillas
Francos
Liceros
Montejo de Tiermes
Retortillo de Soria
Caltojar
Cobertelade
Morón de Almazán
Villalengua
Cervera de la Cañada
Calatayud
Santa Cruz de Grío
Castillejo de Mesleón
Madriguera
Riaza
Riofrío de Riaza
El Muyo
Villacadima
Miedes de Atienza
Barcones
Villasayas
Barahona
Adradas
Monteagudo de las Vicarias
Ariza
Cetina
Alhama de Aragón
Ateca
Mara
Miedes de Aragón
Codos
Aguaviva de la Vega
Santa María de Huerta
Emb. de la Tranquera
Morata de Jiloca
Fuentes de Jiloca
Galve de Sorbe
Pico Grande
Condemios de Arriba
Condemios de Abajo
Atienza
Paredes de Sigüenza
Villarejo
Puerto de Somosierra
Sierra de Ayllón
Cercadillo
Imón
Medinaceli
Salinas de Medinaceli
Arcos de Jalón
Cabolafuente
Nuevalos
Piedra
Acered
Villafeliche
Mainar
Daroca
Santa Cruz
Campillo de Aragón
Cubel
Maiaelrayo
Colmenar de la Sierra
Las Cabezadas
Hiendelaencina
Laina
Mochales
Milmarcos
Montejo de la Sierra
Embalse de El Vado
Congostrina
Embalse de Palmaces
Sigüenza
Barbatona
Alcolea del Pinar
Maranchón
Labros
Santed
Gallocanta
Báguena
Embalse de Puentes Viejas
Tamajón
Veguillas
Negredo
Villaseca de Henares
Algora
La Torresaviñán
Mazarete
Anquela del Ducado
Aragoncillo
Tortuera
Laguna de Gallocanta
Tornos
Buitrago del Lozoya
Lozoyuela
Embalse de El Atazar
Alpedrete de la Sierra
Tortuero
El Berrueco
Cogolludo
Fuencemillán
Mandayona
Jadraque
Almadrones
Riba de Saelices
Cillas
Bello
Calamocha
Odón
Puebla de Beleña
Miralrío
Gajanejos
Alaminos
Abánades
Cobeta
Rillo de Gallo
Molina de Aragón
Caminreal
Monreal del Campo
Torrelaguna
Humanes
Malaguilla
Masegoso de Tajuña
Sacecorbo
Huertahernando
Cordillera Ibérica
Viñuelas
Torre del Burgo
Cifuentes
Gallo
Pozuel del Campo
El Vellón
El Molar
Yunquera de Henares
Torija
Fuentes de la Alcarria
Brihuega
Zaorejas
El Pobo de Dueñas
Sierra
El Casar
Galápagos
Marchamalo
Gárgoles de Abajo
Trillo
Valtablado del Río
Terzaga
Villafranca del Campo
Valdetorres de Jarama
Torrejón del Rey
Atanzón
Guadalajara
Tomellosa
Villanueva de Alcorón
Tordesilos
Ródenas
Fuente el Saz de Jarama
Algete
Budia
Peralveche
Embalse de Entrepeñas
Alustante
Alba
Azuqueca de Henares
Chiloeches
Horche
Chillarón del Rey
Beteta
Peralejos de las Truchas
Checa
Orihuela del Tremedal
Santa Eulalia
Camarma
Armuña de Tajuña
Pareja
Escamilla
Salmerón
Serranía de Cuenca
Orea
Sierra de Albarracín
Pozondón
Los Santos de la Humosa
Alhóndiga
Valdeolivas
Vadillos
Bronchales
La Alcarria
Pozo de Guadalajara
Aranzueque
Valdeconcha
Sacedón
Alcocer
Noguera
Sierra Alta
Cella
Alcalá de Henares
Torrejón de Ardoz
Priego
Cañamares
Escabas
Coslada
San Fernando de Henares
Torres de la Alameda
Loeches
Pastrana
Cañaveruelas
Villaconejos de Trabaque
Fresneda de la Sierra
Albarracín
Gea de Albarracín
Embalse de Buendía
Arcos de la Sierra
San Felipe
Guadalaviar
Fuentenovilla
Sayatón
Buendía
Albalate de las Nogueras
Cañaveras
Villar del Cobo
Velilla de S. Antonio
Campo Real
Mondéjar
Villalba del Rey
Tragacete
Frías de Albarracín
Bezas
Arganda
Valdilecha
Albares
Albalate de Zorita
Tinajas
Terriente
Madrid
Orusco
Gascueña
Torrecilla
Villalba de la Sierra
Huélamo
Montes Universales
Toril
Perales de Tajuña
Villar de Domingo García
Bólliga
Javalón
San Martín de la Vega
Tielmes
Carabaña
Garcinarro
La Peraleja
Guadamejud
Ciudad Encantada
La Toba
Morata de Tajuña
Valdaracete
Brea de Tajo
Estremera
Illana
Saceda del Río
La Ventosa
Losares
Mariana
Laguna del Marquesado
Villarejo de Salvanés
Valdecabras
Ciempozuelos
Chinchón
Barajas de Melo
Huete
Buenache de la Sierra
El Hontanar
Belmonte de Tajo
Fuentidueña de Tajo
Vellisca
Caracenilla
Villar del Saz de Navalón
Chillarón de Cuenca
Valdemoro Sierra
Seseña Nuevo
Colmenar de Oreja
Villaconejos
Loranca del Campo
Salvacañete
Cuenca
Ademuz
Belinchón
Paredes
Naharros
Cabrejas
Puerto de Cabrejas
Júcar
Cañete
Aranjuez
Zarza de Tajo
Tarancón
Carrascosa del Campo
Horcajada de la Torre
Noblejas
Villarrubia de Santiago
Rozalén del Monte
Uclés
Palomares del Campo
Fuentes
Cañada del Hoyo
Fuentelespino de Moya
Landete
Ocaña
Santa Cruz de la Zarza
Villarrubio
Saelices
Altarejos
Reillo
Carboneras de Guadazaón
Villar del Humo
Villatobas
Montalbo
Villarejo-Periesteban
San Lorenzo de la Parrilla
Dosbarrios
Horcajo de Santiago
Villares del Saz
Talayuela
Huerta de Valdecarábanos
Cabezamesada
Villarejo de Fuentes
Cervera del Llano
Valeria
Melgar
Villar de Cañas
Olivares de Júcar
Valera de Abajo
Almodóvar del Pinar
Graballa
La Guardia
Corral de Almaguer
Villamayor de Santiago
Cardenete
Romeral
Lillo
Valverde de Júcar
Mira
Tembleque
Fuentelespino de Haro
La Almarcha
Embalse de Alarcón
Buenache de Alarcón
Enguídanos
Villanueva de Alcardete
Villagordo del Marquesado
Gabaldón
Campillo de Altobuey
Villacañas
La Villa de Don Fadrique
Los Hinojosos
Honrubia
Olmedilla de Alarcón
Fuenterrobles
Quintanar de la Orden
Villaescusa de Haro
Embalse de Contreras
La Puebla de Almoradiel
Santa María del Campo Rus
Cañadajuncosa
Motilla del Palancar
Minglanilla
Villargordo del Cabriel
Miguel Esteban
Belmonte
El Cañavete
Alarcón
Graja de Iniesta
Camporro
El Toboso
Mota del Cuervo
La Alberca de Záncara
El Peral
Madridejos
Quero
Casa de Dulcinea
El Pedernoso
Villanueva de la Jara
Venta del Moro
Consuegra
Villafranca de los Caballeros
Laguna Grande
Las Pedroñas
El Picazo
Rubielos Bajos
Iniesta
Villarta
Alcázar de San Juan
Laguna de Manjavacas
Camuñas
Campo de Criptana
Pedro Muñoz
Las Mesas
El Provencio
San Clemente
Sisante
Casasimarro
Ledaña
Villamalea
Tabaqueros
Puerto Lápice
Herencia
Pantano Muleteros
Casas de Fernando Alonso
Casas de Haro
Quintanar del Rey
Villatoya
Arenales de San Gregorio
Villalgordo del Júcar
Casas-Ibáñez
Las Labores
Socuéllamos
Tarazona de la Mancha
Albore
Villarrobledo
Minaya
Madrigueras
Fuentealbilla
Villarta de S. Juan
Mahora
Alcalá de
Arenas de S. Juan
Argamasilla de Alba
Tomelloso
La Roda
Jorquera
Villavaliente
Valdeganga
Alatoz
Santa Marta
La Gineta
Lagunas de Ruidera
Daimiel
Manzanares
Membrilla
Embalse de Peñarroya
Barrax
Casas del Juan Núñez
La Felipa
Sotuélamos
Munera
Albacete
Hoya-Gonzalo
Higueruela
La Solana
Ruidera
Ossa de Montiel
El Bonillo
Lezuza
La Herrera
Chinchilla de Monte Aragón
Valdepeñas de Calatrava
Ermita de Consolación
Tiriez
Balazote
Laguna del Salobral
Villar de Chinchilla
Bonete
San Carlos del Valle
Carrizosa
El Ballestero
San Pedro
El Salobral
Horna
Corral-Rubio
Pétrola
Laguna de Pétrola
Moral
Pozo Cañada
La Higuera
Castilla
La Mancha
Alcarria

Teruel
Montes Universales
Sierra de Camarena
Sierra de Javalambre
Javalambre 2020
Mosqueruela
Mora de Rubielos
Rubielos de Mora
Penyagolosa 1813
Albocàcer
Castelló de la Plana
El Grao de Castelló
Almassora
Vila-real de los Infantes
Burriana
Benicàssim
Oropesa
Nules
La Vall d'Uixó
Moncofa
Segorbe
Sagunt
Canet d'en Berenguer
El Port de Sagunt
Puçol
Massamagrell
Moncada
Paterna
Burjassot
Meliana
Valencia
Ciudad de las Artes y las Ciencias
Golfo de Valencia
Eivissa 3:15
Palma de Mallorca 6:15
Maó 17:00
Costa del Azahar
Costa Blanca
Manises
Alaquàs
Torrent
Massanassa
Catarroja
El Saler
L'Albufera
Silla
Picassent
Almussafes
Sollana
Sueca
Cullera
Algemesí
Alzira
Carcaixent
Tavernes de la Valldigna
Xàtiva
El Grau
Gandía
Oliva
Denia
Jávea
El Montgó
Cabo de San Antonio
Cabo de la Nao
Benisa
Calpe
Peñón de Ifach
Altea
Benidorm
Villajoyosa
Terra Mítica
Alcoy
Cocentaina
Ontinyent
Ibi
Castalla
Jijona
Villena
Elda
Petrer
Monóvar
San Vicente del Raspeig
San Juan de Alicante
Cabo de las Huertas
Alicante
Marseille
Oran
Elche
Santa Pola
Cabo de Santo Pola
Nueva Tabarca
Crevillente
Callosa de Segura
Orihuela
Dolores
Guardamar del Segura
Rojales
Torrevieja
Pilar de la Horadada
San Pedro del Pinatar
San Javier
Santiago de la Ribera
Torre-Pacheco
Murcia
Molina de Segura
Alcantarilla
Sierra de Espuña
Alhama de Murcia
Totana
Cieza
Jumilla
Yecla
Almansa
Ayora
Hellín
Tobarra
Albacete
Chinchilla de Monte Aragón
Requena
Utiel
Sierra Martés
Buñol
Chiva
Cheste
Villanueva de la Jara
Quintanar del Rey
Tarazona de la Mancha
Madrigueras
Casas-Ibáñez
Minglanilla
Carboneras de Guadazaón
Cañete
Calasparra
Cehegín
Caravaca de la Cruz
Mula
Bullas
Archena
Alguazas
Murcia
Embalse de Contreras
Embalse del Generalísimo
Embalse de Loriguilla
Embalse de Buseo
Embalse de Tous
Emb. de Embarcaderos
Embalse de Camarillas
Embalse de Cenajo
Golfo de Valencia

Peñíscola
3
4
5
1°
2°
A
B
C
40°
39°
90
Is. Columbretes
Islas Columbretes
ISLAS BALEARES
Valldemossa
Banyalbufar
Esporles
Estellencs
Puigpunyent
Sa Dragonera
Andratx
Palma de Mallorca
Calvià
Port d'Andratx
Peguera
Santa Ponça
Magaluf
Barcelona 3:00
Mallorca
Cap de Cala Figuera
Valencia 6:00
Eivissa 2:15
Denia 9:00
Portinatx
Ibiza / Eivissa
Sant Joan Baptista
Pta. Grossa
Sant Miquel
Santa Agnès
Sant Carlos
Tagomago
Es Caná
Sa Conillera
Sant Antoni Abat
Santa Eulària des Riu
Cala Llonga
Sant Rafel
Sant Josep
Eivissa
Palma de Mallorca 2:15
Barcelona 9:30
Valencia 3:15
4:00
Sant Francesc de ses Salines
Es Vedrà
Cap Llentrisca
Punta Portás
S'Espardell
S'Espalmador
0:25
Formentera
Sa Savina
Es Pujols
Sant Ferran
Sant Francesc de Formentera
Nuestra Señora Sa Verge des Pilar
Pta. Rotja
C. de Barbària
Barcelona 9:00
Capo de Cavalleria
Punta Nati
Cala Morell
Fornells
Cap de Favàritx
Ciudadela de Menorca
Es Mercadal
Ferreries
Toro
Cala Galdana
Es Migjorn Gran
Alaior
C. de Artrutx
Son Bou
Maó
Menorca
Sant Climent
Es Castell
Pta. de s'Esperó
Sant Luis
Punta Prima
I. de l'Aire
Palma de Mallorca 7:00
Valencia 16:00
Cap de Formentor
Punta Beca
Port de Pollença
B. de Pollença
Pollença
Cap des Pinar
Alcúdia
Es Port d'Alcúdia
B. d'Alcúdia
Port de Sóller
Fornalutx
Puig Major 1445
Sóller
Deià
Selva
Sa Pobla
C'an Picafort
Cap Ferrutx
Cap des Freu
Morey
Lloseta
Alaró
Bunyola
Inca
Muro
Santa Margalida
Artà
Cala Ratjada
Capdepera
Cuevas de Arta
Marratxí
Sta. Maria del Camí
Sencelles
Sineu
Sant Llorenç des Carctassar
Son Servera
Cala Millor
Petra
Montuïri
Manacor
Punta de n'Amer
Algaida
Monasterio de Cora
Porto Cristo
Cuevas del Drach
Can Pastilla
S'Arenal
Palma Nova
Porreres
Llucmajor
Felanitx
Cales de Mallorca
Cap Enderrocat
Bahía de Palma
Maó 6:30
Campos del Port
San Salvador (Monasterio)
Porto Colom
Cala d'Or
Porto Petro
Cap Blanc
Ses Salines
Santanyí
Colònia de Sant Jordi
Cap de ses Salines
I. des Conills
Parque Nacional de Cabrera
3°
4°

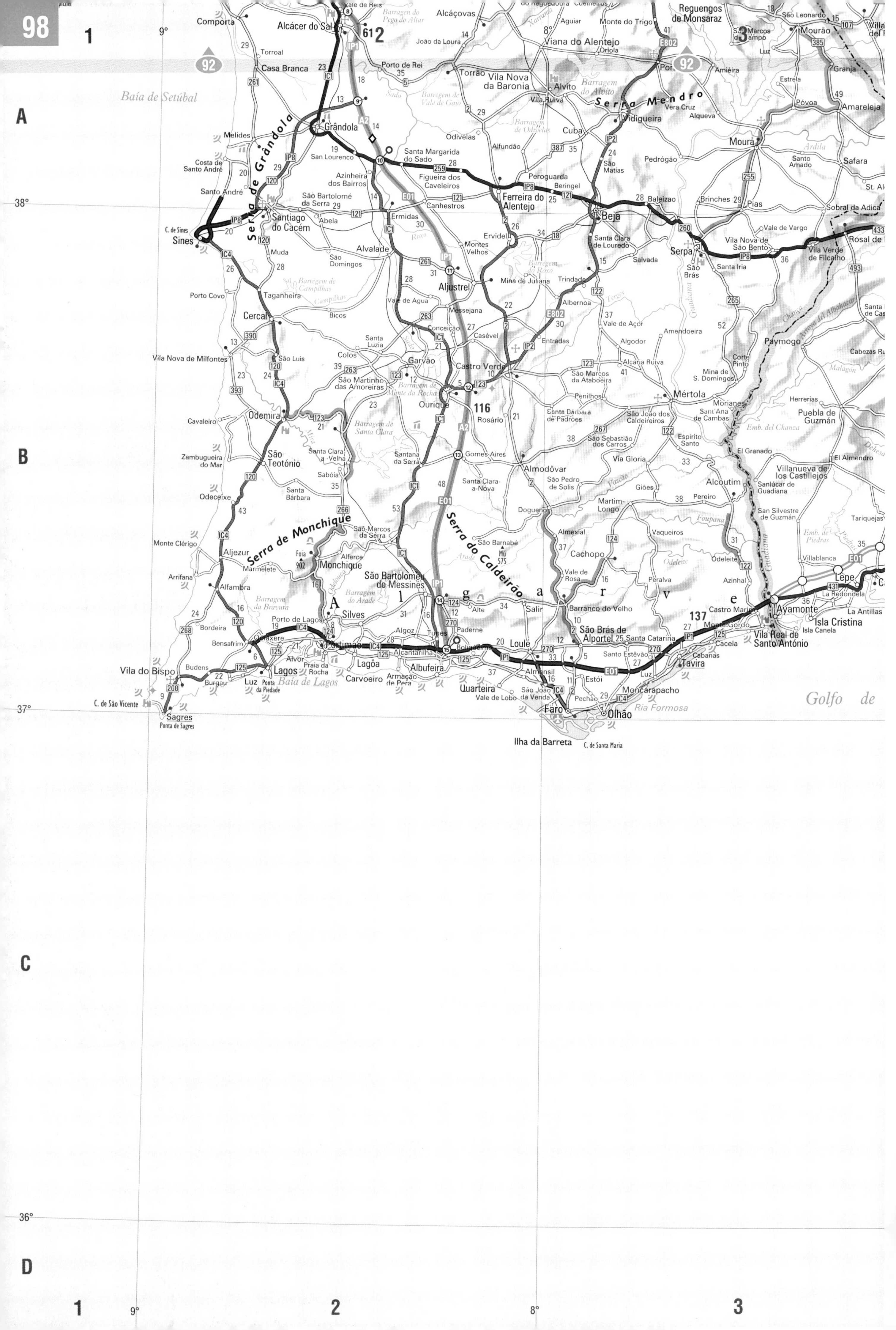
Baía de Setúbal
Comporta
Alcácer do Sal
Alcáçovas
Reguengos de Monsaraz
Mourão
Torroal
Casa Branca
João da Loura
Porto de Rei
Torrão
Vila Nova da Baronia
Viana do Alentejo
Alvito
Aguiar
Monte do Trigo
Oriola
Amieira
Granja
Estrela
Póvoa
Amareleja
Serra Mendro
Vila Ruiva
Vidigueira
Vera Cruz
Alqueva
Grândola
Melides
Costa de Santo André
Santo André
Serra de Grândola
San Lourenço
Santa Margarida do Sado
Odivelas
Alfundão
Cuba
Moura
Pedrógão
Santo Amado
Safara
Azinheira dos Bairros
Figueira dos Caveleiros
Peroguarda
Beringel
São Matias
São Bartolomé da Serra
Ferreira do Alentejo
Baleizao
Brinches
Pias
Sobral da Adica
C. de Sines
Sines
Santiago do Cacém
Abela
Canhestros
Ermidas
Beja
Vale de Vargo
Rosal de
Ervidel
Montes Velhos
Santa Clara de Louredo
Serpa
Vila Nova de São Bento
Vila Verde de Ficalho
Muda
Alvalade
São Domingos
Salvada
São Brás
Santa Iria
Aljustrel
Mina de Juliana
Trindade
Porto Covo
Taganheira
Barragem de Campilhas
Vale de Agua
Albernoa
Cercal
Bicos
Messejana
Vale de Açor
Amendoeira
Conceição
Casével
Entradas
Algodor
Paymogo
Vila Nova de Milfontes
São Luis
Colos
Santa Luzia
Garvão
Castro Verde
Alcaria Ruiva
Corte Pinto
Cabezas R
São Martinho das Amoreiras
São Marcos da Atabodeira
Mina de S. Domingos
Ourique
Penilhos
Mértola
Morianes
Herrerias
Puebla de Guzmán
Cavaleiro
Odemira
Rosário
Santa Bárbara de Padrões
São João dos Caldeireiros
Sant'Ana de Cambas
Zambugueira do Mar
São Teotónio
Santa Clara a-Velha
Santana da Serra
Gomes Aires
Almodôvar
São Sebastião dos Carros
Espirito Santo
El Granado
El Almendro
Via Gloria
Villanueva de los Castillejos
Saboia
Santa Clara-a-Nova
São Pedro de Solis
Alcoutim
Sanlúcar de Guadiana
Odeceixe
Santa Bárbara
Gióes
Pereiro
Martim-Longo
San Silvestre de Guzmán
Tariquejas
Serra de Monchique
São Marcos da Serra
Dogueno
Serra do Caldeirão
Monte Clérigo
Almexial
Vaqueiros
São Barnabé
Aljezur
Foia
Monchique
Alferce
Cachopo
Odeleite
Villablanca
Marmelete
Arrifana
Alfambra
São Bartolomeu de Messines
Vale de Rosa
Peralva
Azinhal
Lepe
Algarve
Silves
Alte
Salir
Barranco do Velho
Castro Marim
Ayamonte
La Redondela
La Antillas
Isla Cristina
Isla Canela
Bordeira
Porto de Lagos
Algoz
Tunes
Paderne
São Brás de Alportel
Santa Catarina
Monte Gordo
Vila Real de Santo António
Bensafrim
Odiáxere
Portimão
Alcantarilha
Loulé
Santo Estêvão
Cacela
Cabanas
Tavira
Vila do Bispo
Budens
Lagos
Alvor
Praia da Rocha
Lagôa
Albufeira
Almansil
Estói
Luz
Burgau
Ponta da Piedade
Baía de Lagos
Carvoeiro
Armação de Pera
Quarteira
Vale de Lobo
São João da Venda
Pechão
Moncarapacho
C. de São Vicente
Sagres
Ponta de Sagres
Faro
Olhão
Ria Formosa
Golfo de
Ilha da Barreta
C. de Santa Maria
38°
37°
36°
9°
8°
A
B
C
D
1
2
3

Sevilla
Huelva
Cádiz
Jerez de la Frontera
Algeciras
La Línea de la Concepción
Gibraltar (U.K.)
Pta. de Europa
Ceuta (España)
Tarifa
Punta Marroqui
Tanger 1:00
Strait of Gibraltar
Bahía de Algeciras
Bahía de Cádiz
Costa de la Luz
Las Palmas de Gran Canaria 48:00
Santa Cruz de Tenerife 53:00
Santa Cruz de la Palma 71:00
Málaga
0:30
Ksar es Seghir
Sierra Morena
Andalucía
Sierra de Aracena
Picos de Aroche
Sierra Norte de Sevilla
Sierra de Hornachuelos
Sierra de los Santos
Serranía de Ronda
Sierra Bermeja
Sierra de Grazalema
Los Alcornocales
Parque Nacional de Doñana
Entorno de Doñana
Jerez de los Caballeros
Oliva de la Frontera
Fregenal de la Sierra
Higuera la Real
Encinasola
Barrancos
Cumbres Mayores
Cumbres de S. Bartolomé
Aracena
Cortegana
Aroche
Jabugo
Almonaster la Real
Zufre
Nerva
Minas de Riotinto
Zalamea la Real
Valverde del Camino
Calañas
Alosno
Tharsis
San Bartolomé de la Torre
Gibraleón
Trigueros
Moguer
Palos de la Frontera
Punta Umbria
Isla de Saltes
Mazagón
El Rompido
Aljaraque
Niebla
La Palma del Condado
Bollullos par del Condado
Almonte
El Rocío
Torre de la Higuera
Fuente de Cantos
Monesterio
Llerena
Usagre
Bienvenida
Zafra
Berlanga
Azuaga
Granja de Torrehermosa
Peñarroya-Pueblonuevo
Fuente Obejuna
Bélmez
Espiel
Villaviciosa de Córdoba
Guadalcanal
Alanís
Cazalla de la Sierra
Constantina
San Nicolás del Puerto
Las Navas de la Concepción
El Pedroso
Santa Olalla
El Real de la Jara
Almadén de la Plata
El Ronquillo
Castilblanco de los Arroyos
Hornachuelos
Almodóvar del Río
Posadas
Palma del Río
Peñaflor
Lora del Río
Fuente Palmera
La Carlota
Écija
Fuentes de Andalucía
Carmona
Cantillana
Villaverde del Río
Brenes
Alcalá del Río
La Rinconada
La Algaba
Guillena
Gerena
Aznalcóllar
Santiponce
Camas
Sanlúcar la Mayor
Mairena de Aljarafe
Coria del Río
La Puebla del Río
Dos Hermanas
Alcalá de Guadaira
El Viso del Alcor
Mairena del Alcor
Marchena
Paradas
El Arahal
Osuna
La Puebla de Cazalla
Utrera
Los Palacios y Villafranca
El Coronil
Morón de la Frontera
Montellano
Las Cabezas de San Juan
Lebrija
Trebujena
Sanlúcar de Barrameda
Chipiona
Rota
El Puerto de Santa María
Puerto Real
San Fernando
Chiclana de la Frontera
Medina Sidonia
Conil de la Frontera
Vejer de la Frontera
Barbate de Franco
Zahara de los Atunes
C. Trafalgar
Los Caños de Meca
Arcos de la Frontera
Bornos
Villamartín
Puerto Serrano
Algodonales
Olvera
Prado del Rey
Grazalema
Ubrique
Ronda
Alcalá de los Gazules
Jimena de la Frontera
Benalup
Castellar de la Frontera
San Roque
Los Barrios
Estepona
Manilva
Casares
Gaucín
Sanlúcar de Barrameda
Alcalá del Valle
Setenil
El Saucejo
Villanueva de S. Juan
Marinaleda
Aguadulce
La Roda de Andalucía
El Rubio
A49
A92
A4
E05
E01
E15
A7
93
99
100
121
131
144
158
198
249
268

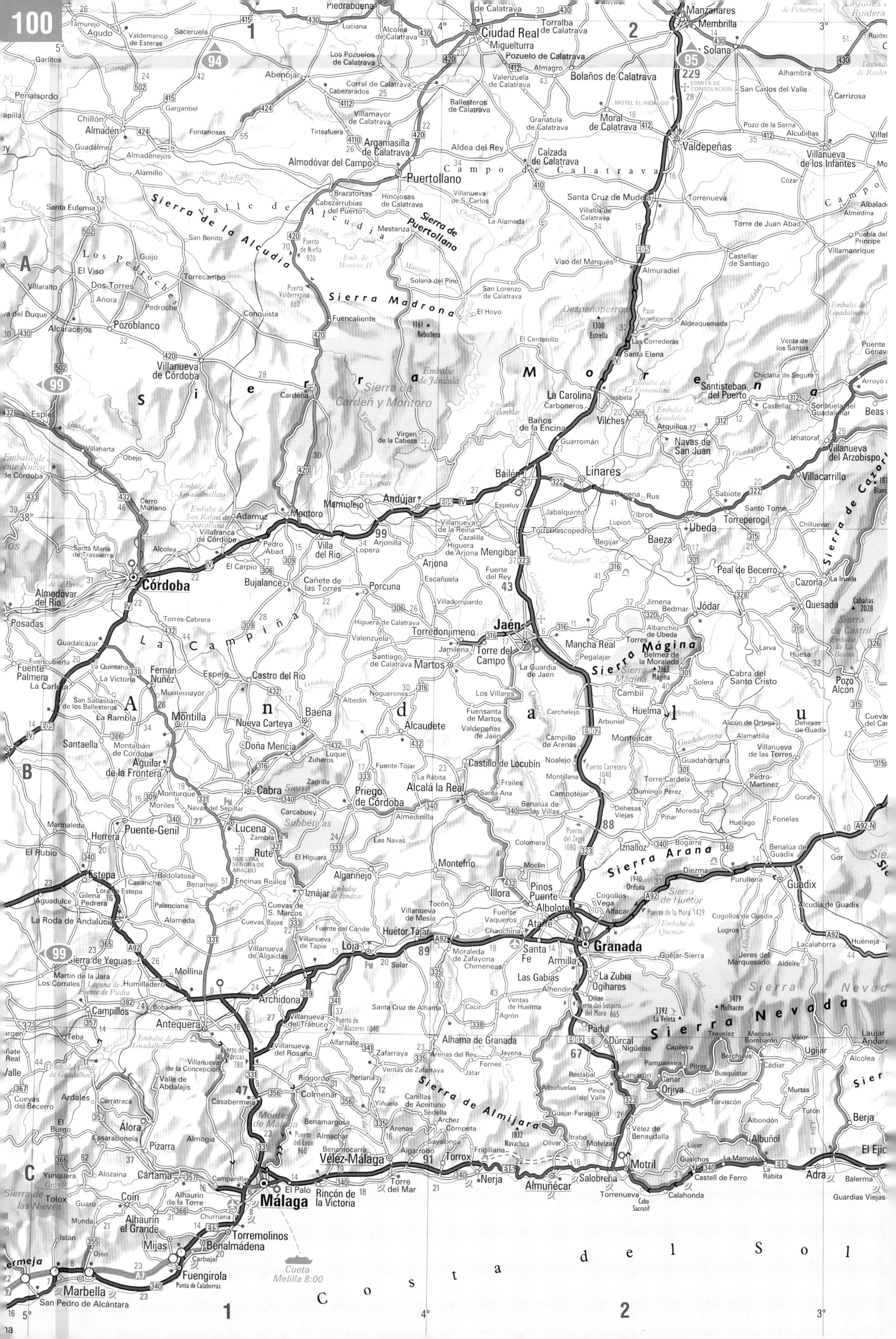

Piedrabuena
Ciudad Real
Miguelturra
Pozuelo de Calatrava
Torralba de Calatrava
Manzanares
Membrilla
La Solana
Tamurejo
Agudo
Valdemanco de Esteras
Saceruela
Luciana
Alcolea de Calatrava
Garlitos
Peñalsordo
Los Pozuelos de Calatrava
Abenójar
Corral de Calatrava
Cabezarados
Almagro
Bolaños de Calatrava
Alhambra
San Carlos del Valle
Carrizosa
Valenzuela de Calatrava
Ballesteros de Calatrava
Moral de Calatrava
Granátula de Calatrava
Chillón
Almadén
Gargantiel
Fontanosas
Villamayor de Calatrava
Tirteafuera
Argamasilla de Calatrava
Aldea del Rey
Calzada de Calatrava
Valdepeñas
Pozo de la Serna
Alcubillas
Villanueva de los Infantes
Guadalmez
Almadenejos
Almodóvar del Campo
Puertollano
Campo de Calatrava
Alamillo
Cózar
Brazatortas
Hinojosas de Calatrava
Villanueva de S. Carlos
Cabezarrubias del Puerto
Santa Cruz de Mudela
Torrenueva
Santa Eufemia
Valle de Alcudia
Sierra de la Alcudia
Sierra de Puertollano
Mestanza
La Alameda
Villalba de Calatrava
Torre de Juan Abad
San Benito
Puerto de Niefla
Almedina
Villamanrique
Guijo
Los Pedroches
El Viso
Dos-Torres
Villaralto
Añora
Torrecampo
Pedroche
Viso del Marqués
Castellar de Santiago
Almuradiel
Solana del Pino
San Lorenzo de Calatrava
Sierra Madrona
El Hoyo
Puerto Valderrepiso
Conquista
Pozoblanco
Alcaracejos
Fuencaliente
Rebollera
Despeñaperros
Estrella
Paso Despeñaperros
Aldeaquemada
Las Correderas
Santa Elena
El Centenillo
Venta de los Santos
Villanueva de Córdoba
Cardeña
Sierra de Cardeña y Montoro
Sierra Morena
Embalse de Jándula
La Carolina
Carboneros
Isabela
Santisteban del Puerto
Chiclana de Segura
Castellar
Sorihuela del Guadalimar
Espiel
Vilches
Arquillos
Navas de San Juan
Baños de la Encina
Guarromán
Virgen de la Cabeza
Villaharta
Obejo
Iznatoraf
Villanueva del Arzobispo
Villacarrillo
Bailén
Linares
Canena
Rus
Sabiote
Torreperogil
Santo Tomé
Chilluevar
Cerro Muriano
Adamuz
Montoro
Marmolejo
Andújar
Espeluy
Jabalquinto
Lupión
Ibros
Úbeda
Baeza
Villanueva de la Reina
Cazalilla
Higuera de Arjona
Mengíbar
Torreblascopedro
Begíjar
Villafranca de Córdoba
Alcolea
Pedro Abad
Villa del Río
Lopera
Arjonilla
Santa María de Trassierra
El Carpio
Córdoba
Almodóvar del Río
Bujalance
Cañete de las Torres
Porcuna
Arjona
Escañuela
Fuerte del Rey
Peal de Becerro
Cazorla
La Iruela
Quesada
Cabañas
Jódar
Jimena
Bedmar
Villadompardo
Posadas
Torres-Cabrera
La Campiña
Higuera de Calatrava
Valenzuela
Torredonjimeno
Jaén
Torre del Campo
Jamilena
Mancha Real
Pegalajar
Torres
Albanchez de Ubeda
Belmez de la Moraleda
Sierra Mágina
Mágina
Guadalcázar
Fuente Palmera
La Carlota
La Quintana
La Victoria
Fernán Núñez
Montemayor
Espejo
Castro del Río
Santiago de Calatrava
Martos
La Guardia de Jaén
Los Villares
Cabra del Santo Cristo
Solera
Pozo Alcón
Huesa
Larva
San Sebastián de los Ballesteros
La Rambla
Montilla
Nueva Carteya
Baena
Albedín
Noguerones
Alcaudete
Fuensanta de Martos
Valdepeñas de Jaén
Carchelejo
Cambil
Arbuniel
Huelma
Alicún de Ortega
Dehesas de Guadix
Santaella
Montalbán de Córdoba
Aguilar de la Frontera
Doña Mencía
Zuheros
Luque
Fuente-Tójar
Castillo de Locubín
Noalejo
Campillo de Arenas
Montejícar
Alamedilla
Villanueva de las Torres
Guadahortuna
Torre Cardela
Pedro-Martínez
Cabra
Zagrilla
Priego de Córdoba
La Rábita
Alcalá la Real
Santa Ana
Frailes
Montillana
Campotéjar
Domingo Pérez
Puerto Carretero
Monturque
Moriles
Navas del Sepillar
Carcabuey
Sierras Subbéticas
Almedinilla
Benalúa de las Villas
Dehesas Viejas
Iznalloz
Piñar
Moreda
Huélago
Fonelas
Gorafe
Marinaleda
Herrera
Puente-Genil
Lucena
Zambra
Rute
Las Navas
Colomera
Puerto del Zegrí
Bogarre
Sierra Arana
Benalúa de Guadix
El Rubio
Estepa
Badolatosa
Casariche
Benamejí
El Higuera
Encinas Reales
Algarinejo
Montefrío
Moclín
Pinos Puente
Illora
Diezma
Purullena
Guadix
Gor
Gilena
Pedrera
Aguadulce
Lora de Estepa
Palenciana
Iznájar
Embalse de Iznájar
Cuevas de S. Marcos
Cuevas Bajas
Tocón
Villanueva de Mesía
Fuente Vaqueros
Chauchina
Atarfe
Albolote
Cogollos-Vega
Alfacar
Sierra de Huétor
Puerto de la Mora
Alcudia de Guadix
La Roda de Andalucía
Alameda
Fuente del Conde
Villanueva de Tapia
Huétor Tájar
Loja
Salar
Moraleda de Zafayona
Chimeneas
Santa Fe
Granada
Armilla
Güéjar-Sierra
Cogollos de Guadix
Lugros
Lacalahorra
Huéneja
Jeres del Marquesado
Aldeire
Sierra de Yeguas
Villanueva de Algaidas
Martín de la Jara
Los Corrales
Laguna de Fuente de Piedra
Mollina
Humilladero
Archidona
Las Gabias
La Zubia
Ogíjares
Alhendín
Sierra Nevada
Mulhacén
Villanueva del Trabuco
Puerto de los Alazores
Santa Cruz de Alhama
Cacín
Ventas de Huelma
Agrón
Dílar
Puerto del Suspiro del Moro
Campillos
Bobadilla
Antequera
Teba
Embalse de Guadalhorce
Puerto de las Pedrizas
Villanueva del Rosario
Alfarnate
Zafarraya
Alhama de Granada
Arenas del Rey
Jayena
Fornes
Játar
Padul
Dúrcal
Nigüelas
La Veleta
Trevélez
Mecina-Bombarón
Válor
Laujar de Andarax
Ugíjar
Cádiar
Capileira
Pampaneira
Pitres
Bérchules
Busquistar
Lanjarón
Cañar
Órgiva
Torvizcón
Murtas
Turón
Alcolea
Villanueva de la Concepción
Valle de Abdalajís
Embalse del Conde de Guadalhorce
Ventas de Zafarraya
Periana
Riogordo
Colmenar
Casabermeja
Ardales
Carratraca
Cuevas del Becerro
Restábal
Albuñuelas
Pinos del Valle
Guajar-Faragüit
Sierra de Almijara
Canillas de Aceituno
Sedella
Archez
Cómpeta
Navachica
Benamargosa
Almáchar
Puerto del León
Montes de Málaga
Yunquera
El Burgo
Álora
Almogía
Pizarra
Casarabonela
Alozaina
Cártama
Campanillas
Benamocarra
Vélez-Málaga
Algarrobo
Sayalonga
Frigiliana
Torrox
Ítrabo
Molvízar
Vélez de Benaudalla
Albondón
Albuñol
Berja
Lújar
Gualchos
Motril
Salobreña
Almuñécar
Nerja
Torre del Mar
Rincón de la Victoria
El Palo
Málaga
Castell de Ferro
La Mamola
La Rábita
Adra
Balerma
Guardias Viejas
El Ejido
Calahonda
Torrenueva
Cabo Sacratif
Tolox
Sierra de las Nieves
Coín
Guaro
Alhaurín de la Torre
Alhaurín el Grande
Churriana
Torremolinos
Benalmádena
Monda
Istán
Ojén
Mijas
Carbajal
Fuengirola
Punta de Calaburras
Marbella
San Pedro de Alcántara
Cueta Melilla 8:00
Costa del Sol

Albacete
Chinchilla de Monte Aragón
Hoya-Gonzalo
La Felipa
Higueruela
Alpera
Almansa
Enguera
Vallada
Moixent
Navalón
La Font de la Figuera
Ontiny
Bocairent
Bañeres
Onil
Castalla
Ibi
Tibi
Munera
Sotuélamos
El Bonillo
Lezuza
Tiriez
Balazote
La Herrera
Villar de Chinchilla
Bonete
Corral-Rubio
Horna
Pozo Cañada
Pétrola
La Higuera
Montealegre del Castillo
Caudete
Villena
Biar
Yecla
Sax
Salinas
Elda
Petrer
Monóvar
Agost
San Vicente del Raspeig
Novelda
Monforte del Cid
Aspe
Crevillente
Elche
Hondón de los Frailes
Pinoso
Jumilla
Casas del Puerto
Fuente-Álamo
Pinilla
Ontur
Albatana
Tobarra
Hellín
Minateda
Agramón
Las Minas
Pozohondo
Alcadozo
Peñas de San Pedro
San Pedro
El Salobral
Robledo
Viveros
El Ballestero
Villanueva de la Fuente
Povedilla
Masegoso
Peñascosa
Alcaraz
Sierra de Alcaraz
Paterna del Madera
Bogarra
Ayna
Liétor
Riopar
Bienservida
Molinicos
Villaverde de Guadalimar
Elche de la Sierra
Génave
Siles
El Arguellite
Yeste
Letur
Socovos
La Puerta de Segura
Orcera
Sierra de Segura
Pontones
Santiago de la Espada
Nerpio
Sierra de Taibilla
El Sabinar
Calasparra
Moratalla
Cieza
Abarán
Blanca
Fortuna
Abanilla
Albatera
Callosa de Segura
Catral
Dolores
Orihuela
Almoradí
Guardamar
Rojales
Benejúzar
Bigastro
Torrevieja
San Miguel de Salinas
Pilar de la Horadada
San Pedro del Pinatar
San Javier
Santiago de la Ribera
Los Alcázares
Torre-Pacheco
Mar Menor
Cartagena
La Unión
Cabo de Palos
Los Nietos
El Algar
Portmán
Escombreras
Archena
Ceutí
Lorquí
Molina de Segura
Santomera
Alguazas
Alcantarilla
Murcia
El Valle
Sangonera la Verde
Librilla
Corvera
Fuente-Álamo de Murcia
Mula
Pliego
Bullas
Cehegín
Caravaca de la Cruz
Archivel
Almudena
Sierra de Espuña
Alhama de Murcia
Aledo
Totana
Lorca
Sierra de la Almenara
Mazarrón
Puerto de Mazarrón
Golfo de Mazarrón
Cabo Tiñoso
Águilas
Cope
Cabo Cope
Pulpí
Puerto Lumbreras
Vélez Rubio
Vélez Blanco
María
Sierra de María
Chirivel
Huéscar
Puebla de Don Fadrique
La Sagra 2381
Castril
Castilleja
Galera
Orce
Cortes de Baza
Benamaurel
Cúllar
Zújar
Baza
Caniles
Sierra de las Estancias
Oria
Albox
Huércal-Overa
Cuevas del Almanzora
Olula del Río
Macael
Purchena
Tíjola
Serón
Cantoria
Zurgena
Vera
Garrucha
Palomares
Antas
Bédar
Los Gallardos
Mojácar
Sorbas
Tabernas
Sierra de los Filabres
Sierra Cabrera
Carboneras
Níjar
Sierra Alhamilla
Sierra de Gádor
Gérgal
Abla
Alhama de Almería
Benahadux
Viator
Huércal de Almería
Almería
Golfo de Almería
Aguadulce
Roquetas de Mar
La Mojonera
Vícar
Félix
Las Negras
Cabo de Gata-Níjar
Sierra del Cabo de Gata
San José
Cabo de Gata
Fernán Pérez
Melilla 7:00
Nador 5:00
Murcia
3
4
5
B
C
2°
1°
37°
38°

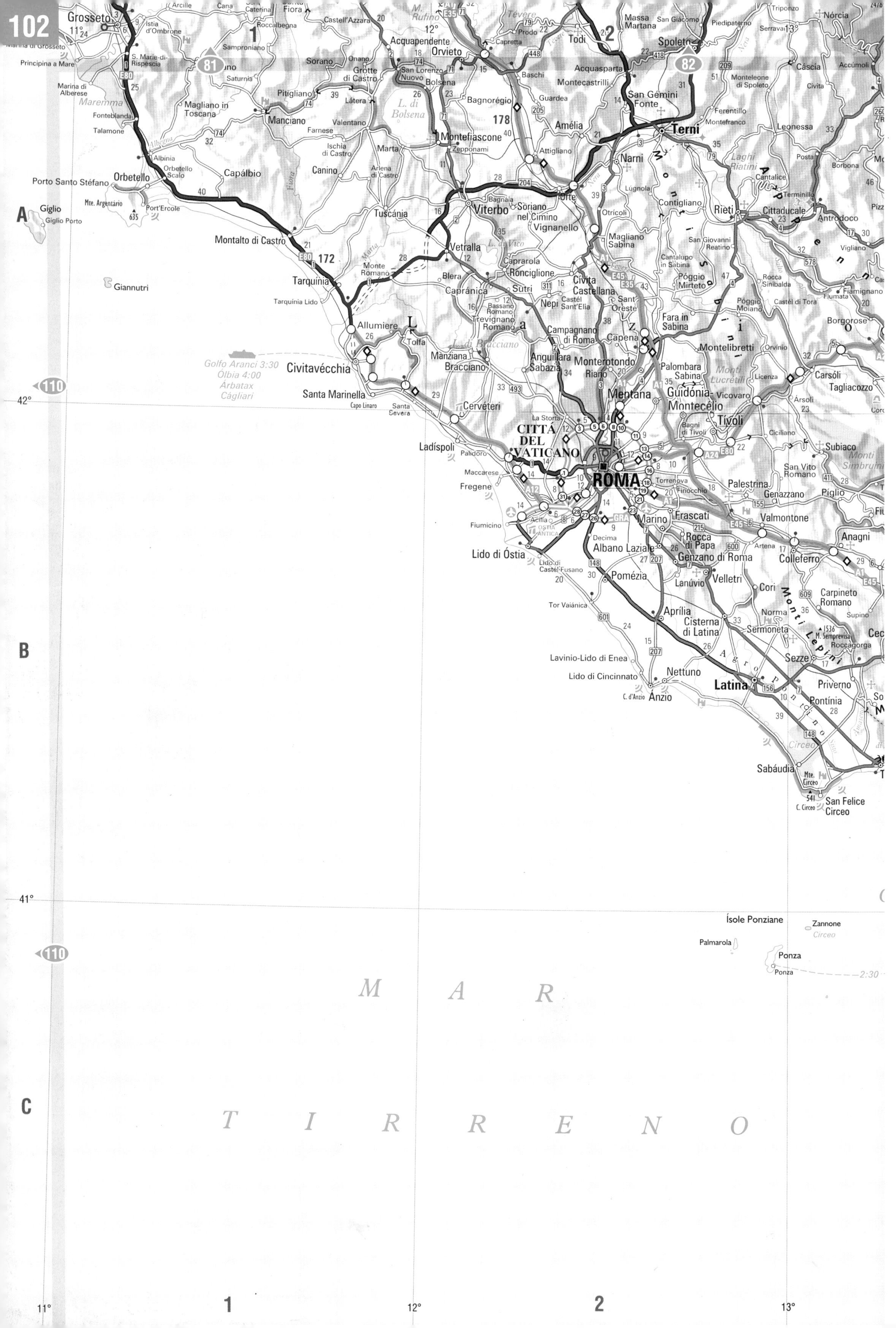

Grosseto
Istia d'Ombrone
Roccalbegna
Arcille
Cana
Santa Caterina
Santa Fiora
Castell'Azzara
M. Rufino
Tevere
Prodo
Todi
Massa Martana
San Giacomo
Piediapaterno
Tripónzo
Nórcia
Serravalle
Marina di Grosseto
Principina a Mare
S. Marie-di-Rispescia
Semproniano
Acquapendente
Orvieto
Capretta
Spoleto
Sorano
Onano
San Lorenzo Nuovo
Grotte di Castro
Baschi
Acquasparta
Montecastrilli
Cáscia
Accúmoli
Saturnia
Marina di Alberese
Maremma
Fonteblanda
Talamone
Magliano in Toscana
Pitigliano
Manciano
Látera
Valentano
Farnese
L. di Bolsena
Bolsena
Bagnorégio
Guardea
San Gémini Fonte
Monteleone di Spoleto
Civita
Ferentillo
Montefranco
Leonessa
Amélia
Terni
Montefiascone
Zepponami
Attigliano
Albinia
Orbetello Scalo
Orbetello
Porto Santo Stéfano
Capálbio
Ischia di Castro
Canino
Marta
Arlena di Castro
Narni
Laghi Riatini
Posta
Borbona
Cantalice
Terminillo
Cittaducale
Antrodoco
Giglio
Giglio Porto
Mte. Argentário
Port'Ercole
Tuscánia
Viterbo
Bagnaia
Soriano nel Cimino
Orte
Lúgnola
Contigliano
Rieti
Vigliano
Otrícoli
Vignanello
Magliano Sabina
San Giovanni Reatino
Cantalupo in Sabina
Póggio Mirteto
Rocca Sinibalda
Castel di Tora
Fiamignano
Fiumata
Montalto di Castro
Vetralla
L. di Vico
Caprarola
Ronciglione
Civita Castellana
Sant'Oreste
Giannutri
Tarquínia
Tarquinia Lido
Monte Romano
Blera
Capránica
Sutri
Nepi
Castel Sant'Elia
Bassano Romano
Trevignano Romano
Fara in Sabina
Póggio Moiano
Borgorose
Allumiere
Tolfa
L. di Bracciano
Manziana
Bracciano
Campagnano di Roma
Capena
Montelibretti
Orvínio
Golfo Aranci 3:30
Ólbia 4:00
Arbatax
Cágliari
Civitavécchia
Anguillara Sabazia
Monterotondo
Riano
Palombara Sabina
Monti Lucretili
Licenza
Carsóli
Tagliacozzo
Santa Marinella
Capo Linaro
Santa Severa
Cervéteri
Mentana
Guidónia-Montecélio
Vicovaro
Ársoli
Tívoli
Bagni di Tívoli
La Storta
CITTÀ DEL VATICANO
Ladíspoli
Palidoro
Ciciliano
Subiaco
Monti Simbruini
Maccarese
Fregene
ROMA
Torrenova
Finocchio
San Vito Romano
Palestrina
Genazzano
Píglio
Fiumicino
Acilia
OSTIA ANTICA
Marino
Frascati
Valmontone
Decima
Rocca di Papa
Artena
Colleferro
Anagni
Lido di Óstia
Lido di Castel Fusano
Albano Laziale
Genzano di Roma
Lanúvio
Velletri
Pomézia
Cori
Carpineto Romano
Tor Vaiánica
Aprília
Cisterna di Latina
Norma
Supino
Sermoneta
M. Semprevisa
Roccagorga
Monti Lepini
Lavinio-Lido di Enea
Lido di Cincinnato
Nettuno
C. d'Anzio
Anzio
Latina
Sezze
Agro Pontino
Priverno
Pontínia
Circeo
Sabáudia
Mte. Circeo
C. Circeo
San Felice Circeo
Ísole Ponziane
Zannone
Palmarola
Ponza
2:30
M A R
T I R R E N O
Appennino Abruzzese
Monti Sabini
Lazio
A
B
C
1
2
11°
12°
13°
42°
41°
81
82
110

3
4
5
A
B
C
14°
15°
42°
41°
82
83
104
106
Téramo
Giulianova
Roseto degli Abruzzi
Pineto
Silvi Marina
Montesilvano
Pescara
Francavilla al Mare
Ortona
Chieti
San Vito Chietino
Lanciano
Vasto
San Salvo
Térmoli
Campomarino
Trémiti
Lésina
Sannicandro Gargánico
Apricena
San Marco in Lámis
San Severo
Torremaggiore
Lucera
Fóggia
Tróia
Ascoli Satriano
Gran Sasso d'Itália
Corno Grande 2912
L'Áquila
Avezzano
Celano
Sulmona
Prátola Peligna
Pópoli
Guardiagrele
Atessa
Casalbordino
Abruzzo
Mte. Amaro 2793
Majella
Roccaraso
Castèl di Sangro
Agnone
Isérnia
Campobasso
Venafro
Cassino
Sora
Frosinone
Alatri
Ferentino
Véroli
Arpino
Isola del Liri
Monte San Giovanni Campano
Ceprano
Pontecorvo
Aquino
Fondi
Terracina
Sperlonga
Fórmia
Gaeta
Minturno
Sessa Aurunca
Monti Aurunci
Golfo di Gaeta
Mondragone
Castél Volturno
Teano
Cápua
Caserta
Maddaloni
Santa Maria Cápua Vétere
Marcianise
Aversa
Giugliano in Campania
Afragola
Acerra
Nola
Avellino
Benevento
Montesárchio
Ariano Irpino
Grottaminarda
Bojano
Piedimonte Matese
Monti del Matese
Morcone
Pozzuoli
Bácoli
NÁPOLI
Torre del Greco
Torre Annunziata
Castellammare di Stábia
Sorrento
Massa Lubrense
Positano
Amalfi
Capri
Anacapri
Ischia
Prócida
Golfo di Nápoli
Pompei
Sarno
Nocera Inferiore
Cava de Tirreni
Salerno
Battipáglia
Éboli
Golfo di Salerno
Agrópoli
Capáccio
Roccadáspide
Campagna
Montella
Monti Picentini
Buccino
Polla
Teggiano
Vallo della Lucánia
Castellabate
Muro Lucano
Ventoténe
Porto Vecchio Cágliari 15:30
Tunis 18:00
Palermo 4:00
Strómboli
Ginostra
Panarea
Lipari
Vulcano
Milazzo

1
2
15°
16°
42°
41°
40°
A
B
C
103
106
186
207
208
Términi
Campomarino
San Salvo
San Salvo Marina
Montenero di Bisàccia
Guglionesi
Lama dei Peligni
Palena
Colledimezzo
Villa Santa Maria
Pescocostanzo
Roccaraso
Capracotta
Agnone
Castèl di Sangro
Carovilli
Trivento
Bagnoli dei Trigno
Isérnia
Carpinone
Frosolone
Campobasso
Larino
Casacalenda
Serracapriola
Chiéuti
Portocannone
San Martino in Pensilis
Lesina
Lago di Lésina
Lago di Varano
Poggio Imperiale
Apricena
Sannicandro Gargánico
Cagnano Varano
Carpino
Ischitella
Rodi Gargánico
Peschici
Vieste
Vico del Gargano
Testa del Gargano
Pugnochiuso
Báia delle Zágare
Gargano
Mattinata
Monte Sant'Ángelo
San Giovanni Rotondo
San Marco in Lámis
Rignano Gargánico
San Severo
San Paolo di Civitate
Torremaggiore
Santa Croce di Magliano
Casalnuovo Monterotaro
Castelnuovo della Dáunia
Manfredónia
Lido di Siponto
Golfo di Manfredónia
Lucera
Fóggia
Amèndola
Zapponeta
Salina di Margherita di Savóia
Margherita di Savóia
Trinitápoli
Barletta
San Ferdinando di Púglia
Cerignola
Andria
Canosa di Púglia
Minervino Murge
Orta Nova
Ascoli Satriano
Candela
Lavello
Melfi
Venosa
Rionero in Vulture
Spinazzola
Palazzo San Gervásio
Genzano di Lucánia
Gravina in Púglia
Acerenza
Irsina
Potenza
Tricárico
Grassano
Tolve
Matese
Monti del Matese
Piedimonte Matese
Bojano
Monti d. Sánnio
Morcone
Benevento
Caserta
Maddaloni
Cápua
Santa Maria Cápua Vétere
Marcianise
Aversa
Acerra
Afragola
Giugliano in Campania
Nola
Avellino
NÁPOLI
Pozzuoli
Portici
Ercolano
Torre del Greco
Torre Annunziata
Castellammare di Stábia
Golfo di Nápoli
Sorrento
Massa Lubrense
Capri
Anacapri
Positano
Amalfi
Praiano
Pompei
Sarno
Nocera Inferiore
Cava de' Tirreni
Salerno
Vietri sul Mare
Pontecagnano
Battipáglia
Éboli
Golfo di Salerno
Campagna
Montecorvino Rovella
Monti Picentini
Solofra
Ariano Irpino
Grottaminarda
Mirabella Eclano
Lacedónia
Montella
Buccino
Muro Lucano
Bella
Avigliano
Picerno
Tito
Polla
Sala Consilina
Padula
Teggiano
Roccadáspide
Capáccio
Agrópoli
Castellabate
Punta Licosa
Vallo della Lucánia
Vallo di Diano
Cilento
Ascea
Pisciotta
Palinuro
C. Palinuro
Camerota
Sapri
Golfo di Policastro
Maratea
Lagonegro
Lauria
Rivello
Viggiano
Moliterno
Marsico Nuovo
Stigliano
San Arcángelo
Senise
Latrónico
Chiaromonte
Francavilla in Sinni
Pollino
Rotonda
Mormanno
Morano Cálabro
Castrovillari
Cassano
Práia a Mare
Scalea
Capo Scalea
Diamante
Belvedere Maríttimo
Sangineto Lido
Cetraro
Roggiano Gravina
Altomonte
Spezzano Albanese
San Marco Argentano
Bisignano
Luzzi
Tunis 18:00
Palermo 4:00
Strómboli
Ginostra
Panarea
Lipari
Vulcano
Milazzo
1:20
0:45

3
4
5
A
B
C
17°
18°
42°
41°
40°
Dubrovnik 7:00
Durrës 0.00
Kérkira 10:00
Igoumenítsa 10:00
Pátrai 16:00
Ancona 12:00
Durrës 8:00
Vlorë 8:00
Kérkira 8:00
Igoumenítsa 9:00
Paoí 7:00
Sami 13:30
Pátrai 13:00
Zákinthos 16:30
Çeşme 30:00
Trani
Bisceglie
Molfetta
Giovinazzo
Santo Spirito
Corato
Terlizzi
Bari
Ruvo di Púglia
Bitonto
Palo del Colle
Bitetto
Sannicandro di Bari
Modugno
Triggiano
Mola di Bari
Capurso
Noicáttaro
Adelfia
Rutigliano
Grumo Áppula
Toritto
Casamássima
Polignano a Mare
Monópoli
Conversano
Acquaviva delle Fonti
Turi
Castellana Grotte
Cassano delle Murge
Sammichele di Bari
Putignano
Savelletri
Fasano
Torre Canne
Rosa Marina
Villanova
Altamura
Gióia del Colle
Noci
Alberobello
Locorotondo
Ostuni
Santéramo in Colle
Cisternino
Carovigno
Torre Guaceto
Martina Franca
Matera
Laterza
Castellaneta
Móttola
Crispiano
Céglie Messápica
San Vito dei Normanni
Bríndisi
Villa Castelli
Ginosa
Palagiano
Massafra
Francavilla Fontana
Canale Reale
Mesagne
Montemésola
Grottáglie
Oria
Latiano
San Pietro Vernótico
Casa l'Abate
Pomárico
Montescaglioso
Bradano
Cellino
Torchiarolo
Lido Azzurro
Táranto
Torre Santa Susanna
S. Marco
Castellaneta Marina
S. Dónaci
Squinzano
Bernalda
Chéradi
San Giórgio Iónico
Monteparano
Fragagnano
Érchie
Trepuzzi
Marina di Ginosa
Talsano
Sava
Guagnano
San Cataldo
Pisticci
Lizzano
Mandúria
San Pancrázio Salentino
Sálice Salentino
Campi Salentina
Surbo
Lecce
Pulsano
Torricella
Lido di Metaponto
Lido Silvana
Avetrana
Véglie
Monteroni di Lecce
Marúggio
San Cesário di Lecce
Vérnole
San Foca
Montalbano Iónico
Leverano
Léquile
Melendugno
Torre dell'Orso
Tursi
Lido di Scanzano
Porto Cesáreo
Copertino
Calimera
Scanzano Jónico
Golfo
di
Táranto
Martano
Policoro
Soleto
Galatina
Lido di Policoro
Nardò
Galátone
Otranto
Rotondella
C. d'Otranto
Nova Siri
Santa Maria al Bagno
Cutrofiano
Maglie
Uggiano la Chiesa
Rocca Imperiale
Gallípoli
Alézio
Collepasso
Poggiardo
Sant'Andrea
Parábita
Nociglia
Santa Cesárea Terme
Oriolo
Montegiordano Marina
Casarano
Diso
Castro
Taviano
Ruffano
Miggiano
Rácale
Tricase
Amendolara
Taurisano
Albidona
Marina di Amendolara
Ugento
Presicce
Alessano
Marina di Novàglie
Trebisacce
Gagliano del Capo
Castrignano del Capo
Marina di Léuca
C. Santa Maria di Léuca
Sibari
C. Trionto
Corigliano Cálabro
Rossano
Crosia
Demétrio
Sila Greca
Cropalati
Mandatoriccio
Cariati
Pta. Fiume Nicá
Longobucco
E55
E90
E843
A14
15
107

1
2
3
A
B
C
D
Agrópoli
Castellabate
Ascea
Palinuro
Camerota
Golfo di Policastro
Sapri
Lagonegro
Lauria
Maratea
Praia a Mare
Scalea
Padula
Montesano sulla Marcellana
Viggiano
Moliterno
San Arcángelo
Latrónico
Senise
Pisticci
Montalbano Iónico
Tursi
Policoro
Scanzano
Rotondella
Nova Siri
Rocca Imperiale
Oriolo
Trebisacce
Amendolara
Castrovillari
Morano Cálabro
Mormanno
Cassano allo Iónio
Sibari
Altomonte
Spezzano Albanese
Roggiano Gravina
Corigliano Cálabro
Rossano
Diamante
Belvedere Maríttimo
Cetraro
Acri
Sila Greca
Bisignano
Luzzi
Montalto Uffugo
Fuscaldo
Páola
Rende
Cosenza
San Lúcido
Sila Grande
La Sila
Amantea
Rogliano
Sila Piccola
Nicastro
Sambiase
Catanzaro
Golfo di Sant'Eufémia
Tiriolo
Pizzo
Vibo Valéntia
Tropea
Filadélfia
Soverato
Serra San Bruno
Mileto
Nicótera
Rosarno
Gióia Tauro
Palmi
Polistena
Taurianova
Cittanova
Guardavalle
Caulónia
Gioiosa Iónica
Siderno
Locri
Bagnara Cálabra
Scilla
Villa San Giovanni
Réggio di Calábria
Aspromonte
Mélito di Porto Salvo
Bovalino Marina
Brancaleone Marina
Messina
Milazzo
Barcellona-Pozzo di Gotto
Patti
Sant'Ágata Militello
Monti Peloritani
Monti Nébrodi
Taormina
Randazzo
Bronte
Ísole Eólie
Strómboli
Panarea
Basiluzzo
Salina
Filicudi
Lípari
Vulcano
40°
39°
38°
15°
16°
104
109
15
Valletta 15:00

Lecce
Surbo
San Cataldo
Lizzano
Pulsano
Mandúria
Torricella
San Pancrázio Salentino
Sálice Salentino
Campi Salentina
Lido di Metaponto
Lido Silvana
Avetrana
Marúggio
Véglie
Monteroni di Lecce
San Foca
San Cesário di Lecce
Vérnole
Melendugno
Torre dell'Orso
Leverano
Léquile
Copertino
Porto Cesáreo
Calimera
Martano
Soleto
Galatina
Nardò
Galátone
Otranto
C. d'Otranto
Uggiano la Chiesa
Santa Maria al Bagno
Cutrofiano
Máglie
Poggiardo
Gallípoli
Sant'Andrea
Alézio
Collepasso
Parábita
Nociglia
Santa Cesárea Terme
Casarano
Diso
Castro
Taviano
Ruffano
Miggiano
Rácale
Taurisano
Tricase
Ugento
Presicce
Alessano
Marina di Nováglie
Gagliano del Capo
Castrignano del Capo
Marina di Léuca
C. Santa Maria di Léuca
Golfo di Táranto
do di Scanzano
no Jónico
Policoro
C. Trionto
Crosia
Cariati
Pta. Fiume Nicá
Campana
Crúcoli
Pta. Alice
Cirò
Cirò Marina
Umbriático
San Nicola dell'Alto
Stróngoli
Giovanni in Fiore
Cotronei
Santa Severina
Roccabernarda
Scandale
Crotone
Mesoraca
Petronà
Cutro
C. Colonna
Crópani
Ísola di Capo Rizzuto
Botricello
C. Rizzuto
MARE IONIO
A
B
C
D
4
5
17°
18°
19°
40°
39°
38°
105
15

Ústica
Nápoli 4:00
Livorno 17:00
Génova 20:00
Cágliari 13:30
2:20
Isola delle Fémmine
C. Gallo
Mondello
Palermo
Golfo di Castellammare
Golfo di Términi Imerese
C. San Vito
San Vito lo Capo
Terrasini
Capaci
Carini
Monreale
Montelepre
P.N Zingaro
M. Sparagio 1110
Scopello
Balestrate
Ficarazzi
Bagheria
Altofonte
Casteldáccia
Misilmeri
Trabia
Términi Imerese
Campofelice di Roccella
Cágliari 11:30
Pizzolungo
Érice
Trápani
Lévanzo
Ísole Égadi
Maréttimo
Favignana
Saline di Trápani e Paceco
Paceco
Valdérice
Castellammare del Golfo
Partinico
San Cipirello
San Guiseppe Jato
Piana degli Albanesi
Bolognetta
Marineo
Cáccamo
Fulgatore
Alcamo
Bosco di Alcamo
Calatafimi
Camporeale
Villafrati
Ciminna
Cerda
Rilievo
Stagnone
Ísole dello Stagnone di Marsala
Vita
Salemi
Gibellina Nuova
Mezzojuso
Rca. Busambra 1613
Montemaggiore Belsito
Vicari
Roccamena
Corleone
Roccapalumba
Caltavuturo
Marsala
Matarocco
Santa Ninfa
Partanna
Salaparuta
Campofiorito
Plla. Imbriaca 718
Prizzi
Lercara Friddi
Ália
Valledolmo
Strasatti
Castelvetrano
Mazara del Vallo
Campobello di Mazara
Santa Margherita di Belice
Sambuca di Sicília
Bisacquino
Chiusa Sclafani
Palazzo Adriano
Santo Stéfano Quisquina
Vallelunga Pratameno
Villalba
Cammarata
Bivona
Mussomeli
Tunis 7:00
Pantelleria 4:45
Granitola-Torretta
C. Granitola
Marinella
Menfi
Caltabellotta
Búrgio
Alessándria della Rocca
M. Cammarata 1578
Cianciana
Casteltérmini
Campofranco
C. S. Marco
Sciacca
Ribera
Cattólica Eraclea
San Biágio Plátani
Montedoro
Serradifalco
Montallegro
Raffadali
Aragona
Racalmuto
Macalube di Aragona
Canicattì
Siciliana
Agrigento
Favara
Castrofilippo
Porto Empédocle
Naro
Camastra
Palma di Montechiaro
Linosa 5:45
Lampedusa 8:15
Canale di Sicilia
Trápani 4:45
Pantelleria
Porto Empédocle 5:45
Linosa
1:45
Ísole Pelágie
(Italia)
Lampione
Lampedusa

Strómboli
Nápoli
Basiluzzo
Panarea
Filicudi
Alicudi
Malfa
Salina
Ísole Eólie
Canneto
Lípari
Vulcano
Capo di Milazzo
Golfo di Milazzo
Milazzo
Golfo di Patti
Capo Calavá
Gioiosa Marea
C. d'Orlando
Brolo
Naso
Patti
Falcone
Barcellona-Pozzo di Gotto
Spadafora
Villafranca Tirrena
Spartà
Torre Faro
Mortelle
Messina
Rometta
Santa Lucia del Mela
Castroreale
Monti Peloritani
M. Poverello 1279
Str. di Messina
Scaletta Zanclea
Ali Terme
Roccalumera
Santa Teresa di Riva
Mandanici
Antillo
Taormina
Giardini Naxos
Cefalù
Santo Stéfano di Camastra
Caronia
Sant'Ágata Militello
Alcara li Fusi
San Fratello
Tusa
Castelbuono
Mistretta
Monti Nébrodi
M. Soro 1847
Longi
Tortorici
Ucria
Floresta
San Piero Patti
Montalbano Elicona
Novara di Sicília
Mazzarrà S. Andrea
Francavilla di Sicilia
Castiglione di Sicilia
Linguaglossa
Randazzo
Santa Doménica Vittória
Cesarò
Capizzi
Geraci Sículo
Petralia Sottana
Gangi
Sperlinga
Troina
Nicosia
Maletto
Bronte
Etna 3323
Passopisciaro
Piedimonte Etneo
Fiumefreddo di Sicília
Máscali
Riposto
Giarre
Zafferana Etnea
Acireale
Aci Catena
Aci Castello
Nicolosi
Trecastagni
Adrano
Biancavilla
Santa Maria di Licodia
Belpasso
Paternò
Misterbianco
Catánia
Golfo di Catánia
Ravenna 35:00
Valletta 11:00
Valletta 15:00
Regalbuto
Centúripe
Agira
Gagliano Castelferrato
Leonforte
Assoro
Villarosa
Calascibetta
Enna
Pergusa
Catenanuova
Alimena
Caltanissetta
Valguarnera Caropepe
Raddusa
Castel di Iúdica
Gerbini
Pietraperzia
Aidone
Piazza Armerina
Ramacca
Barrafranca
Palagonía
Scordia
Mirabella Imbáccari
San Michele di Ganzaria
Mazzarino
Riesi
Caltagirone
Grammichele
Mineo
Militello in Val di Catánia
Lentini
Lago di Lentini
Villasmundo
Capo S. Croce
Augusta
Golfo di Augusta
Francofonte
Melilli
Priolo Gargallo
Sortino
Buccheri
Vizzini
Licodía Eubéa
Niscemi
Butera
Gela
Golfo di Gela
Falconara
San Pietro
Monterosso Almo
M. Lauro 986
Ferla
Solarino
Floridia
Siracusa
Giarratana
Palazzolo Acréide
Monti Iblei
Acate
Chiaramonte Gulfi
Vittória
Cómiso
Ragusa
Canicattini Bagni
Cavagrande del Cassibile
Cassibile
C. Murro di Porco
Avola
Noto
Golfo di Noto
Módica
Scoglitti
Santa Croce Camerina
C. Scarámia
Marina di Ragusa
Donnalucata
Scicli
Rosolini
Íspica
Oasi Faunistica di Vendicari
Marzamemi
Sampieri
Pozzallo
Pachino
C. Passero
Portopalo di C. Passero
Briático
Pizzo
Vibo Valéntia
Tropea
C. Vaticano
M. Poro 710
Mileto
Soriano Cálabro
Nicótera
Íoppolo
Golfo di Gióia
Rosarno
Gióia Táuro
Laureana di Borrello
Polistena
Cinquefrondi
Taurianova
Cittanova
Capo Barbi
Palmi
Seminara
Oppido Mamertina
Bagnara Cálabra
Santa Eufémia d'Aspromonte
Scilla
Villa San Giovanni
Delianuova
Réggio di Calábria
Laganadi
Gambárie
Montalto (M. Cocuzza) 1955
Aspromonte
L'Aspromonte
San Luca
Ardore
Gerace
Pta. di Péllaro
Montebello Iónico
Bagaladi
Lazzaro
Bova
Bova Marina
Staiti
Brancaleone Ma
Mélito di Porto Salvo
C. Spartivento
Gozo
San Dimitri Pt
Victoria (Rabat)
Mgarr
Comino
Catánia 11:00
Reggio di Calábria 15:00
San Pawl il-Bahar
Mellieha
Mosta
Sliema
Valletta
Birkirkara
Rabat
Paola
MALTA
Birzebbugia
Benghisa Pt
Filfla
14° 30'
36°
15°
16°
37°
38°
3
4
5
A
B
C
106
14
15

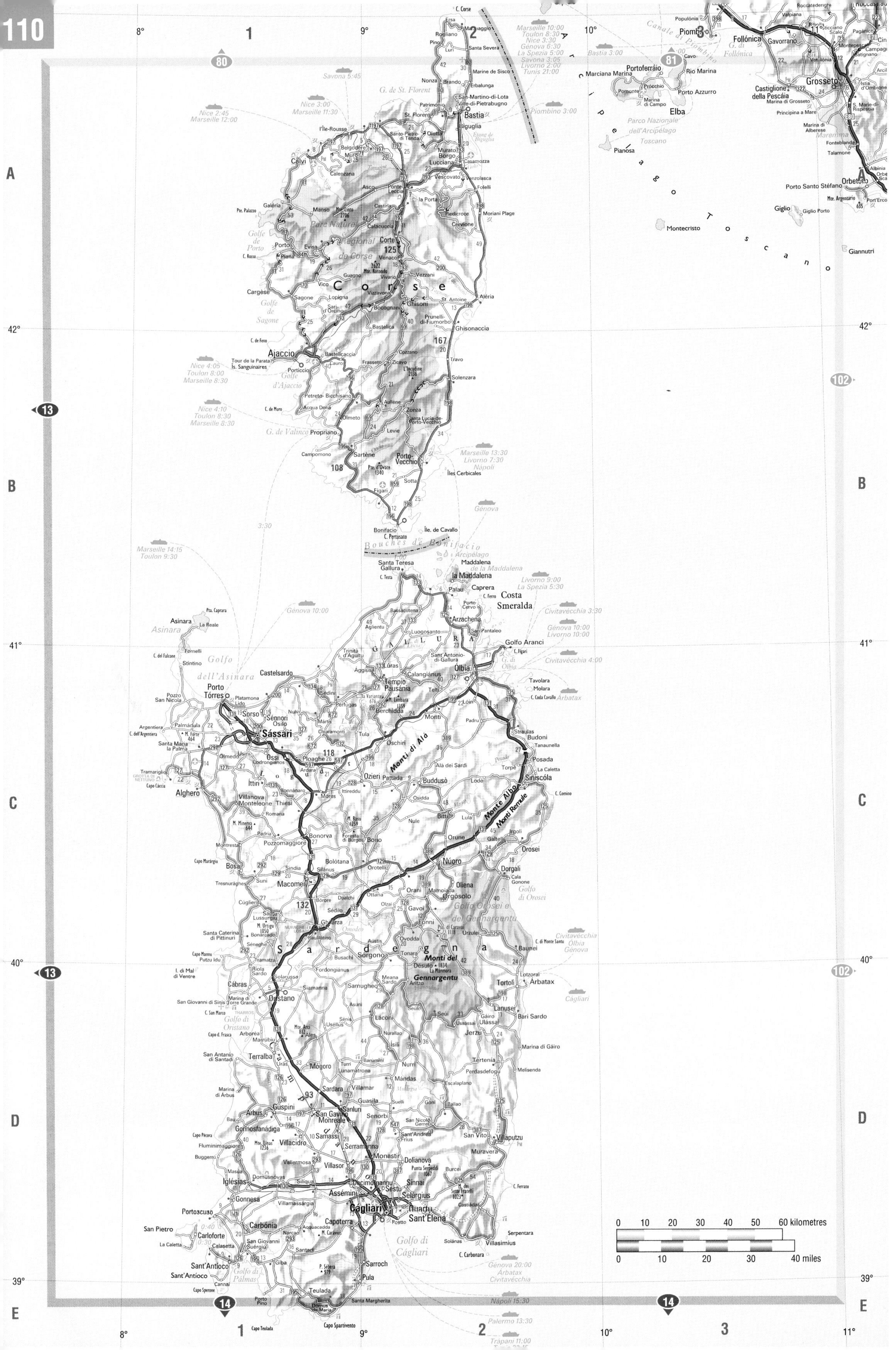

C. Corse
Ersa
Rogliano
Pino
Luri
Santa Severa
Marine de Sisco
Nonza
Brando
Erbalunga
San-Martino-di-Lota
Ville-di-Pietrabugno
Patrimonio
St. Florent
Bastia
Biguglia
G. de St. Florent
Savona 5:45
Nice 3:00
Marseille 11:30
Nice 2:45
Marseille 12:00
Marseille 10:00
Toulon 8:30
Nice 3:30
Gênova 6:30
La Spezia 5:00
Savona 3:05
Livorno 2:00
Tunis 21:00
Piombino 3:00
Bastia 3:00
l'Île-Rousse
Belgodère
Santo-Pietro-di Tenda
Oletta
Murato
Borgo
Lucciana
Casamozza
Calvi
Calenzana
Asco
Ponte Leccia
Vescovato
Venzolasca
Folelli
Galéria
Manso
Mte. Cinto 2706
Castirla
la Porta
Piedicroce
Moriani Plage
Cervione
Parc Naturel Régional de Corse
Calacuccia
Golfe de Porto
Porto
Piana
Evisa
Corte
Venaco
Mte. Rotondo 2622
Vivario
Vezzani
Cargèse
Vico
Guagno
Corse
Aléria
St. Antoine
Ghisoni
Prunelli-di-Fiumorbo
Ghisonaccia
Golfe de Sagone
Sagone
Lopigna
Sari-d'Orcino
Vizzavona
Bocognano
Bastelica
C. de Feno
Ajaccio
Tour de la Parata
Îs. Sanguinaires
Bastelicaccia
Cauro
Porticcio
Golfe d'Ajaccio
Frasseto
Zicavo
Cozzano
L'Incudine 2134
Travo
Solenzara
Nice 4:05
Toulon 8:00
Marseille 8:30
Petreto-Bicchisano
Acqua Doria
C. de Muro
Olmeto
Aullène
Zonza
Santa-Lucia-de-Porto-Vecchio
Nice 4:10
Toulon 8:30
Marseille 8:30
G. de Valinco
Propriano
Levie
Campomoro
Sartène
Porto-Vecchio
Marseille 13:30
Livorno 7:30
Napoli
Îles Cerbicales
Figari
Sotta
Bonifacio
C. Pertusato
Île. de Cavallo
Bouches de Bonifacio
Gênova
3:30
Marseille 14:15
Toulon 9:30
Santa Teresa Gallura
C. Testa
Arcipelago de la Maddalena
Maddalena
la Maddalena
Palau
Caprera
C. Ferro
Costa Smeralda
Livorno 9:00
La Spezia 5:30
Porto Cervo
Civitavècchia 3:30
Gènova 10:00
Livorno 10:00
Civitavècchia 4:00
Gènova 10:00
Asinara
Pta. Caprara
La Reale
Bassacutena
Arzachena
San Pantaleo
Aglientu
Luogosanto
Golfo Aranci
C. Figari
G. di Olbia
Olbia
Fornelli
C. del Falcone
Stintino
Golfo dell'Asinara
Trinità d'Agultu
Gallura
Sant'Antonio-di-Gallura
Aggius
Lùras
Calangiànus
Tempio Pausània
Telti
Tavolara
Molara
C. Coda Cavallo
Arbatax
Castelsardo
Porto Tórres
Platamona Lido
Pozzo San Nicola
Sedini
Perfugas
Berchidda
M. Limbara 1359
Monti
Loiri
Padru
Sorso
Sénnori
Osilo
Nulvi
Sàssari
Chiaramonti
Màrtis
Tula
Argentiera
C. dell'Argentiera
Palmàdula
M. Forte 464
Santa Maria la Palma
Olmedo
Usini
Ossi
Ploaghe
Oschiri
Monti di Alà
Budoni
Tanaunella
Straulas
Posada
Torpè
Alà dei Sardi
Codrongianos
Ardara
Tramariglio
Grotta di Nettuno
Capo Càccia
Alghero
Ittiri
Ozieri
Pattada
Buddusò
Lodè
Siniscola
La Caletta
C. Comino
Bonnànaro
Mores
Ittireddu
Osidda
Villanova Monteleone
Thiesi
Romana
M. Minerva 644
Padria
Pozzomaggiore
M. Rasu 1259
Foresta di Burgos
Bono
Bonorva
Nule
Bitti
Lula
Orune
Monte Albo
Monti Remule
Irgoli
Galtellì
Orosei
Montresta
Capo Marárgiu
Bosa
Sindia
Macomer
Silanus
Bolòtana
Orotelli
Nùoro
Dorgali
Cala Gonone
Golfo di Orosei
Tresnuraghes
Suni
Orani
Mamoiada
Oliena
Orgòsolo
Bòrore
Dualchi
Ottana
Sèdilo
Olzai
Gavoi
Cùglieri
Santu Lussurgiu
Ghilarza
Golfo di Orosei e del Gennargentu
Fonni
M. di Caravai 1118
Urzulei
Santa Caterina di Pittinuri
M. Urtigu 1050
Bonarcado
Paulilàtino
L. Omodeo
Austis
Ovodda
C. di Monte Santu
Civitavècchia
Olbia
Gènova
Capo Mannu
Putzu Idu
Sèneghe
Tramatza
Busachi
Sorgono
Tonara
Sardegna
Monti del Gennargentu
Désulo
La Mármora 1834
Baunei
Lotzorai
Arbatax
Tortolì
I. di Mal di Ventre
Riola Sardo
Solarussa
Fordongiànus
Meana Sardo
Aritzo
Cábras
Siamanna
Samugheo
Cagliari
San Giovanni di Sinis
Marina di Torre Grande
Oristano
C. San Marco
Tharros
Golfo di Oristano
Capo d. Frasca
Arborèa
Asuni
Làconi
Seùlo
Seùi
Ussassai
Gàiro
Ulàssai
Lanusei
Bari Sardo
Marrubiu
Mte. Arci 812
Ales
Sénis
Usellus
Nurallao
Isili
Jerzu
Marina di Gàiro
San Antonio di Santadi
Terralba
Uras
Campidano
Mògoro
Turri
Barumini
Lunamatrona
Nurri
Tertenia
Perdasdefogu
Melisenda
Marina di Arbus
Sardara
Villamar
Màndas
Escalaplano
Arbus
Guspini
San Gavino Monreale
Sanluri
Guasila
Senorbì
Suelli
Goni
Ballao
Bau
Gonnosfanàdiga
Capo Pècora
Villacidro
Samassi
San Nicolò Gerrei
Sant'Andrea Frius
San Vito
Villaputzu
Muravera
Fluminimaggiore
Mte. Linas 1236
Serramanna
Buggerru
Vallermosa
Monastir
Villasor
Dolianova
Punta Serpeddì 1067
Burcei
Iglèsias
Domusnovas
Siliqua
Decimomannu
Sinnai
Sestu
Selargius
M. dei Sette Fratelli 1023
Gonnesa
Assèmini
Castiadas
C. Ferrato
Villamassàrgia
Portoscuso
Carbònia
Cagliari
Quartu Sant'Elena
Poetto
Capoterra
San Pietro
Carloforte
Acquacadda
M. Caravai
Narcao
Golfo di Cagliari
Solànas
Serpentara
Villasimius
C. Carbonara
La Caletta
Calasetta
San Giovanni Suèrgiu
Santadi
Sant'Antìoco
Golfo di Palmas
Giba
P. Sebera 979
Sarroch
Pula
Gènova 20:00
Arbatax
Civitavècchia
Capo Sperone
Teulada
Porto Pino
Domus de Maria
Santa Margherita
Capo Teulada
Capo Spartivento
Nápoli 15:30
Palermo 13:30
Trápani 11:00
Arcipelago Toscano
Canale di Piombino
Piombino
Populònia
Follónica
G. di Follónica
Gavorrano
Marciana Marina
Portoferràio
Rio Marina
Procchio
Pomonte
Marina di Campo
Porto Azzurro
Elba
Parco Nazionale dell'Arcipèlago Toscano
Pianosa
Grosseto
Castiglione della Pescáia
Marina di Grosseto
Principina a Mare
Marina di Alberese
Fonteblanda
Talamone
Orbetello
Porto Santo Stéfano
Mte. Argentario 635
Port'Ercole
Giglio
Giglio Porto
Montecristo
Giannutri
8°
9°
10°
11°
42°
41°
40°
39°
1
2
3
A
B
C
D
E
0 10 20 30 40 50 60 kilometres
0 10 20 30 40 miles

City plans • Plans de villes
Stadtpläne • Piante di città

Motorway	Autoroute
Through route	Route principale
Secondary road	Route secondaire
Dual carriageway	Chaussées séparées
Other road	Autre route
Tunnel	Tunnel
Limited access / pedestrian road	Rue réglementée / rue piétonne
One-way street	Sens unique
Parking	Parc de stationnement
Motorway number	Numéro d'autoroute
National road number	Numéro de route nationale
European road number	Numéro de route européenne
Destination	Destination
Car ferry	Bac passant les autos
Railway	Chemin de fer
Rail/bus station	Gare / gare routière
Underground, metro station	Station de métro
Cable car	Téléférique
Abbey, cathedral	Abbaye, cathédrale
Church of interest	Église intéressante
Synagogue	Synagogue
Hospital	Hôpital
Police station	Police
Post office	Bureau de poste
Tourist information	Office de tourisme
Place of interest	Autre curiosité

Autobahn	Autostrada
Schnellstrasse	Strada d'importanza regionale
Nebenstrasse	Strada d'interesse locale
Zweispurig Schnellstrasse	Strada a carreggiate doppie
Nebenstrecke	Altra strada
Tunnel	Galleria stradale
Beschränkter Zugang / Fussgängerzone	Strada pedonale / a accesso limitato
Einbahnstrasse	Senso unico
Parkplatz	Parcheggio
Autobahnnummer	Numero di autostrada
Nationalstrassennummer	Numero di strada nazionale
Europäische Strassennummer	Numero di strada europea
Ziel	Destinazione
Autofähre	Traghetto automobili
Eisenbahn	Ferrovia
Bahnhof / Busstation	Stazione ferrovia / pullman
U-Bahnstation	Metropolitano
Drahtseilbahn	Funivia
Abtei, Kloster, Kathedrale	Abbazia, duomo
Interessante Kirche	Chiesa da vedere
Synagoge	Sinagoga
Krankenhaus	Ospedale
Polizeiwache	Polizia
Postamt	Ufficio postale
Informationsbüro	Ufficio informazioni turistiche
Sonstige Sehenswürdigkeit	Luogo da vedere

Approach maps • Agglomérations
Carte régionale • Regionalkarte

Toll motorway – with motorway number	Autoroute – avec numéro d'autoroute
Toll-free motorway with European road number	Autoroute avec numéro de route européenne
Motorway services	Aire de service
Motorway junction	Échangeur d'autoroute
Under construction	En construction
Tunnel	Tunnel
Major route dual carriageway / single carriageway	Route principale chausées séparées / chausée sans séparation
Secondary route dual carriageway / single carriageway	Route secondaire chausées séparées / chausée sans séparation
Other road	Autre route
Car ferry	Bac passant les autos
Destination	Destination
Railway	Chemin de fer
Railway station	Gare
Height above sea level – in metres	Altitude – en mètres
Airport	Aéroport principal
Airfield	Autre aéroport
City plan coverage area	Région de plan de ville

Gebührenpflichtige Autobahn – mit Autobahnnummer	Autostrada a pedaggio – con numero
Gebührenfreie Autobahn – Europäische Strassennummer	Autostrada – con numero di strada europea
Autobahnservice	Area di servizio autostradale
Autobahnkreuz	Raccordi autostradali
Im Bau	In construzione
Tunnel	Galleria stradale
Hauptstrecke zweispurige Schnellstrasse	Strada di grande communicazione carreggiata doppia / carreggiata unica
Nebenstrasse zweispurige Schnellstrasse	Strada d'interesse locale carreggiata doppia / carreggiata unica
Nebenstrecke	Altra strada
Autofähre	Traghetto automobili
Ziel	Destinazione
Eisenbahn	Ferrovia
Hauptbahnhof	Stazione ferrovia
Höhe über dem Meeresspiegel	Altezza in metri
Flughafen	Aeroporto
Flugplatz	Aerodromo/campo d'aviazione
Vom Stadtplan abgedecktes Gebiet	Area della pianta della città

Alicante

0 km 0,5

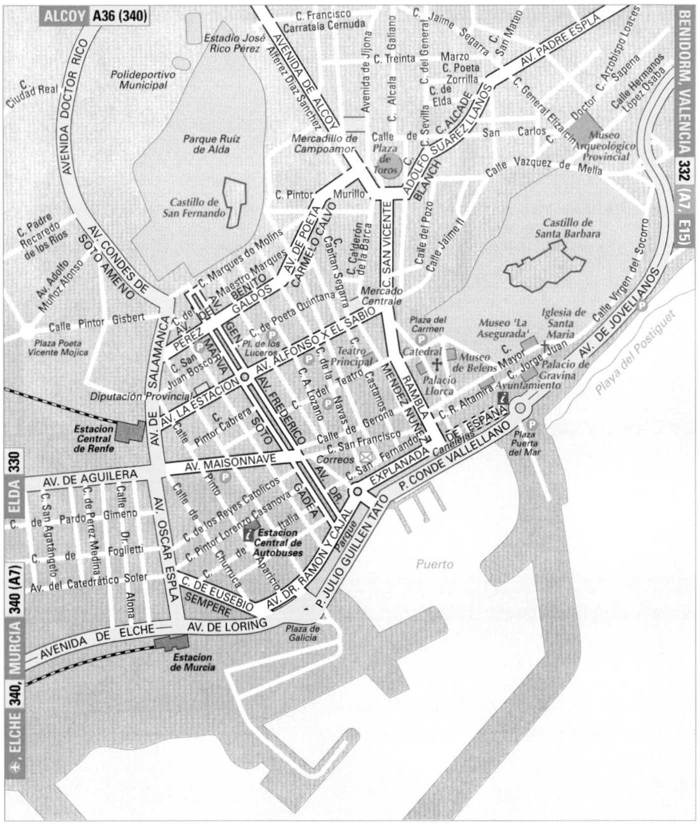

Antwerpen

0 km 1

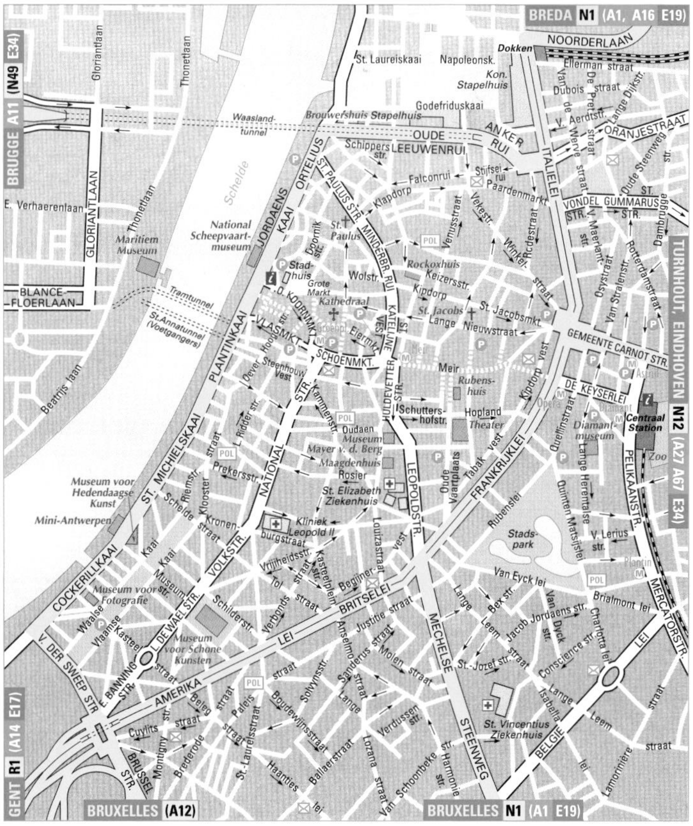

Amsterdam

0 km 2

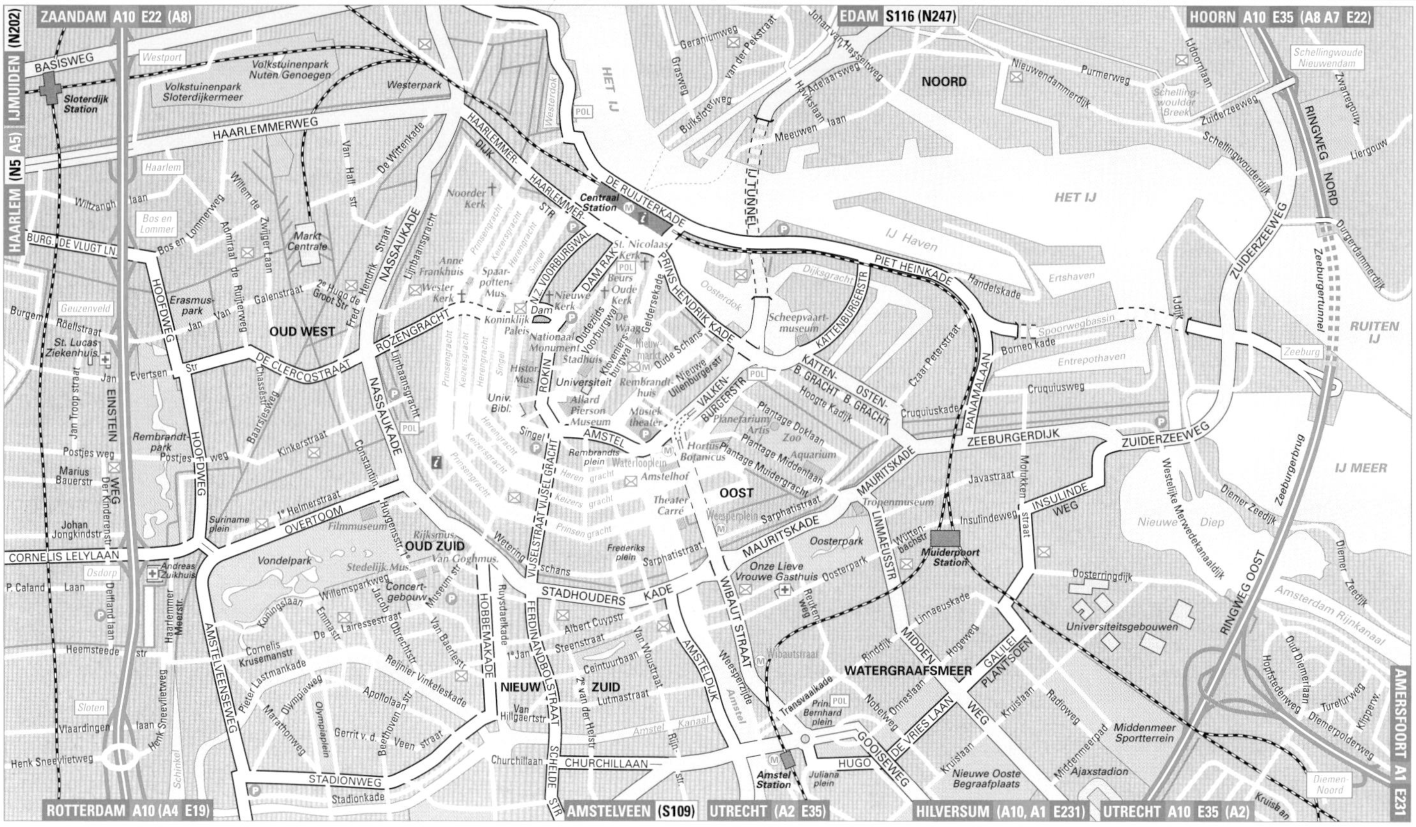

Athínai

0 km 5

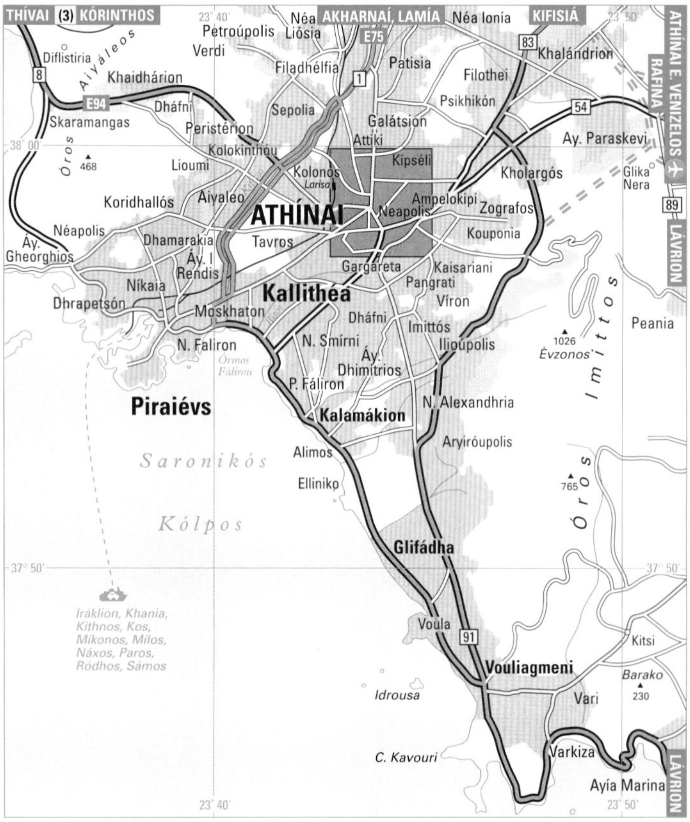

Athínai

0 km 1

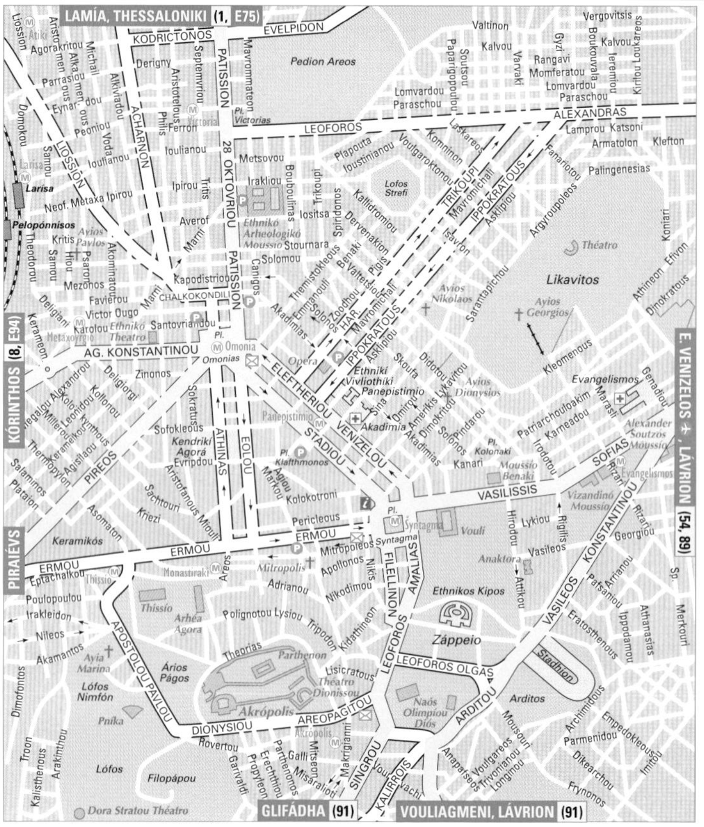

Barcelona

0 km 5

Barcelona

0 km 1

Bruxelles

0 km 1

GENT, OOSTENDE (A10 E40) · ANTWERPEN (A12) · MECHELEN N1 · ANTWERPEN (A1) · BRUXELLES NATIONAL (A201) · LIÈGE (A3 E40) · R21 · NAMUR (A4 E411) · CHARLEROI N5 · MONS N6 · NINOVE N8

Gare du Nord · Jardin Botanique · ST.-JOSSE · Square Ambiorix · Parc du Cinquantenaire · Musées Royaux de Art et d'Histoire · ETTERBEEK · Parc Leopold · Gare du Quartier Leopold · Gare Centrale · Grand Place · Parc de Bruxelles · Palais Royal · Gare du Midi (Eurostar) · ANDERLECHT · ST-GILLES · IXELLES · Boulevard Léopold II · Chaussée de Gand · Chaussée de Ninove · Chaussée de Mons · Chaussée de Louvain · Rue de la Loi · Rue Belliard · Avenue Louise · Boulevard du Midi · Porte de Namur · Porte de Hal · Cimetière St.-Josse · Pl. d. Carabiniers

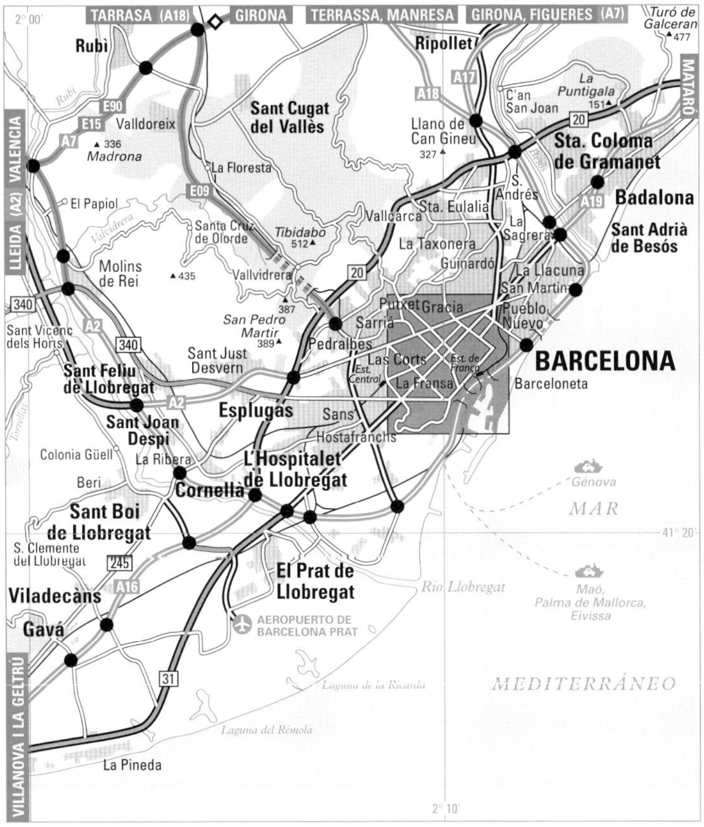

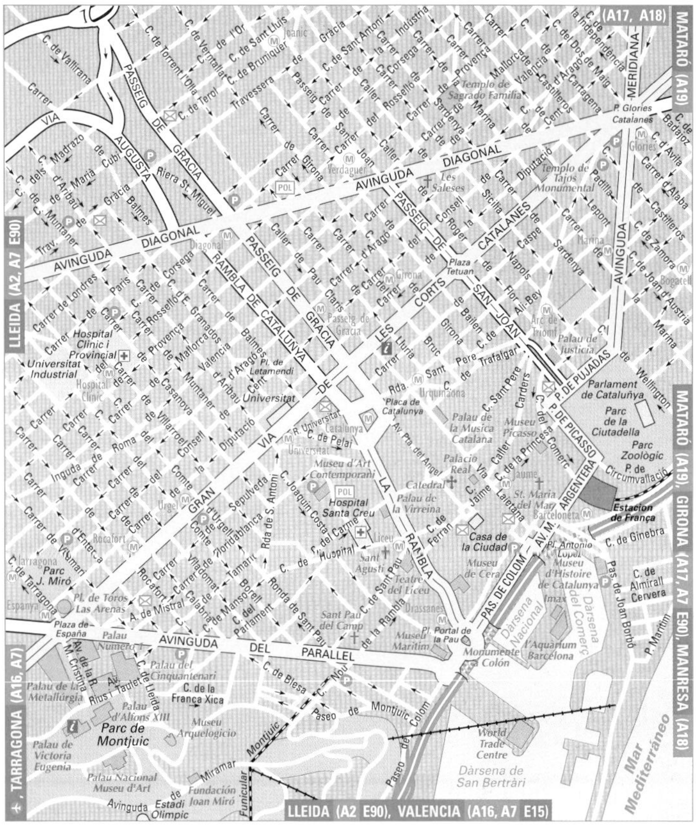

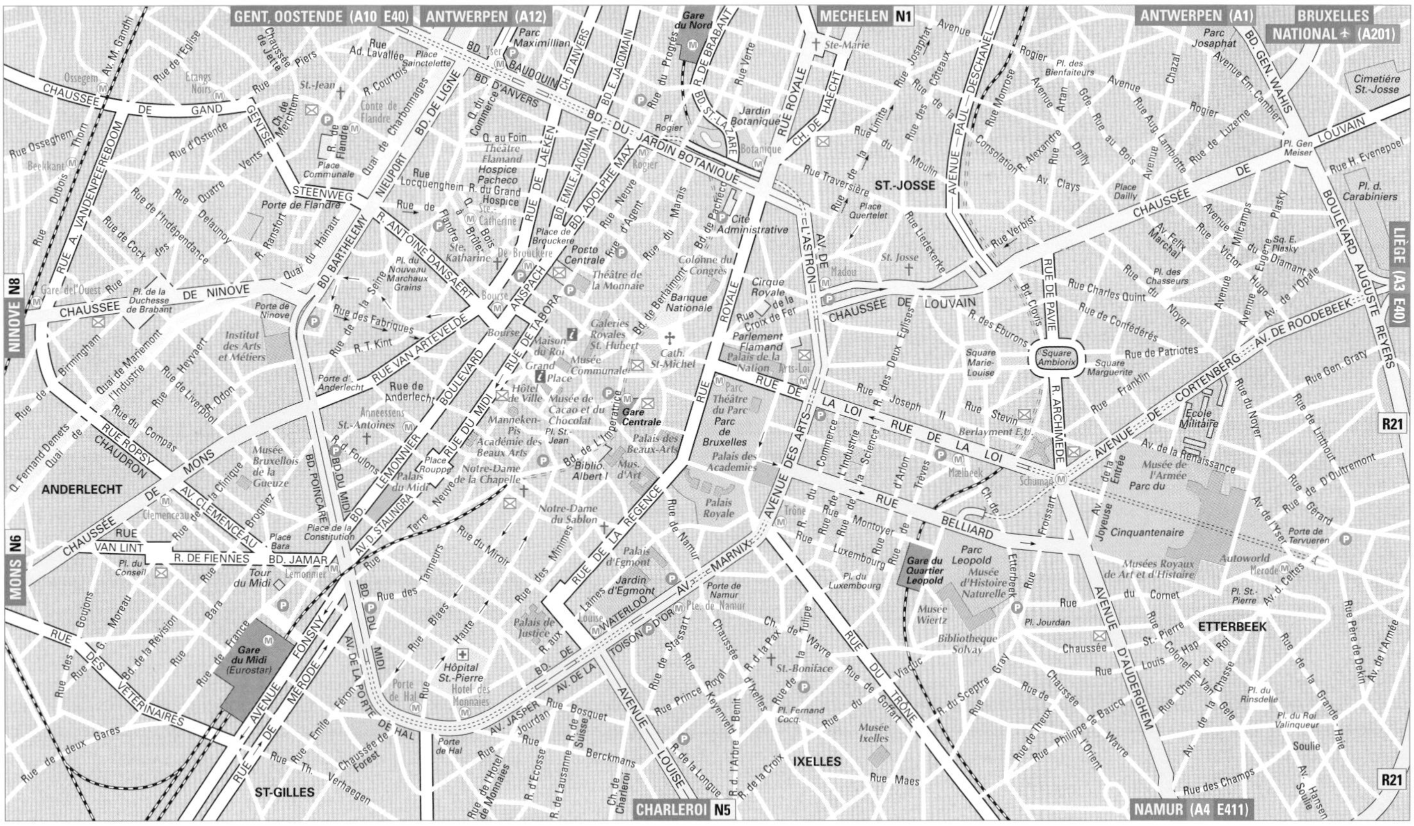

Berlin

0 km 5
HAMBURG (A24), ROSTOCK (A24, A19)
ORANIENBURG, SASSNITZ (96)
HAMBURG (A24, A29)
SZCZECIN (A6)
NAUEN, KYRITZ
BRANDENBURG
FRANKFURT
MAGDEBURG (A10, A2), LEIPZIG (A10, A9)
DRESDEN (A13, E55)
Hennigsdorf
Falkensee
Spandau
Charlottenburg
Tiergarten
Wedding
Reinickendorf
Pankow
Weissensee
Prenzlauer Berg
Mitte
Friedrichshain
Lichtenburg
Kreuzberg
BERLIN
Schöneberg
Neukölln
Treptow
Tempelhof
Steglitz
Zehlendorf
Potsdam
Kleinmachnow
Teltow
Köpenick
Neuenhagen
Schöneiche
Zepernick
Schildow
FLUGHAFEN BERLIN-TEGEL
FLUGHAFEN BERLIN-TEMPELHOF
FLUGHAFEN BERLIN-SCHÖNEFELD

Berlin

0 km 1
ORANIENBURG 96 E251
BERNAU 2
FRANKFURT 1 5
NAUEN 2 5
POTSDAM (A100 A115 E51 1)
TREPTOW (96a)
POTSDAM 1 (A103)
BERLIN-TEMPELHOF 96
BERLIN-SCHÖNEFELD 179
CHARLOTTENBURG
TIERGARTEN
MITTE
KREUZBERG
WILMERSDORF
KURFÜRSTENDAMM
STRASSE DES 17. JUNI
UNTER DEN LINDEN
LEIPZIGER STRASSE
FRIEDRICHSTRASSE
Alexanderplatz
Brandenburger Tor
Reichstag
Potsdamer Pl.
Anhalter Bf.
Zoologischer Garten
Siegessäule
Schloss Bellevue
Checkpoint

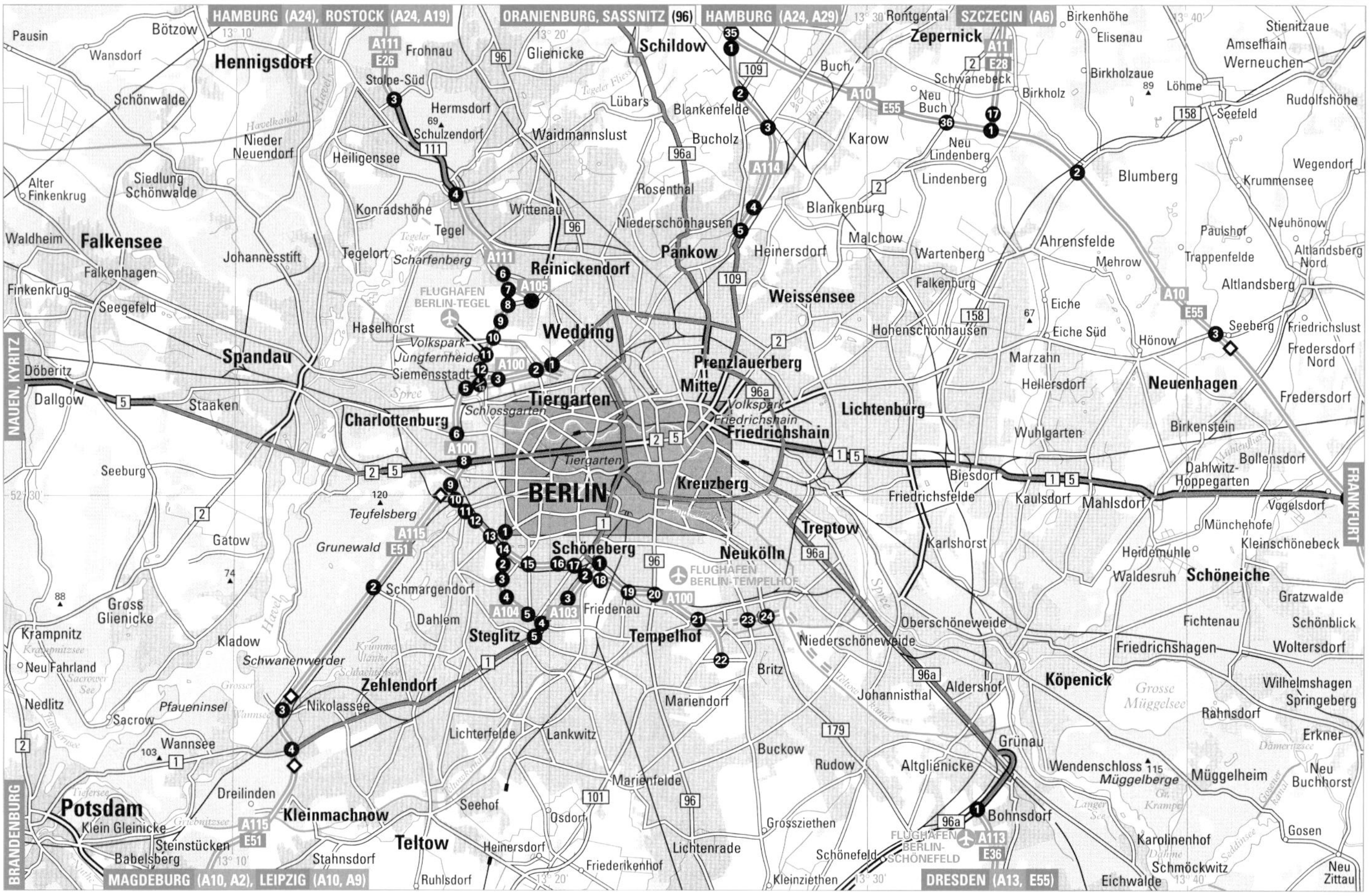

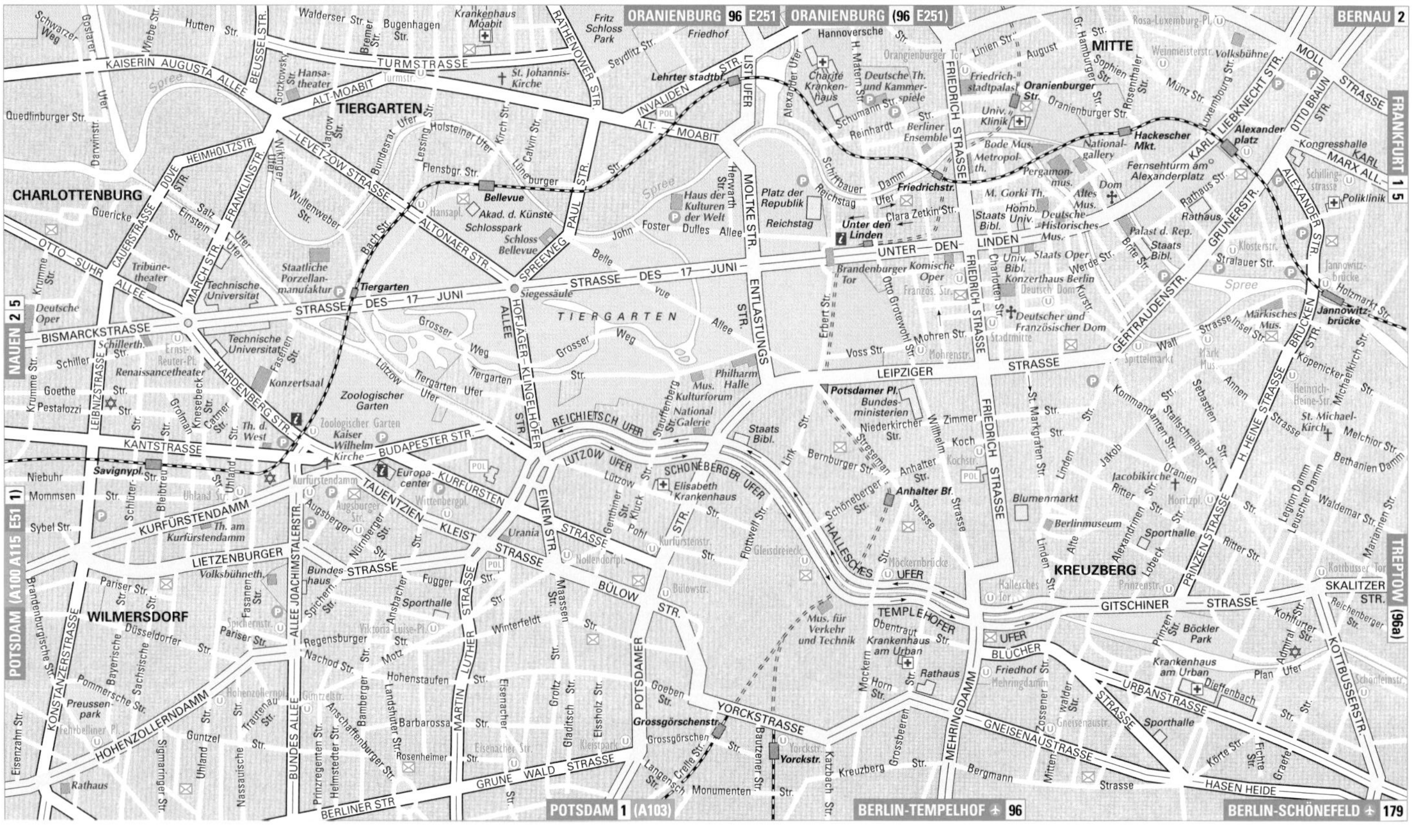

Bordeaux

0 km 5

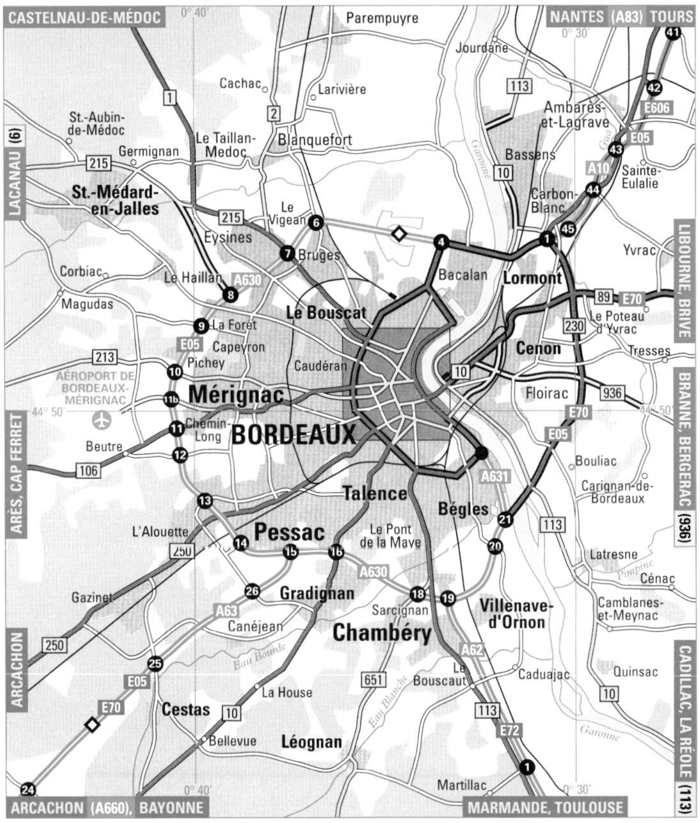

Bordeaux

0 km 1

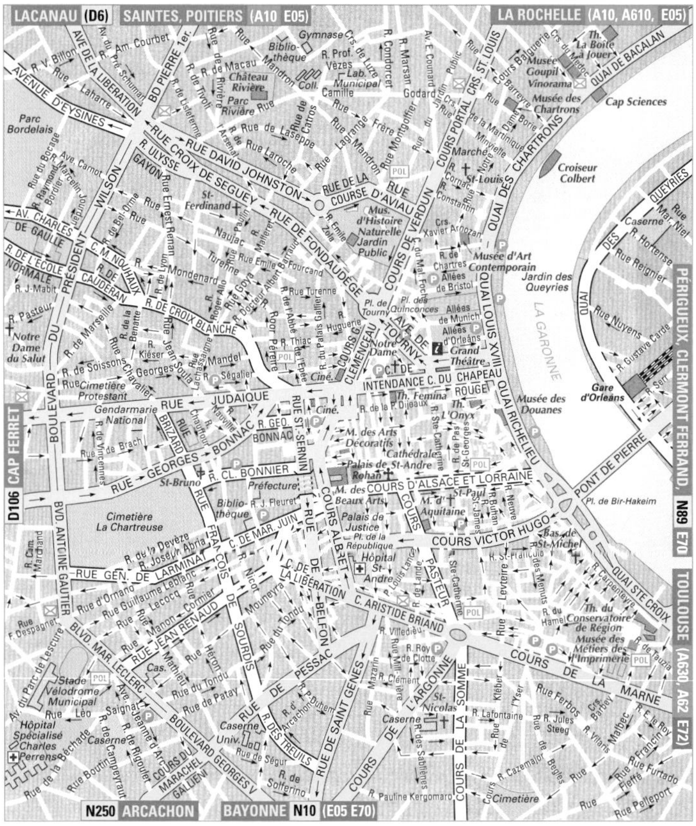

Budapest

0 km 1

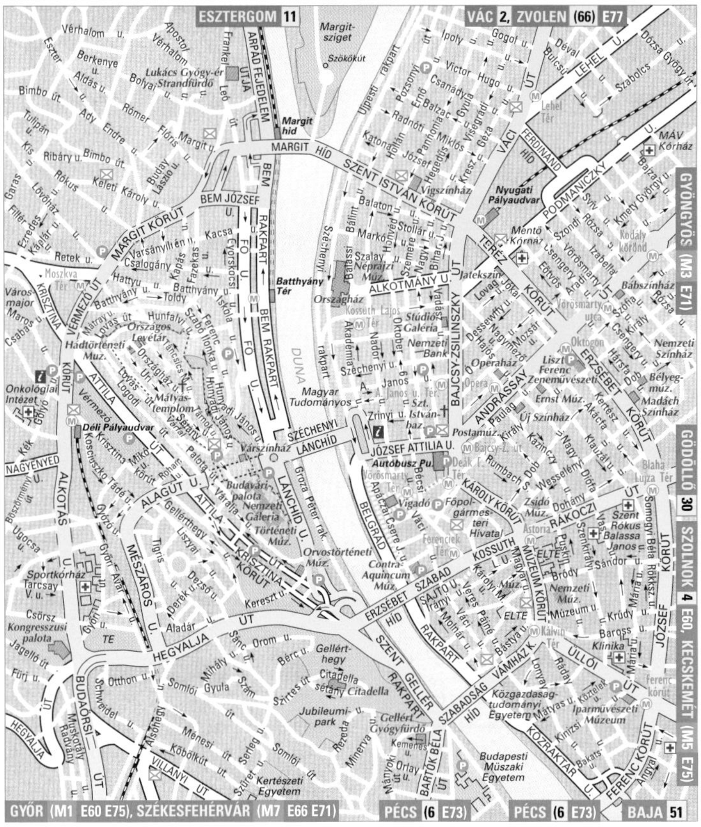

Dublin

0 km 0.5

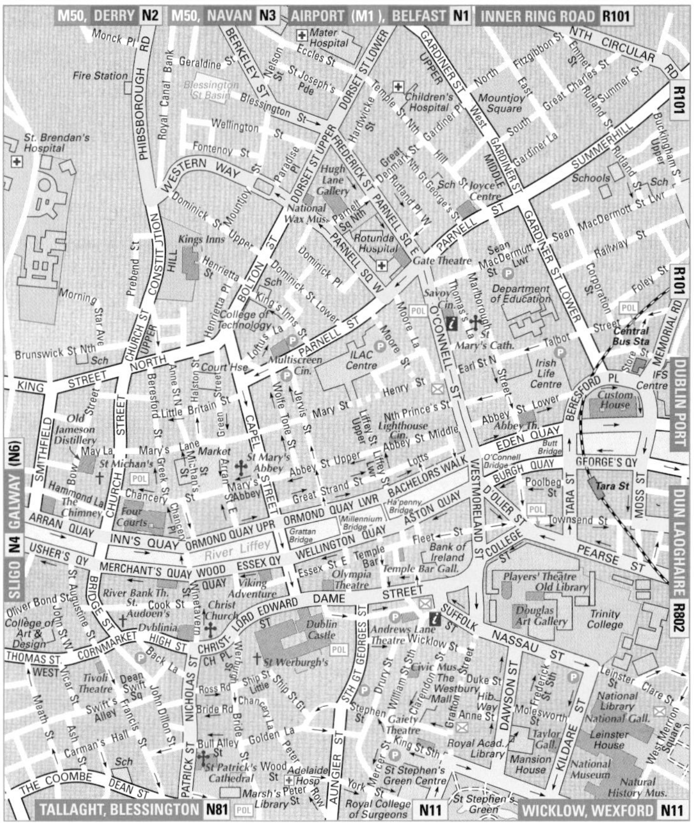

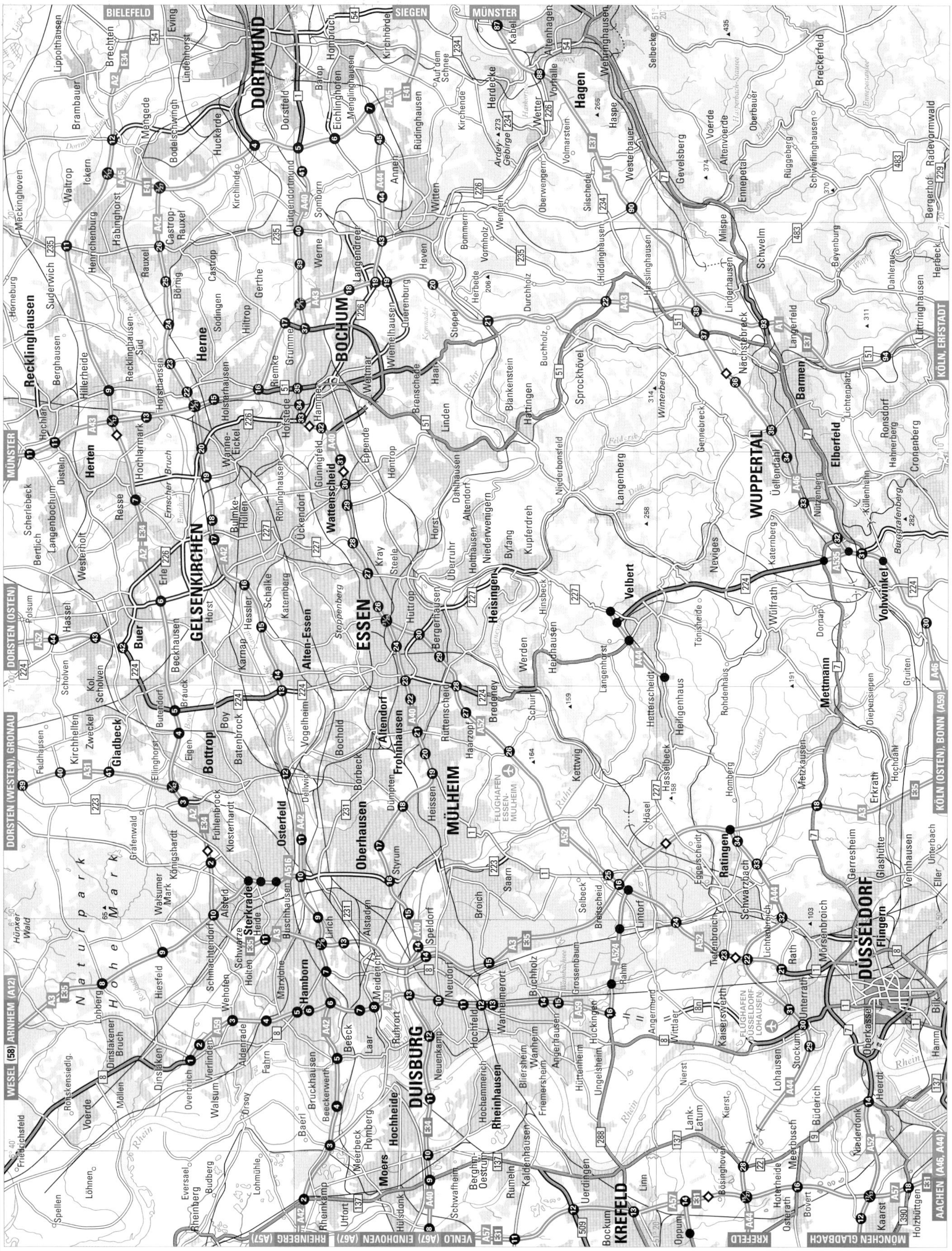

Düsseldorf (Ruhrgebiet)
0 km 5
WESEL (58) ARNHEM (A12)
DORSTEN (WESTEN), GRONAU
DORSTEN (OSTEN)
MÜNSTER
BIELEFELD
SIEGEN
KÖLN, ERFSTADT
KÖLN (OSTEN), BONN (A59)
AACHEN (A46, A44)
MÖNCHEN GLADBACH
KREFELD
VENLO (A67) EINDHOVEN (A67) RHEINBERG (A57)
Naturpark Hohe Mark
DORTMUND
BOCHUM
ESSEN
GELSENKIRCHEN
DUISBURG
MÜLHEIM
Oberhausen
WUPPERTAL
DÜSSELDORF
KREFELD
Recklinghausen
Herne
Herten
Bottrop
Gladbeck
Buer
Hagen
Velbert
Ratingen
Mettmann
Moers
Hochheide
Rheinhausen
Wattenscheid
Sterkrade
Hamborn
Osterfeld
Altendorf
Frohnhausen
Alten-Essen
Heisingen
Barmen
Elberfeld
Vohwinkel
Herdecke
Witten
Hattingen
Sprockhövel
Castrop-Rauxel
Gevelsberg
Schwelm
Dinslaken
Flingern
FLUGHAFEN ESSEN-MÜLHEIM
FLUGHAFEN DÜSSELDORF-LOHAUSEN
Rhein
Ruhr

Düsseldorf

0 km 0.5

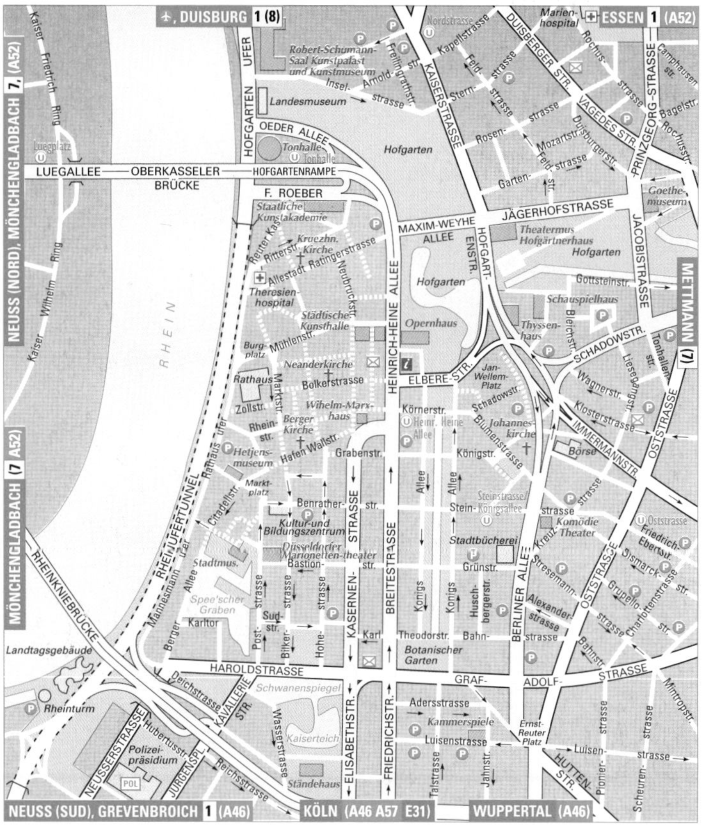

Edinburgh

0 km 0.5

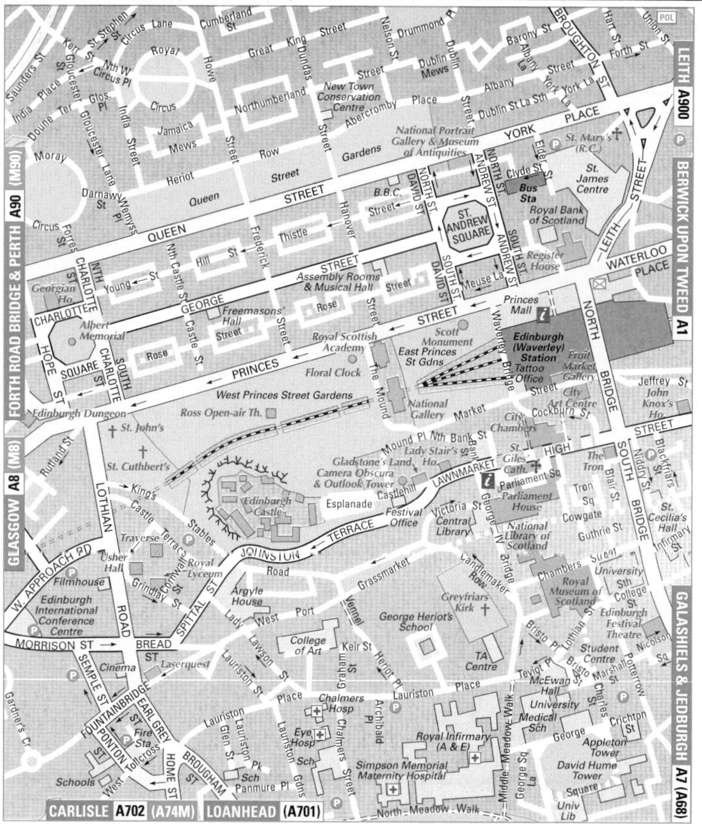

Firenze

0 km 1

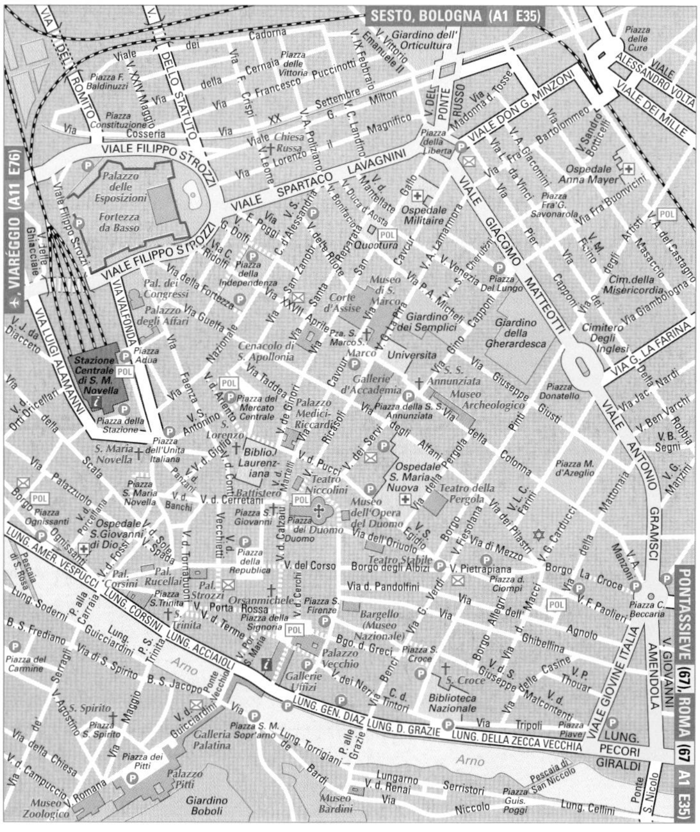

Frankfurt

0 km 0.5

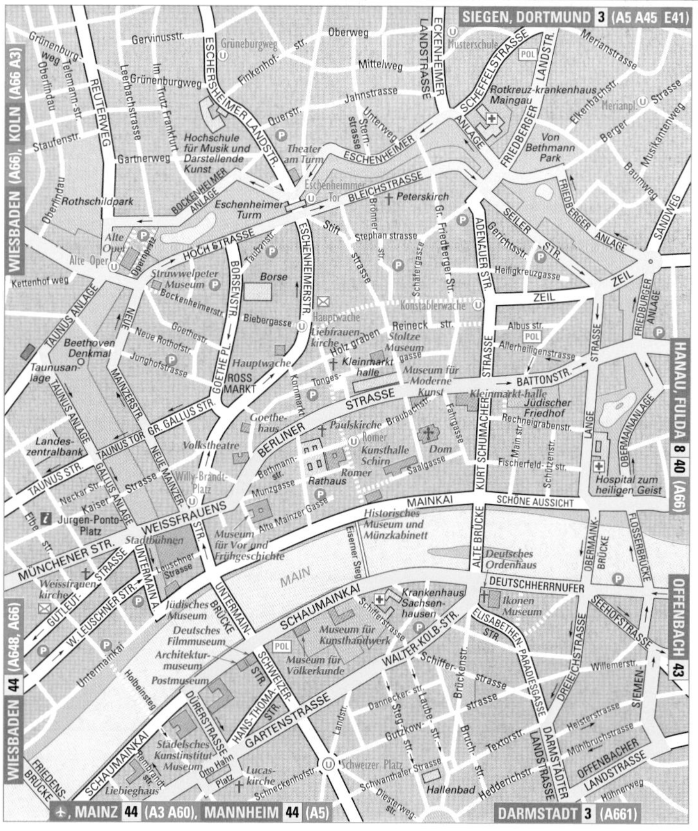

Genève

0 km 1

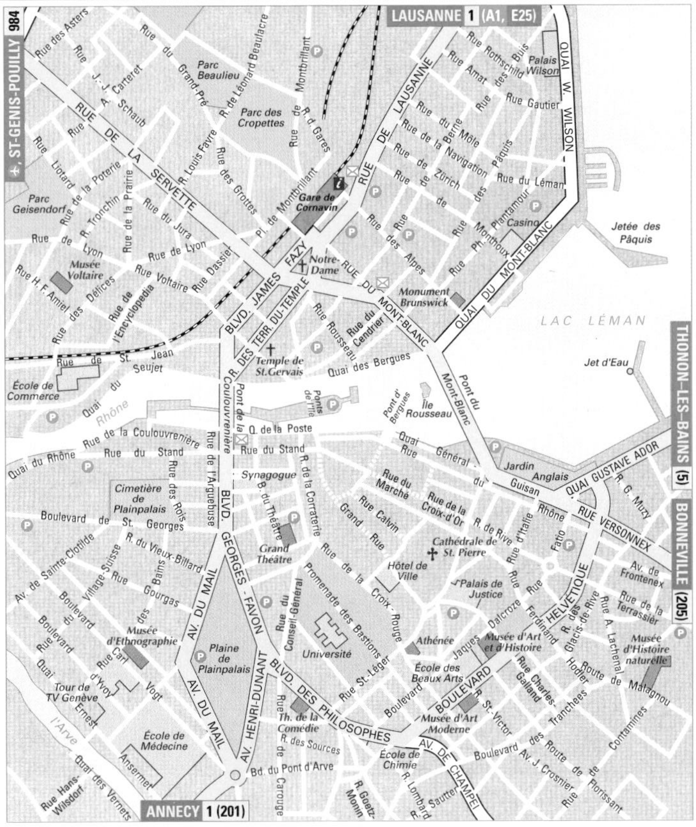

Göteborg

0 km 1

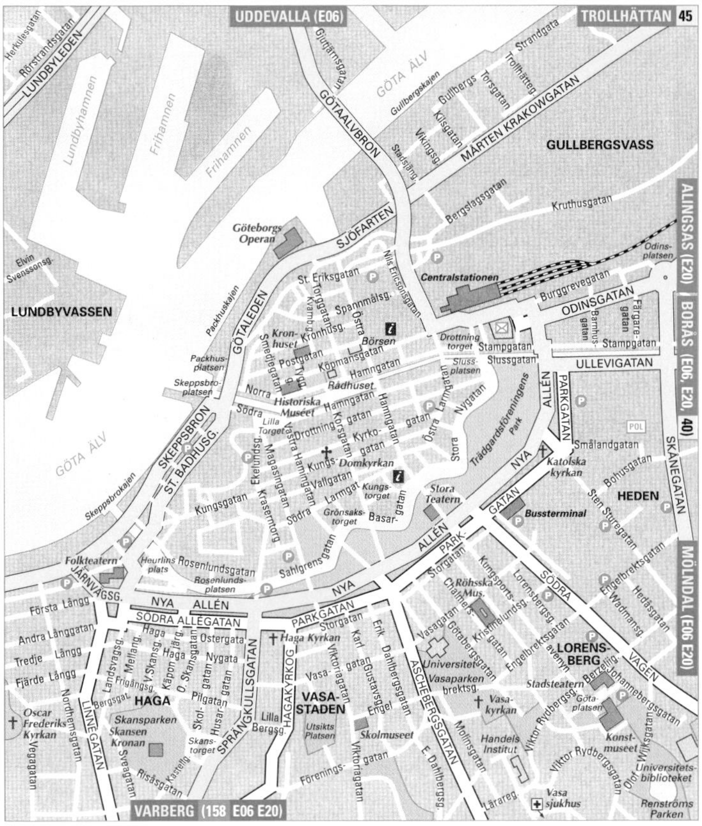

Hamburg

0 km 5

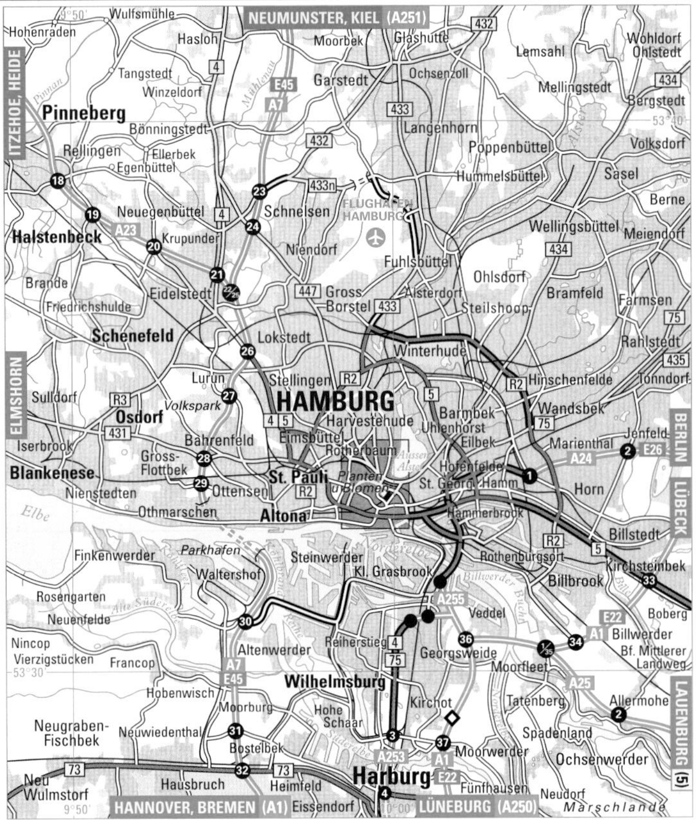

Hamburg

0 km 1

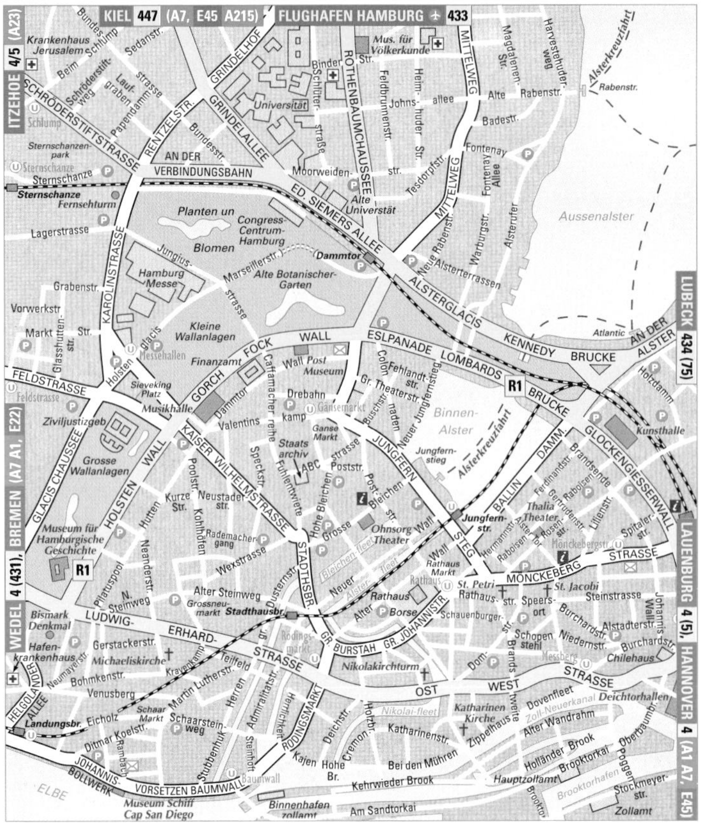

Helsinki

0 km 10

HYVINKÄÄ, HÄMEENLINNA, TAMPERE (3)
TUUSULA, JÄRVENPÄÄ (145)
LAHTI
SALO, TURKU(ÅBO) (1)
PORVOO(BORGÅ), KOTKA (7)
HANKO(HANGÖ) (25)

Järventausta
Ollila
Skogby
Kongo
Linna
Seutula
Ruotsinkylä
Myllykylä
Korso
Maantiekylä
Mäkiniitty
Hanala
Rekola
Nikinmäki
Hindsby
Gesterby
Ketunkorpi
Takkula
Vestra
Keimola
Kivistö
Koivupää
HELSINKI-VANTAAN LENTOASEMA
Harjusuo
Myras
Littjofs
Viirila
Lahnus
Heinässuo
Odilampi
Petas
Vantaanpuisto
Hiekkaharju
Kuninkaanmäki
Immersby
Massby
Veikkola
Siikajärvi
Röylä
Perusmaki
Vantaankoski
Vantaa
Ylästö
Simonkylä
Ita Hakkila
Nuuksio
Gobbacka
Askisto
Niiperi
Martinkylä
Tikkurila
Kaskela
Nybygget
Sotunki
Degermossa
Kolmiranta
Hämeenkylä
Friherrs
Haltiala
Tapanila
Puistola
Hakunila
Västerskog
Haltiavuori
Kaivoksela
Paloheinä
Malmi
TATTARISUO
Brobacka
Rastaala
Laaksolahti
Pakila
Pukinmäki
Rajakylä
Mellunmäki
Östersundom
Kolmpera
Nupuri
Oittaa
Lintuvaara
Konala
Pirkkola
Pihlajamäki
Mellunkylä
Lapinkylä
Lappböle
Västerkulla
Bemböle
Kauniainen
Haaga
Oulunkylä
Myllypuro
Vartiokylä
Grano
Simsalö
Espoo
Esbo
Kilo
Leppävaara
Käpylä
Viikki
Puotila
Vuosaari
Kallvik
Nuljala
Munkkiniemi
Pasila
Herttoniemi
Roihuvuori
Rastila
Tuomarila
Henttaa
Mankkaa
Otaniemi
HELSINKI
Kauklahti
Puolarmetsä
Olari
Tapiola
Lehtisaari
Kulosaari
Tammisalo
Vartiosaari
Sibbo fjärden
Sipoon selkä
Bobäck
Musta Hevonen
Österby
Vehkalahti
Vecklax
Nöykkiö
Hietaniemi
Laajasalo
Jollas
Granlandet
Westend
Masala
Masaby
Espoonlahti
Nokkala
Lauttasaari
Villinki
Trutlandet
Gästerby
Jorvas
Hanskinen
Soukka
Miessaari
Pihlajasaari
Santahamina
Melkki
Vallisaari
Estlotan
Estiluoto
Svinö
Stockholm, Lübeck, Travemünd, Tallinn, Rostock
Kirkkonummi
Kyrkslätt
Gunnarsby
Pentala
Lehtisaaret
Rysäkari
Harmaja
Kuivasaari
Isosaari
Medvastö
Estby

Helsinki

0 km 1

HÄMEENLINNA 3 E12 (3)
HELSINGIN LENTOASEMA (137, 45)
LAHTI 4 E75 (4)
PORVOO 170 (7, E18)
KIRKKONUMMI

Seurasaarentie
Meilahti sairaala
TAKA TÖÖLÖ
Olympiastadion
ALPPIHARJU ÅSHÖJDEN
Sturenkatu
Helsingin katu
Kulosaarensilta
Itäväylä
KULOSAARI BRÄNDÖ
Mäntyniemi
BORTRE TÖLÖ
Agricolankatu
SÖRNÄINEN SÖRNÄS
Hanasaari Hanaholmen
Seurasaari Ulkomuseo
Rajasaari Råholmen
Suomen Kansallisooppera
Kaupunginteatteri
Hämeentie
Sörnäisten rantatie
Mustikkamaa Blåbärslandet
Seurasaari Fölisön
Töölönlahti Tölöviken
Eläintarhanlahti Djurgårdsviken
Sumpasaari Sumparn
Töölön kirkko
Kivelän sairaala
Hesperian sairaala
Finlandiatalo
Sörnäisten satama Sörnäs hamn
Palosaari Paloholmen
Taivalluoto Edesgrundet
Kansallismuseo
Kaupunginmuseo
KLUUVI GLOET
Yliopiston anatominen laitos
Korkeasaari Högholmen
Korkeasaaren eläintarha
Seurasaarenselkä Fölisöfjärden
Eduskuntatalo
Kansallisteatteri
Rautatieasema
Suomen Pankki
LAAJASALO DEGERO
Porsas Grisen
Ourit Örana
Sibelius Akatemia
Postitalo
Tuomiokirkko
Senaatintori
Pohjoissatama Norra hamnen
Suomen Merimuseo
Hylkysaari Vrakholmen
Arkadiankatu
Mannerheimintie
Kaisaniemenkatu
Ateneumin Taidemuseo
Yliopisto
Psykiatrian klinikka
Lapinlahdentie
Amos Andersonin Taidemuseo
Pohjoisesplanadi
Uspenskin katedraali
Katajanokka Skatudden
Kruunuvuorenselkä Kronbergsfjärden
Lapinlahden Silta
Marian sairaala
Vanha Kirkkopuisto
Matkustajaterminaali
Ruoholahdenkatu
Lönnrotinkatu
Saksalainen kirkko
Eteläsatama Södra hamnen
Porkkalankatu
Itämerenkatu
Ruoholahti
Taidehallimuseo
Tähtitorninmäki
Olympiaterminaali
Valkosaari Blekholmen
Katajanoken Skatakobben
LAUTTASAARI DRUMSÖ
Lauttasaaren Silta
Ruoholahti Gräsviken
Hietalahti Sandviken
Johanneksen kirkko
Mannerheim museo
Luoto Klippan
Ryssänsaari Ryssholmen
Mikael Agricola Kirkko
Tehtaankatu
Rakennustaiteen museo
Pikkuluoto Lillklippan
Puolimatkansaari Halvvägsholmen
Vasikkasaari Kalvholmen
Lauttasaarenselkä Drumsöfjärden
LÄNSISATAMA VÄSTRA HAMNEN
Kaivopuisto
Merisatamanranta
Ehrenströmintie

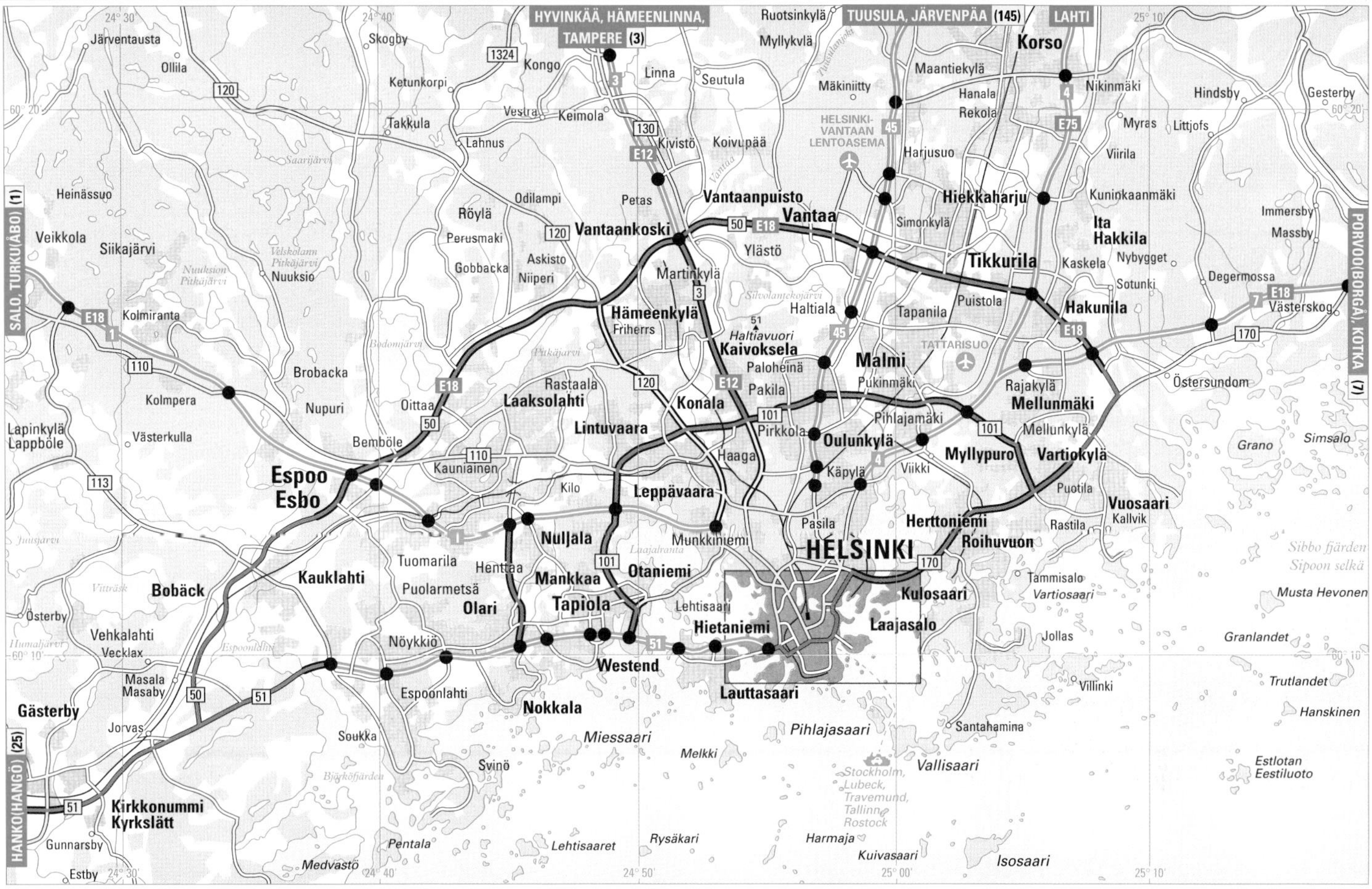

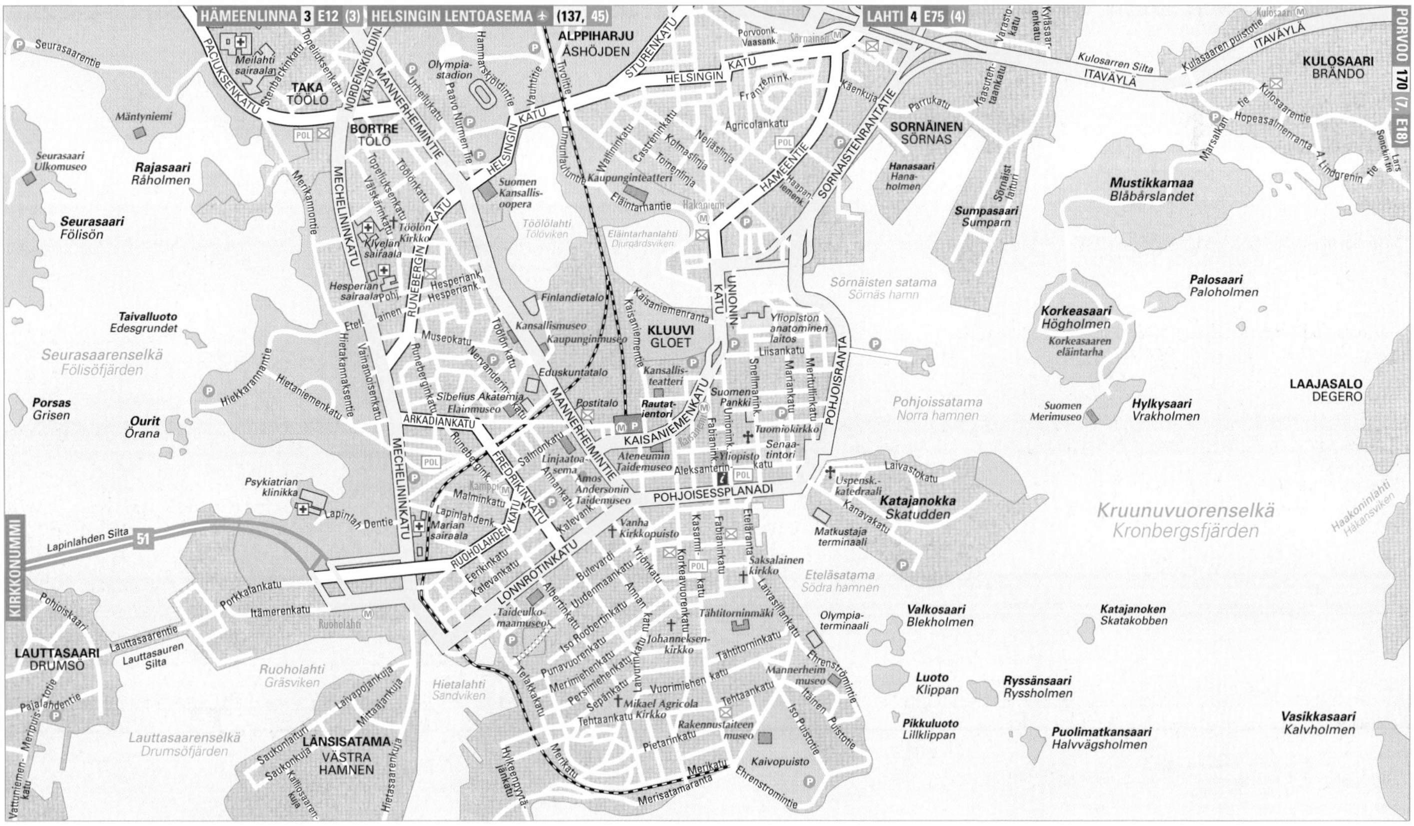

København

0 km 5

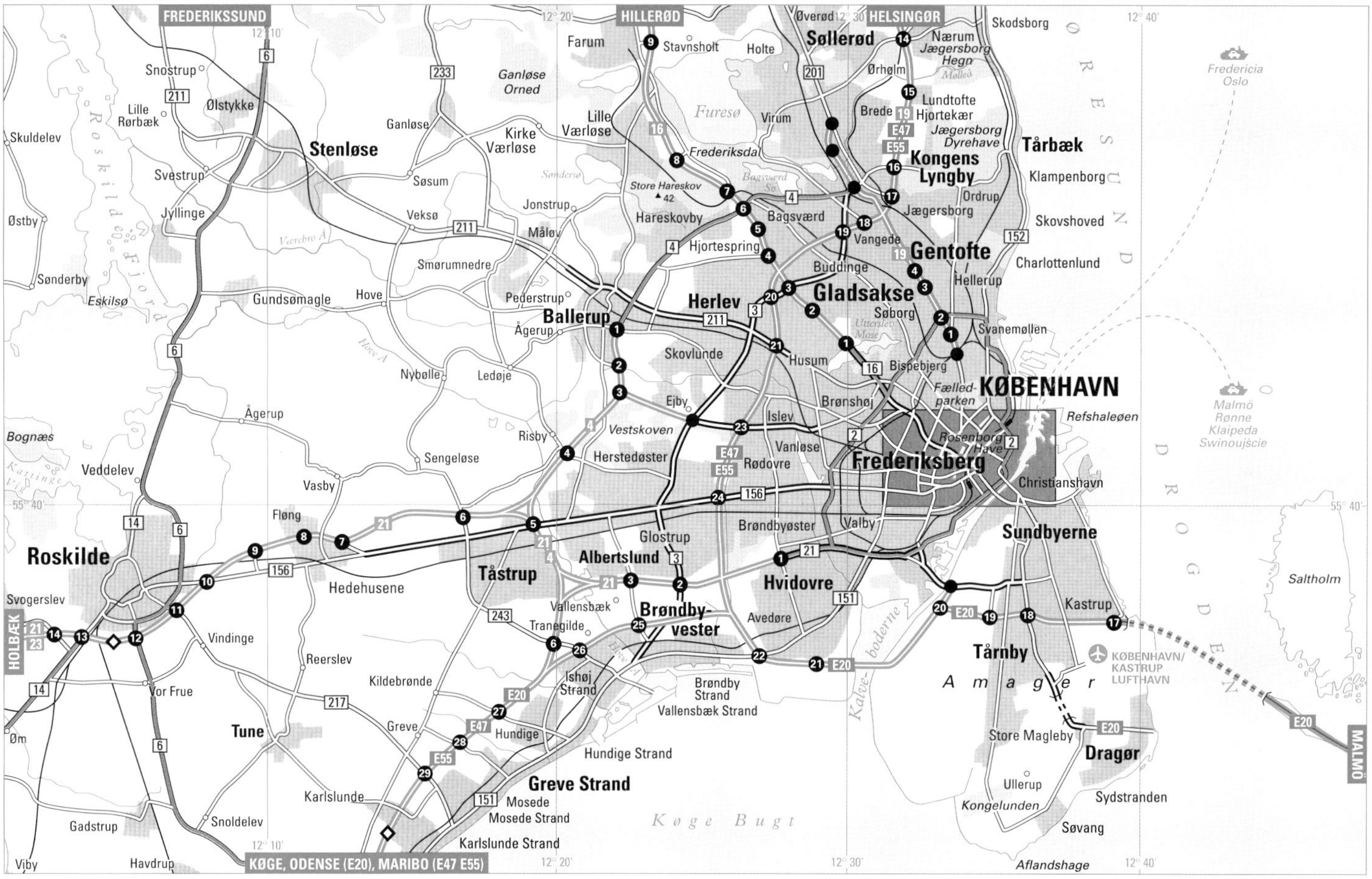

København

0 km 1

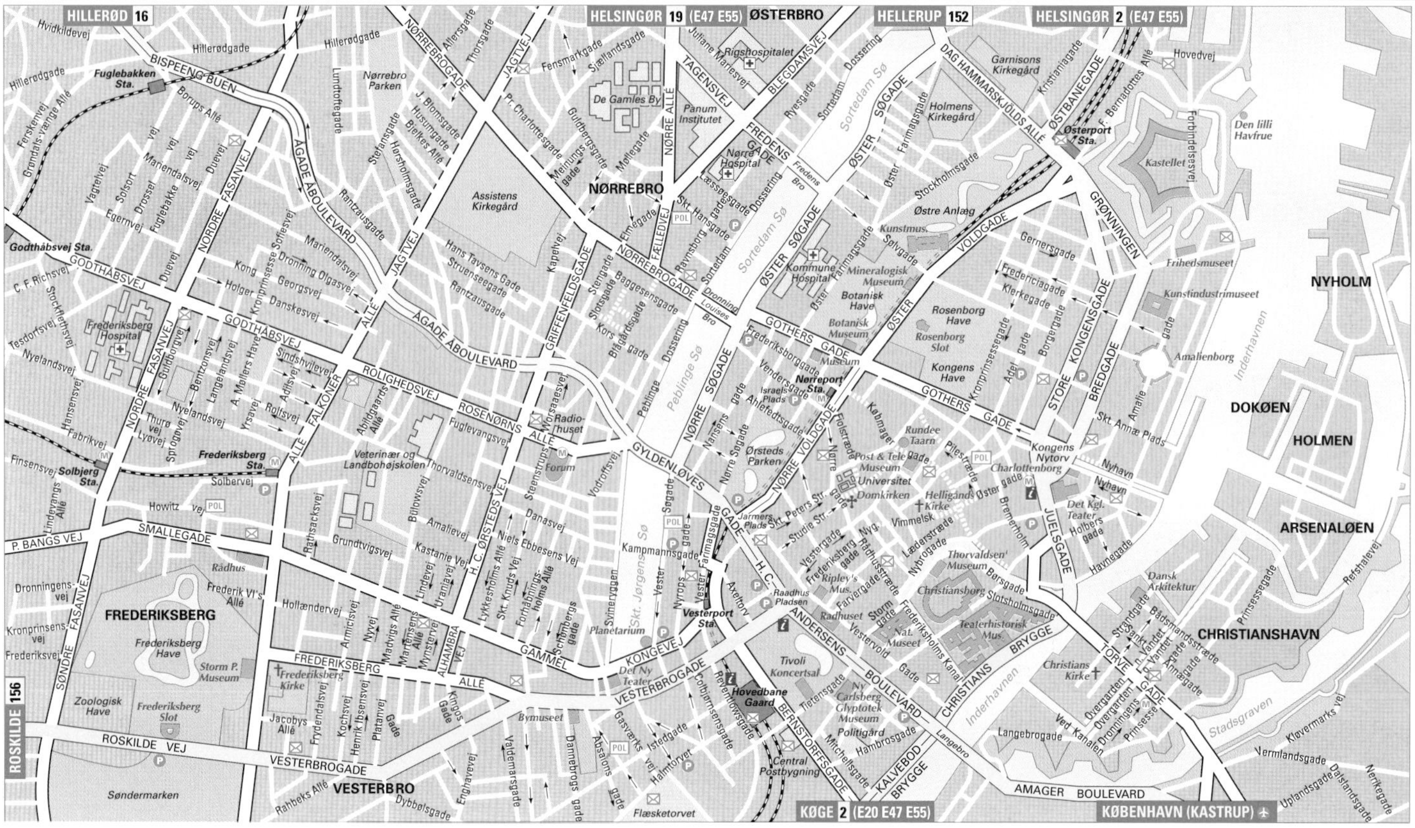

Köln

0 km 1

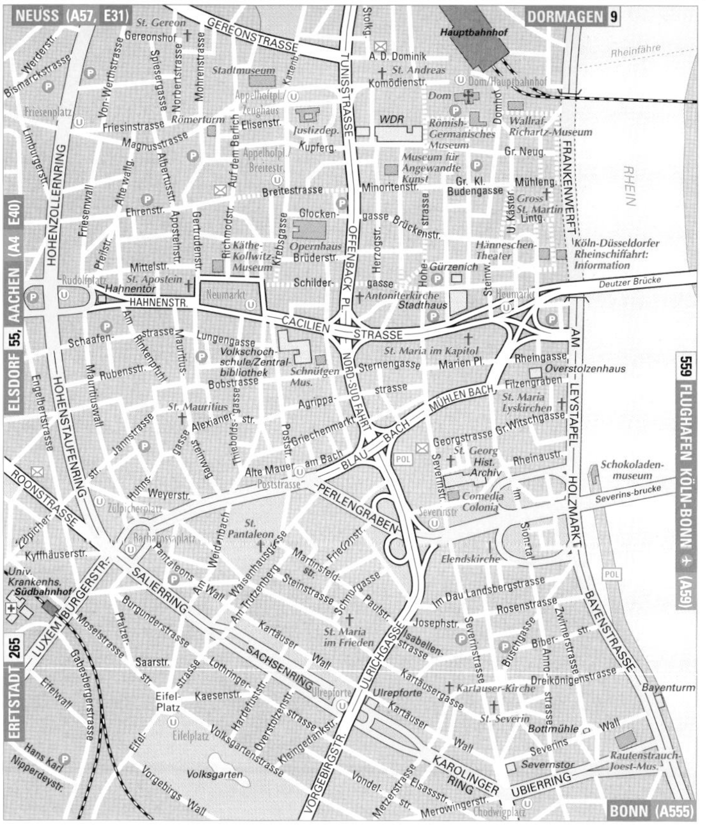

Luxembourg

0 km 0.5

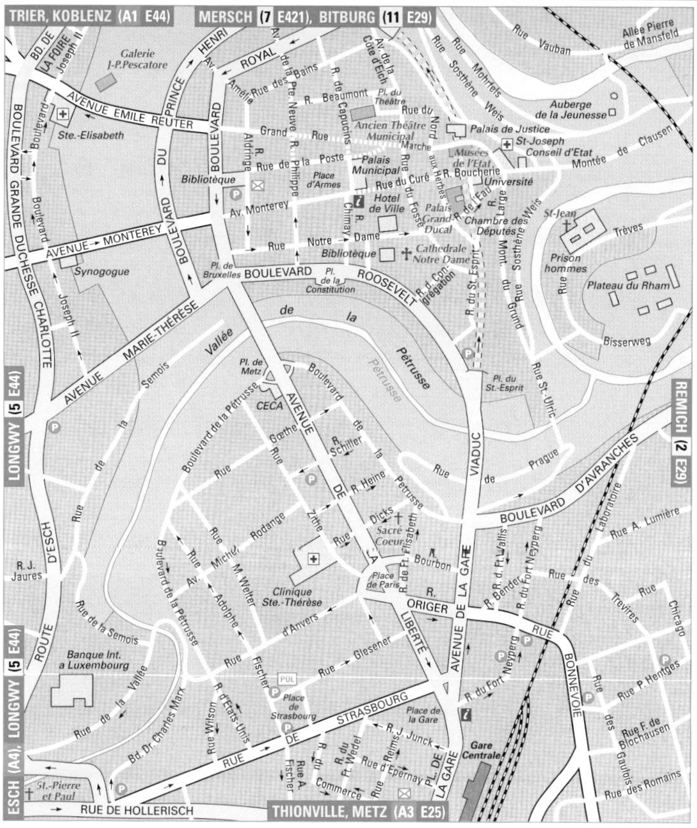

Lisboa

0 km 5

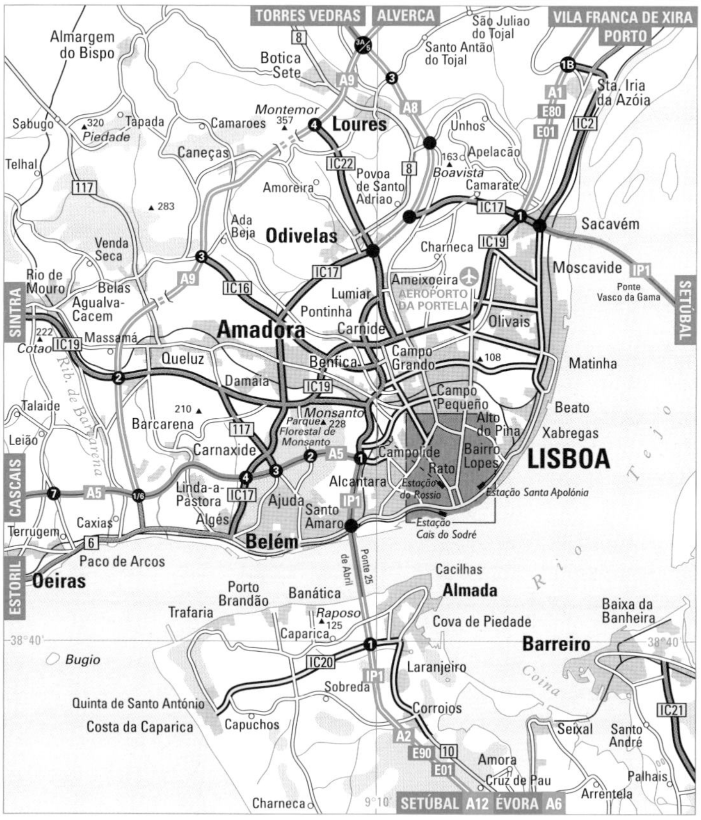

Lisboa

0 km 1

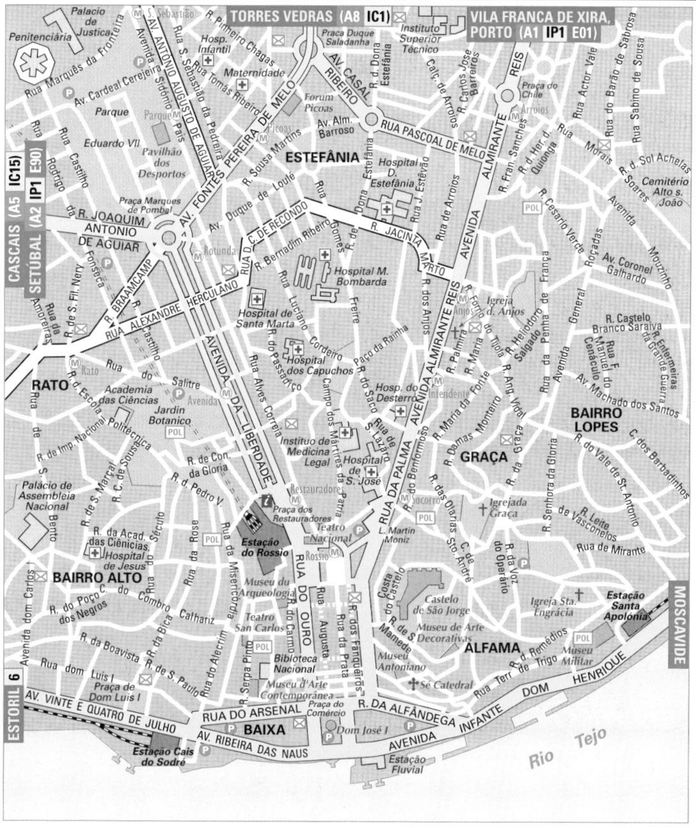

London

0 km 10

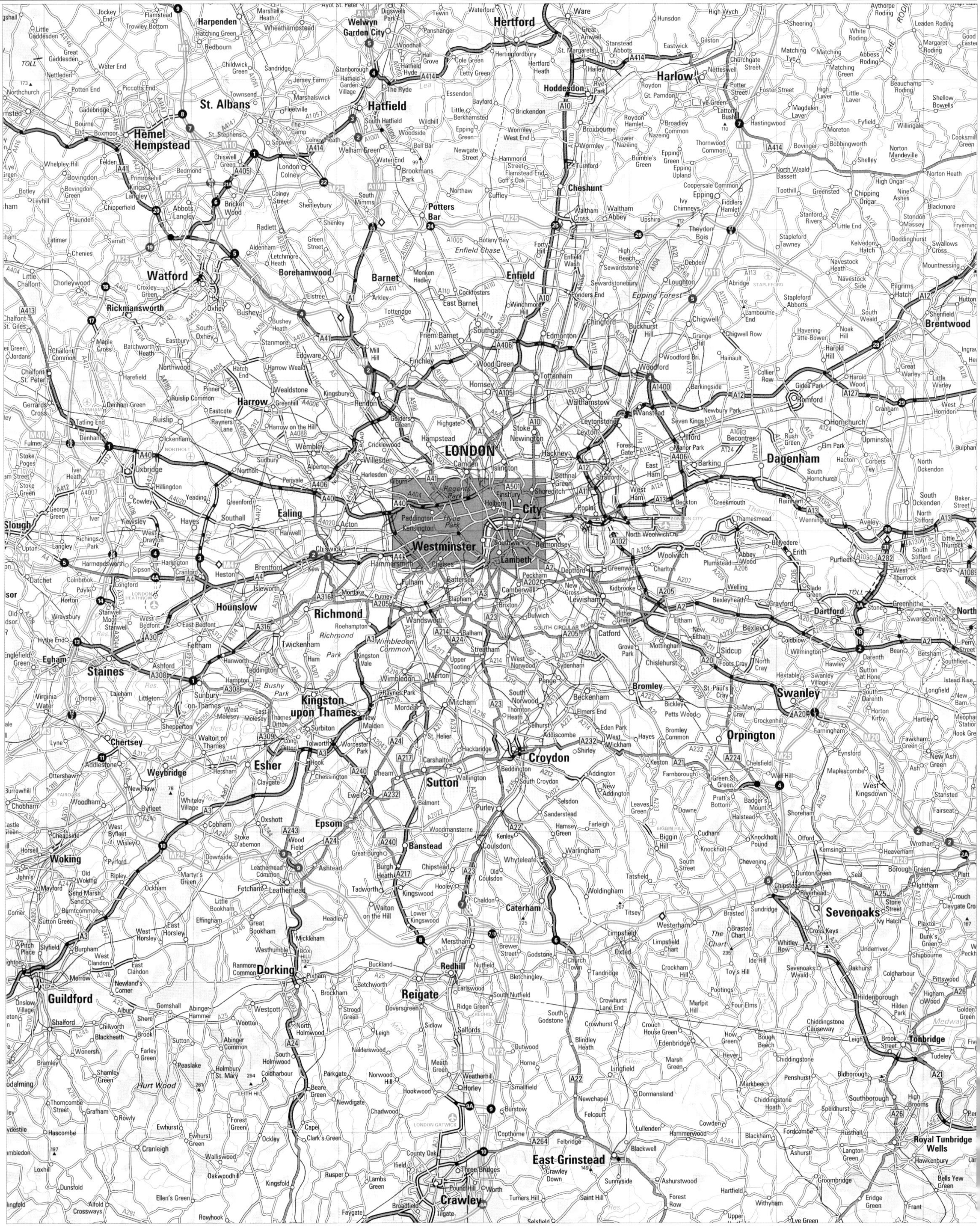

Harpenden
Welwyn Garden City
Hertford
Ware
Harlow
St. Albans
Hatfield
Hoddesdon
Hemel Hempstead
Cheshunt
Potters Bar
Watford
Borehamwood
Barnet
Enfield
Rickmansworth
Brentwood
Harrow
Romford
LONDON
Dagenham
Ealing
City
Slough
Westminster
Lambeth
Hounslow
Richmond
Dartford
Staines
Kingston upon Thames
Swanley
Bromley
Chertsey
Orpington
Esher
Croydon
Weybridge
Sutton
Epsom
Woking
Sevenoaks
Caterham
Dorking
Redhill
Guildford
Reigate
Tonbridge
Royal Tunbridge Wells
East Grinstead
Crawley

London

0 km 2

M1, HENDON A41
A4201 TO A400
M1, CAMDEN TOWN A400
A5203 TO A1
M1, HIGHGATE A1
A1200 TO A1
TOTTENHAM, CAMBRIDGE A10
STRATFORD, WANSTEAD A11
CANNING TOWN, ISLE OF DOGS (A1261) A13
DAGENHAM
M2, GREENWICH A2
CAMBERWELL A202
BRIXTON A203
CLAPHAM A3216
BATTERSEA BRIDGE A3212
PUTNEY BRIDGE A304
M4, HEATHROW A4
UXBRIDGE A4020
A3220 TO A40
OXFORD A40 (M40)

KENSAL RISE
WEST KILBURN
ST. JOHN'S WOOD
MAIDA VALE
WESTBOURNE GREEN
PADDINGTON
BAYSWATER
NOTTING HILL
KENSINGTON
WEST KENSINGTON
SOUTH KENSINGTON
KNIGHTSBRIDGE
BROMPTON
CHELSEA
BELGRAVIA
PIMLICO
MAYFAIR
SOHO
ST. JAMES'S
BLOOMSBURY
HOLBORN
CLERKENWELL
HOXTON
SHOREDITCH
CITY
SOUTHWARK
BOROUGH
NEWINGTON
LAMBETH
KENNINGTON
WALWORTH
BERMONDSEY
REGENT'S PARK
HYDE PARK
KENSINGTON GARDENS

Congestion Charging Zone

Lyon

0 km 5

MÂCON, DIJON (A31)
MÂCON (A6), DIJON (A6, A31)
GENÈVE (A40) & (A432)
CHAMBÉRY, GRENOBLE (A48) & (A432)
VIENNE, VALENCE, MARSEILLE
ST. ETIENNE (A47)
LYON
Villeurbanne
Caluire-et-Cuire
Rillieux-la-Pape
Vaulx-en-Velin
Bron
Vénissieux
St.-Priest
Oullins
Ste.-Foy-lès-Lyon
Meyzieu
Décines-Charpieu
Écully
Limonest
Dardilly
Francheville
Craponne
Chaponost
Brignais
Irigny
Feyzin
Corbas
Mions
Chassieu
Genas
Miribel
AÉRODROME LYON-BRON
Parc de loisirs de Miribel-Jonage

Lyon

0 km 1

MACON, DIJON (A46, A6 E15)
CHAMBÉRY (A43 E70) & (A432)
VALENCE, MARSEILLE (A7 E15)
Gare St.-Paul
PT. LAFAYETTE
COURS LA FAYETTE
RUE GRENETTE
PT. WILSON
RUE CHAMBONNET
PT. DE LA GUILLOTIÈRE
COURS GAMBETTA
GRANDE RUE DE LA GUILLOTIÈRE
Pl. Bellecour
Saône
Rhône

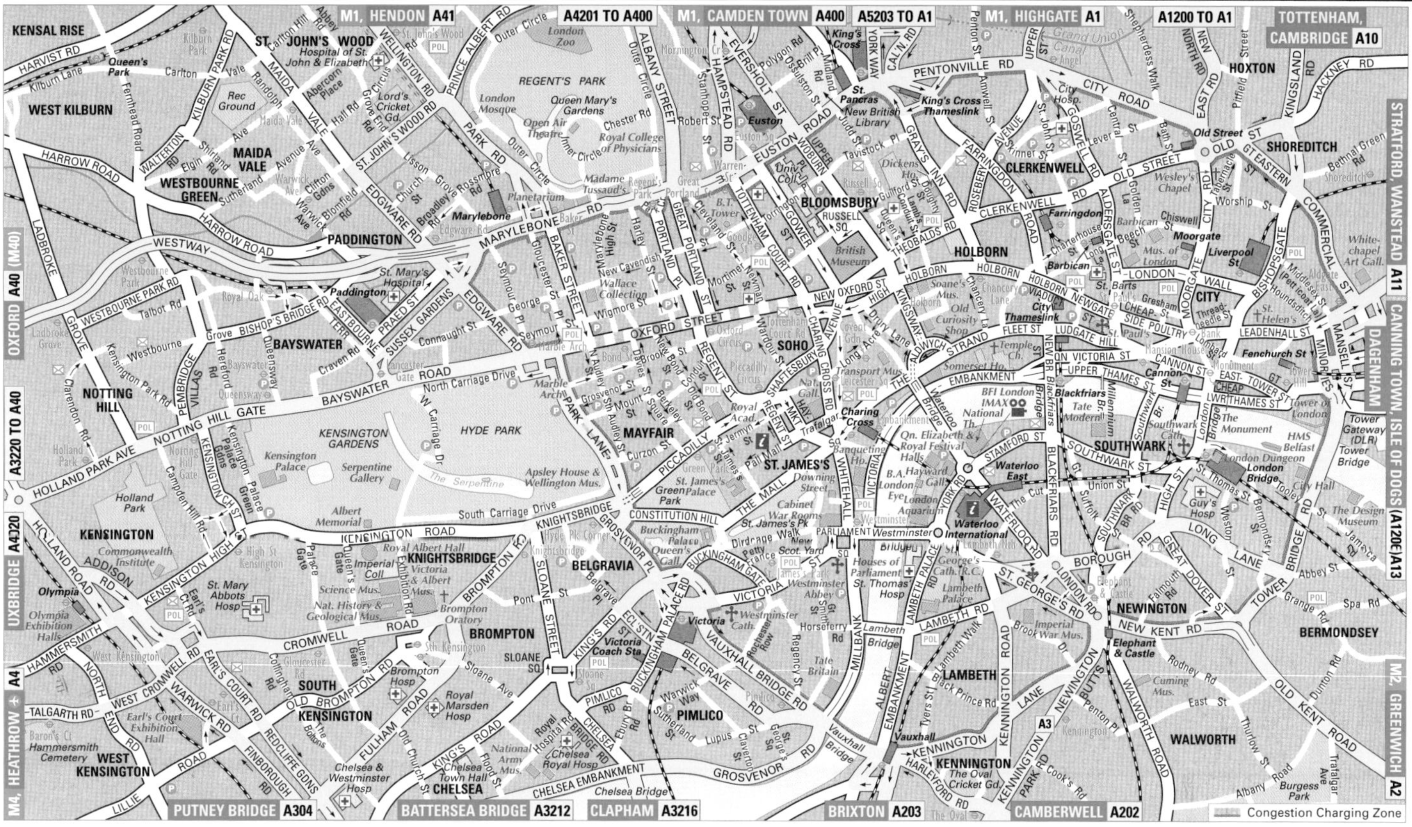

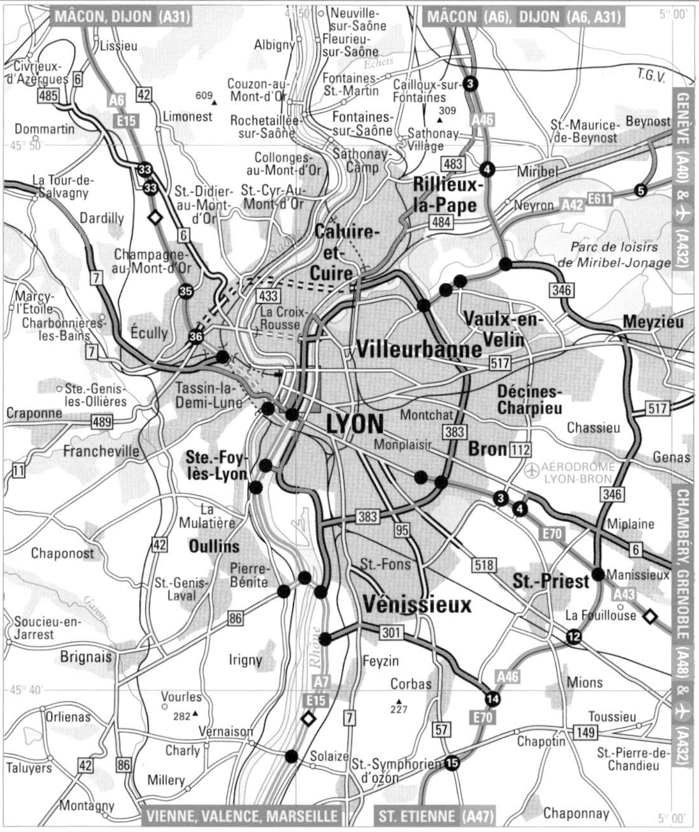

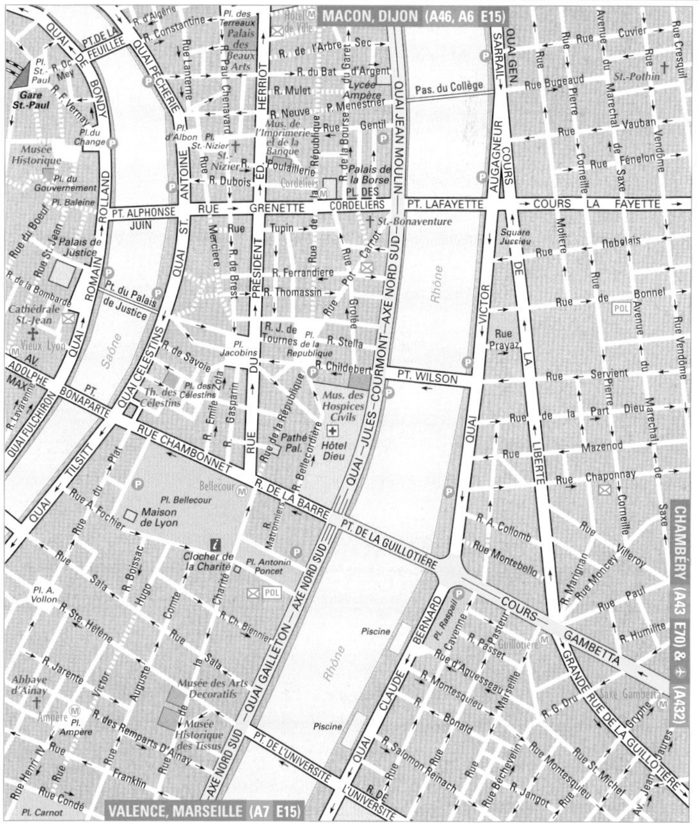

Madrid

0 km 5

Marseille

0 km 0.5

Madrid

0 km 1

LA CORUÑA (NVI, A6) · COLMENAR (607) · BURGOS (NI E05) · (N11, E90) ALCALA (A2)

ARÉVALO M30 (NVI, A6) · TALAVERA DE LA REINA NV E90 · ZARAGOZA (M40, A2 NII E90) · ARGANDA NIII E901 VALENCIA (A3)

TOLEDO M30 (N401) · TOLEDO N401 · ARANJUEZ N IV E05 · ARANJUEZ M30 (N IV)

Templo de Debod · ARGÜELLES · Estación del Norte · UNIVERSIDAD · JUSTICIA · Biblioteca Nacional · Museo Arqueológico · CALLE DE GOYA · CALLE DE ALCALÁ · CALLE DE O'DONNELL · Palacio de los Deportes · IBIZA · Hospital · Jardins Sabatini · Campo del Moro · Palacio Real · PALACIO · Catedral de Nuestra Señora de la Almudena · GRAN VIA · CALLE MAYOR · Plaza Mayor · Puerta del Sol · CORTES · Museo Thyssen-Bornemisza · PASEO DEL PRADO · Museo del Prado · Parque del Retiro · Estanque · Palacio de Velázquez · Palacio de Cristal · Hospital del Niño Jesús · NIÑO JESÚS · CENTRO · CALLE DE SEGOVIA · San Francisco el Grande · Jardín Botánico · La Chopera · Observatorio Astronómico · EMBAJADORES · Centro de Arte Reina Sofía · Estación de Atocha · RETIRO · PASEO REINA CRISTINA · AVENIDA DEL MEDITERRÁNEO · IMPERIAL · ACACIAS · PALOS DE MOGUER · Estación Sur de Autobuses · PACIFICO · RONDA DE TOLEDO · RONDA DE ATOCHA · RONDA DE SEGOVIA · AVENIDA DEL MANZANARES · AVENIDA DE MENÉNDEZ PELAYO · CALLE DEL DOCTOR ESQUERDO · PASEO DE RECOLETOS · CALLE DE SERRANO · CALLE DE ALFONSO XII · CALLE DE BAILÉN · Viveros · Puerta de Segovia

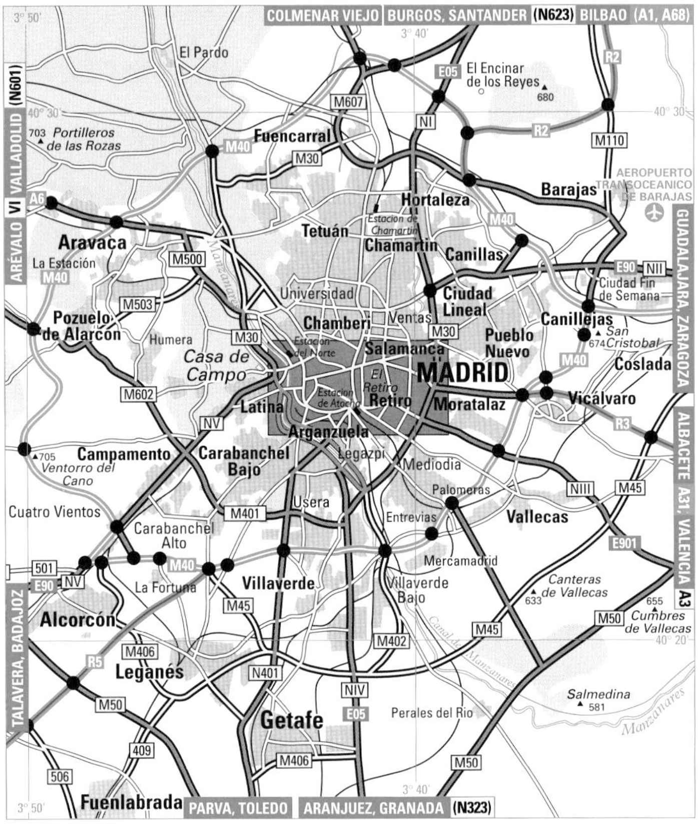

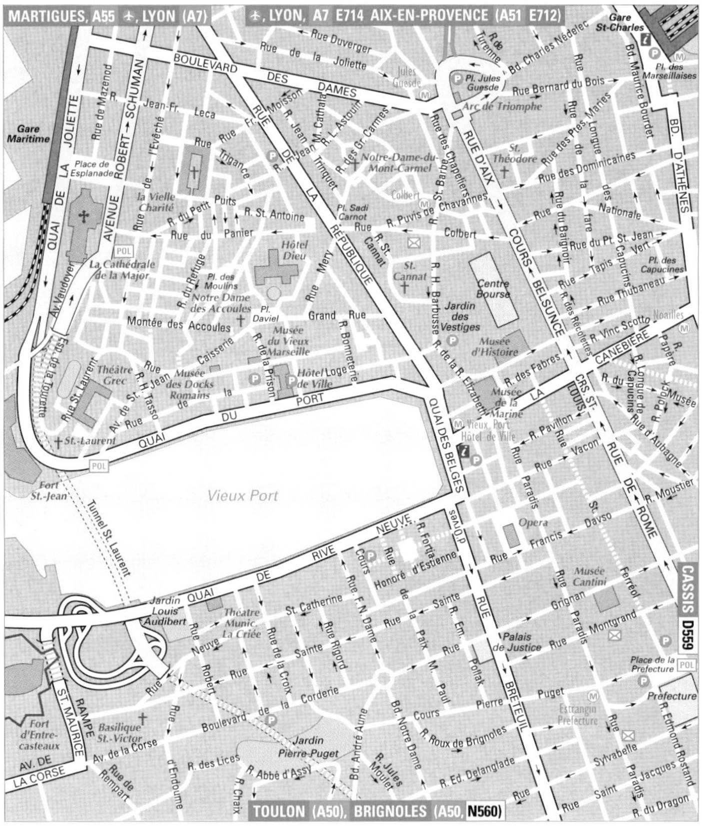

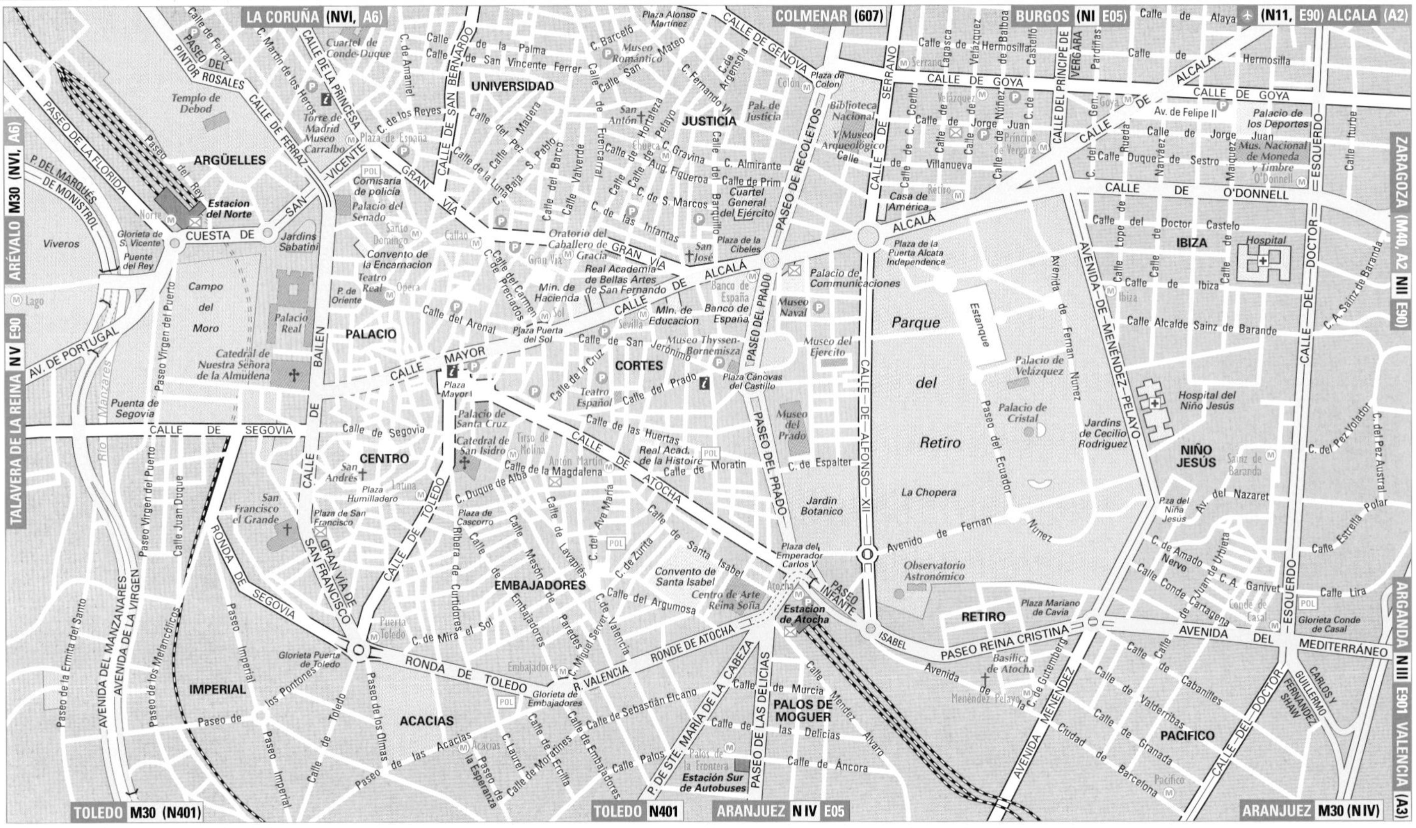

Milano

0 km 5

VARESE, DOMODÓSSOLA (A26, S33)
COMO, ZÜRICH (A2)
LECCO
LECCO (342d)
BERGAMO, BRÉSCIA
NOVARA, TORINO
GÉNOVA, NICE (A10)
PARMA, BOLOGNA

Milano

0 km 1

DOMODÓSSOLA (A8)
VARESE 233
COMO 35 MONZA (36)
BERGAMO 11 (525)
SAN SIRO, MAGENTA 11
LINATE, BRESCIA (11)
ABBIATEGRASSO 494
GENOVA (A7 E62)
PAVIA 35
LODI 9 PARMA (A51, A1)

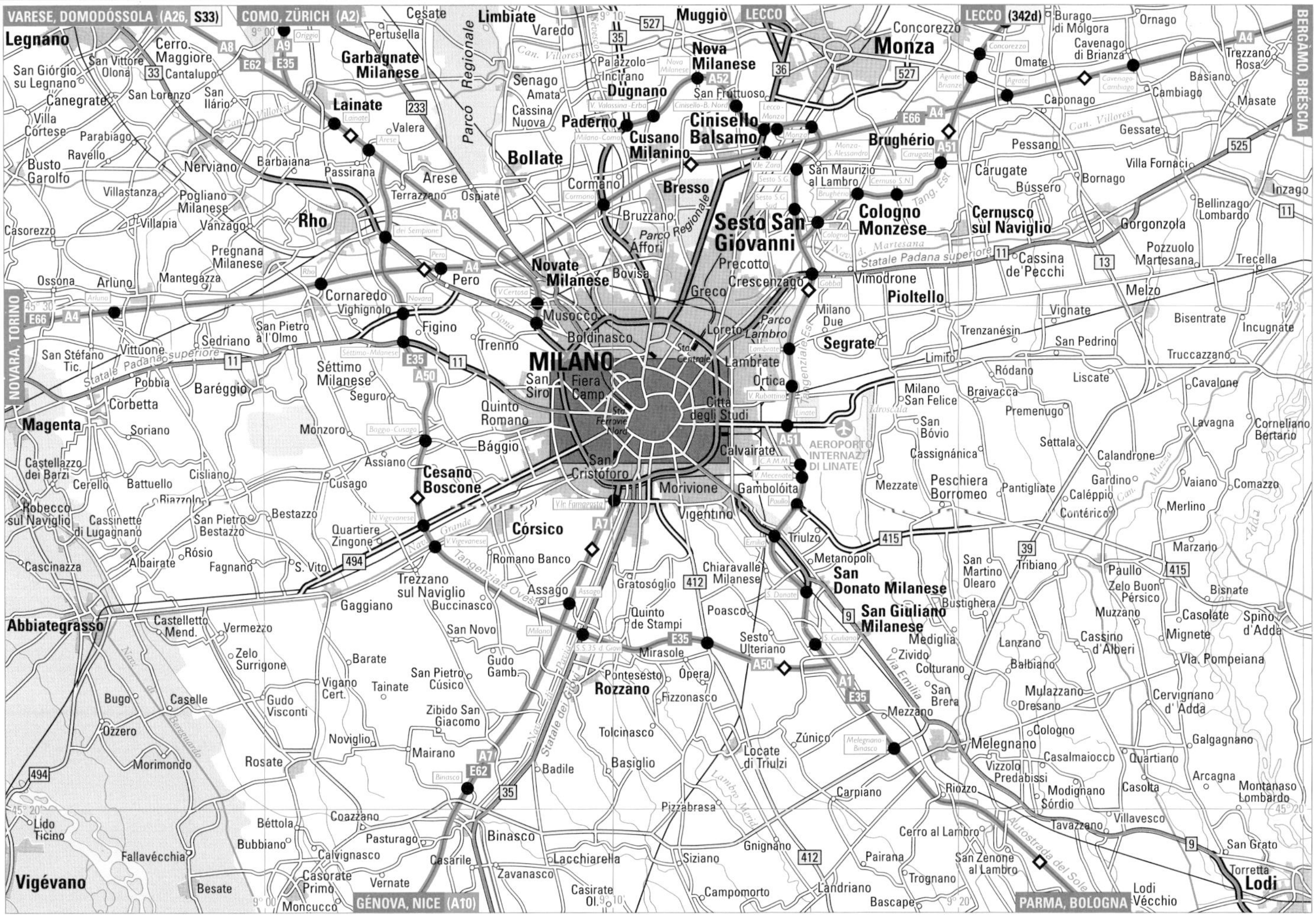

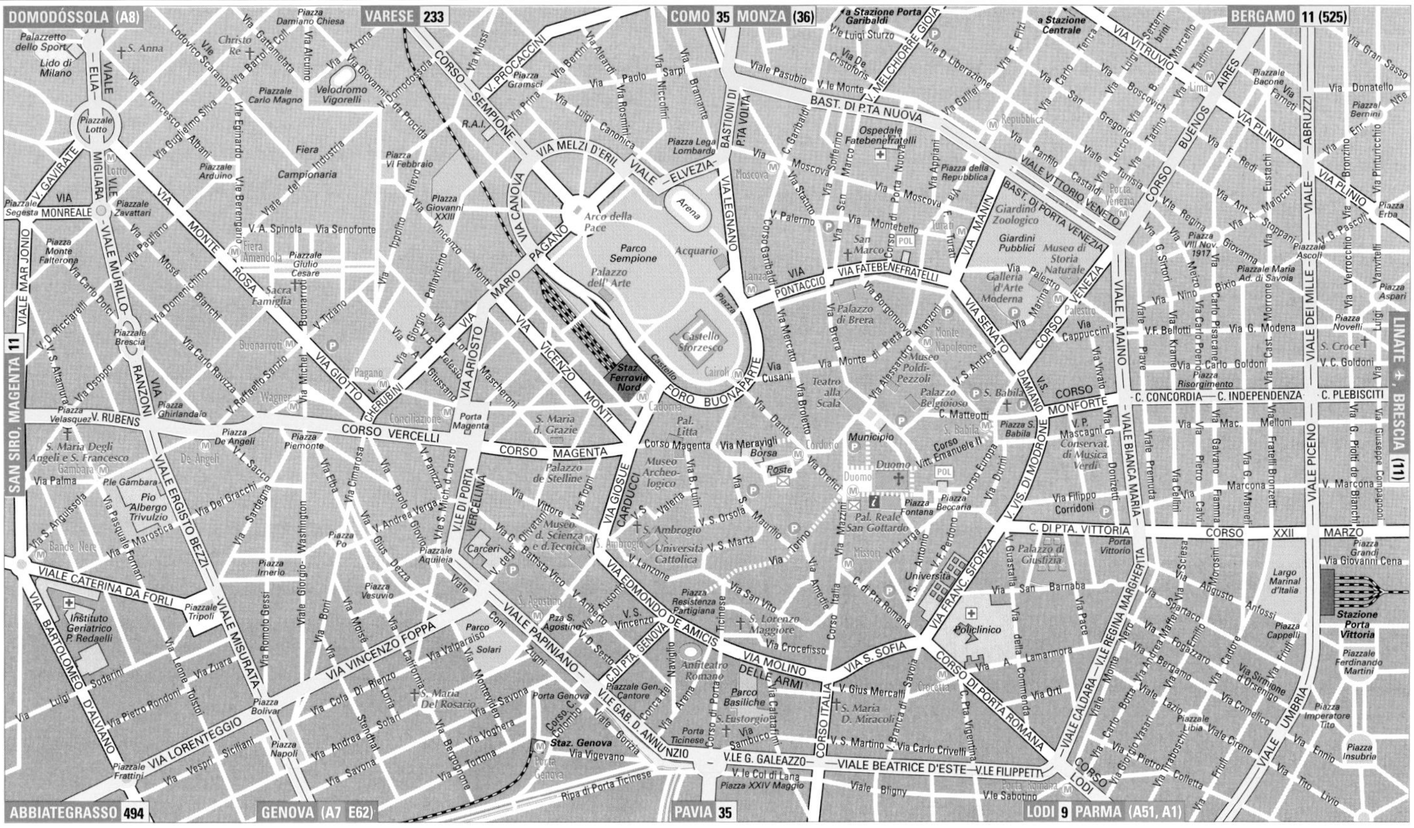

München

0 km 5

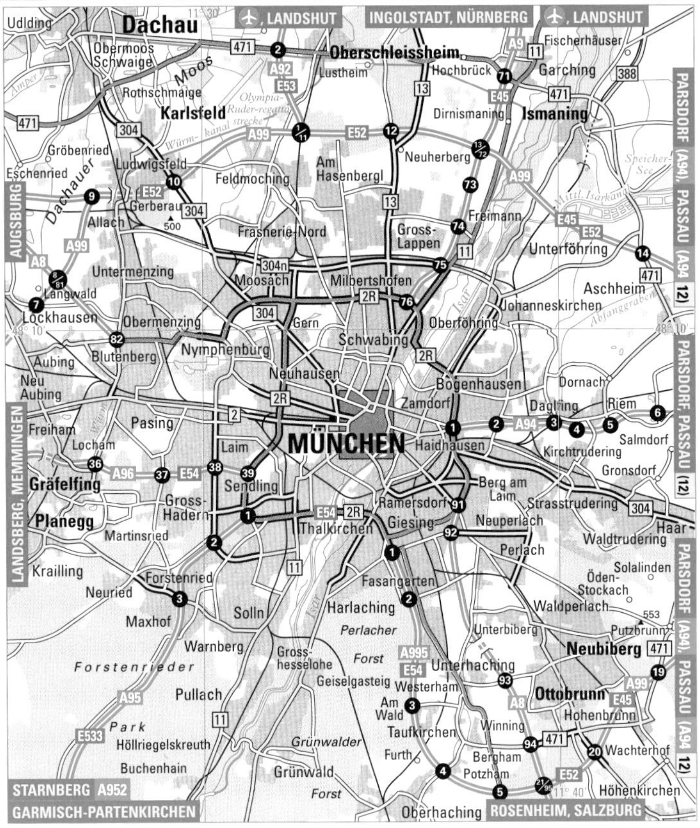

München

0 km 1

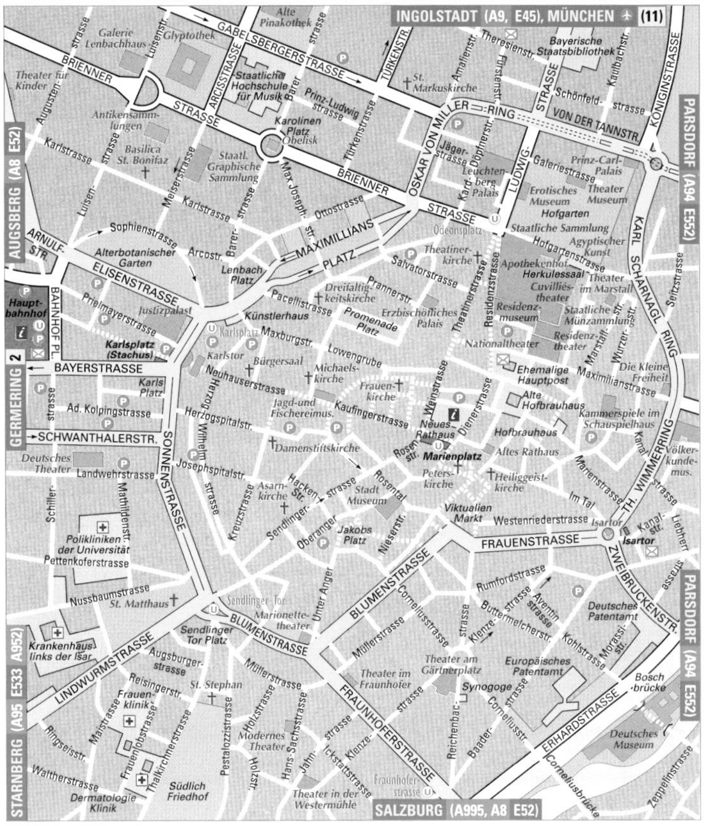

Nápoli

0 km 5

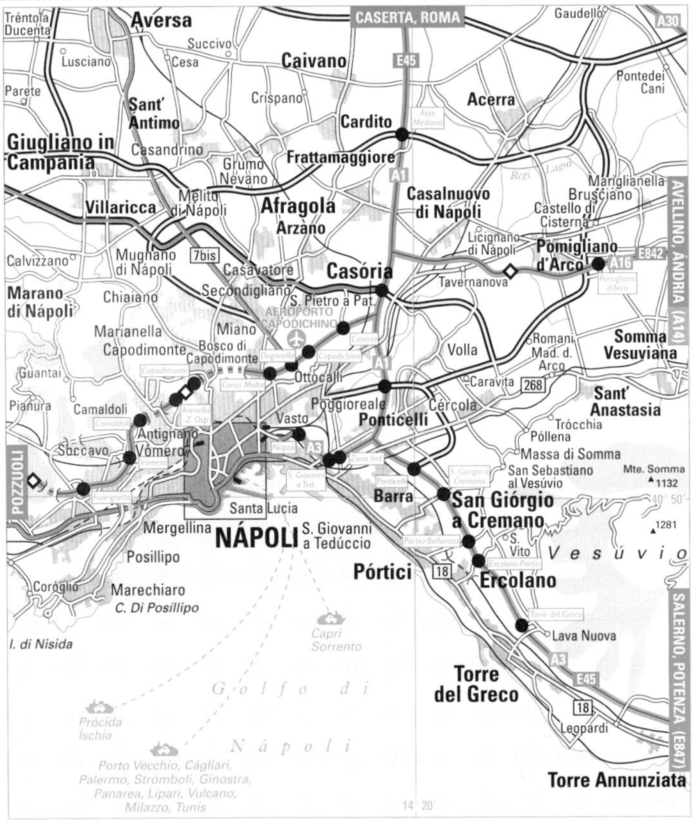

Nápoli

0 km 1

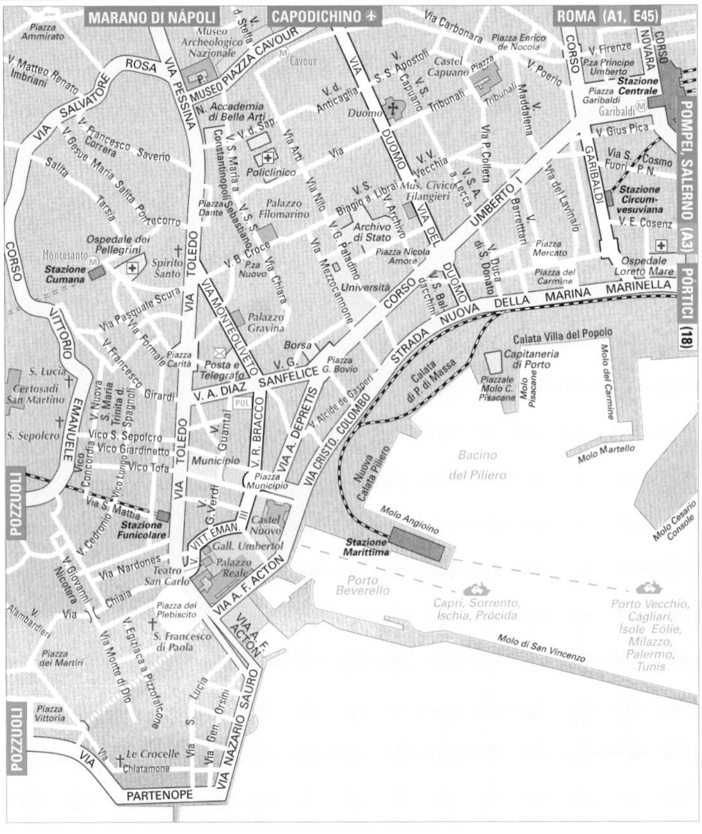

Oslo

0 km 5

BERGEN
GJØVIK, LILLEHAMMER
JESSHEIM, ✈, HAMAR
DRAMMEN, KRISTIANSAND
ASKIM, KARLSTAD
MOSS, FREDRIKSTAD

Nordmarka
Utvika
Bruløkka
Byvann
Heggelielva
Setervann
Sørkedalen
Slakteren
Turter
451
Sandermosen
Slattum
Glosli
Nittedal
Skedsmo-Korset
Skytta
Tryvannshøgda
531
Maridalen
Maridalsvannet
Homledal
By
Bogstadvatn
418
Sognsvatn
Alnsjøen
407
Romas
Vestli
Hvam
Kjeller
Sollihøgda
Holsfjorden
Buruvatn
Holmenkollen
Kjelsås
Skjetten
Lillestrøm
Ila
Stovner
Gorud
Rødtvet
Bærums Verk
Røa
Ris
RING 3
Ullevål
OSLO
RING 2
Høybråten
Strømmen
Rud
Øverskogen
Rustad
Lijordet
Sinsen
Smestad
Skui
Rykkinn
379
Haslum
Ullern
Skøyen
Alna
Toverud
Kolsås
Stabekk
Lysaker
Tøyen
Lørenskog
Sentrum
Storivatn
Bærum
Høvik
Bygdøy
Hovedøya
Ryen
Bryn
363
Lutvatn
Nordre Elvåga
Sylling
Tanum
Sandvika
Fornebu
Lindøya
Oppsal
Bøler
Losby
Rælingen
Ramstadsjøen
Tronstad
Slependen
Snarøya
Ormøya
Bekkelaget
Nøklevatn
Halsjøen
Rustan
Nesøya
Frederikshavn, Helsingborg, København, Hirtshals, Kiel
Nesoddtangen
Lambertseter
Søndre Elvåga
Fløyta
Sandungen
Hvalstad
Semsvann
Nesbru
Østøya
Malmøya
Nordstrand
Østmark-kapellet
Brønnøya
Oksval
Ljabru
Nordbytjernet
Flaskebekk
Bunnefjorden
Skoklefall
Skullerud
Sørsdal
Asker
Oslofjorden
Helvik
Hauketo
Shålsjøen
Krok
Konglungen
Klemetsrud
368
Tonekollen
Sandbakken
Lierskogen
Blakstad
215
Torvvik
Ingierstrand
Mosjøen
Tranby
Dikemark
Kolbotn
Rausjø
Liertoppen
Vollen
Nesodden
Krokhol
Fjellstrand
Bomansvik
Lierbyen
Gjellumvann
Bjerkås
Gjersjøen
Siggerud
Børtervatna
Heggedal
Svartskog
Frogner
Reistad
Svestad
Granerud
Myrvoll
Bru
Slemmestad
Blylaget
134
Oppegård
Binningsvatna
Langen
Nærsnes
10° 20'
10° 30'
10° 40'
10° 50'
11° 00'
60° 00'
59° 50'
E16, E18, E06, 4, 22, 120, 159, 120, 163, 168, 160, 164, 166, 165, 157, 156, 167, 285, 284, 289, 152, 155

Oslo

0 km 0.5

RING 2
RING 2/3, RØA 168
LILLESTRØM 4 (22)
OSLO ✈ 4 (22, E06)
DRAMMEN E18
KARLSTAD E18, FREDRIKSTAD E18 (E06)

Uranienborg kirke
Uranienborgveien
Briskebyveien
Camilla Colletts vei
Oscars gate
Parkveien
Wergelandsveien
Hegdehaugsveien
Welhavens gate
Pilestredet
Rikshospitalet
Ullevålsveien
Vår Frelsers Gravlund
Westye Egebergs gate
Nordre gate
Korsgata
Markveien
Torvald Meyers gate
Rathkes gate
Sverdrups gate
Herslebs gate
Trondheimsveien
Sars gate
Nordraaks gate
Frognerveien
Eckersbergs gate
Odins gate
Gimle
Elisenbergveien
Løvenskiolds gate
Gyldenløves gate
Niels Juels gate
Riddervolds gate
Slotts parken
Det Kongelige Slottet
Wessels gate
Vor Frue hospitalet
Damstredet
Dops gt.
Rosteds gt.
Deichmanns gate
Møllergata
Akerselva
Nordahl Bruns gate
Kunstindustrimus.
St. Olavs gate
St. Olavs kirke
Thor Olsens gate
Fredens borg
Wisesgt.
Hausmanns gate
De Naturhistoriske, Zoologisk, Geologisk museum
Botanisk hage
Botanisk museum
Lakkegata
Bygdøy allé
Frogner kirke
Balders gate
Gabels gate
Colbjørnsens gate
St. Olavs gate
Historisk museum
Kristian IV gate
Deichmanske bibliotek
Maridalsveien
Ostervangsgate
Calmeyers gate
Jens Bjelkes gate
Thomas Heftyes gate
Fritzners gate
Sophus Lies gate
Mogens Thorsens gate
Røde Kors Klinikk
Uranienborg
Oscars gate
Frognerveien
Inkognito gate
Nobelinstituttet
Dronningparken
Frederiks gate
Nasjonalgalleriet
Universitet
Kristian Augusts gate
Keysers gate
Hammersborg tunnelen
Apotekergata
Akersgata
Grubbegata
Youngstorget
Henrik Ibsens gate
Vaterlands tunnelen
Operaen
Brugata
Storgata
Christian Krohgs gate
Vahlsgate
Norby
Lakkegata
Tøyen kirke
Tøyengata
Sørligata
St. Halvard kirke
Smedgata
Borggata
Drammensveien
Ibsen-museet
Nationaltheatret
Det Norske Teater
Johans gate
Universitetsbiblioteket
Arbins gate
Cort Adelers gate
Hansteens gate
Huitfeldts gate
Ruseløkkveien
Stenersen museet
Munkedamsveien
Klingenberggata
Konserthuset
Fridtjof Nansens plass
Kronprinsesse Märthas plass
Vestbanestasjonen
Rådhuset
Rosenkrantz gate
Stortinget
Stortingsgata
Grensen
Karl Johans gate
Domkirke
Biskop Gunnerus' gate
Jernbanetorget
RING 1
Oslo Spektrum
Stenersgata
Grønland
Buss-terminalen
Grønlandsleiret
Akeberg
Tøyenbekken
Platous gate
Schweigaards gate
Hollendergata
Botsfengselsbygningen
Observatoriegata
Terrasse
Parkveien
Frederiks gate
L. Erikssons gate
Frognerkilen
Frogner
Stranda
Filipstadveien
Framnesveien
Dokkveien
Oslotunnelen
Sentralstasjon
Havnegata
Nylandsveien
Bispegata
Dyvekes bro
Prinsens gate
Kongens gate
Nedre Slottsgate
Øvre Slottsgate
Akersgata
Rådhusgata
Christiania torv
Hovedpostkontor
Tollbugata
Dronningens gate
Skippergata
Fred. Olsens gate
Strandgata
Børsen
Teatermuseet
Museet for samtidskunst
Arkitektmuseet
Myntgata
Hjemmefrontmuseet
Akershus Slott og festning
Astrup Fearnley-museet
Akershusstranda
Pipervika
Bjørvika
Bispevika
Havneveien
Oslo gate
Forsvarsmuseet
Festningsgata
Kiel, Hirtshals
Oslofjorden
Frederikshavn, Helsingborg, København

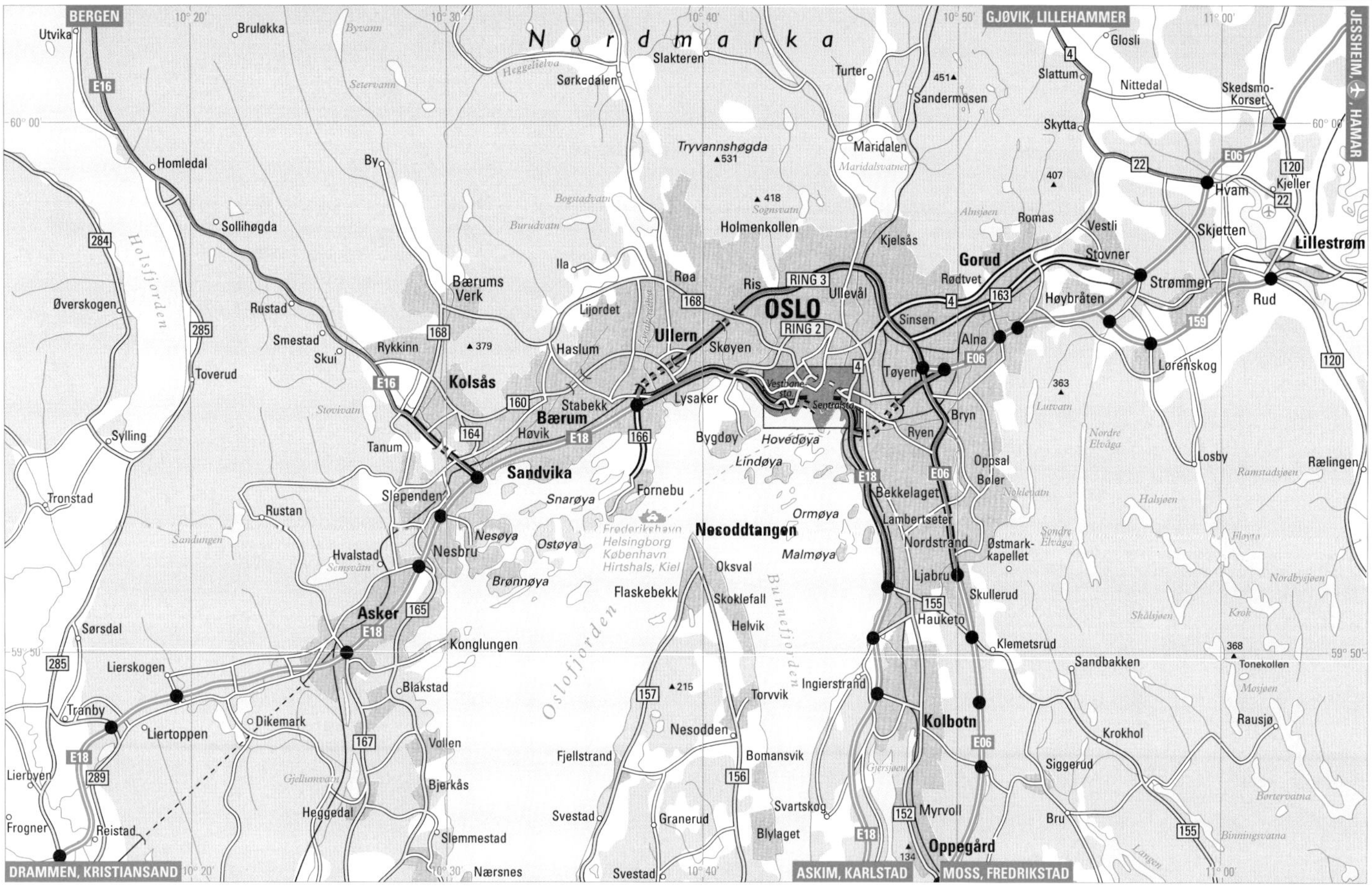

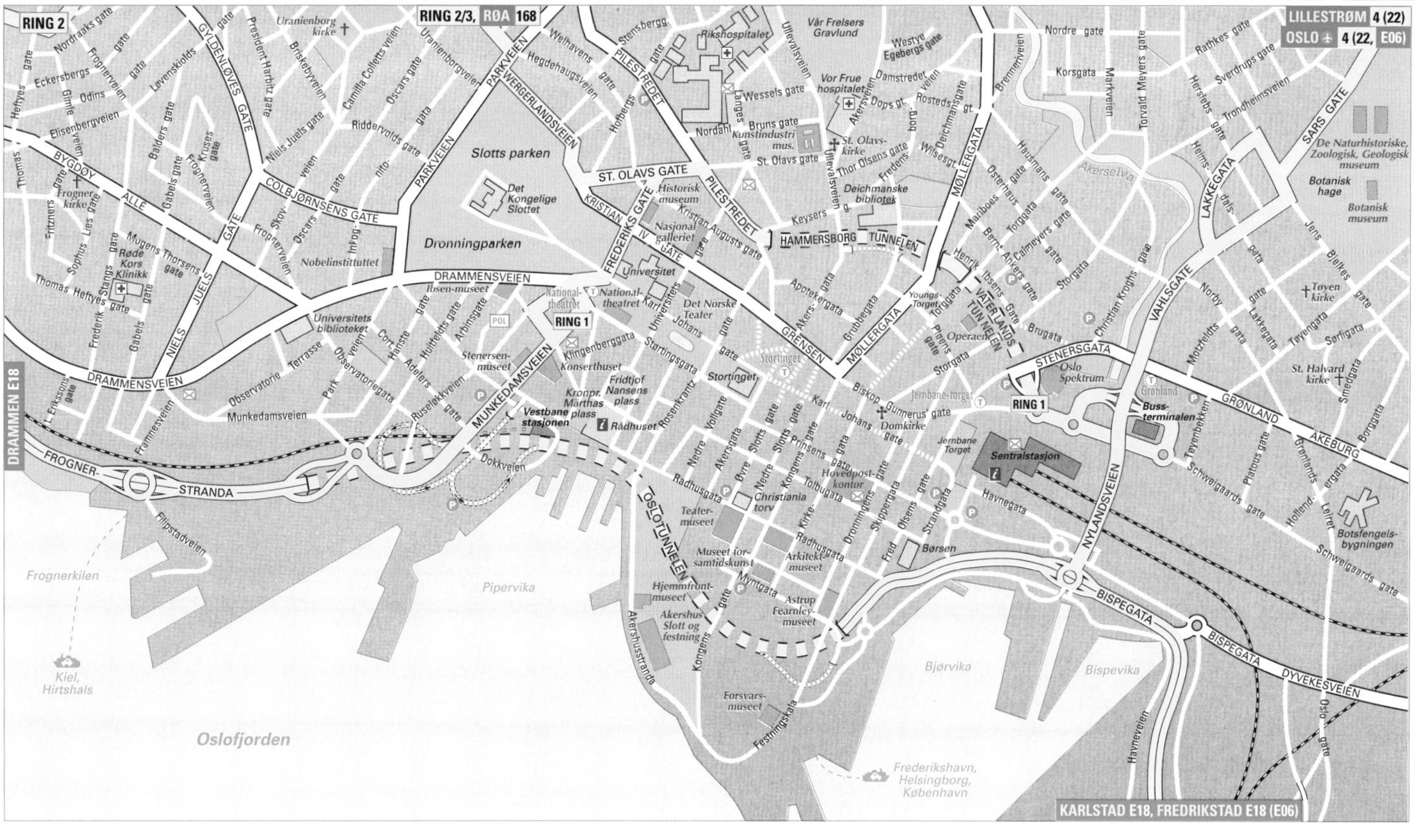

Paris

0 km 5

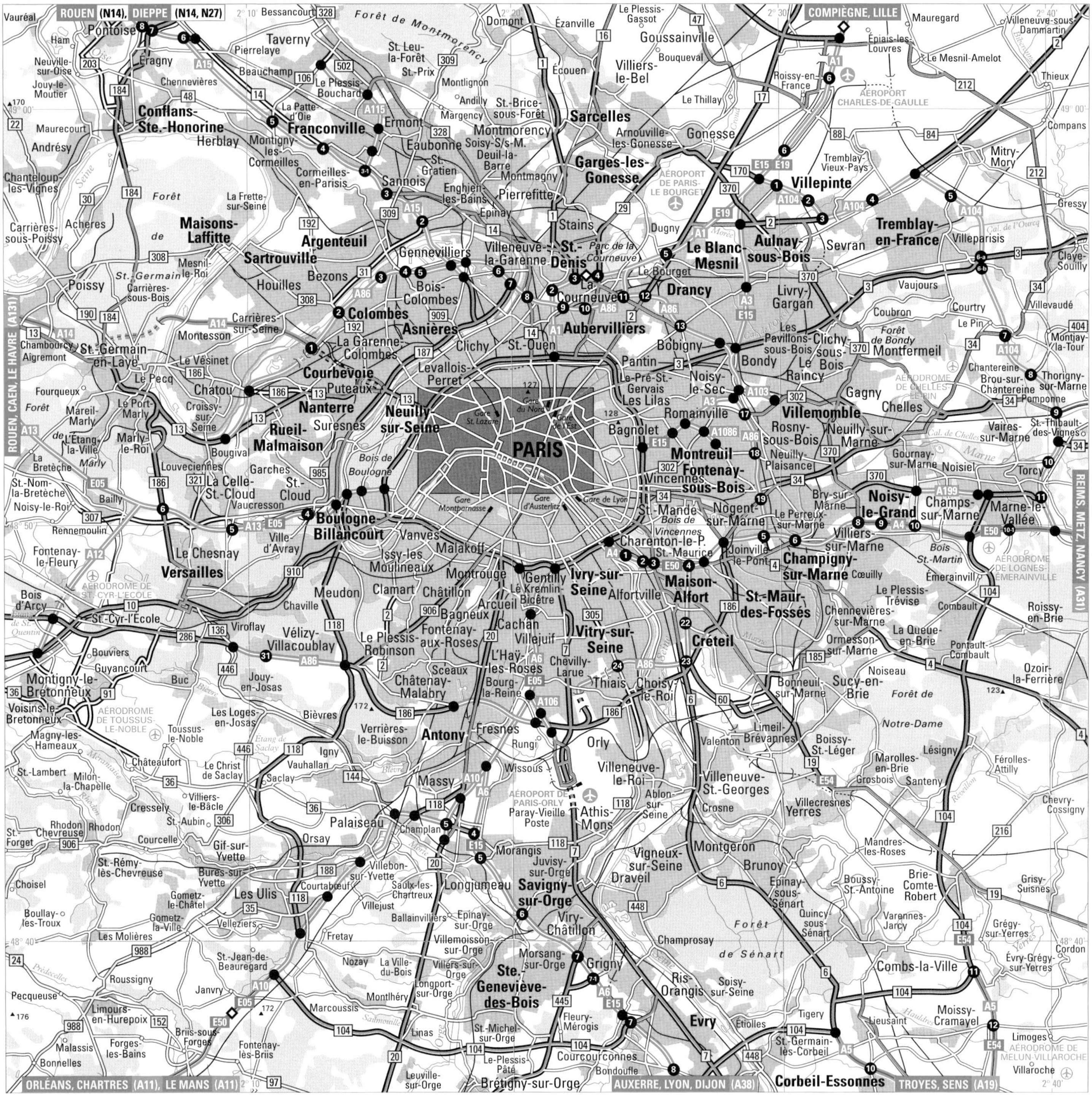
ROUEN (N14), DIEPPE (N14, N27)
COMPIÈGNE, LILLE
ROUEN, CAEN, LE HAVRE (A13)
REIMS, METZ, NANCY (A31)
ORLÉANS, CHARTRES (A11), LE MANS (A11)
AUXERRE, LYON, DIJON (A38)
TROYES, SENS (A19)
PARIS
Forêt de Montmorency
Vauréal
Pontoise
Taverny
Bessancourt
Domont
Ézanville
Le Plessis-Gassot
Goussainville
Mauregard
Villeneuve-sous-Dammartin
Pierrelaye
St.-Leu-la-Forêt
St.-Prix
Écouen
Villiers-le-Bel
Bouqueval
Épiais-lès-Louvres
Le Mesnil-Amelot
Thieux
Neuville-sur-Oise
Ham
Éragny
Jouy-le-Moutier
Beauchamp
Le Plessis-Bouchard
Montlignon
Andilly
St.-Brice-sous-Forêt
Roissy-en-France
AÉROPORT CHARLES-DE-GAULLE
Le Thillay
Chennevières
Conflans-Ste.-Honorine
La Patte-d'Oie
Franconville
Ermont
Margency
Montmorency
Sarcelles
Arnouville-lès-Gonesse
Gonesse
Compans
Maurecourt
Andrésy
Herblay
Montigny-lès-Cormeilles
Eaubonne
Soisy-S/s-M.
Deuil-la-Barre
Garges-lès-Gonesse
Tremblay-Vieux-Pays
Mitry-Mory
Chanteloup-les-Vignes
Cormeilles-en-Parisis
Sannois
St.-Gratien
Montmagny
AÉROPORT DE PARIS-LE BOURGET
Villepinte
Enghien-les-Bains
Pierrefitte
Carrières-sous-Poissy
Achères
Forêt de St.-Germain
La Frette-sur-Seine
Maisons-Laffitte
Argenteuil
Épinay
Stains
Dugny
Aulnay-sous-Bois
Tremblay-en-France
Gressy
Gennevilliers
Villeneuve-la-Garenne
St.-Denis
Parc de la Courneuve
Le Blanc-Mesnil
Sevran
Villeparisis
Claye-Souilly
Poissy
Sartrouville
Mesnil-le-Roi
Carrières-sous-Bois
Houilles
Bezons
Bois-Colombes
La Courneuve
Le Bourget
Drancy
Livry-Gargan
Vaujours
Colombes
Asnières
Aubervilliers
Coubron
Courtry
Villevaudé
Carrières-sur-Seine
Montesson
La Garenne-Colombes
Clichy
St.-Ouen
Bobigny
Les Pavillons-sous-Bois
Clichy-sous-Bois
Forêt de Bondy
Montfermeil
Le Pin
Montjay-la-Tour
Chambourcy
St.-Germain-en-Laye
Aigremont
Le Vésinet
Le Pecq
Courbevoie
Levallois-Perret
Pantin
Bondy
Le Raincy
Chantereine
Brou-sur-Chantereine
Thorigny-sur-Marne
Pomponne
Fourqueux
Chatou
Puteaux
Le Pré-St.-Gervais
Les Lilas
Noisy-le-Sec
AÉRODROME DE CHELLES-LE PIN
Gagny
Chelles
Mareil-Marly
Le Port-Marly
Croissy-sur-Seine
Nanterre
Neuilly-sur-Seine
Gare du Nord
Gare de l'Est
Gare St.-Lazare
Romainville
Villemomble
Rosny-sous-Bois
Neuilly-sur-Marne
Vaires-sur-Marne
St.-Thibault-des-Vignes
L'Étang-la-Ville
Marly-le-Roi
Rueil-Malmaison
Suresnes
Bagnolet
Montreuil
Neuilly-Plaisance
Gournay-sur-Marne
Noisiel
Torcy
La Bretèche
Bougival
Louveciennes
Bois de Boulogne
Fontenay-sous-Bois
Vincennes
St.-Nom-la-Bretèche
Garches
La Celle-St.-Cloud
St.-Cloud
Vaucresson
Bailly
Noisy-le-Roi
St.-Mandé
Bois de Vincennes
Nogent-sur-Marne
Le Perreux-sur-Marne
Bry-sur-Marne
Noisy-le-Grand
Champs-sur-Marne
Marne-la-Vallée
Rennemoulin
Boulogne-Billancourt
Gare Montparnasse
Gare d'Austerlitz
Gare de Lyon
Vanves
Charenton-le-P.
St.-Maurice
Joinville-le-Pont
Villiers-sur-Marne
Champigny-sur-Marne
Bois St.-Martin
Fontenay-le-Fleury
Le Chesnay
Ville-d'Avray
Issy-les-Moulineaux
Malakoff
Montrouge
Gentilly
Ivry-sur-Seine
Maison-Alfort
Cœuilly
AÉRODROME DE LOGNES-ÉMERAINVILLE
Émerainville
Versailles
AÉRODROME DE ST.-CYR-L'ÉCOLE
Meudon
Clamart
Châtillon
Le Kremlin-Bicêtre
Alfortville
St.-Maur-des-Fossés
Le Plessis-Trévise
Bois d'Arcy
Chaville
Arcueil
Bagneux
Cachan
Villejuif
Chennevières-sur-Marne
Combault
Roissy-en-Brie
St.-Cyr-l'École
Viroflay
Vélizy-Villacoublay
Fontenay-aux-Roses
Le Plessis-Robinson
Vitry-sur-Seine
Créteil
La Queue-en-Brie
Ormesson-sur-Marne
Pontault-Combault
Bouviers
Guyancourt
Montigny-le-Bretonneux
Sceaux
L'Haÿ-les-Roses
Chevilly-Larue
Thiais
Choisy-le-Roi
Noiseau
Ozoir-la-Ferrière
Buc
Jouy-en-Josas
Châtenay-Malabry
Bourg-la-Reine
Bonneuil-sur-Marne
Sucy-en-Brie
Forêt de Notre-Dame
Voisins-le-Bretonneux
AÉRODROME DE TOUSSUS-LE-NOBLE
Les Loges-en-Josas
Toussus-le-Noble
Bièvres
Verrières-le-Buisson
Antony
Fresnes
Rungis
Orly
Limeil-Brévannes
Valenton
Boissy-St.-Léger
Magny-les-Hameaux
Igny
Vauhallan
Châteaufort
Le Christ de Saclay
Saclay
Wissous
Villeneuve-le-Roi
Marolles-en-Brie
Grosbois
Santeny
Lésigny
Férolles-Attilly
St.-Lambert
Milon-la-Chapelle
Massy
Villeneuve-St.-Georges
Villiers-le-Bâcle
AÉROPORT DE PARIS-ORLY
Paray-Vieille-Poste
Athis-Mons
Ablon-sur-Seine
Crosne
Yerres
Villecresnes
Cressely
St.-Aubin
Palaiseau
Champlan
Chevry-Cossigny
Rhodon
Chevreuse
St.-Forget
Courcelle
Gif-sur-Yvette
Orsay
Morangis
Juvisy-sur-Orge
Vigneux-sur-Seine
Montgeron
Brunoy
Mandres-les-Roses
St.-Rémy-lès-Chevreuse
Bures-sur-Yvette
Villebon-sur-Yvette
Saulx-les-Chartreux
Longjumeau
Savigny-sur-Orge
Draveil
Épinay-sous-Sénart
Boussy-St.-Antoine
Brie-Comte-Robert
Grisy-Suisnes
Choisel
Gometz-le-Châtel
Les Ulis
Courtabœuf
Villejust
Boullay-les-Troux
Gometz-la-Ville
Velleziers
Ballainvilliers
Épinay-sur-Orge
Viry-Châtillon
Quincy-sous-Sénart
Varennes-Jarcy
Forêt de Sénart
Grégy-sur-Yerres
Cordon
Les Molières
Fretay
Villemoisson-sur-Orge
Champrosay
St.-Jean-de-Beauregard
Nozay
La Ville-du-Bois
Villiers-sur-Orge
Morsang-sur-Orge
Grigny
Ste.-Geneviève-des-Bois
Ris-Orangis
Soisy-sur-Seine
Combs-la-Ville
Évry-Grégy-sur-Yerres
Roussigny
Janvry
Montlhéry
Longpont-sur-Orge
Pecqueuse
Marcoussis
Fleury-Mérogis
Tigery
Moissy-Cramayel
Limours-en-Hurepoix
Briis-sous-Forges
Fontenay-lès-Briis
Linas
St.-Michel-sur-Orge
Évry
Étiolles
Lieusaint
St.-Germain-lès-Corbeil
Limoges
AÉRODROME DE MELUN-VILLAROCHE
Villaroche
Malassis
Bonnelles
Forges-les-Bains
Le Plessis-Pâté
Courcouronnes
Bondoufle
Corbeil-Essonnes
Leuville-sur-Orge
Brétigny-sur-Orge

Paris

0 km 1

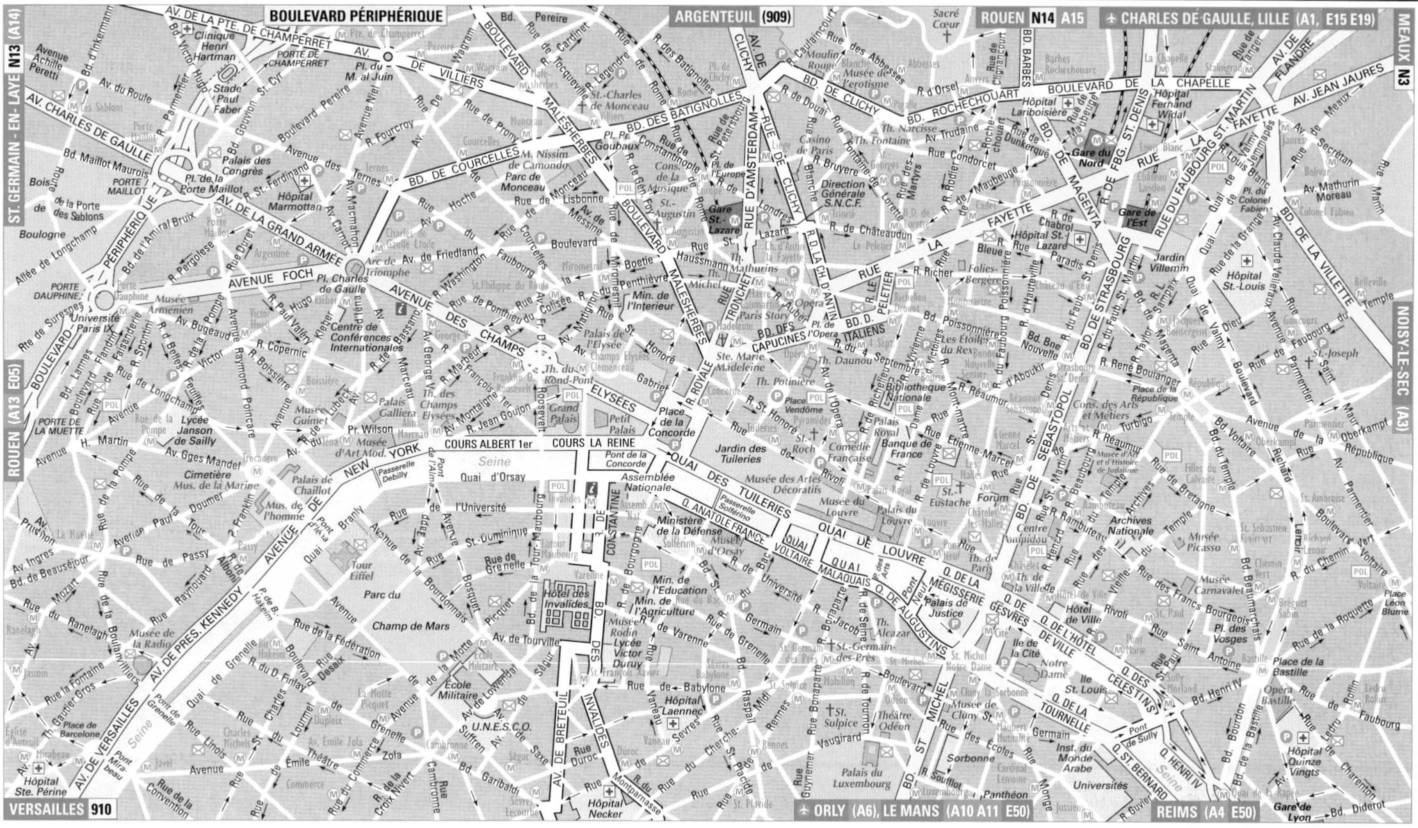

Praha

0 km 5

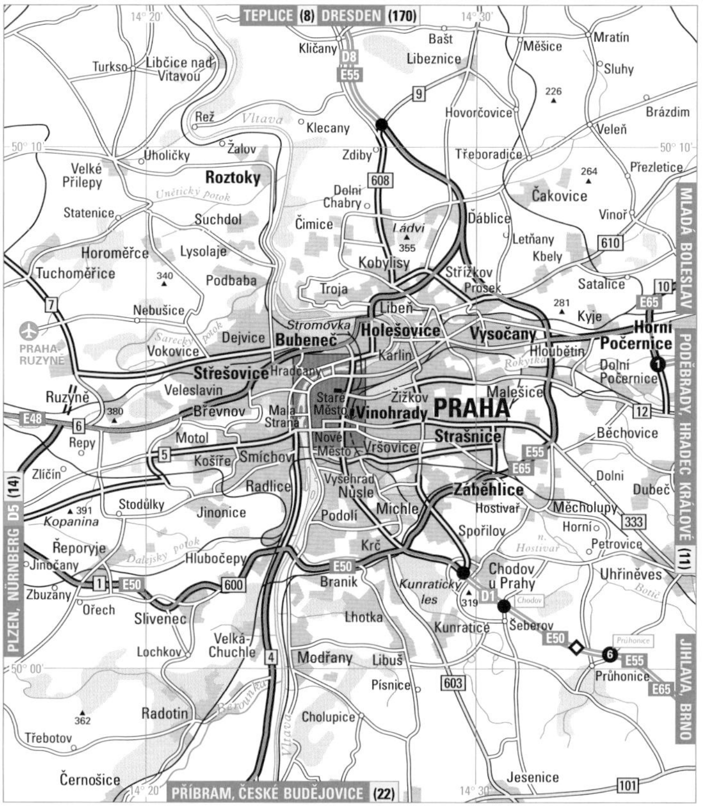

Praha

0 km 1

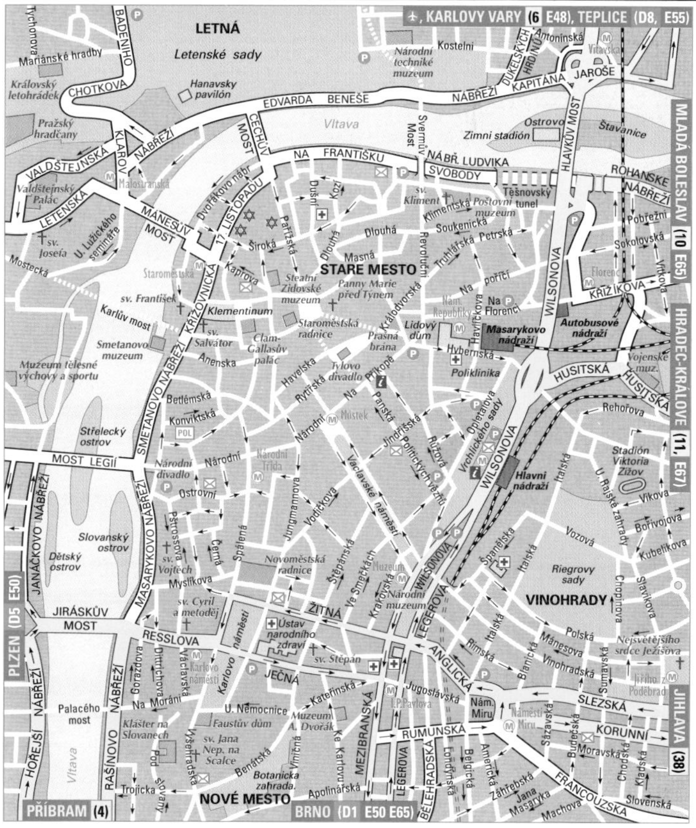

Roma

0 km 5

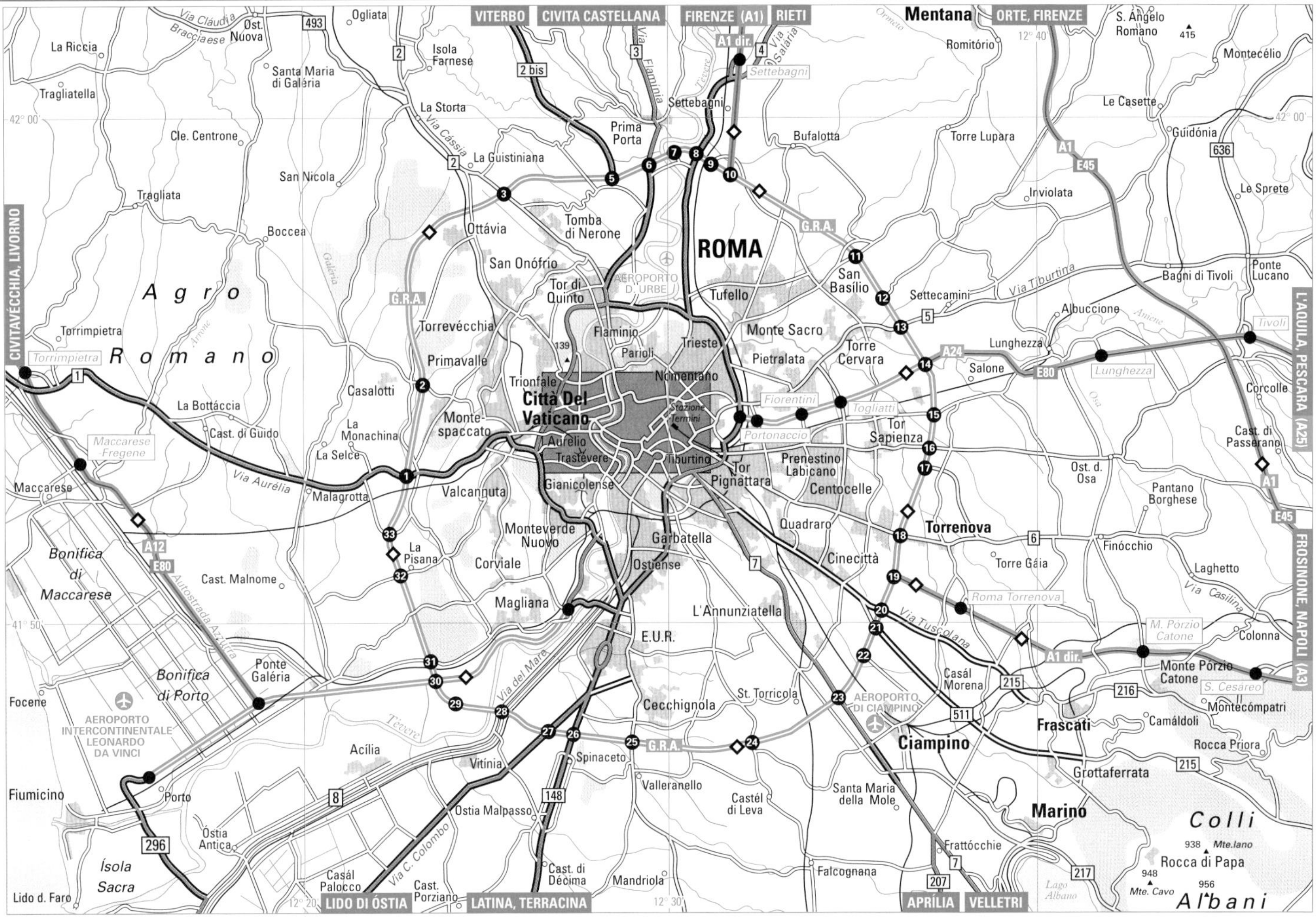

Roma

0 km 1

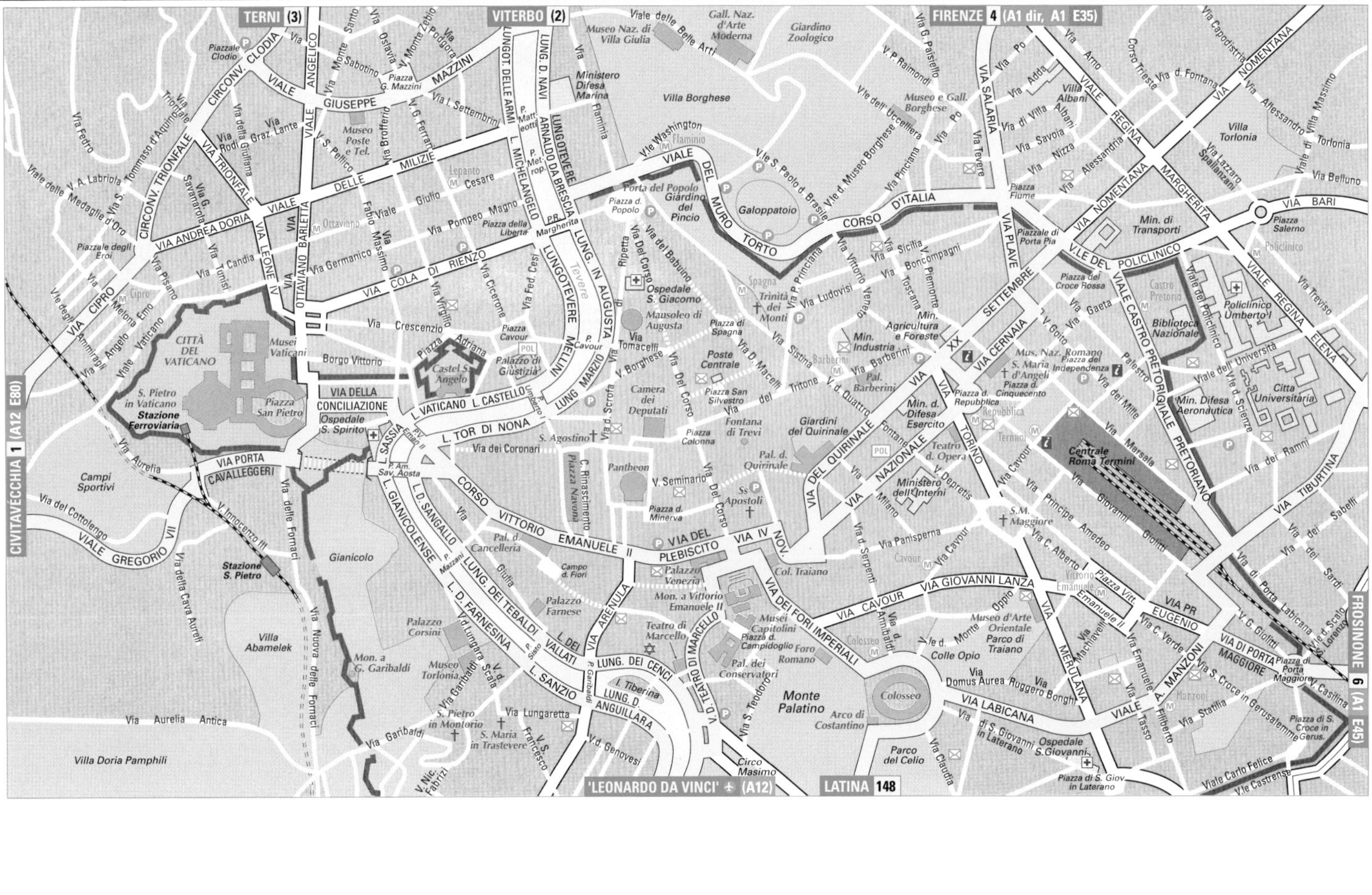

Stockholm

0 km 5

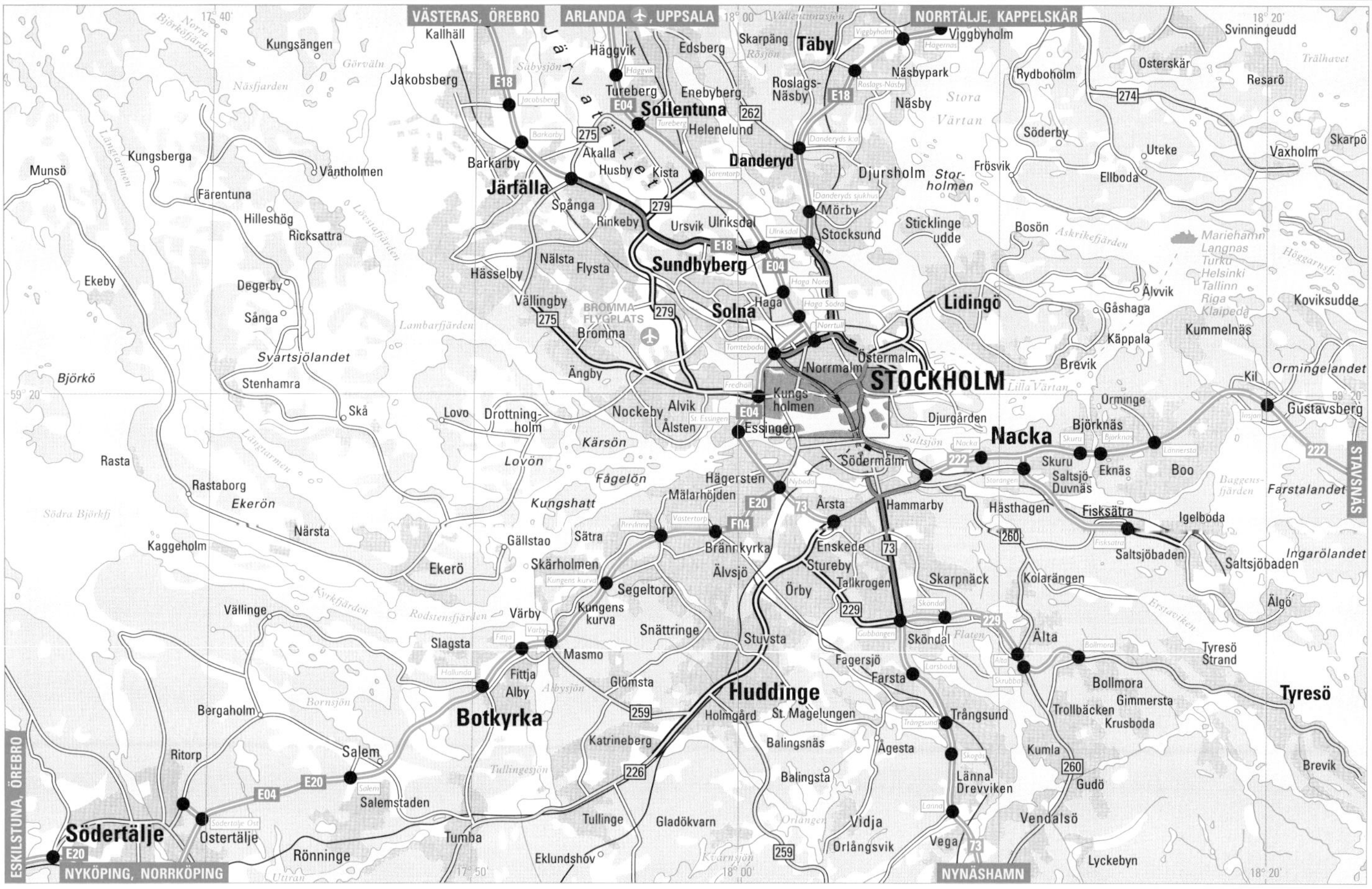

Stockholm

0 km 1

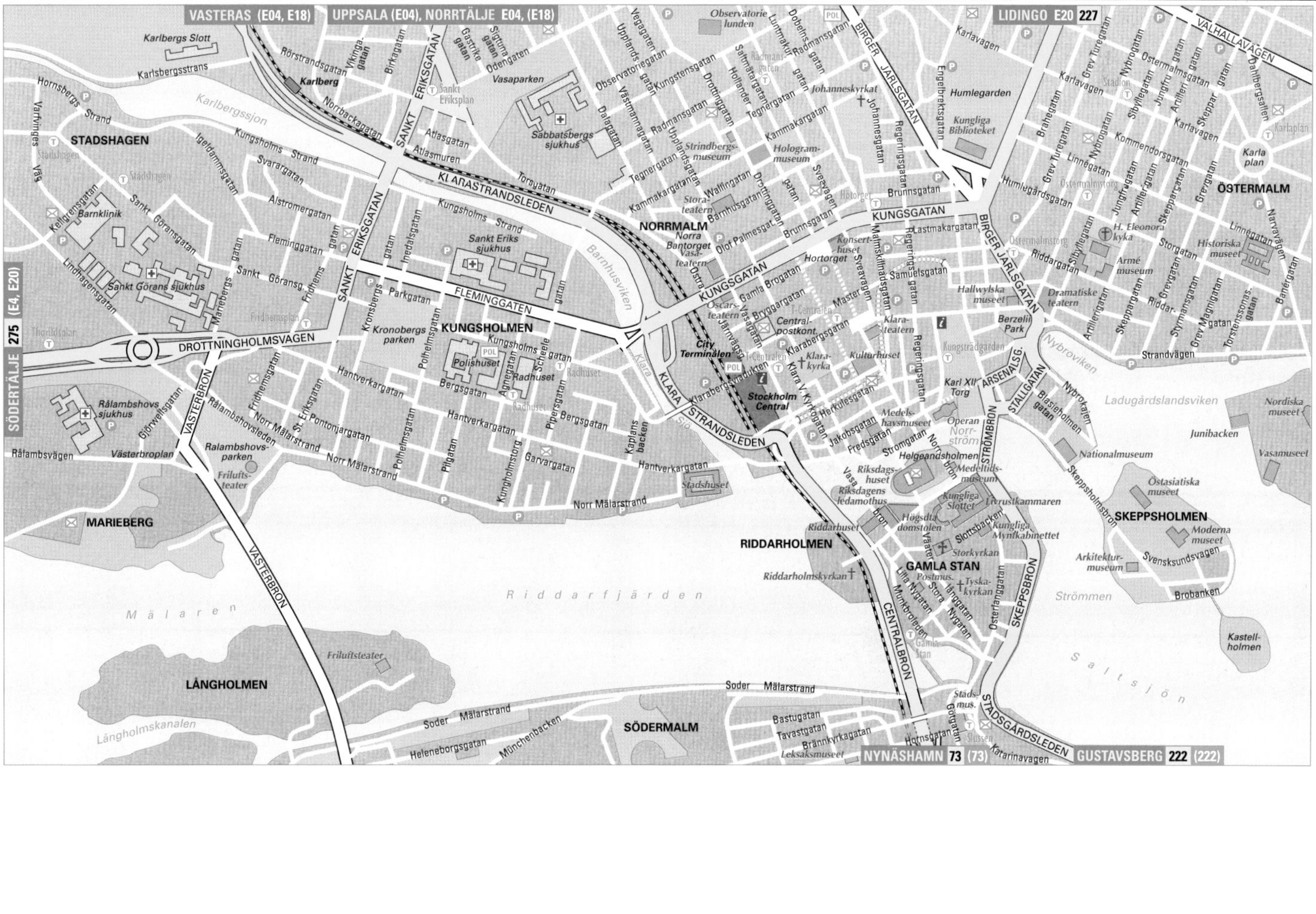

Strasbourg

0 km 5

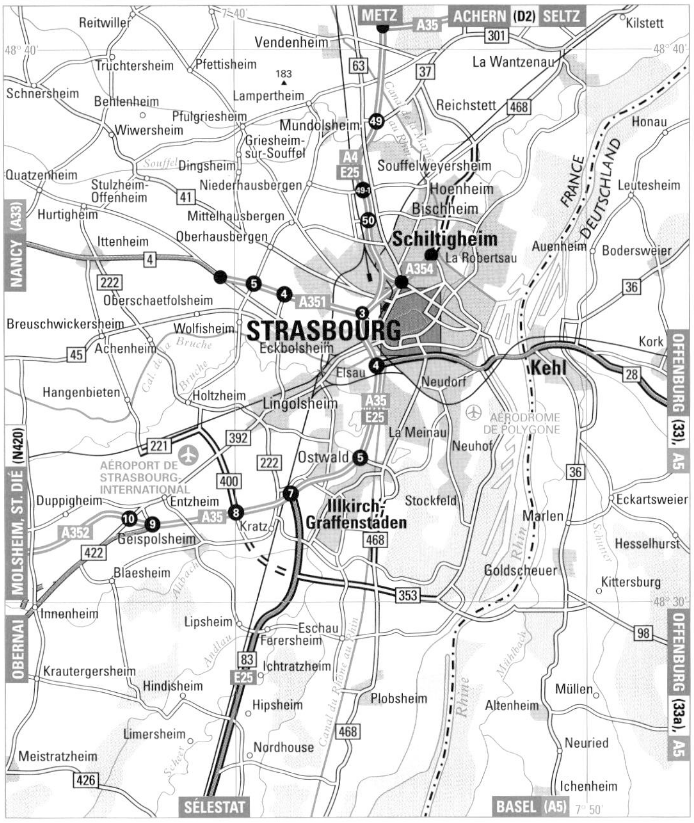

Strasbourg

0 km 0.5

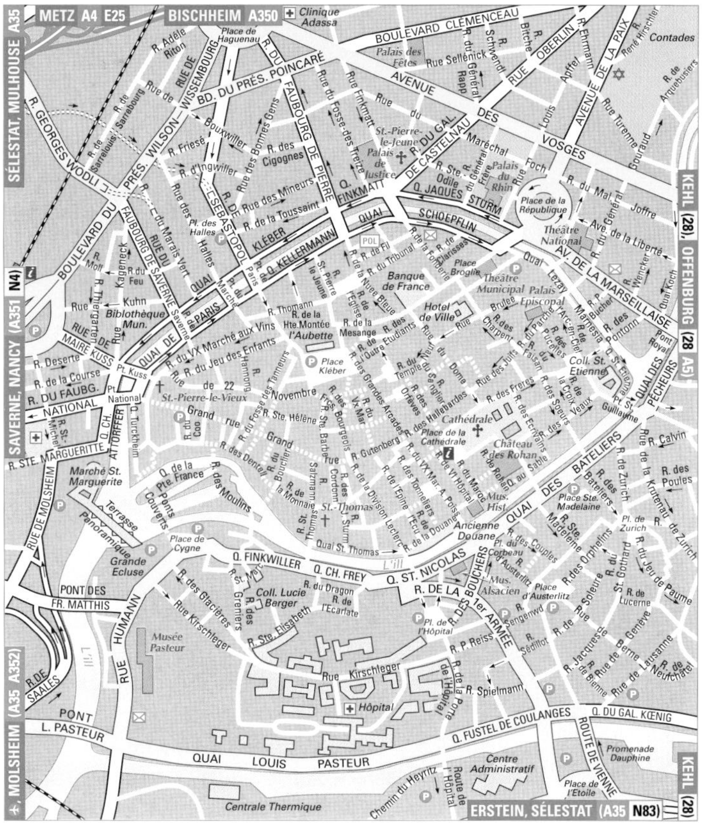

Sevilla

0 km 0.5

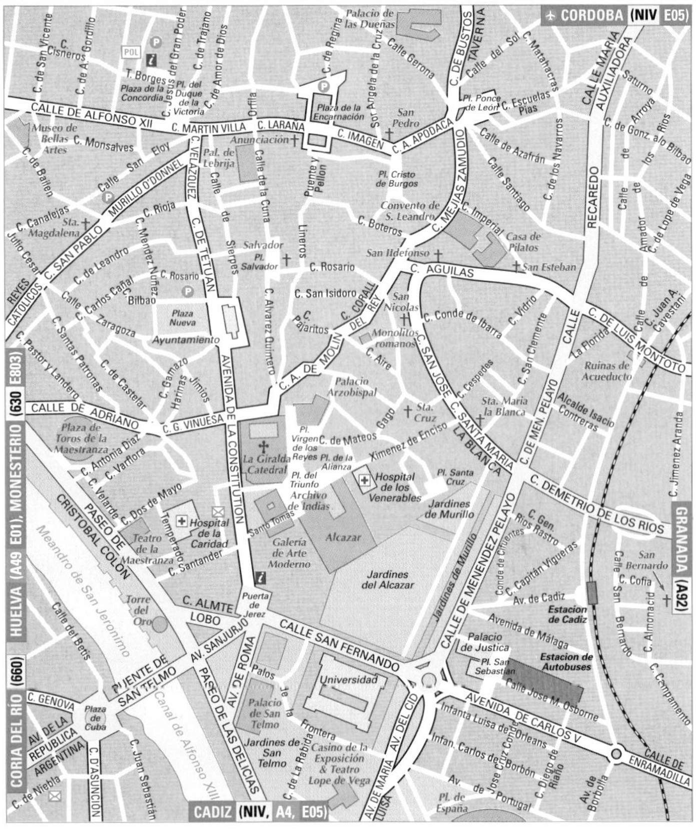

Stuttgart

0 km 0.5

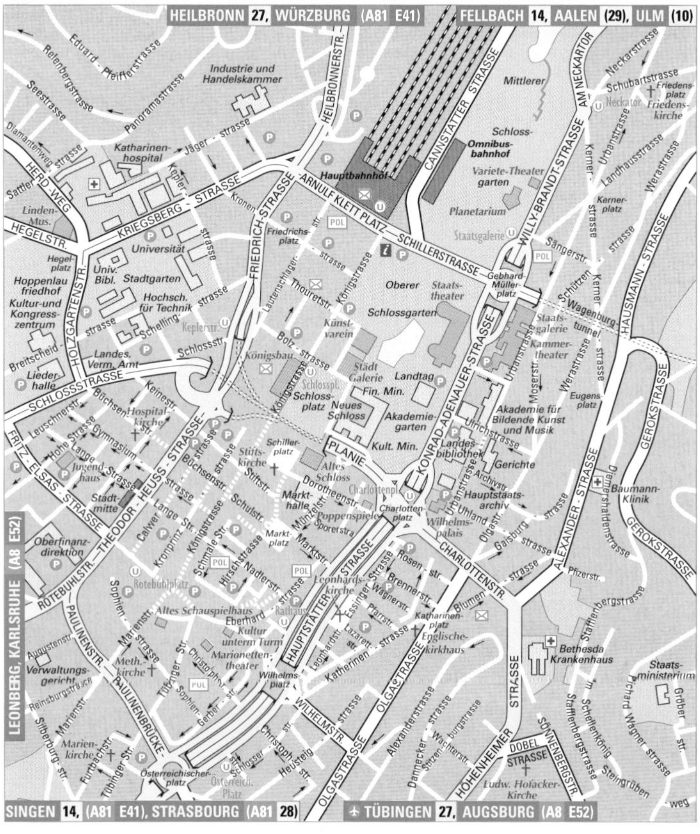

Torino

0 km 5

Bertesseno
Mte. Colombano 658
Moncolombone
Niquidetto
Truc di Miola
Grange
Rossignoli
Robassomero
Malanghero
AEROPORTO DI CASELLE
Volpiano
AOSTA
NOVARA, MILANO
Rivera
Torassi
Castelrosso
S. Giacomo
Caselle Tor.
Léini
Brandizzo
Chivasso
Verolengo
Mte. Arpone 1600
Mte. Lera 1371
la Cassa
Parco Regionale La Mándria
Mompellato
Castello
Rivasacco
Val della Torre
Givoletto
Montelera
Rubbianetta
Bórgaro Torinese
Fornacino
Statale Padana Superiore
Cimena
S. Genésio
Castagneto Po
Colombaro
S. Raffaele
S. Sebastiano da Po
Rubiana
1325 Mte. Curt
Verna
S. Gillio
Mándria
Cast. S. Cristina
Villaretto
Piana di S. Raffaele
Brione
Druento
Venaria
Settimo Torinese
Bussolini Gassinese
Casalborgone
Airali
Grange
Venaria R. Stadio
Bórgaro
Casello
Settimo
Ababadia di Stura
Gássino Torinese
Rivalba
Villár Dora
Almese
1150 Mte. Musinè
Rivera
Savonera
Tangenziale Nord
Castiglione Torinese
SUSA GRENOBLE (A43, A41)
Caselette
S. Pancrazio
Regina Margherita
Grángia
Drubáglio
Cast. di Camerletto
Pianezza
Barca
Bertolla Barca
S. Martino
Berzano di S. Pietro
Almese
S. Ambrógio di Torino
Avigliana
Alpignano
Dora Ripária
Lucento
Parco M. Carrara
S. Máuro Tor
Bardassano
Sciolze
Cinzano
Rivodora
Cordova
670 Superga
Avigliana
Regina Margerhita
Collegno
Vernone
Roccati
Molino
Buttigliere Alta
Rosta
Rivoli
C. So Francia
TORINO
Mongreno
Baldissero Tor.
Pavarolo
Moncucco Torinese
Nevissano
Meana
C. So Allamano
Réaglie
Montaldo Tor.
Avuglione
Sala
Rivata
Reano
Corbiglia
Grugliasco
Parco del Valentino
S. Margherita
Pino Torinese
Marentino
Mombello d'Torino
Castelnuovo Don Bosco
Giaveno
Tetti Neirotti
Paiere
Trana
Villarbasse
Roncáglia
Gérbido
l'Éremo
Andezeno
Arignano
Villa
S. Bernardino
Rivalta di Torino
Doirone
Tangenziale Sud
S. Viu
715 Colle d. Maddalena
Cipresso
Moriondo Tor.
Moranda
Sangano
Dalmassi
Bruino
Beinasco
Mirafiori
Lingotto
Cavoretto
Castelvécchio
Bausone
S. Giovanni
Pratovigero
Mirafiori
Pecetto Tor.
S. Felice
Chieri
Buttigliera d'Asti
Drosso
C. So Unità d'Italia
S. Pietro
S. Giovanni
Mte. S. Giórgio 837
Orbassano
Orbassano
Stupinigi
Moncalieri
Borgaretto
Stupinigi
Mad. d. Scala
Burdini
Allivellatori
Nichelino
Testone
Oviglia
Crivelle
Montegrosso
Piossasco
Piazza
Parco Naturale di Stupinigi
Trofarello
Valle Saúglio
Riva presso Chieri
Cumiana
Candiolo
Dedouche
Moncalieri
Tagliaferro
Pallera
Terrazze
Mago
Cascina Parpáglia
Cambiano
Bianchi
Costa
Gerbole
S.S.20
Valdichiesa
Paschero
Tetti Rolle
Pessione
Volvera
la Loggia
Sántena
Tavernette
Volvera
Candiolo
Sántena
Cast. di S. Salva
Villanova d'Asti
None
Vinovo
Tetti Sapini
Villanova d'A.
Frossasco
None
Brassi
SAVONA
CÚNEO (20)
Tetti Giro
Marocchi
Banna
Corvéglia
ASTI, ALESSÁNDRIA, BRÉSCIA

Torino

0 km 1

CASELLE
IVREA, AOSTA (A5 E612, E25), MILANO (A4 E64)
Stazione Merci Vanchiglia
SUSA (A32 E70)
RIVOLI (25), SUSA (A32 E70)
CHIVASSO (11)
CHIERI (10), ASTI (A21 E70)
CORSO REG. MARGHERITA
PIAZZA DELLA REPUBBLICA
Stazione Autolinee
Porta Palatina
Teatro Romano
Ospedale Maria Adelaide
CORSO REGINA MARGHERITA
Palazzo Reale
Giardino Reale
Armeria Reale
Palacio di Città
Piazza Castello
Palazzo Madama
VIA PIETRO MICCA
Teatro Regio
Teatro Carignano
Palazzo Carignano
Università
Mole Antonelliana
Bibl. Naz.
VIA PO
Università di Studi
Museo Egizio Gall. Sabauda
San Filippo Neri
Piazza S. Carlo
Santa Cristina
Piazza Carlo Emanuele II
Piazza Vittorio Veneto
Ponte Vittorio Emanuele I
Ospedale di S. Giovanni Battista
Piazza Carlo Felice
Stazione Porta Nuova
CORSO VITTORIO EMANUELE II
Tempio Israelitico
Chiesa Evangelica Valdese
Piazza Madama Cristina
Fiume Po
CORSO MONCALIERI
Santa Maria del Monte
Museo Nazionale della Montagna
Parco del Valentino
Ponte Umberto I
Piazza Crimea
PINEROLO (23)
CARIGNANO (20)
MONCALIERI (393), SAVONA (A6 E717)

Warszawa

0 km 1

634
GDAŃSK 7 E77
BIAŁYSTOK 629 (8 E67)
Ogród Zoologiczny
Park Praski
PRAGA
Warszawa Wileńska
Warszawa Wschodnia
NOWE MIASTO
Rynek Starego Miasta
Zamek Królewski
WYBRZEŻE GDAŃSKIE
AL. SOLIDARNOŚCI
MOST ŚLĄSKO-DĄBROWSKI
JANA ZAMOYSKIEGO
Warszawa Stadion
Park Skaryszewski
Stadion Dziesięciolecia
WISŁA
Ogród Saski
Teatr Wielki Opery i Baletu
ŚRÓDMIEŚCIE
Uniwersytet
MOST PONIATOWSKIEGO
AL. GEN. K. ŚWIERCZEWSKIEGO
Pałac Kultury i Nauki
Warszawa Śródmieście
Warszawa Centralna
AL. JEROZOLIMSKIE
Muzeum Narodowe
Warszawa Powiśle
POWIŚLE
Muz. Wojska Polskiego
Most Gen. Zygmunta Berlinga
WŁOCŁAWEK 634 (7, 62)
ŁOWICZ, KONIN 629 (2 E30)
BREST 2 E30
W. Ochota
W. Główna
UJAZDÓW
Politechnika Warszawska
AL. ARMII LUDOWEJ
Filtry
Park Łazienkowski
Stadion „Legia"
WAWELSKA
Park im. Józefa Piłsudskiego
Stadion „A.Z.S."
Stadion „Skra"
Obserwatorium
Astronomiczne
Ogród Botaniczny
KRAKÓW 2 (8, 7, E77)
ŁÓDŹ 2 (14)
OKĘCIE 634
GÓRA KALWARIA 7 (79)

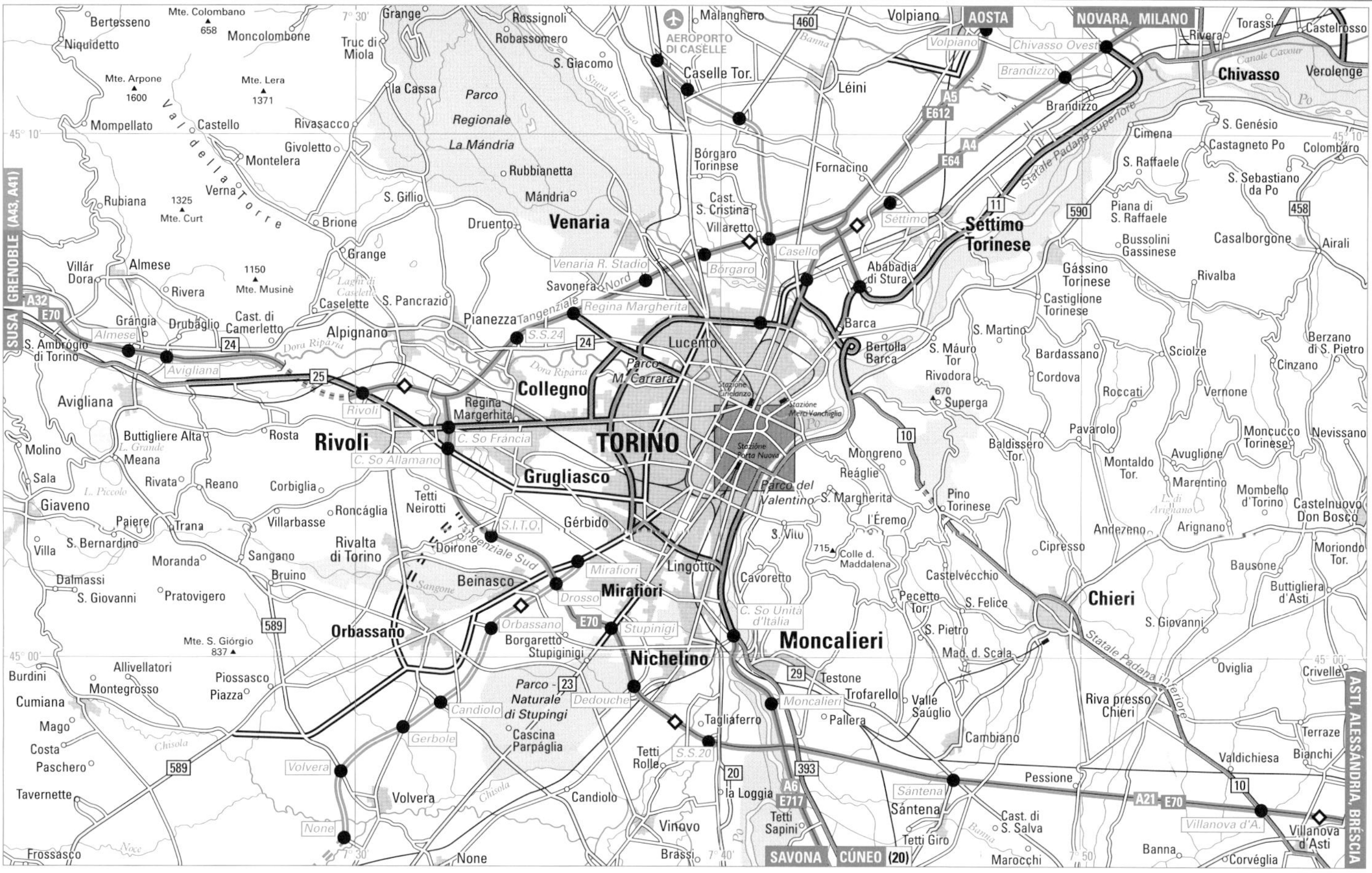

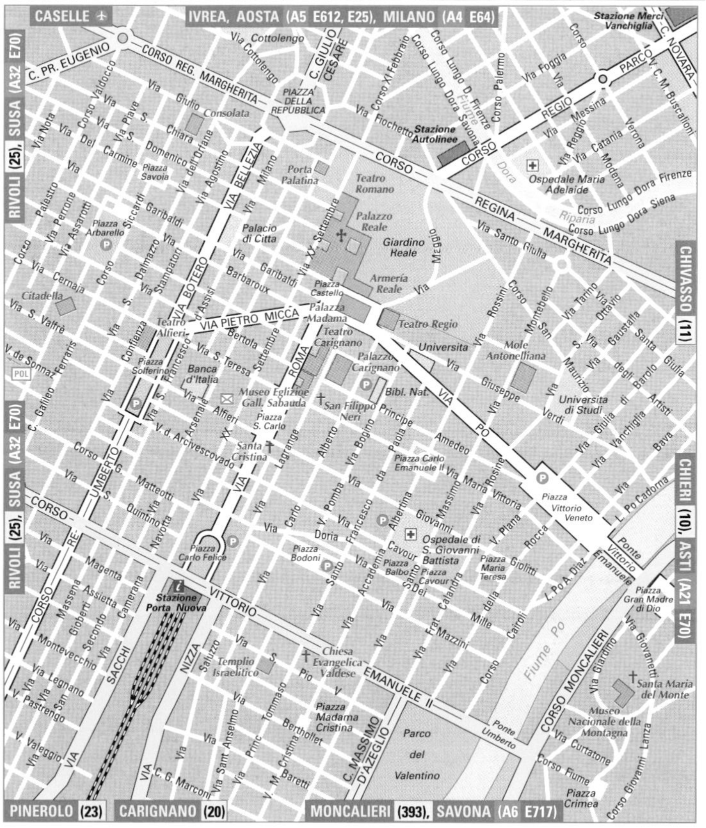

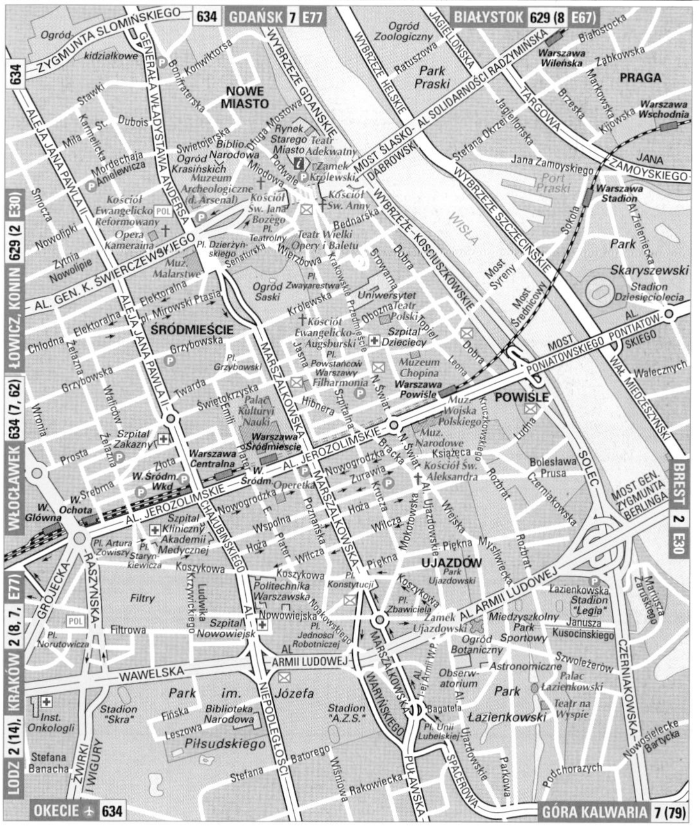

Wien

0 km 1

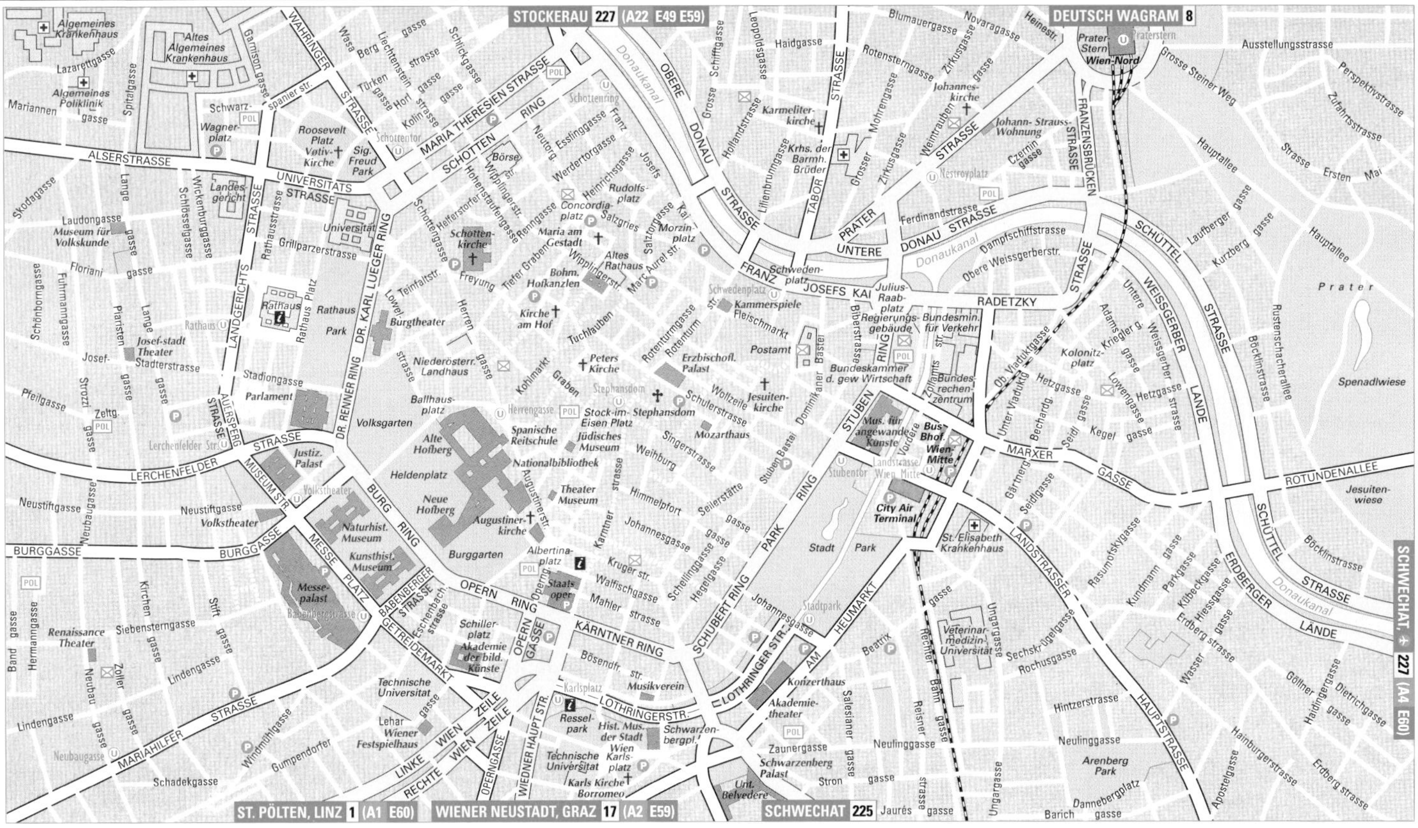

Wien

0 km 5

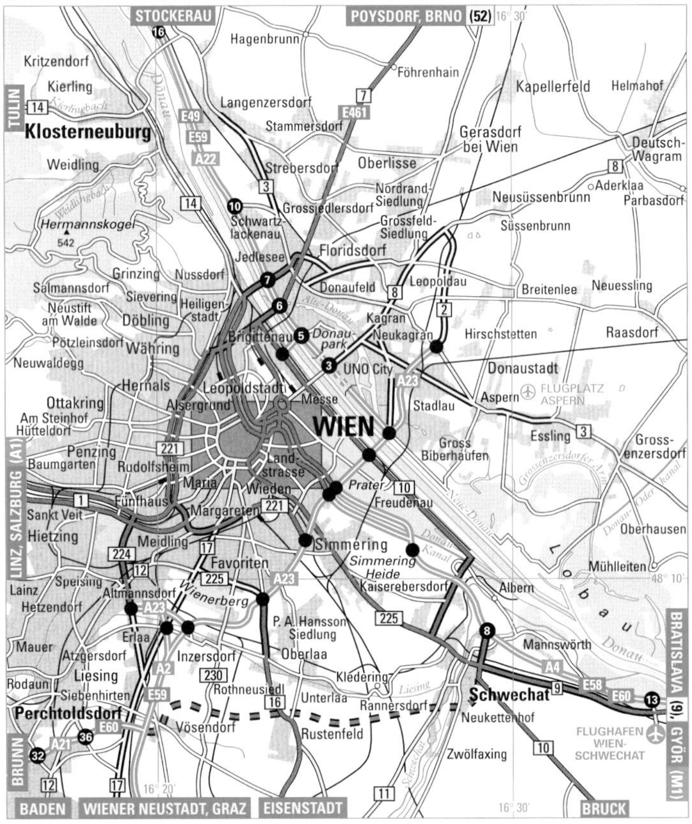

Zürich

0 km 0,5

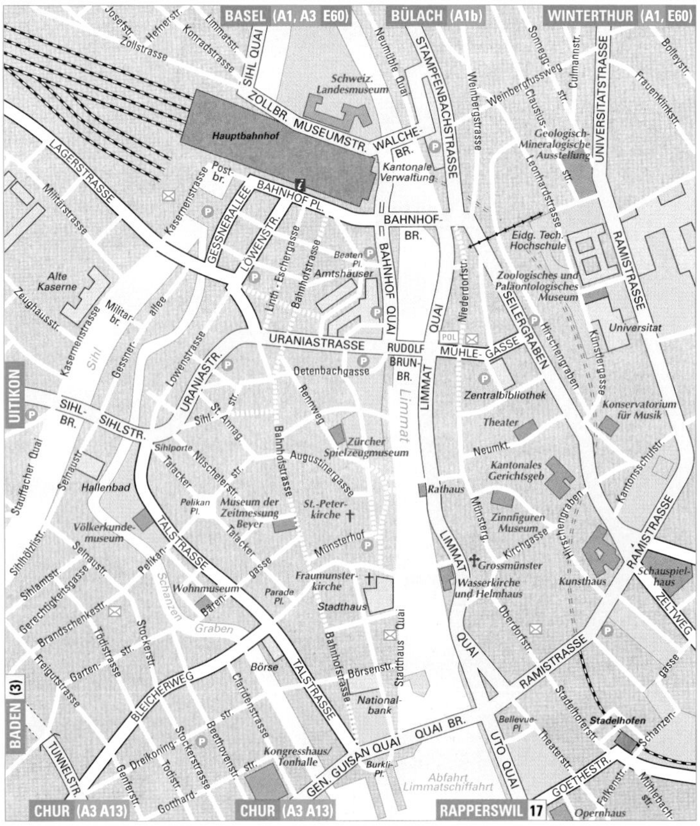

GB	F		D	I
Austria	Autriche	**A**	Österreich	Austria
Albania	Albanie	**AL**	Albanien	Albania
Andorra	Andorre	**AND**	Andorra	Andorra
Belgium	Belgique	**B**	Belgien	Belgio
Bulgaria	Bulgarie	**BG**	Bulgarien	Bulgaria
Bosnia-Hercegovina	Bosnia-Herzegovine	**BIH**	Bosnien-Herzegowina	Bosnia-Herzogovina
Belarus	Belarus	**BY**	Weißrussland	Bielorussia
Switzerland	Suisse	**CH**	Schweiz	Svizzera
Czech Republic	République Tchèque	**CZ**	Tschechische Republik	Repubblica Ceca
Germany	Allemagne	**D**	Deutschland	Germania
Denmark	Danemark	**DK**	Dänemark	Danimarca
Spain	Espagne	**E**	Spanien	Spagna
Estonia	Estonie	**EST**	Estland	Estonia
France	France	**F**	Frankreich	Francia
Finland	Finlande	**FIN**	Finnland	Finlandia
Liechtenstein	Liechtenstein	**FL**	Liechtenstein	Liechtenstein
United Kingdom	Royaume Uni	**GB**	Großbritannien und Nordirland	Regno Unito
Gibraltar	Gibraltar	**GBZ**	Gibraltar	Gibilterra
Greece	Grèce	**GR**	Greichenland	Grecia
Hungary	Hongrie	**H**	Ungarn	Ungheria
Croatia	Croatie	**HR**	Kroatien	Croazia
Italy	Italie	**I**	Italien	Italia
Ireland	Irlande	**IRL**	Irland	Irlanda
Luxembourg	Luxembourg	**L**	Luxemburg	Lussemburgo
Lithuania	Lituanie	**LT**	Litauen	Lituania
Latvia	Lettonie	**LV**	Lettland	Lettonia
Malta	Malte	**M**	Malta	Malta
Monaco	Monaco	**MC**	Monaco	Monaco
Moldavia	Moldavie	**MD**	Moldawien	Moldavia
Macedonia	Macédoine	**MK**	Makedonien	Macedonia
Norway	Norvège	**N**	Norwegen	Norvegia
Netherlands	Pays-Bas	**NL**	Niederlande	Paesi Bassi
Portugal	Portugal	**P**	Portugal	Portogallo
Poland	Pologne	**PL**	Polen	Polonia
Romania	Roumanie	**RO**	Rumanien	Romania
San Marino	Saint-Marin	**RSM**	San Marino	San Marino
Russia	Russie	**RUS**	Russland	Russia
Sweden	Suède	**S**	Schweden	Svezia
Slovak Republic	République Slovaque	**SK**	Slowak Republik	Repubblica Slovacca
Slovenia	Slovénie	**SLO**	Slowenien	Slovenia
Turkey	Turquie	**TR**	Türkei	Turchia
Ukraine	Ukraine	**UA**	Ukraine	Ucraina
Serbia and Montenegro	Serbie et Monténégro	**YU**	Serbien und Montenegro	Serbia e Montenegro

A

A Baña E 86 B2
A Bola E 87 B3
A Cañiza E 87 B2
A Capela E 86 A2
A Coruña E 86 A2
A Estrada E 86 B2
A Fonsagrada E 86 A3
A Guarda E 87 C2
A Gudiña E 87 B3
A Merca E 87 B3
A Peroxa E 86 B3
A Pontenova E 86 A3
A Rúa E 87 B3
A Teixeira E 87 B3
A Veiga E 87 B3
A-Ver-o-Mar P 87 C2
Aabybro DK 38 B2
Aach D 71 A4
Aachen D 50 C2
Aalen D 61 B6
Aalsmeer NL 49 A5
Aalst B 49 C5
Aalten NL 50 B2
Aalter B 49 B4
Äänekoski FIN 3 E19
Aarau CH 70 A3
Aarberg CH 70 A2
Aarburg CH 70 A2
Aardenburg NL 49 B4
Aarschot B 49 C5
Aba H 74 A3
Abádanes E 95 B4
Abades E 94 B2
Abadin E 86 A3
Abádszalók H 75 A5
Abaliget H 74 B3
Abanilla E 96 C1
Abano Terme I 72 C1
Abarán E 101 A4
Abasár H 65 C6
Abbadia San Salvatore I 81 D5
Abbehausen D 43 B5
Abbekäs S 41 D3
Abbeville F 48 C2
Abbey IRL 20 A3
Abbey Town GB 25 D4
Abbeydorney IRL 20 B2
Abbeyfeale IRL 20 B2
Abbeyleix IRL 21 B4
Abbiategrasso I 70 C3
Abbots Bromley GB 27 C4
Abbotsbury GB 29 C5
Abda H 64 C3
Abejar E 89 C4
Abela P 98 B2
Abenberg D 62 A1
Abenójar E 100 A1
Åbenrå DK 39 D2
Abensberg D 62 B2
Aberaeron GB 28 A3
Abercarn GB 29 B4
Aberchirder GB 23 D6
Aberdare GB 29 B4
Aberdaron GB 26 C1
Aberdeen GB 23 D6
Aberdulais GB 28 B4
Aberdyfi GB 26 C1
Aberfeldy GB 25 B4
Aberffraw GB 26 B1
Aberfoyle GB 24 B3
Abergavenny GB 29 B4
Abergele GB 26 B2
Abergynolwyn GB 26 C2
Aberporth GB 28 A3
Abersoch GB 26 C1
Abertillery GB 29 B4
Abertura E 93 B5
Aberystwyth GB 26 C1
Abetone I 81 B4
Abfaltersbach A 72 B2
Abiego E 90 A2
Abild DK 39 E1
Abingdon GB 31 C2
Abington GB 25 C4
Abiul P 92 B2
Abla E 101 B3
Ablis F 58 B2
Abondance F 70 B1
Abony H 75 A5
Aboyne GB 23 D6
Abrantes P 92 B2
Abrest F 68 B3
Abriès F 79 B5
Abrud RO 11 N18
Absdorf A 64 B1
Abtenau A 72 A3
Abtsgmünd D 61 B5
Abusejo E 93 A4
Åby, *Kronoberg* S 40 B4
Åby, *Östergötland* S 37 C3
Åbytorp S 36 B2
Acate I 109 B3
Accadia I 104 A2
Accéglio I 79 B5
Accettura I 104 B3
Acciaroli I 104 B2
Accous F 76 C2
Accrington GB 26 B3
Accúmoli I 82 D2
Acedera E 93 B5
Acehuche E 93 B4
Acered E 95 A5
Acerenza I 104 B2
Acerno I 104 B2
Acerra I 103 C4
Aceuchal E 93 C4
Acharacle GB 24 B2
Achavanich GB 23 C5
Achene B 49 C6
Achenkirch A 72 A1
Achensee A 72 A1
Achenthal A 72 A1
Achern D 61 B4
Acheux-en-Amienois F 48 C3
Achiltibuie GB 22 C3
Achim D 43 B6
Achnasheen GB 22 D3
Achnashellach GB 22 D3
Achosnich GB 24 B1
Aci Castello I 109 B4
Aci Catena I 109 B4
Acilia I 102 B2
Acireale I 109 B4
Acle GB 30 B5
Acquacadda I 110 D1
Acquanegra sul Chiese I 71 C5
Acquapendente I 81 D5
Acquasanta Terme I 82 D2
Acquasparta I 102 A2
Acquaviva I 81 C5
Acquaviva delle Fonti I 105 B3
Acquaviva Picena I 82 D2
Àcqui Terme I 80 B2
Acquigny F 58 A2
Acri I 106 B3
Acs H 64 C4
Acsa H 65 C5
Ácsteszér H 74 A2
Acy-en-Multien F 59 A3
Ada YU 75 C5
Adamuz E 100 A1
Adánd H 74 B3
Adanero E 94 B2
Adapazari TR 16 R22
Adare IRL 20 B3
Adaševci YU 85 A4
Adeanueva de Ebro E 89 B5
Adelboden CH 70 B2
Adelebsen D 51 B5
Adélfia I 105 A3
Adelmannsfelden D 61 B6
Adelsheim D 61 A5
Adelsö S 36 B4
Ademuz E 96 A1
Adenau D 50 C2
Adendorf D 44 B2
Adinkerke B 48 B3
Adjud RO 11 N20
Adliswil CH 70 A3
Admont A 73 A4
Ådneram N 32 B3
Adony H 74 A3
Adorf, *Hessen* D 51 B4
Adorf, *Sachsen* D 52 C2
Adra E 100 C2
Adradas E 89 C4
Adrall E 91 A4
Adrano I 109 B3
Ádria I 81 A6
Adrigole IRL 20 C2
Adwick le Street GB 27 B4
Adzaneta E 96 A2
Æroskøbing DK 39 E3
Aesch CH 70 A2
Affing D 62 B1
Affoltern CH 70 A3
Affric Lodge GB 22 D3
Åfjord N 2 E12
Aflenz Kurort A 73 A5
Afragóla I 103 C4
Afritz A 72 B3
Afyonkarahisar TR 16 S22
Ágasegyháza H 75 B4
Agay F 79 C5
Agazzano I 80 B3
Agde F 78 C2
Agen F 77 B3
Ager E 90 B3
Agerbæk DK 39 D1
Agerskov DK 39 D2
Ageyevo RUS 7 J25
Agger DK 38 C1
Aggersund DK 38 B2
Ággius I 110 C2
Aggsbach Dorf A 63 B6
Aggsbach Markt A 63 B6
Aggtelek H 65 B6
Aghalee GB 19 B5
Agiči BIH 83 B5
Agira I 109 B3
Ağlasun TR 16 T22
Aglientu I 110 B2
Agnières F 79 B4
Agno CH 70 C3
Agnone I 103 B4
Agolada E 86 B2
Agon Coutainville F 57 A4
Ágordo I 72 B2
Agost E 96 C2
Agramón E 101 A4
Agramunt E 91 B4
Agreda E 89 C5
Agrigento I 108 B2
Agrinion GR 15 S17
Agrón E 100 B2
Agrópoli I 104 B1
Agua Longa P 87 C2
Aguadulce, *Almeria* E 101 C3
Aguadulce, *Sevilla* E 100 B1
Agualada E 86 A2
Aguarón E 90 B1
Aguas E 90 A2
Aguas Belas P 92 B2
Aguas de Busot E 96 C2
Aguas de Moura P 92 C2
Águas Frias P 87 C3
Aguas Santas P 87 C2
Aguaviva E 90 C2
Aguaviva de la Vega E 95 A4
Agudo E 94 D2
Águeda P 92 A2
Aguessac F 78 B2
Agugliano I 82 C2
Aguiar P 92 C3
Aguiàr da Beira P 87 D3
Aguilafuente E 94 A2
Aguilar de Campóo E 88 B2
Aguilar de la Frontera E 100 B1
Aguilas E 101 B4
Ahaus D 50 A2
Ahigal E 93 A4
Ahigal de Villarino E 87 C4
Ahillones E 99 A5
Ahlbeck, *Mecklenburg-Vorpommern* D 45 B6
Ahlbeck, *Mecklenburg-Vorpommern* D 45 B6
Ahlen D 50 B3
Ahlhorn D 43 C5
Ahoghill GB 19 B5
Ahrensbök D 44 A2
Ahrensburg D 44 B2
Ahrenshoop D 44 A4
Ahun F 68 B2
Åhus S 41 D4
Aibar E 89 B5
Aich D 62 B3
Aicha D 63 B4
Aichach D 62 B2
Aidone I 109 B3
Aiello Cálabro I 106 B3
Aigen im Mühlkreis A 63 B4
Aigle CH 70 B1
Aignan F 76 C3
Aignay-le-Duc F 59 C5
Aigre F 67 C5
Aigrefeuille-d'Aunis F 66 B4
Aigrefeuille-sur-Maine F 66 A3
Aiguablava E 91 B6
Aiguebelle F 69 C6
Aigueperse F 68 B3
Aigues-Mortes F 78 C3
Aigues-Vives F 78 C1
Aiguilles F 79 B5
Aiguillon F 77 B3
Aigurande F 68 B1
Ailefroide F 79 B5
Aillant-sur-Tholon F 59 C4
Ailly-sur-Noye F 58 A3
Ailly-sur-Somme F 58 A3
Aimargues F 78 C3
Aime F 69 C6
Ainaži LV 6 H19
Ainet A 72 B2
Ainhoa F 76 C1
Ainsa E 90 A3
Airaines F 48 D2
Aird GB 24 B2
Aird Asaig Tairbeart GB 22 D2
Airdrie GB 25 C4
Aire-sur-la-Lys F 48 C3
Aire-sur-l'Adour F 76 C2
Airole I 80 C1
Airolo CH 70 B3
Airvault F 67 B4
Aisey-sur-Seine F 59 C5
Aissey F 69 A6
Aisy-sur-Armançon F 59 C5
Aiterhofen D 62 B3
Aith, *Orkney* GB 23 B6
Aith, *Shetland* GB 22 A7
Aitona E 90 B3
Aitrach D 61 C6
Aiud RO 11 N18
Aix-en-Othe F 59 B4
Aix-en-Provence F 79 C4
Aix-les-Bains F 69 C5
Aixe-sur-Vienne F 67 C6
Aiyion GR 15 S18
Aizenay F 66 B3
Aizkraukle LV 7 H19
Aizpute LV 6 H17
Ajaccio F 110 B1
Ajain F 68 B1
Ajdovščina SLO 72 C3
Ajka H 74 A2
Ajo E 89 A3
Ajofrin E 94 C3
Ajuda P 93 C3
Akasztó H 75 B4
Akçakoca TR 16 R21
Aken D 52 B2
Åkerby S 36 A4
Åkernes N 33 C4
Åkers styckebruk S 36 B4
Åkersberga S 36 B5
Akharnai GR 15 S18
Akhisar TR 16 S20
Åkirkeby DK 41 D4
Akkarfjord N 2 A18
Akkrum NL 42 B2
Åkra N 32 B3
Åkrehamn N 32 B2
Akşehir TR 16 S22
Aktsyabrski BY 7 K21
Åkvåg N 33 C6
Akyazı TR 16 R22
Ala I 71 C6
Alà dei Sardi I 110 C2
Ala di Stura I 70 C2
Alaejos E 88 C1
Alagna Valsésia I 70 C2
Alagón E 90 B1
Alaior, *Menorca* E 97
Alájar E 99 B4
Alakurtti RUS 3 C22
Alameda E 100 B1
Alameda de la Sagra E 94 B3
Alamedilla E 100 B2
Alamillo E 100 A1
Alaminos E 95 B4
Alandroal P 92 C3
Alange E 93 C4
Alanís E 99 A5
Alanno I 103 A3
Alap H 74 B3
Alaquáso E 96 B2
Alar del Rey E 88 B2
Alaraz E 94 B1
Alarcón E 95 C4
Alaró, *Mallorca* E 97
Alaşehir TR 16 S21
Alássio I 80 B2
Alatoz E 96 B1
Alatri I 103 B3
Alavus FIN 3 E18
Alba E 95 B5
Alba I 80 B2
Alba Adriática I 82 D2
Alba de Tormes E 94 B1
Alba de Yeltes E 93 A4
Alba-Iulia RO 11 N18
Albacete E 95 D5
Ålbæk DK 38 B3
Albaida E 96 C2
Albala del Caudillo E 93 B4
Albaladejo E 101 A3
Albalat E 96 B2
Albalate de Cinca E 90 B3
Albalate de las Nogueras E 95 B4
Albalate del Arzobispo E 90 B2
Albalete de Zorita E 95 B4
Alban F 77 C5
Albánchez E 101 B3
Albanchez de Ubeda E 100 B2
Albano Laziale I 102 B2
Albanyà E 91 A5
Albaredo d'Adige I 71 C6
Albares E 95 B3
Albarracín E 95 B5
Albatana E 101 A4
Albatarrec E 90 B3
Albatera E 96 C2
Albbruck D 61 C4
Albedin E 100 B1
Albelda de Iregua E 89 B4
Albenga I 80 B2
Albens F 69 C5
Ålberga, *Södermanland* S 36 B3
Ålberga, *Södermanland* S 37 C3
Albergaria-a-Nova P 87 D2
Albergaria-a-Velha P 92 A2
Albergaria dos Doze P 92 B2
Alberge P 92 C2
Alberic E 96 B2
Albernoa P 98 B3
Alberobello I 105 B4
Alberoni I 72 C2
Albersdorf D 43 A6
Albersloh D 50 B3
Albert F 48 C3
Albertirsa H 75 A4
Albertville F 69 C6
Alberuela de Tubo E 90 B2
Albi F 77 C5
Albidona I 106 B3
Albinia I 102 A1
Albino I 71 C4
Albires E 88 B1
Albisola Marina I 80 B2
Albocácer E 90 C3
Albolote E 100 B2
Albondón E 100 C2
Alborea E 96 B1
Ålborg DK 38 B2
Albox E 101 B3
Albrechtice nad Vitavou CZ 63 A5
Albstadt D 61 B5
Albufeira P 98 B2
Albuñol E 100 C2
Albuñuelas E 100 C2
Alburquerque E 93 B3
Alcácer do Sal P 92 C2
Alcáçovas P 92 C2
Alcadozo E 101 A4
Alcafoces P 93 B3
Alcains P 92 B3
Alcalá de Guadaira E 99 B5
Alcalá de Gurrea E 90 A2
Alcalá de Henares E 95 B3
Alcalá de la Selva E 90 C2
Alcalá de los Gazules E 99 C5
Alcalá de Xivert E 96 A3
Alcalá del Júcar E 96 B1
Alcalá del Río E 99 B5
Alcalá del Valle E 99 C5
Alcalá la Real E 100 B2
Álcamo I 108 B1
Alcampell E 90 B3
Alcanadre E 89 B4
Alcanar E 90 C3
Alcanede P 92 B2
Alcanena P 92 B2
Alcañices E 87 C4
Alcántara E 93 B4
Alcantarilha P 98 B2
Alcantarilla E 101 B4
Alcañiz E 90 B2
Alcara il Fusi I 109 A3
Alcaracejos E 100 A1
Alcaraz E 101 A3
Alcaria Ruiva P 98 B3
Alcarraz E 90 B3
Alcaudete E 100 B1
Alcaudete de la Jara E 94 C2
Alcázar de San Juan E 95 C3
Alcazarén E 88 C2
Alcester GB 29 A6
Alcoba E 94 C2
Alcobaça P 92 B1
Alcobendas E 95 B3
Alcocer E 95 B4
Alcochete P 92 C2
Alcoentre P 92 B2
Alcolea, *Almeria* E 100 C3
Alcolea, *Córdoba* E 100 B1
Alcolea de Calatrava E 94 D2
Alcolea de Cinca E 90 B3
Alcolea de Tajo E 94 C1
Alcolea del Pinar E 95 A4
Alcolea del Rio E 99 B5
Alcollarin E 93 B5
Alconchel E 93 C3
Alconera E 93 C4
Alcontar E 101 B3
Alcora E 96 A2
Alcorcón E 94 B3
Alcorisa E 90 C2
Alcossebre E 96 A3
Alcoutim P 98 B3
Alcover E 91 B4
Alcoy E 96 C2
Alcsútdoboz H 74 A3
Alcubierre E 90 B2
Alcubilla de Avellaneda E 89 C3
Alcubilla de Nogales E 88 B1
Alcubillas E 100 A2
Alcublas E 96 B2
Alcúdia, *Mallorca* E 97
Alcudia de Guadix E 100 B2
Alcuéscar E 93 B4
Aldbrough GB 27 B5
Aldea de Trujillo E 93 B5
Aldea del Cano E 93 B4
Aldea del Fresno E 94 B2
Aldea del Obispo E 93 A4
Aldea del Rey E 100 A2
Aldea Real E 94 A2
Aldeacentenera E 93 B5
Aldeadávila de la Ribera E 87 C4
Aldealcorvo E 94 A3
Aldealuenga de Santa Maria E 89 C3
Aldeamayor de San Martin E 88 C2
Aldeanueva de Barbarroya E 94 C1
Aldeanueva de San Bartolomé E 94 C1
Aldeanueva del Camino E 93 A5
Aldeanueva del Codonal E 94 A2
Aldeapozo E 89 C4
Aldeaquemada E 100 A2
Aldearrubia E 94 A1
Aldeaseca de la Frontera E 94 B1
Aldeasoña E 88 C2
Aldeatejada E 94 B1
Aldeavieja E 94 B2
Aldeburgh GB 30 B5
Aldehuela E 96 A1
Aldehuela de Calatañazor E 89 C4
Aldeia da Serra P 92 C3
Aldeia do Bispo P 93 A4
Aldeia do Mato P 92 B2
Aldeia Gavinha P 92 B1
Aldeire E 100 B2
Aldenhoven D 50 C2
Aldersbach D 62 B4
Aldershot GB 31 C3
Aldudes F 76 C1
Åled S 40 C2
Aledo E 101 B4
Alegria E 89 B4
Aleksa Šantić YU 75 C4
Aleksandrovac, *Srbija* YU 85 B6
Aleksandrovac, *Srbija* YU 85 C6
Aleksandrów Kujawski PL 47 C4
Aleksandrów Łódźki PL 55 B4
Aleksin RUS 7 J25
Ålem S 40 C6
Alençon F 57 B6
Alenquer P 92 B1
Alenya F 91 A5
Aléria F 110 A2
Alès F 78 B3
Áles I 110 D1
Alessándria I 80 B2
Alessándria della Rocca I 108 B2
Alessano I 107 B5
Ålestrup DK 38 C2
Ålesund N 2 E10
Alet-les-Bains F 77 D5
Alexandria GB 24 C3
Alexandria RO 16 Q19
Alexandroúpolis GR 16 R19
Alézio I 105 B5
Alfacar E 100 B2
Alfaiates P 93 A4
Alfajarin E 90 B2
Alfambra E 90 C1
Alfambra P 98 B2
Alfândega da Fé P 87 C4
Alfarela de Jafes P 87 C3
Alfarelos P 92 A2
Alfarim P 92 C1
Alfarnate E 100 C1
Alfaro E 89 B5
Alfarrás E 90 B3
Alfaz del Pi E 96 C2
Alfedena I 103 B4
Alfeizerão P 92 B1
Alfeld, *Bayern* D 62 A2
Alfeld, *Niedersachsen* D 51 B5
Alfena P 87 C2
Alferce P 98 B2
Alfhausen D 43 C4
Alfonsine I 81 B6
Alford, *Aberdeenshire* GB 23 D6
Alford, *Lincolnshire* GB 27 B6
Alforja E 90 B3
Alfoz E 86 A3
Alfreton GB 27 B4
Alfundão P 98 A2
Algaida, *Mallorca* E 97
Algar E 99 C5
Algarås S 35 C6
Ålgård N 32 C2
Algarinejo E 100 B1
Algarrobo E 100 C1
Algatocin E 99 C5
Algeciras E 99 C5
Algemesí E 96 B2
Algés P 92 C1
Algete E 95 B3
Alghero I 110 C1
Älghult S 40 B5
Alginet E 96 B2
Algodonales E 99 C5
Algodor E 94 C3
Algodor P 98 B3
Algora E 95 B4
Algoz P 98 B2
Alguaire E 90 B3
Alguazas E 101 A4
Algutsrum S 40 C6
Algyő H 75 B5
Alhama de Almería E 101 C3
Alhama de Aragón E 89 C5
Alhama de Granada E 100 C2
Alhama de Murcia E 101 B4
Alhambra E 100 A2
Alhandra P 92 C1
Alhaurin de la Torre E 100 C1
Alhaurin el Grande E 100 C1
Alhendin E 100 B2
Alhóndiga E 95 B4
Ali Terme I 109 B4
Alia E 94 C1
Ália I 108 B2
Aliaga E 90 C2
Aliağa TR 16 S20
Alibunar YU 85 A5
Alicante E 96 C2
Alicún de Ortega E 100 B2
Alife I 103 B4
Alija del Infantado E 88 B1
Alijó P 87 C3
Alimena I 109 B3
Alingsås S 35 D4
Alinyà E 91 A4
Aliseda E 93 B4
Alixan F 79 B4
Aljaraque E 99 B3
Aljezur P 98 B2
Aljorra E 101 B4
Aljubarrota P 92 B2
Aljucen E 93 B4
Aljustrel P 98 B2
Alken B 49 C6
Alkmaar NL 42 C1
Alkoven A 63 B5
Allaines F 58 B2
Allaire F 57 C3
Allanche F 68 C2
Alland A 64 B2
Allariz E 87 B3
Allassac F 67 C6
Allauch F 79 C4
Alleen N 33 C4
Allègre F 68 C3
Allemont F 69 C6
Allendale Town GB 25 D5
Allendorf D 51 C4
Allentsteig A 63 B6
Allepuz E 90 C2
Allersberg D 62 A2
Allershausen D 62 B2
Alles E 88 A2
Allevard F 69 C6
Allihies IRL 20 C1
Allingåbro DK 38 C3
Allmannsdorf D 61 C5
Allo E 89 B4
Alloa GB 25 B4
Allogny F 68 A2
Allones, *Eure et Loire* F 58 B2
Allones, *Maine-et-Loire* F 67 A5
Allonnes F 57 C6
Allons F 76 B2
Allos F 79 B5
Allstedt D 52 B1
Alltwalis GB 28 B3
Allumiere I 102 A1
Almaceda P 92 B3
Almacelles E 90 B3
Almachar E 100 C1
Almada P 92 C1
Almadén E 100 A1
Almadén de la Plata E 99 B4
Almadenejos E 100 A1
Almadrones E 95 B4
Almagro E 100 A2
Almajano E 89 C4
Almansa E 96 C1
Almansil P 98 B2
Almanza E 88 B1
Almaraz E 93 B5
Almargen E 99 C5
Almarza E 89 C4
Almásfüzitö H 64 C4
Almassora E 96 B2
Almazán E 89 C4
Almazul E 89 C4
Alme D 51 B4
Almedina E 101 A3
Almedinilla E 100 B1
Almeida E 87 C4
Almeida P 87 D4
Almeirim P 92 B2
Almelo NL 42 C3
Almenar E 90 B3
Almenar de Soria E 89 C4
Almenara E 96 B2
Almendra P 87 D3
Almendral E 93 C4
Almendral de la Cañada E 94 B2
Almendralejo E 93 C4
Almenno San Bartolomeo I 71 C4
Almere NL 42 C2
Almería E 101 C3

Almerimar E 101 C3
Almese I 80 A1
Almexial P 98 B3
Älmhult S 40 C4
Almodôvar P 98 B2
Almodóvar del Campo E 100 A1
Almodóvar del Pinar E 95 C5
Almodóvar del Río E 99 B5
Almofala P 87 D3
Almogia E 100 C1
Almoharin E 93 B4
Almonacid de la Sierra E 89 C5
Almonacid de Toledo E 94 C3
Almonaster la Real E 99 B4
Almondsbury GB 29 B5
Almonte E 99 B4
Almoradí E 96 C2
Almoraima E 99 C5
Almorox E 94 B2
Almoster P 92 B2
Älmsta S 36 B5
Almudena E 101 A4
Almudévar E 90 A2
Almuñécar E 100 C2
Almunge S 36 B5
Almuradiel E 100 A2
Almussafes E 96 B2
Alness GB 23 D4
Alnmouth GB 25 C6
Alnwick GB 25 C6
Álora E 100 C1
Alos d'Ensil E 91 A4
Alosno E 99 B3
Alozaina E 100 C1
Alpbach A 72 A1
Alpedrete de la Sierra E 95 B3
Alpedrinha P 92 A3
Alpen D 50 B2
Alpera E 96 C1
Alphen aan de Rijn NL 49 A5
Alpiarça P 92 B2
Alpignano I 80 A1
Alpirsbach D 61 B4
Alpu TR 16 S22
Alpuente E 96 B1
Alqueva P 98 A3
Alquézar E 90 A3
Als DK 38 C3
Alsasua E 89 B4
Alsdorf D 50 C2
Alselv DK 39 D1
Alsfeld D 51 C5
Alsike S 36 B4
Alsleben D 52 B1
Alsónémedi H 75 A4
Alsótold H 65 C5
Alsóújlak H 74 A1
Alstätte D 50 A2
Alsterbro S 40 C5
Alstermo S 40 C5
Alston GB 25 D5
Alt Ruppin D 45 C4
Alta N 3 B18
Älta S 36 B5
Altamura I 105 B3
Altarejos E 95 C4
Altaussee A 63 C4
Altavilla Irpina I 103 B4
Altavilla Silentina I 104 B2
Altdöbern D 53 B4
Altdorf CH 70 B3
Altdorf D 62 B3
Altdorf bei Nürnberg D 62 A2
Alte P 98 B2
Altea E 96 C2
Altedo I 81 B5
Altenweddingen D 52 A1
Altena D 50 B3
Altenau D 51 B6
Altenberg D 53 C3
Altenberge D 50 A3
Altenbruch D 43 B5
Altenburg D 52 C2
Altenfelden A 63 B4
Altengronau D 51 C5
Altenheim D 60 B3
Altenhundem D 50 B4
Altenkirchen, *Mecklenburg-Vorpommern* D 45 A5
Altenkirchen, *Radom* D 50 C3
Altenkunstadt D 52 C1
Altenmarkt A 63 C5
Altenmarkt D 62 B3
Altenmarkt im Pongall A 72 A3
Altensteig D 61 B4
Altentreptow D 45 B5
Altenwalde D 43 B5
Alter do Chão P 92 B3
Altfraunhofen D 62 B3
Altheim A 63 B4
Altheim D 61 A5
Althofen A 73 B4
Altıntas TR 16 S22
Altkirch F 60 C3
Altlandsberg D 45 C5
Altlewin D 45 C6
Altmannstein D 62 B2
Altmorschen D 51 B5
Altmunster A 63 C4
Altnaharra GB 23 C4
Alto Campoó E 88 A2
Altofonte I 108 A2
Altomonte I 106 B3
Alton, *Hampshire* GB 31 C3
Alton, *Staffordshire* GB 27 C4
Altopáscio I 81 C4
Altötting D 62 B3
Altreichenau D 63 B4
Altshausen D 61 C5
Altstätten CH 71 A4
Altura E 96 B2
Altusried D 61 C6
Alūksne LV 7 H20
Alunda S 36 A5
Alustante E 95 B5
Alva GB 25 B4
Alvaiázere P 92 B2
Alvalade P 98 B2
Älvängen S 35 D4
Alvarenga P 87 D2
Alvares P 92 A2
Alvdal N 2 E12
Älvdalen S 2 F14
Alverca P 92 C1
Alvesta S 40 C4
Alvignac F 77 B4
Alvignano I 103 B4
Alvimare F 58 A1
Alviobeira P 92 B2
Alvito P 98 A3
Älvkarleby S 36 A4
Älvkarleö bruk S 36 A4
Alvor P 98 B2
Alvorge P 92 B2
Alvøy N 32 A2
Älvsbacka S 34 B5
Älvsbyn S 3 D17
Älvsered S 40 B2
Alwernia PL 55 C4
Alwinton GB 25 C5
Alyth GB 25 B4
Alytus LT 6 J19
Alzénau D 51 C5
Alzey D 61 A4
Alzira E 96 B2
Alzonne F 77 C5
Amadora P 92 C1
Åmål S 35 B4
Amalfi I 103 C4
Amaliás GR 15 T17
Amance F 60 C2
Amancey F 69 A6
Amándola I 82 D2
Amantea I 106 B3
Amarante P 87 C2
Amareleja P 98 A3
Amares P 87 C2
Amaseno I 103 B3
Amatrice I 103 A3
Amay B 49 C6
Ambarnyy RUS 3 D23
Ambazac F 67 C6
Amberg D 62 A2
Ambérieu-en-Bugey F 69 C5
Ambérieux-en-Dombes F 69 B4
Ambert F 68 C3
Ambès F 76 A2
Ambjörby S 34 A5
Ambjörnarp S 40 B3
Amble GB 25 C6
Ambleside GB 26 A3
Ambleteuse F 48 C2
Amboise F 67 A5
Ambrières-les-Vallées F 57 B5
Amden CH 71 A4
Amel B 50 C2
Amélia I 102 A2
Amélie-les-Bains-Palalda F 91 A5
Amelinghausen D 44 B2
Amendoa P 92 B2
Amendoeira P 98 B3
Amendolara I 105 C3
Amer E 91 A5
Amerongen NL 49 A6
Amersfoort NL 49 A6
Amersham GB 31 C3
Ames E 86 B2
Amesbury GB 29 B6
Amfilokhia GR 15 S17
Amfípolis GR 15 R18
Amieira, *Évora* P 98 A3
Amieira, *Portalegre* P 92 B3
Amieiro P 92 A2
Amiens F 58 A3
Åminne S 40 B3
Åmli N 33 C5
Amlwch GB 26 B1
Ammanford GB 28 B4
Åmmeberg S 37 C1
Amorbach D 61 A5
Amorebieta E 89 A4
Amorosa P 87 C2
Amorosi I 103 B4
Åmot, *Buskerud* N 33 B6
Åmot, *Telemark* N 33 B4
Åmotfors S 34 B4
Åmotsdal N 33 B5
Amou F 76 C2
Ampezzo I 72 B2
Ampfing D 62 B3
Ampflwang A 63 B4
Amplepuis F 69 C4
Amposta E 90 C3
Ampthill GB 30 B3
Ampudia E 88 C2
Ampuero E 89 A3
Amriswil CH 71 A4
Amstelveen NL 49 A5
Amsterdam NL 42 C1
Amstetten A 63 B5
Amtzell D 61 C5
Amulree GB 25 B4
Amurrio E 89 A4
Amusco E 88 B2
An t-Ob GB 22 D1
Åna-Sira N 32 C3
Anacapri I 103 C4
Anadia P 92 A2
Anadon E 90 C1
Anagni I 102 B3
Ananyiv UA 11 N21
Anascaul IRL 20 B1
Ånäset S 3 D17
Anastaźewo PL 47 C4
Anaya de Alba E 94 B1
Ança P 92 A2
Ancaster GB 27 C5
Ancede P 87 C2
Ancenis F 66 A3
Ancerville F 59 B6
Anchuras E 94 C2
Ancona I 82 C2
Ancora P 87 C2
Ancrum GB 25 C5
Ancy-le-Franc F 59 C5
Andalo I 71 B5
Åndalsnes N 2 E10
Andance F 69 C4
Andau A 64 C3
Andebu N 34 B2
Andeer CH 71 B4
Andelfingen CH 61 C4
Andelot F 59 B6
Andelot-en-Montagne F 69 B5
Andenes N 2 B15
Andenne B 49 C6
Anderlues B 49 C5
Andermatt CH 70 B3
Andernach D 50 C3
Andernos-les-Bains F 76 B1
Anderslöv S 41 D3
Anderstorp S 40 B3
Andijk NL 42 C2
Andoain E 89 A4
Andocs H 74 B2
Andolsheim F 60 B3
Andorra E 90 C2
Andorra La Vella AND 91 A4
Andosilla E 89 B5
Andover GB 31 C2
Andratx, *Mallorca* E 97
Andreapol RUS 7 H23
Andreas GB 26 A1
Andréspol PL 55 B4
Andrest F 76 C3
Andretta I 104 B2
Andrezieux-Bouthéon F 69 C4
Ándria I 104 A3
Andrijevica YU 85 D4
Ándros GR 16 T19
Andrychów PL 65 A5
Andselv N 3 B16
Andújar E 100 A1
Anduze F 78 B2
Åneby N 34 A2
Aneby S 40 B4
Añes E 89 A3
Anet F 58 B2
Anfo I 71 C5
Ang S 40 B4
Anga S 37 D5
Angaïs F 76 C2
Ånge S 2 E14
Angeja P 92 A2
Ängelholm S 41 C2
Ängelsberg S 36 B3
Anger A 73 A5
Angera I 70 C3
Angermünde D 45 B6
Angern A 64 B2
Angers F 67 A4
Angerville F 58 B3
Anghiari I 82 C1
Angle GB 28 B2
Anglès E 91 B5
Anglés, *Tarn* F 77 C5
Angles, *Vendée* F 66 B3
Angles sur l'Anglin F 67 B5
Anglesola E 91 B4
Anglet F 76 C1
Anglure F 59 B4
Angoulême F 67 C5
Angoulins F 66 B3
Angsö S 36 B3
Angües E 90 A2
Anguiano E 89 B4
Anguillara Sabazia I 102 A2
Anguillara Véneta I 72 C1
Anhée B 49 C5
Anholt DK 38 C4
Aniane F 78 C2
Aniche F 49 C4
Änimskog S 35 C4
Anina RO 10 P17
Anizy-le-Château F 59 A4
Anjalankoski FIN 3 F20
Ankaran SLO 72 C3
Ankarsrum S 37 D3
Anklam D 45 B5
Ankum D 43 C4
Anlauftal A 72 A3
Annaberg A 63 C6
Annaberg-Buchholz D 52 C3
Annaberg im Lammertal A 72 A3
Annaburg D 52 B3
Annahütte D 53 B3
Annalong GB 19 B6
Annan GB 25 D4
Anneberg, *Halland* S 35 D4
Anneberg, *Jönköping* S 40 B4
Annecy F 69 C6
Annelund S 35 D5
Annemasse F 69 B6
Annerstad S 40 C3
Annestown IRL 21 B4
Annevoie-Rouillon B 49 C5
Annonay F 69 C4
Annot F 79 C5
Annweiler D 60 A3
Añora E 100 A1
Anould F 60 B2
Anquela del Ducado E 95 B4
Anröchte D 50 B4
Ans DK 39 C2
Ansager DK 39 D1
Ansbach D 61 A6
Anse F 69 C4
Anserœul B 49 C4
Ansfelden A 63 B5
Ansião P 92 B2
Ansó E 76 D2
Ansoain E 89 B5
Anstruther GB 25 B5
Antalya TR 16 T22
Antas E 101 B4
Antegnate I 71 C4
Antequera E 100 B1
Anterselva di Mezzo I 72 B2
Antibes F 79 C6
Antigüedad E 88 C2
Antillo I 109 B4
Antoing B 49 C4
Antonin PL 54 B2
Antrain F 57 B4
Antrim GB 19 B5
Antrodoco I 102 A3
Antronapiana I 70 B3
Antuzede P 92 A2
Antwerpen B 49 B5
Anversa d'Abruzzi I 103 B3
Anvin F 48 C3
Anzat-le-Luguet F 68 C3
Anzi I 104 B2
Ánzio I 102 B2
Anzola d'Emilia I 81 B5
Anzón E 89 C5
Aoiz E 76 D1
Aosta I 70 C2
Apalhão P 92 B3
Apátfalva H 75 B5
Apatin YU 75 C4
Apatity RUS 3 C23
Apc H 65 C5
Apécchio I 82 C1
Apeldoorn NL 50 A1
Apen D 43 B4
Apenburg D 44 C3
Apensen D 43 B6
Apiro I 82 C2
Apolda D 52 B1
Apostag H 75 B3
Äppelbo S 34 A6
Appennino I 82 D2
Appenzell CH 71 A4
Appiano I 71 B6
Appingedam NL 42 B3
Appleby-in-Westmorland GB 26 A3
Applecross GB 22 D3
Appledore GB 28 B3
Appoigny F 59 C4
Apremont-la-Forêt F 60 B1
Aprica I 71 B5
Apricena I 104 A2
Aprigliano I 106 B3
Aprilia I 102 B2
Apt F 79 C4
Apúlia P 87 C2
Aquiléia I 72 C3
Aquilónia I 104 B2
Aquino I 103 B3
Arabayona E 94 A1
Arabba I 72 B1
Aracena E 99 B4
Arad RO 75 B6
Aradac YU 75 C5
Aragona I 108 B2
Aramits F 76 C2
Aramon F 78 C3
Aranda de Duero E 88 C3
Aranda de Moncayo E 89 C5
Arandjelovac YU 85 B5
Aranjuez E 95 B3
Arantzazu E 89 B4
Aranzueque E 95 B3
Aras de Alpuente E 96 B1
Arauzo de Miel E 89 C3
Arazede P 92 A2
Arbas F 77 D3
Árbatax I 110 D2
Arbeca E 90 B3
Arberg D 62 A1
Arbesbach A 63 B5
Arboga S 36 B2
Arbois F 69 B5
Arbon CH 71 A4
Arborea I 110 D1
Arbório I 70 C3
Arbroath GB 25 B5
Arbùcies E 91 B5
Arbuniel E 100 B2
Arbus I 110 D1
Arc-en-Barrois F 59 C5
Arc-et-Senans F 69 A5
Arc-lès-Gray F 69 A5
Arc-sur-Tille F 69 A5
Arcachon F 76 B1
Arce I 103 B3
Arcen NL 50 B2
Arces-Dilo F 59 B4
Arcévia I 82 C1
Archena E 101 A4
Archez E 100 C2
Archiac F 67 C4
Archidona E 100 B1
Archiestown GB 23 D5
Archivel E 101 A4
Arcidosso I 81 D5
Arcille I 81 D5
Arcis-sur-Aube F 59 B5
Arco I 71 C5
Arcones E 94 A3
Arcos E 88 B3
Arcos de Jalón E 95 A4
Arcos de la Frontera E 99 C5
Arcos de la Sierra E 95 B4
Arcos de las Salinas E 96 B1
Arcos de Valdevez P 87 C2
Arcozelo P 92 A3
Arcusa E 90 A3
Arcy-sur-Cure F 59 C4
Ardagh IRL 20 B2
Årdal N 32 B3
Ardala S 35 C5
Ardales E 100 C1
Ardara I 110 C1
Ardara IRL 18 B3
Ardarroch GB 22 D3
Ardbeg GB 24 C1
Ardcharnich GB 22 D3
Ardchyle GB 24 B3
Ardee IRL 19 C5
Arden DK 38 C2
Ardentes F 68 B1
Ardenza I 81 C4
Ardersier GB 23 D4
Ardes F 68 C3
Ardessie GB 22 D3
Ardez CH 71 B5
Ardfert IRL 20 B2
Ardgay GB 23 D4
Ardglass GB 19 B6
Ardgroom IRL 20 C1
Ardhasig GB 22 D2
Ardisa E 90 A2
Ardkearagh IRL 20 C1
Ardlui GB 24 B3
Ardlussa GB 24 B2
Ardón E 88 B1
Ardooie B 49 C4
Ardore I 106 C3
Ardres F 48 C2
Ardrishaig GB 24 B2
Ardrossan GB 24 C3
Are N 32 B2
Åre S 2 E13
Areia Branca P 92 B1
Aremark N 34 B3
Arenales de San Gregorio E 95 C3
Arenas E 100 C1
Arenas de Iguña E 88 A2
Arenas de San Juan E 95 C3
Arenas de San Pedro E 94 B1
Arenas del Rey E 100 C2
Arendal N 33 C5
Arendonk B 49 B6
Arengosse F 76 B2
Arentorp S 35 C4
Arenys de Mar E 91 B5
Arenys de Munt E 91 B5
Arenzano I 80 B2
Areo E 91 A4
Ares E 86 A2
Arès F 76 B1
Ares del Maestrat E 90 C2
Arette F 76 C2
Aretxabaleta E 89 A4
Arevalillo E 94 B1
Arévalo E 94 A2
Arez P 92 B3
Arezzo I 81 C5
Arfeuilles F 68 B3
Argallón E 99 A5
Argamasilla de Alba E 95 C3
Argamasilla de Calatrava E 100 A1
Arganda E 95 B3
Arganil P 92 A2
Argegno I 71 C4
Argelès-Gazost F 76 C2
Argelès-sur-Mer F 91 A6
Argent-sur-Sauldre F 68 A2
Argenta I 81 B5
Argentan F 57 B5
Argentat F 77 A4
Argentera I 79 B5
Argenteuil F 58 B3
Argenthal D 50 D3
Argentiera I 110 C1
Argenton-Château F 67 B4
Argenton-sur-Creuse F 67 B6
Argentona E 91 B5
Argentré F 57 B5
Argentré-du-Plessis F 57 B4
Árgos GR 15 T18
Argostólion GR 15 S17
Argote E 89 B4
Arguedas E 89 B5
Argueil F 58 A2
Arholma S 36 B6
Århus DK 39 C3
Ariano Irpino I 104 A2
Ariano nel Polésine I 82 B1
Aribe E 76 D1
Arienzo I 103 B4
Arild S 41 C2
Arileod GB 24 B1
Arilje YU 85 C5
Arinagour GB 24 B1
Ariño E 90 B2
Arinthod F 69 B5
Arisaig GB 24 B2
Arisgotas E 94 C3
Aritzo I 110 D2
Ariza E 89 C4
Årjäng S 34 B4
Arjeplog S 3 C16
Arjona E 100 B1
Arjonilla E 100 B1
Arkelstorp S 41 C4
Arklow IRL 21 B5
Arkösund S 37 C3
Ärla S 36 B3
Arlanc F 68 C3
Arlanzón E 89 B3
Arlebosc F 78 A3
Arlena di Castro I 102 A1
Arles F 78 C3
Arles-sur-Tech F 91 A5
Arló H 65 B6
Arlon B 60 A1
Armação de Pera P 98 B2
Armadale, *Highland* GB 22 D3
Armadale, *West Lothian* GB 25 C4
Armagh GB 19 B5
Armamar P 87 C3
Armeno I 70 C3
Armenteros E 94 B1
Armentières F 48 C3
Armilla E 100 B2
Armiñón E 89 B4
Armoy GB 19 A5
Armuña de Tajuña E 95 B3
Arnac-Pompadour F 67 C6
Arnage F 57 C6
Arnas F 69 B4
Årnäs S 35 C5
Arnay-le-Duc F 69 A4
Arnborg DK 39 C2
Arnbruck D 62 A3
Arneburg D 44 C4
Arnedillo E 89 B4
Arnedo E 89 B4
Arneguy F 76 C1
Arnés E 90 C3
Årnes N 34 B3
Arnfels A 73 B5
Arnhem NL 50 B1
Arnö S 37 C4
Arnold GB 27 B4
Arnoldstein A 72 B3
Arnsberg D 50 B4
Arnschwang D 62 A3
Arnsdorf D 53 B3
Arnside GB 26 A3
Arnstadt D 51 C6
Arnstein D 51 D5
Arnstorf D 62 B3
Arnum DK 39 D1
Aroche E 99 B4
Áróktő H 65 C6
Arolla CH 70 B2
Arolsen D 51 B5
Arona I 70 C3
Åros N 34 B2
Arosa CH 71 B4
Arosa P 87 C2
Arøsund DK 39 D2
Arouca P 87 D2
Årøysund N 34 B2
Arpajon F 58 B3
Arpajon-sur-Cère F 77 B5
Arpino I 103 B3
Arquata del Tronto I 82 D2
Arques F 48 C3
Arques-la-Bataille F 58 A2
Arquillos E 100 A2
Arraia-Maeztu E 89 B4
Arraiolos P 92 C2
Arrancourt F 60 B2
Arras F 48 C3
Arrasate E 89 A4
Arreau F 77 D3
Arredondo E 89 A3
Arrens-Marsous F 76 D2
Arriate E 99 C5
Arrifana P 98 B2
Arrigorriaga E 89 A4
Arriondas E 88 A1
Arroba de los Montes E 94 C2
Arrochar GB 24 B3
Arromanches-les-Bains F 57 A5
Arronches P 92 B3
Arroniz E 89 B4
Arrou F 58 B2
Arroya E 88 B2
Arroya de Cuéllar E 88 C2
Arroyal E 88 B2
Arroyo de la Luz E 93 B4
Arroyo de San Servan E 93 C4
Arroyo del Ojanco E 100 A3
Arroyomolinos de León E 99 A4
Arroyomolinos de Montánchez E 93 B4
Arruda dos Vinhos P 92 C1
Års DK 38 C2
Ars-en-Ré F 66 B3
Ars-sur-Moselle F 60 A2
Arsac F 76 B2
Arsiè I 72 C1
Arsiero I 71 C6
Årslev DK 39 D3
Ársoli I 102 A3
Årsunda S 36 A3
Artà, *Mallorca* E 97
Arta GR 15 S17
Artajona E 89 B5
Artegna I 72 B3
Arteixo E 86 A2
Artemare F 69 C5
Arten I 72 B1
Artena I 102 B2
Artenay F 58 B2
Artern D 52 B1
Artés E 91 B4
Artesa de Segre E 91 B4
Arth CH 70 A3
Arthez-de-Béarn F 76 C2
Arthon-en-Retz F 66 A3
Arthurstown IRL 21 B5
Artieda E 90 A2
Artix F 76 C2
Artsyz UA 11 N21
Artziniega E 89 A3
Arudy F 76 C2
Arundel GB 31 D3
Årup DK 39 D3
Arveyres F 76 B2
Arvidsjaur S 3 D16
Arvieux F 79 B5
Arvika S 34 B4
Åryd, *Blekinge* S 41 C5
Åryd, *Kronoberg* S 40 C4
Arzachena I 110 B2
Arzacq-Arraziguet F 76 C2
Arzano F 56 C2
Aržano HR 84 C1
Arzberg D 52 C2
Arzignano I 71 C6
Arzila P 92 A2
Arzl im Pitztal A 71 A5
Arzúa E 86 B2
As B 49 B6
Aš CZ 52 C2
Ås N 34 B2
As Neves E 87 B2
As Nogais E 86 B3
As Pontes de García Rodríguez E 86 A3
Aså DK 38 B3
Åsa S 38 B5
Ašanja YU 85 B5
Åsarna S 2 E14
Åsarp S 35 C5
Asasp F 76 C2
Åsbro S 37 C2
Asby S 37 D2
Ascain F 76 C1
Ascea I 104 B2
Ascha D 62 A3
Aschach an der Donau A 63 B5
Aschaffenburg D 51 D5
Aschbach Markt A 63 B5
Ascheberg, *Nordrhein-Westfalen* D 50 B3
Ascheberg, *Schleswig-Holstein* D 44 A2
Aschendorf D 43 B4
Aschersleben D 52 B1
Asciano I 81 C5
Ascó E 90 B3
Áscoli Piceno I 82 D2
Áscoli Satriano I 104 A2
Ascona CH 70 B3
Ascot GB 31 C3
Ascoux F 58 B3
Åseda S 40 B5
Asendorf D 43 C6
Asenovgrad BG 16 Q19
Åsensbruk S 35 C4
Åseral N 33 C4
Asfeld F 59 A5
Åsgårdstrand N 34 B2
Ash, *Kent* GB 31 C5
Ash, *Surrey* GB 31 C3
Åshammar S 36 A3
Ashbourne GB 27 B4
Ashbourne IRL 21 A5
Ashburton GB 28 C4
Ashby de-la-Zouch GB 27 C4
Ashchurch GB 29 B5
Ashford GB 31 C4
Ashington GB 25 C6
Ashley GB 26 C3
Ashmyany BY 7 J19
Ashton Under Lyne GB 26 B3
Ashwell GB 30 B3
Asiago I 71 C6
Asipovichy BY 7 K21
Askam-in-Furness GB 26 A2
Askeaton IRL 20 B3
Asker N 34 B2
Askersund S 37 C1
Askim N 34 B3
Askland N 33 C5
Äsköping S 36 B3
Askøy N 2 F9
Åsljunga S 41 C3
Asnæs DK 39 D4
Ásola I 71 C5
Asolo I 72 C1
Asotthalom H 75 B4
Aspach A 63 B4
Aspang Markt A 73 A6
Aspariegos E 88 C1
Asparn an der Zaya A 64 B2
Aspatria GB 26 A2
Aspberg S 34 B5
Aspe E 96 C2
Aspet F 77 C3
Äspö S 41 C5
Aspres-sur-Buëch F 79 B4
Assafora P 92 C1
Asse B 49 C5
Assel D 43 B6
Asselborn L 50 C1
Assémini I 110 D1
Assen NL 42 C3
Assenede B 49 B4
Assens, *Aarhus Amt.* DK 38 C3
Assens, *Fyns Amt.* DK 39 D2
Assesse B 49 C6
Assisi I 82 C1
Assling D 62 C3
Asso I 71 C4
Ássoro I 109 B3
Assumar P 92 B3
Astaffort F 77 B3
Asten NL 50 B1
Asti I 80 B2
Astorga E 86 B4
Åstorp S 41 C2
Astudillo E 88 B2
Asuni I 110 D1
Asványráró H 64 C3
Aszód H 65 C5
Aszófő H 74 B2
Atalaia P 92 B3
Atalho P 92 C2
Átány H 65 C6
Atanzón E 95 B3
Ataquines E 94 A2
Atarfe E 100 B2
Ateca E 89 C5
Atella I 104 B2
Atessa I 103 A4
Ath B 49 C4
Athboy IRL 19 C5
Athea IRL 20 B2
Athenry IRL 20 A3
Atherstone GB 27 C4
Athies F 59 A3
Athies-sous-Laon F 59 A4
Athinai GR 15 T18
Athleague IRL 20 A3
Athlone IRL 21 A4
Athy IRL 21 B5
Atienza E 95 A4
Atina I 103 B3
Átkár H 65 C5
Åtorp S 36 B1
Åtrå N 33 B5
Åtran S 40 B2
Atri I 103 A3
Atripalda I 103 C4
Attendorn D 50 B3
Attichy F 59 A4
Attigliano I 102 A2
Attigny F 59 A5
Attleborough GB 30 B5
Åtvidaberg S 37 C2
Atzendorf D 52 B1
Au, *Steiermark* A 63 C6
Au, *Vorarlberg* A 71 A4
Au, *Bayern* D 62 B2
Au, *Bayern* D 62 C2
Aub D 61 A6
Aubagne F 79 C4
Aubange B 60 A1
Aubel B 50 C1
Aubenas F 78 B3
Aubenton F 59 A5
Auberive F 59 C6
Aubeterre-sur-Dronne F 67 C5
Aubiet F 77 C3
Aubigné F 67 B4
Aubigny F 66 B3
Aubigny-au-Bac F 49 C4
Aubigny-en-Artois F 48 C3
Aubigny-sur-Nère F 68 A2
Aubin F 77 B5
Aubonne CH 69 B6
Aubrac F 78 B1
Aubusson F 68 C2
Auch F 77 C3
Auchencairn GB 25 D4
Auchinleck GB 24 C3
Auchterarder GB 25 B4
Auchtermuchty GB 25 B4
Auchtertyre GB 22 D3
Audenge F 76 B1
Auderville F 57 A4
Audierne F 56 B1
Audincourt F 70 A1
Audlem GB 26 C3
Audruicq F 48 C3
Audun-le-Roman F 60 A1
Audun-le-Tiche F 60 A1
Aue, *Nordrhein-Westfalen* D 50 B4
Aue, *Sachsen* D 52 C2
Auerbach, *Bayern* D 62 A2
Auerbach, *Sachsen* D 52 C2
Auffach A 72 A2
Augher GB 19 B4
Aughnacloy GB 19 B5
Aughrim IRL 21 B5
Augignac F 67 C5
Augsburg D 62 B1
Augusta I 109 B4
Augustenborg DK 39 E2
Augustfehn D 43 B4
Augustów PL 6 K18
Aukrug D 44 A1
Auldearn GB 23 D5
Aulendorf D 61 C5
Auletta I 104 B2
Aulla I 81 B3
Aullène F 110 B2
Aulnay F 67 B4
Aulnoye-Aymeries F 49 C4
Ault F 48 C2
Aultbea GB 22 D3
Aulum DK 39 C1
Aulus-les-Bains F 77 D4
Auma D 52 C1
Aumale F 58 A2
Aumetz F 60 A1
Aumont-Aubrac F 78 B2
Aunay-en-Bazois F 68 A3
Aunay-sur-Odon F 57 A5
Auneau F 58 B2
Auneuil F 58 A2
Auning DK 39 C3
Aups F 79 C5
Aura D 51 C5
Auray F 56 C3
Aurich D 43 B4
Aurignac F 77 C3
Aurillac F 77 B5
Auriol F 79 C4
Auritz-Burguette E 76 D1
Auronzo di Cadore I 72 B2
Auros F 76 B2
Auroux F 78 B2
Aurskog N 34 B3
Aursmoen N 34 B3
Ausónia I 103 B3
Ausservillgraton A 72 B2
Austad N 33 C4
Austbygda N 33 A5
Aústis I 110 C2
Austmarka N 34 A4
Austre Moland N 33 C5
Austre Vikebygd N 32 B2
Auterive F 77 C4
Autheuil-Authouillet F 58 A2
Authon F 79 B5
Authon-du-Perche F 58 B1
Autol E 89 B5
Autreville F 60 B1
Autrey-lès-Gray F 69 A5
Autun F 69 B4
Auty-le-Châtel F 58 C3
Auvelais B 49 C5
Auvillar F 77 B3
Auxerre F 59 C4
Auxi-le-Château F 48 C3
Auxon F 59 B4
Auxonne F 69 A5
Auxy F 69 B4
Auzances F 68 B2
Auzon F 68 C3
Availles-Limouzine F 67 B5
Avaldsnes N 32 B2
Avallon F 68 A3
Avebury GB 29 B6
Aveiras de Cima P 92 B2
Aveiro P 92 A2
Avelgem B 49 C4
Avellino I 103 C4
Avenches CH 70 B2
Aversa I 103 C4
Avesnes-le-Comte F 48 C3
Avesnes-sur-Helpe F 49 C4

Avesta S 36 A3
Avetrana I 105 B4
Avezzano I 103 A3
Avià E 91 A4
Aviano I 72 B2
Aviemore GB 23 D5
Avigliana I 80 A1
Avigliano I 104 B2
Avignon F 78 C3
Ávila E 94 B2
Avilés E 88 A1
Avintes P 87 C2
Avinyo E 91 B4
Àvio I 71 C5
Avioth F 59 A6
Avis P 92 B3
Avize F 59 B5
Ávola I 109 C4
Avon F 58 B3
Avonmouth GB 29 B5
Avord F 68 A2
Avranches F 57 B4
Avril F 60 A1
Avrillé F 67 A4
Avtovac BIH 84 C3
Awans B 49 C6
Ax-les-Thermes F 91 A4
Axams A 71 A6
Axat F 77 D5
Axbridge GB 29 B5
Axel NL 49 B4
Axminster GB 29 C4
Axvall S 35 C5
Ay F 59 A5
Aya E 89 A4
Ayamonte E 98 B3
Aydın TR 16 T20
Ayelo de Malferit E 96 C2
Ayer CH 70 D2
Ayerbe E 90 A2
Ayette F 48 C3
Ayia GR 15 S18
Aylesbury GB 31 C3
Ayllón E 89 C3
Aylsham GB 30 B5
Ayna E 101 A3
Ayódar E 96 B2
Ayora E 96 B1
Ayr GB 24 C3
Ayron F 67 B5
Aysgarth GB 27 A4
Ayton GB 25 C5
Aytos BG 16 Q20
Ayvacık TR 16 S20
Ayvalık TR 16 S20
Aywaille B 49 C6
Azaila E 90 B2
Azambuja P 92 B2
Azambujeira P 92 B2
Azanja YU 85 B5
Azannes-et-Soumazannes F 60 A1
Azanúy-Alins E 90 B3
Azaruja P 92 C3
Azay-le-Ferron F 67 B6
Azay-le-Rideau F 67 A5
Azcoitia E 89 A4
Azé F 69 B4
Azeiteiros P 92 B3
Azenhas do Mar P 92 C1
Azinhaga P 92 B2
Azinhal P 98 B3
Azinheira dos Bairros P 98 A2
Aznalcázar E 99 B4
Aznalcóllar E 99 B4
Azóia P 92 B2
Azpeitia E 89 A4
Azuaga E 99 A5
Azuara E 90 B2
Azuqueca de Henares E 95 B3
Azur F 76 C1
Azzano Décimo I 72 C2

B

Baad A 71 A5
Baamonde E 86 A3
Baar CH 70 A3
Baarle-Nassau B 49 B5
Baarn NL 49 A6
Babadag RO 11 P21
Babaeski TR 16 R20
Babayevo RUS 7 G24
Babenhausen, *Bayern* D 61 B6
Babenhausen, *Hessen* D 51 D4
Babiak PL 47 C4
Babice PL 55 C4
Babigoszcz PL 45 B6
Babimost PL 53 A5
Babina Greda HR 84 A3
Babócsa H 74 B2
Bábolma H 64 C3
Baborów PL 54 C3
Babót H 64 C3
Babruysk BY 7 K21
Babsk PL 55 B5
Bac GB 22 C2
Bač, *Crna Gora* YU 85 D5
Bač, *Vojvodina* YU 75 C4
Bacares E 101 B3
Bacău RO 11 N20
Baccarat F 60 B2
Bacharach D 50 C3
Bačina YU 85 C6
Bačka Palanka YU 75 C4
Bačka Topola YU 75 C4
Backaryd S 41 C5
Bäckebo S 40 C6
Bäckefors S 35 C4
Bäckhammar S 34 B6
Bački Breg YU 75 C3
Bački-Brestovac YU 75 C4
Bački Monoštor YU 75 C3
Bački Petrovac YU 75 C4
Bački Sokolac YU 75 C4
Backnang D 61 B5
Bačko Gradište YU 75 C5
Bačko Novo Selo YU 75 C4
Bačko Petrovo Selo YU 75 C5
Bácoli I 103 C4
Bacqueville-en-Caux F 58 A2
Bácsalmás H 75 B4
Bácsbokod H 75 B4
Bad Abbach D 62 B3
Bad Aibling D 62 C3
Bad Aussee A 63 C4
Bad Bederkesa D 43 B5
Bad Bentheim D 50 A3
Bad Bergzabern D 60 A3
Bad Berka D 52 C1
Bad Berleburg D 51 B4
Bad Berneck D 52 C1
Bad Bevensen D 44 B2
Bad Bibra D 52 B1
Bad Birnbach D 62 B4
Bad Blankenburg D 52 C1
Bad Bleiberg A 72 B3
Bad Brambach D 52 C2
Bad Bramstedt D 44 B1
Bad Breisig D 50 C3
Bad Brückenau D 51 C5
Bad Buchau D 61 B5
Bad Camberg D 50 C4
Bad Doberan D 44 A3
Bad Driburg D 51 B5
Bad Düben D 52 B2
Bad Dürkheim D 61 A4
Bad Dürrenberg D 52 B2
Bad Dürrheim D 61 B4
Bad Elster D 52 C2
Bad Ems D 50 C3
Bad Endorf D 62 C3
Bad Essen D 51 A4
Bad Fischau A 64 C2
Bad Frankenhausen D 52 B1
Bad Freienwalde D 45 C6
Bad Friedrichshall D 61 A5
Bad Füssing D 63 B4
Bad Gandersheim D 51 B6
Bad Gleichenberg A 73 B5
Bad Goisern A 63 C4
Bad Gottleuba D 53 C3
Bad Grund D 51 B6
Bad Hall A 63 B5
Bad Harzburg D 51 B6
Bad Herrenalb D 61 B4
Bad Hersfeld D 51 C5
Bad Hofgastein A 72 A3
Bad Homburg D 51 C4
Bad Honnef D 50 C3
Bad Hönningen D 50 C3
Bad Iburg D 50 A4
Bad Inner-laterns A 71 A4
Bad Ischl A 63 C4
Bad Karlshafen D 51 B5
Bad Kemmeriboden CH 70 B2
Bad Kissingen D 51 C6
Bad Kleinen D 44 B3
Bad Kohlgrub D 62 C2
Bad König D 61 A5
Bad Königshofen D 51 C6
Bad Köstritz D 52 C2
Bad Kreuzen A 63 B5
Bad Kreuznach D 60 A3
Bad Krozingen D 60 C3
Bad Laasphe D 51 C4
Bad Langensalza D 51 B6
Bad Lauchstädt D 52 B1
Bad Lausick D 52 B2
Bad Lauterberg D 51 B6
Bad Leonfelden A 63 B5
Bad Liebenwerda D 52 B3
Bad Liebenzell D 61 B4
Bad Lippspringe D 51 B4
Bad Meinberg D 51 B4
Bad Mergentheim D 61 A5
Bad Mitterndorf A 72 A3
Bad Münder D 51 A5
Bad Münstereifel D 50 C2
Bad Muskau D 53 B4
Bad Nauheim D 51 C4
Bad Nenndorf D 51 A5
Bad Neuenahr-Ahrweiler D 50 C3
Bad Neustadt D 51 C6
Bad Oeynhausen D 51 A4
Bad Oldesloe D 44 B2
Bad Orb D 51 C5
Bad Peterstal D 61 B4
Bad Pyrmont D 51 B5
Bad Radkersburg A 73 B5
Bad Ragaz CH 71 B4
Bad Rappenau D 61 A5
Bad Reichenhall D 62 C3
Bad Saarow-Pieskow D 53 A4
Bad Sachsa D 51 B6
Bad Säckingen D 70 A2
Bad Salzdetfurth D 51 A6
Bad Salzig D 50 C3
Bad Salzuflen D 51 A4
Bad Salzungen D 51 C6
Bad Sankt Leonhard A 73 B4
Bad Sassendorf D 50 B4
Bad Schandau D 53 C4
Bad Schmiedeberg D 52 B2
Bad Schönborn D 61 A4
Bad Schussenried D 61 B5
Bad Schwalbach D 50 C4
Bad Schwartau D 44 B2
Bad Segeberg D 44 B2
Bad Soden D 51 C4
Bad Soden-Salmünster D 51 C5
Bad Sooden-Allendorf D 51 B5
Bad Sulza D 52 B1
Bad Sülze D 45 A4
Bad Tatzmannsdorf A 73 A6
Bad Tennstedt D 51 B6
Bad Tölz D 62 C2
Bad Urach D 61 B5
Bad Vellach A 73 B4
Bad Vilbel D 51 C4
Bad Vöslau A 64 C2
Bad Waldsee D 61 C5
Bad Wiessee D 62 C2
Bad Wildungen D 51 B5
Bad Wilsnack D 44 C3
Bad Windsheim D 61 A6
Bad Wörishafen D 61 B6
Bad Wurzach D 61 C5
Bad Zwesten D 51 B5
Bad Zwischenahn D 43 B5
Badacsonytomaj H 74 B2
Badajoz E 93 C4
Badalona E 91 B5
Badalucco I 80 C1
Baden A 64 B2
Baden CH 70 A3
Baden-Baden D 61 B4
Bädenas E 90 B1
Badenweiler D 60 C3
Baderna HR 72 C3
Badgastein A 72 A3
Badia Calavena I 71 C6
Badia Polésine I 81 A5
Badia Pratáglia I 81 C5
Badia Tedalda I 82 C1
Bądki PL 47 B4
Badljevina HR 74 C2
Badolato I 106 C3
Badolatosa E 100 B1
Badonviller F 60 B2
Badovinci YU 85 B4
Badules E 90 B1
Bække DK 39 D2
Bækmarksbro DK 39 C1
Baells E 90 B3
Bælum DK 38 C3
Baena E 100 B1
Baesweiler D 50 C2
Baeza E 100 B2
Baflo NL 42 B3
Baga E 91 A4
Bagaladi I 109 A4
Bagenkop DK 39 E3
Baggetorp S 37 B3
Bagh a Chaisteil GB 22 E1
Bagheria I 108 A2
Bagnacavallo I 81 B5
Bagnáia I 102 A2
Bagnara Cálabra I 106 C2
Bagnasco I 80 B2
Bagnères-de-Bigorre F 76 C3
Bagnères-de-Luchon F 77 D3
Bagni del Másino I 71 B4
Bagni di Lucca I 81 B4
Bagni di Rabbi I 71 B5
Bagni di Tivoli I 102 B2
Bagno di Romagna I 81 C5
Bagnoles-de-l'Orne F 57 B5
Bagnoli dei Trigno I 103 B4
Bagnoli di Sopra I 72 C1
Bagnoli Irpino I 104 B2
Bagnolo Mella I 71 C5
Bagnols-en-Forêt F 79 C5
Bagnols-sur-Cèze F 78 B3
Bagnorégio I 102 A2
Bagolino I 71 C5
Bagrationovsk RUS 47 A6
Bagrdan YU 85 B6
Báguena E 95 A5
Bahabón de Esgueva E 88 C3
Bahillo E 88 B2
Báia delle Zágare I 104 A3
Báia Domizia I 103 B3
Baia Mare RO 11 N18
Baiano I 103 C4
Baião P 87 C2
Baiersbronn D 61 B4
Baiersdorf D 62 A2
Baignes-Ste. Radegonde F 67 C4
Baigneux-les-Juifs F 59 C5
Baildon GB 27 B4
Bailén E 100 A2
Băileşti RO 11 P18
Baileux B 49 C5
Bailieborough IRL 19 C5
Bailleul F 48 C3
Baillonville B 49 C6
Bailó E 90 A2
Bain-de-Bretagne F 57 C4
Bains F 78 A2
Bains-les-Bains F 60 B2
Bainton GB 27 B5
Baio E 86 A2
Baiona E 87 B2
Bais F 57 B5
Baiso I 81 B4
Baiuca P 92 A3
Baja H 75 B3
Bajánsenye H 73 B6
Bajina Bašta YU 85 C4
Bajmok YU 75 C4
Bajna H 65 C4
Bajovo Polje YU 84 C3
Bajša YU 75 C4
Bak H 74 B1
Bakar HR 73 C4
Bakewell GB 27 B4
Bakhmach UA 7 L23
Bakio E 89 A4
Bakonybél H 74 A2
Bakonycsernye H 74 A3
Bakonyjákó H 74 A2
Bakonyszentkirály H 74 A2
Bakonyszombathely H 74 A2
Bakov nad Jizerou CZ 53 C4
Bąkowiec PL 55 B6
Baks H 75 B5
Baksa H 74 C3
Bakum D 43 C5
Bala GB 26 C2
Balaguer E 90 B3
Balassa-gyarmat H 65 B5
Balástya H 75 B5
Balatonakali H 74 B2
Balatonalmádi H 74 A3
Balatonboglár H 74 B2
Balatonbozsok H 74 B3
Balatonederics H 74 B2
Balatonfenyves H 74 B2
Balatonföldvár H 74 B2
Balatonfüred H 74 B2
Balatonfűzfő H 74 A3
Balatonkenese H 74 A3
Balatonkiliti H 74 B3
Balatonlelle H 74 B2
Balatonszabadi H 74 B3
Balatonszemes H 74 B2
Balatonszentgyörgy H 74 B2
Balazote E 101 A3
Balbeggie GB 25 B4
Balbigny F 68 C4
Balboa E 86 B4
Balbriggan IRL 19 C5
Balchik BG 16 Q21
Baldock GB 31 C3
Bale HR 82 A2
Baleira E 86 A3
Baleizao P 98 A3
Balen B 49 B6
Balerma E 100 C3
Balestrand N 2 F10
Balestrate I 108 A2
Balfour GB 23 B6
Bälganet S 41 C5
Balıkesir TR 16 S20
Bälinge S 36 B4
Balingen D 61 B4
Balingsta S 36 B4
Balintore GB 23 D5
Baljevac YU 85 C5
Balk NL 42 C2
Balkbrug NL 42 C3
Balla IRL 18 C2
Ballachulish GB 24 B2
Ballaghaderreen IRL 18 C3
Ballancourt-sur-Essonne F 58 B3
Ballantrae GB 24 C3
Ballao I 110 D2
Ballasalla GB 26 A1
Ballater GB 23 D5
Ballen DK 39 D3
Ballenstedt D 52 B1
Ballerias E 90 B2
Balleroy F 57 A5
Ballerup DK 41 D2
Ballesteros de Calatrava E 100 A2
Ballina IRL 18 B2
Ballinalack IRL 19 C4
Ballinamore IRL 19 B4
Ballinascarty IRL 20 C3
Ballinasloe IRL 20 A3
Ballindine IRL 18 C3
Balling DK 38 C1
Ballingarry, *Limerick* IRL 20 B3
Ballingarry, *Tipperary* IRL 21 B4
Ballingeary IRL 20 C2
Ballinhassig IRL 20 C3
Ballinluig GB 25 B4
Ballino I 71 C5
Ballinrobe IRL 18 C2
Ballinskellings IRL 20 C1
Ballinspittle IRL 20 C3
Ballintra IRL 18 B3
Ballivor IRL 21 A5
Ballobar E 90 B3
Ballon F 58 B1
Ballon IRL 21 B5
Ballószög H 75 B4
Ballum DK 39 D1
Ballybay IRL 19 B5
Ballybofey IRL 19 B4
Ballybunion IRL 20 B2
Ballycanew IRL 21 B5
Ballycarry GB 19 B6
Ballycastle GB 19 A5
Ballycastle IRL 18 B2
Ballyclare GB 19 B6
Ballyconneely IRL 18 C1
Ballycotton IRL 20 C3
Ballycroy IRL 18 B2
Ballydehob IRL 20 C2
Ballyferriter IRL 20 B1
Ballygawley GB 19 B4
Ballygowan GB 19 B6
Ballyhaunis IRL 18 C3
Ballyheige IRL 20 B2
Ballyjamesduff IRL 19 C4
Ballylanders IRL 20 B3
Ballylynan IRL 21 B4
Ballymahon IRL 21 A4
Ballymena GB 19 B5
Ballymoe IRL 18 C3
Ballymoney GB 19 A5
Ballymore IRL 21 A4
Ballymote IRL 18 B3
Ballynacorra IRL 20 C3
Ballynagore IRL 21 A4
Ballynahinch GB 19 B6
Ballynure GB 19 B6
Ballyragget IRL 21 B4
Ballysadare IRL 18 B3
Ballyshannon IRL 18 B3
Ballyvaghan IRL 20 A2
Ballyvourney IRL 20 C2
Ballywalter GB 19 B6
Balmaclellan GB 24 C3
Balmaseda E 89 A3
Balme I 70 C2
Balmedie GB 23 D6
Balmuccia I 70 C3
Balna-paling GB 23 D4
Balneario de Panticosa E 76 D2
Balotaszállás H 75 B4
Balsa P 87 C3
Balsareny E 91 B4
Balsorano-Nuovo I 103 B3
Bålsta S 36 B4
Balsthal CH 70 A2
Balta UA 11 M21
Baltanás E 88 C2
Baltar E 87 C3
Baltasound GB 22 A8
Bălţi MD 11 N20
Baltimore IRL 20 C2
Baltinglass IRL 21 B5
Baltiysk RUS 47 A5
Baltów PL 55 B6
Balugães P 87 C2
Balve D 50 B3
Balvi LV 7 H20
Balvicar GB 24 B2
Balya TR 16 S20
Balzo I 82 D2
Bamberg D 62 A1
Bamburgh GB 25 C6
Banatska Palanka YU 85 B6
Banatski Brestovac YU 85 B5
Banatski Despotovac YU 75 C5
Banatski Dvor YU 75 C5
Banatski-Karlovac YU 85 A6
Banatsko Arandjelovo YU 75 B5
Banatsko-Novo Selo YU 85 B5
Banaz TR 16 S21
Banbridge GB 19 B5
Banbury GB 30 B2
Banchory GB 23 D6
Bande B 49 C6
Bande E 87 B3
Bandholm DK 39 E4
Bandırma TR 16 R20
Bandol F 79 C4
Bandon IRL 20 C3
Bañeres E 96 C2
Banff GB 23 D6
Bangor F 66 A1
Bangor, *Down* GB 19 B6
Bangor, *Gwynedd* GB 26 B1
Bangor IRL 18 B2
Banie PL 45 B6
Banja YU 85 C4
Banja Koviljača YU 85 B4
Banja Luka BIH 84 B2
Banja Vručica BIH 84 B2
Banjaloka SLO 73 C4
Banjani YU 85 B4
Banje YU 85 D5
Banjska YU 85 D5
Banka SK 64 B3
Bankekind S 37 C2
Bankend GB 25 C4
Bankeryd S 40 B4
Bankfoot GB 25 B4
Banloc RO 75 C6
Bannalec F 56 C2
Bannes F 59 B4
Bannockburn GB 25 B4
Bañobárez E 87 D4
Bañon E 90 C1
Banon F 79 B4
Baños E 93 A5
Baños de Gigonza E 99 C5
Baños de la Encina E 100 A2
Baños de Molgas E 87 B3
Baños de Rio Tobia E 89 B4
Baños de Valdearados E 89 C3
Bánov CZ 64 B3
Banova Jaruga HR 74 C1
Bánovce nad Bebravou SK 64 B4
Banoviči BIH 84 B3
Banoviči Selo BIH 84 B3
Bánréve H 65 B6
Bansin D 45 B6
Banská Belá SK 65 B4
Banská Bystrica SK 65 B5
Banská Štiavnica SK 65 B4
Banstead GB 31 C3
Banteer IRL 20 B3
Bantry IRL 20 C2
Bantzenheim F 60 C3
Banyalbufar, *Mallorca* E 97
Banyoles E 91 A5
Banyuls-sur-Mer F 91 A6
Bapaume F 48 C3
Bar UA 11 M20
Bar YU 15 Q16
Bar-le-Duc F 59 B6
Bar-sur-Aube F 59 B5
Bar-sur-Seine F 59 B5
Barabhas GB 22 C2
Barači BIH 84 B1
Baracs H 74 B3
Baracska H 74 A3
Barahona E 95 A4
Barajes de Melo E 95 B4
Barakaldo E 89 A4
Baralla E 86 B3
Barañain E 89 B5
Baranavichy BY 7 K20
Báránd H 75 A6
Baranda YU 85 A5
Baranello I 103 B4
Baranów Sandomierski PL 55 C6
Baraqueville F 77 B5
Barasoain E 89 B5
Barbacena P 92 C3
Barbadás E 87 B3
Barbadillo E 94 B1
Barbadillo de Herreros E 89 B3
Barbadillo del Mercado E 89 B3
Barbadillo del Pez E 89 B3
Barban HR 82 A3
Barbarano Vicentino I 71 C6
Barbariga HR 82 B2
Barbastro E 90 A3
Barbate de Franco E 99 C5
Barbatona E 95 A4
Barbâtre F 66 B2
Barbazan F 77 C3
Barbeitos E 86 A3
Barbentane F 78 C3
Barberino di Mugello I 81 B5
Barbezieux-St. Hilaire F 67 C4
Barbonne-Fayel F 59 B4
Barbotan-les-Thermes F 76 C2
Barby D 52 B1
Barca de Alva P 87 C4
Bárcabo E 90 A3
Barcarrota E 93 C4
Barcellona-Pozzo di Gotto I 109 A4
Barcelona E 91 B5
Barcelonette F 79 B5
Barcelos P 87 C2
Bárcena de Pie de Concha E 88 A2
Bárcena del Monasterio E 86 A4
Barchfeld D 51 C6
Barcin PL 46 C3
Barcino PL 46 A2
Bárcis I 72 B2
Barco P 92 A3
Barcones E 89 C4
Barcs H 74 C2
Barcus F 76 C2
Barczewo PL 47 B6
Bardejov SK 10 M17
Bårdesø DK 39 D3
Bardi I 81 B3
Bardney GB 27 B5
Bardo PL 54 C1
Bardolino I 71 C5
Bardonécchia I 79 A5
Bardoňovo SK 65 B4
Barèges F 76 D3
Barenstein D 52 C3
Barentin F 58 A1
Barenton F 57 B5
Barevo BIH 84 B2
Barfleur F 57 A4
Barga I 81 B4
Bargas E 94 C2
Barge I 79 B6
Bargemon F 79 C5
Barghe I 71 C5
Bargoed GB 29 B4
Bargrennan GB 24 C3
Bargteheide D 44 B2
Barham GB 31 C5
Bari I 105 A3
Bari Sardo I 110 D2
Barič Draga HR 83 B4
Barilović HR 73 C5
Barisciano I 103 A3
Barjac F 78 B3
Barjols F 79 C4
Bårkåker N 34 B2
Barkowo, *Dolnosląskie* PL 54 B1
Barkowo, *Pomorskie* PL 46 B3
Bârlad RO 11 N20
Barles F 79 B5
Barletta I 104 A3
Barlinek PL 45 C7
Barmouth GB 26 C1
Barmstedt D 44 B1
Barnard Castle GB 27 A4
Barnarp S 40 B4
Bärnau D 62 A3
Bärnbach A 73 A5
Barneberg D 52 A1
Barnenitz D 45 C4
Barnet GB 31 C3
Barnetby le Wold GB 27 B5
Barneveld NL 49 A6
Barneville-Carteret F 57 A4
Barnoldswick GB 26 B3
Barnowko PL 45 C6
Barnsley GB 27 B4
Barnstädt D 52 B1
Barnstaple GB 28 B3
Barnstorf D 43 C5
Barntrup D 51 B5
Baron F 58 A3
Baronissi I 103 C4
Barqueiro P 92 B2
Barquinha P 92 B2
Barr F 60 B3
Barr GB 24 C3
Barra P 92 A2
Barracas E 96 A2
Barraco E 94 B2
Barrado E 93 A5
Barrafranca I 109 B3
Barranco do Velho P 98 B3
Barrancos P 99 A4
Barrax E 95 C4
Barrbaar D 62 B1
Barre-des-Cevennes F 78 B2
Barreiro P 92 C1
Barreiros E 86 A3
Barrême F 79 C5
Barret-le-Bas F 79 B4
Barrhead GB 24 C3
Barrhill GB 24 C3
Barrio de Nuesra Señora E 88 B1
Barrow-in-Furness GB 26 A2
Barrow upon Humber GB 27 B5
Barrowford GB 26 B3
Barruecopardo E 87 C4
Barruelo de Santullán E 88 B2
Barruera E 90 A3
Barry GB 29 B4
Bårse DK 39 D4
Barsinghausen D 51 A5
Barssel D 43 B4
Barth D 45 A4
Bartholomä D 61 B5
Barton upon Humber GB 27 B5
Bartoszyce PL 47 A6
Barúmini I 110 D1
Baruth D 52 A3
Barvaux B 49 C6
Barver D 43 C5
Barwatd PL 65 A5
Barwice PL 46 B2
Barysaw BY 7 J21
Barzana E 88 A1
Bârzava RO 10 N17
Bárzio I 71 C4
Bas E 91 A5
Bašaid YU 75 C5
Basaluzzo I 80 B2
Basarabeasca MD 11 N21
Basauri E 89 A4
Baschi I 102 A2
Baschurch GB 26 C3
Basconcillos del Tozo E 88 B3
Bascones de Ojeda E 88 B2
Basécles B 49 C4
Basel CH 70 A2
Basélice I 104 A1
Basildon GB 31 C4
Basingstoke GB 31 C2
Baška CZ 65 A4
Baška HR 83 B3
Baška Voda HR 84 C1
Baslow GB 27 B4
Basovizza I 72 C3
Bassacutena I 110 B2
Bassano del Grappa I 72 C1
Bassano Romano I 102 A2
Bassecourt CH 70 A2
Bassella E 91 A4
Bassou F 59 C4
Bassoues F 76 C3
Bassum D 43 C5
Båstad S 41 C2
Bastardo I 82 D1
Bastelica F 110 A2
Bastelicaccia F 110 B1
Bastia F 110 A2
Bastia I 82 C1
Bastogne B 50 C1
Baston GB 30 B3
Bata H 74 B3
Batajnica YU 85 B5
Batalha P 92 B2
Bátaszék H 74 B3
Batea E 90 B3
Batelov CZ 63 A6
Bath GB 29 B5
Bathgate GB 25 C4
Batida H 75 B5
Batignano I 81 D5
Batina HR 74 C3
Bátka SK 65 B6
Batković BIH 85 B4
Batlava YU 85 D6
Batley GB 27 B4
Batočina YU 85 B6
Bátonyterenye H 65 C5
Batrina HR 74 C2
Båtsfjord N 2 A21
Battaglia Terme I 72 C1
Bätterkinden CH 70 A2
Battice B 50 C1
Battipáglia I 104 B1
Battle GB 31 D4
Battonya H 75 B6
Batuša YU 85 B6
Bátya H 75 B3
Baud F 56 C2
Baudour B 49 C4
Baugé F 67 A4
Baugy F 68 A2
Bauma CH 70 A3
Baume-les-Dames F 69 A6
Baumholder D 60 A3
Baunatal D 51 B5
Baunei I 110 C2
Bauska LV 6 H19
Bautzen D 53 B4
Bavanište YU 85 B5
Bavay F 49 C4
Bavilliers F 60 C2
Bavorov CZ 63 A5
Bawdsey GB 31 B5
Bawinkel D 43 C4
Bawtry GB 27 B4
Bayel F 59 B5
Bayeux F 57 A5
Bayındır TR 16 S20
Bayon F 60 B2
Bayonne F 76 C1
Bayons F 79 B5
Bayramiç TR 16 S20
Bayreuth D 52 D1
Bayrischzell D 62 C3
Baza E 101 B3
Bazas F 76 B2
Baziege F 77 C4
Bazoches-les-Gallerandes F 58 B3
Bazoches-sur-Hoëne F 58 B1
Bazzano I 81 B5
Beaconsfield GB 31 C3
Beade E 87 B2
Beadnell GB 25 C6
Beaminster GB 29 C5
Bearsden GB 24 C3
Beas E 99 B4
Beas de Segura E 100 A3
Beasain E 89 A4
Beattock GB 25 C4
Beaubery F 69 B4
Beaucaire F 78 C3
Beaufort F 69 C6
Beaufort IRL 20 B2
Beaufort-en Vallée F 67 A4
Beaugency F 58 C2
Beaujeu, *Alpes-de-Haute-Provence* F 79 B5
Beaujeu, *Rhône* F 69 B4
Beaulac F 76 B2
Beaulieu F 68 A2
Beaulieu GB 31 D2
Beaulieu-sous-la-Roche F 66 B3
Beaulieu-sur-Dordogne F 77 B4
Beaulieu-sur-Mer F 79 C6
Beaulon F 68 B3
Beauly GB 23 D4
Beaumaris GB 26 B1
Beaumesnil F 58 A1
Beaumetz-lès-Loges F 48 C3
Beaumont B 49 C5
Beaumont F 77 B3
Beaumont-de-Lomagne F 77 C3
Beaumont-du-Gâtinais F 58 B3
Beaumont-en-Argonne F 59 A6
Beaumont-Hague F 57 A4
Beaumont-la-Ronce F 67 A5
Beaumont-le-Roger F 58 A1
Beaumont-sur-Oise F 58 A3
Beaumont-sur-Sarthe F 57 B6
Beaune F 69 A4
Beaune-la-Rolande F 58 B3
Beaupréau F 66 A4
Beauraing B 49 C5
Beaurepaire F 69 C5
Beaurepaire-en-Bresse F 69 B5
Beaurières F 79 B4
Beauvais F 58 A3
Beauval F 48 C3
Beauville F 77 B3
Beauvoir-sur-Mer F 66 B2
Beauvoir-sur-Niort F 67 B4
Beba Veche RO 75 B5
Bebertal D 52 A1
Bebington GB 26 B2
Bebra D 51 C5
Bebrina HR 74 C2
Beccles GB 30 B5
Becedas E 93 A5
Beceite E 90 C3
Bečej YU 75 C5
Becerreá E 86 B3
Becerril de Campos E 88 B2
Bécherel F 57 B4
Bechhofen D 61 A6
Bechyně CZ 63 A5
Becilla de Valderaduey E 88 B1
Beckfoot GB 25 D4
Beckingham GB 27 B5
Beckum D 50 B4
Beco P 92 B2

Bécon-les-Granits F 66 A4
Bečov nad Teplou CZ 52 C2
Becsehely H 74 B1
Bedale GB 27 A4
Bedames E 89 A3
Bédar E 101 B4
Bédarieux F 78 C2
Bédarrides F 78 B3
Bedburg D 50 C2
Beddgelert GB 26 B1
Beddingestrand S 41 D3
Bédée F 57 B4
Bedegkér H 74 B3
Bedford GB 30 B3
Będków PL 55 B4
Bedlington GB 25 C6
Bedlno PL 55 A4
Bedmar E 100 B2
Bédoin F 79 B4
Bedónia I 80 B3
Bedretto CH 70 B3
Bedsted DK 38 C1
Bedum NL 42 B3
Bedwas GB 29 B4
Bedworth GB 30 B2
Będzin PL 55 C4
Beek en Donk NL 49 B6
Beekbergen NL 50 A1
Beelen D 50 B4
Beelitz D 52 A2
Beer GB 29 C4
Beerfelde D 45 C6
Beerfelden D 61 A4
Beernem B 49 B4
Beeskow D 53 A4
Beetsterzwaag NL 42 B3
Beetzendorf D 44 C3
Beflelay CH 70 A2
Begaljica YU 85 B5
Bégard F 56 B2
Begejci YU 75 C5
Begijar E 100 B2
Begijnendijk B 49 B5
Begues E 91 B4
Beguildy GB 26 C2
Begur E 91 B6
Beho B 50 C1
Behringen D 51 B6
Beilen NL 42 C3
Beilngries D 62 A2
Beine-Nauroy F 59 A5
Beinwil CH 70 A3
Beiseförth D 51 B5
Beith GB 24 C3
Beiuş RO 11 N18
Beja P 98 A3
Béjar E 93 A5
Békés H 75 B6
Békéscsaba H 75 B6
Bela SK 65 A4
Bela Crkva YU 85 B6
Belá nad Radbuzou CZ 62 A3
Bělá p Bezdězem CZ 53 C4
Bélâbre F 67 B6
Belalcázar E 93 C5
Belanovica YU 85 B4
Bélapátfalva H 65 B6
Belcaire F 77 D4
Bełchatów PL 55 B4
Belchite E 90 B2
Bělčice CZ 63 A4
Belcoo GB 19 B4
Belecke D 51 B4
Beled H 74 A2
Belej HR 83 B3
Beleño E 88 A1
Bélesta F 77 D4
Belev RUS 7 K25
Belfast GB 19 B6
Belford GB 25 C6
Belfort F 60 C2
Belgentier F 79 C4
Belgern D 52 B3
Belgioioso I 71 C4
Belgodère F 110 A2
Belgooly IRL 20 C3
Belgorod RUS 7 L25
Belhade F 76 B2
Beli Manastir HR 74 C3
Belica HR 74 B1
Belin-Béliet F 76 B2
Belinchón E 95 B3
Belišće HR 74 C3
Bělkovice-Lašťany CZ 64 A3
Bell-lloc d'Urgell E 90 B3
Bella I 104 B2
Bellac F 67 B6
Bellágio I 71 C4
Bellananagh IRL 19 C4
Bellano I 71 B4
Bellária I 82 B1
Bellavary IRL 18 C2
Belle-Isle-en-Terre F 56 B2
Belleau F 59 A4
Belleek GB 18 B3
Bellegarde, *Gard* F 78 C3
Bellegarde, *Loiret* F 58 C3
Bellegarde-en-Diois F 79 B4
Bellegarde-en-Marche F 68 C2
Bellegarde-sur-Valserine F 69 B5
Bellême F 58 B1
Bellenaves F 68 B3
Bellentre F 70 C1
Bellevaux F 69 B6
Belleville F 69 B4
Belleville-sur-Vie F 66 B3
Bellevue-la-Montagne F 68 C3
Belley F 69 C5
Bellheim D 61 A4
Bellinge DK 39 D3
Bellingham GB 25 C5
Bellinzago Novarese I 70 C3
Bellinzona CH 70 B4
Bello E 95 B5
Bellpuig d'Urgell E 91 B4
Bellreguart E 96 C2
Bellsbank GB 24 C3
Belltall E 91 B4
Belluno I 72 B2
Bellver de Cerdanya E 91 A4
Bellvis E 90 B3
Bélmez E 99 A5
Belmez de la Moraleda E 100 B2
Belmont GB 22 A8
Belmont-de-la-Loire F 69 B4
Belmont-sur-Rance F 78 C1
Belmonte, *Asturias* E 86 A4
Belmonte, *Cuenca* E 95 C4
Belmonte P 92 A3
Belmonte de San José E 90 C2
Belmonte de Tajo E 95 B3
Belmullet IRL 18 B2
Belœil B 49 C4
Belogradchik BG 15 Q18
Belokorovichi UA 11 L21
Beloljin YU 85 C6
Belorado E 89 B3
Belotič YU 85 B4
Bělotín CZ 64 A3
Belozersk RUS 7 G25
Belp CH 70 B2
Belpasso I 109 B3
Belpech F 77 C4
Belper GB 27 B4
Belsay GB 25 C6
Belsk Duzy PL 55 B5
Beltinci SLO 73 B6
Beltra IRL 18 C2
Belturbet IRL 19 B4
Beluša SK 64 A4
Belušić YU 85 C6
Belvedere Marittimo I 106 B2
Belver de Cinca E 90 B3
Belver de los Montes E 88 C1
Belvès F 77 B3
Belvezet F 78 B2
Belvis de la Jara E 94 C2
Belvis de Monroy E 93 B5
Belyy RUS 7 J23
Belz F 56 C2
Bełżec PL 11 L18
Belzig D 52 A2
Bembibre E 86 B4
Bembridge GB 31 D2
Bemmel NL 50 B1
Bemposta, *Bragança* P 87 C4
Bemposta, *Santarém* P 92 B2
Benabarre E 90 A3
Benacazón E 99 B4
Benaguacil E 96 B2
Benahadux E 101 C3
Benalmádena E 100 C1
Benalúa de Guadix E 100 B2
Benalúa de las Villas E 100 B2
Benalup E 99 C5
Benamargosa E 100 C1
Benamaurel E 101 B3
Benameji E 100 B1
Benamocarra E 100 C1
Benaocaz E 99 C5
Benaoján E 99 C5
Benarrabá E 99 C5
Benasque E 90 A3
Benátky nad Jizerou CZ 53 C4
Benavente E 88 C1
Benavente P 92 C2
Benavides de Órbigo E 88 B1
Benavila P 92 B3
Bendorf D 50 C3
Bene Vagienna I 80 B1
Benedikt SLO 73 B5
Benejama E 96 C2
Benejúzar E 96 C2
Benešov CZ 63 A5
Bénestroff F 60 B2
Benet F 67 B4
Bénévent-l'Abbaye F 67 B6
Benevento I 103 B4
Benfeld F 60 B3
Benfica P 92 B2
Bengtsfors S 35 B4
Beničanci HR 74 C3
Benicarló E 90 C3
Benicássim E 96 A3
Benidorm E 96 C2
Benifaió E 96 B2
Beniganim E 96 C2
Benington GB 27 B6
Benisa E 96 C3
Benkovac HR 83 B4
Benllech GB 26 B1
Benneckenstein D 51 B6
Bénodet F 56 C1
Benquerencia de la Serena E 93 C5
Bensafrim P 98 B2
Bensdorf D 44 C4
Benshausen D 51 C6
Bensheim D 61 A4
Bentley GB 31 C3
Bentwisch D 44 A4
Beočin YU 75 C4
Beograd YU 85 B5
Beragh GB 19 B4
Berane YU 85 D4
Beranga E 89 A3
Berat AL 15 R16
Bérat F 77 C4
Beratzhausen D 62 A2
Bérbaltavár H 74 A1
Berbegal E 90 B2
Berbenno di Valtellina I 71 B4
Berberana E 89 B3
Bercedo E 89 A3
Bercel H 65 C5
Bercenay-le-Hayer F 59 B4
Berceto I 81 B3
Berchem B 49 C4
Berchidda I 110 C2
Berching D 62 A2
Berchtesgaden D 62 C4
Bérchules E 100 C2
Bercianos de Aliste E 87 C4
Berck F 48 C2
Berclaire d'Urgell E 90 B3
Berdoias E 86 A1
Berducedo E 86 A4
Berdún E 90 A2
Berdychiv UA 11 M21
Bere Alston GB 28 C3
Bere Regis GB 29 C5
Bereguardo I 70 C4
Berehove UA 11 M18
Berek BIH 84 A2
Beremend H 74 C3
Berestechko UA 11 L19
Berettyóújfalu H 10 N17
Berezhany UA 11 M19
Berezivka UA 11 N22
Berezna UA 11 L22
Berg D 62 A2
Berg S 37 C3
Berg im Gau D 62 B2
Berga, *Sachsen-Anhalt* D 51 B7
Berga, *Thüringen* D 52 C2
Berga E 91 A4
Berga S 40 B6
Bergama TR 16 S20
Bérgamo I 71 C4
Bergara E 89 A4
Berge, *Brandenburg* D 45 C4
Berge, *Niedersachsen* D 43 C4
Berge, *Telemark* N 33 B5
Berge, *Telemark* N 33 B5
Bergen, *Mecklenburg-Vorpommern* D 45 A5
Bergen, *Niedersachsen* D 44 C1
Bergen, *Niedersachsen* D 44 C2
Bergen N 32 A2
Bergen NL 42 C1
Bergen op Zoom NL 49 B5
Bergerac F 77 B3
Bergères-lés-Vertus F 59 B5
Bergeyk NL 49 B6
Berghausen D 61 B4
Bergheim D 50 C2
Berghem S 40 B2
Bergisch Gladbach D 50 C3
Bergkamen D 50 B3
Bergkvara S 41 C6
Berglern D 62 B2
Bergneustadt D 50 B3
Bergs slussar S 37 C2
Bergshamra S 36 B5
Bergtheim D 61 A6
Bergues F 48 C3
Bergum NL 42 B2
Bergün Bravuogn CH 71 B4
Bergwitz D 52 B2
Berhida H 74 A3
Beringel P 98 A3
Beringen B 49 B6
Berja E 100 C3
Berkeley GB 29 B5
Berkenthin D 44 B2
Berkhamsted GB 31 C3
Berkheim D 61 B6
Berkhof D 43 C6
Berkovići BIH 84 C3
Berkovitsa BG 15 Q18
Berlanga E 99 A5
Berlanga de Duero E 89 C4
Berlevag N 2 A21
Berlikum NL 42 B2
Berlin D 45 C5
Berlstedt D 52 B1
Bermeo E 89 A4
Bermillo de Sayago E 87 C4
Bern CH 70 B2
Bernalda I 105 B3
Bernardos E 94 A2
Bernartice, *Jihočeský* CZ 63 A5
Bernartice, *Východočeský* CZ 53 C5
Bernau, *Baden-Württemberg* D 61 C4
Bernau, *Bayern* D 62 C3
Bernau, *Brandenburg* D 45 C5
Bernaville F 48 C3
Bernay F 58 A1
Bernburg D 52 B1
Berndorf A 64 C2
Berne D 43 B5
Bernecebarati H 65 B4
Bernhardsthal A 64 B2
Bernkastel-Kues D 60 A3
Bernolakovo SK 64 B3
Bernsdorf D 53 B4
Bernstadt D 53 B4
Bernstein A 73 A6
Bernués E 90 A2
Beromünster CH 70 A3
Beroun CZ 53 D4
Berre-l'Etang F 79 C4
Berriedale GB 23 C5
Berriew GB 26 C2
Berrocal E 99 B4
Bersenbrück D 43 C4
Bershad' UA 11 M21
Berthåga S 36 B4
Berthelming F 60 B2
Bertincourt F 48 C3
Bertinoro I 82 B1
Bertogne B 49 C6
Bertrix B 59 A6
Berville-sur-Mer F 58 A1
Berwick-Upon-Tweed GB 25 C5
Berzasca RO 10 P17
Berzence H 74 B2
Berzocana E 93 B5
Besalú E 91 A5
Besançon F 69 A6
Besenfeld D 61 B4
Besenyötelek H 65 C6
Besenyszög H 75 A5
Beshenkovichi BY 7 J21
Besigheim D 61 B5
Běšiny CZ 63 A4
Beška YU 85 A5
Besle F 57 C4
Besnyö H 74 A3
Bessais-le-Fromental F 68 B2
Bessan F 78 C2
Besse-en-Chandesse F 68 C2
Bessé-sur-Braye F 58 C1
Bessèges F 78 B3
Bessines-sur-Gartempe F 67 B6
Best NL 49 B6
Bestorp S 37 C2
Betanzos E 86 A2
Betelu E 89 A5
Bétera E 96 B2
Beteta E 95 B4
Béthenville F 59 A5
Bethesda GB 26 B1
Béthune F 48 C3
Beton-Bazoches F 59 B4
Bettembourg L 60 A2
Betterdorf L 60 A2
Bettna S 37 C3
Béttola I 80 B3
Bettona I 82 C1
Bettyhill GB 23 C4
Betws-y-Coed GB 26 B2
Betxi E 96 B2
Betz F 59 A3
Betzdorf D 50 C3
Beuil F 79 B5
Beulah GB 29 A4
Beuzeville F 58 A1
Bevagna I 82 D1
Bevens-bruk S 37 B2
Beveren B 49 B5
Beverley GB 27 B5
Bevern D 51 B5
Beverstedt D 43 B5
Beverungen D 51 B5
Beverwijk NL 42 C1
Bex CH 70 B2
Bexhill GB 31 D4
Beychevelle F 76 A2
Beykoz TR 16 R21
Beynat F 77 A4
Bezas E 96 A1
Bezau A 71 A4
Bezdan YU 75 C3
Bèze F 69 A5
Bezenet F 68 B2
Bezhetsk RUS 7 H25
Béziers F 78 C2
Bezzecca I 71 C5
Biadki PL 54 B2
Biała, *Łódzkie* PL 55 B4
Biała, *Opolskie* PL 54 C2
Biała Podlaska PL 6 K18
Biała Rawska PL 55 B5
Białaczów PL 55 B5
Biale Błota PL 46 B3
Białobloty PL 54 A2
Białobrzegi PL 55 B5
Białogard PL 46 B1
Białośliwie PL 46 B3
Biały Bór PL 46 B2
Białystok PL 6 K18
Biancavilla I 109 B3
Bianco I 106 C3
Biandrate I 70 C3
Biar E 96 C2
Biarritz F 76 C1
Bias F 76 B1
Biasca CH 70 B3
Biatorbágy H 74 A3
Bibbiena I 81 C5
Bibbona I 81 C4
Biberach, *Baden-Württemberg* D 61 B4
Biberach, *Baden-Württemberg* D 61 B5
Bibinje HR 83 B4
Bibione I 72 C3
Biblis D 61 A4
Bibury GB 29 B6
Biccari I 104 B2
Bicester GB 31 C2
Bichl D 62 C2
Bichlbach A 71 A5
Bicorp E 96 B2
Bicske H 65 C4
Bidache F 76 C1
Bidart F 76 C1
Biddinghuizen NL 42 C2
Biddulph GB 26 B3
Bideford GB 28 B3
Bidford-on-Avon GB 29 A6
Bie S 37 B3
Bieber D 51 C5
Biebersdorf D 53 B4
Biedenkopf D 51 C4
Biel CH 70 A2
Biel E 90 A2
Bielany Wrocławskie PL 54 B1
Bielawa PL 54 C1
Bielawy PL 55 A4
Bielefeld D 51 A4
Biella I 70 C3
Bielsa E 90 A3
Bielsk PL 47 C5
Bielsk Podlaski PL 6 K18
Bielsko-Biała PL 65 A5
Bienenbuttel D 44 B2
Bieniow PL 53 B5
Bienservida E 101 A3
Bienvenida E 99 A4
Bierdzany PL 54 C3
Bierné F 57 C5
Biersted DK 38 B2
Bierun PL 55 C4
Bierutów PL 54 B2
Bierwart B 49 C6
Bierzwina PL 46 B1
Bierzwnik PL 46 B1
Biescas E 90 A2
Biesenthal D 45 C5
Biesiekierz PL 46 A2
Bietigheim-Bissingen D 61 B5
Bièvre B 59 A6
Bieżuń PL 47 C5
Biga TR 16 R20
Bigadiç TR 16 S21
Biganos F 76 B2
Bigas P 87 D3
Bigastro E 96 C2
Bigbury GB 28 C4
Biggar GB 25 C4
Biggin Hill GB 31 C4
Biggleswade GB 30 B3
Bignasco CH 70 B3
Biguglia F 110 A2
Bihać BIH 83 B4
Biharnagybajom H 75 A6
Bijeljani BIH 84 C3
Bijeljina BIH 85 B4
Bijelo Polje YU 85 C4
Bijuesca E 89 C5
Bila Tserkva UA 11 M22
Bilaj HR 83 B4
Bilbao E 89 A4
Bilcza PL 55 C5
Bileća BIH 84 D3
Bilecik TR 16 R22
Biled RO 75 C5
Biłgoraj PL 11 L18
Bilhorod-Dnistrovskyy UA 11 N22
Bilina CZ 53 C3
Bilje HR 74 C3
Billdal S 38 B4
Billerbeck D 50 B3
Billericay GB 31 C4
Billesholm S 41 C2
Billingborough GB 30 B3
Billinge S 41 D3
Billingham GB 27 A4
Billinghay GB 27 B5
Billingsfors S 35 C4
Billingshurst GB 31 C3
Billom F 68 C3
Billund DK 39 D2
Bilopillya UA 7 L24
Bilovec CZ 64 A4
Bilstein D 50 B4
Bilthoven NL 49 A6
Bilzen B 49 C6
Biňa SK 65 C4
Binaced E 90 B3
Binasco I 71 C4
Binbrook GB 27 B5
Binche B 49 C5
Bindlach D 52 D1
Bindslev DK 38 B3
Binefar E 90 B3
Bingen D 50 D3
Bingham GB 27 C5
Bingley GB 27 B4
Binic F 56 B3
Binz D 45 A5
Biograd na Moru HR 83 C4
Bionaz I 70 C2
Bioska YU 85 C4
Birda RO 75 C6
Birdlip GB 29 B5
Birkeland N 33 C5
Birkenfeld, *Baden-Württemberg* D 61 B4
Birkenfeld, *Rheinland-Pfalz* D 60 A3
Birkenhead GB 26 B2
Birkerød DK 41 D2
Birkfeld A 73 A5
Birkirkara M 109 C4
Birmingham GB 27 C4
Birr IRL 21 A4
Birresborn D 50 C2
Birstein D 51 C5
Biržai LT 6 H19
Birzebbugia M 109 C4
Bisáccia I 104 B2
Bisacquino I 108 B2
Bisbal de Falset E 90 B3
Biscarosse F 76 B1
Biscarosse Plage F 76 B1
Biscarrués E 90 A2
Bisceglie I 105 A3
Bischheim F 60 B3
Bischofsheim D 51 C5
Bischofshofen A 72 A3
Bischofswerda D 53 B4
Bischofswiesen D 62 C3
Bischofszell CH 71 A4
Bischwiller F 60 B3
Bisenti I 103 A3
Bishop Auckland GB 27 A4
Bishop's Castle GB 26 C3
Bishop's Stortford GB 31 C4
Bishop's Waltham GB 31 D2
Bishops Lydeard GB 29 B4
Bisignano I 106 B3
Bisingen D 61 B4
Biskupice-Oławskie PL 54 B2
Biskupiec PL 47 B5
Bismark D 44 C3
Bispingen D 44 B1
Bissen L 60 A2
Bissendorf D 50 A4
Bisserup DK 39 D4
Bistango I 80 B2
Bistarac Donje BIH 84 B3
Bistrica BIH 84 B2
Bistrica, *Crna Gora* YU 85 D4
Bistrica, *Srbija* YU 85 C4
Bistrica ob Sotli SLO 73 B5
Bistriţa RO 11 N19
Bisztynek PL 47 A6
Bitburg D 50 D2
Bitche F 60 A3
Bitetto I 105 A3
Bitola MK 15 R17
Bitonto I 105 A3
Bitschwiller F 60 C3
Bitterfeld D 52 B2
Bitti I 110 C2
Biville-sur-Mer F 48 D2
Bivona I 108 B2
Biwer L 60 A2
Bizeljsko SLO 73 B5
Bizovac HR 74 C3
Bjåen N 33 B4
Bjärnum S 41 C3
Bjärred S 41 D3
Bjelland, *Vest-Agder* N 32 C3
Bjelland, *Vest-Agder* N 33 C4
Bjelovar HR 74 C1
Bjerkreim N 32 C3
Bjerreby DK 39 E3
Bjerringbro DK 39 C2
Björbo S 36 B1
Bjørkelangen N 34 B3
Björketorp S 40 B2
Björklinge S 36 A4
Björkö, *Stockholm* S 36 B6
Björkö, *Västra Götaland* S 38 B4
Björköby S 40 B4
Björkvik S 37 C3
Björneborg S 34 B6
Bjørnerod N 35 B3
Bjørnevatn N 3 B21
Björnlunda S 37 B4
Björsäter S 37 C3
Bjurträn S 34 B6
Bjuv S 41 C2
Blace YU 85 C5
Blachownia PL 54 C3
Blackburn GB 26 B3
Blackpool GB 26 B2
Blackstad S 37 D3
Blackwater IRL 21 B5
Blackwaterfoot GB 24 C2
Blacy F 59 B5
Bladåker S 36 A5
Blaenau Ffestiniog GB 26 C2
Blaenavon GB 29 B4
Blaengarw GB 29 B4
Blagaj BIH 83 A5
Blagaj BIH 84 C2
Blagdon GB 29 B5
Blagnac F 77 C4
Blagoevgrad BG 15 Q18
Blaichach D 71 A5
Blain F 66 A3
Blainville-sur-l'Eau F 60 B2
Blair Atholl GB 25 B4
Blairgowrie GB 25 B4
Blajan F 77 C3
Blakeney GB 29 B5
Blakstad N 33 C5
Blâmont F 60 B2
Blanca E 101 A4
Blancos E 87 C3
Blandford Forum GB 29 C5
Blanes E 91 B5
Blangy-sur-Bresle F 58 A2
Blankaholm S 37 D3
Blankenberge B 49 B4
Blankenburg D 51 B6
Blankenfelde D 52 A3
Blankenhain D 52 C1
Blankenheim D 50 C2
Blanquefort F 76 B2
Blansko CZ 64 A2
Blanzac F 67 C5
Blanzy F 69 B4
Blaricum NL 49 A6
Blarney IRL 20 C3
Blascomillán E 94 B1
Blascosancho E 94 B2
Błaszki PL 54 B3
Blatná CZ 63 A4
Blatné SK 64 B3
Blatnice CZ 64 B3
Blatnika BIH 84 B2
Blato HR 84 D1
Blato na Cetini HR 84 C1
Blatten CH 70 B2
Blatzheim D 50 C2
Blaubeuren D 61 B5
Blaufelden D 61 A5
Blaustein D 61 B5
Blaydon GB 25 D6
Blaye F 76 A2
Blaye-les-Mines F 77 B5
Blázquez E 93 C5
Bleckede D 44 B2
Blecua E 90 A2
Bled SLO 73 B4
Bleiburg A 73 B4
Bleichenbach D 51 C5
Bleicherode D 51 B6
Bléneau F 59 C3
Blera I 102 A2
Blérancourt F 59 A4
Bléré F 67 A5
Blesle F 68 C3
Blessington IRL 21 A5
Blet F 68 B2
Bletchley GB 31 C3
Bletterans F 69 B5
Blidö S 36 B5
Blidsberg S 35 D5
Blieskastel D 60 A3
Bligny-sur-Ouche F 69 A4
Blikstorp S 35 C6
Blinja HR 73 C6
Blizanówek PL 54 B3
Bliżyn PL 55 B5
Blois F 58 C2
Blokhus DK 38 B2
Blokzijl NL 42 C2
Blombacka S 34 B5
Blomberg D 51 B5
Blomskog S 34 B4
Blomstermåla S 40 C6
Błonie PL 55 A5
Blonville-sur-Mer F 57 A6
Blötberget S 36 A2
Blovice CZ 63 A4
Bloxham GB 31 B2
Blšany CZ 52 C3
Bludenz A 71 A4
Bludov CZ 64 A2
Blumberg D 61 C4
Blyth, *Northumberland* GB 25 C6
Blyth, *Nottinghamshire* GB 27 B4
Blyth Bridge GB 25 C4
Blythburgh GB 30 B5
Blythe Bridge GB 26 C3
Bo N 33 B6
Bo'ness GB 25 B4
Boa Vista P 92 B2
Boal E 86 A4
Boan YU 85 D4
Boario Terme I 71 C5
Boat of Garten GB 23 D5
Boba H 74 A2
Bobadilla, *Logroño* E 89 B4
Bobadilla, *Málaga* E 100 B1
Bobadilla del Campo E 94 A1
Bobadilla del Monte E 94 B3
Bóbbio I 80 B3
Bóbbio Pellice I 79 B6
Bobigny F 58 B3
Bobingen D 62 B1
Böblingen D 61 B5
Bobolice PL 46 B2
Boboras E 86 B2
Bobowa PL 65 A6
Bobrinets UA 11 M23
Bobrová CZ 64 A2
Bobrovitsa UA 11 L22
Bobrowice PL 53 B5
Bobrówko PL 46 C1
Boca de Huérgano E 88 B2
Bocairent E 96 C2
Bočar YU 75 C5
Bocchigliero I 106 B3
Boceguillas E 89 C3
Bochnia PL 65 A6
Bocholt B 49 B6
Bocholt D 50 B2
Bochov CZ 52 C3
Bochum D 50 B3
Bockara S 40 B6
Bockenem D 51 A6
Bockfliess A 64 B2
Bockhorn D 43 B5
Bočna SLO 73 B4
Bocognano F 110 A2
Boconád H 65 C6
Böcs H 65 B6
Boczów PL 53 A4
Boda, *Stockholm* S 36 A5
Boda, *Värmland* S 34 B5
Boda Glasbruk S 40 C5
Bodafors S 40 B4
Bodajk H 74 A3
Boddam, *Aberdeenshire* GB 23 D7
Boddam, *Shetland* GB 22 B7
Boddin D 44 B3
Bödefeld-Freiheit D 51 B4
Boden S 3 D17
Bodenmais D 62 A4
Bodenteich D 44 C2
Bodenwerder D 51 B5
Bodiam GB 31 C4
Bodinnick GB 28 C3
Bodio CH 70 B3
Bodjani YU 75 C4
Bodmin GB 28 C3
Bodø N 2 C14
Bodonal de la Sierra E 99 A4
Bodrum TR 16 T20
Bodzanów PL 47 C6
Bodzanowice PL 54 C3
Bodzechów PL 55 C6
Bodzentyn PL 55 C5
Boecillo E 88 C2
Boëge F 69 B6
Boën F 68 C3
Bogács H 65 C6
Bogadmindszent H 74 C3
Bogajo E 87 D4
Bogarra E 101 A3
Bogarre E 100 B2
Bogatić YU 85 B4
Bogatynia PL 53 C4
Bogdaniec PL 45 C7
Boge S 37 D5
Bogen D 62 B3
Bogen S 34 A4
Bogense DK 39 D3
Bognanco Fonti I 70 B3
Bognes N 2 B15
Bogno CH 70 B4
Bognor Regis GB 31 D3
Bogoria PL 55 C6
Boguchwaly PL 47 B6
Bogumiłowice PL 55 B4
Boguslav UA 11 M22
Boguszów-Gorce PL 53 C6
Bogutovac YU 85 C5
Bogyiszló H 74 B3
Bohain-en-Vermandois F 49 D4
Böheimkirchen A 64 B1
Bohinjska Bistrica SLO 72 B3
Böhlen D 52 B2
Böhmenkirch D 61 B5
Bohmte D 43 C5
Bohodukhiv UA 7 L24
Bohonal de Ibor E 93 B5
Böhönye H 74 B2
Bohumin CZ 65 A4
Boiro E 86 B2
Bois-d'Amont F 69 B6
Boisseron F 78 C3
Boitzenburg D 45 B5
Boixols E 91 A4
Boizenburg D 44 B2
Bojadła PL 53 B5
Bojano I 103 B4
Bojanowo PL 54 B1
Bøjden DK 39 D3
Bojkovice CZ 64 A3
Bojná SK 64 B4
Bojnice SK 65 B4
Boka YU 75 C5
Böklund D 43 A6
Bokod H 74 A3
Böksholm S 40 B4
Boksitogorsk RUS 7 G23
Bol HR 83 C5
Bolaños de Calatrava E 100 A2
Bolbec F 58 A1
Bölcske H 75 B3
Bolderslev DK 39 E2
Boldog H 65 C5
Boldva H 65 B6
Bolea E 90 A2
Bolekhiv UA 11 M18
Bolesławiec PL 53 B5
Boleszkowice PL 45 C6
Bolewice PL 46 C2
Bolgheri I 81 C4
Bolhrad UA 11 P21
Boliden S 3 D17
Bolimów PL 55 A5
Bolimqueime P 98 B2
Boljevci YU 85 B5
Boljkovci YU 85 B5
Bolkhov RUS 7 K25
Bolków PL 53 C6
Bollebygd S 40 B2
Bollène F 78 B3
Bólliga E 95 B4
Bollnäs S 2 F15
Bollullos E 99 B4
Bollullos par del Condado E 99 B4
Bologna I 81 B5
Bologne F 59 B6
Bolognetta I 108 B2
Bolognola I 82 D2
Bologoye RUS 7 H24
Bolótana I 110 C1
Bolsena I 102 A1
Bolshaya Vradiyevka UA 11 N22
Bolsover GB 27 B4
Bolstad S 35 C4
Bolsward NL 42 B2
Boltaña E 90 A3
Boltenhagen D 44 B3
Boltigen CH 70 B2
Bolton GB 26 B3
Bolu TR 16 R22
Bolvadin TR 16 S22
Bóly H 74 C3
Bolzaneto I 80 B2
Bolzano I 71 B6
Bomba I 103 A4
Bombarral P 92 B1
Bömenzien D 44 C3
Bomlitz D 43 C6
Bømlo N 32 B2
Bøn N 34 A3
Bon-Encontre F 77 B3
Bonaduz CH 71 B4
Bonanza E 99 C4
Boñar E 88 B1
Bonarbridge GB 23 D4
Bonárcado I 110 C1
Bonares E 99 B4
Bonassola I 80 B3
Bonawe GB 24 B2
Bondal N 33 B5
Bondeno I 81 B5
Bondorf D 61 B4
Bondstorp S 40 B3
Bonete E 96 C1
Bonifacio F 110 B2
Bonigen CH 70 B2
Bonin PL 46 A2
Bonn D 50 C3
Bonnánaro I 110 C1
Bonnat F 68 B1
Bonndorf D 61 C4
Bonnétable F 58 B1
Bonnétage F 70 A1
Bonneuil-les-Eaux F 58 A3
Bonneuil-Matours F 67 B5
Bonneval F 58 B2
Bonneval-sur-Arc F 70 C2
Bonneville F 69 B6
Bonnières-sur-Seine F 58 A2
Bonnieux F 79 C4
Bönningheim D 61 A5
Bonny-sur-Loire F 68 A2
Bonnyrigg GB 25 C4
Bono E 90 A3
Bono I 110 C2
Bonorva I 110 C1
Bønsnes N 34 A2
Bonyhád H 74 B3
Boom B 49 B5
Boos F 58 A2
Boostedt D 44 A2
Bootle, *Cumbria* GB 26 A2
Bootle, *Merseyside* GB 26 B2
Bopfingen D 61 B6
Boppard D 50 C3
Boqueixón E 86 B2
Bor CZ 62 A3
Bor S 40 B4
Bor YU 11 P18
Boran-sur-Oise F 58 A3
Borås S 40 B2

Borba P 92 C3
Borbona I 102 A3
Borča YU 85 B5
Borci BIH 84 C3
Borculo NL 50 A2
Bordány H 75 B4
Bordeaux F 76 B2
Bordeira P 98 B2
Bordesholm D 44 A2
Bordighera I 80 C1
Bording DK 39 C2
Bordón E 90 C2
Bore I 81 B3
Borehamwood GB 31 C3
Borek Strzeliński PL 54 C2
Borek Wielkopolski PL 54 B2
Boreland GB 25 C4
Borello I 82 B1
Borensberg S 37 C2
Borgentreich D 51 B5
Börger D 43 C4
Borger NL 42 C3
Borggård S 37 C2
Borghamn S 37 C1
Borghetta di Vara I 81 B3
Borghetto d'Arróscia I 80 B1
Borghetto Santo Spirito I 80 B2
Borgholm S 40 C6
Borghorst D 50 A3
Bórgia I 106 C3
Borgloon B 49 C6
Børglum DK 38 B2
Borgo F 110 A2
Borgo a Mozzano I 81 C4
Borgo alla Collina I 81 C5
Borgo Pace I 82 C1
Borgo San Dalmazzo I 80 B1
Borgo San Lorenzo I 81 C5
Borgo Val di Taro I 81 B3
Borgo Valsugana I 71 B6
Borgo Vercelli I 70 C3
Borgoforte I 81 A4
Borgofranco d'Ivrea I 70 C2
Borgomanero I 70 C3
Borgomasino I 70 C2
Borgonovo Val Tidone I 80 A3
Borgorose I 102 A3
Borgosésia I 70 C3
Borgstena S 35 D5
Borgue GB 24 D3
Borgvik S 34 B4
Borisovka RUS 7 L25
Borja E 89 C5
Bork D 50 B3
Borken D 50 B2
Borkop DK 39 D2
Borkowice PL 55 B5
Borkowo PL 47 C6
Borkum D 42 B3
Borlänge S 36 A2
Bormes-les-Mimosas F 79 C5
Bórmio I 71 B5
Bormujos E 99 B4
Borna D 52 B2
Borne NL 50 A2
Borne Sulinowo PL 46 B2
Bornes P 87 C4
Bornheim D 50 C2
Bornhöved D 44 A2
Börnicke D 45 C4
Bornos E 99 C5
Borobia E 89 C5
Borodino RUS 7 J24
Borohrádek CZ 53 C6
Boronów PL 54 C3
Bórore I 110 C1
Boroszów PL 54 C3
Borota H 75 B4
Boroughbridge GB 27 A4
Borovany CZ 63 B5
Borovichi RUS 7 G23
Borovnica SLO 73 C4
Borovo HR 75 C3
Borovsk RUS 7 J25
Borovy CZ 63 A4
Borowa PL 54 B2
Borowie PL 55 B6
Borox E 94 B3
Borrby S 41 D4
Borre DK 41 E2
Borre N 34 B2
Borredá E 91 A4
Borrenes E 86 B4
Borriol E 96 A2
Borris DK 39 D1
Borris IRL 21 B5
Borris-in-Ossory IRL 21 B4
Borrisokane IRL 20 B3
Borrisoleigh IRL 21 B4
Borrowdale GB 26 A2
Borşa RO 11 N19
Borsdorf D 52 B2
Borsfa H 74 B1
Borský Mikuláš SK 64 B3
Borsodivánka H 65 C6
Borsodnádasd H 65 B6
Bort-les-Orgues F 68 C2
Börte N 33 B4
Borth GB 26 C1
Boruja Kościelne PL 53 A6
Borup DK 39 D4
Boryslav UA 11 M18
Boryspil UA 11 L22
Boryszyn PL 46 C1
Borzęciczki PL 54 B2
Borzęcin PL 55 A5
Borzna UA 7 L23
Borzonasca I 80 B3
Borzyszkowy PL 46 A3
Borzytuchom PL 46 A3
Bosa I 110 C1
Bošáca SK 64 B3
Bosanci HR 73 C5
Bosanska Dubica BIH 74 C1
Bosanska Gradiška BIH 74 C2
Bosanska Kostajnica BIH 74 C1
Bosanska Krupa BIH 83 B5
Bosanski Brod BIH 84 A2
Bosanski Novi BIH 83 A5
Bosanski Petrovac BIH 83 B5
Bosanski Šamac BIH 84 A3
Bosansko Grahovo BIH 83 B5
Bošany SK 64 B4
Bösárkány H 64 C3
Bosau D 44 A2
Bócsa H 75 B4
Boscastle GB 28 C3
Bosco Chiesanuova I 71 C6
Bösdorf D 44 A2
Bösel D 43 B4
Bosham GB 31 D3
Bösingfeld D 51 A5
Boskoop NL 49 A5
Boskovice CZ 64 A2
Bošnjaci HR 84 A3
Bossast E 77 D3
Bossolasco I 80 B2
Boštanj SLO 73 B5
Boston GB 27 C5
Bostrak N 33 B5
Böszénfa H 74 B2
Bot E 90 B3
Botajica BIH 84 B3
Bøte By DK 44 A3
Bothel GB 26 A2
Boticas P 87 C3
Botilsäter S 35 B5
Botoš YU 75 C5
Botoşani RO 11 N20
Botricello I 107 C3
Bottendorf D 51 B4
Bottesford GB 27 C5
Bottnaryd S 40 B3
Bottrop D 50 B2
Botunje YU 85 B6
Boturić YU 85 C5
Bötzingen D 60 B3
Bouaye F 66 A3
Bouça P 87 C3
Boucau F 76 C1
Bouchain F 49 C4
Bouchoir F 58 A3
Boudreville F 59 C5
Boudry CH 70 B1
Bouesse F 67 B6
Bouguenais F 66 A3
Bouhy F 68 A3
Bouillargues F 78 C3
Bouillon B 59 A6
Bouilly F 59 B4
Bouin F 66 B3
Boulay-Moselle F 60 A2
Boulazac F 67 C5
Boule-d'Amont F 91 A5
Bouligny F 60 A1
Boulogne-sur-Gesse F 77 C3
Boulogne-sur-Mer F 48 C2
Bouloire F 58 C1
Bouquemaison F 48 C3
Bourbon-Lancy F 68 B3
Bourbon-l'Archambault F 68 B3
Bourbonne-les-Bains F 60 C1
Bourbourg F 48 C3
Bourbriac F 56 B2
Bourcefranc-le-Chapus F 66 C3
Bourdeaux F 79 B4
Bouresse F 67 B5
Bourg F 76 A2
Bourg-Achard F 58 A1
Bourg-Argental F 69 C4
Bourg-de-Péage F 79 A4
Bourg-de-Thizy F 69 B4
Bourg-de-Visa F 77 B3
Bourg-en-Bresse F 69 B5
Bourg-et-Comin F 59 A4
Bourg-Lastic F 68 C2
Bourg-Madame F 91 A4
Bourg-St. Andéol F 78 B3
Bourg-St. Maurice F 70 C1
Bourganeuf F 68 C1
Bourges F 68 A2
Bourgneuf-en-Retz F 66 A3
Bourgogne F 59 A5
Bourgoin-Jallieu F 69 C5
Bourgtheroulde F 58 A1
Bourgueil F 67 A5
Bourmont F 60 B1
Bourne GB 30 B3
Bournemouth GB 29 C6
Bourneville F 58 A1
Bournezeau F 66 B3
Bourran F 77 B3
Bourret F 77 C4
Bourron-Marlotte F 58 B3
Bourton-on-The-Water GB 29 B6
Boussac F 68 B2
Boussens F 77 C3
Boutersem B 49 C5
Bouttencourt F 48 D2
Bouvières F 79 B4
Bouvron F 66 A3
Bouxwiller F 60 B3
Bouzas E 87 B2
Bouzonville F 60 A2
Bova I 109 B4
Bova Marina I 109 B4
Bovalino Marina I 106 C3
Bovallstrand S 35 C3
Bovec SLO 72 B3
Bóveda E 86 B3
Bóvegno I 71 C5
Bovenau D 44 A1
Bovenden D 51 B5
Bòves I 80 B1
Bovey Tracey GB 28 C4
Bovino I 104 A2
Bøvlingbjerg DK 38 C1
Bovolenta I 72 C1
Bovolone I 71 C6
Bowes GB 27 A4
Bowmore GB 24 C1
Bowness-on-Windermere GB 26 A3
Box GB 29 B5
Boxberg, *Baden-Württemberg* D 61 A5
Boxberg, *Sachsen* D 53 B4
Boxholm S 37 C2
Boxmeer NL 50 B1
Boxtel NL 49 B6
Boyle IRL 18 C3
Božava HR 83 B3
Bozburun TR 16 T21
Bozdoğan TR 16 T21
Božepole Wielkie PL 46 A3
Boževac YU 85 B6
Boži Dar CZ 52 C2
Božice CZ 64 B2
Bozouls F 78 B1
Bozüyük TR 16 S22
Bózzolo I 81 A4
Bra I 80 B1
Braås S 40 B5
Brabrand DK 39 C3
Bracadale GB 22 D2
Bracciano I 102 A2
Bracieux F 67 A6
Bräcke S 2 E14
Brackenheim D 61 A5
Brackley GB 30 B2
Bracklin IRL 19 C5
Bracknell GB 31 C3
Brackwede D 51 B4
Braco GB 25 B4
Brad RO 11 N18
Bradford GB 27 B4
Bradford on Avon GB 29 B5
Bradina BIH 84 C3
Brådland N 32 C3
Brae GB 22 A7
Brædstrup DK 39 D2
Braemar GB 23 D5
Braemore GB 22 D3
Braga P 87 C2
Bragança P 87 C4
Brăila RO 11 P20
Braine F 59 A4
Braine-le-Comte B 49 C5
Braintree GB 31 C4
Braives B 49 C6
Brake D 43 B5
Brakel B 49 C4
Brakel D 51 B5
Bräkne-Hoby S 41 C5
Brålanda S 35 C4
Bralin PL 54 B2
Brallo di Pregola I 80 B3
Bram F 77 C5
Bramafan F 79 C5
Bramberg am Wildkogel A 72 A2
Bramdrupdam DK 39 D2
Bramming DK 39 D1
Brampton GB 25 D5
Bramsche D 43 C4
Branca I 82 C1
Brancaleone Marina I 106 D3
Brancaster GB 30 B4
Brand, *Nieder Östereich* A 63 B6
Brand, *Vorarlberg* A 71 A4
Brand-Erbisdorf D 52 C3
Brandbu N 34 A2
Brande DK 39 D2
Brande-Hornerkirchen D 43 B6
Brandenberg A 72 A1
Brandenburg D 45 C4
Brandis D 52 B2
Brando F 110 A2
Brandomil E 86 A2
Brandon GB 30 B4
Brandshagen D 45 A5
Brandval N 34 A4
Brandýs nad Labem CZ 53 C4
Branice PL 54 C2
Braniewo PL 47 A5
Branik SLO 72 C3
Brankovina YU 85 B4
Branky CZ 64 A3
Branne F 76 B2
Brannenburg-Degerndorf D 62 C3
Brantôme F 67 C5
Branzi I 71 B4
Bras d'Asse F 79 C5
Braslaw BY 7 J20
Braşov RO 11 P19
Brasparts F 56 B2
Brassac, *Charente* F 67 C4
Brassac, *Tarn* F 77 C5
Brassac-les-Mines F 68 C3
Brasschaat B 49 B5
Brastad S 35 C3
Břasy CZ 63 A4
Brąszewice PL 54 B3
Bratislava SK 64 B3
Brattfors S 34 B6
Bratunac BIH 85 B4
Braubach D 50 C3
Braunau A 62 B4
Braunfels D 51 C4
Braunlage D 51 B6
Braunsbedra D 52 B1
Braunschweig D 51 A6
Bray IRL 21 A5
Bray Dunes F 48 B3
Bray-sur-Seine F 59 B4
Bray-sur-Somme F 58 A3
Brazatortas E 100 A1
Brazey-en-Plaine F 69 A5
Brbinj HR 83 B4
Brčko BIH 84 B3
Brdani YU 85 C5
Brdów PL 47 C4
Brea de Tajo E 95 B3
Brécey F 57 B4
Brechen D 50 C4
Brechin GB 25 B5
Brecht B 49 B5
Brecketfeld D 50 B3
Břeclav CZ 64 B2
Brecon GB 29 B4
Brécy F 68 A2
Breda E 91 B5
Breda NL 49 B5
Bredaryd S 40 B3
Breddin D 44 C4
Bredebro DK 39 D1
Bredelar D 51 B4
Bredenfelde D 45 B5
Bredsjö S 36 B1
Bredstedt D 43 A5
Bredsten DK 39 D2
Bree B 49 B6
Bregana HR 73 C5
Breganze I 72 C1
Bregenz A 71 A4
Bréhal F 57 B4
Brehna D 52 B2
Breidenbach F 60 A3
Breil-sur-Roya F 80 C1
Breisach D 60 B3
Breitenbach CH 70 A2
Breitenbach D 51 C5
Breitenberg D 63 B4
Breitenfelde D 44 B2
Breitengussbach D 51 D6
Breivikbotn N 2 A18
Brejning DK 39 D2
Brekken N 2 E12
Brekkestø N 33 C5
Brekstad N 2 E11
Brem-sur-Mer F 66 B3
Bremen D 43 B5
Bremerhaven D 43 B5
Bremervörde D 43 B6
Bremgarten CH 70 A3
Brenderup DK 39 D2
Brenes E 99 B5
Brengova SLO 73 B5
Brenna PL 65 A4
Breno I 71 C5
Brénod F 69 B5
Brensbach D 61 A4
Brentwood GB 31 C4
Brescello I 81 B4
Bréscia I 71 C5
Breskens NL 49 B4
Bresles F 58 A3
Bresnica YU 85 C5
Bressana I 80 A3
Bressanone I 72 B1
Bressuire F 67 B4
Brest BY 6 K18
Brest F 56 B1
Brest HR 72 C3
Brestač YU 85 B4
Brestanica SLO 73 C5
Brestova HR 82 A3
Brestovac HR 74 C2
Bretenoux F 77 B4
Breteuil, *Eure* F 58 B1
Breteuil, *Oise* F 58 A3
Brétigny-sur-Orge F 58 B3
Bretten D 61 A4
Bretteville-sur-Laize F 57 A5
Brettheim D 61 A6
Breuil-Cervinia I 70 C2
Breukelen NL 49 A6
Brevik N 33 B6
Brevik S 36 B5
Breza BIH 84 B3
Brežice SLO 73 C5
Bréziers F 79 B5
Brezna YU 85 C5
Breznica HR 73 B6
Breznica Našička HR 74 C2
Březnice CZ 63 A4
Brezno SK 65 B5
Brezolles F 58 B2
Březová nad Svitavou CZ 64 A2
Brezová pod Bradlom SK 64 B3
Brezovica SK 65 A6
Brezovica SLO 73 B4
Brezovo Polje Selo BIH 84 B3
Briançon F 79 B5
Brianconnet F 79 C5
Briare F 58 C3
Briatexte F 77 C4
Briático I 106 C3
Briaucourt F 59 B6
Bribir HR 73 C4
Bricquebec F 57 A4
Bridge of Cally GB 25 B4
Bridge of Don GB 23 D6
Bridge of Earn GB 25 B4
Bridge of Orchy GB 24 B3
Bridgend, *Argyll & Bute* GB 24 C1
Bridgend, *Bridgend* GB 29 B4
Bridgnorth GB 26 C3
Bridgwater GB 29 B5
Břidličná CZ 64 A3
Bridlington GB 27 A5
Bridport GB 29 C5
Brie-Comte-Robert F 58 B3
Briec F 56 B1
Brienne-le-Château F 59 B5
Brienon-sur-Armançon F 59 C4
Brienz CH 70 B3
Brienza I 104 B2
Brieskow Finkenheerd D 53 A4
Brietlingen D 44 B2
Brieva de Cameros E 89 B4
Briey F 60 A1
Brig CH 70 B3
Brigg GB 27 B5
Brighouse GB 27 B4
Brightlingsea GB 31 C5
Brighton GB 31 D3
Brignogan-Plage F 56 B1
Brignoles F 79 C5
Brigstock GB 30 B3
Brihuega E 95 B4
Brijuni HR 82 B2
Brillon-en-Barrois F 59 B6
Brilon D 51 B4
Brinches P 98 A3
Brindisi I 105 B4
Brinje HR 83 A4
Brinon-sur-Beuvron F 68 A3
Brinon-sur-Sauldre F 68 A2
Brinyan GB 23 B5
Brión E 86 B2
Briones E 89 B4
Brionne F 58 A1
Brioude F 68 C3
Brioux-sur-Boutonne F 67 B4
Briouze F 57 B5
Briscous F 76 C1
Brisighella I 81 B5
Brissac-Quincé F 67 A4
Brissago CH 70 B3
Bristol GB 29 B5
Brive-la-Gaillarde F 67 C6
Briviesca E 89 B3
Brixham GB 29 C4
Brixlegg A 72 A1
Brka BIH 84 B3
Brnaze HR 83 C5
Brněnec CZ 64 A2
Brno CZ 64 A2
Bro S 36 B4
Broad Haven GB 28 B2
Broadclyst GB 29 C4
Broadford GB 22 D3
Broadstairs GB 31 C5
Broadstone GB 29 C5
Broadway GB 29 A6
Broager DK 39 E2
Broaryd S 40 B3
Broby S 41 C4
Brobyværk DK 39 D3
Bročanac BIH 84 C2
Bročanac YU 84 D3
Brocas F 76 B2
Brock D 50 A3
Brockel D 43 B6
Brockenhurst GB 31 D2
Broczyno PL 46 B2
Brod na Kupi HR 73 C4
Brodalen S 35 C3
Brodarevo YU 85 C4
Broddbo S 36 B3
Brodek u Přerova CZ 64 A3
Broden-bach D 50 C3
Brodick GB 24 C2
Brodnica PL 47 B5
Brodnica Graniczna PL 47 A4
Brody PL 47 C6
Brody, *Zielona Góra* PL 53 A5
Brody, *Zielona Góra* PL 53 B4
Brody UA 11 L19
Broglie F 58 B1
Brójce PL 53 A5
Brokind S 37 C2
Brolo I 109 A3
Brome D 44 C2
Bromley GB 31 C4
Bromölla S 41 C4
Bromont-Lamothe F 68 C2
Brömsebro S 41 C5
Bromsgrove GB 29 A5
Bromyard GB 29 A5
Bronchales E 95 B5
Bronco E 93 A4
Brønderslev DK 38 B2
Broni I 80 A3
Brønnøysund N 2 D13
Brøns DK 39 D1
Bronte I 109 B3
Bronzani Mejdan BIH 84 B1
Bronzolo I 71 B6
Broons F 57 B3
Broquies F 78 B1
Brora GB 23 C5
Brørup DK 39 D2
Brösarp S 41 D4
Brostrud N 33 A5
Brotas P 92 C2
Brötjärna S 36 B2
Broto E 90 A2
Brottby S 36 B5
Brou F 58 B2
Brouage F 66 C3
Brough GB 26 A3
Broughshane GB 19 B5
Broughton GB 25 C4
Broughton-in-Furness GB 26 A2
Broumov CZ 54 C1
Broût-Vernet F 68 B3
Brouvelieures F 60 B2
Brouwershaven NL 49 B4
Brovary UA 11 L22
Brovst DK 38 B2
Brownhills GB 27 C4
Brozas E 93 B4
Brozzo I 71 C5
Brtnice CZ 63 A6
Brtonigla HR 72 C3
Bruay-la-Buissière F 48 C3
Bruchhausen-Vilsen D 43 C6
Bruchsal D 61 A4
Bruck, *Bayern* D 62 A3
Brück, *Brandenburg* D 52 A2
Bruck an der Grossglocknerstrasse A 72 A2
Bruck an der Leitha A 64 B2
Bruck an der Mur A 73 A5
Brückl A 73 B4
Bruckmühl D 62 C2
Brue-Auriac F 79 C4
Brüel D 44 B3
Bruen CH 70 B3
Bruère-Allichamps F 68 B2
Bruff IRL 20 B3
Brugg CH 70 A3
Brugge B 49 B4
Brüggen D 50 B2
Brühl D 50 C2
Bruinisse NL 49 B5
Brûlon F 57 C5
Brumano I 71 C4
Brumath F 60 B3
Brummen NL 50 A2
Brumov-Bylnice CZ 64 A4
Brumunddal N 2 F12
Brunau D 44 C3
Brunehamel F 59 A5
Brünen D 50 B2
Brunete E 94 B2
Brunflo S 2 E14
Brunico I 72 B1
Brunkeberg N 33 B5
Brunn D 45 B5
Brunnen CH 70 B3
Brunsbüttel D 43 B6
Brunssum NL 50 C1
Bruntál CZ 64 A3
Brus YU 85 C6
Brušane HR 83 B4
Brusasco I 70 C3
Brusio CH 71 B5
Brusno SK 65 B5
Brusque F 78 C1
Brusson I 70 C2
Brüssow D 45 B6
Brusy PL 46 B3
Bruton GB 29 B5
Bruvno HR 83 B4
Bruvoll N 34 A3
Bruxelles B 49 C5
Bruyères F 60 B2
Bruz F 57 B4
Bruzaholm S 40 B5
Brwinów PL 55 A5
Bryansk RUS 7 K24
Brynamman GB 28 B4
Bryncrug GB 26 C1
Bryne N 32 C2
Brynmawr GB 29 B4
Brzeće YU 85 C5
Brzeg PL 54 C2
Brzeg Dolny PL 54 B1
Brześć Kujawski PL 47 C4
Brzesko PL 65 A6
Brzeszcze PL 65 A5
Brzezie PL 46 B2
Brzeziny, *Łódzkie* PL 55 B4
Brzeziny, *Wielkopolskie* PL 54 B3
Brzeźnica Nowa PL 55 B4
Brzeżno PL 46 B1
Brzotin SK 65 B6
Brzozie Lubawskie PL 47 B5
Bua S 38 B5
Buarcos P 92 A2
Buaveg N 32 B2
Bubbio I 80 B2
Bubry F 56 C2
Bucak TR 16 T22
Bučany SK 64 B3
Buccheri I 109 B3
Buccino I 104 B2
Bucelas P 92 C1
Buch D 62 B3
Buch, *Bayern* D 61 B6
Buchach UA 11 M19
Buchbach D 62 B3
Buchboden A 71 A4
Buchen, *Baden-Württemberg* D 61 A5
Büchen, *Schleswig-Holstein* D 44 B2
Buchenberg D 61 C6
Buchères F 59 B5
Buchholz D 44 B1
Buchloe D 62 B1
Buchlovice CZ 64 A3
Buchlyvie GB 24 B3
Bucholz D 44 B4
Buchs CH 71 A4
Buchy F 58 A2
Bückeburg D 51 A5
Buckfastleigh GB 28 C4
Buckhaven GB 25 B4
Buckie GB 23 D6
Buckingham GB 31 B3
Buckley GB 26 B2
Bückwitz D 44 C4
Bučovice CZ 64 A3
Bucsa H 75 A6
Bucureşti RO 11 P20
Bucy-lés-Pierrepont F 59 A4
Buczek PL 55 B4
Budakalasz H 65 C5
Budakeszi H 75 A3
Budaörs H 75 A3
Budapest H 75 A4
Buddusò I 110 C2
Bude GB 28 C3
Budeč CZ 63 A6
Büdelsdorf D 43 A6
Budens P 98 B2
Budia E 95 B4
Budimlić-Japra BIH 83 B5
Büdingen D 51 C5
Budinšćina HR 73 B6
Budišov CZ 64 A3
Budleigh Salterton GB 29 C4
Budmerice SK 64 B3
Budoni I 110 C2
Búdrio I 81 B5
Budva YU 15 Q16
Budyně nad Ohří CZ 53 C4
Budziszewice PL 55 B4
Budzyń PL 46 C2
Bue N 32 C2
Bueña E 90 C1
Buenache de Alarcón E 95 C4
Buenache de la Sierra E 95 B5
Buenaventura E 94 B2
Buenavista de Valdavia E 88 B2
Buendia E 95 B4
Bueu E 87 B2
Buezo E 89 B3
Bugac H 75 B4
Bugarra E 96 B2
Bugeat F 68 C1
Buggerru I 110 D1
Bugojno BIH 84 B2
Bugyi H 75 A4
Bühl D 61 B4
Bühl, *Bayern* D 71 A5
Bühlertal D 61 B4
Bühlertann D 61 A5
Buia I 72 B3
Builth Wells GB 29 A4
Buis-les-Baronnies F 79 B4
Buitenpost NL 42 B3
Buitrago del Lozoya E 95 B3
Bujalance E 100 B1
Bujaraloz E 90 B2
Buje HR 72 C3
Bujedo E 89 B3
Bük H 74 A1
Buk PL 46 C2
Bükkösd H 74 B2
Bükkzsérc H 65 C6
Bukovci SLO 73 B5
Bukowiec PL 53 A6
Bukowina Tatrzańska PL 65 A6
Bukownica PL 54 B3
Bukowno PL 55 C4
Bülach CH 70 A3
Buldan TR 16 S21
Bulgnéville F 60 B1
Bülkau D 43 B5
Bulkowo PL 47 C6
Bullas E 101 A4
Bulle CH 70 B2
Büllingen B 50 C2
Buna BIH 84 C2
Bunahowen IRL 18 B2
Bunbeg IRL 18 A3
Bunclody IRL 21 B5
Buncrana IRL 19 A4
Bunde, *Niedersachsen* D 43 B4
Bünde, *Nordrhein-Westfalen* D 51 A4
Bundoran IRL 18 B3
Bunessan GB 24 B1
Bungay GB 30 B5
Bunić HR 83 B4
Bunmahon IRL 21 B4
Bunnyconnellan IRL 18 B2
Buño E 86 A2
Buñol E 96 B2
Bunratty IRL 20 B3
Bunsbeek B 49 C5
Buñuel E 89 C5
Bunyola, *Mallorca* E 97
Buonabitácolo I 104 B2
Buonalbergo I 104 A1
Buonconvento I 81 C5
Buonvicino I 106 B2
Burano I 72 C2
Burbach D 50 C4
Burcei I 110 D2
Burdur TR 16 T22
Bureå S 3 D17
Burela E 86 A3
Büren D 51 B4
Büren an der Aare CH 70 A2
Burford GB 29 B6
Burg, *Cottbus* D 53 B4
Burg, *Magdeburg* D 52 A1
Burg, *Schleswig-Holstein* D 43 B6
Burg auf Fehmarn D 44 A3
Burg Stargard D 45 B5
Burgas BG 16 Q20
Burgau A 73 A6
Burgau D 61 B6
Burgau P 98 B2
Burgbernheim D 61 A6
Burgdorf CH 70 A2
Burgdorf D 44 C2
Burgebrach D 62 A1
Bürgel D 52 C1
Burgess Hill GB 31 D3
Burgh le Marsh GB 27 B6
Burghaslach D 61 A6
Burghausen D 62 B3
Burghead GB 23 D5
Burgheim D 62 B2
Búrgio I 108 B2
Burgkirchen D 62 B3
Burgkunstadt D 52 C1
Burglengenfeld D 62 A3
Burgo P 87 D2
Burgoberbach D 61 A6
Burgohondo E 94 B2
Burgos E 88 B3
Burgsinn D 51 C5
Burgstädt D 52 C2
Burgstall D 44 C3
Burgsvik S 6 H16
Burgui E 76 D2
Burguillos E 99 B5
Burguillos de Toledo E 94 C3
Burguillos del Cerro E 93 C4
Burhaniye TR 16 S20
Burhave D 43 B5
Burie F 67 C4
Burjassot E 96 B2
Burk D 61 A6
Burkhardtsdorf D 52 C2
Burlada E 89 B5
Burladingen D 61 B5
Burlage D 43 B4
Burness GB 23 B6
Burnham GB 31 C3
Burnham Market GB 30 B4
Burnham-on-Crouch GB 31 C4
Burnham-on-Sea GB 29 B5
Burniston GB 27 A5
Burnley GB 26 B3
Burntisland GB 25 B4
Burón E 88 A1
Buronzo I 70 C3
Burovac YU 85 B6
Burow D 45 B5
Burravoe GB 22 A7
Burret F 77 D4
Burriana E 96 B2
Burry Port GB 28 B3
Bürs A 71 A4
Bursa TR 16 R21
Burseryd S 40 B3
Bürstadt D 61 A4
Burton GB 26 A3
Burton Agnes GB 27 A5
Burton Bradstock GB 29 C5
Burton Latimer GB 30 B3
Burton upon Stather GB 27 B5
Burton Upon Trent GB 27 C4
Burujón E 94 C2
Burwell GB 30 B4
Burwick GB 23 C6
Bury GB 26 B3
Bury St. Edmunds GB 30 B4
Buryn UA 7 L23
Burzenin PL 54 B3
Busachi I 110 C1
Busalla I 80 B2
Busana I 81 B4
Busano I 70 C2
Busca I 80 B1
Busch D 44 C3
Buševec HR 73 C6
Bushey GB 31 C3
Bushmills GB 19 A5
Bušince SK 65 B5
Buskhyttan S 37 C3
Busko-Zdrój PL 55 C5
Busot E 96 C2
Busovača BIH 84 B2
Busquistar E 100 C2
Bussang F 60 C2
Busseto I 81 B4
Bussière-Badil F 67 C5
Bussière-Poitevine F 67 B5
Bussolengo I 71 C5
Bussoleno I 70 C2
Bussum NL 49 A6
Busto Arsizio I 70 C3
Büsum D 43 A5
Butera I 109 B3
Butgenbach B 50 C2
Butler's Bridge IRL 19 B4
Butryny PL 47 B6
Bütschwil CH 70 A4
Buttermere GB 26 A2
Buttevant IRL 20 B3
Buttstädt D 52 B1
Butzbach D 51 C4
Bützfleth D 43 B6
Bützow D 44 B3
Buxières-les-Mines F 68 B2
Buxtehude D 43 B6
Buxton GB 27 B4
Buxy F 69 B4
Büyükçekmece TR 16 R21
Buzançais F 67 B6
Buzancy F 59 A5
Buzău RO 11 P20
Buzet HR 72 C3
Buzsák H 74 B2
Buzy F 76 C2
By S 36 A3
Byala BG 16 Q19
Byaroza BY 6 K19
Byczyna PL 54 B3
Bydgoszcz PL 47 B4
Bygland N 33 C4
Byglandsfjord N 33 C4
Bykhaw BY 7 K22
Bykle N 33 B4
Bylderup-Bov DK 39 E2
Byrum DK 38 B3
Byšice CZ 53 C4
Byske S 3 D17
Býškovice CZ 64 A3
Byslaw PL 46 B3
Bystré CZ 64 A2
Bystrice, *Středočeský* CZ 65 A4
Bystřice, *Středočeský* CZ 63 A5
Bystřice n Pernštejnem CZ 64 A2
Bystřice pod Hostýnem CZ 64 A3
Bystrzyca Kłodzka PL 54 C1
Bytča SK 65 A4
Bytom PL 54 C3
Bytom Odrzański PL 53 B5
Bytów PL 46 A3
Bzenec CZ 64 B3
Bzince SK 64 B3

C

Cabacos P 92 B2
Cabaj-Čápor SK 64 B4
Cabana E 86 A2
Cabanac-et-Villagrains F 76 B2
Cabañaquinta E 88 A1
Cabanas P 98 B3
Cabañas de Yepes E 95 C3
Cabañas del Castillo E 93 B5
Cabanelles E 91 A5
Cabanes E 96 A3
Cabanillas E 89 B5
Čabar HR 73 C4
Cabasse F 79 C5
Cabdella E 91 A4
Cabeceiras de Basto P 87 C2
Cabeço de Vide P 92 B3
Cabella Ligure I 80 B3
Cabeza del Buey E 93 C5
Cabeza la Vaca E 99 A4
Cabezamesada E 95 C3
Cabezarados E 100 A1
Cabezarrubias del Puerto E 100 A1
Cabezas del Villar E 94 B1
Cabezas Rubias E 99 B3
Cabezón E 88 C2
Cabezón de la Sal E 88 A2
Cabezón de Liébana E 88 A2
Cabezuela E 94 A3
Cabezuela del Valle E 93 A5
Cabo de Gata E 101 C3
Cabo de Palos E 101 B5
Cabolafuenta E 95 A4
Cabourg F 57 A5
Cabra E 100 B1
Cabra P 92 A3
Cabra del Santo Cristo E 100 B2
Cabrach GB 23 D5
Cábras I 110 D1
Cabreiro P 87 C2
Cabreiros E 86 A3
Cabrejas E 95 B4
Cabrela P 92 C2
Cabrillas E 87 D4
Cabuna HR 74 C2
Cacabelos E 86 B4
Čačak YU 85 C5
Cáccamo I 108 B2
Caccuri I 107 B3
Cacela P 98 B3
Cacém P 92 C1
Cáceres E 93 B4
Cachafeiro E 86 B2
Cachopo P 98 B3
Čachtice SK 64 B3
Cacin E 100 B2
Čačinci HR 74 C2
Cadafais P 92 C1
Cadalen F 77 C5
Cadalso E 93 A4
Cadaqués E 91 A6
Cadaval P 92 B1
Cadavedo E 86 A4
Čadavica BIH 84 B1
Čadca SK 65 A4
Cadéac F 77 D3
Cadelbosco di Sopra I 81 B4
Cadenazzo CH 70 B3
Cadenberge D 43 B6
Cadenet F 79 C4
Cadeuil F 66 C4
Cádiar E 100 C2
Cadillac F 76 B2
Cádiz E 99 C4
Čadjavica HR 74 C2
Cadouin F 77 B3
Cadours F 77 C4
Cadrete E 90 B2
Caen F 57 A5
Caerleon GB 29 B5
Caernarfon GB 26 B1
Caerphilly GB 29 B4
Caersws GB 26 C2
Cafede P 92 B3
Caggiano I 104 B2
Cagli I 82 C1
Cágliari I 110 D2
Čaglin HR 74 C2
Cagnano Varano I 104 A2
Cagnes-sur-Mer F 79 C6
Caher IRL 21 B4
Caherciveen IRL 20 C1
Caherdaniel IRL 20 C1
Cahors F 77 B4
Cahul MD 11 P21
Caiazzo I 103 B4
Caion E 86 A2
Cairndow GB 24 B3
Cairnryan GB 24 D2
Cairo Montenotte I 80 B2
Caister-on-Sea GB 30 B5
Caistor GB 27 B5
Caivano I 103 C4
Cajarc F 77 B4
Ćajetina YU 85 C4
Čajniče BIH 84 C4
Čakovec HR 73 B6
Çal TR 16 S21
Cala E 99 B4
Cala d'Or, *Mallorca* E 97
Cala Galdana, *Menorca* E 97
Cala Gonone I 110 C2
Cala Llonga E 97 C4
Cala Millor, *Mallorca* E 97
Cala Ratjada, *Mallorca* E 97
Calabritto I 104 B2
Calaceite E 90 C3
Calacuccia F 110 A2
Calaf E 91 B4
Calafat RO 11 P18
Calafell E 91 B4
Calahonda E 100 C2
Calahorra E 89 B5
Calais F 48 C2
Calalzo di Cadore I 72 B2
Calamocha E 90 C1
Calamonte E 93 C4
Calanais GB 22 C2
Calañas E 99 B4
Calanda E 90 C2
Calangiánus I 110 C2
Călăraşi RO 11 P20
Calascibetta I 109 B3
Calasetta I 110 D1
Calasparra E 101 A4
Calatafimi I 108 B1
Calatayud E 89 C5
Calatorao E 89 C5
Calau D 53 B3
Calbe D 52 B1
Calcena E 89 C5
Calcinelli I 82 C1
Calco I 71 C4
Caldaro sulla strada del vino I 71 B6
Caldarola I 82 C2
Caldas da Rainha P 92 B1
Caldas de Boi E 90 A3
Caldas de Malavella E 91 B5
Caldas de Reis E 86 B2
Caldas de San Jorge P 87 D2
Caldas de Vizela P 87 C2
Caldaso de los Vidrios E 94 B2
Caldbeck GB 26 A2
Caldearenas E 90 A2
Caldelas P 87 C2
Calders E 91 B4
Caldes de Montbui E 91 B5
Caldicot GB 29 B5
Caldirola I 80 B3
Caledon GB 19 B5
Calella, *Barcelona* E 91 B5
Calella, *Girona* E 91 B6
Calenzana F 110 A1
Calera de León E 99 A4
Calera y Chozas E 94 C2
Caleruega E 89 C3
Caleruela E 94 C1
Cales de Mallorca, *Mallorca* E 97
Calestano I 81 B4
Calfsound GB 23 B6
Calgary GB 24 B1
Calimera I 105 B5
Calitri I 104 B2
Calizzano I 80 B2
Callac F 56 B2
Callan IRL 21 B4
Callander GB 24 B3
Callas F 79 C5
Calliano, *Piemonte* I 80 A2
Calliano, *Trentino Alto Adige* I 71 C6
Callington GB 28 C3
Callosa de Ensarriá E 96 C2
Callosa de Segura E 96 C2
Callús E 91 B4
Čalma YU 85 A4
Calmbach D 61 B4
Calne GB 29 B6
Calolziocorte I 71 C4
Calonge E 91 B6
Čalovec SK 64 C3
Calpe E 96 C3
Caltabellotta I 108 B2
Caltagirone I 109 B3
Caltanissetta I 109 B3
Caltavuturo I 108 B2
Caltojar E 89 C4
Caluire-et-Cuire F 69 C4
Caluso I 70 C2
Calvello I 104 B2
Calvi F 110 A1
Calviá, *Mallorca* E 97
Calvisson F 78 C3
Calvörde D 44 C3
Calw D 61 B4
Calzada de Calatrava E 100 A2
Calzada de Valdunciel E 94 A1
Calzadilla de los Barros E 99 A4
Cam GB 29 B5
Camaiore I 81 C4
Camarasa E 90 B3
Camarena E 94 B2
Camarès F 78 C1
Camaret-sur-Aigues F 78 B3
Camaret-sur-Mer F 56 B1
Camarillas E 90 C2
Camariñas E 86 A1
Camarma E 95 B3
Camarzana de Tera E 87 B4
Camas E 99 B4
Camastra I 108 B2
Cambados E 86 B2
Cambarinho P 92 A2
Camberley GB 31 C3
Cambil E 100 B2
Cambo-les-Bains F 76 C1
Camborne GB 28 C2
Cambrai F 49 C4
Cambre E 86 A2
Cambridge GB 30 B4
Cambrils E 91 B4
Cambs D 44 B3
Camburg D 52 B1
Camden GB 31 C3
Cameleño E 88 A2
Camelford GB 28 C3
Çameli TR 16 T21
Camelle E 86 A1
Camerano I 82 C2
Camerino I 82 C2
Camerota I 104 B2
Camigliatello Silano I 106 B3
Caminha P 87 C2
Caminomorisco E 93 A4
Caminreal E 90 C1
Camisano Vicentino I 72 C1
Cammarata I 108 B2
Camogli I 80 B3
Camors F 56 C3
Camp IRL 20 B2
Campagna I 104 B2
Campagnano di Roma I 102 A2
Campagnático I 81 D5
Campan F 76 C3
Campana I 107 B3
Campanario E 93 C5
Campanillas E 100 C1
Campano E 99 C4
Campaspero E 88 C2
Campbeltown GB 24 C2
Campello E 96 C2
Campelos P 92 B1
Campi Bisénzio I 81 C5
Campi Salentina I 105 B5
Campico López E 101 B4
Campiglia Marittima I 81 C4
Campillo de Altobuey E 95 C5
Campillo de Aragón E 95 A5
Campillo de Arenas E 100 B2
Campillo de Llerena E 93 C5
Campillos E 100 B1
Câmpina RO 11 P19
Campli I 82 D2
Campo E 90 A3
Campo de Bacerros E 87 B3
Campo de Caso E 88 A1
Campo de Criptana E 95 C3
Campo Ligure I 80 B2
Campo Lugar E 93 B5
Campo Maior P 93 B3
Campo Molino I 79 B6
Campo Real E 95 B3
Campo Túres I 72 B1
Campobasso I 103 B4
Campobello di Licata I 108 B2
Campobello di Mazara I 108 B1
Campodársego I 72 C1
Campodolcino I 71 B4
Campofelice di Roccella I 108 B2
Campofiorito I 108 B2
Campofórmido I 72 B3
Campofranco I 108 B2
Campofrio E 99 B4
Campogalliano I 81 B4
Campolongo I 72 B2
Campomanes E 88 A1
Campomarino I 103 B5
Camporeale I 108 B2
Camporeggiano I 82 C1
Camporrells E 90 B3
Camporrobles E 96 B1
Campos P 87 C3
Campos del Port, *Mallorca* E 97
Camposa P 87 C2
Camposampiero I 72 C1
Camposanto I 81 B5
Camposines E 90 B3
Campotéjar E 100 B2
Campotosto I 103 A3
Camprodón E 91 A5
Campsegret F 77 B3
Camrose GB 28 B2
Camuñas E 95 C3
Çan TR 16 R20
Can Pastilla, *Mallorca* E 97
C'an Picafort, *Mallorca* E 97
Cana I 81 D5
Cañada del Hoyo E 95 C5
Cañada Rosal E 99 B5
Cañadajuncosa E 95 C4
Čanak HR 83 B4
Çanakkale TR 16 R20
Canal San Bovo I 72 B1
Canale I 80 B1
Canales, *Asturias* E 88 B1
Canales, *Castellón de la Plana* E 96 B2
Canals E 96 C2
Cañamares E 95 B4
Cañamero E 94 C1
Cañar E 100 C2
Cañate la Real E 99 C5
Cañaveral E 93 B4
Cañaveral de León E 99 A4
Cañaveras E 95 B4
Cañaveruelas E 95 B4
Canazei I 72 B1
Cancale F 57 B4
Cancellara I 104 B2
Cancello ed Arnone I 103 B4
Cancon F 77 B3
Canda E 87 B4
Candamil E 86 A3
Candanchu E 76 D2
Candas E 88 A1
Candasnos E 90 B3
Candé F 66 A3
Candela I 104 A2
Candelario E 93 A5
Candeleda E 94 B1
Cándia Lomellina I 70 C3
Candide Casamazzagno I 72 B2
Candin E 86 B4
Candosa P 92 A3
Canecas P 92 C1
Canelli I 80 B2
Canena E 100 A2
Canencia E 94 B3
Canero E 86 A4
Canet de Mar E 91 B5
Canet d'en Berenguer E 96 B2
Canet-Plage F 91 A6
Cañete E 95 B5
Cañete de las Torres E 100 B1
Canfranc E 90 A2
Cangas, *Lugo* E 86 A3
Cangas, *Pontevedra* E 87 B2
Cangas de Narcea E 86 A4
Cangas de Onis E 88 A1
Canha P 92 C2
Canhestros P 98 A2
Canicattì I 108 B2
Canicattini Bagni I 109 B4
Canicosa de la Sierra E 89 C3
Caniles E 101 B3
Canillas de Aceituno E 100 C1
Canino I 102 A1
Canisy F 57 A4
Cañizal E 94 A1
Cañizo E 88 C1
Canjáyar E 101 C3
Cannara I 82 C1
Cánnero Riviera I 70 B3
Cannes F 79 C6
Canneto, *Sicilia* I 109 A3
Canneto, *Toscana* I 81 C4
Canneto sull'Oglio I 81 A4
Cannich GB 22 D4
Cannóbio I 70 B3
Cannock GB 26 C3
Canonbie GB 25 C5
Canosa di Púglia I 104 A3
Cantalapiedra E 94 A1
Cantalejo E 94 A3
Cantalgallo E 99 A4
Cantalice I 102 A2
Cantalpino E 94 A1
Cantalupo in Sabina I 102 A2
Cantanhede P 92 A2
Cantavieja E 90 C2
Čantavir YU 75 C4
Canterbury GB 31 C5
Cantiano I 82 C1
Cantillana E 99 B5
Cantiveros E 94 B2
Cantoria E 101 B3
Cantù I 71 C4
Canvey GB 31 C4
Cany-Barville F 58 A1
Canyet de Mar E 91 B5
Caol GB 24 B2
Cáorle I 72 C2
Caorso I 81 A3
Cap-de-Pin F 76 B2
Cap Ferret F 76 B1
Capáccio I 104 B2
Capaci I 108 A2
Capálbio I 102 A1
Capánnori I 81 C4
Caparde BIH 84 B3
Caparroso E 89 B5
Capbreton F 76 C1
Capdenac-Gare F 77 B5
Capdepera, *Mallorca* E 97
Capel Curig GB 26 B2
Capellades E 91 B4
Capena I 102 A2
Capendu F 77 C5
Capestang F 78 C2
Capestrano I 103 A3
Capileira E 100 C2
Capinha P 92 A3
Ca'Pisani I 82 B1
Capistrello I 103 B3
Capizzi I 109 B3
Čaplje BIH 83 B5
Čapljina BIH 84 C2
Capo di Ponte I 71 B5
Caposile I 72 C2
Capoterra I 110 D1
Cappamore IRL 20 B3
Cappeln D 43 C5
Cappoquin IRL 21 B4
Capracotta I 103 B4
Capránica I 102 A2
Caprarola I 102 A2
Capretta I 82 D1
Capri I 103 C4
Capriati a Volturno I 103 B4
Caprino Veronese I 71 C5
Captieux F 76 B2
Cápua I 103 B4
Capurso I 105 A3
Capvern F 77 C3
Carabaña E 95 B3
Carabias E 88 C3
Caracal RO 11 P19
Caracenilla E 95 B4
Caráglio I 80 B1
Caraman F 77 C4
Caramánico Terme I 103 A4
Caranga E 86 A4
Caranguejeira P 92 B2
Caransebeș RO 11 P18
Carantec F 56 B2
Carapelle I 104 A2
Carasco I 80 B3
Carate Brianza I 71 C4
Caravaca de la Cruz E 101 A4
Caravággio I 71 C4
Carbajal E 100 C1
Carbajo E 93 B3
Carballeda E 86 B3
Carballeda de Avia E 87 B2
Carballo E 86 A2
Carbis Bay GB 28 C2
Carbon-Blanc F 76 B2
Carbonera de Frentes E 89 C4
Carboneras E 101 C4
Carboneras de Guadazaón E 95 C5
Carbonero el Mayor E 94 A2
Carboneros E 100 A2
Carbónia I 110 D1
Carbonin I 72 B2
Carbonne F 77 C4
Carbost, *Highland* GB 22 D2
Carbost, *Highland* GB 22 D2
Carcaboso E 93 A4
Carcabuey E 100 B1
Carcaixent E 96 B2
Carcans F 76 A1
Carcans-Plage F 76 A1
Carção P 87 C4
Carcar E 89 B5
Cárcare I 80 B2
Carcassonne F 77 C5
Carcastillo E 89 B5
Carcedo de Burgos E 89 B3
Carcelén E 96 B1
Carcès F 79 C5
Carchelejo E 100 B2
Çardak TR 16 T21
Cardedeu E 91 B5
Cardeña E 100 A1
Cardenete E 95 C5
Cardeñosa E 94 B2
Cardeto I 109 A4
Cardiff GB 29 B4
Cardigan GB 28 A3
Cardona E 91 B4
Cardosos P 92 B2
Carei RO 11 N18
Carentan F 57 A4
Carentoir F 57 C3
Careri I 106 C3
Carevdar HR 74 B1
Cargèse F 110 A1
Carhaix-Plouguer F 56 B2
Caria P 92 A3
Cariati I 107 B3
Carignan F 59 A6
Carignano I 80 B1
Cariñena E 90 B1
Carini I 108 A2
Cariño E 86 A3
Carinola I 103 B3
Carisbrooke GB 31 D2
Carlabhagh GB 22 C2
Carlepont F 59 A4
Carlet E 96 B2
Carlingford IRL 19 B5
Carlisle GB 25 D5
Carloforte I 110 D1
Carlópoli I 106 B3
Carlow D 44 B2
Carlow IRL 21 B5
Carlton GB 27 C4
Carluke GB 25 C4
Carmagnola I 80 B1
Carmarthen GB 28 B3
Carmaux F 77 B5
Carmena E 94 C2
Cármenes E 88 B1
Carmine I 80 B1
Carmona E 99 B5
Carmonita E 93 B4
Carmyllie GB 25 B5
Carnac F 56 C2
Carndonagh IRL 19 A4
Carnew IRL 21 B5
Carnforth GB 26 A3
Cárnia I 72 B3
Carnlough GB 19 B6
Carno GB 26 C2
Carnon Plage F 78 C2
Carnota E 86 B1
Carnoustie GB 25 B5
Carnwath GB 25 C4
Carolei I 106 B3
Carolinensiel D 43 B4
Carolles F 57 B4
Carona I 71 B4
Caronía I 109 A3
Carovigno I 105 B4
Carovilli I 103 B4
Carpaneto Piacentino I 81 B3
Carpegna I 82 C1
Carpenédolo I 71 C5
Carpentras F 79 B4
Carpi I 81 B4
Carpignano Sésia I 70 C3
Carpineti I 81 B4
Carpineto Romano I 102 B3
Cărpiniș RO 75 C5
Carpino I 104 A2
Carpinone I 103 B4
Carpio E 94 A1
Carquefou F 66 A3
Carqueiranne F 79 C5
Carral E 86 A2
Carranque E 94 B3
Carrapichana P 92 A3
Carrara I 81 B4
Carraroe IRL 20 A2
Carrascalejo E 94 C1
Carrascosa del Campo E 95 B4
Carratraca E 100 C1
Carrazeda de Ansiães P 87 C3
Carrazedo de Montenegro P 87 C3
Carrbridge GB 23 D5
Carregal do Sal P 92 A2
Carreña E 88 A2
Carrick IRL 18 B3
Carrick-on-Shannon IRL 18 C3
Carrick-on-Suir IRL 21 B4
Carrickart IRL 19 A4
Carrickfergus GB 19 B6
Carrickmacross IRL 19 C5
Carrigallen IRL 19 C4
Carrión E 99 B4
Carrión de Calatrava E 94 C3
Carrión de los Condes E 88 B2
Carrizo de la Ribera E 88 B1
Carrizosa E 100 A3
Carro F 79 C4
Carrocera E 88 B1
Carros F 79 C6
Carrouge CH 70 B1
Carrouges F 57 B5
Carrù I 80 B1
Carry-le-Rouet F 79 C4
Carryduff GB 19 B6
Carsóli I 102 A3
Carsphairn GB 24 C3
Cartagena E 101 B5
Cártama E 100 C1
Cartaxo P 92 B2
Cartaya E 98 B3
Carteret F 57 A4
Cartes E 88 A2
Carúnchio I 103 B4
Carviçães P 87 C4
Carvin F 48 C3
Carvoeira P 92 B1
Carvoeiro P 98 B2
Casa Branca, *Portalegre* P 92 C3
Casa Branca, *Setúbal* P 98 A2
Casa Castalda I 82 C1
Casa l'Abate I 105 B5
Casabermeja E 100 C1
Casacalenda I 103 B4
Casaio E 87 B4
Casàl di Principe I 103 B4
Casalarreina E 89 B4
Casalbordino I 103 A4
Casalborgone I 80 A1
Casalbuono I 104 B2
Casalbuttano ed Uniti I 71 C4
Casale Monferrato I 80 A2
Casalécchio di Reno I 81 B5
Casalina I 82 D1
Casalmaggiore I 81 B4
Casalnuovo Monterotaro I 104 A2
Casaloldo I 71 C5
Casalpusterlengo I 71 C4
Casamássima I 105 B3
Casamicciola Terme I 103 C3
Casamozza F 110 A2
Casar de Cáceres E 93 B4
Casar de Palomero E 93 A4
Casarabonela E 100 C1
Casarano I 105 B5
Casarejos E 89 C3
Casares E 99 C5
Casares de las Hurdes E 93 A4
Casariche E 100 B1
Casarrubios del Monte E 94 B2
Casas de Don Pedro E 94 C1
Casas de Fernando Alonso E 95 C4
Casas de Haro E 95 C4
Casas de Juan Gil E 96 B1
Casas de Millán E 93 B4
Casas de Reina E 99 A5
Casas de Ves E 96 B1
Casas del Juan Núñez E 96 B1
Casas del Puerto E 96 C1
Casas del Rio E 96 B1
Casas-Ibáñez E 96 B1
Casas Nuevas E 101 B4
Casasimarro E 95 C4
Casasola E 94 B2
Casasola de Arión E 88 C1
Casasuertes E 88 A2
Casatejada E 93 B5
Casavieja E 94 B2
Casazza I 71 C4
Cascais P 92 C1
Cascante E 89 C5
Cascante del Rio E 96 A1
Cáscia I 82 D2
Casciana Terme I 81 C4
Cáscina I 81 C4
Cáseda E 89 B5
Casekow D 45 B6
Casella I 80 B3
Caselle Torinese I 70 C2
Casemurate I 82 B1
Casenove I 82 D1
Caseres E 90 B3
Caserío Benali E 96 B2
Caserta I 103 B4
Casével P 98 B2
Cashel IRL 21 B4
Casillas E 94 B2
Casillas de Coria E 93 B4
Casina I 81 B4
Casinos E 96 B2
Čáslav CZ 63 A6
Cásola Valsénio I 81 B5
Cásole d'Elsa I 81 C5
Cásoli I 103 A4
Casória I 103 C4
Caspe E 90 B2
Cassà de la Selva E 91 B5
Cassagnas F 78 B2
Cassagnes-Bégonhès F 77 B5
Cassano allo Iónio I 106 B3
Cassano d'Adda I 71 C4
Cassano delle Murge I 105 B3
Cassano Magnago I 70 C3
Cassano Spinola I 80 B2
Cassel F 48 C3
Cassibile I 109 C4
Cassine I 80 B2
Cassino I 103 B3
Cassis F 79 C4
Cassolnovo I 70 C3
Casséjouls F 78 B1
Častá SK 64 B3
Castagnaro I 81 A5
Castagneto Carducci I 81 C4
Castagnola CH 70 B3
Castalla E 96 C2
Castañar de Ibor E 94 C1
Castanheira de Pêra P 92 A2
Cástano Primo I 70 C3
Castasegna CH 71 B4
Castéggio I 80 A3
Casteição P 87 D3
Castejón E 89 B5
Castejón de Monegros E 90 B2
Castejón de Sos E 90 A3
Castejón de Valdejasa E 90 B2
Castèl Baronia I 104 A2
Castel Bolognese I 81 B5
Castel d'Aiano I 81 B4
Castel d'Ario I 71 C5
Castel de Cabra E 90 C2
Castél del Monte I 103 A3
Castel del Piano I 81 D5
Castel di Iúdica I 109 B3
Castel di Rio I 81 B5
Castèl di Sangro I 103 B4
Castél di Tora I 102 A2
Castèl Frentano I 103 A4
Castel San Gimignano I 81 C5
Castèl San Giovanni I 80 A3
Castèl San Pietro Terme I 81 B5
Castél Sant'Elia I 102 A2
Castél Volturno I 103 B3
Castelbuono I 109 B3
Casteldáccia I 108 A2
Casteldelfino I 79 B6
Castelfidardo I 82 C2
Castelfiorentino I 81 C4
Castelforte I 103 B3
Castelfranco Emilia I 81 B5
Castelfranco in Miscano I 104 A2
Castelfranco Véneto I 72 C1
Casteljaloux F 76 B3
Castell Arquato I 81 B3
Castell de Cabres E 90 C3
Castell de Castells E 96 C2
Castell de Ferro E 100 C2
Castellabate I 104 B1
Castellammare del Golfo I 108 A1
Castellammare di Stábia I 103 C4
Castellamonte I 70 C2
Castellana Grotte I 105 B4
Castellane F 79 C5
Castellaneta I 105 B3
Castellaneta Marina I 105 B3
Castellar E 100 A2
Castellar de la Frontera E 99 C5
Castellar de la Ribera E 91 A4
Castellar de Santiago E 100 A2
Castellar del Vallés E 91 B5
Castellarano I 81 B4
Castell'Azzara I 81 D5
Castellbell i Villar E 91 B4
Castelldans E 90 B3
Castelldefels E 91 B4
Castelleone I 71 C4
Castellet E 91 B4
Castelletto di Brenzone I 71 C5
Castellfollit de la Roca E 91 A5
Castellfollit de Riubregos E 91 B4
Castellfort E 90 C2
Castellina in Chianti I 81 C5
Castellina Marittima I 81 C4
Castelló de Farfaña E 90 B3
Castelló de la Plana E 96 B2
Castello d'Empùries E 91 A6
Castello di Fiemme I 71 B6
Castello Tesino I 72 B1
Castelloli E 91 B4
Castellón de Rugat E 96 C2
Castellote E 90 C2
Castellterçol E 91 B5
Castellúcchio I 71 C5
Castellúccio de'Sáuri I 104 A2
Castelluccio Inferiore I 104 C2
Castelmassa I 81 A5
Castelmáuro I 103 B4
Castelmoron-sur-Lot F 77 B3
Castelnau-de-Médoc F 76 A2
Castelnau-de-Montmirail F 77 C4
Castelnau-Magnoac F 77 C3
Castelnau-Montratier F 77 B4
Castelnaudary F 77 C4
Castelnou E 90 B2
Castelnovo ne'Monti I 81 B4
Castelnuovo Berardenga I 81 C5
Castelnuovo della Dàunia I 104 A2
Castelnuovo di Garfagnana I 81 B4
Castelnuovo di Val di Cécina I 81 C4
Castelnuovo Don Bosco I 80 A1
Castelnuovo Scrivia I 80 B2
Castelo Branco, *Bragança* P 87 C4
Castelo Branco, *Castelo Branco* P 92 B3
Castelo de Paiva P 87 C2
Castelo de Vide P 92 B3
Castelo do Neiva P 87 C2
Castelo Mendo P 93 A4
Castelraimondo I 82 C2
Castelsantángelo I 82 D2
Castelsaraceno I 104 B2
Castelsardo I 110 C1
Castelsarrasin F 77 B4
Castelserás E 90 C2
Casteltérmini I 108 B2
Castelvecchio Subéquo I 103 A3
Castelvetrano I 108 B1
Castenédolo I 71 C5
Castets F 76 C1
Castiádas I 110 D2
Castiglion Fibocchi I 81 C5
Castiglion Fiorentino I 81 C5
Castiglioncello I 81 C4
Castiglione I 102 A3
Castiglione Chiavarese I 80 B3
Castiglione d'Adda I 71 C4
Castiglione dei Pepoli I 81 B5
Castiglione del Lago I 81 C6
Castiglione della Pescáia I 81 D4
Castiglione delle Stiviere I 71 C5
Castiglione di Sicilia I 109 B4
Castiglione d'Órcia I 81 C5
Castiglione Messer Marino I 103 B4
Castiglione Messer Raimondo I 103 A3
Castil de Peones E 89 B3
Castilblanco E 94 C1
Castilblanco de los Arroyos E 99 B5
Castilfrío de la Sierra E 89 C4
Castilgaleu E 90 A3
Castilisar E 90 A1
Castilleja E 99 B4
Castillejar E 101 B3
Castillejo de Martin Viejo E 93 A4
Castillejo de Mesleón E 95 A3
Castillejo de Robledo E 89 C3
Castillo de Bayuela E 94 B2
Castillo de Locubin E 100 B2

Castillon-la-Bataille F 76 B2
Castillon-Len-Couserans F 77 D4
Castillonès F 77 B3
Castillonroy E 90 B3
Castilruiz E 89 C4
Castione CH 70 B4
Castions di Strada I 72 C3
Castirla F 110 A2
Castle Cary GB 29 B5
Castle Douglas GB 25 D4
Castlebar IRL 18 C2
Castlebellingham IRL 19 C5
Castleblaney IRL 19 B5
Castlebridge IRL 21 B5
Castlecomer IRL 21 B4
Castlederg GB 19 B4
Castledermot IRL 21 B5
Castleford GB 27 B4
Castleisland IRL 20 B2
Castlemaine IRL 20 B2
Castlemartyr IRL 20 C3
Castlepollard IRL 19 C4
Castlerea IRL 18 C3
Castleton GB 27 B4
Castletown, *Highland* GB 23 C5
Castletown, *Isle of Man* GB 26 A1
Castletown Bearhaven IRL 20 C2
Castletownroche IRL 20 B3
Castlewellan GB 19 B6
Casto I 71 C5
Castrejón E 94 A1
Castrelo del Valle E 87 B3
Castres F 77 C5
Castricum NL 42 C1
Castries F 78 C2
Castrignano del Capo I 107 B5
Castril E 101 B3
Castrillo de Duero E 88 C3
Castrillo de la Vega E 88 C3
Castrillo de Onielo E 88 C2
Castro E 88 A2
Castro I 107 A5
Castro-Caldelas E 87 B3
Castro Daire P 87 D3
Castro de Rey E 86 A3
Castro dei Volsci I 103 B3
Castro del Rio E 100 B1
Castro Laboreiro P 87 B2
Castro Marim P 98 B3
Castro-Urdiales E 89 A3
Castro Verde P 98 B2
Castrocabón E 88 B1
Castrocaro Terme I 81 B5
Castrocontrigo E 87 B4
Castrofilippo I 108 B2
Castrogonzaio E 88 B1
Castrojeriz E 88 B2
Castromonte E 88 C1
Castromudarra E 88 B1
Castronuevo E 88 C1
Castronuño E 88 C1
Castropol E 86 A3
Castroreale I 109 A4
Castroserracin E 88 C3
Castroverde E 86 A3
Castroverde de Campos E 88 C1
Castroverde de Cerrato E 88 C2
Castrovillari I 106 B3
Castuera E 93 C5
Catadau E 96 B2
Cataéggio I 71 B4
Çatalca TR 16 R21
Catánia I 109 B4
Catanzaro I 106 C3
Catanzaro Marina I 106 C3
Catarroja E 96 B2
Catarruchos P 92 A2
Catcleugh GB 25 C5
Catenanuova I 109 B3
Caterham GB 31 C3
Cati E 90 C3
Čatići BIH 84 B3
Catignano I 103 A3
Catillon F 49 C4
Catoira E 86 B2
Caton GB 26 A3
Catral E 96 C2
Catterick GB 27 A4
Cattólica I 82 C1
Cattólica Eraclea I 108 B2
Catton GB 25 D5
Caudebec-en-Caux F 58 A1
Caudete E 96 C2
Caudete de las Fuentes E 96 B1
Caudiel E 96 B2
Caudiès-de-Fenouillèdes F 77 D5
Caudry F 49 C4
Caulkerbush GB 25 D4
Caulnes F 57 B3
Caulónia I 106 C3
Caumont-l'Evente F 57 A5
Caunes-Minervois F 77 C5
Cauro F 110 B1
Caussade F 77 B4
Causse-de-la-Selle F 78 C2
Cauterets F 76 D2
Cava de Tirreni I 103 C4
Cavaglia I 70 C3
Cavaillon F 79 C4
Cavalaire-sur-Mer F 79 C5
Cavaleiro P 98 B2
Cavalese I 71 B6
Cavallermaggiore I 80 B1
Cavallino I 72 C2
Cavan IRL 19 C4
Cavárzere I 72 C2
Cavernais P 92 A3
Cavezzo I 81 B5
Cavignac F 76 A2
Čavle HR 73 C4
Cavo I 81 D4
Cavour I 80 B1
Cawdor GB 23 D5
Çay TR 16 S22
Cayeux-sur-Mer F 48 C2
Caylus F 77 B4
Cayres F 78 B2
Cazalilla E 100 B2
Cazalla de la Sierra E 99 B5
Cazals F 77 B4
Cazanuecos E 88 B1
Cazaubon F 76 C2
Cazaux F 76 B1
Cazères F 77 C4
Cazin BIH 83 B4
Cazis CH 71 B4
Čazma HR 74 C1
Cazo E 88 A1
Cazorla E 100 B3
Cazouls-lès-Béziers F 78 C2
Cea, *León* E 88 B1
Cea, *Orense* E 86 B3
Ceánuri E 89 A4
Ceauce F 57 B5
Cebolla E 94 C2
Čebovce SK 65 B5
Cebreros E 94 B2
Čečava BIH 84 B2
Ceccano I 103 B3
Cece H 74 B3
Cecenowo PL 46 A3
Čechtice CZ 63 A6
Čechtín CZ 64 A1
Cécina I 81 C4
Ceclavin E 93 B4
Cedégolo I 71 B5
Cedeira E 86 A2
Cedillo E 92 B3
Cedillo del Condado E 94 B3
Cedrillas E 90 C2
Cedynia PL 45 C6
Cée E 86 B1
Cefalù I 109 A3
Céggia I 72 C2
Cegléd H 75 A4
Ceglédbercel H 75 A4
Céglie Messápica I 105 B4
Cehegin E 101 A4
Ceilhes-et-Rocozels F 78 C2
Ceinos de Campos E 88 B1
Ceira P 92 A2
Čejč CZ 64 B2
Cela BIH 83 B5
Čelákovice CZ 53 C4
Celano I 103 A3
Celanova E 87 B3
Celbridge IRL 21 A5
Čelebič BIH 83 C5
Celenza Valfortore I 103 B4
Čelić BIH 84 B3
Čelinac BIH 84 B2
Celje SLO 73 B5
Cella E 90 C1
Celldömölk H 74 A2
Celle D 44 C2
Celle Ligure I 80 B2
Celles B 49 C5
Celles-sur-Belle F 67 B4
Cellino San Marco I 105 B4
Celorico da Beira P 92 A3
Celorico de Basto P 87 C2
Cemaes GB 26 B1
Cembra I 71 B6
Čemerno BIH 84 C3
Cenad RO 75 B5
Cencenighe Agordino I 72 B1
Cenei RO 75 C5
Ceneselli I 81 A5
Cenicero E 89 B4
Cenicientos E 94 B2
Censeau F 69 B6
Čenta YU 85 A5
Centallo I 80 B1
Centelles E 91 B5
Cento I 81 B5
Centúripe I 109 B3
Cepeda la Mora E 94 B1
Čepin HR 74 C3
Čepinski Martinci HR 74 C3
Cepovan SLO 72 B3
Ceprano I 103 B3
Čeralije HR 74 C2
Cerami I 109 B3
Cerano I 70 C3
Cérans Foulletourte F 57 C6
Ceraso I 104 B2
Cerbaia I 81 C5
Cerbère F 91 A6
Cercadillo E 95 A4
Cercal, *Lisboa* P 92 B1
Cercal, *Setúbal* P 98 B2
Čerčany CZ 63 A5
Cerceda E 94 B3
Cercedilla E 94 B2
Cercemaggiore I 103 B4
Cercs E 91 A4
Cercy-la-Tour F 68 B3
Cerda I 108 B2
Cerdedo E 86 B2
Cerdeira P 93 A3
Cerdon F 58 C3
Cerea I 71 C6
Ceres GB 25 B5
Ceres I 70 C2
Cerese I 81 A4
Ceresole-Reale I 70 C2
Cereste F 79 C4
Céret F 91 A5
Cerezo de Abajo E 95 A3
Cerezo de Riotirón E 89 B3
Cerfontaine B 49 C5
Cergy F 58 B3
Cerignola I 104 A2
Cérilly F 68 B2
Cerisiers F 59 B4
Cerizay F 67 B4
Çerkezköy TR 16 R20
Cerkije SLO 73 B4
Cerknica SLO 73 C4
Cerkno SLO 72 B3
Cerkwica PL 45 A7
Cerna HR 74 C3
Černá Hora CZ 64 A2
Cernavodă RO 11 P21
Cernay F 60 C3
Cerne Abbas GB 29 C5
Cernégula E 89 B3
Cernik HR 74 C2
Cernóbbio I 70 C4
Černošin CZ 62 A3
Cernovice CZ 63 A5
Cérons F 76 B2
Cerovlje HR 72 C3
Cerovo SK 65 B5
Cerqueto I 82 D1
Cerralbo E 87 D4
Cerreto d'Esi I 82 C1
Cerreto Sannita I 103 B4
Cerrigydrudion GB 26 B2
Cerro Muriano E 100 A1
Certaldo I 81 C5
Certosa di Pésio I 80 B1
Cerva P 87 C3
Cervaro I 103 B3
Cervatos de la Cueza E 88 B2
Červena Řečice CZ 63 A6
Červená-Skala SK 65 B6
Cervená Voda CZ 54 C1
Cerveny Kostelec CZ 53 C6
Cervera E 91 B4
Cervera de la Cañada E 89 C5
Cervera de Pisuerga E 88 B2
Cervera del Llano E 95 C4
Cervera del Rio Alhama E 89 B5
Cervéteri I 102 B2
Cérvia I 82 B1
Cervià de les Garriques E 90 B3
Cervignano del Friuli I 72 C3
Cervinara I 103 B4
Cervione F 110 A2
Cervo E 86 A3
Cervon F 68 A3
Cesana Torinese I 79 B5
Cesarica HR 83 B4
Cesarò I 109 B3
Cesena I 82 B1
Cesenático I 82 B1
Cēsis LV 7 H19
Česká Belá CZ 63 A6
Česká Kamenice CZ 53 C4
Česká Lipa CZ 53 C4
Česká Skalice CZ 53 C6
Česká Třebová CZ 64 A2
České Budějovice CZ 63 B5
České Velenice CZ 63 B5
Český Brod CZ 53 C4
Český Krumlov CZ 63 B5
Český Těšín CZ 65 A4
Česljeva Bara YU 85 B6
Çeşme TR 16 S20
Cessenon F 78 C2
Cesson-Sévigné F 57 B4
Cestas F 76 B2
Čestobrodica YU 85 C5
Cesuras E 86 A2
Cetin Grad HR 73 C5
Cetina E 89 C5
Cetinje YU 15 Q16
Cetraro I 106 B2
Ceuta E 99 D5
Ceuti E 101 A4
Ceva I 80 B2
Cevico de la Torre E 88 C2
Cevico Navero E 88 C2
Cevins F 69 C6
Cévio CH 70 B3
Cewice PL 46 A3
Ceyrat F 68 C3
Ceyzériat F 69 B5
Chaam NL 49 B5
Chabanais F 67 C5
Chabeuil F 79 B4
Chabielice PL 55 B4
Chablis F 59 C4
Châbons F 69 C5
Chabówka PL 65 A5
Chabreloche F 68 C3
Chabris F 67 A6
Chagford GB 28 C4
Chagny F 69 B4
Chagoda RUS 7 G24
Chaherrero E 94 B2
Chailland F 57 B5
Chaillé-les-Marais F 66 B3
Chailles F 67 A6
Chailley F 59 B4
Chalabre F 77 D5
Chalais F 67 C5
Chalamont F 69 C5
Châlette-sur-Loing F 58 B3
Chalindrey F 59 C6
Challacombe GB 28 B4
Challans F 66 B3
Challes-les-Eaux F 69 C5
Chalmazel F 68 C3
Chalmoux F 68 B3
Chalon-sur-Saône F 69 B4
Chalonnes-sur-Loire F 67 A4
Châlons-en-Champagne F 59 B5
Chalupy PL 47 A4
Châlus F 67 C5
Cham CH 70 A3
Cham D 62 A3
Chamberet F 68 C1
Chambéry F 69 C5
Chambilly F 68 B4
Chambley F 60 A1
Chambly F 58 A3
Chambon-sur-Lac F 68 C2
Chambon-sur-Voueize F 68 B2
Chambord F 58 C2
Chamborigaud F 78 B2
Chamboulive F 67 C6
Chamerau D 62 A3
Chamonix-Mont Blanc F 70 C1
Chamoux-sur-Gelon F 69 C6
Champagnac-le-Vieux F 68 C3
Champagney F 60 C2
Champagnole F 69 B5
Champagny-Mouton F 67 B5
Champaubert F 59 B4
Champdeniers-St. Denis F 67 B4
Champdieu F 68 C4
Champdôtre F 69 A5
Champeix F 68 C3
Champéry CH 70 B1
Champigne F 57 C5
Champignelles F 59 C4
Champigny-sur-Veude F 67 A5
Champlitte-et-le-Prelot F 60 C1
Champoluc I 70 C2
Champoly F 68 C3
Champorcher I 70 C2
Champrond-en-Gâtine F 58 B2
Champs-sur-Tarentaine F 68 C2
Champs-sur-Yonne F 59 C4
Champtoceaux F 66 A3
Chamrousse F 79 A4
Chamusca P 92 B2
Chanac F 78 B2
Chanaleilles F 78 B2
Chandler's Ford GB 31 D2
Chandrexa de Queixa E 87 B3
Chañe E 88 C2
Changy F 68 B3
Chantada E 86 B3
Chantelle F 68 B3
Chantenay-St. Imbert F 68 B3
Chanteuges F 78 A2
Chantilly F 58 A3
Chantonnay F 66 B3
Chão de Codes P 92 B2
Chaource F 59 B5
Chapa E 86 B2
Chapareillan F 69 C5
Chapel en le Frith GB 27 B4
Chapelle Royale F 58 B2
Chapelle-St. Laurent F 67 B4
Chard GB 29 C5
Charenton-du-Cher F 68 B2
Charlbury GB 31 C2
Charleroi B 49 C5
Charlestown IRL 18 C3
Charlestown of Aberlour GB 23 D5
Charleville IRL 20 B3
Charleville-Mézières F 59 A5
Charlieu F 68 B4
Charlottenberg S 34 B4
Charlton Kings GB 29 B5
Charly F 59 B4
Charmes F 60 B2
Charmes-sur-Rhône F 78 B3
Charmey CH 70 B2
Charminster GB 29 C5
Charny F 59 C4
Charolles F 69 B4
Chârost F 68 B2
Charquemont F 70 A1
Charrin F 68 B3
Charroux F 67 B5
Chartres F 58 B2
Charzykow PL 46 B3
Chasseneuil-sur-Bonnieure F 67 C5
Chassigny F 59 C6
Château-Arnoux F 79 B5
Château-Chinon F 68 A3
Château-d'Oex CH 70 B2
Château-d'Olonne F 66 B3
Château-du-Loir F 58 C1
Château-Gontier F 57 C5
Château-la-Vallière F 67 A5
Château-Landon F 58 B3
Château-l'Evêque F 67 C5
Château-Porcien F 59 A5
Château-Renault F 58 C1
Château-Salins F 60 B2
Château-Thierry F 59 A4
Châteaubernard F 67 C4
Châteaubourg F 57 B4
Châteaubriant F 57 C4
Châteaudun F 58 B2
Châteaugiron F 57 B4
Châteaulin F 56 B1
Châteaumeillant F 68 B2
Châteauneuf, *Nièvre* F 68 A3
Châteauneuf, *Saône-et-Loire* F 69 B4
Châteauneuf-de-Randon F 78 B2
Châteauneuf-d'Ille-et-Vilaine F 57 B4
Châteauneuf-du-Faou F 56 B2
Châteauneuf-du-Pape F 78 B3
Châteauneuf-en-Thymerais F 58 B2
Châteauneuf la-Forêt F 67 C6
Châteauneuf-le-Rouge F 79 C4
Châteauneuf-sur-Charente F 67 C4
Châteauneuf-sur-Cher F 68 B2
Châteauneuf-sur-Loire F 58 C3
Châteauneuf-sur-Sarthe F 57 C5
Châteauponsac F 67 B6
Châteauredon F 79 B5
Châteaurenard, *Bouches du Rhône* F 78 C3
Châteaurenard, *Loiret* F 59 C3
Châteauroux F 67 B6
Châteauroux-les-Alpes F 79 B5
Châteauvillain F 59 B5
Châtel F 70 B1
Châtel-Censoir F 68 A3
Châtel-de-Neuvre F 68 B3
Châtel-Montagne F 68 B3
Châtel-St. Denis CH 70 B1
Châtel-sur-Moselle F 60 B2
Châtelaillon-Plage F 66 B3
Châtelaudren F 56 B3
Châtelet B 49 C5
Châtelguyon F 68 C3
Châtellerault F 67 B5
Châtelus-Malvaleix F 68 B2
Châtenois F 60 B1
Châtenois-les-Forges F 70 A1
Chatham GB 31 C4
Châtillon I 70 C2
Châtillon-Coligny F 59 C3
Châtillon-en-Bazois F 68 A3
Châtillon-en-Diois F 79 B4
Châtillon-sur Chalaronne F 69 B4
Châtillon-sur-Indre F 67 B6
Châtillon-sur-Loire F 68 A2
Châtillon-sur-Marne F 59 A4
Châtillon-sur-Seine F 59 C5
Châtres F 59 B4
Chatteris GB 30 B4
Chatton GB 25 C6
Chauchina E 100 B2
Chaudes-Aigues F 78 B2
Chaudrey F 59 B5
Chauffailles F 69 B4
Chaulnes F 58 A3
Chaument Gistoux B 49 C5
Chaumergy F 69 B5
Chaumont F 59 B6
Chaumont-en-Vexin F 58 A2
Chaumont-Porcien F 59 A5
Chaumont-sur-Aire F 59 B6
Chaumont-sur-Loire F 67 A6
Chaunay F 67 B5
Chauny F 59 A4
Chaussin F 69 B5
Chauvigny F 67 B5
Chavagnes-en-Paillers F 66 B3
Chavanges F 59 B5
Chaves P 87 C3
Chavignon F 59 A4
Chazelles-sur-Lyon F 69 C4
Chazey-Bons F 69 C5
Cheadle, *Greater Manchester* GB 26 B3
Cheadle, *Staffordshire* GB 27 C4
Cheb CZ 52 C2
Chebsara RUS 7 G26
Checa E 95 B5
Chęciny PL 55 C5
Cheddar GB 29 B5
Cheddleton GB 26 B3
Chef-Boutonne F 67 B4
Chekalin RUS 7 J25
Chekhovo RUS 47 A6
Cheles E 92 C3
Chella E 96 B2
Chelles F 58 B3
Chełm PL 11 L18
Chełmno, *Kujawsko-Pomorskie* PL 47 B4
Chełmno, *Wielkopolskie* PL 54 A3
Chelmsford GB 31 C4
Chełmża PL 47 B4
Cheltenham GB 29 B5
Chelva E 96 B2
Chémery F 67 A6
Chemery-sur-Bar F 59 A5
Chemillé F 67 A4
Chemin F 69 B5
Chemnitz D 52 C2
Chénerailles F 68 B2
Cheniménil F 60 B2
Chenonceaux F 67 A6
Chenôve F 69 A4
Chepstow GB 29 B5
Chera E 96 B2
Cherasco I 80 B1
Cherbourg F 57 A4
Cherchiara di Calàbria I 106 B3
Cherepovets RUS 7 G25
Cherkasy UA 11 M23
Chernihiv UA 11 L22
Chernivtsi UA 11 M19
Chernyakhovsk RUS 6 J17
Chéroy F 59 B3
Cherven BY 7 K21
Chervonohrad UA 11 L19
Cherykaw BY 7 K22
Chesham GB 31 C3
Cheshunt GB 31 C3
Chessy-lès-Pres F 59 B4
Cheste E 96 B2
Chester GB 26 B3
Chester-le-Street GB 25 D6
Chesterfield GB 27 B4
Chevagnes F 68 B3
Chevanceaux F 67 C4
Chevillon F 59 B6
Chevilly F 58 B2
Chew Magna GB 29 B5
Chézery-Forens F 69 B5
Chialamberto I 70 C2
Chiampo I 71 C6
Chianale I 79 B6
Chianciano Terme I 81 C5
Chiaramonte Gulfi I 109 B3
Chiaramonti I 110 C1
Chiaravalle I 82 C2
Chiaravalle Centrale I 106 C3
Chiaréggio I 71 B4
Chiari I 71 C4
Chiaromonte I 104 B3
Chiasso CH 70 C4
Chiàvari I 80 B3
Chiavenna I 71 B4
Chiché F 67 B4
Chichester GB 31 D3
Chiclana de la Frontera E 99 C4
Chiclana de Segura E 100 A2
Chiddingfold GB 31 C3
Chieri I 80 A1
Chiesa in Valmalenco I 71 B4
Chieti I 103 A4
Chieti Scalo I 103 A4
Chiéuti I 103 B5
Chigirin UA 11 M23
Chigwell GB 31 C4
Chillarón de Cuenca E 95 B4
Chillarón del Rey E 95 B4
Chilleurs-aux-Bois F 58 B3
Chillón E 100 A1
Chilluevar E 100 B2
Chiloeches E 95 B3
Chimay B 49 C5
Chimeneas E 100 B2
Chinchilla de Monte Aragón E 96 C1
Chinchón E 95 B3
Chingford GB 31 C4
Chinon F 67 A5
Chióggia I 72 C2
Chiomonte I 79 A5
Chipiona E 99 C4
Chippenham GB 29 B5
Chipping Campden GB 29 A6
Chipping Norton GB 31 C2
Chipping Ongar GB 31 C4
Chipping Sodbury GB 29 B5
Chirac F 78 B2
Chirbury GB 26 C2
Chirens F 69 C5
Chirivel E 101 B3
Chirk GB 26 C2
Chirnside GB 25 C5
Chişinău MD 11 N21
Chisineu Criş RO 10 N17
Chissey-en-Morvan F 69 A4
Chiusa I 71 B6
Chiusa di Pésio I 80 B1
Chiusa Sclàfani I 108 B2
Chiusaforte I 72 B3
Chiusi I 81 C5
Chiva E 96 B2
Chivasso I 70 C2
Chlewiska PL 55 B5
Chludowo PL 46 C2
Chlum u Třeboně CZ 63 B5
Chlumec nad Cidlinou CZ 53 C5
Chmielnik PL 55 C5
Chobienice PL 53 A5
Choceň CZ 53 C6
Choceń PL 47 C5
Chochołow PL 65 A5
Chocianów PL 53 B5
Chociw PL 55 B4
Chociwel PL 45 B7
Choczewo PL 46 A3
Chodaków PL 55 A5
Chodecz PL 47 C5
Chodov CZ 52 C2
Chodzież PL 46 C2
Chojna PL 45 C6
Chojnice PL 46 B3
Chojno PL 46 C2
Chojnów PL 53 B5
Cholet F 66 A4
Chomérac F 78 B3
Chomutov CZ 52 C3
Chop UA 11 M18
Chorges F 79 B5
Chorley GB 26 B3
Chornobyl UA 11 L22
Chortkiv UA 11 M19
Chorzew PL 54 B3
Chorzów PL 54 C3
Choszczno PL 46 B1
Chotcza-Józefów PL 55 B6
Chotěboř CZ 63 A6
Chouilly F 59 A5
Chouto P 92 B2
Chouzy-sur-Cisse F 67 A6
Chozas de Abajo E 88 B1
Chrast, *Vychodočeský* CZ 64 A1
Chrást, *Západočeský* CZ 63 A4
Chrastava CZ 53 C5
Chřibská CZ 53 C4
Christchurch GB 29 C6
Christiansfeld DK 39 D2
Chroberz PL 55 C5
Chropyně CZ 64 A3
Chrudim CZ 53 D5
Chrzanów PL 55 C4
Chtelnica SK 64 B3
Chudovo RUS 7 G22
Chueca E 94 C3
Chulmleigh GB 28 C4
Chur CH 71 B4
Church Stretton GB 26 C3
Churriana E 100 C1
Churwalden CH 71 B4
Chvalšiny CZ 63 B5
Chwaszczyno PL 47 A4
Chynava CZ 53 C4
Chýnov CZ 63 A5
Ciacova RO 75 C6
Ciadîr-Lunga MD 11 N21
Ciadoncha E 88 B3
Cianciana I 108 B2
Ciano d'Enza I 81 B4
Ciążen PL 54 A2
Cibakhaza H 75 B5
Ciborro P 92 C2
Cicagna I 80 B3
Cicciano I 103 C4
Ciçevac YU 85 C6
Ciciliano I 102 B2
Cicognolo I 71 C5
Cidadelhe P 87 D3
Cidones E 89 C4
Ciechanów PL 47 C6
Ciechocinek PL 47 C4
Cielądz PL 55 B5
Ciemnik PL 46 B1
Ciempozuelos E 95 B3
Ciepielów PL 55 B6
Čierny Balog SK 65 B5
Cierp F 77 D3
Cierpice PL 47 C4
Ciervana E 89 A3
Cierznie PL 46 B3
Cieslé PL 47 C6
Cieszyn PL 65 A4
Cieutat F 76 C3
Cieza E 101 A4
Cifer SK 64 B3
Çifteler TR 16 S22
Cifuentes E 95 B4
Cigales E 88 C2
Cigliano I 70 C3
Cillas E 95 B5
Cilleros E 93 A4
Cilleruelo de Arriba E 89 C3
Cilleruelo de Bezana E 88 B3
Cimalmotto CH 70 B3
Cimanes del Tejar E 88 B1
Ciminna I 108 B2
Cimişlia MD 11 N21
Cimolàis I 72 B2
Cîmpulung RO 11 P19
Cinctorres E 90 C2
Cinderford GB 29 B5
Çine TR 16 T21
Činěves CZ 53 C5
Ciney B 49 C6
Cinfães P 87 C2
Cingia de Botti I 81 A4
Cingoli I 82 C2
Cinigiano I 81 D5
Cinobaňa SK 65 B5
Cinq-Mars-la-Pile F 67 A5
Cinquefrondi I 106 C3
Cintegabelle F 77 C4
Cintruénigo E 89 B5
Ciółkowo PL 47 C5
Ciperez E 87 D4
Cirat E 96 A2
Cirella I 106 B2
Cirencester GB 29 B6
Cirey-sur-Vezouze F 60 B2
Ciria E 89 C5
Ciriè I 70 C2
Cirigliano I 104 B3
Cirò I 107 B4
Cirò Marina I 107 B4
Ciry-le-Noble F 69 B4
Cislău RO 11 P20
Cismon del Grappa I 72 C1
Cisneros E 88 B2
Cissac-Médoc F 66 C4
Čista CZ 52 C3
Cisterna di Latina I 102 B2
Cistérniga E 88 C2
Cisternino I 105 B4
Cistierna E 88 B1
Čitluk BIH 84 C2
Citov CZ 53 C4
Città della Pieve I 81 D6
Città di Castello I 82 C1
Città Sant'Angelo I 103 A4
Cittadella I 72 C1
Cittaducale I 102 A2
Cittanova I 106 C3
Ciudad Real E 94 D3
Ciudad Rodrigo E 93 A4
Ciudadela de Menorca, *Menorca* E 97
Cividale del Friuli I 72 B3
Civita I 102 A3
Civita Castellana I 102 A2
Civitanova Alta I 82 C2
Civitanova Marche I 82 C2
Civitavécchia I 102 A1
Civitella di Romagna I 81 B5
Civitella di Tronto I 82 D2
Civitella Roveto I 103 B3
Civray F 67 B5
Çivril TR 16 S21
Cizur Mayor E 89 B5
Cjutadilla E 91 B4
Clabhach GB 24 B1
Clachan GB 22 D2
Clachan na Luib GB 22 D1
Clacton-on-Sea GB 31 C5
Cladich GB 24 B2
Claggan GB 24 B2
Clairvaux-les-Lacs F 69 B5
Clamecy F 68 A3
Claonaig GB 24 C2
Clarecastle IRL 20 B3
Claregalway IRL 20 A3
Claremorris IRL 18 C2
Clarinbridge IRL 20 A3
Clashmore GB 23 D4
Clashmore IRL 21 B4
Claudy GB 19 B4
Clausthal-Zellerfeld D 51 B6
Cláut I 72 B2
Clay Cross GB 27 B4
Claye-Souilly F 58 B3
Cléder F 56 B1
Cleethorpes GB 27 B5
Clefmont F 60 B1
Cléguérec F 56 B2
Clelles F 79 B4
Clenze D 44 C2
Cleobury Mortimer GB 29 A5
Cléon-d'Andran F 78 B3
Cléré-les-Pins F 67 A5
Clères F 58 A2
Clermont F 58 A3
Clermont-en-Argonne F 59 A6
Clermont-Ferrand F 68 C3
Clermont-l'Hérault F 78 C2
Clerval F 69 A6
Clervaux L 50 C2
Cléry-St. André F 58 C2
Cles I 71 B6
Clevedon GB 29 B5
Cleveleys GB 26 B2
Cley GB 30 B5
Clifden IRL 18 C1
Clifford GB 29 A4
Clisson F 66 A3
Clitheroe GB 26 B3
Clogh IRL 21 B4
Cloghan IRL 21 A4
Clogheen IRL 21 B4
Clogher GB 19 B4
Cloghjordan IRL 20 B3
Clohars-Carnoët F 56 C2
Clonakilty IRL 20 C3
Clondalkin IRL 21 A5
Clones IRL 19 B4
Clonmany IRL 19 A4
Clonmel IRL 21 B4
Clonmellon IRL 19 C4
Clonord IRL 21 A4
Clonroche IRL 21 B5
Cloone IRL 19 C4
Cloppenburg D 43 C5
Closeburn GB 25 C4
Clough GB 19 B6
Clova GB 25 B4
Clovelly GB 28 C3
Clowne GB 27 B4
Cloyes-sur-le-Loir F 58 C2
Cloyne IRL 20 C3
Cluis F 68 B1
Cluj-Napoca RO 11 N18
Clun GB 26 C2
Clunes GB 24 B3
Cluny F 69 B4
Cluses F 69 B6
Clusone I 71 C4
Clydach GB 28 B4
Clydebank GB 24 C3
Coachford IRL 20 C3
Coagh GB 19 B5
Coalisland GB 19 B5
Coalville GB 27 C4

Coaña E 86 A4
Cobas E 86 A2
Cobertelade E 89 C4
Cobeta E 95 B4
Cobreces E 88 A2
Coburg D 51 C6
Coca E 94 A2
Cocentaina E 96 C2
Cochem D 50 C3
Cockburnspath GB 25 C5
Cockermouth GB 26 A2
Codigoro I 82 B1
Codogno I 71 C4
Codos E 89 C5
Codróipo I 72 C2
Codrongianos I 110 C1
Coelhoso P 87 C4
Coesfeld D 50 B3
Coevorden NL 42 C3
Cofrentes E 96 B1
Cogeces del Monte E 88 C2
Coggeshall GB 31 C4
Cognac F 67 C4
Cogne I 70 C2
Cognin F 69 C5
Cogolin F 79 C5
Cogollos de Guadix E 100 B2
Cogollos-Vega E 100 B2
Cogolludo E 95 B3
Coimbra P 92 A2
Coin E 100 C1
Coirós E 86 A2
Čoka YU 75 C5
Col SLO 73 C4
Colares P 92 C1
Cölbe D 51 C4
Colbitz D 52 A1
Colchester GB 31 C4
Coldingham GB 25 C5
Colditz D 52 B2
Coldstream GB 25 C5
Colebrooke GB 28 C4
Colera E 91 A6
Coleraine GB 19 A5
Colfiorito I 82 C1
Cólico I 71 B4
Coligny F 69 B5
Colindres E 89 A3
Coll de Nargó E 91 A4
Collado-Mediano E 94 B2
Collado Villalba E 94 B3
Collagna I 81 B4
Collanzo E 88 A1
Collat F 68 C3
Colle di Val d'Elsa I 81 C5
Colle Isarco I 71 B6
Colle Sannita I 103 B4
Collécchio I 81 B4
Colledimezzo I 103 B4
Colleferro I 102 B3
Collelongo I 103 B3
Collepasso I 105 B5
Collepepe I 82 D1
Collesalvetti I 81 C4
Collesano I 108 B2
Colli a Volturno I 103 B4
Collin GB 25 C4
Collinée F 56 B3
Collingham, *Nottinghamshire* GB 27 B5
Collingham, *West Yorkshire* GB 27 B4
Collinghorst D 43 B4
Cóllio I 71 C5
Collobrières F 79 C5
Collon IRL 19 C5
Collooney IRL 18 B3
Colmar F 60 B3
Colmars F 79 B5
Colmenar E 100 C1
Colmenar de la Sierra E 95 A3
Colmenar de Oreja E 95 B3
Colmenar Viejo E 94 B3
Colmonel GB 24 C3
Colne GB 26 B3
Colobraro I 104 B3
Cologna Véneta I 71 C6
Cologne F 77 C3
Cologne al Serio I 71 C4
Colombey-les-Belles F 60 B1
Colombey-les-deux-Églises F 59 B5
Colombres E 88 A2
Colomera E 100 B2
Colomers E 91 A5
Colomiers F 77 C4
Colònia de Sant Jordi, *Mallorca* E 97
Colorno I 81 B4
Colos P 98 B2
Cölpin D 45 B5
Colpy GB 23 D6
Colsterworth GB 30 B3
Coltishall GB 30 B5
Colunga E 88 A1
Colwell GB 25 C5
Colwyn Bay GB 26 B2
Colyford GB 29 C4
Coma-ruga E 91 B4
Comácchio I 82 B1
Combarros E 86 B4
Combeaufontaine F 60 C1
Comber GB 19 B6
Comblain-au-Pont B 49 C6
Combloux F 70 C1
Combourg F 57 B4
Combronde F 68 C3
Comeglians I 72 B2
Comillas E 88 A2
Comines F 49 C4
Cómiso I 109 C3
Comloşu Mare RO 75 C5
Commensacq F 76 B2
Commentry F 68 B2
Commerau D 53 B4
Commercy F 60 B1
Como I 71 C4
Cómpeta E 100 C2
Compiègne F 58 A3
Comporta P 92 C2
Comps-sur-Artuby F 79 C5
Comrat MD 11 N21
Comrie GB 25 B4
Comunanza I 82 D2
Cona, *Emilia Romagna* I 81 B5
Cona, *Veneto* I 72 C2
Concarneau F 56 C2
Conceição P 98 B2
Conches-en-Ouche F 58 B1
Concordia Sagittária I 72 C2
Concordia sulla Sècchia I 81 B4
Concots F 77 B4
Condat F 68 C2
Condé-en-Brie F 59 B4
Condé-sur-l'Escaut F 49 C4
Conde-sur-Marne F 59 A5
Condé-sur-Noireau F 57 B5
Condeixa P 92 A2
Condemios de Abajo E 95 A3
Condemios de Arriba E 95 A3
Condino I 71 C5
Condom F 77 C3
Condove I 80 A1
Condrieu F 69 C4
Conegliano I 72 C2
Conflans-sur-Lanterne F 60 C2
Confolens F 67 B5
Conforto E 86 A3
Cong IRL 18 C2
Congleton GB 26 B3
Congosto E 86 B4
Congosto de Valdavia E 88 B2
Congostrina E 95 A3
Conil de la Frontera E 99 C4
Coningsby GB 27 B5
Coniston GB 26 A2
Conlie F 57 B5
Conliège F 69 B5
Conna IRL 20 B3
Connah's Quay GB 26 B2
Connantre F 59 B4
Connaugh IRL 20 B3
Connaux F 78 B3
Connel GB 24 B2
Connerré F 58 B1
Cononbridge GB 23 D4
Čonoplja YU 75 C4
Conques F 77 B5
Conques-sur-Orbiel F 77 C5
Conquista E 100 A1
Conquista de la Sierra E 93 B5
Consándolo I 81 B5
Consélice I 81 B5
Conselve I 72 C1
Consett GB 25 D6
Consolacão P 92 B1
Constancia P 92 B2
Constanco E 86 A2
Constanţa RO 11 P21
Constanti E 91 B4
Constantina E 99 B5
Consuegra E 95 C3
Consuma I 81 C5
Contarina I 82 A1
Conthey CH 70 B2
Contigliano I 102 A2
Contis-Plage F 76 B1
Contrada I 103 C4
Contres F 67 A6
Contrexéville F 60 B1
Controne I 104 B2
Contursi Termi I 104 B2
Conty F 58 A3
Conversano I 105 B4
Conwy GB 26 B2
Cookstown GB 19 B5
Coole F 59 B5
Coolgreany IRL 21 B5
Cooneen GB 19 B4
Cootehill IRL 19 B4
Cope E 101 B4
Copertino I 105 B5
Copparo I 81 B5
Coppenbrugge D 51 A5
Corabia RO 16 Q19
Córaci I 106 B3
Coralići BIH 83 B4
Corato I 104 A3
Coray F 56 B2
Corbeil-Essonnes F 58 B3
Corbeny F 59 A4
Corbera E 96 B2
Corbie F 58 A3
Corbigny F 68 A3
Corbion B 59 A5
Corbridge GB 25 D5
Corby GB 30 B3
Corconte E 88 A3
Corcubión E 86 B1
Corcumello I 103 A3
Cordenòns I 72 C2
Cordes-sur-Ciel F 77 B4
Córdoba E 100 B1
Cordobilla de Lácara E 93 B4
Cordovado I 72 C2
Corella E 89 B5
Coreses E 88 C1
Corfe Castle GB 29 C5
Corga de Lobão P 87 D2
Cori I 102 B2
Coria E 93 B4
Coria del Rio E 99 B4
Corigliano Cálabro I 106 B3
Corinaldo I 82 C1
Cório I 70 C2
Coripe E 99 C5
CORK IRL 20 C3
Corlay F 56 B2
Corleone I 108 B2
Corleto Monforte I 104 B2
Corleto Perticara I 104 B3
Çorlu TR 16 R20
Cormainville F 58 B2
Cormatin F 69 B4
Cormeilles F 58 A1
Cormery F 67 A5
Cormòns I 72 C3
Cormoz F 69 B5
Cornago E 89 B4
Cornberg D 51 B5
Cornellana E 86 A4
Corneşti MD 11 N21
Corniglio I 81 B4
Cornimont F 60 C2
Corniolo I 81 C5
Cornuda I 72 C2
Cornudella de Montsant E 90 B3
Cornudilla E 89 B3
Cornus F 78 C2
Corpach GB 24 B2
Corps F 79 B4
Corps Nuds F 57 C4
Corral de Almaguer E 95 C3
Corral de Ayllon E 89 C3
Corral de Calatrava E 100 A1
Corral-Rubio E 96 C1
Corrales E 88 C1
Corran GB 24 B2
Corredoiras E 86 A2
Corréggio I 81 B4
Corrèze F 68 C1
Corridónia I 82 C2
Corris GB 26 C2
Corrubedo E 86 B1
Córsico I 71 C4
Corsock GB 25 C4
Corte F 110 A2
Corte de Peleas E 93 C4
Corte Pinto P 98 B3
Corteconception E 99 B4
Cortegaca P 87 D2
Cortegada E 87 B2
Cortegana E 99 B4
Cortemaggiore I 81 B3
Cortemilia I 80 B2
Cortes E 89 C5
Cortes de Aragón E 90 C2
Cortes de Arenoso E 96 A2
Cortes de Baza E 101 B3
Cortes de la Frontera E 99 C5
Cortes de Pallás E 96 B2
Cortiçadas P 92 C2
Cortico P 87 C3
Cortijo de Arriba E 94 C2
Cortijos Nuevos E 101 A3
Cortina d'Ampezzo I 72 B2
Corton GB 30 B5
Cortona I 81 C5
Coruche P 92 C2
Corullón E 86 B4
Corvara in Badia I 72 B1
Corvera E 101 B4
Corwen GB 26 C2
Cosenza I 106 B3
Cosham GB 31 D2
Coslada E 95 B3
Cosne-Cours-sur-Loire F 68 A2
Cosne d'Allier F 68 B2
Cospeito E 86 A3
Cossato I 70 C3
Cossaye F 68 B3
Cossé-le-Vivien F 57 C5
Cossonay CH 69 B6
Costa da Caparica P 92 C1
Costa de Santo André P 98 A2
Costa Nova P 92 A2
Costalpino I 81 C5
Costaros F 78 B2
Costeşti RO 11 P19
Costigliole d'Asti I 80 B2
Costigliole Saluzzo I 80 B1
Coswig, *Sachsen-Anhalt* D 52 B2
Coswig, *Sachsen* D 52 B3
Cotherstone GB 27 A4
Cotronei I 107 B3
Cottbus D 53 B4
Cottenham GB 30 B4
Cottingham GB 27 B5
Coublanc F 60 C1
Couches F 69 B4
Couço P 92 C2
Coucouron F 78 B2
Coucy-le-Château-Auffrique F 59 A4
Couëron F 66 A3
Couhé F 67 B5
Couiza F 77 D5
Coulags GB 22 D3
Coulanges F 68 B3
Coulanges-la-Vineuse F 59 C4
Coulanges-sur-Yonne F 68 A3
Couleuvre F 68 B2
Coulmier-le-Sec F 59 C5
Coulommiers F 59 B4
Coulonges-sur-l'Autize F 67 B4
Coulounieix-Chamiers F 67 C5
Coulport GB 24 B3
Coupar Angus GB 25 B4
Coupéville F 59 B5
Couptrain F 57 B5
Cour-Cheverny F 67 A6
Coura P 87 C2
Courcelles B 49 C5
Courcelles-Chaussy F 60 A2
Courchevel F 70 C1
Courcôme F 67 C5
Courçon F 66 B4
Courgenay CH 70 A2
Courmayeur I 70 C1
Courniou F 78 C1
Cournon-d'Auvergne F 68 C3
Cournonterral F 78 C2
Courpière F 68 C3
Cours-la-Ville F 69 B4
Coursan F 78 C2
Courseulles-sur-Mer F 57 A5
Courson-les-Carrières F 59 C4
Courtalain F 58 B2
Courtenay F 59 B4
Courtomer F 58 B1
Courville F 58 B2
Coussac-Bonneval F 67 C6
Coutances F 57 A4
Couterne F 57 B5
Coutras F 76 A2
Couvet CH 70 B1
Couvin B 49 C5
Couzon F 68 B3
Covadonga E 88 A1
Covaleda E 89 C4
Covarrubias E 89 B3
Covas P 87 C2
Cove GB 22 D3
Coventry GB 30 B2
Coverack GB 28 C2
Covigliáio I 81 B5
Covilhã P 92 A3
Cowbridge GB 29 B4
Cowdenbeath GB 25 B4
Cowes GB 31 D2
Cox F 77 C4
Cózar E 100 A2
Cozes F 66 C4
Cóbh IRL 20 C3
Craco I 105 B3
Craibstone GB 23 D6
Craighouse GB 24 C2
Craignure GB 24 B2
Crail GB 25 B5
Crailsheim D 61 A6
Craiova RO 11 P18
Cramlington GB 25 C6
Cranleigh GB 31 C3
Craon F 57 C5
Craonne F 59 A4
Craponne F 69 C4
Craponne-sur-Arzon F 68 C3
Crathie GB 23 D5
Crato P 92 B3
Craughwell IRL 20 A3
Craven Arms GB 26 C3
Crawford GB 25 C4
Crawinkel D 51 C6
Crawley GB 31 C3
Creag Ghoraidh GB 22 D1
Crecente E 87 B2
Crèches-sur-Saône F 69 B4
Crécy-en-Ponthieu F 48 C2
Crécy-la-Chapelle F 59 B3
Crécy-sur-Serre F 59 A4
Crediton GB 29 C4
Creeslough IRL 19 A4
Creetown GB 24 D3
Creeve GB 19 B5
Creglingen D 61 A6
Creil F 58 A3
Creissels F 78 B2
Crema I 71 C4
Cremeaux F 68 C3
Crémenes E 88 B1
Crémieu F 69 C5
Cremlingen D 51 A6
Cremona I 81 A4
Creney F 59 B5
Črenšovci SLO 73 B6
Créon F 76 B2
Crepaja YU 85 A5
Crépy F 59 A4
Crépy-en-Valois F 59 A3
Cres HR 83 B3
Crescentino I 70 C3
Crespino I 81 B5
Crespos E 94 B2
Cressage GB 26 C3
Cressensac F 77 A4
Crest F 79 B4
Cresta CH 71 B4
Créteil F 58 B3
Creully F 57 A5
Creussen D 62 A2
Creutzwald F 60 A2
Creuzburg D 51 B6
Crevalcore I 81 B5
Crèvecœur-le-Grand F 58 A3
Crevillente E 96 C2
Crévola d'Ossola I 70 B3
Crewe GB 26 B3
Crewkerne GB 29 C5
Criales E 89 B3
Crianlarich GB 24 B3
Criccieth GB 26 C1
Crickhowell GB 29 B4
Cricklade GB 29 B6
Crieff GB 25 B4
Criel-sur-Mer F 48 C2
Crikvenica HR 73 C4
Crillon F 58 A2
Crimmitschau D 52 C2
Crimond GB 23 D7
Crinitz D 53 B3
Cripán E 89 B4
Criquetot-l'Esneval F 57 A6
Crispiano I 105 B4
Crissolo I 79 B6
Cristóbal E 93 A5
Crivitz D 44 B3
Črna SLO 73 B4
Crna Bara, *Srbija* YU 85 B4
Crna Bara, *Vojvodina* YU 75 C5
Crnac HR 74 C2
Crnča YU 85 B4
Crni Lug BIH 83 B5
Crni Lug HR 73 C4
Črni Vrh SLO 73 C4
Crnjelovo Donje BIH 85 B4
Črnomelj SLO 73 C5
Crocketford GB 25 C4
Crocq F 68 C2
Crodo I 70 B3
Croglin GB 25 D5
Crolly IRL 18 A3
Cromarty GB 23 D4
Cromer GB 30 B5
Cronat F 68 B3
Crookhaven IRL 20 C2
Crookstown IRL 20 C3
Croom IRL 20 B3
Cropalati I 106 B3
Crópani I 107 C3
Crosbost GB 22 C2
Crosby GB 26 B2
Crosia I 107 B3
Cross-Hands GB 28 B3
Crossakiel IRL 19 C4
Crosshaven IRL 20 C3
Crosshill GB 24 C3
Crossmolina IRL 18 B2
Crotone I 107 B4
Crottendorf D 52 C2
Crouy F 59 A4
Crowborough GB 31 C4
Crowland GB 30 B3
Crowthorne GB 31 C3
Croyde GB 28 B3
Croydon GB 31 C3
Crozon F 56 B1
Cruas F 78 B3
Cruceni RO 75 B6
Crúcoli I 107 B4
Cruden Bay GB 23 D7
Crudgington GB 26 C3
Cruis F 79 B4
Crumlin GB 19 B5
Cruseilles F 69 B6
Crusheen IRL 20 B3
Cruz de Incio E 86 B3
Črvenka YU 75 C4
Črveny Kamen SK 64 A4
Csabacsüd H 75 B5
Csabrendek H 74 A2
Csákány-doroszló H 73 B6
Csákvár H 74 A3
Csanádapáca H 75 B5
Csanádpalota H 75 B5
Csány H 65 C5
Csanytelek H 75 B5
Csapod H 74 A1
Császár H 74 A3
Császártöltés H 75 B4
Csávoly H 75 B4
Csemö H 75 A4
Csengöd H 75 B4
Csépa H 75 B5
Csepreg H 74 A1
Cserkeszölö H 75 B5
Csernely H 65 B6
Csökmö H 75 A6
Csököly H 74 B2
Csokonyavisonta H 74 B2
Csólyospálos H 75 B4
Csongrád H 75 B5
Csopak H 74 B2
Csorna H 64 C3
Csorvás H 75 B5
Csurgó H 74 B2
Cuacos de Yuste E 93 A5
Cualedro E 87 C3
Cuanca de Campos E 88 B1
Cuba P 98 A3
Cubel E 95 A5
Cubelles E 91 B4
Cubillos E 89 C4
Cubillos del Sil E 86 B4
Cubo de la Solana E 89 C4
Cuckfield GB 31 C3
Cucuron F 79 C4
Cudillero E 86 A4
Cuéllar E 88 C2
Cuenca E 95 B4
Cuers F 79 C5
Cuerva E 94 C2
Cueva de Agreda E 89 C5
Cuevas Bajas E 100 B1
Cuevas del San Clemente E 89 B3
Cuevas de San Marcos E 100 B1
Cuevas del Almanzora E 101 B4
Cuevas del Becerro E 99 C5
Cuevas del Campo E 100 B3
Cuevas del Valle E 94 B1
Cuges-les-Pins F 79 C4
Cúglieri I 110 C1
Cugnaux F 77 C4
Cuijk NL 50 B1
Cuinzier F 69 B4
Cuiseaux F 69 B5
Cuisery F 69 B5
Culan F 68 B2
Culemborg NL 49 B6
Cúllar E 101 B3
Cullaville GB 19 B5
Cullera E 96 B2
Cullivoe GB 22 A7
Cullompton GB 29 C4
Cully CH 70 B1
Culoz F 69 C5
Cults GB 23 D6
Cumbernauld GB 25 C4
Cumbres de San Bartolomé E 99 A4
Cumbres Mayores E 99 A4
Cumiana I 80 B1
Čumić YU 85 B5
Cumnock GB 24 C3
Cúneo I 80 B1
Cunlhat F 68 C3
Čunski HR 82 B3
Cuntis E 86 B2
Cuorgnè I 70 C2
Cupar GB 25 B4
Cupello I 103 A4
Cupra Marittima I 82 C2
Cupramontana I 82 C2
Ćuprija YU 85 C6
Curinga I 106 C3
Currelos E 86 B3
Currie GB 25 C4
Curtea de Argeş RO 11 P19
Curtici RO 75 B6
Curtis E 86 A2
Curtis Santa Eulalia E 86 A2
Čurug YU 75 C5
Cusano Mutri I 103 B4
Cushendall GB 19 A5
Cusset F 68 B3
Cussy-les-Forges F 68 A4
Cutanda E 90 C1
Cutro I 107 B3
Cutrofiano I 105 B5
Cuts F 59 A4
Cuvilly F 58 A3
Cuxhaven D 43 B5
Cvikov CZ 53 C4
Cwmbran GB 29 B4
Cybinka PL 53 A4
Czacz PL 54 A1
Czajków PL 54 B3
Czaplinek PL 46 B2
Czarlin PL 47 A4
Czarna-Dąbrówka PL 46 A3
Czarna Woda PL 47 B4
Czarnca PL 55 C4
Czarne PL 46 B2
Czarnków PL 46 C2
Czarnowo PL 47 B4
Czarnozyly PL 54 B3
Czarny Bór PL 53 C6
Czarny-Dunajec PL 65 A5
Czarny Las PL 54 B2
Czchow PL 65 A6
Czechowice-Dziedzice PL 65 A4
Czempiń PL 54 A1
Czermno PL 55 B5
Czernichow PL 65 A5
Czerniejewo PL 46 C3
Czernikowo PL 47 C4
Czersk PL 46 B3
Czerwieńsk PL 53 A5
Czerwionka-Leszczyny PL 54 C3
Czerwonka PL 47 B6
Czestochowa PL 55 C4
Czeszewo PL 46 C3
Człopa PL 46 B2
Człuchów PL 46 B3

D

Daaden D 50 C3
Dabas H 75 A4
Dąbie PL 54 A3
Dąbki PL 46 A2
Dabo F 60 B3
Dabrowa PL 46 C3
Dąbrowa Górnicza PL 55 C4
Dąbrowa Tarnowska PL 55 C5
Dąbrowice PL 47 C5
Dabrowno PL 47 B6
Dachau D 62 B2
Dačice CZ 63 A6
Dägebüll D 43 A5
Dagmersellen CH 70 A2
Dahlen D 52 B2
Dahlenburg D 44 B2
Dahme D 52 B3
Dahn D 60 A3
Dähre D 44 C2
Dail bho Dheas GB 22 C2
Dailly GB 24 C3
Daimiel E 95 C3
Daingean IRL 21 A4
Đakovica YU 15 Q17
Đakovo HR 74 C3
Dal, *Akershus* N 34 A3
Dal, *Telemark* N 33 B5
Dala-Floda S 36 A1
Dala-Husby S 36 A2
Dala-Järna S 36 A1
Dalaas A 71 A5
Dalabrog GB 22 D1
Dalaman TR 16 T21
Dalarö S 36 B5
Dalbeattie GB 25 D4
Dalby DK 39 D3
Dalby, *Skåne* S 41 D3
Dalby, *Uppsala* S 36 B4
Dale, *Pembrokeshire* GB 28 B2
Dale, *Shetland* GB 22 A7
Dalen, *Akershus* N 34 B3
Dalen, *Telemark* N 33 B5
Daleszyce PL 55 C5
Dalhalvaig GB 23 C5
Dalheim L 60 A2
Dalhem S 37 D5
Dalias E 101 C3
Dalj HR 75 C3
Dalkeith GB 25 C4
Dalkey IRL 21 A5
Dalmally GB 24 B3
Dalmellington GB 24 C3
Dalry, *Dumfries & Galloway* GB 24 C3
Dalry, *North Ayrshire* GB 24 C3
Dalrymple GB 24 C3
Dals Långed S 35 C4
Dals Rostock S 35 C4
Dalsjöfors S 40 B3
Dalskog S 35 C4
Dalston GB 25 D5
Dalstorp S 40 B3
Dalton-in-Furness GB 26 A2
Daluis F 79 B5
Dalum D 43 C4
Dalum S 35 D5
Dalwhinnie GB 24 B3
Damasławek PL 46 C3
Damazan F 76 B3
Dammarie-les-Lys F 58 B3
Dammartin-en-Goële F 58 A3
Damme D 43 C5
Damnica PL 46 A3
Dampierre F 69 A5
Dampierre-sur-Salon F 69 A5
Damüls A 71 A4
Damville F 58 B2
Damvillers F 59 A6
Damwoude NL 42 B2
Danbury GB 31 C4
Dangé-St. Romain F 67 B5
Dångebo S 40 C5
Dangers F 58 B2
Dangeul F 58 B1
Danilovgrad YU 15 Q16
Danischenhagen D 44 A2
Daniszyn PL 54 B2
Danjoutin F 60 C2
Dannas S 40 B3
Dannemarie F 60 C3
Dannemora S 36 A4
Dannenberg D 44 B3
Dánszentmiklós H 75 A4
Dány H 75 A4
Daoulas F 56 B1
Darabani RO 11 M20
Darány H 74 C2
Darda HR 74 C3
Dardesheim D 51 B6
Darfeld D 50 A3
Darfo I 71 C5
Dargiń PL 46 A2
Dargun D 45 B4
Darlington GB 27 A4
Darłowo PL 46 A2
Darmstadt D 61 A4
Darney F 60 B2
Daroca E 95 A5
Darque P 87 C2
Darragh IRL 20 B2
Dartford GB 31 C4
Dartington GB 28 C4
Dartmouth GB 29 C4
Darton GB 27 B4
Daruvar HR 74 C2
Darvas H 75 A6
Darvel GB 24 C3
Darwen GB 26 B3
Dassel D 51 B5
Dassow D 44 B2
Datça TR 16 T20
Datteln D 50 B3
Dattenfeld D 50 C3
Daugard DK 39 D2
Daugavpils LV 7 J20
Daumeray F 57 C5
Daun D 50 C2
Daventry GB 30 B2
Davle CZ 63 A5
Davor HR 74 C2
Davos CH 71 B4
Davyd Haradok BY 7 K20
Dawlish GB 29 C4
Dax F 76 C1
De Haan B 49 B4
De Koog NL 42 B1
De Panne B 48 B3
De Wijk NL 42 C3
Deal GB 31 C5
Deauville F 57 A6
Deba E 89 A4
Debar MK 15 R17
Debe Wielkie PL 55 A6
Dębica PL 55 C6
Dębnica Kaszubska PL 46 A3
Dębno PL 45 C6
Dębołęka PL 54 B3
Dębowa Łaka PL 47 B5
Debrc YU 85 B4
Debrecen H 10 N17
Debrznica PL 53 A5
Debrzno PL 46 B3
Debstedt D 43 B5
Decazeville F 77 B5
Dechtice SK 64 B3
Decima I 102 B2
Decimomannu I 110 D1
Děčín CZ 53 C4
Decize F 68 B3
Decollatura I 106 B3
Decs H 74 B3
Deddington GB 31 C2
Dedelow D 45 B5
Dedemsvaart NL 42 C3
Dédestapolcsány H 65 B6
Dedovichi RUS 7 H21
Deeping St. Nicholas GB 30 B3
Dég H 74 B3
Degaña E 86 B4
Degeberga S 41 D4
Degerfors S 36 B1
Degerhamn S 41 C6
Degernes N 34 B3
Deggendorf D 62 B3
Deggingen D 61 B5
Dego I 80 B2
Degolados P 93 B3
Dehesas de Guadix E 100 B2
Dehesas Viejas E 100 B2
Deia, *Mallorca* E 97
Deining D 62 A2
Deinze B 49 C4
Déiva Marina I 80 B3
Dej RO 11 N18
Deje S 34 B5
Delabole GB 28 C3
Delary S 40 C3
Delbrück D 51 B4
Delden NL 50 A2
Deleitosa E 93 B5
Delekovec HR 74 B1
Delémont CH 70 A2
Delft NL 49 A5
Delfzijl NL 42 B3
Délia I 108 B2
Delianuova I 106 C2
Deliblato YU 85 B6
Deliceto I 104 A2
Delitzsch D 52 B2
Dellach A 72 B3
Delle F 70 A2
Delme F 60 B2
Delmen-horst D 43 B5
Delnice HR 73 C4
Delvin IRL 19 C4
Delvinë AL 15 S17
Demandice SK 65 B4
Demidov RUS 7 J22
Demigny F 69 B4
Demirci TR 16 S21
Demirköy TR 16 R20
Demmin D 45 B5
Demonte I 79 B6
Demyansk RUS 7 H23
Den Burg NL 42 B1
Den Ham NL 42 C3
Den Helder NL 42 C1
Den Oever NL 42 C2
Denain F 49 C4
Denbigh GB 26 B2
Dender-monde B 49 B5
Denekamp NL 42 C3
Denholm GB 25 C5
Denia E 96 C3
Denizli TR 16 T21
Denkendorf D 62 B2
Denklingen D 50 C3
Denny GB 25 B4
Denta RO 75 C6
Déols F 67 B6
Derby GB 27 C4
Dereköy TR 16 R20
Derenberg D 51 B6
Derhaci UA 7 L25
Dermbach D 51 C6
Dermulo I 71 B6
Deronje YU 75 C4
Derry/Londonderry GB 19 B4
Derrygonnelly GB 19 B4
Derrylin GB 19 B4
Dersingham GB 30 B4
Deruta I 82 D1
Dervaig GB 24 B1
Derval F 57 C4
Derventa BIH 84 B2
Dervock GB 19 A5
Desana I 70 C3
Descartes F 67 B5
Desenzano del Garda I 71 C5
Deševa BIH 84 C3
Desimirovac YU 85 B5
Désio I 71 C4
Deskle SLO 72 B3
Desná CZ 53 C5
Dešov CZ 63 B6
Despotovac YU 85 B6
Despotovo YU 75 C4
Dessau D 52 B2
Deštná CZ 63 A5
Destriana E 87 B4
Désulo I 110 C2
Desvres F 48 C2
Deszk H 75 B5
Deta RO 75 C6
Detmold D 51 B4
Dětřichov CZ 64 A3
Dettelbach D 61 A6
Dettingen D 61 B5
Dettwiller F 60 B3
Detva SK 65 B5
Deurne NL 50 B1
Deutsch Wagram A 64 B2
Deutschkreutz A 64 C2
Deutschlandsberg A 73 B5
Deva RO 11 P18
Dévaványa H 75 A5
Devecser H 74 A2
Deventer NL 50 A2
Devil's Bridge GB 28 A4
Devinska Nova Ves SK 64 B2
Devizes GB 29 B6
Devonport GB 28 C3
Devrek TR 16 R22
Devrske HR 83 C4
Dewsbury GB 27 B4
Deza E 89 C4
Dežanovac HR 74 C2
Dezzo I 71 C5
Dhidhimótikhon GR 16 R20
Dhomokós GR 15 S18
Diamante I 106 B2
Dianalund DK 39 D4
Diano d'Alba I 80 B2
Diano Marina I 80 C2
Dicomano I 81 C5
Didcot GB 31 C2
Die F 79 B4
Diebling F 60 A2
Dieburg D 61 A4
Diego del Carpio E 94 B1
Diekirch L 60 A2
Diélette F 57 A4
Diémoz F 69 C5
Dienten am Hochkönig A 72 A2
Diepenbeck B 49 C6
Diepholz D 43 C5
Dieppe F 58 A2
Dierberg D 45 B4
Dierdorf D 50 C3
Dieren NL 50 A2
Dierhagen D 44 A4
Diesdorf D 44 C2
Diessen D 62 C2
Diest B 49 C6
Dietenheim D 61 B6
Dietfurt D 62 A2
Dietikon CH 70 A3
Dietzenbach D 61 A4
Dieue-sur-Meuse F 59 A6
Dieulefit F 79 B4
Dieulouard F 60 B2

Dieuze F 60 B2
Diever NL 42 C3
Diez D 50 C4
Diezma E 100 B2
Differdange L 60 A1
Dignac F 67 C5
Dignano I 72 B2
Digne-les-Bains F 79 B5
Digny F 58 B2
Digoin F 68 B3
Dijon F 69 A5
Diksmuide B 48 B3
Dilar E 100 B2
Dillenburg D 50 C4
Dillingen, *Bayern* D 61 B6
Dillingen, *Saarland* D 60 A2
Dilsen B 50 B1
Dimaro I 71 B5
Dimitrovgrad BG 16 Q19
Dinami I 106 C3
Dinan F 57 B3
Dinant B 49 C5
Dinar TR 16 S22
Dinard F 57 B3
Dingden D 50 B2
Dingelstädt D 51 B6
Dingle IRL 20 B1
Dingle S 35 C3
Dingolfing D 62 B3
Dingtuna S 36 B3
Dingwall GB 23 D4
Dinkelsbühl D 61 A6
Dinkelscherben D 61 B6
Dinklage D 43 C5
Dinslaken D 50 B2
Dinxperlo NL 50 B2
Diö S 40 C4
Diósgyör H 65 B6
Diósjeno H 65 C5
Diou F 68 B3
Dippen GB 24 C2
Dipperz D 51 C5
Dippoldiswalde D 53 C3
Dirdal N 32 C3
Dirksland NL 49 B5
Dirlewang D 61 C6
Dischingen D 61 B6
Disentis CH 70 B3
Diso I 107 A5
Diss GB 30 B5
Dissen D 50 A4
Distington GB 26 A2
Ditzingen D 61 B5
Ditzum D 43 B4
Divača SLO 72 C3
Dives-sur-Mer F 57 A5
Divín SK 65 B5
Divion F 48 C3
Divišov CZ 63 A5
Divonne les Bains F 69 B6
Dixmont F 59 B4
Dizy-le-Gros F 59 A5
Djura S 36 A1
Djurås S 36 A2
Djurmo S 36 A2
Djursdala S 40 B5
Dlouhá Loucka CZ 64 A3
Długowola PL 55 B6
Dmitriyev Lgovskiy RUS 7 K24
Dmitrov RUS 7 H25
Dmitrovsk-Orlovskiy RUS 7 K24
Dno RUS 7 H21
Doade E 86 B3
Dobanovci YU 85 B5
Dobbertin D 44 B4
Dobbiaco I 72 B2
Dobczyce PL 65 A6
Dobele LV 6 H18
Döbeln D 52 B3
Doberlug-Kirchhain D 52 B3
Dobern D 53 B4
Dobersberg A 63 B6
Dobiegniew PL 46 C1
Dobieszyn PL 55 B6
Doboj BIH 84 B3
Dobošnica BIH 84 B3
Doboz H 75 B6
Dobrá CZ 65 A4
Dobra PL 54 B3
Dobra, *Szczecin* PL 45 B6
Dobra, *Szczecin* PL 45 B7
Dobrá Niva SK 65 B5
Dobřany CZ 63 A4
Dobre PL 47 C4
Dobre Miasto PL 47 B6
Dobreta-Turnu-Severin RO 11 P18
Dobri H 74 B1
Dobri Do YU 85 D6
Dobrica YU 75 C5
Dobrich BG 16 Q20
Dobříš CZ 63 A5
Dobro E 89 B3
Dobrodzień PL 54 C3
Döbrököz H 74 B3
Dobromierz PL 53 C6
Dobrosołowo PL 47 C4
Dobroszyce PL 54 B2
Dobrovnik SLO 73 B6
Dobrush BY 7 K22
Dobruška CZ 53 C6
Dobrzany PL 46 B1
Dobrzen Wielki PL 54 C2
Dobrzyca, *Wielkopolskie* PL 46 B2
Dobrzyca, *Wielkopolskie* PL 54 B2
Dobrzyca, *Zachodnio-Pomorskie* PL 46 A1
Dobrzyń nad Wisłą PL 47 C5
Dobšiná SK 65 B6
Dobwalls GB 28 C3
Dochamps B 49 C6
Docking GB 30 B4
Doddington GB 25 C5
Döderhult S 40 B6
Doesburg NL 50 A2
Doetinchem NL 50 B2
Dogliani I 80 B1
Dogueno P 98 B3
Dois Portos P 92 B1
Doische B 49 C5
Dojč SK 64 B3
Dokkedal DK 38 C3
Dokkum NL 42 B2
Dokležovje SLO 73 B6
Doksy CZ 53 C4
Dol-de-Bretagne F 57 B4
Dolancourt F 59 B5
Dolceácqua I 80 C1
Dole F 69 A5
Dølemo N 33 C5
Dolenja vas SLO 73 C4
Dolenjske Toplice SLO 73 C5
Dolfor GB 26 C2
Dolgarrog GB 26 B2
Dolgellau GB 26 C2
Dolianova I 110 D2
Dolice PL 45 B7
Doljani HR 83 B5
Döllach im Mölltal A 72 B2
Dolle D 44 C3
Dollnstein D 62 B2
Dollot F 59 B4
Döllstadt D 51 B6
Dolná Strehová SK 65 B5
Dolné Saliby SK 64 B3
Dolni Benešov CZ 64 A4
Dolni Bousov CZ 53 C5
Dolni Kounice CZ 64 A2
Dolni Kralovice CZ 63 A6
Dolni Újezd CZ 64 A2
Dolni Žandov CZ 52 C2
Dolný Kubín SK 65 A5
Dolo I 72 C2
Dolores E 96 C2
Dolovo YU 85 B5
Dölsach A 72 B2
Dolsk PL 54 A2
Dolwyddelan GB 26 B2
Dolynska UA 11 M23
Domaljevac BIH 84 A3
Domaniç TR 16 S21
Domaniža SK 65 A4
Domanoviči BIH 84 C2
Domašov CZ 54 C2
Domaszék H 75 B4
Domaszków PL 54 C1
Domaszowice PL 54 B3
Domat-Ems CH 71 B4
Domažlice CZ 62 A3
Dombås N 2 E11
Dombasle-sur-Meurthe F 60 B2
Dombegyház H 75 B6
Dombóvár H 74 B3
Domène F 69 C5
Domérat F 68 B2
Domfessel F 60 B3
Domfront F 57 B5
Domfront-en-Champagne F 57 B6
Domingão P 92 B2
Domingo Pérez, *Granada* E 100 B2
Domingo Pérez, *Toledo* E 94 C2
Dömitz D 44 B3
Dommartin F 59 B5
Dommartin-le-Franc F 59 B5
Domme F 77 B4
Dommitzsch D 52 B2
Domodóssola I 70 B3
Domoszló H 65 C6
Dompaire F 60 B2
Dompierre-du-Chemin F 57 B4
Dompierre-sur-Besbre F 68 B3
Dompierre-sur-Mer F 66 B3
Domrémy-la-Pucelle F 60 B1
Dömsöd H 75 A4
Domsure F 69 B5
Dómus de Maria I 110 E1
Domusnóvas I 110 D1
Domžale SLO 73 B4
Don Alvaro E 93 C4
Don Benito E 93 C5
Doña Mencía E 100 B1
Donado E 87 B4
Donaghadee GB 19 B6
Donaueschingen D 61 C4
Donauwörth D 62 B1
Doncaster GB 27 B4
Donegal IRL 18 B3
Donestebe-Santesteban E 76 C1
Donges F 66 A2
Dongo I 71 B4
Donington GB 30 B3
Doniños E 86 A2
Donja Bebrina HR 84 A3
Donja Brela HR 84 C1
Donja Dubica BIH 84 A3
Donja Dubrava HR 74 B1
Donja Kupčina HR 73 C5
Donja Šatornja YU 85 B5
Donja Stubica HR 73 C5
Donje Brišnik BIH 84 C2
Donje Ljupče YU 85 D6
Donje Stative HR 73 C5
Donji-Andrijevci HR 74 C3
Donji Kazanci BIH 83 C5
Donji Koričáni BIH 84 B2
Donji Lapac HR 83 B4
Donji Malovan BIH 84 C2
Donji Miholjac HR 74 C3
Donji Mosti HR 74 B1
Donji Poloj HR 73 C5
Donji-Rujani BIH 83 C5
Donji Srb HR 83 B5
Donji Svilaj BIH 84 A3
Donji Tovarnik YU 85 B4
Donji Vakuf BIH 84 B2
Donnalucata I 109 C3
Donnemarie-Dontilly F 59 B4
Donnersbach A 73 A4
Donnersbachwald A 73 A4
Donnerskirchen A 64 C2
Donorático I 81 C4
Donostia-San Sebastián E 89 A5
Donovaly SK 65 B5
Donzenac F 67 C6
Donzère F 78 B3
Donzy F 68 A3
Doonbeg IRL 20 B2
Doorn NL 49 A6
Dor E 86 A1
Dorchester GB 29 C5
Dørdal N 33 C6
Dordrecht NL 49 B5
Dörenthe D 50 A3
Dores GB 23 D4
Dorf Mecklenburg D 44 B3
Dorfen D 62 B3
Dorfgastein A 72 A3
Dorfmark D 43 C6
Dorgali I 110 C2
Dorking GB 31 C3
Dormagen D 50 B2
Dormánd H 65 C6
Dormans F 59 A4
Dornava SLO 73 B5
Dornbirn A 71 A4
Dornburg D 52 B1
Dorndorf D 51 C6
Dornecy F 68 A3
Dornes F 68 B3
Dornhan D 61 B4
Dornie GB 22 D3
Dornoch GB 23 D4
Dornum D 43 B4
Dorog H 65 C4
Dorogobuzh RUS 7 J23
Dorohoi RO 11 N20
Dorotowo PL 47 B6
Dörpen D 43 C4
Dorsten D 50 B2
Dortan F 69 B5
Dortmund D 50 B3
Doruchów PL 54 B3
Dorum D 43 B5
Dörverden D 43 C6
Dörzbach D 61 A5
Dos Aguas E 96 B2
Dos Hermanas E 99 B5
Dos-Torres E 100 A1
Dosbarrios E 95 C3
Döttlingen D 43 C5
Dottignies B 49 C4
Döttingen CH 70 A3
Douai F 48 C4
Douarnenez F 56 B1
Douchy F 59 C4
Douchy-les-Mines F 49 C4
Doucier F 69 B5
Doudeville F 58 A1
Doué-la-Fontaine F 67 A4
Douglas, *Isle of Man* GB 26 A1
Douglas, *South Lanarkshire* GB 25 C4
Doulaincourt F 59 B6
Doulevant-le-Château F 59 B5
Doullens F 48 C3
Dounby GB 23 B5
Doune GB 24 B3
Dounreay GB 23 C5
Dour B 49 C4
Dourdan F 58 B3
Dourgne F 77 C5
Dournazac F 67 C5
Douro Calvo P 87 D3
Douvaine F 69 B6
Douvres-la-Délivrande F 57 A5
Douzy F 59 A6
Dover GB 31 C5
Dovje SLO 72 B3
Dovre N 2 F11
Downham Market GB 30 B4
Downhill GB 19 A5
Downpatrick GB 19 B6
Doyet F 68 B2
Dozule F 57 A5
Drača YU 85 B5
Dračevo BIH 84 D3
Drachten NL 42 B3
Draga SLO 73 C4
Drăgăşani RO 11 P19
Dragatuš SLO 73 C5
Dragichyn BY 7 K19
Draginja YU 85 B4
Dragocvet YU 85 C6
Dragolovci BIH 84 B2
Dragoni I 103 B4
Dragør DK 41 D2
Dragotina HR 83 A5
Dragotinja BIH 84 A1
Dragozetići HR 82 A3
Draguignan F 79 C5
Drahnsdorf D 52 B3
Drahonice CZ 63 A5
Drahovce SK 64 B3
Dráma GR 16 R19
Drammen N 33 B6
Drangedal N 33 B5
Dransfeld D 51 B5
Dranske D 45 A5
Draperstown GB 19 B5
Drassburg A 64 C2
Drávaszabolcs H 74 C3
Dravograd SLO 73 B5
Drawno PL 46 B1
Drawsko Pomorskie PL 46 B1
Drayton GB 30 B5
Draženov CZ 62 A3
Draževac YU 85 B5
Dražice HR 73 C4
Drebkau D 53 B4
Dreieich D 51 C4
Dreisen D 61 A4
Dren YU 85 C5
Drenovac YU 85 C6
Drenovci HR 84 B3
Drensteinfurt D 50 B3
Dresden D 53 B3
Dretyń PL 46 A2
Dreux F 58 B2
Dřevohostice CZ 64 A3
Drewitz D 52 A2
Drezdenko PL 46 C1
Drežnica HR 83 A4
Drežnik-Grad HR 83 B4
Drietona SK 64 B3
Driffield GB 27 A5
Drimnin GB 24 B2
Drimoleague IRL 20 C2
Dringenberg D 51 B5
Drinić BIH 83 B5
Drinjača BIH 85 B4
Drinovci BIH 84 C2
Drlače YU 85 B4
Drnholec CZ 64 B2
Drniš HR 83 C5
Drnje HR 74 B1
Drnovice CZ 64 A2
Dro I 71 C5
Drøbak N 34 B2
Drobin PL 47 C5
Drochia MD 11 M20
Drochtersen D 43 B6
Drogheda IRL 19 C5
Drohobych UA 11 M18
Droitwich Spa GB 29 A5
Drołtowice PL 54 B2
Dromahair IRL 18 B3
Dromcolliher IRL 20 B3
Dromore, *Down* GB 19 B5
Dromore, *Tyrone* GB 19 B4
Dromore West IRL 18 B3
Dronero I 80 B1
Dronfield GB 27 B4
Drongan GB 24 C3
Dronninglund DK 38 B3
Dronrijp NL 42 B2
Dronten NL 42 C2
Drosendorf A 63 B6
Drösing A 64 B2
Drottningholm S 36 B4
Droué F 58 B2
Drulingen F 60 B3
Drumbeg GB 22 C3
Drumcliff IRL 18 B3
Drumgask GB 23 D4
Drumkeeran IRL 18 B3
Drummore GB 24 D3
Drumnadrochit GB 23 D4
Drumquin GB 19 B4
Drumshanbo IRL 18 B3
Drumsna IRL 19 C4
Drunen NL 49 B6
Druskininkai LT 6 J18
Druten NL 49 B6
Druya BY 7 J20
Družetići YU 85 B5
Drvar BIH 83 B5
Drvenik HR 84 C2
Drwalew PL 55 B6
Drymen GB 24 B3
Drynoch GB 22 D2
Drzewce PL 54 A2
Drzewiany PL 46 B2
Drzewica PL 55 B5
Dualchi I 110 C1
Duas Igrejas P 87 C4
Dub YU 85 C4
Dubá CZ 53 C4
Dubăsari MD 11 N21
Duben D 53 B3
Dübendorf CH 70 A3
Dubí CZ 53 C3
Dubica HR 74 C1
Dublin IRL 21 A5
Dubna RUS 7 H25
Dubňany CZ 64 B3
Dubnica nad Váhom SK 64 B4
Dubník SK 65 C4
Dubno UA 11 L19
Dubodiel SK 64 B4
Dubona YU 85 B5
Dubovac YU 85 B6
Dubovic BIH 83 B5
Dubranec HR 73 C5
Dubrava HR 74 C1
Dubrave BIH 84 B3
Dubravica HR 73 C5
Dubravica YU 85 B6
Dubrovnik HR 84 D3
Dubrovytsya UA 11 L20
Ducey F 57 B4
Duchcov CZ 53 C3
Ducherow D 45 B5
Dučina YU 85 B5
Duclair F 58 A1
Dudar H 74 A2
Duddington GB 30 B3
Duderstadt D 51 B6
Dudeştii Vechi RO 75 B5
Dudley GB 26 C3
Dueñas E 88 C2
Dueville I 72 C1
Duffel B 49 B5
Duffield GB 27 C4
Dufftown GB 23 D5
Duga Poljana YU 85 C5
Duga Resa HR 73 C5
Dugi Rat HR 83 C5
Dugny-sur-Meuse F 59 A6
Dugo Selo HR 73 C6
Dugopolje HR 83 C5
Duino I 72 C3
Duisburg D 50 B2
Dukhovshchina RUS 7 J23
Dukovany CZ 64 A2
Duleek IRL 19 C5
Dülken D 50 B2
Dülmen D 50 B3
Dulovo BG 16 Q20
Dulverton GB 29 B4
Dumbarton GB 24 C3
Dumfries GB 25 C4
Dun Laoghaire IRL 21 A5
Dun-le-Palestel F 67 B6
Dun-les-Places F 68 A4
Dun-sur-Auron F 68 B2
Dun-sur-Meuse F 59 A6
Dunaalmás H 65 C4
Dunabogdány H 65 C5
Dunafalva H 74 B3
Dunaföldvár H 74 B3
Dunaharaszti H 75 A4
Dunajská Streda SK 64 C3
Dunakeszi H 65 C5
Dunakiliti H 64 C3
Dunakömlöd H 74 B3
Dunapataj H 75 B3
Dunaszekcsö H 74 B3
Dunaszentgyorgy H 74 B3
Dunatetétlen H 75 B3
Dunaújváros H 75 B3
Dunavecse H 75 B3
Dunbar GB 25 B5
Dunbeath GB 23 C5
Dunblane GB 25 B4
Dunboyne IRL 21 A5
Dundalk IRL 19 B5
Dundee GB 25 B5
Dundrennan GB 25 D4
Dundrum GB 19 B6
Dunfanaghy IRL 19 A4
Dunfermline GB 25 B4
Dungannon GB 19 B5
Dungarvan IRL 21 B4
Dungiven GB 19 B5
Dunglow IRL 18 B3
Dungourney IRL 20 C3
Duninowo PL 46 A2
Dunkeld GB 25 B4
Dunker S 36 B3
Dunkerque F 48 B3
Dunkineely IRL 18 B3
Dunlavin IRL 21 A5
Dunleer IRL 19 C5
Dunlop GB 24 C3
Dunloy GB 19 A5
Dunmanway IRL 20 C2
Dunmore IRL 18 C3
Dunmore East IRL 21 B5
Dunmurry GB 19 B5
Dunnet GB 23 C5
Dunningen D 61 B4
Dunoon GB 24 C3
Duns GB 25 C5
Dunscore GB 25 C4
Dunsford GB 28 C4
Dunshaughlin IRL 21 A5
Dunstable GB 31 C3
Dunster GB 29 B4
Dunvegan GB 22 D2
Duplek SLO 73 B5
Dupnitsa BG 15 Q18
Durach D 61 C6
Đurakovac YU 85 D5
Durana E 89 B4
Durance F 76 B3
Durango E 89 A4
Durankulak BG 16 Q21
Duras F 76 B3
Durban-Corbières F 78 D1
Dürbheim D 61 B4
Durbuy B 49 C6
Dúrcal E 100 C2
Đurdjenovac HR 74 C3
Đurdjevac HR 74 B2
Đurdjevik BIH 84 B3
Düren D 50 C2
Durham GB 25 D6
Đurinci YU 85 B5
Durlach D 61 B4
Đurmanec HR 73 B5
Durness GB 22 C4
Dürnkrut A 64 B2
Dürrboden CH 71 B4
Dürrenboden CH 70 B3
Durrës AL 15 R16
Durrow IRL 21 B4
Durrus IRL 20 C2
Dursunbey TR 16 S21
Durtal F 57 C5
Durup DK 38 C1
Dusina BIH 84 C2
Dusnok H 75 B3
Dusocin PL 47 B4
Düsseldorf D 50 B2
Dusslingen D 61 B5
Duszniki PL 46 C2
Duszniki-Zdrój PL 54 C1
Dutovlje SLO 72 C3
Duved S 2 E13
Düzce TR 16 R22
Dvor HR 83 A5
Dvorce CZ 64 A3
Dvorníky SK 64 B3
Dvory nad Žitavou SK 64 C4
Dvůr Králové nad Labem CZ 53 C5
Dyatkovo RUS 7 K24
Dybvad DK 38 B3
Dyce GB 23 D6
Dygowo PL 46 A1
Dykehead GB 25 B4
Dymchurch GB 31 C5
Dymer UA 11 L22
Dywity PL 47 B6
Džaniĉi BIH 84 C2
Dziadowa Kłoda PL 54 B2
Działdowo PL 47 B6
Działoszyce PL 55 C5
Działoszyn PL 54 B3
Dziemiany PL 46 A3
Dzierzążnia PL 47 C6
Dzierzgoń PL 47 B5
Dzierzgowo PL 47 B6
Dzierżoniów PL 54 C1
Dzisna BY 7 J21
Dziwnów PL 45 A6
Dzyarzhynsk BY 7 K20
Dzyatlava BY 7 K19

E

Ea E 89 A4
Eaglesfield GB 25 C4
Ealing GB 31 C3
Eardisley GB 29 A4
Earl Shilton GB 30 B2
Earls Barton GB 30 B3
Earlston GB 25 C5
Easington GB 27 B6
Easky IRL 18 B3
East Calder GB 25 C4
East Dereham GB 30 B4
East Grinstead GB 31 C4
East Ilsley GB 31 C2
East Kilbride GB 24 C3
East Linton GB 25 C5
East Markham GB 27 B5
East Wittering GB 31 D3
Eastbourne GB 31 D4
Easter Skeld GB 22 A7
Eastleigh GB 31 D2
Easton GB 29 C5
Eaton Socon GB 30 B3
Eaux-Bonnes F 76 D2
Eauze F 76 C3
Ebberup DK 39 D2
Ebbs A 62 C3
Ebbw Vale GB 29 B4
Ebeleben D 51 B6
Ebeltoft DK 39 C3
Eben im Pongau A 72 A3
Ebene Reichenau A 72 B3
Ebensee A 63 C4
Ebensfeld D 51 C6
Eberbach D 61 A4
Ebergötzen D 51 B6
Ebermann-Stadt D 62 A2
Ebern D 51 C6
Eberndorf A 73 B4
Ebersbach D 53 B4
Ebersberg D 62 B2
Ebersdorf, *Bayern* D 52 C1
Ebersdorf, *Niedersachsen* D 43 B6
Eberstein A 73 B4
Eberswalde D 45 C5
Ebnat-Kappel CH 71 A4
Éboli I 104 B2
Ebrach D 61 A6
Ebreichsdorf A 64 C2
Ebreuil F 68 B3
Ebstorf D 44 B2
Ecclefechan GB 25 C4
Eccleshall GB 26 C3
Eceabat TR 16 R20
Echallens CH 69 B6
Echauri E 89 B5
Echiré F 67 B4
Échirolles F 79 A4
Echourgnac F 76 A3
Echt NL 50 B1
Echte D 51 B6
Echternach L 60 A2
Ecija E 99 B5
Ečka YU 75 C5
Eckartsberga D 52 B1
Eckelshausen D 51 C4
Eckental D 62 A2
Eckernförde D 44 A1
Eckerö FIN 3 F16
Eckington GB 27 B4
Éclaron F 59 B5
Écommoy F 58 C1
Écouché F 57 B5
Ecouis F 58 A2
Ecséd H 65 C5
Ecsegfalva H 75 A5
Écueillé F 67 A6
Ed S 35 C3
Eda S 34 B4
Eda glasbruk S 34 B4
Edam NL 42 C2
Edane S 34 B4
Edderton GB 23 D4
Ede NL 49 A6
Edebäck S 34 A5
Edebo S 36 A5
Edelény H 65 B6
Edelschrott A 73 A5
Edemissen D 44 C2
Edenbridge GB 31 C4
Edenderry IRL 21 A4
Edenkoben D 61 A4
Edesheim D 61 A4
Edewecht D 43 B4
Edgeworthstown IRL 19 C4
Édhessa GR 15 R18
Edinburgh GB 25 C4
Edineţ MD 11 M20
Edirne TR 16 R20
Edland N 33 B4
Edolo I 71 B5
Edremit TR 16 S20
Eds bruk S 37 C3
Edsbro S 36 B5
Edsleskog S 35 B4
Edsvalla S 34 B5
Eekloo B 49 B4
Eemshaven NL 42 B3
Eerbeek NL 50 A2
Eersel NL 49 B6
Eferding A 63 B5
Effiat F 68 B3
Efteløt N 33 B6
Egeln D 52 B1
Eger H 65 C6
Egerbakta H 65 C6
Egernsund DK 39 E2
Egersund N 32 C3
Egerszólát H 65 C6
Egervár H 74 B1
Egg A 71 A4
Egg D 61 B6
Eggedal N 33 A6
Eggenburg A 64 B1
Eggenfelden D 62 B3
Eggesin D 45 B6
Egham GB 31 C3
Éghezée B 49 C5
Egiertowo PL 47 A4
Égletons F 68 C2
Egling D 62 C2
Eglinton GB 19 A4
Eglisau CH 61 C4
Égliseneuve-d'Entraigues F 68 C2
Eglofs D 61 C5
Egmond aan Zee NL 42 C1
Egna I 71 B6
Egremont GB 26 A2
Eğridir TR 16 T22
Egtved DK 39 D2
Eguilles F 79 C4
Eguilly-sous-Bois F 59 B5
Éguzon-Chantôme F 67 B6
Egyek H 65 C6
Egyházasrádóc H 74 A1
Ehekirchen D 62 B2
Ehingen D 61 B5
Ehra-Lessien D 44 C2
Ehrang D 60 A2
Ehrenfriedersdorf D 52 C2
Ehrenhain D 52 C2
Ehrenhausen A 73 B5
Ehringshausen D 51 C4
Ehrwald A 71 A5
Eibar E 89 A4
Eibelstadt D 61 A6
Eibenstock D 52 C2
Eibergen NL 50 A2
Eibiswald A 73 B5
Eichenbarleben D 52 A1
Eichendorf D 62 B3
Eichstätt D 62 B2
Eickelborn D 50 B4
Eidsberg N 34 B3
Eidsfoss N 33 B7
Eidskog N 34 A4
Eidsvoll N 34 A3
Eikefjord N 2 F9
Eikelandsosen N 32 A2
Eiken N 33 C4
Eikstrand N 33 B6
Eilenburg D 52 B2
Eilsleben D 52 A1
Einbeck D 51 B5
Eindhoven NL 49 B6
Einsiedeln CH 70 A3
Einville-au-Jard F 60 B2
Eisenach D 51 C6
Eisenberg, *Rheinland-Pfalz* D 61 A4
Eisenberg, *Thüringen* D 52 C1
Eisenerz A 73 A4
Eisenhüttenstadt D 53 A4
Eisenkappel A 73 B4
Eisenstadt A 64 C2
Eisentratten A 72 B3
Eisfeld D 51 C6
Eisleben D 52 B1
Eislingen D 61 B5
Eitensheim D 62 B2
Eiterfeld D 51 C5
Eitorf D 50 C3
Eivissa E 97 C4
Eixo P 92 A2
Ejby DK 39 D2
Ejea de los Caballeros E 90 A1
Ejstrupholm DK 39 D2
Ejulve E 90 C2
Eke B 49 C4
Ekeby, *Gotland* S 37 D5
Ekeby, *Skåne* S 41 D2
Ekeby, *Uppsala* S 36 A5
Ekeby-Almby S 36 B2
Ekenäs S 35 C5
Ekenässjön S 40 B5
Ekerö S 36 B4
Eket S 41 C3
Eketorp S 41 C6
Ekshärad S 34 A5
Eksjö S 40 B4
El Alamo, *Madrid* E 94 B3
El Alamo, *Sevilla* E 99 B4
El Algar E 101 B5
El Almendro E 98 B3
El Alquián E 101 C3
El Arahal E 99 B5
El Arenal E 94 B1
El Arguellite E 101 A3
El Astillero E 88 A3
El Ballestero E 101 A3
El Barco de Ávila E 93 A5
El Berrón E 88 A1
El Berrueco E 95 B3
El Bodón E 93 A4
El Bonillo E 101 A3
El Bosque E 99 C5
El Bullaque E 94 C2
El Burgo E 100 C1
El Burgo de Ebro E 90 B2
El Burgo de Osma E 89 C3
El Burgo Ranero E 88 B1
El Buste E 89 C5
El Cabaco E 93 A4
El Callejo E 89 A3
El Campillo E 99 B4
El Campillo de la Jara E 94 C1
El Cañavete E 95 C4
El Carpio E 100 B1
El Carpio de Tajo E 94 C2
El Casar E 95 B3
El Casar de Escalona E 94 B2
El Castillo de las Guardas E 99 B4
El Centenillo E 100 A2
El Cerro E 93 A5
El Cerro de Andévalo E 99 B4
El Comenar E 99 C5
El Coronil E 99 B5
El Crucero E 86 A4
El Cubo de Tierra del Vino E 94 A1
El Cuervo E 99 C4
El Ejido E 101 C3
El Escorial E 94 B2
El Espinar E 94 B2
El Frago E 90 A2
El Franco E 86 A4
El Frasno E 89 C5
El Garrobo E 99 B4
El Gastor E 99 C5
El Gordo E 94 C1
El Grado E 90 A3
El Granado E 98 B3
El Grao de Castelló E 96 B3
El Grau E 96 C2
El Higuera E 100 B1
El Hijate E 101 B3
El Hontanar E 96 A1
El Hoyo E 100 A2
El Madroño E 99 B4
El Maillo E 93 A4
El Masnou E 91 B5
El Mirón E 94 B1
El Molar E 95 B3
El Molinillo E 94 C2
El Morell E 91 B4
El Muyo E 89 C3
El Olmo E 88 C3
El Palo E 100 C1
El Pardo E 94 B3
El Payo E 93 A4
El Pedernoso E 95 C4
El Pedroso E 99 B5
El Peral E 95 C5
El Perelló, *Tarragona* E 90 C3
El Perelló, *Valencia* E 96 B2
El Picazo E 95 C4
El Pinell de Bray E 90 B3
El Piñero E 88 C1
El Pla de Santa Maria E 91 B4
El Pobo E 90 C2
El Pobo de Dueñas E 95 B5
El Pont d'Armentera E 91 B4
El Port de la Selva E 91 A6
El Port de Llançá E 91 A6
El Port de Sagunt E 96 B2
El Prat de Llobregat E 91 B5
El Provencio E 95 C4
El Puente E 89 A3
El Puente del Arzobispo E 94 C1
El Puerto E 86 A4
El Puerto de Santa Maria E 99 C4
El Real de la Jara E 99 B4
El Real de San Vincente E 94 B2
El Robledo E 94 C2
El Rocio E 99 B4
El Rompido E 99 B3
El Ronquillo E 99 B4
El Royo E 89 C4
El Rubio E 100 B1
El Sabinar E 101 A3
El Saler E 96 B2
El Salobral E 101 A4
El Saucejo E 99 B5
El Serrat AND 91 A4
El Temple E 90 B2
El Tiemblo E 94 B2
El Toboso E 95 C4
El Tormillo E 90 B2
El Torno E 93 A5
El Valle de las Casas E 88 B1
El Vellón E 95 B3
El Vendrell E 91 B4
El Villar de Arnedo E 89 B4
El Viso E 100 A1
El Viso del Alcor E 99 B5
Élancourt F 58 B2
Elbasan AL 15 R17
Elbeuf F 58 A1
Elbingerode D 51 B6
Elbląg PL 47 A5
Elburg NL 42 C2
Elche E 96 C2
Elche de la Sierra E 101 A3
Elchingen D 61 B6
Elda E 96 C2
Eldena D 44 B3
Eldingen D 44 C2
Elek H 75 B6
Elemir YU 75 C5
Elgin GB 23 D5
Elgoibar E 89 A4
Elgol GB 22 D2
Elie GB 25 B5
Elizondo E 76 C1
Ełk PL 6 K18
Elkhovo BG 16 Q20
Ellenberg D 61 A6
Ellesmere GB 26 C3
Ellesmere Port GB 26 B3
Ellezelles B 49 C4
Ellingen D 62 A1
Ellmau A 72 A2
Ellon GB 23 D6
Ellös S 35 C3
Ellrich D 51 B6
Ellwangen D 61 B6
Elm CH 71 B4
Elm D 43 B6
Elmalı TR 16 T21
Elmshorn D 43 B6
Elmstein D 60 A3
Elne F 91 A5
Elorrio E 89 A4
Előszállás H 74 B3
Éloyes F 60 B2
Elphin GB 22 C3
Els Castells E 91 A4
Elsdorf D 50 C2
Elsenfeld D 61 A5
Elsfleth D 43 B5
Elspeet NL 49 A6
Elst NL 50 B1
Elstead GB 31 C3
Elster D 52 B2
Elsterberg D 52 C2
Elsterwerda D 52 B3
Elstra D 53 B4
Eltmann D 51 D6
Eltville D 50 C4
Elvas P 93 C3
Elven F 56 C3
Elverum N 2 F12

Elvington GB 27 B5
Elxleben D 51 B6
Ely GB 30 B4
Elzach D 61 B4
Elze D 51 A5
Embleton GB 25 C6
Embrun F 79 B5
Embún E 90 A2
Emden D 43 B4
Emet TR 16 S21
Emirdağ TR 16 S22
Emlichheim D 42 C3
Emmaboda S 40 C5
Emmaljunga S 41 C3
Emmeloord NL 42 C2
Emmen CH 70 A3
Emmen NL 42 C3
Emmendingen D 60 B3
Emmer-Compascuum NL 43 C4
Emmerich D 50 B2
Emmern D 51 A5
Emöd H 65 C6
Empoli I 81 C4
Emsbüren D 43 C4
Emsdetten D 50 A3
Emsfors S 40 B6
Emskirchen D 62 A1
Emstek D 43 C5
Emsworth GB 31 D3
Emyvale IRL 19 B5
Encamp AND 91 A4
Encarnaçao P 92 C1
Encinas de Abajo E 94 B1
Encinas de Esgueva E 88 C2
Encinas Reales E 100 B1
Encinasola E 99 A4
Encio E 89 B3
Enciso E 89 B4
Endingen D 60 B3
Endrinal E 93 A5
Endröd H 75 B5
Enebakk N 34 B3
Eneryda S 40 C4
Enese H 64 C3
Enez TR 16 R20
Enfield IRL 21 A5
Eng A 72 A1
Enge-sande D 39 E1
Engelberg CH 70 B3
Engelhartszell A 63 B4
Engelskirchen D 50 C3
Engen D 61 C4
Engerdal N 2 F12
Engesvang DK 39 C2
Enghien B 49 C5
Engstingen D 61 B5
Engter D 43 C5
Enguera E 96 C2
Enguidanos E 96 B1
Enkenbach D 60 A3
Enkhuizen NL 42 C2
Enköping S 36 B4
Enna I 109 B3
Ennezat F 68 C3
Ennigerloh D 50 B4
Enningdal N 35 C3
Ennis IRL 20 B3
Enniscorthy IRL 21 B5
Enniskean IRL 20 C3
Enniskillen GB 19 B4
Ennistimon IRL 20 B2
Enns A 63 B5
Eno FIN 3 E22
Enontekiö FIN 3 B18
Ens NL 42 C2
Enschede NL 50 A2
Ensdorf D 62 A2
Ensisheim F 60 C3
Enstaberga S 37 C3
Enstone GB 31 C2
Entlebuch CH 70 A3
Entrácque I 80 B1
Entradas P 98 B2
Entrains-sur-Nohain F 68 A3
Entrambasaguas E 88 A3
Entrambasmestas E 88 A3
Entraygues-sur-Truyère F 77 B5
Entre-os-Rios P 87 C2
Entrevaux F 79 C5
Entrin Bajo E 93 C4
Entroncamento P 92 B2
Entzheim F 60 B3
Envermeu F 58 A2
Enying H 74 B3
Enzingerboden A 72 A2
Enzklösterle D 61 B4
Épagny F 59 A4
Epalinges CH 70 B1
Epannes F 67 B4
Epe D 50 A3
Epe NL 42 C2
Épernay F 59 A4
Épernon F 58 B2
Epfig F 60 B3
Epierre F 69 C6
Épila E 90 B1
Épinac F 69 B4
Épinal F 60 B2
Episcopia I 104 B3
Epoisses F 69 A4
Eppenbrunn D 60 A3
Eppendorf D 52 C3
Epping GB 31 C4
Eppingen D 61 A4
Epsom GB 31 C3
Epworth GB 27 B5
Eraclea I 72 C2
Eraclea Mare I 72 C2
Erba I 71 C4
Erbach, *Baden-Württemberg* D 61 B5
Erbach, *Hessen* D 61 A4
Erbalunga F 110 A2
Erbendorf D 62 A3
Érchie I 105 B4
Ercolano I 103 C4
Ercsi H 74 A3
Érd H 74 A3
Erdek TR 16 R20
Erdevik YU 85 A4
Erding D 62 B2
Erdőtelek H 65 C6
Erdut HR 75 C4
Erdweg D 62 B2
Ereğli TR 16 R22
Erfde D 43 A6
Erfjord N 32 B3
Erfstadt D 50 C2
Erfurt D 52 C1
Ērgli LV 7 H19
Eriboll GB 22 C4
Érice I 108 A1
Ericeira P 92 C1
Eriksmåla S 40 C5
Eringsboda S 40 C5
Eriswil CH 70 A2
Erkelenz D 50 B2
Erkner D 45 C5
Erkrath D 50 B2
Erla E 90 A2
Erlangen D 62 A2
Erli I 80 B2
Erlsbach A 72 B2
Ermelo NL 49 A6
Ermenonville F 58 A3
Ermezinde P 87 C2
Ermidas P 98 A2
Ermsleben D 52 B1
Erndtebrück D 50 C4
Ernée F 57 B5
Ernestinovo HR 74 C3
Ernstbrunn A 64 B2
Erolzheim D 61 B6
Erquelinnes B 49 C5
Erquy F 56 B3
Erra P 92 C2
Erratzu E 76 C1
Errindlev DK 44 A3
Erro E 76 D1
Ersa F 80 D3
Érsekcsanád H 75 B3
Ersekvadkert H 65 C5
Erstein F 60 B3
Erstfeld CH 70 B3
Ertebølle DK 38 C2
Ertingen D 61 B5
Ervedal, *Coimbra* P 92 A2
Ervedal, *Portalegre* P 92 B3
Ervenik HR 83 B4
Ervidel P 98 B2
Ervy-le-Châtel F 59 B4
Erwitte D 51 B4
Erxleben D 52 A1
Erzsébet H 74 B3
Es Caná E 97 B4
Es Castell, *Menorca* E 97
Es Mercadal, *Menorca* E 97
Es Migjorn Gran, *Menorca* E 97
Es Port d'Alcúdia, *Mallorca* E 97
Es Pujols E 97 C4
Es Soleràs E 90 B3
Esbjerg DK 39 D1
Esbly F 58 B3
Escacena del Campo E 99 B4
Escairón E 86 B3
Escalada E 88 B3
Escalante E 89 A3
Escalaplano I 110 D2
Escalona E 94 B2
Escalona del Prado E 94 A2
Escalonilla E 94 C2
Escalos de Baixo P 92 B3
Escalos de Cima P 92 B3
Escamilla E 95 B4
Escañuela E 100 B1
Escatrón E 90 B2
Esch-sur-Alzette L 60 A1
Eschach D 61 C5
Eschau D 61 A5
Eschede D 44 C2
Eschenau D 62 A2
Eschenbach D 62 A2
Eschenz CH 61 C4
Eschershausen D 51 B5
Eschwege D 51 B6
Eschweiler D 50 C2
Escobasa de Almazán E 89 C4
Escoeuilles F 48 C2
Escombreras E 101 B5
Escos F 76 C1
Escource F 76 B1
Escragnolles F 79 C5
Escrick GB 27 B4
Escurial E 93 B5
Escurial de la Sierra E 93 A5
Esens D 43 B4
Esgos E 87 B3
Esher GB 31 C3
Eskdalemuir GB 25 C4
Eskilhem S 37 D5
Eskilsäter S 35 C5
Eskilstrup DK 39 E4
Eskilstuna S 36 B3
Eskişehir TR 16 S22
Eslarn D 62 A3
Eslava E 89 B5
Eslida E 96 B2
Eslohe D 50 B4
Eslöv S 41 D3
Eşme TR 16 S21
Espalion F 78 B1
Esparragalejo E 93 C4
Esparragosa del Caudillo E 93 C5
Esparragossa de la Serena E 93 C5
Esparreguera E 91 B4
Esparron F 79 C4
Espe N 32 A3
Espedal N 32 C3
Espejo, *Alava* E 89 B4
Espejo, *Córdoba* E 100 B1
Espeland N 32 A2
Espelkamp D 43 C5
Espeluche F 78 B3
Espeluy E 100 A2
Espera E 99 C5
Esperança P 93 B3
Espéraza F 77 D5
Espéria I 103 B3
Espevær N 32 B2
Espiel E 99 A5
Espinama E 88 A2
Espiñaredo E 86 A3
Espinasses F 79 B5
Espinelves E 91 B5
Espinhal P 92 A2
Espinho P 87 C2
Espinilla E 88 A2
Espinosa de Cerrato E 88 C3
Espinosa de los Monteros E 89 A3
Espinoso del Rey E 94 C2
Espirito Santo P 98 B3
Espluga de Francolí E 91 B4
Esplús E 90 B3
Espolla E 91 A5
Espoo FIN 3 F19
Esporles, *Mallorca* E 97
Esposende P 87 C2
Espot E 91 A4
Esquedas E 90 A2
Esquivias E 94 B3
Essen B 49 B5
Essen, *Niedersachsen* D 43 C4
Essen, *Nordrhein-Westfalen* D 50 B3
Essenbach D 62 B3
Essertaux F 58 A3
Essingen D 61 B6
Esslingen D 61 B5
Essoyes F 59 B5
Estacas E 87 B2
Estadilla E 90 A3
Estagel F 78 D1
Estaires F 48 C3
Estang F 76 C2
Estarreja P 87 D2
Estartit E 91 A6
Estavayer-le-Lac CH 70 B1
Este I 72 C1
Esteiro E 86 A2
Estela P 87 C2
Estella E 89 B4
Estellencs, *Mallorca* E 97
Estepa E 100 B1
Estépar E 88 B3
Estepona E 99 C5
Esternay F 59 B4
Esterri d'Aneu E 91 A4
Esterwegen D 43 C4
Estissac F 59 B4
Estivadas E 87 B3
Estivareilles F 68 B2
Estivella E 96 B2
Estói P 98 B3
Estopiñán E 90 B3
Estoril P 92 C1
Estoublon F 79 C5
Estrée-Blanche F 48 C3
Estrées-St. Denis F 58 A3
Estrela P 98 A3
Estremera E 95 B3
Estremoz P 92 C3
Estuna S 36 B5
Esyres F 67 A5
Esztergom H 65 C4
Etables-sur-Mer F 56 B3
Étain F 60 A1
Étalans F 69 A6
Etalle B 60 A1
Étampes F 58 B3
Etang-sur-Arroux F 69 B4
Étaples F 48 C2
Etauliers F 67 C4
Etne N 32 B2
Etoges F 59 B4
Eton GB 31 C3
Etréaupont F 59 A4
Étréchy F 58 B3
Étrépagny F 58 A2
Étretat F 57 A6
Étroeungt F 49 C4
Étroubles I 70 C2
Ettal D 62 C2
Ettelbruck L 60 A2
Etten NL 49 B5
Ettenheim D 60 B3
Ettington GB 29 A6
Ettlingen D 61 B4
Ettringen D 62 B1
Etuz F 69 A5
Etxarri-Aranatz E 89 B4
Etyek H 74 A3
Eu F 48 C2
Euerdorf D 51 C6
Eulate E 89 B4
Eupen B 50 C2
Europoort NL 49 B5
Euskirchen D 50 C2
Eutin D 44 A2
Évaux-les-Bains F 68 B2
Evercreech GB 29 B5
Evergem B 49 B4
Everöd S 41 D4
Eversberg D 51 B4
Everswinkel D 50 B3
Evesham GB 29 A6
Évian-les-Bains F 69 B6
Evisa F 110 A1
Evje N 33 C4
Evolène CH 70 B2
Évora P 92 C3
Evoramonte P 92 C3
Evran F 57 B4
Evrecy F 57 A5
Évreux F 58 A2
Évron F 57 B5
Évry F 58 B3
Ewell GB 31 C3
Ewersbach D 50 C4
Excideuil F 67 C6
Exeter GB 29 C4
Exmes F 57 B6
Exminster GB 29 C4
Exmouth GB 29 C4
Eydehamn N 33 C5
Eye, *Peterborough* GB 30 B3
Eye, *Suffolk* GB 30 B5
Eyemouth GB 25 C5
Eyguians F 79 B4
Eyguières F 79 C4
Eygurande F 68 C2
Eylie F 77 D3
Eymet F 77 B3
Eymoutiers F 68 C1
Eynsham GB 31 C2
Eystrup D 43 C6
Ezaro E 86 B1
Ezcaray E 89 B4
Ezcároz E 76 D1
Ezine TR 16 S20
Ezmoriz P 87 D2

F

Fabara E 90 B3
Fábbrico I 81 B4
Fabero E 86 B4
Fábiánsebestyén H 75 B5
Fåborg DK 39 D3
Fabrègues F 78 C2
Fabriano I 82 C1
Fabrizia I 106 C3
Facha P 87 C2
Facinas E 99 C5
Fačkov SK 65 A4
Fadagosa P 92 B3
Fadd H 74 B3
Faédis I 72 B3
Faenza I 81 B5
Fafe P 87 C2
Fagagna I 72 B3
Făgăras RO 11 P19
Fågelfors S 40 B5
Fågelmara S 41 C5
Fågelsta S 37 C2
Fagerhult S 40 B5
Fagernes N 2 F11
Fagersanna S 35 C6
Fagersta S 36 A2
Fåglavik S 35 C5
Fagnano Castello I 106 B3
Fagnières F 59 B5
Faido CH 70 B3
Fains F 59 B6
Fairford GB 29 B6
Fairlie GB 24 C3
Fajsz H 74 B3
Fakenham GB 30 B4
Fakse DK 39 D5
Fakse Ladeplads DK 41 D2
Falaise F 57 B5
Falcade I 72 B1
Falcarragh IRL 18 A3
Falces E 89 B5
Fălciu RO 11 N21
Falconara I 109 B3
Falconara Marittima I 82 C2
Falcone I 109 A4
Faldingworth GB 27 B5
Falerum S 37 C3
Fălești MD 11 N20
Falkenberg, *Bayern* D 62 A3
Falkenberg, *Brandenburg* D 52 B3
Falkenberg S 40 C2
Falkensee D 45 C5
Falkenstein, *Bayern* D 62 A3
Falkenstein, *Sachsen* D 52 C2
Falkenthal D 45 C5
Falkirk GB 25 B4
Falkland GB 25 B4
Falköping S 35 C5
Fall D 72 A1
Falla S 37 C2
Fallingbostel D 43 C6
Falmouth GB 28 C2
Falset E 90 B3
Fălticeni RO 11 N20
Falun S 36 A2
Fana N 32 A2
Fanano I 81 B4
Fanjeaux F 77 C5
Fano I 82 C2
Fântânele RO 75 B6
Fara in Sabina I 102 A2
Fara Novarese I 70 C3
Faramontanos de Tábara E 88 C1
Farasdues E 90 A1
Fårbo S 40 B6
Fareham GB 31 D2
Färentuna S 36 B4
Färgelanda S 35 C3
Faringdon GB 31 C2
Faringe S 36 B5
Farini I 80 B3
Fariza E 87 C4
Färjestaden S 40 C6
Farkasfa H 73 B6
Farlete E 90 B2
Färlöv S 41 C4
Farmos H 75 A4
Farná SK 65 C4
Farnborough GB 31 C3
Farnese I 102 A1
Farnham GB 31 C3
Farnroda D 51 C6
Faro P 98 B3
Farra d'Alpago I 72 B2
Farranfore IRL 20 B2
Farsala GR 15 S18
Farsø DK 38 C2
Farsund N 32 C3
Farum DK 41 D2
Fårup DK 38 C2
Fasana I 104 B2
Fasano I 105 B4
Fassberg D 44 C2
Fastiv UA 11 L21
Fatesh RUS 7 K24
Fátima P 92 B2
Faucogney-et-la-Mer F 60 C2
Fauguerolles F 76 B3
Faulenrost D 45 B4
Faulquemont F 60 A2
Fauquembergues F 48 C3
Fauske N 2 C14
Fauville-en-Caux F 58 A1
Fauvillers B 60 A1
Favara I 108 B2
Faverges F 69 C6
Faverney F 60 C2
Faversham GB 31 C4
Favignana I 108 B1
Fawley GB 31 D2
Fay-aux-Loges F 58 C3
Fayence F 79 C5
Fayet F 78 C1
Fayl-Billot F 60 C1
Fayón E 90 B3
Fearn GB 23 D5
Fécamp F 58 A1
Feda N 32 C3
Feeny GB 19 B4
Fegen S 40 B3
Fegyvernek H 75 A5
Fehrbellin D 45 C4
Fehring A 73 B6
Feichten A 71 A5
Feiring N 34 A3
Feistritz im Rosental A 73 B4
Feketić YU 75 C4
Felanitx, *Mallorca* E 97
Feld am See A 72 B3
Feldbach A 73 B5
Feldberg D 45 B5
Feldkirch A 71 A4
Feldkirchen in Kärnten A 73 B4
Feldkirchen-Westerham D 62 C2
Felgueiras P 87 C2
Felitto I 104 B2
Félix E 101 C3
Felixstowe GB 31 C5
Felizzano I 80 B2
Felletin F 68 C2
Fellingsbro S 36 B2
Felnac RO 75 B6
Felnémet H 65 C6
Felpéc H 74 A2
Fels am Wagram A 64 B1
Felsberg D 51 B5
Felső-zsolca H 65 B6
Felsönyék H 74 B3
Felsöszentiván H 75 B4
Felsöszentmárton H 74 C2
Felsted DK 39 E2
Feltre I 72 B1
Femsjö S 40 C3
Fenagh IRL 19 B4
Fene E 86 A2
Fenestrelle I 79 A6
Fénétrange F 60 B3
Feneu F 57 C5
Fengersfors S 35 C4
Fenit IRL 20 B2
Fensmark DK 39 D4
Fenwick GB 24 C3
Feolin Ferry GB 24 C1
Ferbane IRL 21 A4
Ferdinandovac HR 74 B2
Ferdinandshof D 45 B5
Fère-Champenoise F 59 B4
Fère-en-Tardenois F 59 A4
Ferentillo I 102 A2
Ferentino I 102 B3
Feria E 93 C4
Feričanci HR 74 C2
Ferla I 109 B3
Ferlach A 73 B4
Ferleiten A 72 A2
Fermil P 87 C3
Fermo I 82 C2
Fermoselle E 87 C4
Fermoy IRL 20 B3
Fernán Nuñéz E 100 B1
Fernán Peréz E 101 C3
Fernancabellero E 94 C3
Fernão Ferro P 92 C1
Fernay-Voltaire F 69 B6
Ferndown GB 29 C6
Ferness GB 23 D5
Fernhurst GB 31 C3
Ferns IRL 21 B5
Ferpècle CH 70 B2
Ferrals-les-Corbières F 78 C1
Ferrandina I 105 B3
Ferrara I 81 B5
Ferrara di Monte Baldo I 71 C5
Ferreira E 86 A3
Ferreira do Alentejo P 98 A2
Ferreira do Zêzere P 92 B2
Ferreras de Abajo E 87 C4
Ferreras de Arriba E 87 C4
Ferreries, *Menorca* E 97
Ferreruela E 90 B1
Ferreruela de Tabara E 87 C4
Ferret CH 70 C2
Ferrette F 70 A2
Ferriere I 80 B3
Ferrière-la-Grande F 49 C4
Ferrières, *Loiret* F 58 B3
Ferrières, *Oise* F 58 A3
Ferrières-sur-Sichon F 68 B3
Ferrol E 86 A2
Ferryhill GB 27 A4
Fertörakos H 64 C2
Fertöszentmiklós H 64 C2
Ferwerd NL 42 B2
Festieux F 59 A4
Feteşti RO 11 P20
Fethard, *Tipperary* IRL 21 B4
Fethard, *Wexford* IRL 21 B5
Fethiye TR 16 T21
Fetsund N 34 B3
Fettercairn GB 25 B5
Feucht D 62 A2
Feuchtwangen D 61 A6
Feudingen D 50 C4
Feuges F 59 B5
Feuquières F 58 A2
Feurs F 69 C4
Fevik N 33 C5
Ffestiniog GB 26 C2
Fiamignano I 102 A3
Fiano I 70 C2
Ficarazzi I 108 A2
Ficarolo I 81 B5
Fichtelberg D 52 C1
Ficulle I 82 D1
Fidenza I 81 B4
Fidjeland N 32 C3
Fieberbrunn A 72 A2
Fier AL 15 R16
Fiera di Primiero I 72 B1
Fiesch CH 70 B3
Fiésole I 81 C5
Fiesso Umbertiano I 81 B5
Figari F 110 B2
Figeac F 77 B5
Figeholm S 40 B6
Figgjo N 32 C2
Figline Valdarno I 81 C5
Figols E 90 A3
Figueira da Foz P 92 A2
Figueira de Castelo Rodrigo P 87 D4
Figueira dos Caveleiros P 98 A2
Figueiredo P 92 B3
Figueiredo de Alva P 87 D3
Figueiró dos Vinhos P 92 B2
Figueres E 91 A5
Figueroles E 96 A2
Figueruela de Arriba E 87 C4
Filadélfia I 106 C3
Fil'akovo SK 65 B5
Filderstadt D 61 B5
Filey GB 27 A5
Filiaşi RO 11 P18
Filiatrá GR 15 T17
Filipstad S 34 B6
Filisur CH 71 B4
Fillan N 2 E11
Filottrano I 82 C2
Filskov DK 39 D2
Filton GB 29 B5
Filtvet N 34 B2
Filzmoos A 72 A3
Finale Emilia I 81 B5
Finale Ligure I 80 B2
Fiñana E 101 B3
Fincham GB 24 C3
Finchingfield GB 31 C4
Findhorn GB 23 D5
Findochty GB 23 D6
Finike TR 16 T22
Finkenberg A 72 A1
Finnea IRL 19 C4
Finnerödja S 37 C1
Finnsnes N 3 B16
Finócchio I 102 B2
Finsjö S 40 B6
Finsland N 33 C4
Finspång S 37 C2
Finsterwalde D 53 B3
Finsterwolde NL 43 B4
Finstown GB 23 B5
Fintona GB 19 B4
Fionnphort GB 24 B1
Fiorenzuola d'Arda I 81 B3
Firenze I 81 C5
Firenzuola I 81 B5
Firmi F 77 B5
Firminy F 69 C4
Firmo I 106 B3
Fischamend Markt A 64 B2
Fischbach A 73 A5
Fischbach D 60 A3
Fischbeck D 44 C4
Fischen D 71 A5
Fishbourne GB 31 D2
Fishguard GB 28 B3
Fiskebäckskil S 35 C3
Fismes F 59 A4
Fisterra E 86 B1
Fitero E 89 B5
Fitjar N 32 B2
Fiuggi I 102 B3
Fiumata I 102 A3
Fiumefreddo Brúzio I 106 B3
Fiumefreddo di Sicilia I 109 B4
Fiumicino I 102 B2
Fivemiletown GB 19 B4
Fivizzano I 81 B4
Fjæra N 32 B3
Fjälkinge S 41 C4
Fjällbacka S 35 C3
Fjärdhundra S 36 B3
Fjellerup DK 38 C3
Fjerritslev DK 38 B2
Fjugesta S 37 C1
Flåbygd N 33 B5
Flaça E 91 A5
Flace F 69 B4
Fladungen D 51 C6
Flåm N 2 F10
Flamatt CH 70 B2
Flamborough GB 27 A5
Flammersfeld D 50 C3
Flassans-sur-Issole F 79 C5
Flatdal N 33 B5
Flateby N 34 B3
Flateland N 33 B4
Flatråker N 32 B2
Flattach A 72 B3
Flatvarp S 37 D3
Flavigny-sur-Moselle F 60 B2
Flavy-le-Martel F 59 A4
Flawil CH 71 A4
Flayosc F 79 C5
Flechtingen D 44 C3
Fleckeby D 43 A6
Fleet GB 31 C3
Fleetmark D 44 C3
Fleetwood GB 26 B2
Flehingen D 61 A4
Flekkefjord N 32 C3
Flen S 37 B3
Flensburg D 39 E2
Fleringe S 37 D5
Flerohopp S 40 C5
Flers F 57 B5
Flesberg N 33 B6
Fleurance F 77 C3
Fleuré F 67 B5
Fleurier CH 69 B6
Fleurus B 49 C5
Fleury, *Hérault* F 78 C2
Fleury, *Yonne* F 59 C4
Fleury-les-Aubrais F 58 C2
Fleury-sur-Andelle F 58 A2
Fleury-sur-Orne F 57 A5
Flieden D 51 C5
Flimby GB 26 A2
Flims CH 71 B4
Flines-lèz-Raches F 49 C4
Flint GB 26 B2
Flirey F 60 B1
Flirsch A 71 A5
Flisby S 40 B4
Fliseryd S 40 B6
Flix E 90 B3
Flixecourt F 48 C3
Flize F 59 A5
Flobecq B 49 C4
Floby S 35 C5
Floda S 35 D4
Flodden GB 25 C5
Flogny-la-Chapelle F 59 C4
Flöha D 52 C3
Flonheim D 61 A4
Florac F 78 B2
Floreffe B 49 C5
Florennes B 49 C5
Florensac F 78 C2
Florentin F 77 C5
Florenville B 59 A6
Flores de Avila E 94 B1
Floresta I 109 B3
Florești MD 11 N21
Florídia I 109 B4
Flórina GR 15 R17
Florø N 2 F9
Flörsheim D 51 C4
Floss D 62 A3
Flühli CH 70 B3
Flumet F 69 C6
Fluminimaggiore I 110 D1
Flums CH 71 A4
Flygsfors S 40 C5
Foča BIH 84 C3
Foça TR 16 S20
Fochabers GB 23 D5
Focşani RO 11 P20
Foel GB 26 C2
Foeni RO 75 C5
Fogdö S 36 B3
Fóggia I 104 A2
Foglianise I 103 B4
Fohnsdorf A 73 A4
Foiano della Chiana I 81 C5
Foix F 77 D4
Fojnica BIH 84 C2
Fojnica BIH 84 C3
Fokino RUS 7 K24
Földeák H 75 B5
Földes H 75 A6
Folgaria I 71 C6
Folgosinho P 92 A3
Folgoso de la Ribera E 86 B4
Folgoso do Courel E 86 B3
Foligno I 82 D1
Folkärna S 36 A3
Folkestone GB 31 C5
Follafoss N 2 E12
Folldal N 2 E12
Follina I 72 C2
Follónica I 81 D4
Foncebadón E 86 B4
Foncine-le-Bas F 69 B6
Fondevila E 87 C2
Fondi I 103 B3
Fondo I 71 B6
Fonelas E 100 B2
Fonfría, *Teruel* E 90 C1
Fonfría, *Zamora* E 87 C4
Fonni I 110 C2
Font-Romeu F 91 A5
Fontaine de Vaucluse F 79 C4
Fontaine-Française F 69 A5
Fontaine-le-Dun F 58 A1
Fontainebleau F 58 B3
Fontan F 80 B1
Fontanarejo E 94 C2
Fontane I 80 B1
Fontanélice I 81 B5
Fontanières F 68 B2
Fontanosas E 100 A1
Fonteblanda I 102 A1
Fontenay-le-Comte F 66 B4
Fontenay-Trésigny F 59 B3
Fontevrault-l'Abbaye F 67 A5
Fontiveros E 94 B2
Fontoy F 60 A1
Fontpédrouse F 91 A5
Fontstown IRL 21 A5
Fonyód H 74 B2
Fonz E 90 A3
Fonzaso I 72 B1
Föppolo I 71 B4
Forbach D 61 B4
Forbach F 60 A2
Forcall E 90 C2
Forcalquier F 79 C4
Forcarei E 86 B2
Forchheim D 62 A2
Forchtenau A 64 C2
Forchtenberg D 61 A5
Ford GB 24 B2
Førde N 32 B2
Førde, *Sogn og Fjordane* N 2 F9
Förderstedt D 52 B1
Førdesfjorden N 32 B2
Fordham GB 30 B4
Fordingbridge GB 29 C6
Fordon PL 47 B4
Fordongiánus I 110 D1
Forenza I 104 B2
Foresta di Búrgos I 110 C1
Forfar GB 25 B5
Forges-les-Eaux F 58 A2
Foria I 104 B2
Forio I 103 C3
Forjães P 87 C2
Forlì I 81 B6
Forlimpopoli I 82 B1
Formazza I 70 B3
Formby GB 26 B2
Formerie F 58 A2
Fórmia I 103 B3
Formígine I 81 B4
Formigliana I 70 C3
Formiguères F 91 A5
Fornalutx, *Mallorca* E 97
Fornelli I 110 C1
Fornells, *Menorca* E 97
Fornelos de Montes E 87 B2
Fornes E 100 C2
Forni Avoltri I 72 B2
Forni di Sopra I 72 B2
Forni di Sotto I 72 B2
Forno, *Piemonte* I 70 C3
Forno, *Piemonte* I 79 A6
Forno Alpi-Graie I 70 C2
Forno di Zoldo I 72 B2
Fornos de Algodres P 92 A3
Fornovo di Taro I 81 B4
Forráskút H 75 B4
Forres GB 23 D5
Forriolo E 87 B3
Fors S 36 A3
Forsand N 32 C3
Forsbacka S 36 A3
Forserum S 40 B4
Forshaga S 34 B5
Forsheda S 40 B3
Forsinain GB 23 C5
Förslöv S 41 C2
Forsmark S 36 A5
Forssa FIN 3 F18
Forssjöbruk S 37 C3
Forst D 53 B4
Forsvik S 37 C1
Fort Augustus GB 22 D4
Fort-Mahon-Plage F 48 C2
Fort William GB 24 B2
Fortanete E 90 C2
Forte dei Marmi I 81 C4
Fortezza I 72 B1
Forth GB 25 C4
Fortrie GB 23 D6
Fortrose GB 23 D4
Fortuna E 101 A4
Fortuneswell GB 29 C5
Fos F 77 D3
Fos-sur-Mer F 78 C3
Fosdinovo I 81 B4
Fosnavåg N 2 E9
Fossacésia I 103 A4
Fossano I 80 B1
Fossato di Vico I 82 C1
Fosse-la-Ville B 49 C5
Fossombrone I 82 C1
Fot H 65 C5
Fouchères F 59 B5
Fouesnant F 56 C1
Foug F 60 B1
Fougères F 57 B4
Fougerolles F 60 C2
Foulain F 59 B6
Fountainhall GB 25 C5
Fouras F 66 C3
Fourchambault F 68 A3
Fourmies F 49 C5
Fournels F 78 B2
Fournols F 68 C3
Fourques F 91 A5
Fourquevaux F 77 C4
Fours F 68 B3
Fowey GB 28 C3
Foxdale GB 26 A1
Foxford IRL 18 C2
Foyers GB 23 D4
Foynes IRL 20 B2
Foz E 86 A3
Foz do Arelho P 92 B1
Foz do Giraldo P 92 B3
Foza I 72 C1
Frabosa Soprana I 80 B1
Frades de la Sierra E 94 B1
Fraga E 90 B3
Fragagnano I 105 B4
Frailes E 100 B2
Fraire B 49 C5
Fraize F 60 B2
Framlingham GB 30 B5
Frammersbach D 51 C5
Framnes N 34 B2
França P 87 C4
Francaltroff F 60 B2
Francavilla al Mare I 103 A4
Francavilla di Sicilia I 109 B4
Francavilla Fontana I 105 B4

Francavilla in Sinni I 104 B3
Francescas F 77 B3
Franco P 87 C3
Francofonte I 109 B3
Francos E 89 C3
Frändefors S 35 C4
Franeker NL 42 B2
Frangy F 69 B5
Frankenau D 51 B4
Frankenberg, *Hessen* D 51 B4
Frankenberg, *Sachsen* D 52 C3
Frankenburg A 63 B4
Frankenfels A 63 C6
Frankenmarkt A 63 C4
Frankenthal D 61 A4
Frankfurt, *Brandenburg* D 45 C6
Frankfurt, *Hessen* D 51 C4
Frankowo PL 47 A6
Františkovy Lázně CZ 52 C2
Franzburg D 45 A4
Frascati I 102 B2
Frasdorf D 62 C3
Fraserburgh GB 23 D6
Frasne F 69 B6
Frasnes-lez-Anvaing B 49 C4
Frasseto F 110 B2
Frastanz A 71 A4
Fratel P 92 B3
Fratta Todina I 82 D1
Frauenau D 63 B4
Frauenfeld CH 70 A3
Frauenkirchen A 64 C2
Frauenstein D 52 C3
Frauental A 73 B5
Frayssinet F 77 B4
Frayssinet-le-Gélat F 77 B4
Frechas P 87 C3
Frechen D 50 C2
Frechilla E 88 B2
Freckenhorst D 50 B3
Fredeburg D 50 B4
Fredelsloh D 51 B5
Fredensborg DK 41 D2
Fredericia DK 39 D2
Frederiks DK 39 C2
Frederikshavn DK 38 B3
Frederikssund DK 39 D5
Frederiksværk DK 39 D5
Fredriksberg S 36 A1
Fredriksdal S 40 B4
Fredrikstad N 34 B2
Fregenal de la Sierra E 99 A4
Fregene I 102 B2
Freiberg D 52 C3
Freiburg, *Baden-Württemberg* D 60 C3
Freiburg, *Niedersachsen* D 43 B6
Freienhagen D 51 B5
Freienhufen D 53 B3
Freihung D 62 A2
Freilassing D 62 C3
Freisen D 60 A3
Freising D 62 B2
Freistadt A 63 B5
Freital D 52 B3
Freixedas P 93 A3
Freixo de Espada à Cinta P 87 C4
Fréjus F 79 C5
Fremdingen D 61 B6
Frenštát pod Radhoštěm CZ 64 A4
Freren D 43 C4
Freshford IRL 21 B4
Freshwater GB 31 D2
Fresnay-sur-Sarthe F 57 B6
Fresne-St. Mamès F 69 A5
Fresneda de la Sierra E 95 B4
Fresneda de la Sierra Tiron E 89 B3
Fresnedillas E 94 B2
Fresnes-en-Woevre F 60 A1
Fresno Alhandiga E 94 B1
Fresno de la Ribera E 88 C1
Fresno de la Vega E 88 B1
Fresno de Sayago E 87 C5
Fresnoy-Folny F 58 A2
Fresnoy-le-Grand F 59 A4
Fressenville F 48 C2
Fréteval F 58 C2
Fretigney F 69 A5
Freudenberg, *Baden-Württemberg* D 61 A5
Freudenberg, *Nordrhein-Westfalen* D 50 C3
Freudenstadt D 61 B4
Freux B 49 D6
Frévent F 48 C3
Freyburg D 52 B1
Freyenstein D 44 B4
Freyming-Merlebach F 60 A2
Freystadt D 62 A2
Freyung D 63 B4
Frias de Albarracin E 95 B5
Fribourg CH 70 B2
Frick CH 70 A3
Fridafors S 41 C4
Fridaythorpe GB 27 A5
Friedberg A 73 A6
Friedberg, *Bayern* D 62 B1
Friedberg, *Hessen* D 51 C4
Friedeburg D 43 B4
Friedewald D 51 C5
Friedland, *Brandenburg* D 53 A4
Friedland, *Mecklenburg-Vorpommern* D 45 B5
Friedland, *Niedersachsen* D 51 B5
Friedrichroda D 51 C6
Friedrichsdorf D 51 C4
Friedrichshafen D 61 C5
Friedrichskoog D 43 A5
Friedrichstadt D 43 A6
Friedrichswalde D 45 B5
Friesach A 73 B4
Friesack D 45 C4
Friesenheim D 60 B3
Friesoythe D 43 B4
Frigiliana E 100 C2
Frillesås S 40 B2
Frinnaryd S 37 D1
Frinton-on-Sea GB 31 C5
Friockheim GB 25 B5
Friol E 86 A3
Fristad S 35 D4
Fritsla S 40 B2
Fritzlar D 51 B5
Frizington GB 26 A2
Frödinge S 40 B6
Froges F 69 C5
Frohburg D 52 B2
Frohnhausen D 50 C4
Frohnleiten A 73 A5
Froissy F 58 A3
Frombork PL 47 A5
Frome GB 29 B5
Frómista E 88 B2
Fröndenberg D 50 B3
Fronsac F 76 B2
Front I 70 C2
Fronteira P 92 B3
Frontenay-Rohan-Rohan F 67 B4
Frontenhausen D 62 B3
Frontignan F 78 C2
Fronton F 77 C4
Fröseke S 40 C5
Frosinone I 103 B3
Frosolone I 103 B4
Frøstrup DK 38 B1
Frosunda S 36 B5
Frouard F 60 B2
Frövi S 36 B2
Fruges F 48 C3
Frutigen CH 70 B2
Frýdek-Místek CZ 65 A4
Frýdlant CZ 53 C5
Frydlant nad Ostravici CZ 65 A4
Frygnowo PL 47 B6
Fryšták CZ 64 A3
Fucécchio I 81 C4
Fuencaliente, *Ciudad Real* E 100 A1
Fuencaliente, *Ciudad Real* E 94 C3
Fuencemillán E 95 B3
Fuendejalón E 89 C5
Fuengirola E 100 C1
Fuenlabrada E 94 B3
Fuenlabrada de los Montes E 94 C2
Fuensalida E 94 B2
Fuensanta E 101 B4
Fuensanta de Martos E 100 B2
Fuente al Olmo de Iscar E 94 A2
Fuente-Alamo E 96 C1
Fuente-Álamo de Murcia E 101 B4
Fuente Dé E 88 A2
Fuente de Cantos E 99 A4
Fuente de Santa Cruz E 94 A2
Fuente del Arco E 99 A5
Fuente del Conde E 100 B1
Fuente del Maestre E 93 C4
Fuente el Fresno E 94 C3
Fuente el Saz de Jarama E 95 B3
Fuente el Sol E 94 A2
Fuente Obejuna E 99 A5
Fuente Palmera E 99 B5
Fuente-Tójar E 100 B1
Fuente Vaqueros E 100 B2
Fuentealbilla E 96 B1
Fuentecén E 88 C3
Fuenteguinaldo E 93 A4
Fuentelapeña E 94 A1
Fuentelcésped E 89 C3
Fuentelespino de Haro E 95 C4
Fuentelespino de Moya E 96 B1
Fuentenovilla E 95 B3
Fuentepelayo E 94 A2
Fuentepinilla E 89 C4
Fuenterroble de Salvatierra E 93 A5
Fuenterrobles E 96 B1
Fuentes E 95 C4
Fuentes de Andalucía E 99 B5
Fuentes de Ebro E 90 B2
Fuentes de Jiloca E 95 A5
Fuentes de la Alcarria E 95 B4
Fuentes de León E 99 A4
Fuentes de Nava E 88 B2
Fuentes de Oñoro E 93 A4
Fuentes de Ropel E 88 B1
Fuentesauco, *Segovia* E 88 C2
Fuentesaúco, *Zamora* E 94 A1
Fuentespalda E 90 C3
Fuentespina E 88 C3
Fuentidueña E 88 C3
Fuentidueña de Tajo E 95 B3
Fuerte del Rey E 100 B2
Fügen A 72 A1
Fuglebjerg DK 39 D4
Fuglevik N 34 B2
Fuhrberg D 44 C1
Fulda D 51 C5
Fulgatore I 108 B1
Fully CH 70 B2
Fulnek CZ 64 A3
Fülöpszállás H 75 B4
Fulpmes A 71 A6
Fumay F 49 D5
Fumel F 77 B3
Funäsdalen S 2 E13
Fundão P 92 A3
Funzie GB 22 A8
Furadouro P 87 D2
Fürstenau, *Niedersachsen* D 43 C4
Fürstenau, *Nordrhein-Westfalen* D 51 B5
Fürstenberg D 45 B5
Fürstenfeld A 73 A6
Fürstenfeldbruck D 62 B2
Fürstenstein D 63 B4
Fürstenwalde D 45 C6
Fürstenwerder D 45 B5
Fürstenzell D 63 B4
Fürth, *Bayern* D 62 A1
Fürth, *Hessen* D 61 A4
Furth im Wald D 62 A3
Furtwangen D 61 B4
Furuby S 40 C5
Furulund S 41 D3
Furusjö S 35 D5
Fusa N 32 A2
Fuscaldo I 106 B3
Fusch an der Grossglocknerstrasse A 72 A2
Fusina I 72 C2
Fusio CH 70 B3
Füssen D 62 C1
Fustiñana E 89 B5
Futog YU 75 C4
Füzesabony H 65 C6
Füzesgyarmat H 75 A6
Fužine HR 73 C4
Fyllinge S 40 C2
Fynshav DK 39 E2
Fyresdal N 33 B5

G

Gaaldorf A 73 A4
Gabaldón E 95 C5
Gabarret F 76 C2
Gabčíkovo SK 64 C3
Gąbin PL 47 C5
Gabriac F 78 B1
Gabrovo BG 16 Q19
Gaby I 70 C2
Gacé F 58 B1
Gacko BIH 84 C3
Gäddede S 2 D14
Gadebusch D 44 B3
Gadmen CH 70 B3
Gádor E 101 C3
Gádoros H 75 B5
Gael F 57 B3
Găeşti RO 11 P19
Gaeta I 103 B3
Gafanhoeira P 92 C2
Gaflenz A 63 C5
Gagarin RUS 7 J24
Gaggenau D 61 B4
Gagliano Castelferrato I 109 B3
Gagliano del Capo I 107 B5
Gagnet S 36 A2
Gagy-vendégi H 65 B6
Gaibanella I 81 B5
Gaildorf D 61 A5
Gaillac F 77 C4
Gaillefontaine F 58 A2
Gaillon F 58 A2
Gainsborough GB 27 B5
Gairloch GB 22 D3
Gairlochy GB 24 B3
Gáiro I 110 D2
Gaj HR 74 C2
Gaj YU 85 B6
Gajanejos E 95 B4
Gajary SK 64 B2
Gajdobra YU 75 C4
Galan F 77 C3
Galanta SK 64 B3
Galapagar E 94 B2
Galápagos E 95 B4
Galaroza E 99 B4
Galashiels GB 25 C5
Galatás GR 15 T18
Galați RO 11 P21
Galatina I 105 B5
Galatone I 105 B5
Galdakao E 89 A4
Galeata I 81 C5
Galende E 87 B4
Galera E 101 B3
Galéria F 110 A1
Galgamácsa H 65 C5
Galgate GB 26 B3
Galgon F 76 B2
Galices P 92 A3
Galinduste E 94 B1
Galisteo E 93 B4
Galków PL 55 B4
Gallarate I 70 C3
Gallardon F 58 B2
Gallegos de Argañán E 93 A4
Gallegos del Solmirón E 94 B1
Galleguillos de Campos E 88 B1
Galleno I 81 C4
Galliate I 70 C3
Gallicano I 81 B4
Gállio I 71 C6
Gallipoli I 105 B4
Gällivare S 3 C17
Gallizien A 73 B4
Gallneukirchen A 63 B5
Gallocanta E 95 B5
Gällstad S 40 B3
Gallur E 89 C5
Galmisdale GB 24 B1
Galmpton GB 29 C4
Galston GB 24 C3
Galta N 32 B2
Galtelli I 110 C2
Galten DK 39 C2
Galtür A 71 B5
Galve de Sorbe E 95 A3
Galveias P 92 B2
Gálvez E 94 C2
Galway IRL 20 A2
Gamaches F 48 D2
Gámbara I 71 C5
Gambárie I 106 C2
Gambassi Terme I 81 C4
Gambatesa I 104 A1
Gambolò I 70 C3
Gaming A 63 C6
Gamla Uppsala S 36 B4
Gamleby S 37 D3
Gamlingay GB 30 B3
Gammelstad S 3 D18
Gammertingen D 61 B5
Gams CH 71 A4
Gamvik N 2 A18
Gan F 76 C2
Gáname E 87 C4
Ganda di Martello I 71 B5
Gandarela P 87 C2
Ganddal N 32 C2
Ganderkesee D 43 B5
Gandesa E 90 B3
Gandía E 96 C2
Gandino I 71 C4
Gandrup DK 38 B3
Ganges F 78 C2
Gånghester S 40 B3
Gangi I 109 B3
Gangkofen D 62 B3
Gannat F 68 B3
Gannay-sur-Loire F 68 B3
Gänserdorf A 64 B2
Ganzlin D 44 B4
Gap F 79 B5
Gara H 75 B4
Garaballa E 96 B1
Garaguso I 104 B3
Garbayuela E 94 C1
Garbhallt GB 24 B2
Garbsen D 43 C6
Garching D 62 B3
Garciaz E 93 B5
Garcihernández E 94 B1
Garcillán E 94 B2
Garcinarro E 95 B4
Garda I 71 C5
Gardanne F 79 C4
Gardeja PL 47 B4
Gardelegen D 44 C3
Gardermoen N 34 A3
Garding D 43 A5
Gardone Riviera I 71 C5
Gardone Val Trómpia I 71 C5
Gárdony H 74 A3
Gardouch F 77 C4
Gards Köpinge S 41 D4
Gårdsjö S 37 C1
Gårdskär S 36 A4
Garein F 76 B2
Garelochhead GB 24 B3
Garéoult F 79 C5
Garešnica HR 74 C1
Garéssio I 80 B2
Garforth GB 27 B4
Gargaliánoi GR 15 T17
Gargaligas E 93 B5
Gargallo E 90 C2
Garganta la Olla E 93 A5
Gargantiel E 100 A1
Gargellen A 71 B4
Gargilesse-Dampierre F 67 B6
Gargnano I 71 C5
Gárgoles de Abajo E 95 B4
Gargrave GB 26 B3
Garitz D 52 B2
Garlasco I 70 C3
Garlieston GB 24 D3
Garlin F 76 C2
Garlitos E 94 D1
Garmisch-Partenkirchen D 71 A6
Garnat-sur-Engièvre F 68 B3
Garpenberg S 36 A3
Garphyttan S 36 B1
Garray E 89 C4
Garrel D 43 C5
Garriguella E 91 A6
Garrison GB 18 B3
Garrovillas E 93 B4
Garrucha E 101 B4
Gars-a-Kamp A 63 B6
Garsdale Head GB 26 A3
Gärsnäs S 41 D4
Garstang GB 26 B3
Gartow D 44 B3
Gartz D 45 B6
Garvagh GB 19 B5
Garvão P 98 B2
Garve GB 22 D4
Garwolin PL 55 B6
Garz D 45 A5
Garzyn PL 54 B1
Gąsawa PL 46 C3
Gåsborn S 34 B6
Gaschurn A 71 B5
Gascueña E 95 B4
Gasny F 58 A2
Gąsocin PL 47 C6
Gastes F 76 B1
Gata E 93 A4
Gata HR 83 C5
Gata de Gorgos E 96 C3
Gatchina RUS 7 G22
Gatehouse of Fleet GB 24 D3
Gátér H 75 B4
Gateshead GB 25 D6
Gátova E 96 B2
Gattendorf A 64 B2
Gatteo a Mare I 82 B1
Gattinara I 70 C3
Gattorna I 80 B3
Gaucín E 99 C5
Gauting D 62 B2
Gava E 91 B5
Gavardo I 71 C5
Gavarnie F 90 A2
Gavi I 80 B2
Gavião P 92 B3
Gavirate I 70 C3
Gävle S 36 A4
Gavoi I 110 C2
Gavorrano I 81 D4
Gavray F 57 B4
Gaweinstal A 64 B2
Gawroniec PL 46 B2
Gaydon GB 30 B2
Gayton GB 30 B4
Gazoldo degli Ippoliti I 71 C5
Gazzuolo I 81 A4
Gbelce SK 65 C4
Gdańsk PL 47 A4
Gdinj HR 84 C1
Gdov RUS 7 G20
Gdów PL 65 A6
Gdynia PL 47 A4
Gea de Albarracin E 95 B5
Geary GB 22 D2
Géaudot F 59 B5
Geaune F 76 C2
Gebesee D 51 B6
Gebze TR 16 R21
Géderlak H 75 B3
Gedern D 51 C5
Gedinne B 49 D5
Gediz TR 16 S21
Gèdre F 76 D3
Gedser DK 44 A3
Gedsted DK 38 C2
Geel B 49 B5
Geesthacht D 44 B2
Geetbets B 49 C6
Gefell D 52 C1
Gehrden D 51 A5
Gehren D 51 C7
Geilenkirchen D 50 C2
Geilo N 2 F11
Geinsheim D 61 A4
Geisa D 51 C5
Geiselhöring D 62 B3
Geiselwind D 61 A6
Geisenfeld D 62 B2
Geisenhausen D 62 B3
Geisenheim D 50 D4
Geising D 53 C3
Geisingen D 61 C4
Geislingen D 61 B5
Geistthal A 73 A5
Geithain D 52 B2
Geithus N 33 B6
Gela I 109 B3
Geldermalsen NL 49 B6
Geldern D 50 B2
Geldrop NL 49 B6
Geleen NL 50 C1
Gelendost TR 16 S22
Gelibolu TR 16 R20
Gelida E 91 B4
Gelnhausen D 51 C5
Gelnica SK 65 B6
Gelsa E 90 B2
Gelse H 74 B1
Gelsenkirchen D 50 B3
Gelsted DK 39 D2
Geltendorf D 62 B2
Gelterkinden CH 70 A2
Gelting D 39 E2
Gelu RO 75 B6
Gelves E 99 B4
Gembloux B 49 C5
Gemeaux F 69 A5
Gémenos F 79 C4
Gemerská Poloma SK 65 B6
Gemerská Ves SK 65 B6
Gemert NL 50 B1
Gemla S 40 C4
Gemlik TR 16 R21
Gemmenich B 50 C1
Gemona del Friuli I 72 B3
Gémozac F 67 C4
Gemund D 50 C2
Gemünden, *Bayern* D 51 C5
Gemünden, *Hessen* D 51 C4
Genappe B 49 C5
Génave E 101 A3
Genazzano I 102 B2
Gençay F 67 B5
Gencsapáti H 74 A1
Gendringen NL 50 B2
Genelard F 69 B4
Genemuiden NL 42 C3
Generalski Stol HR 73 C5
Genevad S 40 C3
Genève CH 69 B6
Genevriéres F 60 C1
Gengenbach D 61 B4
Genillé F 67 A6
Genk B 49 C6
Genlis F 69 A5
Gennep NL 50 B1
Genner DK 39 D2
Gennes F 67 A4
Genola I 80 B1
Génova I 80 B2
Genowefa PL 54 A3
Gensingen D 60 A3
Gent B 49 B4
Genthin D 44 C4
Gentioux F 68 C1
Genzano di Lucánia I 104 B3
Genzano di Roma I 102 B2
Georgenthal D 51 C6
Georgsmarienhütte D 50 A4
Gera D 52 C2
Geraards-bergen B 49 C4
Gerace I 106 C3
Geraci Siculo I 109 B3
Gérardmer F 60 B2
Geras A 63 B6
Gerbéviller F 60 B2
Gerbini I 109 B3
Gerbstedt D 52 B1
Gerena E 99 B4
Geretsried D 62 C2
Gérgal E 101 B3
Gergy F 69 B4
Gerindote E 94 C2
Gerjen H 74 B3
Gerlos A 72 A2
Germay F 59 B6
Germering D 62 B2
Germersheim D 61 A4
Gernika-Lumo E 89 A4
Gernrode D 52 B1
Gernsbach D 61 B4
Gernsheim D 61 A4
Geroda D 51 C5
Gerola Alta I 71 B4
Geroldsgrun D 52 C1
Gerolstein D 50 C2
Gerolzhofen D 61 A6
Gerovo HR 73 C4
Gerrards Cross GB 31 C3
Gerri de la Sal E 91 A4
Gersfeld D 51 C5
Gerstetten D 61 B6
Gersthofen D 62 B1
Gerstungen D 51 C6
Gerswalde D 45 B5
Gerzat F 68 C3
Gerzen D 62 B3
Gescher D 50 B3
Geseke D 51 B4
Geslau D 61 A6
Gespunsart F 59 A5
Gesté F 66 A3
Gestorf D 51 A5
Gesualda I 104 B2
Gesztely H 65 B6
Getafe E 94 B3
Getinge S 40 C2
Getxo E 89 A4
Geversdorf D 43 B6
Gevgelija MK 15 R18
Gevora del Caudillo E 93 C4
Gevrey-Chambertin F 69 A4
Gex F 69 B6
Gey D 50 C2
Geyve TR 16 R22
Gföhl A 63 B6
Ghedi I 71 C5
Gheorgheni RO 11 N19
Ghigo I 79 B6
Ghilarza I 110 C1
Ghisonaccia F 110 A2
Ghisoni F 110 A2
Giardinetto Vécchio I 104 A2
Giardini Naxos I 109 B4
Giarratana I 109 B3
Giarre I 109 B4
Giat F 68 C2
Giaveno I 80 A1
Giazza I 71 C6
Giba I 110 D1
Gibellina Nuova I 108 B1
Gibraleón E 99 B4
Gibraltar GBZ 99 C5
Gic H 74 A2
Gidle PL 55 C4
Giebelstadt D 61 A5
Gieboldehausen D 51 B6
Gielniów PL 55 B5
Gielow D 45 B4
Gien F 58 C3
Giengen D 61 B6
Giens F 79 C5
Giera RO 75 C5
Gieselwerder D 51 B5
Giessen D 51 C4
Gieten NL 42 B3
Giethoorn NL 42 C3
Giffaumont-Champaubert F 59 B5
Gifford GB 25 C5
Gifhorn D 44 C2
Gige H 74 B2
Giglio Porto I 102 A0
Gignac F 78 C2
Gijón E 88 A1
Gilena E 100 B1
Gilford GB 19 B5
Gillberga S 34 B4
Gilleleje DK 41 C2
Gilley F 69 A6
Gilley-sur-Loire F 68 B3
Gillingham, *Dorset* GB 29 B5
Gillingham, *Medway* GB 31 C4
Gilocourt F 59 A3
Gilserberg D 51 C5
Gilsland GB 25 D5
Gilze NL 49 B5
Gimo S 36 A5
Gimont F 77 C3
Ginasservis F 79 C4
Gingelom B 49 C6
Gingst D 45 A5
Ginosa I 105 B3
Ginzling A 72 A1
Giões P 98 B3
Gióia dei Marsi I 103 B3
Gióia del Colle I 105 B3
Gióia Sannitica I 103 B4
Gióia Táuro I 106 C2
Gioiosa Iónica I 106 C3
Gioiosa Marea I 109 A3
Giosla GB 22 C2
Giovinazzo I 105 A3
Girifalco I 106 C3
Giromagny F 60 C2
Girona E 91 B5
Gironcourt-sur-Vraine F 60 B1
Gironella E 91 A4
Gironville-sous-les-Côtes F 60 B1
Girvan GB 24 C3
Gislaved S 40 B3
Gislev DK 39 D3
Gisors F 58 A2
Gissi I 103 A4
Gistad S 37 C2
Gistel B 48 B3
Gistrup DK 38 C3
Giswil CH 70 B3
Giugliano in Campania I 103 C4
Giulianova I 82 D2
Giulvăz RO 75 C5
Giurgiu RO 16 Q19
Give DK 39 D2
Givet F 49 C5
Givors F 69 C4
Givry B 49 C5
Givry F 69 B4
Givry-en-Argonne F 59 B5
Givskud DK 39 D2
Gižalki PL 54 A2
Gizeux F 67 A5
Giżycko PL 6 J17
Gizzeria I 106 C3
Gizzeria Lido I 106 C3
Gjedved DK 39 D2
Gjerlev DK 38 C3
Gjermundshamn N 32 A2
Gjerrild DK 38 C3
Gjerstad N 33 C6
Gjirokastër AL 15 R17
Gjøl DK 38 B2
Gjøvik N 2 F12
Gladbeck D 50 B2
Gladenbach D 51 C4
Glamis GB 25 B5
Glamoč BIH 84 B1
Glamsbjerg DK 39 D3
Gland CH 69 B6
Glandorf D 50 A3
Glanegg A 73 B4
Glanshammar S 36 B2
Glarus CH 70 A4
Glasgow GB 24 C3
Glashütte, *Bayern* D 62 C2
Glashütte, *Sachsen* D 53 C3
Glastonbury GB 29 B5
Glatzau A 73 B5
Glauchau D 52 C2
Glava S 34 B4
Glavatičevo BIH 84 C3
Glavičice BIH 85 B4
Glavnik YU 85 D6
Gledica YU 85 C5
Glein A 73 A4
Gleinstätten A 73 B5
Gleisdorf A 73 A5
Glenamoy IRL 18 B2
Glenarm GB 19 B6
Glenavy GB 19 B5
Glenbarr GB 24 C2
Glenbeigh IRL 20 B2
Glenbrittle GB 22 D2
Glencoe GB 24 B2
Glencolumbkille IRL 18 B3
Glenealy IRL 21 B5
Glenelg GB 22 D3
Glenfinnan GB 24 B2
Glengarriff IRL 20 C2
Glenluce GB 24 D3
Glenrothes GB 25 B4
Glenties IRL 18 B3
Glesien D 52 B2
Gletsch CH 70 B3
Glimåkra S 41 C4
Glin IRL 20 B2
Glina HR 73 C6
Glinde D 44 B2
Glinojeck PL 47 C6
Glinsk IRL 20 A2
Gliwice PL 54 C3
Glödnitz A 73 B4
Gloggnitz A 64 C1
Głogoczów PL 65 A5
Glogonj YU 85 B5
Glogovac YU 85 B5
Głogów PL 53 B6
Głogówek PL 54 C2
Glomel F 56 B2
Glommen S 40 C2
Glommersträsk S 3 D16
Glonn D 62 C2
Glorenza I 71 B5
Gloria P 92 B2
Glossop GB 27 B4
Gloucester GB 29 B5
Głowaczów PL 55 B6
Główczyce PL 46 A3
Glöwen D 44 C4
Głowno PL 55 B4
Gložan YU 75 C4
Głubczyce PL 54 C2
Głuchołazy PL 54 C2
Głuchów PL 55 B5
Głuchowo PL 54 A1
Glücksburg D 39 E2
Glückstadt D 43 B6
Glumina BIH 84 B4
Glumsø DK 39 D4
Glušci YU 85 B4
Glusk BY 7 K21
Głuszyca PL 54 C1
Glyn Neath GB 28 B4
Glyngøre DK 38 C1
Gmünd, *Karnten* A 72 B3
Gmünd, *Nieder Östereich* A 63 B5
Gmund D 62 C2
Gmunden A 63 C4
Gnarrenburg D 43 B6
Gnesau A 72 B3
Gnesta S 37 B4
Gniechowice PL 54 B1
Gniew PL 47 B4
Gniewkowo PL 47 C4
Gniezno PL 46 C3
Gnoien D 45 B4
Gnojnice BIH 84 C2
Gnojno PL 55 C5
Gnosall GB 26 C3
Gnosjö S 40 B3
Goch D 50 B2
Gochsheim D 51 C6
Göd H 65 C5
Godalming GB 31 C3
Goddelsheim D 51 B4
Gódega di Sant'Urbano I 72 C2
Godegård S 37 C2
Godelheim D 51 B5
Goderville F 58 A1
Godiasco I 80 B3
Godič SLO 73 B4
Godkowo PL 47 A5
Godmanchester GB 30 B3
Gödöllö H 65 C5
Gödre H 74 B2
Godshill GB 31 D2
Godzikowice PL 54 C2
Godziszewo PL 47 A4
Goes NL 49 B4
Goetzenbrück F 60 B3
Góglio I 70 B3
Gogolin PL 54 C3
Göhren D 45 A5
Goirle NL 49 B6
Góis P 92 A2
Góito I 71 C5
Goizueta E 89 A5
Gojna Gora YU 85 C5
Gójsk PL 47 C5
Gol N 2 F11
Gola HR 74 B2
Gołańcz PL 46 C3
Gölcük TR 16 R21
Golčův Jenikov CZ 63 A6
Gołczewo PL 45 B6
Goldach CH 71 A4
Goldbach D 51 C5
Goldbeck D 44 C3
Goldberg D 44 B4
Goldenstedt D 43 C5
Gołębiewo PL 47 A4
Golegã P 92 B2
Goleniów PL 45 B6
Golfo Aranci I 110 C2
Golina PL 54 A3
Gölle H 74 B3
Göllersdorf A 64 B2
Golling an der Salzach A 63 C4
Golnice PL 53 B5
Golnik SLO 73 B4
Gölpazarı TR 16 R22
Gols A 64 C2
Golspie GB 23 D5
Golssen D 52 B3
Golub-Dobrzyń PL 47 B5
Golubinci YU 85 B5
Goluchów PL 54 B2
Golzow D 52 A2
Gomagoi I 71 B5
Gómara E 89 C4
Gomaringen D 61 B5
Gomes Aires P 98 B2
Gómezserracin E 88 C2
Gommern D 52 A1
Gomulin PL 55 B4
Gonäs S 36 A2
Goncelin F 69 C5
Gończyce PL 55 B6
Gondomar E 87 B2
Gondomar P 87 C2
Gondrecourt-le-Château F 60 B1
Gondrin F 76 C3
Gönen TR 16 R20
Gonfaron F 79 C5
Goñi E 89 B5
Goni I 110 D2
Gonnesa I 110 D1
Gonnosfanádiga I 110 D1
Gönyü H 64 C3
Gonzaga I 81 B4
Goodrich GB 29 B5
Goodwick GB 28 A2
Gooik B 49 C5
Goole GB 27 B5
Goor NL 50 A2
Göpfritz an der Wild A 63 B6
Goppenstein CH 70 B2
Göppingen D 61 B5
Gor E 100 B3
Góra, *Dolnośląskie* PL 54 B1
Góra, *Mazowieckie* PL 47 C6
Góra Kalwaria PL 55 B6
Gorafe E 100 B2
Gorawino PL 46 B1
Goražde BIH 84 C3
Gordaliza del Pino E 88 B1
Gørding DK 39 D1
Gördola CH 70 B3
Gordon GB 25 C5
Gordoncillo E 88 B1
Gorebridge GB 25 C4
Gorenja Vas SLO 73 B4
Gorenje Jelenje HR 73 C4
Gorey GB 57 A3
Gorey IRL 21 B5
Gorgonzola I 71 C4
Gorica HR 83 B4
Gorican HR 74 B1
Gorinchem NL 49 B5
Goring GB 31 C2
Goritsy RUS 7 H25
Göritz D 45 B5
Gorizia I 72 C3
Górki PL 47 C5
Gorleben D 44 B3

Gorleston-on-sea GB 30 B5
Gørlev DK 39 D4
Görlitz D 53 B4
Górliz E 89 A4
Görmin D 45 B5
Górna Grupa PL 47 B4
Gorna Oryakhovitsa BG 16 Q19
Gornja Gorevnica YU 85 C5
Gornja Klina YU 85 D5
Gornja Ploča HR 83 B4
Gornja Radgona SLO 73 B5
Gornja Sabanta YU 85 C6
Gornja Trešnjevica YU 85 B5
Gornja Tuzla BIH 84 B3
Gornje Polje YU 84 D3
Gornje Ratkovo BIH 84 B1
Gornji Grad SLO 73 B4
Gornji Humac HR 83 C5
Gornji Jasenjani BIH 84 C2
Gornji Kamengrad BIH 83 B5
Gornji Kneginec HR 73 B6
Gornji Kosinj HR 83 B4
Gornji Milanovac YU 85 B5
Gornji Podgradci BIH 84 A2
Gornji Ravno BIH 84 C2
Gornji Sjenicak HR 73 C5
Gornji Vakuf BIH 84 C2
Górno PL 55 C5
Görömböly H 65 B6
Górowo Iławeckie PL 47 A6
Gorran Haven GB 28 C3
Gorredijk NL 42 B3
Gorron F 57 B5
Gorseinon GB 28 B3
Gort IRL 20 A3
Gortin GB 19 B4
Görzke D 52 A2
Gorzkowice PL 55 B4
Górzno PL 47 B5
Gorzów Śląski PL 54 B3
Gorzów Wielkopolski PL 45 C7
Górzyca PL 45 C6
Gorzyce PL 65 A4
Górzyn, *Lubuskie* PL 53 B4
Gorzyń, *Wielkopolskie* PL 46 C1
Gorzyno PL 46 A3
Gosaldo I 72 B1
Gosau A 63 C4
Gosberton GB 30 B3
Gościcino PL 47 A4
Gościęcin PL 54 C3
Gościm PL 46 C1
Gościno PL 46 A1
Gosdorf A 73 B5
Gosforth GB 26 A2
Goslar D 51 B6
Goslice PL 47 C5
Gospič HR 83 B4
Gosport GB 31 D2
Goss Ilsede D 51 A6
Gössäter S 35 C5
Gossau CH 71 A4
Gössnitz D 52 C2
Gössweinstein D 62 A2
Gostkow PL 55 B4
Göstling an der Ybbs A 63 C5
Gostomia PL 46 B2
Gostycyn PL 46 B3
Gostyń PL 54 B2
Gostynin PL 47 C5
Goszczyn PL 55 B5
Göta S 35 C4
Göteborg S 35 D3
Götene S 35 C5
Gotha D 51 C6
Gothem S 37 D5
Gotse Delchev BG 15 R18
Gottersdorf D 62 B3
Göttingen D 51 B5
Götzis A 71 A4
Gouarec F 56 B2
Gouda NL 49 A5
Goudhurst GB 31 C4
Gourdon F 77 B4
Gourgançon F 59 B5
Gourin F 56 B2
Gournay-en-Bray F 58 A2
Gourock GB 24 C3
Gouveia P 92 A3
Gouvy B 50 C1
Gouzeacourt F 49 C4
Gouzon F 68 B2
Govedari HR 84 D2
Govérnolo I 81 A4
Gowarczów PL 55 B5
Gowerton GB 28 B3
Gowidlino PL 46 A3
Gowran IRL 21 B4
Goyatz D 53 A4
Göynük TR 16 R22
Gozdnica PL 53 B5
Gozdowo PL 47 C5
Gozee B 49 C5
Graal-Müritz D 44 A4
Grabenstätt D 62 C3
Grabhair GB 22 C2
Gråbo S 35 D4
Grabovac HR 84 C1
Grabovac YU 85 B5
Grabovci YU 85 B4
Grabow D 44 B3
Grabów PL 55 A4
Grabow nad Pilicą PL 55 B6
Grabów nad Prosną PL 54 B3
Grabowno PL 46 B3
Grabs CH 71 A4
Gračac HR 83 B4
Gračanica BIH 84 B3
Graçay F 68 A1
Grad SLO 73 B6
Gradac HR 84 C2
Gradac, *Crna Gora* YU 85 C4
Gradac, *Srbija* YU 85 C5
Gradačac BIH 84 B3
Gradec HR 73 C6
Gradefes E 88 B1
Grades A 73 B4
Gradil P 92 C1
Gradina HR 74 C2
Gradina YU 85 C4
Gradisca d'Isonzo I 72 C3
Gradište HR 84 A3
Grado E 86 A4
Grado I 72 C3
Grærup Strand DK 39 D1
Græsted DK 41 C2
Grafenau D 63 B4
Gräfenberg D 62 A2
Gräfenhainichen D 52 B2
Grafenschlag A 63 B6
Grafenstein A 73 B4
Gräfenthal D 52 C1
Grafentonna D 51 B6
Grafenwöhr D 62 A2
Grafing D 62 B2
Grafling D 62 B3
Gräfsnäs S 35 C4
Gragnano I 103 C4
Grahovo SLO 72 B3
Graiguenamanagh IRL 21 B5
Grain GB 31 C4
Grainau D 71 A6
Graja de Iniesta E 95 C5
Grajera E 89 C3
Gram DK 39 D2
Gramais A 71 A5
Gramat F 77 B4
Gramatneusiedl A 64 B2
Grambow D 45 B6
Grammichele I 109 B3
Gramzow D 45 B6
Gran N 34 A2
Granada E 100 B2
Granard IRL 19 C4
Grañas E 86 A3
Granátula de Calatrava E 100 A2
Grancey-le-Château F 59 C6
Grand-Champ F 56 C3
Grand Couronne F 58 A2
Grand-Fougeray F 57 C4
Grandas de Salime E 86 A4
Grandcamp-Maisy F 57 A4
Grândola P 98 A2
Grandpré F 59 A5
Grandrieu B 49 C5
Grandrieu F 78 B2
Grandson CH 70 B1
Grandvillars F 70 A1
Grandvilliers F 58 A2
Grañén E 90 B2
Grangärde S 36 A1
Grange IRL 18 B3
Grange-over-Sands GB 26 A3
Grangemouth GB 25 B4
Granges-de Crouhens F 77 D3
Granges-sur-Vologne F 60 B2
Grängesberg S 36 A1
Gräningen D 44 C4
Granitola-Torretta I 108 B1
Granja, *Évora* P 98 A3
Granja, *Porto* P 87 C2
Granja de Moreruela E 88 C1
Granja de Torrehermosa E 99 A5
Gränna S 40 A4
Granollers E 91 B5
Granön S 3 D16
Granowiec PL 54 B2
Granowo PL 54 A1
Gransee D 45 B5
Gransherad N 33 B6
Grantham GB 27 C5
Grantown-on-Spey GB 23 D5
Grantshouse GB 25 C5
Granville F 57 B4
Grasberg D 43 B6
Grasmere GB 26 A2
Grasö S 36 A5
Grassano I 104 B3
Grassau D 62 C3
Grasse F 79 C5
Grassington GB 27 A4
Gråsten DK 39 E2
Grästorp S 35 C4
Gratkorn A 73 A5
Gratwein A 73 A5
Graulhet F 77 C4
Graus E 90 A3
Grávalos E 89 B5
Grave NL 50 B1
Gravedona I 71 B4
Gravelines F 48 B3
Gravellona Toce I 70 C3
's Gravendeel NL 49 B5
's-Gravenhage NL 49 A5
Gravens DK 39 D2
's Gravenzande NL 49 A5
Gravesend GB 31 C4
Graveson F 78 C3
Gravina in Púglia I 105 B3
Gray F 69 A5
Grayrigg GB 26 A3
Grays GB 31 C4
Grayshott GB 31 C3
Grayvoron RUS 7 L24
Graz A 73 A5
Grazalema E 99 C5
Grążawy PL 47 B5
Grazzano Visconti I 80 B3
Greåker N 34 B3
Great Dunmow GB 31 C4
Great Malvern GB 29 A5
Great Torrington GB 28 C3
Great Waltham GB 31 C4
Great Yarmouth GB 30 B5
Grebbestad S 35 C3
Grebenstein D 51 B5
Grębocin PL 47 B4
Greding D 62 A2
Gredstedbro DK 39 D1
Greenhead GB 25 D5
Greenisland GB 19 B6
Greenlaw GB 25 C5
Greenock GB 24 C3
Greenway GB 28 B3
Greenwich GB 31 C4
Grefrath D 50 B2
Greifenburg A 72 B3
Greiffenberg D 45 B5
Greifswald D 45 A5
Grein A 63 B5
Greipstad N 33 C4
Greiz D 52 C2
Grenaa DK 39 C3
Grenade F 77 C4
Grenade-sur-l'Adour F 76 C2
Grenchen CH 70 A2
Grendi N 33 C4
Grenoble F 69 C5
Gréoux-les-Bains F 79 C4
Gresenhorst D 44 A4
Gressoney-la-Trinité I 70 C2
Gressoney-St.-Jean I 70 C2
Gressthal D 51 C6
Gressvik N 34 B2
Gresten A 63 C6
Gretna GB 25 D4
Greussen D 51 B6
Greve in Chianti I 81 C5
Greven, *Mecklenburg-Vorpommern* D 44 B2
Greven, *Nordrhein-Westfalen* D 50 A3
Grevená GR 15 R17
Grevenbroich D 50 B2
Grevenbrück D 50 B4
Grevenmacher L 60 A2
Grevesmühlen D 44 B3
Grevestrand DK 41 D2
Grevie S 41 C2
Greystoke GB 26 A3
Greystones IRL 21 A5
Grez-Doiceau B 49 C5
Grez-en-Bouère F 57 C5
Grèzec F 77 B4
Grezzana I 71 C6
Grgar SLO 72 B3
Grgurevci YU 85 A4
Gries A 71 A6
Gries in Sellrain A 71 A6
Griesbach D 63 B4
Griesheim D 61 A4
Grieskirchen A 63 B4
Griffen A 73 B4
Grignan F 78 B3
Grignano I 72 C3
Grigno I 72 B1
Grignols F 76 B2
Grignon F 69 C6
Grijota E 88 B2
Grijpskerk NL 42 B3
Grillby S 36 B4
Grimaud F 79 C5
Grimbergen B 49 C5
Grimma D 52 B2
Grimmen D 45 A5
Grimmialp CH 70 B2
Grimsås S 40 B3
Grimsby GB 27 B5
Grimslöv S 40 C4
Grimstad N 33 C5
Grimstorp S 40 B4
Grindelwald CH 70 B3
Grindheim N 33 C4
Grindsted DK 39 D1
Griñón E 94 B3
Gripenberg S 37 D1
Gripsholm S 36 B4
Grisolles F 77 C4
Grisslehamn S 36 A5
Gritley GB 23 C6
Grizebeck GB 26 A2
Grndina BIH 84 B1
Gröbming A 72 A3
Gröbzig D 52 B1
Grocka YU 85 B5
Gröditz D 52 B3
Gródki PL 47 B6
Grodków PL 54 C2
Grodziec PL 54 A3
Grodzisk Mazowiecki PL 55 A5
Groenlo NL 50 A2
Groesbeek NL 50 B1
Grohote HR 83 C5
Groitzsch D 52 B2
Groix F 56 C2
Grójec PL 55 B5
Grom PL 47 B6
Gromiljca BIH 84 C3
Grömitz D 44 A2
Gromnik PL 65 A6
Gromo I 71 C4
Gronau, *Niedersachsen* D 51 A5
Gronau, *Nordrhein-Westfalen* D 50 A3
Grönenbach D 61 C6
Grong N 2 D13
Grönhögen S 41 C6
Groningen D 52 B1
Groningen NL 42 B3
Grono CH 71 B4
Grönskåra S 40 B5
Grootegast NL 42 B3
Gropello Cairoli I 70 C3
Grorud N 34 B2
Grósio I 71 B5
Grošnica YU 85 C5
Gross Beeren D 45 C5
Gross Berkel D 51 A5
Gross-botwar D 61 B5
Gross-Dölln D 45 B5
Gross-Gerau D 61 A4
Gross-hartmansdorf D 52 C3
Gross Kreutz D 45 C4
Gross Lafferde D 51 A6
Gross Leutheb D 53 A4
Gross Oesingen D 44 C2
Gross Reken D 50 B3
Gross Sarau D 44 B2
Gross Särchen D 53 B4
Gross Schönebeck D 45 C5
Gross-schweinbarth A 64 B2
Gross Umstadt D 61 A4
Gross Warnow D 44 B3
Gross-Weikersdorf A 64 B1
Gross-Welle D 44 B4
Gross Wokern D 44 B4
Grossalmerode D 51 B5
Grossarl A 72 A3
Grossbodungen D 51 B6
Grossburgwedel D 44 C1
Grosschönau D 53 C4
Grossenbrode D 44 A3
Grossengottern D 51 B6
Grossenhain D 52 B3
Grossenkneten D 43 C5
Grossenlüder D 51 C5
Grossensee D 44 B2
Grossenzersdorf A 64 B2
Grosseto I 81 D5
Grossgerungs A 63 B5
Grossglobnitz A 63 B6
Grosshabersdorf D 62 A1
Grossharras A 64 B2
Grosshöchstetten CH 70 B2
Grosskrut A 64 B2
Grosslohra D 51 B6
Grossmehring D 62 B2
Grossostheim D 61 A5
Grosspertholz A 63 B5
Grosspetersdorf A 73 A6
Grosspostwitz D 53 B4
Grossraming A 63 C5
Grossräschen D 53 B4
Grossrinderfeld D 61 A5
Grossröhrsdorf D 53 B4
Grossschirma D 52 C3
Grosssiegharts A 63 B6
Grosssölk A 72 A3
Grosswarasdorf A 73 A6
Grosswilfersdorf A 73 A5
Grostenquin F 60 B2
Grosuplje SLO 73 C4
Grotli N 2 E10
Grottáglie I 105 B4
Grottaminarda I 104 A2
Grottammare I 82 D2
Grotte di Castro I 102 A1
Grotteria I 106 C3
Gróttole I 104 B3
Grouw NL 42 B2
Grove E 86 B2
Grožnjan HR 72 C3
Grua N 34 A2
Grube D 44 A3
Grubišno Polje HR 74 C2
Grude BIH 84 C2
Grudovo BG 16 Q20
Grudusk PL 47 B6
Grudziądz PL 47 B4
Grue N 34 A4
Gruissan F 78 C2
Grullos E 86 A4
Grumo Áppula I 105 A3
Grums S 34 B5
Grünau im Almtal A 63 C4
Grünberg D 51 C4
Grünburg A 63 C5
Grundau D 51 C5
Gründelhardt D 61 A5
Grundlsee A 63 C4
Grundsund S 35 C3
Grunewald D 53 B3
Grungedal N 33 B4
Grunow D 53 A4
Grünstadt D 61 A4
Gruyères CH 70 B2
Gruža YU 85 C5
Grybów PL 65 A6
Gryfice PL 45 B7
Gryfino PL 45 B6
Gryfów Śląski PL 53 B5
Grymyr N 34 A2
Gryt S 37 D3
Grytgöl S 37 D2
Grythyttan S 36 B1
Grytnäs S 37 C4
Grzmiąca PL 46 B2
Grzybno PL 45 B6
Grzywna PL 47 B4
Gschnitz A 71 A6
Gschwend D 61 B5
Gstaad CH 70 B2
Gsteig CH 70 B2
Guadahortuna E 100 B2
Guadalajara E 95 B3
Guadalaviar E 95 B5
Guadalcanal E 99 A5
Guadalcázar E 100 B1
Guadalix de la Sierra E 94 B3
Guadálmez E 100 A1
Guadalupe E 94 C1
Guadamur E 94 C2
Guadarrama E 94 B2
Guadiaro E 99 C5
Guadix E 100 B2
Guagnano I 105 B4
Guagno F 110 A1
Guajar-Faragüit E 100 C2
Gualchos E 100 C2
Gualdo Tadino I 82 C1
Gualtieri I 81 B4
Guarcino I 103 B3
Guarda P 92 A3
Guardamar del Segura E 96 C2
Guardão P 92 A2
Guardavalle I 106 C3
Guardea I 102 A2
Guárdia I 104 B2
Guárdia Sanframondi I 103 B4
Guardiagrele I 103 A4
Guardiarégia I 103 B4
Guardias Viejas E 101 C3
Guardiola de Bergueda E 91 A4
Guardo E 88 B2
Guareña E 93 C4
Guaro E 100 C1
Guarromán E 100 A2
Guasila I 110 D2
Guastalla I 81 B4
Gúbbio I 82 C1
Guben D 53 B4
Gubin PL 53 B4
Guča YU 85 C5
Gudavac BIH 83 B5
Güderup DK 39 E2
Gudhem S 35 C5
Gudhjem DK 41 D4
Gudovac HR 74 C1
Gudow D 44 B2
Gudvangen N 2 F10
Guebwiller F 60 C3
Guéjar-Sierra E 100 B2
Guéméné-Penfao F 57 C4
Guéméné-sur-Scorff F 56 B2
Güeñes E 89 A3
Guer F 57 C3
Guérande F 66 A2
Guéret F 68 B1
Guérigny F 68 A3
Guesa E 76 D1
Gueugnon F 68 B4
Guglionesi I 103 B4
Gühlen Glienicke D 45 B4
Guia P 92 B2
Guichen F 57 C4
Guidizzolo I 71 C5
Guidónia-Montecélio I 102 B2
Guiglia I 81 B4
Guignes F 58 B3
Guijo E 100 A1
Guijo de Coria E 93 A4
Guijo de Santa Bábera E 93 A5
Guijuelo E 93 A5
Guildford GB 31 C3
Guillaumes F 79 B5
Guillena E 99 B4
Guillestre F 79 B5
Guilsfield GB 26 C2
Guilvinec F 56 C1
Guimarães P 87 C2
Guincho P 92 C1
Guînes F 48 C2
Guingamp F 56 B2
Guipavas F 56 B1
Guisborough GB 27 A4
Guiscard F 59 A4
Guiscriff F 56 B2
Guise F 59 A4
Guisona E 91 B4
Guitiriz E 86 A3
Guîtres F 76 A2
Gujan-Mestras F 76 B1
Gulbene LV 7 H20
Guldborg DK 39 E4
Gullabo S 40 C5
Gullane GB 25 B5
Gullbrandstorp S 40 C2
Gullhaug N 34 B2
Gullringen S 37 D2
Gullspång S 35 C6
Güllük TR 16 T20
Gumiel de Hizán E 88 C3
Gummersbach D 50 B3
Gumünden D 60 A3
Gundelfingen D 60 B3
Gundelfingen D 61 B6
Gundelsheim D 61 A5
Gunderschoffen F 60 B3
Gundertshausen A 62 B3
Gundinci HR 74 C3
Gunja HR 84 B3
Gunnarn S 2 D15
Gunnarskog S 34 B4
Gunnebo S 37 D3
Gunnislake GB 28 C3
Günselsdorf A 64 C2
Guntersblum D 61 A4
Guntersdorf A 64 B2
Guntin E 86 B3
Günzburg D 61 B6
Gunzenhausen D 62 A1
Gurk A 73 B4
Gurrea de Gállego E 90 A2
Gušće HR 74 C1
Gusev RUS 6 J18
Gúspini I 110 D1
Gusselby S 36 B2
Güssing A 73 A6
Gusswerk A 63 C6
Gustav Adolf S 34 A5
Gustavsberg S 36 B5
Gustavsfors S 34 B4
Güstrow D 44 B4
Gusum S 37 C3
Gutcher GB 22 A7
Gutenstein A 64 C1
Gütersloh D 51 B4
Guttannen CH 70 B3
Guttaring A 73 B4
Guttau D 53 B4
Güttingen CH 61 C5
Gützkow D 45 B5
Guzów PL 55 A5
Gvardeysk RUS 6 J17
Gvarv N 33 B6
Gvozd YU 84 D4
Gvozdansko HR 73 C6
Gwda Wielka PL 46 B2
Gwennap GB 28 C2
Gy F 69 A5
Gyál H 75 A4
Gyarmat H 74 A2
Gyé-sur-Seine F 59 B5
Gyékényes H 74 B2
Gylling DK 39 D3
Gyoma H 75 B5
Gyömöre H 74 A2
Gyömrö H 75 A4
Gyón H 75 A4
Gyöngyfa H 74 C2
Gyöngyös H 65 C5
Gyöngyöspata H 65 C5
Gyönk H 74 B3
Györ H 64 C3
Györszemere H 74 A2
Gypsera CH 70 B2
Gysinge S 36 A3
Gyttorp S 36 B1
Gyula H 75 B6
Gyulafirátót H 74 A2
Gyulaj H 74 B3

H

Haacht B 49 C5
Haag, *Nieder Östereich* A 63 B5
Haag, *Ober Östereich* A 63 B4
Haag D 62 B3
Haaksbergen NL 50 A2
Haamstede NL 49 B4
Haan D 50 B3
Haapajärvi FIN 3 E19
Haapsalu EST 6 G18
Haarlem NL 42 C1
Habas F 76 C2
Habay B 60 A1
Habo S 40 B4
Habry CZ 63 A6
Habsheim F 60 C3
Hachenburg D 50 C3
Hacinas E 89 C3
Hacketstown IRL 21 B5
Hackthorpe GB 26 A3
Hadamar D 50 C4
Haddington GB 25 B5
Hadersdorf am Kamp A 63 B6
Haderslev DK 39 D2
Hadleigh, *Essex* GB 31 C4
Hadleigh, *Suffolk* GB 30 B4
Hadlow GB 31 C4
Hadmersleben D 52 B1
Hadsten DK 39 C3
Hadsund DK 38 C3
Hadyach UA 7 L24
Hadžići BIH 84 C3
Hægebostad N 33 C4
Hægeland N 33 C4
Haganj HR 74 C1
Hagby S 40 C6
Hage D 43 B4
Hagen, *Niedersachsen* D 43 B5
Hagen, *Nordrhein-Westfalen* D 50 B3
Hagenbach D 61 A4
Hagenow D 44 B3
Hagetmau F 76 C2
Hagfors S 34 A5
Hagondange F 60 A2
Haguenau F 60 B3
Hahnbach D 62 A2
Hahnslätten D 50 C4
Hahót H 74 B1
Haiger D 50 C4
Haigerloch D 61 B4
Hailsham GB 31 D4
Hainburg A 64 B2
Hainfeld A 64 B1
Hainichen D 52 C3
Hajdúböszörmény H 10 N17
Hajdučica YU 75 C5
Hajdúszoboszló H 75 A6
Hajnáčka SK 65 B5
Hajnówka PL 6 K18
Hajós H 75 B4
Hakkas S 3 C17
Håksberg S 36 A2
Halaszi H 64 C3
Halberstadt D 52 B1
Halberton GB 29 C4
Haldem D 43 C5
Halden N 34 B3
Haldensleben D 52 A1
Halenbeck D 44 B4
Halesowen GB 26 C3
Halesworth GB 30 B5
Halfing D 62 C3
Halhjem N 32 A2
Halifax GB 27 B4
Halkirk GB 23 C5
Hall S 37 D5
Hall in Tirol A 71 A6
Hallabro S 41 C5
Hällabrottet S 37 B2
Halland GB 31 D4
Hällaryd S 41 C4
Hallberga S 36 B3
Hällbybrunn S 36 B3
Halle B 49 C5
Halle, *Nordrhein-Westfalen* D 51 A4
Halle, *Sachsen-Anhalt* D 52 B1
Hålleberga S 40 C5
Hällefors S 36 B1
Hälleforsnäs S 36 B3
Hallein A 62 C4
Hällekis S 35 C5
Hållen S 36 A4
Hallenberg D 51 B4
Hällestad S 37 C2
Hällevadsholm S 35 C3
Hällevik S 41 C4
Hälleviksstrand S 35 C3
Hallingby N 34 A2
Hällnäs S 36 A4
Hallsberg S 37 B2
Hällsta S 36 B3
Hallstahammar S 36 B3
Hallstatt A 72 A3
Hallstavik S 36 A5
Halltorp S 40 C6
Halluin F 49 C4
Hallworthy GB 28 C3
Halmstad S 40 C2
Hals DK 38 B3
Halstead GB 31 C4
Haltdalen N 2 E12
Haltern D 50 B3
Haltwhistle GB 25 D5
Halvarsgårdarna S 36 A2
Halver D 50 B3
Halvrimmen DK 38 B2
Ham F 59 A4
Hamar N 2 F12
Hamarhaug N 32 A2
Hambach F 60 A3
Hambergen D 43 B5
Hambergsund S 35 C3
Hambledon GB 31 D2
Hambuhren D 44 C1
Hamburg D 44 B2
Hamdorf D 43 A6
Hämeenlinna FIN 3 F19
Hameln D 51 A5
Hamersleben D 52 A1
Hamilton GB 24 C3
Hamina FIN 3 F20
Hamm D 50 B3
Hammar S 37 C1
Hammarö S 34 B5
Hamme B 49 B5
Hammel DK 39 C2
Hammelburg D 51 C5
Hammelspring D 45 B5
Hammenhög S 41 D4
Hammerfest N 2 A18
Hammershøj DK 38 C2
Hammerum DK 39 C2
Hamminkeln D 50 B2
Hamnavoe GB 22 A7
Hamneda S 40 C3
Hamont B 49 B6
Hámor H 65 B6
Hamstreet GB 31 C4
Han Knežica BIH 74 C1
Han Pijesak BIH 84 B3
Hanaskog S 41 C4
Hanau D 51 C4
Händelöp S 37 D3
Handlová SK 65 B4
Hanerau-Hademarschen D 43 A6
Hånger S 40 B3
Hanken S 37 C1
Hankensbüttel D 44 C2
Hanko FIN 3 G18
Hannover D 43 C6
Hannut B 49 C6
Hanstedt D 44 B2
Hanstholm DK 38 B1
Hantsavichy BY 7 K20
Hanušovice CZ 54 C1
Haparanda S 3 D19
Haradok BY 7 J21
Harads S 3 C17
Häradsbäck S 40 C4
Harbo S 36 A4
Harboor DK 38 C1
Harburg, *Bayern* D 62 B1
Harburg, *Hamburg* D 44 B1
Hårby DK 39 D3
Harc H 74 B3
Hardegarijp NL 42 B2
Hardegsen D 51 B5
Hardelot Plage F 48 C2
Hardenbeck D 45 B5
Hardenberg NL 42 C3
Harderwijk NL 42 C2
Hardheim D 61 A5
Hardt D 61 B4
Hareid N 2 E10
Haren D 43 C4
Haren NL 42 B3
Harestua N 34 A2
Harfleur F 57 A6
Harg S 36 A5
Hargicourt F 49 D4
Hargnies F 49 C5
Hargshamn S 36 A5
Harkány H 74 C3
Härkeberga S 36 B4
Harkebrügge D 43 B4
Harlech GB 26 C1
Harleston GB 30 B5
Hårlev DK 41 D2
Harlingen NL 42 B2
Harlösa S 41 D3
Harlow GB 31 C4
Härnevi S 36 B4
Härnösand S 2 E15
Haro E 89 B4
Haroldswick GB 22 A8
Háromfa H 74 B2
Haroué F 60 B2
Harpenden GB 31 C3
Harplinge S 40 C2
Harpstedt D 43 C5
Harrogate GB 27 A4
Harrow GB 31 C3
Härryda S 35 D4
Harsefeld D 43 B6
Harsewinkel D 50 B4
Hârşova RO 11 P20
Harstad N 2 B15
Harsum D 51 A5
Harta H 75 B4
Hartberg A 73 A5
Hartburn GB 25 C6
Hartennes F 59 A4
Hartest GB 30 B4
Hartha D 52 B2
Hartland GB 28 C3
Hartlepool GB 27 A4
Hartmanice CZ 63 A4
Hartmannsdorf A 73 A5
Harwell GB 31 C2
Harwich GB 31 C5
Harzgerode D 52 B1
Häselgehr A 71 A5
Haselünne D 43 C4
Haslach D 61 B4
Haslach an der Mühl A 63 B5
Hasle DK 41 D4
Haslemere GB 31 C3
Haslev DK 39 D4
Hasloch D 61 A5
Hasparren F 76 C1
Hasselfelde D 51 B6
Hasselfors S 37 B1
Hasselt B 49 C6
Hasselt NL 42 C3
Hassfurt D 51 C6
Hassleben D 45 B5
Hässleholm S 41 C3
Hasslö S 41 C5
Hassloch D 61 A4
Hästholmen S 37 C1
Hastière-Lavaux B 49 C5
Hastigrow GB 23 C5
Hastings GB 31 D4
Hästveda S 41 C3
Hatfield, *Hertfordshire* GB 31 C3
Hatfield, *South Yorkshire* GB 27 B5
Hatherleigh GB 28 C3
Hathersage GB 27 B4
Hatlestrand N 32 A2
Hattem NL 42 C3
Hatten D 43 B5
Hatten F 60 B3
Hatting DK 39 D2
Hattingen D 50 B3
Hattstadt F 60 B3
Hattstedt D 43 A6
Hatvan H 65 C5
Hatvik N 32 A2
Hau D 50 B2
Haudainville F 59 A6
Hauge N 32 C3
Haugesund N 32 B2
Haughom N 32 C3
Hausdorf A 64 B2
Haukeland N 32 A2
Haukeligrend N 33 B4
Haukipudas FIN 3 D19
Haulerwijk NL 42 B3
Haunersdorf D 62 B3
Hausach D 61 B4
Hausham D 62 C2
Hausmannstätten A 73 B5
Hausvik N 32 C3
Haut-Fays B 49 C6
Hautefort F 67 C6
Hauterives F 69 C5
Hauteville-Lompnès F 69 C5
Hautmont F 49 C4
Hautrage B 49 C4
Hauzenberg D 63 B4
Havant GB 31 D3
Havdrup DK 39 D5
Havelange B 49 C6
Havelberg D 44 C4
Havelte NL 42 C3
Haverfordwest GB 28 B3
Haverhill GB 30 B4
Havering GB 31 C4
Håverud S 35 C4
Havířov CZ 65 A4
Havixbeck D 50 B3
Havlíčkův Brod CZ 63 A6
Havndal DK 38 C3
Havneby DK 39 D1
Havnso DK 39 D4
Havøysund N 2 A19
Havrebjerg DK 39 D4
Havstenssund S 35 C3
Hawes GB 26 A3
Hawick GB 25 C5
Hawkhurst GB 31 C4
Hawkinge GB 31 C5
Haxey GB 27 B5
Hay-on-Wye GB 29 A4
Hayange F 60 A2
Haydon Bridge GB 25 D5
Hayle GB 28 C2
Hayrabolu TR 16 R20
Haysyn UA 11 M21
Hayvoron UA 11 M21
Haywards Heath GB 31 D3
Hazebrouck F 48 C3
Hazlov CZ 52 C2
Heacham GB 30 B4
Headcorn GB 31 C4
Headford IRL 20 A2
Heanor GB 27 B4
Héas F 76 D3
Heathfield GB 31 D4
Hebden Bridge GB 26 B3
Heberg S 40 C2
Heby S 36 B3
Hechingen D 61 B4
Hechlingen D 62 B1
Hecho E 76 D2
Hechtel B 49 B6

Hechthausen D 43 B6
Heckelberg D 45 C5
Heckington GB 27 C5
Hecklingen D 52 B1
Hed S 36 B2
Hedared S 35 D4
Heddal N 33 B6
Hédé F 57 B4
Hede S 2 E13
Hedekas S 35 C3
Hedemora S 36 A2
Hedensted DK 39 D2
Hedersleben D 52 B1
Hedesunda S 36 A4
Hedge End GB 31 D2
Hedon GB 27 B5
Heede D 43 C4
Heek D 50 A3
Heemstede NL 42 C1
Heerde NL 42 C3
's Heerenberg NL 50 B2
Heerenveen NL 42 C2
Heerhugowaard NL 42 C1
Heerlen NL 50 C1
Heeze NL 49 B6
Hegyeshalom H 64 C3
Hegyközség H 74 A1
Heide D 43 A6
Heidelberg D 61 A4
Heiden D 50 B2
Heidenau D 53 C3
Heidenheim D 61 B6
Heidenreichstein A 63 B6
Heikendorf D 44 A2
Heilam GB 22 C4
Heilbad Heiligenstadt D 51 B6
Heilbronn D 61 A5
Heiligenblut A 72 A2
Heiligendamn D 44 A3
Heiligendorf D 44 C2
Heiligengrabe D 44 B4
Heiligenhafen D 44 A2
Heiligenhaus D 50 B2
Heiligenkreuz A 73 B6
Heiligenstadt D 62 A2
Heiloo NL 42 C1
Heilsbronn D 62 A1
Heimburg D 51 B6
Heimdal N 2 E12
Heinerscheid L 50 C2
Heinersdorf D 45 C6
Heining D 63 B4
Heiningen D 61 B5
Heinola FIN 3 F20
Heinsberg D 50 B2
Heist-op-den-Berg B 49 B5
Hejdeby S 37 D5
Hejls DK 39 D2
Hejnice CZ 53 C5
Hel PL 47 A4
Helchteren B 49 B6
Heldburg D 51 C6
Heldrungen D 52 B1
Helechosa E 94 C2
Helensburgh GB 24 B3
Helfenberg A 63 B5
Helgen N 33 B6
Helgeroa N 33 C6
Hellas S 35 C4
Helle N 32 C3
Helleland N 32 C3
Hellendoorn NL 42 C3
Hellenthal D 50 C2
Hellesylt N 2 E10
Hellevoetsluis NL 49 B5
Hellín E 101 A4
Hellvi S 37 D5
Hellvik N 32 C2
Helm-brechts D 52 C1
Helmond NL 49 B6
Helmsdale GB 23 C5
Helmsley GB 27 A4
Helmstedt D 51 A6
Hel'pa SK 65 B5
Helsa D 51 B5
Helsby GB 26 B3
Helsingborg S 41 C2
Helsinge DK 41 C2
Helsingør DK 41 C2
Helsinki FIN 3 F19
Helston GB 28 C2
Hemau D 62 A2
Hemel Hempstead GB 31 C3
Hemer D 50 B3
Héming F 60 B2
Hemmet DK 39 D1
Hemmingstedt D 43 A6
Hemmoor D 43 B6
Hemnes N 34 B3
Hemnesberget N 2 C13
Hemse S 6 H16
Hemsedal N 2 F11
Hemslingen D 43 B6
Hemsworth GB 27 B4
Hen N 34 A2
Henån S 35 C3
Hendaye F 89 A5
Hendek TR 16 R22
Hendungen D 51 C6
Henfield GB 31 D3
Hengelo, Gelderland NL 50 A2
Hengelo, Overijssel NL 50 A2
Hengersberg D 62 B4
Hengoed GB 29 B4
Hénin-Beaumont F 48 C3
Henley-on-Thames GB 31 C3
Henne Strand DK 39 D1
Henneberg D 51 C6
Hennebont F 56 C2
Hennigsdorf D 45 C5
Hennstedt D 43 A6
Henrichemont F 68 A2
Henryków PL 54 C2
Henrykowo PL 47 A6
Henstedt-Ulzburg D 44 B1
Heppenheim D 61 A4
Herad N 32 C3
Herálec CZ 64 A2
Herand N 32 A3
Herbault F 58 C2
Herbern D 50 B3
Herbertstown IRL 20 B3
Herbeumont B 59 A6
Herbignac F 66 A2
Herbisse F 59 B5
Herbitzheim F 60 A3
Herbolzheim D 60 B3
Herborn D 50 C4
Herbrechtingen D 61 B6
Herby PL 54 C3
Herceg-Novi YU 15 Q16
Hercegovać HR 74 C2
Hercegovacka Goleša YU 85 C4
Hercegszántó H 75 C3
Herchen D 50 C3
Heréd H 65 C5
Hereford GB 29 A5
Herefoss N 33 C5
Herencia E 95 C3
Herend H 74 A2
Herent B 49 C5
Herentals B 49 B5
Hérépian F 78 C2
Herfølge DK 39 D5
Herford D 51 A4
Herguijuela E 93 B5
Héric F 66 A3
Héricourt F 70 A1
Héricourt-en-Caux F 58 A1
Hérimoncourt F 70 A1
Heringsdorf D 44 A3
Herisau CH 71 A4
Hérisson F 68 B2
Herk-de-Stad B 49 C6
Herlufmagle DK 39 D4
Hermagor A 72 B3
Hermannsburg D 44 C2
Heřmanův Městec CZ 53 D5
Herment F 68 C2
Hermeskeil D 60 A2
Hermisende E 87 C4
Hermonville F 59 A4
Hermsdorf D 52 C1
Hernani E 89 A5
Hernansancho E 94 B2
Herne D 50 B3
Herne Bay GB 31 C5
Herning DK 39 C1
Heroya N 33 B6
Herramelluri E 89 B3
Herräng S 36 A5
Herre N 33 B6
Herrenberg D 61 B4
Herrera E 100 B1
Herrera de Alcántara E 92 B3
Herrera de los Navarros E 90 B1
Herrera de Pisuerga E 88 B2
Herrera del Duque E 94 C1
Herrerias E 98 B3
Herreros del Suso E 94 B1
Herrestad S 35 C3
Herrhamra S 37 C4
Herrlisheim F 60 B3
Herrljunga S 35 C5
Herrnhut D 53 B4
Herrsching D 62 B2
Hersbruck D 62 A2
Hersby S 36 B5
Herscheid D 50 B3
Herselt B 49 B5
Herstal B 49 C6
Herstmonceux GB 31 D4
Herten D 50 B3
Hertford GB 31 C3
's-Hertogenbosch NL 49 B6
Hervás E 93 A5
Hervik N 32 B2
Herxheim D 61 A4
Herzberg, Brandenburg D 45 C4
Herzberg, Brandenburg D 52 B3
Herzberg, Niedersachsen D 51 B6
Herzebrock D 50 B4
Herzfelde D 45 C5
Herzlake D 43 C4
Herzogen-aurach D 62 A1
Herzogenbuchsee CH 70 A2
Herzogenburg A 63 B6
Herzsprung D 44 B4
Hesby N 32 B2
Hesdin F 48 C3
Hesel D 43 B4
Heskestad N 32 C3
Hesselager DK 39 D3
Hessisch Lichtenau D 51 B5
Hessisch-Oldendorf D 51 A5
Hestra S 40 B3
Heswall GB 26 B2
Hettange-Grande F 60 A2
Hetton-le-Hole GB 25 D6
Hettstedt D 52 B1
Heuchin F 48 C3
Heudicourt-sous-les-Côtes F 60 B1
Heunezel F 60 B2
Heuqueville F 57 A6
Heves H 65 C6
Héviz H 74 B2
Hexham GB 25 D5
Heysham GB 26 A3
Heytesbury GB 29 B5
Hidas H 74 B3
Hieflau A 63 C5
Hiendelaencina E 95 A4
Hiersac F 67 C5
High Bentham GB 26 A3
High Hesket GB 25 D5
High Wycombe GB 31 C3
Highclere GB 31 C2
Highley GB 26 C3
Higuera de Arjona E 100 B2
Higuera de Calatrava E 100 B1
Higuera de la Serena E 93 C5
Higuera de la Sierra E 99 B4
Higuera de Vargas E 93 C4
Higuera la Real E 99 A4
Higuers de Llerena E 93 C4
Higueruela E 96 C1
Híjar E 90 B2
Hilchenbach D 50 B4
Hildburghausen D 51 C6
Hilden D 50 B2
Hilders D 51 C5
Hildesheim D 51 A5
Hilgay GB 30 B4
Hillared S 40 B3
Hille D 51 A4
Hillegom NL 49 A5
Hillerød DK 41 D2
Hillerstorp S 40 B3
Hillesheim D 50 C2
Hillestad N 34 B2
Hillmersdorf D 52 B3
Hillsborough GB 19 B5
Hillswick GB 22 A7
Hilpoltstein D 62 A2
Hiltpoltstein D 62 A2
Hilvarenbeek NL 49 B6
Hilversum NL 49 A6
Himarë AL 15 R10
Himesháza H 74 B3
Himmelberg A 73 B4
Himmelpforten D 43 B6
Himód H 74 A2
Hinckley GB 30 B2
Hindås S 35 D4
Hindelang D 71 A5
Hindelbank CH 70 A2
Hinderavåg N 32 B2
Hindhead GB 31 C3
Hinjosa del Valle E 93 C4
Hinnerup DK 39 C3
Hinneryd S 40 C3
Hinojal E 93 B4
Hinojales E 99 B4
Hinojos E 99 B4
Hinojosa del Duque E 93 C5
Hinojosas de Calatrava E 100 A1
Hinterhornbach A 71 A5
Hinterriss A 71 A6
Hintersee A 63 C4
Hintersee D 45 B6
Hinterstoder A 63 C5
Hintertux A 72 A1
Hinterweidenthal D 60 A3
Hinwil CH 70 A3
Hippolytushoef NL 42 C1
Hirschaid D 62 A1
Hirschau D 62 A2
Hirschfeld D 52 B3
Hirschhorn D 61 A4
Hirsingue F 60 C3
Hirson F 59 A5
Hirtshals DK 38 B2
Hirzenhain D 51 C5
Hishult S 41 C3
Hitchin GB 31 C3
Hittarp S 41 C2
Hittisau A 71 A4
Hitzacker D 44 B3
Hjallerup DK 38 B3
Hjältevad S 40 B5
Hjärnarp S 41 C2
Hjartdal N 33 B5
Hjellestad N 32 A2
Hjelmeland N 32 B3
Hjerkinn N 2 E11
Hjerm DK 38 C1
Hjerpsted DK 39 D1
Hjerting DK 39 D1
Hjo S 35 C6
Hjordkær DK 39 D2
Hjørring DK 38 B3
Hjorted S 37 D3
Hjortkvarn S 37 C2
Hjortsberga S 40 C4
Hjukse N 33 B6
Hjuksebø N 33 B6
Hlinik nad Hronom. SK 65 B4
Hlinsko CZ 64 A1
Hlohovec SK 64 B3
Hluboká nad Vltavou CZ 63 A5
Hlučín CZ 64 A4
Hlukhiv UA 7 L23
Hlyboka UA 11 M19
Hlybokaye BY 7 J20
Hnězdné SK 65 A6
Hnilec SK 65 B5
Hnúšťa SK 65 B5
Hobol H 74 B2
Hobro DK 38 C2
Hobscheid L 60 A1
Hochdonn D 43 A6
Hochdorf CH 70 A3
Hochfelden F 60 B3
Hochspeyer D 60 A3
Höchst im Odenwald D 61 A5
Höchstadt, Bayern D 62 A1
Höchstädt, Bayern D 61 B6
Hochstenbach D 50 C3
Hockenheim D 61 A4
Hoddesdon GB 31 C3
Hodejov SK 65 B6
Hodenhagen D 43 C6
Hodkovice CZ 53 C5
Hódmezövásárhely H 75 B5
Hodnet GB 26 C3
Hodonín CZ 64 B3
Hodslavice CZ 64 A4
Hoedekenskerke NL 49 B4
Hoegaarden B 49 C5
Hoek van Holland NL 49 B5
Hoenderlo NL 50 A1
Hof D 52 C1
Hof N 34 B2
Hofbieber D 51 C5
Hoff GB 26 A3
Hofgeismar D 51 B5
Hofheim, Bayern D 51 C6
Hofheim, Hessen D 51 C4
Hofkirchen im Mühlkreis A 63 B4
Hofors S 36 A3
Höganäs S 41 C2
Högdal S 35 B3
Högfors S 36 B2
Högklint S 37 D5
Högsäter S 35 C4
Högsby S 40 B6
Högsjö S 37 B2
Hogstad S 37 C2
Hőgyész H 74 B3
Hohen Neuendorf D 45 C5
Hohenau A 64 B2
Hohenberg A 63 C6
Hohenbucko D 52 B3
Hohenburg D 62 A2
Hohenems A 71 A4
Hohenhameln D 51 A6
Hohenhausen D 51 A4
Hohenlinden D 62 B2
Hohenlockstedt D 43 B6
Hohenmölsen D 52 B2
Hohennauen D 44 C4
Hohenseeden D 52 A2
Hohentauern A 73 A4
Hohentengen D 61 C4
Hohenwepel D 51 B5
Hohenwestedt D 43 A6
Hohenwutzen D 45 C6
Hohenzieritz D 45 B5
Hohn D 43 A6
Hohne D 44 C2
Hohnstorf D 44 B2
Højer DK 39 E1
Højslev Stby DK 38 C2
Hok S 40 B4
Hohenkirchen D 43 B4
Hökerum S 35 D5
Hökhuvud S 36 A5
Hokksund N 33 B6
Hökön S 40 C4
Hola Pristan UA 11 N23
Holbæk, Aarhus Amt. DK 38 C3
Holbæk, Vestsjællands Amt. DK 39 D4
Holbeach GB 30 B4
Holdenstedt D 44 C2
Holdhus N 32 A2
Holdorf D 43 C5
Holeby DK 44 A3
Hølen N 34 B2
Holešov CZ 64 A3
Holguera E 93 B4
Holíč SK 64 B3
Holice CZ 53 C5
Holice SK 64 C3
Hollabrunn A 64 B2
Hollandstoun GB 23 B6
Høllen N 33 C4
Hollfeld D 52 D1
Hollstadt D 51 C6
Hollum NL 42 B2
Höllviksnäs S 41 D2
Holme-on-Spalding-Moor GB 27 B5
Holmedal N 34 B3
Holmegil N 34 B3
Holmes Chapel GB 26 B3
Holmestrand N 34 B2
Holmfirth GB 27 B4
Holmsbu N 34 B2
Holmsjö S 41 C5
Holmsund S 3 E17
Hölö S 37 B4
Holsbybrunn S 40 B5
Holsljunga S 40 B2
Holstebro DK 39 C1
Holsted DK 39 D1
Holsworthy GB 28 C3
Holt, Norfolk GB 30 B5
Holt, Wrexham GB 26 B3
Holt N 33 C5
Holten NL 50 A2
Holtwick D 50 A3
Holum N 33 C4
Holwerd NL 42 B2
Holycross IRL 21 B4
Holyhead GB 26 B1
Holýšov CZ 62 A4
Holywell GB 26 B2
Holywood GB 19 B6
Holzdorf D 52 B3
Holzhausen D 51 A4
Holzheim D 61 B6
Holzkirchen D 62 C2
Holzminden D 51 B5
Holzthaleben D 51 B6
Homberg, Hessen D 51 B5
Homberg, Hessen D 51 C5
Homburg D 60 A3
Hommelvik N 2 E12
Hommersåk N 32 C2
Hommokmegy H 75 B4
Homokszentgyörgy H 74 B2
Homrogd H 65 B6
Homyel BY 7 K22
Hondarribia E 89 A5
Hondón de los Frailes E 96 C2
Hondschoote F 48 C3
Hönebach D 51 C5
Hønefoss N 34 A2
Honfleur F 57 A6
Høng DK 39 D4
Honiton GB 29 C4
Hönningen D 50 C2
Honningsvåg N 2 A20
Hönö S 38 B4
Honrubia E 95 C4
Hontalbilla E 88 C2
Hontianske-Nemce SK 65 B4
Hontoria de la Cantera E 89 B3
Hontoria de Valdearados E 89 C3
Hontoria del Pinar E 89 C3
Hoofddorp NL 49 A5
Hoogerheide NL 49 B5
Hoogeveen NL 42 C3
Hoogezand-Sappemeer NL 42 B3
Hoogkarspel NL 42 C2
Hoogkerk NL 42 B3
Hoogstede D 42 C3
Hoogstraten B 49 B5
Hook GB 31 C3
Hooksiel D 43 B5
Höör S 41 D3
Hoorn NL 42 C2
Hope GB 26 B2
Hope under Dinmore GB 29 A5
Hopfgarten A 72 A2
Hopfgarten in Defereggen A 72 B2
Hopsten D 43 C4
Hoptrup DK 39 D2
Hora Svatého Sebestiána CZ 52 C3
Horaždóvice CZ 63 A4
Horb am Neckar D 61 B4
Horbelev DK 39 E5
Hørby DK 38 B3
Hörby S 41 D3
Horcajada de la Torre E 95 B4
Horcajo de los Montes E 94 C2
Horcajo de Santiago E 95 C3
Horcajo-Medianero E 94 B1
Horche E 95 B3
Horda S 40 B4
Hořesedly CZ 52 C3
Horezu RO 11 P19
Horgen CH 70 A3
Horgoš YU 75 B4
Hořice CZ 53 C5
Horjul SLO 73 B4
Horka D 53 B4
Hörken S 36 A1
Horki BY 7 J22
Hörle S 40 B4
Horn A 63 B6
Horn D 51 B4
Horn S 37 D2
Horna E 96 C1
Horná Mariková SK 64 A4
Horná Streda SK 64 B3
Horná Štrubna SK 65 B4
Horná Súča SK 64 B3
Hornachos E 93 C4
Hornachuelos E 99 B5
Hornanes N 32 B2
Hornbæk, Aarhus Amt. DK 38 C2
Hornbæk, Frederiksværk DK 41 C2
Hornberg D 61 B4
Hornburg D 51 A6
Horncastle GB 27 B5
Horndal S 36 A3
Horndean GB 31 D2
Horne, Fyns Amt. DK 39 D3
Horne, Ribe Amt. DK 39 D1
Hörnebo S 35 C6
Horneburg D 43 B6
Horní Bečva CZ 64 A4
Horní Benešov CZ 64 A3
Horní Cerekev CZ 63 A6
Horní Jiřetín CZ 52 C3
Horní Lomná CZ 65 A4
Horní Maršov CZ 53 C5
Horní Planá CZ 63 B5
Horní Slavkov CZ 52 C2
Horní Vltavice CZ 63 B4
Horning DK 39 C3
Hörningsholm S 37 B4
Hornnes N 33 C4
Horno D 53 B4
Hornos E 101 A3
Hornoy-le-Bourg F 58 A2
Hornsea GB 27 B5
Hornslet DK 39 C3
Hornstein A 64 C2
Hörnum D 39 E1
Hornum DK 38 C2
Horný Tisovník SK 65 B5
Horodenka UA 11 M19
Horodnya UA 11 L22
Horodok, Khmelnytskyy UA 11 M20
Horodok, Lviv UA 11 M18
Horodyshche UA 11 M22
Horokhiv UA 11 L19
Hořovice CZ 63 A4
Horred S 40 B2
Hörsching A 63 B5
Horsens DK 39 D2
Horsham GB 31 C3
Hørsholm DK 41 D2
Horslunde DK 39 E4
Horšovský Týn CZ 62 A3
Horst NL 50 B2
Horstel D 50 A3
Horsten D 43 B4
Horstmar D 50 A3
Hort H 65 C5
Horta P 87 C3
Horten N 34 B2
Hortezuela E 89 C4
Hortiguela E 89 B3
Hortobágy H 75 A6
Horton in Ribblesdale GB 26 A3
Hørve DK 39 D4
Hörvik S 41 C4
Horwich GB 26 B3
Hösbach D 51 C5
Hosena D 53 B4
Hosenfeld D 51 C5
Hosingen L 50 C2
Hospental CH 70 B3
Hospital IRL 20 B3
Hossegor F 76 C1
Hosszuhetény H 74 B3
Hostal de Ipiés E 90 A2
Hoštálkova CZ 64 A3
Hostalric E 91 B5
Hostens F 76 B2
Hostěradice CZ 64 B2
Hostinné CZ 53 C5
Hostomice CZ 63 A5
Hostouň CZ 62 A3
Hoting S 2 D15
Hotton B 49 C6
Houdain F 48 C3
Houdan F 58 B2
Houdelaincourt F 60 B1
Houeillès F 76 B3
Houffalize B 50 C1
Houghton-le-Spring GB 25 D6
Houlgate F 57 A5
Hounslow GB 31 C3
Hourtin F 66 C3
Hourtin-Plage F 66 C3
Houthalen B 49 B6
Houyet B 49 C5
Hov DK 39 D3
Hova S 35 C6
Høvåg N 33 C5
Hovden N 33 B4
Hove GB 31 D3
Hovedgård DK 39 D2
Hovelhof D 51 B4
Hoven DK 39 D1
Hovingham GB 27 A5
Hovmantorp S 40 C5
Hovsta S 36 B2
Howden GB 27 B5
Höxter D 51 B5
Hoya D 43 C6
Hoya de Santa Maria E 99 B4
Hoya-Gonzalo E 96 C1
Høyanger N 2 F10
Hoyerswerda D 53 B4
Høyjord N 34 B2
Hoylake GB 26 B2
Hoym D 52 B1
Hoyo de Manzanares E 94 B3
Hoyo de Pinares E 94 B2
Hoyocasero E 94 B2
Hoyos E 93 A4
Hoyos del Espino E 94 B1
Hrabušice SK 65 B6
Hradec Králové CZ 53 C5
Hradec nad Moravicí CZ 64 A3
Hrádek CZ 64 B2
Hrádek nad Nisou CZ 53 C4
Hradište SK 65 B4
Hranice, Severomoravský CZ 64 A3
Hranice, Západočeský CZ 52 C2
Hranovnica SK 65 B6
Hrasnica BIH 84 C3
Hrastnik SLO 73 B5
Hrebenka UA 7 L23
Hřensko CZ 53 C4
Hriňová SK 65 B5
Hrochov CZ 64 A2
Hrochův Tynec CZ 53 D5
Hrodna BY 6 K18
Hrodzyanka BY 7 K21
Hronov CZ 53 C6
Hronský Beňadik SK 65 B4
Hrotovice CZ 64 A2
Hrtkovci YU 85 B4
Hrušov SK 65 B5
Hrušovany nad Jevišovkou CZ 64 B2
Hřuštín SK 65 A5
Hrvaćani BIH 84 B2
Hrvace HR 83 C5
Hrymayliv UA 11 M20
Huben A 72 B2
Hückel-hoven D 50 B2
Hückeswagen D 50 B3
Hucknall GB 27 B4
Hucqueliers F 48 C2
Huddersfield GB 27 B4
Huddinge S 36 B4
Huddunge S 36 A3
Hude D 43 B5
Hudiksvall S 2 F15
Huélago E 100 B2
Huélamo E 95 B5
Huelgoat F 56 B2
Huelma E 100 B2
Huelva E 99 B4
Huéneja E 100 B3
Huércal de Almeria E 101 C3
Huércal-Overa E 101 B4
Huerta de Abajo E 89 B3
Huerta de Valdecarabanos E 95 C3
Huerta del Rey E 89 C3
Huertahernando E 95 B4
Huesa E 100 B2
Huesca E 90 A2
Huéscar E 101 B3
Huete E 95 B4
Huétor Tájar E 100 B1
Hüfingen D 61 C4
Hufthamar N 32 A2
Hugh Town GB 28 D1
Huglfing D 62 C2
Huissen NL 50 B1
Huittinen FIN 3 F18
Huizen NL 49 A6
Hulín CZ 64 A3
Hüls D 50 B2
Hulsig DK 38 B3
Hulst NL 49 B5
Hult S 40 B5
Hulterstad S 40 C6
Hultsfred S 40 B5
Humanes E 95 B3
Humberston GB 27 B5
Humble DK 39 E3
Humenné SK 10 M17
Humilladero E 100 B1
Humlebæk DK 41 D2
Humlum DK 38 C1
Hummelsta S 36 B3
Humpolec CZ 63 A6
Humshaugh GB 25 C5
Hundested DK 39 D4
Hundvåg N 32 B2
Hunedoara RO 11 P18
Hünfeld D 51 C5
Hungen D 51 C4
Hungerford GB 31 C2
Hunnebostrand S 35 C3
Hunstanton GB 30 B4
Huntingdon GB 30 B3
Huntley GB 29 B5
Huntly GB 23 D6
Hünxe D 50 B2
Hurbanovo SK 64 C4
Hürbel D 61 B5
Hurdal N 34 A3
Hurezani RO 11 P18
Hurlford GB 24 C3
Hurstbourne Tarrant GB 31 C2
Hurstpierpoint GB 31 D3
Hürth D 50 C2
Hurup DK 38 C1
Husbands Bosworth GB 30 B2
Husby D 39 E2
Husby DK 39 C1
Huşi RO 11 N21
Husina BIH 84 B3
Husinec CZ 63 A4
Husinish GB 22 D1
Huskvarna S 40 B4
Husnes N 32 B2
Hüsten D 50 B3
Hustopeče CZ 64 B2
Hustopeče nad Bečvou CZ 64 A3
Husum D 43 A6
Huta PL 46 C2
Hutovo BIH 84 D2
Hüttenberg A 73 B4
Hüttlingen D 61 B6
Huttoft GB 27 B6
Hutton Cranswick GB 27 B5
Hüttschlag A 72 A3
Huttwil CH 70 A2
Huy B 49 C6
Hval N 34 A2
Hvåle N 33 A6
Hvaler N 35 B3
Hvalpsund DK 38 C2
Hvar HR 83 C5
Hvarnes N 33 B6
Hvidbjerg DK 38 C1
Hvide Sande DK 39 D1
Hvittingfoss N 33 B7
Hybe SK 65 A5
Hycklinge S 37 D2
Hyères F 79 C5
Hyères Plage F 79 C5
Hylestad N 33 B4
Hylke DK 39 D2
Hyllstofta S 41 C3
Hyltebruk S 40 B3
Hynish GB 24 B1
Hynnekleiv N 33 C5
Hythe, Hampshire GB 31 D2
Hythe, Kent GB 31 C5
Hyvinkää FIN 3 F19

I

Iam RO 85 A6
Iaşi RO 11 N20
Ibahernando E 93 B5
Ibarranguelua E 89 A4
Ibbenbüren D 50 A3
Ibeas de Juarros E 89 B3
Ibi E 96 C2
Ibros E 100 A2
Ibstock GB 27 C4
Ichenhausen D 61 B6
Ichnya UA 7 L23
Ichtegem B 49 B4
Ichtershausen D 51 C6
Idanha-a-Novo P 93 B3
Idar-Oberstein D 60 A3
Idd N 35 B3
Idiazábal E 80 B1
Idkerberget S 36 A2
Idön S 36 A5
Idre S 2 F13
Idrija SLO 73 C4
Idritsa RUS 7 H21
Idstein D 50 C4
Idvor YU 75 C5
Iecca Mare RO 75 C5
Ielsi I 103 B4
Ieper B 48 C3
Ierápetra GR 16 U19
Ierissós GR 15 R18
Iesi I 82 C2
Ig SLO 73 C4
Igal H 74 B2
Igea E 89 B4
Igea Marina I 82 B1
Igelfors S 37 C2
Igersheim D 61 A5
Iggesund S 2 F15
Iglesias E 88 B3
Iglésias I 110 D1
Igls A 71 A6
Igneada TR 16 R21
Igny-Comblizy F 59 A4
Igorre E 89 A4
Igoumenitsa GR 15 S17
Igries E 90 A2
Igualada E 91 B4
Igüeña E 86 B4
Iguerande F 68 B4
Iharosberény H 74 B2
Ihl'any SK 65 A6
Ihlienworth D 43 B5
Ihringen D 60 B3
Ihrlerstein D 62 B2
Ii FIN 3 D19
Iisalmi FIN 3 E20
IJmuiden NL 42 C1
IJsselmuiden NL 42 C2
IJzendijke NL 49 B4
Ikast DK 39 C2
Ikervár H 74 A1
il Castagno I 81 C4
Ilandža YU 75 C5
Ilanz CH 71 B4
Ilava SK 64 B4
Iława PL 47 B5
Ilche E 90 B3
Ilchester GB 29 C5
Ilfracombe GB 28 B3
Ílhavo P 92 A2
Ilidža BIH 84 C3
Ilijaš BIH 84 C3
Ilirska Bistrica SLO 73 C4
Ilkeston GB 27 C4
Ilkley GB 27 B4
Illana E 95 B4
Illano E 86 A4
Illar E 101 C3
Illas E 88 A1
Illats F 76 B2
Ille-sur-Têt F 91 A5
Illertissen D 61 B6
Illescas E 94 B3
Illfurth F 60 C3
Illichivsk UA 11 N22
Illiers-Combray F 58 B2
Illkirch-Graffenstaden F 60 B3
Illmersdorf D 52 B3
Illmitz A 64 C2
Íllora E 100 B2
Illueca E 89 C5
Ilmajoki FIN 3 E18
Ilmenau D 51 C6
Ilminster GB 29 C5
Ilok HR 75 C4
Ilomantsi FIN 3 E22
Iłow PL 47 C6
Iłowa PL 53 B5
Iłowo-Osada PL 47 B6
Ilsenburg D 51 B6
Ilshofen D 61 A5
Ilz A 73 A5
Iłża PL 55 B6
Imatra FIN 3 F21
Imielin PL 55 C4
Imingen N 33 A5
Immeln S 41 C4
Immenhausen D 51 B5
Immenstadt D 71 A5
Immingham GB 27 B5
Ímola I 81 B5
Imon E 95 A4
Imotski HR 84 C2
Impéria I 80 C2
Imphy F 68 B3
Imsland N 32 B2
Imst A 71 A5
Inagh IRL 20 B2
Inari FIN 3 B20
Inca, Mallorca E 97
Inchnadamph GB 22 C4
Incinillas E 89 B3
Indija YU 85 A5
Inegöl TR 16 R21
Inerthal CH 70 A3
Infiesto E 88 A1
Ingatorp S 40 B5
Ingedal N 34 B3
Ingelheim D 50 D4
Ingelmunster B 49 C4
Ingelstad S 40 C4
Ingleton GB 26 A3
Ingolfsland N 33 B5
Ingolstadt D 62 B2
Ingrandes, Maine-et-Loire F 66 A4
Ingrandes, Vienne F 67 B5
Ingwiller F 60 B3
Inhulec UA 11 N23
Iniesta E 95 C5
Inishannon IRL 20 C3
Inishcrone IRL 18 B2
Inke H 74 B2
Innellan GB 24 C3
Innerleithen GB 25 C4
Innermessan GB 24 D3
Innertkirchen CH 70 B3
Innervillgraten A 72 B2
Innsbruck A 71 A6
Inowłódz PL 55 B5
Inowrocław PL 47 C4
Ins CH 70 A2
Insch GB 23 D6
Ińsko PL 46 B1
Instow GB 28 B3
Interlaken CH 70 B2
Intragna CH 70 B3
Introbio I 71 C4
Inveralochy GB 23 D7
Inveran GB 23 D4
Inveran IRL 20 A2
Inveraray GB 24 B2
Inverbervie GB 25 B5
Invergarry GB 22 D4
Invergordon GB 23 D4
Invergowrie GB 25 B4
Inverkeilor GB 25 B5
Inverkeithing GB 25 B4
Invermoriston GB 22 D4
Inverness GB 23 D4
Inveruno I 70 C3
Inverurie GB 23 D6
Ioánnina GR 15 S17
Iolanda di Savoia I 81 B5
Ion Corvin RO 11 P20
Ióppolo I 106 C2
İpsala TR 16 R20
Ipswich GB 30 B5
Iráklion GR 16 U19
Irdning A 73 A4
Iregszemcse H 74 B3
Irgoli I 110 C2
Irig YU 85 A4
Ironbridge GB 26 C3

Irpin UA 11 L22
Irrel D 60 A2
Irsina I 104 B3
Irthlingborough GB 30 B3
Iruela E 87 B4
Irún E 89 A5
Irurita E 76 C1
Irurzun E 89 B5
Irvine GB 24 C3
Irvinestown GB 19 B4
Is-sur-Tille F 69 A5
Isaba E 76 D2
Isabela E 100 A2
Isaszeg H 75 A4
Isbister GB 22 A7
Iscar E 88 C2
Ischgl A 71 A5
Íschia I 103 C3
Ischia di Castro I 102 A1
Ischitella I 104 A2
Isdes F 58 C3
Ise N 34 B3
Iselle I 70 B3
Iseltwald CH 70 B2
Isen D 62 B3
Isenbüttel D 44 C2
Iseo I 71 C5
Iserlohn D 50 B3
Isérnia I 103 B4
Isigny-sur-Mer F 57 A4
Ísili I 110 D2
Isla Canela E 98 B3
Isla Cristina E 98 B3
Islares E 89 A3
Isle Of Whithorn GB 24 D3
Isleham GB 30 B4
Ismaning D 62 B2
Isna P 92 B3
Isny D 61 C6
Isoba E 88 A1
Isola F 79 B6
Isola del Gran Sasso d'Itália I 103 A3
Ísola del Liri I 103 B3
Ísola della Scala I 71 C6
Isola delle Fémmine I 108 A2
Ísola di Capo Rizzuto I 107 C4
Isona E 91 A4
Ispagnac F 78 B2
Isparta TR 16 T22
Isperikh BG 16 Q20
Íspica I 109 C3
Isselburg D 50 B2
Issigeac F 77 B3
Issogne I 70 C2
Issoire F 68 C3
Issoncourt F 59 B6
Issoudun F 68 B2
Issum D 50 B2
Issy-l'Evêque F 68 B3
Istán E 100 C1
İstanbul TR 16 R21
Istebna PL 65 A4
Ístia d'Ombrone I 81 D5
Istiaia GR 15 S18
Istok YU 85 D5
Istres, *Bouches du Rhône* F 78 C3
Istvándi H 74 B2
Itoiz E 76 D1
Itrabo E 100 C2
Itri I 103 B3
Ittireddu I 110 C1
Íttiri I 110 C1
Itzehoe D 43 B6
Ivalo FIN 3 B20
Iván H 74 A1
Ivanava BY 7 K19
Ivančice CZ 64 A2
Ivančna Gorica SLO 73 C4
Iváncsa H 74 A3
Ivanec HR 73 B6
Ivanić Grad HR 73 C6
Ivanjica YU 85 C5
Ivanjska BIH 84 B2
Ivanka SK 64 B4
Ivankovo HR 74 C3
Ivano-Frankivsk UA 11 M19
Ivanovice na Hane CZ 64 A3
Ivanska HR 74 C1
Ivatsevichy BY 7 K19
Ivoz Ramet B 49 C6
Ivrea I 70 C2
Ivry-en-Montagne F 69 A4
Ivry-la-Bataille F 58 B2
Ivybridge GB 28 C4
Iwaniska PL 55 C6
Iwiny PL 53 B5
Iwuy F 49 C4
Ixworth GB 30 B4
Izarra E 89 B4
Izbica Kujawska PL 47 C4
Izbište YU 85 A6
Izeda P 87 C4
Izegem B 49 C4
Izernore F 69 B5
Izmayil UA 11 P21
İzmir TR 16 S20
Iznájar E 100 B1
Iznalloz E 100 B2
Iznatoraf E 100 A2
İznik TR 16 R21
Izola SLO 72 C3
Izsák H 75 B4
Izsófalva H 65 B6
Izyaslav UA 11 L20

J

Jabalquinto E 100 A2
Jablanac HR 83 B3
Jablanica BIH 84 C2
Jablonec nad Jizerou CZ 53 C5
Jablonec nad Nisou CZ 53 C5
Jablonica SK 64 B3
Jablonka PL 65 A5
Jabłonna PL 55 A5
Jablonné nad Orlicí CZ 54 C1
Jablonne Podještědí CZ 53 C4
Jablonov nad Turňou SK 65 B6
Jabłonowo Pomorskie PL 47 B5
Jablúnka CZ 64 A3
Jablunkov CZ 65 A4
Jabučje YU 85 B5
Jabugo E 99 B4
Jabuka, *Srbija* YU 85 C4
Jabuka, *Vojvodina* YU 85 B5
Jabukovac HR 73 C6
Jaca E 90 A2
Jáchymov CZ 52 C2
Jacobidrebber D 43 C5
Jade D 43 B5
Jadraque E 95 B4
Jægerspris DK 39 D4
Jaén E 100 B2
Jagare BIH 84 B2
Jagel D 43 A6
Jagenbach A 63 B6
Jagodina YU 85 C6
Jagodnjak HR 74 C3
Jagodzin PL 53 B5
Jagstheim D 61 A6
Jagstzell D 61 A6
Jahodna SK 64 B3
Jajce BIH 84 B2
Ják H 74 A1
Jakabszálbs H 75 B4
Jaklovce SK 65 B6
Jakovlje HR 73 C5
Jakšic HR 74 C2
Jakubany SK 65 A6
Jalance E 96 B1
Jalasjärvi FIN 3 E18
Jalhay B 50 C1
Jaligny-sur-Besbre F 68 B3
Jallais F 66 A4
Jalón E 96 C2
Jâlons F 59 B5
Jamena YU 84 B4
Jamilena E 100 B2
Jämjö S 41 C5
Jamnička Kiselica HR 73 C5
Jamno PL 46 A2
Jamoigne B 59 A6
Jämsä FIN 3 F19
Jämshög S 41 C4
Janakkala FIN 3 F19
Jandelsbrunn D 63 B4
Jänickendorf D 52 A3
Janikowo PL 47 C4
Janja BIH 85 B4
Janjina HR 84 D2
Janki, *Łódzkie* PL 55 B4
Janki, *Mazowieckie* PL 55 A5
Jankov CZ 63 A5
Jankowo Dolne PL 46 C3
Jánoshalma H 75 B4
Jánosháza H 74 A2
Jánoshida H 75 A5
Jánossomorja H 64 C3
Janovice nad Uhlavou CZ 63 A4
Janów PL 55 C4
Janowiec Wielkopolski PL 46 C3
Janowo PL 47 B6
Janville F 58 B2
Janzé F 57 C4
Jarabá SK 65 B5
Jaraczewo PL 54 B2
Jarafuel E 96 B1
Jaraicejo E 93 B5
Jaraíz de la Vera E 93 A5
Jarak YU 85 B4
Jarandilla de la Vera E 93 A5
Jaray E 89 C4
Jard-sur-Mer F 66 B3
Jaren N 34 A2
Jargeau F 58 C3
Jarkovac YU 75 C5
Järlåsa S 36 B4
Jarmen D 45 B5
Järna S 37 B4
Jarnac F 67 C4
Järnforsen S 40 B5
Jarny F 60 A1
Jarocin PL 54 B2
Jaroměř CZ 53 C5
Jaroměřice nad Rokytnou CZ 64 A1
Jaroslav CZ 53 C6
Jaroslavice CZ 64 B2
Jarosław PL 11 L18
Jarosławiec PL 46 A2
Jarošov nad Nežarkou CZ 63 A6
Järpås S 35 C4
Järpen S 2 E13
Jarrow GB 25 D6
Järvenpää FIN 3 F19
Jarvorník CZ 54 C1
Jarzé F 67 A4
Jaša Tomic YU 75 C5
Jasenak HR 73 C5
Jasenica BIH 83 B5
Jasenice HR 83 B4
Jasenovac HR 74 C1
Jasenovo, *Srbija* YU 85 C4
Jasenovo, *Vojvodina* YU 85 B6
Jasień PL 53 B5
Jasienica PL 53 B4
Jasika YU 85 C6
Jasło PL 10 M17
Jasov SK 65 B6
Jásova SK 65 C4
Jasseron F 69 B5
Jastarnia PL 47 A4
Jastrebarsko HR 73 C5
Jastrowie PL 46 B2
Jastrzębia-Góra PL 47 A4
Jastrzębie Zdrój PL 65 A4
Jászals-Lószentgyörgy H 75 A5
Jászapáti H 75 A5
Jászárokszállás H 65 C5
Jászberény H 75 A4
Jászdózsa H 65 C6
Jászfényszaru H 65 C5
Jászjakóhalma H 75 A5
Jászkarajenő H 75 A5
Jászkisér H 75 A5
Jászladány H 75 A5
Jászszentlászló H 75 B4
Jásztelek H 75 A5
Játar E 100 C2
Jatznick D 45 B5
Jaun CH 70 B2
Jausiers F 79 B5
Jávea E 96 C3
Jävenitz D 44 C3
Javerlhac F 67 C5
Javier E 90 A1
Javorani BIH 84 B2
Javorina SK 65 A6
Javron F 57 B5
Jawor PL 53 B6
Jaworzno PL 55 C4
Jaworzyna Śl. PL 54 C1
Jayena E 100 C2
Jażow PL 53 B4
Jebel RO 75 C6
Jebjerg DK 38 C2
Jedburgh GB 25 C5
Jedlinsk PL 55 B6
Jedlnia PL 55 B6
Jedlnia Letnisko PL 55 B6
Jedovnice CZ 64 A2
Jędrychow PL 47 B5
Jędrzejów PL 55 C5
Jedwabno PL 47 B6
Jegłownik PL 47 A5
Jegun F 77 C3
Jēkabpils LV 7 H19
Jektevik N 32 B2
Jelakci YU 85 C5
Jelcz-Laskowice PL 54 B2
Jelenec SK 64 B4
Jelenia Góra PL 53 C5
Jelgava LV 6 H18
Jelka SK 64 B3
Jelling DK 39 D2
Jels DK 39 D2
Jelsa HR 83 C5
Jelsa N 32 B3
Jelšava SK 65 B6
Jemgum D 43 B4
Jemnice CZ 63 A6
Jena D 52 C1
Jenaz CH 71 B4
Jenbach A 72 A1
Jenikow PL 45 B7
Jennersdorf A 73 B6
Jenny S 37 D3
Jerchel D 44 C3
Jeres del Marquesado E 100 B2
Jerez de la Frontera E 99 C4
Jerez de los Caballeros E 99 A4
Jerica E 96 B2
Jerichow D 44 C4
Jerka PL 54 A1
Jermenovci YU 75 C6
Jerslev DK 38 B3
Jerte E 93 A5
Jerup DK 38 B3
Jerxheim D 51 A6
Jerzmanowice PL 55 C4
Jerzu I 110 D2
Jerzwałd PL 47 B5
Jesberg D 51 C5
Jesenice, *Středočeský* CZ 52 C3
Jesenice, *Středočeský* CZ 53 D4
Jesenice SLO 73 B4
Jesenik CZ 54 C2
Jesenké SK 65 B6
Jésolo I 72 C2
Jessen D 52 B2
Jessheim N 34 A3
Jessnitz D 52 B2
Jesteburg D 44 B1
Jeumont F 49 C5
Jeven-stedt D 43 A6
Jever D 43 B4
Jevičko CZ 64 A2
Jevišovice CZ 64 B1
Jevnaker N 34 A2
Jezerane HR 83 A4
Jezero BIH 84 B2
Jezero HR 83 A4
Jeziorany PL 47 B6
Jezów PL 55 B4
Jičín CZ 53 C5
Jičíněves CZ 53 C5
Jihlava CZ 63 A6
Jijona E 96 C2
Jilemnice CZ 53 C5
Jilové CZ 53 C4
Jilové u Prahy CZ 63 A5
Jimbolia RO 75 C5
Jimena E 100 B2
Jimena de la Frontera E 99 C5
Jimera de Libar E 99 C5
Jimramov CZ 64 A2
Jince CZ 63 A4
Jindřichovice CZ 52 C2
Jindřichův Hradec CZ 63 A6
Jirkov CZ 52 C3
Jistebnice CZ 63 A5
Joachimsthal D 45 C5
João da Loura P 98 A2
Jobbágyi H 65 C5
Jochberg A 72 A2
Jódar E 100 B2
Jodoigne B 49 C5
Joensuu FIN 3 E21
Jœuf F 60 A1
Jõgeva EST 7 G20
Johann-georgen-stadt D 52 C2
Johannishus S 41 C5
Johanniskirchen D 62 B3
Johansfors S 40 C5
John o'Groats GB 23 C5
Johnshaven GB 25 B5
Johnstone GB 24 C3
Johnstown IRL 21 B4
Jõhvi EST 7 G20
Joigny F 59 C4
Joinville F 59 B6
Jokkmokk S 3 C16
Jöllenbeck D 51 A4
Jönåker S 37 C3
Jonava LT 6 J19
Jonchery-sur-Vesle F 59 A4
Jondal N 32 A3
Jondalen N 33 B6
Joniškis LT 6 H18
Jönköping S 40 B4
Jønnbu N 33 B6
Jonsered S 35 D4
Jonstorp S 41 C2
Jonzac F 67 C4
Jorba E 91 B4
Jordanów PL 65 A5
Jordanów Ślaski PL 54 C1
Jordanowo PL 53 A5
Jordbro S 36 B5
Jördenstorf D 45 B4
Jordøse DK 39 D3
Jork D 43 B6
Jörn S 3 D17
Jørpeland N 32 B3
Jorquera E 96 B1
Jošan HR 83 B4
Jošanička Banja YU 85 C5
Jošavka BIH 84 B2
Josipdol HR 73 C5
Josipovac HR 74 C3
Jössefors S 34 B4
Josselin F 56 C3
Jøsvafő H 65 B6
Jouarre F 59 B4
Joué-lès-Tours F 67 A5
Joué-sur-Erdre F 66 A3
Joure NL 42 C2
Joutseno FIN 3 F21
Joux-la-Ville F 59 C4
Jouy F 58 B2
Jouy-le-Châtel F 59 B4
Jouy-le-Potier F 58 C2
Joyeuse F 78 B3
Joze F 68 C3
Józefów PL 55 A6
Juan-les-Pins F 79 C6
Juankoski FIN 3 E21
Jübek D 43 A6
Jubera E 89 B4
Jubrique E 99 C5
Jüchsen D 51 C6
Judaberg N 32 B2
Judenburg A 73 A4
Juelsminde DK 39 D3
Jugon-les-Lacs F 57 B3
Juillac F 67 C6
Juillan F 76 C3
Juist D 43 B4
Julianadorp NL 42 C1
Julianstown IRL 19 C5
Jülich D 50 C2
Jullouville F 57 B4
Jumeaux F 68 C3
Jumièges F 58 A1
Jumilhac-le-Grand F 67 C6
Jumilla E 101 A4
Juncosa E 90 B3
Juneda E 90 B3
Jung S 35 C5
Jungingen D 61 B5
Junglinster L 60 A2
Juniville F 59 A5
Junosuando S 3 C18
Junqueira P 87 C3
Juprelle B 49 C6
Jurata PL 47 A4
Jurbarkas LT 6 J18
Jurjevo HR 83 B3
Jūrmala LV 6 H18
Juromenha P 92 C3
Jursla S 37 C3
Jussac F 77 B5
Jussey F 60 C1
Jussy F 59 A4
Juta H 74 B2
Jüterbog D 52 B3
Juuka FIN 3 E21
Juvigny-le-Terte F 57 B4
Juvigny-sous-Andaine F 57 B5
Juzennecourt F 59 B5
Jyderup DK 39 D4
Jyväskylä FIN 3 E19

K

Kaamanen FIN 3 B20
Kaarssen D 44 B3
Kaatscheuvel NL 49 B6
Kaba H 75 A6
Kåbdalis S 3 C16
Kačarevo YU 85 B5
Kačikol YU 85 D6
Kács H 65 C6
Kadan CZ 52 C3
Kadarkút H 74 B2
Kaduy RUS 7 G25
Kågeröd S 41 D3
Kahl D 51 C5
Kahla D 52 C1
Kainach bei Voitsberg A 73 A5
Kaindorf A 73 A5
Kaisersesch D 50 C3
Kaiserslautern D 60 A3
Kaisheim D 62 B1
Kajaani FIN 3 D20
Kajárpéc H 74 A2
Kajdacs H 74 B3
Kakanj BIH 84 B3
Kakasd H 74 B3
Kakolewo PL 54 B1
Kál H 65 C6
Kalabáka GR 15 S17
Kalače YU 85 D5
Kalajoki FIN 3 D18
Kalámai GR 15 T18
Kalbe D 44 C3
Kalce SLO 73 C4
Káld H 74 A2
Kale TR 16 T21
Kalefeld D 51 B6
Kalenić YU 85 C5
Kalesija BIH 84 B3
Kalety PL 54 C3
Kalevala RUS 3 D22
Kalhovd N 33 A5
Kalí HR 83 B4
Kaliningrad RUS 47 A6
Kalinkavichy BY 7 K21
Kalinovac HR 74 B2
Kalinovik BIH 84 C3
Kalinovo SK 65 B5
Kaliska, *Pomorskie* PL 47 A4
Kaliska, *Pomorskie* PL 47 B4
Kalisko PL 55 B4
Kalisz PL 54 B3
Kalisz Pomorski PL 46 B1
Kalix S 3 D18
Kalkan TR 16 T21
Kalkar D 50 B2
Kall D 50 C2
Källby S 35 C5
Kållered S 35 D4
Kållerstad S 40 B3
Kallinge S 41 C5
Kallmünz D 62 A2
Källvik S 37 C4
Kalmar S 40 C6
Kalmthout B 49 B5
Kalná SK 65 B4
Kalocsa H 75 B3
Káloz H 74 B3
Kals A 72 B2
Kalsdorf A 73 B5
Kaltbrunn CH 70 A4
Kaltenbach A 72 A1
Kaltenkirchen D 44 B1
Kaltennordheim D 51 C6
Kaluga RUS 7 J25
Kalundborg DK 39 D4
Kalush UA 11 M19
Kałuszyn PL 55 A6
Kalvehave DK 39 D5
Kalwang A 73 A4
Kalwaria-Zebrzydowska PL 65 A5
Kalyazin RUS 7 H25
Kam H 74 A1
Kamen D 50 B3
Kamenice CZ 64 A1
Kamenice nad Lipou CZ 63 A6
Kameničná SK 64 C4
Kamenný Most SK 65 C4
Kamenny Ujezd CZ 63 B5
Kamenska HR 74 C2
Kamensko HR 84 C1
Kamenz D 53 B4
Kamičak BIH 83 B5
Kamień PL 55 B5
Kamień Krajeński PL 46 B3
Kamień Pomorski PL 45 B6
Kamieniec Zabk PL 54 C1
Kamienka SK 65 A6
Kamienna Góra PL 53 C6
Kamieńsk PL 55 B4
Kaminka UA 11 M23
Kamnik SLO 73 B4
Kamp-Lintfort D 50 B2
Kampen NL 42 C2
Kampinos PL 55 A5
Kampor HR 83 B3
Kamyanets-Podil's'kyy UA 11 M20
Kamyanka-Buz'ka UA 11 L19
Kamýk n Vltavou CZ 63 A5
Kanal SLO 72 B3
Kandalaksha RUS 3 C23
Kandel D 61 A4
Kandern D 60 C3
Kandersteg CH 70 B2
Kandira TR 16 R22
Kandyty PL 47 A6
Kanfanar HR 82 A2
Kangasala FIN 3 F19
Kaniów PL 53 B4
Kanjiža YU 75 B5
Kankaanpää FIN 3 F18
Kannus FIN 3 E18
Kanturk IRL 20 B3
Kapellen A 63 C6
Kapellen B 49 B5
Kapellskär S 36 B6
Kapfenberg A 73 A5
Kapfenstein A 73 B5
Kaplice CZ 63 B5
Kapljuh BIH 83 B5
Kápolna H 65 C6
Kápolnásnyék H 74 A3
Kaposfő H 74 B2
Kaposfüred H 74 B2
Kaposszekcsö H 74 B3
Kaposvár H 74 B2
Kappel D 60 B3
Kappeln D 44 A1
Kappelshamn S 37 D5
Kappl A 71 A5
Kaprun A 72 A2
Kaptol HR 74 C2
Kapuvár H 64 C3
Karabiğa TR 16 R20
Karaburun TR 16 S20
Karacabey TR 16 R21
Karacasu TR 16 T21
Karachev RUS 7 K24
Karácsond H 65 C6
Karád H 74 B2
Karan YU 85 C4
Karancslapujto H 65 B5
Karasjok N 3 B19
Karasu TR 16 R22
Karbenning S 36 A3
Kårberg S 37 C1
Karby D 44 A1
Karby DK 38 C1
Karby S 36 B5
Karcag H 75 A5
Karczew PL 55 A6
Karczów PL 54 C2
Karczowiska PL 53 B6
Kardašova Rečice CZ 63 A5
Karditsa GR 15 S17
Kärdla EST 6 G18
Kardoskút H 75 B5
Kargowa PL 53 A5
Karise DK 41 D2
Káristos GR 16 S19
Karkal TR 16 R21
Karkkila FIN 3 F19
Karl Liebknecht RUS 7 L24
Karlholmsbruk S 36 A4
Karlino PL 46 A1
Karlobag HR 83 B4
Karlovac HR 73 C5
Karlovčic YU 85 B5
Karlovice CZ 54 C2
Karlovo BG 16 Q19
Karlovy Vary CZ 52 C2
Karłowice PL 54 C2
Karlsborg S 37 C1
Karlshamn S 41 C4
Karlshöfen D 43 B6
Karlshus N 34 B2
Karlskoga S 36 B1
Karlskrona S 41 C5
Karlsrud N 33 A5
Karlsruhe D 61 A4
Karlstad S 34 B5
Karlstadt D 51 D5
Karlstetten A 63 B6
Karlstift A 63 B5
Karmacs H 74 B2
Kärna S 35 D3
Karnobat BG 16 Q20
Karojba HR 72 C3
Karow D 44 B4
Karpacz PL 53 C5
Kärrbo S 36 B3
Karrebaeksminde DK 39 D4
Karsin PL 46 B3
Kårsta S 36 B5
Karstädt D 44 B3
Kartitsch A 72 B2
Kartuzy PL 47 A4
Karup DK 39 C2
Karviná CZ 65 A4
Kås DK 38 B2
Kaş TR 16 T21
Kašava CZ 64 A3
Kasejovice CZ 63 A4
Kashin RUS 7 H25
Kašina HR 73 C6
Kasina-Wielka PL 65 A6
Kaskinen FIN 3 E17
Kašperské Hory CZ 63 A4
Kassel D 51 B5
Kastav HR 73 C4
Kaštel-Stari HR 83 C5
Kaštel Zegarski HR 83 B4
Kastellaun D 50 C3
Kastélli GR 16 U18
Kasterlee B 49 B5
Kastl D 62 A2
Kastlösa S 40 C6
Kastorf D 44 B2
Kastoria GR 15 R17
Kastsyukovichy BY 7 K23
Kaszaper H 75 B5
Katerbow D 45 C4
Katerini GR 15 R18
Katlenburg-Lindau D 51 B6
Katovice CZ 63 A4
Katowice PL 55 C4
Katrineholm S 37 C3
Kattarp S 41 C2
Kattilstorp S 35 C5
Katwijk NL 49 A5
Kąty Wrocławskie PL 54 B1
Katymár H 75 B4
Katzenelnbogen D 50 C3
Katzhütte D 52 C1
Kaub D 50 C3
Kaufbeuren D 62 C1
Kauhajoki FIN 3 E18
Kauhava FIN 3 E18
Kaulsdorf D 52 C1
Kaunas LT 6 J18
Kaupanger N 2 F10
Kautokeino N 3 B18
Kautzen A 63 B6
Kavajë AL 15 R16
Kavála GR 16 R19
Kavarna BG 16 Q21
Kävlinge S 41 D3
Kawcze PL 46 A2
Kaxholmen S 40 B4
Kaysersberg F 60 B3
Kazanlŭk BG 16 Q19
Kazár H 65 B5
Kazimierza Wielka PL 55 C5
Kazincbarcika H 65 B6
Kaźmierz PL 46 C2
Kcynia PL 46 B3
Kdyně CZ 62 A4
Keadow IRL 18 B3
Keady GB 19 B5
Kecel H 75 B4
Kecskemét H 75 B4
Kėdainiai LT 6 J18
Kędzierzyn-Koźle PL 54 C3
Keel IRL 18 C1
Keenagh IRL 19 C4
Keerbergen B 49 B5
Kegworth GB 27 C4
Kehl D 60 B3
Kehrigk D 53 A3
Keighley GB 27 B4
Keila EST 6 G19
Keillmore GB 24 C2
Keiss GB 23 C5
Keith GB 23 D6
Kelberg D 50 C2
Kelbra D 52 B1
Kelč CZ 64 A3
Kelchsau A 72 A2
Keld GB 26 A3
Kelebia H 75 B4
Kelemér H 65 B6
Kelheim D 62 B2
Kell D 60 A2
Kellas GB 23 D5
Kellinghusen D 43 B6
Kells GB 19 B5
Kells IRL 19 C5
Kelmis B 50 C2
Kelsall GB 26 B3
Kelso GB 25 C5
Kelsterbach D 51 C4
Keltneyburn GB 24 B3
Kematen A 71 A6
Kemberg D 52 B2
Kemer TR 16 T22
Kemeten A 73 A6
Kemi FIN 3 D19
Kemijärvi FIN 3 C20
Kemnath D 62 A2
Kemnay GB 23 D6
Kemnitz, *Brandenburg* D 52 A2
Kemnitz, *Mecklenburg-Vorpommern* D 45 A5
Kempen D 50 B2
Kempsey GB 29 A5
Kempten D 61 C6
Kemptthal CH 70 A3
Kendal GB 26 A3
Kenderes H 75 A5
Kengyel H 75 A5
Kenilworth GB 30 B2
Kenmare IRL 20 C2
Kenmore GB 25 B4
Kennacraig GB 24 C2
Kenyeri H 74 A2
Kenzingen D 60 B3
Kępice PL 46 A2
Kępno PL 54 B3
Kerava FIN 3 F19
Kerecsend H 65 C6
Kerekegyhaza H 75 B4
Kerepestarcsa H 75 A4
Kérien F 56 B2
Kerkafalva H 73 B6
Kerken D 50 B2
Kerkira GR 15 S16
Kerkrade NL 50 C2
Kerlouan F 56 B1
Kernascléden F 56 B2
Kernhof A 63 C6
Kerns CH 70 B3
Kerpen D 50 C2
Kerrysdale GB 22 D3
Kerta H 74 A2
Kerteminde DK 39 D3
Kerzers CH 70 B2
Keşan TR 16 R20
Kesgrave GB 30 B5
Kesh GB 19 B4
Kesselfall A 72 A2
Kestenga RUS 3 D22
Keswick GB 26 A2
Keszthely H 74 B2
Kétegyháza H 75 B6
Kéthely H 74 B2
Kętrzyn PL 6 J17
Kettering GB 30 B3
Kettlewell GB 26 A3
Kęty PL 65 A5
Ketzin D 45 C4
Keuruu FIN 3 E19
Kevelaer D 50 B2
Kevermes H 75 B6
Kevi YU 75 C4
Keyingham GB 27 B5
Keynsham GB 29 B5
Kežmarok SK 65 A6
Khalkis GR 15 S18
Khaniá GR 16 U19
Kharkiv UA 7 L25
Kharmanli BG 16 R19
Khaskovo BG 16 R19
Kherson UA 11 N23
Khimki RUS 7 J25
Khios GR 16 S20
Khmelnik UA 11 M20
Khmelnytskyy UA 11 M20
Khodoriv UA 11 M19
Kholm RUS 7 H22
Khóra Sfakion GR 16 U19
Khorol UA 11 M23
Khotyn UA 11 M20
Khoyniki BY 11 L21
Khust UA 11 M18
Khvoynaya RUS 7 G24
Kınık TR 16 S20
Kırka TR 16 S22
Kırklareli TR 16 R20
Kızılhisar TR 16 T21
Kiáton GR 15 T18
Kibæk DK 39 C1
Kidderminster GB 26 C3
Kidlington GB 31 C2
Kidsgrove GB 26 B3
Kidwelly GB 28 B3
Kiefersfelden D 62 C3
Kiel D 44 A2
Kielce PL 55 C5
Kiełczygłów PL 55 B4
Kielder GB 25 C5
Kiełpino PL 47 A4
Kielpiny PL 47 B5
Kiernozia PL 55 A4
Kierspe D 50 B3
Kietrz PL 54 C3
Kietz D 45 C6
Kiezmark PL 47 A4
Kifino Selo BIH 84 C3
Kije PL 55 C5
Kijevo HR 83 C5
Kikinda YU 75 C5
Kil N 33 C6
Kil, *Örebro* S 36 B2
Kil, *Värmland* S 34 B5
Kila S 34 B4
Kilb Rabenstein A 63 B6
Kilbaha IRL 20 B2
Kilbeggan IRL 21 A4
Kilberry GB 24 C2
Kilbirnie GB 24 C3
Kilchattan GB 24 C2
Kilchoan GB 24 B1
Kilcock IRL 21 A5
Kilconnell IRL 20 A3
Kilcormac IRL 21 A4
Kilcreggan GB 24 C3
Kilcullen IRL 21 A5
Kilcurry IRL 19 B5
Kildare IRL 21 A5
Kildinstroy RUS 3 B23
Kildonan GB 23 C5
Kildorrery IRL 20 B3
Kilegrend N 33 B5
Kilen N 33 B5
Kilgarvan IRL 20 C2
Kilimli TR 16 R22
Kiliya UA 11 P21
Kilkee IRL 20 B2
Kilkeel GB 19 B5
Kilkelly IRL 18 C3
Kilkenny IRL 21 B4
Kilkieran IRL 20 A2
Kilkinlea IRL 20 B2
Kilkis GR 15 R18
Killadysert IRL 20 B2
Killala IRL 18 B2
Killaloe IRL 20 B3
Killarney IRL 20 B2
Killashandra IRL 19 B4
Killashee IRL 19 C4
Killearn GB 24 B3
Killeberg S 40 C4
Killeigh IRL 21 A4
Killenaule IRL 21 B4
Killimor IRL 20 A3
Killin GB 24 B3
Killinaboy IRL 20 B2
Killinick IRL 21 B5
Killorglin IRL 20 B2
Killucan IRL 21 A4
Killybegs IRL 18 B3
Killyleagh GB 19 B6
Kilmacrenan IRL 19 A4
Kilmacthomas IRL 21 B4
Kilmaine IRL 18 C2
Kilmallock IRL 20 B3
Kilmarnock GB 24 C3
Kilmartin GB 24 B2
Kilmaurs GB 24 C3
Kilmeadan IRL 21 B4
Kilmeedy IRL 20 B3
Kilmelford GB 24 B2
Kilmore Quay IRL 21 B5
Kilmuir GB 23 D4
Kilnaleck IRL 19 C4
Kilninver GB 24 B2
Kilrea GB 19 B5
Kilrush IRL 20 B2
Kilsmo S 37 B2
Kilsyth GB 24 C3
Kiltoom IRL 20 A3
Kilwinning GB 24 C3
Kimasozero RUS 3 D22
Kimi GR 16 S19
Kimovsk RUS 7 J25
Kimratshofen D 61 C6
Kimry RUS 7 H25
Kimstad S 37 C2
Kinbrace GB 23 C5
Kincardine GB 25 B4
Kincraig GB 23 D5
Kindberg A 73 A5
Kindelbruck D 52 B1
King's Lynn GB 30 B4
Kingarrow IRL 18 B3
Kingisepp RUS 7 G21
Kingsbridge GB 28 C4
Kingsclere GB 31 C2
Kingscourt IRL 19 C5
Kingsteignton GB 29 C4
Kingston, *Greater London* GB 31 C3
Kingston, *Moray* GB 23 D5
Kingston Bagpuize GB 31 C2
Kingston upon Hull GB 27 B5
Kingswear GB 29 C4
Kingswood GB 29 B5
Kington GB 29 A4
Kingussie GB 23 D4
Kinloch, *Highland* GB 22 C4
Kinloch, *Highland* GB 22 D2
Kinloch Rannoch GB 24 B3
Kinlochbervie GB 22 C3
Kinlochewe GB 22 D3
Kinlochleven GB 24 B3
Kinlochmoidart GB 24 B2
Kinloss GB 23 D5
Kinlough IRL 18 B3
Kinna S 40 B2
Kinnared S 40 B3
Kinnarp S 35 D5
Kinne-Kleva S 35 C5
Kinnegad IRL 21 A4
Kinnitty IRL 21 A4
Kinrooi B 50 B1
Kinross GB 25 B4
Kinsale IRL 20 C3
Kintarvie GB 22 C2
Kintore GB 23 D6
Kinvarra IRL 20 A3
Kiparissia GR 15 T17
Kipfenburg D 62 B2
Kippen GB 24 B3
Kirberg D 50 C4
Kirchbach in Steiermark A 73 B5
Kirchberg CH 70 A2
Kirchberg, *Baden-Württemberg* D 61 A5
Kirchberg, *Rheinland-Pfalz* D 60 A3
Kirchberg am Wechsel A 64 C1
Kirchberg an der Pielach A 63 B6
Kirchberg im Tirol A 72 A2
Kirchbichl A 72 A2
Kirchdorf, *Bayern* D 63 B4
Kirchdorf, *Mecklenburg-Vorpommern* D 44 B3

Kirchdorf, *Niedersachsen* D 43 C5
Kirchdorf an der Krems A 63 C5
Kirchdorf in Tirol A 72 A2
Kirchenlamitz D 52 C1
Kirchenthumbach D 62 A2
Kirchhain D 51 C4
Kirchheim, *Baden-Württemberg* D 61 B5
Kirchheim, *Bayern* D 61 B6
Kirchheim, *Hessen* D 51 C5
Kirchheim-bolanden D 61 A4
Kirchhundem D 50 B4
Kirchlintein D 43 C6
Kirchschlag A 73 A6
Kirchweidach D 62 B3
Kirchzarten D 60 C3
Kircubbin GB 19 B6
Kirillov RUS 7 G26
Kirishi RUS 7 G23
Kirk Michael GB 26 A1
Kirkbean GB 25 D4
Kirkbride GB 25 D4
Kirkby GB 26 B3
Kirkby Lonsdale GB 26 A3
Kirkby Malzeard GB 27 A4
Kirkby Stephen GB 26 A3
Kirkbymoorside GB 27 A5
Kirkcaldy GB 25 B4
Kirkcolm GB 24 D2
Kirkconnel GB 24 C3
Kirkcowan GB 24 D3
Kirkcudbright GB 24 D3
Kirkehamn N 32 C3
Kirkelly IRL 18 C3
Kirkenær N 34 A4
Kirkenes N 3 B22
Kirkham GB 26 B3
Kirkintilloch GB 24 C3
Kirkkonummi FIN 3 F19
Kirkmichael GB 25 B4
Kirkoswald GB 24 C3
Kirkpatrick Fleming GB 25 C4
Kirkton of Glenisla GB 25 B4
Kirkwall GB 23 C6
Kirkwhelpington GB 25 C6
Kirn D 60 A3
Kirov RUS 7 J24
Kirovohrad UA 11 M23
Kirovsk RUS 3 C23
Kirriemuir GB 25 B5
Kirton GB 30 B3
Kirton in Lindsey GB 27 B5
Kirtorf D 51 C5
Kiruna S 3 C17
Kisa S 37 D2
Kisač YU 75 C4
Kisbér H 74 A3
Kiseljak BIH 84 C3
Kisielice PL 47 B5
Kisköre H 75 A5
Kiskőrös H 75 B4
Kiskunfélegyháza H 75 B4
Kiskunhalas H 75 B4
Kiskunlacháza H 75 A3
Kiskunmajsa H 75 B4
Kisláng H 74 B3
Kisslegg D 61 C5
Kissolt H 75 B4
Kist D 61 A5
Kistanje HR 83 C4
Kistelek H 75 B4
Kisterenye H 65 B5
Kisújszállás H 75 A5
Kisvárda H 11 M18
Kisvejke H 74 B3
Kiszkowo PL 46 C3
Kiszombor H 75 B5
Kitee FIN 3 E22
Kithira GR 15 T18
Kittendorf D 45 B4
Kittilä FIN 3 C19
Kittsee A 64 B3
Kitzbühel A 72 A2
Kitzingen D 61 A6
Kiuruvesi FIN 3 E20
Kivertsi UA 11 L19
Kivik S 41 D4
Kiwity PL 47 A6
Kjellerup DK 39 C2
Kjøllefjord N 2 A20
Kjopmannskjaer N 34 B2
Kl'ačno SK 65 B4
Kladanj BIH 84 B3
Kläden D 44 C3
Klädesholmen S 35 D3
Kladnica YU 85 C5
Kladnice HR 83 C5
Kladno CZ 53 C4
Kladruby CZ 62 A3
Klagenfurt A 73 B4
Klågerup S 41 D3
Klagstorp S 41 D3
Klaipėda LT 6 J17
Klaistow D 52 A2
Klana HR 73 C4
Klanac HR 83 B4
Klanjec HR 73 B5
Klardorf D 62 A3
Klarup DK 38 B3
Klašnice BIH 84 B2
Klässbol S 34 B4
Klášterec nad Ohří CZ 52 C3
Klášťor pod Znievom SK 65 B4
Klatovy CZ 63 A4
Klaus an der Pyhrnbahn A 63 C5
Klazienaveen NL 42 C3
Kłecko PL 46 C3
Kleczew PL 47 C4
Klein Plasten D 45 B4
Klein Sankt Paul A 73 B4
Kleinsölk A 72 A3
Kleinzell A 64 C1
Klejtrup DK 38 C2
Klek YU 75 C5
Klemensker DK 41 D4
Klenak YU 85 B4
Klenci pod Cerchovem CZ 62 A3
Klenica PL 53 B5
Klenje YU 85 B4
Klenovec SK 65 B5
Klenovica HR 83 A3
Klenovnik HR 73 B6
Kleppe N 32 C2
Kleptow D 45 B5
Kletnya RUS 7 K23
Kleve D 50 B2
Klevshult S 40 B4
Klewki PL 47 B6
Kličevac YU 85 B6
Kliening A 73 B4
Klietz D 44 C4
Klikuszowa PL 65 A5
Klimkovice CZ 64 A4
Klimontów PL 55 C6
Klimovichi BY 7 K22
Klin RUS 7 H25
Klinča Sela HR 73 C5
Klingenbach A 64 C2
Klingenberg D 61 A5
Klingenmunster D 61 A4
Klingenthal D 52 C2
Klintehamn S 6 H16
Klintsy RUS 7 K23
Kliny PL 55 B5
Klipley DK 39 E2
Klippan S 41 C3
Klis HR 83 C5
Klitmøller DK 38 B1
Klixbüll D 39 E1
Kljajićevo YU 75 C4
Ključ BIH 83 B5
Klobouky CZ 64 B2
Kłobuck PL 54 C3
Kłodawa, *Lubuskie* PL 45 C7
Kłodawa, *Wielkopolskie* PL 54 A3
Kłodzko PL 54 C1
Kløfta N 34 A3
Klokkarvik N 32 A2
Klokkerholm DK 38 B3
Klokočov SK 65 A4
Kłomnice PL 55 C4
Klonowa PL 54 B3
Kloosterzande NL 49 B4
Kłopot PL 53 A4
Kloštar Ivanić HR 73 C6
Kloster D 45 A5
Kloster DK 39 C1
Klösterle A 71 A5
Klostermansfeld D 52 B1
Klosterneuburg A 64 B2
Klosters CH 71 B4
Kloten CH 70 A3
Klötze D 44 C3
Kluczbork PL 54 C3
Kluczewo PL 46 B2
Kluisbergen B 49 C4
Klundert NL 49 B5
Klutz D 44 B3
Klwów PL 55 B5
Klyetsk BY 7 K20
Knaben N 32 C3
Knapstad N 34 B3
Knäred S 40 C3
Knaresborough GB 27 A4
Knebworth GB 31 C3
Knesebeck D 44 C2
Knesselare B 49 B4
Knežak SLO 73 C4
Kneževi Vinogradi HR 74 C3
Kneževo HR 74 C3
Knić YU 85 C5
Knighton GB 29 A4
Knin HR 83 B5
Knislinge S 41 C4
Knittelfeld A 73 A4
Knivsta S 36 B4
Knock IRL 18 C3
Knocktopher IRL 21 B4
Knokke-Heist B 49 B4
Knowle GB 30 B2
Knurów PL 54 C3
Knutby S 36 B5
Knutsford GB 26 B3
Kobarid SLO 72 B3
København DK 41 D2
Kobenz A 73 A4
Kobersdorf A 64 C2
Kobiernice PL 65 A5
Kobierzyce PL 54 C1
Kobilje SLO 73 B6
Kobiór PL 54 C3
Koblenz CH 61 C4
Koblenz D 50 C3
Kobryn BY 6 K19
Kobylanka PL 45 B6
Kobylin PL 54 B2
Kobyłka PL 55 A6
Kobylniki PL 47 C6
Kocaeli (İzmit) TR 16 R21
Kočani MK 15 R18
Koceljevo YU 85 B4
Kočerin BIH 84 C2
Kočevje SLO 73 C4
Kočevska Reka SLO 73 C4
Kochel am see D 62 C2
Kocs H 64 C4
Kocsér H 75 A4
Kocsola H 74 B3
Koczala PL 46 B3
Kodal N 34 B2
Kodersdorf D 53 B4
Kodrab PL 55 B4
Koekelare B 48 B3
Köflach A 73 A5
Køge DK 41 D2
Kohlberg D 62 A3
Kohtla-Järve EST 7 G20
Köinge S 40 B2
Kojetín CZ 64 A3
Kokava SK 65 B5
Kokkola FIN 3 E18
Kokori BIH 84 B2
Kokoski PL 47 A4
Koksijde B 48 B3
Kola BIH 84 B2
Kola RUS 3 B23
Köla S 34 B4
Kołacin PL 55 B4
Kolari FIN 3 C18
Kolárovo SK 64 C3
Kolašin YU 85 D4
Kolbäck S 36 B3
Kolbacz PL 45 B6
Kolbermoor D 62 C3
Kołbiel PL 55 A6
Kolbnitz A 72 B3
Kolbotn N 34 B2
Kolby Kås DK 39 D3
Kolczewo PL 45 B6
Kolczyglowy PL 46 A3
Kolding DK 39 D2
Kölesd H 74 B3
Kolín CZ 53 C5
Kolind DK 39 C3
Kolinec CZ 63 A4
Koljane HR 83 C5
Kølkær DK 39 C2
Kölleda D 52 B1
Kollum NL 42 B3
Köln D 50 C2
Koło PL 54 A3
Kołobrzeg PL 46 A1
Kolochau D 52 B3
Kolomyya UA 11 M19
Kolonowskie PL 54 C3
Koloveč CZ 62 A4
Kolpino RUS 7 G22
Kolpny RUS 7 K25
Kolrep D 44 B4
Kolsko PL 53 B5
Kolsva S 36 B2
Kolta SK 65 B4
Kolunič BIH 83 B5
Koluszki PL 55 B4
Kolut YU 75 C3
Kølvrå DK 39 C2
Komarica BIH 84 B2
Komárno SK 64 C4
Komárom H 64 C4
Komen SLO 72 C3
Komin HR 84 C2
Komiža HR 83 C5
Komjáti H 65 B6
Komjatice SK 64 B4
Komletinci HR 84 A3
Komló, *Baranya* H 74 B3
Kömlo, *Heves* H 65 C6
Komoča SK 64 C4
Komorniki PL 54 A1
Komorzno PL 54 B3
Komotini GR 16 R19
Konak YU 75 C5
Konakovo RUS 7 H25
Konary PL 55 B6
Konarzyny PL 46 B3
Kondorfa H 74 B1
Kondoros H 75 B5
Kondrovo RUS 7 J24
Kong DK 39 D4
Konga S 40 C5
Kongerslev DK 38 C3
Kongsberg N 33 B6
Kongshamn N 33 C5
Kongsmark DK 39 D1
Kongsvinger N 34 A4
Konice CZ 64 A2
Konie PL 55 B5
Koniecpol PL 55 C4
Königs Wusterhausen D 52 A3
Königsberg D 51 C6
Königsbronn D 61 B6
Königsbrück D 53 B3
Königsbrunn D 62 B1
Königsdorf D 62 C2
Königsee D 52 C1
Königshorst D 45 C4
Königslutter D 51 A6
Königssee D 62 C3
Königstein, *Hessen* D 51 C4
Königstein, *Sachsen* D 53 C4
Königstetten A 64 B2
Königswartha D 53 B4
Königswiesen A 63 B5
Königswinter D 50 C3
Konin PL 54 A3
Koniz CH 70 B2
Konjevići BIH 85 B4
Konjevrate HR 83 C5
Konjic BIH 84 C2
Konjščina HR 73 B6
Könnern D 52 B1
Konnerud N 34 B2
Konopiska PL 54 C3
Konotop PL 53 B5
Konotop UA 7 L23
Końskie PL 55 B5
Konsmo N 33 C4
Konstancin-Jeziorna PL 55 A6
Konstantynów Łódźki PL 55 B4
Konstanz D 61 C5
Kontich B 49 B5
Kontiolahti FIN 3 E21
Konz D 60 A2
Kopčany SK 64 B3
Koper SLO 72 C3
Kopervik N 32 B2
Kópháza H 64 C2
Kopice PL 54 C2
Kopidlno CZ 53 C5
Köping S 36 B2
Köpingebro S 41 D3
Koppang N 2 F12
Kopparberg S 36 B1
Koppom S 34 B4
Koprivna BIH 84 B3
Koprivnica HR 74 B1
Kopřivnice CZ 64 A4
Koprzywnica PL 55 C6
Kopstal L 60 A2
Kopychintsi UA 11 M19
Kopytkowo PL 47 B4
Korbach D 51 B4
Korbecke D 50 B4
Korçë AL 15 R17
Korčula HR 84 D2
Korczyców PL 53 A4
Korenevo RUS 7 L24
Korenita YU 85 B4
Korets UA 11 L20
Korfantów PL 54 C2
Korgen N 2 C13
Korinth DK 39 D3
Kórinthos GR 15 T18
Korita BIH 83 B5
Korita HR 84 D2
Korkuteli TR 16 T22
Körmend H 74 A1
Korne PL 46 A3
Korneuburg A 64 B2
Kornevo RUS 47 A6
Kórnik PL 54 A2
Kornsjø N 35 C3
Környe H 74 A3
Koromačno HR 82 B3
Koronowo PL 46 B3
Körösladány H 75 B6
Köröstarcsa H 75 B6
Korosten UA 11 L21
Korostyshev UA 11 L21
Korsberga, *Jönköping* S 40 B5
Korsberga, *Skaraborg* S 35 C6
Korshavn N 35 B2
Korsnäs S 36 A2
Korsør DK 39 D4
Korsun Shevchenkovskiy UA 11 M22
Kortrijk B 49 C4
Koryčany CZ 64 A3
Koryukovka UA 7 L23
Korzenśko PL 54 B1
Korzybie PL 46 A2
Kosanica YU 85 C4
Kosaya Gora RUS 7 J25
Kösching D 62 B2
Kościan PL 54 A1
Kościelec PL 54 A3
Kościerzyna PL 46 A3
Koserow D 45 A5
Košetice CZ 63 A6
Košice SK 10 M17
Kosjerić YU 85 C4
Koška HR 74 C3
Kosovska Mitrovica YU 85 D5
Kosta S 40 C5
Kostajnica HR 74 C1
Kostajnik YU 85 B4
Kostanjevica SLO 73 C5
Kostelec na Hané CZ 64 A3
Kostelec nad Černými Lesy CZ 53 C4
Kostice CZ 53 C3
Kostkowo PL 47 A4
Kostojevići YU 85 B4
Kostolac YU 85 B6
Kostopil UA 11 L20
Kostów PL 54 B3
Kostrzyn, *Lubuskie* PL 45 C6
Kostrzyn, *Wielkopolskie* PL 46 C3
Koszalin PL 46 A2
Koszęcin PL 54 C3
Kőszeg H 73 A6
Koszwaly PL 47 A4
Koszyce PL 55 C5
Kot SLO 73 C5
Kötelek H 75 A5
Köthen D 52 B1
Kotka FIN 3 F20
Kotomierz PL 47 B4
Kotor YU 15 Q16
Kotor Varoš BIH 84 B2
Kotoriba HR 74 B1
Kotorsko BIH 84 B3
Kotovsk UA 11 N21
Kotraža YU 85 C5
Kötschach A 72 B2
Kötzting D 62 A3
Koudum NL 42 C2
Kouřim CZ 53 C4
Kout na Šumave CZ 62 A4
Kouvola FIN 3 F20
Kovačevac YU 85 B5
Kovačica YU 85 A5
Kovdor RUS 3 C22
Kovel' UA 11 L19
Kovilj YU 75 C5
Kovin YU 85 B5
Kovren YU 85 C4
Kowal PL 47 C5
Kowalewo Pomorskie PL 47 B4
Kowalów PL 45 C6
Kowary PL 53 C5
Köyceğiz TR 16 T21
Kozani GR 15 R17
Kozarac BIH 84 B1
Kozarac HR 73 C5
Kozárovce SK 65 B4
Kozelets UA 11 L22
Kozelsk RUS 7 J24
Kozica HR 84 C2
Koziegłowy PL 55 C4
Kozienice PL 55 B6
Kozina SLO 72 C3
Kozje SLO 73 B5
Kozlu TR 16 R22
Kozluk BIH 85 B4
Koźmin PL 54 B2
Koźminek PL 54 B3
Kozolupy CZ 63 A4
Kożuchów PL 53 B5
Kožuhe BIH 84 B3
Kozyatyn UA 11 M21
Krackow D 45 B6
Krąg PL 46 A2
Kragenæs DK 39 E4
Kragerø N 33 C6
Kragi PL 46 B2
Kragujevac YU 85 B5
Kraiburg D 62 B3
Krajenka PL 46 B2
Krajišnik YU 75 C5
Krajková CZ 52 C2
Krajné SK 64 B3
Krajnik Dolny PL 45 B6
Krakača BIH 83 A4
Kraków PL 55 C4
Krakow am See D 44 B4
Králiky CZ 54 C1
Kraljevica HR 73 C4
Kraljevo YU 85 C5
Kral'ov Brod SK 64 B3
Kral'ovany SK 65 A5
Kralovice CZ 52 D3
Kralupy nad Vltavou CZ 53 C4
Králův Dvůr CZ 63 A5
Kramfors S 2 E15
Kramsach A 72 A1
Kramsk PL 54 A3
Kråmvik N 33 B5
Kranenburg D 50 B2
Kranichfeld D 52 C1
Kranidhion GR 15 T18
Kranj SLO 73 B4
Kranjska Gora SLO 72 B3
Krapanj HR 83 C4
Krapina HR 73 B5
Krapje HR 74 C1
Krapkowice PL 54 C2
Kraselov CZ 63 A4
Krašić HR 73 C5
Kräslava LV 7 J20
Kraslice CZ 52 C2
Krasna PL 55 B5
Krasna Lipa CZ 53 C4
Kraśnik PL 11 L18
Krašnja SLO 73 B4
Krásno SK 65 A4
Krasno Polje HR 83 B4
Krásnohorské Podhradie SK 65 B6
Krasnokutsk UA 7 L24
Krasnozavodsk RUS 7 H26
Krasnystaw PL 11 L18
Krasnyy RUS 7 J22
Krasnyy Kholm RUS 7 G25
Krasocin PL 55 C5
Kraszewice PL 54 B3
Kraszkowice PL 54 B3
Kraubath A 73 A4
Krausnick D 53 A3
Krautheim D 61 A5
Kravaře, *Severočeský* CZ 53 C4
Kraváre, *Severomoravský* CZ 64 A4
Kravarsko HR 73 C6
Kraznějov CZ 63 A4
Krčedin YU 85 A5
Krefeld D 50 B2
Krembz D 44 B3
Kremenchuk UA 11 M23
Kremenets UA 11 L19
Kremmen D 45 C5
Kremna YU 85 C4
Kremnica SK 65 B4
Krempe D 43 B6
Krems A 63 B6
Kremsbrücke A 72 B3
Kremsmünster A 63 B5
Křemže CZ 63 B5
Křenov CZ 64 A2
Krepa PL 54 B3
Krępsko PL 46 B2
Kreševo BIH 84 C3
Kressbronn D 61 C5
Kretinga LT 6 J17
Krettsy RUS 7 G23
Kreuth D 62 C2
Kreuzau D 50 C2
Kreuzlingen CH 61 C5
Kreuztal D 50 C3
Krewelin D 45 C5
Krezluk BIH 84 B2
Krieglach A 73 A5
Kriegsfeld D 60 A3
Kriens CH 70 A3
Krimml A 72 A2
Krimpen aan de IJssel NL 49 B5
Křinec CZ 53 C5
Kristdala S 40 B6
Kristiansand N 33 C5
Kristianstad S 41 C4
Kristiansund N 2 E10
Kristiinankaupunki FIN 3 E17
Kristinehamn S 34 B6
Kriváň SK 65 B5
Križ HR 74 C1
Křižanov CZ 64 A2
Križevci HR 74 B1
Krk HR 83 A3
Krka SLO 73 C4
Krnjača YU 85 B5
Krnjak HR 73 C5
Krnjeuša BIH 83 B5
Krnjevo YU 85 B6
Krnov CZ 54 C2
Krobia PL 54 B1
Kroczyce PL 55 C4
Krøderen N 33 A6
Krokek S 37 C3
Krokom S 2 E14
Krokowa PL 47 A4
Krokstad-elva N 33 B6
Kroksund N 34 B3
Krolevets UA 7 L23
Kroměříž CZ 64 A3
Krommenie NL 42 C1
Krompachy SK 65 B6
Kromy RUS 7 K24
Kronach D 52 C1
Kronshagen D 44 A2
Kronshtadt RUS 7 G21
Kröpelin D 44 A3
Kropp D 43 A6
Kroppenstedt D 52 B1
Kropstädt D 52 B2
Krościenko nad Dunajcem PL 65 A6
Kröslin D 45 A5
Krośnice PL 54 B2
Krośniewice PL 55 A4
Krosno PL 10 M17
Krosno Odrzańskie PL 53 A5
Krostitz D 52 B2
Krotoszyn PL 54 B2
Krottendorf A 73 A5
Krouna CZ 64 A2
Krowiarki PL 54 C3
Kršan HR 73 C4
Krško SLO 73 C5
Krstac YU 84 C3
Krstur YU 75 B5
Křtiny CZ 64 A2
Kruft D 50 C3
Kruishoutem B 49 C4
Krulyewshchyna BY 7 J20
Krumbach A 73 A6
Krumbach D 61 B6
Krün D 71 A6
Krupá CZ 53 C3
Krupa na Vrbasu BIH 84 B2
Krupanj YU 85 B4
Krupina SK 65 B5
Krupka CZ 53 C3
Krupki BY 7 J21
Kruså DK 39 E2
Krušćica BIH 84 B2
Kruševac YU 85 C6
Kruszwica PL 47 C4
Kruszyn PL 47 C5
Krychaw BY 7 K22
Krynica PL 65 A6
Krynica Morska PL 47 A5
Krzęcin PL 46 B1
Krzelów PL 54 B1
Krzepice PL 54 C3
Krzepielów PL 53 B6
Krzeszowice PL 55 C4
Krzeszyce PL 45 C7
Krzynowlaga Mała PL 47 B6
Krzywiń PL 54 B1
Krzyż Wielkopolski PL 46 C2
Krzyżanowice PL 64 A4
Krzyżowa PL 65 A5
Ksiaz Wielkopolski, *Małopolskie* PL 55 C5
Książ Wielkopolski, *Wielkopolskie* PL 54 A2
Ktębowiec PL 46 B2
Kübekháza H 75 B5
Küblis CH 71 B4
Kuchary PL 54 B2
Kuchl A 62 C4
Kucice PL 47 C6
Kuciste HR 84 D2
Kučište YU 85 D5
Kucura YU 75 C4
Kuczbork-Osada PL 47 B6
Kudowa-Zdrój PL 53 C6
Kufstein A 62 C3
Kuggeboda S 41 C5
Kühbach D 62 B2
Kuhmo FIN 3 D21
Kuhmoinen FIN 3 F19
Kuhnsdorf A 73 B4
Kuhstedt D 43 B5
Kuinre NL 42 C2
Kuivastu EST 6 G18
Kukës AL 15 Q17
Kuklin PL 47 B6
Kukljica HR 83 B4
Kukujevci YU 85 A4
Kula TR 16 S21
Kula, *Srbija* YU 85 B6
Kula, *Vojvodina* YU 75 C4
Kuldīga LV 6 H17
Kulen Vakuf BIH 83 B5
Kulina BIH 84 B3
Kulmain D 62 A2
Kulmbach D 52 C1
Kumane YU 75 C5
Kumanovo MK 15 Q17
Kumla S 36 B2
Kumlakyrkby S 36 B3
Kumluca TR 16 T22
Kumrovec HR 73 B5
Kunadacs H 75 B4
Kunágota H 75 B6
Kunbaja H 75 B4
Kunda EST 7 G20
Kundl A 72 A1
Kunfehértó H 75 B4
Kungälv S 35 D3
Kungs-Husby S 36 B4
Kungsängen S 36 B4
Kungsäter S 40 B2
Kungsbacka S 38 B5
Kungsgården S 36 A3
Kungshamn S 35 C3
Kungsör S 36 B3
Kunhegyes H 75 A5
Kunmadaras H 75 A5
Kunovice CZ 64 A3
Kunów PL 55 C6
Kunowo PL 54 B2
Kunštát CZ 64 A2
Kunszállás H 75 B4
Kunszentmárton H 75 B5
Kunszentmiklós H 75 A4
Kunžak CZ 63 A6
Künzelsau D 61 A5
Kuolajärvi RUS 3 C21
Kuopio FIN 3 E20
Kup H 74 A2
Kup PL 54 C2
Kupci YU 85 C6
Kupferzell D 61 A5
Kupinec HR 73 C5
Kupinečki Kraljevac HR 73 C5
Kupinovo YU 85 B5
Kupirovo HR 83 B5
Kupjak HR 73 C4
Kuppenheim D 61 B4
Kupres BIH 84 C2
Küps D 52 C1
Kurd H 74 B3
Kŭrdzhali BG 16 R19
Kuressaare EST 6 G18
Kurikka FIN 3 E18
Kuřim CZ 64 A2
Kurki PL 47 B6
Kurort Oberwiesenthal D 52 C2
Kurort Schmalkalden D 51 C6
Kurort Stolberg D 51 B6
Kurort Wippra D 52 B1
Kurów PL 11 L18
Kurowice PL 55 B4
Kursk RUS 7 L25
Kuršumlija YU 85 C6
Kuršumlijska Banja YU 85 C6
Kürten D 50 B3
Kurzelów PL 55 C4
Kusadak YU 85 B5
Kuşadası TR 16 T20
Kusel D 60 A3
Kusey D 44 C3
Küsnacht CH 70 A3
Kütahya TR 16 S22
Kutenholz D 43 B6
Kutina HR 74 C1
Kutjevo HR 74 C2
Kutná Hora CZ 53 D5
Kutno PL 55 A4
Küttingen CH 70 A3
Kúty SK 64 B3
Kuusamo FIN 3 D21
Kuusankoski FIN 3 F20
Kuvshinovo RUS 7 H24
Kuzmin YU 85 A4
Kuźnia Raciborska PL 54 C3
Kuźnica Czarnkowska PL 46 C2
Kuźnica Żelichowska PL 46 C2
Kværndrup DK 39 D3
Kvänum S 35 C5
Kvås N 33 C4
Kvasice CZ 64 A3
Kvernaland N 32 C2
Kvibille S 40 C2
Kvicksund S 36 B3
Kvidinge S 41 C3
Kvikne N 2 E12
Kvilda CZ 63 A4
Kville S 35 C3
Kvillsfors S 40 B5
Kvinesdal N 32 C3
Kvinlog N 32 C3
Kvinnherad N 32 B3
Kvissel DK 38 B3
Kviteseid N 33 B5
Kvitsøy N 32 B2
Kwakowo PL 46 A3
Kwidzyn PL 47 B4
Kwilcz PL 46 C2
Kyjov CZ 64 D3
Kyle of Lochalsh GB 22 D3
Kyleakin GB 22 D3
Kylerhea GB 22 D3
Kylestrome GB 22 C3
Kyllburg D 50 C2
Kynšperk nad Ohří CZ 52 C2
Kyritz D 44 C4
Kyrksæterøra S 35 C3
Kyrkhult S 41 C4
Kysucké Nové Mesto SK 65 A4
Kyustendil BG 15 Q18
Kyyiv UA 11 L22
Kyyjärvi FIN 3 E19

L

La Adrada E 94 B2
La Alameda E 100 A2
La Alberca E 93 A4
La Alberca de Záncara E 95 C4
La Albergueria de Argañán E 93 A4
La Albuera E 93 C4
La Aldea del Portillo del Busto E 89 B3
La Algaba E 99 B4
La Aliseda de Tormes E 94 B1
La Almarcha E 95 C4
La Almolda E 90 B2
La Almunia de Doña Godina E 89 C5
La Antillas E 98 B3
La Arena E 86 A4
La Aulaga E 99 B4
La Balme-de-Sillingy F 69 C6
La Bañeza E 88 B1
La Barca de la Florida E 99 C5
La Barre-de-Monts F 66 B2
La Barre-en-Ouche F 58 B1
La Barrosa E 99 C4
La Barthe-de-Neste F 77 C3
La Bassée F 48 C3
La Bastide-de-Sèrou F 77 C4
La Bastide-des-Jourdans F 79 C4
La Bastide-Puylaurent F 78 B2
La Bathie F 69 C6
La Baule-Escoublac F 66 A2
La Bazoche-Gouet F 58 B1
La Bégude-de-Mazenc F 78 B3
La Bernerie-en-Retz F 66 A2
La Bisbal d'Empordà E 91 B6
La Boissière F 57 A6
La Bourboule F 68 C2
La Bóveda de Toro E 88 C1
La Brède F 76 B2
La Bresse F 60 B2
La Bridoire F 69 C5
La Brillanne F 79 C4
La Bruffière F 66 A3
La Bussière F 58 C3
La Caillère F 66 B4
La Caletta I 110 C2
La Calmette F 78 C3
La Calzada de Oropesa E 94 C1
La Campana E 99 B5
La Cañada E 94 B2
La Canourgue F 78 B2
La Capelle F 49 D4
La Cardanchosa E 99 A5
La Caridad E 86 A4
La Carlota E 100 B1
La Carolina E 100 A2
La Cava E 90 C3
La Cavalerie F 78 B2
La Celle-en-Moravan F 69 A4
La Celle-St. Avant F 67 A5
La Cerca E 89 B3
La Chaise-Dieu F 68 C3
La Chaize-le-Vicomte F 66 B3
La Chambre F 69 C6
La Chapelaude F 68 B2
La Chapelle-d'Angillon F 68 A2
La Chapelle-en-Aalgaudémar F 79 B5
La Chapelle-en-Vercors F 79 B4
La Chapelle-Glain F 57 C4
La Chapelle-la-Reine F 58 B3
La Chapelle-Laurent F 68 C3
La Chapelle-St. Luc F 59 B5
La Chapelle-sur-Erdre F 66 A3
La Chapelle-Vicomtesse F 58 C2
La Charce F 79 B4
La Charité-sur-Loire F 68 A3
La Chartre-sur-le-Loir F 58 C1
La Châtaigneraie F 67 B4
La Châtre F 68 B1
La Chaussée-sur-Marne F 59 B5
La Chaux-de-Fonds CH 70 A1
La Cheppe F 59 A5
La Chèze F 56 B3
La Ciotat F 79 C4
La Clayette F 69 B4
La Clusaz F 69 C6
La Codosera E 93 B3
La Concha E 88 A3
La Condamine-Châtelard F 79 B5
La Contienda E 99 A4
La Coquille F 67 C5
La Coronada E 93 C5
La Côte-St. André F 69 C5
La Cotinière F 66 C3
La Courtine F 68 C2
La Crau F 79 C5
La Crèche F 67 B4
La Croix F 67 A5
La Croix-Valmer F 79 C5
La Cumbre E 93 B5
La Douze F 77 A3
La Espina E 86 A4
La Estrella E 94 C1
La Farga de Moles E 91 A4
La Fatarella E 90 B3
La Felipa E 95 C5
La Fère F 59 A4
La Ferrière F 66 B3
La Ferrière-en-Parthenay F 67 B4
La-Ferté-Alais F 58 B3
La Ferté-Bernard F 58 B1
La Ferté-Frênel F 58 B1
La Ferté-Gaucher F 59 B4
La Ferté-Imbault F 68 A1
La Ferté-Macé F 57 B5
La Ferté-Milon F 59 A4
La Ferté-St. Aubin F 58 C2
La Ferté-St.Cyr F 58 C2
La Ferté-sous-Jouarre F 59 B4
La Ferté-Vidame F 58 B1
La Ferté Villeneuil F 58 C2
La Feuillie F 58 A2
La Flèche F 57 C5
La Flotte F 66 B3
La Font de la Figuera E 96 C2
La Fouillade F 77 B5
La Fregeneda E 87 D4
La Fresneda E 90 C3
La Fuencubierta E 100 B1
La Fuente de San Esteban E 87 D4
La Fulioala E 91 B4
La Gacilly F 57 C3
La Galera E 90 C3
La Garde-Freinet F 79 C5
La Garnache F 66 B3
La Garriga E 91 B5
La Garrovilla E 93 C4
La Gaubretière F 66 B3
La Gineta E 95 C4
La Granadella, *Alicante* E 96 C3
La Granadella, *Lleida* E 90 B3
La Grand-Combe F 78 B3
La Grande-Croix F 69 C4
La Grande-Motte F 78 C3
La Granja d'Escarp E 90 B3
La Granjuela E 93 C5

La Grave F 79 A5
La Gravelle F 57 B4
La Guardia E 95 C3
La Guardia de Jaén E 100 B2
La Guerche-de-Bretagne F 57 C4
La Guerche-sur-l'Aubois F 68 B2
La Guérinière F 66 B2
La Haba E 93 C5
La Haye-du-Puits F 57 A4
La Haye-Pesnel F 57 B4
La Herlière F 48 C3
La Hermida E 88 A2
La Herrera E 95 D4
La Higuera E 96 C1
La Hiniesta E 88 C1
La Horcajada E 94 B1
La Horra E 88 C3
La Hulpe B 49 C5
La Hutte F 57 B6
La Iglesuela E 94 B2
La Iglesuela del Cid E 90 C2
La Iruela E 100 B3
La Javie F 79 B5
La Jonchère-St. Maurice F 67 B6
La Jonquera E 91 A5
La Lantejuela E 99 B5
La Linea de la Concepción E 99 C5
La Llacuna E 91 B4
La Londe-les-Maures F 79 C5
La Loupe F 58 B2
La Louvière B 49 C5
La Luisiana E 99 B5
La Machine F 68 B3
la Maddalena I 110 B2
La Mailleraye-sur-Seine F 58 A1
La Malène F 78 B2
La Mamola E 100 C2
La Manresana dels Prats E 91 B4
La Masadera E 90 B2
La Mata E 94 C2
La Mata de Ledesma E 87 C5
La Mata de Monteagudo E 88 B1
La Meilleraye-de-Bretagne F 57 C4
La Ménitré F 67 A4
La Mojonera E 101 C3
La Mole F 79 C5
La Molina E 91 A4
La Monnerie-le-Montel F 68 C3
La Morera E 93 C4
La Mothe-Achard F 66 B3
La Mothe-St. Héray F 67 B4
La Motte-Chalançon F 79 B4
La Motte-du-Caire F 79 B5
La Motte-Servolex F 69 C5
La Mudarra E 88 C2
La Muela E 90 B1
La Mure F 79 B4
La Nava E 99 B4
La Nava de Ricomalillo E 94 C2
La Nava de Santiago E 93 B4
La Neuve-Lyre F 58 B1
La Neuveville CH 70 A2
La Nocle-Maulaix F 68 B3
La Nuez de Arriba E 88 B3
La Paca E 101 B4
La Pacaudière F 68 B3
La Palma d'Ebre E 90 B3
La Palma del Condado E 99 B4
La Palme F 78 D2
La Palmyre F 66 C3
La Parra E 93 C4
La Pedraja de Portillo E 88 C2
La Peraleja E 95 B4
La Petit-Pierre F 60 B3
La Pinilla E 101 B4
La Plagne F 70 C1
La Plaza E 86 A4
La Pobla de Lillet E 91 A4
La Pobla de Vallbona E 96 B2
La Pobla Llarga E 96 B2
La Pola de Gordón E 88 B1
la Porta F 110 A2
La Pouëze F 66 A4
La Póveda de Soria E 89 B4
La Preste F 91 A5
La Primaube F 77 B5
La Puebla de Almoradie E 95 C3
La Puebla de Cazalla E 99 B5
La Puebla de los Infantes E 99 B5
La Puebla de Montalbán E 94 C2
La Puebla de Roda E 90 A3
La Puebla de Valdavia E 88 B2
La Puebla de Valverde E 96 A2
La Puebla del Río E 99 B4
La Pueblanueva E 94 C2
La Puerta de Segura E 101 A3
La Punt CH 71 B4
La Quintana E 100 B1
La Quintera E 99 B5
La Rábita, *Granada* E 100 C2
La Rábita, *Jaén* E 100 B1
La Rambla E 100 B1
La Reale I 110 B1
La Redondela E 98 B3
La Réole F 76 B2
La Riera E 86 A4
La Riera de Gaià E 91 B4
La Rinconada E 99 B4
La Rivière-Thibouville F 58 A1
La Robla E 88 B1
La Roca de la Sierra E 93 B2
La Roche CH 70 B2
La Roche-Bernard F 66 A2
La Roche-Canillac F 68 C1
La Roche-Chalais F 67 C5
La Roche Derrien F 56 B2
La Roche-des-Arnauds F 79 B4
La Roche-en-Ardenne B 49 C6
La Roche-en-Brénil F 69 A4
La Roche-Guyon F 58 A2
La Roche-Posay F 67 B5
La Roche-sur-Foron F 69 B6
La Roche-sur-Yon F 66 B3
La Rochebeaucourt-et-Argentine F 67 C5
La Rochefoucauld F 67 C5
La Rochelle F 66 B3
La Rochette F 79 B4
La Roda, *Albacete* E 95 C4
La Roda, *Oviedo* E 86 A4
La Roda de Andalucía E 100 B1
La Roque-Gageac F 77 B4
La Roque-Ste. Marguerite F 78 B2
La Roquebrussanne F 79 C4
La Rubia E 89 C4
La Sagrada E 87 D4
La Salceda E 94 A3
La Salle F 79 B5
la Salute di Livenza I 72 C2
La Salvetat-Peyralès F 77 B5
La Salvetat-sur-Agout F 78 C1
La Sarraz CH 69 B6
La Seca E 88 C2
La Selva del Camp E 91 B4
La Senia E 90 C3
La Serra E 91 B4
La Seu d'Urgell E 91 A4
La Seyne-sur-Mer F 79 C4
La Solana E 95 D3
La Souterraine F 67 B6
La Spézia I 81 B3
La Storta I 102 B2
La Suze-sur-Sarthe F 57 C6
La Teste F 76 B1
La Thuile I 70 C1
La Toba E 95 B5
La Toledana E 94 C2
La Torre de Cabdella E 90 A3
La Torre de Esteban Hambrán E 94 B2
La Torre del l'Espanyol E 90 B3
La Torresaviñán E 95 B4
La Tour d'Aigues F 79 C4
La Tour de Peilz CH 70 B1
La Tour-du-Pin F 69 C5
La Tranche-sur-Mer F 66 B3
La Tremblade F 66 C3
La Trimouille F 67 B6
La Trinité F 56 C2
La Trinité-Porhoët F 56 B3
La Turballe F 66 A2
La Uña E 88 A1
La Unión E 101 B5
La Vall d'Uixó E 96 B2
La Vecilla de Curueño E 88 B1
La Vega, *Asturias* E 88 A1
La Vega, *Asturias* E 88 A1
La Vega, *Cantabria* E 88 A2
La Velilla E 94 A3
La Velles E 94 A1
La Ventosa E 95 B4
La Victoria E 100 B1
La Vid E 89 C3
La Vilavella E 96 B2
La Vilella Baixa E 90 B3
La Villa de Don Fadrique E 95 C3
La Ville Dieu-du-Temple F 77 B4
La Villedieu F 67 B4
La Voulte-sur-Rhône F 78 B3
La Wantzenau F 60 B3
La Yesa E 96 B2
La Zubia E 100 B2
Laa an der Thaya A 64 B2
Laage D 44 B4
Laatzen D 51 A5
Laban IRL 20 A3
Labastide-Murat F 77 B4
Labastide-Rouairoux F 77 C5
Labastide-St. Pierre F 77 C4
Lábatlan H 65 C4
Labenne F 76 C1
Labin HR 82 A3
Łabiszyn PL 46 C3
Lablachère F 78 B3
Lábod H 74 B2
Laboe D 44 A2
Labouheyre F 76 B2
Łabowa PL 65 A6
Labrit F 76 B2
Labros E 95 A5
Labruguière F 77 C5
Labrujo P 87 C2
L'Absie F 67 B4
Lacalahorra E 100 B2
Lacanau F 76 B1
Lacanau-Océan F 76 A1
Lacanche F 69 A4
Lacapelle-Marival F 77 B4
Laćarak YU 85 A4
Lacaune F 78 C1
Laceby GB 27 B5
Lacedónia I 104 A2
Láces I 71 B5
Lachen CH 70 A3
Lachendorf D 44 C2
Lachowice PL 65 A5
Łąck PL 47 C5
Läckeby S 40 C6
Läckö S 35 C5
Lacock GB 29 B5
Láconi I 110 D2
Lacq F 76 C2
Lacroix-Barrez F 77 B5
Lacroix-St. Ouen F 58 A3
Lacroix-sur-Meuse F 60 B1
Łącznik PL 54 C2
Lad H 74 B2
Ladbergen D 50 A3
Lądek-Zdrój PL 54 C1
Ladelund D 39 E2
Ladendorf A 64 B2
Ladignac-le-Long F 67 C6
Ladispoli I 102 B2
Ladoeiro P 93 B3
Ladon F 58 C3
Ladushkin RUS 47 A6
Ladybank GB 25 B4
Laer D 50 A3
Lærdalsøyri N 2 F10
Lafnitz A 73 A6
Lafrançaise F 77 B4
Lagan S 40 C3
Laganadi I 109 A4
Lagares, *Coimbra* P 92 A3
Lagares, *Porto* P 87 C2
Lagaro I 81 B5
Lagartera E 94 C1
Lage D 51 B4
Lägerdorf D 43 B6
Lagg GB 24 C2
Laggan GB 22 D4
Łagiewniki PL 54 C1
Láglio I 71 C4
Lagnieu F 69 C5
Lagny-sur-Marne F 58 B3
Lago, *Calabria* I 106 B3
Lago, *Veneto* I 72 C2
Lagôa P 98 B2
Lagoaça P 87 C4
Lagonegro I 104 B2
Lagos P 98 B2
Lagosanto I 82 B1
Łagów, *Lubuskie* PL 45 C7
Łagów, *Świętokrzyskie* PL 55 C6
Lagrasse F 77 C5
Laguardia E 89 B4
Laguarres E 90 A3
Laguenne F 68 C1
Laguépie F 77 B4
Laguiole F 78 B1
Laguna de Duera E 88 C2
Laguna de Negrillos E 88 B1
Laguna del Marquesado E 95 B5
Lagundo I 71 B6
Lagunilla E 93 A4
Laharie F 76 B2
Lahden D 43 C4
Laheycourt F 59 B6
Lahnstein D 50 C3
Laholm S 40 C3
Lahr D 60 B3
Lahti FIN 3 F19
Laichingen D 61 B5
L'Aigle F 58 B1
Laignes F 59 C5
Laiguéglia I 80 C2
L'Aiguillon-sur-Mer F 66 B3
Laimbach am Ostrong A 63 B6
Laina E 95 A4
Lairg GB 23 C4
Laissac F 78 B1
Láives I 71 B6
Lajkovac YU 85 B5
Lajoskomárom H 74 B3
Lajosmizse H 75 A4
Lak H 65 B6
Lakenheath GB 30 B4
Lakitelek H 75 B5
Lakolk DK 39 D1
Łąkorz PL 47 B5
Lakšárska Nová Ves SK 64 B3
Lakselv N 2 A19
Laktaši BIH 84 B2
L'Albagès E 90 B3
Lalbenque F 77 B4
L'Alcudia E 96 B2
L'Aldea E 90 C3
Lalín E 86 B2
Lalinde F 77 B3
Lalley F 79 B4
Lalling D 62 B4
L'Alpe-d'Huez F 79 A5
Lam D 62 A4
Lama dei Peligni I 103 A4
Lama Mocogno I 81 B4
Lamagistère F 77 B3
Lamarche F 60 B1
Lamarche-sur-Saône F 69 A5
Lamarosa P 92 B2
Lamarque F 76 A2
Lamas P 92 A2
Lamas de Moaro P 87 B2
Lamastre F 78 B3
Lambach A 63 B4
Lamballe F 56 B3
Lamberhurst GB 31 C4
Lambesc F 79 C4
Lambley GB 25 D5
Lambourn GB 31 C2
Lamego P 87 C3
L'Ametlla de Mar E 90 C3
Lamia GR 15 S18
Lammhult S 40 B4
Lamothe-Cassel F 77 B4
Lamothe-Montravel F 76 B3
Lamotte-Beuvron F 58 C3
Lampaul F 56 B0
Lampertheim D 61 A4
Lampeter GB 28 A3
L'Ampolla E 90 C3
Lamprechtshausen A 62 C3
Lamsfeld D 53 B4
Lamspringe D 51 B6
Lamstedt D 43 B6
Lamure-sur-Azergues F 69 B4
Lana I 71 B6
Lanaja E 90 B2
Lanarce F 78 B2
Lanark GB 25 C4
Lancaster GB 26 A3
Lanchester GB 25 D6
Lanciano I 103 A4
Lancing GB 31 D3
Lancova Vas SLO 73 B5
Landau, *Bayern* D 62 B3
Landau, *Rheinland-Pfalz* D 61 A4
Landeck A 71 A5
Landen B 49 C6
Landerneau F 56 B1
Landeryd S 40 B3
Landesbergen D 43 C6
Landete E 96 B1
Landévant F 56 C2
Landévennec F 56 B1
Landivisiau F 56 B1
Landivy F 57 B4
Landl A 62 C3
Landos F 78 B2
Landouzy-la-Ville F 59 A5
Landquart CH 71 B4
Landrecies F 49 C4
Landreville F 59 B5
Landriano I 71 C4
Lands-berg D 52 B2
Landsberg D 62 B1
Landsbro S 40 B4
Landscheid D 50 D2
Landshut D 62 B3
Landskrona S 41 D2
Landstuhl D 60 A3
Lanesborough IRL 19 C4
Lanester F 56 C2
Lanestosa E 89 A3
Langå DK 39 C2
Langa de Duero E 89 C3
Langangen N 33 B6
Långared S 40 B3
Långås S 40 C2
Långasjö S 40 C5
Langau A 63 B6
Langeac F 78 A2
Langeais F 67 A5
Langedijk NL 42 C1
Langeln D 51 B6
Langelsheim D 51 B6
Langemark-Poelkapelle B 48 C3
Langen, *Hessen* D 51 D4
Langen, *Niedersachsen* D 43 B5
Langenau D 61 B6
Langenberg D 51 B4
Langenbruck CH 70 A2
Langenburg D 61 A5
Längenfeld A 71 A5
Langenfeld D 50 B2
Langenlois A 63 B6
Langenlonsheim D 60 A3
Langennaudorf D 52 B3
Langenneufnach D 62 B1
Langenthal CH 70 A2
Langenzenn D 62 A1
Langeoog D 43 B4
Langeskov DK 39 D3
Langesund N 33 B6
Langewiesen D 51 C6
Langförden D 43 C5
Langhagen D 44 B4
Länghem S 40 B3
Langhirano I 81 B4
Langholm GB 25 C5
Langnau CH 70 B2
Langø DK 39 E4
Langogne F 78 B2
Langon F 76 B2
Langquaid D 62 B3
Langreo E 88 A1
Langres F 59 C6
Långserud S 34 B4
Langset N 34 A3
Långshyttan S 36 A3
Langueux F 56 B3
Languidic F 56 C2
Längvik S 36 B5
Langwarden D 43 B5
Langwathby GB 26 A3
Langwedel D 43 C6
Langweid D 62 B1
Langwies CH 71 B4
Lanheses P 87 C2
Lanięta PL 47 C5
Lanildut F 56 B1
Lanjarón E 100 C2
Lanmeur F 56 B2
Lanna, *Jönköping* S 40 B3
Lanna, *Örebro* S 36 B1
Lännaholm S 36 B4
Lannéanou F 56 B2
Lannemezan F 77 C3
Lanneuville-sur-Meuse F 59 A6
Lannilis F 56 B1
Lannion F 56 B2
Lanouaille F 67 C6
Lanškroun CZ 64 A2
Lanslebourg-Mont-Cenis F 70 C1
Lanta F 77 C4
Lantadilla E 88 B2
Lanton F 76 B1
Lantosque F 79 C6
Lanusei I 110 D2
Lanúvio I 102 B2
Lanvollon F 56 B3
Lánycsók H 74 B3
Lanz D 44 B3
Lanza E 86 A2
Lanzada E 86 B2
Lanzahita E 94 B2
Lanžhot CZ 64 B2
Lanzo Torinese I 70 C2
Laole YU 85 B6
Laon F 59 A4
Laons F 58 B2
Lapalisse F 68 B3
Łapczyna Wola PL 55 C4
Lapeyrade F 76 B2
Lapeyrouse F 68 B2
Lapford GB 28 C4
Laplume F 77 B3
Lapoutroie F 60 B3
Lapovo YU 85 B6
Lappeenranta FIN 3 F21
Lapseki TR 16 R20
Lapua FIN 3 E18
L'Áquila I 103 A3
Laracha E 86 A2
Laragh IRL 21 A5
Laragne-Montéglin F 79 B4
l'Arboç E 91 B4
L'Arbresle F 69 C4
Lärbro S 37 D5
Larceveau F 76 C1
Larche, *Alpes-de-Haute-Provence* F 79 B5
Larche, *Corrèze* F 77 A4
Lårdal N 33 B5
Lardosa P 92 B3
Laredo E 89 A3
Largentière F 78 B3
L'Argentière-la-Bessée F 79 B5
Largs GB 24 C3
Lari I 81 C4
Lariño E 86 B1
Larino I 103 B4
Lárisa GR 15 S18
Larkhall GB 25 C4
Larkollen N 34 B2
Larmor-Plage F 56 C2
Larne GB 19 B6
Larochette L 60 A2
Laroque d'Olmes F 77 D4
Laroque-Timbaut F 77 B3
Laroquebrou F 77 B5
Larouco E 87 B3
Larraga E 89 B5
Larrau F 76 C2
Larrazet F 77 C4
Laruns F 76 C2
Larva E 100 B2
Larvik N 33 B7
Las Arenas E 88 A2
Las Cabezadas E 95 A3
Las Cabezas de San Juan E 99 C5
Las Correderas E 100 A2
Las Cuevas de Cañart E 90 C2
Las Gabias E 100 B2
Las Herencias E 94 C2
Las Labores E 95 C3
Las Mesas E 95 C4
Las Minas E 101 A4
Las Navas E 100 B1
Las Navas de la Concepción E 99 B5
Las Navas del Marqués E 94 B2
Las Navillas E 94 C2
Las Negras E 101 C4
Las Pajanosas E 99 B4
Las Pedroñas E 95 C4
Las Planes d'Hostoles E 91 A5
Las Rozas, *Cantabria* E 88 B2
Las Rozas, *Madrid* E 94 B3
Las Uces E 87 C4
Las Veguillas E 94 B1
Las Ventas con Peña Aguilera E 94 C2
Las Ventas de San Julián E 94 B1
Las Villes E 96 A3
Lasarte E 89 A4
Łasin PL 47 B5
Lask PL 55 B4
Łaskarzew PL 55 B6
Laško SLO 73 B5
Laskowice PL 47 B4
Laspaules E 90 A3
Laspuña E 90 A3
Lassan D 45 B5
Lassay-les-Châteaux F 57 B5
Lassigny F 58 A3
Lastovo HR 84 D1
Lastras de Cuéllar E 94 A2
Lästringe S 37 C4
Lastrup D 43 C4
Lastva BIH 84 D3
Latasa E 89 B5
Látera I 102 A1
Laterza I 105 B3
Lathen D 43 C4
Latheron GB 23 C5
Latiano I 105 B4
Latina I 102 B2
Latisana I 72 C3
Látky SK 65 B5
Latowicz PL 55 A6
Latrónico I 104 B3
Latronquière F 77 B5
Latterbach CH 70 B2
Laubach D 51 C4
Laubert F 78 B2
Laucha D 52 B1
Lauchhammer D 53 B3
Lauchheim D 61 B6
Lauda-Königshofen D 61 A5
Laudal N 33 C4
Lauder GB 25 C5
Lauenau D 51 A5
Lauenburg D 44 B2
Lauf D 62 A2
Laufach D 51 C5
Laufen CH 70 A2
Laufen D 62 C3
Lauffen D 61 A5
Laugharne GB 28 B3
Lauingen D 61 B6
Laujar de Andarax E 100 C3
Laukaa FIN 3 E19
Launceston GB 28 C3
Launois-sur-Vence F 59 A5
Laupheim D 61 B5
Lauragh IRL 20 C2
Laureana di Borrello I 106 C3
Laurencekirk GB 25 B5
Laurencetown IRL 20 A3
Laurenzana I 104 B2
Lauria I 104 B2
Laurière F 67 B6
Laurieston GB 24 D3
Laurino I 104 B2
Lausanne CH 69 B6
Laussonne F 78 B3
Lauta D 53 B4
Lautenthal D 51 B6
Lauterach A 71 A4
Lauterbach D 51 C5
Lauterbrunnen CH 70 B2
Lauterecken D 60 A3
Lauterhofen D 62 A2
Lautrec F 77 C5
Lauvvik N 32 C3
Lauzerte F 77 B4
Lauzès F 77 B4
Lauzun F 77 B3
Lavagna I 80 B3
Laval F 57 B5
Lavamünd A 73 B4
Lavardac F 76 B3
Lavaris P 92 A2
Lavarone I 71 C6
Lavau F 59 C3
Lavaur F 77 C4
Lavelanet F 77 D4
Lavello I 104 A2
Lavelsloh D 43 C5
Lavenham GB 30 B4
Laveno I 70 C3
Lavezzola I 81 B5
Laviano I 104 B2
Lavilledieu F 78 B3
Lavinio-Lido di Enea I 102 B2
Lavis I 71 B6
Lavit F 77 C3
Lavoncourt F 60 C1
Lavos P 92 A2
Lavoûter-Chilhac F 68 C3
Lavradio P 92 C1
Lavre P 92 C2
Lavrion GR 16 T19
Lawers GB 24 B3
Ławy PL 45 C6
Laxå S 37 C1
Laxe E 86 A2
Laxey GB 26 A1
Laxford Bridge GB 22 C3
Laxhall S 35 C5
Laxvik S 40 C2
Laza E 87 B3
Lazarevac YU 85 B5
Lazarevo YU 75 C5
Lazise I 71 C5
Łaziska Grn. PL 54 C3
Lazkao E 89 A4
Lázně Bělohrad CZ 53 C5
Lázně Bohdaneč CZ 53 C5
Lázně Kynžvart CZ 52 C2
Lazonby GB 26 A3
Łazy PL 46 A2
Lazzaro I 109 B4
Le Bar-sur-Loup F 79 C5
Le Barp F 76 B2
Le Béage F 78 B3
Le Beausset F 79 C4
Le Bessat F 69 C4
Le Blanc F 67 B6
Le Bleymard F 78 B2
Le Boullay-Mivoye F 58 B2
Le Boulou F 91 A5
Le Bourg F 77 B4
Le Bourg-d'Oisans F 79 A5
Le Bourget-du-Lac F 69 C5
Le Bourgneuf-la-Forêt F 57 B5
Le Bousquet d'Orb F 78 C2
Le Brassus CH 69 B6
Le Breuil F 68 B3
Le Breuil-en-Auge F 57 A6
Le Brusquet F 79 B5
Le Bry CH 70 B2
Le Bugue F 77 B3
Le Buisson F 77 B3
Le Caloy F 76 C2
Le Cap d'Agde F 78 C2
Le Cateau Cambrésis F 49 C4
Le Caylar F 78 C2
Le Cayrol F 78 B1
Le Chambon-Feugerolles F 69 C4
Le Chambon-sur-Lignon F 78 A3
Le Château d'Oléron F 66 C3
Le Châtelard F 69 C6
Le Châtelet F 68 B2
Le Chatelet-en-Brie F 58 B3
Le Chesne F 59 A5
Le Cheylard F 78 B3
Le Collet-de-Deze F 78 B2
Le Conquet F 56 B1
Le Creusot F 69 B4
Le Croisic F 66 A2
Le Crotoy F 48 C2
Le Deschaux F 69 B5
Le Donjon F 68 B3
Le Dorat F 67 B6
Le Faou F 56 B1
Le Faoüet F 56 B2
Le Folgoet F 56 B1
Le Fossat F 77 C4
Le Fousseret F 77 C4
Le Fugeret F 79 B5
Le Gault-Soigny F 59 B4
Le Grand-Bornand F 69 C6
Le-Grand-Bourg F 67 B6
Le Grand-Lucé F 58 C1
Le Grand-Pressigny F 67 B5
Le Grand-Quevilly F 58 A2
Le Grau-du-Roi F 78 C3
Le Havre F 57 A6
Le Hohwald F 60 B3
Le Houga F 76 C2
Le Lardin-St. Lazare F 67 C6
Le Lauzet-Ubaye F 79 B5
Le Lavandou F 79 C5
Le Lion-d'Angers F 57 C5
Le Locle CH 70 A1
Le Loroux-Bottereau F 66 A3
Le Louroux-Béconnais F 66 A4
Le Luc F 79 C5
Le Lude F 57 C6
Le Malzieu-Ville F 78 B2
Le Mans F 57 B6
Le Mas-d'Azil F 77 C4
Le Massegros F 78 B2
Le May-sur-Evre F 66 A4
Le Mayet-de-Montagne F 68 B3
Le Mêle-sur-Sarthe F 58 B1
Le Ménil F 60 B2
Le Merlerault F 57 B6
Le Mesnil-sur-Oger F 59 B5
Le Miroir F 69 B5
Le Molay-Littry F 57 A5
Le Monastier-sur-Gazeille F 78 B2
Le Monêtier-les-Bains F 79 B5
Le Mont-Dore F 68 C2
Le Mont-St. Michel F 57 B4
Le Montet F 68 B3
Le Muret F 76 B2
Le Muy F 79 C5
Le Neubourg F 58 A1
Le Nouvion-en-Thiérache F 49 C4
Le Palais F 66 A1
Le Parcq F 48 C3
Le Péage-de-Roussillon F 69 C4
Le Pellerin F 66 A3
Le Perthus F 91 A5
Le Pertuis F 78 A3
Le Petit-Bornand F 69 C6
Le Poët F 79 B4
Le Poirè-sur-Vie F 66 B3
Le Pont CH 69 B6
Le Pont-de-Montvert F 78 B2
Le Porge F 76 B1
Le Portel F 48 C2
Le Pouldu F 56 C2
Le Pouliguen F 66 A2
le Prese I 71 B5
Le Puy-en-Velay F 78 A2
Le Puy-Ste. Réparade F 79 C4
Le Quesnoy F 49 C4
Le Rayol F 79 C5
Le Rœulx B 49 C5
Le Rouget F 77 B5
Le Rozier F 78 B2
Le Russey F 70 A1
Le Sel-de-Bretagne F 57 C4
Le Sentier CH 69 B6
Le Souquet F 76 C1
Le Teil F 78 B3
Le Teilleul F 57 B5
Le Temple-de-Bretagne F 66 A3
Le Theil F 58 B1
Le Thillot F 60 C2
Le Touquet-Paris-Plage F 48 C2
Le Touvet F 69 C5
Le Translay F 48 D2
Le Tréport F 48 C2
Le Val F 79 C5
Le Val-André F 56 B3
Le Val-d'Ajol F 60 C2
Le Verdon-sur-Mer F 66 C3
Le Vernet F 79 B5
Le Vigan F 78 C2
le Ville I 82 C1
Le Vivier-sur-Mer F 57 B4
Lea GB 27 B5
Leadburn GB 25 C4
Leadhills GB 25 C4
Leap IRL 20 C2
Leatherhead GB 31 C3
Łeba PL 46 A3
Lebach D 60 A2
Lebedyn UA 7 L24
Lebekke B 49 B5
Lébény H 64 C3
Łebno PL 47 A4
Leboreiro E 87 B3
Lębork PL 46 A3
Lebrija E 99 C4
Lebring A 73 B5
Lebus D 45 C6
Lebusa D 52 B3
Leca da Palmeira P 87 C2
Lecce I 105 B5
Lecco I 71 C4
Lécera E 90 B2
Lećevica HR 83 C5
Lech A 71 A5
Lechbruck D 62 C1
Lechlade GB 29 B6
Lechovice CZ 64 B2
Leciñena E 90 B2
Leck D 39 E1
Lectoure F 77 C3
Łęczyca, *Płock* PL 55 A4
Łęczyca, *Szczecin* PL 45 B7
Ledaña E 95 C5
Ledbury GB 29 A5
Lede B 49 C4
Ledeč nad Sazavou CZ 63 A6
Ledenice CZ 63 B5
Ledesma E 87 C4
Lédignan F 78 C3
Lédigos E 88 B2
Ledmore GB 22 C4
Lednice CZ 64 B2
Lednické-Rovné SK 64 A4
Lędyczek PL 46 B2
Lędziny PL 55 C4
Leeds GB 27 B4
Leek GB 26 B3
Leek NL 42 B3
Leenaun IRL 18 C2
Leens NL 42 B3
Leer D 43 B4
Leerdam NL 49 B6
Leerhafe D 43 B4
Leese D 43 C6
Leeuwarden NL 42 B2
Leezen D 44 B2
Leganés E 94 B3
Legau D 61 C6
Legbąd PL 46 B3
Legé F 66 B3
Lège-Cap-Ferret F 76 B1
Legionowo PL 55 A5
Léglise B 60 A1
Legnago I 71 C6
Legnano I 70 C3
Legnaro I 72 C1
Legnica PL 53 B6
Łęgowo PL 47 A4
Legrad HR 74 B1
Léguevin F 77 C4
Legutiano E 89 B4
Lehesten D 52 C1
Lehnice SK 64 B3
Lehnin D 52 A2
Lehrberg D 61 A6
Lehre D 44 C2
Lehrte D 44 C1
Lehsen D 44 B3
Leibnitz A 73 B5
Leicester GB 30 B2
Leiden NL 49 A5
Leidschendam NL 49 A5
Leigh GB 26 B3
Leighlinbridge IRL 21 B5
Leighton Buzzard GB 31 C3
Leignon B 49 C6
Leimen D 61 A4
Leinefelde D 51 B6
Leintwardine GB 29 A5
Leipzig D 52 B2
Leiria P 92 B2
Leirvik N 32 B2
Leisach A 72 B2
Leisnig D 52 B2
Leiston GB 30 B5
Leitholm GB 25 C5
Leitrim IRL 18 C3
Leitza E 89 A5
Leitzkau D 52 A1
Łękawa PL 55 B4
Łękawica PL 65 A5

Lekeitio E 89 A4
Lekenik HR 73 C6
Lekeryd S 40 B4
Łęknica PL 53 B4
Lekunberri E 89 A5
Lekvattnet S 34 A4
Lelkowo PL 47 A6
Lelów PL 55 C4
Lelystad NL 42 C2
Lem, Ringkøbing DK 39 C1
Lem, Viborg Amt. DK 38 C1
Lembach F 60 A3
Lemberg F 60 A3
Lembèye F 76 C2
Lemelerveld NL 42 C3
Lemförde D 43 C5
Lemgo D 51 A4
Lemmer NL 42 C2
Lempdes F 68 C3
Lemvig DK 38 C1
Lemwerder D 43 B5
Lenart SLO 73 B5
Lenartovce SK 65 B6
Lenauheim RO 75 C5
Lencloître F 67 B5
Lend A 72 A3
Lendalfoot GB 24 C3
Lendava SLO 73 B6
Lendery RUS 3 E22
Lendinara I 81 A5
Lendorf A 72 B3
Lendum DK 38 B3
Lengefeld D 52 C3
Lengerich, Niedersachsen D 43 C4
Lengerich, Nordrhein-Westfalen D 50 A3
Lenggries D 62 C2
Lengyeltóti H 74 B2
Lenhovda S 40 C5
Lenk CH 70 B2
Lennartsfors S 34 B3
Lennestadt D 50 B4
Lennoxtown GB 24 C3
Leno I 71 C5
Lénola I 103 B3
Lens B 49 C4
Lens F 48 C3
Lens Lestang F 69 C5
Lensahn D 44 A2
Lentellais E 87 B3
Lentföhrden D 44 B1
Lenti H 74 B1
Lentini I 109 B3
Lenzburg CH 70 A3
Lenzen D 44 B3
Lenzerheide CH 71 B4
Leoben A 73 A5
Leogang A 72 A2
Leominster GB 29 A5
León E 88 B1
Léon F 76 C1
Leonberg D 61 B5
Léoncel F 79 B4
Leonding A 63 B5
Leonessa I 102 A2
Leonforte I 109 B3
Leopoldsburg B 49 B6
Leopoldsdorf im Marchfeld A 64 B2
Leopoldshagen D 45 B5
Leova MD 11 N21
Lepe E 98 B3
Lepenac, Crna Gora YU 85 D4
Lepenac, Srbija YU 85 C5
Lephin GB 22 D2
L'Epine F 79 B4
Lepoglava HR 73 B6
Leppävirta FIN 3 E20
Leppin D 44 C3
Lepsény H 74 B3
Léquile I 105 B5
Lercara Friddi I 108 B2
Lerdal S 35 C3
Leré F 68 A2
Lérici I 81 B3
Lerin E 89 B5
Lerm-et-Musset F 76 B2
Lerma E 88 B3
Lermoos A 71 A5
Lérouville F 60 B1
Lerum S 35 D4
Lervik N 34 B2
Lerwick GB 22 A7
Lés E 77 D3
Les Abrets F 69 C5
Les Aix-d'Angillon F 68 A2
Les Ancizes-Comps F 68 C2
Les Andelys F 58 A2
Les Arcs, Savoie F 70 C1
Les Arcs, Var F 79 C5
Les-Aubiers F 67 B4
Les Baux-de-Provence F 78 C3
Les Bézards F 58 C3
Les Bois CH 70 A1
Les Bordes F 58 C3
Les Borges Blanques E 90 B3
Les Borges del Camp E 91 B4
Les Brunettes F 68 B3
Les Cabannes F 77 D4
Les Contamines-Montjoie F 70 C1
les Coves de Vinroma E 96 A3
Les Déserts F 69 C5
Les Deux-Alpes F 79 B5
Les Diablerets CH 70 B2
Les Echelles F 69 C5
Les Escaldes AND 91 A4
Les Essarts F 66 B3
Les Estables F 78 B3
Les Eyzies-de-Tayac F 77 B4
Les Gets F 70 B1
Les Grandes-Ventes F 58 A2
Les Haudères CH 70 B2
Les Herbiers F 66 B3
Les Hôpitaux-Neufs F 69 B6
Les Lucs-sur-Boulogne F 66 B3
Les Mages F 78 B3
Les Mazures F 59 A5
Les Mées F 79 B4
Les Mureaux F 58 B2
Les Omergues F 79 B4
Les Ormes-sur-Voulzie F 59 B4
Les Orres F 79 B5
Les Pieux F 57 A4
Les Ponts-de-Cé F 67 A4
Les Ponts-de-Martel CH 70 B1
Les Praz F 70 C1
Les Riceys F 59 C5
Les Roches F 69 C4
Les Rosaires F 56 B3
Les Rosiers F 67 A4
Les Rousses F 69 B6
Les Sables-d'Olonne F 66 B3
Les Settons F 68 A4
Les Ternes F 78 A1
Les Thilliers en-Vexin F 58 A2
Les Touches F 66 A3
Les Trois Moûtiers F 67 A5
Les Vans F 78 B3
Les Verrières CH 69 B6
Les Vignes F 78 B2
Lešak YU 85 C5
Lesaka E 89 A5
Lesbury GB 25 C6
L'Escala E 91 A6
Lescar F 76 C2
L'Escarène F 80 C1
Lesce SLO 73 B4
Lescheraines F 69 C6
Lesconil F 56 C1
Lesdins F 59 A4
Lesično SLO 73 B5
Lésina I 103 B5
Lesjaskog N 2 E11
Lesjaverk N 2 E11
Lesjöfors S 34 B6
Leskova Dolina SLO 73 C4
Leskovac YU 15 Q17
Leskovec CZ 64 A3
Leskovec SLO 73 C5
Leskovice CZ 63 A6
Leslie GB 25 B4
Lesmahagow GB 25 C4
Lesmont F 59 B5
Leśna PL 53 B5
Lesneven F 56 B1
Leśnica PL 54 C3
Lešnica YU 85 B4
Leśniów Wielkoplski PL 53 B5
Lesnoye RUS 7 G24
Lesparre-Médoc F 66 C4
Lesponne F 76 C3
L'Espunyola E 91 A4
Lessach A 72 A3
Lessay F 57 A4
Lessebo S 40 C5
Lessines B 49 C4
L'Estany E 91 B5
Lesterps F 67 B5
Leswalt GB 24 D2
Leszno, Mazowieckie PL 55 A5
Leszno, Wielkopolskie PL 54 B1
Leszno Górne PL 53 B5
Letchworth GB 31 C3
Letenye H 74 B1
Letino I 103 B4
Letohrad CZ 54 C1
Letovice CZ 64 A2
Letschin D 45 C6
Letterfrack IRL 18 C2
Letterkenny IRL 19 B4
Lettermacaward IRL 18 B3
Lettoch GB 23 D5
Letur E 101 A3
Letux E 90 B2
Letzlingen D 44 C3
Leucate F 78 D2
Leuchars GB 25 B5
Leuglay F 59 C5
Leuk CH 70 B2
Leukerbad CH 70 B2
Leumrabhagh GB 22 C2
Leuna D 52 B2
Leusden NL 49 A6
Leutenberg D 52 C1
Leuterschach D 61 C6
Leutershausen D 61 A6
Leutkirch D 61 C6
Leuven B 49 C5
Leuze-en-Hainaut B 49 C4
Levádhia GR 15 S18
Levanger N 2 E12
Levanjska Varoš HR 74 C3
Lévanto I 80 B3
Levata I 71 C5
Leven, East Yorkshire GB 27 B5
Leven, Fife GB 25 B5
Leverano I 105 B4
Leverkusen D 50 B2
Levern D 43 C5
Levet F 68 B2
Levice SK 65 B4
Lévico Terme I 71 B6
Levie F 110 B2
Levier F 69 B6
Lévignen F 59 A3
Levinovac HR 74 C2
Levoča SK 65 A6
Levroux F 67 B6
Lewes GB 31 D4
Lewin Brzeski PL 54 C2
Lewisham GB 31 C3
Leyburn GB 27 A4
Leyland GB 26 B3
Leysdown on Sea GB 31 C4
Leysin CH 70 B2
Lezajsk PL 11 L18
Lézardrieux F 56 B2
Lézat-sur-Lèze F 77 C4
Lezay F 67 B4
Lezhë AL 15 R16
Lézignan-Corbières F 78 C1
Lezignan-la-Cèbe F 78 C2
Ležimir YU 85 A4
Lézinnes F 59 C5
Lezoux F 68 C3
Lezuza E 95 D4
Lgov RUS 7 L24
Lhenice CZ 63 B5
Lherm F 77 C4
Lhommaizé F 67 B5
L'Hospitalet F 91 A4
L'Hospitalet de l'Infant E 90 C3
L'Hospitalet de Llobregat E 91 B5
L'Hospitalet-du-Larzac F 78 C2
Lhuître F 59 B5
Liancourt F 58 A3
Liart F 59 A5
Liatorp S 40 C4
Liatrie GB 22 D4
Libáň CZ 53 C5
Libceves CZ 53 C3
Liběchov CZ 53 C4
Liber E 86 B3
Liberec CZ 53 C5
Libiąż PL 55 C4
Libina CZ 64 A3
Libochovice CZ 53 C4
Libourne F 76 B2
Libramont B 60 A1
Librilla E 101 B4
Libros E 96 A1
Licata I 108 B2
Licciana Nardi I 81 B4
Licenza I 102 A2
Liceros E 89 C3
Lich D 51 C4
Lichères-près-Aigremont F 59 C4
Lichfield GB 27 C4
Lichtenau A 63 B6
Lichtenau D 51 B4
Lichtenberg D 52 C1
Lichtenfels D 52 C1
Lichtensteig CH 71 A4
Lichtenstein D 52 C2
Lichtenvoorde NL 50 B2
Lichtervelde B 49 B4
Lička Jesenica HR 83 A4
Lickershamn S 37 D5
Lički Osik HR 83 B4
Ličko Lešce HR 83 B4
Licodia Eubéa I 109 B3
Lida BY 7 K19
Lidečko CZ 64 A4
Lidhult S 40 C3
Lidköping S 35 C5
Lido I 72 C2
Lido Azzurro I 105 B4
Lido degli Estensi I 82 B1
Lido degli Scacchi I 82 B1
Lido della Nazioni I 82 B1
Lido di Camaiore I 81 C4
Lido di Casalbordino I 103 A4
Lido di Castél Fusano I 102 B2
Lido di Cincinnato I 102 B2
Lido di Classe I 82 B1
Lido di Fermo I 82 C2
Lido di Fondi I 103 B3
Lido di Jésolo I 72 C2
Lido di Licola I 103 C4
Lido di Metaponto I 105 B3
Lido di Óstia I 102 B2
Lido di Policoro I 105 B3
Lido di Pomposa I 82 B1
Lido di Savio I 82 B1
Lido di Scanzano I 105 B3
Lido di Siponto I 104 A2
Lido di Squillace I 106 C3
Lido di Volano I 82 B1
Lido Riccio I 103 A4
Lido Silvana I 105 B4
Lidzbark PL 47 B5
Lidzbark Warmiński PL 47 A6
Liebenau A 63 B5
Liebenau D 43 C6
Liebenwalde D 45 C5
Lieberose D 53 B4
Liebling RO 75 C6
Lieboch A 73 B5
Liège B 49 C6
Lieksa FIN 3 E22
Lienen D 50 A3
Lienz A 72 B2
Liepāja LV 6 H17
Lier B 49 B5
Lierbyen N 34 B2
Lierinais F 69 A4
Liesing A 72 B2
Liestal CH 70 A2
Liétor E 101 A4
Lieurey F 58 A1
Liévin F 48 C3
Liezen A 73 A4
Liffol-le-Grand F 60 B1
Lifford IRL 19 B4
Liffré F 57 B4
Ligardes F 77 B3
Lignano Sabbiadoro I 72 C3
Ligne F 66 A3
Lignières F 68 B2
Ligny-en-Barrois F 59 B6
Ligny-le-Châtel F 59 C4
Ligoła Polska PL 54 B2
Ligowo PL 47 C5
Ligueil F 67 A5
Likavka SK 65 A5
Likhoslavl RUS 7 H24
Lild Strand DK 38 B1
L'Île-Bouchard F 67 A5
l'Île-Rousse F 110 A1
Lilienfeld A 63 B6
Lilienthal D 43 B5
Lilla Edet S 35 C4
Lilla Tjärby S 40 C3
Lille B 49 B5
Lille F 49 C4
Lillebonne F 58 A1
Lillehammer N 2 F12
Lillerød DK 41 D2
Lillers F 48 C3
Lillesand N 33 C5
Lillestrøm N 34 B3
Lillkyrka S 36 B4
Lillo E 95 C3
Limanowa PL 65 A6
Limavady GB 19 A5
Limbach-Oberfrohna D 52 C2
Limbaži LV 6 H19
Limbourg B 50 C1
Limburg D 50 C4
Limerick IRL 20 B3
Limes I 71 C5
Limésy F 58 A1
Limmared S 40 B3
Limoges F 67 C6
Limogne-en-Quercy F 77 B4
Limone Piemonte I 80 B1
Limone sul Garda I 71 C5
Limons F 68 C3
Limours F 58 B3
Limoux F 77 C5
Linares E 100 A2
Linares de Mora E 96 A2
Linares de Riofrio E 93 A5
Linas de Broto E 90 A2
Lincoln GB 27 B5
Lind DK 39 C1
Lindau D 71 A4
Lindelse DK 39 E3
Lindenberg D 53 A4
Lindenberg im Allgäu D 61 C5
Lindern D 43 C4
Linderöd S 41 D3
Lindesberg S 36 B2
Lindesnes N 33 D4
Lindholmen S 36 B5
Lindhos GR 16 T21
Lindknud DK 39 D2
Lindlar D 50 B3
Lindö S 37 C3
Lindome S 35 D4
Lindoso P 87 C2
Lindow D 45 C4
Lindsdal S 40 C6
Lindshammar S 40 B5
Lindstedt D 44 C3
Lindved DK 39 D2
Linë CZ 63 A4
Lingen D 43 C4
Linghem S 37 C2
Linguaglossa I 109 B4
Linia PL 46 A3
Linie PL 45 B6
Liniewo PL 47 A4
Linkenheim D 61 A4
Linköping S 37 C2
Linksness GB 23 C5
Linlithgow GB 25 C4
Linneryd S 40 C5
Linnes Hammarby S 36 B4
Linnich D 50 C2
Linslade GB 31 C3
Linthal CH 70 B4
Linyola E 90 B3
Linz A 63 B5
Linz D 50 C3
Lion-sur-Mer F 57 A5
Lioni I 104 B2
Lipany SK 65 A6
Lipar YU 75 C4
Lipari I 109 A3
Lipcani MD 11 M20
Liperi FIN 3 E21
Liphook GB 31 C3
Lipiany PL 45 B6
Lipik HR 74 C2
Lipka PL 46 B3
Lipki Wielkie PL 46 C1
Lipnica PL 46 B3
Lipnica Murowana PL 65 A6
Lipnik PL 55 C6
Lipnik nad Bečvou CZ 64 A3
Lipno, Kujawsko-Pomorskie PL 47 C5
Lipno, Łódzkie PL 54 B3
Liposthey F 76 B2
Lipovac HR 84 A4
Lipovec CZ 64 A2
Lipovets UA 11 M21
Lipovljani HR 74 C1
Lipowina PL 47 A5
Lippborg D 50 B4
Lippó H 74 C3
Lippoldsberg D 51 B5
Lippstadt D 51 B4
Lipsko PL 55 B6
Liptál CZ 64 A3
Liptovská-Lúžna SK 65 B5
Liptovská Osada SK 65 B5
Liptovská-Teplička SK 65 B6
Liptovský Hrádok SK 65 A5
Liptovský Milkuláš SK 65 A5
Lipusz PL 46 A3
Lipůvka CZ 64 A2
Liré F 66 A3
Lisa YU 85 C5
Lisac BIH 84 B2
Lisbellaw GB 19 B4
Lisboa P 92 C1
Lisburn GB 19 B5
Liscannor IRL 20 B2
Lisdoonvarna IRL 20 A2
Lisewo PL 47 B4
Lisia Góra PL 55 C6
Lisięcice PL 54 C2
Lisieux F 57 A6
Liskeard GB 28 C3
L'Isle CH 69 B6
L'Isle-Adam F 58 A3
L'Isle-de-Noé F 77 C3
L'Isle-en-Dodon F 77 C3
L'Isle-Jourdain, Gers F 77 C4
L'Isle-Jourdain, Vienne F 67 B5
L'Isle-sur-la-Sorgue F 79 C4
L'Isle-sur-le Doubs F 69 A6
L'Isle-sur-Serein F 68 A4
Lisle-sur-Tarn F 77 C4
Lismore IRL 21 B4
Lisnaskea GB 19 B4
Lišov CZ 63 A5
Lisów, Lubuskie PL 45 C6
Lisów, Śląskie PL 54 C3
Lisse NL 49 A5
Lissycasey IRL 20 B2
List D 39 D1
Listerby S 41 C5
Listowel IRL 20 B2
Listrac-Médoc F 76 A2
Liszki PL 55 C4
Liszkowo PL 46 B3
Lit S 2 E14
Lit-et-Mixe F 76 B1
Litava SK 65 B5
Litcham GB 30 B4
Litija SLO 73 B4
Litke H 65 B5
Litlabø N 32 B2
Litókhoron GR 15 R18
Litoměřice CZ 53 C4
Litomyšl CZ 64 A2
Litovel CZ 64 A3
Litschau A 63 B6
Little Walsingham GB 30 B4
Littlehampton GB 31 D3
Littleport GB 30 B4
Littleton IRL 21 B4
Litvínov CZ 52 C3
Livarot F 57 B6
Liverno F 77 B4
Liverovici YU 84 D4
Liverpool GB 26 B3
Livigno I 71 B5
Livingston GB 25 C4
Livno BIH 84 C1
Livold SLO 73 C4
Livorno I 81 C4
Livorno Ferraris I 70 C3
Livron-sur-Drôme F 78 B3
Livry-Louvercy F 59 A5
Lixheim F 60 B3
Lizard GB 28 D2
Lizy-sur-Ourcq F 59 A4
Lizzano I 105 B4
Lizzano in Belvedere I 81 B4
Ljig YU 85 B5
Ljosland N 33 C4
Ljubija BIH 83 B5
Ljubinje BIH 84 D3
Ljubljana SLO 73 B4
Ljubno ob Savinji SLO 73 B4
Ljubovija YU 85 B4
Ljubuški BIH 84 C2
Ljugarn S 37 E5
Ljung S 35 D5
Ljunga S 37 C3
Ljungby S 40 C3
Ljungbyhed S 41 C3
Ljungbyholm S 40 C6
Ljungsarp S 40 B3
Ljungsbro S 37 C2
Ljungskile S 35 C3
Ljusdal S 2 F15
Ljusfallshammar S 37 C2
Ljusne S 2 F15
Ljusterö S 36 B5
Ljutomer SLO 73 B6
Lladurs E 91 A4
Llafranc E 91 B6
Llagostera E 91 B5
Llanaelhaiarn GB 26 C1
Llanarth GB 28 A3
Llanbedr GB 26 C1
Llanbedrog GB 26 C1
Llanberis GB 26 B1
Llanbister GB 29 A4
Llanbrynmair GB 26 C2
Llançà E 91 A6
Llandeilo GB 28 B4
Llandissilio GB 28 B3
Llandovery GB 28 B4
Llandrillo GB 26 C2
Llandrindod Wells GB 29 A4
Llandudec F 56 B1
Llandudno GB 26 B2
Llandysul GB 28 A3
Llanelli GB 28 B3
Llanerchymedd GB 26 B1
Llanes E 88 A2
Llanfair Caereinion GB 26 C2
Llanfairfechan GB 26 B2
Llanfyllin GB 26 C2
Llangadog GB 28 B4
Llangefni GB 26 B1
Llangollen GB 26 C2
Llangranog GB 28 A3
Llangurig GB 26 C2
Llanidloes GB 26 C2
Llanilar GB 28 A3
Llanrhystyd GB 28 A3
Llanrwst GB 26 B2
Llansannan GB 26 B2
Llansawel GB 28 A3
Llanstephan GB 28 B3
Llanteno E 89 A3
Llanthony GB 29 B4
Llantrisant GB 29 B4
Llantwit-Major GB 29 B4
Llanuwchllyn GB 26 C2
Llanwddyn GB 26 C2
Llanwrda GB 28 B4
Llanwrtyd Wells GB 29 A4
Llanybydder GB 28 A3
Llanymynech GB 26 C2
Llavorsi E 91 A4
Lleida E 90 B3
Llera E 93 C4
Llerena E 99 A4
Lles E 91 A4
Llessui E 91 A4
Llinars E 91 A4
Lliria E 96 B2
Llivia F 91 A4
Lljezd u Brna CZ 64 A2
Llodio E 89 A4
Lloret de Mar E 91 B5
Llosa de Ranes E 96 B2
Lloseta, Mallorca E 97
Llucena del Cid E 96 A2
Llucmajor, Mallorca E 97
Llutxent E 96 C2
Llwyngwril GB 26 C1
Llyswen GB 29 A4
Lnáře CZ 63 A4
Lniano PL 47 B4
Lo Pagán E 101 B5
Loanhead GB 25 C4
Loano I 80 B2
Loarre E 90 A2
Löbau D 53 B4
Löbejün D 52 B1
Löberöd S 41 D3
Łobez PL 46 B1
Löbnitz D 45 A4
Lobón E 93 C4
Loburg D 52 A2
Łobżenica PL 46 B3
Locana I 70 C2
Locarno CH 70 B3
Loccum D 43 C6
Loče SLO 73 B5
Loch Baghasdail GB 22 D1
Loch nam Madadh GB 22 D1
Lochailort GB 24 B2
Lochaline GB 24 B2
Lochans GB 24 D2
Locharbriggs GB 25 C4
Lochau A 71 A4
Lochcarron GB 22 D3
Lochearnhead GB 24 B3
Lochem NL 50 A2
Loches F 67 A5
Lochgelly GB 25 B4
Lochgilphead GB 24 B2
Lochgoilhead GB 24 B3
Lochinver GB 22 C3
Lochranza GB 24 C2
Ločika YU 85 C6
Lockenhaus A 73 A6
Lockerbie GB 25 C4
Löcknitz D 45 B6
Locmaria F 66 A1
Locmariaquer F 56 C3
Locminé F 56 C3
Locorotondo I 105 B4
Locquirec F 56 B2
Locri I 106 C3
Locronan F 56 B1
Loctudy F 56 C1
Lodares de Osma E 89 C4
Lodě I 110 C2
Lodève F 78 C2
Lodi I 71 C4
Lødingen N 2 B14
Lodosa E 89 B4
Lödöse S 35 C4
Łódź PL 55 B4
Loeches E 95 B3
Løfallstrand N 32 A3
Lofer A 72 A2
Loftahammar S 37 D3
Lofthus N 32 A3
Loftus GB 27 A5
Loga N 32 C3
Logatec SLO 73 C4
Lograto I 71 C5
Logroño E 89 B4
Logrosán E 93 B5
Løgstør DK 38 C2
Løgumgårde DK 39 D1
Løgumkloster DK 39 D1
Lohals DK 39 D3
Lohja FIN 3 F19
Löhlbach D 51 B4
Lohmen, Mecklenburg-Vorpommern D 44 B4
Lohmen, Sachsen D 53 C4
Löhnberg D 50 C4
Lohne, Niedersachsen D 43 C5
Löhne, Nordrhein-Westfalen D 51 A4
Lohr D 51 D5
Lohra D 51 C4
Lohsa D 53 B4
Loiano I 81 B5
Loimaa FIN 3 F18
Loiri I 110 C2
Loitz D 45 B5
Loivos P 87 C3
Loivos do Monte P 87 C3
Loja E 100 B1
Lojanice YU 85 B4
Lojt Kirkeby DK 39 D2
Lok SK 65 B4
Lokca SK 65 A5
Løken N 34 B3
Lokeren B 49 B4
Loket CZ 52 C2
Lokhvitsa UA 7 L23
Løkken DK 38 B2
Løkken N 2 E11
Loknya RUS 7 H22
Lökösháza H 75 B6
Lokot RUS 7 K24
Lokve YU 85 A6
Lollar D 51 C4
L'Olleria E 96 C2
Lölling-Graben A 73 B4
Lom BG 15 Q18
Lom N 2 F11
Lom SK 65 B5
Lombez F 77 C3
Lomello I 80 A2
Łomianki PL 55 A5
Lomma S 41 D3
Lommaryd S 37 D1
Lommatzsch D 52 B3
Lommel B 49 B6
Lommersum D 50 C2
Lomnice CZ 64 A2
Lomnice nad Lužnici CZ 63 A5
Lomnice-nad-Popelkou CZ 53 C5
Łomża PL 6 K18
Lönashult S 40 C4
Lønborg DK 39 D1
Londerzeel B 49 B5
Londinières F 58 A2
London GB 31 C3
Long Bennington GB 27 C5
Long Eaton GB 27 C4
Long Melford GB 30 B4
Long Preston GB 26 A3
Long Sutton GB 30 B4
Longare I 72 C1
Longares E 90 B1
Longarone I 72 B2
Longastrino I 81 B6
Longbenton GB 25 C6
Longchamp-sur-Aujon F 59 B5
Longchaumois F 69 B5
Longeau F 59 C6
Longecourt-en-Plaine F 69 A5
Longeville-les-St. Avold F 60 A2
Longeville-sur-Mer F 66 B3
Longford IRL 19 C4
Longframlington GB 25 C6
Longhope GB 23 C5
Longhorsley GB 25 C6
Longhoughton GB 25 C6
Longi I 109 A3
Longny-au-Perche F 58 B1
Longobucco I 106 B3
Longré F 67 B4
Longridge GB 26 B3
Longroiva P 87 D3
Longtown, Cumbria GB 25 C5
Longtown, Herefordshire GB 29 B5
Longué-Jumelles F 67 A4
Longueau F 58 A3
Longuyon F 60 A1
Longvic F 69 A5
Longvilly B 50 C1
Longwy F 60 A1
Lonigo I 71 C6
Löningen D 43 C4
Lonja HR 74 C1
Lönneberga S 40 B5
Lons-le-Saunier F 69 B5
Lönsboda S 41 C4
Lønstrup DK 38 B2
Looe GB 28 C3
Loon op Zand NL 49 B6
Loone-Plage F 48 B3
Loosdorf A 63 B6
Lopar HR 83 B3
Lopare BIH 84 B3
Lopera E 100 B1
Loppersum NL 42 B3
Łopuszna PL 65 A6
Łopuszno PL 55 C5
Lor F 59 A5
Lora de Estepa E 100 B1
Lora del Río E 99 B5
Loranca del Campo E 95 B4
Lörby S 41 C4
Lorca E 101 B4
Lorch D 50 C3
Lørenfallet N 34 A3
Lørenskog N 34 B2
Loreo I 82 A1
Loreto I 82 C2
Lorgues F 79 C5
Lorica I 106 B3
Lorient F 56 C2
Lorignac F 67 C4
Lörinci H 65 C5
Loriol-sur-Drôme F 78 B3
Lormes F 68 A3
Loro Ciuffenna I 81 C5
Lorqui E 101 A4
Lörrach D 60 C3
Lorrez-le-Bocage F 59 B3
Lorris F 58 C3
Lorup D 43 C4
Łoś PL 55 B5
Los Alcázares E 101 B5
Los Arcos E 89 B4
Los Barios de Luna E 88 B1
Los Barrios E 99 C5
Los Caños de Meca E 99 C4
Los Cerricos E 101 B3
Los Corrales E 100 B1
Los Corrales de Buelna E 88 A2
Los Dolores E 101 B4
Los Gallardos E 101 B4
Los Hinojosos E 95 C4
Los Isidros E 96 B1
Los Molinos E 94 B2
Los Morales E 99 B5
Los Navalmorales E 94 C2
Los Navalucillos E 94 C2
Los Nietos E 101 B5
Los Palacios y Villafranca E 99 B5
Los Pozuelos de Calatrava E 100 A1
Los Rábanos E 89 C4
Los Santos E 93 A5
Los Santos de la Humosa E 95 B3
Los Santos de Maimona E 93 C4
Los Tijos E 88 A2
Los Villares E 100 B2
Los Yébenes E 94 C3
Losacino E 87 C4
Losar de la Vera E 93 A5
Losenstein A 63 C5
Losheim, Nordrhein-Westfalen D 50 C2
Losheim, Saarland D 60 A2
Losne F 69 A5
Løsning DK 39 D2
Lossburg D 61 B4
Losser NL 50 A3
Lossiemouth GB 23 D5
Lössnitz D 52 C2
Loštice CZ 64 A2
Lostwithiel GB 28 C3
Lotorp S 37 C2
Lotyń PL 46 B2
Lotzorai I 110 D2
Louargat F 56 B2
Loudéac F 56 B3
Loudun F 67 A5
Loué F 57 C5
Loughborough GB 27 C4
Loughbrickland GB 19 B5
Loughrea IRL 20 A3
Louhans F 69 B5
Louisburgh IRL 18 C2
Loukhi RUS 3 C23
Loulay F 67 B4
Loulé P 98 B2
Louny CZ 53 C3
Lourdes F 76 C2
Lourenzá E 86 A3
Loures P 92 C1
Loures-Barousse F 77 C3
Louriçal P 92 A2
Lourinhã P 92 B1
Loury F 58 C3
Lousa, Bragança P 87 C3
Lousa, Castelo Branco P 92 B3
Lousã, Coimbra P 92 A2
Lousa, Lisboa P 92 C1
Lousada E 86 B3
Lousada P 87 C2
Louth GB 27 B5
Louverné F 57 B5
Louvie-Juzon F 76 C2
Louviers F 58 A2
Louvigné-du-Désert F 57 B4
Louvois F 59 A5
Lova I 72 C2
Lovasberény H 74 A3
Lovászpatona H 74 A2
Lovech BG 16 Q19
Lövenich D 50 B2
Lóvere I 71 C5
Lövestad S 41 D3
Loviisa FIN 3 F20
Lovinobaňa SK 65 B5
Loviste HR 84 C2
Lovke HR 73 C4
Lövö H 74 A1
Lovosice CZ 53 C4
Lovozero RUS 3 C24
Lovran HR 73 C4
Lovreć HR 84 C1
Lovrenc na Pohorju SLO 73 B5
Lovrin RO 75 C5
Lövstabruk S 36 A4
Löwenberg D 45 C5
Löwenstein D 61 A5
Lowestoft GB 30 B5
Lowick GB 25 C6
Łowicz PL 55 A4
Loxstedt D 43 B5
Loyew BY 11 L22
Lož SLO 73 C4
Loza CZ 63 A4
Loznica YU 85 B4
Lozničko Polje YU 85 B4
Lozorno SK 64 B3
Lozovik YU 85 B6
Lozoya E 94 B3
Lozoyuela E 95 B3
Lozzo di Cadore I 72 B2
Luanco E 88 A1
Luarca E 86 A4
Lubaczów PL 11 L18
Lubań PL 53 B5
Lubanów PL 55 B4
Lubars D 52 A2
Lubasz PL 46 C2
Lubawa PL 47 B5
Lubawka PL 53 C6
Lübbecke D 51 A4
Lübben D 53 B3
Lübbenau D 53 B3
Lubczyna PL 45 B6
Lübeck D 44 B2
Lubenec CZ 52 C3
Lubersac F 67 C6
Lübesse D 44 B3
Lubia E 89 C4
Lubian E 87 B4

Lubiatowo PL 45 B7
Lubichowo PL 47 B4
Lubicz Dolny PL 47 B4
Lubień PL 65 A5
Lubień Kujawski PL 47 C5
Lubienia PL 55 B6
Lubieszewo PL 46 B1
Lubin, *Legnica* PL 53 B6
Lubin, *Szczecin* PL 45 B6
Lublin PL 11 L18
Lubliniec PL 54 C3
Lubmin D 45 A5
Lubniewice PL 46 C1
Lubny UA 11 L23
Lubochnia PL 55 B5
Lubomierz, *Jelenia Góra* PL 53 B5
Lubomierz, *Nowy Secz* PL 65 A6
Lubomino PL 47 A6
Luboń PL 46 C2
L'ubotín SK 65 A6
Lubowidz PL 47 B5
Łubowo, *Wielkopolskie* PL 46 C3
Łubowo, *Zachodnio-Pomorskie* PL 46 B2
Lubraniec PL 47 C4
Lubrín E 101 B3
Lubrza PL 54 C2
Lubsko PL 53 B4
Lübtheen D 44 B3
Lubuczewo PL 46 A3
Luby CZ 52 C2
Lübz D 44 B4
Luc F 78 B2
Luc-en-Diois F 79 B4
Luc-sur-Mer F 57 A5
Lucainena de las Torres E 101 B3
Lucan IRL 21 A5
Lučani YU 85 C5
Lúcar E 101 B3
Luçay-le-Mâle F 67 A6
Lucca I 81 C4
Lucciana F 110 A2
Lucé F 58 B2
Luče SLO 73 B4
Lucena, *Córdoba* E 100 B1
Lucena, *Huelva* E 99 B4
Lucenay-les-Aix F 68 B3
Lucenay-l'Evéque F 69 A4
Lučenec SK 65 B5
Luceni E 90 B1
Lucens CH 70 B1
Lucera I 104 A2
Luceram F 80 C1
Lüchow D 44 C3
Luciana E 94 D2
Lucignano I 81 C5
Lucija SLO 72 C3
Lucka D 52 B2
Luckau D 53 B3
Luckenwalde D 52 A3
Lückstedt D 44 C3
Luco dei Marsi I 103 B3
Luçon F 66 B3
Ludanice SK 64 B4
Ludbreg HR 74 B1
Lüdenscheid D 50 B3
Lüderitz D 44 C3
Lüdersdorf D 44 B2
Ludgershall GB 31 C2
Ludgo S 37 C4
Lüdinghausen D 50 B3
Ludlow GB 29 A5
Ludomy PL 46 C2
Ludvika S 36 A2
Ludweiler Warndt D 60 A2
Ludwigsburg D 61 B5
Ludwigsfelde D 52 A3
Ludwigshafen D 61 A4
Ludwigslust D 44 B3
Ludwigsstadt D 52 C1
Ludza LV 7 H20
Luesia E 90 A1
Luftkurort Arendsee D 44 C3
Lug BIH 84 D3
Lug HR 74 C3
Luga RUS 7 G21
Lugagnano Val d'Arda I 81 B3
Lugano CH 70 B3
Lugau D 52 C2
Lugnas S 35 C5
Lúgnola I 102 A2
Lugny F 69 B4
Lugo E 86 A3
Lugo I 81 B5
Lugoj RO 10 P17
Lugones E 88 A1
Lugros E 100 B2
Luhačovice CZ 64 A3
Luhe D 62 A3
Luino I 70 C3
Luintra E 87 B3
Lújar E 100 C2
Luka nad Jihlavou CZ 63 A6
Lukavac BIH 84 B3
Lukavika BIH 84 B3
Lukovica SLO 73 B4
Lukovit BG 16 Q19
Lukovo HR 83 B3
Lukovo YU 85 C6
Lukovo Šugorje HR 83 B4
Łuków PL 11 L18
Łukowice Brzeskie PL 54 C2
Luksefjell N 33 B6
Łukta PL 47 B6
Lula I 110 C2
Luleå S 3 D18
Lüleburgaz TR 16 R20
Lumbarda HR 84 D2
Lumbier E 90 A1
Lumbrales E 87 D4
Lumbreras E 89 B4
Lumbres F 48 C3
Lummelunda S 37 D5
Lummen B 49 C6
Lumpiaque E 90 B1
Lumsden GB 23 D6
Lun HR 83 B3
Luna E 90 A2
Lunamatrona I 110 D1
Lunano I 82 C1
Lunas F 78 C2
Lund S 41 D3
Lunde DK 39 D1
Lunde N 33 B6
Lunden D 43 A6
Lunderseter N 34 A4
Lunderskov DK 39 D2
Lundsberg S 34 B6
Lüneburg D 44 B2
Lunel F 78 C3
Lünen D 50 B3
Lunéville F 60 B2
Lungern CH 70 B3
Lungro I 106 B3
Luninyets BY 7 K20
Lünne D 43 C4
Lunner N 34 A2
Lunteren NL 49 A6
Lunz am See A 63 C6
Luogosanto I 110 B2
Łupawa PL 46 A3
Lupión E 100 A2
Lupoglav HR 73 C4
Luppa D 52 B2
Luque E 100 B1
Lurago d'Erba I 71 C4
Lúras I 110 C2
Lurcy-Lévis F 68 B2
Lure F 60 C2
Lurgan GB 19 B5
Lury-sur-Arnon F 68 A2
Lušci Palanka BIH 83 B5
Lusévera I 72 B3
Lushnjë AL 15 R16
Lusignan F 67 B5
Lusigny-sur-Barse F 59 B5
Lusnić BIH 84 C1
Luso P 92 A2
Lusówko PL 46 C2
Luss GB 24 B3
Lussac F 76 B2
Lussac-les-Châteaux F 67 B5
Lussac-les-Eglises F 67 B6
Lussan F 78 B3
Lüssow D 44 B4
Lustenau A 71 A4
Luštěnice CZ 53 C4
Lutago I 72 B1
Lutherstadt Wittenberg D 52 B2
Lütjenburg D 44 A2
Lutocin PL 47 C5
Lutomiersk PL 55 B4
Luton GB 31 C3
Lutry CH 70 B1
Lutry PL 47 A6
Lutsk UA 11 L19
Lutter am Barenberge D 51 B6
Lutterworth GB 30 B2
Lututów PL 54 B3
Lützen D 52 B2
Lutzow D 44 B3
Luxembourg L 60 A2
Luxeuil-les-Bains F 60 C2
Luxey F 76 B2
Luz, *Évora* P 98 A3
Luz, *Faro* P 98 B2
Luz, *Faro* P 98 B3
Luz-St-Sauveur F 76 D2
Luzarches F 58 A3
Luže CZ 64 A2
Luzech F 77 B4
Luzern CH 70 A3
Luzino PL 47 A4
Luzy F 68 B3
Luzzi I 106 B3
L'viv UA 11 M19
Lwówek PL 46 C2
Lwówek Śląski PL 53 B5
Lyakhavichy BY 7 K20
Lybster GB 23 C5
Lychen D 45 B5
Lychkova RUS 7 H23
Lyckeby S 41 C5
Lycksele S 3 D16
Lydd GB 31 D4
Lydford GB 28 C3
Lydney GB 29 B5
Lyepyel BY 7 J21
Lykling N 32 B2
Lyme Regis GB 29 C5
Lymington GB 31 D2
Lympne GB 31 C5
Lyndhurst GB 31 D2
Lyneham GB 29 B6
Lyness GB 23 C5
Lyngdal, *Buskerud* N 33 B6
Lyngdal, *Vest-Agder* N 33 C4
Lyngør N 33 C6
Lyngsa DK 38 B3
Lynmouth GB 28 B4
Lynton GB 28 B4
Lyntupy BY 7 J20
Lyon F 69 C4
Lyons-la-Forêt F 58 A2
Lyozna BY 7 J22
Lyrestad S 35 C6
Lysá nad Labem CZ 53 C4
Lysá pod Makytou SK 64 A4
Lysebotn N 32 B3
Lysekil S 35 C3
Lysice CZ 64 A2
Lysomice PL 47 B4
Lyss CH 70 A2
Lystrup DK 39 C3
Lysvik S 34 A5
Łyszkowice PL 55 B4
Lytham St. Anne'S GB 26 B2
Lyuban RUS 7 G22
Lyubertsy RUS 7 J25
Lyuboml' UA 11 L19
Lyubotyn UA 7 M24
Lyubytino RUS 7 G23
Lyudinovo RUS 7 K24

M

Maarheeze NL 49 B6
Maaseik B 50 B1
Maastricht NL 50 C1
Mablethorpe GB 27 B6
Mably F 68 B4
Macael E 101 B3
Maçanet de Cabrenys E 91 A5
Mação P 92 B2
Macau F 76 A2
Maccagno-Agra I 70 B3
Maccarese I 102 B2
Macchiagódena I 103 B4
Macclesfield GB 26 B3
Macduff GB 23 D6
Maceda E 87 B3
Macedo de Cavaleiros P 87 C4
Maceira, *Guarda* P 92 A3
Maceira, *Leiria* P 92 B2
Macelj HR 73 B5
Macerata I 82 C2
Macerata Féltria I 82 C1
Machault F 59 A5
Machecoul F 66 B3
Machrihanish GB 24 C2
Machynlleth GB 26 C2
Macieira P 87 C2
Maciejowice PL 55 B6
Macinaggio F 80 D3
Mackenrode D 51 B6
Mačkovci SLO 73 B6
Macomer I 110 C1
Macon B 49 C5
Mâcon F 69 B4
Macotera E 94 B1
Macroom IRL 20 C3
Macugnaga I 70 C2
Madängsholm S 35 C5
Madaras H 75 B4
Maddaloni I 103 B4
Made NL 49 B5
Madeley GB 26 C3
Maderuelo E 89 C3
Madley GB 29 A5
Madocsa H 75 B3
Madona LV 7 H20
Madonna di Campiglio I 71 B5
Madrid E 94 B3
Madridejos E 95 C3
Madrigal de la Vera E 94 B1
Madrigal de las Altas Torres E 94 A1
Madrigalejo E 93 B5
Madrigalejo de Monte E 88 B3
Madriguera E 89 C3
Madrigueras E 95 C5
Madroñera E 93 B5
Maël-Carhaix F 56 B2
Maella E 90 B3
Maello E 94 B2
Maesteg GB 29 B4
Mafra P 92 C1
Magacela E 93 C5
Magallon E 89 C5
Magaluf, *Mallorca* E 97
Magán E 94 C3
Magaña E 89 C4
Magasa I 71 C5
Magaz E 88 C2
Magdeburg D 52 A1
Magenta I 70 C3
Magesq F 76 C1
Maghera GB 19 B5
Magherafelt GB 19 B5
Maghull GB 26 B3
Magione I 82 C1
Maglaj BIH 84 B3
Maglehem S 41 D4
Magliano de'Marsi I 103 A3
Magliano in Toscana I 102 A1
Magliano Sabina I 102 A2
Maglić YU 75 C4
Máglie I 105 B5
Maglód H 75 A4
Magnac-Bourg F 67 C6
Magnac-Laval F 67 B6
Magnieres F 60 B2
Magnor N 34 B4
Magnuszew PL 55 B6
Magny-Cours F 68 B3
Magny-en-Vexin F 58 A2
Mágocs H 74 B3
Magoute P 92 C1
Maguilla E 93 C5
Maguiresbridge GB 19 B4
Magyarbóly H 74 C3
Magyarkeszi H 74 B3
Magyarszék H 74 B3
Mahide E 87 C4
Mahilyow BY 7 K22
Mahora E 95 C5
Mahovo HR 73 C6
Mähring D 62 A3
Maia E 76 C1
Maia P 87 C2
Maiaelrayo E 95 A3
Maials E 90 B3
Maîche F 70 A1
Máida I 106 C3
Maiden Bradley GB 29 B5
Maiden Newton GB 29 C5
Maidenhead GB 31 C3
Maidstone GB 31 C4
Maienfeld CH 71 A4
Maignelay Montigny F 58 A3
Mailezais F 67 B4
Mailly-le-Camp F 59 B5
Mailly-le-Château F 59 C4
Mainar E 89 C5
Mainbernheim D 61 A6
Mainburg D 62 B2
Mainhardt D 61 A5
Maintal D 51 C4
Maintenon F 58 B2
Mainvilliers F 58 B2
Mainz D 50 C4
Maiorca P 92 A2
Mairena de Aljarafe E 99 B4
Mairena del Alcor E 99 B5
Maisach D 62 B2
Maishofen A 72 A2
Maison-Rouge F 59 B4
Maissau A 64 B1
Maisse F 58 B3
Maizières-lès-Vic F 60 B2
Maja HR 73 C6
Majadahonda E 94 B3
Majadas E 93 B5
Majs H 74 C3
Majšperk SLO 73 B5
Makarska HR 84 C2
Makkum NL 42 B2
Maklár H 65 C6
Makó H 75 B5
Makoszyce PL 54 C2
Makov SK 65 A4
Makovac YU 85 D6
Maków Podhalański PL 65 A5
Makowarsko PL 46 B3
Mala Bosna YU 75 B4
Mala Kladuša BIH 73 C5
Mala Krsna YU 85 B6
Malá Lehota SK 65 B4
Mala Pijace YU 75 B4
Mala Subotica HR 73 B6
Mala Vyska UA 11 M22
Malacky SK 64 B3
Maladzyechna BY 7 J20
Málaga E 100 C1
Malagón E 94 C3
Malaguilla E 95 B3
Malahide IRL 21 A5
Malalbergo I 81 B5
Malanów PL 54 B3
Malaucène F 79 B4
Malaunay F 58 A2
Malaya Vishera RUS 7 G23
Malborghetto I 72 B3
Malbork PL 47 A5
Malborn D 60 A2
Malbuisson F 69 B6
Malcésine I 71 C5
Malchin D 45 B4
Malching D 63 B4
Malchow D 44 B4
Malcocinado E 99 A5
Malczyce PL 54 B1
Maldegem B 49 B4
Maldon GB 31 C4
Małdyty PL 47 B5
Malè I 71 B5
Malemort F 67 C6
Malente D 44 A2
Malerås S 40 C5
Malesherbes F 58 B3
Malestroit F 56 C3
Maletto I 109 B3
Malexander S 37 C2
Malfa I 109 A3
Malgrat de Mar E 91 B5
Malhadas P 87 C4
Mali Lošinj HR 83 B3
Malicorne-sur-Sarthe F 57 C5
Malijai F 79 B5
Malildjoš YU 75 C4
Målilla S 40 B5
Malin IRL 19 A4
Málinec SK 65 B5
Malingsbo S 36 B2
Maliniec PL 54 A3
Malinska HR 83 A3
Maljevac HR 73 C5
Malkara TR 16 R20
Małki PL 47 B5
Malko Tŭrnovo BG 16 Q20
Mallaig GB 22 D3
Mallaranny IRL 18 C2
Mallemort F 79 C4
Mallén E 89 C5
Mallersdorf-Pfaffenberg D 62 B3
Málles Venosta I 71 B5
Malling DK 39 C3
Mallnitz A 72 B3
Mallow IRL 20 B3
Mallwyd GB 26 C2
Malmbäck S 40 B4
Malmberget S 3 C17
Malmédy B 50 C2
Malmesbury GB 29 B5
Malmköping S 36 B3
Malmö S 41 D3
Malmon S 35 D3
Malmslätt S 37 C2
Malnate I 70 C3
Malo I 71 C6
Maloarkhangelsk RUS 7 K25
Małogoszcz PL 55 C5
Maloja CH 71 B4
Małomice PL 53 B5
Måløy N 2 F9
Maloyaroslovets RUS 7 J25
Malpartida E 93 B4
Malpartida de la Serena E 93 C5
Malpartida de Plasencia E 93 B4
Malpas E 90 A3
Malpas GB 26 B3
Malpica P 92 B3
Malpica de Bergantiños E 86 A2
Malpica de Tajo E 94 C2
Malsch D 61 B4
Malšice CZ 63 A5
Malta A 72 B3
Maltat F 68 B3
Maltby GB 27 B4
Malung S 2 F13
Malungsfors S 2 F13
Maluszów PL 45 C7
Maluszyn PL 55 C4
Malva E 88 C1
Malvaglia CH 70 B3
Malveira P 92 C1
Malyn UA 11 L21
Mamarrosa P 92 A2
Mamer L 60 A2
Mamers F 58 B1
Mamirolle F 69 A6
Mammendorf D 62 B2
Mámmola I 106 C3
Mamoiada I 110 C2
Mamonovo RUS 47 A5
Maňa SK 64 B4
Manacor, *Mallorca* E 97
Manavgat TR 16 T22
Mancera de Abajo E 94 B1
Mancha Real E 100 B2
Manchester GB 26 B3
Manching D 62 B2
Manchita E 93 C4
Manciano I 102 A1
Manciet F 76 C3
Mandal N 33 C4
Mandanici I 109 A4
Mándas I 110 D2
Mandatoríccio I 107 B3
Mandayona E 95 B4
Mandelieu-la-Napoule F 79 C5
Mandello del Lário I 71 C4
Mandelsloh D 43 C6
Manderfeld B 50 C2
Manderscheid D 50 C2
Mandino Selo BIH 84 C2
Mandoúdhion GR 15 S18
Mandúria I 105 B4
Mane, *Alpes-de-Haute-Provence* F 79 C4
Mane, *Haute-Garonne* F 77 C3
Manérbio I 71 C5
Mañeru E 89 B5
Manetin CZ 52 D3
Manfredónia I 104 A2
Mangalia RO 16 Q21
Manganeses de la Lampreana E 88 C1
Manganeses de la Polvorosa E 88 B1
Mangen N 34 B3
Mangiennes F 60 A1
Mangotsfield GB 29 B5
Mangualde P 92 A3
Maniago I 72 B2
Manilva E 99 C5
Manisa TR 16 S20
Manises E 96 B2
Mank A 63 B6
Månkarbo S 36 A4
Manlleu E 91 B5
Männedorf CH 70 A3
Mannersdorf am Leithagebirge A 64 C2
Mannheim D 61 A4
Manningtree GB 31 C5
Manoppello I 103 A4
Manorbier GB 28 B3
Manorhamilton IRL 18 B3
Manosque F 79 C4
Manresa E 91 B4
Månsarp S 40 B4
Manschnow D 45 C6
Mansfeld D 52 B1
Mansfield GB 27 B4
Mansilla de Burgos E 88 B3
Mansilla de las Mulas E 88 B1
Manskog S 34 B4
Mansle F 67 C5
Manso F 110 A1
Manteigas P 92 A3
Mantel D 62 A3
Mantes-la-Jolie F 58 B2
Mantes-la-Ville F 58 B2
Manthelan F 67 A5
Mantorp S 37 C2
Mántova I 71 C5
Mänttä FIN 3 E19
Manuel E 96 B2
Manzanal de Arriba E 87 B4
Manzanares E 95 C3
Manzanares el Real E 94 B3
Manzaneda, *León* E 87 B4
Manzaneda, *Orense* E 87 B3
Manzanedo E 88 B3
Manzaneque E 94 C3
Manzanera E 96 A2
Manzanilla E 99 B4
Manzat F 68 C2
Manziana I 102 A2
Manziat F 69 B4
Maó, *Menorca* E 97
Maoča BIH 84 B3
Maqueda E 94 B2
Mara E 89 C5
Maraña E 88 A1
Maranchón E 95 A4
Maranello I 81 B4
Marano I 103 C4
Marano Lagunare I 72 C3
Marans F 66 B4
Maratea I 104 C2
Marateca P 92 C2
Marazion GB 28 C2
Marbach, *Baden-Württemberg* D 61 B5
Marbach, *Hessen* D 51 C5
Marbach F 60 B2
Marbäck S 40 B3
Mårbacka S 34 B5
Marbella E 100 C1
Marboz F 69 B5
Marburg D 51 C4
Marcali H 74 B2
Marčana HR 82 A2
Marcaria I 81 A4
Marcelová SK 64 C4
Marcenat F 68 C2
March GB 30 B4
Marchamalo E 95 B3
Marchaux F 69 A6
Marche-en-Famenne B 49 C6
Marchegg A 64 B2
Marchena E 99 B5
Marchenoir F 58 C2
Marcheprime F 76 B2
Marciac F 76 C3
Marciana Marina I 81 D4
Marcianise I 103 B4
Marcigny F 68 B4
Marcilla E 89 B5
Marcillac-la-Croisille F 68 C2
Marcillac-Vallon F 77 B5
Marcillat-en-Combraille F 68 B2
Marcille-sur-Seine F 59 B4
Marcilloles F 69 C5
Marcilly-le-Hayer F 59 B4
Marcinkowice PL 46 B2
Marciszów PL 53 C6
Marck F 48 C2
Marckolsheim F 60 B3
Marco de Canevezes P 87 C2
Mareham le Fen GB 27 B5
Marek S 37 D2
Marennes F 66 C3
Maresquel F 48 C2
Mareuil F 67 C5
Mareuil-en-Brie F 59 B4
Mareuil-sur-Arnon F 68 B2
Mareuil-sur-Lay F 66 B3
Mareuil-sur-Ourcq F 59 A4
Margam GB 28 B4
Margate GB 31 C5
Margaux F 76 A2
Margerie-Hancourt F 59 B5
Margès F 69 C5
Margherita di Savóia I 104 A3
Margita YU 75 C6
Margone I 70 C2
Margonin PL 46 C3
Marguerittes F 78 C3
Margut F 59 A6
Maria E 101 B3
Maria Neustift A 63 C5
Maria Saal A 73 B4
Mariager DK 38 C2
Mariana E 95 B4
Mariannelund S 40 B5
Marianópoli I 108 B2
Mariánské Lázně CZ 52 D2
Mariapfarr A 72 A3
Mariazell A 63 C6
Maribo DK 39 E4
Maribor SLO 73 B5
Marieberg S 36 B2
Mariefred S 36 B4
Marieholm S 41 D3
Mariembourg B 49 C5
Marienbaum D 50 B2
Marienberg D 52 C3
Marienheide D 50 B3
Mariental D 51 A6
Mariestad S 35 C5
Marigliano I 103 C4
Marignane F 79 C4
Marigny, *Jura* F 69 B5
Marigny, *Manche* F 57 A4
Marigny-le-Châtel F 59 B4
Marija Bistrica HR 73 B6
Marijampolė LT 6 J18
Marín E 87 B2
Marina HR 83 C5
Marina del Cantone I 103 C4
Marina di Acquappesa I 106 B2
Marina di Alberese I 102 A1
Marina di Amendolara I 105 C3
Marina di Árbus I 110 D1
Marina di Campo I 81 D4
Marina di Carrara I 81 B4
Marina di Castagneto-Donorático I 81 C4
Marina di Cécina I 81 C4
Marina di Gáiro I 110 D2
Marina di Ginosa I 105 B3
Marina di Gioiosa Iónica I 106 C3
Marina di Grosseto I 81 D4
Marina di Léuca I 107 B5
Marina di Massa I 81 B4
Marina di Nováglie I 107 B5
Marina di Pisa I 81 C4
Marina di Ragusa I 109 C3
Marina di Ravenna I 82 B1
Marina di Torre Grande I 110 D1
Marina Romea I 82 B1
Marinaleda E 100 B1
Marine de Sisco F 80 D3
Marinella I 108 B1
Marinella di Sarzana I 81 B4
Marineo I 108 B2
Marines F 58 A2
Maringues F 68 C3
Marinha das Ondas P 92 A2
Marinha Grande P 92 B2
Marinhas P 87 C2
Marino I 102 B2
Marjaliza E 94 C3
Markaryd S 40 C3
Markdorf D 61 C5
Markelo NL 50 A2
Market Deeping GB 30 B3
Market Drayton GB 26 C3
Market Harborough GB 30 B3
Market Rasen GB 27 B5
Market Warsop GB 27 B4
Market Weighton GB 27 B5
Markethill GB 19 B5
Markgröningen D 61 B5
Markhausen D 43 C4
Marki PL 55 A6
Markina-Xemein E 89 A4
Markinch GB 25 B4
Märkische Buchholz D 53 A3
Markkleeberg D 52 B2
Marklohe D 43 C6
Marknesse NL 42 C2
Markneukirchen D 52 C2
Markovac YU 85 B6
Markowice PL 54 C3
Markranstädt D 52 B2
Marksuhl D 51 C6
Markt Allhau A 73 A6
Markt Bibart D 61 A6
Markt Erlbach D 62 A1
Markt-heidenfeld D 61 A5
Markt Indersdorf D 62 B2
Markt Rettenbach D 61 C6
Markt Schwaben D 62 B2
Markt-Übelbach A 73 A5
Marktbreit D 61 A6
Marktleuthen D 52 C1
Marktoberdorf D 62 C1
Marktredwitz D 52 C2
Markusica HR 74 C3
Markušovce SK 65 B6
Marl D 50 B3
Marlborough, *Devon* GB 28 C4
Marlborough, *Wiltshire* GB 29 B6
Marle F 59 A4
Marlieux F 69 B5
Marlow D 45 A4
Marlow GB 31 C3
Marma S 36 A4
Marmagne F 69 B4
Marmande F 76 B3
Marmaris TR 16 T21
Marmelete P 98 B2
Marmolejo E 100 A1
Marmoutier F 60 B3
Marnay F 69 A5
Marne D 43 B6
Marnheim D 61 A4
Marnitz D 44 B3
Maroldsweisach D 51 C6
Marolles-les-Braults F 58 B1
Maromme F 58 A2
Marone I 71 C5
Maroslele H 75 B5
Maróstica I 72 C1
Marotta I 82 C2
Marquion F 49 C4
Marquise F 48 C2
Marradi I 81 B5
Marratxi, *Mallorca* E 97
Marrehamn FIN 3 F16
Marrùbiu I 110 D1
Marrum NL 42 B2
Marrupe E 94 B2
Mars-la-Tours F 60 A1
Marsac F 77 C5
Marsac-en-Livradois F 68 C3
Marságlia I 80 B3
Marsala I 108 B1
Marsberg D 51 B4
Marsciano I 82 D1
Marseillan F 78 C2
Marseille F 79 C4
Marseille en Beauvaisis F 58 A2
Mársico Nuovo I 104 B2
Marske-by-the-Sea GB 27 A4
Marson F 59 B5
Märsta S 36 B4
Marstal DK 39 E3
Marstrand S 35 D3
Marta I 102 A1
Martano I 105 B5
Martel F 77 B4
Martelange B 60 A1
Martfeld D 43 C6
Martfű H 75 A5
Martham GB 30 B5
Marthon F 67 C5
Martiago E 93 A4
Martigné-Briand F 67 A4
Martigné-Ferchaud F 57 C4
Martigny CH 70 B2
Martigny-les-Bains F 60 B1
Martigues F 79 C4
Martim-Longo P 98 B3
Martin SK 65 A4
Martin de la Jara E 100 B1
Martin Muñoz de las Posadas E 94 A2
Martina CH 71 B5
Martina Franca I 105 B4
Martinamor E 94 B1
Martinengo I 71 C4
Martinsberg A 63 B6
Martinšćica HR 82 B3
Martinshöhe D 60 A3
Martinsicuro I 82 D2
Martinszell D 61 C6
Mártis I 110 C1
Martofte DK 39 D3
Martonvásár H 74 A3
Martorell E 91 B4
Martos E 100 B2
Martres Tolosane F 77 C3
Marugán E 94 B2
Marúggio I 105 B4
Marvão P 92 B3
Marvejols F 78 B2
Marville F 60 A1
Marwałd PL 47 B5
Marykirk GB 25 B5
Marypark GB 23 D5
Maryport GB 26 A2
Marytavy GB 28 C3
Marzabotto I 81 B5
Marzahna D 52 B2
Marzahne D 45 C4
Marzamemi I 109 C4
Marzocca I 82 C2
Mas de Barberáns E 90 C3
Mas de las Matas E 90 C2
Masa E 88 B3
Máscali I 109 B4
Mascaraque E 94 C3
Mascarenhas P 87 C3
Mascioni I 103 A3
Masegoso E 101 A3
Masegoso de Tajuña E 95 B4
Masera I 70 B3
Masevaux F 60 C2
Masham GB 27 A4
Maside E 87 B2
Maslacq F 76 C2
Maslinica HR 83 C5
Mašlovare BIH 84 B2
Masone I 80 B2
Massa I 81 B4
Massa Fiscáglia I 81 B6
Massa Lombarda I 81 B5
Massa Lubrense I 103 C4
Massa Marittima I 81 C4
Massa Martana I 82 D1
Massafra I 105 B4
Massamagrell E 96 B2
Massanassa E 96 B2
Massarosa I 81 C4
Massat F 77 D4
Massay F 68 A1
Massbach D 51 C6
Masseret F 67 C6
Masseube F 77 C3
Massiac F 68 C3
Massing D 62 B3
Massmechelen B 50 C1
Masty BY 6 K19
Masúa I 110 D1
Masueco E 87 C4
Mašun SLO 73 C4
Maszewo, *Szczecin* PL 45 B7
Maszewo, *Zielona Góra* PL 53 A4
Mata de Alcántara E 93 B4
Matalebreras E 89 C4
Matallana de Torio E 88 B1
Matamala E 89 C4
Mataporquera E 88 B2
Matapozuelos E 88 C2
Mataró E 91 B5
Mataruge YU 85 C4
Mataruška Banja YU 85 C5
Matélica I 82 C2
Matera I 105 B3
Mateševo YU 85 D4
Mátészalka H 11 N18
Matet E 96 B2
Matha F 67 C4
Mathay F 70 A1
Matignon F 57 B3
Matilla de los Caños del Rio E 87 D5
Matlock GB 27 B4
Matosinhos P 87 C2
Matour F 69 B4
Mátraféred H 65 C5
Mátraterenye H 65 B5
Matre N 32 B2
Matrei am Brenner A 71 A6
Matrei in Osttirol A 72 B2
Matrice I 103 B4
Mattarello I 71 B6
Mattersburg A 64 C2
Mattighofen A 62 B4
Mattinata I 104 A3
Mattos P 92 B2
Mattsee A 62 C4
Matulji HR 73 C4
Maubert-Fontaine F 59 A5
Maubeuge F 49 C4
Maubourguet F 76 C3
Mauchline GB 24 C3

Maud GB 23 D6
Mauerkirchen A 62 B4
Mauern D 62 B2
Mauguio F 78 C3
Maulbronn D 61 B4
Maule F 58 B2
Mauléon F 67 B4
Mauléon-Barousse F 77 D3
Mauléon-Licharre F 76 C2
Maulévrier F 67 A4
Maum IRL 18 C2
Maurach A 72 A1
Maure-de-Bretagne F 57 C4
Maureilhan F 78 C2
Mauriac F 68 C2
Mauron F 57 B3
Maurs F 77 B5
Maury F 77 D5
Maussane-les-Alpilles F 78 C3
Mautern A 63 B6
Mautern im Steiermark A 73 A4
Mauterndorf A 72 A3
Mauthausen A 63 B5
Mauthen A 72 B2
Mauvezin F 77 C3
Mauzé-sur-le-Mignon F 67 B4
Maxent F 57 C3
Maxey-sur-Vaise F 60 B1
Maxial P 92 B1
Maxieira P 92 B2
Maxwellheugh GB 25 C5
Mayalde E 94 A1
Maybole GB 24 C3
Mayen D 50 C3
Mayenne F 57 B5
Mayet F 58 C1
Mayorga E 88 B1
Mayres F 78 B3
Mayrhofen A 72 A1
Mazagón E 99 B4
Mazaleón E 90 B3
Mazamet F 77 C5
Mazan F 79 B4
Mazara del Vallo I 108 B1
Mazarambroz E 94 C2
Mazarete E 95 B4
Mazaricos E 86 B2
Mazarrón E 101 B4
Mažeikiai LT 6 H18
Mazères F 77 C4
Mazères-sur-Salat F 77 C3
Mazières-en-Gâtine F 67 B4
Mazin HR 83 B4
Mazuelo E 88 B3
Mazyr BY 7 K21
Mazzarino I 109 B3
Mazzarrà Sant'Andrea I 109 A4
Mazzo di Valtellina I 71 B5
Mchowo PL 47 B6
Mdzewo PL 47 C6
Mealabost GB 22 C2
Mealhada P 92 A2
Meana Sardo I 110 D2
Meaulne F 68 B2
Meaux F 59 B3
Mecerreyes E 89 B3
Mechelen B 49 B5
Mechernich D 50 C2
Mechnica PL 54 C3
Mechterstädt D 51 C6
Mecikal PL 46 B3
Mecina-Bombarón E 100 C2
Meckenbeuren D 61 C5
Meckenheim, *Rheinland-Pfalz* D 50 C3
Meckenheim, *Rheinland-Pfalz* D 61 A4
Meckesheim D 61 A4
Mecseknádasd H 74 B3
Meda I 71 C4
Meda P 87 D3
Medak HR 83 B4
Mede I 80 A2
Medebach D 51 B4
Medelim P 93 A3
Medemblik NL 42 C2
Medena Selista BIH 83 B5
Medesano I 81 B4
Medevi S 37 C1
Medgidia RO 11 P21
Medgyesháza H 75 B6
Medhamn S 34 B5
Mediaş RO 11 N19
Medicina I 81 B5
Medina de las Torres E 99 A4
Medina de Pomar E 89 B3
Medina de Rioseco E 88 C1
Medina del Campo E 88 C2
Medina Sidonia E 99 C5
Medinaceli E 95 A4
Medinilla E 93 A5
Medja YU 75 C5
Medjedja BIH 85 C4
Medulin HR 82 B2
Meduno I 72 B2
Medveda YU 85 B6
Medvedja YU 85 C6
Medvedov SK 64 C3
Medvide HR 83 B4
Medvode SLO 73 B4
Medzev SK 65 B6
Meerane D 52 C2
Meerle B 49 B5
Meersburg D 61 C5
Meeuwen B 49 B6
Mégara GR 15 T18
Megève F 69 C6
Meggenhofen A 63 B4
Mehedeby S 36 A4
Mehun-sur-Yèvre F 68 A2
Meigle GB 25 B4
Meijel NL 50 B1
Meilen CH 70 A3
Meilhan F 76 C2
Meimôa P 93 A3
Meina I 70 C3
Meine D 44 C2
Meinersen D 44 C2
Meinerzhagen D 50 B3
Meiningen D 51 C6
Meira E 86 A3
Meiringen CH 70 B3
Meisenheim D 60 A3
Meissen D 52 B3
Meitingen D 62 B1
Meix-devant-Virton B 60 A1
Męka PL 54 B3
Meka Gruda BIH 84 C3
Mel I 72 B2
Melč CZ 64 A3
Méldola I 82 B1
Meldorf D 43 A6
Melegnano I 71 C4
Melenci YU 75 C5
Melendugno I 105 B5
Melfi I 104 A2
Melgaço P 87 B2
Melgar de Arriba E 88 B1
Melgar de Fernamental E 88 B2
Melgar de Yuso E 88 B2
Melhus N 2 E12
Meliana E 96 B2
Melide CH 70 C3
Melide E 86 B2
Melides P 98 A2
Melilli I 109 B4
Melinovac HR 83 B4
Melisenda I 110 D2
Melisey F 60 C2
Mélito di Porto Salvo I 109 B4
Melk A 63 B6
Melksham GB 29 B5
Mellansel S 3 E16
Mellbystrand S 40 C2
Melle B 49 B4
Melle D 50 A4
Melle F 67 B4
Mellendorf D 43 C6
Mellerud S 35 C4
Mellieha M 109 C4
Mellösa S 37 B3
Mellrichstadt D 51 C6
Mělnické Vtelno CZ 53 C4
Mělník CZ 53 C4
Melón E 87 B2
Melrose GB 25 C5
Mels CH 71 A4
Melsungen D 51 B5
Meltham GB 27 B4
Melton Mowbray GB 30 B3
Melun F 58 B3
Melvaig GB 22 D3
Melvich GB 23 C5
Mélykút H 75 B4
Melzo I 71 C4
Membrilla E 95 D3
Membrio E 93 B3
Memer F 77 B4
Memmelsdorf D 62 A1
Memmingen D 61 C6
Memoria P 92 B2
Mena UA 7 L23
Menàggio I 71 B4
Menai Bridge GB 26 B1
Menasalbas E 94 C2
Menat F 68 B2
Mendavia E 89 B4
Mendaza E 89 B4
Mende F 78 B2
Menden D 50 B3
Mendig D 50 C3
Mendiga P 92 B2
Mendrisio CH 70 C3
Ménéac F 57 B3
Menemen TR 16 S20
Menen B 49 C4
Menetou-Salon F 68 A2
Menfi I 108 B1
Ménfőcsanak H 64 C3
Mengamuñoz E 94 B2
Mengen D 61 B5
Mengeš SLO 73 B4
Mengibar E 100 B2
Mengkofen D 62 B3
Mens F 79 B4
Menslage D 43 C4
Mentana I 102 A2
Menton F 80 C1
Méntrida E 94 B2
Méounes-les-Montrieux F 79 C4
Meppel NL 42 C3
Meppen D 43 C4
Mequinenza E 90 B3
Mer F 58 C2
Mera, *Coruña* E 86 A2
Mera, *Coruña* E 86 A3
Merano I 71 B6
Merate I 71 C4
Mercadillo E 89 A3
Mercatale I 82 C1
Mercatino Conca I 82 C1
Mercato San Severino I 103 C4
Mercato Saraceno I 82 C1
Merching D 62 B1
Merchtem B 49 C5
Merdrignac F 56 B3
Merdžanići BIH 84 C2
Meré E 88 A2
Mere GB 29 B5
Meréville F 58 B3
Merfeld D 50 B3
Méribel F 69 C6
Méribel Motraret F 69 C6
Mérida E 93 C4
Mérignac F 76 B2
Měřín CZ 64 A1
Mering D 62 B1
Merkendorf D 62 A1
Merklin CZ 63 A4
Merksplas B 49 B5
Merlimont Plage F 48 C2
Mern DK 39 D5
Mernye H 74 B2
Mers-les-Bains F 48 C2
Mersch L 60 A2
Merseburg D 52 B1
Merthyr Tydfil GB 29 B4
Mertingen D 62 B1
Mértola P 98 B3
Méru F 58 A3
Merufe P 87 B2
Mervans F 69 B5
Merville F 48 C3
Méry-sur-Seine F 59 B4
Merzig D 60 A2
Mesagne I 105 B4
Mesão Frio P 87 C3
Mesas de Ibor E 93 B5
Meschede D 50 B4
Meschers-sur-Gironde F 66 C4
Meshchovsk RUS 7 J24
Meslay-du-Maine F 57 C5
Mesocco CH 71 B4
Mésola I 82 B1
Mesolóngion GR 15 S17
Mesoraca I 107 B3
Messac F 57 C4
Messancy B 60 A1
Messdorf D 44 C3
Messei F 57 B5
Messejana P 98 B2
Messina I 109 A4
Messini GR 15 T18
Messkirch D 61 C5
Messstetten D 61 B4
Mestanza E 100 A1
Městec Králové CZ 53 C5
Mestlin D 44 B3
Město Albrechtice CZ 54 C2
Město Libavá CZ 64 A3
Město Touškov CZ 63 A4
Mestre I 72 C2
Mesvres F 69 B4
Mesztegnyő H 74 B2
Meta I 103 C4
Metajna HR 83 B4
Metelen D 50 A3
Methlick GB 23 D6
Methóni GR 15 T17
Methven GB 25 B4
Methwold GB 30 B4
Metković HR 84 C2
Metlika SLO 73 C5
Metnitz A 73 B4
Metslawier NL 42 B3
Metten D 62 B3
Mettendorf D 50 D2
Mettet B 49 C5
Mettingen D 50 A3
Mettlach D 60 A2
Mettlen CH 70 B2
Mettmann D 50 B2
Metz F 60 A2
Metzervisse F 60 A2
Metzingen D 61 B5
Meulan F 58 A2
Meung-sur-Loire F 58 C2
Meuselwitz D 52 B2
Meuzac F 67 C6
Mevagissey GB 28 C3
Mexborough GB 27 B4
Meximieux F 69 C5
Mey GB 23 C5
Meyenburg D 44 B4
Meyerhöfen D 43 C5
Meylan F 69 C5
Meymac F 68 C2
Meyrargues F 79 C4
Meyrueis F 78 B2
Meyssac F 77 A4
Meysse F 78 B3
Meyzieu F 69 C4
Mèze F 78 C2
Mézériat F 69 B5
Mežica SLO 73 B4
Mézidon-Canon F 57 A5
Mézières-en-Brenne F 67 B6
Mézières-sur-Issoire F 67 B5
Mézilhac F 78 B3
Mézilles F 59 C4
Mézin F 76 B3
Mezőberény H 75 B6
Mezőcsát H 65 C6
Mezőfalva H 74 B3
Mezőhegyes H 75 B5
Mezőkeresztes H 65 C6
Mezőkomárom H 74 B3
Mezőkövácsháza H 75 B5
Mezőkövesd H 65 C6
Mezőörs H 74 A2
Mézos F 76 B1
Mezőszilas H 74 B3
Mezőtúr H 75 A5
Mezquita de Jarque E 90 C2
Mezzano, *Emilia Romagna* I 82 B1
Mezzano, *Trentino Alto Adige* I 72 B1
Mezzojuso I 108 B2
Mezzoldo I 71 B4
Mezzolombardo I 71 B6
Mgarr M 109 C4
Mglin RUS 7 K23
Miajadas E 93 B5
Mianowice PL 46 A3
Miasteczko Krajeńskie PL 46 B3
Miasteczko Śl. PL 54 C3
Miastko PL 46 A2
Michalovce SK 10 M17
Michałowice PL 55 C4
Michelau D 61 A6
Michelbach D 61 A6
Micheldorf A 63 C5
Michelhausen A 64 B1
Michelsneukirchen D 62 A3
Michelstadt D 61 A5
Michendorf D 52 A3
Michurin BG 16 Q20
Mickleover GB 27 C4
Mid Yell GB 22 A7
Midbea GB 23 B6
Middelburg NL 49 B4
Middelfart DK 39 D2
Middelharnis NL 49 B5
Middelkerke B 48 B3
Middelstum NL 42 B3
Middlesbrough GB 27 A4
Middleton GB 24 B1
Middleton Cheney GB 30 B2
Middleton-in-Teesdale GB 26 A3
Middletown GB 19 B5
Middlewich GB 26 B3
Middlezoy GB 29 B5
Midhurst GB 31 D3
Midleton IRL 20 C3
Midlum D 43 B5
Midsomer Norton GB 29 B5
Midwolda NL 43 B4
Miechów PL 55 C5
Miedes de Aragón E 95 A5
Miedes de Atienza E 95 A3
Międzybodzie Bielskie PL 65 A5
Międzybórz PL 54 B2
Międzychód PL 46 C1
Międzylesie PL 54 C1
Międzyrzec Podlaski PL 11 L18
Międzyrzecz PL 46 C1
Międzywodzie PL 45 A6
Międzyzdroje PL 45 B6
Miejska Górka PL 54 B1
Miélan F 76 C3
Mielec PL 55 C6
Mielęcin PL 45 B6
Mielno, *Warmińsko-Mazurskie* PL 47 B6
Mielno, *Zachodnio-Pomorskie* PL 46 A2
Miengo E 88 A3
Miercurea Ciuc RO 11 N19
Mieres, *Asturias* E 88 A1
Mieres, *Girona* E 91 A5
Mieroszów PL 53 C6
Mierzyn PL 55 B4
Miesau D 60 A3
Miesbach D 62 C2
Mieścisko PL 46 C3
Mieste D 44 C3
Miesterhorst D 44 C3
Mieszków PL 54 A2
Mieszkowice PL 45 C6
Mietków PL 54 C1
Migennes F 59 C4
Miggiano I 107 B5
Migliánico I 103 A4
Migliarino I 81 B5
Migliónico I 105 B3
Mignano Monte Lungo I 103 B3
Migné F 67 B6
Miguel Esteban E 95 C3
Miguelturra E 94 D3
Mihajlovac YU 85 B5
Mihald H 74 B2
Mihaliççık TR 16 S22
Mihályi H 74 A2
Mihla D 51 B6
Mihohnić HR 83 A3
Miholjsko HR 73 C5
Mihovljan HR 73 B5
Mijares E 94 B2
Mijas E 100 C1
Mijoska YU 85 D4
Mike H 74 B2
Mikhnevo RUS 7 J25
Mikkeli FIN 3 F20
Mikleuš HR 74 C2
Mikołajki Pomorskie PL 47 B5
Mikolów PL 54 C3
Mikorzyn PL 54 B3
Mikstat PL 54 B2
Mikulášovice CZ 53 C4
Mikulov CZ 64 B2
Mikulovice CZ 54 C2
Milagro E 89 B5
Miłakowo PL 47 A6
Miland N 33 B5
Milano I 71 C4
Milano Marittima I 82 B1
Milâs TR 16 T20
Milazzo I 109 A4
Mildenhall GB 30 B4
Milejewo PL 47 A5
Milelín CZ 53 C5
Miletić YU 75 C4
Miletićevo YU 75 C6
Mileto I 106 C3
Milevsko CZ 63 A5
Milford IRL 19 A4
Milford Haven GB 28 B2
Milford on Sea GB 31 D2
Milhão P 87 C4
Milići BIH 84 B4
Miličín CZ 63 A5
Milicz PL 54 B2
Milín CZ 63 A5
Militello in Val di Catánia I 109 B3
Miljevina BIH 84 C3
Milkowice PL 53 B6
Millançay F 68 A1
Millares E 96 B2
Millas F 91 A5
Millau F 78 B2
Millesimo I 80 B2
Millevaches F 68 C2
Millom GB 26 A2
Millport GB 24 C3
Millstatt A 72 B3
Millstreet, *Cork* IRL 20 B2
Millstreet, *Waterford* IRL 21 B4
Milltown, *Galway* IRL 18 C3
Milltown, *Kerry* IRL 20 B1
Milltown Malbay IRL 20 B2
Milly-la-Forêt F 58 B3
Milmarcos E 95 A5
Milmersdorf D 45 B5
Milna HR 83 C5
Milnthorpe GB 26 A3
Miločaj YU 85 B5
Milogórze PL 47 A6
Miłomłyn PL 47 B5
Miloševo YU 85 B6
Miłosław PL 54 A2
Milówka PL 65 A5
Miltach D 62 A3
Miltenberg D 61 A5
Milton Keynes GB 31 B3
Milutovac YU 85 C6
Milverton GB 29 B4
Milzyn PL 47 C4
Mimice HR 84 C1
Mimizan F 76 B1
Mimizan-Plage F 76 B1
Mimoň CZ 53 C4
Mina de Juliana P 98 B2
Mina de São Domingos P 98 B3
Minas de Riotinto E 99 B4
Minateda E 101 A4
Minaya E 95 C4
Minde P 92 B2
Mindelheim D 61 B6
Mindelstetten D 62 B2
Minden D 51 A4
Mindszent H 75 B5
Minehead GB 29 B4
Mineo I 109 B3
Minerbe I 71 C6
Minérbio I 81 B5
Minervino Murge I 104 A3
Minglanilla E 96 B1
Mingorria E 94 B2
Minnesund N 34 A3
Miño E 86 A2
Miño de San Esteban E 89 C3
Minsen D 43 B4
Minsk BY 7 K20
Mińsk Mazowiecki PL 55 A6
Minsterley GB 26 C3
Mintlaw GB 23 D6
Minturno I 103 B3
Mionica BIH 84 B3
Mionica YU 85 B5
Mios F 76 B2
Mira E 96 B1
Mira I 72 C2
Mira P 92 A2
Mirabel E 93 B4
Mirabel-aux-Baronnies F 79 B4
Mirabella Eclano I 104 A2
Mirabella Imbáccari I 109 B3
Mirabello I 81 B5
Miradoux F 77 B3
Miraflores de la Sierra E 94 B3
Miralrio E 95 B4
Miramar P 87 C2
Miramare I 82 B1
Miramas F 78 C3
Mirambeau F 67 C4
Miramont-de-Guyenne F 77 B3
Miranda de Arga E 89 B5
Miranda de Ebro E 89 B4
Miranda do Corvo P 92 A2
Miranda do Douro P 87 C4
Mirande F 77 C3
Mirandela P 87 C3
Mirandilla E 93 C4
Mirándola I 81 B5
Miranje HR 83 B4
Mirano I 72 C2
Miravet E 90 B3
Miré F 57 C5
Mirebeau F 67 B5
Mirebeau-sur-Bèze F 69 A5
Mirecourt F 60 B2
Mirepoix F 77 C4
Miribel F 69 C4
Miričina BIH 84 B3
Mirna SLO 73 C5
Miroslav CZ 64 B2
Mirosławice PL 54 C1
Mirosławiec PL 46 B2
Mirošov CZ 63 A4
Mirotice CZ 63 A5
Mirovice CZ 63 A5
Mirow D 45 B4
Mirsk PL 53 C5
Mirzec PL 55 B6
Misilmeri I 108 A2
Miske H 75 B4
Miskolc H 65 B6
Mislinja SLO 73 B5
Missanello I 104 B3
Missillac F 66 A2
Mistelbach A 64 B2
Mistelbach D 62 A2
Misterbianco I 109 B4
Misterhult S 37 D3
Mistretta I 109 B3
Misurina I 72 B2
Mitchelstown IRL 20 B3
Mitilini GR 16 S20
Mittelberg, *Tirol* A 71 B5
Mittelberg, *Vorarlberg* A 71 A5
Mittenwald D 71 A6
Mittenwalde D 52 A3
Mitter-Kleinarl A 72 A3
Mitterback A 63 C6
Mitterdorf im Mürztal A 73 A5
Mittersheim F 60 B2
Mittersill A 72 A2
Mitterskirchen D 62 B3
Mitterteich D 52 D2
Mittweida D 52 C2
Mitwitz D 52 C1
Mizhhir'ya UA 11 M18
Mjällby S 41 C4
Mjöback S 40 B2
Mjölby S 37 C2
Mjøndalen N 33 B7
Mladá Boleslav CZ 53 C4
Mladá Vožice CZ 63 A5
Mladé Buky CZ 53 C5
Mladenovac YU 85 B5
Mladenovo YU 75 C4
Mladikovine BIH 84 B2
Mława PL 47 B6
Mliništé BIH 84 B1
Młodzieszyn PL 55 A5
Młogoszyn PL 55 A4
Młynary PL 47 A5
Mnichóvice CZ 63 A5
Mnichovo Hradiště CZ 53 C4
Mniów PL 55 B5
Mnisek nad Hnilcom SK 65 B6
Mníšek pod Brdy CZ 63 A5
Mniszek PL 55 B5
Mniszków PL 55 B5
Mo, *Hedmark* N 34 A3
Mo, *Telemark* N 33 B4
Mo S 35 C3
Mo i Rana N 2 C14
Moaña E 87 B2
Moate IRL 21 A4
Mocejón E 94 C3
Močenok SK 64 B3
Mochales E 95 A4
Mochowo PL 47 C5
Mochy PL 53 A6
Mockern D 52 A1
Mockfjärd S 36 A1
Möckmühl D 61 A5
Mockrehna D 52 B2
Moclín E 100 B2
Mocsa H 64 C4
Mőcsény H 74 B3
Modane F 70 C1
Modbury GB 28 C4
Módena I 81 B4
Módica I 109 C3
Modigliana I 81 B5
Modlin PL 47 C6
Mödling A 64 B2
Modliszewice PL 55 B5
Modliszewko PL 46 C3
Modogno I 105 A3
Modra SK 64 B3
Modran BIH 84 B3
Modriča BIH 84 B3
Modrý Kamen SK 65 B5
Moëlan-sur-Mer F 56 C2
Moelfre GB 26 B1
Moena I 72 B1
Moerbeke B 49 B4
Moers D 50 B2
Móes P 87 D3
Moffat GB 25 C4
Mogadouro P 87 C4
Mogata S 37 C3
Móggio Udinese I 72 B3
Mogielnica PL 55 B5
Mogilany PL 65 A5
Mogilno PL 46 C3
Mogliano I 82 C2
Mogliano Véneto I 72 C2
Mogor E 87 B2
Mógoro I 110 D1
Moguer E 99 B4
Mohács H 74 C3
Moheda S 40 B4
Mohedas E 93 A4
Mohedas de la Jara E 94 C1
Mohelnice CZ 64 A2
Mohill IRL 19 C4
Möhlin CH 70 A2
Moholm S 35 C6
Mohorn D 52 B3
Mohyliv-Podil's'kyy UA 11 M20
Moi N 32 C3
Moià E 91 B5
Móie I 82 C2
Moimenta da Beira P 87 D3
Moirans F 69 C5
Moirans-en-Montagne F 69 B5
Moisakula EST 7 G19
Moisdon-la-Rivière F 57 C4
Moissac F 77 B4
Moita, *Coimbra* P 92 A2
Moita, *Guarda* P 93 A3
Moita, *Santarém* P 92 B2
Moita, *Setúbal* P 92 C1
Moita dos Ferreiros P 92 B1
Moixent E 96 C2
Mojacar E 101 B4
Mojados E 88 C2
Mojkovac YU 85 D4
Mojmírovce SK 64 B4
Mojtin SK 65 B4
Möklinta S 36 A3
Mokošica HR 84 D3
Mokra Gora YU 85 C4
Mokro Polje HR 83 B5
Mokronog SLO 73 C5
Mokrzyska PL 55 C5
Møkster N 32 A2
Mol B 49 B6
Mol YU 75 C5
Mola di Bari I 105 A4
Molare I 80 B2
Molaretto I 70 C2
Molas F 77 C3
Molassano I 80 B2
Molbergen D 43 C4
Mold GB 26 B2
Moldava nad Bodvou SK 65 B7
Molde N 2 E10
Møldrup DK 38 C2
Moledo do Minho P 87 C2
Molfetta I 105 A3
Molfsee D 44 A2
Molières F 77 B4
Molina de Aragón E 95 B5
Molina de Segura E 101 A4
Molinar E 89 A3
Molinaseca E 86 B4
Molinella I 81 B5
Molinet F 68 B3
Molini di Tures I 72 B1
Molinicos E 101 A3
Molinos de Duero E 89 C4
Molins de Rei E 91 B5
Moliterno I 104 B2
Molkom S 34 B5
Möllbrücke A 72 B3
Mölle S 41 C2
Molledo E 88 A2
Möllenbeck D 45 B5
Mollerussa E 90 B3
Mollet de Perelada E 91 A5
Mollina E 100 B1
Mölln D 44 B2
Molló E 91 A5
Möllösund S 35 C3
Mölltorp S 37 C1
Mölnbo S 37 B4
Mölndal S 35 D4
Mölnlycke S 35 D4
Molompize F 68 C3
Moloy F 69 A4
Molsheim F 60 B3
Moltzow D 45 B4
Molve HR 74 B2
Molveno I 71 B5
Molvizar E 100 C2
Molzbichl A 72 B3
Mombaróccio I 82 C1
Mombeltrán E 94 B1
Mombris D 51 C5
Mombuey E 87 B4
Momchilgrad BG 16 R19
Mommark DK 39 E3
Momo I 70 C3
Monaghan IRL 19 B5
Monar Lodge GB 22 D4
Monasterace Marina I 106 C3
Monasterevin IRL 21 A4
Monasterio de Rodilla E 89 B3
Monastir I 110 D2
Monbahus F 77 B3
Monbazillac F 77 B3
Moncada E 96 B2
Moncalieri I 80 A1
Moncalvo I 80 A2
Monção P 87 B2
Moncarapacho P 98 B3
Moncel-sur-Seille F 60 B2
Monchegorsk RUS 3 C23
Mönchengladbach D 50 B2
Mónchio della Corti I 81 B4
Monchique P 98 B2
Monclar-de-Quercy F 77 C4
Moncofa E 96 B2
Moncontour F 56 B3
Moncoutant F 67 B4
Monda E 100 C1
Mondariz E 87 B2
Mondavio I 82 C1
Mondéjar E 95 B3
Mondello I 108 A2
Mondim de Basto P 87 C3
Mondolfo I 82 C2
Mondoñedo E 86 A3
Mondorf-les-Bains L 60 A2
Mondoubleau F 58 C1
Mondovi I 80 B1
Mondragon F 78 B3
Mondragone I 103 B3
Mondsee A 63 C4
Monéglia I 80 B3
Monegrillo E 90 B2
Monein F 76 C2
Monemvasia GR 15 T18
Mónesi I 80 B1
Monesiglio I 80 B2
Monesterio E 99 A4
Monestier-de-Clermont F 79 B4
Monestiés F 77 B5
Monéteau F 59 C4
Moneygall IRL 21 B4
Moneymore GB 19 B5
Monfalcone I 72 C3
Monfero E 86 A2
Monflanquin F 77 B3
Monflorite E 90 A2
Monforte P 92 B3
Monforte da Beira E 92 B3
Monforte da Beira P 92 B3
Monforte d'Alba I 80 B1
Monforte de Lemos E 86 B3
Monforte de Moyuela E 90 B1
Monforte del Cid E 96 C2
Monghidoro I 81 B5
Mongiana I 106 C3
Monguelfo I 72 B2
Monheim D 62 B1
Moniaive GB 25 C4
Monifieth GB 25 B5
Monikie GB 25 B5
Monistrol-d'Allier F 78 B2
Monistrol de Montserrat E 91 B4
Monistrol-sur-Loire F 68 C4
Mönkebude D 45 B5
Monkton GB 24 C3
Monmouth GB 29 B5
Monnaie F 67 A5
Monnerville F 58 B3
Monnickendam NL 42 C2
Monópoli I 105 B4
Monor H 75 A4
Monóvar E 96 C2
Monpazier F 77 B3
Monreal D 50 C3
Monreal E 89 B5
Monreal del Campo E 95 B5
Monreale I 108 A2
Monroy E 93 B4
Monroyo E 90 C2
Mons B 49 C4
Monsaraz P 92 C3
Monschau D 50 C2
Monségur F 76 B3
Monsélice I 72 C1
Monster NL 49 A5
Mönsterås S 40 B6
Monsummano Terme I 81 C4
Mont-de-Marsan F 76 C2
Mont-Louis F 91 A5
Mont-roig del Camp E 90 B3
Mont-St. Aignan F 58 A2
Mont-St. Vincent F 69 B4
Mont-sous-Vaudrey F 69 B5
Montabaur D 50 C3
Montafia I 80 B2
Montagnac F 78 C2
Montagnana I 71 C6
Montaigu F 66 B3
Montaigu-de-Quercy F 77 B4
Montaiguët-en-Forez F 68 B3
Montaigut F 68 B2
Montaigut-sur-Save F 77 C4
Montalbán E 90 C2
Montalbán de Córdoba E 100 B1
Montalbano Elicona I 109 A4
Montalbano Iónico I 105 B3
Montalbo E 95 C4
Montalcino I 81 C5
Montaldo di Cósola I 80 B3
Montalegre P 87 C3
Montalieu-Vercieu F 69 C5
Montalivet-les-Bains F 66 C3
Montallegro I 108 B2
Montalto delle Marche I 82 D2
Montalto di Castro I 102 A1
Montalto Pavese I 80 B3
Montalto Uffugo I 106 B3
Montalvão P 92 B3
Montamarta E 88 C1
Montana BG 15 Q18
Montana-Vermala CH 70 B2
Montánchez E 93 B4
Montanejos E 96 A2
Montano Antilia I 104 B2
Montans F 77 C4
Montargil P 92 B2
Montargis F 58 C3
Montastruc-la-Conseillère F 77 C4
Montauban F 77 B4
Montauban-de-Bretagne F 57 B3
Montbard F 59 C5
Montbarrey F 69 A5
Montbazens F 77 B5
Montbazon F 67 A5
Montbéliard F 70 A1
Montbenoit F 69 B6
Montbeugny F 68 B3
Montblanc E 91 B4
Montbozon F 69 A6
Montbrison F 68 C4
Montbron F 67 C5
Montbrun-les-Bains F 79 B4
Montceau-les-Mines F 69 B4
Montcenis F 69 B4
Montchanin F 69 B4
Montcornet F 59 A5
Montcuq F 77 B4
Montdardier F 78 C2
Montdidier F 58 A3
Monte-Carlo MC 80 C1
Monte Clara P 92 B3
Monte Clérigo P 98 B2
Monte da Pedra P 92 B3
Monte de Goula P 92 B3
Monte do Trigo P 92 C3
Monte Gordo P 98 B3
Monte Juntos P 92 C3
Monte Porzio I 82 C2
Monte Real P 92 B2
Monte Redondo P 92 B2
Monte Romano I 102 A1
Monte San Giovanni Campano I 103 B3
Monte San Savino I 81 C5
Monte Sant'Ángelo I 104 A2
Monte Vilar P 92 B1
Monteagudo E 101 A4
Monteagudo de las Vicarias E 89 C4
Montealegre E 88 C2
Montealegre del Castillo E 96 C1

Montebello Iónico I 109 B4
Montebello Vicentino I 71 C6
Montebelluna I 72 C2
Montebourg F 57 A4
Montebruno I 80 B3
Montecarotto I 82 C2
Montecassiano I 82 C2
Montecastrilli I 102 A2
Montecatini Terme I 81 C4
Montécchio I 82 C1
Montécchio Emilia I 81 B4
Montécchio Maggiore I 71 C6
Montech F 77 C4
Montechiaro d'Asti I 80 A2
Montecórice I 104 B1
Montecorvino Rovella I 104 B1
Montederramo E 87 B3
Montedoro I 108 B2
Montefalco I 82 D1
Montefalcone di Val Fortore I 104 A2
Montefalcone nel Sànnio I 103 B4
Montefano I 82 C2
Montefiascone I 102 A2
Montefiorino I 81 B4
Montefortino I 82 D2
Montefranco I 102 A2
Montefrio E 100 B2
Montegiordano Marina I 105 B3
Montegiórgio I 82 C2
Montegranaro I 82 C2
Montehermoso E 93 A4
Montejicar E 100 B2
Montejo de la Sierra E 95 A3
Montejo de Tiermes E 89 C3
Monteleone di Púglia I 104 A2
Monteleone di Spoleto I 102 A2
Monteleone d'Orvieto I 82 D1
Montelepre I 108 A2
Montelibretti I 102 A2
Montelier F 79 B4
Montélimar F 78 B3
Montella E 91 A4
Montella I 104 B2
Montellano E 99 B5
Montelupo Fiorentino I 81 C5
Montemaggiore Belsito I 108 B2
Montemagno I 80 B2
Montemayor E 100 B1
Montemayor de Pinilla E 88 C2
Montemésola I 105 B4
Montemilleto I 104 A1
Montemilone I 104 A2
Montemolin E 99 A4
Montemónaco I 82 D2
Montemor-o-Novo P 92 C2
Montemor-o-Velho P 92 A2
Montemurro I 104 B2
Montendre F 67 C4
Montenegro de Cameros E 89 B4
Montenero di Bisáccia I 103 B4
Monteneuf F 57 C3
Monteparano I 105 B4
Montepescali I 81 D5
Montepiano I 81 B5
Montepulciano I 81 C5
Montereale I 102 A3
Montereale Valcellina I 72 B2
Montereau-Faut-Yonne F 59 B3
Monterénzio I 81 B5
Monteroni d'Arbia I 81 C5
Monteroni di Lecce I 105 B5
Monterosso al Mare I 80 B3
Monterosso Almo I 109 B3
Monterosso Grana I 79 B6
Monterotondo I 102 A2
Monterotondo Marittimo I 81 C4
Monterrey E 87 C3
Monterroso E 86 B3
Monterrubio de la Serena E 93 C5
Monterubbiano I 82 C2
Montes Velhos P 98 B2
Montesa E 96 C2
Montesalgueiro E 86 A2
Montesano sulla Marcellana I 104 B2
Montesárchio I 103 B4
Montescaglioso I 105 B3
Montesclaros E 94 B2
Montesilvano I 103 A4
Montespértoli I 81 C5
Montesquieu-Volvestre F 77 C4
Montesquiou F 77 C3
Montestruc-sur-Gers F 77 C3
Montevarchi I 81 C5
Montéveglio I 81 B5
Montfaucon F 66 A3
Montfaucon-d'Argonne F 59 A6
Montfaucon-en-Velay F 69 C4
Montferrat, *Isère* F 69 C5
Montferrat, *Var* F 79 C5
Montfort-en-Chalosse F 76 C2
Montfort-l'Amaury F 58 B2
Montfort-le-Gesnois F 58 B1
Montfort-sur-Meu F 57 B4
Montfort-sur-Risle F 58 A1
Montgai E 90 B3
Montgaillard F 76 C3
Montgenèvre F 79 B5
Montgiscard F 77 C4
Montgomery GB 26 C2
Montguyon F 67 C4
Monthermé F 59 A5
Monthey CH 70 B1
Monthois F 59 A5
Monthureux-sur-Saône F 60 B1
Monti I 110 C2
Monticelli d'Ongina I 81 A3
Montichiari I 71 C5
Monticiano I 81 C5
Montiel E 100 A3
Montier-en-Der F 59 B5
Montieri I 81 C5
Montiglio I 80 A2
Montignac F 77 A4
Montigny-le-Roi F 60 C1
Montigny-lès-Metz F 60 A2
Montigny-sur-Aube F 59 C5
Montijo E 93 C4
Montijo P 92 C2
Montilla E 100 B1
Montillana E 100 B2
Montilly F 68 B3
Montivilliers F 57 A6
Montjaux F 78 B1
Montjean-sur-Loire F 66 A4
Montlhéry F 58 B3
Montlieu-la-Gard F 67 C4
Montlouis-sur-Loire F 67 A5
Montluçon F 68 B2
Montluel F 69 C5
Montmarault F 68 B2
Montmartin-sur-Mer F 57 B4
Montmédy F 59 A6
Montmélian F 69 C6
Montmeyran F 78 B3
Montmirail, *Marne* F 59 B4
Montmirail, *Sarthe* F 58 B1
Montmirat F 78 C3
Montmirey-le-Château F 69 A5
Montmoreau-St. Cybard F 67 C5
Montmorency F 58 B3
Montmorillon F 67 B5
Montmort-Lucy F 59 B4
Montoir-de-Bretagne F 66 A2
Montoire-sur-le-Loir F 58 C1
Montoito P 92 C3
Montolieu F 77 C5
Montório al Vomano I 103 A3
Montoro E 100 A1
Montpellier F 78 C2
Montpezat-de-Quercy F 77 B4
Montpezat-sous-Bouzon F 78 B3
Montpon-Ménestérol F 76 A3
Montpont-en-Bresse F 69 B5
Montréal, *Aude* F 77 C5
Montréal, *Gers* F 76 C3
Montredon-Labessonnié F 77 C5
Montréjeau F 77 C3
Montrésor F 67 A6
Montresta I 110 C1
Montret F 69 B5
Montreuil, *Pas de Calais* F 48 C2
Montreuil, *Seine St. Denis* F 58 B3
Montreuil-aux-Lions F 59 A4
Montreuil-Bellay F 67 A4
Montreux CH 70 B1
Montrevault F 66 A3
Montrevel-en-Bresse F 69 B5
Montrichard F 67 A6
Montricoux F 77 B4
Montrond-les-Bains F 69 C4
Montrose GB 25 B5
Montroy E 96 B2
Monts-sur-Guesnes F 67 B5
Montsalvy F 77 B5
Montsauche-les-Settons F 68 A4
Montseny E 91 B5
Montsoreau F 67 A5
Montsûrs F 57 B5
Montuenga E 94 A2
Montuïri, *Mallorca* E 97
Monturque E 100 B1
Monza I 71 C4
Monzón E 90 B3
Monzón de Campos E 88 B2
Moorbad Lobenstein D 52 C1
Moordorf D 43 B4
Moorslede B 49 C4
Moosburg D 62 B2
Moosburg im Kärnten A 73 B4
Mór H 74 A3
Mora E 94 C3
Móra P 92 C2
Mora S 2 F14
Mora de Rubielos E 96 A2
Móra d'Ebre E 90 B3
Móra la Nova E 90 B3
Moraby S 36 A2
Moradillo de Roa E 88 C3
Morąg PL 47 B5
Mórahalom H 75 B4
Moraime E 86 A1
Morais P 87 C4
Moral de Calatrava E 100 A2
Moraleda de Zafayona E 100 B2
Moraleja E 93 A4
Moraleja del Vino E 88 C1
Morales de Toro E 88 C1
Morales de Valverde E 88 C1
Morales del Vino E 88 C1
Moralina E 87 C4
Morano Cálabro I 106 B3
Mörarp S 41 C2
Morasverdes E 93 A4
Morata de Jalón E 89 C5
Morata de Jiloca E 95 A5
Morata de Tajuña E 95 B3
Moratalla E 101 A4
Moravče SLO 73 B4
Moravec CZ 64 A2
Moraviţa RO 75 C6
Morávka CZ 65 A4
Moravská Třebová CZ 64 A2
Moravské Budějovice CZ 64 A1
Moravské Lieskové SK 64 B3
Moravske Toplice SLO 73 B6
Moravský-Beroun CZ 64 A3
Moravský Krumlov CZ 64 A2
Moravský Svätý Ján SK 64 B3
Morawica PL 55 C5
Morawin PL 54 B3
Morbach D 60 A3
Morbegno I 71 B4
Morbier F 69 B6
Mörbisch am See A 64 C2
Mörbylånga S 40 C6
Morcenx F 76 B2
Morciano di Romagna I 82 C1
Morcone I 103 B4
Morcuera E 89 C3
Mordelles F 57 B4
Moréac F 56 C3
Morebattle GB 25 C5
Morecambe GB 26 A3
Moreda, *Granada* E 100 B2
Moreda, *Oviedo* E 88 A1
Morée F 58 C2
Moreles de Rey E 88 B1
Morella E 90 C2
Moreruela de los Infanzones E 88 C1
Morés E 89 C5
Mores I 110 C1
Morestel F 69 C5
Moret-sur-Loing F 58 B3
Moreton-in-Marsh GB 29 B6
Moretonhampstead GB 28 C4
Moretta I 80 B1
Moreuil F 58 A3
Morez F 69 B6
Mörfelden D 51 D4
Morgano I 72 C2
Morgat F 56 B1
Morges CH 69 B6
Morgex I 70 C2
Morgongåva S 36 B3
Morhange F 60 B2
Morhet B 49 D6
Mori I 71 C5
Morialmé B 49 C5
Morianes P 98 B3
Moriani Plage F 110 A2
Mórichida H 74 A2
Moriles E 100 B1
Morille E 94 B1
Moringen D 51 B5
Morjärv S 3 C18
Morkarla S 36 A4
Mørke DK 39 C3
Mørkøv DK 39 D4
Morkovice-Slížany CZ 64 A3
Morlaàs F 76 C2
Morlaix F 56 B2
Mörlunda S 40 B5
Mormanno I 106 B2
Mormant F 59 B3
Mornant F 69 C4
Morokovo YU 85 D4
Morón de Almazán E 89 C4
Morón de la Frontera E 99 B5
Morović YU 85 A4
Morozzo I 80 B1
Morpeth GB 25 C6
Mörrum S 41 C4
Morsbach D 50 C3
Mörsch D 61 B4
Mörsil S 2 E13
Morsum D 39 E1
Mortagne-au-Perche F 58 B1
Mortagne-sur-Gironde F 66 C4
Mortagne-sur-Sèvre F 66 B4
Mortágua P 92 A2
Mortain F 57 B5
Mortara I 70 C3
Morteau F 69 A6
Mortegliano I 72 C3
Mortelle I 109 A4
Mortemart F 67 B5
Mortimer's Cross GB 29 A5
Mortrée F 57 B6
Mörtschach A 72 B2
Mortsel B 49 B5
Morwenstow GB 28 C3
Moryń PL 47 C6
Morzeszczyn PL 47 B4
Morzewo PL 47 B5
Morzine F 70 B1
Mosalsk RUS 7 J24
Mosbach D 61 A5
Mosby N 33 C4
Mosca P 87 C4
Moscavide P 92 C1
Moščenica HR 73 C6
Moščenice HR 73 C4
Moščenicka Draga HR 73 C4
Mosciano Sant'Ángelo I 82 D2
Mościsko PL 54 C1
Mosina PL 54 A1
Mosjøen N 2 D13
Moskorzew PL 55 C4
Moskva RUS 7 J25
Moslavina Podravska HR 74 C3
Moşniţa Nouă RO 75 C6
Moso in Passiria I 71 B6
Moson-magyaróvár H 64 C3
Mošorin YU 75 C5
Mošovce SK 65 B4
Mosqueruela E 90 C2
Moss N 34 B2
Mössingen D 61 B5
Mosstrand N 33 B5
Most CZ 52 C3
Most na Soči SLO 72 B3
Mosta M 109 C4
Mostar BIH 84 C2
Mosterhamn N 32 B2
Mostki PL 53 A5
Móstoles E 94 B3
Mostová SK 64 B3
Mostowo PL 46 A2
Mostuéjouls F 78 B2
Mosty PL 45 B6
Mostys'ka UA 11 M18
Mota del Cuervo E 95 C4
Mota del Marqués E 88 C1
Motala S 37 C2
Motherwell GB 25 C4
Möthlow D 45 C4
Motilla del Palancar E 95 C5
Motnik SLO 73 B4
Motovun HR 72 C3
Motril E 100 C2
Motta I 71 C6
Motta di Livenza I 72 C2
Motta Montecorvino I 104 A2
Motta Visconti I 70 C3
Mottisfont GB 31 C2
Móttola I 105 B4
Mou DK 38 C3
Mouchard F 69 B5
Moúdhros GR 16 S19
Moudon CH 70 B1
Mougins F 79 C5
Mouilleron en-Pareds F 66 B4
Mouliherne F 67 A5
Moulinet F 80 C1
Moulins F 68 B3
Moulins-Engilbert F 68 B3
Moulins-la-Marche F 58 B1
Moulismes F 67 B5
Moult F 57 A5
Mount Bellew Bridge IRL 20 A3
Mountain Ash GB 29 B4
Mountfield GB 19 B4
Mountmellick IRL 21 A4
Mountrath IRL 21 A4
Mountsorrel GB 30 B2
Moura P 98 A3
Mourão P 92 C3
Mourenx F 76 C2
Mouriés F 78 C3
Mourmelon-le-Grand F 59 A5
Mouronho P 92 A2
Mouscron B 49 C4
Mousehole GB 28 C2
Moussac F 78 C3
Moussey F 60 B2
Mousteru F 56 B2
Moustey F 76 B2
Moustiers-Ste. Marie F 79 C5
Mouthe F 69 B6
Mouthier-Haute-Pierre F 69 A6
Mouthoumet F 77 D5
Moutier CH 70 A2
Moûtiers F 69 C6
Moutiers-les-Mauxfaits F 66 B3
Mouy F 58 A3
Mouzon F 59 A6
Møvik N 32 A2
Moville IRL 19 A4
Moy, *Highland* GB 23 D4
Moy, *Tyrone* GB 19 B5
Moycullen IRL 20 A2
Moyenmoutier F 60 B2
Moyenvic F 60 B2
Mózar E 88 C1
Mozhaysk RUS 7 J25
Mozirje SLO 73 B4
Mözs H 74 B3
Mozzanica I 71 C4
Mramorak YU 85 B5
Mrčajevci YU 85 C5
Mrkonjić Grad BIH 84 B2
Mrkopalj HR 73 C4
Mrmoš YU 85 C6
Mrocza PL 46 B3
Mroczeń PL 54 B2
Mroczno PL 47 B5
Mrozy PL 55 A6
Mrzezyno PL 45 A7
Mšec CZ 53 C3
Mšeno CZ 53 C4
Mstów PL 55 C4
Mstsislaw BY 7 J22
Mszana Dolna PL 65 A6
Mszczonów PL 55 B5
Mtsensk RUS 7 K25
Muć HR 83 C5
Múccia I 82 C2
Much D 50 C3
Much Marcle GB 29 B5
Much Wenlock GB 26 C3
Mücheln D 52 B1
Muchów PL 53 B6
Mucientes E 88 C2
Muckross IRL 20 B2
Muda P 98 B2
Mudanya TR 16 R21
Mudau D 61 A5
Müden D 44 C2
Mudersbach D 50 C3
Mudurnu TR 16 R22
Muel E 90 B1
Muelas del Pan E 87 C5
Muess D 44 B3
Muff IRL 19 A4
Mugardos E 86 A2
Muge P 92 B2
Mügeln, *Sachsen-Anhalt* D 52 B3
Mügeln, *Sachsen* D 52 B3
Múggia I 72 C3
Muğla TR 16 T21
Mugnano I 82 C1
Mugron F 76 C2
Mugueimes E 87 C3
Muhi H 65 C6
Mühlacker D 61 B4
Mühlbach am Hochkönig A 72 A3
Mühlberg, *Brandenburg* D 52 B3
Mühlberg, *Thüringen* D 51 C6
Mühldorf A 72 B3
Mühldorf D 62 B3
Muhleberg CH 70 B2
Mühleim D 61 B4
Muhlen-Eichsen D 44 B3
Mühlhausen, *Bayern* D 62 A1
Mühlhausen, *Thüringen* D 51 B6
Mühltroff D 52 C1
Muhos FIN 3 D20
Muhr A 72 A3
Muine Bheag IRL 21 B5
Muir of Ord GB 23 D4
Muirkirk GB 24 C3
Muirteira P 92 B1
Mukacheve UA 11 M18
Muker GB 26 A3
Mula E 101 A4
Mulben GB 23 D5
Mulegns CH 71 B4
Mules I 71 B6
Mülheim D 50 B2
Mulhouse F 60 C3
Muljava SLO 73 C4
Mullanys Cross IRL 18 B3
Müllheim D 60 C3
Mullhyttan S 36 B1
Mullinavat IRL 21 B4
Mullingar IRL 21 A4
Mullion GB 28 C2
Müllrose D 53 A4
Mullsjö S 35 D5
Mulseryd S 40 B3
Munana E 94 B1
Muñás E 86 A4
Münchberg D 52 C1
Müncheberg D 45 C6
München D 62 B2
Münchhausen D 51 C4
Mundaka E 89 A4
Münden D 51 B5
Munderfing A 63 B4
Munderkingen D 61 B5
Mundesley GB 30 B5
Munera E 95 C4
Mungia E 89 A4
Muñico E 94 B1
Muniesa E 90 B2
Munka-Ljungby S 41 C2
Munkebo DK 39 D3
Munkedal S 35 C3
Munkfors S 34 B5
Munktorp S 36 B3
Münnerstadt D 51 C6
Muñopepe E 94 B2
Muñotello E 94 B1
Münsingen CH 70 B2
Münsingen D 61 B5
Munsö S 36 B4
Münster CH 70 B3
Münster D 50 B3
Münster, *Hessen* D 61 A4
Münster, *Niedersachsen* D 44 C2
Munster F 60 B3
Muntibar E 89 A4
Münzkirchen A 63 B4
Muonio FIN 3 C18
Muotathal CH 70 B3
Mur-de-Barrez F 77 B5
Mur-de-Bretagne F 56 B2
Mur-de-Sologne F 67 A6
Murakeresztúr H 74 B1
Murán SK 65 B6
Murano I 72 C2
Muras E 86 A3
Murat F 78 A1
Murat-sur-Vèbre F 78 C1
Muratlı TR 16 R20
Murato F 110 A2
Murau A 73 A4
Muravera I 110 D2
Murazzano I 80 B2
Murça P 87 C3
Murchante E 89 B5
Murchin D 45 B5
Murcia E 101 B4
Murczyn PL 46 C3
Mureck A 73 B5
Muret F 77 C4
Murg CH 71 A4
Murguia E 89 B4
Muri CH 70 A3
Murias de Paredes E 86 B4
Muriedas E 88 A3
Muriel Viejo E 89 C4
Murillo de Rio Leza E 89 B4
Murillo el Fruto E 89 B5
Murlaggan GB 22 E3
Murmansk RUS 3 B23
Murmashi RUS 3 B23
Murnau D 62 C2
Muro, *Mallorca* E 97
Muro F 110 A1
Muro de Alcoy E 96 C2
Muro Lucano I 104 B2
Murol F 68 C2
Muron F 66 B4
Muros E 86 B1
Muros de Nalón E 86 A4
Murowana Goślina PL 46 C3
Mürren CH 70 B2
Murrhardt D 61 B5
Murska Sobota SLO 73 B6
Mursko Središće HR 73 B6
Murtas E 100 C2
Murten CH 70 B2
Murter HR 83 C4
Murtosa P 87 D2
Murvica HR 83 B4
Murviel-lès-Béziers F 78 C2
Mürzsteg A 63 C6
Murzynowo PL 46 C1
Mürzzuschlag A 63 C6
Musculdy F 76 C2
Muskö S 37 B5
Mušov CZ 64 B2
Musselburgh GB 25 C4
Musselkanaal NL 43 C4
Mussidan F 77 A3
Mussomeli I 108 B2
Musson B 60 A1
Mussy-sur-Seine F 59 C5
Mustafakemalpaşa TR 16 R21
Muszaki PL 47 B6
Muszyna PL 65 A6
Muta SLO 73 B5
Muthill GB 25 B4
Mutné SK 65 A5
Mutriku E 89 A4
Mutterbergalm A 71 A6
Muxia E 86 A1
Muxilka-Ugarte E 89 A4
Muzillac F 66 A2
Mužla SK 65 C4
Muzzano del Turgnano I 72 C3
Mybster GB 23 C5
Myennes F 68 A2
Myjava SK 64 B3
Mykland N 33 C5
Mykolayiv UA 11 N23
Myra N 33 C6
Myresjö S 40 B4
Myrhorod UA 11 M23
Mysen N 34 B3
Mysłakowice PL 53 C5
Myślenice PL 65 A5
Myślibórz PL 45 C6
Mysłowice PL 55 C4
Myszków PL 55 C4
Mytishchi RUS 7 J25
Mýtna SK 65 B5
Mýtne Ludany SK 65 B4

N

N Unnaryd S 40 B3
Naaldwijk NL 49 B5
Naantali FIN 3 F17
Naas IRL 21 A5
Nabais P 92 A3
Nabburg D 62 A3
Načeradec CZ 63 A5
Náchod CZ 53 C6
Nacław PL 46 A2
Nadarzyce PL 46 B2
Nadarzyn PL 55 A5
Nádasd H 74 B1
Nădlac RO 75 B5
Nádudvar H 75 A6
Nadvirna UA 11 M19
Nærbø N 32 C2
Næstved DK 39 D4
Näfels CH 70 A4
Nagel D 52 D1
Nagele NL 42 C2
Nagłowice PL 55 C5
Nagold D 61 B4
Nagore E 76 D1
Nagyatád H 74 B2
Nagybajom H 74 B2
Nagybaracska H 74 B3
Nagybátony H 65 C5
Nagyberény H 74 B3
Nagybörzsöny H 65 C4
Nagycenk H 64 C2
Nagydorog H 74 B3
Nagyfüged H 65 C6
Nagyhersány H 74 C3
Nagyigmánd H 64 C4
Nagyiván H 75 A5
Nagykanizsa H 74 B1
Nagykáta H 75 A4
Nagykonyi H 74 B3
Nagykörös H 75 A4
Nagykörü H 75 A5
Nagylóc H 65 B5
Nagymágocs H 75 B5
Nagymányok H 74 B3
Nagymaros H 65 C4
Nagyoroszi H 65 B5
Nagyrábé H 75 A6
Nagyréde H 65 C5
Nagyszékely H 74 B3
Nagyszénás H 75 B5
Nagyszokoly H 74 B3
Nagytöke H 75 B5
Nagyvázsony H 74 B2
Nagyvenyim H 74 B3
Naharros E 95 B4
Nahe D 44 B2
Naila D 52 C1
Nailloux F 77 C4
Nailsworth GB 29 B5
Naintré F 67 B5
Nairn GB 23 D5
Najac F 77 B4
Nájera E 89 B4
Nak H 74 B3
Nakksjø N 33 B6
Nakło nad Notecią PL 46 B3
Nakskov DK 39 E4
Nalda E 89 B4
Nálepkovo SK 65 B6
Nallihan TR 16 R22
Nalliers F 66 B3
Nalzen F 77 D4
Nalžouské Hory CZ 63 A4
Náměšť nad Oslavou CZ 64 A2
Námestovo SK 65 A5
Namnå N 34 A4
Namsos N 2 D12
Namur B 49 C5
Namysłów PL 54 B2
Nançay F 68 A2
Nanclares de la Oca E 89 B4
Nancy F 60 B2
Nangis F 59 B4
Nannestad N 34 A3
Nant F 78 B2
Nanterre F 58 B3
Nantes F 66 A3
Nanteuil-le-Haudouin F 58 A3
Nantiat F 67 B6
Nantua F 69 B5
Nantwich GB 26 B3
Napajedla CZ 64 A3
Napiwoda PL 47 B6
Nápoli I 103 C4
Naraval E 86 A4
Narberth GB 28 B3
Narbonne F 78 C1
Narbonne-Plage F 78 C2
Narcao I 110 D1
Nardò I 105 B5
Narni I 102 A2
Naro I 108 B2
Naro Fominsk RUS 7 J25
Narón E 86 A2
Narros del Castillo E 94 B1
Narta HR 74 C1
Naruszewo PL 47 C6
Narva EST 7 G21
Narvik N 2 B15
Narzole I 80 B1
Näs S 36 A1
Năsăud RO 11 N19
Nasavrky CZ 64 A1
Nasbinals F 78 B2
Näshull S 40 B5
Našice HR 74 C3
Nasielsk PL 47 C6
Naso I 109 A3
Nassau D 50 C3
Nassenfels D 62 B2
Nassenheide D 45 C5
Nassereith A 71 A5
Nässjö S 40 B4
Nastätten D 50 C3
Näsum S 41 C4
Natalinci YU 85 B5
Nater-Stetten D 62 B2
Naters CH 70 B3
Natters A 71 A6
Nattheim D 61 B6
Nättraby S 41 C5
Naturno I 71 B5
Naucelle F 77 B5
Nauders A 71 B5
Nauen D 45 C4
Naul IRL 19 C5
Naumburg D 52 B1
Naundorf D 52 C3
Naunhof D 52 B2
Naustdal N 2 F9
Nava E 88 A1
Nava de Arévalo E 94 B2
Nava de la Asunción E 94 A2
Nava del Rey E 88 C1
Navacerrada E 94 B2
Navaconcejo E 93 A5
Navafriá E 94 A3
Navahermosa E 94 C2
Navahrudak BY 7 K19
Naval E 90 A3
Navalacruz E 94 B2
Navalcán E 94 B1
Navalcarnero E 94 B2
Navaleno E 89 C3
Navalmanzano E 94 A2
Navalmoral E 94 B2
Navalmoral de la Mata E 93 B5
Navalón E 96 C2
Navalonguilla E 93 A5
Navalperal de Pinares E 94 B2
Navalpino E 94 C2
Navaltalgordo E 94 B2
Navaltoril E 94 C2
Navaluenga E 94 B2
Navalvillar de Pela E 93 B5
Navan IRL 19 C5
Navaperal de Tormes E 94 B1
Navapolatsk BY 7 J21
Navarclés E 91 B4
Navarredonda de Gredos E 94 B1
Navarrenx F 76 C2
Navarrés E 96 B2
Navarrete E 89 B4
Navarrevisca E 94 B2
Navás E 91 B4
Navas de Oro E 94 A2
Navas de San Juan E 100 A2
Navas del Madroño E 93 B4
Navas del Rey E 94 B2
Navas del Sepillar E 100 B1
Navascués E 90 A1
Navasfrias E 93 A4
Nave I 71 C5
Nave de Haver P 93 A4
Nävekvarn S 37 C3
Navelli I 103 A3
Navenby GB 27 B5
Naverstad S 35 C3
Navés E 91 B4
Navezuelas E 94 C1
Navia E 86 A4
Navia de Suarna E 86 B4
Navilly F 69 B5
Navlya RUS 7 K24
Năvodari RO 11 P21
Návpaktos GR 15 S17
Návplion GR 15 T18
Náxos GR 16 T19
Nay F 76 C2
Nazaré P 92 B1
Nazarje SLO 73 B4
Nazilli TR 16 T21
Nazza D 51 B6
Néa Epidhavros GR 15 T18
Néa Moudhaniá GR 15 R18
Neap GB 22 A7
Neath GB 28 B4
Nebljusi HR 83 B4
Neblo SLO 72 B3
Nebolchy RUS 7 G23
Nebra D 52 B1
Nebreda E 89 C3
Nechanice CZ 53 C5
Neckargemünd D 61 A4
Neckarsulm D 61 A5
Neda E 86 A2
Neded SK 64 B3
Nedelišće HR 73 B6
Nederweert NL 50 B1
Nedstrand N 32 B2
Nedvědice CZ 64 A2
Nędza PL 54 C3
Neede NL 50 A2
Needham Market GB 30 B5
Needingworth GB 30 B3
Neermoor D 43 B4
Neeroeteren B 50 B1
Neerpelt B 49 B6
Neesen D 51 A4
Neetze D 44 B2
Nefyn GB 26 C1
Negbina YU 85 C4
Negotin YU 11 P18
Negrar I 71 C5
Negredo E 95 A4
Negreira E 86 B2
Nègrepelisse F 77 B4
Negru Vodă RO 16 Q21
Negueira de Muñiz E 86 A4
Neheim D 50 B3
Neila E 89 B4
Néive I 80 B2
Nejdek CZ 52 C2
Nekla PL 46 C3
Neksø DK 41 D5
Nelas P 92 A3
Nelaug N 33 C5
Nelidovo RUS 7 H23
Nellingen D 61 B5
Nelson GB 26 B3
Neman RUS 6 J18
Nemesgörzsöny H 74 A2
Nemeskér H 74 A1
Nemesnádudvar H 75 B4
Nemesszalók H 74 A2
Németkér H 74 B3
Nemours F 58 B3
Nemška Loka SLO 73 C5
Nemšová SK 64 B4
Nenagh IRL 20 B3
Nenince SK 65 B5
Nenzing A 71 A4
Nepi I 102 A2
Nepomuk CZ 63 A4
Nérac F 77 B3
Neratovice CZ 53 C4
Nerchau D 52 B2
Néré F 67 C4
Neresheim D 61 B6
Nereto I 82 D2
Nerezine HR 82 B3
Nerežišća HR 83 C5
Neringa LT 6 J17
Néris-les-Bains F 68 B2
Nerito I 103 A3
Nerja E 100 C2
Néronde F 69 C4
Nérondes F 68 B2
Nerpio E 101 A3
Nersingen D 61 B6
Nerva E 99 B4
Nervesa della Battáglia I 72 C2
Nervi I 80 B3
Nes NL 42 B2
Nesbyen N 2 F11
Nesflaten N 32 B3
Nesland N 33 B4
Neslandsvatn N 33 C6

Nesle F 59 A3
Nesoddtangen N 34 B2
Nesovice CZ 64 A3
Nesselwang D 61 C6
Nesslau CH 71 A4
Nessmersiel D 43 B4
Nesso I 71 C4
Nesterov UA 11 L18
Nesttun N 32 A2
Nesvady SK 64 C4
Nesvatnstemmen N 33 C5
Nether Stowey GB 29 B4
Netland N 32 C3
Netolice CZ 63 A5
Netphen D 50 C4
Netstal CH 70 A4
Nettancourt F 59 B5
Nettetal D 50 B2
Nettlingen D 51 A6
Nettuno I 102 B2
Neu Darchau D 44 B2
Neu-Isenburg D 51 C4
Neu Kaliss D 44 B3
Neu Lübbenau D 53 A3
Neu-markt am Wallersee A 63 C4
Neu-petershain D 53 B4
Neu-Ravensburg D 61 C5
Neu-Ulm D 61 B6
Neualbenreuth D 52 D2
Neubeckum D 50 B4
Neubrandenburg D 45 B5
Neubruch-hausen D 43 C5
Neubukow D 44 A3
Neuburg D 62 B2
Neuchâtel CH 70 B1
Neudau A 73 A6
Neudietendorf D 51 C6
Neudorf D 61 A4
Neuenbürg, *Baden-Württemberg* D 61 B4
Neuenburg, *Niedersachsen* D 43 B4
Neuendorf D 45 A5
Neuenhagen D 45 C5
Neuenhaus D 42 C3
Neuenkirchen, *Niedersachsen* D 43 B6
Neuenkirchen, *Niedersachsen* D 43 C5
Neuenkirchen, *Nordrhein-Westfalen* D 50 A3
Neuenrade D 50 B3
Neuenwalde D 43 B5
Neuerburg D 50 C2
Neuf-Brisach F 60 B3
Neufahrn, *Bayern* D 62 B2
Neufahrn, *Bayern* D 62 B3
Neufchâteau B 60 A1
Neufchâteau F 60 B1
Neufchâtel-en-Bray F 58 A2
Neufchâtel-sur-Aisne F 59 A5
Neuflize F 59 A5
Neugersdorf D 53 C4
Neuhardenberg D 45 C6
Neuharlingersiel D 43 B4
Neuhaus, *Bayern* D 62 A4
Neuhaus, *Bayern* D 63 B4
Neuhaus, *Niedersachsen* D 43 B6
Neuhaus, *Niedersachsen* D 44 B2
Neuhaus, *Niedersachsen* D 51 B5
Neuhaus a Rennweg D 52 C1
Neuhausen CH 61 C4
Neuhausen ob Eck D 61 C4
Neuhof D 62 A1
Neuhofen an der Krems A 63 B5
Neuillé-Pont-Pierre F 67 A5
Neuilly-en-Thelle F 58 A3
Neuilly-le-Réal F 68 B3
Neuilly-l'Évêque F 59 C6
Neuilly-St. Front F 59 A4
Neukalen D 45 B4
Neukirch D 53 B4
Neukirchen A 62 B4
Neukirchen, *Hessen* D 51 C5
Neukirchen, *Schleswig-Holstein* D 39 E1
Neukirchen-am Grossvenediger A 72 A2
Neukirchen bei Heiligen Blut D 62 A3
Neukloster D 44 B3
Neulengbach A 64 B1
Neulise F 68 C4
Neum BIH 84 D2
Neumagen D 60 A2
Neumarkt D 62 A2
Neumarkt im Hausruckkreis A 63 B4
Neumarkt im Mühlkreis A 63 B5
Neumarkt im Steiermark A 73 A4
Neumarkt Sankt Veit D 62 B3
Neumünster D 44 A1
Neunburg vorm Wald D 62 A3
Neung-sur-Beuvron F 68 A1
Neunkirch, *Luzern* CH 70 A3
Neunkirch, *Schaffhausen* CH 61 C4
Neunkirchen A 64 C2
Neunkirchen, *Nordrhein-Westfalen* D 50 C3
Neunkirchen, *Nordrhein-Westfalen* D 50 C3
Neunkirchen, *Saarland* D 60 A3
Neunkirchen am Brand D 62 A2
Neuötting D 62 B3
Neureut D 61 A4
Neuruppin D 45 C4
Neusäss D 62 B1
Neusiedl A 64 C2
Neuss D 50 B2
Neussargues-Moissac F 68 C2
Neustadt, *Bayern* D 62 A1
Neustadt, *Bayern* D 62 A3
Neustadt, *Bayern* D 62 B2
Neustadt, *Brandenburg* D 44 C4
Neustadt, *Hessen* D 51 C5
Neustadt, *Niedersachsen* D 43 C6
Neustadt, *Rheinland-Pfalz* D 61 A4
Neustadt, *Sachsen* D 53 B4
Neustadt, *Schleswig-Holstein* D 44 A2
Neustadt, *Thüringen* D 52 C1
Neustadt, *Thüringen* D 52 C1
Neustadt-Glewe D 44 B3
Neustift im Stubaital A 71 A6
Neustrelitz D 45 B5
Neutal A 73 A6
Neutrebbin D 45 C6
Neuves-Maisons F 60 B2
Neuvic, *Corrèze* F 68 C2
Neuvic, *Dordogne* F 77 A3
Neuville-aux-Bois F 58 B3
Neuville-de-Poitou F 67 B5
Neuville-les-Dames F 69 B5
Neuville-sur-Saône F 69 C4
Neuvy-le-Roi F 58 C1
Neuvy-St. Sépulchre F 68 B1
Neuvy-Santour F 59 B4
Neuvy-sur-Barangeon F 68 A2
Neuwied D 50 C3
Neuzelle D 53 A4
Névache F 79 A5
Neveklov CZ 63 A5
Nevel RUS 7 H21
Nevers F 68 B3
Nevesinje BIH 84 C3
Névez F 56 C2
Nevlunghavn N 33 C6
New Abbey GB 25 D4
New Aberdour GB 23 D6
New Alresford GB 31 C2
New Costessey GB 30 B5
New Cumnock GB 24 C3
New Galloway GB 24 C3
New Mills GB 27 B4
New Milton GB 31 D2
New Pitsligo GB 23 D6
New Quay GB 28 A3
New Radnor GB 29 A4
New Romney GB 31 D4
New Ross IRL 21 B5
New Scone GB 25 B4
Newark on Trent GB 27 B5
Newbiggin-by-the-Sea GB 25 C6
Newbliss IRL 19 B4
Newborough GB 26 B1
Newbridge IRL 21 A5
Newbridge on Wye GB 29 A4
Newburgh, *Aberdeenshire* GB 23 D6
Newburgh, *Fife* GB 25 B4
Newbury GB 31 C2
Newby Bridge GB 26 A3
Newcastle GB 19 B6
Newcastle Emlyn GB 28 A3
Newcastle-under-Lyme GB 26 B3
Newcastle-Upon-Tyne GB 25 D6
Newcastle West IRL 20 B2
Newcastleton GB 25 C5
Newchurch GB 29 A4
Newent GB 29 B5
Newham GB 31 C4
Newhaven GB 31 D4
Newington GB 31 C5
Newinn IRL 21 B4
Newlyn GB 28 C2
Newmachar GB 23 D6
Newmarket, *Suffolk* GB 30 B4
Newmarket, *Suffolk* GB 22 C2
Newmarket IRL 20 B3
Newmarket-on-Fergus IRL 20 B3
Newport, *Isle of Wight* GB 31 D2
Newport, *Newport* GB 29 B5
Newport, *Pembrokeshire* GB 28 A3
Newport, *Telford & Wrekin* GB 26 C3
Newport, *Mayo* IRL 18 C2
Newport, *Tipperary* IRL 20 B3
Newport-on-Tay GB 25 B5
Newport Pagnell GB 30 B3
Newquay GB 28 C2
Newry GB 19 B5
Newton Abbot GB 29 C4
Newton Arlosh GB 25 D4
Newton Aycliffe GB 27 A4
Newton Ferrers GB 28 C3
Newton Stewart GB 24 D3
Newtonhill GB 23 D6
Newtonmore GB 23 D4
Newtown, *Herefordshire* GB 29 A5
Newtown, *Powys* GB 26 C2
Newtown Cunningham IRL 19 B4
Newtown Hamilton GB 19 B5
Newtown Sands IRL 20 B2
Newtown St. Boswells GB 25 C5
Newtownabbey GB 19 B6
Newtownards GB 19 B6
Newtownbutler GB 19 B4
Newtownmountkennedy IRL 21 A5
Newtownshandrum IRL 20 B3
Newtownstewart GB 19 B4
Nexon F 67 C6
Neyland GB 28 B3
Nibbiano I 80 B3
Nibe DK 38 C2
Nicastro I 106 C3
Niccone I 82 C1
Nice F 79 C6
Nickelsdorf A 64 C3
Nicolosi I 109 B4
Nicosia I 109 B3
Nicótera I 106 C2
Nidda D 51 C5
Nidzica PL 47 B6
Niebla E 99 B4
Nieborów PL 55 A5
Niebüll D 39 E1
Niechanowo PL 46 C3
Niechorze PL 45 A7
Niedalino PL 46 A2
Nieder-Olm D 61 A4
Niederaudorf D 62 C3
Niederaula D 51 C5
Niederbipp CH 70 A2
Niederbronn-les-Bains F 60 B3
Niederfischbach D 50 C3
Niedergörsdorf D 52 B2
Niederkrüchten D 50 B2
Niederndorf A 62 C3
Niedersachs-werfen D 51 B6
Niederstetten D 61 A5
Niederurnen CH 70 A4
Niederwölz A 73 A4
Niedoradz PL 53 B5
Niedzica PL 65 A6
Niegosławice PL 53 B5
Nieheim D 51 B5
Niemcza PL 54 C1
Niemegk D 52 A2
Niemodlin PL 54 C2
Nienburg, *Niedersachsen* D 43 C6
Nienburg, *Sachsen-Anhalt* D 52 B1
Niepołomice PL 55 C5
Nierstein D 61 A4
Niesky D 53 B4
Niestronno PL 46 C3
Nieświń PL 55 B5
Nieszawa PL 47 C4
Nieul-sur-Mer F 66 B3
Nieuw-Amsterdam NL 42 C3
Nieuw-Buinen NL 42 C3
Nieuw-Weerdinge NL 42 C3
Nieuwe Niedorp NL 42 C1
Nieuwe-Pekela NL 42 B3
Nieuwe-schans NL 43 B4
Nieuwegein NL 49 A6
Nieuwerkerken B 49 C6
Nieuwolda NL 42 B3
Nieuwpoort B 48 B3
Nigrita GR 15 R18
Nigüelas E 100 C2
Nijar E 101 C3
Nijemci HR 84 A4
Nijkerk NL 49 A6
Nijlen B 49 B5
Nijmegen NL 50 B1
Nijverdal NL 42 C3
Nikel RUS 3 B22
Nikinci YU 85 B4
Nikitsch A 64 C2
Nikla H 74 B2
Niklasdorf A 73 A5
Nikšić YU 84 D3
Nîmes F 78 C3
Nimis I 72 B3
Nimtofte DK 39 C3
Nin HR 83 B4
Nindorf D 43 A6
Ninemilehouse IRL 21 B4
Ninove B 49 C5
Niort F 67 B4
Niš YU 15 Q17
Nisa P 92 B3
Niscemi I 109 B3
Nissafors S 40 B3
Nissan-lez-Ensérune F 78 C2
Nissedal N 33 B5
Nissumby DK 38 C1
Niton GB 31 D2
Nitra SK 64 B4
Nitrianske-Pravno SK 65 B4
Nitrianske Rudno SK 65 B4
Nitry F 59 C4
Nittedal N 34 A2
Nittenau D 62 A3
Nittendorf D 62 A2
Nivala FIN 3 E19
Nivelles B 49 C5
Nivenskoye RUS 47 A6
Nivnice CZ 64 B3
Nizhyn UA 11 L22
Nižná SK 65 A5
Nižná Boca SK 65 B5
Nižné Repaše SK 65 A6
Nizza Monferrato I 80 B2
Njegůsevo YU 75 C4
Njivice HR 73 C4
Noailles F 58 A3
Noain E 89 B5
Noale I 72 C2
Noalejo E 100 B2
Noblejas E 95 C3
Noceda E 86 B4
Nocera Inferiore I 103 C4
Nocera Terinese I 106 B3
Nocera Umbra I 82 C1
Noceto I 81 B4
Noci I 105 B4
Nociglia I 107 A5
Nodeland N 33 C4
Nödinge S 35 D4
Nods F 69 A6
Noé F 77 C4
Noépoli I 104 B3
Noeux-les-Mines F 48 C3
Noez E 94 C2
Nogales E 93 C4
Nogara I 71 C6
Nogarejas E 87 B4
Nogaro F 76 C2
Nogent F 59 B6
Nogent l'Artaud F 59 B4
Nogent-le-Roi F 58 B2
Nogent-le-Rotrou F 58 B1
Nogent-sur-Seine F 59 B4
Nogent-sur-Vernisson F 58 C3
Nogersund S 41 C4
Noguera E 95 B5
Noguerones E 100 B1
Nohfelden D 60 A3
Noia E 86 B2
Noicáttaro I 105 A3
Noirétable F 68 C3
Noirmoutier-en-l'Île F 66 A2
Noja E 89 A3
Nojewo PL 46 C2
Nokia FIN 3 F18
Nol S 35 D4
Nola I 103 C4
Nolay F 69 B4
Noli I 80 B2
Nombela E 94 B2
Nomeny F 60 B2
Nomexy F 60 B2
Nonancourt F 58 B2
Nonant-le-Pin F 57 B6
Nonántola I 81 B5
Nonaspe E 90 B3
None I 80 B1
Nontron F 67 C5
Nonza F 110 A2
Noordhorn NL 42 B3
Noordwijk NL 49 A5
Noordwijkerhout NL 49 A5
Noordwolde NL 42 C3
Nora S 36 B2
Nørager DK 38 C2
Norberg S 36 A2
Norboda S 36 A5
Nórcia I 82 D2
Nord-Odal N 34 A3
Nordagutu N 33 B6
Nordausques F 48 C3
Nordborg DK 39 D2
Nordby, *Aarhus Amt.* DK 39 D3
Nordby, *Ribe Amt.* DK 39 D1
Norddeich D 43 B4
Norden D 43 B4
Nordenham D 43 B5
Norderhov N 34 A2
Norderney D 43 B4
Norderstapel D 43 A6
Norderstedt D 44 B2
Nordfjordeid N 2 F10
Nordhalben D 52 C1
Nordhausen D 51 B6
Nordheim vor der Rhön D 51 C6
Nordholz D 43 B5
Nordhorn D 43 C4
Nördlingen D 61 B6
Nordmark S 34 B6
Nordstemmen D 51 A5
Nordwalde D 50 A3
Noreña E 88 A1
Noresund N 33 A6
Norg NL 42 B3
Norheimsund N 2 F10
Norie S 41 C4
Norma I 102 B2
Norra Vi S 37 D2
Norrahammar S 40 B4
Nørre Åby DK 39 D2
Nørre Alslev DK 39 E4
Nørre Lyndelse DK 39 D3
Nørre Nebel DK 39 D1
Nørre Snede DK 39 D2
Nørre Vorupør DK 38 C1
Norrent-Fontes F 48 C3
Nørresundby DK 38 B2
Norrhult Klavreström S 40 B5
Norrköping S 37 C3
Norrskedika S 36 A5
Norrtälje S 36 B5
Nors DK 38 B1
Norsbron S 34 B5
Norsholm S 37 C2
Norsjö S 3 D16
Nort-sur-Erdre F 66 A3
Nörten-Hardenberg D 51 B5
North Berwick GB 25 B5
North Charlton GB 25 C6
North Frodingham GB 27 B5
North Kessock GB 23 D4
North Molton GB 28 B4
North Petherton GB 29 B4
North Somercotes GB 27 B6
North Tawton GB 28 C4
North Thoresby GB 27 B5
North Walsham GB 30 B5
Northallerton GB 27 A4
Northampton GB 30 B3
Northeim D 51 B6
Northfleet GB 31 C4
Northleach GB 29 B6
Northpunds GB 22 B7
Northwich GB 26 B3
Norton GB 27 A5
Nortorf D 44 A1
Nörvenich D 50 C2
Norwich GB 30 B5
Norwick GB 22 A8
Nosivka UA 11 L22
Nossa Senhora do Cabo P 92 C1
Nossebro S 35 C4
Nössemark S 34 B3
Nossen D 52 B3
Notaresco I 103 A3
Noto I 109 C4
Notodden N 33 B6
Nottingham GB 27 C4
Nottuln D 50 B3
Nouan-le-Fuzelier F 68 A2
Nouans-les-Fontaines F 67 A6
Nougaroulet F 77 C3
Nouvion F 48 C2
Nouzonville F 59 A5
Nova H 74 B1
Nová Baňa SK 65 B4
Nová Bystrica SK 65 A5
Nová Bystřice CZ 63 A6
Nova Crnja YU 75 C5
Nova Gorica SLO 72 C3
Nova Gradiška HR 74 C2
Nova Levante I 71 B6
Nova Odesa UA 11 N22
Nová Paka CZ 53 C5
Nova Pazova YU 85 B5
Nova Siri I 105 B3
Nova Topola BIH 84 A2
Nova Varoš YU 85 C4
Nova Zagora BG 16 Q19
Novafeltria I 82 C1
Nováky SK 65 B4
Novalaise F 69 C5
Novales E 90 A2
Novalja HR 83 B3
Novara I 70 C3
Novara di Sicilia I 109 A4
Novate Mezzola I 71 B4
Novaya Ladoga RUS 7 F23
Nové Hrady CZ 63 B5
Nové Město SK 64 B3
Nové Město na Moravě CZ 64 A2
Nové Město nad Metují CZ 53 C6
Nové Město pod Smrkem CZ 53 C5
Nové Mitrovice CZ 63 A4
Nové Sady SK 64 B3
Nové Strašeci CZ 53 C3
Nové Zámky SK 64 C4
Novelda E 96 C2
Novellara I 81 B4
Noventa di Piave I 72 C2
Noventa Vicentina I 71 C6
Novés E 94 B2
Noves F 78 C3
Novés de Segre E 91 A4
Novgorod RUS 7 G22
Novhorod-Siverskyy UA 7 L23
Novi Bečej YU 75 C5
Novi di Módena I 81 B4
Novi Kneževac YU 75 B5
Novi Ligure I 80 B2
Novi Marof HR 73 B6
Novi Pazar BG 16 Q20
Novi Pazar YU 85 C5
Novi Sad YU 75 C4
Novi Slankamen YU 85 A5
Novi Travnik BIH 84 B2
Novi Vinodolski HR 83 A3
Novigrad, *Istarska* HR 72 C3
Novigrad, *Zadarsko-Kninska* HR 83 B4
Novigrad Podravski HR 74 B1
Noville B 50 C1
Novion-Porcien F 59 A5
Novo Mesto SLO 73 C5
Novo Miloševo YU 75 B5
Novo Selo BIH 84 A2
Novo Selo, *Kosovo* YU 85 D5
Novo Selo, *Srbija* YU 85 C5
Novohrad-Volynskyy UA 11 L20
Novomirgorod UA 11 M22
Novorzhev RUS 7 H21
Novoselytsya UA 11 M20
Novosil RUS 7 K25
Novosokolniki RUS 7 H21
Novoukrayinka UA 11 M22
Novoveská Huta SK 65 B6
Novovolynsk UA 11 L19
Novozybkov RUS 7 K22
Novska HR 74 C1
Nový Bor CZ 53 C4
Nový Bydžov CZ 53 C5
Novy-Chevrières F 59 A5
Nowy Dwór Mazowiecki PL 47 C6
Nový-Hrozenkov CZ 64 A4
Nový Jičín CZ 64 A4
Nový Knín CZ 63 A5
Novyy Buh UA 11 N23
Nowa Cerekwia PL 54 C2
Nowa Karczma PL 47 A4
Nowa Kościoł PL 53 B5
Nowa Ruda PL 54 C1
Nowa Słupia PL 55 C6
Nowa Sól PL 53 B5
Nowa Wieś PL 47 B5
Nowa-Wieś Wielka PL 47 C4
Nowe PL 47 B4
Nowe Brzesko PL 55 C5
Nowe Grudze PL 55 A4
Nowe Miasteczko PL 53 B5
Nowe Miasto, *Mazowieckie* PL 47 C6
Nowe Miasto, *Mazowieckie* PL 55 B5
Nowe Miasto Lubawskie PL 47 B5
Nowe Miasto nad Wartą PL 54 A2
Nowe Skalmierzyce PL 54 B3
Nowe Warpno PL 45 B6
Nowica PL 47 A5
Nowogard PL 45 B7
Nowogród Bobrzanski PL 53 B5
Nowogrodziec PL 53 B5
Nowosolna PL 55 B4
Nowy Dwór Gdański PL 47 A5
Nowy Korczyn PL 55 C5
Nowy Sącz PL 65 A6
Nowy Staw PL 47 A5
Nowy Targ PL 65 A6
Nowy Tomyśl PL 53 A6
Nowy Wiśnicz PL 65 A6
Noyal-Pontivy F 56 B3
Noyalo F 56 C3
Noyant F 67 A5
Noyelles-sur-Mer F 48 C2
Noyen-sur-Sarthe F 57 C5
Noyers F 59 C4
Noyers-sur-Cher F 67 A6
Noyers-sur-Jabron F 79 B4
Noyon F 59 A3
Nozay F 57 C4
Nuaillé F 66 A4
Nuaillé-d'Aunis F 66 B4
Nubledo E 88 A1
Nuéno E 90 A2
Nuestra Señora Sa Verge des Pilar E 97 C4
Nueva E 88 A2
Nueva Carteya E 100 B1
Nuevalos E 95 A5
Nuits F 59 C5
Nuits-St. Georges F 69 A4
Nule I 110 C2
Nules E 96 B2
Nulvi I 110 C1
Numana I 82 C2
Numansdorp NL 49 B5
Nümbrecht D 50 C3
Nunchritz D 52 B3
Nuneaton GB 30 B2
Nuñomoral E 93 A4
Nunspeet NL 42 C2
Nuoro I 110 C2
Nurallao I 110 D2
Nurmes FIN 3 E21
Nürnberg D 62 A2
Nurri I 110 D2
Nürtingen D 61 B5
Nus I 70 C2
Nusplingen D 61 B4
Nuštar HR 74 C3
Nyáregyháza H 75 A4
Nyárlőrinc H 75 B4
Nyasvizh BY 7 K20
Nybble S 35 B6
Nybøl DK 39 E2
Nyborg DK 39 D3
Nybro S 40 C5
Nybster GB 23 C5
Nyby DK 39 E5
Nye S 40 B5
Nyékládháza H 65 C6
Nyergesujfalu H 65 C4
Nyhammar S 36 A1
Nyhyttan S 36 B1
Nyirád H 74 A2
Nyirbátor H 11 N18
Nyíregyháza H 10 N17
Nyker DK 41 D4
Nykøbing, *Falster* DK 39 E4
Nykøbing, *Vestsjællands Amt.* DK 39 D4
Nykøbing M DK 38 C1
Nyköping S 37 C4
Nykroppa S 34 B6
Nykvarn S 36 B4
Nykyrke S 37 C1
Nylars DK 41 D4
Nymburk CZ 53 C5
Nynäshamn S 37 C4
Nyon CH 69 B6
Nyons F 79 B4
Nýřany CZ 63 A4
Nýrsko CZ 62 A4
Nysa PL 54 C2
Nysäter S 34 B4
Nyskoga S 34 A4
Nysted DK 44 A3
Nystrand N 33 B6
Nyúl H 64 C3

O

O Barco E 86 B4
O Bolo E 87 B3
O Carballiño E 86 B2
O Corgo E 86 B3
Ö Lagnö S 36 B5
O Páramo E 86 B3
O Pedrouzo E 86 B2
O Pino E 86 B2
O Porriño E 87 B2
O Rosal E 87 C2
Oadby GB 30 B2
Oakengates GB 26 C3
Oakham GB 30 B3
Oanes N 32 C3
Obalj BIH 84 C3
Oban GB 24 B2
Obdach A 73 A4
Obejo E 100 A1
Ober Grafendorf A 63 B6
Ober-Morlen D 51 C4
Oberammergau D 62 C2
Oberasbach D 62 A1
Oberau D 62 C2
Oberbruck F 60 C2
Oberdiessbach CH 70 B2
Oberdorf CH 70 A2
Oberdrauburg A 72 B2
Obere Stanz A 73 A5
Oberelsbach D 51 C6
Obergünzburg D 61 C6
Obergurgl A 71 B6
Oberhausen D 50 B2
Oberhof D 51 C6
Oberkirch D 61 B4
Oberkirchen D 51 B4
Oberkochen D 61 B6
Obermassfeld-Grimmenthal D 51 C6
Obernai F 60 B3
Obernberg A 63 B4
Obernburg D 61 A5
Oberndorf D 61 B4
Oberndorf bei Salzburg A 62 C3
Obernkirchen D 51 A5
Oberort A 73 A5
Oberpullendorf A 73 A6
Oberriet CH 71 A4
Oberröblingen D 52 B1
Oberrot D 61 A5
Oberstaufen D 71 A5
Oberstdorf D 71 A5
Obertauern A 72 A3
Obertilliach A 72 B2
Obertraubling D 62 B3
Obertraun A 72 A3
Obertrubach D 62 A2
Obertrum A 62 C4
Oberursel D 51 C4
Obervellach A 72 B3
Oberviechtach D 62 A3
Oberwart A 73 A6
Oberwesel D 50 C3
Oberwinter D 50 C3
Oberwölzstadt A 73 A4
Oberzell D 63 B4
Obice PL 55 C5
Óbidos P 92 B1
Obilić YU 85 D5
Obing D 62 C3
Objat F 67 C6
Objazda PL 46 A3
Oblarn A 73 A4
Obninsk RUS 7 J25
Oborniki PL 46 C2
Oborniki Śląskie PL 54 B1
Obornjača YU 75 C4
Oboyan RUS 7 L25
Obrenovac YU 85 B5
Obrež, *Srbija* YU 85 C6
Obrež, *Vojvodina* YU 85 B4
Obrigheim D 61 A5
Obrov SLO 73 C4
Obrovac HR 83 B4
Obrovac YU 75 C4
Obrovac Sinjski HR 83 C5
Obrzycko PL 46 C2
Obudovac BIH 84 B3
Ocaña E 95 C3
Occhiobello I 81 B5
Occimiano I 80 A2
Očevlja BIH 84 B3
Ochagavía E 76 D1
Ochakiv UA 11 N22
Ochiltree GB 24 C3
Ochla PL 53 B5
Ochotnica-Dolna PL 65 A6
Ochotnica-Górna PL 65 A6
Ochsenfurt D 61 A6
Ochsenhausen D 61 B5
Ochtendung D 50 C3
Ochtrup D 50 A3
Ocieka PL 55 C6
Öckerö S 38 B4
Ocnița MD 11 M20
Očová SK 65 B5
Öcsa H 75 A4
Öcseny H 74 B3
Öcsöd H 75 B5
Octeville F 57 A4
Ocypel PL 47 B4
Ödåkra S 41 C2
Odby DK 38 C1
Odda N 32 A3
Odder DK 39 D3
Ödeborg S 35 C3
Odeceixe P 98 B2
Odechów PL 55 B6
Odeleite P 98 B3
Odemira P 98 B2
Ödemiş TR 16 S20
Odensbacken S 36 B2
Odense DK 39 D3
Odensjö S 40 B4
Oderberg D 45 C6
Oderzo I 72 C2
Odesa UA 11 N22
Ödeshög S 37 C1
Odiáxere P 98 B2
Odie GB 23 B6
Odiham GB 31 C3
Odintsovo RUS 7 J25
Odivelas P 98 A2
Odolanów PL 54 B2
Odón E 95 B5
Odorheiu Secuiesc RO 11 N19
Odoyevo RUS 7 K25
Odrowąz PL 55 B5
Odry CZ 64 A3
Odrzywół PL 55 B5
Ødsted DK 39 D2
Odžaci YU 75 C4
Odžak BIH 84 A3
Oebisfelde D 44 C2
Oederan D 52 C3
Oeding D 50 B2
Oegstgeest NL 49 A5
Oelde D 50 B4
Oelsnitz D 52 C2
Oer-Erkenschwick D 50 B3
Oerlinghausen D 51 B4
Oettingen D 62 B1
Oetz A 71 A5
Oeventrop D 50 B4
Offanengo I 71 C4
Offenbach D 51 C4
Offenburg D 60 B3
Offida I 82 D2
Offingen D 61 B6
Offranville F 58 A2
Ofir P 87 C2
Ofte N 33 B5
Ofterschwang D 71 A5
Oggiono I 71 C4
Ogihares E 100 B2
Ogliastro Cilento I 104 B2
Ogliastro Marina I 104 B1
Ogmore-by-Sea GB 29 B4
Ogna N 32 C2
Ogre LV 6 H19
Ogrodzieniec PL 55 C4
Ogulin HR 73 C5
Ohanes E 101 B3
Ohey B 49 C6
Ohlstadt D 62 C2
Ohrdorf D 44 C2
Ohrdruf D 51 C6
Ohrid MK 15 R17
Öhringen D 61 A5
Oia E 87 B2
Oiã P 92 A2
Oiartzun E 89 A5
Oilgate IRL 21 B5
Oimbra E 87 C3
Oisemont F 48 D2
Oisterwijk NL 49 B6
Ojén E 100 C1
Ojrzeń PL 47 C6
Ojuelos Altos E 99 A5
Okalewo PL 47 B5
Okány H 75 B6
Okehampton GB 28 C3
Okhtyrka UA 7 L24
Oklaj HR 83 C5
Okoč SK 64 C3
Okoličné SK 65 A5
Okonek PL 46 B2
Okonin PL 47 B4
Okřisky CZ 64 A1
Oksa PL 55 C5
Oksbøl DK 39 D1
Oksby DK 39 D1
Okučani HR 74 C2
Okulovka RUS 7 G23
Olagüe E 76 D1
Oland N 33 C5
Olargues F 78 C1
Oława PL 54 C2
Olazagutia E 89 B4
Olbernhau D 52 C3
Ólbia I 110 C2
Olching D 62 B2
Old Deer GB 23 D6

Oldbury GB 29 B5
Oldcastle IRL 19 C4
Oldeberkoop NL 42 C3
Oldeboorn NL 42 B2
Olden N 2 F10
Oldenbrok D 43 B5
Oldenburg, *Niedersachsen* D 43 B5
Oldenburg, *Schleswig-Holstein* D 44 A2
Oldenzaal NL 50 A2
Oldersum D 43 B4
Oldham GB 26 B3
Oldisleben D 52 B1
Oldmeldrum GB 23 D6
Olea E 88 B2
Oleby S 34 A5
Olechów PL 55 B6
Oledo P 92 B3
Olèggio I 70 C3
Oleiros, *Coruña* E 86 A2
Oleiros, *Coruña* E 86 B1
Oleiros P 92 B3
Oleksandriya, *Kirovohrad* UA 11 M23
Oleksandriya, *Rivne* UA 11 L20
Oleksandrovka UA 11 M23
Olen B 49 B5
Ølen N 32 B2
Olenegorsk RUS 3 B23
Olenino RUS 7 H23
Olesa de Montserrat E 91 B4
Oleśnica PL 54 B2
Olešnice CZ 64 A2
Olesno PL 54 C3
Olette F 91 A5
Olevsk UA 11 L20
Olfen D 50 B3
Olgiate Comasco I 70 C3
Olginate I 71 C4
Ølgod DK 39 D1
Olgrinmore GB 23 C5
Olhão P 98 B3
Olhavo P 92 B1
Oliana E 91 A4
Olias del Rey E 94 C3
Oliena I 110 C2
Oliete E 90 C2
Olite E 89 B5
Oliva E 96 C2
Oliva de la Frontera E 99 A4
Oliva de Mérida E 93 C4
Oliva de Plasencia E 93 A4
Olivadi I 106 C3
Olival P 92 B2
Olivar E 100 C2
Olivares E 99 B4
Olivares de Duero E 88 C2
Olivares de Júcar E 95 C4
Oliveira de Azeméis P 87 D2
Oliveira de Frades P 87 D2
Oliveira do Conde P 92 A3
Oliveira do Douro P 87 C2
Oliveira do Hospital P 92 A3
Olivenza E 93 C3
Olivet F 58 C2
Olivone CH 70 B3
Öljehult S 41 C5
Olkusz PL 55 C4
Ollerton GB 27 B4
Ollerup DK 39 D3
Olliergues F 68 C3
Ölmbrotorp S 36 B2
Ölme S 34 B5
Olmedilla de Alarcón E 95 C4
Olmedillo de Roa E 88 C3
Olmedo E 88 C2
Olmedo I 110 C1
Olmeto F 110 B1
Olmillos de Castro E 87 C4
Olmos de Ojeda E 88 B2
Olney GB 30 B3
Ołobok PL 54 B3
Olocau del Rey E 90 C2
Olofström S 41 C4
Olomouc CZ 64 A3
Olonne-sur-Mer F 66 B3
Olonzac F 78 C1
Oloron-Ste. Marie F 76 C2
Olost E 91 B5
Olot E 91 A5
Olovo BIH 84 B3
Olpe D 50 B3
Olsberg D 51 B4
Olsene B 49 C4
Olshammar S 37 C1
Olshanka UA 11 M22
Olshany UA 7 L24
Olszanica PL 53 B5
Olsztyn, *Śląskie* PL 55 C4
Olsztyn, *Warmińsko-Mazurskie* PL 47 B6
Olsztynek PL 47 B6
Olszyna PL 53 B5
Oltedal N 32 C3
Olten CH 70 A2
Olteniţa RO 11 P20
Olula del Rio E 101 B3
Ølve N 32 A2
Olvega E 89 C5
Olvera E 99 C5
Olzai I 110 C2
Omagh GB 19 B4
Omegna I 70 C3
Omiš HR 83 C5
Omišalj HR 73 C4
Ommen NL 42 C3
Omoljica YU 85 B5
On B 49 C6
Oña E 89 B3
Onano I 102 A1
Oñati E 89 A4
Onda E 96 B2
Ondara E 96 C3
Ondarroa E 89 A4
Onesse-et-Laharie F 76 B1
Oneşti RO 11 N20
Onhaye B 49 C5
Onich GB 24 B2
Onil E 96 C2
Onis E 88 A2
Önnestad S 41 C4
Onsala S 38 B5
Ontinyent E 96 C2
Ontur E 101 A4
Onzain F 67 A6
Onzonilla E 88 B1
Oost-Vlieland NL 42 B2
Oostburg NL 49 B4
Oostende B 48 B3
Oosterend NL 42 B2
Oosterhout NL 49 B5
Oosterwolde NL 42 C3
Oosterzele B 49 C4
Oosthuizen NL 42 C2
Oostkamp B 49 B4
Oostmalle B 49 B5
Oostvoorne NL 49 B5
Ootmarsum NL 42 C3
Opalenica PL 53 A6
Opařany CZ 63 A5
Oparić YU 85 C6
Opatija HR 73 C4
Opatów, *Śląskie* PL 54 C3
Opatów, *Świętokrzyskie* PL 55 C6
Opatów, *Wielkopolskie* PL 54 B3
Opatówek PL 54 B3
Opatowiec PL 55 C5
Opava CZ 64 A3
Opeinde NL 42 B3
Oper Thalkirchdorf D 71 A5
Opglabbeerk B 49 B6
Opicina I 72 C3
Oplotnica SLO 73 B5
Opmeer NL 42 C1
Opochka RUS 7 H21
Opočno CZ 53 C6
Opoczno PL 55 B5
Opole PL 54 C2
Oporów PL 55 A4
Opovo YU 85 A5
Oppach D 53 B4
Oppdal N 2 E11
Oppeby, *Östergötland* S 37 C2
Oppeby, *Södermanland* S 37 C3
Oppegård N 34 B2
Oppenau D 61 B4
Oppenberg A 73 A4
Oppenheim D 61 A4
Óppido Lucano I 104 B2
Óppido Mamertina I 106 C2
Opponitz A 63 C5
Oppstad N 34 A3
Oprtalj HR 72 C3
Opsaheden S 34 B5
Ópusztaszer H 75 B5
Opuzen HR 84 C2
Ora I 71 B6
Orada P 92 C3
Oradea RO 10 N17
Oradour-sur-Glane F 67 C6
Oradour-sur-Vayres F 67 C5
Oragonja SLO 72 C3
Orah BIH 84 D3
Orahova BIH 84 B2
Orahovica HR 74 C2
Orahovo BIH 74 C2
Oraison F 79 C4
Orange F 78 B3
Orani I 110 C2
Oranienbaum D 52 B2
Oranienburg D 45 C5
Oranmore IRL 20 A3
Orašac YU 85 B5
Orašje BIH 84 A3
Oravská Lesná SK 65 A5
Oravská Polhora SK 65 A5
Oravské Veselé SK 65 A5
Oravsky-Podzámok SK 65 A5
Orba E 96 C2
Orbacém P 87 C2
Ørbæk DK 39 D3
Orbais F 59 B4
Orbassano I 80 A1
Orbe CH 69 B6
Orbec F 58 A1
Orbetello I 102 A1
Orbetello Scalo I 102 A1
Ørby DK 39 C3
Örbyhus S 36 A4
Orce E 101 B3
Orcera E 101 A3
Orchamps-Vennes F 69 A6
Orchete E 96 C2
Orchies F 49 C4
Orchowo PL 47 C4
Orcières F 79 B5
Ordes E 86 A2
Ordhead GB 23 D6
Ordino AND 91 A4
Ordizia E 89 A4
Orduña E 89 B4
Orea E 95 B5
Orebić HR 84 D2
Örebro S 36 B2
Öregcsertö H 75 B4
Öregrund S 36 A5
Orehoved DK 39 E4
Orel RUS 7 K25
Orellana E 93 B5
Orellana de la Sierra E 93 B5
Ören TR 16 T20
Orestiás GR 16 R20
Organyà E 91 A4
Orgaz E 94 C3
Orgelet F 69 B5
Orgères-en-Beauce F 58 B2
Orgibet F 77 D3
Orgnac-l'Aven F 78 B3
Orgon F 79 C4
Orgósolo I 110 C2
Orhaneli TR 16 S21
Orhangazi TR 16 R21
Orhei MD 11 N21
Oria E 101 B3
Ória I 105 B4
Origny-Ste. Benoite F 59 A4
Orihuela E 96 C2
Orihuela del Tremedal E 95 B5
Oriola P 98 A3
Oriolo I 105 B3
Oriovac HR 74 C2
Orissaare EST 6 G18
Oristano I 110 D1
Öriszentpéter H 73 B6
Ørje N 34 B3
Orjiva E 100 C2
Orkanger N 2 E11
Örkelljunga S 41 C3
Örkény H 75 A4
Orlamünde D 52 C1
Orlane YU 85 D6
Orléans F 58 C2
Orlová CZ 65 A4
Orlovat YU 75 C5
Ormea I 80 B1
Ormelet N 35 B2
Ormemyr N 33 B6
Ormož SLO 73 B6
Ormskirk GB 26 B3
Ornans F 69 A6
Ornäs S 36 A2
Orneta PL 47 A6
Ørnhøj DK 39 C1
Ornö S 37 B5
Örnsköldsvik S 3 E16
Orolik HR 75 C3
Orom YU 75 C4
Oron-la-Ville CH 70 B1
Oronsko PL 55 B5
Oropa I 70 C2
Oropesa, *Castellón de la Plana* E 96 A3
Oropesa, *Toledo* E 94 C1
Orosei I 110 C2
Orosháza H 75 B5
Oroslavje HR 73 B5
Oroszlány H 74 A3
Oroszlo H 74 B3
Orotelli I 110 C2
Orozko E 89 A4
Orphir GB 23 C5
Orpington GB 31 C4
Orreaga-Roncesvalles E 76 C1
Orrefors S 40 C5
Orsa S 2 F14
Orsara di Púglia I 104 A2
Orsay F 58 B3
Orscholz D 60 A2
Orsennes F 67 B6
Orserum S 37 C1
Orsha BY 7 J22
Orsières CH 70 B2
Orsjö S 40 C5
Ørslev DK 39 D4
Orsogna I 103 A4
Orsomarso I 106 B2
Orşova RO 11 P18
Ørsta N 2 E10
Ørsted DK 38 C3
Örsundsbro S 36 B4
Orta Nova I 104 A2
Ortaca TR 16 T21
Orte I 102 A2
Ortenburg D 63 B4
Orth A 64 B2
Orthez F 76 C2
Ortigueira E 86 A3
Ortilla E 90 A2
Ortisei I 72 B1
Orţişoara RO 75 C6
Orton GB 26 A3
Ortona I 103 A4
Ortrand D 53 B3
Orubica HR 74 C2
Ørum DK 38 C2
Orune I 110 C2
Orusco E 95 B3
Orvalho P 92 A3
Orvault F 66 A3
Orvieto I 82 D1
Orvínio I 102 A2
Oryakhovo BG 15 Q18
Orzesze PL 54 C3
Orzinuovi I 71 C4
Orzivécchi I 71 C4
Os, *Hedmark* N 2 E12
Os, *Hedmark* N 34 A3
Os Peares E 86 B3
Osann-Monzelo D 60 A2
Osaonica YU 85 C5
Osbruk S 40 B4
Osby S 41 C3
Oščadnica SK 65 A4
Oschatz D 52 B3
Oschersleben D 52 A1
Óschiri I 110 C2
Osciłowo PL 47 C6
Osdorf D 44 A2
Osečina YU 85 B4
Oseja de Sajambre E 88 A1
Osek CZ 53 C3
Osera de Ebro E 90 B2
Osidda I 110 C2
Osie PL 47 B4
Osieck PL 55 B6
Osieczna PL 54 B1
Osieczno PL 46 B1
Osiek, *Kujawsko-Pomorskie* PL 47 B5
Osiek, *Pomorskie* PL 47 B4
Osiek, *Świętokrzyskie* PL 55 C6
Osiek nad Notecią PL 46 B3
Osielsko PL 47 B4
Osijek HR 74 C3
Osilnica SLO 73 C4
Ósilo I 110 C1
Ósimo I 82 C2
Osinja BIH 84 B2
Osintorf BY 7 J22
Osipaonica YU 85 B6
Osjaków PL 54 B3
Oskamull GB 24 B1
Oskarshamn S 40 B6
Oskarström S 40 C2
Oslany SK 65 B4
Oslavany CZ 64 A2
Ošlje HR 84 D2
Oslo N 34 B2
Ösmo S 37 C4
Osmolin PL 55 A4
Osnabrück D 50 A4
Ośno Lubuskie PL 45 C6
Osoblaha CZ 54 C2
Osor HR 83 B3
Osorno E 88 B2
Øsøyro N 32 A2
Ospedaletti I 80 C1
Ospitaletto I 71 C5
Oss NL 49 B6
Ossa de Montiel E 95 D4
Ossi I 110 C1
Ossun F 76 C2
Ostanå S 41 C4
Ostashkov RUS 7 H23
Östbevern D 50 A3
Østed DK 39 D2
Oster UA 11 L22
Øster Hornum DK 38 C2
Øster Hurup DK 38 C3
Øster-marie DK 41 D5
Øster Tørslev DK 38 C3
Øster Vrå DK 38 B3
Osterburg D 44 C3
Osterburken D 61 A5
Österbybruk S 36 A4
Osterbyhavn DK 38 B4
Österbymo S 37 D2
Ostercappeln D 43 C5
Österfärnebo S 36 A3
Osterfeld D 52 B1
Osterhofen D 62 B4
Osterholz-Scharmbeck D 43 B5
Østerild DK 38 B1
Österlövsta S 36 A4
Ostermiething A 62 B3
Osterode am Harz D 51 B6
Östersund S 2 E14
Östervåla S 36 A4
Östervallskog S 34 B3
Osterwieck D 51 B6
Osterzell D 62 C1
Ostffyasszonyfa H 74 A2
Östhammar S 36 A5
Ostheim F 60 B3
Ostheim vor der Rhön D 51 C6
Osthofen D 61 A4
Ostiano I 71 C5
Ostiglia I 81 A5
Ostiz E 76 D1
Östmark S 34 A4
Ostojićevo YU 75 C5
Ostra I 82 C2
Östra Amtervik S 34 B5
Östra Husby S 37 C3
Östra Ljungby S 41 C3
Östra Ryd S 37 C3
Ostrabby S 41 D3
Ostrach D 61 C5
Ostrau D 52 B3
Ostrava CZ 64 A4
Østre Halsen N 35 B2
Ostrhauderfehn D 43 B4
Ostritz D 53 B4
Ostróda PL 47 B5
Ostroh UA 11 L20
Ostrołęka PL 6 K17
Ostropole PL 46 B2
Ostroróg PL 46 C2
Ostrošovac BIH 83 B4
Ostrov CZ 52 C2
Ostrov RUS 7 H21
Ostrov nad Oslavou CZ 64 A1
Ostrów Mazowiecka PL 6 K17
Ostrów Wielkopolski PL 54 B2
Ostrówek PL 54 B3
Ostrowiec PL 46 A2
Ostrowiec-Świętokrzyski PL 55 C6
Ostrowite PL 47 B5
Ostrowo PL 47 C4
Ostrožac BIH 84 C2
Ostrzeszów PL 54 B2
Ostseebad Kühlungsborn D 44 A3
Ostuni I 105 B4
Osuna E 99 B5
Osvětimany CZ 64 A3
Oswestry GB 26 C2
Oświęcim PL 55 C4
Osztopán H 74 B2
Oteiza E 89 B5
Otelec RO 75 C5
Oteo E 89 A3
Oterbekk N 34 B2
Otero de Herreros E 94 B2
Otero de O Bodas E 87 C4
Othem S 37 D5
Otley GB 27 B4
Otmuchów PL 54 C2
Otočac HR 83 B4
Otok, *Splitsko-Dalmatinska* HR 83 C5
Otok, *Vukovarsko-Srijemska* HR 84 A3
Otoka BIH 83 B5
Otranto I 107 A5
Otrić HR 83 B5
Otrícoli I 102 A2
Otrokovice CZ 64 A3
Ottana I 110 C2
Ottaviano I 103 C4
Ottenby S 41 C6
Ottendorf-Okrilla D 53 B3
Ottenhöfen D 61 B4
Ottenschlag A 63 B6
Ottensheim A 63 B5
Otter Ferry GB 24 B2
Otterbach D 60 A3
Otterbäcken S 35 C6
Otterberg D 60 A3
Otterburn GB 25 C5
Otterndorf D 43 B5
Ottersburg D 43 B6
Ottersweier D 61 B4
Otterup DK 39 D3
Ottery St. Mary GB 29 C4
Ottignies B 49 C5
Ottmarsheim F 60 C3
Ottobeuren D 61 C6
Öttömös H 75 B4
Ottone I 80 B3
Ottweiler D 60 A3
Ötvöskónyi H 74 B2
Otwock PL 55 A6
Ouanne F 59 C4
Ouarville F 58 B2
Oucques F 58 C2
Oud-Beijerland NL 49 B5
Oud Gastel NL 49 B5
Ouddorp NL 49 B4
Oude-Pekela NL 43 B4
Oude-Tonge NL 49 B5
Oudemirdum NL 42 C2
Oudenaarde B 49 C4
Oudenbosch NL 49 B5
Oudenburg B 49 B4
Oudewater NL 49 A5
Oudon F 66 A3
Oughterard IRL 20 A2
Ouguela P 93 B3
Ouistreham F 57 A5
Oulainen FIN 3 D19
Oulchy-le-Château F 59 A4
Oullins F 69 C4
Oulmes F 67 B4
Oulton GB 30 B5
Oulton Broad GB 30 B5
Oulu FIN 3 D19
Oulx I 79 A5
Oundle GB 30 B3
Ourense E 87 B3
Ourique P 98 B2
Ourol E 86 A3
Ouroux-en-Morvan F 68 A3
Ousdale GB 23 C5
Oust F 77 D4
Outeiro P 92 A2
Outeiro de Rei E 86 A3
Outes E 86 B2
Outokumpu FIN 3 E21
Outreau F 48 C2
Outwell GB 30 B4
Ouzouer-le-Marché F 58 C2
Ouzouer-sur-Loire F 58 C3
Ovada I 80 B2
Ovar P 87 D2
Ove DK 38 C2
Ovelgönne D 43 B5
Over-jerstal DK 39 D2
Overath D 50 C3
Overbister GB 23 B6
Øverdinkel NL 50 A3
Överenhörna S 36 B4
Overijse B 49 C5
Överkalix S 3 C18
Overlade DK 38 C2
Överlida S 40 B2
Overpelt B 49 B6
Overton GB 26 C3
Övertorneå S 3 C18
Överum S 37 D3
Ovidiopol UA 11 N22
Oviedo E 88 A1
Oviglio I 80 B2
Ovindoli I 103 A3
Ovodda I 110 C2
Øvre Årdal N 2 F10
Øvre Sirdal N 32 C3
Övre Ullerud S 34 B5
Øvrebygd N 32 C3
Ovruch UA 11 L21
Ovtrup DK 39 D1
Owińska PL 46 C2
Oxelösund S 37 C4
Oxenholme GB 26 A3
Oxford GB 31 C2
Oxie S 41 D3
Oxted GB 31 C4
Øyenkilen N 34 B2
Øyfiell N 33 B5
Øygärdslia N 33 C5
Oykel Bridge GB 22 D4
Øymark N 34 B3
Oyonnax F 69 B5
Øyslebø N 33 C4
Oyten D 43 B6
Øyuvsbu N 33 B4
Ozaeta E 89 B4
Ozalj HR 73 C5
Ożarów PL 55 C6
Ożarów Maz PL 55 A5
Ožbalt SLO 73 B5
Ózd H 65 B6
Ožďany SK 65 B5
Ozieri I 110 C2
Ozimek PL 54 C3
Ozimica BIH 84 B3
Ozora H 74 B3
Ozorków PL 55 B4
Ozzano Monferrato I 80 A2

P

Paal B 49 B6
Pabianice PL 55 B4
Pacanów PL 55 C6
Paceco I 108 B1
Pachino I 109 C4
Pačir YU 75 C4
Pack A 73 A5
Paços de Ferreira P 87 C2
Pacov CZ 63 A6
Pacsa H 74 B2
Pacy-sur-Eure F 58 A2
Paczków PL 54 C2
Padborg DK 39 E2
Padej YU 75 C5
Padene HR 83 B5
Paderborn D 51 B4
Paderne P 98 B2
Padiham GB 26 B3
Padina YU 85 A5
Padinska Skela YU 85 B5
Padornelo P 87 C2
Pádova I 72 C1
Padragkút H 74 A2
Padria I 110 C1
Padrón E 86 B2
Padru I 110 C2
Padstow GB 28 C3
Padul E 100 B2
Padula I 104 B2
Paduli I 104 A1
Paesana I 79 B6
Paese I 72 C2
Pag HR 83 B4
Pagani I 103 C4
Pagánica I 103 A3
Pagánico I 81 D5
Paglieta I 103 A4
Pagny-sur-Moselle F 60 B1
Páhi H 75 B4
Pahl D 62 C2
Paide EST 7 G19
Paignton GB 29 C4
Pailhès F 77 C4
Paimboeuf F 66 A2
Paimpol F 56 B2
Paimpont F 57 B3
Painswick GB 29 B5
Painten D 62 B2
Paisley GB 24 C3
Pajala S 3 C18
Pajares E 88 A1
Pajares de los Oteros E 88 B1
Pajęczno PL 54 B3
Páka H 74 B1
Pakość PL 47 C4
Pakosławice PL 54 C2
Pakoštane HR 83 C4
Pakrac HR 74 C2
Paks H 74 B3
Palacios de la Sierra E 89 C3
Palaciós de la Valduerna E 88 B1
Palacios de Sanabria E 87 B4
Palacios del Sil E 86 B4
Palaciosrubios E 94 A1
Palafrugell E 91 B6
Palagiano I 105 B4
Palagonia I 109 B3
Paláia I 81 C4
Palaiokhóra GR 16 U18
Palaiseau F 58 B3
Palamós E 91 B6
Palanga LT 6 J17
Palanzano I 81 B4
Palárikovo SK 64 B4
Palas de Rei E 86 B3
Palata I 103 B4
Palatna YU 85 C6
Palau I 110 B2
Palavas-les-Flots F 78 C2
Palazuelos de la Sierra E 89 B3
Palazzo Adriano I 108 B2
Palazzo del Pero I 81 C5
Palazzo San Gervásio I 104 B2
Palazzolo Acréide I 109 B3
Palazzolo sull Oglio I 71 C4
Palazzuolo sul Senio I 81 B5
Paldiski EST 6 G19
Pale BIH 84 C3
Palena I 103 B4
Palencia E 88 B2
Palenciana E 100 B1
Palermo I 108 A2
Palestrina I 102 B2
Pálfa H 74 B3
Palfau A 63 C5
Palhaça P 92 A2
Palheiros da Tocha P 92 A2
Palheiros de Quiaios P 92 A2
Palić YU 75 B4
Palidoro I 102 B2
Palinuro I 104 B2
Paliseul B 59 A6
Pallanza I 70 C3
Pallares E 99 A4
Pallaruelo de Monegros E 90 B2
Pallas Green IRL 20 B3
Pallerols E 91 A4
Palling D 62 B3
Palluau F 66 B3
Palma P 92 C2
Palma Campània I 103 C4
Palma de Mallorca, *Mallorca* E 97
Palma del Río E 99 B5
Palma di Montechiaro I 108 B2
Palma Nova, *Mallorca* E 97
Palmanova I 72 C3
Palmela P 92 C2
Palmerola E 91 A5
Palmi I 106 C2
Pälmonostora H 75 B4
Palo del Colle I 105 A3
Palomares E 101 B4
Palomares del Campo E 95 C4
Palomas E 93 C4
Palombara Sabina I 102 A2
Palos de la Frontera E 99 B4
Palotabozsok H 74 B3
Palotás H 65 C5
Pals E 91 B6
Pålsboda S 37 B2
Paluzza I 72 B3
Pamhagen A 64 C2
Pamiers F 77 C4
Pamiętowo PL 46 B3
Pampaneira E 100 C2
Pamparato I 80 B1
Pampilhosa, *Aveiro* P 92 A2
Pampilhosa, *Coimbra* P 92 A3
Pampliega E 88 B3
Pamplona E 89 B5
Panagyurishte BG 16 Q19
Pancalieri I 80 B1
Pančevo YU 85 B5
Pancey F 59 B6
Pancorvo E 89 B3
Pancrudo E 90 C1
Pandino I 71 C4
Pandrup DK 38 B2
Panenský-Týnec CZ 53 C3
Panes E 88 A2
Panevėžys LT 6 J19
Pangbourne GB 31 C2
Panissières F 69 C4
Panki PL 54 C3
Pannes F 58 B3
Panningen NL 50 B1
Pannonhalma H 74 A2
Panschwitz-Kuckau D 53 B4
Pansdorf D 44 B2
Pantano de Cijara E 94 C2
Panticosa E 90 A2
Pantín E 86 A2
Pantoja E 94 B3
Pantón E 86 B3
Panxon E 87 B2
Páola I 106 B3
Paola M 109 C4
Pápa H 74 A2
Papasidero I 106 B2
Pápateszér H 74 A2
Papenburg D 43 B4
Pappenheim D 62 B1
Paprotnia PL 55 A5
Parábita I 105 B5
Paraćin YU 85 C6
Parád H 65 C6
Parada, *Bragança* P 87 C4
Parada, *Viseu* P 92 A2
Paradas E 99 B5
Paradela E 86 B3
Parades de Rubiales E 94 A1
Paradinas de San Juan E 94 B1
Paradiso di Cevadale I 71 B5
Paradyż PL 55 B5
Parainen FIN 3 F18
Parakhino Paddubye RUS 7 G23
Paramé F 57 B4
Páramo E 86 A4
Páramo del Sil E 86 B4
Parandaça P 87 C3
Paravadella E 86 A3
Paray-le-Monial F 68 B4
Parceiros P 92 B2
Parcey F 69 A5
Parchim D 44 B3
Parcice PL 54 B3
Pardilla E 88 C3
Pardubice CZ 53 C5
Paredes E 95 B4
Paredes P 87 C2
Paredes de Coura P 87 C2
Paredes de Nava E 88 B2
Paredes de Siguenza E 95 A4
Pareja E 95 B4
Parennes F 57 B5
Parenti I 106 B3
Parentis-en-Born F 76 B1
Parey D 44 C3
Parfino RUS 7 H22
Parg HR 73 C4
Párga GR 15 S17
Pargny-sur-Saulx F 59 B5
Parigné-l'Évêque F 58 C1
Parikkala FIN 3 F21
Paris F 58 B3
Parisot F 77 B4
Parkano FIN 3 E18
Parknasilla IRL 20 C2
Parla E 94 B3
Parlavá E 91 A6
Parma I 81 B4
Parndorf A 64 C2
Párnica SK 65 A5
Parnu EST 6 G19
Parolis E 101 A3
Parrillas E 94 B1
Parsberg D 62 A2
Parstein D 45 C6
Partakko FIN 3 B20
Partanna I 108 B1
Parthenay F 67 B4
Partinico I 108 A2
Partizani YU 85 B5
Partizánske SK 65 B4
Partney GB 27 B6
Påryd S 40 C5
Parysów PL 55 B6
Parzymiechy PL 54 B3
Paşcani RO 11 N20
Pasewalk D 45 B5
Pašina Voda YU 85 C4
Påskallavik S 40 B6
Pasłęk PL 47 A5
Pašman HR 83 C4
Passage East IRL 21 B5
Passage West IRL 20 C3
Passail A 73 A5
Passais F 57 B5
Passau D 63 B4
Passegueiro P 92 A2
Passignano sul Trasimeno I 82 C1
Passo di Tréia I 82 C2
Passopisciaro I 109 B4
Passow D 45 B6
Passy F 70 C1
Pastavy BY 7 J20
Pástena I 103 B4
Pastrana E 95 B4
Pastrengo I 71 C5
Pasym PL 47 B6
Pásztó H 65 C5
Pata SK 64 B3
Patay F 58 B2
Pateley Bridge GB 27 A4
Paterek PL 46 B3
Paterna E 96 B2
Paterna de Rivera E 99 C5
Paterna del Campo E 99 B4
Paterna del Madera E 101 A3
Paternion A 72 B3
Paternò I 109 B3
Paternópoli I 104 B2
Patersdorf D 62 A3
Paterswolde NL 42 B3
Patna GB 24 C3
Pątnow PL 54 A3
Patos AL 15 R16
Pátrai GR 15 S17
Patrickswell IRL 20 B3
Patrimonio F 110 A2
Patrington GB 27 B5
Pattada I 110 C2
Pattensen, *Niedersachsen* D 44 B2
Pattensen, *Niedersachsen* D 51 A5
Patterdale GB 26 A3
Patti I 109 A3
Páty H 74 A3
Pau F 76 C2
Pauillac F 67 C4
Paularo I 72 B3
Paulhaguet F 68 C3
Paulhan F 78 C2
Paulilátino I 110 C1
Pauliström S 40 B5
Paullo I 71 C4
Paulstown IRL 21 B4
Pausa D 52 C1
Pavia I 71 C4
Pavia P 92 C2
Pavias E 96 B2
Pavilly F 58 A1
Pāvilosta LV 6 H17
Pavino Polje YU 85 C4
Pavullo nel Frignano I 81 B4
Pawłowice, *Opolskie* PL 54 B2
Pawłowice, *Śląskie* PL 65 A4
Payerne CH 70 B1
Paymogo E 98 B3
Payrac F 77 B4
Pazardzhik BG 16 Q19
Pazin HR 72 C3
Paziols F 78 D1
Pčelić HR 74 C2
Peal de Becerro E 100 B2
Peasmarsh GB 31 D4
Peć YU 85 D5
Péccioli I 81 C4
Pécel H 75 A4
Pechao P 98 B3
Pechenga RUS 3 B22
Pechenizhyn UA 11 M19
Pecica RO 75 B6
Pećinci YU 85 B4
Pecka YU 85 B4
Peckelsheim D 51 B5
Pečory RUS 7 H20
Pécs H 74 B3
Pécsvárad H 74 B3
Peczniew PL 54 B3
Pedaso I 82 C2
Pedavena I 72 B1
Pedérobba I 72 C1
Pedersker DK 41 D4
Pedescala I 71 C6
Pedrafita E 86 B3
Pedrajas de San Esteban E 88 C2
Pedralba E 96 B2
Pedralba de la Praderia E 87 B4
Pedraza E 94 A3
Pedreguer E 96 C3
Pedrera E 100 B1
Pedro Abad E 100 B1
Pedro Bernardo E 94 B2
Pedro-Martinez E 100 B2
Pedro Muñoz E 95 C4
Pedroche E 100 A1
Pedrógão P 92 B2
Pedrógão, *Beja* P 98 A3
Pedrógão, *Castelo Branco* P 93 A3
Pedrógão Grande P 92 B2
Pedrola E 90 B1
Pedrosa de Tobalina E 89 B3
Pedrosa del Rey E 88 C1
Pedrosa del Rio Urbel E 88 B3
Pedrosillo de los Aires E 94 B1
Pedrosillo el Ralo E 94 A1
Pędzewo PL 47 B4
Peebles GB 25 C4
Peel GB 26 A1
Peenemünde D 45 A5
Peer B 49 B6
Pega P 93 A3
Pegalajar E 100 B2
Pegau D 52 B2
Peggau A 73 A5

Pegli I 80 B2
Pegnitz D 62 A2
Pego E 96 C2
Pegões-Estação P 92 C2
Pegões Velhos P 92 C2
Pęgów PL 54 B1
Pegswood GB 25 C6
Peguera, *Mallorca* E 97
Peine D 51 A6
Peisey-Nancroix F 70 C1
Peissenberg D 62 C2
Peiting D 62 C1
Peitz D 53 B4
Péjo I 71 B5
Pelagićevo BIH 84 B3
Pelahustán E 94 B2
Pełczyce PL 45 B7
Pelhřimov CZ 63 A6
Pélissanne F 79 C4
Pelkosenniemi FIN 3 C20
Pellegrino Parmense I 81 B3
Pellegrue F 76 B3
Pellérd H 74 B3
Pellestrina I 72 C2
Pellevoisin F 67 B6
Pellizzano I 71 B5
Pello FIN 3 C19
Peloche E 94 C1
Pelplin PL 47 B4
Pelussin F 69 C4
Pély H 75 A5
Pembroke GB 28 B3
Pembroke Dock GB 28 B3
Peña de Cabra E 93 A5
Peñacerrada E 89 B4
Penacova P 92 A2
Peñafiel E 88 C2
Penafiel P 87 C2
Peñaflor E 99 B5
Peñalba de Santiago E 86 B4
Peñalsordo E 93 C5
Penalva do Castelo P 92 A3
Penamacôr P 93 A3
Peñaparda E 93 A4
Peñaranda de Bracamonte E 94 B1
Peñaranda de Duero E 89 C3
Peñarroya de Tastavins E 90 C3
Peñarroya-Pueblonuevo E 99 A5
Peñarrubla E 86 B3
Penarth GB 29 B4
Peñas de San Pedro E 101 A4
Peñascosa E 101 A3
Peñausende E 88 C1
Penc H 65 C5
Pencoed GB 29 B4
Pendeen GB 28 C2
Pendine GB 28 B3
Pendueles E 88 A2
Penedono P 87 D3
Penela P 92 A2
Penhas Juntas P 87 C3
Peniche P 92 B1
Penicuik GB 25 C4
Penig D 52 C2
Penilhos P 98 B3
Peñíscola E 90 C3
Penistone GB 27 B4
Penkridge GB 26 C3
Penkun D 45 B6
Penmarch F 56 C1
Pennabilli I 82 C1
Penne I 103 A3
Penne-d'Agenais F 77 B3
Pennes I 71 B6
Pennyghael GB 24 B1
Peno RUS 7 H23
Penpont GB 25 C4
Penrhyndeudraeth GB 26 C1
Penrith GB 26 A3
Penryn GB 28 C2
Pentraeth GB 26 B1
Penybontfawr GB 26 C2
Penygroes, *Carmarthenshire* GB 28 B3
Penygroes, *Gwynedd* GB 26 B1
Penzance GB 28 C2
Penzberg D 62 C2
Penzlin D 45 B5
Pepeljevac YU 85 C6
Pepinster B 50 C1
Pér H 64 C3
Pera Boa P 92 A3
Perafita P 87 C2
Peraleda de la Mata E 93 B5
Peraleda de San Román E 94 C1
Peraleda del Zaucejo E 93 C5
Perales de Alfambra E 90 C1
Perales de Tajuña E 95 B3
Perales del Puerto E 93 A4
Peralta E 89 B5
Peralta de la Sal E 90 B3
Peralva P 98 B3
Peralveche E 95 B4
Perbál H 65 C4
Perchtoldsdorf A 64 B2
Percy F 57 B4
Perdasdefogu I 110 D2
Perdiguera E 90 B2
Peredo P 87 C4
Peregu Mare RO 75 B5
Pereiro, *Faro* P 98 B3
Pereiro, *Guarda* P 87 D3
Pereiro, *Santarém* P 92 B2
Pereiro de Aguiar E 87 B3
Perelada E 91 A6
Perelejos de las Truchas E 95 B5
Pereña E 87 C4
Pereruela E 88 C1
Pereyaslav-Khmelnytskyy UA 11 L22
Pérfugas I 110 C1
Perg A 63 B5
Pergine Valsugana I 71 B6
Pérgola I 82 C1
Pergusa I 109 B3
Periam RO 75 B5
Periana E 100 C1
Périers F 57 A4
Périgueux F 67 C5
Perino I 80 B3
Perjasica HR 73 C5
Perkáta H 74 A3
Perković HR 83 C5
Perleberg D 44 B3
Perlez YU 75 C5
Pernarec CZ 62 A4
Pernek SK 64 B3
Pernes P 92 B2
Pernes-les-Fontaines F 79 C4
Pernik BG 15 Q18
Pernink CZ 52 C2
Pernitz A 64 C1
Pero Pinheiro P 92 C1
Peroguarda P 98 A2
Pérols F 78 C2
Péronne F 59 A3
Péronnes B 49 C5
Perorrubio E 94 A3
Perosa Argentina I 79 B6
Perozinho P 87 C2
Perpignan F 91 A5
Perranporth GB 28 C2
Perranzabuloe GB 28 C2
Perrecy-les-Forges F 69 B4
Perrero I 79 B6
Perrignier F 69 B6
Perros-Guirec F 56 B2
Persan F 58 A3
Persberg S 34 B6
Persenbeug A 63 B6
Pershore GB 29 A5
Perstorp S 41 C3
Perth GB 25 B4
Pertisau A 72 A1
Pertoča SLO 73 B6
Pertuis F 79 C4
Perućac YU 85 C4
Perúgia I 82 C1
Perušić HR 83 B4
Péruwelz B 49 C4
Pervomaysk UA 11 M22
Perwez B 49 C5
Pesadas de Burgos E 89 B3
Pesaguero E 88 A2
Pésaro I 82 C1
Pescantina I 71 C5
Pescara I 103 A4
Pescasséroli I 103 B3
Peschici I 104 A3
Peschiera del Garda I 71 C5
Péscia I 81 C4
Pescina I 103 A3
Pesco Sannita I 103 B4
Pescocostanzo I 103 B4
Pescopagano I 104 B2
Peshkop AL 15 R17
Pesmes F 69 A5
Pesnica SLO 73 B5
Peso da Régua P 87 C3
Pesquera de Duero E 88 C2
Pessac F 76 B2
Pestovo RUS 7 G24
Pétange L 60 A1
Peteranec HR 74 B1
Peterborough GB 30 B3
Peterculter GB 23 D6
Peterhead GB 23 D7
Peterlee GB 25 D6
Petersfield GB 31 C3
Petershagen, *Brandenburg* D 45 C5
Petershagen, *Brandenburg* D 45 C6
Petershagen, *Nordrhein-Westfalen* D 43 C5
Petershausen D 62 B2
Peterswell IRL 20 A3
Pétervására H 65 B6
Petilia Policastro I 107 B3
Petín E 87 B3
Petkus D 52 B3
Petlovac HR 74 C3
Petlovača YU 85 B4
Petőfiszallás H 75 B4
Petra, *Mallorca* F 97
Petralia Sottana I 109 B3
Petrčane HR 83 B4
Petrella Tifernina I 103 B4
Petrer E 96 C2
Petreto-Bicchisano F 110 B1
Petrich BG 15 R18
Petrijevci HR 74 C3
Petrinja HR 73 C6
Petrodvorets RUS 7 G21
Pétrola E 96 C1
Petronà I 107 B3
Petronell A 64 B2
Petroşani RO 11 P18
Petrovac YU 85 B6
Petrovaradin YU 75 C4
Petrovice BIH 84 B3
Petrovice CZ 53 C3
Pettenbach A 63 C5
Pettigo IRL 19 B4
Petworth GB 31 D3
Peuerbach A 63 B4
Peuntenansa E 88 A2
Pevensey Bay GB 31 D4
Peveragno I 80 B1
Pewsey GB 29 B6
Pewsum D 43 B4
Peyrat-le-Château F 68 C1
Peyrehorade F 76 C1
Peyriac-Minervois F 77 C5
Peyrins F 79 A4
Peyrissac F 67 C6
Peyrolles-en-Provence F 79 C4
Peyruis F 79 B4
Pézarches F 59 B3
Pézenas F 78 C2
Pezinok SK 64 B3
Pezuls F 77 B3
Pfaffenhausen D 61 B6
Pfaffenhofen, *Bayern* D 61 B6
Pfaffenhofen, *Bayern* D 62 B2
Pfaffenhoffen F 60 B3
Pfäffikon CH 70 A3
Pfarrkirchen D 62 B3
Pfeffenhausen D 62 B2
Pfetterhouse F 70 A2
Pforzheim D 61 B4
Pfreimd D 62 A3
Pfronten D 71 A5
Pfullendorf D 61 C5
Pfullingen D 61 B5
Pfunds A 71 B5
Pfungstadt D 61 A4
Pfyn CH 61 C4
Phalsbourg F 60 B3
Philippeville B 49 C5
Philippsreut D 63 B4
Philippsthal D 51 C5
Pınarhisar TR 16 R20
Piacenza I 81 A3
Piacenza d'Adige I 81 A5
Piádena I 81 A4
Piana F 110 A1
Piana Crixia I 80 B2
Piana degli Albanesi I 108 B2
Piana di Monte Verna I 103 B4
Piancastagnáio I 81 D5
Piandelagotti I 81 B4
Pianella, *Abruzzi* I 103 A4
Pianella, *Toscana* I 81 C5
Pianello Val Tidone I 80 B3
Piano I 80 B3
Pianoro I 81 B5
Pians A 71 A5
Pías E 87 B4
Pias P 98 A3
Piaseczno PL 55 A6
Piasek PL 45 C6
Piaski PL 47 A5
Piastów PL 55 A5
Piaszcyna PL 46 A3
Piątek PL 55 A4
Piatra Neamţ RO 11 N20
Piazza al Sérchio I 81 B4
Piazza Armerina I 109 B3
Piazza Brembana I 71 C4
Piazze I 81 D5
Piazzola sul Brenta I 72 C1
Picassent E 96 B2
Piccione I 82 C1
Picerno I 104 B2
Picher D 44 B3
Pickering GB 27 A5
Pico I 103 B3
Picón E 94 C2
Picquigny F 58 A3
Piechowice PL 53 C5
Piecnik PL 46 B2
Piedicavallo I 70 C2
Piedicroce F 110 A2
Piedimonte Etneo I 109 B4
Piedimonte Matese I 103 B4
Piedimulera I 70 B3
Piedipaterno I 82 D1
Piedrabuena E 94 C2
Piedraescrita E 94 C2
Piedrafita E 88 A1
Piedrahita E 94 B1
Piedralaves E 94 B2
Piedras Albas E 93 B4
Piedras Blancas E 88 A1
Piegaro I 82 D1
Piekary Śl. PL 54 C3
Piekoszów PL 55 C5
Pieksämäki FIN 3 E20
Pielenhofen D 62 A2
Pielgrzymka PL 53 B5
Pieniężno PL 47 A6
Pieńsk PL 53 B5
Pienza I 81 C5
Piera E 91 B4
Pieranie PL 47 C4
Pierowall GB 23 B6
Pierre-Buffière F 67 C6
Pierre-de-Bresse F 69 B5
Pierrefeu-du-Var F 79 C5
Pierrefitte-Nestalas F 76 D2
Pierrefitte-sur-Aire F 59 B6
Pierrefonds F 59 A3
Pierrefontaine-les-Varans F 69 A6
Pierrefort F 78 B1
Pierrelatte F 78 B3
Pierrepont F 59 A4
Pierrepont, *Meurthe-et-Moselle* F 60 A1
Piesendorf A 72 A2
Piešťany SK 64 B3
Pieszkowo PL 47 A6
Pieszyce PL 54 C1
Pietarsaari FIN 3 E18
Pietra Ligure I 80 B2
Pietragalla I 104 B2
Pietralunga I 82 C1
Pietramelara I 103 B4
Pietraperzia I 109 B3
Pietrasanta I 81 C4
Pietravairano I 103 B4
Pieve del Cáiro I 80 A2
Pieve di Bono I 71 C5
Pieve di Cadore I 72 B2
Pieve di Cento I 81 B5
Pieve di Soligo I 72 C2
Pieve di Teco I 80 B1
Pieve Santo Stefano I 82 C1
Pieve Torina I 82 C2
Pievepélago I 81 B4
Piglio I 102 B3
Pigna I 80 C1
Pignataro Maggiore I 103 B4
Pijnacker NL 49 A5
Pikalevo RUS 7 G24
Piła PL 46 B2
Pilar de la Horadada E 101 B5
Pilas E 99 B4
Pilastri I 81 B5
Piława PL 55 B6
Piława Górna PL 54 C1
Piławki PL 47 B5
Pilchowice PL 54 C3
Pilica PL 55 C4
Pilis H 75 A4
Piliscaba H 65 C4
Pilisszántó H 65 C4
Pilisvörösvár H 65 C4
Pilos GR 15 T17
Pilsting D 62 B3
Pilszcz PL 54 C2
Pilu RO 75 B6
Pilzno PL 55 D6
Pina de Ebro E 90 B2
Piñar E 100 B2
Pinas F 77 C3
Pincehely H 74 B3
Pinchbeck GB 30 B3
Pińczów PL 55 C5
Pineda de la Sierra E 89 B3
Pineda de Mar E 91 B5
Pinerella I 82 B1
Pinerolo I 79 B6
Pineta Grande I 103 C3
Pineto I 103 A4
Piney F 59 B5
Pinggau A 73 A6
Pinhal Novo P 92 C2
Pinhão P 87 C3
Pinheiro, *Aveiro* P 87 C2
Pinheiro, *Aveiro* P 87 D2
Pinheiro Grande P 92 B2
Pinhel P 87 D3
Pinhoe GB 29 C4
Pinilla E 101 A4
Pinilla de Toro E 88 C1
Pinkafeld A 73 A6
Pinneberg D 44 B1
Pinnow D 53 B4
Pino F 80 D3
Pino de Val E 86 B2
Pino del Río E 88 B2
Pinofranqueado E 93 A4
Pinols F 78 A2
Piñor E 86 B2
Pinos del Valle E 100 C2
Pinos Puente E 100 B2
Pinoso E 96 C1
Pinsk BY 7 K20
Pinto E 94 B3
Pinzano al Tagliamento I 72 B2
Pinzio P 93 A3
Pinzolo I 71 B5
Pióbbico I 82 C1
Piombino I 81 D4
Pionki PL 55 B6
Pionsat F 68 B2
Pióraco I 82 C1
Piornal E 93 A5
Piotrków-Kujawski PL 47 C4
Piotrków Trybunalski PL 55 B4
Piotrkowice PL 55 C5
Piotrowice PL 55 A6
Piotrowo PL 46 C2
Piove di Sacco I 72 C2
Piovene I 71 C6
Piperskärr S 37 D3
Pipriac F 57 C4
Piraiévs GR 15 T18
Piran SLO 72 C3
Piré-sur-Seiche F 57 B4
Pirgos GR 16 T17
Piriac-sur-Mer F 66 A2
Piringsdorf A 73 A6
Pirmasens D 60 A3
Pirna D 53 C3
Pirnmill GB 24 C2
Pirot YU 15 Q18
Pirovac HR 83 C4
Pisa I 81 C4
Pisany F 67 C4
Pisarovina HR 73 C5
Pischelsdorf in der Steiermark A 73 A5
Pişchia RO 75 C6
Pisciotta I 104 B2
Písek CZ 63 A5
Pisogne I 71 C5
Pissos F 76 B2
Pisticci I 105 B3
Pistóia I 81 C4
Piteå S 3 D17
Piteşti RO 11 P19
Pithiviers F 58 B3
Pitigliano I 102 A1
Pitkyaranta RUS 3 F22
Pitlochry GB 25 B4
Pitomača HR 74 C2
Pitres E 100 C2
Pittentrail GB 23 D4
Pitvaros H 75 B5
Pivka SLO 73 C4
Pivnice YU 75 C4
Piwniczna PL 65 A6
Pizarra E 100 C1
Pizzano I 71 B5
Pizzighettone I 71 C4
Pizzo I 106 C3
Pizzoli I 103 A3
Pizzolungo I 108 A1
Plabennec F 56 B1
Placencia E 89 A4
Plaffeien CH 70 B2
Plaisance, *Gers* F 76 C3
Plaisance, *Haute-Garonne* F 77 C4
Plaisance, *Tarn* F 77 C5
Plan E 90 A3
Plan-de-Baix F 79 B4
Plan-d'Orgon F 78 C3
Planá CZ 62 A3
Planá nad Lužnici CZ 63 A5
Plaňany CZ 53 C5
Planchez F 68 A4
Plancoët F 57 B3
Plancy-l'Abbaye F 59 B4
Plandište YU 75 C6
Plánice CZ 63 A4
Planina SLO 73 B5
Planina SLO 73 C4
Plankenfels D 62 A2
Plasencia E 93 A4
Plasenzuela E 93 B4
Plaški HR 83 A4
Plášťovce SK 65 B5
Plasy CZ 63 A4
Platamona Lido I 110 C1
Platania I 106 B3
Plátanos GR 16 U18
Platí I 106 C3
Platičevo YU 85 B4
Platja d'Aro E 91 B6
Plattling D 62 B3
Plau D 44 B4
Plaue, *Brandenburg* D 44 C4
Plaue, *Thüringen* D 51 C6
Plauen D 52 C2
Plavecký Mikuláš SK 64 B3
Plavinas LV 7 H19
Plavna YU 75 C4
Plavnica SK 65 A6
Plavno HR 83 B5
Plavsk RUS 7 K25
Playben F 56 B2
Pléaux F 68 C2
Pleine-Fougères F 57 B4
Pleinfeld D 62 A1
Pleinting D 62 B4
Plélan-le-Grand F 57 C3
Plémet F 56 B3
Pléneuf-Val-André F 56 B3
Plentzia E 89 A4
Plérin F 56 B3
Plešivec SK 65 B6
Plessa D 52 B3
Plessé F 66 A3
Plestin-les-Grèves F 56 B2
Pleszew PL 54 B2
Pleternica HR 74 C2
Plettenberg D 50 B3
Pleubian F 56 B2
Pleumartin F 67 B5
Pleumeur-Bodou F 56 B2
Pleurs F 59 B4
Pleven BG 16 Q19
Plevlja YU 85 C4
Plevnik-Drienové SK 65 A4
Pleyber-Christ F 56 B2
Pliego E 101 B4
Pliešovce SK 65 B5
Plitvička Jezera HR 83 B4
Plitvički Ljeskovac HR 83 B4
Ploaghe I 110 C1
Ploče HR 84 C2
Plochingen D 61 B5
Płock PL 47 C5
Ploemeur F 56 C2
Ploërmel F 56 C3
Plœuc-sur-Lie F 56 B3
Plogastel St. Germain F 56 C1
Plogoff F 56 B1
Ploieşti RO 11 P20
Plombières-les-Bains F 60 C2
Plomin HR 82 A3
Plön D 44 A2
Plonéour-Lanvern F 56 C1
Płonia PL 45 B6
Płońsk PL 47 C6
Plössberg D 62 A3
Płoty PL 45 B7
Plouagat F 56 B2
Plouaret F 56 B2
Plouay F 56 C2
Ploubalay F 57 B3
Ploubazlanec F 56 B2
Ploudalmézeau F 56 B1
Ploudiry F 56 B1
Plouescat F 56 B1
Plouézec F 56 B3
Plougasnou F 56 B2
Plougastel-Daoulas F 56 B1
Plougonven F 56 B2
Plougonver F 56 B2
Plougrescant F 56 B2
Plouguenast F 56 B3
Plouguerneau F 56 B1
Plouha F 56 B3
Plouhinec F 56 B1
Plouigneau F 56 B2
Ploumanach F 56 B2
Plounévez-Quintin F 56 B2
Plouray F 56 B2
Plouzévédé F 56 B1
Plovdiv BG 16 Q19
Plozévet F 56 C1
Plumbridge GB 19 B4
Pluméliau F 56 C3
Plumlov CZ 64 A3
Plungė LT 6 J17
Pluty PL 47 A6
Pluvigner F 56 C3
Plužine BIH 84 C3
Plužine YU 84 C3
Płuznica PL 47 B4
Plymouth GB 28 C3
Plymstock GB 28 C3
Płytnica PL 46 B2
Plyusa RUS 7 G21
Plzeň CZ 63 A4
Pniewy PL 46 C2
Pobes E 89 B4
Poběžovice CZ 62 A3
Pobiedziska PL 46 C3
Pobierowo PL 45 A6
Pobla de Segur E 90 A3
Pobla-Tornesa E 96 A3
Pobladura del Valle E 88 B1
Pobra de Trives E 87 B3
Pobra do Brollón E 86 B3
Pobra do Caramiñal E 86 B2
Pobudje BIH 85 B4
Počátky CZ 63 A6
Poceirão P 92 C2
Pochep RUS 7 K23
Pochinok RUS 7 J23
Pöchlarn A 63 B6
Pociecha PL 55 B5
Pockau D 52 C3
Pocking D 63 B4
Pocklington GB 27 B5
Poda YU 85 D4
Podbořany CZ 52 C3
Podbrdo SLO 72 B3
Podbrezová SK 65 B5
Podčetrtek SLO 73 B5
Poddębice PL 54 B3
Poděbrady CZ 53 C5
Podence P 87 C4
Podensac F 76 B2
Podenzano I 80 B3
Podersdorf am See A 64 C2
Podgaje PL 46 B2
Podgora HR 84 C2
Podgoria PL 55 B6
Podgorač HR 74 C3
Podgorica YU 15 Q16
Podgrad SLO 73 C4
Podhájska SK 65 B4
Podlapača HR 83 B4
Podlejki PL 47 B6
Podlužany SK 65 B4
Podnovlje BIH 84 B3
Podolie SK 64 B3
Podolinec SK 65 A6
Podolsk RUS 7 J25
Podromanija BIH 84 C3
Podturen HR 74 B1
Podujevo YU 85 D6
Podvin CZ 64 B2
Podwilk PL 65 A5
Poetto I 110 D2
Poggendorf D 45 A5
Poggiardo I 107 A5
Poggibonsi I 81 C5
Póggio a Caiano I 81 C5
Poggio Imperiale I 104 A2
Póggio Mirteto I 102 A2
Póggio Moiano I 102 A2
Póggio Renatico I 81 B5
Póggio Rusco I 81 B5
Pöggstall A 63 B6
Pogny F 59 B5
Pogorzela PL 54 B2
Pogorzelice PL 46 A3
Pogrodzie PL 47 A5
Pohorelá SK 65 B6
Pohořelice CZ 64 B2
Pohronská Polhora SK 65 B5
Poiares P 92 A2
Poio E 86 B2
Poirino I 80 B1
Poisson F 68 B4
Poissons F 59 B6
Poissy F 58 B3
Poitiers F 67 B5
Poix-de-Picardie F 58 A2
Poix-Terron F 59 A5
Pokój PL 54 C2
Pokupsko HR 73 C5
Pol E 86 A3
Pol a Charra GB 22 D1
Pola RUS 7 H22
Pola de Allande E 86 A4
Pola de Laviana E 88 A1
Pola de Lena E 88 A1
Pola de Siero E 88 A1
Pola de Somiedo E 86 A4
Polaincourt-et-Clairefontaine F 60 C2
Połajewo PL 46 C2
Polán E 94 C2
Polanica-Zdrój PL 54 C1
Połaniec PL 55 C6
Polanów PL 46 A2
Polatsk BY 7 J21
Polch D 50 C3
Pólczno PL 46 A3
Połczyn-Zdrój PL 46 B2
Polegate GB 31 D4
Poleñino E 90 B2
Polesella I 81 B5
Polessk RUS 6 J17
Polgárdi H 74 A3
Polhov Gradec SLO 73 B4
Police PL 45 B6
Police nad Metují CZ 53 C6
Polička CZ 64 A2
Poličnik HR 83 B4
Policoro I 105 B3
Policzna PL 55 B6
Polignano a Mare I 105 B4
Poligny F 69 B5
Polistena I 106 C3
Políyiros GR 15 R18
Polizzi Generosa I 109 B3
Poljana YU 85 B6
Poljanák HR 83 B4
Poljčane SLO 73 B5
Polje BIH 84 B2
Poljice BIH 83 B5
Poljice BIH 84 B3
Poljna YU 85 C6
Polkowice PL 53 B6
Polla I 104 B2
Pollas E 88 C1
Pöllau A 73 A5
Polleben D 52 B1
Pollença, *Mallorca* E 97
Pollenfeld D 62 B2
Póllica I 104 B2
Polminhac F 77 B5
Polná CZ 63 A6
Polna RUS 7 G21
Polne PL 46 B2
Polomka SK 65 B5
Polonne UA 11 L20
Polperro GB 28 C3
Polruan GB 28 C3
Pöls A 73 A4
Polska Cerekiew PL 54 C3
Poltár SK 65 B5
Põltsamaa EST 7 G19
Polyarny RUS 3 B23
Polyarnyye Zori RUS 3 C23
Polzela SLO 73 B5
Pomarance I 81 C4
Pomarez F 76 C2
Pomárico I 105 B3
Pomáz H 65 C5
Pombal P 92 B2
Pomeroy GB 19 B5
Pomézia I 102 B2
Pomichna UA 11 M22
Pommard F 69 A4
Pommelsbrunn D 62 A2
Pomonte I 81 D4
Pomorie BG 16 Q20
Pompei I 103 C4
Pompey F 60 B2
Pomposa I 82 B1
Poncin F 69 B5
Pondorf D 62 B2
Ponferrada E 86 B4
Poniec PL 54 B1
Ponikva SLO 73 B5
Poniky SK 65 B5
Pons F 67 C4
Ponsacco I 81 C4
Pont-a-Celles B 49 C5
Pont-a-Marcq F 49 C4
Pont-à-Mousson F 60 B2
Pont-Audemer F 58 A1
Pont-Aven F 56 C2
Pont Canavese I 70 C2
Pont-Croix F 56 B1
Pont-d'Ain F 69 B5
Pont-de-Beauvoisin F 69 C5
Pont-de-Buis-lès-Quimerch F 56 B1
Pont-de-Chéruy F 69 C5
Pont de Dore F 68 C3
Pont-de-Labeaume F 78 B3
Pont-de-l'Arche F 58 A2
Pont de Molins E 91 A5
Pont-de-Roide F 70 A1
Pont-de-Salars F 78 B1
Pont de Suert E 90 A3
Pont-de-Vaux F 69 B4
Pont-de-Veyle F 69 B4
Pont-d'Espagne F 76 D2
Pont d'Ouilly F 57 B5
Pont-du-Château F 68 C3
Pont-du-Navoy F 69 B5
Pont-en-Royans F 79 A4
Pont Farcy F 57 B4
Pont-l'Abbé F 56 C1
Pont-l'Évêque F 57 A6
Pont-Remy F 48 C2
Pont-St. Esprit F 78 B3
Pont-St. Mamet F 77 B3
Pont-St. Martin F 66 A3
Pont-St. Martin I 70 C2
Pont-St. Vincent F 60 B2
Pont-Ste-Maxence F 58 A3
Pont Scorff F 56 C2
Pont-sur-Yonne F 59 B4
Pontacq F 76 C2
Pontailler-sur-Saône F 69 A5
Pontão P 92 B2
Pontardawe GB 28 B4
Pontardulais GB 28 B3
Pontarion F 68 C1
Pontarlier F 69 B6
Pontassieve I 81 C5
Pontaubault F 57 B4
Pontaumur F 68 C2
Pontcharra F 69 C6
Pontcharra-sur-Turdine F 69 C4
Pontchâteau F 66 A2
Ponte a Moriano I 81 C4
Ponte Arche I 71 B5
Ponte Cáffaro I 71 C5
Ponte-Caldelas E 87 B2
Ponte da Barca P 87 C2
Ponte de Sor P 92 B2
Ponte dell'Ólio I 80 B3
Ponte di Barbarano I 72 C1
Ponte di Legno I 71 B5
Ponte di Nava I 80 B1
Ponte di Piave I 72 C2
Ponte do Lima P 87 C2
Ponte Felcino I 82 C1
Ponte Gardena I 71 B6
Ponte-Leccia F 110 A2
Ponte nelle Alpi I 72 B2
Ponte San Giovanni I 82 C1
Ponte San Pietro I 71 C4
Ponteareas E 87 B2
Pontebba I 72 B3
Pontecagnano I 104 B1
Ponteceso E 86 A2
Pontecesures E 86 B2
Pontecorvo I 103 B3
Pontedássio I 80 C2
Pontedécimo I 80 B2
Pontedera I 81 C4
Pontedeume E 86 A2
Pontefract GB 27 B4
Ponteginori I 81 C4
Pontelagoscuro I 81 B5
Ponteland GB 25 C6
Pontelandolfo I 103 B4
Pontelongo I 72 C2
Pontenure I 81 B3
Pontenx-les-Forges F 76 B1
Ponterwyd GB 26 C2
Pontevedra E 86 B2
Pontevico I 71 C5
Pontfaverger-Moronvillers F 59 A5
Pontgibaud F 68 C2
Ponticino I 81 C5
Pontigny F 59 C4
Pontijou F 58 C2
Pontínia I 102 B3
Pontinvrea I 80 B2
Pontivy F 56 B3
Pontlevoy F 67 A6
Pontoise F 58 A3
Pontones E 101 A3
Pontonx-sur-l'Abour F 76 C2
Pontoon IRL 18 C2
Pontorson F 57 B4
Pontrémoli I 81 B3
Pontresina CH 71 B4
Pontrhydfendigaid GB 28 A4
Pontrieux F 56 B2
Ponts E 91 B4
Ponts-aux-Dames F 59 B3
Pontvallain F 57 C6
Pontypool GB 29 B4
Pontypridd GB 29 B4
Ponza I 102 C2
Poo E 88 A2
Poole GB 29 C6
Poolewe GB 22 D3
Poperinge B 48 C3
Pópoli I 103 A3
Popovača HR 74 C1
Popow PL 55 A4
Poppel B 49 B6
Poppenhausen, *Bayern* D 51 C6
Poppenhausen, *Hessen* D 51 C5
Poppi I 81 C5
Poprad SK 65 A6
Popučke YU 85 B4
Pópulo P 87 C3
Populónia I 81 D4
Pörböly H 74 B3
Porcuna E 100 B1
Pordenone I 72 C2
Pordic F 56 B3
Poręba PL 55 C4
Poreč HR 72 C3
Pori FIN 3 F17
Porjus S 3 C16
Porkhov RUS 7 H21
Porlezza I 71 B4
Porlock GB 29 B4
Pörnbach D 62 B2
Pornic F 66 A2
Pornichet F 66 A2
Porodin YU 85 B6
Poronin PL 65 A5
Poroszló H 65 C6
Porozina HR 82 A3
Porquerolles F 79 D5
Porrentruy CH 70 A2
Porreres, *Mallorca* E 97
Porretta Terme I 81 B4
Porsgrunn N 33 B6
Porspoder F 56 B1
Port-a-Binson F 59 A4
Port Askaig GB 24 C1
Port Bannatyne GB 24 C2
Port-Barcarès F 78 D2
Port-Camargue F 78 C3
Port Charlotte GB 24 C1
Port d'Andratx, *Mallorca* E 97
Port-de-Bouc F 78 C3
Port-de-Lanne F 76 C1
Port de Pollença, *Mallorca* E 97

Port de Söller, *Mallorca* E 97
Port-des-Barques F 66 C3
Port Ellen GB 24 C1
Port-en-Bessin F 57 A5
Port Erin GB 26 A1
Port Eynon GB 28 B3
Port Glasgow GB 24 C3
Port Henderson GB 22 D3
Port Isaac GB 28 C3
Port-Joinville F 66 B2
Port-la-Nouvelle F 78 C2
Port Logan GB 24 D3
Port Louis F 56 C2
Port Manech F 56 C2
Port Nan Giuran GB 22 C2
Port-Navalo F 66 A2
Port Nis GB 22 C2
Port-St.-Louis-du-Rhône F 78 C3
Port-Ste. Marie F 77 B3
Port St. Mary GB 26 A1
Port-sur-Saône F 60 C2
Port Talbot GB 28 B4
Port-Vendres F 91 A6
Port William GB 24 D3
Portacloy IRL 18 B2
Portadown GB 19 B5
Portaferry GB 19 B6
Portaje E 93 B4
Portalegre P 92 B3
Portarlington IRL 21 A4
Portavadie GB 24 C2
Portavogie GB 19 B6
Portbail F 57 A4
Portbou E 91 A6
Portegrandi I 72 C2
Portel P 98 A3
Portela P 92 A2
Portelo P 87 C4
Portemouro E 86 B2
Port'Ercole I 102 A1
Portes-lès-Valence F 78 B3
Portets F 76 B2
Portezuelo E 93 B4
Portglenone GB 19 B5
Porthcawl GB 28 B4
Porthleven GB 28 C2
Porthmadog GB 26 C1
Porticcio F 110 B1
Portici I 103 C4
Portico di Romagna I 81 B5
Portilla de la Reina E 88 A2
Portillo E 88 C2
Portimao P 98 B2
Portinatx E 97 B4
Portinho da Arrabida P 92 C1
Portishead GB 29 B5
Portknockie GB 23 D6
Portlaoise IRL 21 A4
Portlethen GB 23 D6
Portmagne IRL 20 C1
Portmahomack GB 23 D5
Portman E 101 B5
Portnacroish GB 24 B2
Portnahaven GB 24 C1
Porto F 110 A1
Porto P 87 C2
Porto-Alto P 92 C2
Porto Azzurro I 81 D4
Porto Cerésio I 70 C3
Porto Cervo I 110 B2
Porto Cesáreo I 105 B4
Porto Colom, *Mallorca* E 97
Porto Covo P 98 B2
Porto Cristo, *Mallorca* E 97
Porto d'Ascoli I 82 D2
Porto de Lagos P 98 B2
Porto de Mos P 92 B2
Porto de Rei P 98 A2
Porto do Son E 86 B2
Porto Empédocle I 108 B2
Porto Garibaldi I 82 B1
Porto Petro, *Mallorca* E 97
Porto Pino I 110 E1
Porto Potenza Picena I 82 C2
Porto Recanati I 82 C2
Porto San Giórgio I 82 C2
Porto Sant'Elpidio I 82 C2
Porto Santo Stéfano I 102 A1
Porto Tolle I 82 B1
Porto Tórres I 110 C1
Porto-Vecchio F 110 B2
Portocannone I 103 B5
Portoferráio I 81 D4
Portofino I 80 B3
Portogruaro I 72 C2
Portomaggiore I 81 B5
Portomarin E 86 B3
Porton GB 29 B6
Portonovo E 87 B2
Portopalo di Capo Passero I 109 C4
Portør N 33 C6
Portoscuso I 110 D1
Portovénere I 81 B3
Portpatrick GB 24 D2
Portreath GB 28 C2
Portree GB 22 D2
Portroe IRL 20 B3
Portrush GB 19 A5
Portsall F 56 B1
Portsmouth GB 31 D2
Portsoy GB 23 D6
Portstewart GB 19 A5
Portugalete E 89 A4
Portumna IRL 20 A3
Porvoo FIN 3 F19
Porzuna E 94 C2
Posada, *Oviedo* E 88 A1
Posada, *Oviedo* E 88 A2
Posada, *Sardegna* I 110 C2
Posada de Valdeón E 88 A2
Posadas E 99 B5
Poschiavo CH 71 B5
Posedarje HR 83 B4
Positano I 103 C4
Possagno I 72 C1
Posseck D 52 C2
Possesse F 59 B5
Pössneck D 52 C1
Posta I 102 A3
Posta Piana I 104 A2
Postal I 71 B6
Postbauer-Heng D 62 A2
Posterholt NL 50 B2
Postioma I 72 C2
Postira HR 83 C5
Postojna SLO 73 C4
Postoloprty CZ 53 C3
Postomino PL 46 A2
Posušje BIH 84 C2
Potenza I 104 B2
Potenza Picena I 82 C2
Potes E 88 A2
Potigny F 57 B5
Potkrajci YU 85 C4
Potočari BIH 85 B4
Potoci BIH 83 B5
Potoci BIH 84 C2
Potony H 74 C2
Potries E 96 C2
Potsdam D 45 C5
Potštát CZ 64 A3
Pottenbrunn A 63 B6
Pottendorf A 64 C2
Pottenstein A 64 C2
Pottenstein D 62 A2
Potters Bar GB 31 C3
Pöttmes D 62 B2
Pöttsching A 64 C2
Potworów PL 55 B5
Pouancé F 57 C4
Pougues-les-Eaux F 68 A3
Pouilly-en-Auxois F 69 A4
Pouilly-sous Charlieu F 68 B4
Pouilly-sur-Loire F 68 A2
Poujol-sur-Orb F 78 C2
Poullaouen F 56 B2
Poulton-le-Fylde GB 26 B3
Poundstock GB 28 C3
Pourcy F 59 A4
Pourrain F 59 C4
Pouy-de-Touges F 77 C4
Pouyastruc F 76 C3
Pouzauges F 66 B4
Pova de Santa Iria P 92 C1
Považská Bystrica SK 65 A4
Povedilla E 101 A3
Povlja HR 84 C1
Povljana HR 83 B4
Póvoa, *Beja* P 98 A3
Póvoa, *Santarém* P 92 B2
Póvoa de Lanhosa P 87 C2
Póvoa de Varzim P 87 C2
Póvoa e Meadas P 92 B3
Powidz PL 46 C3
Poyales del Hoyo E 94 B1
Poynton GB 26 B3
Poyntz Pass GB 19 B5
Poysdorf A 64 B2
Poza de la Sal E 89 B3
Pozaldez E 88 C2
Pozán de Vero E 90 A3
Požarevac YU 85 B6
Požega HR 74 C2
Požega YU 85 C5
Poznań PL 46 C2
Pozo Alcón E 100 B3
Pozo Cañada E 101 A4
Pozo de Guadalajara E 95 B3
Pozo de la Serna E 100 A2
Pozoantiguo E 88 C1
Pozoblanco E 100 A1
Pozohondo E 101 A4
Pozondón E 95 B5
Poźrzadło Wielkie PL 46 B1
Pozuel del Campo E 95 B5
Pozuelo de Alarcón E 94 B3
Pozuelo de Calatrava E 100 A2
Pozuelo de Zarzón E 93 A4
Pozuelo del Páramo E 88 B1
Pozzallo I 109 C3
Pozzomaggiore I 110 C1
Pozzuoli I 103 C4
Pozzuolo I 81 C5
Prabuty PL 47 B5
Prača BIH 84 C3
Prachatice CZ 63 A4
Prada E 87 B3
Pradelle F 79 B4
Pradelles F 78 B2
Prades E 90 B3
Prades F 91 A5
Pradła PL 55 C4
Prado E 88 A1
Prado P 87 C2
Prado del Rey E 99 C5
Pradoluengo E 89 B3
Præstø DK 39 D5
Pragelato I 79 A5
Pragersko SLO 73 B5
Prägraten A 72 A2
Praha CZ 53 C4
Prahecq F 67 B4
Praia P 92 B1
Práia a Mare I 106 B2
Praia da Rocha P 98 B2
Praia da Viera P 92 B2
Praia de Mira P 92 A2
Praiano I 103 C4
Pralboino I 71 C5
Pralognan-la-Vanoise F 70 C1
Pranjani YU 85 B5
Prapatnica HR 83 C5
Praszka PL 54 B3
Prat de Compte E 90 C3
Prata I 81 C4
Prata di Pordenone I 72 C2
Pratau D 52 B2
Pratdip E 90 B3
Pratella I 103 B4
Prato I 81 C5
Prátola Peligna I 103 A3
Pratola Serra I 103 C4
Prats-de-Mollo-la-Preste F 91 A5
Prauthoy F 59 C6
Pravia E 86 A4
Praxmar A 71 A6
Prayssac F 77 B4
Prazzo I 79 B6
Pré-en-Pail F 57 B5
Prebold SLO 73 B5
Précy-sur-Thil F 69 A4
Predáppio I 81 B5
Predazzo I 72 B1
Předin CZ 63 A6
Preding A 73 B5
Predjame SLO 73 C4
Predlitz A 72 A3
Predmeja SLO 72 C3
Predoi I 72 A2
Prees GB 26 C3
Preetz D 44 A2
Préfailles F 66 A2
Pregarten A 63 B5
Pregrada HR 73 B5
Preiļi LV 7 H20
Preitenegg A 73 B4
Prekaja BIH 83 B5
Preko HR 83 B4
Preljina YU 85 C5
Prelog HR 74 B1
Prelošćica HR 74 C1
Přelouč CZ 53 C5
Prem SLO 73 C4
Premantura HR 82 B2
Prémery F 68 A3
Prémia I 70 B3
Premià de Mar E 91 B5
Premnitz D 44 C4
Prémont F 49 C4
Prenzlau D 45 B5
Preodac BIH 83 B5
Přerov CZ 64 A3
Prerow D 45 A4
Presencio E 88 B3
Presicce I 107 B5
Presly F 68 A2
Prešov SK 10 M17
Pressac F 67 B5
Pressath D 62 A2
Pressbaum A 64 B2
Prestatyn GB 26 B2
Prestebakke N 35 C3
Presteigne GB 29 A4
Přeštice CZ 63 A4
Preston, *Lancashire* GB 26 B3
Preston, *Scottish Borders* GB 25 C5
Prestonpans GB 25 C5
Prestwick GB 24 C3
Prettin D 52 B2
Preturo I 103 A3
Pretzchendorf D 52 C3
Pretzier D 44 C3
Pretzsch D 52 B2
Preuilly-sur-Claise F 67 B5
Prevalje SLO 73 B4
Prevenchères F 78 B2
Préveranges F 68 B2
Préveza GR 15 S17
Prevršac HR 73 C6
Prezid HR 73 C4
Priaranza del Bierzo E 86 B4
Priay F 69 B5
Pribeta SK 64 C4
Priboj BIH 84 B3
Priboj YU 85 C4
Příbor CZ 64 A4
Příbram CZ 63 A5
Pribylina SK 65 A5
Přibyslav CZ 63 A6
Pričević YU 85 B4
Pridjel BIH 84 B3
Priego E 95 B4
Priego de Córdoba E 100 B1
Priekule LV 6 H17
Prien D 62 C3
Prienai LT 6 J18
Prievidza SK 65 B4
Prigradica HR 84 D1
Prigrevica YU 75 C4
Prijeboj HR 83 B4
Prijedor BIH 83 B5
Prijepolje YU 85 C4
Prilep MK 15 R17
Priluka BIH 84 C1
Primda CZ 62 A3
Primel-Trégastel F 56 B2
Primišje HR 73 C5
Primorsk, *Kaliningrad* RUS 47 A6
Primorsk, *Severo-Zapadnyy* RUS 3 F21
Primošten HR 83 C4
Primstal D 60 A2
Princes Risborough GB 31 C3
Princetown GB 28 C3
Principina a Mare I 102 A1
Priolo Gargallo I 109 B4
Priora E 88 B2
Priozersk RUS 3 F22
Prisoje BIH 84 C2
Pristen RUS 7 L25
Priština YU 85 D6
Pritzerbe D 44 C4
Pritzier D 44 B3
Pritzwalk D 44 B4
Privas F 78 B3
Priverno I 102 B3
Privlaka, *Vukovarsko-Srijemska* HR 74 C3
Privlaka, *Zadarska* HR 83 B4
Prizna HR 83 B3
Prizren YU 15 Q17
Prizzi I 108 B2
Prnjavor BIH 84 B2
Prnjavor HR 73 C5
Prnjavor YU 85 B4
Proaza E 86 A4
Probstzella D 52 C1
Probus GB 28 C3
Prócchio I 81 D4
Prochowice PL 53 B6
Prócida I 103 C4
Prodo I 82 D1
Proença-a-Nova P 92 B3
Proença-a-Velha P 93 A3
Profondeville B 49 C5
Prokuplje YU 15 Q17
Propriano F 110 B1
Prosec CZ 64 A2
Prösen D 52 B3
Prosenjakovci SLO 73 B6
Prostějov CZ 64 A3
Prószków PL 54 C2
Proszowice PL 55 C5
Protić BIH 84 B1
Protivanov CZ 64 A2
Protivín CZ 63 A5
Prötzel D 45 C5
Provins F 59 B4
Prozor BIH 84 C2
Prudhoe GB 25 D6
Prudnik PL 54 C2
Pruggern A 72 A3
Prüm D 50 C2
Pruna E 99 C5
Prunelli-di-Fiumorbo F 110 A2
Prunetta I 81 B4
Pruniers F 68 B2
Prusice PL 54 B1
Pruské SK 64 A4
Pruszcz PL 47 B4
Pruszcz Gdański PL 47 A4
Pruszków PL 55 A5
Prutz A 71 A5
Prüzen D 44 B4
Pruzhany BY 6 K19
Pružina SK 65 A4
Pryluky UA 7 L23
Pryzlęg PL 45 C7
Przechlewo PL 46 B3
Przecław PL 55 C6
Przedbórz PL 55 B4
Przedecz PL 47 C4
Przejęslav PL 53 B5
Przemków PL 53 B5
Przemocze PL 45 B6
Przemyśl PL 11 M18
Przerąb PL 55 B4
Przewodnik PL 47 B4
Przewóz PL 53 B4
Przezmark PL 47 B5
Przodkowo PL 47 A4
Przybiernów PL 45 B6
Przyborowice PL 47 C6
Przybyszew PL 55 B5
Przybyszów PL 55 B4
Przylęg PL 46 C1
Przysucha PL 55 B5
Przytóczna PL 46 C1
Przytyk PL 55 B5
Przywidz PL 47 A4
Psary PL 54 B3
Pskov RUS 7 H21
Pszczew PL 46 C1
Pszczółki PL 47 A4
Pszczyna PL 65 A4
Pszów PL 54 C3
Ptolemais GR 15 R17
Ptuj SLO 73 B5
Puch A 62 C4
Puchberg am Schneeberg A 64 C1
Puchheim D 62 B2
Púchov SK 64 A4
Pučišća HR 83 C5
Puck PL 47 A4
Puçol E 96 B2
Puconci SLO 73 B6
Pudasjärvi FIN 3 D20
Puderbach D 50 C3
Puebla de Albortón E 90 B2
Puebla de Alcocer E 93 C5
Puebla de Beleña E 95 B3
Puebla de Don Fadrique E 101 B3
Puebla de Don Rodrigo E 94 C2
Puebla de Guzmán E 98 B3
Puebla de la Calzada E 93 C4
Puebla de la Reina E 93 C4
Puebla de Lillo E 88 A1
Puebla de Obando E 93 B4
Puebla de Sanabria E 87 B4
Puebla de Sancho Pérez E 93 C4
Puebla del Maestre E 99 A4
Puebla del Principe E 100 A3
Puente Almuhey E 88 B2
Puente de Domingo Flórez E 86 B4
Puente de Génave E 101 A3
Puente de Montañana E 90 A3
Puente del Congosto E 94 B1
Puente Duero E 88 C2
Puente-Genil E 100 B1
Puente la Reina E 89 B5
Puente la Reina de Jaca E 90 A2
Puente Mayorga E 99 C5
Puente Viesgo E 88 A3
Puentelarra E 89 B3
Puertas, *Asturias* E 88 A2
Puertas, *Salamanca* E 87 C4
Puerto de Mazarrón E 101 B4
Puerto de San Vicente E 94 C1
Puerto de Santa Cruz E 93 B5
Puerto-Lápice E 95 C3
Puerto Lumbreras E 101 B4
Puerto Moral E 99 B4
Puerto Real E 99 C4
Puerto Rey E 94 C1
Puerto Seguro E 87 D4
Puerto Serrano E 99 C5
Puertollano E 100 A1
Puget-Sur-Argens F 79 C5
Puget-Théniers F 79 C5
Puget-ville F 79 C5
Pugnochiuso I 104 A3
Puig Reig E 91 B4
Puigcerdà E 91 A4
Puigpunyent, *Mallorca* E 97
Puillon F 76 C2
Puimichel F 79 C5
Puimoisson F 79 C5
Puiseaux F 58 B3
Puisieux F 48 C3
Puisserguier F 78 C2
Puivert F 77 D5
Pujols F 76 B2
Pukanec SK 65 B4
Pukavik S 41 C4
Pukë AL 15 Q16
Pula HR 82 B2
Pula I 110 D1
Puławy PL 10 L17
Pulborough GB 31 D3
Pulfero I 72 B3
Pulgar E 94 C2
Pulheim D 50 B2
Pulkau A 64 B1
Pulpi E 101 B4
Pulsano I 105 B4
Pulsnitz D 53 B4
Pułtusk PL 6 K17
Pumpsaint GB 28 A4
Punat HR 83 A3
Punta Marina I 82 B1
Punta Prima, *Menorca* E 97
Punta Sabbioni I 72 C2
Punta Umbria E 99 B4
Puntas de Calnegre E 101 B4
Puolanka FIN 3 D20
Puračić BIH 84 B3
Purbach am Neusiedler See A 64 C2
Purchena E 101 B3
Purfleet GB 31 C4
Purgstall A 63 B6
Purkersdorf A 64 B2
Purmerend NL 42 C1
Purullena E 100 B2
Pushkin RUS 7 G22
Pushkino RUS 7 H25
Püspökladány H 75 A6
Pusté Ulany SK 64 B3
Pustelnik PL 55 A6
Pustoshka RUS 7 H21
Puszcza Mariańska PL 55 B5
Puszczykowo PL 54 A1
Pusztamagyaród H 74 B1
Pusztamonostor H 75 A4
Pusztaszabolcs H 74 A3
Pusztavám H 74 A3
Putanges-Pont-Ecrepin F 57 B5
Putbus D 45 A5
Putignano I 105 B4
Putlitz D 44 B4
Putnok H 65 B6
Putte B 49 B5
Puttelange-aux-Lacs F 60 A2
Putten NL 49 A6
Puttgarden D 44 A3
Püttlingen D 60 A2
Putzu Idu I 110 C1
Puy-Guillaume F 68 C3
Puy-l'Évêque F 77 B4
Puylaroque F 77 B4
Puylaurens F 77 C5
Puymirol F 77 B3
Puyôo F 76 C2
Puyrolland F 67 B4
Pwllheli GB 26 C1
Pyetrikaw BY 7 K21
Pyhäjärvi FIN 3 E19
Pyla-sur-Mer F 76 B1
Pyriatyn UA 7 L23
Pyrzyce PL 45 B6
Pysely CZ 63 A5
Pyskowice PL 54 C3
Pytalovo RUS 7 H20
Pyzdry PL 54 A2

Q

Quakenbrück D 43 C4
Quargnento I 80 B2
Quarré-les-Tombes F 68 A3
Quarteira P 98 B2
Quartu Sant'Élena I 110 D2
Quatre-Champs F 59 A5
Quedlinburg D 52 B1
Queensferry, *Edinburgh* GB 25 C4
Queensferry, *Flintshire* GB 26 B2
Queige F 69 C6
Queipo E 99 B4
Queixans E 91 A4
Quel E 89 B4
Queljada P 87 C2
Quemada E 89 C3
Queralbs E 91 A5
Quercianella I 81 C4
Querfurt D 52 B1
Quérigut F 91 A5
Quero E 95 C3
Quero I 72 C1
Querqueville F 57 A4
Quesada E 100 B2
Questembert F 56 C3
Quettehou F 57 A4
Quevauvillers F 58 A3
Quevy B 49 C5
Quiaois P 92 A2
Quiberon F 66 A1
Quiberville F 58 A1
Quickborn D 44 B1
Quiévrain B 49 C4
Quillan F 77 D5
Quillebeuf F 58 A1
Quimper F 56 B1
Quimperlé F 56 C2
Quincampoix F 58 A2
Quincoces de Yuso E 89 B3
Quincy F 68 A2
Quinéville F 57 A4
Quingey F 69 A5
Quinson F 79 C5
Quinssaines F 68 B2
Quinta-Grande P 92 C2
Quintana de la Serena E 93 C5
Quintana del Castillo E 86 B4
Quintana del Marco E 88 B1
Quintana del Puenta E 88 B2
Quintana-Martin Galindez E 89 B3
Quintanaortuño E 88 B3
Quintanapalla E 89 B3
Quintanar de la Orden E 95 C3
Quintanar de la Sierra E 89 C3
Quintanar del Rey E 95 C5
Quintanilla de la Mata E 88 C3
Quintanilla de Onésimo E 88 C2
Quintanilla de Somoza E 87 B4
Quintanilla del Coco E 89 C3
Quintas de Valdelucio E 88 B2
Quintela P 87 D3
Quintin F 56 B3
Quinto E 90 B2
Quinzano d'Oglio I 71 C5
Quiroga E 86 B3
Quismondo E 94 B2
Quissac F 78 C2
Quistello I 81 A4

R

Raab A 63 B4
Raabs an der Thaya A 63 B6
Raahe FIN 3 D19
Raalte NL 42 C3
Raamsdonksveer NL 49 B5
Rab HR 83 B3
Rabac HR 82 A3
Rábade E 86 A3
Rábafüzes H 73 B6
Rábahidvég H 74 A1
Rabanales E 87 C4
Rábapatona H 64 C3
Rabapordány H 64 C3
Rabastens F 77 C4
Rabastens-de-Bigorre F 76 C3
Rabat M 109 C4
Rabča SK 65 A5
Rabe YU 75 B5
Rabi CZ 63 A4
Rabino PL 46 B1
Rabka PL 65 A5
Rača, *Srbija* YU 85 B6
Rača, *Srbija* YU 85 C6
Rácale I 105 C5
Rácalmás H 75 A3
Racalmuto I 108 B2
Racconigi I 80 B1
Rače SLO 73 B5
Rachecourt-sur-Marne F 59 B6
Raciąż PL 47 C6
Racibórz PL 54 C3
Račinovci HR 84 B3
Ráckeve H 75 A3
Racławice PL 55 C5
Racławice Śląskie PL 54 C2
Racot PL 54 A1
Råda, *Skaraborg* S 35 C5
Råda, *Värmland* S 34 A5
Radalj YU 85 B4
Rădăuți RO 11 N19
Radda in Chianti I 81 C5
Raddusa I 109 B3
Radeberg D 53 B3
Radebeul D 52 B3
Radeburg D 53 B3
Radeče SLO 73 B5
Radekhiv UA 11 L19
Radenci SLO 73 B6
Radenthein A 72 B3
Radevormwald D 50 B3
Radicófani I 81 D5
Radicóndoli I 81 C5
Radišići BIH 84 C2
Radizel SLO 73 B5
Radków PL 54 C1
Radlje ob Dravi SLO 73 B5
Radłów PL 55 C5
Radmer an der Stube A 73 A4
Radnice CZ 63 A4
Radohova BIH 84 B2
Radolfzell D 61 C4
Radom PL 55 B6
Radomice PL 47 C5
Radomin PL 47 B5
Radomsko PL 55 B4
Radomyshl UA 11 L21
Radomyśl Wielki PL 55 C6
Radošina SK 64 B3
Radošovce SK 64 B3
Radostowo PL 47 B6
Radoszewice PL 54 B3
Radoszyce PL 55 B5
Radotín CZ 53 D4
Radovljica SLO 73 B4
Radowo Wielkie PL 46 B1
Radstadt A 72 A3
Radstock GB 29 B5
Raduc HR 83 B4
Radviliškis LT 6 J18
Radzanów, *Mazowieckie* PL 47 C6
Radzanów, *Mazowieckie* PL 55 B5
Radziejów PL 47 C4
Radziejowice PL 55 A5
Radzovce SK 65 B5
Radzyń Chełmiński PL 47 B4
Raeren B 50 C2
Raesfeld D 50 B2
Raffadali I 108 B2
Ragachow BY 7 K22
Ragály H 65 B6
Raglan GB 29 B5
Ragnitz A 73 B5
Ragusa I 109 C3
Rahden D 43 C5
Råholt N 34 A3
Raiano I 103 A3
Raigada E 87 B3
Rain D 62 B1
Rainbach im Mühlkreis A 63 B5
Rainham GB 31 C4
Rairiz de Veiga E 87 B3
Raisdorf D 44 A2
Raisio FIN 3 F18
Raiva, *Aveiro* P 87 C2
Raiva, *Coimbra* P 92 A2
Raja Jooseppi RUS 3 B21
Rajcza PL 65 A5
Rajec SK 65 A4
Rajec-Jestřebí CZ 64 A2
Rajecké Teplice SK 65 A4
Rajevo Selo HR 84 B3
Rajhrad CZ 64 A2
Rajić HR 74 C2
Rajka H 64 C3
Rakaca H 65 B6
Rakek SLO 73 C4
Rakhiv UA 11 M19
Rakitna SLO 73 C4
Rakkestad N 34 B3
Rákóczifalva H 75 A5
Rakoniewice PL 53 A6
Rakoszyce PL 54 B1
Raková SK 65 A4
Rakovac BIH 84 A2
Rakovica HR 83 B4
Rakovník CZ 53 C3
Rakow D 45 A5
Raków PL 55 C6
Rakvere EST 7 G20
Ralja YU 85 B5
Ramacastañas E 94 B1
Ramacca I 109 B3
Ramales de la Victoria E 89 A3
Rambervillers F 60 B2
Rambouillet F 58 B2
Rambucourt F 60 B1
Ramdala S 41 C5
Ramerupt F 59 B5
Ramingstein A 72 A3
Ramirás E 87 B2
Ramiswil CH 70 A2
Ramkvilla S 40 B4
Ramme DK 38 C1
Rämmen S 34 A6
Ramnäs S 36 B3
Ramnes N 34 B2
Râmnicu Vâlcea RO 11 P19
Ramonville-St. Agne F 77 C4
Rampside GB 26 A2
Ramsau D 62 C3
Ramsbeck D 51 B4
Ramsberg S 36 B2
Ramsey, *Cambridgeshire* GB 30 B3
Ramsey, *Isle of Man* GB 26 A1
Ramseycleuch GB 25 C4
Ramsgate GB 31 C5
Ramstein-Meisenbach D 60 A3
Ranalt A 71 A6
Rånåsfoss N 34 A3
Rance B 49 C5
Ránchio I 82 C1
Randaberg N 32 B2
Randalstown GB 19 B5
Randan F 68 B3
Randazzo I 109 B3
Randegg A 63 B5
Randers DK 38 C3
Randin E 87 C3
Rânes F 57 B5
Rångedala S 35 D5
Ranis D 52 C1
Rankweil A 71 A4
Rånnaväg S 40 B3
Ränneslöv S 40 C3
Rannoch Station GB 24 B3
Ransäter S 34 B5
Ransbach-Baumbach D 50 C3
Ransta S 36 B3
Ranua FIN 3 D20
Ranum DK 38 C2
Ranvalhal P 92 B1
Raon-l'Étape F 60 B2
Ráossi I 71 C6
Rapallo I 80 B3
Rapla EST 6 G19
Rapness GB 23 B6
Rapolano Terme I 81 C5
Rapolla I 104 B2
Raposa P 92 B2
Rapperswil CH 70 A3
Raša HR 82 A3
Rasal E 90 A2
Rascafria E 94 B3
Rasdorf D 51 C5
Raseiniai LT 6 J18
Rašica SLO 73 C4
Rasines E 89 A3
Raška YU 85 C5
Rasquera E 90 B3
Rássina I 81 C5
Rastatt D 61 B4
Rastede D 43 B5
Rastenberg D 52 B1
Rastošnica BIH 84 B3
Rastovac YU 84 D3
Rasueros E 94 A1
Rasy PL 55 B4
Raszków PL 54 B2
Rataje YU 85 C6
Rätansbyn S 2 E14
Rateče SLO 72 B3
Ratekau D 44 B2
Ratež SLO 73 C5
Rathangan IRL 21 A5
Rathcoole IRL 21 A5
Rathcormack IRL 20 B3
Rathdrum IRL 21 B5
Rathebur D 45 B5
Rathenow D 44 C4
Rathfriland GB 19 B5
Rathkeale IRL 20 B3
Rathmelton IRL 19 A4
Rathmolyon IRL 21 A5
Rathmore IRL 20 B2
Rathmullan IRL 19 A4
Rathnew IRL 21 B5
Rathvilly IRL 21 B5
Ratibořské Hory CZ 63 A5
Ratingen D 50 B2
Ratková SK 65 B6
Ratkovo YU 75 C4
Ratne UA 11 L19
Ratoath IRL 21 A5
Rattelsdorf D 51 C6
Ratten A 73 A5
Rattray GB 25 B4
Rättvik S 2 F14
Ratzeburg D 44 B2
Rätzlingen D 44 C3
Raucourt-et-Flaba F 59 A5
Raufoss N 2 F12
Rauland N 33 B5
Raulhac F 77 B5
Rauma FIN 3 F17
Raunds GB 30 B3
Rauris A 72 A3
Rautavaara FIN 3 E21
Rauzan F 76 B2
Rava-Rus'ka UA 11 L18
Ravanusa I 108 B2
Ravča HR 84 C2
Ravels B 49 B5
Rävemåla S 40 C5
Ravenglass GB 26 A2
Ravenna I 82 B1
Ravensburg D 61 C5
Rävlanda S 40 B2
Ravna Gora HR 73 C4
Ravne na Koroškem SLO 73 B4
Ravnište YU 85 C6
Ravnje YU 85 B4
Ravno BIH 84 D2
Ravno Selo YU 75 C4
Rawa Mazowiecka PL 55 B5
Rawicz PL 54 B1
Rawtenstall GB 26 B3
Rayleigh GB 31 C4
Ražana YU 85 B4
Ražanac HR 83 B4
Razboj BIH 84 A2
Razbojna YU 85 C6
Razes F 67 B6
Razgrad BG 16 Q20
Razkrižje SLO 73 B6
Razo E 86 A2
Reading GB 31 C3
Réalmont F 77 C5
Rebais F 59 B4
Reboly RUS 3 E22
Rebordelo P 87 C3
Recanati I 82 C2
Recas E 94 B3
Recaş RO 10 P17
Recco I 80 B3
Recess IRL 18 C2
Recey-sur-Ource F 59 C5
Recezinhos P 87 C2
Rechnitz A 73 A6
Rechytsa BY 7 K22
Recke D 43 C4
Recklinghausen D 50 B3
Recoaro Terme I 71 C6
Recogne B 59 A6

Recoules-Prévinquières F 78 B1
Recsk H 65 C6
Recz PL 46 B1
Red Point GB 22 D3
Reda PL 47 A4
Redange L 60 A1
Redcar GB 27 A4
Redditch GB 29 A6
Redefin D 44 B3
Redhill GB 31 C3
Redics H 73 B6
Redkino RUS 7 H25
Redland GB 23 B5
Redlin D 44 B4
Redon F 57 C3
Redondela E 87 B2
Redondo P 92 C3
Redruth GB 28 C2
Redzikowo PL 46 A3
Reepham GB 30 B5
Rees D 50 B2
Reeth GB 27 A4
Reetz D 44 B3
Reftele S 40 B3
Regalbuto I 109 B3
Regen D 62 B4
Regensburg D 62 A3
Regenstauf D 62 A3
Reggello I 81 C5
Réggio di Calábria I 109 A4
Réggio nell'Emília I 81 B4
Reggiolo I 81 B4
Reghin RO 11 N19
Régil E 89 A4
Regna S 37 C2
Regniéville F 60 B1
Regny F 69 C4
Rego da Leirosa P 92 A2
Regöly H 74 B3
Regueiro E 86 B2
Reguengo, *Portalegre* P 92 B3
Reguengo, *Santarém* P 92 B2
Reguengos de Monsaraz P 92 C3
Rehau D 52 C2
Rehburg D 43 C6
Rehden D 43 C5
Rehna D 44 B3
Reichelsheim D 61 A4
Reichelshofen D 61 A6
Reichenau A 64 C1
Reichenbach, *Sachsen* D 52 C2
Reichenbach, *Sachsen* D 53 B4
Reichenfels A 73 A4
Reichensachsen D 51 B6
Reichertshofen D 62 B2
Reichshoffen F 60 B3
Reiden CH 70 A2
Reigada E 86 A4
Reigada P 87 D4
Reigate GB 31 C3
Reillanne F 79 C4
Reillo E 95 C5
Reims F 59 A5
Reinach CH 70 A3
Reinbek D 44 B2
Reinberg D 45 A5
Reinfeld D 44 B2
Reinheim D 61 A4
Reinosa E 88 A2
Reinstorf D 44 B3
Reisach A 72 B3
Reiss GB 23 C5
Rejmyre S 37 C2
Rekavice BIH 84 B2
Rekovac YU 85 C6
Relleu E 96 C2
Rém H 75 B4
Remagen D 50 C3
Rémalard F 58 B1
Rembercourt-aux-Pots F 59 B6
Remedios P 92 B1
Remels D 43 B4
Remich L 60 A2
Rémilly F 60 A2
Remiremont F 60 C2
Remolinos E 90 B1
Remoulins F 78 C3
Remscheid D 50 B3
Rémuzat F 79 B4
Renaison F 68 B3
Renazé F 57 C4
Renchen D 61 B4
Rencurel F 79 A4
Rende I 106 B3
Rendsburg D 43 A6
Renedo E 88 C2
Renens CH 69 B6
Renfrew GB 24 C3
Reni UA 11 P21
Rennerod D 50 C4
Rennertshofen D 62 B2
Rennes F 57 B4
Rennes-les-Bains F 77 D5
Rennweg A 72 A3
Rens DK 39 E2
Rentería E 89 A5
Répcelak H 74 A2
Requena E 96 B1
Réquista F 77 B5
Rerik D 44 A3
Resana I 72 C1
Resarö S 36 B5
Resende P 87 C3
Résia (Reschen) I 71 B5
Reşiţa RO 10 P17
Resko PL 46 B1
Resnik YU 85 B5
Ressons-sur-Matz F 58 A3
Restábal E 100 C2
Resuttano I 109 B3
Retamal E 93 C4
Retford GB 27 B5
Rethel F 59 A5
Rethem D 43 C6
Réthimnon GR 16 U19
Retie B 49 B6
Retiers F 57 C4
Retków PL 53 B6
Retortillo E 87 D4
Retortillo de Soria E 89 C3
Retournac F 68 C4
Rétság H 65 C5
Rettenegg A 73 A5
Retuerta del Bullaque E 94 C2
Retz A 64 B1
Retzbach D 61 A5
Reuden D 52 A2
Reuilly F 68 A2
Reus E 91 B4
Reusel NL 49 B6
Reuterstadt Stavenhagen D 45 B4
Reuth D 62 A3
Reutlingen D 61 B5
Reutte A 71 A5
Reuver NL 50 B2
Revel F 77 C4
Revello I 80 B1
Revenga E 94 B2
Revest-du-Bion F 79 B4
Révfülöp H 74 B2
Revigny-sur-Ornain F 59 B5
Revin F 59 A5
Řevnice CZ 63 A5
Řevničov CZ 53 C3
Revo I 71 B6
Revúca SK 65 B6
Rewa PL 47 A4
Rewal PL 45 A7
Reyero E 88 B1
Rezé F 66 A3
Rēzekne LV 7 H20
Rezovo BG 16 R21
Rezzato I 71 C5
Rezzoáglio I 80 B3
Rhaunen D 60 A3
Rhayader GB 29 A4
Rheda-Wiedenbrück D 50 B4
Rhede, *Niedersachsen* D 43 B4
Rhede, *Nordrhein-Westfalen* D 50 B2
Rheinau D 60 B3
Rheinbach D 50 C2
Rheinberg D 50 B2
Rheine D 50 A3
Rheinfelden D 70 A2
Rheinsberg D 45 B4
Rhêmes-Notre-Dame I 70 C2
Rhenen NL 49 B6
Rhens D 50 C3
Rheydt D 50 B2
Rhiconich GB 22 C4
Rhinow D 44 C4
Rhiw GB 26 C1
Rho I 70 C4
Rhoden D 51 B5
Rhondda GB 29 B4
Rhosllanerchrugog GB 26 B2
Rhosneigr GB 26 B1
Rhossili GB 28 B3
Rhubodach GB 24 C2
Rhuddlan GB 26 B2
Rhyl GB 26 B2
Rhynie GB 23 D6
Riala S 36 B5
Riallé F 66 A3
Riaño E 88 B1
Riano I 102 A2
Rians F 79 C4
Rianxo E 86 B2
Riaza E 95 A3
Riba E 89 A3
Riba de Saelices E 95 B4
Riba-Roja de Turia E 96 B2
Riba-roja d'Ebre E 90 B3
Ribadavia E 87 B2
Ribadeo E 86 A3
Ribadesella E 88 A1
Ribaflecha E 89 B4
Ribaforada E 89 C5
Ribare YU 85 B6
Ribariće YU 85 D5
Ribe DK 39 D1
Ribeauvillé F 60 B3
Ribécourt-Dreslincourt F 59 A3
Ribeira da Pena P 87 C3
Ribeira de Piquín E 86 A3
Ribemont F 59 A4
Ribera I 108 B2
Ribera de Cardós E 91 A4
Ribera del Fresno E 93 C4
Ribérac F 67 C5
Ribes de Freser E 91 A5
Ribesalbes E 96 A2
Ribiers F 79 B4
Ribnica BIH 84 B3
Ribnica SLO 73 C4
Ribnica YU 85 C5
Ribnica na Potorju SLO 73 B5
Ribnik HR 73 C5
Rîbniţa MD 11 N21
Ribnitz-Damgarten D 44 A4
Ribolla I 81 D5
Říčany, *Jihomoravský* CZ 64 A2
Říčany, *Středočeský* CZ 53 D4
Riccia I 103 B4
Riccione I 82 B1
Ricco Del Golfo I 81 B3
Richebourg F 59 B6
Richelieu F 67 A5
Richisau CH 70 A3
Richmond, *Greater London* GB 31 C3
Richmond, *North Yorkshire* GB 27 A4
Richtenberg D 45 A4
Richterswil CH 70 A3
Rickling D 44 A2
Rickmansworth GB 31 C3
Ricla E 89 C5
Riddarhyttan S 36 B2
Ridderkerk NL 49 B5
Riddes CH 70 B2
Ridjica YU 75 C4
Riec-sur-Bélon F 56 C2
Ried A 63 B4
Ried im Oberinntal A 71 A5
Riedenburg D 62 B2
Riedlingen D 61 B5
Riedstadt D 61 A4
Riegersburg A 73 B5
Riego de la Vega E 88 B1
Riego del Camino E 88 C1
Riello E 88 B1
Riemst B 49 C6
Rienne B 49 D5
Riénsena E 88 A2
Riesa D 52 B3
Riese Pio X I 72 C1
Riesi I 109 B3
Riestedt D 52 B1
Rietberg D 51 B4
Rieti I 102 A2
Rietschen D 53 B4
Rieumes F 77 C4
Rieupeyroux F 77 B5
Rieux F 77 C4
Riez F 79 C5
Rīga LV 6 H19
Riggisberg CH 70 B2
Rignac F 77 B5
Rignano Gargánico I 104 A2
Rigolato I 72 B2
Rigside GB 25 C4
Rigutino I 81 C5
Riihimäki FIN 3 F19
Rijeka HR 73 C4
Rijen NL 49 B5
Rijkevorsel B 49 B5
Rijssen NL 50 A2
Rilić BIH 84 C2
Rilievo I 108 B1
Rillo de Gallo E 95 B5
Rimavská Baňa SK 65 B5
Rimavská Seč SK 65 B6
Rimavská Sobota SK 65 B6
Rimbo S 36 B5
Rimforsa S 37 C2
Rímini I 82 B1
Rîmnicu Sărat RO 11 P20
Rimogne F 59 A5
Rimpar D 61 A5
Rimske Toplice SLO 73 B5
Rincón de la Victoria E 100 C1
Rincón de Soto E 89 B5
Ringarum S 37 C3
Ringaskiddy IRL 20 C3
Ringe DK 39 D3
Ringkøbing DK 39 C1
Ringsted DK 39 D4
Ringwood GB 29 C6
Rinkaby S 41 D4
Rinkabyholm S 40 C6
Rinlo E 86 A3
Rinn A 71 A6
Rinteln D 51 A5
Rio E 86 B3
Rio do Coures P 92 B2
Rio Douro P 87 C3
Rio Frio P 92 C2
Rio frio de Riaza E 95 A3
Rio Maior P 92 B2
Rio Marina I 81 D4
Rio Tinto P 87 C2
Riobo E 87 B2
Riodeva E 96 A1
Riofrio E 94 B2
Riofrio de Aliste E 87 C4
Riogordo E 100 C1
Rioja E 101 C3
Riola I 81 B5
Riola Sardo I 110 D1
Riolobos E 93 B4
Riom F 68 C3
Riom-ès-Montagnes F 68 C2
Riomaggiore I 81 B3
Rion-des-Landes F 76 C2
Rionegro del Puente E 87 B4
Rionero in Vúlture I 104 B2
Riopar E 101 A3
Riós E 87 C3
Rioseco E 88 A1
Rioseco de Tapia E 88 B1
Riotord F 69 C4
Riotorto E 86 A3
Rioz F 69 A6
Ripač BIH 83 B4
Ripacándida I 104 B2
Ripanj YU 85 B5
Ripatransone I 82 D2
Ripley GB 27 B4
Ripoll E 91 A5
Ripon GB 27 A4
Riposto I 109 B4
Risan YU 15 Q16
Risca GB 29 B4
Rischenau D 51 B5
Riscle F 76 C2
Rišňovce SK 64 B3
Risør N 33 C6
Risøyhamn N 2 B14
Ritterhude D 43 B5
Riva del Garda I 71 C5
Riva Ligure I 80 C1
Rivanazzano I 80 B3
Rivarolo Canavese I 70 C2
Rivarolo Mantovano I 81 A4
Rive-de-Gier F 69 C4
Rivedoux-Plage F 66 B3
Rivello I 104 B2
Rivergaro I 80 B3
Rives F 69 C5
Rivesaltes F 78 D1
Rivignano I 72 C3
Rivne UA 11 L20
Rivoli I 80 A1
Rivolta d'Adda I 71 C4
Rixheim F 60 C3
Rixo S 35 C3
Rjukan N 33 B5
Rø DK 41 D4
Rö S 36 B5
Roa E 88 C3
Roa N 34 B2
Roade GB 30 B3
Roager DK 39 D1
Roaldkvam N 32 B3
Roanne F 68 B4
Robakowo PL 47 B4
Róbbio I 70 C3
Röbel D 45 B4
Roberton GB 25 C5
Robertville B 50 C2
Robin Hood's Bay GB 27 A5
Robleda E 93 A4
Robledillo de Trujillo E 93 B5
Robledo, *Albacete* E 101 A3
Robledo, *Orense* E 86 B4
Robledo de Chavela E 94 B2
Robledo del Buey E 94 C2
Robledo del Mazo E 94 C2
Robledollano E 93 B5
Robles de la Valcueva E 88 B1
Robliza de Cojos E 87 D5
Robres E 90 B2
Robres del Castillo E 89 B4
Rocafort de Queralt E 91 B4
Rocamadour F 77 B4
Rocca di Mezzo I 103 A3
Rocca di Papa I 102 B2
Rocca Imperiale I 105 B3
Rocca Priora I 82 C2
Rocca San Casciano I 81 B5
Rocca Sinibalda I 102 A2
Roccabernarda I 107 B3
Roccabianca I 81 A4
Roccadáspide I 104 B2
Roccagorga I 102 B3
Roccalbegna I 81 D5
Roccalumera I 109 B4
Roccamena I 108 B2
Roccamonfina I 103 B3
Roccanova I 104 B3
Roccapalumba I 108 B2
Roccapassa I 102 A3
Roccaraso I 103 B4
Roccasecca I 103 B3
Roccastrada I 81 C5
Roccatederighi I 81 C5
Roccella Iónica I 106 C3
Rocchetta Sant'António I 104 A2
Rocester GB 27 C4
Rochdale GB 26 B3
Roche-lez-Beaupré F 69 A6
Rochechouart F 67 C5
Rochefort B 49 C6
Rochefort F 66 C4
Rochefort-en-Terre F 57 C3
Rochefort-Montagne F 68 C2
Rochefort-sur-Nenon F 69 A5
Rochemaure F 78 B3
Rocheservière F 66 B3
Rochester, *Medway* GB 31 C4
Rochester, *Northumberland* GB 25 C5
Rochlitz D 52 B2
Rociana del Condado E 99 B4
Rockenhausen D 60 A3
Rockhammar S 36 B2
Rockneby S 40 C6
Ročko Polje HR 73 C4
Rocroi F 59 A5
Roda de Bara E 91 B4
Roda de Ter E 91 B5
Rodach D 51 C6
Rodalben D 60 A3
Rødberg N 33 A5
Rødby DK 44 A3
Rødbyhavn DK 44 A3
Rødding, *Sonderjyllands Amt.* DK 39 D2
Rødding, *Viborg Amt.* DK 38 C1
Rödeby S 41 C5
Rodeiro E 86 B3
Rødekro DK 39 D2
Roden NL 42 B3
Ródenas E 95 B5
Rodenkirchen D 43 B5
Rödental D 52 C1
Rödermark D 51 D4
Rodewisch D 52 C2
Rodez F 77 B5
Ródhos GR 16 T21
Rodi Gargánico I 104 A2
Roding D 62 A3
Rødkærsbro DK 39 C2
Rodoňá E 91 B4
Rødvig DK 41 D2
Roermond NL 50 B1
Roesbrugge B 48 C3
Roeschwoog F 61 B4
Roeselare B 49 C4
Roetgen D 50 C2
Roffiac F 78 A2
Röfors S 37 C1
Rofrano I 104 B2
Rogač HR 83 C5
Rogačica YU 85 B4
Rogalinek PL 54 A1
Rogaška Slatina SLO 73 B5
Rogatec SLO 73 B5
Rogatica BIH 84 C4
Rogatyn UA 11 M19
Rogätz D 52 A1
Roggendorf D 44 B3
Roggiano Gravina I 106 B3
Roghadal GB 22 D2
Rogliano F 80 D3
Rogliano I 106 B3
Rognes F 79 C4
Rogny-les-7-Ecluses F 59 C3
Rogowo PL 46 C3
Rogóz PL 47 A6
Rogoznica HR 83 C4
Rogoźnica PL 53 B6
Rogoźno PL 46 C2
Rohan F 56 B3
Röhlingen D 61 B6
Rohožnik SK 64 B3
Rohr D 51 C6
Rohr im Gebirge A 63 C6
Rohrbach A 63 B4
Rohrbach-lès-Bitche F 60 A3
Rohrberg D 44 C3
Röhrnbach D 63 B4
Roisel F 59 A4
Roja LV 6 H18
Rojales E 96 C2
Rokiciny PL 55 B4
Rokietnica PL 46 C2
Rokiškis LT 7 J19
Rokitki PL 53 B5
Rokitno RUS 7 L24
Rokycany CZ 63 A4
Rolampont F 59 C6
Rold DK 38 C2
Røldal N 32 B3
Rolde NL 42 C3
Rolfstorp S 40 B2
Rollag N 33 A6
Rollán E 94 B1
Rolle CH 69 B6
Roma I 102 B2
Roma S 37 D5
Romagnano Sésia I 70 C3
Romagné F 57 B4
Romakloster S 37 D5
Roman RO 11 N20
Romana I 110 C1
Romanèche-Thorins F 69 B4
Romano di Lombardia I 71 C4
Romans-sur-Isère F 79 A4
Romanshorn CH 71 A4
Rombas F 60 A2
Romeán E 86 B3
Romenay F 69 B5
Romeral E 95 C3
Römerstein D 61 B5
Rometta I 109 A4
Romford GB 31 C4
Romhány H 65 C5
Römhild D 51 C6
Romilly-sur-Seine F 59 B4
Romny UA 7 L23
Romodan UA 11 M23
Romont CH 70 B1
Romorantin-Lanthenay F 68 A1
Romrod D 51 C5
Romsey GB 31 D1
Rømskog N 34 B3
Rønbjerg DK 38 C1
Roncal E 76 D2
Ronce-les-Bains F 66 C3
Ronchamp F 60 C2
Ronchi dei Legionari I 72 C3
Ronciglione I 102 A2
Ronco Canavese I 70 C2
Ronco Scrivia I 80 B2
Ronda E 99 C5
Rønde DK 39 C3
Rönnäng S 35 D3
Rønne DK 41 D4
Ronneburg D 52 C2
Ronneby S 41 C5
Rönneshytta S 37 C2
Ronninge S 36 B4
Rönö S 37 C3
Ronov nad Doubravou CZ 63 A6
Ronse B 49 C4
Roosendaal NL 49 B5
Roosky IRL 19 C4
Ropczyce PL 55 C6
Ropeid N 32 B3
Roquebillière F 79 B6
Roquebrun F 78 C2
Roquecourbe F 77 C5
Roquefort F 76 B2
Roquemaure F 78 B3
Roquesteron F 79 C6
Roquetas de Mar E 101 C3
Roquetes E 90 C3
Roquevaire F 79 C4
Rørbæk DK 38 C2
Rore BIH 83 B5
Röro S 35 D3
Røros N 2 E12
Rorschach CH 71 A4
Rørvig DK 39 D4
Rørvik N 2 D12
Rörvik S 40 B4
Rosà I 72 C1
Rosa Marina I 105 B4
Rosal de la Frontera E 98 B3
Rosalina Mare I 72 C2
Rosans F 79 B4
Rosário P 98 B2
Rosarno I 106 C2
Rosbach D 50 C3
Rosche D 44 C2
Rościszewo PL 47 C5
Roscoff F 56 B2
Roscommon IRL 18 C3
Roscrea IRL 21 B4
Rosdorf D 51 B5
Rose I 106 B3
Rosegg A 73 B4
Rosehall GB 22 D4
Rosehearty GB 23 D6
Rosel GB 57 A3
Rosell E 90 C3
Roselló E 90 B3
Rosendal N 32 B3
Rosenfeld D 61 B4
Rosenfors S 40 B5
Rosenheim D 62 C3
Rosenow D 45 B5
Rosenthal D 45 B4
Rosersberg S 36 B4
Roses E 91 A6
Roseto degli Abruzzi I 103 A4
Roseto Valfortore I 104 A2
Rosheim F 60 B3
Rosia I 81 C5
Rosice CZ 64 A2
Rosières-en-Santerre F 58 A3
Rosignano Maríttimo I 81 C4
Rosignano Solvay I 81 C4
Roşiori-de-Vede RO 11 P19
Roskhill GB 22 D2
Roskilde DK 39 D5
Röslau D 52 C1
Roslavl RUS 7 K23
Roslev DK 38 C1
Rosmaninhal P 93 B3
Rosmult IRL 21 B4
Rosnowo PL 46 A2
Rosolini I 109 C3
Rosova YU 85 C4
Rosoy F 59 B4
Rosporden F 56 C2
Rosquete P 92 B2
Rosrath D 50 C3
Ross-on-Wye GB 29 B5
Rossa CH 71 B4
Rossano I 106 B3
Rossas, *Aveiro* P 87 D2
Rossas, *Braga* P 87 C2
Rossdorf D 51 C6
Rossett GB 26 B3
Rosshaupten D 62 C1
Rossiglione I 80 B2
Rossignol B 60 A1
Rossla D 52 B1
Rosslare IRL 21 B5
Rosslare Harbour IRL 21 B5
Rosslau D 52 B2
Rosslea GB 19 B4
Rossleben D 52 B1
Rossoszyca PL 54 B3
Rosswein D 52 B3
Röstånga S 41 C3
Roštár SK 65 B6
Rostock D 44 A4
Rostrenen F 56 B2
Rosyth GB 25 B4
Röszke H 75 B5
Rot am See D 61 A6
Rota E 99 C4
Rota Greca I 106 B3
Rotella I 82 D2
Rotenburg, *Hessen* D 51 C5
Rotenburg, *Niedersachsen* D 43 B6
Roth, *Bayern* D 62 A2
Roth, *Rheinland-Pfalz* D 50 C3
Rothbury GB 25 C6
Rothemühl D 45 B5
Rothen-kempenow D 45 B6
Röthenbach D 62 A2
Rothenburg D 53 B4
Rothenburg ob der Tauber D 61 A6
Rothéneuf F 57 B4
Rothenstein D 62 B2
Rotherham GB 27 B4
Rothes GB 23 D5
Rothesay GB 24 C2
Rothwell GB 30 B3
Rotnes N 34 A2
Rotonda I 104 C3
Rotondella I 105 B3
Rotova E 96 C2
Rott, *Bayern* D 62 C1
Rott, *Bayern* D 62 C3
Rottach-Egern D 62 C2
Röttenbach D 62 A2
Rottenbuch D 62 C1
Rottenburg, *Baden-Württemberg* D 61 B4
Rottenburg, *Bayern* D 62 B3
Rottenmann A 73 A4
Rotterdam NL 49 B5
Rotthalmünster D 63 B4
Rottingdean GB 31 D3
Röttingen D 61 A5
Rottleberode D 51 B6
Rottne S 40 B4
Rottneros S 34 B5
Rottofreno I 80 A3
Rottweil D 61 B4
Rötz D 62 A3
Roubaix F 49 C4
Roudnice nad Labem CZ 53 C4
Roudouallec F 56 B2
Rouen F 58 A2
Rouffach F 60 C3
Rougé F 57 C4
Rougemont F 69 A6
Rougemont le-Château F 60 C2
Rouillac F 67 C4
Rouillé F 67 B5
Roujan F 78 C2
Roulans F 69 A6
Roundwood IRL 21 A5
Rousinov CZ 64 A2
Roussac F 67 B6
Rousses F 78 B2
Roussillon F 69 C4
Rouvroy-sur-Audry F 59 A5
Rouy F 68 A3
Rovaniemi FIN 3 C19
Rovato I 71 C4
Rovensko pod Troskami CZ 53 C5
Roverbella I 71 C5
Rovereto I 71 C6
Röverhagen D 44 A4
Roverud N 34 A4
Rovigo I 81 A5
Rovinj HR 82 A2
Rovišće HR 74 C1
Rów PL 45 C6
Rowy PL 46 A3
Royal Leamington Spa GB 30 B2
Royal Tunbridge Wells GB 31 C4
Royan F 66 C3
Royat F 68 C3
Roybon F 69 C5
Roybridge GB 24 B3
Roye F 58 A3
Røykenvik N 34 A2
Royos E 101 B3
Royston GB 30 B3
Rozadas E 86 A4
Rožaj YU 85 D5
Rozalén del Monte E 95 C4
Różańsko PL 45 C6
Rožanstvo YU 85 C4
Rozay-en-Brie F 59 B3
Roždalovice CZ 53 C5
Rozdilna UA 11 N22
Rozental PL 47 B5
Rozhyshche UA 11 L19
Rožmitál pod Třemšínem CZ 63 A4
Rožňava SK 65 B6
Rožnov pod Radhoštěm CZ 64 A4
Rozoy-sur-Serre F 59 A5
Rozprza PL 55 B4
Roztoky CZ 53 C4
Rozvadov CZ 62 A3
Rozzano I 71 C4
Ruanes E 93 B5
Rubbestadneset N 32 B2
Rubi E 91 B5
Rubiá E 86 B4
Rubiacedo de Abajo E 89 B3
Rubielos Bajos E 95 C4
Rubielos de Mora E 96 A2
Rubiera I 81 B4
Rucandio E 89 B3
Rud, *Akershus* N 34 A3
Rud, *Buskerud* N 33 A7
Ruda PL 54 B3
Ruda S 40 B6
Ruda Maleniecka PL 55 B5
Ruda Pilczycka PL 55 C5
Ruda Śl. PL 54 C3
Rudabánya H 65 B6
Ruden A 73 B4
Rudersberg D 61 B5
Rudersdorf A 73 A6
Rüdersdorf D 45 C5
Ruderting D 63 B4
Rüdesheim D 50 D3
Rudkøbing DK 39 E3
Rudmanns A 63 B6
Rudna CZ 53 C4
Rudna PL 53 B6
Rudnik, *Kosovo* YU 85 D5
Rudnik, *Srbija* YU 85 B5
Rudniki, *Opolskie* PL 54 B3
Rudniki, *Śląskie* PL 55 C4
Rudno, *Dolnosląskie* PL 54 B1
Rudno, *Pomorskie* PL 47 B4
Rudnya RUS 7 J22
Rudo BIH 85 C4
Rudolstadt D 52 C1
Rudowica PL 53 B5
Rudozem BG 16 R19
Ruds Vedby DK 39 D4
Rudskoga S 35 B6
Rudston GB 27 A5
Rudy PL 54 C3
Rue F 48 C2
Rueda E 88 C2
Rueda de Jalón E 90 B1
Ruelle-sur-Touvre F 67 C5
Ruerrero E 88 B3
Ruffano I 107 B5
Ruffec F 67 B5
Rufina I 81 C5
Rugby GB 30 B2
Rugeley GB 27 C4
Rugles F 58 B1
Rugozero RUS 3 D23
Rühen D 44 C2
Ruhla D 51 C6
Ruhland D 53 B3
Ruhle D 43 C4
Ruhpolding D 62 C3
Ruhstorf D 63 B4
Ruidera E 95 D4
Ruillé-sur-le-Loir F 58 C1
Ruinen NL 42 C3
Ruiselede B 49 B4
Rulles B 60 A1
Rülzheim D 61 A4
Rum H 74 A1
Ruma YU 85 A4
Rumboci BIH 84 C2
Rumburk CZ 53 C4
Rumenka YU 75 C4
Rumia PL 47 A4
Rumigny F 59 A5
Rumilly F 69 C5
Rumney GB 29 B4
Rumont F 59 B6
Rumy PL 47 B6
Runa P 92 B1
Runcorn GB 26 B3
Rungsted DK 41 D2
Runhällen S 36 A3
Runowo PL 47 A6
Ruokolahti FIN 3 F21
Ruoms F 78 B3
Ruoti I 104 B2
Rupa HR 73 C4
Ruppichteroth D 50 C3
Rupt-sur-Moselle F 60 C2
Rus E 100 A2
Ruse BG 16 Q20
Ruše SLO 73 B5
Ruševo HR 74 C3
Rush IRL 21 A5
Rushden GB 30 B3
Rusiec PL 54 B3
Rusinowo, *Zachodnio-Pomorskie* PL 46 B1
Rusinowo, *Zachodnio-Pomorskie* PL 46 B2
Ruski Krstur YU 75 C4
Ruskington GB 27 B5
Rusovce SK 64 B3
Rüsselsheim D 51 D4
Russi I 81 B6
Rust A 64 C2
Rustrel F 79 C4
Ruszki PL 55 A5
Ruszów PL 53 B5
Rute E 100 B1
Rüthen D 51 B4
Rutherglen GB 24 C3
Ruthin GB 26 B2
Ruthven GB 23 D4
Ruthwell GB 25 D4
Rüti CH 70 A3
Rutigliano I 105 A4
Rutoši YU 85 C4
Rutuna S 37 C4
Ruurlo NL 50 A2
Ruvo del Monte I 104 B2
Ruvo di Púglia I 105 A3
Ružic HR 83 C5
Ružomberok SK 65 A5
Ruzsa H 75 B4
Ry DK 39 C2
Rybany SK 64 B4
Rybina PL 47 A5
Rybinsk RUS 7 G26
Rybnik PL 54 C3
Rychliki PL 47 B5
Rychlocice PL 54 B3
Rychnov nad Kněžnou CZ 54 C1
Rychnowo PL 47 B6
Rychtal PL 54 B2
Rychwał PL 54 A3
Ryczywół, *Mazowieckie* PL 55 B6
Ryczywól, *Wielkopolskie* PL 46 C2
Ryd S 40 C4
Rydaholm S 40 C4
Rydal S 40 B2
Rydbo S 36 B5
Rydboholm S 40 B2
Ryde GB 31 D2
Rydöbruk S 40 C3
Rydsgård S 41 D3
Rydsnäs S 37 D2
Rydultowy PL 54 C3
Rydzyna PL 54 B1
Rye GB 31 D4
Rygge N 34 B2
Ryjewo PL 47 B4
Rykene N 33 C5
Rylsk RUS 7 L24
Rymań PL 46 B1
Rýmařov CZ 64 A3
Rynarzewo PL 46 B3
Ryomgård DK 39 C3
Rypin PL 47 B5
Ryssby S 40 C4
Rytel PL 46 B3
Rytro PL 65 A6
Rywociny PL 47 B6
Rzeczenica PL 46 B3
Rzeczniów PL 55 B6
Rzeczyca PL 55 B5
Rzęgnowo PL 47 B6
Rzejowice PL 55 B4
Rzemień PL 55 C6
Rzepin PL 45 C6
Rzesznikowo PL 46 B1
Rzeszów PL 10 L17
Rzgów PL 55 B4
Rzhev RUS 7 H24

S

Sa Pobla, *Mallorca* E 97
Sa Savina E 97 C4
Saal, *Bayern* D 51 C6
Saal, *Bayern* D 62 B2
Saalbach A 72 A2
Saalburg D 52 C1
Saales F 60 B3
Saalfeld D 52 C1
Saalfelden am Steinernen Meer A 72 A2
Saanen CH 70 B2
Saarbrücken D 60 A2
Saarburg D 60 A2

Saarijärvi FIN 3 E19
Saarlouis D 60 A2
Saas-Fee CH 70 B2
Šabac YU 85 B4
Sabadell E 91 B5
Sabáudia I 102 B3
Sabbioneta I 81 B4
Sabero E 88 B1
Sabiñánigo E 90 A2
Sabiote E 100 A2
Sablé-sur-Sarthe F 57 C5
Sables-d'Or-les-Pins F 56 B3
Sabóia P 98 B2
Saborsko HR 83 A4
Sabres F 76 B2
Sabrosa P 87 C3
Sabugal P 93 A3
Săcălaz RO 75 C6
Sacecorbo E 95 B4
Saceda del Rio E 95 B4
Sacedón E 95 B4
Săcele RO 11 P19
Saceruela E 94 D2
Sachsenburg A 72 B3
Sachsenhagen D 43 C6
Sacile I 72 C2
Sacramenia E 88 C3
Sada E 86 A2
Sádaba E 90 A1
Saddell GB 24 C2
Sadernes E 91 A5
Sadki PL 46 B3
Sadkowice PL 55 B5
Sadów PL 53 A4
Sadská CZ 53 C4
Sæbøvik N 32 B2
Sæby DK 38 B3
Saelices E 95 C4
Saelices de Mayorga E 88 B1
Saerbeck D 50 A3
Særslev DK 39 D3
Sætre N 34 B2
Saeul L 60 A1
Sævareid N 32 A2
Safara P 98 A3
Säffle S 34 B4
Saffron Walden GB 31 B4
Safonovo RUS 7 J23
Säfsnäs S 36 A1
Şag RO 75 C6
Sagard D 45 A5
S'Agaro E 91 B6
Sagone F 110 A1
Sagres P 98 C2
Ságújfalu H 65 B5
Sagunt E 96 B2
Sagvåg N 32 B2
Ságvár H 74 B3
Sagy F 69 B5
Sahagún E 88 B1
Šahy SK 65 B4
Saignelégier CH 70 A1
Saignes F 68 C2
Saillagouse F 91 A5
Saillans F 79 B4
Sains F 59 A4
St. Affrique F 78 C1
St.-Agnan F 68 B3
St. Agnant F 66 C4
St. Agrève F 78 A3
St. Aignan F 67 A6
St. Aignan-sur-Roë F 57 C4
St. Alban-sur-Limagnole F 78 B2
St. Amand-en-Puisaye F 68 A3
St. Amand-les-Eaux F 49 C4
St. Amand-Longpré F 58 C2
St. Amand-Montrond F 68 B2
St. Amans F 78 B2
St. Amans-Soult F 77 C5
St. Amant-Roche-Savine F 68 C3
St. Amarin F 60 C2
St.-Ambroix F 78 B3
St. Amé F 60 B2
St. Amour F 69 B5
St. André-de-Corcy F 69 C4
St. Andre-de-Cubzac F 76 B2
St. André-de-l'Eure F 58 B2
St. André-de-Sangonis F 78 C2
St. Andre-de-Valborgne F 78 B2
St. André-les-Alpes F 79 C5
St. Angel F 68 C2
St. Anthème F 68 C3
St. Antoine-de-Ficalba F 77 B3
St. Antönien CH 71 B4
St. Antonin-Noble-Val F 77 B4
St. Août F 68 B1
St. Armant-Tallende F 68 C3
St. Arnoult F 58 B2
St. Astier F 77 A3
St. Auban F 79 C5
St.-Aubin CH 70 B1
St. Aubin F 69 A5
St. Aubin GB 57 A3
St. Aubin-d'Aubigné F 57 B4
St. Aubin-du-Cormier F 57 B4
St. Aubin-sur-Aire F 59 B6
St. Aubin-sur-Mer F 57 A5
St. Aulaye F 67 C5
St. Avit F 68 C2
St. Avold F 60 A2
St. Aygulf F 79 C5
St. Bauzille-de-Putois F 78 C2
St-Béat F 77 D3
St. Benim-d'Azy F 68 B3
St. Benoît-du-Sault F 67 B6
St. Benoît-en-Woëvre F 60 B1
St. Berthevin F 57 B5
St. Blaise-la-Roche F 60 B3
St. Blin F 59 B6
St. Bonnet F 79 B5
St. Bonnet-de-Joux F 69 B4
St. Bonnet-le-Château F 68 C4
St. Bonnet-le-Froid F 69 C4
St. Brévin-les-Pins F 66 A2
St. Briac-sur-Mer F 57 B3
St. Brice-en-Coglès F 57 B4
St. Brieuc F 56 B3
St. Bris-le-Vineux F 59 C4
St. Broladre F 57 B4
St. Calais F 58 C1
St. Cannat F 79 C4
St. Cast-le-Guildo F 57 B3
St. Céré F 77 B4
St. Cergue CH 69 B6
St. Cergues F 69 B6
St. Cernin F 77 A5
St. Chamant F 77 A4
St. Chamas F 79 C4
St. Chamond F 69 C4
St. Chély-d'Apcher F 78 B2
St. Chély-d'Aubrac F 78 B1
St. Chinian F 78 C1
St. Christol-lès-Alès F 78 B3
St. Christoly-Médoc F 66 C4
St. Christophe-du-Ligneron F 66 B3
St. Christophe-en-Brionnais F 69 B4
St. Ciers-sur-Gironde F 67 C4
St. Clair-sur-Epte F 58 A2
St. Clar F 77 C3
St. Claud F 67 C5
St. Claude F 69 B5
St. Come-d'Olt F 78 B1
St. Cosme-en-Vairais F 58 B1
St. Cyprien, *Dordogne* F 77 B4
St-Cyprien, *Pyrenées-Orientales* F 91 A6
St. Cyr-sur-Loire F 67 A5
St. Cyr-sur-Mer F 79 C4
St. Cyr-sur-Methon F 69 B4
St. Denis F 58 B3
St. Denis-d'Oléron F 66 B3
St. Denis-d'Orques F 57 B5
St. Didier F 69 B4
St. Didier-en-Velay F 69 C4
St. Dié F 60 B2
St. Dizier F 59 B5
St. Dizier-Leyrenne F 67 B6
St. Efflam F 56 B2
St. Égrève F 69 C5
St. Eloy-les-Mines F 68 B2
St. Émilion F 76 B2
St. Esteben F 76 C1
St. Estèphe F 67 C4
St. Étienne F 69 C4
St. Etienne-de-Baigorry F 76 C1
St. Étienne-de-Cuines F 69 C6
St. Etienne-de-Fursac F 67 B6
St. Etienne-de-Montluc F 66 A3
St. Etienne-de-St. Geoirs F 69 C5
St. Étienne-de-Tinée F 79 B5
St. Étienne-du-Bois F 69 B5
St. Étienne-du-Rouvray F 58 A2
St. Etienne-les-Orgues F 79 B4
St. Fargeau F 59 C4
St. Félicien F 78 A3
St. Felix-de-Sorgues F 78 C1
St. Félix-Lauragais F 77 C4
St. Firmin F 79 B5
St. Florent F 110 A2
St. Florent-le-Vieil F 66 A3
St. Florent-sur-Cher F 68 B2
St. Florentin F 59 C4
St. Flour F 78 A2
St. Flovier F 67 B6
St. Fort-sur-le-Né F 67 C4
St. Fulgent F 66 B3
St. Galmier F 69 C4
St-Gaudens F 77 C3
St. Gaultier F 67 B6
St. Gély-du-Fesc F 78 C2
St. Genest-Malifaux F 69 C4
St. Gengoux-le-National F 69 B4
St. Geniez F 79 B5
St. Geniez-d'Olt F 78 B1
St. Genis-de-Saintonge F 67 C4
St.-Genis-Pouilly F 69 B6
St. Genix-sur-Guiers F 69 C5
St. Georges Buttavent F 57 B5
St. Georges-d'Aurac F 68 C3
St. Georges-de-Commiers F 79 A4
St. Georges-de-Didonne F 66 C4
St. Georges-de-Luzençon F 78 B1
St. Georges-de Mons F 68 C2
St. Georges-de-Reneins F 69 B4
St. Georges d'Oléron F 66 C3
St. Georges-en-Couzan F 68 C3
St. Georges-lès-Baillargeaux F 67 B5
St. Georges-sur-Loire F 67 A4
St. Georges-sur-Meuse B 49 C6
St. Geours-de-Maremne F 76 C1
St. Gérand-de-Vaux F 68 B3
St. Gérand-le-Puy F 68 B3
St. Germain F 60 C2
St. Germain-Chassenay F 68 B3
St. Germain-de-Calberte F 78 B2
St. Germain-de-Confolens F 67 B5
St. Germain-de-Joux F 69 B5
St. Germain-des-Fossés F 68 B3
St. Germain-du-Bois F 69 B5
St. Germain-du-Plain F 69 B4
St. Germain-du Puy F 68 A2
St. Germain-en-Laye F 58 B3
St. Germain-Laval F 68 C4
St. Germain-Lembron F 68 C3
St. Germain-les-Belles F 67 C6
St.-Germain-Lespinasse F 68 B3
St. Germain-l'Herm F 68 C3
St. Gervais-d'Auvergne F 68 B2
St. Gervais-les-Bains F 70 C1
St. Gervais-sur-Mare F 78 C2
St. Gildas-de-Rhuys F 66 A2
St. Gildas-des-Bois F 66 A2
St. Gilles, *Gard* F 78 C3
St. Gilles, *Ille-et-Vilaine* F 57 B4
St. Gilles-Croix-de-Vie F 66 B3
St. Gingolph F 70 B1
St-Girons, *Ariège* F 77 D4
St. Girons, *Landes* F 76 C1
St. Girons-Plage F 76 C1
St. Gobain F 59 A4
St. Guénolé F 56 C1
St. Helier GB 57 A3
St. Herblain F 66 A3
St. Hilaire, *Allier* F 68 B3
St. Hilaire, *Aude* F 77 C5
St. Hilaire-de-Riez F 66 B3
St. Hilaire-de-Villefranche F 67 C4
St. Hilaire-des-Loges F 67 B4
St. Hilaire-du-Harcouët F 57 B4
St. Hilaire-du-Rosier F 79 A4
St. Hippolyte, *Aveyron* F 77 B5
St. Hippolyte, *Doubs* F 70 A1
St. Hippolyte-du-Fort F 78 C2
St. Honoré-les-Bains F 68 B3
St. Hubert B 49 C6
St. Imier CH 70 A2
St. Izaire F 78 C1
St. Jacques-de-la-Lande F 57 B4
St. Jacut-de-la-Mer F 57 B3
St. James F 57 B4
Saint Jaume d'Enveja E 90 C3
St. Jean-Brévelay F 56 C3
St. Jean-d'Angély F 67 C4
St. Jean-de-Belleville F 69 C6
St. Jean-de-Bournay F 69 C5
St. Jean-de-Braye F 58 C2
St. Jean-de-Côle F 67 C5
St. Jean-de-Daye F 57 A4
St. Jean de Losne F 69 A5
St. Jean-de-Luz F 76 C1
St. Jean-de-Maurienne F 69 C6
St. Jean-de-Monts F 66 B2
St. Jean-d'Illac F 76 B2
St. Jean-du-Bruel F 78 B2
St. Jean-du-Gard F 78 B2
St. Jean-en-Royans F 79 A4
St. Jean-la-Riviere F 79 C6
St. Jean-Pied-de-Port F 76 C1
St. Jean-Poutge F 77 C3
St. Jeoire F 69 B6
St. Joachim F 66 A2
St. Jorioz F 69 C6
St. Joris Winge B 49 C5
St. Jouin-de-Marnes F 67 B4
St. Juéry F 77 C5
St. Julien-Chapteuil F 78 A3
St. Julien-de-Vouvantes F 57 C4
St. Julien-du-Sault F 59 B4
St. Julien-du-Verdon F 79 C5
St. Julien-en-Born F 76 B1
St. Julien-en-Genevois F 69 B6
St. Julien la-Vêtre F 68 C3
St. Julien-l'Ars F 67 B5
St. Julien-Mont-Denis F 69 C6
St. Julien-sur-Reyssouze F 69 B5
St. Junien F 67 C5
St. Just F 78 B3
St. Just-en-Chaussée F 58 A3
St. Just-en-Chevalet F 68 C3
St. Just-St. Rambert F 69 C4
St. Justin F 76 C2
St. Lary-Soulan F 77 D3
St. Laurent-d'Aigouze F 78 C3
St. Laurent-de-Chamousset F 69 C4
St. Laurent-de-Condel F 57 A5
St. Laurent-de-la-Cabrerisse F 78 C1
St-Laurent-de-la-Salanque F 78 D1
St. Laurent-des-Autels F 66 A3
St. Laurent-du-Pont F 69 C5
St. Laurent-en-Caux F 58 A1
St. Laurent-en-Grandvaux F 69 B5
St. Laurent-Médoc F 76 A2
St. Laurent-sur-Gorre F 67 C5
St. Laurent-sur-Mer F 57 A5
St. Laurent-sur-Sèvre F 66 B4
St. Leger B 60 A1
St. Léger-de-Vignes F 68 B3
St. Léger-sous-Beuvray F 68 B4
St. Léger-sur-Dheune F 69 B4
St. Léonard-de-Noblat F 67 C6
St. Lô F 57 A4
St. Lon-les-Mines F 76 C1
St. Louis F 60 C3
St. Loup F 68 B3
St. Loup-de-la-Salle F 69 B4
St. Loup-sur-Semouse F 60 C2
St. Lunaire F 57 B3
St. Lupicin F 69 B5
St. Lyphard F 66 A2
St. Lys F 77 C4
St. Macaire F 76 B2
St. Maclou F 58 A1
St. Maixent-l'École F 67 B4
St. Malo F 57 B3
St. Mamet-la-Salvetat F 77 B5
St. Mandrier-sur-Mer F 79 C4
St. Marcel, *Drôme* F 78 B3
St. Marcel, *Saône-et-Loire* F 69 B4
St. Marcellin F 69 C5
St. Marcellin sur Loire F 68 C4
St. Marcet F 77 C3
St. Mards-en-Othe F 59 B4
St. Mars-la-Jaille F 66 A3
St. Martin-d'Ablois F 59 B4
St. Martin-d'Auxigny F 68 A2
St. Martin-de-Belleville F 69 C6
St. Martin-de-Bossenay F 59 B4
St. Martin-de-Crau F 78 C3
St. Martin-de-Londres F 78 C2
St. Martin-de-Queyrières F 79 B5
St. Martin-de-Ré F 66 B3
St.-Martin-de-Valamas F 78 B3
St. Martin-d'Entraunes F 79 B5
St. Martin des Besaces F 57 A5
St. Martin-d'Estreaux F 68 B3
St. Martin-d'Hères F 69 C5
St. Martin-du-Frêne F 69 B5
St. Martin-en-Bresse F 69 B5
St.-Martin-en-Haut F 69 C4
St. Martin-la-Méanne F 68 C1
St. Martin-sur-Ouanne F 59 C4
St. Martin-Valmeroux F 77 A5
St. Martin-Vésubie F 79 B6
St.-Martory F 77 C3
St. Mathieu F 67 C5
St. Mathieu-de-Tréviers F 78 C2
St. Maurice CH 70 B1
St. Maurice-Navacelles F 78 C2
St. Maurice-sur-Moselle F 60 C2
St. Maximin-la-Ste. Baume F 79 C4
St. Méard-de-Gurçon F 76 B3
St. Médard-de-Guizières F 76 A2
St. Médard-en-Jalles F 76 B2
St. Méen-le-Grand F 57 B3
St. Menges F 59 A5
St. Město CZ 54 C1
St. M'Hervé F 57 B4
St. Michel F 59 A5
St. Michel, *Gers* F 77 C3
St. Michel-Chef-Chef F 66 A2
St. Michel-de-Maurienne F 69 C6
St. Michel-en-Grève F 56 B2
St. Michel-en-l'Herm F 66 B3
St. Michel-Mont-Mercure F 66 B4
St. Mihiel F 60 B1
St. Montant F 78 B3
St. Moritz CH 71 B4
St. Nazaire F 66 A2
St. Nazaire-en-Royans F 79 A4
St. Nazaire-le-Désert F 79 B4
St. Nectaire F 68 C2
St. Nicolas-de-Port F 60 B2
St. Nicolas-de-Redon F 57 C3
St. Nicolas-du-Pélem F 56 B2
St. Niklaas B 49 B5
St. Omer F 48 C3
St. Pair-sur-Mer F 57 B4
Saint-Palais F 76 C1
St. Palais-sur-Mer F 66 C3
St. Pardoux-la-Rivière F 67 C5
St. Paul-Cap-de-Joux F 77 C4
St-Paul-de-Fenouillet F 77 D5
St.-Paul-de-Varax F 69 B5
St. Paul-le-Jeune F 78 B3
St. Paul-lès-Dax F 76 C1
St. Paul-Trois-Châteaux F 78 B3
St. Paulien F 78 A2
St. Pé-de-Bigorre F 76 C2
St. Pée-sur-Nivelle F 76 C1
St. Péravy-la-Colombe F 58 C2
St. Péray F 78 B3
St. Père-en-Retz F 66 A2
St. Peter Port GB 56 A3
St. Philbert-de-Grand-Lieu F 66 A3
St. Pierre F 78 C1
St. Pierre-d'Albigny F 69 C6
St. Pierre-d'Allevard F 69 C6
St. Pierre-de-Chartreuse F 69 C5
St. Pierre-de-Chignac F 77 A3
St. Pierre-de-la-Fage F 78 C2
St. Pierre-d'Entremont F 69 C5
St. Pierre-d'Oléron F 66 C3
St. Pierre-Eglise F 57 A4
St. Pierre-en-Port F 58 A1
St. Pierre-le-Moûtier F 68 B3
St. Pierre Montlimart F 66 A3
St. Pierre-Quiberon F 66 A1
St. Pierre-sur-Dives F 57 A5
St. Pierreville F 78 B3
St. Pieters-Leeuw B 49 C5
St. Plancard F 77 C3
St. Poix F 57 C4
St-Pol-de-Léon F 56 B2
St. Pol-sur-Mer F 48 B3
St. Pol-sur-Ternoise F 48 C3
St. Polgues F 68 C3
St. Pons-de-Thomières F 78 C1
St. Porchaire F 67 C4
St. Pourçain-sur-Sioule F 68 B3
St. Priest F 69 C4
St. Privat F 77 A5
St. Quay-Portrieux F 56 B3
St. Quentin F 59 A4
St. Quentin-la-Poterie F 78 B3
St. Quentin-les-Anges F 57 C5
St. Rambert-d'Albon F 69 C4
St. Rambert-en-Bugey F 69 C5
St. Raphaël F 79 C5
St. Rémy-de-Provence F 78 C3
St. Rémy-du-Val F 57 B6
St. Remy-en-Bouzemont F 59 B5
St-Renan F 56 B1
St. Révérien F 68 A3
St. Riquier F 48 C2
St. Romain-de-Colbosc F 58 A1
St. Rome-de-Cernon F 78 B1
St. Rome-de-Tarn F 78 B1
St Sadurní d'Anoia E 91 B4
St. Saëns F 58 A2
St. Sampson GB 56 A3
St. Samson-la-Poterie F 58 A2
St. Saturnin-de-Lenne F 78 B2
St. Saturnin-lès-Apt F 79 C4
St. Sauflieu F 58 A3
St. Saulge F 68 A3
St. Sauveur, *Finistère* F 56 B2
St. Sauveur, *Haute-Saône* F 60 C2
St. Sauveur-de-Montagut F 78 B3
St. Sauveur-en-Puisaye F 59 C4
St. Sauveur-en-Rue F 69 C4
St. Sauveur-le-Vicomte F 57 A4
St. Sauveur-Lendelin F 57 A4
St. Sauveur-sur-Tinée F 79 B6
St. Savin, *Gironde* F 76 A2
St. Savin, *Vienne* F 67 B5
St. Savinien F 67 C4
St. Savournin F 79 C4
St. Seine-l'Abbaye F 69 A4
St. Sernin-sur-Rance F 77 C5
St. Sevan-sur-Mer F 57 B3
St. Sever F 76 C2
St. Sever-Calvados F 57 B4
St. Sorlin-d'Arves F 69 C6
St. Soupplets F 58 A3
St. Sulpice F 77 C4
St. Sulpice-Laurière F 67 B6
St. Sulpice-les-Feuilles F 67 B6
St. Symphorien F 76 B2
St. Symphorien-de-Lay F 69 C4
St. Symphorien d'Ozon F 69 C4
St. Symphorien-sur-Coise F 69 C4
St-Thégonnec F 56 B2
St. Thiébault F 60 B1
St. Trivier-de-Courtes F 69 B5
St. Trivier sur-Moignans F 69 B4
St. Trojan-les-Bains F 66 C3
St. Tropez F 79 C5
St. Truiden B 49 C6
St. Vaast-la-Hougue F 57 A4
St. Valérien F 59 B4
St. Valery-en-Caux F 58 A1
St. Valéry-sur-Somme F 48 C2
St. Vallier, *Drôme* F 69 C4
St. Vallier, *Saône-et-Loire* F 69 B4
St. Vallier-de-Thiey F 79 C5
St. Varent F 67 B4
St. Vaury F 68 B1
St. Venant F 48 C3
Saint Vincent I 70 C2
St. Vincent-de-Tyrosse F 76 C1
St. Vit F 69 A5
St. Vith B 50 C2
St. Vivien-de-Médoc F 66 C3
St. Yan F 68 B4
St. Yorre F 68 B3
St. Yrieix-la-Perche F 67 C6
Ste. Adresse F 57 A6
Ste. Anne F 58 B1
Ste. Anne-d'Auray F 56 C3
Ste. Croix CH 69 B6
Ste. Croix-Volvestre F 77 C4
Ste. Engrâce F 76 C2
Ste. Enimie F 78 B2
Ste. Foy-de-Peyrolières F 77 C4
Ste. Foy-la-Grande F 76 B3
Ste. Foy l'Argentiere F 69 C4
Ste. Gauburge-Ste. Colombe F 58 B1
Ste. Gemme la Plaine F 66 B3
Ste. Geneviève F 58 A3
Ste. Hélène F 76 B2
Ste. Hélène-sur-Isère F 69 C6
Ste. Hermine F 66 B3
Ste. Jalle F 79 B4
Ste. Livrade-sur-Lot F 77 B3
Ste-Marie-aux-Mines F 60 B3
Ste. Marie-du-Mont F 57 A4
Ste. Maure-de-Touraine F 67 A5
Ste. Maxime F 79 C5
Ste-Ménéhould F 59 A5
Ste. Mère-Église F 57 A4
Ste. Ode B 49 C6
Ste-Savine F 59 B5
Ste. Sévère-sur-Indre F 68 B2
Ste. Sigolène F 69 C4
Ste. Suzanne F 57 B5
Ste. Tulle F 79 C4
Sainteny F 57 A4
Saintes F 67 C4
Stes-Maries-de-la-Mer F 78 C3
Saintfield GB 19 B6
Saissac F 77 C5
Saja E 88 A2
Sajan YU 75 C5
Šajkaš YU 75 C5
Sajókaza H 65 B6
Sajószentpéter H 65 B6
Sajóvámos H 65 B6
Šakiai LT 6 J18
Sakskobing DK 39 E4
Sakule YU 85 A5
Sala S 36 B3
Šal'a SK 64 B3
Sala Baganza I 81 B4
Sala Consilina I 104 B2
Salakovac YU 85 B6
Salamanca E 94 B1
Salamis GR 15 T18
Salandra I 104 B3
Salaparuta I 108 B1
Salar E 100 B1
Salardú E 90 A3
Salas E 86 A4
Salas de los Infantes E 89 B3
Salau F 77 D4
Salavaux CH 70 B2
Salbertrand I 79 A5
Salbohed S 36 B3
Salbris F 68 A2
Salce E 86 B4
Salching D 62 B3
Salcombe GB 28 C4
Saldaña E 88 B2
Saldus LV 6 H18
Sale I 80 B2
Saleby S 35 C5
Salem D 61 C5
Salemi I 108 B1
Salen, *Highland* GB 24 B2
Salen, *Highland* GB 24 B2
Sälen S 2 F13
Salernes F 79 C5
Salerno I 104 B1
Salers F 68 C2
Salford GB 26 B3
Salgótarján H 65 B5
Salgueiro P 92 B3
Sali HR 83 C4
Sálice Salentino I 105 B4
Salientes E 86 B4
Salies-de-Béarn F 76 C2
Salies-du-Salat F 77 C3
Salignac-Eyvigues F 77 B4
Saligney-sur-Roudon F 68 B3
Salihli TR 16 S21
Salihorsk BY 7 K20
Salinas, *Alicante* E 96 C2
Salinas, *Huesca* E 90 A3
Salinas de Medinaceli E 95 A4
Salinas de Pisuerga E 88 B2
Saline di Volterra I 81 C4
Salins-les-Bains F 69 B5
Salir P 98 B2
Salisbury GB 29 B6
Salla A 73 A4
Salla FIN 3 C21
Sallachy GB 23 C4
Sallanches F 70 C1
Sallent E 91 B4
Sallent de Gállego E 76 D2
Salles F 76 B2
Salles-Curan F 78 B1
Salles-sur-l'Hers F 77 C4
Sallins IRL 21 A5
Salmerón E 95 B4
Salmiech F 77 B5
Salmoral E 94 B1
Salo FIN 3 F18
Salò I 71 C5
Salobreña E 100 C2
Salon-de-Provence F 79 C4
Salonta RO 10 N17
Salorino E 93 B3
Salornay-sur-Guye F 69 B4
Salorno I 71 B6
Salou E 91 B4
Šalovci SLO 73 B6
Salses-le-Chateau F 78 D1
Salsomaggiore Terme I 81 B3
Salt E 91 B5
Saltara I 82 C1
Saltash GB 28 C3
Saltburn-by-the-Sea GB 27 A5
Saltcoats GB 24 C3
Saltfleet GB 27 B6
Salto P 87 C3
Saltrød N 33 C5
Saltsjöbaden S 36 B5
Saltvik S 40 B6
Saludécio I 82 C1
Salussola I 70 C3
Saluzzo I 80 B1
Salvacañete E 96 A1
Salvada P 98 B3
Salvagnac F 77 C4
Salvaleon E 93 C4
Salvaterra de Magos P 92 B2
Salvaterra do Extremo P 93 B4
Salvatierra, *Avila* E 89 B4
Salvatierra, *Badajoz* E 93 C4
Salvatierra de Santiago E 93 B4
Salviac F 77 B4
Salz-hemmendorf D 51 A5
Salzburg A 62 C4
Salzgitter D 51 A6
Salzgitter Bad D 51 A6
Salzhausen D 44 B2
Salzkotten D 51 B4
Salzmünde D 52 B1
Salzwedel D 44 C3
Samadet F 76 C2
Samassi I 110 D1
Samatan F 77 C3
Sambiase I 106 C3
Sambir UA 11 M18
Samborowo PL 47 B5
Sambuca di Sicilia I 108 B2
Samedan CH 71 B4
Samer F 48 C2
Sámi GR 15 S17
Sammichele di Bari I 105 B3
Samnaun CH 71 B5
Samobor HR 73 C5
Samoëns F 70 B1
Samogneux F 59 A6
Samokov BG 15 Q18
Samora Correia P 92 C2
Šamorín SK 64 B3
Samos E 86 B3
Samoš YU 75 C5
Samper de Calanda E 90 B2
Sampéyre I 79 B6
Sampieri I 109 C3
Sampigny F 60 B1
Samplawa PL 47 B5
Samproniano I 81 D5
Samtens D 45 A5
Samugheo I 110 D1
San Adrián E 89 B5
San Agustín E 101 C3
San Agustin de Guadalix E 95 B3
San Alberto I 82 B1
San Amaro E 87 B2
San Andrés del Rabanedo E 88 B1
San Antolin de Ibias E 86 A4
San Arcángelo I 104 B3
San Asensio E 89 B4
San Bartolomé de la Torre E 99 B3
San Bartolomé de las Abiertas E 94 C2
San Bartolomé de Pinares E 94 B2
San Bartolomeo in Galdo I 104 A2
San Benedetto del Tronto I 82 D2
San Benedetto in Alpe I 81 C5
San Benedetto Po I 81 A4
San Benito E 100 A1
San Benito de la Contienda E 93 C3
San Biágio Plátani I 108 B2
San Biágio Saracinisco I 103 B3
San Bonifacio I 71 C6
San Calixto E 99 B5
San Cándido I 72 B2
San Carlo CH 70 B3

San Carlo I 108 B2
San Carlos del Valle E 100 A2
San Casciano dei Bagni I 81 D5
San Casciano in Val di Pesa I 81 C5
San Cataldo, *Puglia* I 105 B5
San Cataldo, *Sicilia* I 108 B2
San Cebrián de Castro E 88 C1
San Cesário di Lecce I 105 B5
San Chirico Raparo I 104 B3
San Cibrao das Viñas E 87 B3
San Cipirello I 108 B2
San Ciprián E 86 A3
San Clemente E 95 C4
San Clodio E 86 B3
San Colombano al Lambro I 71 C4
San Costanzo I 82 C2
San Crisóbal de Entreviñas E 88 B1
San Cristóbal de la Polantera E 88 B1
San Cristóbal de la Vega E 94 A2
San Cristovo E 87 C3
San Damiano d'Asti I 80 B2
San Damiano Macra I 79 B6
San Daniele del Friuli I 72 B3
San Demétrio Corone I 106 B3
San Demétrio nè Vestini I 103 A3
San Donà di Piave I 72 C2
San Dónaci I 105 B4
San Donato Val di Comino I 103 B3
San Emiliano E 88 B1
San Enrique E 99 C5
San Esteban E 86 A4
San Esteban de Gormaz E 89 C3
San Esteban de la Sierra E 93 A5
San Esteban de Litera E 90 B3
San Esteban de Valdueza E 86 B4
San Esteban del Molar E 88 C1
San Esteban del Valle E 94 B2
San Fele I 104 B2
San Felice Circeo I 102 B3
San Felice sul Panaro I 81 B5
San Felices E 88 B3
San Felices de los Gallégos E 87 D4
San Ferdinando di Púglia I 104 A3
San Fernando E 99 C4
San Fernando de Henares E 95 B3
San Fili I 106 B3
San Foca I 105 B5
San Fratello I 109 B3
San Gavino Monreale I 110 D1
San Gémini Fonte I 102 A2
San Germano Vercellese I 70 C3
San Giácomo, *Trentino Alto Adige* I 72 B1
San Giácomo, *Umbria* I 82 D1
San Gimignano I 81 C5
San Ginésio I 82 C2
San Giórgio a Liri I 103 B3
San Giórgio del Sánnio I 104 A1
San Giorgio della Richinvelda I 72 B2
San Giórgio di Lomellina I 70 C3
San Giórgio di Nogaro I 72 C3
San Giorgio di Piano I 81 B5
San Giórgio Iónico I 105 B4
San Giovanni a Piro I 104 B2
San Giovanni Bianco I 71 C4
San Giovanni di Sinis I 110 D1
San Giovanni in Croce I 81 A4
San Giovanni in Fiore I 106 B3
San Giovanni in Persiceto I 81 B5
San Giovanni Reatino I 102 A2
San Giovanni Rotondo I 104 A2
San Giovanni Suérgiu I 110 D1
San Giovanni Valdarno I 81 C5
San Giuliano Terme I 81 C4
San Giustino I 82 C1
San Godenzo I 81 C5
San Gregorio Magno I 104 B2
San Guiseppe Jato I 108 B2
San Javier E 101 B5
San Jorge P 92 B2
San José E 101 C3
San Juan E 89 B3
San Juan de Alicante E 96 C2
San Juan de la Nava E 94 B2
San Justo de la Vega E 86 B4
San Lazzaro di Sávena I 81 B5
San Leo I 82 C1
San Leonardo de Yagüe E 89 C3
San Leonardo in Passiria I 71 B6
San Lorenzo a Merse I 81 C5
San Lorenzo al Mare I 80 C1
San Lorenzo Bellizzi I 106 B3
San Lorenzo de Calatrava E 100 A2
San Lorenzo de El Escorial E 94 B2
San Lorenzo de la Parrilla E 95 C4
San Lorenzo di Sebato I 72 B1
San Lorenzo in Campo I 82 C1
San Lorenzo Nuovo I 102 A1
San Lourenco P 98 A2
San Luca I 106 C3
San Lúcido I 106 B3
San Marcello I 82 C2
San Marcello Pistoiese I 81 B4
San Marcial E 88 C1
San Marco I 104 B1
San Marco Argentano I 106 B3
San Marco dei Cavoti I 104 A1
San Marco in Lámis I 104 A2
San Marino RSM 82 C1
San Martin de Castañeda E 87 B4
San Martín de la Vega E 95 B3
San Martin de la Vega del Alberche E 94 B1
San Martin de Luiña E 86 A4
San Martin de Montalbán E 94 C2
San Martin de Oscos E 86 A4
San Martin de Pusa E 94 C2
San Martin de Unx E 89 B5
San Martín de Valdeiglesias E 94 B2
San Martin del Tesorillo E 99 C5
San Martino di Campagna I 72 B2
San Martino di Castrozza I 72 B1
San-Martino-di-Lota F 110 A2
San Martino in Pénsilis I 103 B5
San Mateo de Gallego E 90 B2
San Máuro Forte I 104 B3
San Michele all'Adige I 71 B6
San Michele di Ganzaria I 109 B3
San Michele Mondovì I 80 B1
San Miguel de Aguayo E 88 A2
San Miguel de Bernuy E 88 C3
San Miguel de Salinas E 96 D2
San Miguel del Arroyo E 88 C2
San Millán de la Cogolla E 89 B4
San Miniato I 81 C4
San Muñoz E 87 D4
San Nicola dell'Alto I 107 B3
San Nicolás del Puerto E 99 B5
San Nicolò I 81 B5
San Nicolò Gerrei I 110 D2
San Pablo de los Montes E 94 C2
San Pancrázio Salentino I 105 B4
San Pantaleo I 110 B2
San Páolo di Civitate I 104 A2
San Pawl il-Bahar M 109 C4
San Pedro, *Albacete* E 101 A3
San Pedro, *Oviedo* E 86 A4
San Pedro de Alcántara E 100 C1
San Pedro de Cadeira P 92 B1
San Pedro de Ceque E 87 B4
San Pedro de Latarce E 88 C1
San Pedro de Merida E 93 C4
San Pedro de Valderaduey E 88 B2
San Pedro del Arroyo E 94 B2
San Pedro del Pinatar E 101 B5
San Pedro del Romeral E 88 A3
San Pedro Manrique E 89 B4
San Pellegrino Terme I 71 C4
San Piero a Sieve I 81 C5
San Piero in Bagno I 81 C5
San Piero Patti I 109 A3
San Pietro I 109 B3
San Pietro in Casale I 81 B5
San Pietro in Gu I 72 C1
San Pietro in Palazzi I 81 C4
San Pietro in Volta I 72 C2
San Pietro Vara I 80 B3
San Pietro Vernótico I 105 B4
San Polo d'Enza I 81 B4
San Quirico d'Órcia I 81 C5
San Rafael del Rio E 90 C3
San Remo I 80 C1
San Román de Cameros E 89 B4
San Roman de Hernija E 88 C1
San Román de la Cuba E 88 B2
San Roman de los Montes E 94 B2
San Romao P 92 C3
San Roque E 99 C5
San Roque de Riomera E 88 A3
San Rufo I 104 B2
San Sabastián de los Ballesteros E 100 B1
San Salvador de Cantamuda E 88 B2
San Salvo I 103 A4
San Salvo Marina I 103 A4
San Sebastián de los Reyes E 95 B3
San Sebastiano Curone I 80 B3
San Secondo Parmense I 81 B4
San Severino Marche I 82 C2
San Severino Lucano I 104 B3
San Severo I 104 A2
San Silvestre de Guzmán E 98 B3
San Sosti I 106 B3
San Stéfano di Cadore I 72 B2
San Stino di Livenza I 72 C2
San Telmo E 99 B4
San Tirso de Abres E 86 A3
San Valentino alla Muta I 71 B5
San Venanzo I 82 D1
San Vicente de Alcántara E 93 B3
San Vicente de Arana E 89 B4
San Vicente de la Barquera E 88 A2
San Vicente de la Sonsierra E 89 B4
San Vicente de Toranzo E 88 A3
San Vietro E 87 C4
San Vigilio I 72 B1
San Vincente del Raspeig E 96 C2
San Vincenzo I 81 C4
San Vito I 110 D2
San Vito al Tagliamento I 72 C2
San Vito Chietino I 103 A4
San Vito dei Normanni I 105 B4
San Vito di Cadore I 72 B2
San Vito lo Capo I 108 A1
San Vito Romano I 102 B2
Sanaigmore GB 24 C1
Sânandrei RO 75 C6
Sanary-sur-Mer F 79 C4
Sancergues F 68 A2
Sancerre F 68 A2
Sancey-le-Long F 69 A6
Sanchiorian E 94 B2
Sanchonuño E 88 C2
Sancoins F 68 B2
Sancti-Petri E 99 C4
Sancti-Spiritus E 93 A4
Sand, *Hedmark* N 34 A3
Sand, *Rogaland* N 32 B3
Sandane N 2 F10
Sandanski BG 15 R18
Sandared S 40 B2
Sandau D 44 C4
Sandbach D 63 B4
Sandbach GB 26 B3
Sandbank GB 24 C3
Sandbanks GB 29 C6
Sandby DK 39 E4
Sande D 43 B5
Sande N 34 B2
Sandefjord N 34 B2
Sandeid N 32 B2
Sandersleben D 52 B1
Sandes N 33 C4
Sandesneben D 44 B2
Sandhead GB 24 D3
Sandhem S 35 D5
Sandhorst D 43 B4
Sandhurst GB 31 C3
Sandıklı TR 16 S22
Sandillon F 58 C3
Sandl A 63 B5
Sandnes N 32 C2
Sandness GB 22 A7
Sandnessjøen N 2 C13
Sando E 87 D4
Sandomierz PL 55 C6
Sándorfalva H 75 B5
Sandown GB 31 D2
Sandoysund N 35 B2
Sandrigo I 72 C1
Sandsele S 2 D15
Sandsjöfors S 40 B4
Sandvig-Allinge DK 41 D4
Sandvika, *Akershus* N 34 B2
Sandvika, *Nord-Trøndelag* N 2 E13
Sandviken S 36 A3
Sandvikvåy N 32 B2
Sandwich GB 31 C5
Sandy GB 30 B3
Sangatte F 48 C2
Sangerhausen D 52 B1
Sangineto Lido I 106 B2
Sangonera la Verde E 101 B4
Sangüesa E 90 A1
Sanguinet F 76 B1
Sanica BIH 83 B5
Sanitz D 44 A4
Sankt Aegyd am Neuwalde A 63 C6
Sankt Andrä A 73 B4
Sankt Andreasberg D 51 B6
Sankt Anna S 37 C3
Sankt Anna am Aigen A 73 B5
Sankt Anton am Arlberg A 71 A5
Sankt Anton an der Jessnitz A 63 C6
Sankt Augustin D 50 C3
Sankt Blasien D 61 C4
Sankt Englmar D 62 A3
Sankt Gallen A 63 C5
Sankt Gallen CH 71 A4
Sankt Gallenkirch A 71 A4
Sankt Georgen A 63 B5
Sankt Georgen D 61 B4
Sankt Georgen am Reith A 63 C5
Sankt Georgen ob Judenburg A 73 A4
Sankt Georgen ob Murau A 73 A4
Sankt Gilgen A 63 C4
Sankt Goar D 50 C3
Sankt Goarshausen D 50 C3
Sankt Ingbert D 60 A3
Sankt Jacob A 73 B4
Sankt Jakob in Defereggen A 72 B2
Sankt Johann a Tauern A 73 A4
Sankt Johann am Wesen A 63 B4
Sankt Johann im Pongau A 72 A3
Sankt Johann in Tirol A 72 A2
Sankt Katharein an der Laming A 73 A5
Sankt Kathrein am Hauenstein A 73 A5
Sankt Lambrecht A 73 A4
Sankt Leonhard am Forst A 63 B6
Sankt Leonhard im Pitztal A 71 A5
Sankt Lorenzen A 72 B2
Sankt Marein, *Steiermark* A 73 A5
Sankt Marein, *Steiermark* A 73 A5
Sankt Margarethen im Lavanttal A 73 B4
Sankt Margrethen CH 71 A4
Sankt Michael A 73 A5
Sankt Michael im Burgenland A 73 A6
Sankt Michael im Lungau A 72 A3
Sankt Michaelisdonn D 43 B6
Sankt Niklaus CH 70 B2
Sankt Nikolai im Sölktal A 73 A4
Sankt Olof S 41 D4
Sankt Oswald D 63 B4
Sankt Paul A 73 B4
Sankt Paul F 79 B5
Sankt Peter D 61 B4
Sankt Peter am Kammersberg A 73 A4
Sankt Peter-Ording D 43 A5
Sankt-Peterburg RUS 7 G22
Sankt Pölten A 63 B6
Sankt Radegund A 73 A5
Sankt Ruprecht an der Raab A 73 A5
Sankt Salvator A 73 B4
Sankt Stefan A 73 B4
Sankt Stefan an der Gail A 72 B3
Sankt Stefan im Rosental A 73 B5
Sankt Valentin A 63 B5
Sankt Veit an der Glan A 73 B4
Sankt Veit an der Gölsen A 63 B6
Sankt Veit in Defereggen A 72 B2
Sankt Wendel D 60 A3
Sankt Wolfgang A 63 C4
Sankt Wolfgang D 62 B3
Sanlúcar de Barrameda E 99 C4
Sanlúcar de Guadiana E 98 B3
Sanlúcar la Mayor E 99 B4
Sanluri I 110 D1
Sânmihaiu Roman RO 75 C6
Sänna S 37 C1
Sannazzaro de'Burgondi I 80 A2
Sanne D 44 C3
Sannicandro di Bari I 105 A3
Sannicandro Gargánico I 104 A2
Sânnicolau Mare RO 75 B5
Sannidal N 33 C6
Sanniki PL 47 C5
Sanok PL 11 M18
Sanquhar GB 25 C4
Sansepolcro I 82 C1
Sanski Most BIH 83 B5
Sant Agusti de Lluçanès E 91 A5
Sant Antoni Abat E 97 C4
Sant Antoni de Calonge E 91 B6
Sant Boi de Llobregat E 91 B5
Sant Carles de la Ràpita E 90 C3
Sant Carlos E 97 B4
Sant Celoni E 91 B5
Sant Climent, *Menorca* E 97
Sant Feliu E 91 B5
Sant Feliu de Codines E 91 B5
Sant Feliu de Guíxols E 91 B6
Sant Feliu Sasserra E 91 B5
Sant Ferran E 97 C4
Sant Francesc de Formentera E 97 C4
Sant Francesc de ses Salines E 97 C4
Sant Hilari Sacalm E 91 B5
Sant Hipòlit de Voltregà E 91 A5
Sant Jaume dels Domenys E 91 B4
Sant Joan Baptista E 97 B4
Sant Joan de les Abadesses E 91 A5
Sant Jordi E 90 C3
Sant Josep E 97 C4
Sant Juliá de Loria AND 91 A4
Sant Llorenç de Morunys E 91 A4
Sant Llorenç des Carctassar, *Mallorca* E 97
Sant Llorenç Savall E 91 B5
Sant Luis, *Menorca* E 97
Sant Martí de Llemaná E 91 A5
Sant Martí de Maldá E 91 B4
Sant Marti Sarroca E 91 B4
Sant Mateu E 90 C3
Sant Miquel E 97 B4
Sant Pau de Seguries E 91 A5
Sant Pere de Riudebitles E 91 B4
Sant Pere Pescador E 91 A6
Sant Pere Sallavinera E 91 B4
Sant Quirze de Besora E 91 A5
Sant Rafel E 97 C4
Sant Ramon E 91 B4
Sant Vincenç de Castellet E 91 B4
Santa Agnès E 97 B4
Santa Amalia E 93 B4
Santa Ana, *Cáceres* E 93 B5
Santa Ana, *Jaén* E 100 B2
Santa Ana de Pusa E 94 C2
Santa Barbara E 90 C3
Santa Barbara de Casa E 98 B3
Santa Bárbara de Padrões P 98 B3
Santa Catarina P 98 B3
Santa Caterina di Pittinuri I 110 C1
Santa Caterina Villarmosa I 109 B3
Santa Cesárea Terme I 107 A5
Santa Clara-a-Nova P 98 B2
Santa Clara-a-Velha P 98 B2
Santa Clara de Louredo P 98 B3
Santa Coloma de Farners E 91 B5
Santa Coloma de Gramenet E 91 B5
Santa Coloma de Queralt E 91 B4
Santa Colomba de Curueño E 88 B1
Santa Colomba de Somoza E 86 B4
Santa Comba E 86 A2
Santa Comba Dão P 92 A2
Santa Comba de Rossas P 87 C4
Santa Cristina I 71 C4
Santa Cristina de la Polvorosa E 88 B1
Santa Croce Camerina I 109 C3
Santa Croce di Magliano I 103 B4
Santa Cruz E 86 A2
Santa Cruz P 92 B1
Santa Cruz de Alhama E 100 B2
Santa Cruz de Campezo E 89 B4
Santa Cruz de Grio E 89 C5
Santa Cruz de la Salceda E 89 C3
Santa Cruz de la Sierra E 93 B5
Santa Cruz de la Zarza E 95 C3
Santa Cruz de Moya E 96 B1
Santa Cruz de Mudela E 100 A2
Santa Cruz de Paniagua E 93 A4
Santa Cruz del Retamar E 94 B2
Santa Cruz del Valle E 94 B1
Santa Doménica Talao I 106 B2
Santa Doménica Vittória I 109 B3
Santa Elena E 100 A2
Santa Elena de Jamuz E 88 B1
Santa Eufemia E 100 A1
Santa Eufémia d'Aspromonte I 106 C2
Santa Eulalia E 95 B5
Santa Eulália P 93 C3
Santa Eulalia de Oscos E 86 A3
Santa Eulàlia des Riu E 97 C4
Santa Fe E 100 B2
Santa Fiora I 81 D5
Santa Gertrude I 71 B5
Santa Giustina I 72 B2
Santa Iria P 98 B3
Santa Leocadia P 87 C2
Santa Lucia-de-Porto-Vecchio F 110 B2
Santa Lucia del Mela I 109 A4
Santa Luzia P 98 B2
Santa Maddalena Vallalta I 72 B2
Santa Magdalena de Polpis E 90 C3
Santa Margalida, *Mallorca* E 97
Santa Margarida P 92 B2
Santa Margarida do Sado P 98 A2
Santa Margaridao de Montbui E 91 B4
Santa Margherita I 110 E1
Santa Margherita di Belice I 108 B2
Santa Margherita Ligure I 80 B3
Santa Maria CH 71 B5
Santa Maria E 90 A2
Santa Maria al Bagno I 105 B4
Santa Maria Cápua Vétere I 103 B4
Santa Maria da Feira P 87 D2
Santa Maria de Cayón E 88 A3
Santa Maria de Corco E 91 A5
Santa Maria de Huerta E 95 A4
Santa Maria de la Alameda E 94 B2
Santa Maria de las Hoyas E 89 C3
Santa Maria de Mercadillo E 89 C3
Santa Maria de Nieva E 101 B4
Santa Maria de Trassierra E 100 B1
Santa Maria del Cami, *Mallorca* E 97
Santa Maria del Campo E 88 B3
Santa Maria del Campo Rus E 95 C4
Santa Maria del Páramo E 88 B1
Santa Maria del Taro I 80 B3
Santa Maria della Versa I 80 B3
Santa Maria di Licodia I 109 B3
Santa Maria-di-Rispéscia I 81 D5
Santa Maria la Real de Nieva E 94 A2
Santa Maria Maggiore I 70 B3
Santa Maria Ribarredonda E 89 B3
Santa Marina del Rey E 88 B1
Santa Marinella I 102 A1
Santa Marta, *Albacete* E 95 C4
Santa Marta, *Badajoz* E 93 C4
Santa Marta de Magasca E 93 B4
Santa Marta de Penaguião P 87 C3
Santa Marta de Tormes E 94 B1
Santa Ninfa I 108 B1
Santa Olalla, *Huelva* E 99 B4
Santa Olalla, *Toledo* E 94 B2
Santa Pau E 91 A5
Santa Pola E 96 C2
Santa Ponça, *Mallorca* E 97
Santa Severa F 80 D3
Santa Severa I 102 A1
Santa Severina I 107 B3
Santa Sofia I 81 C5
Santa Suzana, *Évora* P 92 C3
Santa Suzana, *Setúbal* P 92 C2
Santa Teresa di Riva I 109 B4
Santa Teresa Gallura I 110 B2
Santa Uxía E 86 B2
Santa Valburga I 71 B5
Santa Vittória in Matenano I 82 C2
Santacara E 89 B5
Santadi I 110 D1
Santaella E 100 B1
Sant'Ágata dei Goti I 103 B4
Sant'Ágata di Ésaro I 106 B2
Sant'Ágata di Púglia I 104 A2
Sant'Agata Feltria I 82 C1
Sant'Ágata Militello I 109 A3
Santana, *Évora* P 92 C2
Santana, *Setúbal* P 92 C1
Santana da Serra P 98 B2
Sant'Ana de Cambas P 98 B3
Santana do Mato P 92 C2
Sant'Anastasia I 103 C4
Santander E 88 A3
Sant'Andrea Frius I 110 D2
Sant'Ángelo dei Lombardi I 104 B2
Sant'Angelo in Vado I 82 C1
Sant'Angelo Lodigiano I 71 C4
Sant'Antioco I 110 D1
Sant'Antonio-di-Gallura I 110 C2
Santanyí, *Mallorca* E 97
Santarcángelo di Romagna I 82 B1
Santarém P 92 B2
Santas Martas E 88 B1
Sant'Caterina I 81 D5
Santed E 95 A5
Sant'Egidio alla Vibrata I 82 D2
Sant'Elia a Pianisi I 103 B4
Sant'Elia Fiumerapido I 103 B3
Santelices E 88 A3
Sant'Elpidio a Mare I 82 C2
Santéramo in Colle I 105 B3
Santervas de la Vega E 88 B2
Santhià I 70 C3
Santiago de Alcántara E 93 B3
Santiago de Calatrava E 100 B1
Santiago de Compostela E 86 B2
Santiago de la Espade E 101 A3
Santiago de la Puebla E 94 B1
Santiago de la Ribera E 101 B5
Santiago de Litem P 92 B2
Santiago del Campo E 93 B4
Santiago do Cacém P 98 B2
Santiago do Escoural P 92 C2
Santiago Maior P 92 C3
Santibáñez de Béjar E 93 A5
Santibáñez de la Peña E 88 B2
Santibáñez de Murias E 88 A1
Santibáñez de Vidriales E 87 B4
Santibáñez el Alto E 93 A4
Santibáñez el Bajo E 93 A4
Santillana E 88 A2
Santiponce E 99 B4
Santisteban del Puerto E 100 A2
Santiuste de San Juan Bautiste E 94 A2
Santiz E 94 A1
Sant'Ilario d'Enza I 81 B4
Santo Aleixo P 98 A3
Santo Amado P 98 A3
Santo Amaro P 92 C3
Santo André P 98 A2
Santo Domingo E 93 C3
Santo Domingo de la Calzada E 89 B4
Santo Domingo de Silos E 89 C3
Santo Estêvão, *Faro* P 98 B3
Santo Estêvão, *Santarém* P 92 C2
Santo-Pietro-di Tenda F 110 A2
Santo Spirito I 105 A3
Santo Stefano d'Aveto I 80 B3
Santo Stéfano di Camastra I 109 A3
Santo Stefano di Magra I 81 B3
Santo Stéfano Quisquina I 108 B2
Santo Tirso P 87 C2
Santo Tomé E 100 A2
Santok PL 46 C1
Santomera E 101 A4
Santoña E 89 A3
Sant'Oreste I 102 A2
Santotis E 88 A2
Santovenia, *Burgos* E 89 B3
Santovenia, *Zamora* E 88 C1
Santpedor E 91 B4
Santu Lussurgiu I 110 C1
Santutzi E 89 A3
Sanxenxo E 86 B2
Sanza I 104 B2
São Aleixo P 92 C3
São Barnabé P 98 B2
São Bartolomé da Serra P 98 A2
São Bartolomeu de Messines P 98 B2
São Bento P 87 C2
São Brás P 98 B3
São Brás de Alportel P 98 B3
São Braz do Reguedoura P 92 C2
São Cristóvão P 92 C2
São Domingos P 98 B2
São Geraldo P 92 C2
São Jacinto P 92 A2

São João da Madeira P 87 D2
São João da Pesqueira P 87 C3
São João da Ribeira P 92 B2
São João da Serra P 87 D2
São João da Venda P 98 B3
São João dos Caldeireiros P 98 B3
São Julião P 92 B3
São Leonardo P 92 C3
São Luis P 98 B2
São Manços P 92 C3
São Marcos da Ataboeira P 98 B3
Saõ Marcos da Serra P 98 B2
São Marcos de Campo P 92 C3
São Martinho da Cortiça P 92 A2
São Martinho das Amoreiras P 98 B2
São Martinho do Porto P 92 B1
São Matias, *Beja* P 98 A3
São Matias, *Évora* P 92 C2
São Miguel d'Acha P 92 A3
São Miguel de Machede P 92 C3
São Pedro da Torre P 87 C2
São Pedro de Muel P 92 B1
São Pedro de Solis P 98 B3
São Pedro do Sul P 87 D2
São Romão P 92 C2
São Sebastião dos Carros P 98 B3
São Teotónio P 98 B2
São Torcato P 87 C2
Saorge F 80 C1
Sapanca TR 16 R22
Sapataria P 92 C1
Sápes GR 16 R19
Sapiãos P 87 C3
Sappada I 72 B2
Sapri I 104 D2
Sarajevo BIH 84 C3
Saramon F 77 C3
Sarandës AL 15 S17
Saranovo YU 85 B5
Saraorci YU 85 B6
Saray TR 16 R20
Sarayköy TR 16 T21
Sarbia PL 46 C2
Sarbinowo, *Zachodnio-Pomorskie* PL 45 C6
Sarbinowo, *Zachodnio-Pomorskie* PL 46 A1
Sárbogárd H 74 B3
Sarcelles F 58 A3
Sarche I 71 B5
Sardoal P 92 B2
Sardón de Duero E 88 C2
Sare F 76 C1
S'Arenal, *Mallorca* E 97
Šarengrad HR 75 C4
Sarentino I 71 B6
Sarezzo I 71 C5
Sargans CH 71 A4
Sári H 75 A4
Sari-d'Orcino F 110 A1
Sarıgöl TR 16 S21
Sarilhos Grandes P 92 C2
Sariñena E 90 B2
Sárisáp H 65 C4
Sarıyer TR 16 R21
Sarkad H 75 B6
Sárkeresztes H 74 A3
Sárkeresztúr H 74 A3
Şarköy TR 16 R20
Sarlat-la-Canéda F 77 B4
Sarliac-sur-l'Isle F 67 C5
Sármellék H 74 B2
Särna S 2 F13
Sarnadas P 92 B3
Sarnano I 82 C2
Sarnen CH 70 B3
Sarnesfield GB 29 A5
Sárnico I 71 C4
Sarno I 103 C4
Sarnonico I 71 B6
Sarnow D 45 B5
Sarny UA 11 L20
Särö S 38 B4
Saronno I 70 C4
Sárosd H 74 A3
Šarovce SK 65 B4
Sarpsborg N 34 B3
Sarracín E 88 B3
Sarral E 91 B4
Sarralbe F 60 A3
Sarrancolin F 77 D3
Sarras F 69 C4
Sarre I 70 C2
Sarre-Union F 60 B3
Sarreaus E 87 B3
Sarrebourg F 60 B3
Sarreguemines F 60 A3
Sárrétudvari H 75 A6
Sarria E 86 B3
Sarrià de Ter E 91 A5
Sarrión E 96 A2
Sarroca de Lleida E 90 B3
Sarroch I 110 D2
Sarron F 76 C2
Sàrsina I 82 C1
Sarstedt D 51 A5
Sárszentlörinc H 74 B3
Sárszentmihaly H 74 A3
Sárszentmiklós H 74 B3
Sarteano I 81 D5
Sartène F 110 B1
Sartilly F 57 B4
Sartirana Lomellina I 80 A2
Sárvár H 74 A1
Sarzana I 81 B3
Sarzeau F 66 A2
Sarzedas P 92 B3
Sas van Gent NL 49 B4
Sasamón E 88 B2
Sásd H 74 B3
Sasino PL 46 A3
Sássari I 110 C1
Sassello I 80 B2
Sassenberg D 50 B4
Sassetta I 81 C4
Sassnitz D 45 A5
Sasso d'Ombrone I 81 D5
Sasso Marconi I 81 B5
Sassocorvaro I 82 C1
Sassoferrato I 82 C1
Sassoleone I 81 B5
Sassuolo I 81 B4
Sástago E 90 B2
Šaštinske Stráže SK 64 B3
Satão P 87 D3
Såtenäs S 35 C4
Säter S 36 A2
Sätila S 40 B2
Satillieu F 69 C4
Satnica Đakovačka HR 74 C3
Sátoraljaújhely H 10 M17
Satow D 44 B3
Sätra-brunn S 36 B3
Satrup D 43 A6
Satteins A 71 A4
Satu Mare RO 11 N18
Saturnia I 102 A1
Saucats F 76 B2
Saucelle E 87 C4
Sauda N 32 B3
Saudasjøen N 32 B3
Sauerlach D 62 C2
Saugues F 78 B2
Sauherad N 33 B6
Saujon F 66 C4
Sauland N 33 B5
Saulces Monclin F 59 A5
Saulgau D 61 B5
Saulgrub D 62 C2
Saulieu F 69 A4
Sault F 79 B4
Sault-Brénaz F 69 C5
Sault-de-Navailles F 76 C2
Saulx F 60 C2
Saulxures-sur-Moselotte F 60 C2
Saulzais-le-Potier F 68 B2
Saumos F 76 B1
Saumur F 67 A4
Saundersfoot GB 28 B3
Saurat F 77 D4
Sáuris I 72 B2
Sausset-les-Pins F 79 C4
Sauteyrargues F 78 C2
Sauvagnat F 68 C2
Sauve F 78 C2
Sauveterre-de-Béarn F 76 C2
Sauveterre-de-Guyenne F 76 B2
Sauviat-sur-Vige F 67 C6
Sauxillanges F 68 C3
Sauzé-Vaussais F 67 B5
Sauzet, *Drôme* F 78 B3
Sauzet, *Lot* F 77 B4
Sauzon F 66 A1
Sava I 105 B4
Savarsin RO 11 N18
Savci SLO 73 B6
Säve S 35 D3
Savelletri I 105 B4
Savelli I 107 B3
Savenay F 66 A3
Saverdun F 77 C4
Saverne F 60 B3
Savières F 59 B4
Savigliano I 80 B1
Savignac-les-Eglises F 67 C5
Savignano Irpino I 104 A2
Savignano sul Rubicone I 82 B1
Savigny-sur-Braye F 58 C1
Saviñán E 89 C5
Savines-le-lac F 79 B5
Savino Selo YU 75 C4
Savio I 82 B1
Sävja S 36 B4
Šavnik YU 85 D4
Savognin CH 71 B4
Savona I 80 B2
Savonlinna FIN 3 F21
Sävsjö S 40 B4
Sävsjöström S 40 B5
Savudrija HR 72 C3
Sawbridgeworth GB 31 C4
Sawtry GB 30 B3
Sax E 96 C2
Saxdalen S 36 A1
Saxilby GB 27 B5
Saxmundham GB 30 B5
Saxthorpe GB 30 B5
Sayalonga E 100 C1
Sayatón E 95 B4
Sayda D 52 C3
Sázava, *Jihomoravský* CZ 64 A1
Sázava, *Středočeský* CZ 63 A5
Scaër F 56 B2
Scafa I 103 A4
Scalasaig GB 24 B1
Scalby GB 27 A5
Scalea I 106 B2
Scaletta Zanclea I 109 A4
Scalloway GB 22 A7
Scamblesby GB 27 B5
Scandale I 107 B3
Scandiano I 81 B4
Scandicci I 81 C5
Scandolara Ravara I 81 A4
Scanno I 103 B3
Scansano I 102 A1
Scanzano Jónico I 105 B3
Scarborough GB 27 A5
Scardovari I 82 B1
Scardoy GB 22 D4
Scarinish GB 24 B1
Scarperia I 81 C5
Scarriff IRL 20 B3
Scey-sur-Saône et St. Albin F 60 C1
Sch-en-feld D 62 A3
Schachendorf A 73 A6
Schaffhausen CH 61 C4
Schafstädt D 52 B1
Schafstedt D 43 A6
Schäftlarn D 62 C2
Schagen NL 42 C1
Schalkau D 51 C7
Schangnau CH 70 B2
Schapbach D 61 B4
Scharbeutz D 44 A2
Schärding A 63 B4
Scharnitz A 71 A6
Scharrel D 43 B4
Schattendorf A 64 C2
Scheemda NL 42 B3
Scheessel D 43 B6
Schéggia I 82 C1
Scheibbs A 63 B6
Scheibenberg D 52 C2
Scheidegg D 61 C5
Scheifling A 73 A4
Scheinfeld D 61 A6
Schelklingen D 61 B5
Schenefeld, *Schleswig-Holstein* D 43 A6
Schenefeld, *Schleswig-Holstein* D 44 B1
Schenklengsfeld D 51 C5
Scherfede D 51 B5
Schermbeck D 50 B2
Scherpenzeel NL 49 A6
Schesslitz D 52 D1
Scheveningen NL 49 A5
Schiedam NL 49 B5
Schieder-Schwalenberg D 51 B5
Schierling D 62 B3
Schiers CH 71 B4
Schildau D 52 B2
Schillingen D 60 A2
Schillingsfürst D 61 A6
Schilpário I 71 B5
Schiltach D 61 B4
Schiltigheim F 60 B3
Schio I 71 C6
Schirmeck F 60 B3
Schirnding D 52 C2
Schkeuditz D 52 B2
Schkölen D 52 B1
Schlabendorf D 53 B3
Schladen D 51 A6
Schladming A 72 A3
Schlangen D 51 B4
Schleiden D 50 C2
Schleiz D 52 C1
Schleswig D 43 A6
Schleusingen D 51 C6
Schlieben D 52 B3
Schliengen D 60 C3
Schliersee D 62 C2
Schlitz D 51 C5
Schloss Neuhans D 51 B4
Schlossvippach D 52 B1
Schlotheim D 51 B6
Schluchsee D 61 C4
Schlüchtern D 51 C5
Schmallenberg D 50 B4
Schmelz D 60 A2
Schmidmühlen D 62 A2
Schmiedeberg D 53 C3
Schmiedefeld D 51 C6
Schmirn A 72 A1
Schmölln, *Brandenburg* D 45 B6
Schmölln, *Sachsen* D 52 C2
Schnaittach D 62 A2
Schneeberg D 52 C2
Schneizlreuth D 62 C3
Schneverdingen D 44 B1
Schöder A 73 A4
Schoenburg B 50 C2
Schollene D 44 C4
Schöllkrippen D 51 C5
Schomberg D 61 B4
Schönach D 62 B3
Schönau, *Baden-Württemberg* D 60 C3
Schönau, *Bayern* D 62 B3
Schönbeck D 45 B5
Schönberg, *Bayern* D 63 B4
Schönberg, *Mecklenburg-Vorpommern* D 44 B2
Schönberg, *Schleswig-Holstein* D 44 A2
Schönebeck D 52 A1
Schöneck D 52 C2
Schönecken- D 50 C2
Schönermark D 45 B5
Schönewalde D 52 B3
Schongau D 62 C1
Schöngrabern A 64 B2
Schönhagen D 51 B5
Schönhausen D 44 C4
Schöningen D 51 A6
Schönkirchen D 44 A2
Schönsee D 62 A3
Schöntal D 61 A5
Schönthal D 62 A3
Schonungen D 51 C6
Schönwalde D 44 A2
Schoondijke NL 49 B4
Schoonebeek NL 42 C3
Schoonhoven NL 49 B5
Schopfheim D 60 C3
Schöppenstedt D 51 A6
Schörfling A 63 C4
Schorndorf D 61 B5
Schortens D 43 B4
Schotten D 51 C5
Schramberg D 61 B4
Schraplau D 52 B1
Schrattenberg A 64 B2
Schrecksbach D 51 C5
Schrems A 63 B6
Schrobenhausen D 62 B2
Schröcken A 71 A5
Schrozberg D 61 A5
Schruns A 71 A4
Schüpfheim CH 70 B3
Schüttorf D 50 A3
Schwaan D 44 B4
Schwabach D 62 A2
Schwäbisch Gmünd D 61 B5
Schwäbisch Hall D 61 A5
Schwabmünchen D 62 B1
Schwadorf A 64 B2
Schwagstorf D 43 C4
Schwaigern D 61 A5
Schwalmstadt D 51 C5
Schwanberg A 73 B5
Schwanden CH 70 B4
Schwandorf D 62 A3
Schwanebeck D 52 B1
Schwanenstadt A 63 B4
Schwanewede D 43 B5
Schwanfeld D 61 A6
Schwangau D 62 C1
Schwarmstedt D 43 C6
Schwarz-heide D 53 B3
Schwarza D 51 C6
Schwarzach im Pongau A 72 A3
Schwarzach im Gebirge A 63 C6
Schwarzenau A 63 B6
Schwarzenbach D 52 C1
Schwarzenbach am Wald D 52 C1
Schwarzenbek D 44 B2
Schwarzenberg D 52 C2
Schwarzenburg CH 70 B2
Schwaz A 72 A1
Schwechat A 64 B2
Schwedt D 45 B6
Schwei D 43 B5
Schweich D 60 A2
Schweighausen D 60 B3
Schweinfurt D 51 C6
Schweinitz D 52 B3
Schweinrich D 45 B4
Schwelm D 50 B3
Schwemsal D 52 B2
Schwendt A 62 C3
Schwenningen D 61 B4
Schwepnitz D 53 B3
Schwerin D 44 B3
Schwerte D 50 B3
Schwetzingen D 61 A4
Schwyz CH 70 A3
Sciacca I 108 B2
Scicli I 109 C3
Ściechów PL 45 C6
Scigliano I 106 B3
Scilla I 106 C2
Ścinawa PL 53 B6
Scionzier F 69 B6
Scoglitti I 109 C3
Scole GB 30 B5
Sconser GB 22 D2
Scopello, *Piemonte* I 70 C3
Scopello, *Sicilia* I 108 A1
Scordia I 109 B3
Scorzè I 72 C2
Scotch Corner GB 27 A4
Scotter GB 27 B5
Scourie GB 22 C3
Scousburgh GB 22 B7
Scrabster GB 23 C5
Screeb IRL 20 A2
Scremerston GB 25 C6
Scritto I 82 C1
Scunthorpe GB 27 B5
Scuol CH 71 B5
Scúrcola Marsicana I 103 A3
Seaford GB 31 D4
Seaham GB 25 D6
Seahouses GB 25 C6
Seascale GB 26 A2
Seaton GB 29 C4
Sebazac-Concourès F 77 B5
Sebečevo YU 85 C5
Seben TR 16 R22
Sebersdorf A 73 A5
Sebezh RUS 7 H21
Sebnitz D 53 C4
Seborga I 80 C1
Seč, *Vychodočeský* CZ 63 A6
Seč, *Západočeský* CZ 63 A4
Sečanj YU 75 C5
Secemin PL 55 C4
Seckau A 73 A4
Seclin F 49 C4
Secondigny F 67 B4
Seda P 92 B3
Sedan F 59 A5
Sedano E 88 B3
Sedbergh GB 26 A3
Sedella E 100 C1
Séderon F 79 B4
Sedgefield GB 27 A4
Sedico I 72 B2
Sédilo I 110 C1
Sédini I 110 C1
Sedlarica HR 74 C2
Sedlčany CZ 63 A5
Sedlec-Prčice CZ 63 A5
Sedlice CZ 63 A4
Sędziejowice PL 55 B4
Sędziszów PL 55 C5
Sędziszów Małapolski PL 55 C6
Seebach F 60 B3
Seeboden A 72 B3
Seefeld, *Brandenburg* D 45 C5
Seefeld, *Niedersachsen* D 43 B5
Seefeld in Tirol A 71 A6
Seehausen, *Sachsen-Anhalt* D 44 C3
Seehausen, *Sachsen-Anhalt* D 52 A1
Seeheim-Jugenheim D 61 A4
Seelbach D 60 B3
Seelow D 45 C6
Seelze D 43 C6
Seerhausen D 52 B3
Sées F 57 B6
Seesen D 51 B6
Seeshaupt D 62 C2
Seewalchen A 63 C4
Seferihisar TR 16 S20
Sefkerin YU 85 A5
Segerstad S 34 B5
Segesd H 74 B2
Segmon S 34 B5
Segonzac F 67 C4
Segorbe E 96 B2
Segovia E 94 B2
Segré F 57 C5
Ségur-les-Villas F 68 C2
Segura E 89 B4
Segura P 93 B3
Segura de León E 99 A4
Segura de los Baños E 90 C2
Segurrilla E 94 B2
Sehnde D 44 C1
Seia P 92 A3
Seiches-sur-le-Loir F 57 C5
Seifhennersdorf D 53 C4
Seignelay F 59 C4
Seijo E 87 C2
Seilhac F 67 C6
Seilles B 49 C6
Seinäjoki FIN 3 E18
Seissan F 77 C3
Seitenstetten Markt A 63 B5
Seixal P 92 C1
Seiz A 73 A4
Seizthal A 73 A4
Sejerslev DK 38 C1
Seksna RUS 7 G26
Selárgius I 110 D2
Selb D 52 C2
Selby GB 27 B4
Selca HR 84 C1
Selce HR 73 C4
Selçuk TR 16 T20
Selde DK 38 C2
Selenča YU 75 C4
Selestat F 60 B3
Seleuš YU 85 A5
Selevac YU 85 B5
Selgua E 90 B3
Selice SK 64 B3
Seligenstadt D 51 C4
Seligenthal D 51 C6
Selizharovo RUS 7 H23
Seljord N 33 B5
Selkirk GB 25 C5
Sellano I 82 D1
Selles-St.-Denis F 68 A1
Selles-sur-Cher F 67 A6
Sellières F 69 B5
Sellin D 45 A5
Sellye H 74 C2
Selm D 50 B3
Selnica ob Dravi SLO 73 B5
Selongey F 59 C6
Selonnet F 79 B5
Selow D 44 B3
Selsey GB 31 D3
Selsingen D 43 B6
Selters D 50 C3
Seltso RUS 7 K24
Seltz F 61 B4
Selva, *Mallorca* E 97
Selva di Cadore I 72 B2
Selva di Val Gardena I 72 B1
Selvik N 34 B2
Selvino I 71 C4
Selyatyn UA 11 N19
Sem N 34 B2
Semeljci HR 74 C3
Semenovka, *Chernihiv* UA 7 K23
Semenovka, *Kremenchuk* UA 11 M23
Semič SLO 73 C5
Semide F 59 A5
Semide P 92 A2
Semily CZ 53 C5
Seminara I 106 C2
Semlac RO 75 B5
Semmen-stedt D 51 A6
Šempeter SLO 73 B5
Semriach A 73 A5
Semur-en-Auxois F 69 A4
Sena E 90 B2
Sena de Luna E 88 B1
Senarpont F 58 A2
Sénas F 79 C4
Senčanski Trešnjevac YU 75 C4
Sencelles, *Mallorca* E 97
Senčur SLO 73 B4
Senden, *Bayern* D 61 B6
Senden, *Nordrhein-Westfalen* D 50 B3
Sendenhorst D 50 B3
Sendim P 87 C4
Senec SK 64 B3
Seneffe B 49 C5
Séneghe I 110 C1
Senés E 101 B3
Senez F 79 C5
Senftenberg D 53 B4
Sengwarden D 43 B5
Senica SK 64 B3
Senice na Hané CZ 64 A3
Senigállia I 82 C2
Senirkent TR 16 S22
Sénis I 110 D1
Senise I 104 B3
Senj HR 83 B3
Senlis F 58 A3
Sennan S 40 C2
Sennecey-le-Grand F 69 B4
Sennen GB 28 C2
Senno BY 7 J21
Sènnori I 110 C1
Sennwald CH 71 A4
Sennybridge GB 29 B4
Senohrad SK 65 B5
Senonches F 58 B2
Senones F 60 B2
Senorbì I 110 D2
Senovo SLO 73 B5
Senožeče SLO 73 C4
Senožeti SLO 73 B4
Sens F 59 B4
Sens-de-Bretagne F 57 B4
Senta YU 75 C5
Senterada E 90 A3
Šentilj SLO 73 B5
Šentjernej SLO 73 C5
Šentjur SLO 73 B5
Seoane E 86 B3
Seon CH 70 A3
Sépeaux F 59 C4
Sépey CH 70 B2
Sepino I 103 B4
Sępólno Krajeńskie PL 46 B3
Seppenrade D 50 B3
Seppois F 70 A2
Septeuil F 58 B2
Sepúlveda E 88 C3
Sequals I 72 B2
Sequeros E 93 A4
Seraincourt F 59 A5
Seraing B 49 C6
Seravezza I 81 C4
Sered' SK 64 B3
Seredka RUS 7 G21
Seregélyes H 74 A3
Seregno I 71 C4
Sérent F 56 C3
Serfaus A 71 A5
Sergiyev Posad RUS 7 H26
Seriate I 71 C4
Sérifontaine F 58 A2
Sérignan F 78 C2
Serik TR 16 T22
Serina I 71 C4
Sermaises F 58 B3
Sermaize-les-Bains F 59 B5
Sérmide I 81 B5
Sermoneta I 102 B2
Sernache de Bonjardim P 92 B2
Sernancelhe P 87 D3
Serón E 101 B3
Serón de Najima E 89 C4
Serooskerke NL 49 B4
Seròs E 90 B3
Serpa P 98 B3
Serpukhov RUS 7 J25
Serra de Outes E 86 B2
Serra San Bruno I 106 C3
Serra San Quirico I 82 C2
Serracapriola I 103 B5
Serrada E 88 C2
Serradifalco I 108 B2
Serradilla E 93 B4
Serradilla del Arroyo E 93 A4
Serradilla del Llano E 93 A4
Sérrai GR 15 R18
Serramanna I 110 D1
Serramazzoni I 81 B4
Serranillos E 94 B2
Serrapetrona I 82 C2
Serrastretta I 106 B3
Serravalle, *Piemonte* I 70 C3
Serravalle, *Umbria* I 82 D2
Serravalle di Chienti I 82 C1
Serravalle Scrivia I 80 B2
Serre I 104 B2
Serrejón E 93 B5
Serres F 79 B4
Serrières F 69 C4
Sersale I 106 B3
Sertã P 92 B2
Sertig Dörfli CH 71 B4
Servance F 60 C2
Serverette F 78 B2
Servian F 78 C2
Serviers F 78 B3
Servigliano I 82 C2
Serzedelo P 87 C2
Ses Salines, *Mallorca* E 97
Seseña E 95 B3
Sesimbra P 92 C1
Seskinore GB 19 B4
Sesma E 89 B4
Sessa Aurunca I 103 B3
Sesta Godano I 80 B3
Šestanovac HR 84 C1
Sestao E 89 A4
Sestino I 82 C1
Sesto I 72 B2
Sesto Calende I 70 C3
Sesto Fiorentino I 81 C5
Sesto San Giovanni I 71 C4
Séstola I 81 B4
Sestri Levante I 80 B3
Sestriere I 79 B5
Sestroretsk RUS 3 F22
Sestu I 110 D2
Sesvete HR 73 C6
Setcases E 91 A5
Sète F 78 C2
Setenil E 99 C5
Šetonje YU 85 B6
Setskog N 34 B3
Séttimo Torinese I 80 A1
Settimo Vittone I 70 C2
Settle GB 26 A3
Setúbal P 92 C2
Seubersdort D 62 A2
Seùi I 110 D2
Seùlo I 110 D2
Seurre F 69 B5
Sevel DK 38 C1
Sevenoaks GB 31 C4
Sever do Vouga P 87 D2
Sévérac-le-Château F 78 B2
Severin HR 73 C5
Severomorsk RUS 3 B23
Séveso I 71 C4
Ševětin CZ 63 A5
Sévigny F 59 A5
Sevilla E 99 B5
Sevilla la Nueva E 94 B2
Sevilleja de la Jara E 94 C2
Sevlievo BG 16 Q10
Sevnica SLO 73 B5
Sevojno YU 85 C4
Sevrier F 69 C6
Sevsk RUS 7 K24
Sexdrega S 40 B3
Seyches F 76 B3
Seyda D 52 B2
Seyitgazi TR 16 S22
Seyne F 79 B5
Seynes F 78 B3
Seyssel F 69 C5
Sežana SLO 72 C3
Sézanne F 59 B4
Sezulfe P 87 C3
Sezze I 102 B3
Sfântu Gheorghe RO 11 P19
Sforzacosta I 82 C2
Sgarasta Mhor GB 22 D1
Shaftesbury GB 29 B5
Shaldon GB 29 C4
Shanagolden IRL 20 B2
Shanklin GB 31 D2
Shap GB 26 A3
Sharpness GB 29 B5
Shawbury GB 26 C3
Shchekino RUS 7 J25
Shchigry RUS 7 L25
Shchors UA 11 L22
Sheerness GB 31 C4
Sheffield GB 27 B4
Shefford GB 31 B3
Shenfield GB 31 C4
Shepetivka UA 11 L20
Shepshed GB 27 C4
Shepton Mallet GB 29 B5
Sherborne GB 29 C5
Shercock IRL 19 C5
Sheringham GB 30 B5
Shiel Bridge GB 22 D3
Shieldaig GB 22 D3
Shillelagh IRL 21 B5
Shimsk RUS 7 G22
Shipston-on-Stour GB 29 A6
Shklow BY 7 J22
Shkodër AL 15 Q16
Shoeburyness GB 31 C4
Shoreham-by-Sea GB 31 D3
Shostka UA 7 L23
Shotley Gate GB 31 C5
Shpola UA 11 M22
Shrewsbury GB 26 C3
Shugozero RUS 7 G24
Shumen BG 16 Q20
Siabost GB 22 C2
Sianów PL 46 A2
Siauges-St.-Romain F 78 A2
Šiauliai LT 6 J18
Sibari I 106 B3
Sibbhult S 41 C4
Šibenik HR 83 C4
Sibinj HR 74 C2
Sibiu RO 11 P19
Sibnica YU 85 B5
Sibsey GB 27 B6
Siculiana I 108 B2
Šid YU 85 A4
Siddeburen NL 42 B3
Siderno I 106 C3
Sidhirókastron GR 15 R18
Sidmouth GB 29 C4
Sidzina PL 65 A5
Siebenlehn D 52 B3
Siedlce PL 6 K18
Siedlice PL 46 B1
Siedlinghausen D 51 B4
Siedlisko PL 46 C2
Sieg-hartskirchen A 64 B2
Siegburg D 50 C3
Siegen D 50 C4
Siegenburg D 62 B2
Siegsdorf D 62 C3
Siekierki PL 45 C6
Sielpia PL 55 B5
Siemiany PL 47 B5
Siena I 81 C5
Sieniawka PL 53 C4
Siennica PL 55 A6
Sienno PL 55 B6
Sieradz PL 54 B3
Sieraków, *Śląskie* PL 54 C3
Sieraków, *Wielkopolskie* PL 46 C2
Sierakowice PL 46 A3
Sierck-les-Bains F 60 A2
Sierentz F 60 C3
Sierning A 63 B5
Sierpc PL 47 C5
Sierra de Fuentes E 93 B4
Sierra de Luna E 90 A2
Sierra de Yeguas E 100 B1
Sierre CH 70 B2
Siestrzeń PL 55 A5
Sietamo E 90 A2
Siewierz PL 55 C4
Sigdal N 33 A6
Sigean F 78 C1
Sighetu-Marmatiei RO 11 N18
Sighişoara RO 11 N19
Sigillo I 82 C1
Sigmaringen D 61 B5
Signa I 81 C5
Signes F 79 C4
Signy-l'Abbaye F 59 A5
Signy-le-Petit F 59 A5
Sigogne F 67 C4
Sigtuna S 36 B4
Sigueiro E 86 B2
Sigüenza E 95 A4
Sigües E 90 A1
Sigulda LV 6 H19
Siilinjärvi FIN 3 E20
Sikenica SK 65 B4
Siklós H 74 C3
Sikórz PL 47 C5
Silandro I 71 B5
Silánus I 110 C1
Šilbaš YU 75 C4
Silbersted D 43 A6
Şile TR 16 R21
Siles E 101 A3
Silgueiros P 92 A3
Siliqua I 110 D1
Silistra BG 11 P20
Silivri TR 16 R21
Siljan N 33 B6
Silkeborg DK 39 C2
Silla E 96 B2
Sillamäe EST 7 G20
Sillé-le-Guillaume F 57 B5
Silleda E 86 B2
Sillenstede D 43 B4
Sillerud S 34 B4
Sillian A 72 B2
Silloth GB 25 D4
Silno PL 46 B3
Silnowo PL 46 B2
Silo HR 83 A3
Sils E 91 B5
Šilute LT 6 J17
Silvaplana CH 71 B4
Silvares P 92 A3
Silverdalen S 40 B5
Silvermines IRL 20 B3
Silverstone GB 30 B2
Silverton GB 29 C4
Silves P 98 B2
Silvi Marina I 103 A4
Simandre F 69 B4
Šimanovci YU 85 B5
Simard F 69 B5
Simat de Valldigna E 96 B2
Simav TR 16 S21
Simbach, *Bayern* D 62 B3
Simbach, *Bayern* D 62 B4
Simbário I 106 C3
Simeria RO 11 P18
Simićevo YU 85 B6
Simlångsdalen S 40 C3
Simmerath D 50 C2
Simmerberg D 61 C5
Simmern D 50 D3
Simo FIN 3 D19
Šimonovce SK 65 B6
Simonsbath GB 28 B4
Simonstorp S 37 C3
Simontornya H 74 B3
Simplon CH 70 B3
Simrishamn S 41 D4
Sinaia RO 11 P19
Sinalunga I 81 C5
Sinarcas E 96 B1
Sindal DK 38 B3
Sindelfingen D 61 B5
Sindia I 110 C1
Sines P 98 B2
Sineu, *Mallorca* E 97
Singen D 61 C4
Singleton GB 31 D3
Siniscóla I 110 C2
Sinj HR 83 C5
Sinlabajos E 94 A2
Sinn D 50 C4
Sinnai I 110 D2
Sinnes N 32 C3
Sins CH 70 A3
Sinsheim D 61 A4
Sint Annaland NL 49 B5
Sint Annaparochie NL 42 B2
Sint Athonis NL 50 B1
Sint Nicolaasga NL 42 C2
Sint Oedenrode NL 49 B6

Sintra P 92 C1
Sinzheim D 61 B4
Sinzig D 50 C3
Siófok H 74 B3
Sion CH 70 B2
Sion Mills GB 19 B4
Siorac-en-Périgord F 77 B3
Šipanska Luka HR 84 D2
Šipovo BIH 84 B2
Sira N 32 C3
Siracusa I 109 B4
Siret RO 11 N20
Sirevåg N 32 C2
Sirig YU 75 C4
Sirmione I 71 C5
Sirok H 65 C6
Široké SK 65 B6
Široki Brijeg BIH 84 C2
Sirolo I 82 C2
Siruela E 94 D1
Sisak HR 73 C6
Sisante E 95 C4
Šišljavić HR 73 C5
Sissach CH 70 A2
Sissonne F 59 A4
Sistelo P 87 C2
Sisteron F 79 B4
Sistiana I 72 C3
Sitges E 91 B4
Sitia GR 16 U20
Sittard NL 50 B1
Sittensen D 43 B6
Sittingbourne GB 31 C4
Sitzenroda D 52 B2
Sivac YU 75 C4
Siverić HR 83 C5
Sivrihisar TR 16 S22
Sixt-Fer-à-Cheval F 70 B1
Siziano I 71 C4
Sizun F 56 B1
Sjenica YU 85 C5
Sjöbo S 41 D3
Sjømarken S 40 B2
Sjørring DK 38 C1
Sjötofta S 40 B3
Sjötorp S 35 C5
Sjuntorp S 35 C4
Skadovsk UA 11 N23
Skælskør DK 39 D4
Skærbæk DK 39 D1
Skafså N 33 B5
Skagen DK 38 B3
Skagersvik S 35 C6
Skała PL 55 C4
Skała-Podilska UA 11 M20
Skalat UA 11 M19
Skalbmierz PL 55 C5
Skålevik N 33 C5
Skalica SK 64 B3
Skalité SK 65 A4
Skalná CZ 52 C2
Skals DK 38 C2
Skanderborg DK 39 C2
Skåne-Tranås S 41 D3
Skånes-Fagerhult S 41 C3
Skånevik N 32 B2
Skänninge S 37 C2
Skanör med Falsterbo S 41 D2
Skåpafors S 35 B4
Skępe PL 53 A5
Skara S 35 C5
Skarberget N 2 B15
Skärblacka S 37 C2
Skare N 32 B3
Skåre S 34 B5
Skärhamn S 35 D3
Skarnes N 34 A3
Skarp Salling DK 38 C2
Skärplinge S 36 A4
Skarrild DK 39 D1
Skärstad S 40 B4
Skarszewy PL 47 A4
Skårup DK 39 D3
Skaryszew PL 55 B6
Skarżysko-Kamienna PL 55 B5
Skarzysko Ksiazece PL 55 B5
Skatøy N 33 C6
Skattkärr S 34 B5
Skave DK 39 C1
Skawina PL 65 A5
Skebobruk S 36 B5
Skebokvarn S 37 B3
Skedala S 40 C2
Skedevi S 37 C2
Skedsmokorset N 34 A3
Skee S 35 C3
Skegness GB 27 B6
Skela YU 85 B5
Skelani BIH 85 C4
Skellefteå S 3 D17
Skelleftehamn S 3 D17
Skelmersdale GB 26 B3
Skelmorlie GB 24 C3
Skelund DK 38 C3
Skender Vakuf BIH 84 B2
Skene S 40 B2
Skępe PL 47 C5
Skepplanda S 35 D4
Skeppshult S 40 B3
Skerries IRL 19 C5
Ski N 34 B2
Skibbereen IRL 20 C2
Skien N 33 B6
Skierniewice PL 55 B5
Skillingaryd S 40 B4
Skillinge S 41 D4
Skillingmark S 34 B4
Skinnardal S 37 B5
Skinnskatteberg S 36 B2
Skipness GB 24 C2
Skipsea GB 27 B5
Skipton GB 26 B3
Skiptvet N 34 B3
Skivarp S 41 D3
Skive DK 38 C2
Skjærhalden N 35 B3
Skjeberg N 34 B3
Skjeggedal N 32 A3
Skjeljavik N 32 B2
Skjern DK 39 D1
Skjold N 32 B2
Skjoldastraumen N 32 B2
Skjolden N 2 F10
Skjønhaug N 34 B3
Škocjan SLO 73 C5
Skoczów PL 65 A4
Skodborg DK 39 D2
Škofja Loka SLO 73 B4
Škofljica SLO 73 C4
Skoghall S 34 B5
Skogstorp, *Halland* S 40 C2
Skogstorp, *Södermanland* S 36 B3
Skoki PL 46 C3
Skokloster S 36 B4
Sköldinge S 37 B3
Skole UA 11 M18
Skollenborg N 33 B6
Sköllersta S 36 B2
Skomlin PL 54 B3
Skopje MK 15 Q17
Skoppum N 34 B2
Skórcz PL 47 B4
Skorogoszcz PL 54 C2
Skoroszów PL 54 B2
Skørping DK 38 C2
Skotfoss N 33 B6
Skotniki PL 55 B4
Skotselv N 33 B6
Skotterud N 34 B4
Skottorp S 40 C2
Skovby DK 39 E2
Skövde S 35 C5
Skovsgård DK 38 B2
Skrad HR 73 C4
Skradin HR 83 C4
Skradnik HR 73 C5
Skrdlovice CZ 64 A1
Skrea S 40 C2
Skruv S 40 C5
Skrwilno PL 47 B5
Skrydstrup DK 39 D2
Skućani BIH 84 C1
Skudeneshavn N 32 B2
Skui N 34 B2
Skulsk PL 47 C4
Skultorp S 35 C5
Skultuna S 36 B3
Skuodas LT 6 H17
Skurup S 41 D3
Skuteč CZ 64 A1
Skutskär S 36 A4
Skvyra UA 11 M21
Skwierzyna PL 46 C1
Skýcov SK 65 B4
Skyllberg S 37 C1
Skyttorp S 36 A4
Sládkovičovo SK 64 B3
Slagelse DK 39 D4
Slagharen NL 42 C3
Slaidburn GB 26 B3
Slane IRL 19 C5
Slangerup DK 41 D2
Slano HR 84 D2
Slantsy RUS 7 G21
Slaný CZ 53 C4
Slap SLO 72 B3
Šlapanice CZ 64 A2
Slatina BIH 84 C2
Slatina HR 74 C2
Slatina RO 11 P19
Slatina YU 85 C5
Slatiňany CZ 64 A1
Slatinice CZ 64 A3
Slattum N 34 B2
Slavičin CZ 64 A3
Slavkov CZ 64 B3
Slavkov u Brna CZ 64 A2
Slavkovica YU 85 B5
Slavonice CZ 63 B6
Slavonski Brod HR 74 C3
Slavonski Kobas HR 74 C2
Slavošovce SK 65 B6
Slavskoye RUS 47 A6
Slavuta UA 11 L20
Sława, *Lubuskie* PL 53 B6
Sława, *Zachodnio-Pomorskie* PL 46 B1
Slawharad BY 7 K22
Sławków PL 55 C4
Sławno, *Wielkopolskie* PL 46 C3
Sławno, *Zachodnio-Pomorskie* PL 46 A2
Sławoborze PL 46 B1
Sl'ažany SK 64 B4
Sleaford GB 27 C5
Sledmere GB 27 A5
Sleights GB 27 A5
Slemmestad N 34 B2
Ślesin PL 47 C4
Sliač SK 65 B5
Sliema M 109 C4
Sligo IRL 18 B3
Slite S 37 D5
Slitu N 34 B3
Sliven BG 16 Q20
Śliwice PL 47 B4
Slobozia RO 11 P20
Slochteren NL 42 B3
Slöinge S 40 C2
Słomniki PL 55 C5
Slonim BY 7 K19
Słońsk PL 45 C6
Slottsbron S 34 B5
Slough GB 31 C3
Slovenj Gradec SLO 73 B5
Slovenska Bistrica SLO 73 B5
Slovenská L'upča SK 65 B5
Slovenská-Ves SK 65 A6
Slovenské Darmoty SK 65 B5
Slovenske Konjice SLO 73 B5
Słubice PL 45 C6
Sluderno I 71 B5
Sluis NL 49 B4
Šluknov CZ 53 B4
Slunj HR 83 A4
Słupca PL 54 A2
Słupiec PL 54 C1
Słupsk PL 46 A3
Slutsk BY 7 K20
Smålandsstenar S 40 B3
Smardzewo PL 53 A5
Smarhon BY 7 J20
Smarje SLO 73 B5
Šmarjeta SLO 73 C5
Šmartno SLO 73 B4
Smečno CZ 53 C4
Smedby S 40 C6
Smědec CZ 63 B5
Smederevo YU 85 B5
Smederevska Palanka YU 85 B5
Smedjebacken S 36 A2
Smęgorzów PL 55 C6
Smeland N 33 C5
Smidary CZ 53 C5
Śmigiel PL 54 A1
Smila UA 11 M22
Smilde NL 42 C3
Smiřice CZ 53 C5
Smithfield GB 25 D5
Śmitowo PL 46 B2
Smögen S 35 C3
Smogulec PL 46 B3
Smolenice SK 64 B3
Smolensk RUS 7 J23
Smoljan BG 16 R19
Smolník SK 65 B6
Smuka SLO 73 C4
Smygehamn S 41 D3
Smykow PL 55 B5
Snainton GB 27 A5
Snaith GB 27 B4
Snaptun DK 39 D3
Snarum N 33 A6
Snedsted DK 38 C1
Sneek NL 42 B2
Sneem IRL 20 C2
Snejbjerg DK 39 C1
Snihurivka UA 11 N23
Šnjegotina BIH 84 B2
Snøde DK 39 D3
Snogebaek DK 41 D5
Snyatyn UA 11 M19
Soave I 71 C6
Sober E 86 B3
Sobernheim D 60 A3
Soběslav CZ 63 A5
Sobienie Jeziory PL 55 B6
Sobota, *Dolnośląskie* PL 53 B5
Sobota, *Łódzkie* PL 55 A4
Sobotište SK 64 B3
Sobotka CZ 53 C5
Sobótka, *Dolnośląskie* PL 54 C1
Sobótka, *Wielkopolskie* PL 54 B2
Sobra HR 84 D2
Sobrado, *Coruña* E 86 A2
Sobrado, *Lugo* E 86 B3
Sobral da Adica P 98 A3
Sobral de Monte Argraço P 92 C1
Sobreira Formosa P 92 B3
Søby DK 39 E3
Soca SLO 72 B3
Sočanica YU 85 C5
Sochaczew PL 55 A5
Socol RO 85 B6
Socovos E 101 A4
Socuéllamos E 95 C4
Sodankylä FIN 3 C20
Soderåkra S 40 C6
Söderbärke S 36 A2
Söderby-Karl S 36 B5
Söderfors S 36 A4
Söderhamn S 2 F15
Söderköping S 37 C3
Södertälje S 36 B4
Södingberg A 73 A5
Södra Finnö S 37 C3
Södra Ny S 34 B5
Södra Råda S 35 B6
Södra Sandby S 41 D3
Södra Vi S 40 B5
Sodražica SLO 73 C4
Sodupe E 89 A3
Soengas P 87 C2
Soest D 50 B4
Soest NL 49 A6
Sofiya BG 15 Q18
Şofronea RO 75 B6
Sögel D 43 C4
Sogliano al Rubicone I 82 B1
Sogndalsfjøra N 2 F10
Søgne N 33 C4
Söğüt TR 16 R22
Soham GB 30 B4
Sohland D 53 B4
Sohren D 60 A3
Soignies B 49 C5
Soissons F 59 A4
Söjtör H 74 B1
Sokal' UA 11 L19
Söke TR 16 T20
Sokna N 33 A6
Sokndal N 32 C3
Soko BIH 84 B3
Sokolac BIH 84 C3
Sokółka PL 6 K18
Sokolov CZ 52 C2
Sokołów Podlaski PL 6 K18
Sokołowo PL 54 A3
Sola N 32 C2
Solana de los Barros E 93 C4
Solana del Pino E 100 A1
Solares E 88 A3
Solarino I 109 B4
Solarussa I 110 D1
Solas GB 22 D1
Solber-gelva N 34 B2
Solberga S 40 B4
Solčany SK 64 B4
Solčava SLO 73 B4
Solda I 71 B5
Sölden A 71 B6
Solec Kujawski PL 47 B4
Solec n. Wisła PL 55 B6
Soleils F 79 C5
Solenzara F 110 B2
Solera E 100 B2
Solesmes F 49 C4
Soleto I 105 B5
Solgne F 60 B2
Solheimsvik N 32 B3
Solignac F 67 C5
Solihull GB 27 C4
Solin HR 83 C5
Solingen D 50 B3
Solivella E 91 B4
Solkan SLO 72 C3
Söll A 72 A2
Sollana E 96 B2
Sollebrunn S 35 C4
Sollefteå S 2 E15
Sollen-tuna S 36 B4
Sollenau A 64 C2
Sóller, *Mallorca* E 97
Sollested DK 39 E4
Solliès-Pont F 79 C5
Sollihøgda N 34 B2
Solnechnogorsk RUS 7 H25
Solnice CZ 54 C1
Solofra I 103 C4
Solomiac F 77 C3
Solopaca I 103 B4
Solórzano E 89 A3
Solothurn CH 70 A2
Solre-le-Château F 49 C5
Solsona E 91 B4
Solt H 75 B4
Soltau D 44 C1
Soltsy RUS 7 G22
Soltszentimre H 75 B4
Soltvadkert H 75 B4
Solumsmoen N 33 B6
Solva GB 28 B2
Sölvesborg S 41 C4
Solymár H 65 C4
Soma TR 16 S20
Somain F 49 C4
Somberek H 74 B3
Sombernon F 69 A4
Sombor YU 75 C4
Sombreffe B 49 C5
Someren NL 50 B1
Somero FIN 3 F18
Somersham GB 30 B3
Somerton GB 29 B5
Sominy PL 46 A3
Somma Lombardo I 70 C3
Sommariva del Bosco I 80 B1
Sommatino I 108 B2
Somme-Tourbe F 59 A5
Sommeilles F 59 B5
Sommen S 37 C1
Sommepy-Tahure F 59 A5
Sömmerda D 52 B1
Sommerfeld D 45 C5
Sommersted DK 39 D2
Sommesous F 59 B5
Sommières F 78 C3
Sommières-du-Clain F 67 B5
Somo E 88 A3
Somogyfajsz H 74 B2
Somogyjád H 74 B2
Somogysámson H 74 B2
Somogysárd H 74 B2
Somogyszil H 74 B3
Somogyszob H 74 B2
Somogyvár H 74 B2
Somontin E 101 B3
Somosiero E 95 A3
Somoskőújfalu H 65 B5
Sompolno PL 47 C4
Sompuis F 59 B5
Son N 34 B2
Son NL 49 B6
Son Bou, *Menorca* E 97
Son Servera, *Mallorca* E 97
Sonceboz CH 70 A2
Soncillo E 88 B3
Soncino I 71 C4
Sondalo I 71 B5
Sondeled N 33 C6
Sønder Bjert DK 39 D2
Sønder Felding DK 39 D1
Sønder Hygum DK 39 D1
Sønder Omme DK 39 D1
Sønderborg DK 39 E2
Sønderho DK 39 D1
Sondershausen D 51 B6
Sondersø DK 39 D3
Søndervig DK 38 C1
Søndre Enningdal Kappel N 35 C3
Sondrio I 71 B4
Soneja E 96 B2
Songe N 33 C6
Songeons F 58 A2
Sonkovo RUS 7 H25
Sönnarslöv S 41 D4
Sonneberg D 52 C1
Sonnefeld D 52 C1
Sonnewalde D 52 B3
Sonnino I 102 B3
Sonogno CH 70 B3
Sonsbeck D 50 B2
Sonseca E 94 C3
Sonstorp S 37 C2
Sonta YU 75 C4
Sontheim D 61 B6
Sonthofen D 71 A5
Sontra D 51 B5
Sopelana E 89 A4
Sopje HR 74 C2
Šoporňa SK 64 B3
Sopot PL 47 A4
Sopot YU 85 B5
Sopron H 64 C2
Šor YU 85 B4
Sora I 103 B3
Soragna I 81 B4
Sorano I 102 A1
Sorbara I 81 B5
Sorbas E 101 B3
Sórbolo I 81 B4
Sordal N 33 C4
Sordale GB 23 C5
Sore F 76 B2
Sörenberg CH 70 B3
Soresina I 71 C4
Sorèze F 77 C5
Sorges F 67 C5
Sórgono I 110 C2
Sorgues F 78 B3
Soria E 89 C4
Soriano Cálabro I 106 C3
Soriano nel Cimino I 102 A2
Sorihuela del Guadalimar E 100 A2
Sorisdale GB 24 B1
Sormás H 74 B1
Sorø DK 39 D4
Soroca MD 11 M21
Sorrento I 103 C4
Sorsele S 2 D15
Sorso I 110 C1
Sort E 91 A4
Sortavala RUS 3 F22
Sortino I 109 B4
Sortland N 2 B14
Sørum N 34 A2
Sørumsand N 34 B3
Sorunda S 37 B4
Sörup D 43 A6
Sorvik S 36 A2
Sos F 76 B3
Sos del Rey Católico E 90 A1
Sösdala S 41 C3
Sošice HR 73 C5
Sośnica PL 46 B2
Sośnicowice PL 54 C3
Sośno PL 46 B3
Sosnovyy Bor RUS 7 G21
Sosnowiec PL 55 C4
Sospel F 80 C1
Šoštanj SLO 73 B5
Sotillo de Adrada E 94 B2
Sotillo de la Ribera E 88 C3
Sotin HR 75 C4
Sotkamo FIN 3 D21
Soto de la Marina E 88 A3
Soto de los Infantes E 86 A4
Soto de Real E 94 B3
Soto de Ribera E 88 A1
Soto del Barco E 86 A4
Soto y Amío E 88 B1
Sotobañado y Priorato E 88 B2
Sotoserrano E 93 A4
Sotresgudo E 88 B2
Sotrondio E 88 A1
Sotta F 110 B2
Sottomarina I 72 C2
Sottrum D 43 B6
Sotuelamos E 95 C4
Souain F 59 A5
Soual F 77 C5
Soucy F 59 B4
Soudron F 59 B5
Souesmes F 68 A2
Soufflenheim F 60 B3
Souflion GR 16 R20
Souillac F 77 B4
Souilly F 59 A6
Soulac-sur-Mer F 66 C3
Soulaines-Dhuys F 59 B5
Soultz-Haut-Rhin F 60 C3
Soultz-sous-Forêts F 60 B3
Soumagne B 50 C1
Soumoulou F 76 C2
Souppes-sur-Loing F 58 B3
Souprosse F 76 C2
Sourdeval F 57 B5
Soure P 92 A2
Sournia F 77 D5
Souro Pires P 87 D3
Sours F 58 B2
Sousceyrac F 77 B5
Sousel P 92 C3
Soustons F 76 C1
Soutelo de Montes E 86 B2
South Brent GB 28 C4
South Cave GB 27 B5
South Hayling GB 31 D3
South Molton GB 28 B4
South Ockendon GB 31 C4
South Petherton GB 29 C5
South Shields GB 25 D6
South Tawton GB 28 C4
South Woodham Ferrers GB 31 C4
Southam GB 30 B2
Southampton GB 31 D2
Southborough GB 31 C4
Southend GB 24 C2
Southend-on-Sea GB 31 C4
Southport GB 26 B2
Southwell GB 27 B5
Southwold GB 30 B5
Souto P 92 A3
Souto da Carpalhosa P 92 B2
Soutochao E 87 C3
Souvigny F 68 B3
Souzay-Champigny F 67 A4
Soverato I 106 C3
Soveria Mannelli I 106 B3
Sövestad S 41 D3
Sovetsk RUS 6 J17
Sovići BIH 84 C2
Sovicille I 81 C5
Sowerby GB 27 A4
Soyaux F 67 C5
Søyland N 32 C2
Spa B 50 C1
Spadafora I 109 A4
Spaichingen D 61 B4
Spakenburg NL 49 A6
Spalding GB 30 B3
Spálené Poříčí CZ 63 A4
Spalt D 62 A1
Spangenberg D 51 B5
Spangereid N 33 C4
Spantekow D 45 B5
Sparanise I 103 B4
Sparkær DK 38 C2
Sparkford GB 29 B5
Sparreholm S 37 B3
Spartà I 109 A4
Spárti GR 15 T18
Spas-Demensk RUS 7 J24
Spean Bridge GB 24 B3
Speicher D 60 A2
Speichersdorf D 62 A2
Speke GB 26 B3
Spello I 82 D1
Spenge D 51 A4
Spennymoor GB 25 D6
Spentrup DK 38 C3
Sperenberg D 52 A3
Sperlinga I 109 B3
Sperlonga I 103 B3
Spetalen N 34 B2
Speyer D 61 A4
Spezzano Albanese I 106 B3
Spezzano della Sila I 106 B3
Spiddle IRL 20 A2
Spiegelau D 63 B4
Spiekeroog D 43 B4
Spiez CH 70 B2
Spigno Monferrato I 80 B2
Spijk NL 42 B3
Spijkenisse NL 49 B5
Spilamberto I 81 B5
Spilimbergo I 72 B2
Spilsby GB 27 B6
Spinazzola I 104 B3
Spincourt F 60 A1
Spind N 32 C3
Spindleruv-Mlyn CZ 53 C5
Spinoso I 104 B2
Špišić Bukovica HR 74 C2
Spišská Belá SK 65 A6
Spišská Nová Ves SK 65 B6
Spišská Stará Ves SK 65 A6
Spišské-Hanušovce SK 65 A6
Spišské Podhradie SK 65 B6
Spišské Vlachy SK 65 B6
Spišský-Štvrtok SK 65 B6
Spital A 63 C5
Spital am Semmering A 63 C6
Spittal an der Drau A 72 B3
Spittle of Glenshee GB 25 B4
Spitz A 63 B6
Spjærøy N 35 B2
Spjald DK 39 C1
Spjelkavik N 2 E10
Spjutsbygd S 41 C5
Split HR 83 C5
Splügen CH 71 B4
Spodsbjerg DK 39 E3
Spofforth GB 27 B4
Spoleto I 82 D1
Spoltore I 103 A4
Spondigna I 71 B5
Sponvika N 35 B3
Spornitz D 44 B3
Spotorno I 80 B2
Spraitbach D 61 B5
Sprakensehl D 44 C2
Spręcowo PL 47 B6
Spremberg D 53 B4
Spresiano I 72 C2
Sprimont B 49 C6
Springe D 51 A5
Sproatley GB 27 B5
Spydeberg N 34 B3
Spytkowice PL 65 A5
Squillace I 106 C3
Squinzano I 105 B5
Sračinec HR 73 B6
Srbac BIH 84 A2
Srbica YU 85 D5
Srbobran YU 75 C4
Srebrenica BIH 85 B4
Srebrenik BIH 84 B3
Središče SLO 73 B6
Śrem PL 54 A2
Sremska Mitrovica YU 85 B4
Sremski Karlovci YU 75 C4
Srní CZ 63 A4
Srnice Gornje BIH 84 B3
Srock PL 55 B4
Środa Śląska PL 54 B1
Środa Wielkopolski PL 54 A2
Srpska Crnja YU 75 C5
Srpski Itebej YU 75 C5
Srpski Miletić YU 75 C4
St. Abb's GB 25 C5
St. Agnes GB 28 C2
St. Albans GB 31 C3
St. Andrews GB 25 B5
St. Asaph GB 26 B2
St. Athan GB 29 B4
St. Austell GB 28 C3
St. Bees GB 26 A2
St. Blazey GB 28 C3
St. Clears GB 28 B3
St. Columb Major GB 28 C3
St. David'S GB 28 B2
St. Dogmaels GB 28 A3
St. Enoder GB 28 C3
St. Fillans GB 24 B3
St. Harmon GB 29 A4
St. Helens GB 26 B3
St. Issey GB 28 C3
St. Ives, *Cambridgeshire* GB 30 B3
St. Ives, *Cornwall* GB 28 C2
St. Johnstown IRL 19 B4
St. Just GB 28 C2
St. Keverne GB 28 C2
St. Leonards GB 31 D4
St. Margaret's-at-Cliffe GB 31 C5
St. Margaret's Hope GB 23 C6
St. Mary's GB 23 C6
St. Mawes GB 28 C2
St. Monance GB 25 B5
St. Neots GB 30 B3
St. Teath GB 28 C3
Staatz A 64 B2
Staberdorf D 44 A3
Stabroek B 49 B5
Stachy CZ 63 A4
Stade D 43 B6
Staden B 49 C4
Stadl an der Mur A 72 A3
Stadskanaal NL 42 C3
Stadtallendorf D 51 C5
Stadthagen D 51 A5
Stadtilm D 52 C1
Stadtkyll D 50 C2
Stadtlauringen D 51 C6
Stadtlengsfeld D 51 C6
Stadtlohn D 50 B2
Stadtoldendorf D 51 B5
Stadtroda D 52 C1
Stadtsteinach D 52 C1
Stäfa CH 70 A3
Staffanstorp S 41 D3
Staffelstein D 51 C6
Staffin GB 22 D2
Stafford GB 26 C3
Stainach A 73 A4
Staindrop GB 27 A4
Staines GB 31 C3
Stainville F 59 B6
Stainz A 73 B5
Staithes GB 27 A5
Staiti I 106 D3
Stäket S 36 B4
Stalać YU 85 C6
Štalcerji SLO 73 C4
Stalden CH 70 B2
Stalham GB 30 B5
Stallarholmen S 36 B4
Ställberg S 36 B1
Ställdalen S 36 B1
Stallhofen A 73 A5
Stalowa Wola PL 11 L18
Stamford GB 30 B3
Stamford Bridge GB 27 B5
Stams A 71 A5
Stamsried D 62 A3
Stamsund N 2 B13
Stanford le Hope GB 31 C4
Stange N 2 F12
Stanghella I 72 C1
Stanhope GB 25 D5
Stanišić YU 75 C4
Stanisławów PL 55 A6
Staňkov CZ 62 A4
Stankovci HR 83 C4
Stanley GB 25 D6
Stans CH 70 B3
Stansted Mountfitchet GB 31 C4
Stanzach A 71 A5
Stapar YU 75 C4
Staphorst NL 42 C3
Staplehurst GB 31 C4
Stąporków PL 55 B5
Stara Baška HR 83 B3
Stara Fužina SLO 72 B3
Stara Kamienica PL 53 C5
Stara Kiszewa PL 47 B4
Stará L'ubovňa SK 65 A6
Stara Moravica YU 75 C4
Stara Novalja HR 83 B3
Stara Pazova YU 85 B5
Stará Turá SK 64 B3
Stara Zagora BG 16 Q19
Starachowice PL 55 B6
Staraya Russa RUS 7 H22
Stärbsnäs S 36 B6
Starčevo YU 85 B5
Stare Dłutowo PL 47 B5
Staré Hamry CZ 65 A4
Stare Jabłonki PL 47 B6
Staré Město CZ 64 A3
Stare Pole PL 47 A5
Stare Sedlo CZ 63 A5
Stare Strącze PL 53 B6
Stargard Szczeciński PL 45 B7
Stari Banovci YU 85 B5
Stari Gradac HR 74 C2
Stari Jankovci HR 75 C3
Stari Majdan BIH 83 B5
Stari-Mikanovci HR 74 C3
Starigrad, *Ličko-Senjska* HR 83 B3
Starigrad, *Splitsko-Dalmatinska* HR 83 C5
Starigrad-Paklenica HR 83 B4
Staritsa RUS 7 H24
Starkenbach A 71 A5
Starnberg D 62 C2
Staro Petrovo Selo HR 74 C2
Staro Selo HR 73 C5
Staro Selo YU 85 B6
Starodub RUS 7 K23
Starogard PL 46 B1
Starogard Gdański PL 47 B4
Starokonstyantyniv UA 11 M20
Stary Brzozów PL 55 A5
Stary Dzierzgoń PL 47 B5
Starý Hrozenkov CZ 64 B3
Stary Jaroslaw PL 46 A2
Stary Plzenec CZ 63 A4
Stary Sącz PL 65 A6
Starý Smokovec SK 65 A6
Staryy Chartoriysk UA 11 L19
Staškov SK 65 A4
Stassfurt D 52 B1
Staszów PL 55 C6
Stathelle N 33 B6
Staufen D 60 C3
Staunton GB 29 B5
Štavalj YU 85 C5
Stavanger N 32 C2
Stavby S 36 A5
Staveley GB 27 B4
Stavelot B 50 C1
Stavenisse NL 49 B5
Stavern N 33 C7
Stavnäs S 34 B4
Stavoren NL 42 C2
Stavsnäs S 36 B5
Stawiszyn PL 54 B3
Steane N 33 B5
Stechelberg CH 70 B2
Štěchovice CZ 63 A5
Stechow D 44 C4
Steckborn CH 61 C4
Stede Broek NL 42 C2
Steeg A 71 A5
Steenbergen NL 49 B5
Steenvoorde F 48 C3
Steenwijk NL 42 C3
Štefanje HR 74 C1
Steffisburg CH 70 B2
Stegaurach D 62 A1
Stege DK 41 E2
Stegelitz D 45 B5
Stegersbach A 73 A6
Stegna PL 47 A5
Steimbke D 43 C6
Stein GB 22 D2
Stein an Rhein CH 61 C4
Steinach A 71 A6
Steinach, *Baden-Württemberg* D 61 B4
Steinach, *Bayern* D 51 C6
Steinach, *Thüringen* D 52 C1
Steinau, *Bayern* D 51 C5
Steinau, *Niedersachsen* D 43 B5
Steinbeck D 45 C5
Steinberg am Rofan A 72 A1
Steindorf A 73 B4
Steinen D 60 C3
Steinfeld A 72 B3
Steinfeld D 43 C5
Steinfurt D 50 A3
Steingaden D 62 C1
Steinhagen D 51 A4
Steinheid D 52 C1
Steinheim, *Bayern* D 61 B6
Steinheim, *Nordrhein-Westfalen* D 51 B5
Steinhöfel D 45 C6
Steinhorst D 44 C2
Steinigtwolmsdorf D 53 B4
Steinkjer N 2 D12
Steinsholt N 33 B6
Stekene B 49 B5
Stelle D 44 B2
Stellendam NL 49 B5
Stenay F 59 A6
Stenberga S 40 B5
Stendal D 44 C3
Stenhammar S 35 C5
Stenhamra S 36 B4
Stenhousemuir GB 25 B4
Stenløse DK 41 D2
Stensätra S 36 A3
Stenstorp S 35 C5
Stenstrup DK 39 D3
Stenungsund S 35 C3
Štěpánov CZ 64 A3
Stephanskirchen D 62 C3
Stepnica PL 45 B6
Stepojevac YU 85 B5
Sterbfritz D 51 C5
Sternberg D 44 B3
Šternberk CZ 64 A3
Sterup D 44 A1
Stęszew PL 54 A1
Štěti CZ 53 C4
Stevenage GB 31 C3
Stewarton GB 24 C3
Steyerburg D 43 C6
Steyning GB 31 D3
Steyr A 63 B5
Stężyca PL 46 A3
Stezzano I 71 C4
Stia I 81 C5
Stibb Cross GB 28 C3
Sticciano Scalo I 81 D5
Stidsvig S 41 C3
Stiens NL 42 B2
Stige DK 39 D3
Stigen S 35 C4
Stigliano I 104 B3
Stigtomta S 37 C3
Stillington GB 27 A4
Stilo I 106 C3
Stintino I 110 C1
Stio I 103 C5
Štip MK 15 R18
Stirling GB 25 B4
Štítnik SK 65 B6
Štíty CZ 64 A2
Stjärnhov S 37 B4
Stjärnsund S 36 A3
Stjørdalshalsen N 2 E12
Stobnica PL 55 B4
Stobno PL 46 B2
Stobreč HR 83 C5
Stochov CZ 53 C3
Stockach D 61 C5
Stockalp CH 70 B3
Stockaryd S 40 B4
Stockbridge GB 31 C2
Stockerau A 64 B2

Stockheim D 52 C1
Stockholm S 36 B5
Stockport GB 26 B3
Stocksbridge GB 27 B4
Stockton-on-Tees GB 27 A4
Stod CZ 62 A4
Stoer GB 22 C3
Stoholm DK 38 C2
Stoke Ferry GB 30 B4
Stoke Fleming GB 29 C4
Stoke Mandeville GB 31 C3
Stoke-on-Trent GB 26 B3
Stokesley GB 27 A4
Stokke N 34 B2
Stokkemarke DK 39 E4
Stokken N 33 C5
Stokmarknes N 2 B14
Štoky CZ 63 A6
Stolac BIH 84 C2
Stolberg D 50 C2
Stolin BY 11 L20
Stollberg D 52 C2
Stöllet S 34 A5
Stollhamm D 43 B5
Stolno PL 47 B4
Stolpen D 53 B4
Stolzenau D 43 C6
Ston HR 84 D2
Stonařov CZ 63 A6
Stone GB 26 C3
Stonehaven GB 25 B5
Stonehouse GB 25 C4
Stony Stratford GB 30 B3
Stopanja YU 85 C6
Stopnica PL 55 C5
Storå S 36 B2
Store GB 23 B6
Store Damme DK 41 E2
Store Heddinge DK 41 D2
Store Herrestad S 41 D3
Store Levene S 35 C4
Store Skedvi S 36 A2
Store Vika S 37 C4
Storebø N 32 A2
Storebro S 40 B5
Støren N 2 E12
Storfjord N 3 B17
Storfors S 34 B6
Storkow, *Brandenburg* D 53 A3
Storkow, *Mecklenburg-Vorpommern* D 45 B6
Storlien S 2 E13
Stornara I 104 A2
Stornoway GB 22 C2
Storo I 71 C5
Storozhynets UA 11 M19
Storrington GB 31 D3
Storuman S 2 D15
Storvik S 36 A3
Storvreta S 36 B4
Štós SK 65 B6
Stössen D 52 B1
Stotel D 43 B5
Stötten D 62 C1
Stotternheim D 52 B1
Stourbridge GB 26 C3
Stourport-on-Severn GB 29 A5
Støvring DK 38 C2
Stow GB 25 C5
Stow-on-the-Wold GB 29 B6
Stowbtsy BY 7 K20
Stowmarket GB 30 B5
Straach D 52 B2
Strabane GB 19 B4
Strachan GB 23 D6
Strachur GB 24 B2
Strackholt D 43 B4
Stradbally IRL 20 B1
Stradella I 80 A3
Straelen D 50 B2
Stragari YU 85 B5
Strakonice CZ 63 A4
Strålsnäs S 37 C2
Stralsund D 45 A5
Stranda, *Møre og Romsdal* N 2 E10
Stranda, *Nord-Trøndelag* N 2 E12
Strandby DK 38 B3
Strandebarm N 32 A3
Strandhill IRL 18 B3
Strandlykkja N 34 A3
Strandvik N 32 A2
Strangford GB 19 B6
Strängnäs S 36 B4
Strångsjö S 37 C3
Strání CZ 64 B3
Stranice SLO 73 B5
Stranorlar IRL 19 B4
Stranraer GB 24 D2
Strasatti I 108 B1
Strasbourg F 60 B3
Strasburg D 45 B5
Strašice CZ 63 A4
Strass im Steiermark A 73 B5
Stråssa S 36 B2
Strassburg A 73 B4
Strasskirchen D 62 B3
Strasswalchen A 63 C4
Stratford-upon-Avon GB 29 A6
Strathaven GB 24 C3
Strathdon GB 23 D5
Strathkanaird GB 22 D3
Strathpeffer GB 23 D4
Strathy GB 23 C5
Strathyre GB 24 B3
Stratinska BIH 84 B1
Stratton GB 28 C3
Straubing D 62 B3
Straulas I 110 C2
Straupitz D 53 B4
Strausberg D 45 C5
Straussfurt D 51 B7
Strawczyn PL 55 C5
Straž nad Nezárkou CZ 63 A5
Straža SLO 73 C5
Straža YU 85 B6
Strážnice CZ 64 B3
Strážný CZ 63 B4
Štrbské Pleso SK 65 A6
Strečno SK 65 A4
Street GB 29 B5
Strehla D 52 B3
Strekov SK 65 C4
Strem A 73 A6
Stremska-Rača YU 85 B4
Strengberg A 63 B5
Stresa I 70 C3
Streuldorf D 51 C6
Strib DK 39 D2
Striberg S 36 B1
Stříbro CZ 62 A3
Strichen GB 23 D6
Strigno I 71 B6
Štrigova HR 73 B6
Strijen NL 49 B5
Strimasund S 2 C14
Strizivojna HR 74 C3
Strmica HR 83 B5
Strmilov CZ 63 A6
Ströhen D 43 C5
Strokestown IRL 18 C3
Stromberg, *Nordrhein-Westfalen* D 50 B4
Stromberg, *Rheinland-Pfalz* D 60 A3
Stromeferry GB 22 D3
Stromness GB 23 C5
Strömsberg S 36 A4
Strömsfors S 37 C3
Strömsnäsbruk S 40 C3
Strömstad S 35 C3
Strömsund, *Jämtland* S 2 E14
Strömsund, *Västerbotten* S 2 D15
Stronachlachar GB 24 B3
Strongoli I 107 B4
Stronie Śląskie PL 54 C1
Strontian GB 24 B2
Stroppiana I 70 C3
Stroud GB 29 B5
Stroża PL 65 A5
Strücklingen D 43 B4
Struer DK 38 C1
Strugi Krasnyye RUS 7 G21
Strumica MK 15 R18
Strumien PL 65 A4
Struy GB 22 D4
Stružec HR 74 C1
Stryków PL 55 B4
Stryn N 2 F10
Stryy UA 11 M18
Strzałkowo PL 54 A2
Strzegocin PL 47 C6
Strzegom PL 53 C6
Strzegowo PL 47 C6
Strzelce PL 55 A4
Strzelce Krajeńskie PL 46 C1
Strzelce Kurowo PL 46 C1
Strzelce Opolskie PL 54 C3
Strzelin PL 54 C2
Strzelno PL 47 C4
Strzepcz PL 47 A4
Strzybnica PL 54 C3
Strzygi PL 47 B5
Stubal YU 85 C5
Stubbekøbing DK 39 E5
Stuben A 71 A5
Stubenberg A 73 A5
Stubline YU 85 B5
Studená CZ 63 A6
Studenci HR 84 C2
Studenica YU 85 C5
Studenka CZ 64 A4
Studenzen A 73 A5
Studienka SK 64 B3
Studland GB 29 C6
Studley GB 29 A6
Studzienice PL 46 A3
Stuer D 44 B4
Stuhr D 43 B5
Stukenbrock D 51 B4
Stülpe D 52 A3
Stupava SK 64 B3
Stupnik HR 73 C5
Stupsk PL 47 B6
Sturkö S 41 C5
Sturminster Newton GB 29 C5
Štúrovo SK 65 C4
Sturton GB 27 B5
Stuttgart D 61 B5
Stvolny CZ 52 C3
Styri N 34 A3
Stysö S 38 B4
Suances E 88 A2
Subbiano I 81 C5
Subiaco I 102 B3
Subotica YU 75 B4
Subotište YU 85 B4
Sučany SK 65 A4
Suceava RO 11 N20
Sucha-Beskidzka PL 65 A5
Suchacz PL 47 A5
Suchań PL 45 B7
Suchdol nad Lužnice CZ 63 B5
Suchedniów PL 55 B5
Suchorze PL 46 A3
Suchteln D 50 B2
Sucina E 101 B5
Suckow D 44 B3
Sućuraj HR 84 C2
Sudbury GB 30 B4
Süderbrarup D 44 A1
Süderlügum D 39 E1
Sudoměřice u Bechyně CZ 63 A5
Sudovec HR 73 B6
Sudzha RUS 7 L24
Sueca E 96 B2
Suelli I 110 D2
Sugenheim D 61 A6
Sugères F 68 C3
Sugny B 59 A5
Suhl D 51 C6
Suhlendorf D 44 C2
Suho Polje BIH 85 B4
Suhopolje HR 74 C2
Şuhut TR 16 S22
Šuica BIH 84 C2
Suippes F 59 A5
Sukhinichi RUS 7 J24
Sukošan HR 83 B4
Sükösd H 75 B3
Suków PL 55 C5
Šul'a SK 65 B5
Suldalsosen N 32 B3
Suldrup DK 38 C2
Sulechów PL 53 A5
Sulęcin PL 45 C7
Sulęczyno PL 46 A3
Sulejów PL 55 B4
Sulejówek PL 55 A6
Sulgen CH 71 A4
Sulibórz PL 46 B1
Sulina RO 11 P21
Sulingen D 43 C5
Suliszewo PL 46 B1
Sulitjelma N 2 C15
Sułkowice PL 65 A5
Sully-sur-Loire F 58 C3
Sulmierzyce, *Łódzkie* PL 55 B4
Sulmierzyce, *Wielkopolskie* PL 54 B2
Sulmona I 103 A3
Sułoszowa PL 55 C4
Sulów PL 54 B2
Sulsdorf D 44 A3
Sülysáp H 75 A4
Sülz D 61 B4
Sulzbach, *Baden-Württemberg* D 61 A5
Sulzbach, *Baden-Württemberg* D 61 B5
Sulzbach, *Bayern* D 61 A5
Sulzbach, *Saarland* D 60 A3
Sulzbach-Rosenberg D 62 A2
Sülze D 44 C2
Sulzfeld D 51 C6
Sumartin HR 84 C1
Sumburgh GB 22 B7
Sümeg H 74 B2
Sumiswald CH 70 A2
Šumná CZ 64 B1
Šumperk CZ 64 A2
Šumvald CZ 64 A3
Sumy UA 7 L24
Sunbilla E 76 C1
Sünching D 62 B3
Sund S 34 D3
Sundby DK 38 C1
Sunde N 32 B2
Sunde bru N 33 C6
Sunderland GB 25 D6
Sundern D 50 B4
Sundhultsbrunn S 37 D1
Sunds DK 39 C2
Sundsvall S 2 E15
Suni I 110 C1
Sunja HR 74 C1
Sunnansjö S 36 A1
Sunndalsøra N 2 E11
Sunne S 34 B5
Sunnemo S 34 B5
Sunnersberg S 35 C5
Suomussalmi FIN 3 D21
Suoyarvi RUS 3 E23
Super Sauze F 79 B5
Supetar HR 83 C5
Supetarska Draga HR 83 B3
Supino I 102 B3
Šuplja Stijena YU 84 C4
Surahammar S 36 B3
Šurany SK 64 B4
Surazh BY 7 J22
Surazh RUS 7 K23
Surbo I 105 B5
Surčin YU 85 B5
Surgères F 67 B4
Surhuisterveen NL 42 B3
Súria E 91 B4
Surin F 67 B5
Sursee CH 70 A3
Surte S 35 D4
Surwold D 43 C4
Sury-le-Comtal F 69 C4
Susa I 70 C2
Šušara YU 85 B6
Susch CH 71 B5
Susegana I 72 C2
Süsel D 44 A2
Sušice CZ 63 A4
Šušnjevica HR 73 C4
Sussen D 61 B5
Susurluk TR 16 S21
Susz PL 47 B5
Sütçüler TR 16 T22
Sutivan HR 83 C5
Sutjeska YU 75 C5
Sutri I 102 A2
Sutton GB 31 C3
Sutton Coldfield GB 27 C4
Sutton-in-Ashfield GB 27 B4
Sutton-on-Sea GB 27 B6
Sutton-on-Trent GB 27 B5
Sutton Scotney GB 31 C2
Sutton Valence GB 31 C4
Suvaja BIH 83 B5
Suvereto I 81 C4
Suvorov RUS 7 J25
Suwałki PL 6 J18
Suze-la-Rousse F 78 B3
Suzzara I 81 B4
Svalöv S 41 D3
Svanberga S 36 B5
Svaneke DK 41 D5
Svanesund S 35 C3
Svängsta S 41 C4
Svanskog S 34 B4
Svappavaara S 3 C17
Svarstad N 33 B6
Svartå, *Örebro* S 36 B1
Svärta, *Södermanland* S 37 C4
Svärtinge S 37 C3
Svätý Jur SK 64 B3
Svätý Peter SK 64 C4
Svedala S 41 D3
Sveg S 2 E14
Sveindal N 33 C4
Sveio N 32 B2
Svejbæk DK 39 C2
Svelvik N 34 B2
Svendborg DK 39 D3
Svene N 33 B6
Svenljunga S 40 B3
Svennevad S 37 B2
Svenstrup DK 38 C2
Švermov CZ 53 C4
Sveti Ivan Zabno HR 74 C1
Sveti Ivan Zelina HR 73 C6
Sveti Rok HR 83 B4
Světlá nad Sázavou CZ 63 A6
Svetlyy RUS 47 A6
Svetvinčenat HR 82 A2
Švica HR 83 B4
Svidník SK 10 M17
Švihov CZ 63 A4
Svilajnac YU 85 B6
Svilengrad BG 16 R20
Svindal N 34 B3
Svinná SK 64 B4
Svinninge DK 39 D4
Svinninge S 36 B5
Svishtov BG 16 Q19
Svislach BY 6 K19
Svit SK 65 A6
Svitavy CZ 64 A2
Svitlovodsk UA 11 M23
Svodin SK 65 C4
Svolvær N 2 B14
Svortland N 32 B2
Svratka CZ 64 A2
Svrčinovec SK 65 A4
Svullrya N 34 A4
Svyetlahorsk BY 7 K21
Swadlincote GB 27 C4
Swaffham GB 30 B4
Swanage GB 29 C6
Swanley GB 31 C4
Swanlinbar IRL 19 B4
Swansea GB 28 B4
Swarzędz PL 46 C3
Swatragh GB 19 B5
Świątki PL 47 B6
Świdnica, *Wałbrzych* PL 54 C1
Świdnica, *Zielona Góra* PL 53 B5
Świdnik PL 11 L18
Świdwin PL 46 B1
Świebodzice PL 53 C6
Świebodzin PL 53 A5
Świecie PL 47 B4
Świedziebnia PL 47 B5
Świeradów Zdrój PL 53 C5
Świerki PL 54 C1
Świerzawa PL 53 B5
Świerzno PL 45 B6
Święta PL 45 B6
Świeta Anna PL 55 C4
Świętno PL 53 A6
Swifterbant NL 42 C2
Swindon GB 29 B6
Swineshead GB 30 B3
Swinford IRL 18 C3
Świnoujście PL 45 B6
Swinton GB 25 C5
Swobnica PL 45 B6
Swords IRL 21 A5
Swornegacie PL 46 B3
Sya S 37 C2
Syasstroy RUS 7 F23
Sycewice PL 46 A2
Sychevka RUS 7 J24
Syców PL 54 B2
Sycowice PL 53 A5
Sydnes N 32 B2
Syfteland N 32 A2
Syke D 43 C5
Sylling N 34 B2
Symbister GB 22 A7
Symington GB 25 C4
Symonds Yat GB 29 B5
Sypniewo, *Kujawsko-Pomorskie* PL 46 B3
Sypniewo, *Wielkopolskie* PL 46 B2
Sysslebäck S 2 F13
Szabadbattyán H 74 A3
Szabadegyháza H 74 A3
Szabadszállás H 75 B4
Szadek PL 54 B3
Szajol H 75 A5
Szakály H 74 B3
Szakcs H 74 B3
Szakmár H 75 B4
Szalánta H 74 C3
Szałas PL 55 B5
Szalkszentmárton H 75 B4
Szalonna H 65 B6
Szamocin PL 46 B3
Szamotuły PL 46 C2
Szany H 74 A2
Szarvas H 75 B5
Szarvaskő H 65 C6
Szászvár H 74 B3
Százhalombatta H 74 A3
Szczawa PL 65 A6
Szczawnica PL 65 A6
Szczecin PL 45 B6
Szczecinek PL 46 B2
Szczekociny PL 55 C4
Szczerców PL 55 B4
Szczucin PL 55 C6
Szczuczarz PL 46 B2
Szczurkowo PL 47 A6
Szczurowa PL 55 C5
Szczyrk PL 65 A5
Szczytna PL 54 C1
Szczytno PL 6 K17
Szczyty PL 54 B3
Szécsény H 65 B5
Szederkény H 74 C3
Szedres H 74 B3
Szeged H 75 B5
Szeghalom H 75 A6
Szegvár H 75 B5
Székesfehérvár H 74 A3
Székkutas H 75 B5
Szekszárd H 74 B3
Szemplino Czarne PL 47 B6
Szemud PL 47 A4
Szendehely H 65 C5
Szendrö H 65 B6
Szentendre H 65 C5
Szentes H 75 B5
Szentgotthárd H 73 B6
Szentlászló H 74 B2
Szentlörinc H 74 B2
Szentmártonkáta H 75 A4
Szenyér H 74 B2
Szeremle H 74 B3
Szerep H 75 A6
Szigetszentmiklós H 75 A4
Szigetvár H 74 B2
Szikáncs H 75 B5
Szikszó H 65 B6
Szil H 74 A2
Szilvásvárad H 65 B6
Szklarska Poreba PL 53 C5
Szlichtyngowa PL 53 B6
Szob H 65 C4
Szolnok H 75 A5
Szombathely H 74 A1
Szorosad H 74 B3
Szpetal Graniczny PL 47 C5
Szprotawa PL 53 B5
Szreńsk PL 47 B6
Sztum PL 47 B5
Sztutowo PL 47 A5
Szubin PL 46 B3
Szücsi H 65 C5
Szulmierz PL 47 C6
Szulok H 74 B2
Szumanie PL 47 C5
Szwecja PL 46 B2
Szydłów, *Łódzkie* PL 55 B4
Szydłów, *Świętokrzyskie* PL 55 C6
Szydłowiec PL 55 B5
Szydlowo, *Mazowieckie* PL 47 B6
Szydłowo, *Wielkopolskie* PL 46 B2
Szymanów PL 55 A5
Szynkielów PL 54 B3
Szynwald PL 55 D6

T

Tab H 74 B3
Tabanera la Luenga E 94 A2
Tabaqueros E 96 B1
Tábara E 88 C1
Tabenera de Cerrato E 88 B2
Taberg S 40 B4
Tabernas E 101 B3
Tabiano Bagni I 81 B4
Taboada E 86 B3
Taboadela E 87 B3
Tábor CZ 63 A5
Táborfalva H 75 A4
Taborište HR 73 C6
Tábua P 92 A2
Tabuaco P 87 C3
Tabuenca E 89 C5
Tabuyo del Monte E 87 B4
Täby S 36 B5
Tác H 74 A3
Tachov CZ 62 A3
Tadcaster GB 27 B4
Tadley GB 31 C2
Tafalla E 89 B5
Taganheira P 98 B2
Tågarp S 41 D2
Tággia I 80 C1
Tagliacozzo I 102 A3
Táglio di Po I 82 A1
Tagnon F 59 A5
Tahal E 101 B3
Tahitótfalu H 65 C5
Tailfingen D 61 B5
Taillis F 57 B4
Tain GB 23 D4
Tain-l'Hermitage F 78 A3
Taipadas P 92 C2
Taivalkoski FIN 3 D21
Takene S 34 B5
Takovo YU 85 B5
Taksony H 75 A4
Tal E 86 B2
Tal-Y-Llyn GB 26 C2
Talachyn BY 7 J21
Talamello I 82 C1
Talamone I 102 A1
Talant F 69 A4
Talarrubias E 94 C1
Talaván E 93 B4
Talavera de la Reina E 94 C2
Talavera la Real E 93 C4
Talayuela E 93 B5
Talayuelas E 96 B1
Talgarth GB 29 B4
Talgje N 32 B2
Talhadas P 92 A2
Táliga E 93 C3
Talizat F 78 A2
Tálla I 81 C5
Talladale GB 22 D3
Tallaght IRL 21 A5
Tallard F 79 B5
Talloires F 69 C6
Tallinn EST 6 G19
Tallow IRL 21 B3
Talmay F 69 A5
Talmont-St. Hilaire F 66 B3
Talmont-sur-Gironde F 66 C4
Talne UA 11 M22
Talsano I 105 B4
Talsi LV 6 H18
Talvik N 2 A18
Talybont GB 26 C2
Tamajón E 95 B3
Tamame E 88 C1
Tamames E 93 A4
Tamarit de Mar E 91 B4
Tamarite de Litera E 90 B3
Tamariu E 91 B6
Tamási H 74 B3
Tambach-Dietharz D 51 C6
Tameza E 86 A4
Tammisaari FIN 3 F18
Tampere FIN 3 F18
Tamsweg A 72 A3
Tamurejo E 94 D2
Tamworth GB 27 C4
Tana N 2 A21
Tañabueyes E 89 B3
Tanakajd H 74 A1
Tananger N 32 C2
Tanaunella I 110 C2
Tancarville F 58 A1
Tånga S 41 C2
Tangelic H 74 B3
Tangerhütte D 44 C3
Tangermünde D 44 C3
Taninges F 69 B6
Tann D 51 C6
Tanna D 52 C1
Tannadice GB 25 B5
Tannåker S 40 C3
Tännäs S 2 E13
Tannay, *Ardennes* F 59 A5
Tannay, *Nièvre* F 68 A3
Tannenbergsthal D 52 C2
Tännesberg D 62 A3
Tannheim A 71 A5
Tanowo PL 45 B6
Tanum S 35 C3
Tanumshede S 35 C3
Tanus F 77 B5
Tanvald CZ 53 C5
Taormina I 109 B4
Tapa EST 7 G19
Tapfheim D 62 B1
Tapia de Casariego E 86 A4
Tápióbicske H 75 A4
Tápiógyörgye H 75 A4
Tápióság H 75 A4
Tápiószecsö H 75 A4
Tápiószele H 75 A4
Tápiószentmárton H 75 A4
Tapolca H 74 B2
Tapolcafö H 74 A2
Tar HR 72 C3
Taradell E 91 B5
Taramundi E 86 A3
Tarancón E 95 B3
Táranto I 105 B4
Tarare F 69 C4
Tarascon F 78 C3
Tarascon-sur-Ariège F 77 D4
Tarashcha UA 11 M22
Tarazona E 89 C5
Tarazona de la Mancha E 95 C5
Tarbena E 96 C2
Tarbert GB 24 C2
Tarbert IRL 20 B2
Tarbes F 76 C3
Tarbet GB 24 B3
Tarbolton GB 24 C3
Tarcento I 72 B3
Tarčin BIH 84 C3
Tarczyn PL 55 B5
Tardajos E 88 B3
Tardelcuende E 89 C4
Tardets-Sorholus F 76 C2
Tardienta E 90 B2
Targon F 76 B2
Târgovişte RO 11 P19
Târgu-Jiu RO 11 P18
Târgu Mureş RO 11 N19
Târgu Ocna RO 11 N20
Târgu Secuiesc RO 11 P20
Tarifa E 99 C5
Tariquejas E 99 B3
Tarján H 65 C4
Tárkány H 64 C4
Tarland GB 23 D6
Tarłów PL 55 B6
Tarm DK 39 D1
Tarmstedt D 43 B6
Tärnaby S 2 D14
Tarnalelesz H 65 B6
Tarnaörs H 65 C6
Tărnăveni RO 11 N19
Tarnobrzeg PL 55 C6
Tarnos F 76 C1
Tarnów, *Gorzów Wielkopolski* PL 45 C6
Tarnów, *Tarnów* PL 55 C5
Tarnowo Podgórne PL 46 C2
Tarnowskie Góry PL 54 C3
Tärnsjö S 36 A3
Tarouca P 87 C3
Tarp D 43 A6
Tarquinia I 102 A1
Tarquinia Lido I 102 A1
Tarragona E 91 B4
Tàrrega E 91 B4
Tarrenz A 71 A5
Tårs, *Nordjyllands* DK 38 B3
Tårs, *Storstrøms* DK 39 E4
Tarsia I 106 B3
Tartas F 76 C2
Tartu EST 7 G20
Tarusa RUS 7 J25
Tarves GB 23 D6
Tarvisio I 72 B3
Täsch CH 70 B2
Tasov CZ 64 A2
Tasovčići BIH 84 C2
Tåstrup DK 41 D2
Tát H 65 C4
Tata H 65 C4
Tatabánya H 74 A3
Tataháza H 75 B4
Tatarbunary UA 11 P21
Tatárszentgyörgy H 75 A4
Tatranská-Lomnica SK 65 A6
Tau N 32 B2
Tauberbischofsheim D 61 A5
Taucha D 52 B2
Taufkirchen D 62 B3
Taufkirchen an der Pram A 63 B4
Taulé F 56 B2
Taulignan F 78 B3
Taulov DK 39 D2
Taunton GB 29 B4
Taunusstein D 50 C4
Tauragė LT 6 J18
Taurianova I 106 C3
Taurisano I 107 B5
Tauste E 90 B1
Tauves F 68 C2
Tavankut YU 75 B4
Tavannes CH 70 A2
Tavarnelle val di Pesa I 81 C5
Tavas TR 16 T21
Tavaux F 69 A5
Taverna I 106 B3
Taverne CH 70 B3
Tavernelle I 82 C1
Tavernes de la Valldigna E 96 B2
Tavérnola Bergamasca I 71 C5
Taverny F 58 A3
Tavescan E 91 A4
Taviano I 105 C5
Tavira P 98 B3
Tavistock GB 28 C3
Tavnik YU 85 C5
Tavşanlı TR 16 S21
Tayinloan GB 24 C2
Taynuilt GB 24 B2
Tayport GB 25 B5
Tázlár H 75 B4
Tazones E 88 A1
Tczew PL 47 A4
Tczów PL 55 B6
Teangue GB 22 D3
Teano I 103 B4
Teba E 100 C1
Tebay GB 26 A3
Techendorf A 72 B3
Tecklenburg D 50 A3
Tecko-matorp S 41 D3
Tecuci RO 11 P20
Tefenni TR 16 T21
Tegelsmora S 36 A4
Tegernsee D 62 C2
Teggiano I 104 B2
Tegoleto I 81 C5
Teichel D 52 C1
Teignmouth GB 29 C4
Teillay F 57 C4
Teisendorf D 62 C3
Teistungen D 51 B6
Teixeiro E 86 A2
Tejada de Tiétar E 93 A5
Tejado E 89 C4
Tejares E 94 B1
Tejn DK 41 D4
Tekirdağ TR 16 R20
Tekovské-Lužany SK 65 B4
Telavåg N 32 A1
Telč CZ 63 A6
Telese Terme I 103 B4
Telford GB 26 C3
Telfs A 71 A6
Telgárt SK 65 B6
Telgte D 50 B3
Tellingstedt D 43 A6
Telšiai LT 6 J18
Telti I 110 C2
Teltow D 45 C5
Tembleque E 95 C3
Temelin CZ 63 A5
Temerin YU 75 C4
Temiño E 89 B3
Témpio Pausánia I 110 C2
Temple Sowerby GB 26 A3
Templederry IRL 20 B3
Templemore IRL 21 B4
Templin D 45 B5
Temse B 49 B5
Ten Boer NL 42 B3
Tenay F 69 C5
Tenbury Wells GB 29 A5
Tenby GB 28 B3
Tence F 78 A3
Tende F 80 B1
Tenhult S 40 B4
Tenja (Sv. Ana) HR 74 C3
Tenneville B 49 C6
Tensta S 36 A4
Tenterden GB 31 C4
Teo E 86 B2
Teora I 104 B2
Teplá CZ 52 D2
Teplice CZ 53 C3
Teplička nad Váhom SK 65 A4
Ter Apel NL 43 C4
Tera E 89 C4
Téramo I 103 A3
Terborg NL 50 B2
Terchová SK 65 A5
Terebovlya UA 11 M19
Teremia Mare RO 75 C5
Terena P 92 C3
Teresa de Cofrentes E 96 B1
Terešov CZ 63 A4
Terezino Polje HR 74 C2
Tergnier F 59 A4
Teriberka RUS 3 B24
Terlizzi I 105 A3
Termas de Monfortinho P 93 A4
Terme di Súio I 103 B3
Terme di Valdieri I 79 B6
Termens E 90 B3
Termes F 78 B2
Términi Imerese I 108 B2
Terminillo I 102 A2
Térmoli I 103 B5
Termonfeckin IRL 19 C5
Ternberg A 63 C5
Terndrup DK 38 C3
Terneuzen NL 49 B4
Terni I 102 A2
Ternitz A 64 C2
Ternopil UA 11 M19
Terracina I 102 B3
Terralba I 110 D1
Terranova di Pollino I 104 C3
Terranova di Sibari I 106 B3
Terras do Bouro P 87 C2
Terrasini I 108 A2
Terrassa E 91 B5
Terrasson-la-Villedieu F 77 A4
Terrazos E 89 B3
Terriente E 95 B5
Terrugem P 92 C3
Tertenia I 110 D2
Teruel E 90 C1
Tervola FIN 3 C19
Tervuren B 49 C5
Terzaga E 95 B5
Tešanj BIH 84 B2
Tesáske-Mlyňany SK 65 B4
Teslić BIH 84 B2
Tessin D 44 A4
Tessy-sur-Vire F 57 B4
Tét H 74 A2
Tetbury GB 29 B5
Teterchen F 60 A2
Teterow D 45 B4
Teteven BG 16 Q19
Tetiyev UA 11 M21
Tetovo MK 15 Q17
Tettau D 52 C1
Tettnang D 61 C5
Teublitz D 62 A3
Teuchern D 52 B2
Teulada E 96 C3
Teulada I 110 E1
Teupitz D 52 A3
Teutschenthal D 52 B1
Tevel H 74 B3
Teviothead GB 25 C5
Tewkesbury GB 29 B5
Thale D 52 B1
Thalfang D 60 A2
Thalgau A 63 C4
Thalkirch CH 71 B4
Thalmässing D 62 A2
Thalwil CH 70 A3
Thame GB 31 C3
Thann F 60 C3
Thannhausen D 61 B6
Thaon-les-Vosges F 60 B2
Tharandt D 52 C3
Tharsis E 99 B3
Thatcham GB 31 C2
Thaxted GB 31 C4
Thayngen CH 61 C4
The Barony GB 23 B5
The Mumbles GB 28 B4
Theale GB 31 C2
Thedinghausen D 43 C6
Theessen D 52 A2
Themar D 51 C6
Thénezay F 67 B4
Thenon F 77 A4
Therouanne F 48 C3
Thessaloniki GR 15 R18
Thetford GB 30 B4
Theux B 50 C1
Thézar-les-Corbières F 78 C1
Thèze F 76 C2
Thiberville F 58 A1
Thibie F 59 B5
Thiéblemont-Farémont F 59 B5
Thiendorf D 53 B3
Thiene I 71 C6
Thierrens CH 70 B1
Thiers F 68 C3
Thiesi I 110 C1
Thiessow D 45 A5
Thiezac F 77 A5
Thionville F 60 A2
Thiron-Gardais F 58 B1
Thirsk GB 27 A4
Thisted DK 38 C1
Thivai GR 15 S18
Thivars F 58 B2
Thiviers F 67 C5
Thizy F 69 B4
Tholen NL 49 B5
Tholey D 60 A3
Thomas Street IRL 20 A3
Thomastown IRL 21 B4
Thônes F 69 C6
Thonnance-les-Joinville F 59 B6
Thonon-les-Bains F 69 B6
Thorame-Haute F 79 B5
Thorens-Glières F 69 C6
Thorigny-sur-Oreuse F 59 B4
Thörl A 73 A5
Thornaby on Tees GB 27 A4
Thornbury GB 29 B5
Thorne GB 27 B5
Thornhill, *Dumfries & Galloway* GB 25 C4
Thornhill, *Stirling* GB 24 B3
Thornthwaite GB 26 A2
Thornton Dale GB 27 A5
Thouarcé F 67 A4
Thouars F 67 B4
Thrapston GB 30 B3
Threlkeld GB 26 A2
Thrumster GB 23 C5

Thueyts F 78 B3
Thuin B 49 C5
Thuir F 91 A5
Thumau D 52 C1
Thun CH 70 B2
Thuret F 68 C3
Thurey F 69 B5
Thüringen A 71 A4
Thurins F 69 C4
Thürkow D 45 B4
Thurles IRL 21 B4
Thurmaston GB 30 B2
Thurø By DK 39 D3
Thursby GB 25 D4
Thurso GB 23 C5
Thury-Harcourt F 57 B5
Thusis CH 71 B4
Thyborøn DK 38 C1
Thyregod DK 39 D2
Tibi E 96 C2
Tibro S 35 C6
Tidaholm S 35 C5
Tidan S 35 C6
Tidersrum S 37 D2
Tiedra E 88 C1
Tiefenbach D 62 A3
Tiefencastel CH 71 B4
Tiefenort D 51 C6
Tiefensee D 45 C5
Tiel NL 49 B6
Tielmes E 95 B3
Tielt B 49 B4
Tienen B 49 C5
Tiengen D 61 C4
Tiercé F 57 C5
Tierga E 89 C5
Tiermas E 90 A1
Tierp S 36 A4
Tierrantona E 90 A3
Tighina MD 11 N21
Tighnabruaich GB 24 C2
Tignes F 70 C1
Tigy F 58 C3
Tihany H 74 B2
Tijnje NL 42 B2
Tijola E 101 B3
Tikhvin RUS 7 G23
Til Châtel F 69 A5
Tilburg NL 49 B6
Tilh F 76 C2
Tillac F 76 C3
Tillberga S 36 B3
Tille F 58 A3
Tillicoultry GB 25 B4
Tilloy Bellay F 59 A5
Tilly-sur-Seulles F 57 A5
Tim DK 39 C1
Timau I 72 B3
Timbákion GR 16 U19
Timişoara RO 75 C6
Timmele S 35 D5
Timmendorfer Strand D 44 B2
Timmernabben S 40 C6
Timmersdala S 35 C5
Timoleague IRL 20 C3
Timolin IRL 21 B5
Timsfors S 40 C3
Timsgearraidh GB 22 C1
Tinajas E 95 B4
Tinalhas P 92 B3
Tinchebray F 57 B5
Tineo E 86 A4
Tinglev DK 39 E2
Tingsryd S 40 C4
Tingstäde S 37 D5
Tingvoll N 2 E11
Tinnoset N 33 B6
Tinos GR 16 T19
Tintagel GB 28 C3
Tinténiac F 57 B4
Tintern GB 29 B5
Tintigny B 60 A1
Tione di Trento I 71 B5
Tipperary IRL 20 B3
Tiptree GB 31 C4
Tiranë AL 15 R16
Tirano I 71 B5
Tiraspol MD 11 N21
Tire TR 16 S20
Tires I 71 B6
Tiriez E 101 A3
Tirig E 90 C3
Tiriolo I 106 C3
Tirnavos GR 15 S18
Tirrénia I 81 C4
Tirschenreuth D 62 A3
Tirstrup DK 39 C3
Tirteafuera E 100 A1
Tishono RUS 47 A6
Tisno HR 83 C4
Tišnov CZ 64 A2
Tisovec SK 65 B5
Tisselskog S 35 C4
Tistedal N 34 B3
Tistrup DK 39 D1
Tisvildeleje DK 39 C5
Tiszaalpár H 75 B4
Tiszabö H 75 A5
Tiszadorogma H 65 C6
Tiszaföldvár H 75 B5
Tiszafüred H 65 C6
Tiszajenö H 75 A5
Tiszakécske H 75 B5
Tiszakeszi H 65 C6
Tiszakürt H 75 B5
Tiszanána H 75 A5
Tiszaörs H 75 A5
Tiszaroff H 75 A5
Tiszasüly H 75 A5
Tiszasziget H 75 B5
Tiszaszölös H 75 A5
Titaguas E 96 B1
Titel YU 75 C5
Titisee-Neustadt D 61 C4
Tito I 104 B2
Titova Korenica HR 83 B4
Titling D 63 B4
Tittmoning D 62 B3
Titz D 50 B2
Tived S 37 C1
Tiverton GB 29 C4
Tivisa E 90 B3
Tivoli I 102 B2
Tjæreborg DK 39 D1
Tjällmo S 37 C2
Tjome N 34 B2
Tjonnefoss N 33 C5
Tjörnarp S 41 D3
Tkon HR 83 C4
Tlmače SK 65 B4
Tłuchowo PL 47 C5
Tlumačov CZ 64 A3
Tóalmas H 75 A4
Toano I 81 B4
Toba D 51 B6
Tobarra E 101 A4
Tobercurry IRL 18 B3
Tobermore GB 19 B5
Tobermory GB 24 B1
Toberonochy GB 24 B2
Tobha Mor GB 22 D1
Tobo S 36 A4
Tocane-St. Apre F 67 C5
Tocha P 92 A2
Tocina E 99 B5
Töcksfors S 34 B3
Tocón E 100 B2
Todi I 82 D1
Todmorden GB 26 B3
Todorici BIH 84 B2
Todtmoos D 61 C4
Todtnau D 60 C3
Toén E 87 B3
Tofta, Gotland S 37 D5
Tofta, Skaraborg S 35 C5
Tofte N 34 B2
Töftedal S 35 C3
Tofterup DK 39 D1
Toftlund DK 39 D2
Töfü H 74 B3
Tokarnia PL 55 C5
Tokary PL 54 B3
Tokod H 65 C4
Tököl H 75 A3
Tolastadh bho Thuath GB 22 C2
Toledo E 94 C2
Tolentino I 82 C2
Tolfa I 102 A1
Tolg S 40 B4
Tolkmicko PL 47 A5
Tolko PL 47 A6
Tollarp S 41 D3
Tollered S 35 D4
Tøllose DK 39 D4
Tolmachevo RUS 7 G21
Tolmezzo I 72 B3
Tolmin SLO 72 B3
Tolna H 74 B3
Tolnanémedi H 74 B3
Tolob GB 22 B7
Tolosa E 89 A4
Tolosa P 92 B3
Tolox E 100 C1
Tolpuddle GB 29 C5
Tolva E 90 A3
Tolve I 104 B3
Tomar P 92 B2
Tomaševac YU 75 C5
Tomašica BIH 83 B5
Tomášikovo SK 64 B3
Tomašouka BY 6 L18
Tomášovce SK 65 B5
Tomaszów Mazowiecki PL 55 B5
Tomatin GB 23 D5
Tombeboeuf F 77 B3
Tomdoun GB 22 D3
Tomelilla S 41 D3
Tomellosa E 95 B4
Tomelloso E 95 C3
Tomiño E 87 C2
Tomintoul GB 23 D5
Tomislavgrad BIH 84 C2
Tomisław PL 53 B5
Tomisławice PL 47 C4
Tomnavoulin GB 23 D5
Tompa H 75 B4
Tompaládony H 74 A1
Tomter N 34 B2
Tona E 91 B5
Tonara I 110 C2
Tonbridge GB 31 C4
Tondela P 92 A2
Tønder DK 39 E1
Tongeren B 49 C6
Tongue GB 23 C4
Tönisvorst D 50 B2
Tonnay-Boutonne F 67 C4
Tonnay-Charente F 66 C4
Tonneins F 77 B3
Tonnerre F 59 C4
Tönning D 43 A5
Tønsberg N 34 B2
Tonstad N 32 C3
Toomyvara IRL 20 B3
Toormore IRL 20 C2
Topares E 101 B3
Topas E 94 A1
Toplița RO 11 N19
Topola YU 85 B5
Topoľčany SK 64 B4
Topoľčianky SK 65 B4
Topolje HR 73 C6
Topólka PL 47 C4
Topoľníky SK 64 C3
Toponár H 74 B2
Toporów PL 53 A5
Topsham GB 29 C4
Topusko HR 73 C5
Toques E 86 B3
Tor Vaiánica I 102 B2
Torà E 91 B4
Toral de los Guzmanes E 88 B1
Toral de los Vados E 86 B4
Torbalı TR 16 S20
Torbjörntorp S 35 C5
Torbole I 71 C5
Torchiarolo I 105 B5
Torcross GB 29 C4
Torcy-le-Petit F 58 A2
Torda YU 75 C5
Tørdal N 33 B5
Tordehumos E 88 C1
Tordera E 91 B5
Tordesillas E 88 C1
Tordesilos E 95 B5
Töre S 3 D18
Töreboda S 35 C6
Toreby DK 39 E4
Torekov S 41 C2
Torella dei Lombardi I 104 B2
Torellò E 91 A5
Toreno E 86 B4
Torfou F 66 A3
Torgau D 52 B3
Torgelow D 45 B6
Torgueda P 87 C3
Torhamn S 41 C5
Torhout B 49 B4
Torigni-sur-Vire F 57 A5
Torija E 95 B3
Toril E 95 B5
Torino I 80 A1
Toritto I 105 B3
Torkovichi RUS 7 G22
Torla E 90 A2
Tormestorp S 41 C3
Tórmini I 71 C5
Tornada P 92 B1
Tornal'a SK 65 B6
Tornavacas E 93 A5
Tornby DK 38 B2
Tornesch D 43 B6
Torness GB 23 D4
Torniella I 81 C5
Tornimparte I 103 A3
Torning DK 39 C2
Tornio FIN 3 D19
Tornjoš YU 75 C4
Tornos E 95 B5
Toro E 88 C1
Törökszentmiklós H 75 A5
Toropets RUS 7 H22
Torpè I 110 C2
Torphins GB 23 D6
Torpoint GB 28 C3
Torpsbruk S 40 B4
Torquay GB 29 C4
Torquemada E 88 B2
Torralba de Burgo E 89 C4
Torralba de Calatrava E 94 C3
Torrão P 98 A2
Torre Annunziata I 103 C4
Torre Canne I 105 B4
Torre Cardela E 100 B2
Torre das Vargens P 92 B3
Torre de Coelheiros P 92 C3
Torre de Dom Chama P 87 C3
Torre de Juan Abad E 100 A2
Torre de la Higuera E 99 B4
Torre de Miguel Sesmero E 93 C4
Torre de Moncorvo P 87 C3
Torre de Santa Maria E 93 B4
Torre del Bierzo E 86 B4
Torre del Burgo E 95 B3
Torre del Campo E 100 B2
Torre del Greco I 103 C4
Torre del Lago Puccini I 81 C4
Torre del Mar E 100 C1
Torre dell'Orso I 105 B5
Torre do Terranho P 87 D3
Torre Faro I 109 A4
Torre la Ribera E 90 A3
Torre los Negros E 90 C1
Torre Orsáia I 104 B2
Torre-Pacheco E 101 B5
Torre Péllice I 79 B6
Torre Santa Susanna I 105 B4
Torreblacos E 89 C4
Torreblanca E 96 A3
Torreblascopedro E 100 A2
Torrecaballeros E 94 A2
Torrecampo E 100 A1
Torrecilla E 95 B4
Torrecilla de la Jara E 94 C2
Torrecilla de la Orden E 94 A1
Torrecilla del Pinar E 88 C2
Torrecilla en Cameros E 89 B4
Torrecillas de la Tiesa E 93 B5
Torredembarra E 91 B4
Torredonjimeno E 100 B2
Torregrosa E 90 B3
Torreira P 87 D2
Torrejón de Ardoz E 95 B3
Torrejón de la Calzada E 94 B3
Torrejón del Rey E 95 B3
Torrejon el Rubio E 93 B4
Torrejoncillo E 93 B4
Torrelaguna E 95 B3
Torrelapaja E 89 C5
Torrelavega E 88 A2
Torrelobatón E 88 C1
Torrelodones E 94 B3
Torremaggiore I 104 A2
Torremanzanas E 96 C2
Torremayor E 93 C4
Torremezzo di Falconara I 106 B3
Torremocha E 93 B4
Torremolinos E 100 C1
Torrenieri I 81 C5
Torrenostra E 96 A3
Torrenova I 102 B2
Torrent E 96 B2
Torrente de Cinca E 90 B3
Torrenueva, *Ciudad Real* E 100 A2
Torrenueva, *Granada* E 100 C2
Torreorgaz E 93 B4
Torreperogil E 100 A2
Torres E 100 B2
Torres-Cabrera E 100 B1
Torres de la Alameda E 95 B3
Torres Novas P 92 B2
Torres Vedras P 92 B1
Torresandino E 88 C3
Torrevieja E 96 D2
Torri del Benaco I 71 C5
Torricella I 105 B4
Torridon GB 22 D3
Torriglia I 80 B3
Torrijos E 94 C2
Tørring DK 39 D2
Torrita di Siena I 81 C5
Torroal P 98 A2
Torroella de Montgri E 91 A6
Torrox E 100 C2
Torrskog S 34 B4
Torsåker S 36 A3
Torsang S 36 A2
Torsås S 41 C6
Torsby S 34 A4
Torshälla S 36 B3
Torslanda S 35 D3
Torsminde DK 39 C1
Törtel H 75 A4
Tórtoles E 94 B1
Tórtoles de Esgueva E 88 C2
Tortoli I 110 D2
Tortona I 80 B2
Tórtora I 104 C2
Tortoreto Lido I 82 D2
Tortorici I 109 A3
Tortosa E 90 C3
Tortosendo P 92 A3
Tortuera E 95 B5
Tortuero E 95 B3
Toruń PL 47 B4
Torup S 40 C3
Torver GB 26 A2
Tørvikbygde N 32 A3
Torviscón E 100 C2
Torzhok RUS 7 H24
Torzym PL 53 A5
Toscelanor-Maderno I 71 C5
Tosno RUS 7 G22
Tossa de Mar E 91 B5
Tosse F 76 C1
Tösse S 35 C4
Tossicia I 103 A3
Tostedt D 43 B6
Tószeg H 75 A5
Toszek PL 54 C3
Totana E 101 B4
Totebo S 37 D3
Tôtes F 58 A2
Tótkomlós H 75 B5
Totlandsvik N 32 B3
Totnes GB 28 C4
Tótszerdahely H 74 B1
Totton GB 31 D2
Touça P 87 C3
Toucy F 59 C4
Toul F 60 B1
Toulon F 79 C4
Toulon-sur-Allier F 68 B3
Toulon-sur-Arroux F 68 B4
Toulouse F 77 C4
Tourcoing F 49 C4
Tourlaville F 57 A4
Tournai B 49 C4
Tournan-en-Brie F 58 B3
Tournay F 76 C3
Tournon-d'Agenais F 77 B3
Tournon-St. Martin F 67 B5
Tournon-sur-Rhône F 78 A3
Tournus F 69 B4
Touro E 86 B2
Touro P 87 D3
Tourouvre F 58 B1
Tourriers F 67 C5
Tours F 67 A5
Tourteron F 59 A5
Tourves F 79 C4
Toury F 58 B2
Touvedo P 87 C2
Touvois F 66 B3
Toužim CZ 52 C2
Tovačov CZ 64 A3
Tovariševo YU 75 C4
Tovarnik HR 75 C4
Tovdal N 33 C5
Tovrljane YU 85 C6
Towcester GB 30 B3
Town Yetholm GB 25 C5
Trabada E 86 A3
Trabadelo E 86 B4
Trabanca E 87 C4
Trabazos E 87 C4
Traben-Trarbach D 60 A3
Trabia I 108 B2
Tradate I 70 C3
Trädet S 35 D5
Trafaria P 92 C1
Tragacete E 95 B5
Tragwein A 63 B5
Traiguera E 90 C3
Trainel F 59 B4
Traisen A 63 B6
Traismauer A 64 B1
Traitsching D 62 A3
Tralee IRL 20 B2
Tramacastilla de Tena E 90 A2
Tramagal P 92 B2
Tramariglio I 110 C1
Tramatza I 110 C1
Tramelan CH 70 A2
Tramonti di Sopra I 72 B2
Tramore IRL 21 B4
Trana I 80 A1
Tranås S 37 C1
Tranbjerg DK 39 C3
Tranby N 34 B2
Trancoso P 87 D3
Tranebjerg DK 39 D3
Tranekær DK 39 E3
Tranemo S 40 B3
Tranent GB 25 C5
Tranevåg N 32 C3
Trani I 104 A3
Trans-en-Provence F 79 C5
Tranvik S 36 B5
Trápani I 108 A1
Trappes F 58 B3
Traryd S 40 C3
Trasacco I 103 B3
Trasierra E 99 A4
Träslövsläge S 40 B2
Trasmiras E 87 B3
Traspinedo E 88 C2
Trate SLO 73 B5
Trauchgau D 62 C1
Traun A 63 B5
Traunreut D 62 C3
Traunstein D 62 C3
Traunwalchen D 62 C3
Tråvad S 35 C5
Travemünde D 44 B2
Traversétolo I 81 B4
Travnik BIH 84 B2
Travnik SLO 73 C4
Travo I 80 B3
Trawsfynydd GB 26 C2
Trbovlje SLO 73 B5
Trbušani YU 85 C5
Trebaň F 68 B3
Třebařov CZ 64 A2
Trebatsch D 53 A4
Trebbin D 52 A3
Třebechovice pod Orebem CZ 53 C5
Trebel D 44 B2
Třebenice CZ 53 C3
Trebeurden F 56 B2
Třebíč CZ 64 A1
Trebinje BIH 84 D3
Trebisacce I 106 B3
Trebitz D 52 B2
Trebnje SLO 73 C5
Třeboň CZ 63 A5
Třebovice CZ 64 A2
Trebsen D 52 B2
Trebujena E 99 C4
Trecastagni I 109 B4
Trecate I 70 C3
Trecenta I 81 A5
Tredegar GB 29 B4
Tredózio I 81 B5
Treffen A 72 B3
Treffort F 69 B5
Treffurt D 51 B6
Trefnant GB 26 B2
Tregaron GB 28 A4
Trégastel-Plage F 56 B2
Tregnago I 71 C6
Tregony GB 28 C3
Tréguier F 56 B2
Trégunc F 56 C2
Treharris GB 29 B4
Tréia I 82 C2
Treignac F 68 C1
Treignat F 68 B2
Treignes B 49 C5
Treis-Karden D 50 C3
Trekanten S 40 C6
Trélazé F 67 A4
Trelech GB 28 B3
Trélissac F 67 C5
Trelleborg S 41 D3
Trélon F 49 C5
Trélou-sur-Marne F 59 A4
Tremblay-le-Vicomte F 58 B2
Tremés P 92 B2
Tremezzo I 71 C4
Třemošná CZ 63 A4
Tremp E 90 A3
Trenčianska Stankovce SK 64 B3
Trenčianska Turná SK 64 B4
Trenčianske Teplá SK 64 B4
Trenčianske Teplice SK 64 B4
Trenčín SK 64 B4
Trendelburg D 51 B5
Trensacq F 76 B2
Trent D 45 A5
Trento I 71 B6
Treorchy GB 29 B4
Trepča YU 85 D5
Trept F 69 C5
Trepuzzi I 105 B5
Trescore Balneário I 71 C4
Tresenda I 71 B5
Tresigallo I 81 B5
Trešnjevica YU 85 C6
Tresnurághes I 110 C1
Trespaderne E 89 B3
Třešť CZ 63 A6
Trestina I 82 C1
Tretower GB 29 B4
Trets F 79 C4
Tretten N 2 F12
Treuchtlingen D 62 B1
Treuen D 52 C2
Treuenbrietzen D 52 A2
Treungen N 33 B5
Trevelez E 100 C2
Trevi I 82 D1
Trevi nel Lázio I 102 B3
Treviana E 89 B3
Treviglio I 71 C4
Trevignano Romano I 102 A2
Treviso I 72 C2
Trévoux F 69 C4
Treysa D 51 C5
Trézelles F 68 B3
Trezzo sull'Adda I 71 C4
Trhová Kamenice CZ 64 A1
Trhové Sviny CZ 63 B5
Triacastela E 86 B3
Triaize F 66 B3
Triaucourt-en-Argonne F 59 B6
Tribanj Kruščica HR 83 B4
Triberg D 61 B4
Tribsees D 45 A4
Tribuče SLO 73 C5
Tricarico I 104 B3
Tricase I 107 B5
Tricésimo I 72 B3
Trie-sur-Baïse F 77 C3
Trieben A 73 A4
Triebes D 52 C2
Triepkendorf D 45 B5
Trier D 60 A2
Trieste I 72 C3
Triggiano I 105 A3
Triglitz D 44 B4
Trignac F 66 A2
Trigueros E 99 B4
Trigueros del Valle E 88 C2
Trijebine YU 85 C4
Trikkala GR 15 S17
Trilj HR 83 C5
Trillo E 95 B4
Trilport F 59 B3
Trim IRL 21 A5
Trimdon GB 25 D6
Trindade, *Beja* P 98 B3
Trindade, *Bragança* P 87 C3
Třinec CZ 65 A4
Tring GB 31 C3
Trinità d'Agultu I 110 C1
Trinitápoli I 104 A3
Trino I 70 C3
Trinta P 92 A3
Triora I 80 C1
Tripolis GR 15 T18
Triponzo I 82 D1
Triptis D 52 C1
Triste E 90 A2
Trittau D 44 B2
Trivento I 103 B4
Trivero I 70 C3
Trivigno I 104 B2
Trn BIH 84 B2
Trnava HR 74 C3
Trnava SK 64 B3
Trnovec SK 64 B3
Trnovo BIH 84 C3
Trnovska vas SLO 73 B5
Troarn F 57 A5
Trochtelfingen D 61 B5
Trœnse DK 39 D3
Trofa P 87 C2
Trofaiach A 73 A5
Trofors N 2 D13
Trogir HR 83 C5
Trøgstad N 34 B3
Tróia I 104 A2
Troia P 92 C2
Troina I 109 B3
Trois-Ponts B 50 C1
Troisdorf D 50 C3
Troisvierges L 50 C2
Trojane SLO 73 B4
Trojanów PL 55 B6
Troldhede DK 39 D1
Trollhättan S 35 C4
Trolog BIH 84 C1
Tromello I 70 C3
Tromøy N 33 C5
Tromsø N 3 B16
Trondheim N 2 E12
Tronget F 68 B3
Trönninge S 40 C2
Trönningeby S 40 B2
Tronzano-Vercellese I 70 C3
Trôo F 58 C1
Troon GB 24 C3
Tropea I 106 C2
Tropy Sztumskie PL 47 B5
Trosa S 37 C4
Trosly-Breuil F 59 A4
Trossingen D 61 B4
Trostberg D 62 B3
Trostyanets UA 7 L24
Trouville-sur-Mer F 57 A6
Trowbridge GB 29 B5
Troyes F 59 B5
Trpanj HR 84 C2
Trpezi YU 85 D5
Trpinja HR 74 C3
Tršće HR 73 C4
Tršice CZ 64 A3
Trstená SK 65 A5
Trstenci BIH 84 A2
Trstenik, *Kosovo* YU 85 D5
Trstenik, *Srbija* YU 85 C6
Trsteno HR 84 D2
Trstice SK 64 B3
Trstin SK 64 B3
Trubchevsk RUS 7 K23
Trubia E 88 A1
Trubjela YU 84 D3
Truchas E 87 B4
Trujillanos E 93 C4
Trujillo E 93 B5
Trumieje PL 47 B5
Trun CH 70 B3
Trun F 57 B6
Truro GB 28 C2
Trusetal D 51 C6
Truskavets' UA 11 M18
Trustrup DK 39 C3
Trutnov CZ 53 C5
Tryserum S 37 C3
Trysil N 2 F13
Tryszczyn PL 46 B3
Trzcianka PL 46 B2
Trzciel PL 46 C1
Trzcińsko Zdrój PL 45 C6
Trzebiatów PL 45 A7
Trzebiel PL 53 B4
Trzebielino PL 46 A3
Trzebień PL 53 B5
Trzebiez PL 45 B6
Trzebinia PL 55 C4
Trzebnica PL 54 B2
Trzebnice PL 53 B6
Trzeciewiec PL 47 B4
Trzemeszno PL 46 C3
Trzemeszno-Lubuskie PL 46 C1
Trzetrzewina PL 65 A6
Tržič SLO 73 B4
Tschagguns A 71 A4
Tschernitz D 53 B4
Tsebrykove UA 11 N22
Tsvetkovo UA 11 M22
Tsyelyakhany BY 7 K19
Tua P 87 C3
Tuam IRL 20 A3
Tubbergen NL 42 C3
Tubilla del Lago E 89 C3
Tübingen D 61 B5
Tubize B 49 C5
Tučapy CZ 63 A5
Tučepi HR 84 C2
Tuchan F 78 D1
Tüchen D 44 B4
Tuchola PL 46 B3
Tuchomie PL 46 A3
Tuczno PL 46 B2
Tuddal N 33 B5
Tudela E 89 B5
Tudela de Duero E 88 C2
Tudweiliog GB 26 C1
Tuejar E 96 B1
Tuffé F 58 B1
Tufsingdalen N 2 E12
Tuhaň CZ 53 C4
Tui E 87 B2
Tukums LV 6 H18
Tula I 110 C1
Tula RUS 7 J25
Tulcea RO 11 P21
Tul'chyn UA 11 M21
Tulette F 78 B3
Tuliszków PL 54 A3
Tulla IRL 20 B3
Tullamore IRL 21 A4
Tulle F 68 C1
Tullins F 69 C5
Tulln A 64 B2
Tullow IRL 21 B5
Tułowice PL 54 C2
Tulsk IRL 18 C3
Tumba S 36 B4
Tummel Bridge GB 24 B3
Tun S 35 C4
Tuna, *Kalmar* S 40 B6
Tuna, *Uppsala* S 36 A5
Tuna Hästberg S 36 A2
Tunes P 98 B2
Tungelsta S 37 B5
Tunnerstad S 40 A4
Tunstall GB 30 B5
Tuohikotti FIN 3 F20
Tuoro sul Trasimeno I 82 C1
Tupadły PL 47 C4
Tupanari BIH 84 B3
Tupik RUS 7 J23
Tuplice PL 53 B4
Tura H 65 C5
Turanj HR 83 C4
Turany SK 65 A5
Turbe BIH 84 B2
Turbenthal CH 70 A3
Turcia E 88 B1
Turčianske Teplice SK 65 B4
Turcifal P 92 B1
Turckheim F 60 B3
Turda RO 11 N18
Turégano E 94 A3
Turek PL 54 A3
Türgovishte BG 16 Q20
Turgutlu TR 16 S20
Turi I 105 B4
Turís E 96 B2
Túrje H 74 B2
Turka UA 11 M18
Túrkeve H 75 A5
Türkheim D 62 B1
Turku FIN 3 F18
Turleque E 95 C3
Turňa nad Bodvou SK 65 B6
Turnberry GB 24 C3
Turnhout B 49 B5
Türnitz A 63 C6
Turnov CZ 53 C5
Turnu RO 75 B6
Turnu Măgurele RO 16 Q19
Turón E 100 C2
Turoszów PL 53 C4
Turowo PL 47 B6
Turquol P 92 B1
Turri I 110 D1
Turries F 79 B5
Turriff GB 23 D6
Tursi I 105 B3
Turtmann CH 70 B2
Turze PL 54 B2
Turzovka SK 65 A4
Tusa I 109 B3
Tuscánia I 102 A1
Tušilovic HR 73 C5
Tuszyn PL 55 B4
Tutin YU 85 D5
Tutow D 45 B5
Tutrakan BG 11 P20
Tuttlingen D 61 C4
Tutzing D 62 C2
Tuzla BIH 84 B3
Tvååker S 40 B2
Tvärskog S 40 C6
Tvedestrand N 33 C5
Tver RUS 7 H24
Tversted DK 38 B3
Tving S 41 C5
Tvrdošin SK 65 A5
Tvrdošovce SK 64 B4
Twardogóra PL 54 B2
Twatt GB 23 B5
Twello NL 50 A2
Twimberg A 73 B4
Twist D 43 C4
Twistringen D 43 C5
Tworóg PL 54 C3
Twyford, *Hampshire* GB 31 C2
Twyford, *Wokingham* GB 31 C3
Tyachiv UA 11 M18
Tychówka PL 46 B2
Tychowo PL 46 B2
Tychy PL 54 C3
Tyec nad Labem CZ 53 C5
Tygelsjö S 41 D2
Tylstrup DK 38 B2
Tymbark PL 65 A6
Tymowa PL 65 A6
Týn nad Vltavou CZ 63 A5
Tyndrum GB 24 B3
Týnec nad Sázavou CZ 63 A5
Tynemouth GB 25 C6
Tyngsjö S 34 A5
Týniště nad Orlicí CZ 53 C6
Tynset N 2 E12
Tyresö S 36 B5
Tyringe S 41 C3
Tyrislöt S 37 C3
Tyristrand N 34 A2
Tyrrellspass IRL 21 A4
Tysnes N 32 A2
Tyssedal N 32 A3
Tystberga S 37 C4
Tysvær N 32 B2
Tywyn GB 26 C1
Tzummarum NL 42 B2

U

Ub YU 85 B5
Ubby DK 39 D4
Úbeda E 100 A2
Überlingen D 61 C5
Ubidea E 89 A4
Ubli HR 84 D1
Ubrique E 99 C5
Ucero E 89 C3
Uchaud F 78 C3
Uchte D 43 C5
Uckerath D 50 C3
Uckfield GB 31 D4
Uclés E 95 C4
Ucria I 109 A3
Udbina HR 83 B4
Uddebo S 40 B3
Uddeholm S 34 A5
Uddevalla S 35 C3
Uddheden S 34 B4
Uden NL 49 B6
Uder D 51 B6
Udiča SK 65 A4
Údine I 72 B3
Udvar H 74 C3
Ueckermünde D 45 B6
Uelsen D 42 C3
Uelzen D 44 C2
Uetendorf CH 70 B2
Uetersen D 43 B6
Uetze D 44 C2
Uffculme GB 29 C4
Uffenheim D 61 A6
Ugarana E 89 A4
Ugento I 107 B5
Ugerldse DK 39 D4
Uggerslev DK 39 D3
Uggiano la Chiesa I 107 A5
Ugijar E 100 C2
Ugine F 69 C6
Uglejevik BIH 84 B4
Uglenes N 32 A2
Uglich RUS 7 H26
Ugljane HR 83 C5
Ugod H 74 A2
Uherské Hradiště CZ 64 A3
Uherský Brod CZ 64 A3
Uherský Ostroh CZ 64 B3
Uhingen D 61 B5
Uhlířské-Janovice CZ 63 A6
Uhřiněves CZ 53 C4
Uhyst D 53 B4
Uig GB 22 D2
Uitgeest NL 42 C1
Uithoorn NL 49 A5
Uithuizen NL 42 B3
Uithuizermeeden NL 42 B3
Uivar RO 75 C5
Ujazd, *Łódzkie* PL 55 B4
Ujazd, *Opolskie* PL 54 C3
Ujhartyán H 75 A4
Újkígyós H 75 B6
Ujpetre H 74 C3
Ujście PL 46 B2
Ujsolt H 75 B4
Újszász H 75 A5
Ujué E 89 B5
Ukanc SLO 72 B3
Ukmergė LT 6 J19
Ukna S 37 C3
Ul'anka SK 65 B5
Ulássai I 110 D2
Ulbster GB 23 C5
Ulceby GB 27 B5
Ulcinj YU 15 R16
Uldum DK 39 D2
Ulefoss N 33 B6
Uleila del Campo E 101 B3
Ulfborg DK 39 C1
Uljma YU 85 A6
Ullapool GB 22 D3
Ullared S 40 B2
Ullatun N 32 B3
Ulldecona E 90 C3
Ulldemolins E 90 B3
Ullerslev DK 39 D3
Ullervad S 35 C5
Üllés H 75 B4
Üllo H 75 A4
Ullvi S 36 B3
Ulm D 61 B5
Ulme P 92 B2
Ulmen D 50 C2
Ulog BIH 84 C3
Ulricehamn S 35 D5
Ulrichstein D 51 C5
Ulrika S 37 C2
Ulrum NL 42 B3
Ulsberg N 2 E12
Ulsta GB 22 A7
Ulsted DK 38 B3
Ulstrup, *Vestsjællands Amt.* DK 39 D3
Ulstrup, *Viborg Amt.* DK 39 C2
Ulubey TR 16 S21
Uluborlu TR 16 S22
Ulverston GB 26 A2
Umag HR 72 C3
Uman UA 11 M22
Umba RUS 3 C24
Umbértide I 82 C1
Umbrìatico I 107 B3
Umčari YU 85 B5
Umeå S 3 E17
Umhausen A 71 A5
Umka YU 85 B5
Umljanovic HR 83 C5
Unapool GB 22 C3

Uncastillo E 90 A1
Undenäs S 37 C1
Unecha RUS 7 K23
Unešić HR 83 C5
Úněšov CZ 62 A4
Ungheni MD 11 N20
Unhais da Serra P 92 A3
Unhošt CZ 53 C4
Unichowo PL 46 A3
Uničov CZ 64 A3
Uniejów PL 54 B3
Unisław PL 47 B4
Unkel D 50 C3
Unken A 62 C3
Unna D 50 B3
Unnaryd S 40 C3
Unquera E 88 A2
Unter Langkampfen A 72 A2
Unter-steinbach D 61 A6
Unterach A 63 C4
Unterägeri CH 70 A3
Unterammergau D 62 C2
Unterhaching D 62 B2
Unteriberg CH 70 A3
Unterkochen D 61 B6
Unterlaussa A 63 C5
Unterlüss D 44 C2
Untermünkheim D 61 A5
Unterschächen CH 70 B3
Unterschleissheim D 62 B2
Unterschwaningen D 62 A1
Untersiemau D 51 C6
Unterweissenbach A 63 B5
Unterzell D 62 A3
Upavon GB 29 B6
Úpice CZ 53 C6
Upphärad S 35 C4
Uppingham GB 30 B3
Upplands-Väsby S 36 B4
Uppsala S 36 B4
Upton-upon-Severn GB 29 A5
Ur F 91 A4
Uras I 110 D1
Uraz PL 54 B1
Urbánia I 82 C1
Urbino I 82 C1
Urçay F 68 B2
Urda E 94 C3
Urdax E 76 C1
Urdilde E 86 B2
Urdos F 76 D2
Urk NL 42 C2
Úrkút H 74 A2
Urla TR 16 S20
Urlingford IRL 21 B4
Urnäsch CH 71 A4
Uroševac YU 15 Q17
Urracal E 101 B3
Urries E 90 A1
Urroz E 89 B5
Ursensollen D 62 A2
Urshult S 40 C4
Uršna Sela SLO 73 C5
Urszulewo PL 47 C5
Ury F 58 B3
Urziceni RO 11 P20
Urzulei I 110 C2
Usagre E 93 C4
Uşak TR 16 S21
Ušće YU 85 C5
Usedom D 45 B5
Useldange L 60 A1
Usellus I 110 D1
Ushakovo RUS 47 A6
Usingen D 51 C4
Usini I 110 C1
Usk GB 29 B5
Uskedal N 32 B2
Uslar D 51 B5
Úsov CZ 64 A3
Usquert NL 42 B3
Ussássai I 110 D2
Ussé F 67 A5
Usséglio I 70 C2
Ussel, *Cantal* F 78 A1
Ussel, *Corrèze* F 68 C2
Usson-du-Poitou F 67 B5
Usson-en-Forez F 68 C3
Usson-les-Bains F 77 D5
Ust Luga RUS 7 G21
Ustaritz F 76 C1
Úštěk CZ 53 C4
Uster CH 70 A3
Ústí CZ 64 A3
Ústí nad Labem CZ 53 C4
Ústí nad Orlicí CZ 53 D6
Ustibar BIH 85 C4
Ustikolina BIH 84 C3
Ustiprača BIH 84 C4
Ustka PL 46 A3
Ustroń PL 65 A4
Ustronie Morskie PL 46 A1
Ustyuzhna RUS 7 G25
Uszód H 74 B3
Utåker N 32 B2
Utebo E 90 B2
Utena LT 7 J19
Utery CZ 62 A4
Utiel E 96 B1
Utö S 37 C5
Utrecht NL 49 A6
Utrera E 99 B5
Utrillas E 90 C2
Utsjoki FIN 3 B20
Utstein kloster N 32 B2
Uttendorf A 72 A2
Uttenweiler D 61 B5
Utterslev DK 39 E4
Uttoxeter GB 27 C4
Utvälinge S 41 C2
Uusikaarlepyy FIN 3 E18
Uusikaupunki FIN 3 F17
Uvac BIH 85 C4
Úvaly CZ 53 C4
Uvdal N 33 A5
Uzdin YU 75 C5
Uzdowo PL 47 B6
Uzel F 56 B3
Uzerche F 67 C6
Uzès F 78 B3
Uzhhorod UA 11 M18
Uzhok UA 11 M18
Užice YU 85 C4
Uznach CH 70 A3
Üzümköprü TR 16 R20

V

Vaas F 58 C1
Vaasa FIN 3 E17
Vaasen NL 50 A1
Vabre F 77 C5
Vác H 65 C5
Vacha D 51 C6
Váchartyán H 65 C5
Väckelsång S 40 C4
Vacqueyras F 78 B3
Vad S 36 A2
Vada I 81 C4
Väddö S 36 B5
Väderstad S 37 C1
Vadheim N 2 F9
Vadillo de la Sierra E 94 B1
Vadillos E 95 B4
Vadla N 32 B3
Vado I 81 B5
Vado Lígure I 80 B2
Vadsø N 2 A21
Vadstena S 37 C1
Vadum DK 38 B2
Vaduz FL 71 A4
Væggerløse DK 44 A3
Vafos N 33 C6
Vág H 74 A2
Vaggeryd S 40 B4
Vaglia I 81 C5
Váglio Basilicata I 104 B2
Vagney F 60 B2
Vagnhärad S 37 C4
Vagnsunda S 36 B5
Vagos P 92 A2
Vaiano I 81 C5
Vaiges F 57 B5
Vaihingen D 61 B4
Vaillant F 59 C6
Vailly-sur-Aisne F 59 A4
Vailly-sur Sauldre F 68 A2
Vairano Scalo I 103 B4
Vaison-la-Romaine F 79 B4
Vaite F 60 C1
Väjern S 35 C3
Vajszló H 74 C2
Vál H 74 A3
Val de San Lorenzo E 86 B4
Val de Santo Domingo E 94 B2
Val d'Esquières F 79 C5
Val-d'Isère F 70 C1
Val-Suzon F 69 A4
Val Thorens F 69 C6
Valaam RUS 3 F22
Valada P 92 B2
Valadares P 87 C2
Valado P 92 B1
Valandovo MK 15 R18
Valaská SK 65 B5
Valaská Belá SK 65 B4
Valaská Dubová SK 65 A5
Valašská Polanka CZ 64 A3
Valašské Klobouky CZ 64 A4
Valašské Meziříčí CZ 64 A3
Valberg F 79 B5
Vålberg S 34 B5
Valbo S 36 A4
Valbom P 87 C2
Valbondione I 71 B5
Valbonnais F 79 B4
Valbuena de Duero E 88 C2
Vâlcani RO 75 C5
Valdagno I 71 C6
Valdahon F 69 A6
Valdaracete E 95 B3
Valday RUS 7 H23
Valdealgorfa E 90 C2
Valdecaballeros E 94 C1
Valdecabras E 95 B4
Valdecarros E 94 B1
Valdeconcha E 95 B4
Valdeflores E 99 B4
Valdefresno E 88 B1
Valdeganga E 95 C5
Valdelacasa E 93 A5
Valdelacasa de Tajo E 94 C1
Valdelarco E 99 B4
Valdelosa E 94 A1
Valdeltormo E 90 C3
Valdelugeros E 88 B1
Valdemanco de Esteras E 100 A1
Valdemarsvik S 37 C3
Valdemorillo E 94 B2
Valdemoro E 94 B3
Valdemoro Sierra E 95 B5
Valdenoceda E 89 B3
Valdeobispo E 93 A4
Valdeolivas E 95 B4
Valdepeñas E 100 A2
Valdepeñas de Jaén E 100 B2
Valdepiélago E 88 B1
Valdepolo E 88 B1
Valderas E 88 B1
Valdérice I 108 A1
Valderrobres E 90 C3
Valderrueda E 88 B2
Valdestillas E 88 C2
Valdetorres E 93 C4
Valdetorres de Jarama E 95 B3
Valdeverdeja E 94 C1
Valdevimbre E 88 B1
Valdieri I 80 B1
Valdilecha E 95 B3
Valdobbiádene I 72 C1
Valdocondes E 89 C3
Valdoviño E 86 A2
Vale de Açor, *Beja* P 98 B3
Vale de Açor, *Portalegre* P 92 B3
Vale de Agua P 98 B2
Vale de Cambra P 87 D2
Vale de Lobo P 98 B2
Vale de Prazeres P 92 A3
Vale de Reis P 92 C2
Vale de Rosa P 98 B3
Vale de Santarém P 92 B2
Vale de Vargo P 98 B3
Vale do Peso P 92 B3
Valea lui Mihai RO 11 N18
Valega P 87 D2
Valéggio sul Mincio I 71 C5
Valeiro P 92 C2
Valença P 87 B2
Valençay F 67 A6
Valence, *Charente* F 67 C5
Valence, *Drôme* F 78 B3
Valence d'Agen F 77 B3
Valence-d'Albigeois F 77 B5
Valence-sur-Baise F 77 C3
Valencia E 96 B2
Valencia de Alcántara E 93 B3
Valencia de Don Juan E 88 B1
Valencia de las Torres E 93 C4
Valencia de Mombuey E 99 A3
Valencia del Ventoso E 99 A4
Valenciennes F 49 C4
Valensole F 79 C4
Valentano I 102 A1
Valentigney F 70 A1
Valentine F 77 C3
Valenza I 80 A2
Valenzuela E 100 B1
Valenzuela de Calatrava E 100 A2
Våler N 34 B2
Valera de Abajo E 95 C4
Valeria E 95 C4
Valestrand N 32 B2
Valevåg N 32 B2
Valfabbrica I 82 C1
Valflaunes F 78 C2
Valga EST 7 H20
Valgorge F 78 B3
Valgrisenche I 70 C2
Valguarnera Caropepe I 109 B3
Valhelhas P 92 A3
Valjevo YU 85 B4
Valka LV 7 H19
Valkeakoski FIN 3 F19
Valkenburg NL 50 C1
Valkenswaard NL 49 B6
Valkó H 65 C5
Vall d'Alba E 96 A2
Valla S 37 B3
Vallada E 96 C2
Vallado E 86 A4
Valladolid E 88 C2
Vallåkra S 41 D2
Vallata I 104 A1
Vallberga S 40 C3
Valldemossa, *Mallorca* E 97
Valle N 33 B4
Valle Castellana I 82 D2
Valle de Abdalajís E 100 C1
Valle de Cabuérniga E 88 A2
Valle de la Serena E 93 C5
Valle de Matamoros E 93 C4
Valle de Santa Ana E 93 C4
Valle Mosso I 70 C3
Valledolmo I 108 B2
Vallelado E 88 C2
Vallelunga Pratameno I 108 B2
Vallendar D 50 C3
Vallentuna S 36 B5
Valleraugue F 78 B2
Vallermosa I 110 D1
Vallet F 66 A3
Valletta M 109 C4
Valley GB 26 B1
Vallfogona de Riucorb E 91 B4
Valli del Pasúbio I 71 C6
Vallo della Lucánia I 104 B2
Valloire F 69 C6
Vallombrosa I 81 C5
Vallon-Pont-d'Arc F 78 B3
Vallorbe CH 69 B6
Vallouise F 79 B5
Valls E 91 B4
Vallstena S 37 D5
Valmadrid E 90 B2
Valmiera LV 7 H19
Valmojado E 94 B2
Valmont F 58 A1
Valmontone I 102 B2
Valö S 36 A5
Valognes F 57 A4
Valonga P 92 A2
Valongo P 87 C2
Válor E 100 C2
Valoria la Buena E 88 C2
Valozhyn BY 7 J20
Valpaços P 87 C3
Valpelline I 70 C2
Valpiana I 81 C4
Valpovo HR 74 C3
Valras-Plage F 78 C2
Valréas F 78 B3
Vals CH 71 B4
Vals-les-Bains F 78 B3
Valsavarenche I 70 C2
Välse DK 39 E4
Valsequillo E 93 C5
Valsonne F 69 C4
Valstagna I 72 C1
Valtablado del Rio E 95 B4
Valtice CZ 64 B2
Valtiendas E 88 C3
Valtierra E 89 B5
Valtopina I 82 C1
Valtorta I 71 C4
Valtournenche I 70 C2
Valverde E 89 C5
Valverde de Burguillos E 93 C4
Valverde de Júcar E 95 C4
Valverde de la Vera E 93 A5
Valverde de la Virgen E 88 B1
Valverde de Llerena E 99 A5
Valverde de Mérida E 93 C4
Valverde del Camino E 99 B4
Valverde del Fresno E 93 A4
Vamberk CZ 54 C1
Vamdrup DK 39 D2
Vammala FIN 3 F18
Vámosmikola H 65 C4
Vámosszabadi H 64 C3
Vanault-les-Dames F 59 B5
Vandel DK 39 D2
Vandenesse F 68 B3
Vandenesse-en-Auxois F 69 A4
Vandóies I 72 B1
Väne-Åsaka S 35 C4
Vänersborg S 35 C4
Vänersnäs S 35 C4
Vänge S 36 B4
Vangsnes N 2 F10
Vännäs S 3 E16
Vannes F 56 C3
Vansbro S 34 A6
Vanse N 32 C3
Vantaa FIN 3 F19
Vanyarc H 65 C5
Vaour F 77 B4
Vapnyarka UA 11 M21
Vaprio d'Adda I 71 C4
Vaqueiros P 98 B3
Vara S 35 C4
Varacieux F 69 C5
Varades F 66 A3
Varages F 79 C4
Varaldsøy N 32 A2
Varallo I 70 C3
Varano de'Melegari I 81 B4
Varaždin HR 73 B6
Varaždinske Toplice HR 73 B6
Varazze I 80 B2
Varberg S 40 B2
Varde DK 39 D1
Vardø N 2 A22
Vardomb H 74 B3
Varel D 43 B5
Varėna LT 6 J19
Varengeville-sur-Mer F 58 A1
Varenna I 71 B4
Varennes-en-Argonne F 59 A6
Varennes-le-Grand F 69 B4
Varennes-St. Sauveur F 69 B5
Varennes-sur-Allier F 68 B3
Varennes-sur-Amance F 60 C1
Vareš BIH 84 B3
Varese I 70 C3
Varese Ligure I 80 B3
Vârfurile RO 11 N18
Vårgårda S 35 C4
Vargas E 88 A3
Vargas P 92 B2
Vargön S 35 C4
Varhaug N 32 C2
Variaş RO 75 B5
Variaşu Mic RO 75 B6
Varilhes F 77 C4
Varin SK 65 A4
Väring S 35 C5
Váriz P 87 C4
Varkaus FIN 3 E20
Värmlands Bro S 34 B5
Värmskog S 34 B4
Varna BG 16 Q20
Varna YU 85 B4
Värnamo S 40 B4
Varnhem S 35 C5
Varnsdorf CZ 53 C4
Värö S 40 B2
Varoška Rijeka BIH 83 A5
Városlöd H 74 A2
Várpalota H 74 A3
Varreddes F 59 B3
Vars F 79 B5
Varsi I 81 B3
Varsseveld NL 50 B2
Vårsta S 36 B4
Vartofta S 35 C5
Varvarin YU 85 C6
Vårvik S 34 B4
Várvölgy H 74 B2
Varzi I 80 B3
Varzjelas P 92 A2
Varzo I 70 B3
Varzy F 68 A3
Vasad H 75 A4
Väse S 34 B5
Vašica YU 85 A4
Vasilevichi BY 7 K21
Väskinde S 37 D5
Vaskút H 75 B3
Vaslui RO 11 N20
Vassieux-en-Vercors F 79 B4
Vassmolösa S 40 C6
Vassy F 57 B5
Västerås S 36 B3
Västerby S 36 A2
Västerfärnebo S 36 B3
Västerhaninge S 36 B5
Västervik S 37 D3
Vasto I 103 A4
Västra Ämtervik S 34 B5
Västra-Bodarne S 35 D4
Västra Karup S 41 C2
Vasvár H 74 A1
Vasylkiv UA 11 L22
Vát H 74 A1
Vatan F 68 A1
Vatin YU 75 C6
Vatnås N 33 B6
Vätö S 36 B5
Vatra-Dornei RO 11 N19
Vatry F 59 B5
Vattholma S 36 A4
Vättis CH 71 B4
Vauchamps F 59 B4
Vauchassis F 59 B4
Vaucouleurs F 60 B1
Vaudoy-en-Brie F 59 B4
Vaulen N 32 C2
Vaulruz CH 70 B1
Vaulx Vraucourt F 48 C3
Vaumas F 68 B3
Vausseroux F 67 B4
Vauvenargues F 79 C4
Vauvert F 78 C3
Vauvillers F 60 C2
Vaux-sur-Sure B 60 A1
Vawkavysk BY 6 K19
Vaxholm S 36 B5
Växjö S 40 C4
Våxtorp S 41 C3
Vayrac F 77 B4
Važec SK 65 A5
Veberöd S 41 D3
Vechelde D 51 A6
Vechta D 43 C5
Vecinos E 94 B1
Vecsés H 75 A4
Vedavågen N 32 B2
Veddige S 40 B2
Vedersø DK 39 C1
Vedeseta I 71 C4
Vedevåg S 36 B2
Vedra E 86 B2
Vedum S 35 C4
Veendam NL 42 B3
Veenendaal NL 49 A6
Vega, *Asturias* E 88 A1
Vega, *Asturias* E 88 A1
Vega de Espinareda E 86 B4
Vega de Infanzones E 88 B1
Vega de Pas E 88 A3
Vega de Valcarce E 86 B4
Vega de Valdetronco E 88 C1
Vegadeo E 86 A3
Vegårshei N 33 C5
Vegas de Coria E 93 A4
Vegas del Condado E 88 B1
Vegby S 40 B3
Veggli N 33 A6
Veghel NL 49 B6
Véglie I 105 B4
Veguillas E 95 B3
Vegusdal N 33 C5
Veikåker N 33 A6
Veinge S 40 C3
Vejbystrand S 41 C2
Vejen DK 39 D2
Vejer de la Frontera E 99 C5
Vejle DK 39 D2
Vejprty CZ 52 C3
Vela Luka HR 83 D5
Velada E 94 B2
Velayos E 94 B2
Velbert D 50 B3
Velburg D 62 A2
Velden, *Bayern* D 62 A2
Velden, *Bayern* D 62 B3
Velden am Worther See A 73 B4
Velefique E 101 B3
Velen D 50 B3
Velenje SLO 73 B5
Veles MK 15 R17
Velesevec HR 73 C6
Velešin CZ 63 B5
Velestino GR 15 S18
Velez Blanco E 101 B3
Vélez de Benaudalla E 100 C2
Vélez-Málaga E 100 C1
Vélez Rubio E 101 B3
Veli Lošinj HR 83 B3
Veliki Radinci YU 85 A4
Velika HR 74 C2
Velika Drenova YU 85 C6
Velika Gorica HR 73 C6
Velika Grdevac HR 74 C2
Velika Greda YU 75 C6
Velika Ilova BIH 84 B2
Velika Kladuša BIH 73 C5
Velika Kopanica HR 74 C3
Velika Krsna YU 85 B5
Velika Obarska BIH 85 B4
Velika Pisanica HR 74 C2
Velika Plana YU 85 B5
Velika Zdenci HR 74 B2
Velike Lašče SLO 73 C4
Veliki Gaj YU 75 C6
Veliki Popović YU 85 B6
Velikiye Luki RUS 7 H22
Veliko Orašje YU 85 B6
Veliko Selo YU 85 B6
Veliko Tŭrnovo BG 16 Q19
Velilla de San Antonio E 95 B3
Velilla del Río Carrió E 88 B2
Velizh RUS 7 J22
Veljun HR 73 C5
Velká Bíteš CZ 64 A2
Velka Hled'scbe CZ 52 D2
Velká Lomnica SK 65 A6
Velká nad Veličkou CZ 64 B3
Velké Bystřice CZ 64 A3
Velké Heraltice CZ 64 A3
Velké Karlovice CZ 64 A4
Vel'ké Leváre SK 64 B3
Velké Losiny CZ 54 C2
Velké Meziříčí CZ 64 A2
Velké Pavlovice CZ 64 B2
Vel'ké Rovné SK 65 A4
Vel'ké Uherce SK 65 B4
Vel'ké Zálužie SK 64 B3
Vel'ke'Kostol'any SK 64 B3
Vel'ký Blahovo SK 65 B6
Velky Bor CZ 63 A4
Vel'ký Cetin SK 64 B4
Vel'ký Krtiš SK 65 B5
Vel'ký Meder SK 64 C3
Velky Ujezd CZ 64 A3
Vellahn D 44 B2
Vellberg D 61 A5
Velles F 67 B6
Velletri I 102 B2
Vellinge S 41 D3
Vellisca E 95 B4
Velliza E 88 C2
Vellmar D 51 B5
Velp NL 50 A1
Velten D 45 C5
Velvary CZ 53 C4
Vemb DK 39 C1
Veme N 34 A2
Véménd H 74 B3
Vemmedrup DK 39 D5
Vena S 40 B5
Venaco F 110 A2
Venafro I 103 B4
Venarey-les-Laumes F 69 A4
Venaria I 70 C2
Venasca I 80 B1
Venčane YU 85 B5
Vence F 79 C6
Venda Nova, *Coimbra* P 92 A2
Venda Nova, *Leiria* P 92 B2
Vendas Novas P 92 C2
Vendays-Montalivet F 66 C3
Vendel S 36 A4
Vendelso S 36 B5
Vendeuil F 59 A4
Vendeuvre-sur-Barse F 59 B5
Vendœuvres F 67 B6
Vendôme F 58 C2
Venelles F 79 C4
Veness GB 23 B6
Venézia I 72 C2
Venialbo E 88 C1
Vénissieux F 69 C4
Venlo NL 50 B2
Venn Green GB 28 C3
Vennesla N 33 C4
Vennesund N 2 D13
Venosa I 104 B2
Venray NL 50 B1
Vent A 71 B5
Venta de Baños E 88 C2
Venta de los Santos E 100 A2
Venta del Moro E 96 B1
Venta las Ranas E 88 A1
Ventanueva E 86 A4
Ventas de Huelma E 100 B2
Ventas de Zafarraya E 100 C1
Ventavon F 79 B4
Ventimíglia I 80 C1
Ventnor GB 31 D2
Ventosa de la Sierra E 89 C4
Ventosilla E 89 C4
Ventspils LV 6 H17
Venturina I 81 C4
Venzolasca F 110 A2
Venzone I 72 B3
Vép H 74 A1
Vera E 101 B4
Vera Cruz P 98 A3
Vera de Bidasoa E 76 C1
Vera de Moncayo E 89 C5
Verbánia I 70 C3
Verberie F 58 A3
Verbicaro I 106 B2
Verbier CH 70 B2
Vercel-Villedieu-le-Camp F 69 A6
Vercelli I 70 C3
Verchen D 45 B4
Vercheny F 79 B4
Verclause F 79 B4
Verdalsøra N 2 E12
Verden D 43 C6
Verdens Ende N 35 B2
Verdille F 67 C4
Verdú E 91 B4
Verdun F 59 A6
Verdun-sur-Garonne F 77 C4
Verdun-sur-le-Doubs F 69 B5
Veresegyház H 65 C5
Verfeil F 77 C4
Vergato I 81 B5
Vergel E 96 C3
Vergeletto CH 70 B3
Verges E 91 A6
Vergiate I 70 C3
Vergt F 77 A3
Verín E 87 C3
Veringenstadt D 61 B5
Verkhovye RUS 7 K25
Verl D 51 B4
Vermand F 59 A4
Vermelha P 92 B1
Vermenton F 59 C4
Vern-d'Anjou F 57 C5
Vernago I 71 B5
Vernante I 80 B1
Vernantes F 67 A5
Vernár SK 65 B6
Vernasca I 81 B3
Vernayaz CH 70 B2
Vernazza I 81 B3
Verneřice CZ 53 C4
Vernet F 77 C4
Vernet-les-Bains F 91 A5
Verneuil F 59 A4
Verneuil-sur-Avre F 58 B1
Vernier CH 69 B6
Vérnio I 81 B5
Vérnole I 105 B5
Vernon F 58 A2
Vernoux-en-Vivarais F 78 B3
Veróce H 65 C5
Véroia GR 15 R18
Verolanuova I 71 C5
Véroli I 103 B3
Verona I 71 C6
Verpelét H 65 C6
Verrès I 70 C2
Verrey-sous-Salmaise F 69 A4
Verrières F 67 B5
Versailles F 58 B3
Versam CH 71 B4
Verseg H 65 C5
Versmold D 50 A4
Versoix CH 69 B6
Verteillac F 67 C5
Vértesacsa H 74 A3
Vertou F 66 A3
Vertus F 59 B4
Verviers B 50 C1
Vervins F 59 A4
Verwood GB 29 C6
Veryan GB 28 C3
Veržej SLO 73 B6
Verzuolo I 80 B1
Verzy F 59 A5
Vescovato F 110 A2
Vése H 74 B2
Veselí nad Lužnicí CZ 63 A5
Veselí nad Moravou CZ 64 B3
Veseliy BG 16 Q20
Vésime I 80 B2
Vesoul F 60 C2
Vespolate I 70 C3
Vessigebro S 40 C2
Vestbygd N 32 C3
Vestenanova I 71 C6
Vester Husby S 37 C3
Vester Nebel DK 39 D2
Vester Torup DK 38 B2
Vester Vedsted DK 39 D1
Vesterøhavn DK 38 B3
Vestervig DK 38 C1
Vestfossen N 33 B6
Vestmarka N 34 B3
Vestone I 71 C5
Vesyegonsk RUS 7 G25
Veszprém H 74 A2
Veszprémvarsány H 74 A2
Vésztő H 75 B6
Vetlanda S 40 B5
Vetovo HR 74 C2
Vetralla I 102 A2
Větrný Jeníkov CZ 63 A6
Vétroz CH 70 B2
Vetschau D 53 B4
Vetto I 81 B4
Vetulónia I 81 D4
Veules-les-Roses F 58 A1
Veulettes-sur-Mer F 58 A1
Veum N 33 B5
Veurne B 48 B3
Veverská Bítýška CZ 64 A2
Vevey CH 70 B1
Vex CH 70 B2
Veynes F 79 B4
Veyre-Monton F 68 C3
Veyrier F 69 C6
Vézelay F 68 A3
Vézelise F 60 B2
Vézenobres F 78 B3
Vezins F 67 A4
Vézins-de-Lévézou F 78 B1
Vezza di Óglio I 71 B5
Vezzani F 110 A2
Vezzano I 71 B6
Vezzano sul Cróstolo I 81 B4
Via Gloria P 98 B3
Viadana I 81 B4
Viana E 89 B4
Viana do Alentejo P 98 A2
Viana do Bolo E 87 B3
Viana do Castelo P 87 C2
Vianden L 60 A2
Viaréggio I 81 C4
Viator E 101 C3
Vibble S 37 E5
Vibo Valéntia I 106 C3
Viborg DK 38 C2
Vibraye F 58 B1
Vic E 91 B5
Vic-en-Bigorre F 76 C3
Vic-Fézensac F 76 C3
Vic-le-Comte F 68 C3
Vic-sur-Aisne F 59 A4
Vic-sur-Cère F 77 B5
Vicar E 101 C3
Vicarello I 81 C4
Vicari I 108 B2
Vicchio I 81 C5
Vicdessos F 77 D4
Vicenza I 71 C6
Vichy F 68 B3
Vickan S 38 B5
Vickerstown GB 26 A2
Vico F 110 A1
Vico del Gargano I 104 A2
Vico Equense I 103 C4
Vicopisano I 81 C4
Vicosoprano CH 71 B4
Vicovaro I 102 A2
Victoria (Rabat) M 109 C4
Vidago P 87 C3
Vidauban F 79 C5
Vide P 92 A3
Videbæk DK 39 C1
Videm SLO 73 C4
Videseter N 2 F10
Vidigueira P 98 A3
Vidin BG 15 Q18
Vidlin GB 22 A7
Vidzy BY 7 J20
Viechtach D 62 A3
Vieille-Brioude F 68 C3
Vieira P 92 B2
Vieira do Minho P 87 C2
Vieiros P 92 C3
Vielha E 90 A3
Vielle-Aure F 77 D3
Viellevigne F 66 B3
Vielmur-sur-Agout F 77 C5
Viels Maison F 59 B4
Vielsalm B 50 C1
Vienenburg D 51 B6
Vienne F 69 C4
Vieritz D 44 C4
Viernheim D 61 A4
Vierraden D 45 B6
Viersen D 50 B2
Vierville-sur-Mer F 57 A5
Vierzon F 68 A2
Vieselbach D 52 C1
Vieste I 104 A3
Vieteren B 48 C3
Vietri di Potenza I 104 B2
Vietri sul Mare I 104 B1
Vieux-Boucau-les-Bains F 76 C1
Vif F 79 A4
Vig DK 39 D4
Vigásio I 71 C5
Vigaun A 63 C4
Vigeland N 33 C4
Vigeois F 67 C6
Vigévano I 70 C3
Viggianello I 104 C3
Viggiano I 104 B2
Vigliano I 102 A3
Vigmostad N 33 C4
Vignale I 80 A2
Vignanello I 102 A2
Vigneulles-lès-Hattonchâtel F 60 B1
Vignola I 81 B5
Vignory F 59 B6
Vignoux-sur Barangeon F 68 A2
Vigo E 87 B2
Vigo di Fassa I 72 B1
Vigone I 80 B1
Vigrestad N 32 C2
Vihiers F 67 A4
Viitasaari FIN 3 E19
Vik, *Rogaland* N 32 C2
Vik S 41 D4
Vika S 36 A2
Vikajärvi FIN 3 C20
Vikane N 34 B2
Vikedal N 32 B2
Vikeland N 33 C4
Viken S 41 C2
Viker N 34 A2
Vikersund N 33 B6
Vikeså N 32 C3
Vikevåg N 32 B2
Vikingstad S 37 C2
Vikja, *Sogn og Fjordane* N 2 F10
Vikmanshyttan S 36 A2
Vikøy N 32 A3
Viksta S 36 A4
Vila Boim P 92 C3
Vila Chã de Ourique P 92 B2
Vila de Cruces E 86 B2
Vila de Rei P 92 B2
Vila do Bispo P 98 B2
Vila do Conde P 87 C2
Vila Flor P 87 C3
Vila Franca das Navas P 92 A3
Vila Franca de Xira P 92 C1
Vila Fresca P 92 C1
Vila Nogueira P 92 C1
Vila Nova da Baronia P 98 A2
Vila Nova de Cerveira P 87 C2
Vila Nova de Famalicão P 87 C2
Vila Nova de Foz Côa P 87 C3
Vila Nova de Gaia P 87 C2
Vila Nova de Milfontes P 98 B2
Vila Nova de Ourém P 92 B2
Vila Nova de Paiva P 87 D3
Vila Nova de São Bento P 98 B3
Vila Pouca de Aguiar P 87 C3
Vila Praja de Ancora P 87 C2
Vila Real P 87 C3
Vila-real de los Infantes E 96 B2
Vila Real de Santo António P 98 B3
Vila-Rodona E 91 B4
Vila Ruiva P 98 A3
Vila Seca P 92 A2
Vila Velha de Ródão P 92 B3

Vila Verde, *Braga* P 87 C2
Vila Verde, *Lisboa* P 92 B1
Vila Verde de Filcalho P 98 B3
Vila Viçosa P 92 C3
Viladamat E 91 A6
Viladrau E 91 B5
Vilafranca del Maestrat E 90 C2
Vilafranca del Penedès E 91 B4
Vilagarcia de Arousa E 86 B2
Vilajuiga E 91 A6
Vilamarin E 86 B3
Vilamartin de Valdeorras E 86 B3
Vilanova de Castelló E 96 B2
Vilanova de Sau E 91 B5
Vilanova i la Geltrú E 91 B4
Vilapedre E 86 A3
Vilar de Santos E 87 B3
Vilar Formosa P 93 A4
Vilarandelo P 87 C3
Vilardevós E 87 C3
Vilasantar E 86 A2
Vilaseca E 91 B4
Vilassar de Mar E 91 B5
Vilches E 100 A2
Vildbjerg DK 39 C1
Vilémov CZ 63 A6
Vileyka BY 7 J20
Vilhelmina S 2 D15
Viljandi EST 7 G19
Villa Castelli I 105 B4
Villa Cova de Lixa P 87 C2
Villa de Peralonso E 87 C4
Villa del Prado E 94 B2
Villa del Rio E 100 B1
Villa di Chiavenna I 71 B4
Villa Minozzo I 81 B4
Villa San Giovanni I 109 A4
Villa Santa Maria I 103 B4
Villa Santina I 72 B2
Villabáñez E 88 C2
Villablanca E 98 B3
Villablino E 86 B4
Villabona E 89 A4
Villabragima E 88 C1
Villabuena del Puente E 88 C1
Villacadima E 95 A3
Villacañas E 95 C3
Villacarriedo E 88 A3
Villacarrillo E 100 A2
Villacastín E 94 B2
Villach A 72 B3
Villacidro I 110 D1
Villaconejos E 95 B3
Villaconejos de Trabaque E 95 B4
Villada E 88 B2
Villadangos del Páramo E 88 B1
Villadecanes E 86 B4
Villadepera E 87 C4
Villadiego E 88 B2
Villadompardo E 100 B1
Villadóssola I 70 B3
Villaeles de Valdavia E 88 B2
Villaescusa de Haro E 95 C4
Villafáfila E 88 C1
Villafeliche E 95 A5
Villaflores E 94 A1
Villafrades de Campos E 88 B2
Villafranca, *Avila* E 94 B1
Villafranca, *Navarra* E 89 B5
Villafranca de Córdoba E 100 B1
Villafranca de los Barros E 93 C4
Villafranca de los Caballeros E 95 C3
Villafranca del Bierzo E 86 B4
Villafranca di Verona I 71 C5
Villafranca in Lunigiana I 81 B3
Villafranca-Montes de Oca E 89 B3
Villafranca Tirrena I 109 A4
Villafranco del Campo E 95 B5
Villafranco del Guadalquivir E 99 B4
Villafrati I 108 B2
Villafrechós E 88 C1
Villafruela E 88 C3
Villagarcia de las Torres E 99 A4
Villaggio Mancuso I 106 B3
Villagonzalo E 93 C4
Villagotón E 86 B4
Villagrains F 76 B2
Villaharta E 100 A1
Villahermosa E 100 A3
Villaherreros E 88 B2
Villahoz E 88 B3
Villaines-la-Juhel F 57 B5
Villajoyosa E 96 C2
Villalago I 103 B3
Villalba E 86 A3
Villalba I 108 B2
Villalba de Calatrava E 100 A2
Villalba de Guardo E 88 B2
Villalba de la Sierra E 95 B4
Villalba de los Alcores E 88 C2
Villalba de los Barros E 93 C4
Villalba del Alcor E 99 B4
Villalba del Rey E 95 B4
Villalcampo E 87 C4
Villalcázar de Sirga E 88 B2
Villalengua E 89 C5
Villalgordo del Júcar E 95 C4
Villalgordo del Marquesado E 95 C4
Villalmóndar E 89 B3
Villalón de Campos E 88 B1
Villalonga E 96 C2
Villalonso E 88 C1
Villalpando E 88 C1
Villaluenga E 94 B3
Villalumbroso E 88 B2
Villálvaro E 89 C3
Villamalea E 96 B1
Villamanán E 88 B1
Villamanín E 88 B1
Villamanrique E 100 A3
Villamanrique de la Condesa E 99 B4
Villamanta E 94 B2
Villamantilla E 94 B2
Villamar I 110 D1
Villamartin E 99 C5
Villamartin de Campos E 88 B2
Villamartin de Don Sancho E 88 B1
Villamassárgia I 110 D1
Villamayor E 88 A1
Villamayor de Calatrava E 100 A1
Villamayor de Campos E 88 C1
Villamayor de Santiago E 95 C4
Villamblard F 77 A3
Villamejil E 86 B4
Villamesías E 93 B5
Villaminaya E 94 C3
Villamor de los Escuderos E 94 A1
Villamoronta E 88 B2
Villamuelas E 94 C3
Villamuriel de Cerrato E 88 C2
Villandraut F 76 B2
Villanova I 105 B4
Villanova d'Asti I 80 B1
Villanova del Battista I 104 A2
Villanova Mondovì I 80 B1
Villanova Monteleone I 110 C1
Villante E 88 B3
Villantério I 71 C4
Villanubla E 88 C2
Villanueva de Alcardete E 95 C3
Villanueva de Alcorón E 95 B4
Villanueva de Algaidas E 100 B1
Villanueva de Argaña E 88 B3
Villanueva de Bogas E 94 C3
Villanueva de Córdoba E 100 A1
Villanueva de Gállego E 90 B2
Villanueva de la Concepcion E 100 C1
Villanueva de la Fuente E 101 A3
Villanueva de la Jara E 95 C5
Villanueva de la Reina E 100 A2
Villanueva de la Serena E 93 C5
Villanueva de la Sierra E 93 A4
Villanueva de la Vera E 94 B1
Villanueva de las Manzanas E 88 B1
Villanueva de las Peras E 88 C1
Villanueva de las Torres E 100 B2
Villanueva de los Castillejos E 98 B3
Villanueva de los Infantes E 100 A3
Villanueva de Mesia E 100 B2
Villanueva de Nía E 88 B2
Villanueva de Oscos E 86 A4
Villanueva de San Carlos E 100 A2
Villanueva de San Juan E 99 B5
Villanueva de Tapia E 100 B1
Villanueva de Valdegovia E 89 B3
Villanueva del Aceral E 94 A2
Villanueva del Arzobispo E 100 A3
Villanueva del Campo E 88 C1
Villanueva del Duque E 100 A1
Villanueva del Fresno E 93 C3
Villanueva del Huerva E 90 B1
Villanueva del Rey E 99 A5
Villanueva del Rio E 99 B5
Villanueva del Rio y Minas E 99 B5
Villanueva del Rosario E 100 C1
Villanueva del Trabuco E 100 B1
Villány H 74 C3
Villaputzu I 110 D2
Villaquejida E 88 B1
Villaquilambre E 88 B1
Villaquiran de los Infantes E 88 B2
Villar de Barrio E 87 B3
Villar de Cañas E 95 C4
Villar de Chinchilla E 96 C1
Villar de Ciervo E 87 D4
Villar de Domingo Garcia E 95 B4
Villar de los Navarros E 90 B1
Villar de Rena E 93 B5
Villar del Arzobispo E 96 B2
Villar del Buey E 87 C4
Villar del Cobo E 95 B5
Villar del Humo E 95 C5
Villar del Pedroso E 94 C1
Villar del Rey E 93 B4
Villar del Rio E 89 B4
Villar del Saz de Navalón E 95 B4
Villar Perosa I 79 B6
Villaralto E 100 A1
Villarcayo E 89 B3
Villard-de-Lans F 79 A4
Villardeciervos E 87 C4
Villardefrades E 88 C1
Villarejo E 95 A3
Villarejo de Fuentes E 95 C4
Villarejo de Orbigo E 88 B1
Villarejo de Salvanes E 95 B3
Villarejo-Periesteban E 95 C4
Villares del Saz E 95 C4
Villaretto I 79 A6
Villargordo del Cabriel E 96 B1
Villarino E 87 C4
Villarino de Conso E 87 B3
Villarluengo E 90 C2
Villarobe E 89 B3
Villarosa I 109 B3
Villarramiel E 88 B2
Villarrasa E 99 B4
Villarreal de San Carlos E 93 B4
Villarrin de Campos E 88 C1
Villarrobledo E 95 C4
Villarroya de la Sierra E 89 C5
Villarroya de los Pinares E 90 C2
Villarrubia de los Ojos E 95 C3
Villarrubia de Santiago E 95 C3
Villarrubio E 95 C4
Villars-les-Dombes F 69 B5
Villarta E 95 C5
Villarta de los Montes E 94 C2
Villarta de San Juan E 95 C3
Villasana de Mena E 89 A3
Villasandino E 88 B2
Villasante E 89 A3
Villasarracino E 88 B2
Villasayas E 89 C4
Villasdardo E 87 C4
Villaseca de Henares E 95 B4
Villaseca de la Sagra E 94 C3
Villaseco de los Gamitos E 87 C4
Villaseco de los Reyes E 87 C4
Villasequilla de Yepes E 94 C3
Villasimius I 110 D2
Villasmundo I 109 B4
Villasor I 110 D1
Villastar E 96 A1
Villastellone I 80 B1
Villatobas E 95 C3
Villatorp E 94 B1
Villatoya E 96 B1
Villavaliente E 96 B1
Villavelayo E 89 B4
Villavella E 87 B3
Villaver de de Guadalimar E 101 A3
Villaverde del Rio E 99 B5
Villaviciosa E 88 A1
Villaviciosa de Córdoba E 100 A1
Villaviciosa de Odón E 94 B3
Villavieja de Yeltes E 87 D4
Villayón E 86 A4
Villé F 60 B3
Ville-di-Pietrabugno F 110 A2
Ville-sous-la-Ferté F 59 B5
Ville-sur-Illon F 60 B2
Ville-sur-Tourbe F 59 A5
Villebois-Lavalette F 67 C5
Villecerf F 59 B3
Villecomtal F 77 B5
Villedieu-les-Poêles F 57 B4
Villedieu-sur-Indre F 67 B6
Villefagnan F 67 B5
Villefontaine F 69 C5
Villefort F 78 B2
Villefranche-d'Albigeois F 77 C5
Villefranche-d'Allier F 68 B2
Villefranche-de-Lauragais F 77 C4
Villefranche-de-Lonchat F 76 B3
Villefranche-de-Panat F 78 B1
Villefranche-de-Rouergue F 77 B5
Villefranche-du-Périgord F 77 B4
Villefranche-sur-Cher F 68 A1
Villefranche-sur-Mer F 79 C6
Villefranche-sur-Saône F 69 B4
Villegenon F 68 A2
Villel E 96 A1
Villemaur-sur-Vanne F 59 B4
Villemur-sur-Tarn F 77 C4
Villena E 96 C2
Villenauxe-la-Grande F 59 B4
Villenave-d'Ornon F 76 B2
Villeneuve CH 70 B1
Villeneuve F 77 B5
Villeneuve-d'Ascq F 49 C4
Villeneuve-de-Berg F 78 B3
Villeneuve-de-Marsan F 76 C2
Villeneuve-de-Rivière F 77 C3
Villeneuve-la-Guyard F 59 B4
Villeneuve-l'Archevêque F 59 B4
Villeneuve-le-Comte F 58 B3
Villeneuve-lès-Avignon F 78 C3
Villeneuve-les-Corbières F 78 D1
Villeneuve-St. Georges F 58 B3
Villeneuve-sur-Allier F 68 B3
Villeneuve-sur-Lot F 77 B3
Villeneuve-sur-Yonne F 59 B4
Villeréal F 77 B3
Villerias E 88 C2
Villeromain F 58 C2
Villers-Bocage, *Calvados* F 57 A5
Villers-Bocage, *Somme* F 48 D3
Villers-Bretonneux F 58 A3
Villers-Carbonnel F 59 A3
Villers-Cotterêts F 59 A4
Villers-Farlay F 69 B5
Villers-le-Gambon B 49 C5
Villers le Lac F 70 A1
Villers-sur-Mer F 57 A6
Villersexel F 69 A6
Villerupt F 60 A1
Villerville F 57 A6
Villeseneux F 59 B5
Villetrun F 58 C2
Villetta Barrea I 103 B3
Villeurbanne F 69 C4
Villeveyrac F 78 C2
Villevocance F 69 C4
Villiers-St. Benoit F 59 C4
Villiers-St. Georges F 59 B4
Villingen D 61 B4
Villmar D 50 C4
Villoldo E 88 B2
Villoria E 94 B1
Vilnius LT 7 J19
Vils A 71 A5
Vils DK 38 C1
Vilsbiburg D 62 B3
Vilseck D 62 A2
Vilshofen D 63 B4
Vilshult S 41 C4
Vilusi YU 84 D3
Vilvestre E 87 C4
Vilvoorde B 49 C5
Vimeiro P 92 B1
Vimercate I 71 C4
Vimianzo E 86 A1
Vimieiro P 92 C3
Vimioso P 87 C4
Vimmerby S 40 B5
Vimoutiers F 57 B6
Vimperk CZ 63 A4
Vimy F 48 C3
Vinadi CH 71 B5
Vinadio I 79 B6
Vinaixa E 90 B3
Vinarós E 90 C3
Vinay F 69 C5
Vinberg S 40 C2
Vinca F 91 A5
Vinča YU 85 B5
Vinchiaturo I 103 B4
Vinci I 81 C4
Vindeby DK 39 D3
Vindeln S 3 D16
Vinderup DK 38 C1
Vindsvik N 32 B3
Vinets F 59 B5
Vineuil F 67 A6
Vinga RO 75 B6
Vingåker S 37 B2
Vingrau F 78 D1
Vinhais P 87 C4
Vinica HR 73 B6
Vinica SK 65 B5
Vinica SLO 73 C5
Vinicka YU 85 D4
Viniegra de Arriba E 89 B4
Vinje, *Sør-Trøndelag* N 2 E11
Vinje, *Telemark* N 33 B4
Vinkovci HR 74 C3
Vinninga S 35 C5
Vinnytsya UA 11 M21
Vinon-sur-Verdon F 79 C4
Vinslöv S 41 C3
Vintrosa S 36 B1
Viñuela de Sayago E 88 C1
Viñuelas E 95 B3
Vinuesa E 89 C4
Vinzelberg D 44 C3
Viöl D 43 A6
Viola I 80 B1
Violay F 69 C4
Vipava SLO 72 C3
Vipiteno I 71 B6
Vipperow D 45 B4
Vir BIH 84 C2
Vir HR 83 B4
Vira CH 70 B3
Vire F 57 B5
Vireux F 49 C5
Virgen A 72 A2
Virgen de la Cabeza E 100 A1
Virginia IRL 19 C4
Virieu F 69 C5
Virieu-le-Grand F 69 C5
Virje HR 74 B1
Virklund DK 39 C2
Virovitica HR 74 C2
Virsbo S 36 B3
Virserum S 40 B5
Virton B 60 A1
Virtsu EST 6 G18
Viry F 69 B6
Vis HR 83 C5
Visbek D 43 C5
Visby DK 39 D1
Visby S 37 D5
Visé B 50 C1
Višegrad BIH 85 C4
Viserba I 82 B1
Viseu P 92 A3
Visiedo E 90 C1
Viskafors S 40 B2
Visland N 32 C3
Vislanda S 40 C4
Visnes N 32 B2
Višnja Gora SLO 73 C4
Višnjan HR 73 C3
Višnové CZ 64 B2
Visnums-Kil S 34 B6
Viso del Marqués E 100 A2
Visoko BIH 84 C3
Visoko SLO 73 B4
Visone I 80 B2
Visp CH 70 B2
Vissefjärda S 40 C5
Visselhövede D 43 C6
Vissenbjerg DK 39 D3
Visso I 82 D2
Vistabella del Maestrat E 96 A2
Vita I 108 B1
Vitanje SLO 73 B5
Vitanovac YU 85 C5
Viterbo I 102 A2
Vitez BIH 84 B2
Vitigudino E 87 C4
Vitina BIH 84 C2
Vitis A 63 B6
Vitkov CZ 64 A3
Vitkovac YU 85 C5
Vitomirica YU 85 D5
Vitoria Gasteiz E 89 B4
Vitré F 57 B4
Vitrey-sur-Mance F 60 C1
Vitry-en-Artois F 48 C3
Vitry-le-François F 59 B5
Vitry-sur-Seine F 58 B3
Vitsand S 34 A4
Vitsyebsk BY 7 J22
Vittangi S 3 C17
Vittaryd S 40 C3
Vitteaux F 69 A4
Vittel F 60 B1
Vittinge S 36 B4
Vittória I 109 C3
Vittório Véneto I 72 C2
Vittsjö S 41 C3
Viù I 70 C2
Viul N 34 A2
Vivario F 110 A2
Viveiro E 86 A3
Vivel del Rio Martin E 90 C2
Viver E 96 B2
Viverols F 68 C3
Viveros E 101 A3
Viviers F 78 B3
Vivonne F 67 B5
Vivy F 67 A4
Vize TR 16 R20
Vizille F 79 A4
Viziñada HR 72 C3
Viziru RO 11 P20
Vizovice CZ 64 A3
Vizvár H 74 B2
Vizzavona F 110 A2
Vizzini I 109 B3
Vlachovice CZ 64 A3
Vlachovo SK 65 B6
Vláchovo Březi CZ 63 A4
Vladimirci YU 85 B4
Vladimirovac YU 85 A5
Vladislav CZ 64 A1
Vlagtwedde NL 43 B4
Vlajkovac YU 85 A6
Vlasenica BIH 84 B3
Vlašim CZ 63 A5
Vlatkoviči BIH 84 B2
Vledder NL 42 C3
Vlissingen NL 49 B4
Vlorë AL 15 R16
Vlotho D 51 A4
Vnanje Gorice SLO 73 C4
Vobarno I 71 C5
Voćin HR 74 C2
Vöcklabruck A 63 B4
Vöcklamarkt A 63 C4
Vodanj YU 85 B5
Voderady SK 64 B3
Vodice, *Istarska* HR 73 C4
Vodice, *Šibenska* HR 83 C4
Vodice SLO 73 B4
Vodňany CZ 63 A5
Vodnjan HR 82 B2
Vodskov DK 38 B3
Voe GB 22 A7
Voerså DK 38 B3
Voghera I 80 B3
Vogogna I 70 B3
Vogošća BIH 84 C3
Vogüé F 78 B3
Vohburg D 62 B2
Vohenstrauss D 62 A3
Vöhl D 51 B4
Vöhrenbach D 61 B4
Vöhringen D 61 B6
Void-Vacon F 60 B1
Voiron F 69 C5
Voise F 58 B2
Voisey F 60 C1
Voiteg RO 75 C6
Voiteur F 69 B5
Voitsberg A 73 A5
Vojens DK 39 D2
Vojka YU 85 B5
Vojlovica YU 85 B5
Vojnić HR 73 C5
Vojnice SK 65 C4
Vojnik SLO 73 B5
Vojvoda Stepa YU 75 C5
Volargne I 71 C5
Volary CZ 63 B4
Volče SLO 72 B3
Volda N 2 E10
Volendam NL 42 C2
Volga RUS 7 G26
Volkach D 61 A6
Völkermarkt A 73 B4
Volkhov RUS 7 G23
Völklingen D 60 A2
Volkmarsen D 51 B5
Vollenhove NL 42 C2
Vollore-Montagne F 68 C3
Vollsjö S 41 D3
Volodymyr-Volyns'kyy UA 11 L19
Volokolamsk RUS 7 H24
Vólos GR 15 S18
Volosovo RUS 7 G21
Volovets UA 11 M18
Volta Mantovana I 71 C5
Voltággio I 80 B2
Volterra I 81 C4
Voltri I 80 B2
Volturara Áppula I 104 A2
Volturara Irpina I 104 B1
Volvic F 68 C3
Volyně CZ 63 A4
Vónitsa GR 15 S17
Vönöck H 74 A2
Vonsild DK 39 D2
Voorschoten NL 49 A5
Vorau A 73 A5
Vorbasse DK 39 D2
Vorchdorf A 63 C4
Vorden NL 50 A2
Vordernberg A 73 A4
Vordingborg DK 39 D4
Voreppe F 69 C5
Vorey F 68 C3
Vorgod DK 39 C1
Vormsund N 34 A3
Voronezh UA 7 L23
Võru EST 7 H20
Voss N 2 F10
Votice CZ 63 A5
Voué F 59 B5
Vouillé F 67 B5
Voulx F 59 B3
Voussac F 68 B3
Vouvray F 67 A5
Vouvry CH 70 B1
Vouzela P 92 A2
Vouziers F 59 A5
Voves F 58 B2
Voy GB 23 B5
Voynitsa RUS 3 D22
Voznesensk UA 11 N22
Vrå DK 38 B2
Vrå S 40 C3
Vráble SK 64 B4
Vračenovići YU 84 D3
Vračev Gaj YU 85 B6
Vraćevsnica YU 85 B5
Vrådal N 33 B5
Vrana HR 83 B3
Vranduk BIH 84 B2
Vrångö S 38 B4
Vrani RO 85 A6
Vranić YU 85 B5
Vraniči BIH 84 C3
Vranja HR 73 C4
Vranjak BIH 84 B3
Vranje YU 15 Q17
Vranov nad Dyje CZ 64 B1
Vranovice CZ 64 B2
Vransko SLO 73 B4
Vrapčići BIH 84 C2
Vratimov CZ 64 A4
Vratsa BG 15 Q18
Vrbanja HR 84 B3
Vrbanjci BIH 84 B2
Vrbas YU 75 C4
Vrbaška BIH 74 C2
Vrbnik, *Primorsko-Goranska* HR 83 A3
Vrbnik, *Zadarsko-Kninska* HR 83 B5
Vrbno p. Pradědem CZ 54 C2
Vrboska HR 83 C5
Vrbov SK 65 A6
Vrbovce SK 64 B3
Vrbové SK 64 B3
Vrbovec HR 73 C6
Vrbovski YU 85 B5
Vrbovsko HR 73 C5
Vrchlabí CZ 53 C5
Vrčin YU 85 B5
Vrdy CZ 63 A6
Vrebac HR 83 B4
Vreden D 50 A2
Vrela YU 85 D5
Vreoci YU 85 B5
Vretstorp S 37 B1
Vrginmost HR 73 C5
Vrgorac HR 84 C2
Vrhnika SLO 73 C4
Vrhovine HR 83 B4
Vrhpolje YU 85 B4
Vriezenveen NL 42 C3
Vrigne-aux-Bois F 59 A5
Vrigstad S 40 B4
Vrlika HR 83 C5
Vrmbaje YU 85 C5
Vrnjačka Banja YU 85 C5
Vrnograč BIH 73 C5
Vron F 48 C2
Vroomshoop NL 42 C3
Vroutek CZ 52 C3
Vrpolje HR 74 C3
Vršac YU 85 A6
Vrsar HR 82 A2
Vrsi HR 83 B4
Vrtoče BIH 83 B5
Vrútky SK 65 A4
Všeruby CZ 62 A3
Všestary CZ 53 C5
Vsetin CZ 64 A3
Vuča YU 85 D5
Vučitrn YU 85 D5
Vučkovica YU 85 C5
Vught NL 49 B6
Vuillafans F 69 A6
Vukovar HR 75 C4
Vulcan RO 11 P18
Vulcanești MD 11 P21
Vuolijoki FIN 3 D20
Vuzenica SLO 73 B5
Vy-lès Lure F 60 C2
Vyartsilya RUS 3 E22
Vyazma RUS 7 J24
Vyborg RUS 3 F21
Výčapy CZ 64 A1
Výčapy-Opatovce SK 64 B4
Východna SK 65 A5
Vydrany SK 64 B3
Vyerkhnyadzvinsk BY 7 J20
Vyhne SK 65 B4
Vylkove UA 11 P21
Vynohradiv UA 11 M18
Vyshniy Volochek RUS 7 H24
Vyškov CZ 64 A3
Vysoká nad Kysucou SK 65 A4
Vysoké Mýto CZ 53 D6
Vysokovsk RUS 7 H25
Vyšší Brod CZ 63 B5

W

Waabs D 44 A1
Waalwijk NL 49 B6
Waarschoot B 49 B4
Wabern D 51 B5
Wąbrzeźno PL 47 B4
Wąchock PL 55 B6
Wachow D 45 C4
Wachów PL 54 C3
Wächtersbach D 51 C5
Wackersdorf D 62 A3
Waddington GB 27 B5
Wadebridge GB 28 C3
Wadelsdorf D 53 B4
Wädenswil CH 70 A3
Wadern D 60 A2
Wadersloh D 50 B4
Wadlew PL 55 B4
Wadowice PL 65 A5
Wagenfeld D 43 C5
Wageningen NL 49 B6
Waghäusel D 61 A4
Waging D 62 C3
Wagrain A 72 A3
Wągrowiec PL 46 C3
Wahlsdorf D 52 B3
Wahlstedt D 44 B2
Wahrenholz D 44 C2
Waiblingen D 61 B5
Waidhaus D 62 A3
Waidhofen an der Thaya A 63 B6
Waidhofen an der Ybbs A 63 C5
Waimes B 50 C2
Wainfleet All Saints GB 27 B6
Waizenkirchen A 63 B4
Wakefield GB 27 B4
Wałbrzych PL 53 C6
Walchensee D 62 C2
Walchsee A 62 C3
Wałcz PL 46 B2
Wald CH 70 A3
Wald-Michelbach D 61 A4
Waldaschaff D 51 D5
Waldbach A 73 A5
Waldböckelheim D 60 A3
Waldbröl D 50 C3
Waldeck D 51 B5
Waldenburg D 52 C2
Waldfischbach-Burgalben D 60 A3
Waldheim D 52 B3
Waldkappel D 51 B5
Waldkirch D 60 B3
Waldkirchen D 63 B4
Waldkirchen am Wesen A 63 B4
Waldkraiburg D 62 B3
Waldmohr D 60 A3
Waldmünchen D 62 A3
Waldring A 62 C3
Waldsassen D 52 C2
Waldshut D 61 C4
Waldstatt CH 71 A4
Waldwisse F 60 A2
Walenstadt CH 71 A4
Walentynów PL 55 B6
Walichnowy PL 54 B3
Walincourt F 49 C4
Walkenried D 51 B6
Walkeringham GB 27 B5
Wallasey GB 26 B2
Walldürn D 61 A5
Wallenfells D 52 C1
Wallenhorst D 43 C5
Wallers F 49 C4
Wallersdorf D 62 B3
Wallerstein D 61 B6
Wallingford GB 31 C2
Wallitz D 45 B4
Walls GB 22 A7
Wallsbüll D 39 E2
Walmer GB 31 C5
Walsall GB 27 C4
Walshoutem B 49 C6
Walsrode D 43 C6
Waltenhofen D 61 C6
Waltershausen D 51 C6
Waltham Abbey GB 31 C4
Waltham on the Wolds GB 30 B3
Walton-on-Thames GB 31 C3
Walton-on-the-Naze GB 31 C5
Wamba E 88 C2
Wanderup D 43 A6
Wandlitz D 45 C5
Wanfried D 51 B6
Wangen im Allgäu D 61 C5
Wangerooge D 43 B4
Wangersen D 43 B6
Wängi CH 70 A3
Wanna D 43 B5
Wansford GB 30 B3
Wantage GB 31 C2
Wanzleben D 52 A1
Waplewo PL 47 B6
Wapnica PL 46 B1
Wapno PL 46 C3
Warburg D 51 B5
Wardenburg D 43 B5
Ware GB 31 C3
Waregem B 49 C4
Wareham GB 29 C5
Waremme B 49 C6
Waren D 45 B4
Warendorf D 50 B3
Warga NL 42 B2
Warin D 44 B3
Wark GB 25 C5
Warka PL 55 B6
Warkworth GB 25 C6
Warlubie PL 47 B4
Warminster GB 29 B5
Warnemünde D 44 A4
Warnow D 44 B3
Warnsveld NL 50 A2
Warrenpoint GB 19 B5
Warrington GB 26 B3
Warsingsfehn D 43 B4
Warsow D 44 B3
Warstein D 51 B4
Warszawa PL 55 A6
Warta PL 54 B3
Wartberg A 63 C5
Warth A 71 A5
Warwick GB 30 B2
Warza D 51 C6
Wasbister GB 23 B5
Washington GB 25 D6
Wąsosz PL 54 B1
Wasselonne F 60 B3
Wassen CH 70 B3
Wassenaar NL 49 A5
Wasserauen CH 71 A4
Wasserburg D 62 B3
Wassertrüdingen D 61 A6
Wassy F 59 B5
Wasungen D 51 C6
Watchet GB 29 B4
Waterford IRL 21 B4
Watergrasshill IRL 20 B3
Waterloo B 49 C5
Waterville IRL 20 C1
Watford GB 31 C3
Wathlingen D 44 C2
Watten F 48 C3
Watten GB 23 C5
Wattens A 72 A1
Watton GB 30 B4
Wattwil CH 71 A4
Waunfawr GB 26 B1
Wavignies F 58 A3
Wavre B 49 C5
Wearhead GB 25 D5
Wechadlow PL 55 C5
Wedel D 43 B6
Wedemark D 43 C6
Weedon Bec GB 30 B2
Weener D 43 B4
Weert NL 50 B1
Weesp NL 49 A6
Weeze D 50 B2
Weferlingen D 52 A1
Wegeleben D 52 B1
Weggis CH 70 A3
Węgierska-Górka PL 65 A5
Wegliniec PL 53 B5
Węgorzyno PL 46 B1
Węgrzynice PL 53 A5
Wegscheid D 63 B4
Wehdel D 43 B5
Wehr D 60 C3
Weibersbrunn D 61 A5
Weichering D 62 B2
Weida D 52 C2
Weiden D 62 A3
Weidenberg D 52 D1
Weidenhain D 52 B2
Weidenstetten D 61 B5
Weierbach D 60 A3
Weikersheim D 61 A5
Weil D 62 B1
Weil am Rhein D 60 C3
Weil der Stadt D 61 B4
Weilburg D 50 C4
Weilerswist D 50 C2
Weilheim, *Baden-Württemberg* D 61 B5
Weilheim, *Bayern* D 62 C2

Weilmünster D 51 C4
Weiltensfeld A 73 B4
Weimar D 52 C1
Weinberg D 61 A6
Weinfelden CH 61 C5
Weingarten, *Baden-Württemberg* D 61 A4
Weingarten, *Baden-Württemberg* D 61 C5
Weinheim D 61 A4
Weinstadt D 61 B5
Weismain D 52 C1
Weissbriach A 72 B3
Weissenbach A 71 A5
Weissenberg D 53 B4
Weissenbrunn D 52 C1
Weissenburg D 62 A1
Weissenfels D 52 B1
Weissenhorn D 61 B6
Weissenkirchen A 63 B6
Weissensee D 52 B1
Weissenstadt D 52 C1
Weisskirchen im Steiermark A 73 A4
Weisstannen CH 71 B4
Weisswasser D 53 B4
Weitendorf D 44 B4
Weitersfeld A 64 B1
Weitersfelden A 63 B5
Weitnau D 61 C6
Weitra A 63 B5
Weiz A 73 A5
Wejherowo PL 47 A4
Welkenraedt B 50 C1
Wellaune D 52 B2
Wellin B 49 C6
Wellingborough GB 30 B3
Wellington, *Somerset* GB 29 C4
Wellington, *Telford & Wrekin* GB 26 C3
Wellingtonbridge IRL 21 B5
Wells GB 29 B5
Wells-next-the-Sea GB 30 B4
Wels A 63 B5
Welschenrohr CH 70 A2
Welshpool GB 26 C2
Welver D 50 B3
Welwyn Garden City GB 31 C3
Welzheim D 61 B5
Welzow D 53 B4
Wem GB 26 C3
Wembury GB 28 C3
Wemding D 62 B1
Wenden D 50 C3
Wendisch Rietz D 53 A4
Wendlingen D 61 B5
Weng A 63 B4
Weng bei Admont A 63 C5
Wengen CH 70 B2
Wenigzell A 73 A5
Wennigsen D 51 A5
Wenns A 71 A5
Wenzenbach D 62 A3
Weppersdorf A 64 C2
Werben D 44 C3
Werbig D 52 B3
Werdau D 52 C2
Werder D 45 C4
Werdohl D 50 B3
Werfen A 72 A3
Werkendam NL 49 B5
Werl D 50 B3
Werlte D 43 C4
Wermelskirchen D 50 B3
Wermsdorf D 52 B2
Wernberg Köblitz D 62 A3
Werne D 50 B3
Werneck D 51 D6
Werneuchen D 45 C5
Wernigerode D 51 B6
Wertach D 61 C6
Wertheim D 61 A5
Wertingen D 62 B1
Weseke D 50 B2
Wesel D 50 B2
Wesenberg D 45 B4
Wesendorf D 44 C2
Wesołowo PL 47 B6
Wesselburen D 43 A5
Wesseling D 50 C2
West Bridgford GB 27 C4
West Bromwich GB 27 C4
West Haddon GB 30 B2
West Kilbride GB 24 C3
West Linton GB 25 C4
West Lulworth GB 29 C5
West Mersea GB 31 C4
West-Terschelling NL 42 B2
West Woodburn GB 25 C5
Westbury, *Shropshire* GB 26 C3
Westbury, *Wiltshire* GB 29 B5
Westbury-on-Severn GB 29 B5
Westendorf A 72 A2
Westensee D 44 A1
Westerbork NL 42 C3
Westerburg D 50 C3
Westerhaar NL 42 C3
Westerholt D 43 B4
Westerkappeln D 50 A3
Westerland D 39 E1
Westerlo B 49 B5
Westerstede D 43 B4
Westheim D 62 A1
Westhill GB 23 D6
Westkapelle B 49 B4
Westkapelle NL 49 B4
Westminster GB 31 C3
Weston GB 26 C3
Weston-super-Mare GB 29 B5
Westport IRL 18 C2
Westruther GB 25 C5
Westward Ho! GB 28 B3
Wetheral GB 25 D5
Wetherby GB 27 B4
Wetter, *Hessen* D 51 C4
Wetter, *Nordrhein-Westfalen* D 50 B3
Wetteren B 49 B4
Wettin D 52 B1
Wettringen D 50 A3
Wetzikon CH 70 A3
Wetzlar D 51 C4
Wewelsfleth D 43 B6
Wexford IRL 21 B5
Weybridge GB 31 C3
Weyer Markt A 63 C5
Weyerbusch D 50 C3
Weyersheim F 60 B3
Weyhe D 43 C5
Weyhill GB 31 C2
Weymouth GB 29 C5
Weyregg A 63 C4
Węzyska PL 53 A4
Whalton GB 25 C6
Whauphill GB 24 D3
Wheatley GB 31 C2
Whickham GB 25 D6
Whipsnade GB 31 C3
Whitburn GB 25 C4
Whitby GB 27 A5
Whitchurch, *Hampshire* GB 31 C2
Whitchurch, *Herefordshire* GB 29 B5
Whitchurch, *Shropshire* GB 26 C3
White Bridge GB 23 D4
Whitegate IRL 20 C3
Whitehaven GB 26 A2
Whitehead GB 19 B6
Whithorn GB 24 D3
Whitley Bay GB 25 C6
Whitstable GB 31 C5
Whittington GB 26 C3
Whittlesey GB 30 B3
Wiązów PL 54 C2
Wiązowna PL 55 A6
Wick GB 23 C5
Wickede D 50 B3
Wickford GB 31 C4
Wickham GB 31 D2
Wickham Market GB 30 B5
Wicklow IRL 21 B5
Wicko PL 46 A3
Widawa PL 54 B3
Widdrington GB 25 C6
Widecombe in the Moor GB 28 C4
Widemouth GB 28 C3
Widnes GB 26 B3
Widuchowo PL 45 B6
Więcbork PL 46 B3
Wiefelstede D 43 B5
Wiehe D 52 B1
Wiehl D 50 C3
Wiek D 45 A5
Większyce PL 54 C3
Wiele PL 46 B3
Wieleń PL 46 C2
Wielgie, *Łódzkie* PL 54 B3
Wielgie, *Mazowieckie* PL 55 B6
Wielgomłyny PL 55 B4
Wielichowo PL 53 A6
Wieliczka PL 65 A6
Wielka Łąka PL 47 B4
Wielowies PL 54 C3
Wieluń PL 54 B3
Wien A 64 B2
Wiener Neustadt A 64 C2
Wiepke D 44 C3
Wierden NL 42 C3
Wieren D 44 C2
Wieruszów PL 54 B3
Wierzbica PL 55 B6
Wierzbie PL 54 B3
Wierzbięcin PL 45 B7
Wierzchowo PL 46 B2
Wierzchucino PL 47 A4
Wierzchy PL 54 B3
Wies A 73 B5
Wiesau D 62 A3
Wiesbaden D 50 C4
Wieselburg A 63 B6
Wiesen CH 71 B4
Wiesenburg D 52 A2
Wiesenfelden D 62 A3
Wiesensteig D 61 D5
Wiesentheid D 61 A6
Wiesloch D 61 A4
Wiesmath A 64 C2
Wiesmoor D 43 B4
Wietmarschen D 43 C4
Wietze D 44 C1
Wigan GB 26 B3
Wiggen CH 70 B2
Wigston GB 30 B2
Wigton GB 25 D4
Wigtown GB 24 D3
Wijchen NL 50 B1
Wijhe NL 42 C3
Wijk bij Duurstede NL 49 B6
Wil CH 70 A4
Wilamowice PL 65 A5
Wilczęta PL 47 A5
Wilczkowice PL 55 A4
Wilczna PL 54 A3
Wilczyn PL 47 C4
Wildalpen A 63 C5
Wildbad D 61 B4
Wildberg, *Baden-Württemberg* D 61 B4
Wildberg, *Brandenburg* D 45 C4
Wildegg CH 70 A3
Wildendürnbach A 64 B2
Wildeshausen D 43 C5
Wildon A 73 B5
Wilfersdorf A 64 B2
Wilga PL 55 B6
Wilhelmsburg A 63 B6
Wilhelmsburg D 45 B5
Wilhelmsdorf D 61 C5
Wilhelmshaven D 43 B5
Willebadessen D 51 B5
Willebroek B 49 B5
Wilhermsdorf D 62 A1
Willich D 50 B2
Willingen D 51 B4
Willington GB 25 D6
Willisau CH 70 A3
Wilmslow GB 26 B3
Wilsdruff D 52 B3
Wilster D 43 B6
Wilsum D 42 C3
Wilton GB 29 B6
Wiltz L 50 D1
Wimborne Minster GB 29 C6
Wimereux F 48 C2
Wimmenau F 60 B3
Wimmis CH 70 B2
Wincanton GB 29 B5
Winchcombe GB 29 B6
Winchelsea GB 31 D4
Winchester GB 31 C2
Windermere GB 26 A3
Windischeschenbach D 62 A3
Windischgarsten A 63 C5
Windorf D 63 B4
Windsbach D 62 A1
Windsor GB 31 C3
Windygates GB 25 B4
Wingene B 49 B4
Wingham GB 31 C5
Winkleigh GB 28 C4
Winklern A 72 B2
Winnenden D 61 B5
Winnigstedt D 51 A6
Winnweiler D 60 A3
Winschoten NL 43 B4
Winsen, *Niedersachsen* D 44 B2
Winsen, *Niedersachsen* D 44 C1
Winsford GB 26 B3
Wińsko PL 54 B1
Winslow GB 31 C3
Winsum, *Friesland* NL 42 B2
Winsum, *Groningen* NL 42 B3
Winterberg D 51 B4
Winterfeld D 44 C3
Winterswijk NL 50 B2
Winterthur CH 70 A3
Wintzenheim F 60 B3
Winzer D 62 B4
Wipperdorf D 51 B6
Wipperfürth D 50 B3
Wirksworth GB 27 B4
Wisbech GB 30 B4
Wischhafen D 43 B6
Wishaw GB 25 C4
Wisła PL 65 A4
Wisła Wielka PL 65 A4
Wislica PL 55 C5
Wismar D 44 B3
Wisniewo PL 47 B6
Wiśniowa PL 65 A6
Wissant F 48 C2
Wissembourg F 60 A3
Wissen D 50 C3
Witanowice PL 65 A5
Witham GB 31 C4
Withern GB 27 B6
Withernsea GB 27 B6
Witkowo PL 46 C3
Witmarsum NL 42 B2
Witney GB 31 C2
Witnica PL 45 C6
Witonia PL 55 A4
Witry-les-Reims F 59 A5
Wittdün D 43 A5
Wittelsheim F 60 C3
Witten D 50 B3
Wittenberge D 44 B3
Wittenburg D 44 B3
Wittenheim F 60 C3
Wittichenau D 53 B4
Wittighausen D 61 A5
Wittingen D 44 C2
Wittislingen D 61 B6
Wittlich D 50 D2
Wittmannsdorf A 73 B5
Wittmund D 43 B4
Wittorf D 43 B6
Wittstock D 44 B4
Witzenhausen D 51 B5
Wiveliscombe GB 29 B4
Wivenhoe GB 31 C4
Władysławowo PL 47 A4
Wleń PL 53 B5
Włocławek PL 47 C5
Włodawa PL 11 L18
Włodzimierzów PL 55 B4
Włosień PL 53 B5
Włostow PL 55 C6
Włoszczowa PL 55 C4
Wöbbelin D 44 B3
Woburn GB 31 C3
Wodzisław PL 55 C5
Wodzisław Śląski PL 65 A4
Woerden NL 49 A5
Wœrth F 60 B3
Wohlen CH 70 A3
Woippy F 60 A2
Wojciechy PL 47 A6
Wojcieszow PL 53 C5
Wojkowice Kościelne PL 55 C4
Wojnicz PL 65 A6
Woking GB 31 C3
Wokingham GB 31 C3
Wola Jachowa PL 55 C5
Wola Niechcicka PL 55 B4
Wolbórz PL 55 B4
Wolbrom PL 55 C4
Wołczyn PL 54 B3
Woldegk D 45 B5
Wolf's Castle GB 28 B3
Wolfach D 61 B4
Wolfegg D 61 C5
Wolfen D 52 B2
Wolfenbüttel D 51 A6
Wolfersheim D 51 C4
Wolfhagen D 51 B5
Wolfratshausen D 62 C2
Wolfsberg A 73 B4
Wolfsburg D 44 C2
Wolfshagen D 45 B5
Wolfstein D 60 A3
Wolfurt A 71 A4
Wolgast D 45 A5
Wolhusen CH 70 A3
Wolin PL 45 B6
Wolka PL 55 B5
Wolkenstein D 52 C3
Wolkersdorf A 64 B2
Wöllersdorf A 64 C2
Wollin D 52 A2
Wöllstadt D 51 C4
Wolmirstedt D 52 A1
Wolnzach D 62 B2
Wołów PL 54 B1
Wolsztyn PL 53 A6
Wolvega NL 42 C2
Wolverhampton GB 26 C3
Wolverton GB 30 B3
Wombwell GB 27 B4
Woodbridge GB 30 B5
Woodhall Spa GB 27 B5
Woodstock GB 31 C2
Wookey Hole GB 29 B5
Wool GB 29 C5
Woolacombe GB 28 B3
Wooler GB 25 C5
Woolwich GB 31 C4
Wooperton GB 25 C6
Worb CH 70 B2
Worbis D 51 B6
Worcester GB 29 A5
Wördern A 64 B2
Wörgl A 72 A2
Workington GB 26 A2
Worksop GB 27 B4
Workum NL 42 C2
Wörlitz D 52 B2
Wormer NL 42 C1
Wormhout F 48 C3
Wormit GB 25 B5
Worms D 61 A4
Worpswede D 43 B5
Wörrstadt D 61 A4
Wörschach A 73 A4
Worsley GB 26 B3
Wörth, *Bayern* D 61 A5
Wörth, *Bayern* D 62 A3
Wörth, *Bayern* D 62 B3
Wörth, *Rheinland-Pfalz* D 61 A4
Worthing GB 31 D3
Woudsend NL 42 C2
Woumen B 48 B3
Woźniki PL 55 C4
Wragby GB 27 B5
Wrangle GB 27 B6
Wręczyca Wlk. PL 54 C3
Wredenhagen D 45 B4
Wremen D 43 B5
Wrentham GB 30 B5
Wrexham GB 26 B3
Wriedel D 44 B2
Wriezen D 45 C6
Wrist D 43 B6
Wróblewo, *Mazowieckie* PL 47 C6
Wróblewo, *Wielkopolskie* PL 46 C2
Wrocki PL 47 B5
Wrocław PL 54 B2
Wronki PL 46 C2
Wroxham GB 30 B5
Września PL 54 A2
Wrzosowo PL 46 A1
Wschowa PL 53 B6
Wulfen, *Nordrhein-Westfalen* D 50 B3
Wulfen, *Sachsen-Anhalt* D 52 B1
Wulkau D 44 C4
Wünnenberg D 51 B4
Wünsdorf D 52 A3
Wunsiedel D 52 C2
Wunstorf D 43 C6
Wuppertal D 50 B3
Wurmannsquick D 62 B3
Würselen D 50 C2
Wurzbach D 52 C1
Würzburg D 61 A5
Wurzen D 52 B2
Wust D 45 C4
Wusterhausen D 44 C4
Wustrau-Altfriesack D 45 C4
Wustrow D 44 A4
Wuustwezel B 49 B5
Wye GB 31 C4
Wyględów PL 55 B6
Wyk D 43 A5
Wykroty PL 53 B5
Wylye GB 29 B6
Wymiarki PL 53 B5
Wymondham GB 30 B5
Wyrzysk PL 46 B3
Wyśmierzyce PL 55 B5
Wysoka, *Dolnośląskie* PL 53 B5
Wysoka, *Wielkopolskie* PL 46 B3
Wyszanów PL 54 B3
Wyszogród PL 47 C6

X

Xanten D 50 B2
Xánthi GR 16 R19
Xàtiva E 96 C2
Xeraco E 96 B2
Xert E 90 C3
Xerta E 90 C3
Xertigny F 60 B2
Xinzo de Limia E 87 B3
Xove E 86 A3
Xubia E 86 A2
Xunqueira de Ambia E 87 B3
Xunqueira de Espadañedo E 87 B3

Y

Y Felinheli GB 26 B1
Yablanitsa BG 16 Q19
Yahotyn UA 11 L22
Yalova TR 16 R21
Yalvaç TR 16 S22
Yambol BG 16 Q20
Yampil UA 11 M21
Yarcombe GB 29 C4
Yaremcha UA 11 M19
Yarm GB 27 A4
Yarmouth GB 31 D2
Yarrow GB 25 C4
Yartsevo RUS 7 J23
Yasinya UA 11 M19
Yatağan TR 16 T21
Yate GB 29 B5
Yatton GB 29 B5
Yavoriv UA 11 M18
Yaxley GB 30 B3
Ybbs A 63 B6
Ybbsitz A 63 C5
Ydby DK 38 C1
Yddal N 32 A2
Yealmpton GB 28 C4
Yebra de Basa E 90 A2
Yecla E 96 C1
Yecla de Yeltes E 87 D4
Yelnya RUS 7 J23
Yelsk BY 11 L21
Yelverton GB 28 C3
Yenice TR 16 S20
Yenihisar TR 16 T20
Yenişehir TR 16 R21
Yenne F 69 C5
Yeovil GB 29 C5
Yepes E 95 C3
Yerseke NL 49 B5
Yerville F 58 A1
Yeşilova TR 16 T21
Yesnogorsk RUS 7 J25
Yeste E 101 A3
Yezerishche BY 7 J21
Ygos-St. Saturnin F 76 C2
Ygrande F 68 B2
Yiannitsa GR 15 R18
Yiñuela E 100 C1
Yithion GR 15 T18
Ylitornio FIN 3 C18
Ylivieska FIN 3 D19
Ymonville F 58 B2
Yngsjö S 41 D4
York GB 27 B4
Youghal IRL 21 C4
Yport F 58 A1
Yssingeaux F 68 C4
Ystad S 41 D3
Ystalyfera GB 28 B4
Ystebrød N 32 C2
Ystradgynlais GB 28 B4
Ytre Arna N 2 F9
Ytre Enebakk N 34 B3
Yukhnov RUS 7 J24
Yunak TR 16 S22
Yuncos E 94 B3
Yunquera E 100 C1
Yunquera de Henares E 95 B3
Yushkozero RUS 3 D23
Yverdon-les-Bains CH 70 B1
Yvetot F 58 A1
Yvignac F 57 B3
Yvoir B 49 C5
Yvonand CH 70 B1
Yxnerum S 37 C3
Yzeure F 68 B3

Z

Zaamslag NL 49 B4
Zaanstad NL 42 C1
Žabalj YU 75 C5
Zabar H 65 B6
Žabari YU 85 B6
Zabiče SLO 72 C4
Zabierzów PL 55 C4
Ząbki PL 55 A6
Ząbkowice Śląskie PL 54 C1
Zablaće HR 83 C4
Zablaće YU 85 C5
Žabljak YU 85 C4
Žabno PL 55 C5
Zabok HR 73 B5
Žabokreky SK 64 B4
Zabor PL 53 B5
Žabrdje BIH 84 B3
Zábřeh CZ 64 A2
Zabrežje YU 85 B5
Zabrze PL 54 C3
Zabrzeź PL 65 A6
Zadar HR 83 B4
Zadzim PL 54 B3
Zafarraya E 100 C1
Zafferana Etnea I 109 B4
Zafra E 93 C4
Žaga SLO 72 B3
Zagajica YU 85 B6
Żagań PL 53 B5
Zaglav HR 83 C4
Zaglavak YU 85 C4
Zagnanśk PL 55 C5
Zagorc SLO 73 B4
Zagorićani BIH 84 C2
Zagorje SLO 73 B4
Zagórów PL 54 A2
Zagradje YU 85 B5
Zagreb HR 73 C5
Zagrilla E 100 B1
Zagvozd HR 84 C2
Zagwiździe PL 54 C2
Zagyvarekas H 75 A5
Zagyvaróna H 65 B5
Zahara E 99 C5
Zahara de los Atunes E 99 C5
Zahinos E 93 C4
Zahna D 52 B2
Záhoří CZ 63 A5
Zahrádka CZ 63 A6
Zahrensdorf D 44 B2
Zaidin E 90 B3
Zaječar YU 15 Q18
Zákamenné SK 65 A5
Zákány H 74 B1
Zákányszék H 74 B3
Zákinthos GR 15 T17
Zakliczyn PL 65 A6
Zakopane PL 65 A5
Zakroczym PL 47 C6
Zakrzew PL 55 B6
Zakrzewo PL 47 C4
Zákupy CZ 53 C4
Zalaapáti H 74 B2
Zalabaksa H 74 B1
Zalaegerszeg H 74 B1
Zalakomár H 74 B2
Zalakoppány H 74 B2
Zalalövő H 74 B1
Zalamea de la Serena E 93 C5
Zalamea la Real E 99 B4
Zalaszentgrót H 74 B2
Zalaszentiván H 74 B1
Zalău RO 11 N18
Zalavár H 74 B2
Zalcsie PL 55 B4
Zaldibar E 89 A4
Žalec SLO 73 B5
Zalesie PL 47 B6
Zalewo PL 47 B5
Zalishchyky UA 11 M19
Zalla E 89 A3
Zaltbommel NL 49 B6
Zamárdi H 74 B2
Zamarte PL 46 B3
Zamberk CZ 54 C1
Zambra E 100 B1
Zambugueira do Mar P 98 B2
Zámoly H 74 A3
Zamora E 88 C1
Zamość PL 11 L18
Zamoście PL 55 B4
Zams A 71 A5
Zandhoven B 49 B5
Žandov CZ 53 C4
Zandvoort NL 42 C1
Zánka H 74 B2
Zaorejas E 95 B4
Zaovine YU 85 C4
Zapadnaya Dvina RUS 7 H23
Zapfend D 51 C6
Zapole PL 54 B3
Zapolyarnyy RUS 3 B22
Zapponeta I 104 A2
Zaprešić HR 73 C5
Zaragoza E 90 B2
Zarasai LT 7 J20
Zarautz E 89 A4
Zarcilla de Ramos E 101 B4
Żarki PL 55 C4
Žarnovica SK 65 B4
Zarnow PL 55 B5
Zarnowiec PL 47 A4
Zarošice CZ 64 A2
Żarów PL 54 C1
Zarren B 48 B3
Zarrentin D 44 B2
Żary PL 53 B5
Zarza Capilla E 93 C5
Zarza de Alange E 93 C4
Zarza de Granadilla E 93 A4
Zarza de Tajo E 95 B3
Zarza la Mayor E 93 B4
Zarzadilla de Totana E 101 B4
Zarzuela del Monte E 94 B2
Zarzuela del Pinar E 94 A2
Zas E 86 A2
Zasavica YU 85 B4
Zasieki PL 53 B4
Zásmuky CZ 53 D5
Žatec CZ 52 C3
Zaton HR 84 D3
Zatonie PL 53 B5
Zator PL 55 D4
Zauchwitz D 52 A3
Zavala BIH 84 D2
Zavalje BIH 83 B4
Zavattarello I 80 B3
Zavidovići BIH 84 B3
Zavlaka YU 85 B4
Zawady PL 55 B5
Zawadzkie PL 54 C3
Zawdy PL 54 B3
Zawidów PL 53 B5
Zawiercie PL 55 C4
Zawoja PL 65 A5
Zawonia PL 54 B2
Žažina HR 73 C6
Zázrivá SK 65 A5
Zbarazh UA 11 M19
Zbąszyń PL 53 A5
Zbąszynek PL 53 A5
Zbehy SK 64 B4
Zbiersk PL 54 B3
Zbiroh CZ 63 A4
Zblewo PL 47 B4
Zbójno PL 47 B5
Zbrachlin PL 47 B4
Zbraslav CZ 53 D4
Zbraslavice CZ 63 A6
Ždala HR 74 B2
Ždánice CZ 64 A3
Ždár nad Sázavou CZ 64 A1
Zdenci HR 74 C2
Ždiar SK 65 A6
Zdice CZ 63 A4
Zdirec nad Doubravou CZ 64 A1
Zdolbuniv UA 11 L20
Zdounky CZ 64 A3
Zdravinje YU 85 C6
Zduńska Wola PL 54 B3
Zduny, *Łódzkie* PL 55 A4
Zduny, *Wielkopolskie* PL 54 B2
Żdżary PL 55 B5
Zdziechowice, *Opolskie* PL 54 B3
Zdziechowice, *Wielkopolskie* PL 54 A2
Zdziszowice PL 54 C3
Zeberio E 89 A4
Žebrák CZ 63 A4
Zebreira P 93 B3
Zebrzydowa PL 53 B5
Zechlin D 45 B4
Zechlinerhütte D 45 B4
Zederhaus A 72 A3
Žednik YU 75 C4
Zeebrugge B 49 B4
Zehdenick D 45 C5
Zehren D 52 B3
Zeil D 51 C6
Zeist NL 49 A6
Zeithain D 52 B3
Zeitz D 52 B2
Želatava CZ 63 A6
Żelazno, *Dolnośląskie* PL 54 C1
Żelazno, *Pomorskie* PL 46 A3
Zele B 49 B5
Zelenoborskiy RUS 3 C23
Zelenogorsk RUS 3 F21
Zelenograd RUS 7 H25
Zelenogradsk RUS 6 J17
Železná Ruda CZ 63 A4
Železnice CZ 53 C5
Železnik YU 85 B5
Zelezniki SLO 73 B4
Železny Brod CZ 53 C5
Zelhem NL 50 A2
Želiezovce SK 65 B4
Zelkowo PL 46 A3
Zell CH 70 A2
Zell, *Baden-Württemberg* D 60 C3
Zell, *Baden-Württemberg* D 61 B4
Zell, *Rheinland-Pfalz* D 50 C3
Zell am See A 72 A2
Zell am Ziller A 72 A1
Zell an der Pram A 63 B4
Zell bei Zellhof A 63 B5
Zella-Mehlis D 51 C6
Zellerndorf A 64 B1
Zellingen D 61 A5
Želovce SK 65 B5
Żelów PL 55 B4
Zeltweg A 73 A4
Zelzate B 49 B4
Zemberovce SK 65 B4
Zembrzyce PL 65 A5
Zemianske-Kostol'any SK 65 B4
Zemitz D 45 B5
Zemné SK 64 C3
Zemst B 49 C5
Zemun YU 85 B5
Zemunik Donji HR 83 B4
Zenica BIH 84 B2
Zennor GB 28 C2
Žepa BIH 85 C4
Žepče BIH 84 B3
Zepponami I 102 A2
Zerbst D 52 B2
Zerf D 60 A2
Żerków PL 54 A2
Zermatt CH 70 B2
Zernez CH 71 B5
Zerpenschleuse D 45 C5
Zestoa E 89 A4
Zetel D 43 B4
Zeulenroda D 52 C1
Zeven D 43 B6
Zevenaar NL 50 B2
Zevenbergen NL 49 B5
Zévio I 71 C6
Zgierz PL 55 B4
Zgorzelec PL 53 B5
Zgošća BIH 84 B3
Zhabinka BY 6 K19
Zharkovskiy RUS 7 J23
Zhashkiv UA 11 M22
Zheleznogorsk RUS 7 K24
Zhizdra RUS 7 K24
Zhlobin BY 7 K22
Zhmerynka UA 11 M21
Zhodzina BY 7 J21
Zhovtneve UA 11 N23
Zhukovka RUS 7 K23
Zhytomyr UA 11 L21
Žiar nad Hronom SK 65 B4
Zicavo F 110 B2
Zickhusen D 44 B3
Zidani Most SLO 73 B5
Ziddorf D 45 B4
Židlochovice CZ 64 A2
Ziębice PL 54 C2
Ziegendorf D 44 B3
Ziegenrück D 52 C1
Zieleniec, *Dolnośląskie* PL 54 C1
Zieleniec, *Zachodnio-Pomorskie* PL 46 B1
Zielona PL 47 B5
Zielona Góra PL 53 B5
Zielonka PL 55 A6
Zieluń-Osada PL 47 B5
Ziemetshausen D 61 B6
Zierenberg D 51 B5
Zierikzee NL 49 B4
Ziersdorf A 64 B1
Zierzow D 44 B3
Ziesar D 52 A2
Ziesendorf D 44 B4
Ziethen D 45 C5
Žihle CZ 52 C3
Žilina SK 65 A4
Ziltendorf D 53 A4
Zimna Woda PL 47 B6
Zimnicea RO 16 Q19
Zinal CH 70 B2
Zinasco I 80 A3
Zingst D 45 A4
Zinkgruvan S 37 C2
Žinkovy CZ 63 A4
Zinnowitz D 45 A5
Zirc H 74 A2
Žiri SLO 73 B4
Zirl A 71 A6
Zirndorf D 62 A1
Žirovnica YU 85 B6
Žirovnice CZ 63 A6
Zisterdorf A 64 B2
Zitište YU 75 C5
Zittau D 53 C4
Živaja HR 74 C1
Živinice BIH 84 B3
Zlatar HR 73 B6
Zlatar Bistrica HR 73 B6
Zlate Hory CZ 54 C2
Zlaté Klasy SK 64 B3
Zlaté Moravce SK 65 B4
Zlatná na Ostrove SK 64 C3
Zlatniky SK 64 B4
Zlatograd BG 16 R19
Žlebič SLO 73 C4
Zlín CZ 64 A3
Złocieniec PL 46 B2
Złoczew PL 54 B3
Zlonice CZ 53 C4
Złotniki Kujawskie PL 47 C4
Złotoryja PL 53 B5
Złotów PL 46 B3
Złoty Stok PL 54 C1
Zlutice CZ 52 C3
Zmajevac BIH 83 B5
Zmajevo YU 75 C4
Żmigród PL 54 B1
Zmijavci HR 84 C2
Žminj HR 82 A2
Znamyanka UA 11 M23
Żnin PL 46 C3
Znojmo CZ 64 B2
Zöblitz D 52 C3
Zocca I 81 B4
Zoetermeer NL 49 A5
Zofingen CH 70 A2
Zogno I 71 C4
Zohor SK 64 B2
Zolling D 62 B2
Zolochiv UA 11 M19
Zolotonosha UA 11 M23
Zomba H 74 B3
Zomergem B 49 B4
Zoñán E 86 A3
Zonguldak TR 16 R22
Zonhoven B 49 C6
Zonza F 110 B2
Zörbig D 52 B2
Zorita E 93 B5
Żory PL 54 C3
Zossen D 52 A3
Zottegem B 49 C4
Zoutkamp NL 42 B3
Zovi Do BIH 84 C3
Zreče SLO 73 B5
Zrenjanin YU 75 C5
Žrnovica HR 83 C5
Zruč nad Sázavou CZ 63 A6
Zsámbék H 74 A3
Zsámbok H 75 A4
Zsana H 75 B4
Zschopau D 52 C3
Zuberec SK 65 A5
Zubieta E 89 A5
Zubin Potok YU 85 D5
Zubiri E 76 D1
Zubtsov RUS 7 H24
Zucaina E 96 A2
Zudar D 45 A5
Zuera E 90 B2
Zufre E 99 B4
Zug CH 70 A3
Zuheros E 100 B1
Zuidhorn NL 42 B3
Zuidlaren NL 42 B3
Zuidwolde NL 42 C3
Zújar E 101 B3
Żukowo PL 47 A4
Žuljana HR 84 D2
Žulová CZ 54 C2
Zülpich D 50 C2
Zumaia E 89 A4
Zumárraga E 89 A4
Zundert NL 49 B5
Županja HR 84 A3
Zurgena E 101 B3
Zürich CH 70 A3
Żuromin PL 47 B5
Zurzach CH 61 C4
Zusmarshausen D 61 B6
Zusow D 44 B3
Züssow D 45 B5
Žuta Lovka HR 83 B4
Zutphen NL 50 A2
Žužemberk SLO 73 C4
Zvečan YU 85 D5
Zvenyhorodka UA 11 M22
Zvikovské Podhradí CZ 63 A5
Zvolen SK 65 B5
Zvolenská Slatina SK 65 B5
Zvornik BIH 85 B4
Zwartsluis NL 42 C3
Zweibrücken D 60 A3
Zweisimmen CH 70 B2
Zwettl A 63 B6
Zwettl an der Rodl A 63 B5
Zwickau D 52 C2
Zwiefalten D 61 B5
Zwieryn PL 46 C1
Zwierzno PL 47 A5
Zwiesel D 63 A4
Zwieselstein A 71 B6
Zwoleń PL 55 B6
Zwolle NL 42 C3
Zwönitz D 52 C2
Zychlin PL 55 A4
Zydowo, *Wielkopolskie* PL 46 C3
Zydowo, *Zachodnio-Pomorskie* PL 46 A2
Żyrardów PL 55 A5
Żytno PL 55 C4
Żywiec PL 65 A5